D0388129

Turkey

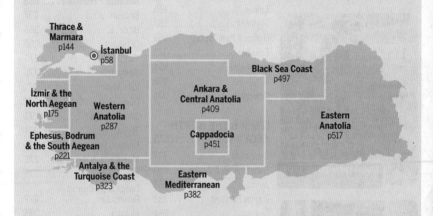

Thrace & Marmara
p144

İstanbul
p58

İzmir & the North Aegean
p175

Western Anatolia
p287

Ephesus, Bodrum & the South Aegean
p221

Antalya & the Turquoise Coast
p323

Ankara & Central Anatolia
p409

Cappadocia
p451

Eastern Mediterranean
p382

Black Sea Coast
p497

Eastern Anatolia
p517

THIS EDITION WRITTEN AND RESEARCHED BY

James Bainbridge, Brett Atkinson, Steve Fallon, Jessica Lee,
Virginia Maxwell, Hugh McNaughtan, John Noble

Contents

LOKUM (TURKISH DELIGHT)

PEREKOTYPOLE/SHUTTERSTOCK ©

VIACHESLAV LOPATIN/SHUTTERSTOCK ©

ISTANBUL P58

Contents

LEVENT BARIN/EYEEM/GETTY IMAGES ©

ISTANBUL P58

ON THE ROAD

ALANYA P384

ISTANBUL P58

Contents

SPECIAL FEATURES

Welcome to Turkey

A richly historical land with some of the best cuisine you will ever taste, scenery from beaches to mountains and the great city of İstanbul.

Epic History

From the ancient port city of Ephesus (Efes) to the soaring Byzantine dome of Aya Sofya, Turkey has more than its fair share of world-famous ruins and monuments. A succession of historical figures and empires – including the Romans, Byzantines and Ottomans – have all left their mark on this former stopover along the Silk Road. Experiencing their legacy takes you from the closeted quarters of the sultan and his harem in İstanbul's sprawling Topkapı Palace to the romantic and mysterious Lycian ruins on Mediterranean beaches.

Lyrical Landscapes

Turkey's diverse landscapes, from Aegean olive groves to eastern steppe, provide a lyrical setting for its many great ruins. The country's most magical scenery is to be found in Asian Anatolia, where beautiful vistas are provided by the vertiginous Mediterranean coastline, Cappadocia's otherworldly 'fairy chimney' rock formations and wavy valleys, the alpine pastures of the Kaçkar Mountains, and golden beaches such as 18km-long Patara. Whether you settle down with a çay to enjoy the view across mountain-ringed Lake Eğirdir or explore the hilly hinterland, Turkey's landscape will leave a lasting impression.

Activities Galore

Turkey offers activities to suit every temperament, from outdoors adventure to cultural enrichment. Watery fun includes diving, windsurfing, rafting and canyoning in mountain gorges, kayaking over Kekova's sunken ruins, and traditional *gület* cruises on the Mediterranean and Aegean. Or take to the air with Ölüdeniz' thrilling paragliding flights or a hot-air balloon ride over Cappadocia. For a fresh angle on stunning Turkish scenery, trek to highland pastures or walk part of the Lycian Way trail. In town, take a culinary course, soak in the hamam or hit İstanbul's Grand Bazaar to buy a carpet or flat-weave kilim rug.

Culinary Exploration

The best thing about sampling Turkey's delicious specialties – ranging from meze on a Mediterranean harbour to a pension breakfast featuring ingredients fresh from the kitchen garden – is that they take you to the heart of Turkish culture. For the sociable and family-orientated Turks, gathering together and eating well is a time-honoured ritual. So deepen your understanding of Turkey by getting stuck into olive-oil-lathered Aegean vegetables or spicy Anatolian kebaps, drinking a tulip-shaped glass of çay and contemplating some baklava for dessert.

Why I Love Turkey

By James Bainbridge, Writer

My first visit to Turkey was 20 years ago, when I finished a European rail odyssey in İstanbul, discovering the Blue Mosque and Sultanahmet's sights. I'll never forget drinking çay on my hostel's roof terrace, scribbling in my notebook and watching the ferries cross over to Asia. Wanting to visit somewhere between the continents, I jumped on a boat to the Princes' Islands, where an old man gave me a lift in his horse-drawn *fayton* (carriage). It was my first taste of the Turkish friendliness and hospitality I've been experiencing ever since.

For more about our writers, see p640.

Above: Ferries on the Bosphorus, İstanbul (p58)

Turkey

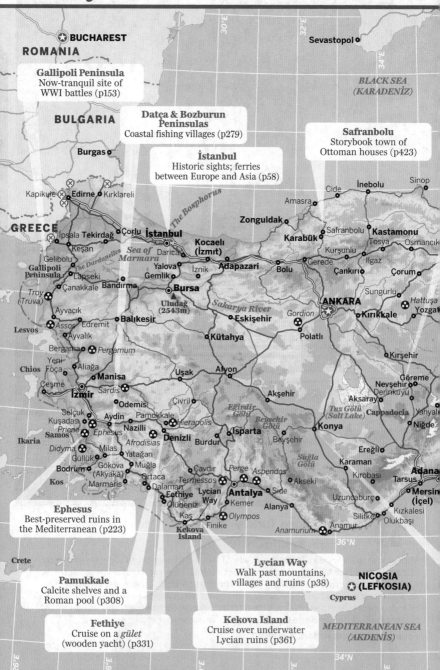

Gallipoli Peninsula
Now-tranquil site of
WWI battles (p153)

**Datça & Bozburun
Peninsulas**
Coastal fishing villages (p279)

Safranbolu
Storybook town of
Ottoman houses (p423)

İstanbul
Historic sights; ferries
between Europe and Asia (p58)

Ephesus
Best-preserved ruins in
the Mediterranean (p223)

Pamukkale
Calcite shelves and a
Roman pool (p308)

Lycian Way
Walk past mountains,
villages and ruins (p38)

Fethiye
Cruise on a *gület*
(wooden yacht) (p331)

Kekova Island
Cruise over underwater
Lycian ruins (p361)

ROMANIA

BUCHAREST

Sevastopol

BLACK SEA
(KARADENİZ)

BULGARIA

Burgas

Kapıkule Edirne Kırklareli

GREECE

İpsala Tekirdağ Çorlu **İstanbul**

Keşan

Gelibolu

Gallipoli
Peninsula Lapseki

Troy
(Truva) Çanakkale Bandırma

Ayvacık

Lesvos Assos Edremit

Ayvalık

Bergama *Pergamum*

Chios Yeni
Foça Aliağa

Çeşme **İzmir** *Sardis*

Odemiş

Selçuk Aydın

Kuşadası

Priene *Ephesus* Nazilli

Samos

Ikaria Didyma Milas

Güllük

Bodrum Gökova Muğla
(Akyaka)

Kos Marmaris Ortaca Dalaman

Fethiye Lycian
Ölüdeniz Way

Kaş Kemer

Finike

Kekova
Island

Crete

Cide İnebolu Sinop

Amasra

Zonguldak Safranbolu Kastamonu

Karabük Tosya Osmancık

Kurşunlu Ilgaz

Gerede Çankırı Çorum

Bolu

Sungurlu

ANKARA Hattuşa
Yozgat

Eskişehir Gordion Kırıkkale

Kütahya Polatlı

Uşak Afyon Kırşehir

Akşehir Göreme
Nevşehir

Aksaray Derinkuyu

Çivril Tuz Gölü Cappadocia
(Salt Lake) Yahyalı

Pamukkale Egirdir
Gölü Konya Niğde

Hierapolis Beyşehir
Gölü

Denizli Isparta Ereğli

Afrodisias Burdur Beyşehir Karaman

Yatağan Suğla
Gölü Kırobası

Çavdır *Perge* *Aspendos* Adana

Termessos **Antalya** Akseki Tarsus

Side Uzunçaburç Mersin
(İçel)

Olympos Alanya Silifke Kızkalesi

Anamurium Olukbaşı

Anamur

NICOSIA
(LEFKOSIA)

Cyprus

MEDITERRANEAN SEA
(AKDENİZ)

The Bosphorus

Kocaeli
(İzmit)

Darıca

Yalova İznik Adapazarı

Gemlik

Bursa

Uludağ
(2543m) *Sakarya River*

Sea of
Marmara

The Dardanelles

N 0 ▬▬▬▬▬ 200 km
0 ▬▬▬▬▬ 100 miles

RUSSIA

Grozny

Ani
Eerie ruins of a former
Armenian capital (p543)

Sukhumi

Cappadocia
Surreal fairy chimneys
and cave dwellings (p451)

Kaçkar Mountains
Hike through high-
altitude pastures (p523)

Kutaisi

GEORGIA

TBILISI ✪

Sumela Monastery
Cliff-face monastery
surveys valleys (p514)

Batumi
Sarp ⊗
Hopa ⊗
Türközü ⊗
Aktaş ⊗

Vanadzor

Bafra

Samsun

Trabzon   Rize
Artvin
Mt Kaçkar
(Kaçkar Dağı)
(3937m) ▲
Yusufeli
Çıldır
Gölü
Göle
Ani
Gyumri
ARMENIA
YEREVAN

Ünye
Giresun
Ordu
Sumela
Monastery
Kars
Sarıkamış

Amasya
Reşadiye
Gümüşhane
Kelkit River
Bayburt
Tortum
Çoruh River
Kağızman
Iğdır
Lake
Sevan

Niksar
Turhal   Tokat
Koyulhisar
Suşehri
Refahiye
Karasu River
Pasinler
Horasan
Ağrı River
Tuzluca
Mt Ararat
(Ağrı Dağı)
(5137m) ▲
Gürbulak ⊗

Sivas
Zara
Erzincan
Tercan
Erzurum
Ağrı
Doğubayazıt
Bazargan

Kızılırmak River
Şarkışla
Divriği
Tunceli
Patnos
Muradiye

Kayseri
Gürün
Keban
Dam
Bingöl
Mt Nemrut
(Nemrut Dağı)
(3050m) ▲
Muş
Lake Van
(Van Gölü)
Çaldıran
Özalp
IRAN

Elazığ
Murat River
Tatvan
Van
Gürpınar

Göksun
Elbistan
Karakaya Dam
Malatya
Bitlis
Baykan
Gevaş
Başkale
Sero

Doğanşehir
Nemrut Dağı
(Mt Nemrut)
(2106m) ▲
Batman
Siirt
Çatak
Hakkâri
Esendere ⊗
Yüksekova

Kahramanmaraş
Gölbaşı
Kahta
Atatürk
Dam
Siverek
Kurtalan
Diyarbakır
Şırnak
Mt Cilo
(Cilo Dağı)
(4168m) ▲

Kozan
Adıyaman
Hilvan
Viranşehir
Mardin
Tigris River

GAZİANTEP
(ANTEP)
Karatepe ✪
Birecik
Şanlıurfa
(Urfa) ✪
Qamishle
Nussaybin

Osmaniye
Ceyhan
Kilis
Barak ⊗
Harran ✪
Ceylanpınar ⊗
Mosul

İskenderun
Elbeyli ⊗
Akçakale

Antakya
(Hatay)
Öncüpınar ⊗
Erbil

Reyhanlı
Bab al-Hawa ⊗
Lake
al-Assad
Nemrut Dağı (Mt Nemrut)
Giant stone heads litter
a mountain (p550)
Kirkük

Yayladağı

Lattakia

Deir ez-Zur

Konya
Dervishes whirl at the
Mevlâna Festival (p442)

ELEVATION

IRAQ

Tripoli
LEBANON
Aleppo
(Halab)
Palmyra
SYRIA
Euphrates River

3000m
2500m
2000m
1500m
1000m
700m
500m
200m
100m
0

BEIRUT ✪

Turkey's
Top 19

Crossing Between Continents

1 In İstanbul, you can board a commuter ferry (p608) and flit between Europe and Asia in under an hour. Every day, a flotilla takes locals up the Bosphorus and over the Sea of Marmara, sounding sonorous horns as it goes. Morning services share the waterways with diminutive fishing boats and massive container ships, all accompanied by flocks of shrieking seagulls. At sunset, the tapering minarets and Byzantine domes of the Old City are thrown into relief against a dusky pink sky – it's the city's most magical sight.

Cappadocia

2 Cappadocia's hard-set honey-comb landscape looks sculpted by a swarm of genius bees. The truth – the effects of erosion on rock formed of ash from megalithic volcanic eruptions – is only slightly less cool. Humans have also left their mark here, in the Byzantine frescoes in rock-cut churches and in the bowels of complex underground cities. These days, Cappadocia (p451) is all about good times: fine wine, local dishes and five-star caves; horse riding, valley hikes and hot-air ballooning. There's enough to keep you buzzing for days.

1

2

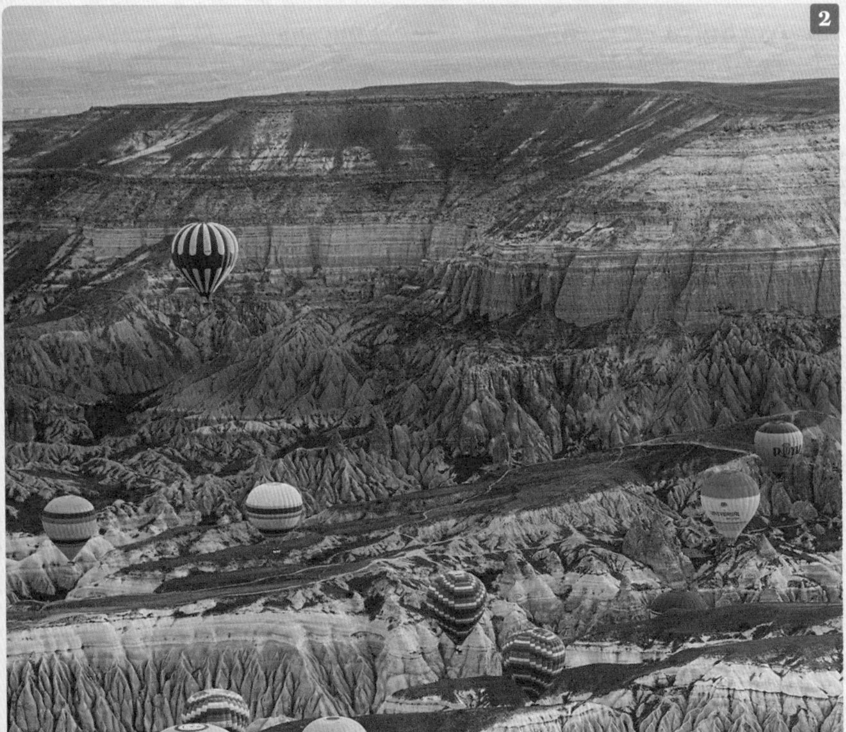

Aya Sofya

3 Even in mighty İstanbul, nothing beats the Aya Sofya (p66), or Church of the Divine Wisdom, which was for centuries the greatest church in Christendom. Emperor Justinian had it built in the 6th century, as part of his mission to restore the greatness of the Roman Empire; gazing up at the floating dome, it's hard to believe this fresco-covered marvel didn't single-handedly revive Rome's fortunes. Glittering mosaics depict biblical scenes and ancient figures such as Empress Zoe, one of only three standalone Byzantine empresses.

Ephesus

4 Undoubtedly the most famous of Turkey's countless ancient sites, and considered the best-preserved ruins in the Mediterranean, Ephesus (Efes; p226) is a powerful tribute to Greek artistry and Roman architectural prowess. A stroll down the marble-coated Curetes Way provides myriad photo opportunities – not least the Library of Celsus with its two storeys of columns, and the Terrace Houses, their vivid frescoes and sophisticated mosaics giving insight into the daily lives of the city's elite. Right: Library of Celsus (p227)

Lycian Way

5 Acclaimed as one of the world's top 10 long-distance walks, the Lycian Way (p334) follows signposted paths for 500km between Fethiye and Antalya. This is the Teke Peninsula, once the stamping ground of the ancient and mysterious Lycian civilisation. The route leads through pine and cedar forests in the shadow of mountains rising almost 3000m, passing villages, stunning coastal views and an embarrassment of ruins at ancient cities such as Pınara, Xanthos, Letoön and Olympos. Walk it in sections (unless you have plenty of time and stamina).

PGFACTORY/GETTY IMAGES ©

Beaches

6 Turkey's beaches are world famous, offering a summer mix of sun, sand and azure waters. Topping the list are Mediterranean and Aegean beauties such as Kaputaş (p348), a tiny cove with dazzling shallows near Kalkan, and Patara, Turkey's longest beach. Many of the finest Mediterranean *plajlar* (beaches) dot the Lycian Way footpath, while stretches of Aegean sand offer activities such as windsurfing in Alaçatı, Akyaka and Gökçeada. The Black Sea coast also has its charms, and the beaches around the historic towns of Amasra and Sinop are perennially popular with Turkish tourists.

Kekova Island

7 Cruise to the underwater ruins fringing this Mediterranean isle or stay beneath the Crusader fortress in neighbouring Kaleköy ('Castle Village'), its pensions, fish restaurants and Lycian sarcophagi reached by boat or the Lycian Way footpath. Kekova Island (p361) is skirted by the remains of Lycian Simena, which was submerged following a series of severe earthquakes in the 2nd century AD. From a kayak or glass-bottomed boat, you can see shattered amphorae, building foundations, staircases and moorings disappearing into the Mediterranean depths.

Ani

8 Ani (p543) is a truly exceptional site. Historically intriguing, culturally compelling and scenically magical, this ghost city floating in a sea of grass looks like a movie set. Lying in blissful isolation right at the Armenian border, the site exudes an eerie ambience. Before its decline following a Mongol sacking in 1236, Ani was a thriving city, a Silk Road entrepôt and capital of the Armenian kingdom from 961 to 1046. The ruins include several notable churches as well as a cathedral built between 987 and 1010. Above right: Church of the Redeemer (p543)

Hamams

9 At many hamams in Turkey, plenty of extras are on offer: bath treatments, facials, pedicures and so on. However, we recommend you stick with the tried and true hamam experience – a soak and a scrub followed by a good (and optional) pummelling. After this cleansing ritual and cultural experience, the world (and your body) will never feel quite the same again; do leave time to relax with a çay afterwards. For a truly memorable hamam, seek out a soak in Antalya's atmospheric old quarter or historic Sultanahmet, İstanbul (p107).

/ GETTY IMAGES ©

NEIL OVERY/GETTY IMAGES ©

Gület Cruising

10 Known locally as a 'blue voyage' (*mavi yolculuk*), a cruise lasting four days and three nights on a *gület* (traditional wooden sailing boat; pictured) along the western Mediterranean's Turquoise Coast is the highlight of many a trip to Turkey. The cruises offer opportunities to explore isolated beaches, watch sunsets and truly get away from it all, offshore and offline – a rare treat nowadays. The usual route is Fethiye (p331) to Olympos, stopping at Mediterranean highlights such as Butterfly Valley, though aficionados say the Fethiye to Marmaris route is even prettier.

Gallipoli Peninsula

11 The narrow stretch of land (p153) guarding the entrance to the much-contested Dardanelles is a beautiful area, where pine trees roll across hills above Eceabat's backpacker hang-outs and Kilitbahir's castle. Touring the peaceful countryside is a poignant experience for many: memorials and cemeteries mark the spots where, a century ago, young men from far away fought and died in gruelling conditions. The passionate guides do a good job of evoking the futility and tragedy of the Gallipoli campaign, one of WWI's worst episodes.

Meyhanes

12 Say *şerefe* (cheers) to Efes-drinking Turks in a *meyhane* (tavern). A raucous night mixing meze with rakı (anise spirit) and live music is a time-honoured Turkish activity. Melon, white cheese and fish go particularly well with the *aslan sütü* (lion's milk; the clear rakı turns white when added to water) and the soundtrack ranges from romantic ballads to *fasıl,* lively local gypsy music. A great place to sample Turkish nightlife is Beyoğlu, İstanbul (p123), where the *meyhane* precincts around İstiklal Caddesi heave with people on Friday and Saturday nights.

Bazaar Shopping

13 Turkey's markets range from İstanbul's clamorous Grand Bazaar (p85) to its colourful, fragrant Spice Bazaar; and from the traditional shadow puppets in Bursa's *kapalı çarşı* (covered market) to the mixed sack of Ottoman tiles, nargiles (water pipes) and Spider-Man suits in Antalya's İki Kapılar Hanı. To take home the finest Turkish carpets you need a sultan's fortune, but don't be discouraged. Find something you like, drink some çay with the shopkeeper, and accept that you might not bag the best deal but at least you'll have honed your haggling skills. Below: Grand Bazaar (p85), İstanbul

Sumela Monastery

14 The cliff-face location of Sumela Monastery (p514) is more than matched by the Black Sea hinterland's verdant scenery. The gently winding road to the Byzantine monastery twists past riverside fish restaurants, and your journey from nearby Trabzon may be pleasantly hindered by a herd of sheep en route to fresh pastures. The last few kilometres afford tantalising glimpses across pine-covered valleys of Sumela's honey-coloured walls, and the final approach on foot leads up a forest path to the rock-cut retreat. Sumela is set to reopen after restoration is completed in 2017.

Nemrut Dağı
(Mt Nemrut)

15 One man's megalomania echoes across the centuries atop Nemrut Dağı's (p550) exposed summit, home to a 1st-century BC king's monumental burial ground. An emerging sunrise coaxes shadows from the mountain's giant sculpted heads, and as dawn breaks the finer details of the landscape below are added. As you huddle against the chill of a new morning, a warming glass of çay could not be more welcome. And when your time on the summit is complete, don't miss the Roman bridge crossing the nearby Cendere River.

Pamukkale

16 Famed for its intricate series of travertines (p308; calcite shelves), and crowned by the ruined Roman and Byzantine spa city of Hierapolis, the 'Cotton Castle' – a bleach-white mirage by day and alien ski slope by night – is one of Turkey's most unusual treasures. Explore ruins such as the Roman theatre and soak your feet in the thermal water filling the crystal travertines, then tiptoe down to Pamukkale village past a line of the saucer-shaped formations. An optional extra is a dunk in Hierapolis' Antique Pool amid toppled marble columns.

Whirling Dervishes

17 The *sema* (whirling dervish ceremony) crackles with spiritual energy as the robe-clad dervishes spin, a constellation of dancers performing this trance-like ritual. The ceremony begins and ends with chanted passages from the Koran and is rich with symbolism; the dervishes' felt hats represent their tombstones, as the dance signifies relinquishing earthly life to be reborn in mystical union with God. You can see a *sema* in locations including İstanbul, Cappadocia, Bursa and Konya; Konya's Mevlâna Museum (p443) gives insight into the mystical Mevlevi, the original whirling dervishes.

Datça & Bozburun Peninsulas

18 These mountainous peninsulas (p279), stretching lazily from Marmaris towards the Greek island of Symi, form a scenic dividing line between the Aegean and Mediterranean. From *gület*-building Bozburun village to the ruins of Knidos at the tip of the Datça Peninsula, the adjoining fingers of land mix holiday charm with rustic tranquility. Eski Datça (Old Datça) has cobbled lanes and bougainvillea-draped stone houses, while Selimiye is an up-and-coming village with good restaurants. Top right: Knidos (p282)

Safranbolu

19 Listed for eternal preservation by Unesco in 1994, Safranbolu (p423) is Turkey's prime example of an Ottoman town brought back to life. Domestic tourists full of nostalgia descend here to stay in half-timbered houses that seem torn from the pages of a children's storybook. And the magic doesn't end there. Sweets and saffron vendors line the cobblestone alleyways, and artisans and cobblers ply their centuries-old trades beneath medieval mosques. When the summer storms light up the night sky, the fantasy is complete.

Need to Know

For more information, see Survival Guide (p589)

Currency
Türk Lirası (Turkish lira; ₺)

Language
Turkish, Kurdish

Visas
For stays of up to 90 days, most Western nationalities either don't require visas or should purchase one in advance from www.evisa.gov.tr.

Money
ATMs are widely available. Credit and debit cards are accepted by most businesses in cities and tourist areas.

Mobile Phones
Most foreign phones work on international roaming. Local SIM cards are widely available and cost from ₺65, including ₺35 credit. Data bundles cost from ₺20 for 1GB. Networks block unregistered foreign phones after 120 days.

Time
Eastern European Summer Time all year round (GMT/UTC plus three hours)

When to Go

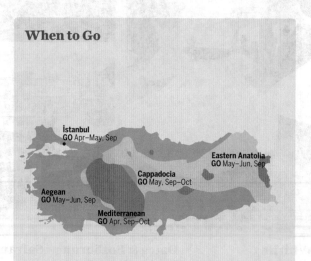

İstanbul
GO Apr–May, Sep

Eastern Anatolia
GO May–Jun, Sep

Cappadocia
GO May, Sep–Oct

Aegean
GO May–Jun, Sep

Mediterranean
GO Apr, Sep–Oct

Desert, dry climate
Warm to hot summers, mild winters
Mild to hot summers, cold winters

High Season
(Jun–Aug)

➡ Prices and temperatures highest

➡ Expect crowds, book ahead

➡ Turkish school holidays mid-June to mid-September

➡ Christmas–New Year and Easter also busy

Shoulder
(May & Sep)

➡ Fewer crowds, apart from around Kurban Bayramı holiday (currently late August/early September)

➡ Warm spring and autumn temperatures, especially in the southwest

Low Season
(Oct–Apr)

➡ October is autumn; spring starts in April

➡ Accommodations in tourist areas close or offer discounts

➡ High season in ski resorts

➡ İstanbul's low season is November to March

Useful Websites

Lonely Planet (www.lonely planet.com/turkey) Destination information, hotel bookings, traveller forum and more.

Turkey Travel Planner (www.turkeytravelplanner.com) Useful travel info.

Turkish Cultural Foundation (www.turkishculture.org) Culture and heritage; useful for archaeological sites.

Go Turkey (www.goturkey.com) Official tourism portal.

Good Morning Turkey (www.goodmorningturkey.com) Turkish news in English and Turkish.

All About Turkey (www.allaboutturkey.com) Multilingual introduction.

Important Numbers

Turkey country code	☑90
International access code from Turkey	☑00
Ambulance	☑112
Fire	☑110
Police	☑155

Exchange Rates

Australia	A$1	₺2.12
Canada	C$1	₺2.14
Europe	€1	₺3.31
Japan	¥100	₺2.60
New Zealand	NZ$1	₺1.95
UK	£1	₺3.99
USA	US$1	₺2.95

For current exchange rates see www.xe.com.

Daily Costs

Budget: Less than ₺150

➡ Dorm bed: €7–24

➡ İstanbul–Gallipoli Peninsula bus ticket: ₺45

➡ *Balık ekmek* (fish kebap): ₺8–10

➡ Beer: ₺7–12

Midrange: ₺150–350

➡ Double room ₺90–180

➡ Double in İstanbul and Bodrum: €90–200

➡ İstanbul–Cappadocia flight: from ₺50

➡ Fish and meze meal: ₺40

➡ Boat day trip: ₺35

Top end: More than ₺350

➡ Double room: more than ₺180

➡ Double in İstanbul and Bodrum: more than €200

➡ Four-day *gület* cruise: €200–300

➡ Hot-air balloon flight: €160–175

➡ Car hire per day: from €20

Opening Hours

We've provided summer high-season opening hours in our coverage; hours will generally decrease in the shoulder and low seasons. The following are standard opening hours.

Information 8.30am-noon and 1.30-5pm Monday to Friday

Eating 11am-10pm

Drinking 4pm-late

Nightclubs 11pm-late

Shopping 9am-6pm Monday to Friday (longer in tourist areas and big cities – including weekend opening)

Government departments, offices and banks 8.30am-noon and 1.30-5pm Monday to Friday

Arriving in Turkey

Atatürk International Airport (p136; İstanbul) Metro and tram to Sultanahmet (₺8, 6am to midnight, one hour); Havataş bus to Taksim Meydanı (₺11, 4am to 1am, 45 minutes); taxi to Sultanahmet (₺45, 35 minutes), taxi to Beyoğlu (₺55, 45 minutes).

Sabiha Gökçen International Airport (p136; İstanbul) Havataş bus to Taksim Meydanı (₺14, 3.30am to 1am, 1½ hours), from where a funicular (₺4) and tram (₺4) travel to Sultanahmet (30 minutes); Havataş bus to Kadıköy (₺9, 4am to 1am, one hour); taxi to Sultanahmet (₺155, 1¼ hours) and Beyoğlu (₺140, one hour).

Büyük İstanbul Otogarı (p136; İstanbul) The metro service between Aksaray and Atatürk International Airport runs to Zeytinburnu (₺4), from where trams continue to Sultanahmet and Kabataş/Taksim (₺4, one hour total); a taxi to Sultanahmet or Taksim Meydanı costs about ₺35 (30 minutes).

Getting Around

Bus Generally efficient and good value. Frequent services between major cities and tourist spots. Often fewer services in winter.

Air Domestic flights reduce travel time. More route choices if flying to/from İstanbul.

Train The growing network of high-speed services offers rapid routes across Anatolia. The bus is often quicker than normal trains.

Car A great way to explore rural areas, with rental operators in cities and airports. Drive on the right. Petrol is expensive.

Ferry Regular services cross the Sea of Marmara and link parts of the Aegean coast.

For much more on **getting around**, see p604

First Time Turkey

For more information, see Survival Guide (p589)

Checklist

➡ Check your passport will be valid for at least six months after entering Turkey.

➡ Check if you need a visa and purchase it at www.evisa.gov.tr.

➡ Inform your credit-card provider of your travel plans.

➡ Check travel vaccinations are up to date.

➡ Book flights and hire car online.

➡ Book accommodation for popular areas.

➡ Organise airport transfer.

What to Pack

➡ Passport

➡ Photocopy of passport – to take out and about

➡ Paper copy of e-visa

➡ Credit and debit cards

➡ Bank's contact details

➡ Back-up euros/dollars

➡ Oral rehydration salts

➡ Conservative clothing for mosque visits

➡ Toilet roll/paper

➡ Soap or hand sanitiser

➡ Chargers and adaptor

➡ Insurer's contact details

Top Tips for Your Trip

➡ Turkey is like a few countries rolled into one; the east is sparsely populated and devoutly Muslim, whereas much of the Aegean, Mediterranean and İstanbul are more Westernised.

➡ Turkey is predominantly Muslim, but certainly tolerant and welcoming to non-Muslims.

➡ Tourist areas are mostly well developed and the infrastructure runs efficiently.

➡ Turkey is a nationalistic country: Turkish flags and portraits of founding father Atatürk abound; be respectful, as Turks are extremely proud.

➡ Make an effort to get off the beaten track; village hospitality and home cooking are memorable experiences.

➡ Suicide bombers have brought negative publicity, but Turkey remains largely safe.

➡ Marches and demonstrations are a regular occurence, but best avoided as they can lead to clashes with the police.

What to Wear

İstanbul and the Aegean and Mediterranean resort towns are used to Western dress, including bikinis on the beach and short skirts in nightclubs. In eastern and central Anatolia, people are conservative; even men should stick to long trousers. In staunchly Islamic cities such as Erzurum, even T-shirts and sandals are inadvisable. Women do not need to cover their head unless they enter a mosque. To decrease the likelihood of receiving unwanted attention from local men with misconceptions about Western women's 'availability', dress on the conservative side throughout Turkey.

Sleeping

It's generally unnecessary to book accommodation in advance. However, if you are visiting a popular place such as İstanbul or Bodrum in high season, it's worth reserving well ahead. Turkey has a range of accommodation options to suit every budget; see p590 for more information.

Islam & Ramazan

Turkey is predominantly Islamic, but tolerant of other religions and lifestyles. This is especially true in western Turkey, where there are as many bars as mosques and it is sometimes easy to forget you are in an Islamic country. Do bear in mind, however, that Ramazan, the holy month when Muslims fast between dawn and dusk, currently falls in May and June. Cut the locals some slack; they might be grumpy if they are fasting in hot weather. Don't eat, drink or smoke in public during the day, and if you aren't a fasting Muslim, don't go to an *iftar* (evening meal to break the fast) tent for cheap food.

Bargaining

Haggling is common in bazaars, as well as for out-of-season accommodation and long taxi journeys. In other instances, you're expected to pay the stated price.

Tipping

Turkey is fairly European in its approach to tipping and you won't be pestered for baksheesh. Tipping is customary in restaurants, hotels and taxis; optional elsewhere.

Restaurants A few coins in budget eateries; 10% to 15% of the bill in midrange and top-end establishments.

Hotel porter Give 3% of the room price in midrange and top-end hotels only.

Taxis Round up metered fares to the nearest 50 kuruş.

MATT MUNRO/LONELY PLANET ©

Language

English is widely spoken in İstanbul and touristy parts of western Turkey; less so in eastern and central Anatolia, where knowing a few Turkish phrases, covering relevant topics such as accommodation, is invaluable. Learning a few Turkish phrases is also appreciated by Turks. Turkish is fun to learn as pronunciation is easy. Learning Turkish is more useful than Kurdish, as most Kurds speak Turkish (but not vice versa). Many Turks speak German.

Etiquette

Religion Dress modestly and be respectful around mosques.

Restaurants Generally, whoever extended the invitation to eat together picks up the bill.

Alcohol Bars are common, but public drinking and inebriation are less acceptable away from tourist towns.

Greetings Turks value respect; when meeting a group of people, shake hands with all, male and female.

Relationships Do not be overly tactile with your partner in public; beware miscommunications with locals.

Politics Use tact; criticising Turkish nationalism can land you in prison.

Shopping Visiting the bazaar, be prepared to haggle and drink tea with shopkeepers.

Queues Turks can be pushy in public situations; be assertive.

What's New

New Museums

Set to open in 2017, the Troy Museum (p170) will be a stunning showcase of the treasures of past centuries, while Ankara's new Erimtan Archaeology & Arts Museum (p414) houses an astounding collection of mostly Roman artefacts. The capital's Museum of Anatolian Civilisations (p411) is now fully renovated, with its entire collection on display, and the new Bodrum Maritime Museum (p260) explores the peninsula's maritime past through finely crafted scale models of boats.

Ephesus

Plans have been approved to dredge a canal from the ancient harbour of Ephesus (Efes) to the Aegean, allowing visitors to arrive by boat and restoring the city's original identity as a port. (p226)

Ottoman Palace Kitchens

Topkapı Palace's huge kitchens (p80), which once prepared lavish imperial feasts, have reopened after painstaking renovations. Likewise, Dolmabahçe Palace's kitchens now house İstanbul's Palace Collections Museum (p99).

Museum Pass

In addition to İstanbul, discount cards now cover museums and sights in Cappadocia (including Göreme Open-Air Museum), the Aegean (including Ephesus and Pergamum), the Mediterranean, and the whole of Turkey. (p592)

Ephesus Museum

Selçuk's museum of artefacts from Ephesus has reopened following renovations, displaying works such as the phallic effigy of Priapus and two multi-breasted marble statues of Artemis. (p234)

Activities

New offerings include a children's Grand Bazaar scavenger hunt (p108), a hop-on, hop-off Golden Horn ferry tour (p105), Culinary Backstreets' İzmir walking tour (p203), and Cappadocia's Cappadox arts festival in May (p465).

İstanbul Regeneration

The historic Balat neighbourhood (p90) on the Golden Horn is being revitalised; Tophane (p93) has become a design precinct; and on İstanbul's Asian side, once-dishevelled Yeldeğirmeni (p99) has gained cultural cred.

Hiking

The world's longest cable car, Bursa's 8.2km Teleferik (p301), whisks fresh-air fiends up Uludağ (2543m). Apollonia Lodge in Boğazcık village gives Lycian Way hikers a stop-off between Kaş and Üçağız (p360).

Architectural Triumphs

Stunning restorations include Istanbul's Nuruosmaniye Mosque (p90), the Grand Synagogue of Edirne (p147) and Antakya's Church of St Peter (p406), while İstanbul's tile-encrusted Hünkâr Kasrı pavilion (p89) is now open to the public.

For more recommendations and reviews, see lonelyplanet.com/Turkey

If You Like...

Bazaars

Centuries ago, Seljuk and Ottoman traders travelled the Silk Road, stopping at caravanserais to do business. The tradition is still alive and so is haggling in Turkey's labyrinthine bazaars.

Grand Bazaar Hone your bargaining skills in İstanbul's original and best shopping mall. (p85)

Kapalı Çarşı Bursa's 14th-century Old Mirrored Market houses shadow-puppet shops. (p293)

Spice Bazaar Jewel-like *lokum* (Turkish delight) and pyramids of spices provide eye candy at İstanbul's fragrant bazaar. (p89)

Kemeraltı Market İzmir's labyrinthine bazaar features shops, eateries, artisans' workshops, mosques, coffeehouses, tea gardens and synagogues. (p199)

Hamams

Hamams are also known as Turkish baths, a name coined by Europeans introduced to their steamy pleasures by the Ottomans. Have a massage or just soak in the calming atmosphere.

Sefa Hamamı This restored 13th-century gem in Kaleiçi (Old Antalya) retains many of its Seljuk features. (p367)

Kılıç Ali Paşa Hamamı The service matches the stunning interior of this restored 16th-century İstanbul hamam. (p107)

Yeni Kaplıca 'New thermal bath' is actually Bursa's oldest, founded by the 6th-century Byzantine emperor Justinian I. (p296)

Kelebek Turkish Bath Spa Cappadocia's most luxurious hamam experience, with a full range of spa-style added extras. (p458)

Beaches

Turkey is surrounded by the Mediterranean, the Aegean, the Black Sea and the Sea of Marmara, offering numerous beaches for reclining by the 'wine-dark sea' (as Homer called the Aegean).

Kaputaş The pale sandy cove and brilliant azure waters near Kalkan look brochure-perfect. (p348)

Kabak Take a steep ride or follow the Lycian Way down to this Mediterranean beach hideaway. (p342)

Patara One of the Mediterranean's longest beaches, with 18km of white sand, ruins and sea turtles. (p347)

Ayazma A ruined Greek Orthodox monastery overlooks Bozcaada's best beach. (p177)

Gökçeada You might have the little-visited Aegean island's beaches to yourself. (p172)

Kızkalesi Warm water invites you to swim to the 12th-century Byzantine fortress just offshore. (p393)

History

Turks are proud of their long, eventful history, and it's easy to share their enthusiasm at the country's mosques and palaces, ruins and museums.

Topkapı Palace İstanbul's historic significance can be felt everywhere, but particularly in the greatest Ottoman palace. (p76)

Gallipoli Peninsula Poignant memorials and cemeteries recall the battles fought here in WWI. (p154)

Kayaköy Places like this ghost town recall the Greeks displaced by a century-old population exchange. (p339)

Zelve Open-Air Museum Turkey's many Christian sites include these rock-cut monasteries in a Cappadocian valley. (p467)

Hattuşa Explore off the beaten track to the capitals of Anatolian civilisations, including the Hittite HQ. (p428)

Food & Drink

Turkey has epicurean indulgence nailed, from street snacks to gourmet restaurants. Not only does every region offer local dishes, you can sample them in individualistic eateries and panoramic terraces.

Cappadocia Home Cooking Sample true home-style Cappadocian cooking, surrounded by the family's organic garden in a valley village. (p483)

Limon Aile Lokantası On the Bodrum Peninsula, Limon offers an original take on the much-loved Aegean meze-and-seafood experience. (p271)

Alex's Place One of the hole-in-the-wall cocktail bars taking over in fashionable Beyoğlu, İstanbul. (p124)

Hatay Sultan Sofrası The mezes and spicy kebaps are good examples of Antakya's Syrian and Arab culinary influences. (p408)

Zeytin Bağı Overlooking the Bay of Edremit, this foodie retreat serves what may be Turkey's best breakfast. (p184)

Activities

Turkey's many outdoor activities make the most of its beautiful and diverse terrain, from mountain ranges to beaches – and çay and baklava, or Efes beer and meze, await afterwards.

Walking Opportunities range from half-day wanders through

Top: Diving, Kaş (p354)
Bottom: Süleymaniye Mosque (p85), one of İstanbul's architectural triumphs

Cappadocia's valleys to 500km Mediterranean trails. (p37)

Saklıkent Gorge The 18km-long fissure near Fethiye is Turkey's top spot for canyoning. (p344)

Water Sports On the Aegean and Mediterranean, diving, windsurfing, kiteboarding, canoeing and waterskiing are on offer. (p40)

Yusufeli Northeastern Anatolia's activity capital offers adrenaline-pumping white-water rafting and mountain walking. (p532)

Kekova Island Sea kayak over walls, shattered amphorae and other remains of the Lycian 'sunken city'. (p361)

Uludağ National Park The ski resort above Bursa is one of several across the country. (p301)

Ruins

Whether in a city centre or atop a craggy cliff, the country's ruins bring out the historical romantic in you. Excavations continue at many, giving new glimpses of ancient history.

Ephesus (Efes) The best-preserved classical city in the eastern Mediterranean evokes daily life in Roman times. (p226)

Nemrut Dağı Atop Mt Nemrut are the toppled heads of statues built by a 1st-century-BC king. (p550)

Pergamum The Hellenistic theatre is a vertigo-inducing marvel and the Asclepion was Rome's pre-eminent medical centre. (p192)

Ani The 10th-century Armenian capital features fascinating remnants of ancient cultures, from Georgian to Zoroastrian. (p543)

Landscape

Apart from a toe sticking into Europe, Turkey is part of Asia, so it should come as no surprise that its landscapes are varied and stunning.

Cappadocia The fairy chimneys (rock formations) and smooth valleys are best explored on foot or horseback. (p451)

Mt Ararat Turkey's highest peak (5137m) is typical of northeastern Anatolia's rugged scenery. (p549)

Amasra to Sinop A great drive takes you past Black Sea beaches and green hills. (p500)

Behramkale The hillside village has dreamy views of the Aegean coast. (p180)

Eğirdir Gölü The mountain-ringed Anatolian lake, like those at Bafa and İznik, is among Turkey's unsung glories. (p315)

Datça & Bozburun Peninsulas Raw landscape dividing the Aegean and Mediterranean, riddled with coves and pine forests. (p279)

Nemrut Dağı Mountain-top stone heads gaze at the Anti-Taurus Range. (p550)

Ala Dağlar National Park Waterfalls crash down limestone cliffs in the Taurus Mountains. (p488)

Architecture

Turkey's legacy of mighty empires has left a bounty of imposing buildings: palaces, mosques, churches, monasteries and caravansaries are a few of the ancient structures evoking bygone eras.

Aya Sofya The greatest surviving Byzantine building, just one of the glorious edifices in Sultanahmet, İstanbul. (p66)

İshak Paşa Palace Perched above the steppe, this 18th-century pile mixes Seljuk, Ottoman, Georgian, Persian and Armenian styles. (p546)

Ulu Cami & Darüşşifası Stone portal carvings so intricate that locals say they prove the existence of God. (p438)

Safranbolu From this heritage town to the Aegean's old Greek villages, boutique hotels occupy Ottoman mansions. (p423)

İstanbul Naval Museum The exhibition hall, displaying 19th-century rowboats, is among İstanbul's attractive contemporary gallery and museum buildings. (p99)

Museums

In a country marked by great dynasties, from Hittite hill men to Ottoman sultans, every self-respecting town has a museum to preserve its local history.

İstanbul Archaeology Museums İstanbul's museums range from long-standing institutions like this complex in Gülhane Park to contemporary galleries. (p83)

Göreme Open-Air Museum Only in surreal Cappadocia could a valley of rock-cut Byzantine churches be called a museum. (p454)

Museum of Anatolian Civilisations Ankara's star attraction examines the ancient civilisations that warred and waned on the surrounding steppe. (p411)

Ephesus Museum Selçuk's fine collection contains artefacts from Ephesus, including the famous effigy of phallic god Priapus. (p234)

Amasra (p498)

Museum of Underwater Archaeology Housed in Bodrum's 15th-century Castle of St Peter, it displays bounty from ancient shipwrecks. (p259)

İzmir Museum of History & Art One of Turkey's richest repositories of artefacts, including stunning sculptures from the Aegean's ancient sites. (p199)

Hatay Archaeology Museum Reopened in new premises that do justice to Antakya's great collection of classical mosaics. (p405)

Cities

Turks are a regionalist bunch; they will invariably tell you their town is *en çok güzel* (the most beautiful) – but these are the best places to experience urban Turkey.

İstanbul The world's only city on two continents, the megacity was once the capital of empires. (p58)

Antalya The classically beautiful and stylishly modern gateway to the Turkish Riviera. (p365)

İzmir Turkey's third-largest city is right on the Aegean; its *kordon* (seafront promenade) is a joy. (p198)

Antakya (Hatay) The site of the biblical Antioch has a distinctively Arabic feel. (p405)

Konya The Anatolian boomtown is historical and mystical with its Seljuk architecture and whirling dervish heritage. (p442)

Boutique Hotels

From half-timbered Ottoman mansions to Greek stone houses, Turkey's architectural gems are increasingly being converted into small, one-off hotels. These distinctive properties offer a local experience with a stylish twist.

Kelebek Hotel Take up residence in a fairy chimney and experience troglodyte life in luxury. (p460)

Alaçatı Scores of the Aegean village's stone Greek houses have been converted into boutique digs. (p217)

Safranbolu Among rocky bluffs, the fairy-tale town is an idyllic setting for hotels in Ottoman piles. (p425)

White Garden Pansion A smattering of boutique hotels adds further charm to Antalya's Roman-Ottoman old quarter. (p369)

Nişanyan Hotel A 19th-century renovated stone house in the hill village of Şirince near Ephesus. (p242)

Month by Month

January

The dead of winter. Even İstanbul's streets are empty of crowds, local and foreign, and snow closes eastern Anatolia's mountain passes and delays buses. Accommodation in tourist areas is mostly closed.

🎉 New Year's Day

A surrogate Christmas takes place across the Islamic country, with decorations, exchanges of gifts and greeting cards. Celebrations begin on New Year's Eve and continue through this public holiday. Over Christmas and New Year, accommodation fills up and prices rise.

March

As in the preceding months, you might have sights to yourself outside the country's top destinations, and you can get discounts at accommodation options that are open.

☆ İzmir European Jazz Festival

This jazz festival fills the Aegean city with a high-profile lineup of European and local performers. Gigs, workshops, seminars and a garden party make this a lively time for jazz lovers to visit. (p206)

🎉 Çanakkale Naval Victory

On 18 March Turks descend on the Gallipoli (Gelibolu) Peninsula and Çanakkale to celebrate what they call the Çanakkale Naval Victory – and commemorate the WWI campaign's 130,000 fatalities. The area, particularly the Turkish memorials in the southern peninsula, is thronged with visitors. (p165)

🍴 Mesir Festival, Manisa

An altogether different way of marking the spring equinox, Manisa's Unesco-protected festival celebrates *Mesir macunu* (Mesir paste), a scrumptious treat made from dozens of spices that once cured Süleyman the Magnificent's mother of illness. Takes place over a week around 21 March. (p213)

April

Spring. April and May are high season in İstanbul and shoulder season elsewhere. Not a great month to get a tan in northern Turkey, but you can enjoy balmy, breezy weather in the southwest.

🍴 Alaçatı Herb Festival

The Alaçatı Herb Festival is a great time to visit the culinary-minded Aegean town, home to many fine restaurants and boutique hotels. The festival celebrates the unique local herbs, with many opportunities to enjoy the dishes they flavour. (p217)

🎉 İstanbul Tulip Festival

İstanbul's parks and gardens are resplendent with tulips, which originated in Turkey before being exported to the Netherlands during the Ottoman era. Multicoloured tulips are often planted to resemble the Turks' cherished 'evil eye'. Flowers bloom from late March or early April. (p108)

☆ İstanbul Film Festival

For a filmic fortnight, cinemas around town host a packed program of Turkish and international films and events. An excellent crash course in Turkish cinema, but book ahead. (p108)

🎎 Anzac Day, Gallipoli Peninsula

On 25 April the WWI battles for the Dardanelles are commemorated and the Allied soldiers remembered. Antipodean pilgrims sleep at Anzac Cove before the dawn services; a busy time on the peninsula. (p160)

May

Another good month to visit. Shoulder season continues outside İstanbul, with attendant savings, but spring is flirting with summer and the Aegean and Mediterranean beaches are heating up.

🏄 Windsurfing, Alaçatı

In Turkey's windsurfing centre, Alaçatı, the season begins in mid-May. The protected Aegean bay hosts the Windsurf World Cup in August and the season winds down in early November, when many of the eight resident schools close. (p218)

◉ Ruins, Mosques, Palaces & Museums

This is your last chance until September to see the main attractions at famous Aegean and Mediterranean sights such as Ephesus without major crowds, which can become almost unbearable at the height of summer.

🏃 Dedegöl Mountaineering Festival, Eğirdir

Dedegöl Mountaineering Festival sees Eğirdir's mountaineering club scramble up Mt Dedegöl (2998m), now spring is thawing the Taurus Mountains. Register to join the free two-day event (19 May), which includes a night at the base camp. (p317)

☆ International Bursa Festival

The International Bursa Festival, the city's 2½-week music and dance jamboree, features diverse regional and world music, plus an international headliner or two. Free performances are offered and tickets for top acts are around ₺40. Begins in mid-May. (p297)

🎎 Cappadox Festival, Uçhisar

Cappadocia's three-day arts festival merges music, nature walks, art exhibitions, yoga and gastronomy into an extravaganza of Turkish contemporary culture, highlighting the area's natural beauty. (p465)

June

Summer. Shoulder season in İstanbul and high season

elsewhere until the end of August. Expect sizzling temperatures, inflexible hotel prices and crowds at sights – often avoided by visiting early, late or at lunchtime.

🎎 Çamlıhemşin Ayder Festival, Ayder

Held over the first or second weekend in June, this popular early-summer festival highlights Hemşin culture with folk dance and music. It also features northeast Turkey's bloodless form of bullfighting, *boğa güreşleri*, in which two bulls push at each other until one backs off. (p531)

☆ İstanbul Music Festival

Probably Turkey's most important arts festival, featuring performances of opera, dance, orchestral concerts and chamber recitals. Acts are often internationally renowned and the action takes place at atmosphere-laden venues such as Aya İrini, the Byzantine church in the Topkapı Palace grounds. (p108)

🎎 Historic Kırkpınar Oil Wrestling Festival, Edirne

In a sport dating back over 650 years, brawny *pehlivan* (wrestlers) from across Turkey rub themselves from head to foot with olive oil and grapple. Late June or early July. (p149)

July

This month and August turn the Aegean and Mediterranean tourist heartlands into sun-

and-fun machines, and temperatures peak across the country. The blue skies bring out the best in the hot-blooded Turkish personality.

🏃 Mountain Walking

Between the Black Sea coast and the Anatolian steppe, the snow clears from the passes in the Kaçkar Mountains (Kaçkar Dağları), allowing multiday treks and sublime *yaylalar* (highland pastures) views in July and August. www.cultureroutesinturkey.com.

☆ Music Festivals

Turkey enjoys a string of summer music jamborees, including highbrow festivals in İstanbul, Bursa and İzmir. The cities host multiple pop, rock, jazz and dance music events, while summer playgrounds such as Alaçatı and the Bodrum Peninsula turn into mini-Ibizas. June to August.

August

Even at night, the weather is hot and humid; pack sun cream and anti-mosquito spray. Walking and activities are best tackled early in the morning or at sunset.

🎇 Cappadocian Festivals

Two festivals take place in the land of fairy chimneys (rock formations). A summer series of chamber music concerts are held in the valleys and, from 16 to 18 August, sleepy Hacıbektaş comes alive with the annual pilgrimage of Bektaşi dervishes. (p459)

Top: Kaçkar Mountains (p523)
Bottom: Competitors in the Historic Kırkpınar Oil-Wrestling Festival, Edirne (p149)

September

İstanbul's second high season begins; elsewhere, it's shoulder season – temperatures, crowds and prices lessen. Accommodation and activities, such as boat trips, begin winding down for the winter.

☆ Aspendos Opera & Ballet Festival

The internationally acclaimed Aspendos Opera & Ballet Festival takes place in this atmospheric Roman theatre near Antalya (June or late August and September). (p376)

🏃 Diving

The water is warmest from May to October and you can expect water temperatures of 25°C in September. Turkey's scuba-diving centre is Kaş on the Mediterranean, with operators also found in Marmaris, Bodrum, Kuşadası and Ayvalık on the Aegean.

🎭 İstanbul Biennial

The city's major visual-arts shindig, considered to be one of the world's most prestigious biennials, takes place from mid-September to mid-November in odd-numbered years. Venues around town host the internationally curated event. (p109)

☆ Sunsplash Festival, Bodrum

Held on Xuma Beach, Yalıkavak, at the tip of the Bodrum Peninsula, this popular mid-September music festival toasts the end of Bodrum's busy summer season with an eclectic mix of electronic, world and jazz DJs and musicians. (p271)

October

Autumn is truly here; outside İstanbul, many accommodation options have shut for the winter. Good weather is unlikely up north, but the Mediterranean and Aegean experience fresh, sunny days.

☆ Akbank Jazz Festival

Every October, İstanbul celebrates its love of jazz with this eclectic lineup of local and international performers. Going for over 25 years, it's the older sibling of July's İstanbul Jazz Festival. (p109)

🏃 Walking

The weather in eastern Anatolia has already become challenging by this time of year, but in the southwest, autumn and spring are the best seasons to enjoy the scenery without too much sweat on your brow. See www.trekkingin turkey.com and www.cari antrail.com.

November

Even on the coastlines, summer is a distant memory. Rain falls on İstanbul and the Black Sea, southern resort towns are deserted and eastern Anatolia is ensnarled in snow.

🎭 Karagöz Festival, Bursa

A week of performances celebrate the city's Karagöz shadow-puppetry heritage, with local and international puppeteers and marionette performers. Held in November of odd years. (p297)

December

Turks fortify themselves against the cold with hot çay and hearty kebaps. Most of the country is chilly and wet or icy, although the western Mediterranean is milder and day walks there are viable.

🏃 Ski Season

Hit the slopes: the Turkish ski season begins at half a dozen resorts across the country, including Cappadocia's Erciyes Dağı (Mt Erciyes), Uludağ (near Bursa), Palandöken (near Erzurum) and Sarıkamış, near Kars. Late November to early April.

☉ Snow in Anatolia

If you're really lucky, after skiing on Erciyes Dağı, you could head west and see central Cappadocia's fairy chimneys looking even more magical under a layer of snow. Eastern Anatolia is also covered in a white blanket, but temperatures are brutally low.

Itineraries

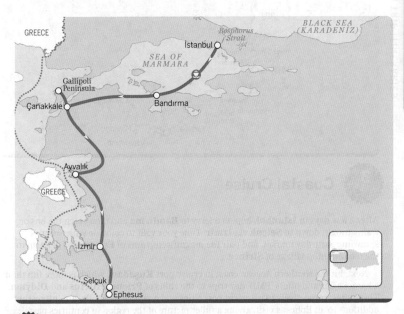

10 DAYS Classic Turkey

Most first-time visitors to Turkey arrive with two ancient names on their lips: İstanbul and Ephesus. This journey across the Sea of Marmara and down the Aegean coast covers both.

You'll need at least three days in **İstanbul** to even scrape the surface of its millennia of history. The top three sights are the Aya Sofya, Topkapı Palace and the Blue Mosque, but there's a sultan's treasury of other sights and activities, including a cruise up the Bosphorus, nightlife around İstiklal Caddesi, and the Grand Bazaar.

From İstanbul, instead of schlepping out to the city's main otogar (bus station), hop on a ferry to Bandırma. From there, you can catch a bus or train straight down to Selçuk (for Ephesus) via İzmir, but it's more interesting to head west to **Çanakkale**, a lively student town on the Dardanelles. A tour of the nearby **Gallipoli Peninsula's** poignant WWI battlefields is a memorable experience.

From Çanakkale, it's a 3½-hour bus ride to **Ayvalık**, with its tumbledown old Greek quarter and fish restaurants. Finally, another bus journey (via İzmir) reaches **Selçuk**, a pleasantly rustic town and the base for visiting glorious **Ephesus (Efes)**, the best-preserved classical city in the eastern Mediterranean.

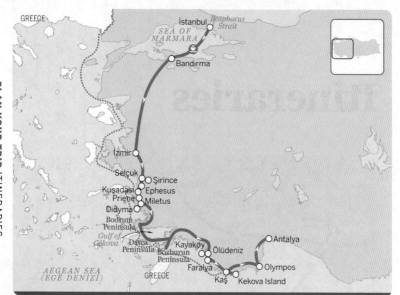

Coastal Cruise

3 WEEKS

After a few days in **İstanbul**, hop on a ferry to **Bandırma** and then catch the bus or train straight down to **Selçuk** via **İzmir**. Time your visit to coincide with Selçuk's sprawling Saturday market, and pair the magnificent ruins of **Ephesus** with a trip to the mountaintop village of **Şirince**.

Next, hit the southern Aegean coast in cruise port **Kuşadası**, which is more fun than a karaoke bar and offers 'PMD' day trips to the ruins of **Priene**, **Miletus** and **Didyma**. These sites, respectively two ancient port cities and a temple to Apollo, are interesting additions to an Ephesus visit, giving a fuller picture of the region in centuries past. Spend a day or two nibbling calamari and sipping cocktails on the chichi **Bodrum Peninsula** and cross the Gulf of Gökova by ferry to the **Datça Peninsula**. With their fishing villages and rugged hinterland of forested mountains, Datça and the adjoining Bozburun Peninsula are excellent for revving up a scooter or just putting your feet up.

Continuing along the Mediterranean coast, beautiful **Ölüdeniz** is the spot to paraglide from atop Baba Dağ (Mt Baba; 1960m) or lie low on a beach towel. While in the area, consider basing yourself in secluded **Kayaköy** with its ruined Greek town. You're now within kicking distance of the 509km-long Lycian Way. Hike for a day through superb countryside to overnight in heavenly **Faralya**, overlooking Butterfly Valley; further inroads along the trail will definitely top your 'next time' list.

Also on the Lycian Way, laid-back **Kaş**' pretty harbourside square buzzes nightly with friendly folk enjoying the sea breeze, views, fresh meze and a beer or two. One of Turkey's most beguiling boat trips departs from here, taking in the sunken Lycian city at **Kekova Island**. From Kaş, it's a couple of hours to **Olympos**, famous for the naturally occurring Chimaera flames and beach treehouses.

A 1½-hour bus journey reaches the city of **Antalya**. Its Roman-Ottoman quarter, Kaleiçi, is worth a wander, against the backdrop of a jaw-dropping mountain range. From Antalya you can fly back to İstanbul or take a nine-hour bus ride across the plains to Cappadocia.

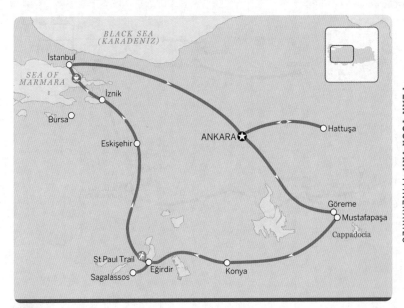

 Cappadocia Meander

From İstanbul, catch a bus or hop on the fast train to **Ankara**, the Turkish capital. The political town is no match for that show-stealer on the Bosphorus, but two key sights here give an insight into Turkish history, ancient and modern: the Anıt Kabir, Atatürk's hilltop mausoleum, and the Museum of Anatolian Civilisations, a restored 15th-century *bedesten* (covered market) packed with finds from the surrounding steppe. Tying in with the latter, a detour east takes in the isolated, evocative ruins of **Hattuşa**, which was the Hittite capital in the late Bronze Age.

Leave three days to explore Cappadocia, based in a cave hotel in **Göreme**, the travellers' hang-out surrounded by valleys of fairy chimneys. The famous rock formations line the roads to sights including Göreme Open-Air Museum's rock-cut frescoed churches and the Byzantine underground cities at Kaymaklı and Derinkuyu. Among the hot-air balloon trips, valley walks and horse riding, schedule some time to just sit and appreciate the fantastical landscape in çay-drinking villages such as **Mustafapaşa**, with its stone-carved Greek houses and 18th-century church.

Fly straight back to İstanbul or, if you have enough time and a penchant for Anatolia's mountains and steppe, continue by bus. Stop in **Konya** for lunch en route to **Eğirdir**, and tour the turquoise-domed Mevlâna Museum, containing the tomb of the Mevlâna (whirling dervish) order's 13th-century founder. Lakeside Eğirdir, with its road-connected island and crumbling old Greek quarter ringed by beaches and the Taurus Mountains (Toros Dağları), is a serene base for walking a section of the **St Paul Trail**. Possible day trips include the stunning ruins of **Sagalassos**, a Greco-Roman city at 1500m in the Taurus Mountains.

From Eğirdir, you can catch a bus back to İstanbul or fly from nearby Isparta. If spending your last night in Anatolian tranquility appeals more than the hustle-bustle of İstanbul, head to lakeside **İznik**, its Ottoman tile-making heritage on display between Roman-Byzantine walls. You will have to change buses in Eskişehir or Bursa to get there, while the final leg of the journey is a ferry across the Sea of Marmara to İstanbul.

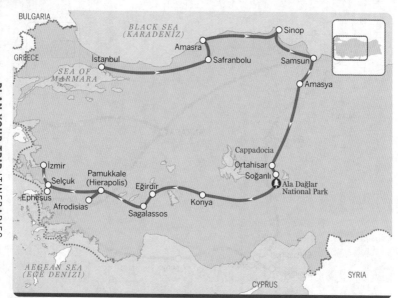

Anatolian Circle

3 WEEKS

Begin with a few days among mosques, palaces and some 14 million folk in **İstanbul**, former capital of the Ottoman and Byzantine empires. Next, head east to **Safranbolu**, with its winding streets of Ottoman mansions, before turning north to **Amasra**, where Turkish holidaymakers wander the Byzantine castle and eat fresh fish on the two harbours. Amasra is the beginning of the drive through rugged hills to **Sinop**, another pretty Black Sea port town and the birthplace of Greek philosopher Diogenes the Cynic.

Next, it's a six-hour bus journey via Samsun to **Amasya**, with its Ottoman houses, Pontic tombs and castle. Take it all in from a terrace by the Yeşilırmak River, and drink several tulip-shaped glasses of çay, before another long bus ride across the Anatolian steppe to Cappadocia. This enchanting land of fairy chimneys and cave churches is wholeheartedly back on the beaten track, but you can escape the tour buses by exploring the valleys on foot or horseback. Likewise, Göreme and Ürgüp are the usual bases, but you could stay in a less-touristy village such as **Ortahisar**, with its craggy castle. South of central Cappadocia, see rock-cut churches without the crowds in **Soğanlı**, where Byzantine monastic settlements occupy two valleys. Then head into the **Ala Dağlar National Park** for some of Turkey's most breathtaking scenery in the Taurus Mountains (Toros Dağları).

Konya, its magnificent mosques recalling its stint as capital of the Seljuk sultanate of Rum, makes a convenient lunch stop en route to Eğirdir. Lakeside **Eğirdir** has views of the Taurus Mountains and little-visited local sights such as **Sagalassos**, a ruined Greco-Roman city at an altitude of 1500m. There are more impressive classical ruins at **Hierapolis**, an ancient spa city overlooking the village of **Pamukkale** from atop the travertines, a mountain of calcite shelves. Nearby **Afrodisias**, once a Roman provincial capital, is equally incredible; you might have the 30,000-seat stadium to yourself.

From Denizli (near Pamukkale), it's just a few hours' journey by bus or train to **Selçuk**, base for visiting **Ephesus**. From Selçuk, you can fly back to İstanbul from nearby **İzmir**, or continue overland via our Classic Turkey itinerary.

Plan Your Trip

Turkey's Outdoors

Whether you want to sail over archaeological remains, tackle challenging summits or explore the countryside on horseback, Turkey offers superb playgrounds for active travellers from aspiring kayakers to dedicated skiers. Safety standards are good too, provided you stick to reputable operators with qualified, English-speaking staff.

Walking & Trekking

Walking in Turkey is increasingly popular among both Turks and travellers, and a growing number of local and foreign firms offer walking holidays here. The country is blessed with numerous mountains, from the Taurus ranges in the southwest to the Kaçkars in the northeast, which all provide fabulous hiking opportunities. Hiking is also the best way to visit villages and sights rarely seen by holidaymakers, and it will give you a taste of life in rural Turkey.

Hiking options range from challenging multi-day hikes, such as the 500km Saint Paul trail from Perge near Antalya, through rural western Anatolia, and ending near Lake Eğirdir, to gentle afternoon strolls, such as in Cappadocia.

For more information on hiking in Turkey, visit Trekking in Turkey (www.trekkinginturkey.com) and Culture Routes in Turkey (www.cultureroutesinturkey.com).

Safety Advice

Bar a few well-known and well-maintained trails, most are not signposted and it's recommended to hire a guide, or at least seek local advice before setting off.

Weather conditions can fluctuate quickly between extremes, so come prepared and check the local conditions.

Top Regions

Antalya & the Turquoise Coast
The Western Mediterranean offers the widest array of activities, including sea-kayaking, boat trips, diving, two waymarked walking trails, canyoning, rafting and paragliding.

Cappadocia
Excellent for a half- or full-day hike, with a surreal landscape of curvy valleys and fairy chimneys. There are also mountain-walking opportunities, horse-riding, and skiing on Erciyes Dağı (Mt Erciyes).

Eastern Anatolia
Head to the eastern wilds, especially the northern part, for mountain walking, white-water rafting, horse-riding, skiing, snowboarding and cross-country skiing.

South Aegean
Bring your swimming trunks to the more-popular stretch of the Aegean, where operators in spots such as Bodrum, Marmaris and Akyaka offer boat trips galore and water sports including diving, waterskiing, windsurfing and kite-boarding.

Day Walks

For half- and full-day walks, Cappadocia is unbeatable, with a dozen valleys that are easily negotiated on foot, around Göreme as well as the Ihlara Valley. These walks, one to several hours in length with minor gradients, are perfectly suited to casual walkers and even families. The fairy chimneys are unforgettable, and walking is the best way to do the landscapes and sights justice – and discover areas that travellers usually don't reach. After all, there aren't many places in the world where you can walk between a string of ancient, rock-cut churches in a lunar landscape.

Long-Distance Trails

Culture Routes in Turkey has developed two iconic waymarked trails, the Lycian Way and St Paul Trail, plus several new long-distance routes, which range from the Evliya Çelebi Way – tracing the route of the famed Ottoman traveller – to the Carian Trail in the south Aegean. The routes are best tackled in spring or autumn and don't have to be walked in their entirety; it's easy to bite off a small chunk. See the website (www.culturerou tesinturkey.com) for information, guidebooks and maps covering the trails.

Lycian Way

The Lycian Way covers 509km between Fethiye and Antalya, partly inland, partly along the coast of ancient Lycia, via Patara, Kalkan, Kaş, Finike, Olympos and Tekirova. Highlights include stunning coastal views, pine and cedar forests, laid-back villages, ruins of ancient cities, Mt Olympos and Baba Dağ. Kate Clow, who established the trail, describes it in detail in the walking guide *The Lycian Way*.

HOT-AIR BALLOONING

One of Turkey's most iconic outdoor experiences is floating above Cappadocia's undulating waves of rock valleys in a hot-air balloon. The experience is a pricey one and requires a seriously early morning wake-up call but the rolling views of the moonscape below are judged worth it by most travellers. Balloon flights are year-round but are weather dependent.

St Paul Trail

The St Paul Trail extends 500km north, from Perge, 10km east of Antalya, to Yalvaç, northeast of Eğirdir Gölü (Lake Eğirdir). Partly following the route walked by St Paul on his first missionary journey in Asia Minor, it's more challenging than the Lycian Way, with more ascents. Along the way you'll pass canyons, waterfalls, forests, a medieval paved road, Roman baths and an aqueduct, and numerous quaint villages.

St Paul Trail, by Kate Clow and Terry Richardson, describes the trail in detail. Eğirdir is a good place to base yourself, with an activities centre geared towards walking the trail.

Mountain Walks

Turkey is home to some seriously good mountain walking.

Mt Ararat Turkey's highest mountain, the majestic and challenging 5137m Mt Ararat, near the Armenian border, is one of the region's top climbs and can be tackled in five days (including acclimatisation) from nearby Doğubayazıt. You'll need to be cashed up and patient with all the bureaucracy – the mandatory permit needed to climb was not being issued during 2015 and 2016.

Kaçkar Mountains In northeastern Anatolia, the Kaçkars offer lakes, forests and varied flora, at altitudes from about 2000m to 3937m. There are numerous possible routes, ranging from a few hours to multi-day treks crossing the high passes over the mountain range.

Cappadocia The starkly beautiful Ala Dağlar National Park (part of the Taurus Mountains) in southern Cappadocia offers superb multi-day trekking opportunities, while 3268m Hasan Dağı (Mt Hasan) can be summited in one challenging day.

Horse Riding

There are numerous opportunities to get on the saddle in Turkey but Cappadocia is Turkey's top spot for riding with numerous good riding tracks criss-crossing the marvellous landscapes. Local outfits offer guided rides from one-hour jaunts to multi-day trips. Elsewhere, there are some excellent horse-riding opportunities in the countryside around Fethiye and Antalya (along part of the St Paul Trail), and multi-day riding journeys along the trail of the Evliya Çelebi Way.

Above: White-water rafting on the Manavgat River, near Side (p378)

Right: Horse riding, Nevşehir (p471)

MARK READ/LONELY PLANET ©

Water Sports

Lounging on a white-sand beach is certainly tempting, but there are many opportunities to dip your toes in the sea.

Scuba Diving

OK, the Red Sea it ain't, but where else in the world can you swim over amphorae and broken pottery from ancient shipwrecks? Turkey also offers a wide choice of reefs, drop-offs and caves. The waters are generally calm, with no tides or currents, and visibility averages 20m (not too bad by Mediterranean standards). Pelagics are rare, but small reef species are prolific. Here you can mingle with groupers, dentex, moray eels, sea bream, octopus and parrot fish, as well as the occasional amberjack, barracuda and ray. You don't need to be a strong diver; there are sites for all levels of proficiency. For experienced divers, there are superb expanses of red coral to explore (usually under 30m of water).

The standard of diving facilities is high, and you'll find professional dive centres with qualified, English-speaking instructors. Most centres are affiliated with internationally recognised dive organisations. Compared with other countries, diving in Turkey is pretty cheap, and it's a great place to learn. Most dive companies offer introductory dives for beginners and reasonably priced open-water certification courses.

While it is possible to dive all year, the best time is May to October when the water is warmest (you can expect up to 25°C in September).

Top Dive Spots

Kaş is Turkey's scuba-diving hub, with excellent Mediterranean dive sites and numerous operators. On the Aegean coast, Marmaris, Bodrum, Kuşadası and Ayvalık also have a reputation for good diving.

Sea Kayaking & Canoeing

Maps clearly show the tortuous coastline in the western Mediterranean area, with its secluded coves, deep blue bays, pine-clad mountains, islands shimmering in the distance and laid-back villages. Paddling is the best way to comfortably access pristine terrain – some inaccessible by road – and experience the breathtaking scenery of the aptly named Turquoise Coast. You might see flying fish and turtles, and if you're really lucky, frolicking dolphins.

Day trips are the norm, but longer tours can be organised with overnight camping under the stars on deserted beaches. They should include transfers, guides, gear and meals. There are also paddling spots on the Aegean coast, including Akyaka.

Top Paddling Spots

Kekova Sunken City (p359) This magical spot, with Lycian ruins partly submerged 6m below the sea, perfectly lends itself to a sea-kayaking tour from Kaş. This superb day excursion, suitable for all fitness levels, allows you to glide over underwater walls, foundations and staircases submerged by 2nd-century earthquakes, clearly visible through crystal-clear waters.

Patara (p345) Canoeing trips on the Xanthos River offer a unique opportunity to glide past jungle-like riverbanks and discover a rich ecosystem, with birds, crabs and turtles. Ending your journey on Patara beach, Turkey's longest, adds to the appeal.

Canyoning

Canyoning is a mix of climbing, hiking, abseiling, swimming and some serious jumping or plunging – down waterfalls, river gorges, and water-polished chutes in natural pools. Experience is not usually necessary, but water confidence and reasonable fitness are advantageous. Expect adventure centres offering canyoning to provide wetsuits, helmets and harnesses, and outings to be led by a qualified instructor. The 18km-long Saklıkent Gorge (p344), southeast of Fethiye, features leaping into natural pools, swimming through narrow passages, scrambling over rocks and abseiling down waterfalls.

White-Water Rafting

Stick to the more reputable operators, as it's important to choose one with the experience, skills and equipment to run a safe and exciting expedition. Your guide should give you a comprehensive safety talk and paddle training before you launch off downstream. Top rafting spots:

Çoruh River (p526) Although much of the river's white-water rafting has already been curtailed by dam-building, the Çoruh and its tributaries (the İspir and Barhal Rivers) still offer some thrills and spills for rafters for now. Yusufeli (the main base for organising trips) and the town's surrounding area is set to be flooded when the Yusufeli Dam opens in

2019 after which local rafting operators think rafting will only be possible on the Barhal River.

Çamlıhemşin (p526) On the other side of the Kaçkars, offering gentle rapids and impressive scenery.

Köprülü Kanyon (p378) Between Antalya and Side, on the Turquoise Coast, the Köprülü Kanyon is one of Turkey's most popular white-water rafting spots. Trips (usually two or three hours) are offered by a number of rafting operators.

Saklıkent Gorge (p344) An 18km-long gorge near Fethiye, which offers rafting (rather than white-water rafting).

Zamantı River In Cappadocia's Ala Dağlar National Park.

Boat Trips

For a boat trip along the Aegean or Mediterranean coast, there are endless possibilities, ranging from day trips – out of pretty much everywhere with a harbour, from Ayvalık in the north Aegean all the way around the coast to Alanya in the eastern Mediterranean – to chartering a graceful *gület* (traditional wooden yacht) for a few days of cruising. The most popular *gület* route is between Demre (Kale; near Olympos) and Fethiye.

Windsurfing & Kitesurfing

The PWA (Professional Windsurfers Association) World Cup takes place in Alaçatı, on the Çeşme Peninsula. With constant, strong breezes (up to 25 knots) and a 2km-long beach with shallows and calm water conditions from mid-May to early November, Alaçatı is a world-class windsurfing destination. It's also an ideal place to learn, with English-speaking instructors and an array of classes available, and a prime kitesurfing spot. Alternatively, Akyaka (near Marmaris) is increasingly popular for windsurfing and kite-boarding.

Winter Sports

Turkey is not just a summer destination. It's still little known outside Turkey that winter sports are widely available here, notably excellent skiing (*kayak* in Turkish).

Skiing

Don't expect the Alps, but powder junkies will be genuinely surprised at the quality

> **PARAGLIDING**
>
> Picture yourself gracefully drifting over the velvety indigo of the sea, feeling the caress of the breeze... Paragliding from the slopes of Baba Dağ (1960m) in Ölüdeniz, which has consistently excellent uplifting thermals from late April to early November, is top notch. For beginners, local operators offer tandem flights, for which no training or experience is required. You just have to run a few steps and the rest is entirely controlled by the pilot, to whom you're attached with a harness. Parasailing is also available in Ölüdeniz, while Kaş and Pamukkale are also popular for paragliding.

of Turkey's infrastructure and the great snow conditions from December to April. Whether you're a seasoned or novice *kayakcı* (skier), there are options galore. Most ski resorts have been upgraded in recent years and feature good facilities, including well-equipped hotels – and at lower prices than many Western European resorts.

Most hotels offer daily and weekly packages including lift passes and full board. Equipment rental and tuition are available, though English-speaking instructors are hard to find. Most resorts cater to snowboarders, and some offer cross-country skiing and snowshoeing.

Ski Resorts

Uludağ (p301) Near Bursa, this major resort has chain hotels and a gondola from the city's outskirts. On winter weekends it's popular with İstanbullu snow bunnies.

Palandöken A major resort on the outskirts of Erzurum (www.skiingturkey.com/resorts/palandoken.html).

Sarıkamış Surrounded by vast expanses of pines, this resort near Kars has deep, dry powder (http://www.skiingturkey.com/resorts/sarikamis.html).

Davraz Dağı Mt Davraz rises between three lakes near Eğirdir, offering Nordic and downhill skiing and snowboarding.

Erciyes Dağı Above Kayseri in the Cappadocia region, Mt Erciyes offers excellent ski-runs for all skiing abilities.

Plan Your Trip

Eat & Drink Like a Local

In Turkey, meals are events to be celebrated. The national cuisine is made memorable by the use of fresh seasonal ingredients and a local expertise in grilling meat and fish that has been perfected over centuries. Here, kebaps are succulent, mezes are made daily, and freshly caught fish is expertly cooked over coals and served unadorned, accompanied by Turkey's famous aniseed-flavoured drink, rakı. When you eat out here, you're sure to finish your meal replete and satisfied.

The Year in Food

Spring (Mar–May)
Kalkan (turbot), *levrek* (sea bass), *mezgit* (whiting) and *karides* (shrimp) are in plentiful supply, as are salads featuring artichoke, broad beans, radish and cucumber; strawberries and green plums.

Summer (Jun–Aug)
Sardalya (sardines) and *ıstakoz* (lobster) are summer treats. Meze spreads draw on freshly harvested artichoke, broad bean and walnut. Seasonal salads feature cucumber, corn and tomato; watermelon and fig start their four-month seasons.

Fall (Sep–Nov)
Locals celebrate the start of the four-month *hamsi* (anchovy), *palamut* (bonito) and *lüfer* (bluefish) seasons, plus the short *çupra* (gilthead sea bream) season. Pomegranates appear in October and are plentiful until the end of February.

Winter (Dec–Feb)
The best season for fish; December is known for its *hamsi* and January for *istavrit* (horse mackerel), *lüfer* and *palamut*. Chestnuts are harvested and roasted on street corners.

What to Eat

Local produce makes its way from ground to table quickly here, ensuring freshness and flavour.

Mezes

Mezes (small, tapas-like dishes) aren't just a type of dish, they're a whole eating experience. If you eat in a local household, your host may put out a few lovingly prepared mezes for guests to nibble on before the main course is served. In *meyhanes* (taverns), waiters heave around enormous trays full of cold mezes that customers can choose from – hot mezes are ordered from the menu. Mezes are usually vegetable-based, though seafood dishes can also feature.

Meat

Overall, the Turks are huge meat eaters, which can be a problem if you're a vegetarian. Beef, lamb, mutton, liver and chicken are prepared in a number of ways. The most famous of these is the kebap – *şiş* and döner – but köfte, *saç kavurma* (stir-fried cubed meat dishes) and *güveç* (meat and vegetable stews cooked in a terracotta pot) are just as common.

The most popular sausage in Turkey is the spicy beef *sucuk*. Garlicky *pastırma* (pressed beef preserved in spices) is regularly used as an accompaniment to egg dishes; it's occasionally served with warm hummus (chickpea, tahini and lemon dip) as a meze.

Fish

Fish is wonderful here, but can be pricey. In a *balık restoran* (fish restaurant) you should always try to do as the locals do and choose your own fish from the display. After doing this, the fish will be weighed, and the price computed at the day's per-kilogram rate.

Popular species include *hamsi* (anchovy), *lüfer* (bluefish), *kalkan* (turbot), *levrek* (sea bass), *lahos* (white grouper), *mezgit* (whiting), *çipura* (gilthead bream) and *palamut* (bonito).

Vegetables & Salads

Turks love vegetables, eating them fresh in summer and pickling them for winter (*türşu* means pickled vegetables). There are two particularly Turkish ways of preparing vegetables: the first is known as *zeytinyağlı* (sautéed in olive oil) and the second *dolma* (stuffed with rice or meat).

Simplicity is the key to Turkish *salata* (salads), with crunchy fresh ingredients being adorned with a shake of oil and vinegar at the table and eaten with gusto as a meze or as an accompaniment to a meat or fish main course.

Sugar, Spice & Everything Nice

Turks don't usually finish their meal with a dessert, preferring to serve fruit as a finale. Most of them love a mid-afternoon sugar hit, though, and will often pop into a *muhallebici* (milk-pudding shop), *pastane* (cake shop) or *baklavacı* (baklava shop) for a piece of syrup-drenched baklava, a plate of chocolate-crowned profiteroles or a *fırın sütlaç* (rice pudding) tasting of milk, sugar and just a hint of exotic spices. Other Turkish sweet specialties worth sampling are *kadayıf*, dough soaked in syrup and topped with a layer of *kaymak* (clotted cream); *künefe*, layers of *kadayıf* cemented together with sweet cheese, doused in syrup and

served hot with a sprinkling of pistachio; and *katmer*, thin layers of pastry filled with *kaymak* and pistachio and served hot.

What to Drink
Alcoholic Drinks

Turkey's most beloved tipple is rakı, a grape spirit infused with aniseed. Similar to Greek ouzo, it's served in long thin glasses and is drunk neat or with water, which turns the clear liquid chalky white; if you want to add ice *(buz)*, do so after adding water, as dropping ice straight into rakı kills its flavour.

Bira (beer) is also popular. The local drop, Efes, is a perky pilsener that comes in bottles and cans and on tap.

Turkey grows and bottles its own *şarap* (wine), which has greatly improved in quality over the past decade but is quite expensive due to high government taxes. If you want red wine ask for *kırmızı şarap;* for white ask for *beyaz şarap.* Popular local varietals include *boğazkere,* a strong-bodied red; *kalecik karası,* an elegant red with an aroma of vanilla and cocoa; *emir,* a light and floral white; and *narince,* a fruity yet dry white.

Nonalcoholic Drinks

Drinking çay is the national pastime, and the country's cup of choice is made with leaves from the Black Sea region. Sugar cubes are the only accompaniment and you'll find these are needed to counter the effects of long brewing, although you can always try asking for it *açık* (weaker).

The wholly chemical *elma çay* (apple tea) is caffeine-free and only for tourists – locals wouldn't be seen dead drinking the stuff.

Türk kahve (Turkish coffee) is a thick and powerful brew drunk in a couple of short sips. If you order a cup, you will be asked how sweet you like it – *çok şekerli* means 'very sweet', *orta şekerli* 'middling', *az şekerli* 'slightly sweet' and *şekersiz or sade* 'not at all'.

Ayran is a refreshing drink made by whipping yoghurt with water and salt; it's the traditional accompaniment to kebaps.

Sahlep is a hot milky drink that takes off the winter chill. Made from wild orchid bulbs, it's reputed to be an aphrodisiac.

Food Experiences

Keen on the idea of a gastronomic odyssey? You've come to the right country.

Meals of a Lifetime

Asitane (p117) & **Deraliye** (p115) İstanbul restaurants that research and recreate Ottoman dishes devised for the sultans.

Cappadocia Home Cooking (p483) Cooking classes and rustic meals enjoyed in a family home on the edge of the Ayvalı Gorge.

Lâl Girit Mutfağı (p190) Magnificent Cretanstyle mezes made in Cunda using recipes from a beloved grandmother.

Okyanus Balık Evi (p503) Black Sea seafood restaurant with a strict 'only in season' policy and an unusual meze selection.

Orfoz (p266) Often cited as one of Turkey's best seafood restaurants, this Bodrum institution serves unusual and delectable dishes.

Zeytin Bağı (p184) Gets our vote for the best Turkish breakfast in the country, with Bay of Edremit views an added extra.

Cheap Treats

Balık ekmek Grilled fish fillets stuffed into bread with salad and a squeeze of lemon; sold at stands next to ferry docks around the country.

Simit Bread ring studded with sesame seeds; sold in bakeries and by street vendors.

Midye dolma Mussels stuffed with spiced rice and sold by street vendors.

Döner kebap Lamb cooked on a revolving upright skewer then thinly sliced and served in bread with salad and a sprinkling of sumac.

Gözleme Thin savoury pancakes filled with cheese, spinach, mushroom or potato; particularly popular in central Anatolia.

Ayvalık tost Toasted sandwich crammed with cheese, spicy sausage, pickles, tomatoes, ketchup, mayonnaise and anything else its creator can think of; named after the North Aegean town where it was invented.

Dare to Try

Kokoreç Seasoned lamb/mutton intestines stuffed with offal, grilled over coals and served in bread; sold at kokoreçis (kokoreç stands).

Boza Viscous tonic made from water, sugar and fermented barley that has a reputation for building up strength and virility. Best sampled at historic Vefa Bozacısı (p122) in İstanbul.

İşkembe or kelle paça çorba Tripe or sheep's trotter soup; the former is reputed to be a hangover cure.

Şalgam suyu Sour, crimson-coloured juice made by boiling turnips and adding vinegar; particularly popular in the eastern Mediterranean city of Mersin.

Tavuk göğsü Sweet milk pudding made with chicken breast meat.

Söğüş Poached tongue, cheek and brain served cold in bread with chopped onion, parsley, mint, tomato, cumin and hot chilli flakes. A specialty of İzmir.

Local Specialities

İstanbul

It's the national capital in all but name and Turks relocate here from every corner of the country, meaning that regional cuisines are well represented within the local restaurant scene. The Syrian-influenced dishes of Turkey's southeast are particularly fashionable at the moment, but the number one choice when it comes to dining out is almost inevitably a Black Sea–style fish restaurant or *meyhane* (tavern). The only dishes that can be said to be unique to the city are those served at Ottoman restaurants where the rich concoctions enjoyed by the sultans and their courtiers are recreated.

Thrace & Marmara

In Marmara – and especially in its capital, Edirne – liver reigns supreme and is usually served deep-fried with crispy fried chillies and a dollop of yoghurt. Dishes in Thrace are dominated by fish rather than offal, and the locals are fond of sweet treats such as Gökçeada island's *efi badem* (sugar-dusted biscuits made with almond, butter and flour). In recent years, local wineries here have been producing some of the country's most impressive vintages and can be visited by following the Thracian Wine Route (p153).

Above: Meze dishes on display

Right: *Imam bayıldı* (famous aubergine dish)

POPULAR DISHES
....

acılı ezme spicy tomato and onion paste

Adana kebap spicy *köfte* wrapped around a flat skewer and grilled

alinazik eggplant puree with yoghurt and ground *köfte*

balık ekmek fish sandwich

beyti sarma spicy ground meat baked in bread and served with yoghurt

börek sweet or savoury filled pastry

büryan lamb slow-cooked in a pit

çacık yoghurt dip with garlic and mint

çiğ köfte raw ground lamb mixed with pounded bulgur and spices

çoban salatası salad of tomato, cucumber, onion and sweet pepper

döner kebap lamb cooked on a revolving upright skewer, then thinly sliced

fava salatası mashed broad-bean salad

fıstıklı kebap minced lamb studded with pistachios

gözleme filled savoury pancake

haydari yoghurt dip with roasted eggplant and garlic

hünkâr beğendi lamb or beef stew served on a mound of rich eggplant puree

imam bayıldı aubergine (eggplant), onion, tomato and peppers slow-cooked in olive oil

içli köfte ground lamb and onion with a bulgur coating

işkembe çorbası tripe soup

İskender (Bursa) kebap *döner* served on a bed of pide and yoghurt topped with to-mato and burnt butter sauces

karıışık izgara mixed grilled lamb

The Aegean

Mezes made with seafood, freshly picked vegetables, wild herbs and locally produced olive oil are the backbone of Turkish Aegean cuisine, providing a delicious inducement for visitors. Fish dominates menus on the coast, but inland villagers love their lamb, serving it in unusual forms such as *keşkek* (lamb mince and coarse, pounded wheat). The island of Bozcada is dotted with picturesque vineyards supplying its well-regarded local wineries with grapes, and wines from the İzmir region are starting to develop a national profile.

Western & Central Anatolia

Turkey's heartland has a cuisine dominated by kebaps. Regional specialties that have become national treasures include the rich and addictive İskender, or Bursa, kebap (döner lamb on a bed of crumbled pide, topped with yoghurt, hot tomato sauce and browned butter) and the *tokat*

kebap (skewers of lamb and sliced eggplant hung vertically, grilled, then baked in a wood-fired oven and served with roasted garlic). Both take their names from the cities where they originated. Popular sweets include *kestane şekeri* (candied chestnuts).

The Mediterranean

The eastern Mediterranean is home to three towns with serious foodie credentials: Silifke, Adana and Antakya. Silifke is known for its yoghurt, Adana for its eponymously titled kebap (minced beef or lamb mixed with powdered red pepper then grilled on a skewer and dusted with slightly sour sumac) and Antakya for its wealth of Syrian-influenced dips, salads, croquettes and desserts. The best-loved of these desserts is *künefe,* layers of vermicelli-like noodles cemented together with sweet cheese, doused in sugar syrup and served hot with a sprinkling of pistachio. Both gooey and crispy, it's dangerously addictive – consider yourself warned.

kısır bulgar salad

kokoreç seasoned, grilled lamb/mutton intestines

köfte meatballs; *izgara köfte* means grilled meatballs

kuru fasulye haricot beans cooked in a spicy tomato sauce

lahmacun thin and crispy Arabic-style pizza topped with minced lamb

mantı ravioli stuffed with meat and topped with yoghurt, tomato and butter

mercimek çorbası lentil soup

muhammara dip of walnuts, bread, tahini, olive oil and lemon juice

pastırma pressed beef preserved in spices

patlıcan kebap cubed or minced lamb grilled with aubergine (eggplant)

patlıcan kızartması fried aubergine (eggplant) with tomato

perde pilavi chicken and rice cooked in pastry

pide Turkish pizza

piyaz white-bean salad

sigara böreği deep-fried cigar-shaped pastries filled with white cheese

şiş kebap small pieces of lamb grilled on a skewer

su böreği lasagne-like layered pastry laced with white cheese and parsley

tavuk şiş small boneless chicken pieces grilled on a skewer

testi kebap lamb or chicken slow-cooked in a sealed terracotta pot

tokat kebap lamb cubes grilled with potato, tomato, aubergine (eggplant) and garlic

Urfa kebap a mild version of the Adana kebap

yaprak sarma/yaprak dolması vine leaves stuffed with rice and herbs

Black Sea

Hamsı (anchovies) are loved with a passion along the Black Sea coast. Generations of Karadeniz (Black Sea) cooks have used this slim silver fish in breads, soups and pilafs, thrown them on the grill or dusted them with flour before snap-frying them. It's not the only culinary reason to head here, though. *Muhlama* (cornmeal cooked with butter and cheese), *karalahana çorbası* (collard soup) and the decadently rich *Laz böreği* (flaky pastry layered with custard and hazelnuts) are other dishes that demand gastronomic investigation. Also of note are the hazelnuts grown around Ordu and the black tea grown in Rize.

Northeastern Anatolia

Fruits of the forest and field are on show in this far-flung corner of the country. Flowery honey from small producers is slathered on bread and topped with ultra-creamy *kaymak* (clotted cream) in a breakfast ritual that is now being emu-lated across the country, and *kaz* (goose) and lamb are roasted or stewed in dishes reminiscent of those served in neighbouring Iran, Georgia and Armenia. In Kars, milk from animals grazed on rich steppe grasses is used to make many delicious varieties of cheese. Unusual drinks include *reyhane,* made from purple basil.

Southeastern Anatolia

Top of this region's foodie list is Gaziantep (Antep), destination of choice for lovers of pistachio. The local examples are plump and flavoursome, showcased in the city's famous baklava and *katmer* (thin pastry sheets layered with clotted cream and nuts, topped with pistachio, baked and served straight from the oven). Also notable is Şanlıurfa (Urfa), home to *urfa kebap* (skewered lamb with tomatoes, sliced onion and hot peppers) and the country's best examples of the Arabic-influenced wafer-thin pizza known as *lahmacun*. Other regional treats include sweet apricots from Malatya.

Gözleme (savoury pancake)

How to Eat & Drink

Like all countries with great national cuisines, Turkey has rules and rituals around where and when to eat.

When to Eat

Kahvaltı (breakfast) Usually eaten at home or in a hotel, although *böreks* (sweet or savoury filled pastries) and *simits* (sesame-encrusted bread rings) are popular eat-on-the-run alternatives.

Öğle yemeği (lunch) Usually eaten at a cafe, *lokanta* (eatery serving ready-made food) or fast-food stand around noon.

Akşam yemeği (dinner) The main meal of the day, eaten with family and/or friends around 6pm (rural areas) and 7.30pm to 8pm (cities).

Where to Eat

Balık restoran Fish restaurant.

Hazır yemek lokantası (often abbreviated to *lokanta*) Eatery serving ready-made meals.

Kebapçı Kebap restaurant.

Köfteci *Köfte* (meatball) restaurant.

Meyhane Tavern where mezes, grilled meats and fish are enjoyed; live music is sometimes performed.

Ocakbaşı Kebap restaurant where customers watch meat being grilled over coals.

Pideci Pizza restaurant.

Menu Decoder

Ana yemekler Main courses; usually meat or fish dishes.

Bira Beer; the most popular local tipple is Efes Pilsen.

Dolma Something stuffed with rice and/or meat.

İçmekler Drinks.

Meze Small tapas-like hot or cold dish eaten at the start of a meal.

Porsiyon Portion, helping. *Yarım porsiyon* is a half-portion.

(Kırmızı/Beyaz) Şarap (Red/White) Wine.

Servis ücreti Service charge.

Su Water; *maden suyu* is mineral water.

Tatlı(lar) Sweets; often baklava, stewed fruit or a milk-based pudding.

Zeytinyağlı Food cooked in olive oil.

Plan Your Trip

Travel with Children

Çocuklar (children) are the beloved centrepiece of family life in Turkey, and your children will be welcomed wherever they go. Your journey will be peppered with exclamations of *Maşallah* (glory be to God) and your children will be clutched into the adoring arms of strangers.

Turkey for Kids

Travelling in family-focused Turkey is a blessing with kids big and small – waiters play with babies, strangers entertain and indulge at every turn, and free or discounted entry to sights is common. Do bear in mind, however, that facilities are often lacking and safety consciousness rarely meets Western norms.

Children's Highlights

Accommodation

Cave hotels, Cappadocia (p459) These offer novel accommodation, as do Olympos tree houses and Kabak's beach retreats.

Activities

Tandem paragliding, Ölüdeniz (p342) One of many western Mediterranean spots where you can mix beach-based fun and water sports with more dramatic activities.

Resorts, Bodrum (p256) Holiday complexes and beaches around the pretty town, along with Kuşadası and Marmaris' water parks, make the Aegean a good option for a relaxed seaside holiday.

Best Regions for Kids

İstanbul
Ice cream by the Bosphorus, ferry rides, the thrill of the Grand Bazaar, magnificent palaces and atmospheric ruins.

Ephesus, Bodrum & the South Aegean
Ruins such as Ephesus for older children, plus beaches for kids of all ages. Holiday spots like Kuşadası, Bodrum, Marmaris and Akyaka offer plenty of sights, facilities, resorts, water parks and sports, with less touristy coastline nearby.

Antalya & the Turquoise Coast
Water sports and activities from tandem paragliding to sea kayaking over submerged ruins. With younger children, holiday towns like Kaş offer picturesque lanes and sandy beaches.

Cappadocia
The fantastical landscape of fairy chimneys (rock formations) and underground cities will thrill older children, as will cave accommodation. A safe, relaxing rural area with activities including horse riding, hot-air ballooning and walking.

İzmir & the North Aegean
More Aegean beaches. İzmir's *kordon* (seafront) is a child-friendly promenade – spacious, flat, pretty and offering numerous eating options.

Horse riding, Cappadocia (p458) A memorable
way to see the rocky valleys, as is hot-air ballooning.

Walking (p37) Teenagers will enjoy exploring Cappadocia or the Kaçkar Mountains.

Cooking courses Available in locations such as
İstanbul.

Historic Sites

Major sights For older children and teenagers,
Turkey offers intriguing and romantic relics, from
Ephesus to Ani, Pergamum and Afrodisias.

Hippodrome, İstanbul (p74) Ruins such as this
Byzantine race track offer plenty of space for toddlers to expend energy.

Basilica Cistern, İstanbul (p70) Children will
love the creepy atmosphere of this subterranean
cavern, with walkways suspended over the water.

Cappadocia (p451) Exploring the fairy chimneys,
caves and underground cities will prove memorable for older kids.

Turquoise Coast (p323) At Mediterranean spots
such as Patara and Kekova, you can mix ruins with
the beach, boat trips and sea kayaking.

Museums

Rahmi M Koç Museums, İstanbul (p106) and
Ankara (p414) Interactive museums with planes,
trains and automobiles on display.

Bodrum Maritime Museum (p260) Scale models
of boats and a collection of 6000 shells.

İstanbul Naval Museum (p99) Its large hall of
ornate caïque rowboats is a knockout.

Ephesus Museum (p234), **Selçuk** Displays bring
the ancient world of Ephesus to life.

Transport

Ferries Popular in İstanbul and İzmir.

Funiculars and antique tram, İstanbul (p138)
Novel ways to climb Beyoğlu's hills.

Teleferik, Bursa (p301) The world's longest cable
car climbs 8.2km up Uludağ (Great Mountain;
2543m).

Carriage rides, Princes' Islands (p142) *Fayton*
(horse-drawn carriage) rides and bikes are offered
on İstanbul's islands.

Treats

Sweet treats (p43) Turkey does these as well as
it does kebaps – including baklava, *dondurma* (ice
cream) and *lokum* (Turkish delight).

Planning

Accommodation

➡ Many hotels in all price ranges have family
suites.

➡ Self-catering apartments and villas are
common in tourist areas such as Bodrum.

➡ Cots are increasingly common; many hotels
will organise one with advance notice.

➡ Resorts offer kids' clubs, and hotels in tourist
areas may be able to arrange babysitting.

Eating

➡ Children's menus are uncommon outside
tourist areas, but restaurants will often prepare
special dishes for children.

➡ High chairs are by no means common, but
can sometimes be found in tourist areas (apart
from İstanbul).

Facilities

➡ Public baby-changing facilities are rare, but
found in some chain restaurants.

➡ Breastfeeding in public is uncommon; best to
do so in a private or discreet place.

➡ Seaside towns and cities often have
playgrounds, but check the equipment for safety.

Getting Around

➡ Buses often lack functioning toilets, but they
normally stop every few hours.

➡ Free travel for children on public transport
within cities, and discounts on longer journeys,
are common.

➡ Most car-rental companies can provide baby
seats for a small extra charge.

Exploring the Göreme Open-Air Museum (p454), Cappadocia

➡ Dangerous drivers and uneven surfaces make using strollers an extreme sport.

➡ A 'baby backpack' is useful for walking around sights.

Health

➡ In hot, moist climates, any wound or break in the skin may lead to infection. The area should be cleaned and then kept dry and clean.

➡ Encourage your child to avoid dogs and other mammals because of the risk of rabies and other diseases.

➡ For children and pregnant or breastfeeding women, double-check drugs and dosages prescribed for travel by doctors and pharmacists, as they may be unsuitable. The same applies to practitioners in Turkey.

➡ Some information on the suitability of drugs and recommended dosage can be found on travel-health websites.

Products

➡ Double-check the suitability of prescriptions your children are given while in Turkey.

➡ Pasteurised UHT milk is sold in cartons everywhere, but fresh milk is harder to find.

➡ Consider bringing a supply of baby food – what little you find here, your baby will likely find inedible – or it will just be mashed banana.

➡ Migros supermarkets have the best range of baby food.

➡ Most supermarkets stock formula (although it is very expensive) and vitamin-fortified rice cereal.

➡ Disposable *bebek bezi* (nappies or diapers) are readily available.

➡ The best nappies are Prima and Huggies, sold in pharmacies and supermarkets; don't bother with cheaper local brands.

Resources

➡ Lonely Planet's *Travel with Children* has practical information and advice.

Safety

➡ In hotels and other buildings, look out for open power points.

➡ Many taps are unmarked and reversed (cold on the left, hot on the right).

On the street, watch for:

➡ Turkey's notorious drivers, particularly those on pavement-mounting mopeds.

➡ Crudely covered electric mains.

➡ Open stairwells.

➡ Serious potholes.

➡ Open drains.

➡ Carelessly secured building sites.

Regions at a Glance

Given Turkey's vast scale, it makes sense to focus your travels on one or two regions. This need not confine you to one part of the country – domestic flights are an affordable way to cross the Anatolian steppe in a few hours. A visit to mighty İstanbul can easily be paired with a bus or train to western Turkey's many highlights, or a flight east for off-the-beaten-track adventures. While there are many constants throughout Turkey and the food is certainly excellent everywhere, this is an incredibly diverse country offering varied experiences. Each region has its own charms, so choose wisely and you could find yourself hiking across snowy mountains in wild northeastern Anatolia, sauntering through cosmopolitan İstanbul or sunbathing on a Mediterranean beach.

İstanbul

History
Nightlife
Shopping

Imperial Grandeur

The megacity formerly known as Constantinople and Byzantium was the capital of a series of empires. The Aya Sofya, a church-turned-mosque-turned-museum, is the grandest remnant of the Byzantine Empire; Ottoman landmarks include the Blue Mosque and Topkapı Palace.

Beyoğlu Bars

Beyoğlu is an exhilarating melting pot between the dusk and dawn calls to prayer, when up-for-it crowds swirl through its hole-in-the-wall cocktail bars, rooftop watering holes, pedestrian precincts and bohemian nightclubs.

Markets & Bazaars

The city's famous bazaars include the sprawling Grand Bazaar, the fragrant Spice Bazaar, and the Arasta Bazaar with its carpet and ceramics stores. There are markets and malls galore, including Kadıköy's food market on the Asian side. Neighbourhoods worth visiting include Çukurcuma for antiques and collectables, and Galata for fashion.

p58

Thrace & Marmara

Military History
Architecture
Aegean Culture

WWI Battlefields

Over 100,000 soldiers died on the now-tranquil Gallipoli Peninsula, a pilgrimage site for Australians, New Zealanders and Turks. Touring the memorials, battlefields and trenches that dot the beaches and hills is simply heart-wrenching.

Ottoman Finery

Edirne's Ottoman gems include Selimiye Camii, one of the finest works of the great architect Mimar Sinan, while Çanakkale's Ottoman old town has mosques, hamams and a 19th-century clock tower.

Greek Connections

Turkey's northwest corner is famous for the ruined classical city of Troy, which traded with the Greeks until the Trojan War. The wooden horse used in the Brad Pitt movie *Troy* stands on Çanakkale seafront. A ferry ride from Gallipoli or Çanakkale reaches Gökçeada, with its slow-paced Aegean lifestyle and Greek heritage including hilltop villages.

p144

İzmir & the North Aegean

History
Slow Travel
Food

Multicultural Footsteps

Many peoples have left their mark here. Ayvalık and Bozcaada town's old Greek quarters resonate with memories of the population exchange with Greece, while İzmir has Sephardic synagogues and Levantine architecture. Going further back, the hilltop ruins of Pergamum are some of Turkey's finest, and numerous, less-visited sites are found on the Biga Peninsula.

Village Life

Outside the summer tourist season, life has an alluringly slow rural pace in laid-back spots such as Bozcaada island, the Biga Peninsula, Behramkale, Ayvalık and Bergama. Changing seasons and weekly markets are still the main events.

Meze & Seafood

This is the place to try a classic Turkish feast of meze, *balık* (fish) and rakı (anise spirit) on a seafront terrace. If the fish prices seem steep, stick to the olive oil–soaked mezes.

p175

Ephesus, Bodrum & the South Aegean

History
Nightlife
Sun & Surf

Classical Sites

Romans once bustled along the Curetes Way at Ephesus, Turkey's most visited ruins. Less-frequented sites include eerie Priene, a hilltop Ionian city; Miletus, an ancient port; Didyma's Temple of Apollo, once the world's second-largest temple; and Knidos, a Dorian port on the Datça Peninsula.

Sundowners in Style

Bodrum's tourist machine has created a mean nightlife, with waterfront bar-clubs on its twin bays. Another sexy Bodrum Peninsula sundowner spot is Göltürkbükü, the summer playground of İstanbul's jet set.

Hidden Beaches

The Datça and Bozburun peninsulas hide secluded coves and azure waters, while *gület* (traditional wooden yacht) cruises discover unspoilt parts of the coastline between Marmaris and Fethiye. The Bodrum Peninsula's busier beaches are also excellent for swimming and water sports.

p221

PLAN YOUR TRIP REGIONS AT A GLANCE

Western Anatolia

History
Ruins
Activities

Ancient Empires

Bursa was the Ottoman capital before Constantinople, İznik's weathered stone gates and Aya Sofya recall its Byzantine greatness, and the Phrygian Valley's rock-hewn monuments survive from the distant Phrygian era. Meanwhile, Eskişehir mixes its pastel-painted Ottoman quarter with today's lively cultural scene and nightlife.

Mountaintop Relics

Hierapolis, a ruined spa city, famously stands atop Pamukkale's glistening white travertines. Quieter sites include Sagalassos, a Pisidian-Hellenistic-Roman city in the Taurus Mountains, and Afrodisias, a grand provincial Roman capital.

Hiking

Two long-distance hiking paths, the Phrygian Way and St Paul Trail, respectively wind through the Phrygian Valley, and over the Taurus Mountains from the Mediterranean to Western Anatolia's serene Lake District. Above Bursa, Uludağ ('Great Mountain'; 2543m) is ideal for summer walks.

p287

Antalya & the Turquoise Coast

Beaches
Hiking
Ruins

Sand & Sights

Patara, Turkey's longest beach, and the Dalyan area both offer a diverse menu of sand, ancient ruins and nesting sea turtles. Likewise, as well as its beach, Olympos is famed for its Lycian ruins and the naturally occurring flames of the Chimaera. In Ölüdeniz, see the stunning beach and lagoon from above on a tandem paragliding flight.

Historic Footsteps

The Western Mediterranean region's two long-distance waymarked footpaths, the Lycian Way and St Paul Trail, name-check historical folk who passed through. The former trail crosses the Teke Peninsula, littered with sepulchres and sarcophagi left millennia ago by the Lycians.

Lyrical Lycian Relics

The trademark funerary monuments of the Lycian civilisation nestle in the secluded coves and wrinkly cliff faces of spectacular spots such as Xanthos, Pınara and Kaleköy.

p323

Eastern Mediterranean

History
Cuisine
Biblical Legacies

Surreal Sights

History has a fairytale quality here: Kızkalesi Castle (Maiden's Castle) seemingly floats offshore, Zeus is said to have imprisoned hydra-headed Typhon in the Gorge of Hell, and Anemurium's sprawling and eerily quiet Roman-Byzantine ruins stretch 500m down to a pebble beach with mammoth city walls scaling the mountainside above.

Arab Influences

Antakya is a Turkish and Arab culinary melting pot. The city's influences from nearby Syria include lemon wedges and mint, which accompany kebaps and local specialities.

Paul's Footsteps

The early Christian and Old Testament sites in Tarsus include St Paul's ruined house, where pilgrims drink from the well. Paul and Peter both preached in Antakya (the biblical Antioch), and Silifke's Church of St Thekla recalls Paul's early follower.

p382

Ankara & Central Anatolia

History
Architecture
Ruins

Momentous Events

This is where Alexander the Great cut the Gordion knot, King Midas turned everything to gold, Atatürk began his revolution, the whirling dervishes first whirled, and Julius Caesar uttered his famous line: '*Veni, vidi, vici*' ('I came, I saw, I conquered').

Ottoman Heritage

Safranbolu and Amasya are Ottoman heritage towns, with boutique hotels occupying their half-timbered, black-and-white houses.

Iconic Sights

Gordion's Phrygian tomb (circa 700 BC) might be the world's oldest wooden structure, and Hattuşa was the Hittite capital over 3000 years ago. Locals say the doorways of Divriği's 780-year-old mosque complex, with their exploding stone stars, are so intricately carved that their craftmanship proves the existence of God.

p409

Cappadocia

History
Activities
Landscapes

Byzantine Christians

Cappadocia was a refuge for Byzantine Christians, who carved monastic settlements into the rock, left frescoes on the cave walls and hid from Islamic armies in underground cities.

Hiking

This is one of Turkey's best regions for going walkabout, with options ranging from gentle saunters through the dreamy valleys to serious missions. South of leafy Ihlara Valley, Mt Hasan (3268m) and the Ala Dağlar National Park are both challenging.

Rock Formations

Cappadocia's lava-formed tuff cliff faces and surreal 'fairy chimneys' are riddled with caves. Some are occupied by centuries-old churches, others by full-time cave-dwellers. Many are now hotels, offering an experience of the troglodyte lifestyle in comfort and style. A memorable way to appreciate the surreal rocky canyons is from above, on a dawn hot-air balloon flight.

p451

Black Sea Coast

History
Slow Travel
Scenery

History

Anatolia's north coast was once the Kingdom of Pontus, and Ottoman Greeks tried to create a post-WWI Pontic state here. Impressive ruins include Sumela, the Byzantine monastery clinging to a cliff face, and Trabzon's 13th-century church-turned-mosque Aya Sofya.

Local Experiences

The Karadeniz (Black Sea) offers experiences unknown to non-Turkish holidaymakers, such as sipping çay in tea-producing Rize; wandering Amasra and Sinop's ancient fortifications; staying in Ordu and Ünye's old Greek and Armenian quarters; and discovering the rugged *yaylalar* (mountain pastures) above Ordu.

Dramatic Coastline

The winding road from Amasra to Sinop is Turkey's answer to California's Hwy 1, and there are more coastal vistas around Yason Burnu (Cape Jason), with its chapel marking the spot where Jason and the Argonauts passed by in search of the golden fleece.

p497

Eastern Anatolia

Ruins
Activities
Landscapes

Remote Outposts

Medieval Armenian and Georgian churches dot the steppe and valleys; isolated Ani was an Armenian capital and Silk Road trading centre. Near the Iranian border, mountainside İshak Paşa Palace is worthy of *One Thousand and One Nights*, and atop Nemrut Dağı (Mt Nemrut), the toppled stone heads are a legendary sight.

Outdoor Adventure

Yusufeli is a white-water rafting and trekking centre, with more rapids, day hikes and multiday trails found across the Kaçkar Mountains around Çamlıhemşin.

Alpine Scenery

In the Kaçkars and around Şavşat and Ardanuç, villages, ruins and traditional wooden houses nestle in the *yaylalar* (highland pastures): the beginnings of the Caucasus region, which stretches east to the Caspian Sea and north to Russia.

p517

On the Road

İstanbul

POP 14.6 MILLION

Best Places to Eat

➡ Antiochia (p118)

➡ Çiya Sofrası (p121)

➡ Develi Baklava (p116)

➡ Eleos (p120)

➡ Hayvore (p117)

Best Places to Sleep

➡ Hotel Empress Zoe (p111)

➡ Hotel Ibrahim Pasha (p111)

➡ Karaköy Rooms (p113)

➡ Louis Appartements (p113)

➡ Marmara Guesthouse (p110)

Why Go?

Some ancient cities are the sum of their monuments. But others, such as İstanbul, factor a lot more into the equation. Here, you can visit Byzantine churches and Ottoman mosques in the morning, shop in chic boutiques during the afternoon and party at bars and clubs throughout the night. In the space of a few minutes you can hear the evocative strains of the call to prayer issuing from the Old City's tapering minarets, the sonorous horn of a crowded commuter ferry crossing between Europe and Asia, and the strident cries of a street hawker selling fresh seasonal produce. Put simply, this marvellous metropolis is an exercise in sensory seduction like no other.

Ask locals to describe what they love about İstanbul and they'll shrug, give a small smile and say merely that there is no other place like it. Spend a few days here, and you'll know exactly what they mean.

When to Go
İstanbul

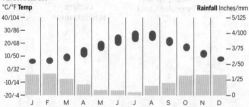

Apr Sunshine and balmy breezes usher in the colourful İstanbul Tulip Festival.

Jun & Jul Venues around town host high-profile classical, jazz and contemporary music festivals.

Sep Heat disperses and locals enjoy the season for *lüfer* (bluefish), a favourite local fish.

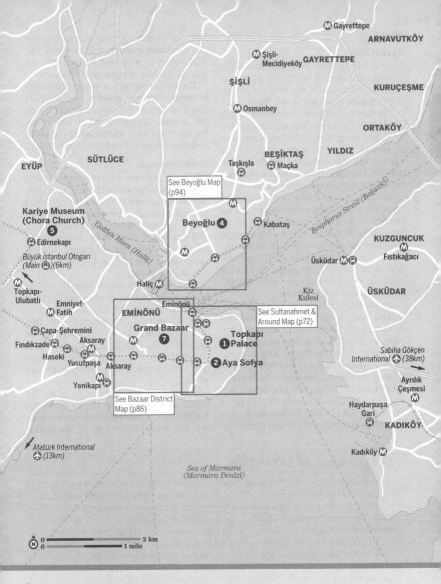

İstanbul Highlights

1 Topkapı Palace (p76)
Uncovering the secrets of the seraglio in this opulent palace.

2 Aya Sofya (p66)
Marvelling at the interior of one of the world's truly great buildings.

3 Hamams (p107)
Surrendering to the steam.

4 Beyoğlu (p122) Drinking at a rooftop bar, then dining at one of the many restaurants.

5 Kariye Museum (Chora Church; p92) Admiring the Byzantine mosaics.

6 Ferry trip (p138)
Journeying along the mighty Bosphorus, up the Golden Horn or to the Princes' Islands.

7 Grand Bazaar (p85)
Losing yourself in the hidden caravanserais and labyrinthine lanes.

8 Contemporary art galleries (p99) Contemplating the cutting edge.

9 Çay bahçesi (p121)
Kicking back with the locals at a traditional tea garden.

History

Byzantium

Legend tells us that the city of Byzantium was founded around 667 BC by a group of colonists from Megara, northwest of Athens. It was named after their leader, Byzas.

The new colony quickly prospered, largely due to its ability to levy tolls and harbour fees on ships passing through the Bosphorus, then as now an important waterway. A thriving marketplace was established and the inhabitants lived on traded goods and the abundant fish stocks in the surrounding waters.

In 512 BC Darius, emperor of Persia, captured the city during his campaign against the Scythians. Following the retreat of the Persians in 478 BC, the town came under the influence and protection of Athens and joined the Athenian League. Though this was a turbulent relationship, Byzantium stayed under Athenian rule until 355 BC, when it gained independence.

By the end of the Hellenistic period, Byzantium had formed an alliance with the Roman Empire. It retained its status as a free state, and kept this even after being officially incorporated into the Roman Empire in AD 79 by Vespasian. Life was relatively uneventful until the city's leaders made a big mistake: they picked the wrong side in a Roman war of succession following the death of Emperor Pertinax in AD 193. When Septimius Severus emerged victorious over his rival Pescennius Niger, he mounted a three-year siege of the city, eventually massacring Byzantium's citizens, razing its walls and burning it to the ground. Ancient Byzantium was no more.

The new emperor was aware of the city's important strategic position, and soon set about rebuilding it. Severus named his new city Augusta Antonina and it was subsequently ruled by a succession of emperors, including the great Diocletian (r 284–305).

Constantinople

Diocletian had decreed that after his retirement, the government of the Roman Empire should be overseen by co-emperors Galerius in the east (Augusta Antonina) and Constantine in the west (Rome). This resulted in a civil war, which was won by Constantine in AD 324 when he defeated Licinius, Galerius' successor, at Chrysopolis (the present-day suburb of Üsküdar).

With his victory, Constantine (r 324–37) became sole emperor of a reunited empire. He also became the first Christian emperor, though he only formally converted on his deathbed. To solidify his power he summoned the First Ecumenical Council at Nicaea (İznik) in 325, establishing the precedent of the emperor's supremacy in Church affairs.

Constantine also decided to move the capital of the empire to the shores of the Bosphorus, where the line between the Eastern and Western divisions of the empire

---

GREAT PALACE OF BYZANTIUM

Constantine the Great built the Great Palace soon after he declared Constantinople to be the capital of the Roman Empire in AD 330. Successive Byzantine leaders left their mark by adding to it, and the complex eventually consisted of hundreds of buildings over six levels. These included throne rooms, audience chambers, churches, chapels, stadiums and thermal baths, all enclosed by walls and set in terraced parklands stretching from the Hippodrome over to Hagia Sofia (Aya Sofya) and down the slope, ending at the sea walls on the Sea of Marmara. The palace was finally abandoned after the Fourth Crusade sacked the city in 1204, and its ruins were pillaged and filled in after the Conquest, becoming the foundations of much of Sultanahmet and Cankurtaran.

Various pieces of the Great Palace have been uncovered – many by budding hotelier 'archaeologists'. The mosaics in the Great Palace Mosaic Museum (Map p71; ☑0212-518 1205; http://ayasofyamuzesi.gov.tr/en/museum-great-palace-mosaics; Torun Sokak; ₺15; ⊙9am-7pm mid-Apr–Sep, to 5pm Oct–mid-Apr, last entry 30min before closing; ⛐Sultanahmet) once graced the floor of the complex, and excavations at the Sultanahmet Archaeological Park (Map p72; Kabasakal Caddesi; ⛐Sultanahmet), near Aya Sofya, have uncovered other parts of the palace. Controversially, some of these excavations were subsumed into a new extension of the neighbouring luxury Four Seasons Hotel before public outcry stalled the project.

For more information, check out www.byzantium1200.com, which has computer-generated images that bring ancient Byzantium to life.

had previously been drawn. He built a new, wider circle of walls around the site of Byzantium and laid out a magnificent city within. The city was dedicated on 11 May 330 as New Rome, but soon came to be called Constantinople.

The city continued to grow under the rule of the emperors. Theodosius II (r 408–50), threatened by the forces of Attila the Hun, ordered that an even wider, more formidable circle of walls be built around the city. Encircling all seven hills of the city, the walls were completed in 413, only to be brought down by a series of earthquakes in 447. They were hastily rebuilt in a mere two months – the rapid approach of Attila and the Huns acting as a powerful stimulus. The Theodosian walls successfully held out invaders for the next 757 years and still stand today, though they are in an increasingly dilapidated state of repair.

Theodosius II died in 450 and was succeeded by a string of emperors, including the most famous of all Byzantine emperors, Justinian the Great. From 565 to 1025, a succession of warrior emperors kept invaders such as the Persians and the Avars at bay. Though the foreign armies often managed to get as far as Chalcedon (the present-day suburb of Kadıköy), none were able to breach Theodosius' land walls.

In 1071 Emperor Romanus IV Diogenes (r 1068–1071) led his army to eastern Anatolia to do battle with the Seljuk Turks, who had been forced out of Central Asia by the encroaching Mongols. However, at Manzikert (Malazgirt) the Byzantines were disastrously defeated, the emperor captured and imprisoned, and the former Byzantine heartland of Anatolia thus thrown open to Turkish invasion and settlement.

As Turkish power was consolidated to the east of Constantinople, the power of Venice – always a maritime and commercial rival to Constantinople – grew in the West. This coincided with the launch of the First Crusade and the arrival in Constantinople of the first of the Crusaders in 1096.

In 1204 soldiers of the Fourth Crusade led by Enrico Dandolo, Doge of Venice, attacked and ransacked the city. They then ruled it with an ally, Count Baldwin of Flanders, until 1261, when soldiers under Michael VIII Palaiologos, a Byzantine aristocrat in exile who had risen to become co-emperor of Nicaea, successfully recaptured it. The Byzantine Empire was restored.

İstanbul

Two decades after Michael reclaimed Constantinople, a Turkish warlord named Ertuğrul died in the village of Söğüt near Nicaea. He left his son Osman, who was known as Gazi (Warrior for the Faith), a small territory. Osman's followers became known in the Empire as Osmanlıs and in the West as the Ottomans.

Osman died in 1324 and was succeeded by his son Orhan. In 1326 Orhan captured Bursa, made it his capital and took the title of sultan. His son Murat I (r 1362–89) took Adrianople (Edirne) in 1371.

Murat's son Beyazıt (r 1389–1402) unsuccessfully laid siege to Constantinople in 1394, then defeated a Crusader army 100,000 strong on the Danube in 1396. Though temporarily checked by the armies of Tamerlane and a nasty war of succession between Beyazıt's four sons that was eventually won by Mehmet I (r 1413–21), the Ottomans continued to grow in power and size. By 1440 the Ottoman armies under Murat II (r 1421–51) had taken Thessalonica, unsuccessfully laid siege to Constantinople and Belgrade, and battled Christian armies for Transylvania. It was at this point in history that Mehmet II 'the Conqueror' (r 1451–81) came to power and vowed to attain the ultimate prize – Constantinople.

The Byzantines had closed the mouth of the Golden Horn with a heavy chain to prevent Ottoman boats from sailing in and attacking the city walls on the northern side. Not to be thwarted, Mehmet marshalled his boats at a cove (where Dolmabahçe Palace now stands) and had them transported overland by night on rollers, up the valley (present site of the Hilton Hotel) and down the other side into the Golden Horn at Kasımpaşa. Catching the Byzantine defenders by surprise, he soon had the Golden Horn under control.

The last great obstacle was provided by the city's mighty walls. No matter how heavily Mehmet's cannons battered them, the Byzantines rebuilt the walls by night and, come daybreak, the impetuous young sultan would find himself back where he'd started. Finally, he received a proposal from a Hungarian cannon founder called Urban who had come to help the Byzantine emperor defend Christendom against the infidels. Finding that the Byzantine emperor had no money, Urban was quick to discard his religious convictions and instead offered to make Mehmet the most enormous cannon

İstanbul

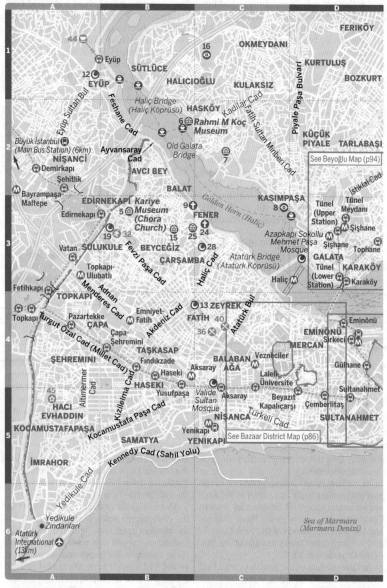

ever seen. Mehmet gladly accepted and the mighty cannon breached the western walls, allowing the Ottomans into the city. On 28 May 1453 the final attack began, and by the evening of the 29th the Turks were in complete control of the city. The last Byzantine emperor, Constantine XI Palaiologos, died fighting on the walls.

Seeing himself as the successor to great emperors such as Constantine and Justinian, the 21-year-old conqueror at once began to rebuild and repopulate the city. Aya

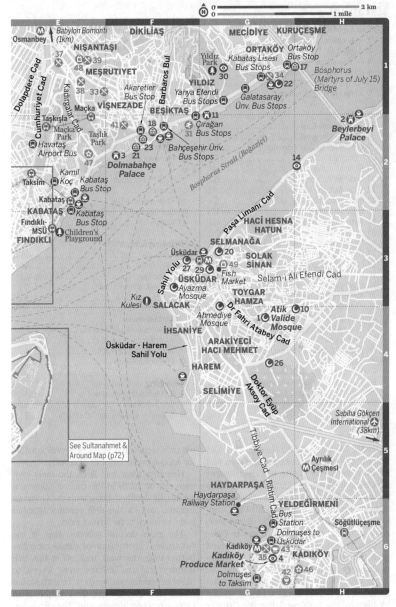

Sofya was converted to a mosque; a new mosque, the Fatih (Conqueror) Camii, was built on the fourth hill; and the Eski Saray (Old Palace) was constructed on the third hill, followed by a new palace (Topkapı) on Sarayburnu a few years later. The city walls were repaired and a new fortress, Yedikule, was built. İstanbul, as it began to be known, became the new administrative, commercial and cultural centre of the ever-growing Ottoman Empire.

İstanbul

Under Mehmet's rule, Greeks who had fled the city were encouraged to return and an imperial decree calling for resettlement was issued; Muslims, Jews and Christians all took up his offer and were promised the right to worship as they pleased. The Genoese, who had fought with the Byzantines, were pardoned and allowed to stay in Galata, though the fortifications that surrounded their settlement were torn down. Only Galata Tower was allowed to stand.

Mehmet died in 1481 and was succeeded by Beyazıt II (r 1481–1512), who was ousted by his son, the ruthless Selim the Grim (r 1512–20), famed for executing seven grand viziers and numerous relatives during his relatively short reign.

The building boom that Mehmet kicked off was continued by his successors, with Süleyman the Magnificent (r 1520–66) and his architect Mimar Sinan being responsible for an enormous amount of construction.

However, what had been the most civilised city on earth in the time of Süleyman eventually declined along with the Ottoman Empire, and by the 19th century İstanbul had lost much of its former glory.

The city's decline reflected that of the sultanate. The concept of democracy, imported from the West, took off in the 19th century and the sultans were forced to make concessions towards it. In 1876 Sultan Abdül Hamid II allowed the creation of an Ottoman constitution and the first-ever Ottoman parliament. By 1908 the Committee for Union and Progress (CUP), better known as the Young Turks, they forced the sultan to abdicate, reinstated the constitution and assumed governance of the empire.

One of the factors leading to the the Young Turks' decision to ally themselves with the Central Powers in WWI was their fear that the Allies (particularly Russia) coveted İstanbul. Unfortunately, the alliance led to their political demise when the Central Powers were defeated. The Young Turks' leaders resigned, fled İstanbul and went into exile, leaving the city to be occupied by British, French and Italian troops placed there in accordance with the Armistice of Mudros, which ended Ottoman participation in the war. The city was returned to Ottoman rule under the 1923 Treaty of Lausanne, which defined the borders of the modern Turkish state.

After the Republic was founded in 1923, the new government was set up in Ankara. Robbed of its status as the capital of a vast empire, İstanbul lost much of its wealth and atmosphere. The city's streets and neighbourhoods decayed, its infrastructure was neither maintained nor improved and little economic development occurred there for the next half-century.

The Recent Past

The weak economic position of İstanbul was reflected in the rest of the country, and this led to growing dissatisfaction with a succession of governments. There were military coups in 1960 and 1971, and the late 1960s and 1970s were characterised by left-wing activism and political violence. This reached a shocking crescendo on 1 May (May Day) 1977, when there was a flare-up between rival political factions at a huge demonstration in Taksim Meydanı (Taksim Sq). Security forces intervened and approximately 40 protesters were killed.

Under the presidency of economist Turgut Özal, the 1980s saw a free-market-led economic and tourism boom. Özal's government also presided over a great increase in urbanisation, with trainloads of people from eastern Anatolia making their way to İstanbul in search of jobs in the booming industrial sector. The city's infrastructure couldn't cope back then and is still catching up, despite nearly four decades of large-scale municipal works being undertaken.

National elections in April 1999 brought in a coalition government led by Bülent Ecevit's left-wing Democratic Left Party. After years under the conservative right of the Refah Partisi, the election result heralded a shift towards European-style social democracy. Unfortunately for the new government, there was a spectacular collapse of the Turk-ish economy in 2001, leading to its electoral defeat in 2002. The victorious party was the moderate Adalet ve Kalkınma Partisi (Justice and Development Party; AKP), led by phoenix-like Recep Tayyip Erdoğan. In İstanbul, candidates from the AKP were elected into power in most municipalities, including the powerful Fatih Municipality, which includes Eminönü. Subsequent elections have had the same result.

The Gezi Park protests of 2013 was an influential event in conteporary politics. These protests, which were staged in and around Taksim Meydanı, were initially a public response to a plan to redevelop the park, on the northeastern edge of the square, but transformed into a much larger protest by İstanbullus against what they saw as an increasingly autocratic and undemocratic Turkish government. Called in to disperse the crowd, police used tear gas and water cannons, which led to violent clashes, 8000 injuries, at least four deaths and thousands of arrests.

After Gezi, local authorities cracked down on any political demonstrations that were seen as antigovernment and made any large assemblies in or around Taksim Meydanı illegal. Local media outlets seen to be antigovernment were also targeted, with some being forceably closed or taken over by the government. Many İstanbul-based writers, journalists and editors were charged with serious crimes, including membership of a terror organisation, espionage and revealing confidential documents. Charges under Article 301 of the Turkish penal code, which make it a punishable offence to insult Turkishness or various official Turkish institutions (including the president), were prevalent.

A coup d'état staged by a small faction of the military in July 2016 was defeated when members of the public took to the streets to defend the democratically elected AKP government. Official reprisals against anyone suspected of being a coup perpetrator or supporter were draconian, with thousands of İstanbullus arrested, media outlets closed down and universities and schools purged. Unsurprisingly, tourist arrivals to the city plunged as a result of the turmoil and the local economy is still reeling as a result.

◎ Sights

İstanbul is the world's only city to straddle two continents, separated by the Sea of Marmara. You'll spend most of your time on the European side exploring Sultanahmet's sights and Beyoğlu's restaurants and bars, but a trip to the city's Asian side is highly recommended for the scenic ferry ride between the two shores and for the fascinating glimpse into local life that a visit to suburbs such as Kadıköy and Üsküdar imparts.

◉ Sultanahmet & Around

Many visitors to İstanbul never make it out of Sultanahmet. And while this is a shame, it's hardly surprising. After all, not many cities have such a concentration of historic sights, shopping precincts, hotels and eateries within easy walking distance. Ideally suited to exploration by foot, the neighbourhood is a showcase of the city's glorious past, crammed as it is with mosques, palaces, churches and houses dating from Roman, Byzantine and Ottoman periods.

★**Aya Sofya**   MUSEUM
(Hagia Sophia; Map p72; ☑0212-522 1750, 0212-522 0989; http://ayasofyamuzesi.gov.tr/en; Aya Sofya Meydanı 1; adult/child under 12yr ₺40/free; ⊗9am-7pm Tue-Sun mid-Apr–mid-Oct, to 5pm mid-Oct–mid-Apr, last entry 1hr before closing; 🚇Sultanahmet) There are many important monuments in İstanbul, but this venerable structure – which was commissioned by the great Byzantine emperor Justinian, consecrated as a church in 537, converted to a mosque by Mehmet the Conqueror in 1453 and declared a museum by Atatürk in 1935 – surpasses the rest due to its innovative architectural form, rich history, religious importance and extraordinary beauty.

➡ **Ground Floor**
As you enter the building and walk into the inner narthex, look up to see a brilliant mosaic of *Christ as Pantocrator* (Ruler of All) above the third and largest door (the Imperial Door). Through this is the building's main space, famous for its dome, huge nave and gold mosaics.

The focal point at this level is the apse, with its magnificent 9th-century mosaic of the *Virgin and Christ Child*. The mosaics above the apse once depicted the archangels Gabriel and Michael; today only fragments remain.

The Byzantine emperors were crowned while seated on a throne placed within the omphalion, the section of inlaid marble in the main floor.

Ottoman additions to the building include a *mimber* (pulpit) and *mihrab* (prayer niche indicating the direction of Mecca); large 19th-century medallions inscribed with gilt Arabic letters; a curious elevated kiosk known as the *hünkar mahfili;* and an ornate library behind the omphalion.

Looking up towards the northeast (to your left if you are facing the apse), you should be able to see three mosaics at the base of the northern tympanum (semicircle) beneath the dome, although they have recently been obscured by a scaffold-

---

İSTANBUL IN...

Two Days
With only two days, you'll need to get cracking! On day one, visit the Blue Mosque (p75), Aya Sofya (above) and the Basilica Cistern (p70) in the morning, grab a quick lunch in Hocapaşa Sokak in Sirkeci and then follow our walking tour (p114) of the Grand Bazaar (p85) in the afternoon. Head to Beyoğlu in the evening.

Day two should be devoted to Topkapı Palace (p76) and the Bosphorus. Spend the morning at the palace, then board one of the private excursion boats at Eminönü or the hop-on/hop-off service at Kabataş for a Bosphorus cruise. Afterwards, walk up through Galata to İstiklal Caddesi (p92) and have a drink at a rooftop bar before dinner nearby.

Four Days
Follow the two-day itinerary, and on your third day visit the İstanbul Archaeology Museums (p83) or Museum of Turkish & Islamic Arts (p76) in the morning, have lunch in or around the Grand Bazaar and then visit the Süleymaniye Mosque (p85) in the afternoon. For dinner, head back across Galata Bridge to Beyoğlu. Day four could be devoted to contemporary art galleries and Orhan Pamuk's Museum of Innocence (p96) in Beyoğlu, or to a ferry trip up the Golden Horn to Eyüp. At night, the bar, restaurant and club scenes on the other side of Galata Bridge once again await.

Aya Sofya

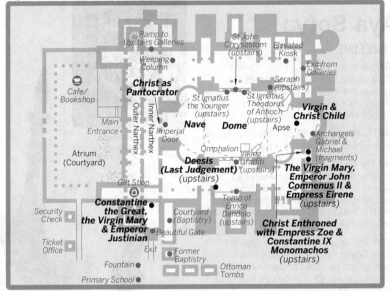

Map labels:
Ramp to Upstairs Galleries
St John Chrysostom (upstairs)
Elevated Kiosk
Weeping Column
Exit from Galleries
Cafe/Bookshop
Christ as Pantocrator
St Ignatius the Younger (upstairs)
St Ignatius Theodorus of Antioch (upstairs)
Seraph (upstairs)
Virgin & Christ Child
Main Entrance
Outer Narthex
Inner Narthex
Imperial Door
Nave
Dome
Apse
Archangels Gabriel & Michael (fragments)
Atrium (Courtyard)
Omphalion
Viking Graffiti (upstairs)
Deesis (Last Judgement) (upstairs)
The Virgin Mary, Emperor John Comnenus II & Empress Eirene (upstairs)
Gift Shop
Security Check
Constantine the Great, the Virgin Mary & Emperor Justinian
Courtyard (Baptistry)
Tomb of Enrico Dandolo (upstairs)
Christ Enthroned with Empress Zoe & Constantine IX Monomachos (upstairs)
Ticket Office
Beautiful Gate
Exit
Former Baptistry
Fountain
Ottoman Tombs
Primary School

ing tower used in restoration works. These are 9th-century portraits of St Ignatius the Younger, St John Chrysostom and St Ignatius Theodorus of Antioch. To their right, on one of the pendentives (concave triangular segments below the dome), is a 14th-century mosaic of the face of a seraph (six-winged angel charged with the caretaking of God's throne).

In the side aisle at the bottom of the ramp to the upstairs galleries is a column with a worn copper facing pierced by a hole. According to legend, the pillar, known as the Weeping Column, was blessed by St Gregory the Miracle Worker and putting one's finger into the hole is said to lead to ailments being healed if the finger emerges moist.

➤ **Upstairs Galleries**

To access the galleries, walk up the switchback ramp at the northern end of the inner narthex. In the south gallery (straight ahead and then left through the 6th-century marble door) are the remnants of a magnificent *Deesis* (Last Judgement). This 13th-century mosaic depicts Christ with the Virgin Mary on his right and John the Baptist on his left.

Further on, at the eastern (apse) end of the gallery, an 11th-century mosaic depicts *Christ Enthroned with Empress Zoe and Constantine IX Monomachos.*

To the right of Zoe and Constantine is a 12th-century mosaic depicting *The Virgin Mary, Emperor John Comnenus II and Empress Eirene.* The emperor, who was known as 'John the Good', is on the Virgin's left and the empress, who was known for her charitable works, is to her right. Their son Alexius, who died soon after the portrait was made, is depicted next to Eirene.

➤ **Exiting the Building**

As you leave the inner narthex, be sure to look back to admire the 10th-century mosaic of *Constantine the Great, the Virgin Mary and the Emperor Justinian* on the lunette of the inner doorway. Constantine (right) is offering the Virgin, who holds the Christ Child, the city of İstanbul; Justinian (left) is offering her Aya Sofya.

Just after you exit the building through the Beautiful Gate, a magnificent bronze gate dating from the 2nd century BC, there is a doorway on the left. This leads into a small courtyard that was once part of a 6th-century baptistry. In the 17th century the baptistry was converted into a tomb for Sultans Mustafa I and İbrahim I. The huge stone basin displayed in the courtyard is the original font.

On the opposite side of Aya Sofya Meydanı are the **Baths of Lady Hürrem**

Aya Sofya

TIMELINE

537 Emperor Justinian, depicted in one of the church's famous **mosaics ❶**, presides over the consecration of Byzantium's new basilica, Hagia Sophia (Church of the Holy Wisdom).

557 The huge **dome ❷**, damaged during an earthquake, collapses and is rebuilt.

843 The second Byzantine Iconoclastic period ends and figurative **mosaics ❸** begin to be added to the interior. These include a depiction of the Empress Zoe and her third husband, Emperor Constantine IX Monomachos.

1204 Soldiers of the Fourth Crusade led by the Doge of Venice, Enrico Dandolo, conquer and ransack Constantinople. Dandolo's **tomb ❹** is eventually erected in the church whose desecration he presided over.

1453 The city falls to the Ottomans; Mehmet II orders that Hagia Sophia be converted to a mosque and renamed Aya Sofya.

1577 Sultan Selim II is buried in a specially designed tomb, which sits alongside the **tombs ❺** of four other Ottoman Sultans in Aya Sofya's grounds.

1847–49 Sultan Abdül Mecit I orders that the building be restored and redecorated; the huge **Ottoman Medallions ❻** in the nave are added.

1935 The mosque is converted into a museum by order of Mustafa Kemal Atatürk, president of the new Turkish Republic.

2009 The face of one of the four **seraphs ❼** is uncovered during major restoration works in the nave.

2012 Restoration of the exterior walls and western upper gallery commences.

TOP TIPS

Bring binoculars if you want to properly view the mosaic portraits in the apse and under the dome.

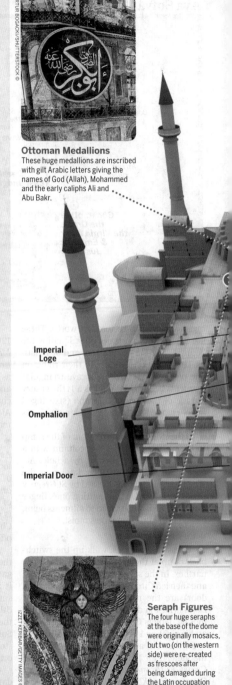

Ottoman Medallions
These huge medallions are inscribed with gilt Arabic letters giving the names of God (Allah), Mohammed and the early caliphs Ali and Abu Bakr.

Imperial Loge

Omphalion

Imperial Door

Seraph Figures
The four huge seraphs at the base of the dome were originally mosaics, but two (on the western side) were re-created as frescoes after being damaged during the Latin occupation (1204–61).

Dome
Soaring 56m from ground level, the dome was originally covered in gold mosaics but was decorated with calligraphy during the 1847–49 restoration works overseen by Swiss-born architects Gaspard and Giuseppe Fossati.

Christ Enthroned with Empress Zoe and Constantine IX Monomachos
This mosaic portrait in the upper gallery depicts Zoe, one of only three Byzantine women to rule as empress in their own right.

Ottoman Tombs
The tombs of five Ottoman sultans and their families are located in Aya Sofya's southern corner and can be accessed via Babıhümayun Caddesi. One of these occupies the church's original Baptistry.

Aya Sofya Tombs

Former Baptistry

Muvakkithane (place where prayer hours were determined)

Exit

Ablutions Fountain

Primary School

Main Entrance

Grave of Enrico Dandolo
The Venetian doge died in 1205, only one year after he and his Crusaders had stormed the city. A 19th-century marker in the upper gallery indicates the probable location of his grave.

Constantine the Great, the Virgin Mary and Emperor Justinian
This 11th-century mosaic shows Constantine (right) offering the Virgin Mary the city of Constantinople. Justinian (left) is offering her Hagia Sophia.

(Ayasofya Hürrem Sultan Hamamı), built between 1556 and 1557. Designed by Sinan, the hamam was commissioned by Süleyman the Magnificent in the name of his wife Hürrem Sultan, known to history as Roxelana.

Aya Sofya Tombs
TOMB

(Aya Sofya Müzesi Padişah Türbeleri; Map p72; ☏ 0212-522 1750; http://ayasofyamuzesi.gov.tr/en; Babıhümayun Caddesi; ⊘ 9am-5pm; ⊕ Sultanahmet) FREE Part of the Aya Sofya complex but entered via Babıhümayun Caddesi, these tombs are the final resting places of five 16th- and 17th-century sultans – Mehmet III, Selim II, Murat III, İbrahim I and Mustafa I – most of whom are buried with members of their families. The ornate interior decoration in the tombs features the very best Ottoman tile work, calligraphy and decorative paintwork.

Mehmet III's tomb dates from 1608 and Murat III's from 1599; both are adorned with particularly beautiful İznik tiles. Next to Murat's tomb is that of his five children, who died in a plague epidemic; this was designed by Sinan and has simple but beautiful painted decoration.

Selim II's tomb, which was designed by Sinan and built in 1577, is particularly poignant, as it houses the graves of five of his sons, murdered on the same night in December 1574 to ensure the peaceful succession of the oldest, Murat III. It also houses the graves of 19 of Murat's sons, murdered in January 1595 to ensure Mehmet III's succession. They were the last of the royal princes to be murdered by their siblings – after this, the younger brothers of succeeding sultans were confined to the *kafes* (cage) in Topkapı Palace instead.

The fifth tomb is Aya Sofya's original baptistry, converted to a mausoleum for sultans İbrahim I and Mustafa I during the 17th century.

ℹ CLOSING DAYS
....

Plan your sightseeing around the major attractions' weekly closing days:

Monday Aya Sofya (p66), Carpet Museum, Dolmabahçe Palace (p98)

Tuesday Topkapı Palace (p76; including Harem and Aya İrini)

Thursday Dolmabahçe Palace

Sunday Grand Bazaar (p85)

Carpet Museum
MUSEUM

(Halı Müzesi; Map p72; ☏ 0212-518 1330; www.halimuzesi.com; cnr Babıhümayun Caddesi & Soğukçeşme Sokak; ₺10; ⊘ 9am-6pm Tue-Sun mid-Apr–mid-Oct, to 4pm mid-Oct–mid-Apr; ⊕ Sultanahmet or Gülhane) Housed in an *imaret* (soup kitchen) added to the Aya Sofya complex in the 18th century, this museum is entered through a spectacular baroque gate and gives the visitor an excellent overview of the history of Anatolian carpet making. The carpets, which have been sourced from mosques throughout the country, date from the 14th to 20th centuries.

There are three galleries, each entered through Tardis-like humidity-controlled entrances. The first, in the *me'kel* (dining hall), features early Anatolian-era carpets with geometric and abstract designs; these are sometimes called Holbein carpets in honour of Dutch artist Hans Holbein the Younger, who often depicted them in his paintings. Also here are examples of the best-known type of Turkish carpets: Uşak (Ushak) carpets of the 16th and 17th centuries.

The second gallery, in the *aşhane* (kitchen), displays rugs with central and eastern Anatolian motifs including star-shaped medallions and keyholes; the latter is said to have been inspired by the mosque *mihrab* (panels decode the many symbols' meanings). Don't miss the particularly fine red-and-yellow 19th-century Hereke rug, on the left at the end of the room, from the Mustafa Mosque in Sirkeci.

The third gallery, in the *fodlahane* (bakery), is the most impressive, with huge 17th- and 18th-century Uşak carpets from the Süleymaniye Mosque and another 19th-century example from the Blue Mosque. The latter is also a late example of a *saf* prayer rug; several people could pray side by side in a *saf* (line) on its multiple *mihrab* decorations.

★ Basilica Cistern
CISTERN

(Yerebatan Sarnıçı; Map p72; ☏ 0212-512 1570; www.yerebatan.com; Yerebatan Caddesi; ₺20; ⊘ 9am-6.30pm mid-Apr–Sep, to 5.30pm Nov–mid-Apr; ⊕ Sultanahmet) This subterranean structure was commissioned by Emperor Justinian and built in 532. The largest surviving Byzantine cistern in İstanbul, it was constructed using 336 columns, many of which were salvaged from ruined temples and feature fine carved capitals. Its symmetry and sheer grandeur of conception are quite breathtaking, and its cavernous depths make a great retreat on summer days.

Sultanahmet

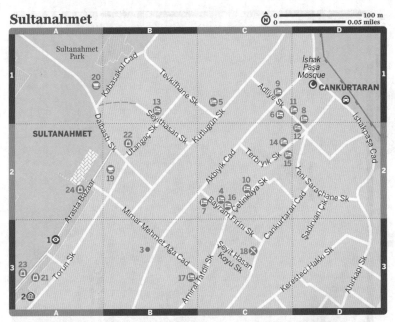

Sultanahmet

Like most sites in İstanbul, the cistern has an unusual history. It was originally known as the Basilica Cistern because it lay underneath the Stoa Basilica, one of the great squares on the first hill. Designed to service the Great Palace and surrounding buildings, it was able to store up to 80,000 cu metres of water delivered via 20km of aqueducts from a reservoir near the Black Sea, but was closed when the Byzantine emperors relocated from the Great Palace. Forgotten by the city authorities some time before the Conquest, it wasn't rediscovered until 1545, when scholar Petrus Gyllius was researching Byzantine antiquities in the city and was told by local residents that they were able to obtain water by lowering buckets into a dark space below their basement floors. Some were even catching fish this way. Intrigued, Gyllius explored the neighbourhood and finally accessed the cistern through one

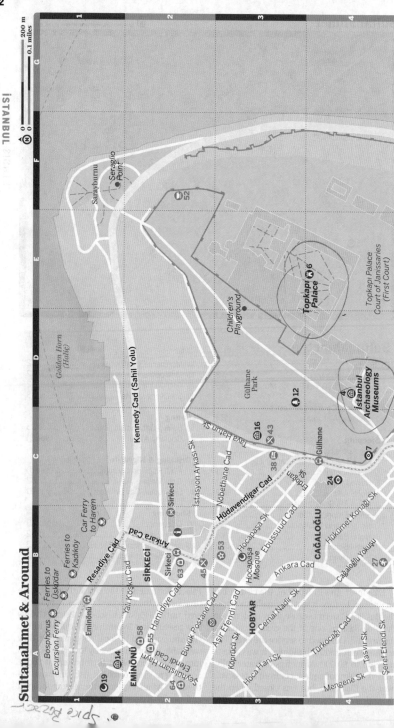

ISTANBUL

Sultanahmet & Around

Spice Bazaar

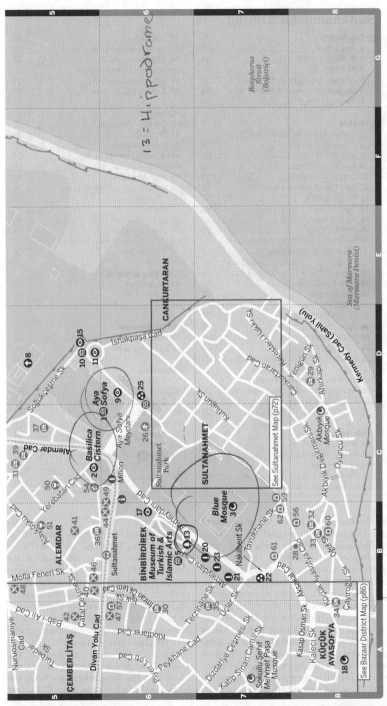

ISTANBUL HIGHLIGHTS

13 = Hippodrome

Grand Bazaar

Bosphorus Strait (Boğazı)

Sea of Marmara (Marmara Denizi)

CANKURTARAN

Kennedy Cad (Sahil Yolu)

Ishakpaşa Cad

8

10 📷 15
11 ⊙

Soğukçeşme Sk

Aya Sofya

9 ⊙
1 📷

Aya Sofya Meydanı

25

Milion

SULTANAHMET

Kutlugün Sk

Cankurtaran Cad

Keresteci Hakkı Sk

29

Ahırkapı Sk

Akbıyık Mosque

Akbıyık Değirmeni Sk

Oyuncu Sk

Basilica Cistern

2 ⊙

Alemdar Cad

Sultanahmet Park

26

See Sultanahmet Map (p72)

37

31 39

50

Yerebatan Cad

54

49

44

f

ALEMDAR

Atikalışöku Cad

41

51

17

Blue Mosque

3 ⊙

Tavukhane Sk

Nakilbent Sk

62 56

59

32

Molla Feneri Sk

46

36

Sultanahmet

BINBIRDIREK

Museum of Turkish & Islamic Arts

5

13
20

21

23

22

33

60

Küçük Ayasofya Cad

61

28

Oğul Sk

48

ÇEMBERLİTAŞ

Çatal Çeşme Sk

İmran Öktem Cad

30

47 57

Işık Sk

Klodfarer Cad

35

Üçler Sk

Terzihane Sk

See Bazaar District Map (p86)

34

KÜÇÜK AYASOFYA

Çayıroğlu Sk

Nuruosmaniye Cad

Türbedar Sk

Bab-ı Ali Cad

42

Divan Yolu Cad

Peykhane Cad

Dizdariye Çeşmesi Sk

Piyer Loti Cad

Katip Sinan Camii Sk

Sokollu Şehit Mehmet Paşa Mosque

Kasap Osman Sk

Kaleci Sk

18 ⊙

Amvadani Cad

Binbirdirek Meydanı Sk

Bosphorus Strait (Boğazı)

Sultanahmet & Around

of the basements. Even after his discovery, the Ottomans (who referred to the cistern as Yerebatan Saray) didn't treat the so-called Underground Palace with the respect it deserved – it became a dumping ground for all sorts of junk, as well as corpses.

The cistern was cleaned and renovated in 1985 by the İstanbul Metropolitan Municipality and opened to the public in 1987. It's now one of the city's most popular tourist attractions. Walking along its raised wooden platforms, you'll feel water dripping from the vaulted ceiling and see schools of ghostly carp patrolling the water – it certainly has bucketloads of atmosphere.

Hippodrome   PARK

(Atmeydanı; Map p72; Atmeydanı Caddesi; ☐ Sultanahmet) The Byzantine emperors loved nothing more than an afternoon at the chariot races, and this rectangular arena alongside Sultanahmet Park was their venue of choice. In its heyday, it was decorated by obelisks and statues, some of which remain in place today. Re-landscaped in more recent years, it is one of the city's most popular meeting places and promenades.

Originally the arena consisted of two levels of galleries, a central spine, starting boxes and the semicircular southern end known as the **Sphendone** (Map p72; Nakilbent

Sokak; 🚇 Sultanahmet), parts of which still stand. The galleries that once topped this stone structure were damaged during the Fourth Crusade and ended up being totally dismantled in the Ottoman period; many of the original columns were used in the construction of the Süleymaniye Mosque.

The Hippodrome was the centre of Byzantium's life for 1000 years and of Ottoman life for another 400 years, and has been the scene of countless political dramas. In Byzantine times, the rival chariot teams of 'Greens' and 'Blues' had separate sectarian connections. Support for a team was akin to membership of a political party, and a team victory had important effects on policy. Occasionally, Greens and Blues joined forces against the emperor, as was the case in AD 532 when a chariot race was disturbed by protests against Justinian's high tax regime. This escalated into the Nika riots (so called after the protesters' cry of *Nika!*, or Victory!), which led to tens of thousands of protesters being massacred in the Hippodrome by imperial forces. Not surprisingly, chariot races were banned for some time afterwards.

Ottoman sultans also kept an eye on activities in the Hippodrome. If things were going badly in the empire, a surly crowd gathering here could signal the start of a disturbance, then a riot, then a revolution. In 1826 the slaughter of the corrupt janissary corps (the sultan's personal bodyguards) was carried out here by the reformer Sultan Mahmut II. In 1909 there were riots here that caused the downfall of Abdül Hamit II.

Despite the ever-present threat of the Hippodrome being the scene of their downfall, emperors and sultans sought to outdo one another in beautifying it, and adorned the centre with statues from the far reaches of the empire. Unfortunately, many priceless statues carved by ancient masters have disappeared from their original homes here. Chief among those responsible for such thefts were the soldiers of the Fourth Crusade, who invaded Constantinople, a Christian ally city, in 1204.

Near the northern end of the Hippodrome, the little gazebo with beautiful stonework is known as Kaiser Wilhelm's Fountain. The German emperor paid a state visit to Sultan Abdül Hamit II in 1898, and presented this fountain to the sultan and his people as a token of friendship in 1901. The monograms on the dome's interior feature Abdül Hamit's *tuğra* (calligraphic signature) and the first letter of Wilhelm's name, representing their political union.

The immaculately preserved pink granite Obelisk of Theodosius in the centre was carved in Egypt during the reign of Thutmose III (r 1549–1503 BC) and erected in the Amon-Re temple at Karnak. Theodosius the Great (r 379–95) had it brought from Egypt to Constantinople in AD 390. On the marble podium below the obelisk, look for the carvings of Theodosius, his wife, his sons, state officials and bodyguards watching the chariot-race action from the *kathisma* (imperial box).

South of the obelisk is a strange column coming up out of a hole in the ground. Known as the Spiral Column, it was once much taller and was topped by three serpents' heads. Originally cast to commemorate a victory of the Hellenic confederation over the Persians in the battle of Plataea, it stood in front of the Temple of Apollo at Delphi (Greece) from 478 BC until Constantine the Great had it brought to his new capital city around AD 330. Though badly damaged in Byzantine times, the serpents' heads survived until the early 18th century. Now all that remains of them is one upper jaw, which was discovered in a basement of Aya Sofya and is housed in the İstanbul Archaeology Museums (p83).

After sacking Aya Sofya in 1204, the soldiers of the Fourth Crusade tore all the plates from the Rough-Stone Obelisk, at the Hippodrome's southern end, in the mistaken belief that they were solid gold (in fact, they were gold-covered bronze). The Crusaders also stole the famous Triumphal Quadriga (team of four horses cast in bronze) and placed it atop the main door of Venice's Basilica di San Marco; replicas are now located there, as the originals were moved into the basilica for safekeeping.

★ Blue Mosque   MOSQUE
(Sultanahmet Camii; Map p72; ☎ 0545 577 1899; www.bluemosque.co; Hippodrome; ⊗ closed to non-worshippers during 6 daily prayer times; 🚇 Sultanahmet) İstanbul's most photogenic building was the grand project of Sultan Ahmet I (r 1603–17), whose tomb is located on the north side of the site facing Sultanahmet Park. The mosque's wonderfully curvaceous exterior features a cascade of domes and six slender minarets. Blue İznik tiles adorn the interior and give the building its unofficial but commonly used name.

With the mosque's exterior, the architect, Sedefkâr Mehmet Ağa, managed to orchestrate a visual wham-bam effect similar to that of nearby star Aya Sofya's interior. Its curves are voluptuous; it has six minarets (more than any other mosque at the time it was built); and its courtyard is the biggest of all of the Ottoman mosques. The interior has a similarly grand scale: the İznik tiles number in the tens of thousands; there are 260 windows; and the central prayer space is huge.

To best grasp the mosque's design, enter the complex via the Hippodrome rather than from Sultanahmet Park. Once inside the courtyard, which is the same size as the mosque's interior, you'll appreciate the building's perfect proportions.

The mosque is such a popular attraction that admission is controlled in order to preserve its sacred atmosphere. Only worshippers are admitted through the main door; visitors must use the south door (follow the signs). The mosque is closed to nonworshippers during the six daily prayer times: two hours before dawn, dawn, midday, afternoon, sunset and right before the last light of the day.

★ Museum of Turkish & Islamic Arts   MUSEUM

(Türk ve İslam Eserleri Müzesi; Map p72; www.tiem. gov.tr; Atmeydanı Caddesi 46, Hippodrome; adult/child under 12yr ₺25/free; ⊙9am-5pm Nov–mid-Apr, to 7pm mid-Apr–Oct, last entry 30min before closing; ⓐSultanahmet) This Ottoman palace was built in 1524 for İbrahim Paşa, childhood friend, brother-in-law and grand vizier of Süleyman the Magnificent. Recently renovated, it has a magnificent collection of artefacts, including exquisite calligraphy and one of the world's most impressive antique carpet collections. Some large-scale carpets have been moved from the upper rooms to the Carpet Museum (p70), but the collection remains a knockout with its palace carpets, prayer rugs and glittering artefacts such as a 17th-century Ottoman incense burner.

Born in Greece, İbrahim Paşa was captured in that country as a child and sold as a slave into the imperial household in İstanbul. He worked as a page in Topkapı Palace, where he became friendly with Süleyman, who was the same age. When his friend became sultan, İbrahim was made in turn chief falconer, chief of the royal bedchamber and grand vizier. This palace was bestowed on him by Süleyman the year before he was

given the hand of Süleyman's sister, Hadice, in marriage. Alas, the fairy tale was not to last for poor İbrahim. His wealth, power and influence on the monarch became so great that others wishing to influence the sultan became envious, chief among them Süleyman's powerful wife, Haseki Hürrem Sultan (Roxelana). After a rival accused İbrahim of disloyalty, Roxelana convinced her husband that İbrahim was a threat and Süleyman had him strangled in 1536.

Artefacts in the museum's collection date from the 8th to the 19th century and come from across the Middle East. They include *müknames* (scrolls outlining an imperial decree) featuring the sultan's *tuğra* (calligraphic signature); Iranian book binding from the Safavid period (1501–1722); 12th- and 13th-century wooden columns and doors from Damascus and Cizre; Holbein, Lotto, Konya, Uşhak, Iran and Caucasia carpets; and even a cutting of the Prophet's beard. Sections of the Hippodrome walls can be seen near the entrance.

Little Aya Sofya   MOSQUE

(Küçük Aya Sofya Camii, SS Sergius & Bacchus Church; Map p72; Küçük Ayasofya Caddesi; ⊙sunrise-sunset; ⓐSultanahmet, Çemberlitaş) **FREE** Justinian and his wife Theodora built this little church between 527 and 536, just before Justinian built Aya Sofya. You can still see their monogram worked into some of the frilly white capitals. The building is one of the most beautiful Byzantine structures in the city despite being converted into a mosque in the early 16th century and having many of its original features obscured during an extensive restoration in 2007.

★ Topkapı Palace   PALACE

(Topkapı Sarayı; Map p72; ☑0212-512 0480; www. topkapisarayi.gov.tr; Babıhümayun Caddesi; palace adult/child under 12yr ₺40/free, Harem adult/child under 6yr ₺25/free; ⊙9am-6.45pm Wed-Mon mid-Apr–Oct, to 4.45pm Nov–mid-Apr, last entry 45min before closing; ⓐSultanahmet) Topkapı is the subject of more colourful stories than most of the world's museums put together. Libidinous sultans, ambitious courtiers, beautiful concubines and scheming eunuchs lived and worked here between the 15th and 19th centuries when it was the court of the Ottoman empire. A visit to the palace's opulent pavilions, jewel-filled Treasury and sprawling Harem gives a fascinating glimpse into their lives.

Topkapı Palace (Topkapı Sarayı)

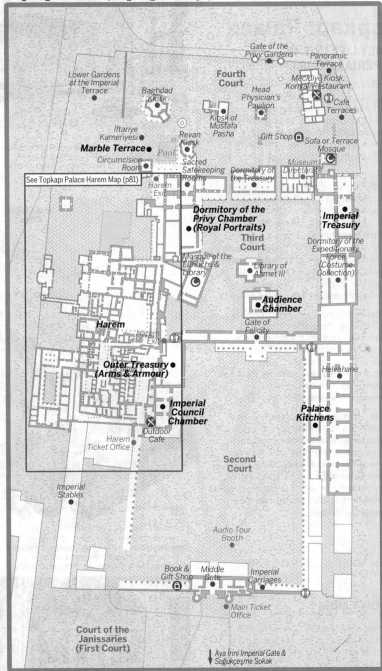

Gate of the Privy Gardens

Panoramic Terrace

Fourth Court

Lower Gardens of the Imperial Terrace

Baghdad Kiosk

Head Physician's Pavilion

Macidiye Kiosk; Konyalı Restaurant

Cafe Terraces

İftariye Kameriyesi

Marble Terrace

Revan Kiosk

Kiosk of Mustafa Pasha

Gift Shop

Sofa or Terrace Mosque

Circumcision Room

Pool

Sacred Safekeeping Rooms

Dormitory of the Treasury

Museum Directorate

See Topkapı Palace Harem Map (p81)

Harem Exit

Dormitory of the Privy Chamber (Royal Portraits)

Imperial Treasury

Third Court

Dormitory of the Expeditionary Force (Costume Collection)

Mosque of the Eunuchs & Library

Library of Ahmet III

Harem

Audience Chamber

Harem Exit

Gate of Felicity

Helvahane

Outer Treasury (Arms & Armour)

Imperial Council Chamber

Outdoor Cafe

Palace Kitchens

Harem Ticket Office

Second Court

Imperial Stables

Audio Tour Booth

Book & Gift Shop

Middle Gate

Imperial Carriages

Main Ticket Office

Court of the Janissaries (First Court)

Aya İrini Imperial Gate & Soğukçeşme Sokak

Topkapı Palace
DAILY LIFE IN THE IMPERIAL COURT

A visit to this opulent palace compound, with its courtyards, harem and pavilions, offers a fascinating glimpse into the lives of the Ottoman sultans. During its heyday, royal wives and children, concubines, eunuchs and servants were among the 4000 people living within Topkapı's walls.

The sultans and their families rarely left the palace grounds, relying on courtiers and diplomats to bring them news of the outside world. Most visitors would go straight to the magnificent **Imperial Council Chamber ❶**, where the sultan's grand vizier and Dîvân (Council) regularly met to discuss affairs of state and receive foreign dignitaries. Many of these visitors brought lavish gifts and tributes to embellish the **Imperial Treasury ❷**.

After receiving any guests and meeting with the Dîvân, the grand vizier would make his way through the ornate **Gate of Felicity ❸** into the Third Court, the palace's residential quarter. Here, he would brief the sultan on the deliberations and decisions of the Dîvân in the colonnaded **Audience Chamber ❹**.

Meanwhile, day-to-day domestic chores and intrigues would be underway in the **Harem ❺** and servants would be preparing feasts in the massive **Palace Kitchens ❻**. Amid all this activity, the **Marble Terrace ❼** was a tranquil retreat where the sultan would come to relax, look out over the city and perhaps regret his sequestered lifestyle.

DON'T MISS

There are spectacular views from the terrace above the Konyalı Restaurant and also from the Marble Terrace in the Fourth Court.

Harem
The sultan, his mother and the crown prince had sumptuously decorated private apartments in the Harem. The most beautiful of these are the Twin Kiosks (pictured), which were used by the crown prince. ...

Harem Ticket Office

Middle Gate

Aya İrini

Imperial Gate

Imperial Council Chamber
This is where the Dîvân (Council) made laws, citizens presented petitions and foreign dignitaries were presented to the court. The sultan sometimes eavesdropped on proceedings through the window with the golden grille.

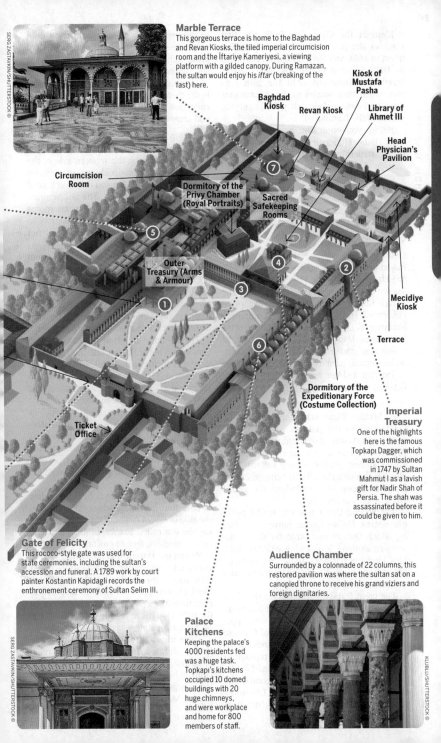

Marble Terrace
This gorgeous terrace is home to the Baghdad and Revan Kiosks, the tiled imperial circumcision room and the İftariye Kameriyesi, a viewing platform with a gilded canopy. During Ramazan, the sultan would enjoy his *iftar* (breaking of the fast) here.

Kiosk of Mustafa Pasha

Baghdad Kiosk

Revan Kiosk

Library of Ahmet III

Head Physician's Pavilion

Circumcision Room

Dormitory of the Privy Chamber (Royal Portraits)

Sacred Safekeeping Rooms

Outer Treasury (Arms & Armour)

Mecidiye Kiosk

Terrace

Ticket Office

Dormitory of the Expeditionary Force (Costume Collection)

Imperial Treasury
One of the highlights here is the famous Topkapı Dagger, which was commissioned in 1747 by Sultan Mahmut I as a lavish gift for Nadir Shah of Persia. The shah was assassinated before it could be given to him.

Gate of Felicity
This rococo-style gate was used for state ceremonies, including the sultan's accession and funeral. A 1789 work by court painter Kostantin Kapidagli records the enthronement ceremony of Sultan Selim III.

Palace Kitchens
Keeping the palace's 4000 residents fed was a huge task. Topkapı's kitchens occupied 10 domed buildings with 20 huge chimneys, and were workplace and home for 800 members of staff.

Audience Chamber
Surrounded by a colonnade of 22 columns, this restored pavilion was where the sultan sat on a canopied throne to receive his grand viziers and foreign dignitaries.

Mehmet the Conqueror built the first stage of the palace shortly after the Conquest in 1453, and lived here until his death in 1481. Subsequent sultans lived in this rarefied environment until the 19th century, when they moved to the ostentatious European-style palaces they built on the shores of the Bosphorus.

Before you enter the palace's Imperial Gate (Bab-ı Hümayun), take a look at the ornate structure in the cobbled square just outside. This is the rococo-style **Fountain of Sultan Ahmet III** (Map p72; Babıhümayun Caddesi), built in 1728 by the sultan who so favoured tulips.

The main ticket office is in the First Court, just before the gate to the Second Court.

➡ **First Court**

Pass through the **Imperial Gate** (cnr Babıhümayun Caddesi & Soğukçeşme Sokak; Map p72; 🚇 Sultanahmet) into the First Court, which is known as the Court of the Janissaries or the Parade Court. On your left is the Byzantine church of Hagia Eirene, more commonly known as **Aya İrini** (Hagia Eirene, Church of the Divine Peace; Map p72; ☎ 0212-512 0480; http://topkapisarayi.gov.tr/en/hagia-irene-0; 1st Court, Topkapı Palace; adult/child under 6yr ₺20/free; ⏰ 9am-7pm Wed-Mon Apr–mid-Oct, to 5pm mid-Oct–Mar; 🚇 Sultanahmet).

➡ **Second Court**

The Middle Gate (Ortakapı or Bab-üs Selâm) led to the palace's Second Court, used for the business of running the empire. In Ottoman times, only the sultan and the *valide sultan* (mother of the sultan) were allowed through the Middle Gate on horseback. Everyone else, including the grand vizier, had to dismount.

The Second Court has a beautiful park-like setting. Unlike typical European palaces, which feature one large building with outlying gardens, Topkapı is a series of pavilions, kitchens, barracks, audience chambers, kiosks and sleeping quarters built around a central enclosure.

The great **Palace Kitchens** on the right (east) as you enter have reopened following years of restoration. They hold a small portion of Topkapı's vast collection of Chinese celadon porcelain, valued by the sultans for its beauty but also because it was reputed to change colour if touched by poisoned food.

On the left (west) side of the Second Court is the ornate **Imperial Council Chamber** (Dîvân-ı Hümâyûn). The council met here to discuss matters of state, and the sultan sometimes eavesdropped through the gold grille high in the wall. The room to the right showcases clocks from the palace collection.

North of the Imperial Council Chamber is the **Outer Treasury**, where an impressive collection of Ottoman and European arms and armour is displayed.

➡ **Harem**

The entrance to the Harem is beneath the Tower of Justice on the western side of the Second Court. If you decide to visit – and we highly recommend that you do – you'll need to buy a dedicated ticket. The visitor route through the Harem changes when rooms are closed for restoration or stabilisation, so some of the areas mentioned here may not be open during your visit.

As popular belief would have it, the Harem was a place where the sultan could engage in debauchery at will. In more prosaic reality, these were the imperial family quarters, and every detail of Harem life was governed by tradition, obligation and ceremony. The word 'harem' literally means 'forbidden' or 'private'.

The sultans supported as many as 300 concubines in the Harem, although numbers were usually lower than this. Upon entering the Harem, the girls would be schooled in Islam and in Turkish culture and language, as well as the arts of make-up, dress, comportment, music, reading, writing, embroidery and dancing. They then entered a meritocracy, first as ladies-in-waiting to the sultan's concubines and children, then to the *valide sultan* and finally – if they were particularly attractive and talented – to the sultan himself.

The sultan was allowed by Islamic law to have four legitimate wives, who received the title of *kadın* (wife). If a wife bore him a son she was called *haseki sultan;* if she bore him a daughter, *haseki kadın.*

Ruling the Harem was the *valide sultan,* who often owned large landed estates in her own name and controlled them through black eunuch servants. Able to give orders directly to the grand vizier, her influence on the sultan, on his wives and concubines, and on matters of state was often profound.

The earliest of the 300-odd rooms in the Harem were constructed during the reign of Murat III (r 1574–95); the harems of previous sultans were at the now-demolished Eski Sarayı (Old Palace), near present-day Beyazıt Meydanı.

Topkapı Palace Harem

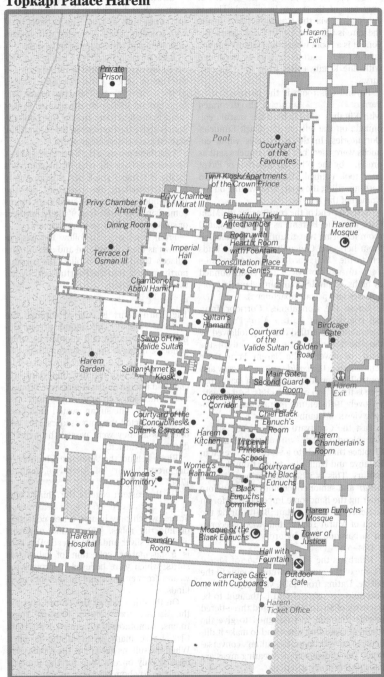

Harem Exit

Private Prison

Pool

Courtyard of the Favourites

Twin Kiosk/Apartments of the Crown Prince

Privy Chamber of Murat III

Privy Chamber of Ahmet III

Beautifully Tiled Antechamber

Dining Room

Room with Hearth; Room with Fountain

Harem Mosque

Terrace of Osman III

Imperial Hall

Consultation Place of the Genies

Chamber of Abdül Hamit I

Sultan's Hamam

Courtyard of the Valide Sultan

Birdcage Gate

Salon of the Valide Sultan

Golden Road

Harem Garden

Sultan Ahmet's Kiosk

Main Gate; Second Guard Room

Harem Exit

Concubines Corridor

Courtyard of the Concubines & Sultan's Consorts

Chief Black Eunuch's Room

Harem Kitchen

Imperial Princes School

Harem Chamberlain's Room

Women's Hamam

Courtyard of the Black Eunuchs

Women's Dormitory

Black Eunuchs Dormitories

Harem Eunuchs' Mosque

Harem Hospital

Mosque of the Black Eunuchs

Tower of Justice

Laundry Room

Hall with Fountain

Carriage Gate; Dome with Cupboards

Outdoor Cafe

Harem Ticket Office

The Harem complex has six floors, but only one of these can be visited. This is approached via the Carriage Gate. Inside the gate is the Dome with Cupboards. Beyond it is a room where the Harem's eunuch guards were stationed. This is decorated with fine Kütahya tiles from the 17th century.

Beyond this room is the narrow Courtyard of the Black Eunuchs, also decorated with Kütahya tiles. Behind the marble colonnade on the left are the Black Eunuchs' Dormitories. In the early days white eunuchs were used, but black eunuchs sent as presents by the Ottoman governor of Egypt later took control. As many as 200 lived here, guarding the doors and waiting on the women of the Harem.

At the far end of the courtyard is the Main Gate into the Harem, as well as a guard room featuring two gigantic gilded mirrors. From here, the Concubines' Corridor leads left to the Courtyard of the Concubines and Sultan's Consorts. This is surrounded by baths, a laundry fountain, a laundry, dormitories and private apartments.

Across the Concubines' Corridor from the courtyard is Sultan Ahmet's Kiosk, decorated with a tiled chimney, followed by the Apartments of the Valide Sultan, the centre of power in the Harem. From these ornate rooms the *valide sultan* oversaw and controlled her huge 'family'. Of particular note is the Salon of the Valide Sultan with its lovely 19th-century murals featuring bucolic views of İstanbul.

Past the Courtyard of the Valide Sultan is a splendid reception room with a large fireplace that leads to a vestibule covered in Kütahya and İznik tiles dating from the 17th century. This is where the princes, *valide sultan* and senior concubines waited before entering the handsome Imperial Hall for an audience with the sultan. Built during the reign of Murat III, the hall was redecorated in baroque style by order of Osman III (r 1754–57).

Nearby is the Privy Chamber of Murat III, one of the most sumptuous rooms in the palace. Dating from 1578, virtually all of its decoration is original and is thought to be the work of Sinan. The restored three-tiered marble fountain was designed to give the sound of cascading water and to make it difficult to eavesdrop on the sultan's conversations. The gilded canopied seating areas are later 18th-century additions.

Continue to the Privy Chamber of Ahmed III and peek into the adjoining dining room built in 1705. The latter is lined with wooden panels decorated with images of flowers and fruits painted in lacquer.

Back through the Privy Chamber of Murat III are two of the most beautiful rooms in the Harem – the Twin Kiosk/Apartments of the Crown Prince. These two rooms date from around 1600; note the painted canvas dome in the first room and the fine İznik tile panels above the fireplace in the second. The stained glass is also noteworthy.

Past these rooms is the Courtyard of the Favourites. Over the edge of the courtyard (really a terrace) you'll see a large empty pool. Overlooking the courtyard are the tiny windows of the many small dark rooms comprising the *kafes* (cage) where brothers or sons of the sultan were imprisoned.

From here, you can follow the passage known as the Golden Road and exit into the palace's Third Court, or follow the corridor north and exit into the Fourth Court by the Circumcision Room.

➤ Third Court

The Third Court is entered through the Gate of Felicity. The sultan's private domain, it was staffed and guarded by white eunuchs. Inside is the Audience Chamber, constructed in the 16th century but refurbished in the 18th century. Important officials and foreign ambassadors were brought to this little kiosk to conduct the high business of state. The sultan, seated on a huge divan, inspected the ambassadors' gifts and offerings as they were passed through the doorway on the left.

Right behind the Audience Chamber is the pretty Library of Ahmet III, built in 1719.

On the eastern edge of the Third Court is the Dormitory of the Expeditionary Force, which now houses a rich collection of imperial robes, kaftans and uniforms worked in silver and gold thread. Also here is a fascinating collection of talismanic shirts, which were believed to protect the wearer from enemies and misfortunes of all kinds.

On the other side of the Third Court are the Sacred Safekeeping Rooms. These rooms, sumptuously decorated with İznik tiles, house many relics of the Prophet. When the sultans lived here, the rooms were opened only once a year, for the imperial family to pay homage to the memory of the

Prophet on the 15th day of the holy month of Ramazan.

Next to the sacred Safekeeping Rooms is the **Dormitory of the Privy Chamber**, which houses an exhibit of portraits of 36 sultans. The highlight is a wonderful painting of the *Enthronement Ceremony of Sultan Selim III* (1789) by Konstantin Kapidagli.

➡ Imperial Treasury

Located on the eastern edge of the Third Court, Topkapı's Treasury features an incredible collection of objects made from or decorated with gold, silver, rubies, emeralds, jade, pearls and diamonds. The building itself was constructed during Mehmet the Conqueror's reign in 1460 and was used originally as reception rooms.

The second of the four rooms exhibits non-Ottoman objects received as gifts or spoils of war, for example a glittering zinc jug with golden adornments from Tabriz, Iran. The tiny Indian figures, mainly made from seed pearls, are also well worth seeking out. The Treasury's most famous exhibit, the Topkapı Dagger, is in the fourth room. The object of the criminal heist in Jules Dassin's 1964 film *Topkapi*, the dagger features three enormous emeralds on the hilt and a watch set into the pommel. Near it is the Kaşıkçı (Spoonmaker's) Diamond, a teardrop-shaped 86-carat rock surrounded by dozens of smaller stones. First worn by Mehmet IV at his accession to the throne in 1648, it's one of the largest diamonds in the world.

➡ Fourth Court

Pleasure pavilions occupy the palace's Fourth Court. These include the **Mecidiye Kiosk**, which was built by Abdül Mecit (r 1839–61) according to 19th-century European models. Beneath this is the Konyalı restaurant, which offers wonderful views from its terrace but is let down by the quality and price of its food. Up steps from the Mecidiye Kiosk is the **Head Physician's Pavilion**. Interestingly, the head physician was always one of the sultan's Jewish subjects. On this terrace you will also find the **Kiosk of Mustafa Pasha**, sometimes called the Sofa Köşkü. During the reign of Ahmet III, the Tulip Garden outside the kiosk was filled with the latest varieties of the flower.

Up the stairs at the end of the Tulip Garden is the **Marble Terrace**, a platform with a decorative pool, three pavilions and the whimsical **İftariye Kameriyesi**, a small structure commissioned by İbrahim I ('the Crazy') in 1640 as a picturesque place to break the fast of Ramazan.

Murat IV built the **Revan Kiosk** in 1636 after reclaiming the city of Yerevan (now in Armenia) from Persia. In 1639 he constructed the **Baghdad Kiosk**, one of the last examples of classical palace architecture, to commemorate his victory over that city. Notice its superb İznik tiles, painted ceiling and mother-of-pearl and tortoiseshell inlay. The small **Circumcision Room** (Sünnet Odası) was used for the ritual that admits Muslim boys to manhood. Built by İbrahim I in 1640, the outer walls of the chamber are graced by particularly beautiful tile panels.

★ İstanbul Archaeology Museums　　　　　　　　MUSEUM

(İstanbul Arkeoloji Müzeleri; Map p72; ☎0212-520 7740; www.istanbularkeoloji.gov.tr; Osman Hamdi Bey Yokuşu Sokak, Gülhane; adult/child under 12yr ₺20/free; ☉9am-7pm, last entry 6pm; 🚇Gülhane) This superb museum showcases archaeological and artistic treasures from the Topkapı collections. Housed in three buildings, its exhibits include ancient artefacts, classical statuary and an exhibition tracing İstanbul's history. There are many highlights, but the sarcophagi from the Royal Necropolis of Sidon are particularly striking.

The complex has three main parts: the Museum of the Ancient Orient (Eski Şark Eserler Müzesi), the Archaeology Museum (Arkeoloji Müzesi) and the Tiled Pavilion (Çinili Köşk). These museums house the palace collections formed during the late 19th century by museum director, artist and archaeologist Osman Hamdi Bey. The complex can be easily reached by walking down the slope from Topkapı's First Court, or by walking up the hill from the main gate of Gülhane Park.

➡ Museum of the Ancient Orient

Located immediately on the left after you enter the complex, this 1883 building has a collection of pre-Islamic items gathered from the expanse of the Ottoman Empire. Highlights include a series of large blue-and-yellow glazed-brick panels that once lined the processional street and the Ishtar gate of ancient Babylon. These depict real and mythical animals such as lions, dragons and bulls.

➡ Archaeology Museum

On the opposite side of the column-filled courtyard to the Museum of the Ancient

İSTANBUL SIGHTS

ÜSKÜDAR

A working-class suburb with a conservative population, Üsküdar isn't blessed with the restaurants, bars and cafes that give Kadıköy such a vibrant and inclusive edge, but it does have one very big asset: an array of magnificent imperial mosques. Foremost among these is the **Atik Valide Mosque** (Atik Valide Camii; Map p62; Valide Imaret Sokak; ⊜ Üsküdar, Ⓜ Üsküdar), designed by Sinan for the Valide Sultan Nurbanu, wife of Selim II (the Sot) and mother of Murat III. Dating from 1583, it has retained most of the buildings in its original *külliye* (mosque complex) and has a commanding location on Üsküdar's highest hill. The nearby **Çinili Mosque** (Çinili Camii, Tiled Mosque; Map p62; Çinili Hamam Sokak; ⊜ Üsküdar, Ⓜ Üsküdar) is dwarfed in comparison, but is notable for the multi-coloured İznik tiles that adorn its interior. Slightly further up the hill is one of the few architecturally notable modern mosques in the city, the **Şakirin Mosque** (Map p62; cnr Huhkuyusu Caddesi & Dr Burhanettin Üstünel Sokak; ☐ 6, 9A, 11P, 11V, 12A, 12C). Designed by Hüsrev Tayla and featuring an interior by Zeynap Fadıllıoğlu, it is located opposite the Zeynep Kamil Hospital on the road to Kadıköy.

Down by the *iskele* (ferry dock) are the **Mihrimah Sultan Mosque** (Mihrimah Sultan Camii; Map p62; Paşa Limanı Caddesi; ⊜ Üsküdar, Ⓜ Üsküdar), a Sinan design from 1547–48 that was commissioned by the daughter of Süleyman the Magnificent; and the **Yeni Valide Mosque** (Yeni Valide Camii, New Queen Mother's Mosque; Map p62; Demokrasi Meydanı; ⊜ Üsküdar, Ⓜ Üsküdar), commissioned by Ahmet III for his mother. South of the *iskele* is yet another Sinan design: the diminutive 1580 **Şemsi Ahmed Paşa Mosque** (Şemsi Paşa Camii, Kuskonmaz Camii; Map p62; Paşa Limanı Caddesi; ⊜ Üsküdar, Ⓜ Üsküdar). Next to this is the popular **Mistanbul Hancı Cafe** (Map p62; Sahil Yolu 12; ⊙ 9am-midnight; ⊜ Üsküdar, Ⓜ Üsküdar), a waterside *çay bahçesi* (tea garden) where you can enjoy a tea, coffee or soft drink while admiring the view and watching the ever-present group of anglers trying their luck in the choppy waters below. Before leaving the suburb, consider purchasing some of the unusual and delicious *lokum* (Turkish delight) sold at **Şekerci Aytekin Erol Caferzade** (p134) in the Balıkçılar Çarşısı (Fish Market) off Hakimiyeti Milliye Caddesi.

To get here from Kadıköy, take bus 12 or 12A from the bus station in front of the Turyol *iskele*, or one of the many dolmuşes (minibuses that stop anywhere along their prescribed routes) picking up passengers nearby. From Üsküdar, ferries travel back to Eminönü, Karaköy, Kabataş and Beşiktaş.

Females should bring a scarf or shawl to use as a head covering while visiting the mosques, and all visitors should dress appropriately (ie, no shorts, short skirts or skimpy tops).

Orient is this imposing neoclassical building, which was wrapped in scaffolding and tarpaulin and undergoing renovation when we visited. It houses an extensive collection of classical statuary and sarcophagi plus a sprawling exhibit documenting İstanbul's history.

The museum's major treasures are sarcophagi from sites including the Royal Necropolis of Sidon (Side in modern-day Lebanon), unearthed in 1887 by Osman Hamdi Bey. The extraordinary *Alexander Sarcophagus* and *Mourning Women Sarcophagus* were not on display when we visited. However, some good pieces from the statuary collection are exhibited on the way into the museum, including a marble head of Alexander from Pergamum.

On the 1st floor, a fascinating albeit dusty exhibition called **İstanbul Through the Ages** traces the city's history through its neighbourhoods during different periods: Archaic, Hellenistic, Roman, Byzantine and Ottoman. On the 2nd floor is the museum's 'Anatolia and Troy Through the Ages' exhibition; on the 3rd, the 'Neighbouring Cultures of Anatolia, Cyprus, Syria and Palestine' exhibition was closed at the time of writing.

When we visited, a separate entrance led to an impressive collection of ancient grave-cult sarcophagi from Syria, Lebanon, Thessalonica and Ephesus, including impressive **anthropoid sarcophagi** from Sidon. Three halls are filled with the amazingly detailed stelae and sarcophagi, most dating from between AD 140 and 270. Many of the sarcophagi look like tiny temples or residential buildings; don't miss the Sidamara Sarcophagus from Konya with its interlocking horses' legs and playful cherubs. The last room in this section contains Roman floor mosaics and examples of Anatolian architecture from antiquity.

➜ Tiled Pavilion

The last of the complex's museum buildings is this handsome pavilion, constructed in 1472 by order of Mehmet the Conqueror. The portico, which has 14 marble columns, was constructed during the reign of Sultan Abdül Hamit I (1774–89) after the original burned down in 1737.

On display here are Seljuk, Anatolian and Ottoman tiles and ceramics dating from the end of the 12th century to the beginning of the 20th century. The collection includes İznik tiles from the period between the mid-14th and 17th centuries when that city produced the finest coloured tiles in the world. When you enter the central room you can't miss the stunning *mihrab* from the İbrahim Bey İmâret in Karaman, built in 1432.

Gülhane Park   PARK

(Gülhane Parkı; Map p72; ◷ 7am-10pm; 🚇 Gülhane) Gülhane Park was once the outer garden of Topkapı Palace, accessible only to the royal court. These days crowds of locals come here to picnic under the many trees, promenade past the formally planted flowerbeds, and enjoy wonderful views of the Bosphorus, Sea of Marmara and Princes' Islands from the Set Üstü Çay Bahçesi on the park's northeastern edge. The park is especially lovely during the İstanbul Tulip Festival (p108), when tulips are arranged to resemble *nazar boncuk* 'evil eye' charms.

Green-fingered beautification has brought improvements to walkways and amenities, and the park has seen the opening of the İstanbul Museum of the History of Science & Technology in Islam (İstanbul İslam Bilim ve Teknoloji Tarihi Müzesi; Map p72; ☑0212-528 8065; www.ibttm.org; Has Ahırlar Binaları; adult/child under 12yr ₺10/free; ◷9am-6.30pm Wed-Mon mid-Apr–Oct, to 4.30pm Nov–mid-Apr, last entry 30min before closing; 🚇Gülhane).

Next to the southern entrance is the Alay Köşkü (Parade Kiosk), now open to the public as the Ahmet Hamdi Tanpınar Literature Museum Library (Ahmet Hamdi Tanpınar Edebiyat Müze Kütüphanesi; Map p72; ☑0212-520 2081; ◷10am-7pm Mon-Sat; 🚇Gülhane) FREE.

Across the street and 100m downhill from the park's main gate is an outrageously curvaceous rococo gate leading into the precincts of what was once the grand vizierate, or Ottoman prime ministry, known in the West as the Sublime Porte (Map p72; Alemdar Caddesi; 🚇Gülhane) thanks to this flamboyant entrance. Today the buildings beyond the gate hold various offices of the İstanbul provincial government (the Vilayeti).

◉ Bazaar District

Crowned by the city's first and most evocative shopping mall – the famous Grand Bazaar (Kapalı Çarşı) – the Bazaar District is also home to two of the grandest of all Ottoman buildings, the Süleymaniye and Beyazıt Mosques.

★ Grand Bazaar   MARKET

(Kapalı Çarşı, Covered Market; Map p128; www.kapalicarsi.org.tr; ◷8.30am-7pm Mon-Sat, last entry 6pm; 🚇Beyazıt Kapalıçarşı) The colourful and chaotic Grand Bazaar is the heart of İstanbul's Old City and has been so for centuries. Starting as a small vaulted *bedesten* (warehouse) built by order of Mehmet the Conqueror in 1461, it grew to cover a vast area as lanes between the *bedesten,* neighbouring shops and *hans* (caravanserais) were roofed and the market assumed the sprawling, labyrinthine form that it retains today.

When here, be sure to peep through doorways to discover hidden *hans*, veer down narrow lanes to watch artisans at work and wander the main thoroughfares to differentiate treasures from tourist tack. It's obligatory to drink lots of tea, compare price after price and try your hand at the art of bargaining. Allow at least three hours for your visit; some travellers spend three days!

★ Süleymaniye Mosque   MOSQUE

(Map p86; Professor Sıddık Sami Onar Caddesi; Ⓜ Vezneciler) The Süleymaniye crowns one of İstanbul's seven hills and dominates the Golden Horn, providing a landmark for the entire city. Though it's not the largest of the Ottoman mosques, it is certainly one of the grandest and most beautiful. It's also unusual in that many of its original *külliye* (mosque complex) buildings have been retained and sympathetically adapted for reuse.

Commissioned by Süleyman I, known as 'the Magnificent', the Süleymaniye was the fourth imperial mosque built in İstanbul

Bazaar District

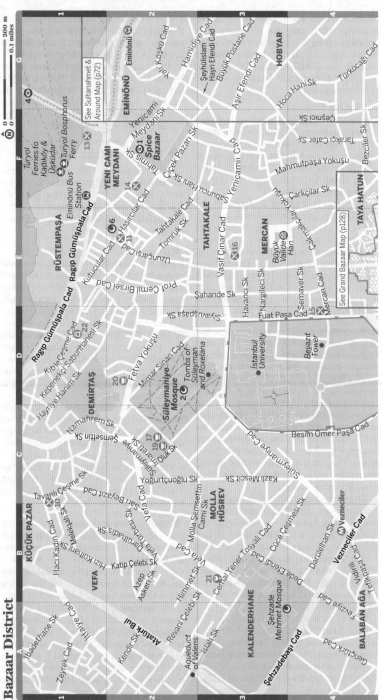

Map labels:

İbadethane Sk
Zeyrek Cad
İtfaiye Cad
Kendiri Sk
Aqueduct of Valens
İslan Sk
Revani Çelebi Sk
Atatürk Bul
Şehzadebaşı Cad
KALENDERHANE
Şehzade Mehmet Mosque
Himmet Sk
21
Cerhal Yener Tosyali Cad
Dede Efendi Cad
Vidinli Cad
Tefkipaşa Cad
Feyziye Cad
Gençtürk Cad
BALABAN AĞA
Vezneciler Cad
M Vezneciler
Darülilhan Sk
Cüce Çeşmesi Sk
MOLLA HÜSREV
Molla Şemsettin Cami Sk
Kazil Mescit Sk
Süleymaniye Cad
Besim Ömer Paşa Cad
Yoğurtçuoğlu Sk
Vefa Cad
Sarı Beyazit Cad
Vefa Türbesi Sk
Darülhadis Sk
Katip Çelebi Sk
Azep Askeri Sk
VEFA
Melekşah Sk
Hızır Külhanı Sk
Hacı Kadın Cad
Tavanlı Çeşme Sk
10
KÜÇÜK PAZAR
Namahrem Sk
Şemsettin Sk
Süleymaniye Sk
Tiryaki Sk
17
19
11
Olluk Sk
20
Fetva Yokuşu
Mimar Sinan Cad
Tombs of Süleyman and Roxelana
Süleymaniye Mosque
2
İstanbul University
Beyazit Tower
Hayriye Hanım Sk
Kepenekçi Sabunhanesi Sk
Kıble Çeşme Cad
DEMİRTAŞ
22
Ragıp Gümüşpala Cad
RÜSTEMPAŞA
Eminönü Bus Station
Turyol Ferries to Kadıköy & Üsküdar
Turyol Bosphorus Ferry
4
See Sultanahmet & Around Map (p72)
13
YENİ CAMİ MEYDANI
14
Tahmis Sk
Hasırcılar Cad
6
11
Kutucular Cad
Uzunçarşı Cad
Tahtakale Cad
Tomruk Cad
Prof Cemil Birsel Cad
Şahande Sk
Siyavuşpaşa Sk
Havancı Sk
Fuat Paşa Cad
Nargileci Sk
Semaver Sk
Vasıf Çınar Cad
TAHTAKALE
Yenicami Cad
Sabuncu Han Sk
Çiçek Pazarı Sk
Spice Bazaar
1
Yenicami Meydanı Sk
EMİNÖNÜ
Eminönü M
4
Yalı Köşkü Cad
Hamidiye Cad
Şeyhülislam Hayri Efendi Cad
Büyük Postane Cad
HOBYAR
Aşir Efendi Cad
Hoca Hanı Sk
Türkocağı Cad
Çeşnici Sk
Tarakçı Cafer Sk
Bezciler Sk
Mahmutpaşa Yokuşu
Çarkçılar Sk
Çakmakçılar Yokuşu
MERCAN
Büyük Valide Han
16
15
Mercan Cad
See Grand Bazaar Map (p128)
TAYA HATUN

Scale:
200 m
0.1 miles
N

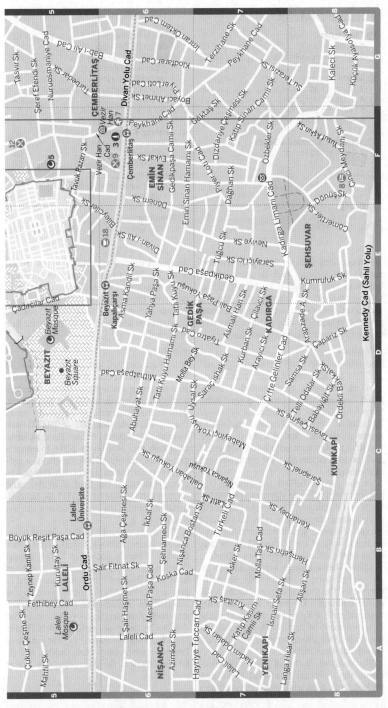

Bazaar District

and it certainly lives up to its patron's nickname. The mosque and its surrounding buildings were designed by Mimar Sinan, the most famous and talented of all imperial architects. Sinan's *türbe* (tomb) is just outside the mosque's walled garden, next to a disused *medrese* (seminary) building.

➡ **Mosque**

The mosque was built between 1550 and 1557. Its setting and plan are particularly pleasing, featuring gardens and a three-sided forecourt with a central domed ablutions fountain. The four minarets with their 10 beautiful *şerefes* (balconies) are said to represent the fact that Süleyman was the fourth of the Osmanlı sultans to rule the city and the 10th sultan after the establishment of the empire.

In the garden behind the mosque is a terrace offering lovely views of the Golden Horn and Bosphorus. The street underneath once housed the mosque complex's *arasta* (street of shops), which was built into the retaining wall of the terrace. Close by was a five-level *mülazim* (preparatory school).

Inside, the building is breathtaking in its size and pleasing in its simplicity. Sinan incorporated the four buttresses into the walls of the building – the result is wonderfully 'transparent' (ie open and airy) and highly reminiscent of Aya Sofya, especially as the dome is nearly as large as the one that crowns the Byzantine basilica.

The *mihrab* (niche in a minaret indicating the direction of Mecca) is covered in fine İznik tiles, and other interior decoration includes window shutters inlaid with mother-of-pearl, gorgeous stained-glass windows, painted *muqarnas* (corbels with honeycomb detail), a spectacular persimmon-coloured floor carpet, painted pendentives and medallions featuring fine calligraphy.

➡ **Külliye**

Süleyman specified that his mosque should have the full complement of public services: *imaret* (soup kitchen), *medrese*, hamam, *darüşşifa* (hospital) etc. Today the *imaret*, with its charming garden courtyard, houses the **Dârüzziyafe** (Map p86; ☑ 0212-511 8414; www.daruzziyafe.com.tr; ⊙ 11am-11pm; Ⓜ Vezneciler) cafe and is a lovely place to enjoy a çay. On its right-hand side (north) is a *tabhane* (inn for travelling dervishes) that was being restored at the time of writing, and on its left-hand side (south) is Lale Bahçesi, (p122) a popular tea garden set in a sunken courtyard.

The main entrance to the mosque is accessed from Professor Sıddık Sami Onar Caddesi, formerly known as Tiryaki Çarşışı (Market of the Addicts). The buildings here once housed three *medreses* and a primary school; they're now home to the Süleymaniye Library and a raft of popular streetside *fasulye* (bean) restaurants that used to be teahouses selling opium (hence the street's former name). On the corner of Professor Sıddık Sami Onar Caddesi and Şifahane Sokak is the *darüşşifa,* also under restoration.

The still-functioning **Süleymaniye Hamamı** is on the eastern side of the mosque.

➡ **Tombs**

To the right (southeast) of the main entrance is the cemetery, home to the octagonal tombs of Süleyman and his wife Haseki Hürrem Sultan (Roxelana). The tile work surrounding the entrances to both is superb and the ivory-inlaid panels in Süleyman's tomb are lovely.

➡ **Surrounding Area**

The streets surrounding the mosque are home to what may well be the most extensive concentration of Ottoman timber houses on the historical peninsula, many of which are currently being restored as part of an urban regeneration project. To see some of these, head down Felva Yokuşu (between the *tabhane* and Sinan's tomb) and then veer right into Namahrem Sokak and Ayrancı Sokak. One of the many Ottoman-era houses here was once occupied by Mimar Sinan; it now houses a cafe.

Alternatively, from Professor Siddık Sami Onar Caddesi head southwest into narrow Ayşekadin Hamamı Sokak (it's hidden in the middle of the souvenir stands) and follow it and Kayserili Ahmetpaşa Sokak down through the Molla Hüsrev district, which is slowly being restored as part of the Süleymaniye Urban Regeneration Project. Kayserili Ahmetpaşa Sokak is home to a number of pretty timber houses built in the late 19th and early 20th centuries.

Rüstem Paşa Mosque   MOSQUE
(Rüstem Paşa Camii; Map p86; Hasırcılar Caddesi, Rüstem Paşa; 🚇 Eminönü) Nestled in the middle of the busy Tahtakale shopping district, this diminutive mosque is a gem. Dating from 1560, it was designed by Sinan for Rüstem Paşa, son-in-law and grand vizier of Süleyman the Magnificent. A showpiece of the best Ottoman architecture and tile work, it is thought to have been the prototype for Sinan's greatest work, the Selimiye Camii in Edirne.

The mosque is easy to miss because it's not at street level. There's a set of access stairs on Hasırcılar Caddesi and another on the small street that runs right (north) off Hasırcılar Caddesi towards the Golden Horn. At the top of the stairs, there's a terrace and the mosque's colonnaded porch. You'll immediately notice the exquisite panels of İznik tiles set into the mosque's facade.

The interior is covered in more tiles and features a lovely dome, supported by four tiled pillars.

The preponderance of tiles was Rüstem Paşa's way of signalling his wealth and influence, with İznik tiles being particularly expensive and desirable. It may not have assisted his passage into the higher realm though, because by all accounts he was a loathsome character. His contemporaries dubbed him Kehle-i-Ikbal (the Louse of Fortune) because he was found to be infected with lice on the eve of his marriage to Mihrimah, Süleyman's favourite daughter. He is best remembered for plotting with Roxelana to turn Süleyman against his favourite son, Mustafa. They were successful and Mustafa was strangled in 1553 on his father's orders.

⭐ **Spice Bazaar**   MARKET
(Mısır Çarşısı, Egyptian Market; Map p86; 📞 212-513 6597; www.misircarsisi.org; ⊗ 8am-7.30pm; 🚇 Eminönü) Vividly coloured spices are displayed alongside jewel-like *lokum* (Turkish delight) at this Ottoman-era marketplace, providing eye candy for the thousands of tourists and locals who make their way here every day. Stalls also sell caviar, dried herbs, honey, nuts and dried fruits. The number of stalls selling tourist trinkets increases annually, yet this remains a great place to stock up on edible souvenirs, share a few jokes with vendors and marvel at the well-preserved building.

New Mosque   MOSQUE
(Yeni Camii; Map p72; Yenicamii Meydanı Sokak, Eminönü; 🚇 Eminönü) Only in İstanbul would a 400-year-old mosque be called 'new'. Constructed between 1597 and 1665, its design references both the Blue Mosque and the Süleymaniye Mosque, with a large forecourt and a square sanctuary surmounted by a series of semidomes crowned by a grand dome. The interior is richly decorated with gold leaf, İznik tiles and carved marble.

Hünkâr Kasrı   MUSEUM
(Hünkâr Mahfili; Map p72; Arpacılar Caddesi 29, Eminönü; ⊗ 9am-5pm Mon-Sat during exhibitions; 🚇 Eminönü) **FREE** Built over a grand archway attached to the New Mosque, this small *kasrı* (pavilion) or *mahfili* (loge) dates from the same period and functioned as a waiting area and retreat for the sultans. It comprises a salon, bedchamber and toilet and is decorated with exquisite İznik tiles throughout. Entry is via an extremely long and wide

staircase that is now ulitised by the İstanbul Ticaret Odası (Chamber of Commerce) as a temporary exhibition space.

Galata Bridge
BRIDGE

(Galata Köprüsü; Map p86; 🚇 Eminönü, Karaköy) To experience İstanbul at its most magical, walk across the Galata Bridge at sunset. At this time, the historic Galata Tower is surrounded by shrieking seagulls, the mosques atop the seven hills of the city are silhouetted against a soft red-pink sky and the evocative scent of apple tobacco wafts out of the nargile cafes under the bridge.

⊙ Western Districts

A showcase of İstanbul's ethnically diverse and endlessly fascinating history, this neighbourhood to the west of the Historic Peninsula contains synagogues built by the Jews in Balat and churches constructed by the Greeks in Fener. In recent times migrants from eastern Turkey have settled here, attracted by the vibrant Wednesday street market in Fatih and the presence of two important Islamic pilgrimage sites: the tombs of Mehmet the Conqueror and Ebu Eyüp el-Ensari.

Fatih Mosque
MOSQUE

(Fatih Camii, Mosque of the Conqueror; Map p62; Fevzi Paşa Caddesi, Fatih; 🚌 28 from Eminönü, 87 from Taksim) The Fatih was the first great imperial mosque built in İstanbul following the Conquest. Mehmet the Conqueror chose to locate it on the hilltop site of the ruined Church of the Apostles, burial place of Constantine and other Byzantine emperors. Mehmet decided to be buried here as well; his tomb is behind the mosque and is inevitably filled with worshippers.

Fethiye Museum
MUSEUM

(Fethiye Müzesi, Church of Pammakaristos; Map p62; 📞 0212-635 1273; http://ayasofyamuzesi. gov.tr/en; Fethiye Caddesi, Çarşamba; ₺5; ⊙ 9am-7pm mid-Apr–late Oct, to 5pm late Oct–mid-Apr; 🚌 99, 99A, 99Y from Eminönü, 55T from Taksim) Not long after the Conquest, Mehmet the Conqueror visited this 13th-century church to discuss theological questions with the Patriarch of the Orthodox Church. They talked in the southern side chapel known as the parecclesion, which is decorated with gold mosaics and is now open as a small museum.

The church was endowed by a nephew of Emperor Michael VIII Palaeologos and

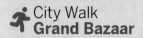

🏃 City Walk
Grand Bazaar

START ÇEMBERLİTAŞ TRAM STOP
END SAHAFLAR ÇARŞISI
LENGTH 1KM; THREE HOURS

There are thousands of shops in the bazaar, and this can be overwhelming for the first-time visitor. By following this suggested itinerary, you should be able to develop an understanding of the bazaar's history, its layout and its important position as the hub of the surrounding retail precinct.

Start at the tram stop next to the tall column known as ❶ **Çemberlitaş** (p114). From here, walk down Vezir Han Caddesi and you will soon come to the entrance to the Vezir Han, a *han* (caravanserai) built between 1659 and 1660 by the Köprülüs, a distinguished Ottoman family. Five of its members served as *vezir* (grand vizier) to the sultan, hence its name. In Ottoman times, this *han* would have offered travelling merchants accommodation and a place to do business. Though gold manufacturers still work here, the *han* is in a sadly dilapidated state. Look for the *tuğra* (monogram or crest) of the sultan over the main gateway.

Continue walking down Vezir Han Caddesi until you come to a cobbled pedestrianised street on your left. Walk along this until you reach the baroque-style ❷ **Nuruosmaniye Mosque** (Nuruosmaniye Camii, Light of Osman Mosque; Vezir Han Caddesi, Beyazıt; 🚇 Çemberlitaş). Next to it is one of the major entrances to the Grand Bazaar, the Nuruosmaniye Kapısı (Nuruosmaniye Gate; Gate 1), which is adorned by an imperial *tuğra*.

Head into brightly lit Kalpakçılar Caddesi, the busiest street in the bazaar. Originally named after the *kalpakçılars* (makers of fur hats) who had their stores here, it's now full of jewellers. Walk a short distance and then turn right into Sandal Bedestenı Sokak before veering left into Ağa Sokak, which takes you into the oldest part of the bazaar, the ❸ **İç (Inner) Bedesten**, where most of the bazaar's antique stores are located.

Exiting the İç Bedesten from its north door, head to the first cross street, ❹ **Halıcılar Sokak**, where popular bath ware and textile shops are located.

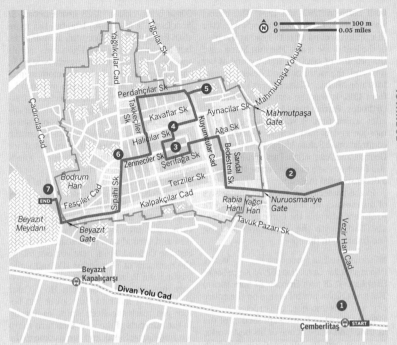

Walking east (right) you will come to Kuyumcular Caddesi (Street of the Jewellers). Turn left and walk past the little kiosk in the middle of the street. Built in the 19th century and known as the Oriental Kiosk, this was once home to the most famous *muhallebici* (milk-pudding shop) in the district. A little further down, on the right-hand side of the street, is the pretty **5 Zincirli (Chain) Han**.

From Kuyumcular Caddesi, turn sharp left into Perdahçılar Sokak (Street of the Polishers) and left again into Takkeçiler Sokak (Street of the Skullcap Makers), home to marble *sebils* (public drinking fountains).

Turn right into Zenneciler Sokak (Street of the Clothing Sellers) and you will soon come

to a junction with another of the bazaar's major thoroughfares: Sipahi Sokak (Street of the Cavalry Soldiers). **6 Şark Kahvesi** (p122), a traditional coffeehouse, is on the corner.

Turn left into Sipahi Sokak and walk until you return to Kalpakçılar Caddesi. Turn right and exit the bazaar from the Beyazıt Kapısı (Beyazıt Gate; Gate 7). Turn right again and then left into the first passage on the left, where you'll find the **7 Sahaflar Çarşısı** (p114), a book and paper market established in Byzantine times. At the centre of its shady courtyard is a bust of İbrahim Müteferrika (1674–1745), who printed the first book in Turkey in 1732.

built between 1292 and 1294. The chapel was endowed by the benefactor's wife (the inscription around Christ's head at the base of the half dome reads 'The nun Maria gave the promise of salvation in the name of her husband, the victorious and deserving pro-tostrator Michael Glabas Ducas') and dates from 1315. It was the seat of the Christian Orthodox Patriarchate from 1455 to 1587, after which time it was converted into a mosque and named Fethiye (Conquest) to commemorate Sultan Murat III's victories in Georgia and Azerbaijan. Part of the building still functions as a mosque, while this part is a deconsecrated museum.

In the paracclesion, the most impressive of the mosaics are the **Pantokrator and 12 Prophets** adorning the dome, and the **Deesis (Christ with the Virgin and St John the Baptist)** in the apse.

Mihrimah Sultan Mosque
MOSQUE

(Mihrimah Sultan Camii; Map p62; Ali Kuşçu Sokak, Edirnekapı; 28 from Eminönü, 87 from Taksim) The great Sinan put his stamp on the entire city and this mosque, constructed in the 1560s next to the Edirnekapı section of the historic land walls, is one of his best works. Commissioned by Süleyman the Magnificent's favourite daughter, Mihrimah, it features a wonderfully light and airy interior with delicate stained-glass windows and an unusual 'birdcage' chandelier.

★ Kariye Museum (Chora Church)
MUSEUM

(Kariye Müzesi; Map p62; 0212-631 9241; www.choramuseum.com; Kariye Camii Sokak 18, Edirnekapı; adult/child ₺30/free; ⏰9am-7pm mid-Apr-late Oct, to 5pm late Oct-mid-Apr, last entry

30min before closing; 28 from Eminönü, 87 from Taksim, Ayvansaray) İstanbul has more than its fair share of Byzantine monuments, but few are as drop-dead gorgeous as this mosaic- and fresco-laden church. Nestled in the shadow of Theodosius II's monumental land walls and now a museum overseen by the curators of Aya Sofya, it receives a fraction of the visitor numbers that its big sister the famous Aya Sofya attracts but offers equally fascinating insights into Byzantine art. Parts of the museum were closed for renovation at the time of writing; check which are open before visiting.

The best way to get to this part of town is to catch the Haliç (Golden Horn) ferry (p105) from Eminönü to Ayvansaray and walk up the hill along Dervişzade Sokak, turn right into Eğrikapı Mumhane Caddesi and then almost immediately left into Şişhane Caddesi. From here you can follow the remnants of Theodosius II's land walls, passing the Palace of Constantine Porphyrogenitus on your way. From Hoca Çakır Caddesi, veer left into Vaiz Sokak just before you reach the steep stairs leading up to the ramparts of the wall, then turn sharp left into Kariye Sokak and you'll come to the museum.

The building was originally known as the Church of the Holy Saviour Outside the Walls (Chora literally means 'country'), reflecting the fact that when it was first built it was located outside the original city walls constructed by Constantine the Great.

What you see today isn't the original church. Instead, it was reconstructed at least five times, most significantly in the

---

DON'T MISS

İSTIKLAL CADDESI

Once called the Grand Rue de Pera but renamed İstiklal in the early years of the Republic, Beyoğlu's premier boulevard **İstiklal Caddesi** (Independence Ave; Map p94; Taksim, Şişhane) is a perfect metaphor for 21st-century Turkey, being an exciting mix of modernity and tradition. Contemporary boutiques and cutting-edge cultural centres are housed in its grand 19th-century buildings, and an antique tram traverses its length alongside crowds of pedestrians making their way to the bustling cafes, bistros and bars for which Beyoğlu is known.

At the boulevard's northern end is frantically busy **Taksim Meydanı**, the symbolic heart of the modern city and the scene of often-violent protests in recent years. Another square, Galatasaray Meydanı, is at the boulevard's midpoint, close to Beyoğlu's much-loved **Fish Market** (p130) and **Çiçek Pasajı** (Flower Passage; Map p94; Taksim). At its southern end is Tünel Meydanı and the relatively tranquil district of Galata, home to atmospheric lanes and traces of a fortified settlement built by Genoese merchants in the 13th century.

11th, 12th and 14th centuries. Virtually all of the interior decoration – the famous mosaics and the less renowned but equally striking frescos – dates from circa 1320 and was funded by Theodore Metochites, a poet and man of letters who was *logothetes,* the official responsible for the Byzantine treasury, under Emperor Andronikos II (r 1282–1328). One of the museum's most wonderful mosaics, found above the door to the nave in the inner narthex, depicts Theodore offering the church to Christ.

Today the Chora consists of five main architectural units: the nave, the two-storied structure (annex) added to the north, the inner and the outer narthexes and the chapel for tombs (parecclesion) to the south. In 2013 a second major restoration commenced. This ongoing process is happening in stages, and involves closure of parts of the museum; first the nave and the two-storey annexes on the northern side of the building, followed by the inner narthex, and finally the outer narthex and parecclesion. As the parecclesion has the finest frescos, it may not be worth visiting the church during the final stage.

➡ **Mosaics**

Most of the interior is covered with mosaics depicting the lives of Christ and the Virgin Mary. Look out for the *Khalke Jesus,* which shows Christ and Mary with two donors: Prince Isaac Comnenos and Melane, daughter of Byzantine emperor Michael VIII Palaiologos. This is under the right dome in the inner narthex. On the dome itself is a stunning depiction of Jesus and his ancestors *(The Genealogy of Christ).* On the narthex's left dome is a serenely beautiful mosaic of *Mary and the Baby Jesus Surrounded by her Ancestors.*

In the nave are three mosaics: *Christ; Mary and the Baby Jesus;* and the *Dormition of the Blessed Virgin (Assumption)* – turn around to see the latter, as it's over the main door you just entered. The 'infant' being held by Jesus is actually Mary's soul.

➡ **Frescos**

To the right of the nave is the **parecclesion,** a side chapel built to hold the tombs of the church's founder and his relatives, close friends and associates. This is decorated with frescos that deal with the themes of death and resurrection, depicting scenes taken from the Old Testament. The striking painting in the apse known as the *Anastasis* shows a powerful Christ raising Adam

and Eve out of their sarcophagi, with saints and kings in attendance. The gates of hell are shown under Christ's feet. Less majestic but no less beautiful are the frescos adorning the dome, which show Mary and 12 attendant angels. On the ceiling between this dome and the apse, the Last Judgement strikingly depicts this scene from the Book of Revelation in dazzling white with gilt accents, with the rolling up of heaven represented by a coiling motif surrounded by the choirs of heaven.

Patriarchal Church of St George CHURCH
(St George in the Phanar; Map p62; ☑ 0212-531 9670; www.ec-patr.org; Sadrazam Ali Paşa Caddesi, Fener; ⊙ 8.30am-4.30pm; 🚌 99, 99A, 99Y from Eminönü, 55T from Taksim) Dating from 1836, this church is part of the Greek Patriarchate compound. Inside the church are artefacts including Byzantine mosaics, religious relics and a wood-and-inlay patriarchal throne. The most eye-catching feature is an ornately carved wooden iconostasis (screen of icons) that was restored and lavishly gilded in 1994.

Yavuz Sultan Selim Mosque MOSQUE
(Sultan Selim Camii, Mosque of Yavuz Selim; Map p62; Yavuz Selim Caddesi, Çarşamba; ⊙ tomb 9am-5pm; 🚌 99, 99A, 99Y from Eminönü, 55T from Taksim) The sultan to whom this mosque was dedicated (Süleyman the Magnificent's father, Selim I, known as 'the Grim') is famous for having killed two of his brothers, six of his nephews and three of his own sons in order to assure his succession and that of Süleyman. He did, however, lay the groundwork for his son's imperial success and, to this day, İstanbullus love his mosque.

◉ **Beyoğlu & Around**

The high-octane hub of eating, drinking and entertainment in the city, Beyoğlu is where visitors and locals come in search of good restaurants and bars, live-music venues, hip hotels and edgy boutiques. Built around the major boulevard of İstiklal Caddesi, it incorporates a mix of bohemian residential districts such as Çukurcuma and Cihangir, bustling entertainment enclaves such as Asmalımescit, and historically rich pockets such as Tophane, Galata and Karaköy that have morphed into style centres.

If you have the time, it makes sense to spread your exploration of this neighbourhood over two days. The first day could

Beyoğlu

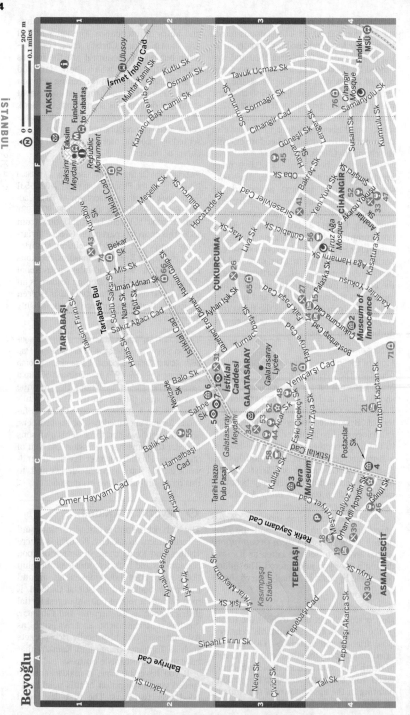

200 m
0.1 miles

G

İsmet İnönü Cad

Ulusoy

TAKSİM

Funicular
to Kabataş

Taksim
Meydanı

Republic
Monument

Muhtar Kamil Sk

Kutlu Sk

Osmanlı Sk

Kazancı Başı Camii Sk

Tavuk Uçmaz Sk

Sormagir Sk

Cihangir Cad

76

Cihangir
Mosque

Samanyolu Sk

Kumrulu Sk

Fındıklı-
MSÜ

F

Taksim
Meydanı

70

İstiklal Cad

Meşelik Sk

Bilirci Sk

Oba Sk

45

Güneşli Sk

Bakraç Sk

41

Sıraselviler Cad

Günek Sk

Yeni Yuva Sk

56

Firuz Ağa
Mosque

Ağa Hamamı Sk

52

Anahtar Sk

Akarsu Yokuşu

Şimşirci Sk

33

47

CİHANGİR

Kaşatura Sk

Kadıliler Yokuşu

E

43

Kurabiye
Sk

Bekar
Sk

74

Mis Sk

İmam Adnan Sk

Hasnun Galip Sk

Gazeteci Erol Dernek Sk

Hocazade Sk

Mağ Sk

Liva Sk

Gülbahçe Sk

ÇUKURCUMA

26

65

Ayhan Işık Sk

Falik Paşa Cad

Çukurcuma Cad

Bostanbaşı Cad

21

14

15

Museum of
Innocence

D

TARLABAŞI

Tarlabaşı Bul

Taksim Fırını Sk

Susılı Saksı Sk

Nane Sk

Sakız Ağacı Cad

İstiklal Cad

Turnacıbaşı Sk

31

Galatasaray
Lycée

Galatasaray
Caddesi

67

Yeniçarşı Cad

Hayriye Cad

71

Tomtom Kaptan Sk

C

Ömer Hayyam Cad

Balık Sk

Hamalbaşı
Cad

55

Nevizade
Sk

Balo Sk

Sahne
Sk

5

6

7

10

GALATASARAY

Galatasaray
Meydanı

34

53

62

48

44

Acara Sk

Nur-i Ziya Sk

Eski Çiçekçi Sk

İstiklal Cad

Postaclar
Sk

4

60

46

Gönül Sk

B

Aynalı Çeşme Cad

Işık Çık

Tarihi Hazzo
Pulo Pasajı

58

Kallavi Sk

3

Pera
Museum

Meşrutiyet Cad

Refik Saydam Cad

Meşr

18

19

Omar Adil Anaydın Sk

39

Balyoz Sk

ASMALIMESCIT

Kuyu Sk

30

A

Hakim Sk

Bahriye Cad

Sipahi Fırını Sk

Neva Sk

Çivici Sk

TEPEBAŞI

Kasımpaşa
Stadium

Işık Sk

Askerler Meydanı Sk

Tepebaşı Cad

Tali Sk

Tepebaşı Akarca Sk

1

2

3

4

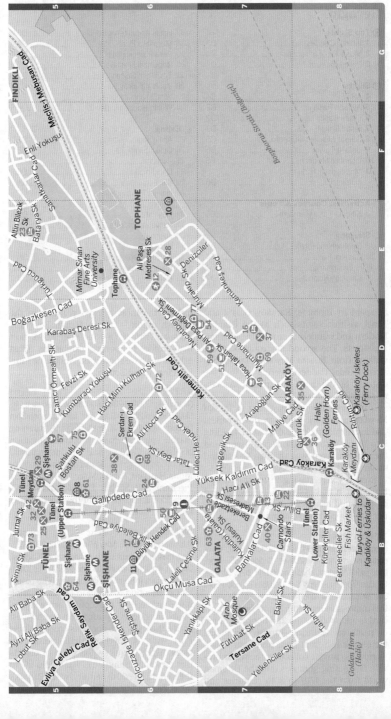

Beyoğlu

be spent in Tophane, Karaköy, Galata and Tünel, visiting sights such as the İstanbul Modern and wandering around the fascinating streets. The second day could be spent walking from Taksim Meydanı (Taksim Sq) along İstiklal Caddesi, veering off into the districts of Cihangir, Çukurcuma, Asmalımescit and Tepebaşı.

If you only have one day, start in Taksim Meydanı and work your way down İstiklal Caddesi, exploring the Balık Pazarı, heading into Tepebaşı to visit the Pera Museum and then making your way through Galata and down to Karaköy.

Even if you're staying in another neighbourhood, it makes sense to follow the lead of locals and head here every night for dinner, bar-hopping and clubbing.

★ **Pera Museum**   MUSEUM
(Pera Müzesi; Map p94; ☑ 0212-334 9900; www.peramuseum.org; Meşrutiyet Caddesi 65, Tepebaşı; adult/student/child under 12yr ₺20/10/free; ☉ 10am-7pm Tue-Thu & Sat, to 10pm Fri, noon-6pm Sun; Ⓜ Şişhane, ⓓ Tünel) There's plenty to see at this impressive museum, but its major drawcard is undoubtedly the 2nd-floor exhibition of paintings featuring Turkish Orientalist themes. Drawn from Suna and İnan Kıraç's world-class private collection, the works provide fascinating glimpses into the Ottoman world from the 17th to 20th centuries and

include the most beloved painting in the Turkish canon – Osman Hamdı Bey's *The Tortoise Trainer* (1906). Other floors host high-profile temporary exhibitions (past exhibitions have showcased Warhol, de Chirico, Picasso and Botero).

ARTER   GALLERY
(Map p94; ☑ 0212-708 5800; www.arter.org.tr; İstiklal Caddesi 211; ☉ 11am-7pm Tue-Thu, noon-8pm Fri-Sun; Ⓜ Şişhane, ⓓ Tünel) **FREE** A stunning marble spiral staircase, prominent location on İstiklal Caddesi and an international exhibition program featuring the likes of Mona Hatoum, Sarkis, Marc Quinn, Patricia Piccinini and Sophia Pompéry make this four-floor art space one of the most prestigious art venues in town.

★ **Museum of Innocence**   MUSEUM
(Masumiyet Müzesi; Map p94; ☑ 0212-252 9738; www.masumiyetmuzesi.org; Çukurcuma Caddesi, Dalgıç Çıkmazı 2; adult/student ₺25/10; ☉ 10am-6pm Tue-Sun, to 9pm Thu; ⓓ Tophane) The painstaking attention to detail in this fascinating museum/piece of conceptual art will certainly provide every amateur psychologist with a theory or two about its creator, Nobel Prize–winning novelist Orhan Pamuk. Vitrines display a quirky collection of objects that evoke the minutiae of İstanbullu life in the mid- to late 20th century, when Pamuk's novel *The Museum of Innocence* is set.

Occupying a modest 19th-century timber house, the museum relies on its vitrines, which are reminiscent of the work of American artist Joseph Cornell, to retell the story of the love affair of Kemal and Füsun, the novel's protagonists. These displays are both beautiful and moving. Some, such as the installation using 4213 cigarette butts, are as strange as they are powerful.

Pamuk's 'Modest Manifesto for Museums' is reproduced on a panel on the ground floor. In it he asserts: 'The resources that are channeled into monumental, symbolic museums should be diverted to smaller museums that tell the stories of individuals'. The individuals in this case are fictional, of course, and their story is evoked in a highly nostalgic fashion, but in creating this museum Pamuk has put his money where his mouth is and come out triumphant.

Hiring an audio guide (₺5) provides an invaluable commentary and is highly recommended.

Galata Mevlevi Museum MUSEUM
(Galata Mevlevihanesi Müzesi; Map p94; www.galatamevlevihanesimuzesi.gov.tr; Galipdede Caddesi 15, Tünel; ₺10; ⊙9am-4pm Tue-Sun; Ⓜ Şişhane, ⓀTünel) The *semahane* (whirling-dervish hall) at the centre of this *tekke* (dervish lodge) was erected in 1491 and renovated in 1608 and 2009. It's part of a complex including a *meydan-ı şerif* (courtyard), *çeşme* (drinking fountain), *türbesi* (tomb) and *hamuşan* (cemetery). The oldest of six historic Mevlevihaneleri (Mevlevi *tekkes*) remaining in İstanbul, the complex was converted into a museum in 1946.

The Mevlevi *tarika* (order), founded in the central Anatolian city of Konya during the 13th century, flourished throughout the Ottoman Empire. Like several other orders, the Mevlevis stressed the unity of humankind before God, regardless of creed.

Taking their name from the great Sufi mystic and poet Celaleddin Rumi (1207–73), called Mevlana (Our Leader) by his disciples, Mevlevis seek to achieve mystical communion with God through a *sema* (ceremony) involving chants, prayers, music and a whirling dance. This *tekke's* first *şeyh* (sheikh) was Şemaî Mehmed Çelebi, a grandson of the great Mevlana.

Dervish orders were banned in the early days of the Turkish Republic because of their ultraconservative religious politics. Although the ban has been lifted, only a handful of functioning *tekkes* remain in İstanbul, including this one and the İstanbul Bilim Sanat Kültür ve Eğitim Derneği in Fatih. Konya remains the heart of the Mevlevi order.

Beneath the *semahane* is an interesting exhibit that includes displays of Mevlevi

WORTH A TRIP

DOLMABAHÇE PALACE

These days it's fashionable for architects and critics influenced by the less-is-more aesthetic of the Bauhaus masters to sneer at buildings such as Dolmabahçe Palace (Dolmabahçe Sarayı; Map p62; ☏ 0212-327 2626; www.millisaraylar.gov.tr; Dolmabahçe Caddesi, Beşiktaş; adult Selâmlık ₺30, Harem ₺20, joint ticket ₺40; ⏰ 9am-4pm Tue, Wed & Fri-Sun; ⊠ Kabataş). However, the crowds that throng to this imperial pleasure palace with its neoclassical exterior and over-the-top interior clearly don't share that disdain, flocking here to visit its Selâmlık (Ceremonial Suites), Harem and Veliaht Dairesi (Apartments of the Crown Prince). The latter is home to the National Palaces Painting Museum (Milli Saraylar Resim Müzesi; Map p62; ☏ 0212-236 9000; www.millisaraylar.gov.tr; Dolmabahçe Caddesi, Beşiktaş; admission ₺20; ⏰ 9am-4pm Tue, Wed & Fri-Sun; ⊠ Akaretler, ⊠ Kabataş).

More rather than less was certainly the philosophy of Sultan Abdül Mecit I (r 1839–61), who decided to move his imperial court from Topkapı to a lavish new palace on the shores of the Bosphorus. For a site he chose the *dolma bahçe* (filled-in garden) where his predecessors, Sultans Ahmet I and Osman II, had filled in a little cove in order to create a royal park complete with wooden pleasure kiosks and pavilions.

Abdül Mecit commissioned imperial architects Nikoğos and Garabed Balyan to construct an Ottoman-European palace that would impress everyone who set eyes on it. Traditional Ottoman palace architecture was eschewed – there are no pavilions here, and the palace turns its back to the splendid view rather than celebrating it. The designer of the Paris Opera was brought in to do the interiors, which perhaps explains their exaggerated theatricality. Construction was completed in 1854, and the sultan and his family moved in two years later. Though it had the wow factor in spades, Abdül Mecit's extravagant project precipitated the empire's bankruptcy and signalled the beginning of the end for the Osmanlı dynasty. During the early years of the republic, Atatürk used the palace as his İstanbul base and died here on 10 November 1938.

The tourist entrance to the palace grounds is the ornate imperial gate, with an equally ornate clock tower just inside. Sarkis Balyan designed the tower between 1890 and 1895 for Sultan Abdül Hamit II (r 1876–1909). There is an outdoor cafe near here with premium Bosphorus views and reasonable prices (yes, really).

Set in well-tended gardens, the palace is divided into three sections: the Selâmlık, Harem and Veliaht Dairesi. Entry is via a compulsory and dreadfully rushed guided tour (up to 50 people per group), which focuses on the Selâmlık but visits parts of the Harem as well; you can visit the National Palaces Paintings Museum independently. In busy periods English-language tours leave every 10 minutes or so; during quiet times every 25 minutes is more likely.

Note that visitor numbers in the palace are limited to 3000 per day and this ceiling is often reached on weekends and holidays – come midweek if possible, and even then be prepared to queue (often for long periods and in full sun). If you arrive before 3pm (summer) or 2pm (winter), you must buy a combined ticket to tour both the Selâmlık and Harem; after those times you can take only one tour; we recommend the Selâmlık for its huge chandeliers and crystal staircase made by Baccarat. Note, admission here is not covered by the Museum Pass İstanbul.

Just outside the gate, the Dolmabahçe Mosque (Dolmabahçe Camii) on Muallim Naci Caddesi was designed by Nikoğos Balyan and completed in 1853.

---

clothing, turbans and accessories. The *mahfiller* (upstairs floor) houses the *tekke*'s collection of traditional musical instruments, calligraphy and *ebru* (paper marbling).

The *hamuşan* is full of stones with graceful Ottoman inscriptions, including the tomb of Galip Dede, the 17th-century Sufi poet whom the street is named after. The

shapes atop the stones reflect the headgear of the deceased, each hat denoting a different religious rank.

Museum of Turkish Jews MUSEUM
(500 Yil Vakfi Türk Musevileri, The Quincentennial Foundation Museum of Turkish Jews; Map p94; ☏ 0212-292 6333; www.muze500.com; Büyük

Hendek Caddesi 39, Şişhane; adult/child under 12yr ₺20/free; ⊙10am-4pm Mon-Thu, to 1pm Fri, to 2pm Sun; Ⓜ Şişhane, ᵮ Tünel) Housed in a building attached to the Neve Shalom synagogue near the Galata Tower, this museum was established in 2001 to commemorate the 500th anniversary of the arrival of the Sephardic Jews in the Ottoman Empire, and moved to its current location in 2014. The imaginatively curated and chronologically arranged interactive collection comprises photographs, video, sound recordings and objects that document the history of the Jewish people in Turkey. Visitors must have photo ID with them to enter.

Galata Tower TOWER

(Galata Kulesi; Map p94; www.galatakulesi.org; Galata Meydanı, Galata; adult/child under 12yr ₺25/5; ⊙9am-8.30pm; ᵮ Karaköy, ᵮ Tünel) The cylindrical Galata Tower stands sentry over the approach to 'new' İstanbul. Constructed in 1348, it was the tallest structure in the city for centuries and it still dominates the skyline north of the Golden Horn. Its vertiginous upper balcony offers 360-degree views of the city, but we're not convinced that the view (though spectacular) justifies the steep admission cost.

Be warned that queues can be long and the viewing balcony can get horribly overcrowded. An elevator goes most of the way to the top, but there is one flight of stairs to climb.

İstanbul Modern GALLERY

(İstanbul Modern Sanat Müzesi; Map p94; ☑0212-334 7300; www.istanbulmodern.org; Meclis-i Mebusan Caddesi, Tophane; adult/student/child under 12yr ₺25/14/free; ⊙10am-6pm Tue, Wed & Fri-Sun, to 8pm Thu; ᵮ Tophane) This large, lavishly funded and innovative museum has an extensive collection of Turkish art and also stages a constantly changing and uniformly excellent program of mixed-media exhibitions by high-profile local and international artists. Its permanent home is next to the Bosphorus in Tophane, but the massive Galataport redevelopment project currently underway means that it will temporarily relocate to another site in Beyoğlu some time in 2016/17.

⊙ Beşiktaş

Palace Collections Museum MUSEUM

(Saray Koleksiyonları Müzesi; Map p62; ☑0212-236 9000; www.millisaraylar.gov.tr; Beşiktaş Caddesi, Beşiktaş; adult/child ₺5/2; ⊙9am-5pm Tue-Sun; ᵮ Akaretler, ᵮ Kabataş) Occupying the warehouse-like Dolmabahçe Palace kitchens, this museum exhibits items used in the royal palaces and pavilions during the late Ottoman Empire and early Turkish Republic. It is a fascinating hotchpotch of some 5000 objects, including palace portraits and photos, teasets, tiled Islamic wall inscriptions, prayer rugs and embroidery. Hereke carpets and **Yıldız Porselen Fabrikası** (Yıldız Porcelain Factory; Map p62; ☑0212-260 2370; www.millisaraylar.gov.tr; Yıldız Parkı, Yıldız; adult/child & student ₺5/1; ⊙9am-6pm Mon-Fri; ᵮ Kabataş Lisesi) porcelain are also here.

İstanbul Naval Museum MUSEUM

(İstanbul Deniz Müzesi; Map p62; ☑0212-327 4345; www.denizmuzeleri.tsk.tr; Beşiktaş Caddesi 6, Beşiktaş; adult/student & child ₺6.50/free; ⊙9am-5pm Mon-Fri, 10am-6pm Sat & Sun mid-May–mid-Oct, 9am-5pm Tue-Sun mid-Oct–mid-May; ᵮ Bahçeşehir Ünv.) Established over a century ago to celebrate and commemorate Turkish naval history, this museum has been undergoing a prolonged and major renovation. Its architecturally noteworthy copper-clad exhibition hall opened in 2013 and showcases a spectacular collection of 19th-century imperial caïques, ornately decorated wooden rowboats used by the royal household. Temporary exhibitions take place in the downstairs gallery.

⊙ Kadıköy

In recent years locals have been decamping from the European side of town to Asia in ever-increasing numbers, setting up home in the suburbs that are strung south from the Bosphorus (Martyrs of July 15) Bridge. Of these, bustling Kadıköy and its annex Moda are of the most interest to visitors, being home to İstanbul's best produce market, great eateries, convivial cafes, grunge bars and a progressive vibe.

★ Kadıköy Produce Market MARKET

(Kadıköy Pazarı; Map p62; streets around Güneşlibahçe Sokak; ⊙Mon-Sat; ᵮ Kadıköy) An aromatic, colourful and alluring showcase of the best fresh produce in the city, the Kadıköy Pazarı is foodie central for locals and is becoming an increasingly popular destination for tourists. Equally rewarding to explore independently or on a guided culinary walk, it's small enough to retain a local feel yet large enough to support a variety of specialist traders.

Getting here involves crossing from Europe to Asia and is best achieved on a ferry – from the deck you'll be able to admire the domes and minarets studding the skylines of both shores and watch seagulls swooping overhead. Once you've arrived, cross Rihtim Caddesi in front of the main *iskele* (ferry dock) and walk up Muvakkithane Caddesi or Yasa Caddesi to reach the centre of the action. The best produce shops are in Güneşlibahçe Sokak – you'll see fish glistening on beds of crushed ice, displays of seasonal fruits and vegetables, combs of amber-hued honey, tubs of tangy pickles, bins of freshly roasted nuts and much, much more.

Eating and drinking opportunities in and around the bazaar are plentiful: creamy yoghurt and honey at **Honeyci** (Map p62; ☑0533 515 8888; www.honeyci.com.tr; Güneşli Bahçe Sokak 28; yogurt & honey tub ₺5; ☺9am-10pm; ☑; ☑Kadıköy), regional Anatolian specialities at Çiya Sofrası (p121), the catch of the day at **Kadı Nimet Balıkçılık** (Map p62; ☑0216-348 7389; www.kadinimet.com; Serasker Caddesi 10a; mezes ₺9-25; ☺11am-11pm; ✴☑; ☑Kadıköy), indulgent cakes at Baylan Pastanesi (p121) and the city's best Turkish coffee at Fazıl Bey (p125). For gifts to take home, consider *lokum* (Turkish Delight) from Ali Muhiddin Hacı Bekir (p130), coffee from Fazıl Bey or olive-oil soap from one of the herbalists in Güneşlibahçe Sokak.

For a serious immersion into the local food culture, sign up for a walk with İstanbul Eats (p109), Turkish Flavours (p109) or İstanbul on Food (p109) – all three companies pride themselves on knowing the best local places to eat and shop.

🏃 Activities

🏃 Bosphorus Ferry Tours

Divan Yolu and İstiklal Caddesi are always awash with people, but neither is the city's major thoroughfare. That honour goes to the mighty Bosphorus Strait, which joins the Sea of Marmara (Marmara Denizi) with the Black Sea (Karadeniz), 32km north of the Galata Bridge. Over the centuries the Bosphorus has been crossed by conquering armies, intrepid merchants and many an adventurous spirit. These days, thousands of İstanbullus commute along it; fishing vessels try their luck in its waters; huge tankers and container ships make a stately progress down its central channel; and tourists ride the excursion ferries that ply its length. On one side is Europe, on the other Asia – both shores are lined with historic *yalıs* (seafront mansions) and have loads of attractions. As a result, a day spent exploring by ferry and/or bus is enormously rewarding.

Eminönü to Beşiktaş

Hop onto the boat at the Boğaz Iskelesi (Bosphorus Ferry Dock) on the Eminönü quay near the Galata Bridge. It's always a good idea to arrive 30 minutes or so before the scheduled departure time and manoeuvre your way to the front of the queue that builds near the doors leading to the dock. When these open and the boat can be boarded, you'll need to move fast to score a good seat. The best spots are on the sides of the upper deck at the bow or stern.

The Asian shore is to the right side of the ferry as it cruises up the strait; Europe is to the left. When you start your trip, watch out for the small island of **Kız Kulesi**, just off the Asian shore near Üsküdar. One of the city's most distinctive landmarks, this 18th-century structure has functioned as a lighthouse, quarantine station and restaurant. It also featured in the 1999 James Bond film *The World Is Not Enough*.

KADIKÖY STREET ART

Kadıköy is the centre of the city's street-art scene, and the streets of the Yeldeğirmeni district near the *iskele* (ferry dock) are where many local and visiting artists hang out; head to Karakolhane Sokak near the railway tracks, Misak-ı Milli Sokak, İzzettin Sokak and Macit Erbudak Sokak to see their work. Other examples are on or near Moda Caddesi: look for murals by Adekan next to the Gerekli Şeyler bookshop and on the side of the tennis courts in Hüseyin Bey Sokak off Osman Yeki Üngör Sokak; for the mural by Canavar in the square next to the Mopaş supermarket on Dr Esat Işık Caddesi; and also for the mural by Yabanci on the side of the Greek school in Neşe Sokağı. When wandering through the streets you'll also see interesting tagging by Yok ('nothing' in Turkish).

Just before the first stop at Beşiktaş, you'll pass the grandiose Dolmabahçe Palace (p98), built on the European shore of the Bosphorus by Sultan Abdül Mecit between 1843 and 1854.

Beşiktaş to Kanlica

After a brief stop at Beşiktaş, **Çırağan Palace** (Çırağan Sarayı; Map p62; Çırağan Caddesi 84, Ortaköy; 🚌 Çırağan), once home to Sultan Abdül Aziz and now a luxury hotel, looms up on the left. Next to it on the left is the Four Seasons Hotel; on the right is the long yellow building occupied by the prestigious Galatasaray University. Across the strait on the Asian shore is the **Fethi Ahmed Paşa Yalı** (Map p62; Kuzguncuk; 🚌 15 from Üsküdar), a wide white building with a red-tiled roof that was built in the pretty suburb of Kuzguncuk in the late 18th century. The word *yalı* comes from the Greek word for 'coast', and describes the summer residences along the Bosphorus built by Ottoman aristocracy and foreign ambassadors in the 17th, 18th and 19th centuries, now all protected by the country's heritage laws.

A little further along on your left is the recently restored **Ortaköy Mosque** (Ortaköy Camii, Büyük Mecidiye Camii; Map p62; İskele Meydanı, Ortaköy; 🚌 Ortaköy). The mosque's dome and two minarets are dwarfed by the adjacent **Bosphorus (Martyrs of July 15) Bridge**, opened in 1973 on the 50th anniversary of the founding of the Turkish Republic.

Under the bridge on the European shore are two huge *yalıs:* the red-roofed **Hatice Sultan Yalı** (Map p62; Ortaköy; 🚌 22 & 25E from Kabataş, 22RE & 40 from Beşiktaş, 40, 40T & 42T from Taksim), once the home of Sultan Murad V's daughter, Hatice; and the **Fehime Sultan Yalı** (Map p62; Ortaköy; 🚌 22 & 25E from Kabataş, 22RE & 40 from Beşiktaş, 40, 40T & 42T from Taksim), home to Hatice's sister Fehime. Both are undergoing massive restorations and will be transformed into a luxury hotel. On the Asian side is the ornate **Beylerbeyi Palace** (Beylerbeyi Sarayı; Map p62; 🚌 0212-327 2626; www.millisaraylar.gov.tr; Abdullah Ağa Caddesi, Beylerbeyi; adult/student/child under 7yr ₺20/₺5/free; ⊙ 9am-4.30pm Tue, Wed & Fri-Sun Apr-Oct, to 3.30pm Nov-Mar; 🚌 15 from Üsküdar) – look for its whimsical marble bathing pavilions on the shore; one was for men, the other for the women of the harem.

Past the small village of Çengelköy on the Asian side is the imposing **Kuleli Military School** (Map p140; Çengelköy; 🚌 15, 15E, 15H, 15KÇ, 15M, 15N, 15P, 15ŞN, 15T, 15U from Üsküdar, 15F from Kadıköy), built in 1860 and immortalised in İrfan Orga's wonderful memoir *Portrait of a Turkish Family*. Look out for its two 'witch hat' towers.

Almost opposite Kuleli on the European shore is **Arnavutköy** (Albanian Village), which boasts a number of gabled Ottoman-era wooden houses and Greek Orthodox churches. On the hill above it are buildings formerly occupied by the American College for Girls. Its most famous alumni was Halide Edib Adıvar, who wrote about the years she spent here in her 1926 work *The Memoir of Halide Edib*. The building is now part of the prestigious Robert College.

Arnavutköy runs straight into the glamorous suburb of **Bebek**, known for its upmarket shopping and chic cafe-bars such as **Lucca** (Map p140; 🚌 0212-257 1255; www. luccastyle.com; Cevdetpaşa Caddesi 51b, Bebek; ⊙ 10am-2am; 🚌 22, 22B & 25E from Kabataş, 22RE & 40 from Beşiktaş, 40, 40T & 42T from Taksim). It also has the most glamorous Starbucks in the city (right on the water, and with a lovely terrace). Bebek's shops surround a small park and the Ottoman Revivalist–style **Bebek Mosque** (Map p140; 🚌 22, 22B & 25E from Kabataş, 22RE & 40 from Beşiktaş, 40, 40T & 42T from Taksim); to the east of these is the ferry dock, to the south is the **Egyptian consulate building** (Map p140; Bebek; 🚌 22 & 25E from Kabataş, 22RE & 40 from Beşiktaş, 40, 40T & 42T from Taksim), thought by some critics to be the work of Italian architect Raimondo D'Aronco. This gorgeous art nouveau mini-palace was built for Emine Hanım, mother of the last khedive (viceroy) of Egypt, Abbas Hilmi II. It's the white building with two mansard towers and an ornate wrought-iron fence.

Opposite Bebek on the Asian shore is **Kandilli**, the 'Place of Lamps', named after the lamps that were lit here to warn ships of the particularly treacherous currents at the headland. Among the many *yalıs* here is the huge red **Kont Ostrorog Yalı** (Map p140; Kandilli; 🚌 15, 15F & 15T from Üsküdar), built in the 19th century by Count Leon Ostorog, a Polish adviser to the Ottoman court; Pierre Loti visited here when he visited İstanbul in the 1890s. A bit further on, past Kandilli, is the long white **Kıbrıslı ('Cypriot') Yalı** (Map p140; Kandilli; 🚌 15, 15E, 15H, 15KÇ, 15M, 15N, 15P, 15ŞN, 15T, 15U from Üsküdar, 14R & 15YK from Kadıköy), which dates from 1760.

Next to the Kıbrıslı are the **Büyük Göksu Deresi** (Great Heavenly Stream) and **Küçük Göksu Deresi** (Small Heavenly Stream), two brooks that descend from the Asian hills into the Bosphorus. Between them is a fertile delta, grassy and shady, which the Ottoman elite thought perfect for picnics. Foreign residents referred to it as 'The Sweet Waters of Asia'. If the weather was good, the sultan joined the picnic, and did so in style. Sultan Abdül Mecit's answer to a simple picnic blanket was **Küçüksu Kasrı** (Map p140; ☑0216-332 3303; Küçüksu Caddesi, Küçüksu; adult/student/child under 7yr ₺5/1/ free; ☉9am-4.30pm Tue, Wed & Fri-Sun Apr-Oct, to 3.30pm Nov-Mar; 🚍15, 15E, 15H, 15KÇ, 15M, 15N, 15P, 15ŞN, 15T, 15U from Üsküdar, 14R & 15YK from Kadıköy, 🚢Kabataş), an ornate hunting lodge built in 1856–57. Earlier sultans had wooden kiosks here, but architect Nikoğos Balyan designed a rococo gem in marble for his monarch. You'll see its ornate cast-iron fence, boat dock and wedding-cake exterior from the ferry.

Close to the Fatih Sultan Mehmet Bridge are the majestic fortress structures of **Rumeli Hisarı** (Fortress of Europe; Map p140; ☑0212-263 5305; Yahya Kemal Caddesi 42, Rumeli Hisarı; ₺10; ☉9am-noon & 12.30-4pm Thu-Tue; 🚍22 & 25E from Kabataş, 22RE & 40 from Beşiktaş, 40, 40T & 42T from Taksim) and **Anadolu Hisarı** (Fortress of Anatolia; Map p140; Anadolu Hisarı; 🚍15, 15KÇ & 15ŞN from Üsküdar, 15F from Kadıköy). Mehmet the Conqueror had Rumeli Hisarı built in a mere four months in 1452, in preparation for his siege of Byzantine Constantinople. For its location, he chose the narrowest point of the Bosphorus, opposite Anadolu Hisarı, which Sultan Beyazıt I had built in 1394. By doing so, Mehmet was able to control all traffic on the strait, cutting the city off from resupply by sea.

To speed Rumeli Hisarı's completion, Mehmet ordered each of his three viziers to take responsibility for one of the three main towers. If his tower's construction was not completed on schedule, the vizier would pay with his life. Not surprisingly, the work was completed on time. The useful military life of the mighty fortress lasted less than one year. After the conquest of Constantinople, it was used as a glorified Bosphorus toll booth for a while, then as a barracks, a prison and finally as an open-air theatre.

Within Rumeli Hisarı's walls are park-like grounds, an open-air theatre and the minaret of a ruined mosque. Steep stairs (with no barriers, so beware!) lead up to the ramparts and towers; the views of the Bosphorus are magnificent. Just next to the fortress is a clutch of cafes and restaurants, the most popular of which is **Sade Kahve** (Map p140; ☑0212-263 8800; www.sadekahve.com.tr; Yahya Kemal Caddesi 20a, Rumeli Hisarı; breakfast plates ₺5-12, gözleme & börek ₺14-15; ☉7am-midnight; 🚍22 & 25E from Kabataş, 22RE & 40 from Beşiktaş, 40, 40T & 42T from Taksim).

Between Rumeli Hisari and the **Fatih Sultan Mehmet Bridge** is an eccentric-looking turreted building known locally as the Perili Köşk (Haunted Mansion). Properly referred to as the Yusuf Ziya Pasha mansion, the building's construction kicked off around 1910 but was halted in 1914 when the Ottoman Empire was drawn into WWI and all of its construction workers were forced to quit their jobs and enlist in the army. Work on the 10-storey building came to a standstill and it remained empty, leading to its 'Haunted Mansion' tag. Eighty years later, work finally resumed and the finished building became the home of **Borusan Contemporary** (Map p140; ☑0212-393 5200; www.borusancontemporary.com; Perili Köşk, Baltalimanı Hisar Caddesi 5, Rumeli Hisarı; adult/student/child under 12yr ₺10/5/free; ☉10am-8pm Sat & Sun; 🚍22 & 25E from Kabataş, 22RE & 40 from Beşiktaş, 40, 40T & 42T from Taksim), a cultural centre.

The ferry doesn't stop at Rumeli Hisarı; you can either leave the ferry at Kanlıca and catch a taxi across the Fatih Bridge (this will cost around ₺25 including the bridge toll) or you can visit on your way back to town from Sarıyer. Though Anadolu Hisarı is not open as a museum, visitors are free to wander about its ruined walls.

There are many architecturally and historically important *yalıs* in and around Anadolu Hisarı. These include the **Köprülü Amcazade Hüseyin Paşa Yalı** (Map p140; Anadolu Hisarı; 🚍15, 15KÇ & 15ŞN from Üsküdar, 15F from Kadıköy), a cantilevered box-like structure built for one of Mustafa II's grand viziers in 1698. The oldest *yalı* on the Bosphorus, it is currently undergoing a major renovation. Next door, the **Zarif Mustafa Paşa Yalı** (Map p140; Anadolu Hisarı; 🚍15, 15KÇ & 15ŞN from Üsküdar, 15F from Kadıköy) was built in the early 19th century by the official coffee-maker to Sultan Mahmud II. Look for its upstairs salon, which juts out over the water and is supported by unusual curved timber struts.

Almost directly under the Fatih Bridge on the European shore is the huge stone four-storey **Tophane Müşiri Zeki Paşa Yalı** (Map p140; Rumeli Hisarı; 🚌22 & 25E from Kabataş, 22RE & 40 from Beşiktaş, 40, 40T & 42T from Taksim), a mansion built in the early 20th century for a field marshall in the Ottoman army. Later, it was sold to Sabiha Sultan, daughter of Mehmet VI, the last of the Ottoman sultans, and her husband İmer Faruk Efendi, grandson of Sultan Abdül Aziz. When the sultanate was abolished in 1922, Mehmet walked from this palace onto a British warship, never to return to Turkey.

Past the bridge on the Asian side is **Kanlıca**, the ferry's next stop. This charming village is famous for the rich and delicious yoghurt produced here, which is sold on the ferry and in two cafes on the shady waterfront square. The small **Gâzi İskender Paşa Mosque** (Map p140; Kanlıca; ⛴Kanlıca) in the square dates from 1560 and was designed by Mimar Sinan. There are excellent views of a number of *yalıs* as the ferry arrives and departs here.

High on a promontory above Kanlıca is **Hıdiv Kasrı** (Khedive's Villa; Map p140; www.beltur.com.tr; Çubuklu Yolu 32, Çubuklu; 🕘9am-10pm; ⛴Kanlıca) **FREE**, a gorgeous art nouveau villa built by the last khedive of Egypt as a summer residence for use during his family's annual visits to İstanbul. You can see its square white tower (often flying a Turkish flag) from the ferry.

Kanlica to Sariyer

On the opposite shore is the wealthy suburb of Emirgan, home to the impressive **Sakıp Sabancı Museum** (Map p140; ☎0212-277 2200; www.sakipsabancimuzesi.org; Sakıp Sabancı Caddesi 42, Emirgan; adult/student/child under 14yr ₺20/10/free, Wed free; 🕘10am-5.30pm Tue, Thu & Fri-Sun, to 7.30pm Wed; 🚌22 & 25E from Kabataş, 22RE & 40 from Beşiktaş, 40, 40T & 42T from Taksim). This museum has a permanent collection showcasing Ottoman manuscripts and calligraphy, but is best known for its blockbuster temporary exhibitions. The permanent collection occupies a 1925 mansion designed by Italian architect Edouard De Nari for the Egyptian Prince Mehmed Ali Hasan, and the temporary exhibitions are staged in an impressive modern extension designed by local firm Savaş, Erkel and Çırakoğlu.

On the hill above Emirgan is **Emirgan Korusu (Woods)**, a huge public reserve that is particularly beautiful in April, when it is carpeted with thousands of tulips.

North of Emirgan, there's a ferry dock near the small yacht-lined cove of **İstinye**. Nearby, on a point jutting out from the European shore, is the suburb of **Yeniköy**. This was a favourite summer resort for the Ottomans, as indicated by the cluster of lavish 18th- and 19th-century *yalıs* around the ferry dock. The most notable of these is the frilly white **Ahmed Afif Paşa Yalı** (Map p140; Yeniköy; 🚌25E from Kabataş, 40B from Beşiktaş, 40T & 42T from Taksim), designed by Alexandre Vallaury, architect of the Pera Palas Hotel in Beyoğlu, and built in the late 19th century.

On the opposite shore is the village of **Paşabahçe**, famous for its glassware factory. A bit further on is the fishing village of **Beykoz**, which has a graceful ablutions fountain, the İshak Ağa Çeşmesi, dating from 1746, near the village square. Much of the land along the Bosphorus shore north of Beykoz is a military zone.

Originally called Therapia for its healthy climate, the little cove of **Tarabya** on the European shore has been a favourite summer watering place for İstanbul's well-to-do for centuries, though modern developments such as the multistorey Grand Hotel Tarabya right on the promontory have poisoned much of its charm. For an account of Therapia in its heyday, read Harold Nicolson's 1921 novel *Sweet Waters*. Nicolson, who is best known as Vita Sackville-West's husband, served as the third Secretary in the British embassy in Constantinople between 1912 and 1914, the years of the Balkan Wars, and clearly knew Therapia well. In the novel, the main character, Eirene, who was based on Vita, spent her summers here.

North of the village are some of the old summer embassies of foreign powers. When the heat and fear of disease increased in the warm months, foreign ambassadors would retire to palatial residences, complete with lush gardens, on this shore. The region for such embassy residences extended north to the village of Büyükdere, notable for its churches, summer embassies and the **Sadberk Hanım Museum** (Map p140; ☎0212-242 3813; www.sadberkhanimmuzesi.org.tr; Piyasa Caddesi 27-29, Büyükdere; adult/student ₺7/2; 🕘10am-4.30pm Thu-Tue; 🅿; ⛴Sarıyer). Named after the wife of the late Vehbi Koç, founder of Turkey's foremost commercial empire, this museum is housed in two late 19th-century *yalıs* and is a showcase of both Turkish-Islamic artefacts collected by Mrs Koç and antiquities from the noted Hüseyin Kocabaş collection. Objects include İznik and Kütahya ceramics, Ottoman silk textiles and needlework, and an exquisite collection of diadems from the Mycenaean, Archaic and Classical periods. Labels are in English and Turkish, and there's an excellent gift shop. To get here, alight from the ferry at Sarıyer and walk left (south) from the ferry dock for approximately 10 minutes.

The residents of Sarıyer, the next village up from Büyükdere on the European shore, have traditionally made a living by fishing and it is still possible to see fisherfolk mending their nets and selling their catch north of the dock.

Sarıyer to Anadolu Kavaği

From Sarıyer, it's a short trip to Rumeli Kavağı, a sleepy place where the only excitement comes courtesy of the arrival and departure of the ferry. South of the town lies the shrine of the Muslim saint Telli Baba, reputed to be able to find suitable husbands for young women who pray there.

Anadolu Kavağı, on the opposite shore, is where the Long Bosphorus Tour finishes its journey. Once a fishing village, its local economy now relies on the tourism trade and its main square is full of mediocre fish restaurants and their touts.

Perched above the village are the ruins of Anadolu Kavağı Kalesi (Yoros Kalesi; Map p140; Anadolu Kavağı; ⓢ Anadolu Kavağı), a medieval castle overlooking both the Black Sea and the Bosphorus. The castle originally had eight massive towers in its walls, but little of the original structure has survived. First built by the Byzantines, it was restored and reinforced by the Genoese in the 1300s, and later by the Ottomans. An archaeological excavation is currently underway and as a result access is limited. There are, however, great views of the recently opened Yavuz Sultan Selim (Third) Bridge. It takes 30 to 50 minutes to walk up to the fortress from the town. Alternatively, taxis wait near the fountain in the town square just east of the ferry dock; they charge around ₺20 for the return trip with 30 minutes waiting time. Restaurants and *çay bahçesi* (tea gardens) along the walking route serve overpriced food and drink.

Long Bosphorus Tour (Uzun Boğaz Turu) Most day trippers take this ferry operated by İstanbul Şehir Hatları (İstanbul City Routes; ☑ 153; www.sehirhatlari.com.tr). It travels the entire length of the strait in a 95-minute one-way trip and departs from the *iskele* (ferry dock) at Eminönü daily at 10.35am and returns from Anadolu Kavağı at 3pm. A return (çift) ticket costs adult/under six years/ child six to 11 years ₺25/free/12.50; a one-way (tek yön) ticket costs ₺15/free/7.50. The ferry stops at Beşiktaş, Kanlıca (Map p140), Sarıyer (Map p140), Rumeli Kavağı (Map p140) and Anadolu Kavağı (Map p140). It's not possible to get on and off the ferry at stops along the way using the same ticket.

Short Bosphorus Tour (Kısa Boğaz Turu) From early March to May and from mid-September to October, İstanbul Şehir Hatları (p104) offers a two-hour tour leaving Eminönü daily at 2.30pm, picking up passengers in Ortaköy 20 minutes later. It travels as far as the Fatih Sultan Mehmet Bridge before returning to Eminönü. Tickets cost adult/child under six years/ child six to 11 years ₺12/free/6. From November to early March the service is limited to Saturdays, Sundays and holidays.

Hop-Off Palace Tour Departing from the *iskele* behind the petrol station at Kabataş, this tour operated by Dentur Avrasya (☑ 444 6336; www.denturavrasya.com) costs ₺15, leaves four times daily at 12.45pm, 1.45pm, 2.45pm and 3.45pm, and allows passengers to alight at Emirgan (Map p140), Küçüksu (Map p140) Kasrı and Beylerbeyi (Map p62) Palace and reboard on the same ticket. It would be very rushed to make three stops in one afternoon but two stops is achievable. Be aware that Küçüksu Kasrı and Beylerbeyi Palace close at 3.30pm (winter) and 4.30pm (summer). Dentur Avrasya also operates one long and short tour each day from Kabataş (check website for details).

Excursion Tours A number of companies offer short tours from Eminönü travelling to Anadolu Hisarı and back without stopping; of these Turyol is probably the most reputable. Its boats leave from the dock on the western side of the Galata Bridge hourly from 10am to 6pm. Boats operated by other companies leave from near the Boğaz İskelesi and from near the Haliç İskelesi. The entire trip takes about 90 minutes and tickets usually cost ₺12.

Bus All bus tickets and commuter ferry trips cost ₺4 (₺2.30 with an İstanbulkart).
➔ **From Sarıyer** Buses 25E and 40 head south to Emirgan.
➔ **From Emirgan** Buses 22, 22RE and 25E head to Kabataş, and 40, 40T and 42T go to Taksim.

All travel via Rumeli Hisarı, Bebek, Ortaköy, Yıldız and Beşiktaş.

⮕ From Anadolu Kavağı Bus 15A leaves from the square straight ahead from the ferry terminal en route to Kavacık. Get off at Kanlıca to visit Hıdiv Kasrı or transfer to bus 15 at Beykoz, which will take you south to Üsküdar via Çengelköy, the Küçüksu stop (for Küçüksu Kasrı) and the Beylerbeyi Sarayı stop (for Beylerbeyi). Bus 15F and 15BK take the same route but continue to Kadıköy.

> ### ℹ LONG BOSPHORUS TOUR
> If you buy a return ticket on the Long Bosphorus Tour (p104), you'll be forced to spend three hours in the tourist-trap village of Anadolu Kavağı. It's much better to buy a one-way ticket and alight there, at Sarıyer or at Kanlıca and make your way back to İstanbul by bus. Alternatively, take the Dentur Avraysa hop-on/hop-off tour from Kabataş.

🏃 Golden Horn Ferry Tour

Few visitors to İstanbul have heard about the ferry route up and down the length of the Golden Horn (Haliç). Until recently, this stretch of water to the north of the Galata Bridge was heavily polluted and its suburbs offered little to tempt travellers. All that's changing these days, with the Haliç suburbs being gentrified and beautification works (including the creation of many parks) being undertaken along both sides of the waterway. The ferry trip to Eyüp offers magnificent views of the imperial mosques atop the Old City's hills, glimpses of the historic city walls, and panoramas of ancient suburbs including Fener, Balat and Ayvansaray. On the opposite shore, vistas include Ottoman *mezarlıgıs* (cemeteries) and the remnants of Ottoman arsenals and naval docks.

Üsküdar to Kasımpaşa

After departing from Üsküdar on the Asian side, the ferry stops at the Haliç *iskelesis* (Golden Horn ferry docks) at **Karaköy** (Map p94) and Eminönü. The Karaköy *iskele* is on the northern side of the Galata Bridge, before the large Kadıköy *iskele*. The Eminönü *iskele* is on the western side of the Galata Bridge behind a car park next to the bus station. From Eminönü, the ferry passes underneath the Haliç Metro Bridge and the Atatürk (aka Unkapanı) Bridge before stopping at **Kasımpaşa** (Map p62) on the opposite side of the Golden Horn. This area is where the Ottoman imperial naval yards were located between the 16th and early 20th centuries, and some of the original building stock remains. The palace-like building to the left of the *iskele* is the 19th-century **Bahriye Nezareti** (Map p62; ⊠Kasimpaşa), where the Ministry for the Navy was once based. It is currently undergoing a major restoration. On the hill above is an 18th-century building with a

clock tower. This was originally the Naval Academy but was converted to a hospital in the 1850s; French soldiers were treated here during the Crimean War.

There are plans to redevelop the shipyards here into a huge complex including shops, hotels and restaurants, although locals seem sceptical that this will go ahead in the near future.

Kasımpaşa to Hasköy

As the ferry makes its way to the next stop, Hasköy (Map p62), you can see the fascinating Western District suburbs of **Fener** and **Balat** on the western (left) shore.

Fener is the traditional home of the city's Greek population, and although few Greeks are resident these days, a number of important Greek Orthodox sites remain. The prominent red-brick building with domed tower on the hill is the **Phanar Greek Orthodox College** (Megali School, Great School, Kırmızı Mektep; Map p62; Sancaktar Caddesi, Fener; 🚌99, 99A, 99Y from Eminönü, 55T from Taksim), the oldest house of learning in İstanbul. The school has been housed in Fener since before the Conquest – the present building dates from 1881–83. Sadly, it currently has a total enrolment of less than 100 students.

From this point, there are good views of the Yavuz Sultan Selim Mosque (p93) on the ridgeline and the Gothic Revival **Church of St Stephen of the Bulgars** (Sveti Stefan Church; Map p62; Mürsel Paşa Caddesi 85, Fener; 🚌99, 99A, 99Y from Eminönü, 55T from Taksim) on the waterfront, which has distinctive gilded copolas.

The next suburb, Balat, was once home to a large proportion of İstanbul's Jewish population but is now crowded with migrants from the east of the country.

Passing the derelict remains of the original Galata Bridge on its way, the ferry then docks at Hasköy (Map p62). For centuries a small, predominantly Jewish, village, Hasköy became home to a naval shipyard and a sultan's hunting ground in the Ottoman period. Today it has two sights of interest to visitors: the Rahmi M Koç Museum (Rahmi M Koç Müzesi; Map p62; ☑ 0212-369 6600; www.rmk-museum.org.tr; Hasköy Caddesi 5, Hasköy; museum adult/student/child under 7yr ₺15/6/free, steam-tug cruise ₺5/3/free, submarine adult/student ₺7/5, planetarium ₺2; ☉ 10am-5pm Tue-Fri, to 6pm Sat & Sun Oct-Mar, to 7pm Sat & Sun Apr-Sep; ☻Hasköy), which is located directly to the left of the ferry stop (Hasköy İskelesi); and Aynalıkavak Kasrı (Aynalıkavak Pavilion; Map p62; ☑ 0212-256 9750; www.millisaraylar.gov.tr; Aynalıkavak Caddesi, Hasköy; adult/student ₺5/1; ☉ 9am-4.30pm Tue, Wed & Fri-Sun Apr-Oct, to 3.30pm Nov-Mar; ☐47, 47E, 47N from Eminönü, 36T, 54K, 54HT from Taksim), a short walk away. This ornate 18th-century imperial hunting pavilion is set in a pretty garden and now houses a collection of historic musical instruments. To get there, walk southeast (right) along Hasköy Caddesi, veer left into Okmeydanı Caddesi and then right into Sempt Konağı Sokak, which runs into Kasimpaşa-Hasköy Caddesi.

A number of historic cemeteries cling to the hills behind Hasköy. These include the Hasköy Musevi Mezarlıgı (Map p62; ☻Sütlüce), where many generations of Jewish İstanbullus have been buried.

Hasköy to Eyüp

The ferry's next stop is at Ayvansaray on the opposite shore. From Ayvansaray (Map p62), you can visit the Kariye Museum (Chora Church; p92) or walk up to Edirnekapı to see a well-preserved section of the historic city walls. It's possible to see part of the wall structure from the ferry.

From Ayvansaray, the ferry crosses to Sütlüce (Map p62) and then returns to the western shore to terminate at Eyüp (Map p62). This conservative suburb is built around the Eyüp Sultan Mosque (Eyüp Sultan Camii, Mosque of the Great Eyüp; Map p62; Camii Kebir Sokak, Eyüp; ☉ tomb 9.30am-4.30pm; ☐99, 99A, 99Y from Eminönü, 55T from Taksim; ☻Eyüp), one of the most important religious sites in Turkey. After visiting, head to the Pierre Loti Café (Map p62; Gümüşsuyu Balmumcu Sokak 1, Eyüp; ☉ 8am-midnight; ☻Eyüp), where you can stop for a tea or coffee and enjoy panoramic views.

GETTING THERE & AWAY

You can explore the Golden Horn in half a day by boarding the ferry in Karaköy or Eminönü, alighting once at either Hasköy (for the Rahmi M Koç Museum) or Eyüp (for the Eyüp Sultan Mosque) and then reboarding a ferry for the return trip. If you have a full day, you could visit both of these sights and also visit Aynalıkavak Kasrı before or after visiting the Rahmi M Koç Museum. Another good option is to alight at Ayvansaray on your return trip, follow the historic land walls up the hill and visit the Kariye Museum (Chora Church).

Ferry İstanbul Şehir Hatları (p104) Operates the commuter Haliç ferry service. It departs Üsküdar hourly from 7.30am to 8.45pm and travels up the Golden Horn to Eyüp, picking up most passengers in Karaköy and Eminönü; the last ferry returns from Eyüp at 7.45pm (8.45pm on Sunday). The trip takes 55 minutes (35 minutes from Eminönü) and tickets cost ₺4 (₺2.30 with an İstanbulkart). If you alight, you'll need to pay a new fare for the next leg. Note that all passengers must alight at Eyüp. Check online for timetable and fare updates.

Dentur Avraysa (p104) offers a hop-on, hop-off tour (₺15) departing from Beşiktaş at 10am, noon, 2pm, 4pm and 6pm, stopping at Kabataş (where most people board), Hasköy, Eyüp and the Miniatürk theme park in Sütlüce before making the return trip. Check online for schedule updates.

Bus All bus tickets cost ₺4 (₺2.30 with an İstanbulkart).
➟ **From Eyüp** Buses 36CE, 44B, 48E, 99, 99Y and 399B/C travel to Eminönü from the Necip Fazıl Kısaküre stop in front of the ferry via Balat, Fener and Karaköy. Bus 39C travels to Aksaray via Edirnekapı, allowing you to stop and visit the Kariye Museum (Chora Church).
➟ **From Hasköy** Buses 36T, 54K or 54HT travel to Taksim. Buses 47, 47E or 47N travel to Eminönü.

🏃 Hamams

Succumbing to a soapy scrub in a steamy hamam is one of İstanbul's quintessential experiences. Not everyone feels comfortable with baring all (or most) of their body in public, though. If you include yourself in this group, a number of the city's spas offer private hamam treatments.

Ayasofya Hürrem
Sultan Hamamı   HAMAM
(Map p72; ☑ 0212-517 3535; www.ayasofya hamami.com; Aya Sofya Meydanı 2; bath treat-

ments €85-170, massages €40-75; ⊙ 8am-10pm; ⓢ Sultanahmet) This meticulously restored twin hamam dating to 1556 offers the most luxurious traditional bath experience in the Old City. Designed by Mimar Sinan, it was built just across the road from Aya Sofya by order of Süleyman the Magnificent and named in honour of his wife Hürrem Sultan, commonly known as Roxelana.

The building's three-year, US$13 million restoration, completed in 2011, was closely monitored by heritage authorities and the end result is wonderful: it retains Sinan's austere design but endows it with an understated modern luxury. There are separate baths for males and females, both with a handsome *soğukluk* (entrance vestibule) surrounded by wooden change cubicles.

Treatments are expert and the surrounds are exceptionally clean. The basic 35-minute bath treatment costs €85 and includes a scrub and soap massage, olive-oil soap and a personal *kese* (coarse cloth mitten used for exfoliation). Book ahead in high season. In warm weather, a cafe and restaurant operate on the outdoor terrace.

★ **Kılıç Ali Paşa Hamamı**   HAMAM
(Map p94; ☑ 0212-393 8010; http://kilicali pasahamami.com; Hamam Sokak 1, off Kemeraltı Caddesi, Tophane; traditional hamam ritual ₺170; ⊙ women 8am-4pm, men 4.30-11.30pm; ⓢ Tophane) It took seven years to develop a conservation plan for this 1580 Mimar Sinan–designed building and complete the meticulous restoration. Fortunately, the result was well worth waiting for. The hamam's interior is simply stunning and the place is run with total professionalism, ensuring a clean and enjoyable Turkish bath experience. Services include a traditional hamam ritual (₺170) and massage (from ₺140).

Cağaloğlu Hamamı   HAMAM
(Map p72; ☑ 0212-522 2424; www.cagaloglu hamami.com.tr; Prof Kazım İsmail Gürkan Caddesi 24; bath, scrub & massage packages €40-120, self-service €30; ⊙ 8am-10pm; ⓢ Sultanahmet) Built in 1741 by order of Sultan Mahmut I, this gorgeous hamam offers separate baths for men and women and a range of bath services that are – alas – overpriced considering how quick and rudimentary the wash, scrub and massage treatments are. Consider signing up for the self-service treatment (€30) only.

Çemberlitaş Hamamı   HAMAM
(Map p86; ☑ 0212-522 7974; www.cemberlitas hamami.com; Vezir Han Caddesi 8, Çemberlitaş; self-service ₺70, bath, scrub & soap massage ₺115; ⊙ 6am-midnight; ⓢ Çemberlitaş) There won't be too many times in your life when you'll get the opportunity to have a Turkish bath in a building dating back to 1584, so now might well be the time to do it – particularly as this twin hamam was designed by the great architect Sinan and is among the most beautiful in the city.

The building was commissioned by Nurbanu Sultan, wife of Selim II and mother of Murat III. Both of its bath chambers have a huge marble *sıcaklık* (circular marble heat platform) and a gorgeous dome with glass apertures. The *camekan* (entrance hall) for men is original, but the women's version is new.

It costs ₺75 to add an oil massage to the standard bath package, but all massages and treatments here are perfunctory, so we'd suggest giving this a miss and opting for the cheaper self-serve option. Tips are meant to be covered in the treatment price and there's a 20% discount for ISIC student-card holders.

Mihrimah Sultan Hamamı   HAMAM
(Map p62; ☑ 0212-523 0487; www.mihrimah sultanhamami.com; Fevzi Paşa Caddesi 333, Edirnekapı; bath ₺25, incl scrub & massage ₺45; ⊙ men 7am-11pm, women 9am-8pm; ⓢ 28 from Eminönü, 87 from Taksim) Visit this restored hamam for an affordable and authentic experience. It lacks the architectural beauty of its counterparts in Sultanahmet, but is satisfyingly clean and has a friendly neighbourhood atmosphere. There are separate sections for men and women.

**Four Seasons Istanbul
at the Bosphorus**   SPA
(Map p62; ☑ 0212-381 4000; www.fourseasons. com/bosphorus; Çırağan Caddesi 28, Beşiktaş; 30/45/60min hamam experience €125/155/185; ⊙ 9am-9pm; ⓢ Bahçeşehir Ünv. or Çırağan) With its luxury-hotel setting, this spa has wow factor in spades, including a stunning indoor pool area, steam room, sauna and relaxation lounge. Facials and massages, from deep tissue to hot stone, are available and the gorgeous marble hamam is perfect if you're looking for an indulgent Turkish bath experience. The hamam and treatment packages include full access to the spa facilities.

🏃 Tours

★ İstanbul Walks
WALKING
(Map p72; ☑ 0554 335 6622, 0212-516 6300; www.istanbulwalks.com; 1st fl, Şifa Hamamı Sokak 1; tours adult €35-75, child under 2/7yr free/30% discount; 🚇 Sultanahmet) Specialising in cultural tourism, this company is run by history buffs and offers a large range of guided walking tours conducted by knowledgeable English-speaking guides. Tours concentrate on İstanbul's various neighbourhoods, but there are also tours of major monuments, a Turkish coffee trail, and a Bosphorus and Golden Horn cruise by private boat.

★ Urban Adventures
CULTURAL
(☑ 0535 022 2003; www.urbanadventures.com; tours from €27) This highly professional outfit runs a number of cultural tours including a 3½-hour night tasting walk in Beyoğlu and a dinnertime visit to Small Projects İstanbul, an NGO working to support Syrian refugees in the city. All proceeds from the latter tour go to the charity.

★ Alternative City Tours
TOURS
(www.alternativecitytours.com; tour per group of up to 6 people €150 plus lunch) Having lived in İstanbul for many years, New York–born photographer Monica Fritz recently made the decision to share some of the many secrets she has learned about the city with fellow shutterbugs. Her informed and enjoyable tour portfolio covers the European and Asian shores and beyond, and she provides plenty of cultural and historical context.

Artwalk İstanbul
WALKING
(☑ 0537 797 7525; www.artwalkistanbul.com; group tours per person ₺75-100, private tours by negotiation; ☺ Apr-Dec) Saliha Yavuz and her small team of curators, artists and critics offer guided English-language visits to commercial and artist-run galleries, as well as artists' studios, providing an excellent introduction to the city's vibrant contemporary-art scene. Tours concentrate on neighbourhoods, with gallery walks in Galata, Tophane, Taksim and Nişantaşı, and a tour of artists' studios in Kadıköy.

Les Arts Turcs
CULTURAL
(Map p72; ☑ 0212-527 6859; www.lesartsturcs.com; 3rd fl, Incili Cavus Sokak 19, Alemdar; ₺70; 🚇 Sultanahmet) This long-established cultural tourism outfit based near the Basilica Cistern offers twice-weekly opportunities to attend a *sema* (whirling-dervish ceremony) at the EMAV Silivrikapı Mevlana Cultural Center in Fatih on Thursdays at 8pm. The ticket cost includes a 15-minute Q&A session in English, a guide and minivan transfers to/from Sultanahmet.

🎉 Festivals & Events

İstanbul Film Festival
FILM
(http://film.iksv.org/en) If you're keen to view the best in Turkish film and bump into a few local film stars while doing so, this is the event to attend. Held in the first half of April in cinemas around town, it's hugely popular. The program includes retrospectives and recent releases from Turkey and abroad.

İstanbul Tulip Festival
CULTURAL
(☺ April) FREE The tulip (*lale* in Turkish) is one of İstanbul's traditional symbols, and the local government celebrates this fact by planting over 10 million of them annually. These bloom in April, endowing almost every street and park with vivid spring colours and wonderful photo opportunities.

Chill-Out Festival
MUSIC
(www.chilloutfest.com) A two-day event in May featuring a concept stage, cultural and artistic activities, yoga programs and plenty of music (everything from soul to funk to world beats). It's held at Life Park in Sarıyer on the Bosphorus.

İstanbul Music Festival
MUSIC
(http://muzik.iksv.org/en) The city's premier arts festival includes performances of opera, dance, orchestral concerts and chamber recitals. Acts are often internationally renowned and the action takes place in June at atmosphere-laden venues such as Aya İrini (p80) in Sultanahmet and the **Süreyya Opera House** (Map p62; ☑ 0216-346 1531; www.sureyyaoperasi.org; Gen Asim Gündüz (Bahariye) Caddesi 29; 🚇 Kadıköy) in Kadıköy.

İstanbul Jazz Festival
MUSIC
(http://caz.iksv.org/en) Held from late June to late July each year, this is an exhilarating hybrid of conventional jazz, electronica, drum and bass, world music and rock. Venues include Salon in Şişhane, and parks around the city.

COOKING COURSES & TOURS

Ask İstanbullus what makes their city special and the answer usually comes straight from their stomachs. The local cuisine has a fan club as numerous as it is vociferous, and its members enjoy nothing better than introducing visitors to the foods, eateries and provedores of the city. In short, this is a dream destination for everyone who loves to eat, cook and shop for food, particularly as plenty of cooking courses and food-focused walking tours are on offer, including the following:

Cooking Alaturka (Map p71; ☑0212-458 5919; www.cookingalaturka.com; Akbıyık Caddesi 72a, Cankurtaran; classes per person incl meal €65; ☉10.30am & 4.30pm by reservation Mon-Sat; ⊠Sultanahmet) Runs popular classes suitable for all skill levels.

İstanbul Eats (http://istanbuleats.com; tours per person US$75-125) Fantastic food tours and a one-day cooking class in the fascinating Kurtuluş neighbourhood.

İstanbul on Food (☑0538 966 7671; http://istanbulonfood.com; tour US$100) A newly launched company offering food tours.

Turkish Flavours (☑0532 218 0653; www.turkishflavours.com; tours per person US$80-125) Walking tours and excellent cooking classes held in a private residence on the Asian side of town. If requested, the course can focus on a Sephardic menu.

Urban Adventures (opposite) A variety of food tours.

İstanbul Biennial
ART

(http://bienal.iksv.org/en) The city's major visual-arts shindig takes place from mid-September to mid-November in odd-numbered years. An international curator or panel of curators nominates a theme and puts together a cutting-edge program that is then exhibited in a variety of venues around town.

Akbank Jazz Festival
MUSIC

(Akbank Caz Festivali; www.akbanksanat.com) This older sister to the International İstanbul Jazz Festival is a boutique event, with a program featuring traditional and avant-garde jazz, as well as Middle Eastern fusions and a special program of young jazz. It's held in October each year, and venues are scattered around town.

İstanbul Design Biennial
DESIGN

(http://bienal.iksv.org/en) A relatively new addition to the İKSV's stellar calendar of festivals, this themed event sees the city's design community celebrating its profession and critically discussing its future. It's held between October and November in even-numbered years.

Sleeping

Every accommodation style is available in İstanbul. You can live like a sultan in a world-class luxury hotel, bunk down in a dorm bed or settle into a stylish boutique establishment. The secret is to choose the neighbourhood that best suits your interests and then look for accommodation that will suit your style and budget – there are loads of options to choose from.

Sultanahmet & Around

Sultanahmet is the heart of Old İstanbul and the city's premier sightseeing area, so hotels here and in the adjoining neighbourhoods to the east (Cankurtaran), south (Küçük Ayasofya) and northwest (Binbirdirek, Çemberlitaş, Alemdar and Cağaloğlu) are supremely convenient. The area's main drawbacks are carpet touts and the dearth of decent bars and restaurants. Some Cankurtaran hotels can also be noisy, with loud music coming from the bars and hostels on Akbıyık Caddesi. Early in the morning you may be woken by the call to prayer issuing from mosques such as İshak Paşa Mosque (at the northeastern end of Akbıyık Caddesi).

★Marmara Guesthouse
PENSION $

(Map p71; ☑0212-638 3638; www.marmaraguesthouse.com; Terbıyık Sokak 15, Cankurtaran; d €65-85, tr €80-100, f €95-115; ☯❄☎; ⊠Sultanahmet) Few of Sultanahmet's family-run pensions can compete with the Marmara's cleanliness, comfort and thoughtful details. Owner Elif and team go out of their way to welcome guests, offering advice aplenty and serving a delicious breakfast on the vine-covered, sea-facing roof terrace. Rooms have four-poster beds with Turkish hangings, good bathrooms (small in some cases) and double-glazed windows.

Members of the same family operate the similarly impressive **Saruhan Hotel** (Map p86; ☑ 0212-458 7608; www.saruhanhotel.com; Cinci Meydanı Sokak 34, Kadırga; s/d/f €70/75/105; ⊖ ✳ @ 🕱; 🖰 Çemberlitaş) in the predominantly residential pocket of Kadırga.

★ **Hotel Alp Guesthouse** HOTEL $
(Map p71; ☑ 0212-517 7067; www.alpguesthouse.com; Adliye Sokak 4, Cankurtaran; s/d €55/80; ⊖ ✳ 🕱; 🖰 Sultanahmet) This wooden building lives up to its location in Sultanahmet's premier small-hotel enclave, offering attractive, well-priced single, double, triple and family rooms. Bathrooms are small but very clean, and there are plenty of amenities. The roof terrace is one of the best in this area, with great sea views, comfortable indoor and outdoor seating, and free tea and coffee.

★ **Hotel Şebnem** HOTEL $
(Map p71; ☑ 0212-517 6623; www.sebnemhotel.net; Adliye Sokak 1, Cankurtaran; s €50, d €70-80, tr/f €90/110; ⊖ ✳ @ 🕱; 🖰 Sultanahmet) An appealing sense of simplicity and intimacy pervades the Şebnem. Antiques dot the 15 smart rooms, which have wooden floors, modern bathrooms and comfortable beds; two have a private courtyard garden. The large terrace upstairs has a cafe-bar and views over the Sea of Marmara.

★ **Metropolis Hostel** HOSTEL $
(Map p71; ☑ 0212-518 1822; www.metropolishostel.com; Terbıyık Sokak 24, Cankurtaran; dm €15-16, d €60-65, s/d/tw/tr without bathroom €44/46/49/68; P ⊖ ✳ 🕱; 🖰 Sultanahmet) Located in a quiet street where a good night's sleep is assured, the friendly Metropolis offers four- to six-bed dorms, including a female-only en suite option with six beds and sweeping Sea of Marmara views. The rooftop terrace has a bar and sea views to equal many pricier hotels, and the busy entertainment program includes summer barbecues and belly dancing.

Showers and toilets are clean but in limited supply, and the steep stairs could be challenging for some travellers.

Ahmet Efendi Evi PENSION $
(Map p72; ☑ 0212-518 8465; www.ahmetefendievi.com; Keresteci Hakkı Sokak 23, Cankurtaran; s €45-65, d €50-80, f €70-95; P ⊖ ✳ 🕱; 🖰 Sultanahmet) Mr Ahmet's House has an appealing home-away-from-home feel and is a great choice for families, with a warm welcome from hostess Gönül and family. In a predominantly residential area (a rarity in Sultanahmet), its nine rooms of various sizes have modern decor and fittings; one has a terrace with views of the Blue Mosque and Sea of Marmara.

Hotel Nomade BOUTIQUE HOTEL $
(Map p72; ☑ 0212-513 8173; www.hotelnomade.com; Ticarethane Sokak 15, Alemdar; s/d/tr €40/45/70; P ⊖ ✳ 🕱; 🖰 Sultanahmet) Designer style and budget pricing don't often go together, but the Nomade bucks the trend. Just a few steps off busy Divan Yolu, it offers simple rooms that some guests find too small – request the largest possible. Everyone loves the roof-terrace bar, though (smack-bang in front of Aya Sofya).

Hotel Grand Peninsula HOTEL $
(Map p71; ☑ 0212-458 7710; www.grandpeninsula hotel.com; Cetinkaya Sokak 3, Cankurtaran; d €50-65, s/tr/f €40/80/90; P ⊖ ✳ 🕱) A sister hotel to nearby **Peninsula** (Map p71; ☑ 0212-458 6850; www.hotelpeninsula.com; Adliye Sokak 6, Cankurtaran; d €35-50, tr €60, f €65-100; ⊖ ✳ @ 🕱; 🖰 Sultanahmet) and **Hanedan** (Map p71; ☑ 0212-516 4869; www.hanedanhotel.com; Adliye Sokak 3, Cankurtaran; s €45, d €50-55, tr €70, f €85-95; ⊖ ✳ @ 🕱; 🖰 Sultanahmet), the Grand Peninsula was renovated in 2016, resulting in a pleasant property with scattered carpets and appealing decorative touches. The small doubles certainly live up to their name, but the large doubles, such as 304, are comfortable budget options.

Breakfast is served on the roof terrace with a view of the city's Asian side and Princes' Islands.

Cheers Hostel HOSTEL $
(Map p72; ☑ 0212-526 0200; www.cheershostel.com; Zeynep Sultan Camii Sokak 21, Sultanahmet; dm €15-24, d €60-70, tr €90-105, f €135; P ⊖ ✳ @ 🕱; 🖰 Gülhane) These five- to 10-bed dorms are worlds away from the impersonal barrack-like spaces in bigger hostels. Bright and airy, they feature wooden floorboards, rugs, lockers and comfortable beds. Cheers is a little basic in places, but has an

excellent central position and a cosy rooftop bar with a great view and, in winter, an open fire.

Big Apple Hostel

HOSTEL $

(Map p71; ☑ 0212-517 7931; www.hostelbigapple. com; Bayram Fırını Sokak 12, Cankurtaran; dm €15-45, r €30-75; ☻ ❄ @ ☎; ⛟ Sultanahmet) It may lack a traveller vibe, but the compensations at this comfortable hostel include six-bed air-conditioned dorms (including a female-only option) with comfortable beds and private bathroom, as well as hotel-style private rooms with satellite TV, fridge and bathroom. Added to this is a rooftop bar-breakfast room with sea views.

Zeynep Sultan Hotel

HOTEL $

(Map p72; ☑ 0212-514 5001; www.zeynep sultanhotel.com; Zeynep Sultan Camii Sokak 25, Alemdar; s/d/tr €50/60/75; ☏ ☻ ❄ ☎; ⛟ Sultanahmet, Gülhane) There aren't many hotels in the world that can boast a Byzantine chapel in the basement, but the Zeynep Sultan can. Its 22 renovated rooms have a modern, white look and include fridges, tea and coffee facilities, and attractive marble finish in the bathrooms. Breakfast is served on the rear terrace with Aya Sofya views.

★ Sirkeci Mansion

HOTEL $$

(Map p72; ☑ 0212-528 4344; www.sirkeci mansion.com; Taya Hatun Sokak 5, Sirkeci; s €110-247, d €149-247, tr €199, f €209-224; ☻ ❄ ☎ ☒; ⛟ Gülhane) Travellers love this terrific-value hotel overlooking Gülhane Park, with its impeccably clean, well-sized and amenity-laden rooms, some with park-facing balconies. It has a restaurant where a lavish breakfast is served, an indoor pool and a hamam. Top marks go to the attention to detail, the helpful staff and the complimentary entertainment program, which includes walking tours and afternoon teas.

★ Hotel Empress Zoe

BOUTIQUE HOTEL $$

(Map p71; ☑ 0212-518 2504; www.emzoe.com; Akbıyık Caddesi 10, Cankurtaran; s €60-90, d €140-160, tr €150, ste €180-300; ☻ ❄ ☎; ⛟ Sultanahmet) Named after the feisty Byzantine empress, this is one of İstanbul's most impressive boutique hotels. The four buildings house 26 diverse rooms. The enticing garden suites overlook a 15th-century hamam and the gorgeous flower-filled courtyard where breakfast is served in warm weather. You can enjoy an early evening drink there,

ⓘ ACCOMMODATION

Hotels here are busy, so you should book your room as far in advance as possible, particularly if you are visiting during the high season (Easter–May, September–October and Christmas/ New Year). Recent years have seen significant fluctuations in tourist numbers in İstanbul, so most hotels now use yield management systems when setting their rates. This means that in quiet times prices can drop dramatically (sometimes by as much as 50%) and in busy times they can skyrocket. As a result, you should treat our prices as a guide only – it is possible that the price you are quoted will be quite different. Note that most hotels in İstanbul set their prices in euros, and we have listed them as such here.

or while admiring the sea view from the terrace.

★ Hotel Amira

BOUTIQUE HOTEL $$

(Map p72; ☑ 0212-516 1640; www.hotelamira. com; Mustafapaşa Sokak 43, Küçük Ayasofya; r €129-159; ☻ ❄ @ ☎) A consistent performer, Amira has 32 attractive rooms with Ottoman flourishes. It's a relaxing haven after a long day of sightseeing, complete with tea and coffee, slippers, a safe and bottled water aplenty. Adding further appeal are the attentive service, a spa, a roof terrace overlooking the Little Aya Sofya and the Sea of Marmara, and complimentary afternoon tea in served in the sunken lounge.

The only difference between standard and deluxe rooms is size, with poky bathrooms in the former.

★ Hotel Ibrahim Pasha

BOUTIQUE HOTEL $$

(Map p72; ☑ 0212-518 0394; www.ibrahimpasha. com; Terzihane Sokak 7, Sultanahmet; r standard/ deluxe €125/175; ☻ ❄ @ ☎; ⛟ Sultanahmet) Cultural tomes are piled in reception and throughout the 24 rooms of this exemplary design hotel, which also has a comfortable lounge with open fire, and a terrace bar with knockout views of the nearby Blue Mosque and Hippodrome. Rooms are gorgeous but some are small, with more space in the deluxe options and those in the new section.

Hotel Alilass
DESIGN HOTEL $$
(Map p71; ☑ 0212-516 8860; www.hotelalilass. com; Bayram Fırını Sokak 9, Cankurtaran; s €60-90, d €70-100; ☺ ✳ 🛜; 🚇 Sultanahmet) This well-priced design hotel has 22 small but stylish rooms, with low-hanging lights, black-and-white photos of Old İstanbul, and bathrooms featuring Ottoman tiles and glass walls. Facilities include a lobby cafe, roof terrace and conservatory-like breakfast room in the back garden.

Hotel Uyan
HOTEL $$
(Map p71; ☑ 0212-518 9255; www.uyanhotel. com; Utangaç Sokak 25, Cankurtaran; r €99-150, f/ste €180/200; ℗ ☺ ✳ @ 🛜; 🚇 Sultanahmet) The Uyan's quietly elegant decor nods towards Ottoman style, but never goes over the top in its antique furniture, prints and monochromatic floral bedspreads. Rooms are comfortable and mostly of a decent size; the exceptions are the budget singles (€60), which are tiny but serviceable. Breakfast is enjoyed in the top-floor space or on the terrace that has Blue Mosque and sea views.

Ottoman Hotel Imperial
HOTEL $$
(Map p72; ☑ 0212-513 6151; www.ottoman hotelimperial.com; Caferiye Sokak 6; r from €100; ☺ ✳ @ 🛜; 🚇 Sultanahmet) This four-star hotel is in a wonderfully quiet location just outside the Topkapı Palace walls. Its large and comfortable rooms have plenty of amenities, including minibars and coffee machines, and are decorated with Ottoman-style objets d'art; opt for one facing the neighbouring Aya Sofya or in the rear annexe. No roof terrace, but on-site Matbah (p116) restaurant is excellent.

Osman Han Hotel
HOTEL $$
(Map p71; ☑ 0212-458 7702; www.osmanhanhotel. com; Çetinkaya Sokak 1, Cankurtaran; s/d standard €160/170, deluxe €180/190; ☺ ✳ 🛜; 🚇 Sultanahmet) Amenity levels at this friendly little hotel are high: rooms have comfortable beds, minibars, tea and coffee facilities, and satellite TV, while the breakfast room and terrace have sea views. The main difference between standard and deluxe rooms is space, with cramped bathrooms in the former category. The ground-floor rooms (single/double €130/140) are right next to reception.

Weekend rates are €10 higher per room.

Dersaadet Hotel
HOTEL $$
(Map p72; ☑ 0212-458 0760; www.hotelder saadet.com; Kapıağası Sokak 5, Küçük Ayasofya; s

from €70, d €84-152, ste €180-200; ☺ ✳ @ 🛜; 🚇 Sultanahmet) Dersaadet means 'Place of Happiness' in Turkish – and guests are inevitably happy at this well-run place with Ottoman-style decor and Sea of Marmara views throughout. A restored mansion, its 17 comfortable rooms include a sumptuous penthouse suite. Amenities include a lift and a terrace with panoramic views.

Arcadia Blue Hotel
HOTEL $$
(Map p72; ☑ 0212-516 9696; www.hotelarcadia blue.com; İmran Öktem Caddesi 1, Bindirbirek; r economy/standard/sea view/deluxe from €63/108/129/171; ℗ ✳ 🛜; 🚇 Sultanahmet) This modern hotel has memorable views of Aya Sofya, the Blue Mosque, the Bosphorus and the Sea of Marmara from its roof-terrace bar-restaurant, and a ground-floor cafe where complimentary afternoon tea is served. There's also a hamam and a gym. Rooms are extremely comfortable; all are a good size but the sea-view options are worth their higher price tag.

Emine Sultan Hotel & Suites
BOUTIQUE HOTEL $$
(Map p72; ☑ 0212-458 4666; www.eminesultan hotel.com; Kapıağası Sokak 6, Cankurtaran; s €55-115, d €60-125, tr/q €145/160; ℗ ☺ ✳ @ 🛜; 🚇 Sultanahmet) This tall wooden building, topped with covered and open terraces on the 4th and 5th floors, has 16 small, faintly kitschy rooms with pretty cream-and-pink decor, and sea views in some cases.

Sarı Konak Hotel
BOUTIQUE HOTEL $$
(Map p71; ☑ 0212-638 6258; www.istanbulhotel sarikonak.com; Mimar Mehmet Ağa Caddesi 26, Cankurtaran; r €104-134, tr/f/ste €154/234/234; ℗ ☺ ✳ @ 🛜; 🚇 Sultanahmet) Guests here enjoy relaxing on the roof terrace with its Sea of Marmara and Blue Mosque views, but also take advantage of the comfortable lounge and courtyard downstairs. With Ottoman touches and prints of Old İstanbul, bedrooms are similarly impressive from the attractive standard rooms upwards.

Four Seasons Istanbul at Sultanahmet
HOTEL $$$
(Map p71; ☑ 0212-402 3000; www.fourseasons. com/istanbul; Tevkifhane Sokak 1, Cankurtaran; r from €400; ℗ ✳ @ 🛜; 🚇 Sultanahmet) This luxurious hotel has an excellent position near Aya Sofya and the Blue Mosque, with views of both and of the Bosphorus from its rooftop bar-restaurant. Facilities include a spa and an excellent restaurant in the leafy

inner courtyard, while even the entry-level superior rooms are serene havens with original Turkish artworks and handwoven kilims (pileless woven rugs).

▐ Beyoğlu

★ Louis Appartements
HOTEL $

(Map p94; ☑ 0212-293 4052; www.louis.com. tr/galata; İlk Belediye Caddesi 10, Şişhane; d/ste €90/200; ⊜ ❄ @ ☎; M Şişhane, ⛴ Tünel) The top-floor suite at this meticulously maintained and keenly priced hotel near the Galata Tower is the knockout option among the 12 suites and rooms on offer. All have a large bed, TV/DVD player, ironing set-up and kitchenette equipped with appliances, including an espresso machine. Decor is understated but pleasing; staff are helpful. An optional breakfast costs €9 per person.

Rapunzel Hostel
HOSTEL $

(Map p94; ☑ 0212-292 5034; www.rapunzel istanbul.com; Bereketzade Camii Sokak 3, Galata; dm €14-24, s €35, tw €40-70; ❄ @ ☎; M Şişhane, ⛴ Tünel) This intimate hostel near Galata Tower is blessed with informed, friendly and enthusiastic staff, making it a great choice for budget travellers. Dorms and rooms are small but have air-con, clean private bathrooms, reading lights and power points; mixed and female dorms also have lockers. There's a cosy TV room and a roof terrace with view of the Historical Peninsula.

World House Hostel
HOSTEL $

(Map p94; ☑ 0212-293 5520; www.worldhouse istanbul.com; Galipdede Caddesi 85, Galata; dm €9-22, d €36-68, tr €48-78; @ ☎; M Şişhane, ⛴ Tünel) Tucked behind the Latife Cafe, this long-standing and justly popular hostel is close to Beyoğlu's entertainment strips but not too far from the sights in Sultanahmet. Nonstandard hostel features include double-glazed windows and an in-house *lokanta* (serving ready-made food; lunch ₺10). All dorms are mixed (the best are in the front building) and bathrooms are clean (one shower/toilet for every nine beds).

★ Casa di Bava
BOUTIQUE HOTEL $$

(Map p94; ☑ 0538-377 3877; www.casadibava istanbul.com; Bostanbaşı Caddesi 28, Çukurcuma; economy ste €140, 1-bedroom apt €180, 2-bedroom penthouse €320; ⊜ ❄ ❄; M Taksim) The two-bedroom penthouse apartment at this recently opened suite hotel is an absolute knockout, and the 11 one-bedroom apartments in the 1880s building are im-

pressive, too. All are stylishly decorated and well appointed, with original artworks, fully equipped kitchenettes and washing machines. The basement suites are smaller and less expensive; all have daily maid service. In-room breakfast costs €6 per person.

★ Karaköy Rooms
BOUTIQUE HOTEL $$

(Map p94; ☑ 0212-252 5422; http://karakoyrooms. com; Galata Şarap İskelesi Sokak 10, Karaköy; standard r €80-130, studio €130-200; ⊜ ❄ ☎; ⛴ Karaköy) Occupying five floors above one of the city's best-loved restaurants, this splendid hotel has only 10 rooms – book well in advance. The double and deluxe rooms are spacious, comfortable, well-equipped and offer exceptional value for money. The pricier studios are enormous, with well-equipped kitchenettes. Decor is super-stylish throughout and the breakfast (served in the restaurant) is lavish and delicious.

★ TomTom Suites
BOUTIQUE HOTEL $$

(Map p94; ☑ 0212-292 4949; www.tomtomsuites. com; Tomtom Kaptan Sokak 18, Tophane; standard ste €150-170, deluxe ste €170-325; ⊜ ❄ @ ☎; ⛴ Tophane) We're more than happy to beat the drum about this hotel, occupying a former Franciscan nunnery off İstiklal Caddesi. Its contemporary decor is understated but elegant, levels of service are high and the suites are spacious and beautifully appointed. A delicious and generous breakfast is served in the rooftop restaurant with its panoramic view. Sadly, dinner is considerably less impressive.

★ Witt Istanbul Hotel
BOUTIQUE HOTEL $$

(Map p94; ☑ 0212-293 1500; www.wittistanbul. com; Defterdar Yokuşu 26, Cihangir; d ste €125-285, terrace ste €195-450; ❄ @ ☎; M Taksim, ⛴ Tophane) Showcasing nearly as many designer features as an issue of *Monocle* magazine, this stylish apartment hotel in Cihangir offers spacious suites with seating area, CD/DVD player, espresso machine, king-size bed and swish bathroom. Most have kitchenettes and a few have panoramic terraces (there's also a communal rooftop terrace). It's a short but steep climb from the Tophane tram stop.

Marmara Pera
HOTEL $$

(Map p94; ☑ 0212-251 4646; www.themarmara hotels.com; Meşrutiyet Caddesi 1, Tepebaşı; r/f/ste €120/240/300; P ⊜ ❄ @ ❄ ❄; M Şişhane, ⛴ Tünel) A great location in the midst of Beyoğlu's major entertainment enclave makes this high-rise modern hotel an excellent choice. Added extras include a health club, a tiny outdoor pool, a truly fabulous buffet breakfast spread (€15 per person) and the fashionable Mikla (p123) rooftop bar and restaurant. Rooms with a sea view are approximately 30% more expensive.

Bankerhan Hotel
BOUTIQUE HOTEL $$
(Map p94; ☑ 0212-243 5617; www.bankerhan.com; Banker Sokağı 2, Galata; standard s/d €79/99, tw €120, king & loft r €120-129; ❄ ❄ @ ⚡; ☐ Karaköy) Budget and boutique aren't concepts that sit comfortably together, but this recently opened hotel on the edge of Galata and Karaköy can legitimately claim to be both. The owners have a notable contemporary-art collection that is scattered throughout the building, and the 36 rooms are both stylish and comfortable. The cheapest options are cramped – upgrade if possible.

Vault Karaköy
BOUTIQUE HOTEL $$
(Map p94; ☑ 212-244 6434; www.thehousehotel. com; Bankalar Caddesi 5, Karaköy; s €109-209, d €134-234, ste €159-959; ❄ @ ⚡; Ⓜ Şişhane, ☐ Karaköy) This flagship property of İstanbul's fashionable House Hotel group is a stylish and evocative meld of old and new. Occupying a grand bank building complete with vaults (hence the name), facilities include a gym, hamam, lobby bar-restaurant and rooftop lounge. Rooms are comfortable and well equipped (opt for a deluxe if possible, as classic and superior rooms are slightly cramped).

Istanbul Place Apartments
APARTMENT $$
(☑ 0506 449 3393; http://istanbulplace.com; apt 1-bed €80-121, 2-bed €109-230, 3-bed €115-270; ❄ ⚡) Operated by a British-Turkish couple, this apartment-rental company has nine well-appointed and beautifully presented properties in historic buildings across Galata and Taksim.

Hamamhane
BOUTIQUE HOTEL $$
(Map p94; ☑ 0212-293 4963; www.hamamhane. com; Çukurcuma Caddesi 45, Çukurcuma; studio €110, f & ste €140; ❄ ❄ @ ⚡; ☐ Tophane) Çukurcuma is one of the few enclaves in Beyoğlu to retain an authentic neighbourhood feel, so it's a great spot for a city sojourn. Each of the spacious studios and suites at this keenly priced hotel come with a fully equipped kitchenette and clothes washer/dryer. Decor is Ikea-stylish and there's an extremely pleasant ground-floor dining room and terrace.

It's worth noting that the owners have plans to renovate and open the adjoining hamam. While this occurs, construction noise and dust may be a problem.

★ Pera Palace Hotel
HISTORIC HOTEL $$$
(Map p94; ☑ 0212-377 4000; www.perapalace. com; Meşrutiyet Caddesi 52, Tepebaşı; r €150-325, ste €330-550; ℗ ❄ ❄ @ ⚡ ❄ ❄; Ⓜ Şişhane) This famous hotel underwent a €23-million restoration in 2010 and the result is simply splendiferous. Rooms are luxurious and extremely comfortable, and facilities include an atmospheric bar and lounge (the latter often closed for private functions), spa, gym and restaurant. The most impressive feature of all is the service, which is both friendly and efficient. Breakfast costs €25.

✗ Eating

✗ Sultanahmet & Around

Sultanahmet's lovely settings and great views are too often accompanied by disappointing meals. That said, we've eaten our way through the neighbourhood and, fortunately, there are a few gems to be found.

If you're in the Sirkeci neighbourhood at lunchtime, join the locals in Hocapaşa Sokak, a pedestrianised street lined with cheap eateries. Here, *lokantas* offer *hazır yemek* (ready-made dishes), *köftecis* dish out flavoursome meatballs, *kebapçıs* grill meat to order and *pidecis* serve piping-hot pides (Turkish-style pizza). For more about eating in Sirkeci, check http://sirkeci restaurants.com.

The Küçük Ayasofya neighbourhood is another good option for more authentic and affordable eateries.

Sefa Restaurant
TURKISH $
(Map p72; ☑ 0212-520 0670; www.sefarestaurant. com.tr; Nuruosmaniye Caddesi 11, Cağaloğlu; portions ₺8-14, kebaps ₺20; ⊙ 7am-5pm; ⚡; ☐ Sultanahmet) Describing its cuisine as Ottoman, this popular place offers *hazır yemek* (ready-made dishes) and kebaps at reasonable prices. You can order from an English menu, but at busy times you may find it easier to just pick daily specials from the bain-marie. Try to arrive early-ish for lunch because many dishes run out by 1.30pm. No alcohol.

Erol Lokantası
TURKISH $
(Map p72; ☑ 0212-511 0322; Çatal Çeşme Sokak 3, Cağaloğlu; portions ₺5.50-15.50; ⊙ 11am-9pm

Mon-Sat; ✆; 🚇 Sultanahmet) One of Sultanahmet's last *lokantas* (eateries serving ready-made food), Erol wouldn't win any awards for its interior design but might for its warm welcome and food. The dishes in the bain-marie are made fresh daily using seasonal ingredients by the Erol family members, who have collectively put in several decades in the kitchen.

Çiğdem Pastanesi
CAFE $

(Map p72; Divan Yolu Caddesi 62a; pastries ₺1.50-7.50, cakes ₺3-10; ⏱ 7.30am-11.30pm; 🚇 Sultanahmet) Strategically located on the main drag between Aya Sofya Meydanı and the Grand Bazaar, Çiğdem has been tempting locals since 1961 with its mouth-watering window display of gateaux and pastries. Pop in for a quick tea (₺2.50) or coffee (flat white ₺7.50) accompanied by *börek* (filled pastries), baklava or *tavuk göğsü* (a dessert made from milk, rice and pounded chicken breast).

Karadeniz Aile Pide ve Kebap Salonu
PIDE, KEBAP $

(Map p72; ✆ 0212-522 9191; www.karadenizpide.net; Hacı Tahsinbey Sokak 7, off Divan Yolu Caddesi; pides ₺16-24, kebaps ₺18-32; ⏱ 11am-10pm; 🚇 Sultanahmet) Serving tasty pides and kebaps since 1985, the original Karadeniz (Black Sea)–style pide joint in this enclave is a hit with local shopkeepers. You can claim a table in the utilitarian interior (women usually sit upstairs) or on the lane. No alcohol.

Make sure that you don't get this place confused with those nearby, which have cheekily used versions of its name but are nowhere near as good. This one is on the street corner.

Tarihi Sultanahmet Köftecisi Selim Usta
KÖFTE $

(Map p72; ✆ 0212-520 0566; www.sultanahmetkoftesi.com; Divan Yolu Caddesi 12; köfte ₺16, beans ₺7, çorba ₺5; ⏱ 11am-10pm; 🚇 Sultanahmet) Not to be confused with the nearby Meşhur Sultanahmet Köftecisi, this no-frills place near the Sultanahmet tram stop is the most famous eatery in the Old City. It has been serving its slightly rubbery *ızgara köfte* (grilled meatballs) and bean salad to ultra-loyal locals since 1920, and shows no sign of losing its custom – there's often a queue outside.

Sedef İskender
KEBAP $

(Map p72; ✆ 0212-516 2420; www.sedefdoner.com; Divan Yolu Caddesi 21b; döner ₺13; ⏱ 11am-10pm; 🚇 Sultanahmet) Locals swear that Sedef serves Sultanahmet's best döner kebap (spit-roasted lamb slices), and keep the chef busy shaving thin slices of meat or chicken with his enormous knife. A portion stuffed into fresh bread *(yarım ekmek)* makes a great lunch, but the food is not fresh later in the day. Eat in the cafeteria at the back or order a cheaper *paket* (takeaway).

Gülhane Kandil Tesisleri
TURKISH $

(Map p72; ✆ 0212-444 6644; www.beltur.istanbul; Gülhane Park; sandwiches ₺6.50-16.50, all-day breakfast plates ₺22, mains ₺19; ⏱ 11am-10pm; 🚇 Gülhane) In spring, the perfume from a profusion of hyacinths blooming in Gülhane Park wafts over the outdoor tables of this garden cafe, which is built into the park's historic walls. It's a lovely spot, when the weather is kind, for breakfast, a light lunch or a coffee break (Turkish coffee ₺5, çay ₺2.50).

★ Deraliye
OTTOMAN $$$

(Map p72; ✆ 0212-520 7778; www.deraliyerestaurant.com; Ticarethane Sokak 10; mains ₺34-64; ⏱ 11am-10pm; 🍷✆; 🚇 Sultanahmet) Starting with a complimentary glass of palate-titillating pomegranate-flower juice, Deraliye offers a taste of the sumptuous dishes once served in the great Ottoman palaces. The menu gives a potted history of each dish, so you can live out your royal banquet fantasies by ordering the goose kebap served to Süleyman the Magnificent or Mehmet II's favourite lamb stew.

★ Cooking Alaturka
TURKISH $$$

(Map p71; ✆ 0212-458 5919; www.cookingalaturka.com; Akbıyık Caddesi 72a, Cankurtaran; set lunch or dinner ₺65; ⏱ lunch 1-3pm & dinner 7-9pm by reservation Mon-Sat; 🍷✆; 🚇 Sultanahmet) One of the Sultanahmet area's best dining experiences, this hybrid cooking school–restaurant serves a set four- or five-course menu of Turkish home cooking, regional Anatolian specialities and Ottoman classics. Sampling dishes such as *imam bayıldı* ('the imam fainted'; eggplant, onion, tomato and peppers slow-cooked in olive oil) with a glass of local wine is a wonderful way to experience authentic Turkish cuisine.

★ Balıkçı Sabahattin
SEAFOOD $$$

(Map p71; ✆ 0212-458 1824; www.balikcisabahattin.com; Şeyit Hasan Koyu Sokak 1, Cankurtaran; mezes ₺10-40, fish ₺40-60; ⏱ 11am-10pm; ✆; 🚇 Sultanahmet) Balıkçı Sabahattin is an enduring favourite with discerning Turks from near and far, who enjoy the limited menu of meze and seafood, including fish from red mullet to sole. This is Sultanahmet's most prestigious restaurant and its best food, although the service can be harried. You'll dine under a leafy canopy in the garden (one section smoking, the other nonsmoking).

Matbah
OTTOMAN $$$

(Map p72; ☑0212-514 6151; www.matbah restaurant.com; Ottoman Hotel Imperial, Caferiye Sokak 6/1; mezes ₺15-23, mains ₺29-61; ☉noon-10.30pm; ☎☑; ☒Sultanahmet) One of a growing number of İstanbul restaurants specialising in so-called Ottoman palace cuisine, Matbah offers dishes that were devised centuries ago in the royal kitchens of Constantinople. The menu changes with the season and features unusual ingredients such as goose, quail, quince and molasses. Try the sailor's roll starter (seven cheeses wrapped in filo, fried and drizzled with honey).

✖ Bazaar District

★ Develi Baklava
SWEETS $

(Map p86; ☑0212-512 1261; Hasırcılar Caddesi 89, Eminönü; portions ₺10-12; ☉7am-7pm Mon-Sat; ☒Eminönü) As with many things Turkish, there's a ritual associated with eating baklava. Afficionados don't use a knife and fork. Instead, they turn their baklava upside down with the help of an index finger and thumb, and pop it into the mouth. To emulate them, head to this famous shop close to the Spice Bazaar. It's one of the city's best *baklavacıs* (baklava shops).

★ Fatih Damak Pide
PIDE $

(Map p62; ☑0212-521 5057; www.fatihdamakpide. com; Büyük Karaman Caddesi 48, Fatih; pides ₺17-25; ☉7am-11pm; ⓜVezneciler) It's worth making the trek to this *pideci* overlooking the Fatih İtfaiye Park near the Aqueduct of Valens. Its reputation for making the best Karadeniz (Black Sea)–style pide on the historic peninsula is well deserved and the pots of tea served with meals are a nice touch (the first pot is free, subsequent pots are charged).

★ Bereket Döner
KEBAP $

(Map p86; Hacı Kadın Caddesi, cnr Tavanlı Çeşme Sokak, Küçük Pazar; döner sandwiches from ₺3.50; ☉11am-8pm Mon-Sat; ⓜHaliç) The best döner *ekmek* (sandwich) in the district – maybe even the city – can be found at this local eatery in the rundown Küçük Pazar shopping

strip between Eminönü and Atatürk Bulvarı. Definitely worth the trek.

Gazientep Burç Ocakbaşı
KEBAP $

(Map p128; Parçacılar Sokak 12, off Yağlıkçılar Caddesi, Grand Bazaar; kebaps ₺15-20; ☉noon-4pm Mon-Sat; ☒Beyazıt-Kapalı Çarşı) The *usta* (grill master) at this simple place presides over a charcoal grill where choice cuts of meats are cooked to perfection. You can claim a stool, or ask for a *dürüm* (meat wrapped in bread) kebap to go. We particularly recommend the spicy Adana kebap and the delectable *dolması* (eggplant and red peppers stuffed with rice and herbs).

Dönerci Şahin Usta
KEBAP $

(Map p128; ☑0212-526 5297; www.donercisahin usta.com; Kılıççılar Sokak 9, Nuruosmaniye; döner kebap from ₺9; ☉11am-3pm Mon-Sat; ☒Çemberlitaş) Turks take family, football and food seriously. And when it comes to food, few dishes are sampled and assessed as widely as the humble döner kebap. Ask any shopkeeper in the Grand Bazaar about who makes the best döner in the immediate area, and you are likely to get the same answer: 'Şahin Usta, of course!'. Takeaway only.

Pak Pide & Pizza Salonu
PIDE $

(Map p86; ☑0212-513 7664; Paşa Camii Sokak 16, Mercan; pides ₺9-14; ☉11am-3pm Mon-Sat; ☒Eminönü) Finding this worker's *pideçisi* (Turkish pizza parlour) is an adventure in itself, as it's hidden in the steep narrow lanes behind the Büyük Valide Han. Fortunately, your quest will pay off when you try the fabulous pides, which are served straight from the oven.

Dürümcü Raif Usta
KEBAP $

(Map p86; ☑0212-528 4910; Küçük Yıldız Han Sokak 6, Mahmutpaşa; dürüm kebap ₺10-12; ☉11.30am-6pm Mon-Sat; ☒Çemberlitaş) The assembly line of staff assisting the *usta* (grill master) at this place attests to the excellence and popularity of its Adana or Urfa *dürüm kebap* (Adana or Urfa kebap, raw onion and parsley wrapped in *lavaş* bread). Note that the Adana is spicy; Urfa isn't.

Meşhur Dönercı Hacı Osman'ın Yeri
KEBAP $

(Map p86; Fuat Paşa Caddesi 16, Mercan; döner kebap from ₺4.50; ☉11am-5pm Mon-Sat; ☒Beyazıt-Kapalı Çarşı) This döner stand, occupying an elegant Ottoman *sebil* (fountain) outside the Ali Paşa Camii on the corner of Mercan Caddesi, is hugely popular with local shopkeepers and shoppers as well as students from nearby İstanbul University.

Bena Dondurmaları
DESSERTS, ICE CREAM **$**
(Map p86; ☑ 0212-520 5440; Gazı Atik Ali Paşa Camii 12b, Çemberlitaş; ice cream per scoop ₺1, desserts ₺3-5; ☻ 10am-6pm Mon-Sat; ☑ Çemberlitaş) There's inevitably an afternoon queue in front of this tiny *dondurma* (Turkish ice cream) shop In the courtyard of the Atik Ali Paşa Camii. Though the *dondurma* is an undeniable draw, we tend to opt for the *fırın sütlaç* (rice pudding) or decadent *trileçe* (creamy sponge cake with a caramel topping).

Eminönü Balık Ekmek (Fish Sandwich) Boats
SEAFOOD **$**
(Map p86; fish sandwiches ₺8; ☻ 8am-10pm; ☑ Eminönü) Come here to sample the city's best-loved street food, accompanied by *turşucusu* (pickles, ₺2) or *şalgam* (sour turnip juice, ₺2) purchased from one of the vendors nearby.

Sur Ocakbaşı
KEBAP **$$**
(Map p62; ☑ 0212-533 8088; www.surocakbasi. com; İtfaiye Caddesi 27, Fatih; kebaps ₺15-30; ☻ 11am-1am; Ⓜ Vezneciler) Indulge in some peerless people-watching while enjoying the grilled meats at this popular place in the Women's Bazaar. The square is always full of locals shopping or enjoying a gossip, and tourists were a rare sight before Anthony Bourdain filmed a segment of *No Reservations* here and blew Sur's cover.

There are plenty of options on offer: consider the mixed Sur kebap plate (₺30), *içli köfte* (deep-fried lamb and onion meatballs with a bulgur coating, ₺4), *çiğ köfte* (meat pounded with spices and eaten raw, ₺10) and *lahmacun* (thin, meat-topped pizza, ₺5). There's no alcohol, but there's homemade *ayran* (yoghurt drink).

Hamdi Restaurant
KEBAP **$$**
(Map p86; ☑ 0212-444 6463; www.hamdi restorant.com.tr; Kalçın Sokak 11, Eminönü; mezes ₺11.50-26, kebaps ₺28-50; ☻ noon-midnight; Ⓟ ❊ ♿; ☑ Eminönü) One of the city's best-loved restaurants, this place near the Spice Bazaar is owned by Hamdi Arpacı, who started out as a street-food vendor in the 1960s. His tasty Urfa-style kebaps were so popular that he soon graduated from his modest stand to this building, which has views of the Old City, Golden Horn and Galata from its top-floor terrace.

The food is excellent. Try the *yoğurtlu şakşuka* (yoghurt meze with fried eggplant, peppers and potato), the *içli köfte* (meatballs rolled in bulgur) and the *lahmacun* (thin, meat-topped pizza) followed by any of the kebaps and you'll leave replete and happy – extremely replete if you finish with the house-made baklava, *katmer* (flaky pastry stuffed with pistachios and clotted cream) or *künefe* (layers of *kadayif* – dough soaked in syrup and topped with a layer of clotted cream – cemented together with sweet cheese, doused in syrup and served hot with a sprinkling of pistachio). Any place this good is always going to be busy, so make sure you book, and don't forget to request a rooftop table with a view (outside if the weather is hot).

One slight caveat: staff work hard and are clearly encouraged to turn tables over as fast as possible. Don't expect much personal service, and be prepared for little time between courses.

There's another branch on the rooftop of the Radisson Blu Hotel in Beyoğlu (p119).

✕ Western Districts

Head to the Vodina Caddesi area for a mix of hip cafes, excellent restaurants, neighbourhood bakeries and supermarkets catering to locals.

★ Asitane
OTTOMAN **$$$**
(Map p62; ☑ 0212-635 7997; www.asitane restaurant.com; Kariye Oteli, Kariye Camii Sokak 6, Edirnekapı; starters ₺18-28, mains ₺58; ☻ noon-10.30pm; ♿; ☑ 28 from Eminönü, 87 from Taksim, ☑ Ayvansaray) This elegant restaurant next to the Kariye Museum (Chora Church) serves Ottoman dishes devised for the palace kitchens at Topkapı, Edirne and Dolmabahçe. Its chefs have been tracking down historic recipes for years, and the menu is full of versions that will tempt most modern palates, including vegetarian.

✕ Beyoğlu & Around

★ Hayvore
LOKANTA **$**
(Map p94; ☑ 0212-245 7501; www.hayvore.com; Turnacıbaşı Sokak 4, Galatasaray; soups ₺6-10, pides ₺16-23, portions ₺10-20; ☻ 11.30am-11pm; ❊ ☜ ♿; Ⓜ Taksim) Notable *lokantas* (traditional eateries serving ready-made dishes) are few and far between in modern-day Beyoğlu, so the existence of this bustling place next to the Galatasaray Lycée is to be

wholeheartedly celebrated. Specialising in Black Sea cuisine, its delicious leafy greens, pilafs, *hamsi* (fresh anchovy) dishes, soups and pides (Turkish-style pizza) are best enjoyed at lunch – go early to score a table.

★Karaköy Güllüoğlu   SWEETS, BÖREK $

(Map p94; ☑0212-293 0910; www.karakoygulluoglu. com; Katlı Otopark, Kemankeş Caddesi, Karaköy; portion baklava ₺8-17, portion börek ₺7.50-8; ⊙7am-11pm Sun-Thu, 8am-11.30pm Fri & Sat; ⊞; ⊠Karaköy) This much-loved *baklavacı* (baklava shop) opened in 1949 and was the first İstanbul branch of a business established in Gaziantep in the 1820s. A family feud has since led to the opening of other Güllüoğlu offshoots around town, but this remains the best. Pay for a *porsiyon* (portion) of whatever takes your fancy at the register, then order at the counter.

The most popular baklava flavours are *fıstıklı* (pistachio) and *cevizli* (walnut), and many regulars order a serve of *kaymak* (clotted cream) on the side. A glass of tea will take the edge off the sweetness. Note that the *börek* (filled pastry) here is good too.

Savoy Pastanesi   CAFE $

(Map p94; ☑0212-249 1818; www.savoypastanesi. com; Sıraselviler Caddesi 91a, Cihangir; börek ₺7, millefeuille ₺7.50; ⊙7am-11pm Mon-Sat; ⊞⊞; ⊠Taksim) İstanbul has many businesses that have attained iconic status and Savoy is undoubtedly one of them. Down the hill from

---

THE GREAT SINAN

None of today's star architects come close to having the influence over a city that Mimar Koca Sinan had over Constantinople during his 50-year career.

Born in 1497, Sinan was a recruit to the *devşirme*, the annual intake of Christian youths into the janissaries. He became a Muslim (as all such recruits did) and eventually took up a post as a military engineer in the corps. Süleyman the Magnificent appointed him the chief of the imperial architects in 1538.

Sinan designed a total of 321 buildings, 85 of which are still standing in İstanbul. He died in 1588 and is buried in a self-designed *türbe* (tomb) located in one of the corners of the Süleymaniye Mosque, the building that many believe to be his greatest work.

Taksim Meydanı, it was established in 1950 and is known for its delicious cakes (especially the decadently creamy millefeuille), milk puddings, biscuits and *börek*. Sit upstairs or on the streetside terrace.

Mavra   CAFE $

(Map p94; ☑0212-252 7488; Serdar-ı Ekrem Caddesi 31, Galata; breakfast ₺16-32, sandwiches ₺12-24, pastas ₺18-22; ⊙9.30am-1am; ⊞⊡; ⊠Şişhane, ⊠Tünel) Serdar-ı Ekrem Caddesi is one of the most interesting streets in Galata, full of ornate 19th-century apartment blocks and avant-garde boutiques. Mavra was the first of the cafes to open on the strip, and remains one of the best, offering simple food and drinks amid decor that is thrift-shop chic.

Helvetia Lokanta   TURKISH $

(Map p94; ☑0212-245 8780; General Yazgan Sokak 8a, Tünel; mixed plates ₺12.50-15; ⊙noon-10pm Mon-Sat; ⊡; ⊠Şişhane, ⊠Tünel) This tiny *lokanta* with its open kitchen is popular with locals, who head here to enjoy the freshly prepared, vegetarian-friendly fare. Choose up to five of the home-style dishes for your plate and enjoy them in the relaxed dining space. No alcohol, and cash only.

★Antiochia   SOUTHEASTERN ANATOLIA $$

(Map p94; ☑0212-244 0820; www.antiochia concept.com; General Yazgan Sokak 3, Tünel; mezes & salads ₺13-18, pides ₺21-22, kebaps ₺24-52; ⊙noon-midnight Mon-Sat; ❄⊞⊞; ⊠Tünel) Dishes from the southeastern city of Antakya (Hatay) are the speciality here. Cold mezes feature olives and wild herbs, and hot choices include delicious *içli köfte* (ground lamb and onion with a bulgar coating)and *özel peyniri* (special fried cheese). Kebaps are exceptional – try the succulent *şiş et* (grilled lamb). Set-menu dinners offer excellent value and there's a 20% discount at lunch, when pides reign supreme.

★Karaköy Lokantası   TURKISH $$

(Map p94; ☑0212-292 4455; www.karakoylokantasi. com; Kemankeş Caddesi 37a, Karaköy; mezes ₺10-24, lunch portions ₺13-25, mains ₺28-55; ⊙noon-4pm & 6pm-midnight Mon-Sat, 6pm-midnight Sun; ❄⊞; ⊠Karaköy) Known for its gorgeous tiled interior, genial owner and bustling vibe, Karaköy Lokantası serves tasty and well-priced food to its loyal local clientele. It functions as a *lokanta* (eatery serving ready-made food) during the day, but at night it morphs into a *meyhane* (tavern), with slightly higher prices. Bookings are essential for dinner.

★Zübeyir Ocakbaşı
KEBAP $$

(Map p94; ✐0212-293 3951; Bekar Sokak 28; mezes ₺10, kebaps ₺28-38; ⊘noon-midnight; ✸✿; ⓂTaksim) Every morning the chefs at this popular *ocakbaşı* (grill house) prepare fresh, top-quality meat – spicy chicken wings and Adana kebaps, flavoursome ribs, pungent liver kebaps and well-marinated lamb *şiş* kebaps (roast skewered meat) – to be grilled over handsome copper-hooded barbecues that night. The offerings are famous throughout the city, so booking a table is essential.

Hamdi Restaurant Pera
KEBAP $$

(Map p94; ✐0212-377 2500; http://hamdi.com.tr/en/pera; Radisson Blu Hotel, Refik Saydam Caddesi 19, Tepebaşı; mezes ₺11.50-26, kebaps ₺28-50; ✸➡; ⓂŞişhane, ⓉTünel) The swish new Beyoğlu branch of this much-loved Eminönü restaurant (p117) has a terrace with a panoramic view of the Golden Horn.

Dandin
CAFE $$

(Map p94; ✐0212-245 3369; www.dandin.co; Kılıçalipaşa Mescidi Sokak 17a, Karaköy; sandwiches ₺21-26, cakes ₺8-15; ⊘10am-11pm Sun-Thu, to midnight Fri & Sat; ✸✿⚇; ⓉTophane) A decadent array of cakes, pastries and trifles provide the headline act at this happening cafe, with savoury treats, including pizzas and sandwiches, supplying a trusty backup. The loft-like white space, with its hanging brass lamps and huge tiled counter, is a lovely environment in which to enjoy them accompanied by fresh juice, good espresso coffee or herbal tea.

Çukurcuma 49
PIZZA $$

(Map p94; ✐0212-249 0048; Turnacıbaşı Caddesi 49, Çukurcuma; pizzas ₺18-40; ⊘10.30am-10.30pm; ✸✿⚇➡; ⓂTaksim) A hipster vibe, mellow jazz soundtrack and Italian-style pizzas are the drawcards at this neighbourhood favourite. We're fans of the cheap 'desperate house wine' (an extremely quaffable red from Yunatçılar winery on the Aegean island of Bozcaada) and also of the pizza with thyme, mozzarella and *pastırma* (pressed beef preserved in spices).

Check the Facebook feed for details of weekly live jazz sessions.

Karaköy Gümrük
MODERN TURKISH $$

(Map p94; ✐0212-244 2252; http://karakoygumruk.com.tr; Gümrük Sokak 4, Karaköy; snacks & small plates ₺22-45, mains ₺23-52; ⊘10am-midnight Mon-Sat; ✸✿; ⓉKaraköy) An exemplar of the casually stylish restaurant model that has been trending in İstanbul for a few years now, Gümrük has a menu that changes each day according to what's fresh at the market. Dishes are often clever twists on classic Turkish street food – think beautifully presented pilafs, flavourful offal dishes and a delectable *balık ekmek* (fish sandwich).

Journey
CAFE $$

(Map p94; ✐0212-244 8989; www.journeycihangir.com; Akarsu Yokuşu 21a, Cihangir; sandwiches ₺19-22, salads ₺19-24, mains ₺18-44; ⊘9am-2am Tue-Sun, to 1am Mon; ✿⚇➡; ⓂTaksim) This laid-back lounge cafe located in the expat enclave of Cihangir serves a great range of Mediterranean comfort foods, including sandwiches, soups, pizzas and pastas. Many of the dishes use organic produce, and vegetarian, vegan and gluten-free options are on offer. Locals have been known to claim the front couch for breakfast and stay put until closing time.

Sofyalı 9
TURKISH $$

(Map p94; ✐0212-252 3810; www.sofyali.com.tr; Sofyalı Sokak 9, Asmalımescit; mezes ₺5.50-26, mains ₺26-52; ⊘1pm-midnight Sun-Thu, to 2am Fri & Sat; ✸⚇➡; ⓂTaksim, ⓉTünel) Tables at this *meyhane* are hot property on a Friday or Saturday night, when locals flock here to enjoy the tasty food and convivial atmosphere. Regulars tend to stick to mezes, choosing cold dishes from the waiter's tray and ordering *kalamar tava* (fried calamari), *folyoda ahtapot* (grilled octopus in foil) and *Anavut ciğeri* (Albanian fried liver) from the menu.

Kafe Ara
CAFE $$

(Map p94; ✐0212-245 4105; http://kafeara.com; Tosbağ Sokak 2, Galatasaray; sandwiches ₺24-34, pastas ₺26-28, mains ₺26-40; ⊘7.30am-11pm Mon-Thu, to 1am Fri, 10.30am-1am Sat, 10.30am-11pm Sun; ✿⚇; ⓂŞişhane, ⓉTünel) This casual cafe occupies a converted garage in a lane opposite the Galatasaray Lycée and is named after legendary local photographer Ara Güler, whose photographs of the city adorn the walls. It serves an array of well-priced salads, sandwiches and Turkish comfort food. Enjoying Sunday brunch (₺35) at one of the lane tables is particularly pleasant. No alcohol.

★Cuma
MODERN TURKISH $$$

(Map p94; ✐0212-293 2062; www.cuma.cc; Çukurcuma Caddesi 53a, Çukurcuma; breakfast plate ₺42, lunch dishes ₺19-34, dinner mains ₺30-36;

⊘9am-11pm Mon-Sat, to 8pm Sun; 🔊🖉🖈;
Ⓜ Taksim) Banu Tiryakioğulları's laid-back
foodie oasis in the heart of Çukurcuma has
one of the most devoted customer bases in
the city. Tables are on the leafy terrace or in
the atmospheric upstairs dining space, and
the healthy, seasonally driven menu is heavy
on flavour and light on fuss – breakfast is
particularly delicious (we love the fruit
smoothies and house-baked bread).

★Eleos   MEYHANE $$$
(Map p94; ✉ 0212-244 9090; www.eleosrestaurant.
com; 2nd fl, İstiklal Caddesi 231, Tünel; mezes ₺10-
30, mains from ₺30; ⊘2.30pm-midnight; 🟦🛜🖈;
Ⓜ Şişhane, 🚇Tünel) Hidden upstairs in the
shabby Hıdivyal Palas building, Eleos trans-
ports its diners from Beyoğlu to the Greek
islands. Stylish blue-and-white decor and a
fabulous Bosphorus view set the scene, and
the food seals the deal – colourful mezes
featuring plenty of herbs and garlic, tender
octopus and calamari, perfectly grilled fish,
and fresh fruit to finish. Advance bookings
essential.

★Neolokal   MODERN TURKISH $$$
(Map p94; ✉ 0212-244 0016; www.neolokal.com;
1st fl, SALT Galata, Bankalar Caddesi 11, Karaköy;
mains ₺42-62; ⊘6-11pm Tue-Sun; 🟦🛜; 🚇Kar-
aköy) Chef Maksut Aşkar opened this swish
eatery in late 2014 and has been wowing local and international diners with his exciting
twists on traditional Turkish food ever since.
Utilising ingredients listed on the Slow Food
Foundation's Ark of Taste, his refined and
delicious dishes are enjoyed alongside the
spectacular Old City views offered by both
the dining room and terrace.

The restaurant is accessed via a staircase
in the ground-floor cafe – sadly, the food
served there is nowhere near as impressive
as its upstairs counterpart.

Meze by Lemon Tree   MODERN TURKISH $$$
(Map p94; ✉ 0212-252 8302; www.mezze.com.
tr; Meşrutiyet Caddesi 83b, Tepebaşı; mezes ₺14-
39, mains ₺40-56, 4-course degustation menu
for 2 ₺196; ⊘6pm-midnight; 🟦🖉; Ⓜ Şişhane,
🚇Tünel) Chef Gençay Üçok creates some of
the most interesting and delicious modern
Turkish food seen in the city and serves it
in an intimate restaurant opposite the Pera
Palace Hotel. Regulars tend to opt for the de-
gustation menu, or choose from the wonder-
ful array of hot and cold mezes, rather than
ordering mains. Bookings essential.

✗ Beşiktaş, Ortaköy & Nişantaşı

The student and professional population
ensures plenty of eateries in Beşiktaş and
Ortaköy. On weekends in Ortaköy, locals
flock to the *kümpir* (stuffed baked potatoes)
and waffle stands behind Ortaköy Mosque
or to branches of the chains Kitchenette and
House Cafe. Inland from the main square,
kebapçıs (kebap restaurants) and other af-
fordable eateries are found in the lanes and
Muallim Naci Caddesi. Likewise in Beşiktaş,
affordable seafood restaurants, attracting
students and middle-class locals, sit near the
fish market between Ortabahçe Caddesi and
the streets leading east to Barbaros Bulvarı.
Head to affluent Nişantaşı to sample the fin-
est contemporary Turkish cuisine.

Pare Baklava Bar   SWEETS $
(Map p62; ✉ 0212-236 5920; www.parebaklavabar.
com; Şakayık Sokak 32, Nişantaşı; ⊘8am-9pm
Mon-Sat, 10am-4pm Sun; 🟦🛜; Ⓜ Osmanbey)
Billing itself as Turkey's first-ever baklava
bar, this bijou business flies in top-grade
baklava and *katmer* (flaky pastry stuffed
with pistachios and clotted cream) from Ga-
ziantep every day. Choose from the artfully
arranged display and settle back to enjoy a
few pieces with a glass of tea or a well-made
coffee.

Kantın   MODERN ANATOLIAN $$
(Map p62; ✉ 0212-219 3114; www.kantin.biz;
Maçka Caddesi 35a, Milli Reasürans Pasajı 16 ve
60, Nişantaşı; mains ₺15-44; ⊘11am-5pm Mon,
to 11.30pm Tue-Sat; Ⓜ Osmanbey) An early
and much-loved adopter of the Slow Food
philosophy, 'Canteen' remains one of İstan-
bul's best bistros (and high-end takeaways).
Chef-owner Semsa Denizsel, a pioneer of
the farm-to-table approach in Turkey, serves
'new İstanbul cuisine', reflecting the city's
melting-pot heritage of Turkish, Greek,
Armenian and Jewish home cooking. Only
local and seasonal produce is used and the
menu changes regularly.

Hünkar   ANATOLIAN $$
(Map p62; ✉ 0212-225 4665; www.hunkarlokantasi.
com; Mim Kemal Öke Caddesi 21, Nişantaşı; meze
₺10, mains ₺35; ⊘noon-10.30pm; 🖉; Ⓜ Osman-
bey) If you decide to spend a day or half-day
shopping in Nişantaşı, consider taking a
break and eating at Hünkar, one of the city's
best *lokantas* (eateries serving ready-made
food). In business since 1950, it serves all the
classic mezes and grilled-meat dishes.

Alancha MODERN TURKISH $$$
(Map p62; ☑0212-261 3535; http://en.alancha.com; Maçka Kempinski Residence, Şehit Mehmet Sokak 9, Maçka; menu ₺240; ☺7.30-10pm; Ⓜ Osmanbey) Alancha's designer decor is as striking as its colourful and artfully arranged dinner dishes, which range from servings of wild sea bass to filet mignon. Go for the Anatolian tasting menu, which features a dozen courses prepared with artisan ingredients from the seven regions of Anatolia, starting with stuffed mussels and continuing through pistachio kebap to baklava and *lokum* (Turkish Delight). Wine pairing costs ₺160.

Banyan ASIAN $$$
(Map p62; ☑0212-259 9060; www.banyan restaurant.com; 2nd fl, Salhane Sokak 3, Ortaköy; sushi ₺40, mains ₺80; ☺noon-midnight; ☑; ☒Kabataş Lisesi) The menu here travels around Asia, featuring Thai, Japanese, Indian, Vietnamese and Chinese dishes, and including soups, sushi, satays and salads. Banyan claims to serve food for the soul, and you can enjoy it with exceptional views of the Ortaköy Mosque and Bosphorus (Martyrs of July 15) Bridge, or linger over a sunset cocktail (₺60) at the open-fronted terrace bar.

Vogue INTERNATIONAL $$$
(Map p62; ☑0212-227 4404; www.vogue restaurant.com; 13th fl, A Blok, BJK Plaza, Spor Caddesi 92, Akaretler, Beşiktaş; starters ₺26-50, mains ₺30-75; ☺noon-2am; ☑; ☒Akaretler) This sophisticated bar-restaurant in a Beşiktaş office block opened in 1997, and feels like it has been going strong since Atatürk was lodging in the nearby Dolmabahçe Palace. A menu of pasta, seafood, sushi, lamb shanks and roast duck, the panoramic Bosphorus views and its various molecular cocktails make Vogue a favourite haunt of the Nişantaşı power-broker set.

✖ **Kadiköy**

Baylan Pastanesi SWEETS $
(Map p62; ☑0216-336 2881; www.baylanpastanesi. com.tr; Muvakkithane Caddesi 9; parfaits ₺16-19, cakes ₺16; ☺7am-10pm; ☒Kadıköy) The front window and interior of this Kadıköy cake shop, which opened in 1961, have stood the test of time and so too has its popularity. Regulars tend to order a decadent ice-cream sundae or a pile of chocolate and caramel profiteroles, but an espresso coffee and plate of house-made macaroons (₺14) is a tempting alternative.

★ **Çiya Sofrası** ANATOLIAN $$
(Map p62; ☑0216-330 3190; www.ciya.com. tr; Güneşlibahçe Sokak 43; portions ₺12-30; ☺11.30am-10pm; ❄☑☒; ☒Kadıköy) Known throughout the culinary world, Musa Dağdeviren's *lokanta* (eatery serving ready-made food) showcases dishes from regional Turkey and is a wonderful place to sample treats such as *lahmacun* (Arabic-style pizza), *içli köfte* (meatballs rolled in bulgar and fried) and *perde pılavı* (chicken and rice in pastry casing). No alcohol, but the homemade *şerbet* (sweet fruit drink) is a delicious accompaniment.

Vegetarians are very well catered for here, but should avoid Çiya's adjoining *kebapçı* (kebaps ₺18 to ₺40), which sells a huge variety of tasty meat dishes.

Cibalikapı SEAFOOD $$$
(☑0216-348 9363; www.cibalikapibalikcisi.com; Moda Caddesi 163a, Moda; mezes ₺8-20, fish mains from ₺24; ☺noon-midnight; ❄; ☒Kadıköy) Generally acknowledged as one of the city's best fish restaurants, Cibalikapı has two branches: one on the Golden Horn and the other here in Moda. Super-fresh mezes and seafood are enjoyed in the pleasant dining room or on the garden terrace. If you go with a large appetite the daily degustation (₺180 for two persons) is good value.

The other branch is next to Kadir Has University in Fener on the Golden Horn.

🍷 **Drinking & Nightlife**

🍷 **Sultanahmet & Around**

Most Sultanahmet restaurants are licensed, while streets such as Şeftali Sokak (near the Basilica Cistern), the adjoining İncili Çavuş Sokak and, down in Cankurtaran, Akbıyık Caddesi are good hunting grounds for bars. Few are on a par with those in Beyoğlu, but do not despair. Why not substitute tobacco or caffeine for alcohol and visit one of the atmospheric *çay bahçesis* dotted around the neighbourhood?

Set Üstü Çay Bahçesi TEA GARDEN
(Map p72; Gülhane Park; ☺7am-10pm; ☒Gülhane) Come to this terraced tea garden to watch the ferries plying the route from Europe to Asia while enjoying an excellent pot of tea (for one/two ₺10/15) accompanied by hot water (such a relief after the usual fiendishly strong Turkish brew). Fast food (₺3 to ₺10) including *tost* (toasted cheese sandwich)

and *köfte ekmek* (Turkish meatballs in bread) is available.

Derviş Aile Çay Bahçesi
TEA GARDEN

(Map p71; cnr Dalbastı Sokak & Kabasakal Caddesi; ⏰7am-midnight Apr-Oct; 🚇Sultanahmet) Superbly located directly opposite the Blue Mosque, the Derviş beckons patrons with its comfortable cane chairs and shady trees. Efficient service, reasonable prices and peerless people-watching opportunities make it a great place for a leisurely çay (₺3), nargile (₺22), *tost* (toasted sandwich; ₺7) and a game of backgammon.

Cafe Meşale
NARGILE CAFE

(Map p71; Arasta Bazaar, cnr Dalbastı & Torun Sokaks, Cankurtaran; ⏰24hr; 🚇Sultanahmet) Located in a sunken courtyard behind the Blue Mosque, Meşale is a tourist trap par excellence, but still has loads of charm. Generations of backpackers have joined locals in claiming one of its cushioned benches and enjoying a tea and nargile. It has sporadic live Turkish music and a bustling vibe in the evening.

Kybele Cafe
BAR, CAFE

(Map p72; ☎0212-511 7766; www.kybelehotel.com; Yerebatan Caddesi 23; ⏰7.30am-11.30pm; 🚇Sultanahmet) The hotel lounge bar–cafe close to the Basilica Cistern is chock-full of antique furniture, richly coloured rugs and old etchings and prints, but its signature style comes courtesy of the hundreds of colourful glass lights hanging from the ceiling.

A'YA Rooftop Lounge
BAR

(Map p71; ☎0212-402 3000; www.fourseasons.com/istanbul; Four Seasons Istanbul at Sultanahmet, Tevkifhane Sokak 1, Cankurtaran; ⏰4pm-late; 🚇Sultanahmet) Open in summer, this rooftop bar has a full-on view of Aya Sofya, Ayasofya Hürrem Sultan Hamamı and the Bosphorus, while the Blue Mosque is only partially obscured. Cocktails (₺49), meze (₺30) and an impressive selection of spirits add to the appeal. In winter, sit downstairs in the lounge bar or courtyard garden.

Cihannüma
BAR

(Map p72; ☎0212-512 0207; www.cihannumaistanbul.com; And Hotel, Yerebatan Caddesi 18; ⏰noon-midnight; 🚇Sultanahmet) We don't recommend eating at this rooftop hotel restaurant near Aya Sofya, but the view from its narrow balcony and glass-sheathed dining room is one of the Old City's best (spot Aya Sofya, the Blue Mosque, Topkapı Palace, Galata Tower and the Bosphorus (Martyrs of July 15) Bridge), so it's a great choice for a scenic afternoon drink or sundowner.

🍺 Bazaar District

★Mimar Sinan Teras Cafe
NARGILE CAFE

(Map p86; ☎0212-514 4414; Mimar Sinan Han, Fetva Yokuşu 34-35, Süleymaniye; ⏰8am-1am; 🛜; Ⓜ Vezneciler) A magnificent panorama of the city can be enjoyed from the spacious outdoor terrace of this popular student cafe in a ramshackle building located in the shadow of Süleymaniye Mosque. Head here during the day or in the evening to admire the view over a coffee, unwind with a nargile or enjoy a glass of çay and game of backgammon.

★Erenler Nargile ve Çay Bahçesi
TEA GARDEN

(Map p86; Yeniçeriler Caddesi 35, Beyazıt; ⏰7am-midnight; 🚇Beyazıt-Kapalı Çarşı) Set in the vine-covered courtyard of the Çorlulu Ali Paşa Medrese, this nargile cafe near the Grand Bazaar is the most atmospheric in the Old City.

Vefa Bozacısı
BOZA BAR

(Map p86; ☎0212-519 4922; www.vefa.com.tr; 66 Vefa Caddesi, Molla Hüsrev; boza ₺3; ⏰8am-midnight; Ⓜ Vezneciler) This famous *boza* bar was established in 1876 and locals still flock here to drink the viscous tonic, which is made from water, sugar and fermented barley and has a slight lemony tang. Topped with dried chickpeas and a sprinkle of cinnamon, it has a reputation for building up strength and virility, and tends to be an acquired taste.

In summer, the bar also serves *şıra,* a fermented grape juice.

Şark Kahvesi
CAFE

(Oriental Coffee Shop; Map p128; ☎0212-512 1144; Yağlıkçılar Caddesi 134, Grand Bazaar; ⏰8.30am-7pm Mon-Sat; 🚇Beyazıt-Kapalı Çarşı) The Şark's arched ceiling betrays its former existence as part of a bazaar street – years ago some enterprising *kahveci* (coffeehouse owner) walled up several sides and turned it into a cafe. Located on one of the bazaar's major thoroughfares, it's popular with both stallholders and tourists, who enjoy tea, coffee (Turkish, espresso and filter) or a cold drink.

Lale Bahçesi
TEA GARDEN

(Map p86; Şifahane Caddesi 2, Süleymaniye; ⏰9am-11pm; Ⓜ Vezneciler) Make your way down the stairs into the sunken courtyard opposite the Süleymaniye Mosque to discover this outdoor teahouse, which is popular with students from the nearby theological college and İstanbul University, who head here to enjoy çay and nargiles.

Beyoğlu

There are hundreds of bars in Beyoğlu, with the major bar strips being Balo, Nevizade, Gönül and Sofyalı Sokaks. As a rule, drinks are much cheaper at street-level venues than at rooftop bars. Note that many of the Beyoğlu clubs close over the warmer months (June to September), when the party crowd moves down to Turkey's southern coasts.

★Federal Coffee Company CAFE

(Map p94; ☎0212-245 0903; www.federal.coffee; Küçük Hendek Caddesi 7, Galata; ⏲8am-midnight; 📶; Ⓜ Şişhane, 🚊Tünel) Our favourite of the recent tsunami of coffee roasteries to open in the city, the Federal Coffee Company advertises itself as an 'Australian Coffee Roaster' and visitors from Down Under will certainly feel at home when sipping a perfectly executed espresso-style coffee in its stylish surrounds. Couches, reading materials and wi-fi make it a perfect caffeine-fuelled workspace.

Dem TEAHOUSE

(Map p94; ☎0212-293 9792; www.demkarakoy.com; Hoca Tahsin Sokak 17, Karaköy; ⏲10am-11pm; 🚊Tophane) As far from a traditional *çay bahçesi* as one can imagine, Dem serves 60 types of freshly brewed tea in fine china cups and with milk on request. A selection of panini, wraps, cakes and scones is also on offer, and everything is served on streetside tables or under the ultra-chic Zettel'z 5 light fitting in the main space.

★Unter BAR

(Map p94; ☎0212-244-5151; www.unter.com.tr; Kara Ali Kaptan Sokak 4, Karaköy; ⏲9am-midnight Tue-Thu & Sun, to 2am Fri & Sat; 📶; 🚊Tophane) This scenester-free zone epitomises the new Karaköy style: it's glam without trying too hard, and has a vaguely arty vibe. Ground-floor windows open to the street in fine weather, allowing the action to spill outside during busy periods.

Good cocktails and decent wine by the glass are major draws here, as is the varied food menu (breakfast ₺18 to ₺32, mains ₺27 to ₺48).

360 BAR

(Map p94; ☎0533 691 0360; www.360istanbul.com; 8th fl, İstiklal Caddesi 163; ⏲noon-2am Sun-Thu, to 4am Fri & Sat; 📶; Ⓜ Şişhane, 🚊Tünel) İstanbul's most famous bar, and deservedly so. If you can score one of the bar stools on the terrace you'll be happy indeed – the view is truly extraordinary. It morphs into a club after midnight on Friday and Saturday, when a cover charge of ₺50 applies (this includes one drink). The food is overpriced and underwhelming – don't bother with dinner.

★Manda Batmaz COFFEE

(Map p94; Olivia Geçidi 1a, off İstiklal Caddesi; ⏲10am-11pm; Ⓜ Şişhane, 🚊Tünel) Bored with the brouhaha over modern-day coffee culture? Don't care where your beans have been roasted, or whether your barista's tattoos are on show? If so, this tiny coffee shop is for you. Serving Beyoğlu's best Turkish coffee for over two decades, its cups of ultra-thick and aromatic coffee are much cheaper than the indifferently made lattes ubiquitous elsewhere.

Fil CAFE

(Map p94; ☎0212-243 1994; www.filbooks.net; Ali Paşa Değirmeni Sokak 1, Karaköy; ⏲10am-10pm Tue-Sun; 🚊Karaköy) Dedicated to photography books, creative workshops and coffee, this bookshop-cafe in Karaköy is crammed into two floors of a small space that has been stylishly fitted out with a marble bar, comfortable banquettes and upstairs work desks. Staff are extremely friendly and there's an inclusive vibe. There are also cakes (₺15 to ₺16) and sandwiches (₺12 to ₺14) on offer.

★Mikla BAR

(Map p94; ☎0212-293 5656; www.miklarestaurant.com; Marmara Pera Hotel, Meşrutiyet Caddesi 15, Tepebaşı; ⏲from 6pm Mon-Sat summer only; Ⓜ Şişhane, 🚊Tünel) It's worth overlooking the occasional bit of uppity service at this stylish rooftop bar to enjoy excellent cocktails and what could well be the best view in İstanbul. In winter the drinking action moves to the bar in the upmarket restaurant one floor down.

CUE İstiklal CLUB

(Map p94; ☎0536 460 7137; 5th fl, Yeniçarşı Caddesi 38, Galatasaray; cover varies; ⏲10pm-4am Tue-Sat; Ⓜ Şişhane, 🚊Tünel) A magnificent view, large dance floor, decent sound system and well-made cocktails are the draws at this popular temple to electronica. Check its Twitter and Facebook feeds for who is playing/spinning the deep-house, techno and tech-house soundtrack.

Karabatak
CAFE

(Map p94; ☑0212-243 6993; www.karabatak.com; Kara Ali Kaptan Sokak 7, Karaköy; ☺8.30am-10pm Mon-Fri, 9.30am-10pm Sat & Sun; ☜; ☒Tophane) Importing dark-roasted Julius Meinl coffee from Vienna, Karabatak's baristas use it to conjure up some of Karaköy's best brews. The outside seating is hotly contested, but the quiet tables inside can be just as alluring. Choose from filter, espresso or Turkish coffee and order a panino or sandwich if you're hungry.

Kronotrop
CAFE

(Map p94; ☑0212-249 9271; www.kronotrop.com. tr/en; Firuzağa Cami Sokak 2b, Cihangir; ☺7.30am-9pm Mon-Fri, 10am-10pm Sat, 10am-9pm Sun; ☜; ☒Taksim) Specialty coffee bars have proliferated in İstanbul in recent years, spearheaded by businesses such as this hip place opposite the Firuz Ağa Mosque in Cihangir. Owned by noted restaurateur Mehmet Gürs, it sources beans from across the globe and roasts them in a purpose-built facility in nearby Maslak. Choose from espresso, cold-drip, filtered, Aeropress, Chemex and traditional Turkish varieties.

Geyik
BAR, CAFE

(Map p94; ☑0532 773 0013; Akarsu Yokuşu 22, Cihangir; ☺10am-2am; ☒Taksim) A hybrid coffee roastery and cocktail bar? Yep, you read that correctly. Run by one-time Turkish barista champion Serkan İpekli and mixologist Yağmur Engin, this ultra-fashionable place is popular with coffee aficionados during the day and barflies at night. On Friday and Saturday evenings it's so crowded that the action spills out of the wood-panelled interior onto the street.

Indigo
CLUB

(Map p94; ☑0212-244 8567; http://indigo-istanbul. com; 1st-5th fl, 309 Akarsu Sokak, Galatasaray; cover varies; ☺11.30pm-5am Fri & Sat, closed summer; ☒Şişhane, ☒Tünel) Its popularity has waxed and waned over the years, but Beyoğlu's four-floor electronic-music temple is back in big-time favour with the city's dance-music enthusiasts. The program spotlights top-notch local and visiting DJs or live acts, focusing on house, tech house and tech disco, with an occasional electro-rock number thrown into the mix. Smokers congregate on the upstairs terrace.

Kloster
CLUB

(Map p94; ☑0533 258 9393; http://kloster.com. tr; Kamer Hatun Caddesi 10; cover varies; ☺10pm-6am Wed-Sat; ☒Taksim) Three floors, three different stages and a famous rooftop terrace make this temple to electronica the largest club in the city. There are regular appearances by European DJs; check the Facebook feed for details.

Cihangir 21
BAR

(Map p94; ☑0212-251 1626; Coşkun Sokak 21, Cihangir; ☺9.30am-2.30am; ☜; ☒Taksim) The great thing about this neighbourhood place is its inclusiveness – the regulars include black-clad boho types, besuited professionals, expat loafers and quite a few characters who defy categorisation. There's beer on tap (Efes and Miller), a smokers' section and a bustling feel after work hours; it's quite laidback during the day.

5 Kat
BAR

(Map p94; ☑0212-293 3774; www.5kat.com; 5th fl, Soğancı Sokak 7, Cihangir; ☺5pm-2am Mon-Fri, 10am-2am Sat, 11am-2am Sun; ☜; ☒Taksim) This İstanbul institution has been around for over two decades and is a great alternative for those who can't stomach the style overload at many of the high-profile Beyoğlu bars. In winter drinks are served in the boudoir-style bar on the 5th floor; in summer action moves to the outdoor roof terrace. Both have great Bosphorus views.

Leb-i Derya
BAR

(Map p94; ☑0212-293 4989; www.lebiderya.com; 6th fl, Kumbaracı İş Hanı, Kumbaracı Yokuşu 57, Galata; ☺4pm-2am Mon-Thu, to 3am Fri, 10am-3am Sat, to 2am Sun; ☜; ☒Şişhane, ☒Tünel) On the top floor of a dishevelled building off İstiklal, Leb-i Derya has wonderful views across to the Old City and down the Bosphorus, meaning that seats on the small outdoor terrace or at the bar are highly prized. Many people enjoy the pricey modern Mediterranean food on offer, but we aren't impressed, so only recommend it as a bar.

Alex's Place
BAR

(Map p94; Gönül Sokak 7, Asmalımescit; ☺6pm-1am Tue-Sat; ☒Şişhane, ☒Tünel) A hole-in-the-wall speakeasy in the heart of the Asmalımescit entertainment precinct, this place is beloved of local bohemians who work in the arts and cultural sectors. American owner Alex Waldman is passionate about cocktails and his craft creations have been known to convert beer and wine drinkers alike.

🍷 Ortaköy & Kuruçeşme

The stretch of Bosphorus shoreline between Ortaköy and Kuruçeşme is often referred to as the Golden Mile, a reference to its string of high-profile waterfront nightclubs. Clubs are best visited during summer, when they open nightly and their waterside terraces are truly magical party venues. A night here won't suit everyone, though: drinks are pricey, club restaurants poor quality and pricey, entrance policies can be inconsistent, and door staff notoriously rude and tip-hungry.

There's usually a cover charge Friday and Saturday nights, but you can often avoid this with a restaurant booking.

🍷 Kadiköy

★ Fazıl Bey
COFFEE

(Map p62; ☑ 0216-450 2870; www.fazilbey.com; Serasker Caddesi 1; ⊙ 8am-11pm; 🚊 Kadıköy) Making the call as to who makes the best Turkish coffee in İstanbul is no easy task, but our vote goes to Fazıl Bey, the best-loved *khavehan* (coffeeshop) on Serasker Caddesi. Enjoying a cup while watching the passing parade of shoppers has kept locals entertained for decades. There are other, less atmospheric, branches in Tavus Sokak and Bağdat Caddesi.

Arkaoda
BAR, CAFE

(Map p62; ☑ 0216-418 0277; www.arkaoda.com; Kadife Sokak 18; ⊙ noon-2am; 🛜; 🚊 Kadıköy) A hub of indie music and art, this relaxed place hosts concerts, DJ sets, festivals, parties, themed markets and film screenings. The comfortable couches in the upstairs lounge are a great spot to while away the daytime hours with a coffee or tea; evening action moves to the rear courtyard, which is covered in winter.

Karga Bar
BAR

(Map p62; ☑ 0216-449 1725; www.karga.com.tr; Kadife Sokak 16; ⊙ 11am-2am; 🛜; 🚊 Kadıköy) Multi-storey Karga is one of the most famous bars in the city, offering cheap drinks, alternative music (DJs and live acts) and avant-garde art on its walls. It's not signed well – look for the small black bird.

☆ Entertainment

It's rare to have a week go by without a range of special events, festivals and performances being staged in İstanbul. Locals adore listening to live music (jazz is a particular favourite), attend multiplex cinemas on a regular basis and support a small but thriving number of local theatre, opera and dance companies.

Biletix
BOOKING SERVICE

(☑ 0216-556 9800; www.biletix.com) The number-one web-based resource when sourcing tickets for concerts and events across the city.

★ Babylon Bomonti
LIVE MUSIC

(Map p140; ☑ 0212-334 0190; www.babylon.com. tr; Tarihi Bomonti Bira Fabrikası, Birahane Sokak 1, Bomonti; 🚇 Osmanbey) **FREE** İstanbul's pre-eminent live-music venue has been packing the crowds in since 1999 and shows no sign of losing its mojo, especially now that it has moved to a larger space in an atmospheric old beer factory in the upmarket arts enclave of Bomonti, reasonably close to the Osmanbey metro stop.

Borusan Art
PERFORMING ARTS

(Borusan Sanat; Map p94; ☑ 0212-705 8700; www.borusansanat.com/en; İstiklal Caddesi 160a; 🚇 Şişhane, 🚠 Tünel) An exciting privately funded cultural centre on İstiklal, Borusan Art is housed in a handsome building and hosts classical, jazz, world and new music concerts in its music hall. The occasional dance performance is included in its schedule.

Garajistanbul
CULTURAL CENTRE

(Map p94; ☑ 0212-244 4499; www.garajistanbul. org; Kaymakem Reşat Bey Sokak 11a, Galatasaray; 🚇 Şişhane, 🚠 Tünel) This performance space occupies a former parking garage in a narrow street behind İstiklal Caddesi and is about as edgy as the city's performance scene gets. It hosts contemporary dance performances, poetry readings, theatrical performances and live music (especially jazz).

Nardis Jazz Club
JAZZ

(Map p94; ☑ 0212-244 6327; www.nardisjazz.com; Kuledibi Sokak 14, Galata; cover varies; ⊙ 9.30pm-12.30am Mon-Thu, 10.30pm-1.30am Fri & Sat, closed Jul & Aug; 🚇 Şişhane, 🚠 Tünel) Named after a Miles Davis track, this intimate venue near the Galata Tower is run by jazz guitarist Önder Focan and his wife Zuhal. Performers include gifted amateurs, local jazz luminaries and visiting international artists. It's small, so you'll need to book if you want a decent table. There's a limited dinner/snack menu.

Salon LIVE MUSIC
(Map p94; ☑ 0212-334 0700; www.saloniksv.com; Ground fl, İstanbul Foundation for Culture & Arts, Sadi Konuralp Caddesi 5, Şişhane; ⊘ Oct-May; Ⓜ Şişhane, ⊟ Tünel) This intimate performance space in the İstanbul Foundation for Culture & Arts (İKSV) building hosts live contemporary music (classical, jazz, rock, alternative and world music) as well as theatrical and dance performances. Check its Facebook and Twitter feeds for program details and book through Biletix or the venue's box office.

Vodafone Arena STADIUM
(İnönü Stadyumu; Map p62; www.vodafonearena.com.tr; Kadırgalar Caddesi 1, Beşiktaş; ⊟ Kabataş) This is the home of one of the top football clubs in Turkey's Super League (Süper Lig), Beşiktaş (the Black Eagles). Matches usually take place at the weekend, often on a Saturday night, between August and May. Tickets are sold at the stadium on the day of the match, but most fans buy them in advance through Biletix.

🛍 Shopping

İstanbullus have perfected the practice of shopping over centuries, and most visitors to the city are quick to follow their lead. Historic bazaars, colourful street markets and an ever-expanding portfolio of modern shopping malls cater to every desire and make sourcing a souvenir or two both easy and satisfying.

🛍 Sultanahmet & Around

The best shopping in Sultanahmet is found in and around the **Arasta Bazaar** (Map p71; off Torun Sokak; ⊟ Sultanahmet), a historic arcade of shops that was once part of the *külliye* (mosque complex) of the Blue Mosque (Sultanahmet Camii). Some of Turkey's best-known rug and ceramics dealers have shops in the surrounding streets.

★ **Jennifer's Hamam** BATHWARES, HOMEWARES
(Map p72; ☑ 0212-516 3022; www.jennifershamam. com; Öğül Sokak 20; ⊘ 8.30am-9pm Apr-Oct, to 7pm Nov-Mar; ⊟ Sultanahmet) Owned by Canadian Jennifer Gaudet, this shop stocks top-quality hamam items, including towels, robes and *peştemals* (bath wraps) produced

---

SEEING THE DERVISHES WHIRL

If you thought the Hare Krishnas or the Harlem congregations were the only religious groups to celebrate their faith through music and movement, think again. Those sultans of spiritual spin known as the 'whirling dervishes' have been twirling their way to a higher plane ever since the 13th century and show no sign of slowing down.

There are a number of opportunities to see dervishes whirling in İstanbul. The best known of these is the weekly ceremony in the *semahane* (whirling-dervish hall) in the Galata Mevlevi Museum (Galata Mevlevihanesi Müzesi; Map p94; www.galatamevlevi hanesimuzesi.gov.tr; Galipdede Caddesi 15, Tünel; ₺70; ⊘ performances 5pm Sun; Ⓜ Şişhane, ⊟ Tünel) in Tünel. This one-hour ceremony is held on Sunday at 5pm and costs ₺70 per person. Come early to buy your ticket.

Another much longer and more authentic ceremony is held at the EMAV Silivrikapı Mevlana Cultural Center (EMAV Silivrikapı Mevlana Kültür Merkezi; Map p62; ☑ 0212-588 5780; www.emav.org; Yeni Tavanlı Çeşme Sokak 6, Silivrikapı; ⊟ Çapa-Şehremini) on Thursday evening between 7.30pm and 11pm. This includes a Q&A session (in Turkish), prayers and a *sema* (ceremony). You'll need to sit on the ground for a long period. Admission is by donation. Those wishing to have an English-language introduction to the *sema*, be accompanied by a guide and be taken there and back by minibus from Sultanahmet should book through Les Arts Turcs (p108).

For a more touristy experience, the Hodjapasha Culture Centre (Map p72; ☑ 0212-511 4626; www.hodjapasha.com; Hocapaşa Hamamı Sokak 3b, Sirkeci; performances adult ₺70-80, child under 12yr ₺40-50; ⊟ Sirkeci), housed in a beautifully converted 15th-century hamam near Eminönü, presents whirling-dervish performances at least three evenings per week throughout the year.

Remember that the ceremony is a religious one – by whirling, the adherents believe they are attaining a higher union with God. So don't talk, leave your seat or take flash photographs while the dervishes are spinning or chanting.

using certified organic cotton and silk on old-style shuttled looms. It also sells natural soaps and *keses* (coarse cloth mittens used for exfoliation). Prices are set; no bargaining. This is the main showroom; there is another branch in the Arasta Bazaar (Map p71; Arasta Bazaar 135; ⊘8.30am-9pm Apr-Oct, to 7pm Nov-Mar; ⬓Sultanahmet).

★**Özlem Tuna**   JEWELLERY, HOMEWARES
(Map p72; ☑0212-527 9285; www.ozlemtuna.com; 5th fl, Nemlizade Han, Ankara Caddesi 65, Eminönü; ⊘9am-6pm Mon-Fri; ⬓Sirkeci) A leader in Turkey's contemporary-design movement, Özlem Tuna produces super-stylish jewellery and homewares and sells them from her atelier overlooking Sirkeci train station. Her pieces use forms and colours that reference İstanbul's history and culture (tulips, seagulls, Byzantine mosaics, *nazar boncuk* 'evil eye' charms) and include hamam bowls, coffee and teasets, coasters, rings, earrings, cufflinks and necklaces.

★**Galeri Kayseri**   BOOKS
(Map p72; ☑0212-516 3366; www.galerikayseri. com; Divan Yolu Caddesi 11 & 58; ⊘9am-8pm; ⬓Sultanahmet) Peddling literature since 1996, these twin shops stock a well-presented selection of English-language novels, history books, maps and coffee-table tomes on Turkey, and have knowledgable staff on hand to recommend a good holiday read. The second, smaller, shop is on the opposite side of the road half a block closer to Aya Sofya.

Cocoon   CARPETS, TEXTILES
(Map p72; ☑0212-518 0338; www.yastk.com; Küçük Ayasofya Caddesi 17; ⊘9am-6pm; ⬓Sultanahmet) Sultanahmet is thickly carpeted with rug and textile shops but Cocoon is worth a look. Felt hats, felt-and-silk scarves, rugs, cushion covers and textiles from Central Asia are artfully displayed.

There's a second branch selling hamam items in the Arasta Bazaar (Map p71; Arasta Bazaar 93; ⊘9am-7pm; ⬓Sultanahmet).

Mehmet Çetinkaya
Gallery   CARPETS, JEWELLERY
(Map p72; ☑0212-517 1603, 0212-517 6808; www.cetinkayagallery.com; Tavukhane Sokak 5-7; ⊘9am-8pm; ⬓Sultanahmet) Mehmet Çetinkaya is one of the country's foremost experts on antique oriental carpets and kilims. Built over a Byzantine well, his flagship store-cum-gallery stocks items

of artistic and ethnographic significance, and is full of treasures including carpets, kilims, textiles and jewellery. A branch in the Arasta Bazaar (Map p71; Arasta Bazaar 58; ⊘9am-8pm; ⬓Sultanahmet) sells textiles and antique jewellery.

İznik Classics   CERAMICS
(Map p71; ☑0212-516 8874; www.iznikclassics. com; Utangaç Sokak 17; ⊘9am-8pm, closes 6.30pm winter; ⬓Sultanahmet) İznik Classics is one of the best places in town to source hand-painted collector-item ceramics made with real quartz and using metal oxides for pigments. Admire the range here or at branches in the Arasta Bazaar (Map p72; ☑0212-517 3608; Arasta Bazaar 119; ⊘9am-8pm, to 6.30pm winter; ⬓Sultanahment) and Grand Bazaar (Map p128; ☑0212-520 2568; www. iznikclassics.com; Şerifağa Sokak 188, İç Bedesten, Grand Bazaar; ⊘8.30am-7pm Mon-Sat; ⬓Beyazıt-Kapalı Çarşı). The shop next door at number 13 sells Kütahya ceramics, including tiles, plates and bowls.

Khaftan   ART, ANTIQUES
(Map p72; ☑0212-458 5425; Nakilbent Sokak 16; ⊘9am-7pm; ⬓Sultanahmet) Gleaming Russian icons, delicate calligraphy (old and new), ceramics, *karagöz* (shadow-puppet theatre) puppets, Ottoman prints and contemporary paintings are all on show in this attractive shop.

🏛 Bazaar District

The city's two most famous shopping destinations – the Grand and Spice Bazaars – are in this district. In between the two is the vibrant local shopping neighbourhood of Tahtakale.

★**Epoque**   ANTIQUES
(Map p128; ☑0212-527 7865; Sandal Bedesten Sokak 38, Grand Bazaar; ⊘8.30am-7pm Mon-Sat; ⬓Beyazıt-Kapalı Çarşı) Serious antique shoppers should make their way to this old-fashioned business near the bazaar's Nuruosmaniye Gate. Silver candlesticks and trays, enamelled cigarette cases, jewellery, watches and an extraordinary range of icons are on offer in the elegant shop. The elderly owner and sales members are happy to welcome browsers.

★**Necef Antik & Gold**   JEWELLERY
(Map p128; ☑0212-513 0372; necefantik@outlook. com; Şerifağa Sokak 123, İç Bedesten, Grand Bazaar; ⊘8.30am-7pm Mon-Sat; ⬓Beyazıt-Kapalı Çarşı)

Grand Bazaar

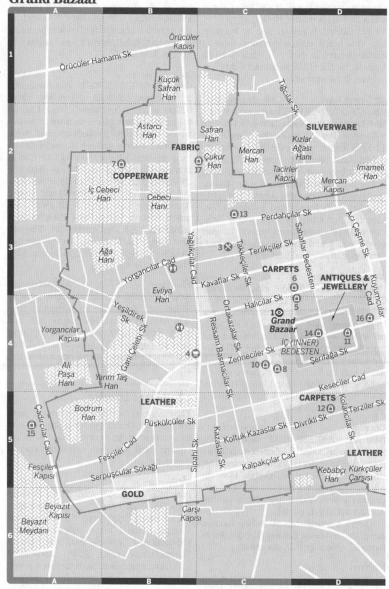

Owner Haluk Botasun has been handcrafting 24-carat gold jewellery in his tiny İç Bedesten store for decades, producing attractive pieces in Byzantine and Ottoman styles. The earrings and cufflinks featuring delicate mosaics are particularly desirable.

★ **Abdulla Natural Products**   TEXTILES, BATHWARE
(Map p128; ☑ 0212-527 3684; www.abdulla.com; Halıcılar Sokak 60, Grand Bazaar; ⊙ 8.30am-7pm Mon-Sat; ☒ Beyazıt-Kapalı Çarşı) The first of the Western-style designer stores to appear

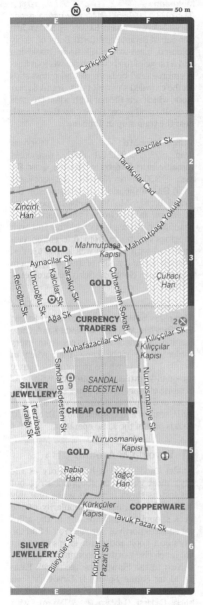

Grand Bazaar

★**Altan Şekerleme**   FOOD & DRINKS
(Map p86; ☎0212-522 5909; Kıble Çeşme Caddesi 68, Eminönü; ⏱8am-7pm Mon-Sat, 9am-6pm Sun; Ⓜ Haliç) Kids aren't the only ones who like candy stores. İstanbullus of every age have been coming to this shop in the Küçük Pazar (Little Bazaar) precinct below the Süleymaniye Mosque since 1865, lured by its cheap and delectable *lokum* (Turkish Delight), *helva* (sweet made from sesame seeds) and *akide* (hard candy).

Derviş   TEXTILES
(Map p128; ☎0212-528 7883; www.dervis.com; Halıcılar Sokak 51, Grand Bazaar; ⏱8.30am-7pm Mon-Sat; 🚇Beyazıt-Kapalı Çarşı) Raw cotton and silk *peştemals* (bath wraps) share shelf space here with traditional Turkish dowry vests and engagement dresses. If these don't take your fancy, the pure olive-oil soaps and old hamam bowls are sure to step into the breach. There's another branch (Map p128; ☎0212-528 7883; www.dervis.com; Cebeci Han 10, Grand Bazaar; ⏱8.30am-7pm Mon-Sat; 🚇Beyazıt-Kapalı Çarşı) off Yağlıçılar Caddesi.

Dhoku   CARPETS
(Map p128; ☎0212-527 6841; www.dhoku.com; Tekkeçiler Sokak 58-60, Grand Bazaar; ⏱8.30am-7pm Mon-Sat; 🚇Beyazıt-Kapalı Çarşı) One of the new generation of rug stores opening in the bazaar, Dhoku (meaning 'texture') sells artfully designed wool kilims in resolutely

in this ancient marketplace, Abdulla sells top-quality cotton bed linen and towels, hand-spun woollen throws from eastern Turkey, cotton *peştemals* (bath wraps) and pure olive-oil soap.

modernist designs. Its sister store, **Ethni-Con** (Map p128; ☑ 0212-527 6841; www.ethnicon.com; Tekkeçiler Sokak 58-60, Grand Bazaar; ☺ 8.30am-7pm Mon-Sat; 🚇 Beyazıt-Kapalı Çarşı), opposite Dhoku, sells similarly stylish rugs in vivid colours.

Vakko İndirim
FASHION & ACCESSORIES

(Vakko Sale Store; Map p72; Sultan Hamamı Caddesi 8a, Eminönü; ☺ 10am-6.30pm Mon-Sat; 🚇 Eminönü) This remainder outlet of İstanbul's famous fashion store should be on the itinerary of all bargain hunters. Top-quality men's and women's clothing – often stuff that's been designed and made in Italy – is sold here for a fraction of its original price.

Ümit Berksoy
JEWELLERY

(Map p128; ☑ 0212-522 3391; İnciler Sokak 2-6, Grand Bazaar; ☺ 8.30am-7pm Mon-Sat; Ⓜ Vezneciler, 🚇 Beyazıt-Kapalı Çarşı) Jeweller Ümit Berksoy handcrafts gorgeous Byzantine-style rings, earings and necklaces using gold and old coins at his tiny atelier just outside the İç Bedesten. He also creates contemporary pieces.

Ali Muhıddin Hacı Bekir
FOOD

(Map p72; ☑ 0212-522 8543; www.hacibekir.com.tr; Hamidiye Caddesi 33, Eminönü; ☺ 9am-7.30pm; 🚇 Eminönü) Many people think that this historic shop, which has been operated by members of the same family for over 200 years, is the best place in the city to buy *lokum* (Turkish Delight). Choose from *sade* (plain), *cevizli* (walnut), *fıstıklı* (pistachio), *badem* (almond) or *roze* (rose water). There are other branches in **Beyoğlu** (Map p94; ☑ 0212-244 2804; www.hacibekir.com.tr; İstiklal Caddesi 83; Ⓜ Taksim) and **Kadıköy** (Map p62; ☑ 0216-336 1519; Muvakkithane Caddesi 6; ☺ 8am-8pm; 🚊 Kadıköy).

Hafız Mustafa
FOOD

(Map p72; ☑ 0212-513 3610; www.hafizmustafa.com; Hamidiye Caddesi 84, Eminönü; ☺ 8am-8pm Mon-Sat, 9am-8pm Sun; 🚇 Eminönü) 🖋 Located opposite Ali Muhıddin Hacı Bekir, Hafız Mustafa sells excellent *lokum*. You can buy a small bag of freshly made treats to sample, plus gift boxes to take home. Best of all, staff are happy to let you taste before buying (within reason, of course). There are other branches in **Sirkeci** (Map p72; ☑ 0212-527 6654; www.hafizmustafa.com; Muradiye Caddesi 51, Sirkeci; börek ₺5, baklava ₺6-7.50, puddings ₺6; ☺ 9am-6pm; 🕿; 🚇 Sirkeci) and **Sultanahmet** (Map p72; ☑ 0212-514 9068; Divan Yolu Caddesi 14, Sultanahmet; ☺ 9am-6pm; 🕿; 🚇 Sultanahmet).

Mekhann
TEXTILES

(Map p128; ☑ 0212-519 9444; www.mekhann.com; Divrikli Sokak 49, Grand Bazaar; ☺ 8.30am-7pm Mon-Sat; 🚇 Beyazıt-Kapalı Çarşı) Bolts of richly coloured, hand-woven silk from Uzbekistan and a range of finely woven shawls join finely embroidered bedspreads and pillow slips on the crowded shelves of this Grand Bazaar store, which sets the bar high when it comes to quality and price. There's another branch near the tram stop in Tophane.

Muhlis Günbattı
TEXTILES

(Map p128; ☑ 0212-511 6562; www.muhlisgunbatti.com.tr; Perdahçılar Sokak 48, Grand Bazaar; ☺ 8.30am-7pm Mon-Sat; 🚇 Beyazıt-Kapalı Çarşı) One of the most famous stores in the Grand Bazaar, Muhlis Günbattı specialises in *suzani* fabrics from Uzbekistan. These beautiful bedspreads, tablecloths and wall hangings are made from fine cotton embroidered with silk. As well as the textiles, it stocks a small range of antique Ottoman fabrics and clothing richly embroidered with gold.

Yazmacı Necdet Danış
TEXTILES

(Map p128; Yağlıkçılar Caddesi 57, Grand Bazaar; ☺ 8.30am-7pm Mon-Sat; 🚇 Beyazıt-Kapalı Çarşı) Fashion designers and buyers from every corner of the globe know that, when in İstanbul, this is where to come to source top-quality textiles. It's crammed with bolts of fabric of every description – shiny, simple, sheer and sophisticated – as well as *peştemals,* scarves and clothes. Murat Danış next door is part of the same operation.

🏛 Beyoğlu & Around

İstiklal Caddesi has a long history as the city's most glamorous shopping strip, but has lost its sheen in recent years, probably due to the phenomenal popularity of the sleek shopping malls opening in the affluent suburbs north of Beyoğlu. You'll find the city's best book and music shops here, but not much else worthy of comment.

Next to the Flower Passage (Çiçek Pasajı), along Şahne Sokak, is Beyoğlu's **Fish Market** (Balık Pazarı; Map p94; Şahne Sokak, off İstiklal Caddesi, Galatasaray; Ⓜ Taksim), with stalls selling fruit, vegetables, caviar, pickles and other produce. Leading off the Fish Market is the neoclassical **Avrupa Pasajı** (European Passage; Map p94; Ⓜ Taksim), a pretty passageway with a handful of shops selling tourist wares and antique prints. Aslıhan

Pasajı, nearby, is a two-storey arcade bursting with secondhand books.

The streets around Tünel Meydanı and Galata Kulesi Meydanı are being colonised by avant-garde fashion and homeware designers and make for exciting shopping. Between the two squares is Galipdede Caddesi, home to a major concentration of musical-instrument shops.

Antique stores can be found dotting the narrow winding streets of Çukurcuma, and small fashion ateliers are scattered across Tophane and the expat enclave of Cihangir. All three areas are well worth a wander.

★Hiç   HOMEWARES, HANDICRAFTS
(Map p94; ✆0212-251 9973; www.hiccrafts.com; Lüleci Hendek Caddesi 35, Tophane; ⊙10.30am-7pm Mon-Sat; 🚊Tophane) Interior designer Emel Güntaş is one of İstanbul's style icons and this recently opened contemporary crafts shop in Tophane is a favourite destination for the city's design mavens. The stock includes cushions, carpets, kilims (pileless woven rugs), silk scarves, lamps, furniture, glassware, porcelain and felt crafts. Everything here is artisan-made and absolutely gorgeous.

★Nahıl   HANDICRAFTS, BATHWARE
(Map p94; ✆0212-251 9085; www.nahil.com.tr; Bekar Sokak 17, Taksim; ⊙10am-7pm Mon-Sat; 🚇Taksim) The felting, lacework, embroidery, all-natural soaps and soft toys in this lovely shop are made by economically disadvantaged women in Turkey's rural areas. All profits are returned to them, ensuring that they and their families have better lives.

★NYKS   HOMEWARES
(Map p94; ✆0212-252 6957; www.nyks.com.tr; Serdar-ı Ekrem Sokak 49/1a, Galata; 🚇Şişhane, 🚊Tünel) Olive-oil candles scented with mint, thyme, bay leaf, pine, lavender, cedar, bergamot, rosemary and green mandarin are presented in gorgeous copper, marble, glass and ceramic containers and offered at this cute shop on one of the city's most attractive shopping streets. Well priced and unusual, they are excellent souvenirs to take home or give to friends and family.

Eyüp Sabri Tuncer   BEAUTY
(Map p94; ✆0212-244 0098; www.eyupsabri tuncer.com; Mumhane Caddesi 10, Karaköy; ⊙10am-7pm; 🚊Karaköy) Turks of every age adore the colognes and beauty products produced by this local company, which was

established in 1923. Its *doğal zeytınyağlı* (natural olive oil) body balms and soaps are wonderfully inexpensive considering their quality.

A La Turca   CARPETS, ANTIQUES
(Map p94; ✆0212-245 2933; www.alaturcahouse. com; Faik Paşa Caddesi 4, Çukurcuma; ⊙10.30am-7.30pm Mon-Sat; 🚇Taksim) Antique Anatolian kilims and textiles are stacked alongside top-drawer Ottoman antiques in this fabulous shop in Çukurcuma. This is the best area in the city to browse for antiques and curios, and A La Turca is probably the most interesting of its retail outlets. Ring the doorbell to gain entrance.

Antijen Design   CLOTHING
(Map p94; ✆0212-251 8614; www.niluferkaraca. com.tr; Yenicarşı Caddesi 9, Galatasaray; ⊙10am-7pm Mon-Sat; 🚇Taksim) Local designer Nilüfer Karaca creates sculptural pieces in muted tones that customers can purchase off the rack or have made to measure in two or three days. Her form-hugging summer frocks and statement winter coats are particularly desirable.

Arzu Kaprol   CLOTHING
(Map p94; ✆0212-252 7571; www.arzukaprol. net; Serdar-ı Ekrem Sokak 22, Galata; 🚇Şişhane, 🚊Tünel) Arzu Kaprol is Parisian-trained and lauded throughout Turkey for her exciting designs. Her collections of women's clothing and accessories feature in Paris Fashion Week and are stocked by international retailers, including Harrods in London. This store showcases her sleek prêt-à-porter range.

Misela   FASHION & ACCESSORIES
(Map p94; ✆0212-243 5300; www.miselaistanbul. com; Meşrutiyet Caddesi 107e, Tepebaşı; ⊙11am-7pm Mon-Thu, to 8pm Fri, noon-8pm Sat; 🚇Şişhane, 🚊Tünel) No self-respecting local fashionista would be without a chic handbag designed by local gal Serra Türker. Quality materials and skill are the hallmarks, for which you will pay accordingly.

Hamm   HOMEWARES
(Map p94; ✆0533 234 1122; www.hamm.com.tr; Boğazkesen Caddesi 71a, Tophane; ⊙10am-7pm Mon-Sat, 11am-5pm Sun; 🚊Tophane) Its location on Boğazkesen Caddesi, near the Tophane tram stop, is one of Beyoğlu's style hubs, and Hamm is a great place to garner an understanding of contemporary Turkish style. It showcases furniture, lighting and homewares designed and made in İstanbul.

MATT MUNRO/LONELY PLANET ©

1. Pots for sale, Grand Bazaar (p85) 2. Grand Bazaar (p85)
3. Spice Bazaar (p89) 4. Lamps on display, Grand Bazaar (p85)

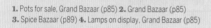

İstanbul's Bazaars

Turks have honed the ancient arts of shopping and bargaining over centuries. In İstanbul, the city's Ottoman-era bazaars are as much monuments as marketplaces, spaces showcasing architecture and atmosphere that are nearly as impressive as the artisan wares offered for sale.

The Grand Bazaar

One of the world's oldest and best-loved shopping malls, the Grand Bazaar, has been luring shoppers into its labyrinthine lanes and hidden *hans* (caravanserais) ever since Mehmet the Conqueror ordered its construction in 1461. Come here to purchase carpets and kilims, bathwares, jewellery and textiles. Be sure to investigate its fabulous fast-food opportunities too.

The Spice Bazaar

Seductively scented and inevitably crammed with shoppers, this building opposite the Eminönü ferry docks has been selling goods to stock household pantries since the 17th century, when it was the last stop for the camel caravans that travelled the legendary Spice Routes from China, Persia and India. These days it's a great place to source dried fruit and spices.

The Arasta Bazaar

In the shadow of the Blue Mosque, this elongated open arcade of shops has a laid-back atmosphere that stands in stark contrast to the crowded and noisy Grand and Spice Bazaars. Come for carpets and kilims, bathwares, ceramics and textiles.

Produce Markets

İstanbul is blessed with fabulous fresh produce markets. Consider visiting the following markets:

➡ **Kadıköy Produce Market** (p99)

➡ **Balık Pazarı, Beyoğlu** (İstiklal Caddesi, Galatasaray; 🚋Kabataş, then funicular to Taksim)

➡ **Kadınlar Pazarı, Zeyrek** (İtfaiye Caddesi, Fatih; 🚋Aksaray)

Selda Okutan
JEWELLERY

(Map p94; ☑0212-514 1164; www.seldaokutan. com; Ali Paşa Değirmeni Sokak 10a, Tophane; ⊙10am-7pm Mon-Sat; 🚇Tophane) Selda Okutan's sculptural pieces featuring tiny naked figures have the local fashion industry all aflutter. Come to her design studio in Tophane to see what all the fuss is about.

Hafız Mustafa
SWEETS

(Map p94; İstiklal Caddesi 35, Taksim; ⊙8am-1am; 🚇Taksim) The Beyoğlu branch of this much-loved sweets store, signed as 'Hakkı Zade', is close to Taksim Meydanı.

Opus3a
MUSIC

(Map p94; ☑0212-251 8405; www.opus3a.com; Cihangir Caddesi 3a, Cihangir; ⊙11am-8.30pm, to 9.30pm Jun-Aug; 🚇Taksim) Those keen to supplement their CD or vinyl collections with some Turkish music should head to this large shop in Cihangir, where knowledgable English-speaking staff can steer you towards the best local classical, jazz, alternative and pop recordings.

🛍 Beşiktaş, Nişantaşı & Kuruçeşme

Serious shoppers, visiting celebs, public-relations professionals and the city's gilded youth gravitate towards upmarket Nişantaşı, which is located about 2km north of Taksim Meydanı and accessed via the metro (Osmanbey stop). International fashion and design shops are found in the streets surrounding the main artery, Teşvikiye Caddesi, which prompts some locals to refer to that area as Teşvikiye. Nişantaşı is one of İstanbul's major fashion hubs, especially Abdi İpekçi Caddesi, where Turkish and international designers can be found.

Gönül Paksoy
CLOTHING

(Map p62; ☑0212-236 0209; gonulpaksoy@gmail. com; Demet Apt 4a, Akkavak Sokak, Nişantaşı; ⊙10am-7pm Tue-Sat, from 1pm Mon; 🚇Osmanbey) Paksoy creates and sells pieces that transcend fashion and step into art. In fact, her work was once the subject of an exhibition at İstanbul's Rezan Haş Gallery. Her distinctive clothing is handmade using naturally dyed fabrics (mainly silk, linen, cotton, cashmere, goat hair and wool) and often decorated with vintage beads.

She also creates and sells delicate silk and cotton knits and exquisite jewellery based on traditional Ottoman designs.

Lokum Istanbul
FOOD

(☑0212-257 1052; www.lokumistanbul.com; Kuruçeşme Caddesi 19, Kuruçeşme; ⊙9am-8pm Mon-Fri, from 10am Sat & Sun; 🚇Kuruçeşme) *Lokum* (Turkish Delight) is elevated to the status of artwork at this boutique. Owner and creator Zeynep Keyman brings back the delights, flavours, knowledge and beauty of Otto-man-Turkish products, including colourful and chunky pomegranate and pistachio *lokum* (pick up a small box for ₺65), *akide* candies (traditional boiled lollies), cologne water and scented candles. The gorgeous packaging makes these treats perfect gifts.

Zorlu Center
SHOPPING CENTRE

(Map p140; ☑0212-924 0124; www.zorlucenter. com; Beşiktaş; 🚇Gayrettepe) Comprising a shopping mall, residential development and performing arts centre, the Zorlu Center draws people with its upmarket shops, concerts featuring local and international artists, food chains (including Eataly and Jamie's Italian) and a 14-screen cinema complex.

🛍 Üsküdar

Şekerci Aytekin Erol Caferzade
FOOD

(Map p62; ☑0216-337 1337; www.caferzade.com.tr; Atlas Sokak 21; ⊙8am-9pm; 🚢Üsküdar, 🚇Üsküdar) One of the major draws in Üsküdar's bustling Fish Market (Balıkçılar Çarşısı), this sweets shop has been supplying locals with their regular fixes of *lokum* (Turkish delight) since 1945 and is known for unusual flavours such as *narlı çifte kavrulmuş fıstıklı* (pomegranate and pistachio). It also sells a huge range of colourful *akide* (hard candy).

ℹ Information

DANGERS & ANNOYANCES

➡ Recently, political tensions within the country and the region have led to a violent, ultimately unsuccessful military coup d'état. There have also been terrorist incidents including bomb attacks in areas and facilities frequented by tourists. Visitors should monitor their country's travel advisories and stay alert at all times.

➡ Always employ common sense when exploring city neighbourhoods. Be particularly careful near the historic city walls, as these harbour vagrants and people with substance-abuse problems – don't walk here alone or after dark.

➡ As a pedestrian, always give way to vehicles; the sovereignty of the pedestrian is recognised in law but not out on the street. Footpaths

❶ MUSEUM PASS

Most visitors spend at least three days in İstanbul and cram as many museum visits as possible into their stay, so purchasing a **Museum Pass İstanbul** (http://www.muze. gov.tr/en/museum-card) is worth considering. Valid for 120 hours (five days) from the first museum you visit, it costs ₺85 and allows one entrance to each of Topkapı Palace and Harem, Aya Sofya, Aya İrini, the İstanbul Archaeology Museums, the Museum of Turkish and Islamic Arts, the Great Palace Mosaics Museum, the Kariye Museum (Chora Church), Galata Mevlevi Museum, Fethiye Museum, Rumeli Hisarı, Yıldız Sarayı and the İstanbul Museum of the History of Science & Technology in Islam. Purchased individually, admission fees to these sights will cost ₺260, so the pass represents a possible saving of ₺175. It sometimes allows you to bypass ticket queues too.

As well as giving entry to these government-operated museums, the pass also provides discounts on entry to privately run museums such as the Museum of Innocence, the Pera Museum and the Rahmi M Koç Museum.

The pass can be purchased through some hotels and from the ticket offices of all of the museums it covers.

(sidewalks) and road surfaces are often in a poorly maintained state and some shops have basements that are accessed from the footpath via steep steps without barriers – watch where you are walking!

MEDICAL SERVICES

Standards of food hygiene are generally high in İstanbul and visitors experience few food-related illnesses. To be safe, treat street food with caution and if you dine in a *lokanta* (restaurant serving ready-made food) make sure you choose dishes that look hot and freshly prepared.

Tap water in İstanbul is chlorinated, but is still not guaranteed to be safe (many locals don't drink it). Spring water is cheap and sold everywhere in 330mL, 1.5L and 3L plastic bottles.

Turkey doesn't have reciprocal health-care arrangements with other countries, so having travel insurance is highly advisable.

For minor problems it's customary to ask at a chemist/pharmacy *(eczane)* for advice. Many pharmacists speak English and will prescribe treatment on the spot. Drugs requiring a prescription in Western countries are often sold over the counter (except for the most dangerous or addictive ones) and will often be cheaper too. Make sure that you know the generic name of your medicine; the commercial name may not be the same in Turkey.

Most doctors in Turkey speak English and half of all the physicians in İstanbul are women. If a woman visits a male doctor, it's customary for her to have a companion present during any physical examination or treatment.

Though they are expensive, it's probably easiest to visit one of the private hospitals listed here if you need medical care when in İstanbul. Their standard of care is generally quite high and you will have no trouble finding staff who speak

English. Both accept credit-card payments and will charge around ₺300 for a standard consultation.

American Hospital (Amerikan Hastenesi; ☑ 0212-444 3777, 0212-311 2000; www. americanhospitalistanbul.com; Güzelbahçe Sokak 20, Nişantaşı; ⊗24hr; Ⓜ Osmanbey) Pediatric, dental and many other clinics.

Memorial Hospital (☑ 0212-444 7888, 0212-314 6666; www.memorial.com.tr/en; Piyalepaşa Bulvarı, Şişli; Ⓜ Şişli) Emergency department, eye centre and pediatric clinic.

MONEY

ATMs are widespread. Credit cards accepted at most shops, hotels and upmarket restaurants.

POST

Central Post Office (Merkez Postane; Map p72; ☑ 444 1788; www.ptt.gov.tr; Büyük Postane Caddesi; ⊗8.30am-5pm; 🚇 Sirkeci) The international parcel service is on the right as you enter. You will also find ATMs here.

TOURIST INFORMATION

The Ministry of Culture & Tourism (www.turizm. gov.tr) currently operates three tourist information offices or booths in the city and has booths at both international airports. In our experience, the Sirkeci office is the most helpful and the Sultanahmet office is the least helpful.

Tourist Office – Atatürk International Airport (☑ 0212-465 3547; International Arrivals Hall, Atatürk International Airport; ⊗9am-9pm)

Tourist Office – Sabiha Gökçen International Airport (☑ 0216-588 8794; ⊗8am-7pm)

Tourist Office – Sirkeci Train Station (Map p72; ☑ 0555 675 2674, 0212-511 5888; Sirkeci Gar, Ankara Caddesi, Sirkeci; ⊗9.30am-6pm mid-Apr–Sep, 9am-5.30pm Oct–mid-Apr; 🚇 Sirkeci)

❶ TELEPHONE CODES

If you are in European İstanbul and wish to call a number in Asian İstanbul, you must dial 0216 before the number. If you are in Asian İstanbul and wish to call a number in European İstanbul, use 0212. Do not use a prefix (that is, don't use the 0212/6) if you are calling a number on the same shore.

Tourist Office – Sultanahmet (Map p72; ☏ 0212-518 8754; Hippodrome, Sultanahmet; ⊙ 8.30am-6.30pm mid-Apr–Sep, 9am-5.30pm Oct–mid-Apr; ☖ Sultanahmet)

Tourist Office – Taksim (Map p94; ☏ 0212-233 0592; www.kulturturizm.gov.tr; Ground fl, Seyran Apartmanı, Mete Caddesi, Taksim; ⊙ 9.30am-6pm mid-Apr–Sep, 9am-5.30pm Oct–mid-Apr; Ⓜ Taksim)

❶ Getting There & Away

It's the national capital in all but name, so getting to İstanbul is easy. There are currently two international airports and a new and improved third airport is due to open in 2018. When it does, Atatürk International Airport will be retired from use. There is one *otogar* (bus station) from which national and international services arrive and depart. At the time of writing there were no international rail connections, but this situation may change when upgrades to rail lines throughout the country are completed and when the security situation in Turkey's east and in Syria improves.

Flights, cars and tours can be booked online at www.lonelyplanet.com/bookings.

AIR

Atatürk International Airport

The city's main airport, **Atatürk International Airport** (IST, Atatürk Havalimanı; Map p140; ☏ +90 444 9828; www.ataturkairport.com), is located in Yeşilköy, 23km west of Sultanahmet. The international terminal (Dış Hatlar) and domestic terminal (İç Hatlar) operate at or close to capacity, which has prompted the Turkish Government to announce construction of a new, much larger, airport 50km north of the city centre. The first stage of the new airport's construction is due to be completed by 2018 but the facility won't be fully operational until 2025.

The airport has car-rental desks, exchange offices, stands of mobile-phone companies, a 24-hour pharmacy, ATMs and a PTT (post office) at the international arrivals area. A 24-hour supermarket is located on the walkway to the metro.

Left luggage A booth to your right as you exit customs offers luggage storage and charges ₺20 per suitcase or backpack per 24 hours; it's open around the clock.

Tourist information There's a small office in the international arrivals hall that is open from 9am to 9pm. It provides maps and advice.

Sabiha Gökçen International Airport

The city's second international airport, **Sabiha Gökçen International Airport** (SAW, Sabiha Gökçen Havalimanı; ☏ 0216-588 8888; www.sgairport.com), is at Pendik/Kurtköy on the Asian side of the city.

It has ATMs, car-rental desks, stands of mobile-phone companies, exchange offices, a mini-market and a PTT in the international arrivals hall.

Left luggage A booth in the international arrivals hall offers luggage storage.

Tourist information There's a small office in the international arrivals hall that is open from 9am to 7pm. It provides maps and advice.

BUS

The **Büyük İstanbul Otogarı** (Big İstanbul Bus Station; ☏ 0212-658 0505; www.otogaristanbul.com) is the city's main bus station for both intercity and international routes. Often called simply 'the Otogar' (Bus Station), it's located at Esenler in the municipality of Bayrampaşa, about 10km west of Sultanahmet. The metro service between Aksaray and Atatürk International Airport stops here (Otogar stop). From the Otogar you can take the metro to Zeytinburnu and then easily connect with a tram (₺4) to Sultanahmet or Kabataş/Taksim. If you're going to Beyoğlu, bus 830 leaves from the centre of the Otogar every 15 minutes between 6am and 10.50pm and takes approximately one hour to reach Taksim Meydanı. The trip costs ₺4 and is slower than the metro/tram alternative. A taxi will cost approximately ₺35 to both Sultanahmet and Taksim.

There's a second, much smaller, otogar at Alibeyköy, where buses from central Anatolia (including Ankara and Cappadocia) stop en route to Esenler. From here passengers can take a *servis* (service bus) to Taksim; the transfer is included in the ticket cost. The only problem with this option is that service drivers rarely speak English and passengers sometimes have to wait for a *servis* – it's probably easier to go to Esenler. Note that no *servises* go to Sultanahmet.

The city's third otogar is in Ataşehir, on the Asian side at the junction of the O-2 and O-4 motorways. From Ataşehir, *servises* transfer passengers to Asian suburbs, including Kadıköy and Üsküdar.

TRAIN

At the time of writing, no international train services were leaving İstanbul; the daily Bosfor

Ekspresi service to Bucharest via Sofia was by bus between İstanbul and Sofia and then by train between Sofia and Bucharest. It departs at 10pm daily (₺65 to Sofia, ₺125 to Bucharest).

A fast-train service operates between Ankara and Pendik, 20km southeast of Kadıköy on the Asian side of the city. This takes approximately 3½ hours and ticket prices start at ₺70. Unfortunately, Pendik is difficult to access. You'll need to take the metro from Sirkeci to Ayrılık Çeşmesi and then change to the M4 metro and travel to the end of the line at Kartal. From Kartal bus 17B and taxis travel the last 6km to Pendik Garı. There are future plans to extend the M4 to Pendik and Kaynarca, but a timetable for this has yet to be announced.

ⓘ Getting Around

➡ *Jetons* (ticket tokens) can be purchased from ticket machines or offices at tram stops, *iskelesi* and funicular and metro stations, but it's much cheaper and easier to use an İstanbulkart.

➡ You must have an İstanbulkart to use a bus.

➡ Pay the driver when you take a dolmuş (shared minibus); fares vary according to destination and length of trip.

➡ Ticket prices are usually the same on public and private ferry services; İstanbulkarts can be used on some private ferries, but not all.

➡ İstanbulkarts cannot be used to pay for Bosphorus ferry tours.

TO/FROM ATATÜRK INTERNATIONAL AIRPORT

Airport Bus

If you are staying in Beyoğlu, the **Havataş airport bus** (Map p62; 📞 444 2656; http://havatas.com) from Atatürk International Airport is probably the most convenient option. This departs from outside the arrivals hall. Buses leave every 30 minutes between 4am and 1am; the trip takes between 40 minutes and one hour, depending on traffic. Tickets cost ₺11 and the bus stops in front of the Point Hotel on Cumhuriyet Caddesi, close to Taksim Meydanı. Note that signage on the buses and at stops sometimes reads 'Havaş' rather than 'Havataş'.

A public bus service (96T) travels from a stop next to the Havataş buses outside the arrivals hall and travels to Taksim Meydanı (₺4, two hours, six daily); check the İETT website (www.iett.istanbul/en) for departure times. To travel on this bus, you must have an İstanbulkart. These are available at the machines at the metro-station entrance on the lower ground floor.

Hotel Shuttles

Many hotels will provide a free pick-up service from Atatürk International Airport if you stay with them for three nights or more. There are also a number of very slow shuttle-bus services from hotels to the airport for your return trip; these cost around ₺25..Check details with your hotel.

Metro & Tram

There's an efficient metro service between the airport and Yenikapı, from where you can connect to the M2 metro to Hacıosman. This stops at Vezneciler in the Bazaar District, and in Şişhane and Taksim in Beyoğlu en route. Another service, the Marmaray to Ayrılık Çeşmesi, stops at Sirkeci near the Eminönü ferry docks and in Üsküdar on the Asian shore en route.

To get to Sultanahmet, alight from the metro at Zeytinburnu, from where it's easy to connect with the tram to Sultanahmet, Eminönü and Kabataş. From Kabataş, there's a funicular to Taksim Meydanı (Taksim Sq). Note that if you are going to the airport from the city centre you

---

ⓘ İSTANBULKARTS

İstanbul's public-transport system is excellent, and one of its major strengths is the İstanbulkart, a rechargeable travel card similar to London's Oyster Card, Hong Kong's Octopus Card and Paris' Navigo.

İstanbulkarts are simple to operate. As you enter a bus or pass through the turnstile at a ferry dock or metro station, swipe your card for entry and the fare will automatically be deducted from your balance. The cards offer a considerable discount on fares (₺2.20 to ₺2.45 according to the destination, as opposed to the usual ₺4, with additional transfers within a two-hour journey window: ₺1.75 for the first transfer, ₺1.60 for the second and ₺1.40 for all subsequent transfers). They can also be used to pay for fares for more than one traveller (one swipe per person per ride).

The cards can be purchased from machines at metro and funicular stations for a non-refundable charge of ₺10, which includes ₺4 in credit. If you buy yours from a street kiosk near a tram or bus stop (look for an 'Akbil', 'Dolum Noktası' or 'İstanbulkart' sign), you will pay ₺8 for one with a plastic cover, or ₺7 without. These won't include any credit.

Cards can be recharged with amounts between ₺5 and ₺150 at kiosks or at machines at ferry docks, metro and bus stations.

should take the Bağcilar service rather than the Cevizlibağ one, which terminates before Zeytinburnu.

The metro station is on the lower ground floor beneath the international departures hall – follow the 'Metro/Subway' signs down the escalators and through the underground walkway. You'll need to purchase a *jeton* (ticket token; ₺4) for each individual metro trip or purchase and recharge an İstanbulkart (travel card; ₺10, including ₺4 credit) from the machines at the metro entrance. Services depart every six to 10 minutes from 6am until midnight. If you get off the metro at Zeytinburnu, the tram platform is right in front of you. You'll need to buy another token (₺4) to pass through the turnstiles.

Taxi

A taxi from the airport costs around ₺45 to Sultanahmet, ₺55 to Beyoğlu and ₺80 to Kadıköy.

TO/FROM SABIHA GÖKÇEN INTERNATIONAL AIRPORT

Airport Bus

Havataş (p137) airport buses travel from the airport to Taksim Meydanı between 3.30am and 1am. There are also services to Kadıköy between 4am and 1am. Tickets cost ₺14 to Taksim (1½ hours) and ₺9 to Kadıköy (one hour). If you're heading towards the Old City from Taksim, you can take the funicular from Taksim to Kabataş (₺4) followed by the tram from Kabataş to Sultanahmet (₺4). From Kadıköy, ferries travel to Eminönü (₺4).

Hotel Shuttle

Hotels rarely provide free pick-up services from Sabiha Gökçen. Shuttle-bus services from hotels to the airport cost up to ₺75 but are infrequent – check details with your hotel. The trip can take up to two hours, so allow plenty of time.

Taxi

Taxis from this airport to the city are expensive. To Beyoğlu you'll be looking at around ₺140; to Sultanahmet around ₺155.

BUS

The bus system in İstanbul is extremely efficient, though traffic congestion in the city means that bus trips can be very long. The introduction of Metrobüs lines (where buses are given dedicated traffic lanes) aims to relieve this problem, but these tend to service residential suburbs out of the city centre and are thus of limited benefit to travellers. The major bus stands are underneath Taksim Meydanı and at Beşiktaş, Kabataş, Eminönü, Kadıköy and Üsküdar, with most services running between 6am and 11pm. Destinations and main stops on city bus routes are shown on a sign on the right (kerb) side of the bus (*otobüs*), or on the electronic display at its front. You must have an İstanbulkart before boarding.

The most useful bus lines for travellers are those running along both sides of the Bosphorus and the Golden Horn, those in the Western Districts and those between Üsküdar and Kadıköy.

FERRY

The most enjoyable way to get around town is by ferry. Crossing between the Asian and European shores, up and down the Golden Horn and Bosphorus, and over to the Princes' Islands, these vessels are as efficient as they are popular with locals. Some are operated by the government-owned İstanbul Şehir Hatları; others by private companies, including **Dentur Avrasya** (☑ 444 6336; www.denturavrasya.com) and **Turyol** (☑ 0212-251 4421; www.turyol.com). Timetables are posted at *iskelesi* (ferry docks).

On the European side, the major ferry docks are at the mouth of the Golden Horn (Eminönü and Karaköy), at Beşiktaş and next to the tram stop at Kabataş, 2km past the Galata Bridge.

The ferries run to two annual timetables: winter (mid-September to May) and summer (June to mid-September). Tickets are cheap (usually ₺4) and it's possible to use an İstanbulkart on most routes.

There are also *deniz otobüsü* and *hızlı feribot* (seabus and fast ferry) services, but these ply routes that are of less interest to the traveller and are also more expensive than the conventional ferries. For more information, check **İstanbul Deniz Otobüsleri** (İDO; ☑ 0850 222 4436; www.ido.com.tr).

Routes

Ferries ply the following useful two-way routes:

→ Beşiktaş–Kadıköy
→ Beşiktaş–Üsküdar
→ Eminönü–Anadolu Kavağı (Bosphorus Cruise)
→ Eminönü–Kadıköy
→ Eminönü–Üsküdar
→ Kabataş–Kadıköy
→ Kabataş–Kadıköy–Kınaılada–Burgazada–Heybeliada–Büyükada (Princes' Islands ferry)
→ Kabataş–Üsküdar
→ Karaköy–Kadıköy (some stop at Haydarpaşa)
→ Karaköy–Üsküdar
→ Sarıyer–Rumeli Kavağı–Anadolu Kavağı
→ Üsküdar–Karaköy–Eminönü–Kasımpaşa–Hasköy–Ayvansaray–Sütlüce–Eyüp (Golden Horn Ferry)

There are also limited services to, from and between the Bosphorus suburbs.

FUNICULAR & CABLE CAR

There are two funiculars (*funiküleri*) and two cable cars (*teleferic*) in the city. All are short trips and İstanbulkarts can be used.

A funicular called the Tünel carries passengers between Karaköy, at the base of the Galata

Bridge (Galata Köprüsü), to Tünel Meydanı, at one end of İstiklal Caddesi. The service operates every five minutes between 7am and 10.45pm and a *jeton* costs ₺4.

The second funicular carries passengers from Kabataş, at the end of the tramline, to Taksim Meydanı, where it connects to the metro. The service operates every five minutes from 6am to midnight and a *jeton* costs ₺4.

A cable car runs between the waterside at Eyüp and the Pierre Loti Café (8am to 10pm). Another travels between Maçka (near Taksim) and the İstanbul Technical University in Taşkışla (8am to 7pm). *Jetons* for each cost ₺4.

METRO

Metro services depart every five minutes between 6am and midnight. *Jetons* cost ₺4 and İstanbulkarts can be used.

One line (the M1A) connects Yenikapı, southwest of Sultanahmet, with the airport. This stops at 16 stations, including Aksaray and the Otogar, along the way.

Another line (the M2) connects Yenikapı with Taksim, stopping at three stations along the way: Vezneciler, near the Grand Bazaar; on the new bridge across the Golden Horn (Haliç); and at Şişhane, near Tünel Meydanı in Beyoğlu. From Taksim it travels northeast to Hacıosman via nine stations. A branch line, the M6, connects one of these stops, Levent, with Boğaziçi Üniversitesi near the Bosphorus.

A fourth line, known as the Marmaray, connects Kazlıçeşme, west of the Old City, with Ayrılık Çeşmesi, on the city's Asian side. This travels via a tunnel under the Sea of Marmara, stopping at Yenikapı, Sirkeci and Üsküdar en route and connecting with the M4 metro running between Kadıköy and Kartal. A small number of İstanbullus refuse to use this tunnel link, believing that safety standards were compromised during its construction so as to expedite its opening.

TAXI

İstanbul is full of yellow taxis. Some drivers are lunatics, others are con artists; most are neither. If you're caught with the first category and you're about to go into meltdown, say '*yavaş!*' (slow down!). Drivers in the con-artist category tend to prey on tourists. All taxis have digital meters and must run them, but some of these drivers ask for a flat fare, or pretend the meter doesn't work so they can gouge you at the end of the trip. The best way to counter this is to tell them no meter, no ride. Avoid the taxis waiting for fares near Aya Sofya Meydanı – we have received reports of rip-offs.

Taxi fares are very reasonable and rates are the same during both day and night. It costs around ₺15 to travel between Beyoğlu and Sultanahmet.

Few taxis have seat belts. If you take a taxi from the European side of the city to the Asian side over one of the Bosphorus bridges, it is your responsibility to cover the toll (₺4.75). The driver will add this to your fare. There is no toll when crossing from Asia to Europe.

TRAM

An excellent *tramvay* (tramway) service runs from Bağcılar, in the city's west, to Zeytinburnu (where it connects with the metro from the airport) and on to Sultanahmet and Eminönü. It then crosses the Galata Bridge to Karaköy (to connect with the Tünel) and Kabataş (to connect with the funicular to Taksim Meydanı). A second service runs from Cevizlibağ, closer to Sultanahmet on the same line, through to Kabataş. Both services run every five minutes from 6am to midnight. The fare is ₺4; *jetons* are available from machines on every tram stop and İstanbulkarts can be used.

A small antique tram travels the length of İstiklal Caddesi in Beyoğlu from a stop near Tünel Meydanı to Taksim Meydanı (7am to 10.20pm). Electronic tickets (₺4) can be purchased from the ticket office at the Tünel funicular, and İstanbulkarts can be used.

Another small tram line follows a loop through Kadıköy and the neighbouring suburb of Moda every 10 minutes between 6.55am and 9.20pm. *Jetons* cost ₺4 and İstanbulkarts can be used.

AROUND İSTANBUL

Princes' Islands

Most İstanbullus refer to the Princes' Islands as 'The Islands' (Adalar). Lying 20km southeast of the city in the Sea of Marmara, the islands are a popular destination for a day escape from the city but are oppressively crowded between May and October, when visitors can number up to 50,000 per day on weekends. Five of the nine islands in the group are populated, but most visitors head to the two largest, Büyükada and Heybeliada.

The islands have been populated since the 4th century BC, acquiring their present name in the 6th century AD after coming into the possession of the Byzantine prince, Justin. The first Greek Orthodox monastery was established in 846 and regular ferry services from İstanbul began in 1846. Wealthy İstanbullus then began to purchase holiday villas here. Büyükada and Burgaza were popular with families of Greek and Jewish heritage; Heybeliada was predominantly Greek.

Around İstanbul

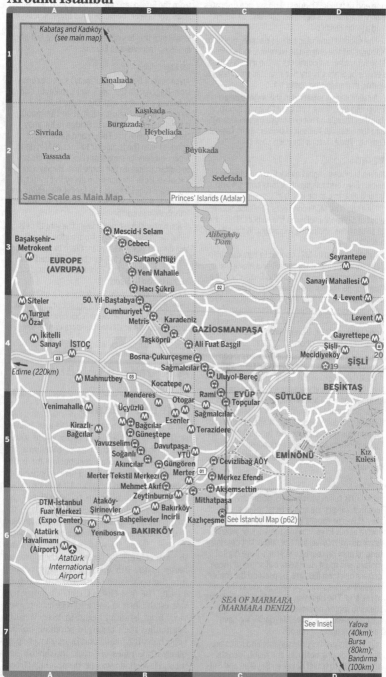

Kabataş and Kadıköy
(see main map)

Kınalıada

Kaşıkada
Burgazada   Heybeliada

Sivriada

Yassıada

Büyükada

Sedefada

Same Scale as Main Map

Princes' Islands (Adalar)

Başakşehir–
Metrokent

Mescid-i Selam

Cebeci

EUROPE
(AVRUPA)

Sultançiftliği

Yeni Mahalle

Hacı Şükrü

Alibeyköy
Dam

Seyrantepe

Sanayi Mahallesi

Siteler

Turgut
Özal

İkitelli
Sanayi

İSTOÇ

50. Yıl-Baştabya
Cumhuriyet
Metris

Karadeniz

GAZİOSMANPAŞA

Taşköprü

Ali Fuat Başgil

4. Levent

Levent

Gayrettepe

Şişli-
Mecidiyeköy

Bosna-Çukurçeşme

Edirne (220km)

Mahmutbey

Sağmalcılar

Uluyol-Bereç

Kocatepe

Menderes

Otogar

Rami

Topçular

SİŞLİ
20

ŞİŞLİ

BEŞİKTAŞ

SÜTLÜCE

Yenimahalle

Üçyüzlü

Bağcılar

Esenler

Sağmalcılar

Terazidere

EYÜP

Kirazlı-
Bağcılar

Güneştepe

Yavuzselim

Davutpaşa-
YTÜ

Soğanlı

Akıncılar

Güngören

Merter

Cevizlibağ AÖY

Merkez Efendi

EMİNÖNÜ

Kız
Kulesi

Merter Tekstil Merkezi

Mehmet Akıf

Zeytinburnu

Aksemsettin

Mithatpaşa

DTM-İstanbul
Fuar Merkezi
(Expo Center)

Ataköy-
Şirinevler

Bahçelievler

Bakırköy-
İncirli

Kazlıçeşme

See İstanbul Map (p62)

Atatürk
Havalimanı
(Airport)

Yenibosna

BAKIRKÖY

Atatürk
International
Airport

SEA OF MARMARA
(MARMARA DENİZİ)

See Inset

Yalova
(40km);
Bursa
(80km);
Bandırma
(100km)

Around İstanbul

The islands are best visited in the warmer months. Many restaurants and most hotels are closed between November and April; and ferry services are occasionally cancelled due to poor weather, resulting in visitors being stranded overnight without accommodation.

Adalar Belediyesi (Princes' Islands Municipality; ☑ 0216-382 3382; www.adalar.bel.tr; ⛴ from Kabataş) Has an English-language website that includes tourist information and *fayton* (horse-drawn carriage) prices.

❶ Getting There & Away

On summer weekends, board the ferry and grab a seat at least half an hour before departure time unless you want to stand the whole way. From the right side of the ferry you can view the various islands en route. Heading towards the Sea of Marmara, passengers are treated to fine views of Topkapı Palace, Aya Sofya and the Blue Mosque on the right and Kız Kulesi, Haydarpaşa train station and the distinctive minaret-style clock towers of Marmara University on the left. After a quick stop at Kadıköy, the ferry makes its way to the first island in the group, Kınalıada (30 minutes), then to Burgazada (15 minutes), to Heybeliada (15 minutes), the second-largest island, and to Büyükada (10 minutes), the largest island in the group.

Be sure to check the websites of all companies as schedules and routes change regularly.

Dentur Avrasya (p104) Operates regular small ferries stopping at Büyükada and Heybeliada (₺6); these leave from the dock behind the gas station at Kabataş.

İDO (☑ 0850-222 4436; www.ido.com.tr) Offer two daily fast catamaran ferry services from Kabataş (₺11 *jeton* or ₺8.60 on İstanbulkart).

Istanbul Şehir Hatları (p104) Runs at least eight ferry services daily to the islands from 6.50am to 11pm (to 9pm June to mid-September) from Kabataş. These depart from the Adalar İskelesi (Adalar Ferry Dock). The most useful departure times for day trippers are 8.40am and 10.40am (8.30am, 9.30am and 10.30am from June to mid-September). The trip costs ₺5.50 (₺4.40 with an İstanbulkart) to the islands and the same for each leg between the islands and for the return trip. Ferries return to İstanbul every two hours or so. Last ferries leave Büyükada at 6.15pm and 8.20pm and Heybeliada at 6.30pm and 8.35pm (9.15pm and 10.15pm from Büyükada and 9.30pm and 10.30pm from June to mid-September).

Turyol (☑ 0212-251 4421; http://turyol.com) Operates small ferry services between three and five times per day from both Karaköy and Eminönü to Büyükada (₺6).

❶ Getting Around

One of the wonderful things about the Princes' Islands is that they are car-free zones. The main forms of transport are motorised carts, bicycles and *faytons* (horse-drawn carriages). The name *fayton* comes from the mythical Phaeton, son of the sun god Helios.

Heybeliada

Heybeliada (Heybeli for short) is the prettiest island in the Adalar group, replete with ornate 19th-century timber villas and offering gorgeous sea views from myriad viewpoints. It's extremely popular with day trippers from İstanbul, who flock here on weekends to walk in the pine groves and swim from the tiny, and usually crowded, beaches. The island's major landmarks are the hilltop Hagia Triada Monastery, which is perched above a picturesque line of poplar trees in a spot that has been occupied by a Greek monastery since Byzantine times, and

the Deniz Lisesi (Turkish Navel Academy), which was founded in 1824 and which you'll see to the left of the ferry dock as you arrive.

The delightful walk from the *iskele* (ferry dock) up to the Merit Halki Palace hotel at the top of Refah Şehitleri Caddesi passes a host of large wooden villas set in lovingly tended gardens. Many laneways and streets lead to picnic spots and lookout points.

Perched above a picturesque line of poplar trees in a spot that has been occupied by a Greek monastery since Byzantine times, **Hagia Triada Monastery** (Aya Triada; ☑ 0216-351 8563; Ümit Tepesi; ☺ daily by appointment; ⓢ Heybeliada) is an 1844 complex that housed a Greek Orthodox theological school until 1971, when it was closed on the government's orders; the Ecumenical Orthodox Patriarchate is waging an ongoing campaign to have it reopened. There's a small church with an ornate altar and an internationally renowned library that houses many old and rare manuscripts.

🛏 Sleeping & Eating

Heybeliada has only a few hotels, with the best being the upmarket **Merit Halki Palace** (☑ 0216-351 0025; www.merithotels.com; Refah Şehitleri Caddesi 94; @ 🗟 🕿 ; ⓢ Heybeliada).

Heyamola Ada Lokantası TURKISH $$
(☑ 0216-351 1111; www.heyamolaadalokantasi.com; Mavi Marmara Yalı Caddesi 30b; mezes ₺10-22, salads ₺10-14, mains ₺22-40; ☺ 9am-11pm, closed Mon Nov-Apr; ⓢ Heybeliada) Opposite the İDO ferry dock, this busy place wows customers with a generous array of vegetable, yoghurt and seafood mezes. Those unsure of what to order can rely on the mixed meze plates (small/large ₺30/50) followed by a couple of hot seafood dishes. In summer there's sometimes live music on weekend nights.

❶ Getting Around

Bicycles are available for rent in several of the town's shops (per hour/day ₺10/30). The *fayton* stand is on Araba Meydanı behind the Atatürk statue. Hire one for a one-hour tour of the island (*büyük turu*, ₺63) or a 25-minute tour (*küçük turu*, ₺50).

Büyükada

The largest island in the Adalar group, Büyükada (Great Island) is impressive viewed from the ferry: gingerbread villas climb up the slopes of the hill and the bulbous twin cupolas of the Splendid Palas

Hotel provide an unmistakable landmark. There's plenty to keep visitors occupied for a full day, with an excellent museum showcasing every aspect of island life, streets dotted with handsome 19th-century timber villas, heavily wooded pine forests with walking tracks, a spectacularly located Greek Orthodox monastery and a number of clean beaches.

You'll disembark the ferry at the island's attractive Ottoman Revival–style *iskele* (ferry dock) building, which dates from 1915 and features attractive Kütahya tiles. The museum, monastery, forests and beaches are a pleasant, although often uphill, walk or a short *fayton* (horse-drawn carriage) ride away.

Sights & Activities

Büyükada has some good swimming beaches, but you'll need to pay for the privilege of using them. Try Nakibey, Yörükali and Viranbağ, where you'll pay between ₺20 and ₺40 per day per person (this will include use of a sun lounge and umbrella).

Museum of the Princes' Islands   MUSEUM
(Adalar Müzesi; ☎0216-382 6430; www.adalar-muzesi.org; Yılmaz Türk Caddesi; adult/student ₺5/3, Wed free; ⊙9am-6pm Tue-Sun Apr-Oct, to 5pm Nov-Mar; ⊠Büyükada) Relegated to an isolated site next to Aya Nikola Beach on the southeastern side of the island, this excellent museum is often overlooked by visitors but we highly recommend making the effort to get here. Multimedia exhibits focus on the history and culture of the Adalar and cover every aspect of island life, including geology, flora, religious heritage, food, architecture, music, festivals and literature. Interpretative panels and videos are in both Turkish and English, and there are objects galore to admire.

Church and Monastery of St George   MONASTERY
(Aya Yorgi Kilise ve Manastırı; ⊠Büyükada) There's not a lot to see at this Greek Orthodox monastery complex located on a 203m-high hill known as Yücetepe, but the panoramic views from the monastery terrace make the hour-long trek worthwhile. A small and gaudy church is the only building of note, so most visitors spend their time at the pleasant Yücetepe Kır Gazinosu restaurant. Its outdoor tables have views to İstanbul and the nearby islands of Yassıada and Sivriada.

Sleeping & Eating

You'll need to book ahead if you want to stay overnight in summer. Both the heritage-listed Splendid Palas Hotel (☎0216-382 6950; www.splendidhotel.net; 23 Nisan Caddesi 53; r €145, with sea views €175-200; ⊛⊜⊠; ⊠Büyükada) and the More Guesthouse (☎0507 792 9500; http://morecafepansiyon.com; Malul Gazi Caddesi 2; r with/without bathroom €100/90, ste €130; ⊛⊜⊠; ⊠Büyükada) in Büyükada are open year-round.

Yücetepe Kır Gazinosu Restaurant   TURKISH $
(☎0216-382 1333; Monastery of St George; mains ₺14-20; ⊙daily Apr-Oct, Sat & Sun only Nov-Mar) This simple place has benches and chairs on a terrace overlooking the sea and İstanbul. Dishes are simple but good – the *köfte* (meatballs) are particularly tasty. You can also enjoy a beer or glass of tea here. It's at the very top of the hill where the Monastery of St George is located.

Teras Restaurant   TURKISH $$
(Eskibağ Teras; ☎0535 521 2724; Halık Koyu Beach; brunch ₺35, mains from ₺30; ⊙10am-11pm; ⊞; ⊠Büyükada) Overlooking Büyükada's longest beach, Teras is a fabulous spot for a leisurely year-round weekend brunch or summer dinner (arrive before sunset). Brunch includes favourites such as *menemen* (scrambled eggs with peppers, tomatoes and sometimes cheese) and *börek* (filled pastry); dinner features spit-roast lamb and ultra-fresh fish. It's a five-minute walk from Luna Park (take the road near the donkey park); a *fayton* costs ₺45.

Prinkipo   MEYHANE $$$
(☎0216-382 3591; Gülistan Caddesi 11; set menu incl alcohol ₺125; ⊙11am-midnight; ⊠Büyükada) Operated by local character Fıstık Ahmet, this long-standing favourite near the port is known for its excellent mezes and lavish pourings of alcohol (it's not the type of place that will appeal to teetotallers). Bookings essential during summer, especially on Friday and Saturday nights when there is live music.

Getting Around

Bicycles are available for rent in several of the town's shops (per hour/day ₺10 /30), and shops on the market street can provide picnic supplies. The *fayton* stand is to the left of the clock tower. Hire one for a 70-minute tour of the town, hills and shore (*büyük turu*, ₺95) or a shorter tour (*küçük turu*, ₺80). It costs ₺35 to the Museum of the Princes' Islands.

Thrace & Marmara

Best Places to Eat

➡ Barba Yorgo Taverna (p174)

➡ Kilye Suvla Lokanta (p161)

➡ Mustafanın Kayfesi (p173)

➡ Sardalya (p165)

➡ Umurbey Winehouse (p153)

Best Places to Sleep

➡ Anemos Hotel (p173)

➡ Hotel Casa Villa (p161)

➡ Gallipoli Houses (p161)

➡ Limon Hostel (p150)

➡ Son Vapur Konuk Evi (p172)

Why Go?

Grand narratives have unfolded in this corner of Turkey for millenniums, leaving an extraordinary archaeological site (Troy), a city of Ottoman buildings (Edirne), historically significant battlefields (Gallipoli) and a culturally fascinating and physically beautiful island outpost (Gökçeada) for visitors to explore. It was here that Alexander the Great crossed the Hellespont on his conquering march to Persia, and where the Achaeans (Greeks) and Trojans fought the war immortalised by Homer in the *Iliad*. Mehmet II launched his campaign to conquer Constantinople from the Ottoman capital of Edirne, and nearly 500 years later Allied forces landed on the Gallipoli (Gelibolu) Peninsula, triggering a bloody stand-off with Turkish troops that would drag on for nine long months and help to define the modern nations of Turkey, Australia and New Zealand. History continues to echo, but there is an increasingly contemporary verve in the student bars of Çanakkale and the vineyards of Thrace.

When to Go
Edirne

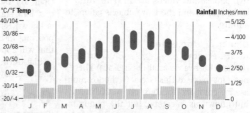

Apr & May
Multicoloured wildflowers carpet hillsides on the Gallipoli Peninsula.

May & Jun
Organic black cherries and semi-deserted beaches on Gökçeada island.

Aug Locals party on Çanakkale's waterfront during the Troia Festival.

EDIRNE

☎ 0284 / POP 173,000

Capital of the Ottoman empire before Mehmet II conquered Constantinople, Edirne is blessed with imperial building stock, a notable culinary heritage and a lingering and much-cherished sense of civic grandeur. Close to the Greek and Bulgarian borders, the city has a European flavour that is best appreciated in summer, when locals party on the banks of the Tunca and Meriç Rivers and cheer on the contestants at the world-famous Kırkpınar oil-wrestling festival (p149).

History

Emperor Hadrian made Hadrianopolis (later Adrianople) the main centre of Roman Thrace in the early 2nd century AD. In the

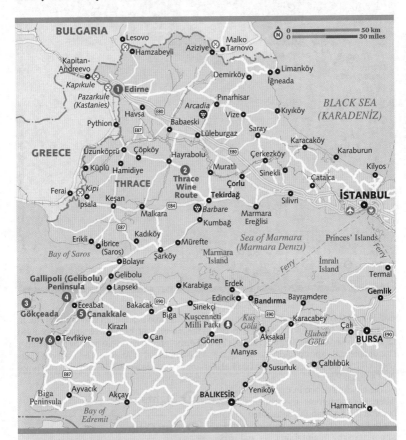

Thrace & Marmara Highlights

❶ Selimiye Mosque (p146) Visiting this exquisite World Heritage–listed building in the former Ottoman capital of Edirne.

❷ Thrace Wine Route (p153) Sampling local wine and food at vineyards among stunning scenery.

❸ Gökçeada (p171) Investigating the fascinating Greek heritage and windswept landscape on this Aegean island.

❹ Gallipoli (Gelibolu) Peninsula (p153) Walking in the footsteps of WWI soldiers and contemplating the horrors of war.

❺ Çanakkale (p164) Lazing away an afternoon while admiring the view over the Dardanelles at a waterfront çay bahçesi (tea garden).

❻ Ruins of Troy (p170) Exploring the many layers of ancient history at this ancient archaeological site.

Edirne

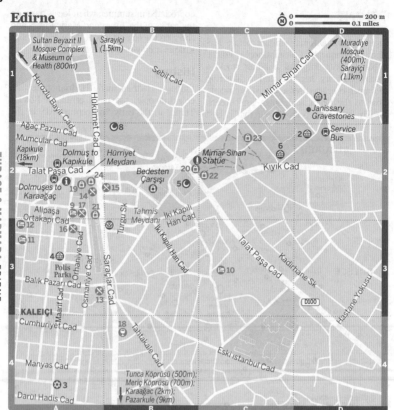

N 0 — 200 m
0 — 0.1 miles

mid-14th century the nascent Ottoman state began to grow in size and power, and in 1363 its army crossed the Dardanelles, skirted Constantinople and captured Adrianople, renaming it Edirne and making it the third capital of the Ottoman Empire.

The city functioned in this role until 1453, when Constantinople was conquered and became the new capital. Subsequent sultans continued to acknowledge Edirne's historical importance by maintaining its industries and preserving its buildings. It was briefly occupied by imperial Russian troops in 1829, during the Greek War of Independence, and in 1878, during the Russo-Turkish War of 1877–78, but remained relatively unscathed by these events. Its role as a fortress defending Ottoman Constantinople and eastern Thrace during the Balkan Wars of 1912–13 was more significant, and it suffered heavy losses of life and property at this time.

When the Ottoman Empire collapsed after WWI, the Allies handed Thrace to the Greeks and declared İstanbul an international city. In the summer of 1920 Greek armies occupied Edirne, only to be driven back by forces under the command of Atatürk. The Treaty of Lausanne (1923) ceded Edirne and eastern Thrace to the Turks.

⊙ Sights

⊙ City Centre

Selimiye Mosque MOSQUE
(Selimiye Camii; Map p146) Of all the achievements of Ottoman architect Mimar Koca Sinan (1497–1588), whose best-known buildings adorn İstanbul's skyline and include the magnificent Süleymaniye Mosque, this exquisite mosque is believed by many to be the greatest. Built between 1569 and 1575 by order of Sultan Selim II at Edirne's highest point, the mosque features four striking 71m-high minarets and was positioned in the centre of an extensive *külliye* (mosque complex), which

Edirne

THRACE & MARMARA EDIRNE

included a *medrese* (Islamic school of higher studies), *darül Hadis* (Hadith school) and *arasta* (arcade of shops).

The main entrance is through the western courtyard, home to a lovely marble *şadırvan* (ablution fountain). Inside, the broad, lofty dome – at 31.3m, marginally wider than that of İstanbul's Aya Sofya – is supported by eight pillars, arches and external buttresses, creating a surprisingly spacious interior. As they only bear a portion of the dome's weight, the walls are sound enough to hold dozens of windows, the light from which brings out the interior's colourful calligraphic decorations.

Unesco added the mosque and its *külliye* to its World Heritage list in 2011.

Grand Synagogue of Edirne   SYNAGOGUE
(Map p146; Maarif Caddesi 75) FREE Reopened after a 36-year closure and a five-year US$2.5 million restoration project, Edirne's Grand Synagogue is the sole reminder of when a community of more than 20,000 Sephardic Jews lived in the city. Built in 1906 to replace 13 smaller synagogues destroyed in the Great Fire of Edirne in 1903, the elegant building features a delicately hued arched roof and beautifully tiled floors.

When the synagogue was first constructed it could house up to 1200 worshippers. Its vibrant yellow exterior now shines amid the fading wooden houses and boxy apartment buildings of Edirne's former Jewish Quarter. Edirne's Jewish population now numbers in single figures, but the synagogue has been consecrated for religious purposes in addition to being considered a museum.

Edirne Turkish & Islamic Art Museum   MUSEUM
(Edirne Türk-İslam Eserleri Müzesi; Map p146; ☑0284-225 5748; Selimiye Mosque; ₺5; ⊙9am-5pm) The small rooms of the elegant *darül Hadis* (Hadith school) in the northeastern corner of the Selimiye Mosque's courtyard house an eclectic collection of Ottoman-era artefacts, including calligraphy, weaponry, glass, woodwork, ceramics, costumes and jewellery. Some of the rooms feature mannequins in ethnographic-style displays; our favourite is the Circumcision Room (check out the look on the young boy's face!). The handsome Tekke Works Room displays Dervish-related Korans, prayer rugs and musical instruments.

Selimiye Foundation Museum   MUSEUM
(Selimiye Vakıf Müzesi; Map p146; ☑0284-212 1133; Selimiye Mosque complex; ⊙9am-5pm Tue-Sun) FREE This museum is housed in a handsome building in the Selimye Mosque's *külliye* (mosque complex; in a *medrese* in the southeastern corner of the courtyard). It showcases a collection of art and artefacts drawn from mosques and religious buildings in and around Edirne.

Edirne Archaeology & Ethnography Museum   MUSEUM
(Edirne Arkeoloji ve Etnografya Müzesi; Map p146; ☑0284-225 1120; Kadır Paşa Mektep Sokak 7; ₺5; ⊙9am-5.30pm) This museum has two sections: one archaeological and the other ethnographic. Archaeological highlights include Thracian funerary steles. The ethnographic section showcases carpets, embroidery, textiles, calligraphy and jewellery; don't miss the objects decorated in the Edirnekâri style,

a lacquering technique developed locally during the Ottoman era. The museum is located behind the Selimiye Mosque.

Üç Şerefeli Mosque MOSQUE

(Üç Şerefeli Cami; Map p146; Hükümet Caddesi) Edirne's *merkez* (town centre) is visually dominated by this mosque, which was built by order of Sultan Murat II between 1437 and 1447 and has four strikingly different minarets. Its name refers to the *üc şerefeli* (three balconies) on the tallest minaret; the second tallest has two balconies and the remaining two have one balcony each.

Old Mosque MOSQUE

(Eski Camii; Map p146; Muaffıklarhane Sokak) Though not as prominent on Edirne's skyline as the Selimiye and Üç Şerefeli Mosques, the Eski (Old) Mosque is an important landmark in the city and has a large and loyal local congregation. Built between 1403 and 1414, it is the oldest of the city's imperial mosques and features a square, fortress-like form and an arcaded portico topped with a series of small domes. Inside, there are huge calligraphic inscriptions on the walls.

The mosque originally had an extensive *külliye* (mosque complex), but today only its handsome *bedesten* (covered bazaar) remains. This comprises 36 strongrooms covered by 14 domes in two rows of seven. The *bedesten* was the centre of commercial activity in Edirne in the 15th century and the strongrooms were needed to secure valuable goods including jewellery, armour and carpets. Today its stores sell merchandise that is considerably less impressive.

Kaleiçi HISTORIC SITE

Roughly translated, *kaleiçi* means 'inside the castle'. In Edirne it is used to describe the old streets to the south of Talat Paşa Caddesi and west of Saraçlar Caddesi. Dating from the medieval period, this is the heart of the old city and it retains a number of ornately decorated timber houses dating from the 18th, 19th and early 20th centuries, as well as a couple of handsome stone civic buildings.

When exploring, look out for the **Kırkpınar Evi** (Kırkpınar House; Map p146; ☑ 0284-212 8622; www.kirkpinar.org; Maarif Caddesi; ⊙ 10am-noon & 2-6pm) opposite Polis Parkı (Police Park). Its collection of memorabilia associated with oil wrestling is drab, but the building itself is a good example of Edirne's traditional houses. Some of these have undergone recent restoration (the Mihran Hanım Konağı in Gazipaşa Caddesi is a good example), but many are in a

sad state of disrepair. Other interesting buildings include the police station in Maarif Caddesi and the recently restored Great Synagogue on Manyas Caddesi, which was built in 1906 and has now been reopened to the public.

Muradiye Mosque MOSQUE

(Muradiye Camii; Mimar Sinan Caddesi) Built for Sultan Murat II between 1426 and 1436, this mosque interestingly once housed a Mevlevi (whirling dervish) lodge. The mosque's T-shaped plan has twin *eyvans* (vaulted halls), an unusual cupola, fine İznik tiles covering the interior walls and striking calligraphy on the exterior. It's an easy 15-minute walk northeast of Selimiye Mosque.

⊙ North of the Centre

Sultan Beyazıt II Mosque Complex MOSQUE

(Beyazıt II Camii ve Külliyesi; Beyazıt Caddesi, Yıldırım Beyazıt Mahallesi) Standing in splendid isolation on the banks of the Tunca River, this complex was commissioned by Sultan Beyazıt II and built between 1484 and 1488. The mosque's design lies between two other Edirne mosques: its prayer hall has one large dome, similar to the Selimiye, but it also has a courtyard and fountain like the Üç Şerefeli. The *külliye* (mosque complex) includes a *tabhane* (hostel), *tımarhane* (asylum), *tip medresesi* (medical school) and *darüşşifa* (hospital).

The complex is a 10-minute taxi ride (₺15) from the centre or a longish but pleasant walk down Horozlu Bayır Sokak and across the Yalnıgöz and Sultan Beyazıt II Bridges. The Yalnıgöz (Lonely Arch, or Lone Eye) dates from 1570 and was designed by Mimar Sinan; the Beyazıt II dates from 1488. Alternatively, dolmuşes (minibuses; ₺2.50) to Yenimaret ('Y. Maret') leaving from opposite the tourist office pass the complex.

Museum of Health MUSEUM

(Sağlık Müzesi; ☑ 0284-224 0922; www.saglik muzesi-en.trakya.edu.tr; Sultan Beyazıt II mosque complex, Beyazıt Caddesi, Yıldırım Beyazıt Mahallesi; ₺5; ⊙ 9am-5.30pm) The extremely beautiful *darüşşifa* (hospital) and *tip medresesi* (medical school) in the Sultan Beyazıt II mosque complex now house this museum tracing the history of Islamic medicine. Overseen by Trakya Üniversitesi, the museum highlights innovative treatments developed and utilised in the hospital and medical school here from 1488 to 1909. Mannequins dressed as Ottoman-era doctors, patients and medical students are used in scenes illustrating various medical procedures, and interpretative panels explain the connection between the hospital's physical design and treatments.

Sarayiçi
HISTORIC SITE

It was here, in the 15th century, that Sultan Murat II built the Eski Sarayı (Old Palace). Little remains of this grand structure, which was blown up just before the Russo-Turkish War of 1877–78 to prevent the Russians capturing weapons stored inside. Fortunately, the kitchens where Ottoman palace cuisine was developed have been rebuilt and today an area that was once the sultans' private hunting reserve is home to a modern stadium where the famous Kırkpınar oil-wrestling festival is held.

Near the stadium, which is flanked by bronze sculptures of wrestling *başpehlivan* (champions), stands the Adalet Kasrı (Justice Hall; 1561), a stone tower with a conical roof that dates from the time of Süleyman the Magnificent (r 1520-66). In front of it are two square columns: on the Seng-i Hürmet (Stone of Respect) to the right, people would place petitions to the sultan, while the Seng-i İbret (Stone of Warning) on the left displayed the heads of high-court officers who had managed to anger the sultan.

Behind the Adalet Kasrı is the small Fatih Köprüsü (Conqueror Bridge; 1452). Across it and on the right is a sombre Balkan Wars memorial; straight ahead and to the left are the scattered ruins of the Eski Sarayı.

To get here, walk north along Hükümet Caddesi and cross the Tunca River on Saraçhane Köprüsü (Saddler's Bridge; 1451); or head north on Mimar Sinan Caddesi and Saray Yolu, and cross the river on Kanumi/Saray Köprüsü (Kanumi/Palace Bridge), which was designed by Mimar Sinan in 1560. Alternatively, it's a scenic 1km walk along the road to the north of the river from the Sultan Beyazıt II mosque complex.

☉ South of the Centre

In fine weather, the social scene in Edirne moves to the banks of the Tunca and Meriç Rivers, a 20- to 25-minute walk from the tourist office on Hürriyet Meydanı. To join the party, follow Saraçlar Caddesi past the stadium and cross the Tunca Köprüsü, an Ottoman stone humpback bridge dating back to 1615, and then the longer and extremely graceful Meriç Köprüsü, built in 1847.

Other options to detour south of the river include in a phaeton (horse-drawn carriage), or by renting a bicycle for a few hours. Both are available at the southern end of Saraçlar Caddesi, Edirne's pedestrians-only main shopping street.

THRACE & MARMARA EDIRNE

KIRKPINAR OIL-WRESTLING FESTIVAL

The testosterone-charged Tarihi Kırkpınar Yağlı Güreş Festivali (Historic Kırkpınar Oil-Wrestling Festival; http://kirkpinar.org; ☉ Jun or Jul) is famous throughout Turkey and attracts enormous crowds to Edirne for one week in late June or early July every year.

The crowds come to cheer on muscular men skimpily clad in *kispet* (tight leather shorts) and lathered in olive oil, who attempt to wrestle their opponents to the ground or to lift them above their shoulders. And no, this is not a headline event on the international gay festival circuit – it's serious, ultra-macho sport, Turkish style.

According to local legend, the festival's origins go back to 1363, when the Ottoman sultan Orhan Gazi sent his brother Süleyman Paşa along with 40 men to conquer the Byzantine fortress at Domuz. The soldiers were all keen wrestlers, and after their victory they challenged each other to bouts. Two of them were so evenly matched that they fought for days without any clear result, until both of them finally dropped dead. When the bodies were buried under a nearby fig tree, a spring mysteriously appeared. The site was given the name Kırkpınar (40 Springs), in the wrestlers' honour.

The annual three-day contest has been held in Sarayiçi on the outskirts of Edirne since the birth of the republic, and is now preceded by four days of wrestling-themed festivities. Wrestlers, who are classed not by weight but by height, age and experience, compete in 13 categories – from *minik* (toddler) to *baş* (first class) – and dozens of matches take place simultaneously in the Sarayiçi stadium. Bouts are now capped at 30 or 40 minutes, after which they enter 'sudden death' one-fall-wins overtime. When all the fights are decided, prizes are awarded for conduct and technique, as well as the coveted and hotly contested *başpehlivan* (head wrestler) title.

Entry to the first day of the wrestling is free; tickets are required for the next two. There's a ticket box at the venue, or you can purchase tickets from Biletix (www.biletix.com). Note that accommodation in and around the city over this week fills up fast.

🛏 Sleeping

★ Limon Hostel
HOSTEL $

(Map p146; ☑ 0284-214 5577; www.facebook.
com/limonhostel; Türkocağı Arka Sokak 14; r per
person ₺20; ✳ 🛜) Simple but spotless shared
rooms are enlivened by colourful arty decor
at this recent opening a short walk from
good cafes and restaurants. There's not
much English spoken, but the friendly owners are super keen to make guests welcome.
The sheltered inner courtyard – dotted with
plants and umbrellas – is a great place for
catching up with other travellers.

Sarı Pansiyon
PENSION $

(Map p146; ☑ 0284-212 4080; www.saripansiyon.
com; Mehmet Karagöz Sokak 17; s/d without bathroom ₺45/90; @ 🛜) Named for its daffodil-
yellow exterior, this unassuming place offers
simple rooms with single beds and satellite
TV. Shared bathrooms are clean, with 24-hour
hot water. The location is convenient but is
opposite a school, so it can be noisy in the
morning. Though the owner doesn't speak
English, he will happily use a translation program on his computer to communicate.

Efe Hotel
HOTEL $$

(Map p146; ☑ 0284-213 6080; www.efehotel.com;
Maarif Caddesi 13; s/d ₺100/150; ✳ @ 🛜) A time-
warp feel dominates at this old-timer on busy
(read: noisy) Maarif Caddesi. Rooms have a
nanna-esque decor with worn furniture and
fittings, and the basement bar-restaurant
where breakfast is served has carpet that
must have been fashionable in the 1970s. It's
clean, though, and the English-speaking man-
ager goes out of his way to be helpful.

★ Hotel Edirne Palace
HOTEL $$$

(Map p146; ☑ 0284-214 7474; www.hoteledirne
palace.com; Vavlı Cami Sokak 4; r €50-75; ✳ @ 🛜)
Tucked into the quiet backstreets below the
Old Mosque, this modern business hotel offers comfortable, bright and impeccably clean
rooms with a good range of amenities. The
staff are extremely helpful and breakfast is
better than average, with interesting egg dishes and freshly baked pastries. It's definitely
the best sleeping option in the city centre.

🍴 Eating

The city centre is full of *ciğercisi* (liver restaurants) serving the city's signature dish, *tava
ciğer* (thinly sliced calf's liver deep-fried and
eaten with crispy fried red chillies), usually enjoyed with a chaser of *ayran* (yoghurt
drink). Other local specialities include *badem*
ezmesi (marzipan) and *gaziler helva* (veteran's helva), a rich concoction of butter, flour,
milk, sugar and almonds.

A wide assortment of eateries lie along
Saraçlar and Maarif Caddesis. Most of the
riverside restaurants south of the centre are
open only in summer and are often booked
solid at weekends.

Köfteci Osman
TURKISH $

(Map p146; ☑ 0284-214 1717; www.edirnelikofte
ciosman.com; Saraçlar Caddesi 3; ciğer or köfte ₺15;
⏰ 11am-10pm) Widely recommended by locals
for its tasty *tava ciğer* (thinly sliced calf's liver deep fried and eaten with crispy fried red
chillies) and *köfte* (meatballs), Osman has a
prime location at the top of the city's main pedestrian drag, so it's easy to locate. Efficient
waiters ensure that the indoor and outdoor
tables turn over quickly.

Balıkçım Yasem
SEAFOOD $

(Map p146; ☑ 0284-225 4247; Balık Pazarı Caddesi
9; fish sandwiches ₺5, cooked fish ₺10-15; ⏰ 8am-
9pm) Appropriately located near the fish fountain just off Saraçlar Caddesi, this tiny eatery
next to the city's busiest fishmonger cooks up
fresh catch of the day and serves it to a constant stream of customers. Take away or eat at
one of the five tables on the street.

Niyazi Usta
KEBAP $$

(Map p146; ☑ 0284-213 3372; www.cigerciniyazi
usta.com.tr; Alipaşa Ortakapı Caddesi 5/2; portions/
half-portions ₺16/10; ⏰ 9am-9pm) This bright,
modern and very friendly joint is perhaps the
best place in town to try a *porsyon* (portion)
of *tava ciğer* (thinly sliced calf's liver deep
fried and eaten with crispy fried red chillies).
Wash it down with a glass of *ayran* (yoghurt
drink) or *şalgam* (sour turnip juice).

Balkan Piliç
TURKISH $$

(Map p146; ☑ 0284-225 2155; Saraçlar Caddesi 14;
portions ₺5-14; ⏰ 11am-4pm Mon-Sat) The *piliç*
(chicken) roasting in the window signals the
house speciality at this extremely popular
esnaf lokanta (eatery serving ready-made
food). Order a *porsyon* (portion) with a side
order of *pilav* (plain rice or rice cooked with
bulgur or lentils). Alternatively, choose from
the daily changing array of meat and vegetable stews in the bain-marie.

Patio Cafe & Restaurant
CAFE $$

(Map p146; www.patiocaferestaurant.com; Aziziiye
Sokak 5; mains ₺20-35; ⏰ 8am-10pm) Concealed
behind a narrow doorway, Patio's spacious
inner courtyard is one of Edirne's most

relaxing places to eat and drink. Beer, wine and cocktails complement a menu combining Turkish flavours – try the chargrilled octopus – with international salads and pasta, and if the weather is cooler a roof slides across to enclose the alfresco area. Good freshly squeezed juices too.

Drinking & Nightlife

There are *çay bahçesi* (tea gardens) all over town. The most popular are near the Tunca Köprüsü and Meriç Köprüsü (bridges) south of the centre, in the Polis Parkı on Maarif Caddesi and around the Mimar Sinan statue in the city centre. Most of the bar action is in the northern side streets between Saraçlar and Maarif Caddesis or along the street joining the two bridges.

Çalgılı Meyhane PUB
(Map p146; ☑ 0284-213 8945; Saraçlar Caddesi; ⊙ 9pm-late) A boozy atmosphere, friendly staff and live *halk meziği* (folk music) five days per week are the attractions at this traditional tavern. Basic *meyhane* (pub) food is available, but it's fine to stick with drinks only; a huge tankard of ice-cold Efes costs a mere ₺15. Be sure to tip the musicians before you leave.

Kahverengi BAR
(Map p146; ☑ 0284-214 4210; www.kahverengibistro.com; Orhaniye Caddesi 14; ⊙ 10am-3am) Its laid-back ambience, pleasant outdoor deck and bargain snack-and-beer combo deals make Kahverengi popular with a youthful local clientele. Efes beer is the tipple of choice, but there are also imported beers and robust cocktails on offer. Pretty good music, and Edirne's smattering of hipsters were on board when we dropped by too.

Shopping

Traditional Edirne souvenirs include *meyve sabunu* (fruit-shaped soaps) and *badem ezmesi* (marzipan).

Keçecizade FOOD & DRINKS
(Map p146; ☑ 0284-212 1261; www.kececizade.com; Saraçlar Caddesi 50; ⊙ 9am-8pm) Edirne's residents are particularly partial to sweet treats, as is evident by the huge number of *şekerlemes* (sweet shops) scattered through the city. Keçecizade is one of two popular local chains specialising in *lokum* (Turkish delight) and *badem ezmesi* (Turkish delight), and is a good place to sample both. There's another branch (Map p146; ☑ 0284-225 2681; www.kececizade.com; Belediye Dükkanları (Eski Camii Karşısı) 4; ⊙ 9am-8pm) opposite the Old Mosque.

Arslanzade FOOD & DRINKS
(Map p146; www.arslanzade.com.tr; Belediye Dükkanları (Eski Camii Karşısı) 2; ⊙ 10am-8pm) Arslanzade produces *badem ezmesi* (marzipan) and *lokum* (Turkish delight) but also offers delicious *devâ-i misk helvası* (a sweet made with sugar, egg white and 41 different spices) and *kallavi kurabiye* (biscuit made with pistachio, saffron and honey).

Ali Paşa Covered Bazaar BAZAAR
(Map p146; ⊙ 7am-sunset) Mimar Sinan designed this long and highly atmospheric bazaar in 1569. Inside, Turkuaz (Map p146; ☑ 0284-214 1171; Ali Paşa Çarşısı 125; ⊙ 7am-sunset) is one of the best spots in the city to buy *meyve sabunu* (fruit-shaped soap).

Selimiye Arastası MARKET
(Selimiye Arcade; Map p146; ⊙ sunrise-sunset) Also known as the Kavaflar Arastası (Cobblers' Arcade), this historic market below the Selimiye Mosque was part of the original *külliye* (mosque complex). Shops include branches of Arslanzade and Keçecizade sweets chains.

ℹ Information

Tourist Office (Map p146; ☑ 0284-213 9208; edirnetourisminformation@gmail.com; Hürriyet Meydanı 17; ⊙ 8.30am-noon & 1-5.30pm) Very helpful, with English-language brochures and a city map.

ℹ Getting There & Away

BUS & DOLMUŞ
Edirne's otogar (bus station) is 9km southeast of the centre on the access road to the E80. *Servis* (service) buses provided by the bus companies provide free transfers between the otogar and the city centre for ticketed passengers. From Edirne, the service bus (Map p146) departs from outside the ramshackle *çay bahçesi* on the outer southwest corner of the Selimiye Mosque complex approximately 45 minutes before ticketed departure times. A taxi between the otogar and the city centre costs around ₺35.

Dolmuşes service the city and also travel to the Bulgarian and Greek borders.

Çanakkale (₺40, four hours) At least four buses daily on Truva (www.truvaturizm.com) and Metro (www.metroturizm.com.tr).

İstanbul (₺30, 2¾ hours) Frequent buses to the Büyük Otogar in Esenler on Metro, Ulusoy and Nilüfer. Demand is high, so book ahead.

Kapıkule (₺10, 25 minutes) Dolmuşes run to this Bulgarian border crossing, 18km northwest, from a **stop** (Map p146) near the Şekerbank

WORTH A TRIP

SANCAKLAR CAMII

Cutting-edge architects are rarely given commissions to design religious buildings in modern-day Turkey, and as a result most contemporary mosques are uninspired pastiches of Ottoman-era structures. The extraordinary Sancaklar Camii (Sancaklar Mosque) near Büyükçekmece Lake in Thrace is a notable exception to this rule. Designed by Emre Arolat Architects and built between 2011 and 2012, its most striking feature is a subterranean interior that manages to be theatrical and deeply contemplative at the same time.

To get here, take the O-3 (tolled) and E80 from İstanbul. Before reaching Büyükçekmece, exit towards Alkent. Turn right, pass through the Alkent 200 residences and make your way to the Toskana Vadisi Evleri housing development; the mosque is on the edge of this, opposite the Toskana Çarşısı (Market).

branch opposite the tourist office on Talat Paşa Caddesi.

Pazarkule The nearest Greek border post is 9km southwest of Edirne. Catch a dolmuş to Karaağac (₺4, 15 minutes) from the **stop** (Map p146) on the southern side of Talat Paşa Caddesi near the tourist office and tell the driver that you want to go to Pazarkule.

Sofia, Bulgaria (₺30 to ₺65, 5½ to 6½ hours) Five services daily on Metro Turizm.

TRAIN

Edirne train station is 4km southeast of the Eski Cami and is known as Kapıkule in schedules. To get to the station from the centre, dolmuşes and city buses travel southeast on Talat Paşa Caddesi (including bus 3). Get off near the Migros Supermarket and walk down İstasyon Caddesi. A taxi costs around ₺15.

İstanbul

At the time of writing, track work was being undertaken on the Edirne to İstanbul section and connecting bus transfers were being utilised. Check under 'International Trains' on www.tcdd.gov.tr for the latest update.

Europe

The *Bosfor Ekspresi* leaves Edirne at 2.52am for Bucharest (Romania) travelling via Sofia and Plovdiv in Bulgaria en route.

TEKİRDAĞ

📞 0282 / POP 183,000

Overlooking an attractive bay on the northern shore of the Sea of Marmara, Tekirdağ features a bustling waterfront area complete with parks, playgrounds and *çay bahçesi*. Though definitely not worth a trip in itself, the waterfront and a scattering of timber houses dating from the 18th century make the town a reasonable pit stop en route to/from Greece or the Gallipoli Peninsula.

👁 Sights

Tekirdağ Archaeological & Ethnographic Museum MUSEUM
(Tekirdağ Arkeoloji ve Etnografya Müzesi; 📞 0282-261 2082; Rakoczi Caddesi 1; ⊙ 9am-5pm Tue-Sun) **FREE** Housed in the Tekirdağ Vali Konağı (Governor's Mansion), a fine Ottoman Revival–style building dating from 1927, this modest museum gives a fascinating glimpse into the history of Thrace. The most striking exhibit is the setting of marble furniture and silver plates from the Naip tumulus (burial mound) dating back to the late 4th century BC; this would have formed a celebratory setting for the serving of wine.

To get here from the tourist office, walk west along the waterfront for about 1km, cross Atatürk Bulvarı and walk up the steep flight of stairs to Vali Konağı Caddesi. The museum is to the right.

Rákóczi Museum MUSEUM
(Rakoczi Müzesi; 📞 0282-263 8577; Hikmet Çevik Sokak 21; ₺3; ⊙ 9am-noon & 1-5pm Tue-Sun) This house museum is a shrine to Prince Ferenc (Francis) II Rákóczi (1676–1735), who led the first Hungarian uprising against the Habsburgs between 1703 and 1711. Forced into exile, the Transylvanian was given asylum by Sultan Ahmet III in 1720 and lived in this pretty 18th-century timber *konak* (mansion) for a number of years. The *konak's* interior fittings are good-quality reproductions, as the originals were returned to Kassa in Hungary (now Košice in Slovakia). Displays include portraits, weapons and letters.

The museum is west of the Tekirdağ Archaeological & Ethnographic Museum, on the opposite side of the road.

🛏 Sleeping & Eating

The row of restaurants opposite the waterfront serve the city's famous *Tekirdağ köftesi* (bullet-shaped *köfte* served with a spicy red sauce).

Golden Yat Hotel   HOTEL $$
(☑0282-261 1054; www.goldenyat.com; Yalı Caddesi 21; s ₺110-130, d ₺150-170; ❄ 🔊) This 1970s-era block opposite the waterfront claims three-star status but is looking increasingly worn each time we visit. Front rooms can be noisy, but the quieter and slightly cheaper options at the rear are smaller and darker. The best hotel in town.

★ Umurbey Winehouse   TAPAS, TURKISH $$$
(☑0282-260 1379; www.umurbeyvineyards.com; Atatürk Bulvarı; tapas ₺8-17, mains ₺16-30; ⊙3pm-midnight) This eatery near the ocean-front in Tekirdağ belongs to Umurbey Vine-yards. Located around 800m down the hill from the bus station, the main focus of the menu is shared tapas – try the tasting plate (₺17) or the local cheeses (₺25) – and tasty pasta, grilled meat and salmon.

Wine flights (from ₺15 to ₺20) sampling Umurbey's cabernet, merlot and sauvignon blanc varietals are available, and ask about visiting the rustic Umurbey Şarapları vine-yard, around 16km southwest of Tekirdağ en route to Çanakkale.

Özcanlar   KÖFTE $$
(☑0282-263 4088; www.ozcanlarkofte.com; Liman Karşısı 68, Atatürk Bulvarı; köfte ₺15-30; ⊙10am-10pm) The most popular of various *köfte* (meat-ball) restaurants overlooking the waterfront,

Özcanlar has been serving up a limited range of soups, meat dishes and local desserts since 1953. Tables on the outdoor terrace fill fast, as the cafeteria-style dining room can be noisy.

❶ Getting There & Away

The otogar (bus station) is located 1km northeast of the main waterfront promenade. Arriving by bus from İstanbul (₺17, 2½ hours) or Edirne (₺20, two hours), it's an easy walk down Çiftlikönü Caddesi. Buses to/from Eceabat (₺35, three hours) and Çanakkale (₺30, 3½ hours) travel via both the otogar and the waterfront and can be flagged down along Atatürk Caddesi.

Dolmuşes travel throughout the town and its outlying suburbs. Tickets cost ₺2.50 and can be purchased from the driver.

GALLIPOLI PENINSULA
☑0286

Today, the Gallipoli (Gelibolu) Peninsula battle-fields are protected landscapes covered in pine forests and fringed by beaches and coves. However, the battles fought here in 1915 are still alive in Turkish and foreign memories and hold important places in the Turkish, Australian and New Zealand national narra-tives. Australians and New Zealanders view the peninsula, now protected as the Gallipoli Historical National Park, as a place of pilgrim-age, and visit in their tens of thousands each year; they are outnumbered by Turks who, drawn by the legend of the courageous 57th

---

THRACE WINE ROUTE

Vines have been cultivated in Thrace (Trakya) since ancient times. In his epic poem the *Iliad*, Homer wrote about the honey-sweet black wine produced here. Generations of local farmers have capitalised on the region's rich soil, flat geography and benign climate to grow grapes for wine production.

Inspired by Italy's Strade del Vino (Wine Roads) network, the Thrace Wine Route aims to entice visitors to Thracian vineyards, to enjoy local gastronomy, investigate regional heritage and admire the area's stunning scenery. The route passes through mountains, forests and a variety of micro-climates surrounded by three seas (Sea of Marmara, the Aegean Sea and the Black Sea).

Guided tours of vineyards are offered from the first 'bud breaks' in late April to the harvest in October. Book ahead for tours, vineyard restaurants and on-site accommoda-tion. The highly regarded Arcadia Vineyards, an hour's drive southeast of Edirne, is worth a detour en route to/from İstanbul or the Gallipoli Peninsula.

Many vineyards along the wine route have restaurants and cafes where local wine and food are matched. Both Arcadia (☑0533 514 1490; www.arcadiavineyards.com; ⊙by ap-pointment) and Barbare (☑0212-257 0700; www.barbarewines.com; ⊙by appointment) have worthwhile restaurants, and other vineyards offer summer dining. You'll also find excel-lent food and wine matches at the Umurbey Winehouse in nearby Tekirdağ. Booking ahead at vineyard restaurants is recommended.

Gallipoli (Gelibolu) Peninsula

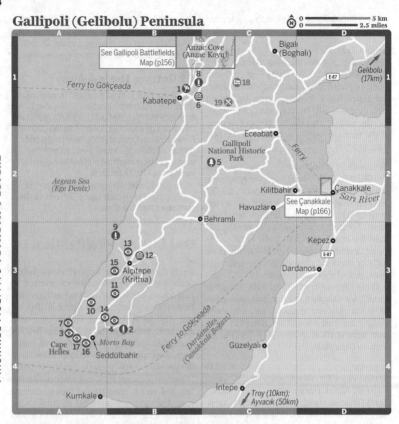

Gallipoli (Gelibolu) Peninsula

regiment and its commander, Mustafa Kemal (the future Atatürk), also travel here in ever-increasing numbers to pay their respects.

The most convenient bases for visiting the battlefields are Eceabat on the western shore of the Dardanelles, and Çanakkale on the eastern shore, accessed via car ferry (25 minutes) from Eceabat; Çanakkale is the more

exciting destination, with better cafes, bars and restaurants. Also worth considering as a base is the unspoiled island of Gökçeada, a 75-minute car-ferry ride from Kabatepe. Very few options exist in the battlefield area itself.

Having your own transport will maximise your opportunities for exploration and is highly recommended. Rental-car options abound in Çanakkale. Alternatively, from Çanakkale or Eceabat you can hire a private guide with transport or join an organised bus tour of the battlefields.

Many tour companies offer one-day tours from İstanbul that involve 10 to 12 hours travel time in a minibus. We do not recommend these as they are exhausting and we have received reports of drivers exceeding speed limits and driving dangerously so as to minimise time on the road.

History

Less than 1500m wide at its narrowest point, the Strait of Çanakkale (Çanakkale Boğazı), better known to English-speakers as the Dardanelles or the Hellespont, has always offered the best opportunity for travellers – and armies – to cross between Europe and Asia Minor.

King Xerxes I of Persia forded the strait with a bridge of boats in 481 BC, as did Alexander the Great a century and a half later. In Byzantine times it was the first line of defence for Constantinople, but by 1402 the strait was under the control of the Ottoman Sultan Beyazıt I (r 1390–1402), which allowed his armies to conquer the Balkans. Beyazıt's great-grandson Mehmet the Conqueror fortified the strait as part of his grand plan to conquer Constantinople (1453), building eight separate fortresses. The strait remained fortified after he defeated the Byzantines, signalling to foreign powers that this strategic sea passage was firmly in Ottoman hands.

The Ottomans remained neutral at the outbreak of WWI, but in October 1914 they joined the Central Powers and closed the Dardanelles, blocking the Allies' major supply route between Britain, France and their ally Russia. In response, the First Lord of the British Admiralty, Winston Churchill, decided that it was vitally important that the Allies take control of both the strait and the Bosphorus, which meant capturing İstanbul. His Allied partners agreed, and in March 1915 a strong Franco-British fleet attempted to force the Dardanelles. It was defeated on 18 March in what the Turks commemorate as the Çanakkale Naval Victory (Çanakkale Deniz Zaferi).

Undaunted, the Allies devised another strategy to capture the strait. On 25 April, British, Australian, New Zealand and Indian troops landed on the Gallipoli Peninsula, in a diversionary manoeuvre, French troops landed at Kum Kale near Çanakkale. The landings on the peninsula were a disaster for the Allies, with the British 29th Division suffering horrendous losses at Cape Hellas and the Anzac troops landing at a relatively inaccessible beach north of their planned landing point near Gaba Tepe (Kabatepe). Rather than overcoming the Turkish defences and swiftly making their way across the peninsula to the strait (the planned objective), the Allies were hemmed in by their enemy, forced to dig trenches for protection and stage bloody assaults to try and improve their position. After nine months of ferocious combat but little headway, the Allied forces withdrew in December 1915 and January 1916.

The Gallipoli campaign – in Turkish the Çanakkale Savaşı (Battle of Çanakkale) – resulted in a total of more than half a million casualties, of which 130,000 were deaths. The British Empire saw the loss of some 36,000 lives, including 8700 Australians and 2700 New Zealanders. French casualties numbered 47,000 (making up over half the entire French contingent); 8800 Frenchmen died. Half the 500,000 Ottoman troops were casualties, with almost 86,700 killed.

◉ Sights

Gallipoli Historical National Park (Gelibolu Yarımadası Tarihi Milli Parkı; Map p154; http://gytmp.milliparklar.gov.tr) encompasses 33,500 hectares of the peninsula. There are currently 40 Allied war cemeteries at Gallipoli, and at least 20 Turkish ones. The principal battles took place on the peninsula's western shore, around Anzac Cove (Anzac Koyu), 12km northwest of Eceabat, and in the hills east of the cove. If you wish to identify a particular grave when you are here, the Commonwealth War Graves Commission website (www.cwgc.org) is a useful resource.

There are several different signage systems in use: Turkish highway signs; national-park administration signs; and wooden signs posted by the Commonwealth War Graves Commission. This can lead to confusion because the foreign and Turkish troops used different names for the battlefields, and the park signs don't necessarily agree with those erected by the highway department. We've used both English and Turkish names.

◉ Northern Peninsula

About 3km north of Eceabat, the road to Kabatepe heads west into the park.

Gallipoli Battlefields

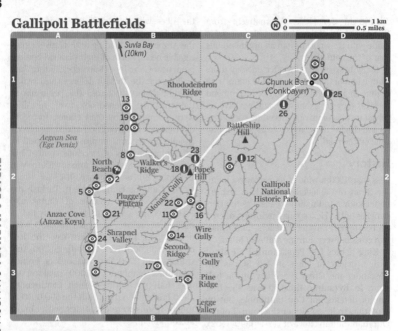

Gallipoli Battlefields

◉ Sights

1 57 Alay Cemetery	....	B2
2 Anzac Commemorative Site	....	B2
3 Anzac Cove (Anzac Koyu)	....	A3
4 Arıburnu Cemetery	....	A2
5 Arıburnu Sahil Anıtı	....	A2
6 Baby 700 Cemetery	....	C2
7 Beach (Hell Spit) Cemetery	....	A3
8 Canterbury Cemetery	....	B2
9 Chunuk Bair New Zealand		
Cemetery & Memorial	....	D1
10 Conkbayırı Atatürk Anıtı	....	D1
11 Courtney's & Steele's Post		
Cemetery	....	B2
12 Düztepe Monument	....	C2
13 Embarkation Pier Cemetery	....	B1

14 Johnston's Jolly	....	B3
15 Kanlısırt Kitabesi	....	B3
16 Kesikdere Cemetery	....	B2
17 Lone Pine Cemetery	....	B3
Mesudiye Topu	....	(see 6)
18 Nek	....	B2
19 New Zealand No 2 Outpost		
Cemetery	....	B1
20 No 2 Outpost Cemetery	....	B1
21 Plugge's Plateau Cemetery	....	B2
22 Quinn's Post Cemetery	....	B2
23 Sergeant Mehmet Monument	....	B2
24 Shrapnel Valley Cemetery	....	A3
25 Suyatağı Anıtı	....	D1
26 Talat Göktepe Monument	....	C1

Gallipoli Simulation Centre

The extremely impressive and informative Gallipoli Simulation Centre (Çannakale Destanı Tanıtım Merkezi; Map p154; ☎0284-810 0050; http://canakkaledestani.milliparklar.gov.tr; Kabatepe; ₺20; ☺9.30-11am & 1.30-5pm), roughly 1km east of the village of Kabatepe, is a great place to start your tour if you're travelling independently. It comprises 11 gallery rooms in which high-tech 3D simulation equipment takes the viewer on a historical journey through the Gallipoli naval and land campaigns. Events are presented from both Turkish and Allied points of view, and the technology allows visitors to choose their presentation language and to interact with the display. Improved historical displays were added in 2015 for the 100th commemoration of the WWI battles in 1915. There's a small cafe in which you can recover if it all gets a bit too realistic.

Kabatepe Village

The small harbour here was probably the object of the Allied landing on 25 April 1915. In the predawn dark it is possible that uncharted currents swept the Allies' landing craft northwards to the steep cliffs of Arıburnu – a bit of bad luck that may have sealed the campaign's fate from the start. Today there's little in Kabatepe except for a camping ground, a cafe and a dock for ferries to Gökçeada island. Just north of the promontory is the stretch of sand known as Brighton Beach (Map p154), a favourite swimming spot for Anzac troops during the campaign. Today, it's the only officially sanctioned swimming spot on the peninsula. A small Gelibolu Milli Parkı (Gallipoli National Park) office here sells maps, souvenirs and snacks.

Anzac Cove

A short drive north along the coastal road from Brighton Beach takes you to Beach (Hell Spit) Cemetery (Map p156). Before it, a rough track cuts inland to Lone Pine (1.5km) and, across the road from the car park at the cemetery, another track heads inland to Shrapnel Valley Cemetery (Map p156) and Plugge's Plateau Cemetery (Map p156).

Following the road for another 400m from the turn-off, or taking the footpath from Beach Cemetery past the WWII bunker, brings you to Anzac Cove (Map p156). This now extremely narrow stretch of sand beneath and just south of the Arıburnu cliffs was where the ill-fated Allied landing began on 25 April 1915. Ordered to advance inland, the Allied forces at first gained some ground but later in the day met with fierce resistance from the Ottoman forces under the leadership of Mustafa Kemal, who had foreseen where they would land and disobeyed an order to send his troops further south to Cape Helles.

In August of the same year a major offensive was staged in an attempt to advance beyond the beach up to the ridges of Chunuk Bair and Sarı Bair (Yellow Slope). It resulted in the battles at Lone Pine and the Nek, the bloodiest of the campaign, but little progress was made.

Another 300m along is the Arıburnu Sahil Anıtı (Arıburnu Coastal Memorial; Map p156), a moving Turkish monument inscribed with Atatürk's famous words of peace and reconciliation, spoken in 1934:

> To us there is no difference between the Johnnies and the Mehmets…You, the mothers, who sent your sons from faraway countries, wipe away your tears; your sons are now lying in our bosom…After having lost their lives in this land, they have become our sons as well.

Just beyond the memorial is Arıburnu Cemetery (Map p156) and, 750m further north, Canterbury Cemetery (Map p156). Between them is the Anzac Commemorative Site (Anzac Tören Alanı; Map p156) at North Beach, where dawn services are held on Anzac Day (25 April). This is where the much-photographed Anzac monument is located. From it, look up towards the cliffs and you can easily make out the image in the sandy cliff face nicknamed 'the Sphinx' by young diggers (Aussie infantrymen) who had arrived from Australia via Egypt.

Less than 1km further along the seaside road on the right-hand side are the cemeteries at No 2 Outpost (Map p156), set back inland from the road, and New Zealand No 2 Outpost (Map p156). The Embarkation Pier Cemetery (Map p156) is 200m beyond the New Zealand No 2 Outpost on the left.

Towards Lone Pine

Returning to the Gallipoli Simulation Centre, around 1km east of Kabatepe, you should then follow the signs to Lone Pine, just under 3km uphill.

En route, the first monument you'll come to is Mehmetçiğe Derin Saygı Anıtı (Map p154), on the right-hand side of the road about 1km from the junction. It's dedicated to 'Mehmetçik' (Little Mehmet, the Turkish 'tommy' or 'digger'), who carried a Kiwi soldier to safety.

Another 1200m brings you to the Kanlısırt Kitabesi (Bloody Ridge Inscription; Map p156), a memorial that describes the battle of Lone Pine from the Turkish viewpoint.

Lone Pine

Lone Pine (Kanlısırt; Map p156), 400m uphill from Kanlısırt Kitabesi, is perhaps the most moving of all the Anzac cemeteries. Australian forces captured the Turkish positions here on the afternoon of 6 August 1915. During the battle, which was staged in an area the size of a soccer field, more than 4000 men died and thousands more were injured. The trees that once shaded the cemetery were swept away by a forest fire in 1994, leaving only one: a lone pine planted from the seed of the original solitary tree, that stood here at the beginning of the battle and gave the battlefield its name.

Explore the tombstones, which carry touching epitaphs. The cemetery includes the grave of the youngest soldier to die here, a boy of just 14. You can view the remains of trenches just behind the parking area.

From here, it's 3km up the one-way road to the New Zealand Memorial at Chunuk Bair.

Johnston's Jolly to Quinn's Post

Progressing up the hill from Lone Pine, the ferocity of the battles becomes more apparent; at some points the trenches are only a few metres apart. The order to attack meant certain death to those who followed it, and virtually all did as they were ordered on both sides.

The road marks what was the thin strip of no-man's land between the two sides' trenches, as it continues to the cemeteries Johnston's Jolly (Kırmızı Sırt; Map p156), 200m on the right beyond Lone Pine, Courtney's & Steele's Post (Map p156), roughly the same distance again, and Quinn's Post (Map p156), 100m uphill.

57 Alay & Kesikdere Cemeteries

About 1km uphill from Lone Pine, across the road from the Little Mehmet statue, is the cemetery (57 Alay Şehitliği; Map p156) and monument for the Ottoman 57th Regiment, which was led by Mustafa Kemal and almost completely wiped out on 25 April while halting the Anzac attempt to advance to the high ground of Chunuk Bair.

The statue of an old man showing his granddaughter the battle sites represents Hüseyin Kaçmaz, who fought in the Balkan Wars, the Gallipoli campaign and at the fateful Battle of Dumlupınar during the War of Independence. He died in 1994 aged 111, the last surviving Turkish Gallipoli veteran.

Down some steps from here, the Kesikdere Cemetery (Map p156) contains the remains of another 1115 Turkish soldiers from the 57th and other regiments.

Sergeant Mehmet Monument & the Nek

About 100m uphill past the 57th Alay Cemetery, a road goes west to the Sergeant Mehmet Monument (Map p156), dedicated to the Turkish sergeant who fought with rocks and his fists after he ran out of ammunition, and the Nek (Map p156). It was at the Nek on the morning of 7 August 1915 that the 8th (Victorian) and 10th (Western Australian) Regiments of the third Light Horse Brigade vaulted out of their trenches into fire and were cut down before they reached the enemy line, an episode immortalised in Peter Weir's 1981 film *Gallipoli*.

Baby 700 Cemetery & Mesudiye Topu

About 200m uphill on the right from the access road to the Nek is the Baby 700 Cemetery (Map p156) and the Ottoman cannon called the Mesudiye Topu (Map p156). Named after its height above sea level in feet, Baby 700 was the limit of the initial attack, and the graves here are mostly dated 25 April.

Düztepe & Talat Göktepe Monuments

The Düztepe Monument (Map p156), uphill from the Baby 700 Cemetery, marks the spot where the Ottoman 10th Regiment held the

---

WALKING THE BATTLEFIELDS

The best way to explore the battlefields is undoubtedly in the footsteps of the original combatants. Walking the hills and gullies of this landscape offers a glimpse into the physical challenges that faced troops in 1915. It also allows you to enjoy the wonderful views and landscape of the national park.

The Australian Goverrnment's Department of Veterans Affairs website (www.anzacsite. gov.au) includes details of a one-day walk exploring the main area held by Anzac troops during the campaign. This starts in North Beach, includes sites such as Anzac Cove and Lone Pine, and ends on the high ground near the Nek and Walker's Ridge. Walk instructions, downloadable audio commentary and plenty of historical information is available on the website. For a New Zealand perspective see www.ngatapuwae.govt.nz for audio guides, maps and an excellent downloadable smartphone app that really brings to life the history of the battlefields.

Crowded House Tours (p160) offers several walking tours. Expert guides lead a number of trails including a one-day tour of the battlefields of the Anzac sector; a half-day 'New Zealand Trail' following the advance of NZ troops to Chunuk Bair; and a full-day walk around the Helles sector following the paths of British troops. Guides will try to accommodate special interests, including visiting particular graves. The cost depends on how many walkers are in the group and includes lunch and transport to/from the start and finish points from Eceabat or Çanakkale.

Walkers should be sure to bring sturdy shoes, as the terrain can be steep and difficult in parts. Hats and sunblock are essential in the warmer months; a rain jacket is useful at other times of the year. Don't forget water and food.

line. Views of the Dardanelles and the surrounding countryside are superb. About 1km further on is a monument (Map p156) to a more recent casualty of Gallipoli: Talat Göktepe, chief director of the Çanakkale Forestry District, who died fighting the devastating forest fire of 1994.

Chunuk Bair & Around

At the top of the hill, some 500m past the Talat Göktepe Monument, a right turn at the T-junction takes you east to the Suyatağı Anıtı (Watercourse Monument; Map p156). Having stayed awake for four days and nights, Mustafa Kemal spent the night of 9 August here, directing part of the counterattack to the Allied offensive.

Back at the T-junction, turn left for Chunuk Bair (known as Conk Bayiri in Turkish), the first objective of the Allied landing in April 1915, and now the site of the Chunuk Bair New Zealand Cemetery & Memorial (Conkbayırı Yeni Zelanda Mezarlığı ve Anıtı; Map p156) and the Conkbayırı Atatürk Anıtı (Conkbayırı Atatürk Memorial; Map p156), a huge statue of the Turkish hero.

As the Anzac troops made their way up the scrub-covered slopes on 25 April, Mustafa Kemal brought up the 57th Infantry Regiment and gave them his famous order: 'I am not ordering you to attack, I am ordering you to die. In the time it takes us to die, other troops and commanders will arrive to take our places'.

Chunuk Bair was also at the heart of the struggle for the peninsula from 6 to 10 August 1915, when some 16,000 men died on this ridge. The Allied attack from 6 to 7 August, which included the New Zealand Mounted Rifle Brigade and a Maori contingent, was deadly, but the attack on the following day was of a ferocity which, according to Mustafa Kemal, 'could scarcely be described'.

⊙ Southern Peninsula

From Kabatepe it's about 12km to the village of Alçıtepe, formerly known as Krithia. A few metres north of the village's main intersection is the Salim Mutlu War Museum (Salim Mutlu Müsezi; Map p154; admission ₺2; ⊙8am-8pm), a hodgepodge of rusty finds from the battlefields, giving a sense of just how much artillery was fired. At the main intersection, a sign points right to the Turkish Sargı Yeri Cemetery (Map p154), approximately 1.5km away, with its enormous statue of 'Mehmet' and solid Nuri Yamut Monument (Map p154). Take the first left for the Twelve Tree Copse

Cemetery (Map p154), 2km away, and the Pink Farm Cemetery (Map p154), 3km away.

From Pink Farm, the road passes the Lancashire Landing Cemetery (Map p154). Turn right 1km before Seddülbahir village for the Cape Helles British Memorial (Map p154), a commanding stone obelisk honouring the 20,000-plus Britons and Australians who perished in this area and have no known graves. The initial Allied attack was two-pronged: in addition to the landing at Anzac Cove in the north, there was a landing on 'V' Beach at the tip of the peninsula. Yahya Çavuş Şehitliği (Sergeant Yahya Cemetery; Map p154) remembers the Turkish officer who led the resistance to the Allied landing here, and who caused heavy casualties. 'V' Beach Cemetery (Map p154) is visible 500m downhill.

North of Seddülbahir, the road divides; the left fork leads to the Skew Bridge Cemetery (Map p154), followed by the Redoubt Cemetery (Map p154). Turn right and head east, following signs for Abide or Çanakkale Şehitleri Anıtı at Morto Bay, and you'll pass the French War Memorial & Cemetery (Map p154). French troops, including a regiment of Africans, attacked Kumkale on the Asian shore in March 1915 with complete success, then re-embarked and landed in support of their British comrades-in-arms at Cape Helles, where they were virtually wiped out. The rarely visited French cemetery is extremely moving, with rows of metal crosses and five white-concrete ossuaries each containing the bones of 3000 soldiers.

The Çanakkale Şehitleri Anıtı (Çanakkale Martyrs' Memorial; Map p154), also known as the Abide (Monument), is a gigantic stone structure that commemorates all the Turkish soldiers who fought and died at Gallipoli.

En route back to Eceabat and Çanakkale, a massive fortress dominates tiny Kilitbahir. Although closed for restoration at the time of research, the spectacular exterior is worth a look. Built by Mehmet the Conqueror in 1452 and given a grand seven-storey interior tower a century later by Süleyman the Magnificent, it and Çimenlik Kalesi in Çanakkale ensured that the Ottomans retained control of the Dardenelles.

☞ Tours

Guided tours are popular ways to explore the battlefields. Recommended tour providers generally offer three-hour morning tours and five- or six-hour afternoon tours, including transport by minibus and guide. Most also include lunch.

THRACE & MARMARA GALLIPOLI PENINSULA

GALLIPOLI BACKGROUND RESEARCH

Peter Weir's 1981 film *Gallipoli* is a classic of Australian cinema and is well worth viewing. In 2014 Australian–New Zealand actor Russell Crowe released his directorial debut, *The Water Diviner*. The film tells the story of an Australian father who makes his way to Turkey to ascertain the fate of his three sons, all missing in action after the Battle of Gallipoli.

Reading at least one of following books before your visit will allow you to make the most of your time here:

Gallipoli (2001) Award-winning Australian historian and journalist Les Carlyon's book is highly regarded by military historians and is a gripping, magnificently written account of the campaign.

Gallipoli Battlefield Guide (Çanakkale Muharebe Alanları Gezi Rehberi; 2006) The English-language version of this reference book by Gürsel Göncü and Şahin Doğan is still available at some bookshops in Çanakkale and Eceabat.

Gallipoli (2011) Military historian Peter Hart, an oral historian at the Imperial War Museum's sound archive, focuses on the contribution of British troops to the campaign.

Gallipoli (1956) This classic by the Australian-born foreign correspondent Alan Moorehead was re-released in a Perennial Classics edition in 2002.

Gallipoli – The New Zealand Story (1998) Written by respected New Zealand military historian Christopher Pugsley.

Gallipoli (2015) Written by popular Australian author Peter Fitzsimons for the 100th anniversary of the WWI campaign.

★ **Crowded House Tours** TOURS
(✆ 0286-814 1565; www.crowdedhousegallipoli.com; Zubeyde Hanim Meydani 28, Eceabat) Based at spacious new premises right on the Eceabat waterfront, this is the most professional of the tour companies operating on the Gallipoli Peninsula and is heartily recommended, especially if you can join a tour led by the affable and extremely knowledgable Bülent 'Bill' Yilmaz Korkmaz. Its core offering is an afternoon tour of the main Anzac battlefields and cemeteries (€25).

Other options include a morning tour of Cape Helles (€30), a morning snorkelling excursion around a WWI shipwreck at Anzac Cove (€15), an afternoon tour by boat of the Anzac landing sites (₺50), and two-day Gallipoli and Troy packages from İstanbul (prices on application).

Bülent Korkmaz also leads walking tours of the battlefields.

Kenan Çelik TOURS
(✆ 0286-217 7468; www.kcelik.com; half-/full-day small-group tours €120/150) One of Turkey's foremost experts on the Gallipoli campaign, Kenan Çelik has retired from his position as lecturer in English language and literature at Çanakkale Onsekiz Mart University and now conducts private tours of the battlefields. He offers full-day tours concentrating on significant Anzac or Turkish sites, and can also cover Suvla Bay and Cape Helles.

There's an extra charge of €50/100 if transport is required.

Hassle Free Travel Agency TOURS
(✆ 0286-213 5969; www.anzachouse.com; Cumhuriyet Meydanı 59, Çanakkale) Operating from its base in Çanakkale, this long-standing company offers a half-day tour of the Anzac battlefields and cemeteries (€40) and a package including a boat trip to the Anzac landing beaches, a snorkel at Anzac Cove and a visit to the Gallipoli Simulation Centre (€50). It also offers Gallipoli and Troy tours with onward transport to İstanbul or Selçuk/Ephesus.

☆ Festivals & Events

Two dates attract the largest crowds each year: the Turkish naval victory in the Dardanelles is commemorated on 18 March in Çanakkale, and the Allied landings are commemorated on 25 April.

Anzac Day COMMEMORATION
(◷ 25 Apr) A sombre mood prevails at the dawn service marking the anniversary of the WWI landing of the Australian and New Zealand Army Corps (Anzacs) at Gallipoli, which attracts up to ten thousand travellers from Australia and New Zealand each year.

🛏 Sleeping & Eating

There are really no places to eat around the Gallipoli battlefields. An essential stop en route for breakfast or lunch is at the excellent Doyuranlar Aile Çay ve Gözleme for tea and *gözleme* (savoury Turkish pancakes).

★**Gallipoli Houses**   BOUTIQUE HOTEL **$$$**
(Map p154; ☑0286-814 2650; www.thegallipoli houses.com; Kocadere; s €55-75, d €65-85; ☉mid-Mar–mid-Nov; 🕸) Located in a farming village within the Gallipoli Historical National Park, this is the intelligent accommodation choice when visiting the peninsula. The 10 rooms are split between the original stone house and a purpose-built section with countryside views. Note that there is usually a minimum stay of two nights and that children under the age of 10 are not accommodated.

Rooms are spacious and comfortable, and there is a pleasant bar area where guests can enjoy a drink and chat before dinner (€17.50). Eric, the Belgian cohost, and his Turkish wife, Ozlem, are equally at ease preparing home-cooked Turkish cuisine as tailoring a battlefields itinerary. Lunch boxes are also available.

Doyuranlar Aile Çay ve Gözleme   TURKISH **$**
(Map p154; ☑0286-814 1652; mains ₺7-12; ☉from 7.30am; 🕿) The village women in charge of this roadside eatery and *çay bahçesi* (tea garden) midway between Eceabat and Kabatepe serve up huge breakfast platters, *köfte* (meatballs) and *menemen* (eggs scrambled with white cheese, tomatoes and peppers). Regulars opt for the house speciality: crisp and delicious *gözleme* (savoury pancakes) washed down with a glass of *ayran* (yoghurt drink).

ℹ Information

Visit Gallipoli (www.gallipoli.gov.au) is full of useful information.

ℹ Getting There & Around

With your own transport you can easily tour the northern battlefields in a day. Cars can be rented in Çanakkale and Eceabat. Trying to do both the northern and southern parts of the peninsula is possible within one day, provided you get a very early start. Without your own transport, a guided tour is the most time-efficient means of exploring the area.

DOLMUŞ

The only regular public-transport options on the peninsula are the dolmuş between Eceabat and Kilitbahir (₺2, every 45 minutes) and the dolmuş between Eceabat and Kabatepe (₺4, 15 minutes). The latter meets ferries from Gökçeada

year-round and makes more frequent runs in the summer months. There are usually a couple of dolmuşes each day from Kilitbahir to Seddülbahir and Alçıtepe, but the timetable changes frequently.

FERRY

Gestaş (☑0286-444 0752; www.gdu.com.tr) operates ferries across the Dardanelles between Çanakkale and Eceabat and Çanakkale and Kilitbahir. They also cross the Aegean between Kabatepe and Gökçeada.

TAXI

A taxi between Kabatepe and Eceabat will cost approximately ₺50.

ECEABAT

☑0286 / POP 5630

Eceabat (ancient Maydos) is an unremarkable waterfront town on the southern shore of the Dardanelles. It is notable only for its proximity to the main Gallipoli battlefields and for its ferry link to Çanakkale. Ferries dock by the main square (Cumhuriyet Meydanı), which is ringed by hotels, restaurants, ATMs, a post office, bus-company offices, and dolmuş and taxi stands.

🛏 Sleeping & Eating

★**Hotel Casa Villa**   BOUTIQUE HOTEL **$$**
(☑0286-814 1320; www.otelcasavilla.com; Çamburnu Sokak 75; r ₺160; 🕸🕿) Casa Villa maximises its hilltop location above Eceabat with excellent views from elegantrooms, and plenty of outdoor furniture makes it easy to enjoy the ocean and town vistas. Breakfast – served in a sunny glass conservatory – is one of western Turkey's best; treats such as freshly cooked *sigara böreği* (deep-fried pastries with cheese) and omelettes are offered most mornings.

Hotel Crowded House   HOTEL **$$**
(☑0286-810 0041; www.hotelcrowdedhouse.com; Hüseyin Avni Sokak 4; s/d/tr €30/40/50; 🕸@🕿) Crowded House has modern rooms with comfortable beds and clean bathrooms. A simple breakfast is included in the room charge, and there's a courtyard restaurant at the rear where other meals (including summer barbecues) are offered. Downstairs is crammed with Australian and NZ memorabilia.

★**Kilye Suvla Lokanta**   MODERN TURKISH **$$**
(☑0286-814 1000; www.suvla.com.tr; Suvla Winery, Çınarlıdere 11; mains ₺15-28; ☉lokanta noon-3pm, tasting room & concept store 8.30am-5.30pm; 🍴) Suvla's 60 hectares of certified organic vineyards are located near Kabatepe on the

EITAN SIMANOR / GETTY IMAGES ©

1. Lone Pine cemetery (p157) 2. Anzac Cove (p157)
3. Cape Helles British Memorial (p159)

Gallipoli Battlefields

Pilgrimage is the oldest – and often the most rewarding – form of travel. In Turkey there are a number of ancient pilgrimage destinations, but only one dates from modern times and draws both local and international visitors: the pine-scented peninsula where the bloody Gallipoli campaign of WWI unfolded.

Cemeteries

There were almost 130,000 Turkish and Allied deaths at Gallipoli and the battlefields are home to more than 60 meticulously maintained cemeteries. Places for contemplation and commemoration include the Allied cemeteries at Beach (Hell Spit), Arıburnu (Anzac Cove), Lone Pine, Chunuk Bair and V Beach; and the Turkish 57 Alay (57th Regiment) and Kesikdere cemeteries.

Memorials

Gallipoli is a place where bravery and sacrifice are honoured and where the narratives of modern nations have been forged. The most famous memorial on the peninsula is the Arıburnu Sahil Anıtı (Arıburnu Coastal Memorial), which records Atatürk's famous words of peace and reconciliation between the 'Johnnies' and the 'Mehmets'. Other memorials include the stone obelisk at Cape Helles that commemorates the 20,000-plus Britons and Australians who perished on the southern peninsula and have no known graves.

Landing Beaches

Few places are so closely associated with national identity as Anzac Cove, where Australian and New Zealand troops landed on 25 April 1915. Today, the annual Anzac Day dawn service is held at nearby North Beach. Casualties at Anzac Cove were relatively minor, as opposed to those incurred on the five beaches at Cape Helles – most notably V and W Beaches – where thousands of deaths occurred.

opposite side of the peninsula, but its winery, complete with restaurant, tasting room and produce store, is on Eceabat's outskirts. Worth a dedicated visit, it offers an impressive menu with modern twists on Turkish classics such as *köfte* (meatballs), plus fresh salads and Turkish-style pizzas. Try the goat's cheese ravioli with a zingy local sauvignon blanc.

❶ Getting There & Away

ÇANAKKALE

Gestaş (☑ 0286-444 0752; www.gdu.com.tr) ferries cross the Dardanelles between Eceabat and Çanakkale in both directions (per person/car ₺3/30, 25 minutes) every hour on the hour between 7am and midnight, and roughly every two hours after that. The ticket box is right next to where passengers embark.

Bus tickets can be purchased from the **Truva** (Cumhuriyet Meydanı; ⊙ 8am-10pm) and **Metro** (Cumhuriyet Meydanı; ⊙ 8am-10pm) offices on the ground floor of the Grand Eceabat Hotel building opposite the port.

KABATEPE

In summer regular dolmuşes run to Kabatepe ferry dock (₺4, 15 minutes); in winter they only meet the ferries. If asked, the dolmuş will drop you at the **Gallipoli Simulation Centre** (p156), 750m southeast of the bottom of the road up to Lone Pine and Chunuk Bair.

KILITBAHIR

Dolmuşes run to Kilitbahir every 45 minutes (₺2, 10 minutes).

İSTANBUL

Buses services run to İstanbul: those to the Büyük Otogar in Esenler leave regularly (₺45, five hours); those to Ataşehir Otogar near Kadıköy on the Asian side are less frequent. **Truva Turizm** (Map p166; ☑ 0286-212 2222; www.truvaturizm.com) offers the best service.

ÇANAKKALE

☑ 0286 / POP 123,000

If you thought Çanakkale was worth visiting only as a launching point for Gallipoli's battlefields, think again. The presence of the highly regarded Çanakkale Onsekiz Mart University endows this small city with a sizeable student population that loves nothing more to eat, drink and party in the atmospheric cobbled lanes around the *saat kulesi* (clock tower; 1897) and along the sweeping *kordon* (waterfront promenade). Joining their revelries is a highlight of any visit.

The undisputed hub of the region, Çanakkale is replete with mythological associations.

It was from the ancient town of Abydos immediately north that Leander swam across the Hellespont every night to see his love, Hero; and it was in the Dardanelles that Helle, the daughter of Athamas, was drowned in the legend of the Golden Fleece, giving the waterway its ancient name. Close by are the remnants of ancient Troy, immortalised by Homer in his epic poem the *Iliad*.

⊙ Sights & Activities

Dardanelles Straits Naval Command Museum   MUSEUM

(Çanakkale Boğaz Komutanliği Deniz Müzesi; Map p166; ☑ 0286-213 1730; Çimenlik Sokak; ₺7; ⊙ 9am-noon & 1.30-5pm Tue-Sun) At the southern end of the *kordon* (waterfront promenade) a park lies dotted with guns, cannons and military artefacts. Near the park entrance is this small military museum containing exhibits on the Gallipoli battles and some war relics. Museum ticket-holders can also board the replica of the *Nusrat* mine-layer, which played a significant role in the Çanakkale Naval Victory, and visit Çimenlik Kalesi (built by order of Mehmet the Conqueror in 1452) located behind the park.

Kent Müzesi   MUSEUM

(City Museum; Map p166; ☑ 0286-214 3417; www.canakkalekentmuzesi.com; Fetvane Sokak 31; ⊙ 10am-7pm Tue-Sun Apr-Aug, to 5pm Sep-May) **FREE** The lives of Çanakkale's residents since Ottoman times are the focus of this small museum, which has drawn on oral histories for the content of many of its display panels. There are photographs, newspaper articles and a few artefacts on show. Ask for the English-translation texts to get the most out of the exhibitions.

Trojan Horse   MONUMENT

(Map p166) Wolfgang Petersen's 2004 movie *Troy* had a big impact on the Çanakkale region, including boosting visitor numbers to the archaeological site and endowing the northern stretch of the waterfront promenade with this wooden horse, which was used in the film shoot. There are information displays and a model of the ancient city underneath.

Yalı Hamam   HAMAM

(Map p166; Çarşı Caddesi 5; full treatments ₺50; ⊙ 8am-11pm) Women may not feel comfortable in this 17th-century hamam, as it is a mixed facility and the attendants are male. That said, it's clean, the *göbektaşı* (raised platform used for massage) is piping hot and the massage will please those who like a bit of a pummel.

✿ Festivals & Events

Çanakkale Naval Victory COMMEMORATION
(Çanakkale Deniz Zaferi; ☉ 18 Mar) Turks celebrate this WWI Dardanelles naval victory on 18 March.

Troia Festival CULTURAL
(Troia Festivali; ☉ mid-Aug) Parades, concerts and exhibitions take over the *kordon* (waterfront promenade) and big-name Turkish music acts perform at free concerts in Cumhuriyet Meydanı for five days mid-August.

Hellespont & Dardanelles Swim SPORTS
(www.swimhellespont.com; ☉ 30 Aug) On Turkey's Victory Day, the Dardanelles Strait is closed to maritime traffic for 1½ hours when swimmers race the 4.5km from Eceabat to Çanakkale.

🛏 Sleeping

If you'll be in town during major events (p160) book well in advance and be prepared to pay a premium. Weekends – especially from mid-March to mid-June and during September – are very popular with Turkish visitors, so try to visit on a weekday, and definitely book ahead for accommodation from Friday to Sunday.

Anzac House Hostel HOSTEL $
(Map p166; ☎ 0286-213 5969; www.anzac house.com; Cumhuriyet Meydanı 59; dm/s/d/tw ₺30/50/80/80; ❋ ☎) Operated by the excellent Hassle Free Tours, Çanakkale's only backpacker hostel has been made-over to re-emerge as the area's best option for budget travellers. Not all the simple rooms have windows, but they are well kept. Tours around the battlefields, Troy and further afield are all on tap downstairs, and Çanakkale's best bars and cafes are nearby.

Pansiyon Egem PENSION $
(Map p166; ☎ 0286-213 2623; www.egempansiyon. com; Kemalyeri Sokak 9; s/d from ₺60/100; ❋ ☎) Following a makeover under new owners, this is a good-value option in an interesting area of the old town close to cafes and restaurants. Decor is crisp, white and modern; the brand-new bathrooms are spotless; and the young English-speaking team at reception usually bring an open mind to negotiations on rates. Not all rooms have windows.

Anzac Hotel HOTEL $$
(Map p166; ☎ 0286-217 7777; www.anzachotel. com; Saat Kulesi Meydanı 8; s €25-30, d €33-40; ❋ ☎) An extremely professional management team ensures that this renovated and keenly priced hotel opposite the clock tower is well maintained and has high levels of service. Rooms are a good size, include tea- and coffee-making facilities and have double-glazed windows. The convivial bar on the mezzanine shows the movies *Gallipoli* and *Troy* nightly.

Hotel Kervansaray BOUTIQUE HOTEL $$
(Map p166; ☎ 0286-217 8192; www.otelkervan saray.com; Fetvane Sokak 13; s/d from €45/50; ❋ ☎) In an Ottoman house once owned in the early 20th century by a judge, the Kervansaray is one of Çanakkale's more historic accommodation options. The smell of yesteryear may permeate the older rooms, but the dowdiness is kind of fun. Rooms in the newer section have bath-tubs instead of showers. The garden en route is a little oasis.

Hotel Limani HOTEL $$$
(Map p166; ☎ 0286-217 2908; www.hotellimani. com; Yalı Caddesi 12; s/d ₺160/260; ❋ ☎) Overlooking the harbour, the Limani deserves its reputation as Çanakkale's best top-end hotel. Rooms are on the small side, but are comfortable and have pretty decor. It's worth paying extra for land or sea views, as the budget alternatives are windowless. The downstairs restaurant-bar serves decent meals and a mighty fine buffet breakfast.

Hotel des Etrangers BOUTIQUE HOTEL $$$
(Map p166; ☎ 0286-214 2424; www.hoteldes etrangers.com.tr; Yalı Caddesi 25-27; r €90-100; ❋ ☎) This historic hotel is an atmospheric sleeping choice offering eight rooms with whitewashed wooden floors, inlaid timber ceilings and tasteful country-style furniture. The four rooms at the front are larger and have small balconies overlooking the harbour and bustling Yalı Caddesi. Note that windows aren't double glazed and the location can be noisy. Heinrich Schliemann, who led the first excavation of Troy, once stayed here.

🍴 Eating

★ Sardalya SEAFOOD $
(Map p166; Küçük Hamam Sokak 24b; snacks from ₺6; ☉ 8am-11pm) Named after a type of fish, the no-frills Sardalya is a popular local joint serving everything from *balık ekmek* (fish sandwiches) to plates of fried mussels or calamari, and deep-fried sardines with salad. Pull up a seat at the counter and chat with the locals between tasty mouthfuls, or ask for takeaway and stroll the short distance to the waterfront.

Çonk Coffee CAFE $
(Map p166; Kemalyeri Sokak 3; snacks from ₺3; ☉ 8am-10pm) A display of old radios, cameras

Çanakkale

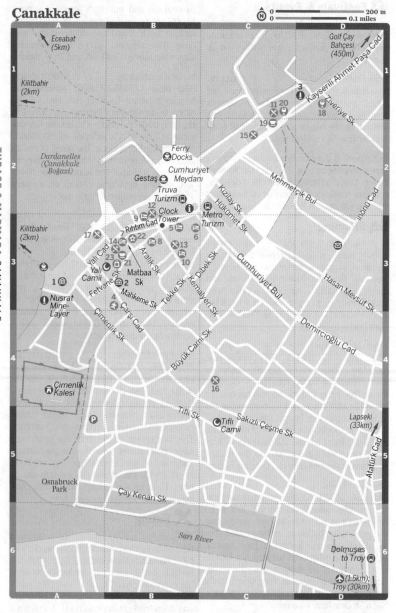

and photographs adorns the walls of this small and extremely friendly cafe, which serves Turkish and espresso coffee, hot dogs, sandwiches and the city's best *tostu* (toasted sandwiches). Brilliant freshly squeezed orange juice too.

Hüsmanoğlu Babalığın Torunları   SWEETS $
(Map p166; ☏0286-217 7733; Yalı Caddesi 29; per kg ₺20; ☉8am-7pm) One of the best places in town for *peynir helvası* (a dessert of flour or semolina, butter and sugar).

Çanakkale

Assos Cafe   CAFE $$
(Map p166; ☑0532 784 6484; Kayserili Ahmet Paşa Caddesi 27; meals ₺13-27; ☺8am-2am; ☜) Head to this hang-out near the Trojan Horse for a hamburger, fajitas or pizza washed down with cold beer. Louder as the night gets older, the music is indie and Western rather than Turkish pop. Regulars like to meet up with friends, use the free wi-fi and play *tavla* (backgammon). Look forward to a decent range of Turkish and international beers.

Yalova   SEAFOOD $$
(Map p166; ☑0286-217 1045; www.yalovarestaurant.com; Gümrük Sokak 7; mezes ₺8-22, mains ₺25-40) Locals have been coming here for slap-up meals since 1940. A two-storey place on the *kordon*, it serves seafood that often comes straight off the fishing boats moored out the front. Head upstairs to choose from the meze and fish displays, and be sure to quaff some locally produced Suvla wine with your meal.

Kavala   SEAFOOD $$
(Kavala Balık Lokantası; Map p166; ☑0284-214 3519; www.canakkalekavala.com; Kayserili Ahmet Paşa Caddesi 5; mezes ₺8-22, mains ₺20-40; ☺8am-midnight) The outdoor terrace of this extremely friendly place on the northern stretch of the *kordon* is always packed with locals, so you should book ahead to secure a table or be prepared to sit inside. The decor is Greek-island style, but the food is traditional Turkish, with all the usual meze and fish standards on offer.

Cafe du Port   INTERNATIONAL $$
(Map p166; ☑0286-217 2908; Yalı Caddesi 12; mains ₺22-28; ☺8am-11pm) The restaurant at

Hotel Limani is popular for good reason. The glass-fronted building on the *kordon* (waterfront promenade) is stylish and inviting; the chefs are the most versatile in Çanakkale; and the service is brilliant. Specialities include steaks, salads, pastas, and whatever else inspires the manager during his regular Istanbul sojourns. If nothing else, settle in for an end-of-day mojito.

🍷 Drinking & Entertainment

Çanakkale's student population ensures a healthy cafe, bar and club scene. Fetvane Sokak near the clock tower has so many bars and clubs that locals call it Barlar Sokağı (Bar St). The city is unusual in that many of the *çay bahçesis* and cafes along the *kordon* serve alcohol as well as tea.

★Yalı Hanı   TEA GARDEN, BAR
(Map p166; Fetvane Sokak 26; ☺8am-10pm, closed winter) Hidden in the wisteria-covered courtyard of a late 19th-century caravanserai is this atmospheric hybrid *çay bahçesi* (tea garden) and bar that doubles as a performance and film-festival venue. It's a favourite haunt of boho types, who linger over glasses of wine and earnest conversation after checking out the art exhibitions that are often held in the upstairs space.

Golf Çay Bahçesi   TEA GARDEN
(Gazi Bulvarı; ☺8am-10pm) One of the best spots to be when the sun sets over the Dardanelles, Golf has a huge outdoor terrace where you can enjoy a beer or a glass of tea while admiring the view. It's just past the northern end of

the *kordon* (waterfront promenade), near the Necip Paşa Mosque.

Helles Cafe
BAR

(Map p166; Kayserili Ahmet Paşa Caddesi 29a; ☺8am-2am) Turkish craft beer in Çanakkale – who'd have thought? The Helles Cafe increases its friendly ambience and alfresco appeal along the *kordon* by serving craft brews from the Gara Guzu brewery in the southwestern city of Muğla. Beers include a hoppy amber ale and a Belgian-tinged blonde ale, both decent tipples if Efes is tasting a little bland.

Akava Lounge
BAR

(Map p166; www.akava.com.tr; Kayserili Ahmet Paşa Caddesi 24a; ☺8am-2am) Çanakkale's hippest place also features the city's longest and most well-stocked bar. Regulars crowd in for cocktails served amid colourful street art and wall murals, and the international menu features pizza, pasta, steaks, salads and Mexican dishes. There's a bigger-than-usual range of beers on tap, and even a few flavourful and interesting international bottled brews.

Bayramefendi Osmanlı Kahvecisi
CAFE

(Map p166; Kayserili Ahmet Paşa Caddesi; coffee from ₺4; ☺8am-midnight) The city's most popular cafe is this colourful, wood-lined homage to coffee prepared many ways. Some of Çanakkale's hipsters idle away afternoons by chatting and smoking here. Try to secure an outside table for ocean breezes along the *kordon* – and look for the retro 'moustache' logo adorning everything from signage to coffee cups.

Joker Bar
LIVE MUSIC, BAR

(Map p166; www.jokerbarcanakkale.com; Matbaa Sokak 3; concerts ₺25-35; ☺noon-1am) Cold beer, outdoor seating and the opportunity to see up and coming bands from around the country combine at one of Çanakkale's best smaller music venues. Local students crowd in for gigs that usually kick off around 8pm on Friday and Saturday nights. The surrounding Matbaa Sokak laneway is also packed with other pubs, cafes and restaurants.

🛍 Shopping

Kepenek Keramik
CERAMICS

(Map p166; www.kepenekkeramik.com; Yalı Hanı 28/30, Fetvane Sokak; ☺10am-6pm) Çanakkale has a long history of ceramics manufacturing, and the designs at Kepenek are often interesting updates on this established tradition. Highlights of the store's well-priced range include robust terracotta kitchenware enlivened with vibrant and colourful glazes, and rustic

and compact figurines that make excellent gifts and souvenirs. The little Trojan horses – complete with wheels – are particularly cool.

ℹ Information

Tourist office (Map p166; ☑0284-217 1187; İskele Meydanı 67; ☺8.30am-5.30pm Mon-Fri, 10am-12.30 & 1.30-4pm Sat & Sun) Strategically located between the ferry pier and the clock tower, this helpful office can supply city maps, information about Gallipoli battlefields and dolmuş timetables.

ℹ Getting There & Around

AIR

Anadolu Jet (www.anadolujet.com), operated by Turkish Airlines, flies to/from Ankara daily (from ₺115, 90 minutes). A municipal minibus meets flights at **Çanakkale Airport** (☑0286-213 1021; www.canakkale.dhmi.gov.tr) and travels into the city centre (₺3); by taxi it's around ₺30

BUS

The easiest way to get to/from Çanakkale on public transport is by bus. The city's new otogar (bus station) is around 7km east of the centre, but many buses pick up and drop off at the ferry dock. If not, local bus 9 (₺2) trundles down the hill to the city centre. **Metro Turizm** (Map p166; ☑0286-213 1260; www.metroturizm.com.tr) and **Truva Turizm** (p164) offer the most frequent service schedules, but other companies also service the city.

Ankara (₺70, 10 hours) One daily on Truva and two on Metro.

Bursa (₺40, 4½ hours) At least four daily on both Truva and Metro.

Edirne (₺40, 4½ hours) At least two daily on both Truva and Metro.

İstanbul (₺55, six hours) Services to Büyük Otogar in Esenler on the city's European side (Metro and Truva) and to Ataşehir Otogar near Kadıköy on the Asian side (Truva).

İzmir (₺45, 5¾ hours) Via Ayvalık (₺30, 3¼ hours) Frequent services on both Truva and Metro.

BOAT

Ferry services are all handled by **Gestaş** (Map p166; ☑0286-444 0 752; www.gdu.com.tr), which has a modern and spacious ticket office and waiting room in Çanakkale.

Ferries depart from the main **ferry** (Map p166) dock and further **south** (Map p166) along the waterfront.

Bozcaada (₺10, passenger ferry only) Departs Saturday at 8am, returning at 5pm.

Eceabat (₺3/35 per person/car, 25 minutes) Departs every hour on the hour between 5am and midnight, and every one to two hours after that.

Gökçeada (₺10, passenger ferry only). Departs 8am Monday and 7.30pm Friday, returning from Gökçeada at 6pm on Thursday and Sunday. More regular vehicular ferries to Gökçeada depart from Kapatepe on the western side of the Gallipoli Peninsula (accessible via Eceabat).

Kilitbahir (₺2/30 per person/car, 20 minutes) Departs every 30 to 60 minutes between 7.30am and 12.30am from either the main pier or the smaller pier to the south.

DOLMUŞ

Dolmuşes to Troy (Map p166) (₺5, 35 minutes, hourly) leave on the half-hour between 9.30am and 5pm from a station at the northern end of the bridge over the Sarı River in Çanakkale and drop passengers at the archaeological site's car park. During summer, the first dolmuş departs Çanakkale at 7.30am and the last departure back from Troy leaves at 8.15pm.

TROY (TRUVA)

☑ 0286

While not the most dramatic of Turkey's ancient sites, Troy is testament to the importance of myth to the human experience. Some imagination is needed to reconstruct the city's former splendour, but a decent guide will quickly bring to life the place that set the scene for Homer's *Iliad*. Troy is a popular destination for weekending school parties; try to visit mid-week.

History

This area was first inhabited during the early Bronze Age (late 4th millennium BC). The walled cities called Troy I to Troy V (3000–1700 BC) had cultures similar to that of the Bronze Age, but Troy VI (1700–1250 BC) took on a different, Mycenae-influenced character, doubling in size and trading prosperously with the region's Greek colonies. By the time of Troy VI, the city probably covered the entire plateau, making it one of the largest towns in the Aegean region. An earthquake brought down the city walls in 1350 BC, but these were rebuilt. There is evidence of widespread fire and slaughter around 1250 BC (Troy VII), which leads many historians to believe that this is when the Trojan War occurred. What is known of the economic and political history of the Aegean region in this period suggests that the real cause of the war was intense commercial rivalry between Troy and the mercantile Mycenaean kingdom, the prize being control of the Dardanelles and lucrative trade with the Black Sea.

The city was abandoned by the end of the 2nd millennium BC but was reoccupied by Greek settlers from Lemnos in the 8th century BC (Troy VIII, 700–85 BC). In 188 BC it was identified by the Romans as the Ilion of Homer and recognised as the mother city of Rome (Ilium Novum), and was granted exemption from taxes. The city prospered under Roman rule and survived a severe earthquake in the early 6th century. Abandoned once again in the 9th century, it was reoccupied in the later Byzantine period and not finally deserted until well into the Ottoman period.

The archaeological site was added to Unesco's World Heritage list in 1998. In the Unesco citation, the ruins are described as the most significant demonstration of the first contact between the civilisations of Anatolia and the Mediterranean world.

Discovering Troy

Up until the 19th century, many historians doubted whether ancient Troy had ever existed. One man who was convinced of its existence – to an almost obsessive level – was the German businessman Heinrich Schliemann (1822–90), who in 1870 received permission from the Ottoman government to excavate a hill near the village of Hisarlık, which archaeologists had previously identified as a possible site for the city.

Schliemann was more of an eager treasure hunter than a methodical archaeologist and he quickly tore open the site, uncovering the remains of a ruined city, which he confidently identified as the Troy of Homeric legend. He also found a great cache of gold artefacts that he named 'Priam's Treasure'.

In his haste, Schliemann failed to appreciate that Troy was not a single city but rather a series of settlements built one on top of the other over the course of about 2500 years. Subsequent archaeologists have identified the remains of nine separate Troys, large sections of which were damaged during Schliemann's hot-headed pursuit of glory. Furthermore, it was soon established that his precious treasures were not from the time of Homer's Troy, but from the much earlier Troy II.

Schliemann's dubious approach continued after the excavation, when he smuggled part of 'Priam's Treasure' out of the Ottoman Empire. Much was displayed in Berlin, where it was seized by Soviet troops at the end of WWII. Following decades of denials about their whereabouts, the treasures were eventually found hidden away in the Pushkin Museum in Moscow, where they remain today.

Troy (Truva)

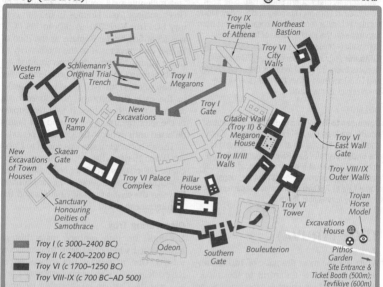

Troy IX Temple of Athena
Northeast Bastion
Troy VI City Walls
Western Gate
Schliemann's Original Trial Trench
Troy II Megarons
Troy I Gate
Troy II Ramp
New Excavations
Citadel Wall (Troy II) & Megaron House
Troy VI East Wall Gate
New Excavations of Town Houses
Skaean Gate
Troy II/III Walls
Troy VIII/IX Outer Walls
Troy VI Palace Complex
Pillar House
Trojan Horse Model
Sanctuary Honouring Deities of Samothrace
Troy VI Tower
Excavations House
Odeon
Southern Gate
Bouleuterion
Pithos Garden
Site Entrance & Ticket Booth (500m); Tevfikiye (600m)

Troy I (c 3000–2400 BC)
Troy II (c 2400–2200 BC)
Troy VI (c 1700–1250 BC)
Troy VIII-IX (c 700 BC–AD 500)

Located nearby in the village of Tevfikiye, the spectacular new Troy Museum is scheduled to open in mid-2017, but delays may see this date pushed out. At the time of writing there was speculation that the treasures in Moscow's Pushkin Museum could be returned to Turkey for display at Troy, but ongoing diplomatic tensions between Ankara and Moscow regarding the situation in Syria make this unforeseeable for the near future.

⊙ Sights

Ruins of Troy ARCHAEOLOGICAL SITE
(🖉 0286-283 0536; adult/child under 12yr ₺25/free; ⊙ 8am-7.30pm Apr-Oct, to 5pm Nov-Mar) If you come to Troy expecting a rebuilt ancient city along the lines of Ephesus, you'll be disappointed. The site resembles an overgrown archaeological dig and it's very difficult to imagine what the ancient city would have looked like. Fortunately, an informative audio guide (₺10) helps to evoke the ancient city for those who are visiting without a tour guide.

As you approach the ruins, take the stone steps up on the right. These bring you out on top of what was the outer wall of Troy VIII/IX, from where you can gaze on the fortifications of the east wall gate and tower of Troy VI.

Go back down the steps and follow the boardwalk to the right, between thick stone walls and up a knoll, from where you can look

at some original (as well as some reconstructed) red-brick walls of Troy II/III. The curved protective roof above them is the same shape and height as the Hisarlık mound before excavations began in 1874.

Continue following the path, past the northeast bastion of the heavily fortified city of Troy VI, the site of a Graeco-Roman Troy IX Temple of Athena and further walls of Troy II/III. You can make out the stone foundations of a megaron (building with porch) from the same era.

Next, beyond traces of the wall of Early/Middle Troy (Troy I south gate) are more remains of megarons of Troy II, which were inhabited by a literal 'upper class' while the poor huddled on the plains.

The path then sweeps past Schliemann's original trench, which cut straight through all the layers of the city. Signs point out the nine city strata in the trench's 15m-high sides.

Just round the corner is a stretch of wall from what is believed to have been the two-storey-high Troy VI Palace Complex, followed by traces from Troy VIII/IX of a sanctuary to unknown deities. Later, a new sanctuary was built on the same site, apparently honouring the deities of Samothrace. Eventually, the path passes in front of the Roman Odeon, where concerts were held and, to the right, the Bouleuterion (Council Chamber), bringing you back to where you started.

☞ Tours

Gallipoli Peninsula tour companies including Hassle Free (p160) and Crowded Ho (p160) use Tours (p160) run half-day guided tours of Troy for around €35. Both will also organise a full-day program, including a morning at Troy, lunch in Eceabat and an afternoon on the Gallipoli battlefields for around €75. Local guide Uran Savaş (📞0542 263 4839; uransa vas17@hotmail.com) speaks excellent English and conducts private tours of the archaeological site (₺150).

🛏 Sleeping & Eating

Troia Pension   PENSION $

(📞0286-283 0571; www.troiapension.com; Truva Mola Noktası, Tevfikiye; camp/campervan sites without breakfast €15, s/d €30/50; ❄🤖) This simple place is a short walk from the ruins, behind a cafe and souvenir store. Run by tour guide Uran Savaş, it offers four twin rooms and powered sites for visitors with tents or campervans. There are squeaky-clean showers and toilets as well as a facility for changing toilet water in vans. Meals are available in the cafe.

❶ Getting There & Away

Dolmuşes to Troy (₺5, 35 minutes, hourly) leave on the half-hour between 9.30am and 5pm from a station at the northern end of the bridge over the Sarı River in Çanakkale and drop passengers at the archaeological site's car park. During summer, the first dolmuş departs Çanakkale at 7.30am and the last departure back from Troy leaves at 8.15pm. The tourist information office has a handy flyer with the latest timings.

GÖKÇEADA

📞 0286 / POP 8640

'Heavenly Island' is a spectacular Aegean outpost 11 nautical miles from the Gallipoli Peninsula. On weekends and holidays during the summer months it is popular with residents of İstanbul and İzmir, who are drawn by its unspoiled landscape, sandy beaches and Greek-influenced culture. At other times of the year it is a tranquil place where visitors are rare and the surroundings are bucolic.

It's a mystery to us why Gökçeada isn't more popular as a base for those visiting the nearby Gallipoli battlefields. A ferry links the island with Kabatepe at the heart of the Gallipoli Peninsula, carries both cars and passengers and takes only 75 minutes. There is a small but alluring range of accommodation options on offer and plenty of opportunities for swimming, windsurfing, trekking and cultural tourism.

History

Gökçeada was once a predominantly Greek (Rum) island known as Imbros or İmroz. During WWI it was an important base for the Gallipoli campaign; indeed, Allied commander General Ian Hamilton stationed himself at the village of Aydıncık (then Kefalos) on the island's southeastern coast. Along with its smaller island neighbour to the south, Bozcaada, Gökçeada was ceded to the new Turkish Republic in 1923 as part of the Treaty of Lausanne but was exempted from the population exchange, retaining a predominantly Greek population. However, in 1946 the Turkish authorities installed the first wave of Turkish settlers from the Black Sea region, starting a clear but unstated process of 'Turkification' that reached its height in the 1960s and 1970s when up to 6000 Turks from the mainland – many from the east – were relocated here. Greek schools were forceably closed, Greek churches were desecrated and 90% of the island's cultivatable land was appropriated from Greek residents, most of whom had no choice but to leave. In 1970 the island was renamed Gökçeada by the Turkish government. These days, there are approximately 200 Greek residents, most of whom are elderly.

◉ Sights

The main sights of interest are the area's villages. Heading west from Gökçeada town, better known as Merkez (Centre), you'll pass Zeytinli (Aya Theodoros) after 3km, Tepeköy (Agridia), another 7km on, and Dereköy (Shinudy), another 5km west. All were built on hillsides overlooking the island's central valley to avoid pirate raids. Many of the stone houses in these villages are deserted and falling into disrepair. However, thanks to a few enthusiastic and entrepreneurial residents of Greek heritage in Zeytinli and Tepeköy, the villages are discovering the benefits of small-scale tourism and some former residents and their families are returning.

Kaleköy   VILLAGE

Perched on the hillside above the harbour at Kaleköy is 'High Kaleköy' (formerly Kastro), a pretty village built around a ruined Genoese fortress. Overlooking the Aegean island of Samothrace (Samothraki), most of its buildings date from the time when its residents were Greek; all were forced out in the 1960s and 1970s. There's a disused church, a charming coffee shop, a couple of restaurants, a number of pensions and two boutique hotels.

Gökçeada

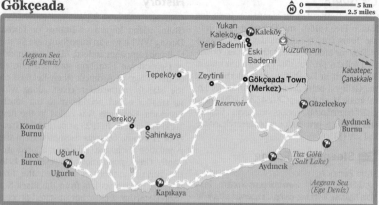

A dolmuş (minibus) links both it and the harbour with Merkez.

Down on the harbour, the beach and nearby fish restaurants are popular with touring Turks. The coastline between Kaleköy and Kuzulimanı forms a *sualtı milli parkı* (national marine park).

Eski Bademli   VILLAGE

Hilltop Greek village Eski Bademli (Old Bademli) looks down on rather ugly Yeni Bademli (New Bademli) and over the valley to the Aegean. The village has cobbled lanes, old stone houses and plenty of almond trees (*bademli* is the Turkish word for almond).

◉ Beaches

The sand beach at **Aydıncık** is the best on the island. It is adjacent to **Tuz Gölü** (Salt Lake), a favourite shelter for pink flamingos between November and March. The lake is rich in sulphur and reputed to be good for the skin. Further west there are good beaches at **Kapıkaya** and **Uğurlu**.

✨ Festivals & Events

Greek Easter   RELIGIOUS

Many former residents return to the island for Easter celebrations. Accommodation can be very difficult to secure.

Festival of the Virgin Mary   RELIGIOUS

(Panayia; ◉15 Aug) Church services and feasts to celebrate the Virgin Mary.

🛏 Sleeping

Most accommodation is centred around Kaleköy and Merkez, and there are also characterful options in Greek villages such as Zeytinli

and Tepeköy. In summer it's not unusual for locals to approach and offer you a spare room in their house (*ev pansiyonu*) for considerably less than the prices charged by pensions and hotels. Many establishments close during the low season.

🛏 Merkez & Eski Bademli

Taylan Hotel   HOTEL $

(☎0286-887 2451; omertaylanada@hotmail.com; Atatürk Caddesi, Merkez; s/d ₺60/90; ❄🛜) On the main street in Merkez, this place has seen better days, but it's clean, the management is friendly (though not bilingual) and there's a bustling downstairs restaurant.

Hotel Kale Palace   HOTEL $$

(☎0286-888 0021; www.hotelkalepalace.com; Atatürk Caddesi 54, Merkez; s/d/tr ₺100/150/200; ❄🛜) You'll look in vain for any skerrick of character, but this modern monolith offers spacious, well-maintained three-star rooms at reasonable prices. Very little English is spoken. Good location near restaurants and public transport to explore the rest of the island.

★ Son Vapur Konuk Evi   BOUTIQUE HOTEL $$$

(☎0286-887 2085; Eski Bademli; r ₺250-300) Cascading down a hillside in Eski Bademli, Son Vapur's boutique charm includes colourful if slightly rustic rooms, and a characterful ambience courtesy of the friendly family owners. Rugs and antiques create a cosy, welcoming vibe, and the astounding views from the terrace of Son Vapur's Ada Vapuru restaurant (open July to September) include the imposing profile of the Greek island of Samothrace.

⌂ Yukarı Kaleköy

★ **Anemos Hotel**   BOUTIQUE HOTEL **$$$**
(✍ 0286-887 3729; www.anemos.com.tr; Yukarı Kaleköy 98, Yukarı Kaleköy; basic/standard/superior r ₺280/360/430; ✴ 🛜 🕸) *Anemos* means 'wind' in Turkish, and this hotel brought the winds of change to Gökçeada. It's responsible for introducing the concept of the boutique hotel and has attracted clients from the mainland who would previously have headed to style-setting Bodrum for their vacations. Ground-floor basic rooms are smallish; standards are spacious; and superiors are large (some have private terraces). All are well appointed.

Castle   BOUTIQUE HOTEL **$$$**
(✍ 0554 676 5155; www.hotelthecastle.com; Yukarı Kaleköy 29-30, Yukarı Kaleköy; r from ₺250; ✷ May-Nov; ✴ 🛜) Most of the old houses on the island were built using the golden-hued stone you'll see scattered across the landscape. High in Yukarı Kaleköy, with wonderful views, this charming hotel incorporates two old Greek houses that were built this way. There are five good-size standard rooms that sleep three, and four larger suites sleeping four. All have kitchenettes.

⌂ Aydıncık

Şen Camping   CAMPING GROUND **$**
(✍ 0286-898 1020; Aydıncık; campsites per person ₺15; ✷ May-Sep) The water almost laps the tent sites at this camping ground. Though it's looking a bit rundown, the place is neat and all sites include bathroom use. The restaurant and cafe-bar are popular in high season. If you're keen to windsurf, there's equipment for hire and an in-house instructor.

Gökçeada Sörf
Eğitim Merkezi Oteli   RESORT **$$$**
(Gökçeada Surf Training Centre Hotel; ✍ 0286-898 1022; www.surfgokceada.com; Aydıncık; s/d ₺200/330; ✷ May-Sep; ✴ 🛜) They take windsurfing seriously here, and offer guests six-lesson packages over three to four days (₺480). Surrounded by gardens that lead straight to the sandy beach, 46 rooms have tiled floors and sand-coloured walls. The beach cafe-bar and restaurant are definite draws.

⌂ Zeytinli & Tepeköy

Pansyon Agridia   PENSION **$$**
(✍ 0286-887 2138; www.facebook.com/dimitris. assanakis; Tepeköy; s/d €30/40) Owner Dimitris Assanakis is extremely proud of his white-washed pension perched on the village's highest point. There are three simply decorated rooms with good beds; a double and twin share a bathroom and the second twin has an en suite. All can be hot in summer, but the balcony with its magnificent view over the valley well and truly compensates.

Zeytinali Hotel   BOUTIQUE HOTEL **$$$**
(✍ 0286-887 3707; www.zeytindalihotel.com; Zeytinliköy 168, Zeytinli; s/d ₺240/300; ✷ May-Oct; ✴ 🛜) Two rebuilt Greek stone houses at the top of the old village showcase island style and comfort. The 16 rooms – each named after a Greek god – have satellite TVs and views of the village or the sea; wi-fi is only available in the lobby and on the terrace. The ground-floor restaurant is popular with day trippers.

✗ Eating

✗ Merkez

Balbadem Cafe   CAFE **$**
(Yesilada Sokak 8, Merkez; snacks & mains ₺8-18; ✷ 7am-11pm) Framed by grape arbours, our favourite cafe in Merkez is concealed in an old stone house a short walk from the main square. Colourful tables fill Balbadem's shaded verandah; there's an excellent range of teas and coffees; and don't be surprised if the friendly posse of local cats patiently lines up while you're tucking into the *köy kahvaltı* (village-style breakfast; ₺18).

Meydanı Pastanesi   PASTICCERIA **$**
(✍ 0286-887 4420; www.efibadem.com.tr/meydani; Atatürk Caddesi 31, Merkez; tea & efi badem ₺3; ✷ 6am-11pm) Every visitor to Gökçeada makes their way to the island's most popular cafe at some stage, lured by its famous creation, the *efi badem*. A sugar-dusted biscuit made with almonds, butter and flour, it is the perfect accompaniment to a glass of tea. Pastries, other biscuits and slices of pizza are also available.

✗ Kaleköy

★ **Mustafanın Kayfesi**   CAFE **$$**
(✍ 0286-887 2063; www.mustafaninkayfesi.com; Kaleköy; breakfast plates ₺20; ✷ 9am-9pm) Look for the free-standing bell tower of the Ayia Marina church to find this welcoming cafe, which is tucked into the adjacent garden. The village-style breakfast is delicious, and the Turkish coffee is the best on the island. In the late afternoon, a nargile (water pipe) and coffee combo really hits the spot.

Yakamoz
TURKISH, SEAFOOD **$$**

(☑0286-887 2057; www.gokceadayakamoz.com; Yukarı Kaleköy; mains ₺25-35; ☉11am-3pm & 6-10pm) For a sundowner with million-dollar views over the water, head to the terrace restaurant at the Yakamoz Motel.

✖ Zeytinli & Tepeköy

Nostos Cafe
CAFE **$**

(Zeytinli; coffee & cake ₺10; ☉10am-9pm) Established in 1860, and still run by descendants of the original owners, this cafe in the Greek hilltop village of Zeytinli is a brilliant spot for a cup of robust *dibek* coffee. The house-made lemonade is very refreshing, and sweet treats include silky *panacotta* and crème caramel. Linger to admire the interesting heritage black-and-white photographs of island life.

★ Barba Yorgo Taverna
AEGEAN **$$**

(☑0286-887 4247; www.barbayorgo.com; Tepeköy; mains ₺25-30; ☉noon-3pm & 6-11pm May-Sep) A good time is assured at this atmospheric village restaurant overlooking vineyards and the 1780 Ayios Yioryios church. The menu includes goat stew, wonderfully tender octopus and platefuls of meze, all washed down with carafes of the house-made wine. Baba Yorgo produces a knock-your-socks-off retsina, an eminently quaffable red blend and a more sophisticated organic cabernet sauvignon.

🛍 Shopping

Gökçeada is one of only nine Turkish Cittaslow (www.cittaslowturkiye.org) cities and is committed to producing organic foodstuffs. At the forefront of this endeavour is local organic farm Elta-Ada (☑0216-336 2376; www.elta-ada.com.tr). Shops around the main square in Merkez sell local products including artisan-made soap, olive oil, jams, honey and *dibek* coffee. The best of these is Ada Rüzgarı (☑0286-887 2496; www.adaruzgari.com; Suluoğlu İş Merkezi 24b, Merkez; ☉8am-10pm).

ℹ Information

Facilities such as a bank, ATMs and a post office are found 6km inland at Merkez, where most of the island's population lives.

The **tourist office** (☑0286-887 3005; Cumhuriyet Meydanı; ☉9am-2pm & 3-7pm) is in a timber kiosk next to the main dolmuş stop in Merkez. Opening hours can be haphazard.

ℹ Getting There & Away

Check the **Gestaş** (p161) website or with your hotel for ferry departure times as these change according to the season.

FERRIES

Gallipoli Peninsula Ferries cross between Kabatepe and Gökçeada (per person/car ₺3/35, 75 minutes). Services run three times daily each way from September to May, five times daily in June and July, and more regularly in August.

Çanakkale Ferries (per person ₺10, 1½ hours) leave Çanakkale at 8am Monday and 7.30pm Friday, and return from Gökçeada on Thursday and Sunday at 6pm. At the time of writing this was a passenger-only ferry, so if you have your own transport you'll need to travel to the island from Kabatepe.

ℹ Getting Around

CAR

Note that the only petrol station is 2km from Merkez on the Kuzulimanı road. There are three car-hire companies on the island, including **Gökçeada-Rent-A-Car** (☑0286-887 2417; Atatürk Caddesi 84), in Merkez, which charges around ₺150 per day for a small car.

DOLMUŞ

Ferries dock at Kuzulimanı, from where you can take a dolmuş to Merkez (₺3, 15 minutes, eight per day). Change at Merkez to continue to Kaleköy, 5km further north (₺2, 25 minutes). Some of the Kaleköy dolmuşes stop in Yeni Bademli and Yukarı Kaleköy en route.

TAXI

It costs around ₺350 to hire a taxi for half a day and tour the island. The following are approximate costs for short trips:

Kuzulimanı–Merkez ₺20, 10 minutes

Kuzulimanı–Kaleköy ₺30, 20 minutes

Kuzulimanı–Yukarı Kaleköy ₺40, 25 minutes

Merkez–Kaleköy ₺15, five minutes

Merkez–Zeytinli ₺20, 10 minutes

Merkez–Tepeköy ₺25, 20 minutes

Merkez–Aydıncık ₺30, 15 minutes

İzmir & the North Aegean

Best Places to Eat

➡ Lǎl Girit Mutfağı (p190)
➡ Asma Yaprağı (p218)
➡ Zeytin Bağı (p184)
➡ Horasan (p216)

Best Places to Sleep

➡ Assos Alarga (p181)
➡ Taş Otel (p217)
➡ Swissôtel Büyük Efes (p207)
➡ Nar Konak (p181)
➡ Assosyal Otel (p181)

Why Go?

An extraordinary number of attractions are waiting to be discovered along the short stretch of coast between the Dardanelles and the Çeşme Peninsula. There are sandy beaches aplenty, and innumerable scenic viewpoints from where the Greek islands of Lesbos and Chios appear to float on the sparkling Aegean Sea.

There are also plenty of reminders of the region's importance in antiquity, most notably the extraordinary Acropolis and Askeplion at Bergama (Pergamum), the evocative ruins of Teos and the spectacularly sited Temple of Athena at Behramkale (Assos).

But as wonderful as these beaches and ruins are – not to mention the compelling attractions on offer in the urbane city of İzmir – most people who visit this part of the country say their most lasting memories are of the bittersweet traces of Greek heritage that have influenced the local cuisine and architecture and enriched the lives of its inhabitants.

When to Go

İzmir

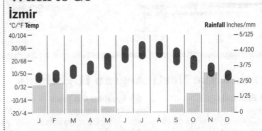

Apr Alaçatı hosts a foodie celebration of Aegean *ot* (wild greens).

Jun The International İzmir Festival brings music to the region.

Sep Bozcaada celebrates the grape harvest at its wine festival.

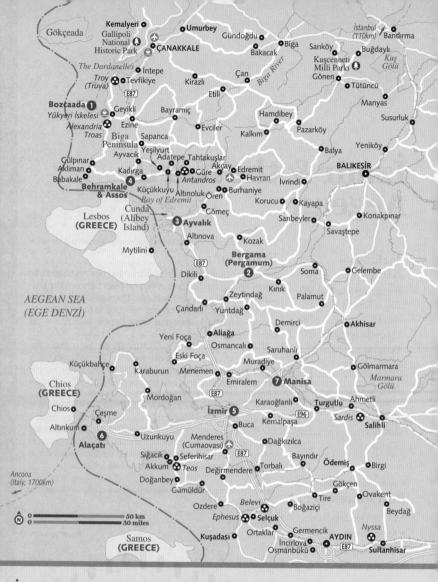

İzmir & the North Aegean Highlights

❶ Bozcaada (p177)
Enjoying fine wine, fresh fish and Greek-style mezes on an island escape.

❷ Bergama (Pergamum) (p190) Exploring one of Turkey's most magnificent ancient sites.

❸ Ayvalık's Old Town (p184) Wandering the atmospheric backstreets of this Greek neighbourhood.

❹ Behramkale & Assos (p180) Admiring the glorious sea views from the Temple of Athena.

❺ İzmir (p198) Losing yourself in the labyrinthine

lanes of the historic Kemeraltı Market.

❻ Alaçatı (p217) Partying with the glitterati in the glamour town of the Çeşme Peninsula.

❼ Manisa (p212)
Marvelling at the beauty of the 16th-century Muradiye Mosque.

Bozcaada

📞 0286 / POP 2754

Windswept Bozcaada (Tenedos in Greek) is a hugely popular weekend and summer destination for residents of İstanbul, Çanakkale and İzmir. A showcase of rustic Aegean style, it's more down to earth than Alaçatı and Bodrum but is still crowded and expensive in the high season. Most of the action occurs in Merkez (or Bozcaada Town), which has an atmospheric historic Greek quarter full of brightly painted houses that have been converted into boutique hotels, B&Bs, tavernas and bars.

The island is small – just under 40 sq km – with sandy beaches and picturesque vineyards. These supply the grapes for Bozcaada's boutique wineries, whose vintages can be sampled at cellar doors and in the many Greek-style tavernas in Merkez.

Many businesses shut down outside the high season (mid-June to mid-September); between November and March the island is as quiet as a graveyard. Information about the island is available at http://en.bozcaadareh beri.com and www.gobozcaada.com.

◎ Sights & Activities

The best swimming beaches are on the southern side of the island and include **Akvaryum** (Aquarium), **Ayazma** and **Sulubahçe**. All are jam-packed during summer. Ayazma is by far the most popular and best equipped (umbrellas and deckchair hire ₺10 per day), boasting several tavernas. It's also the location of the small Greek Orthodox **Aya Paraskevi Monastery** (Ayazma Monastery; Map p178; Ayazma Beach). **Çayır Beach** on the northern side of the island is a popular windsurfing and kitesurfing destination.

Bozcaada Castle   CASTLE
(Bozcaada Kalesi; Map p178; ₺5; ⊙10am-1pm & 2-6pm) It is generally thought that Bozcaada's colossal fortress dates to Byzantine times, but it has been significantly rebuilt by the Venetians, Genoese and Ottomans. Over the dry moat and within the double walls are traces of a mosque, ammunition stores, a barracks, an infirmary and Roman pillars. It sits right next to the ferry terminal.

Bozcaada Museum   MUSEUM
(Bozcaada Yerel Tarih Araştırma Merkezi; 📞0532-215 6033; http://bozcaadamuzesi.net; Lale Sokak 7; adult/student & child ₺10/5; ⊙10am-8pm late

Apr–late Oct) Located 100m west of the ferry terminal in the old Greek district, this small museum and local-history research centre is a treasure trove of island curios: maps, prints, photographs, seashells and day-to-day artefacts.

Church of St Mary   CHURCH
(Meryem Ana Kilisesi, Teodoku Eastern Orthodox Church; 20 Eylül Caddesi 42/a) This 19th-century church in the old Greek neighbourhood to the west of the fortress is one of only two remaining Greek Orthodox churches on the island (there were originally over 30). Its distinctive bell tower was built in 1865. The church opens for mass on Sunday mornings at 8am but is closed at other times.

🛌 Sleeping

It's sensible to book your accommodation in advance, especially between June and September. Most hotels and pensions are in Merkez, with many options in the old Greek quarter around the Church of St Mary. Light sleepers should be warned that this quarter is noisy well into the wee small hours; for a quieter option consider the Turkish quarter on the hill behind the castle. Many businesses only open for the high season.

★**Latife Hanım Konağı**   BOUTIQUE HOTEL $
(Madam Latife Mansion; 📞0286-690 0030; www. latifehanimkonagi.com; Atatürk Caddesi 23; d/ste ₺260/750; ❉ 🛜) The island's most stylish hotel occupies a meticulously restored century-old house near the Church of St Mary in the Greek quarter. Standard rooms are tastefully decorated with white bedspreads and kilims, but are small. Views from the 2nd-floor roof terrace, where breakfast is served, are commanding. The hotel has a private beach elsewhere on the island. Excellent value.

Kale Pansiyon   PENSION $
(Castle Pension; 📞0286-697 8840; www.kale pansiyon.net; İnönü Caddesi 69; basement d/tr ₺150/200, d/tr ₺220/270; ⊙mid-Jun–mid-Sep; ❉ 🛜) Reached via a steep climb from the old Greek quarter, and with commanding views over the town, the family-run 'Castle' offers simple but clean rooms; those in the basement are darker but cheaper. There's a friendly host and a lovely garden to have breakfast in. Of its two pink-coloured houses, the one on the right has better bathrooms. There's a 15% discount for cash payments.

Bozcaada

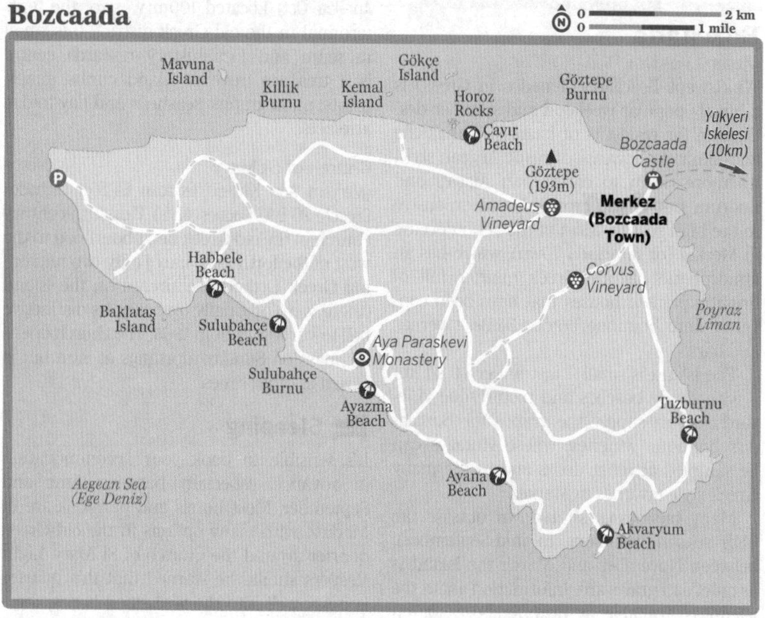

Kaikias Otel BOUTIQUE HOTEL $$
(☎0532 363 2697; www.kaikias.com; Eskici Sokak 1; s ₺300, d ₺400-500, ste ₺900; ⊙mid-Jun–mid-Sep; ❄📶) Overlooking a tiny square near the castle, this 20-room hotel in two buildings has attractive, sometimes quirky, decor and a variety of room types. The standard rooms are cramped – opt for a VIP room or suite if possible. The terrace right on the water is a major drawcard, but the in-house cafe means that noise is a given.

Bademlik Otel B&B $$
(☎0535 825 6812; www.bademlikotel.com; Asmalı Fırın Sokak 19; d ₺275-325, tr ₺425-475; P❄📶) Opened in 2015, this designer B&B in the Turkish quarter near the castle offers five rooms with white walls, minimal furniture and pretty but cramped tiled bathrooms. Breakfast is served on the attractive front terrace.

Eating

Local specialities include *kurabiye* (biscuits) made with *bademli* (almonds) and *sakızlı* (mastic); *oğlak kapama* (goat meat stewed with lettuce and fennel); and *domates reçeli* (tomato jam).

Many of the island's eateries and cafes are open for the high season only. Others open their doors only at weekends and on Wednesdays, when a produce market is held in Hamam Sokak between the *iskele* (dock) and the Alaybay Mosque.

Çiçek Pastanesi CAFE $
(☎0286-690 0053; www.renklisen.com; Cumhuriyet Meydanı 17; ⊙7am-11pm) Its location in a pretty square near the Alaybey Mosque is only one of the attractions of this friendly cafe and bakery, which was established in 1959. There are indoor tables, but the choice seating is outside under the trees. The *poğaças* (savoury pastries) and biscuits are delicious (try the *Tenedos kurabiye* or the *acıbadem kurabiye,* which are made with almonds).

Cabalı Meyhane AEGEAN $$
(☎0286-697 0118; Kazanlar Sokak 12; fish price per kg; ⊙noon-2am May-Sep) A premium location right on the water in the shadow of Bozcaada Castle gives this eatery an edge over the competition, but it's the party atmosphere and excellent Greek-style seafood and mezes that are the major draw here.

Cafe at Lisa's CAFE $$
(☎0286-697 0182; Cami Sokak 1; pizzas & pastas ₺19-28, cakes ₺12; ⊙10am-1am Apr-Nov; 📶) Australian Lisa Lay opened this casual cafe in an

old bakery near the *iskele* two decades ago, and has built a loyal clientele of expats and island visitors since this time. The limited menu includes cake, toasted sandwiches, pasta and pizza. Grab an outside table beneath the big tree.

Boruzan SEAFOOD $$
(📞 0286-697 8414; www.boruzanrestoran.com; Liman İçi; mezes ₺10-25, mains ₺20-40; ⏱ 9am-1am) Our favourite of the fish restaurants by the *liman* (harbour), blue-and-white Boruzan offers a wide range of mezes made with produce from the restaurant's own vegetable patch, as well as simple seafood dishes such as *kalamar tava* (grilled squid). A branch opens in summer at Ayazma Beach.

 Drinking & Nightlife

Polente BAR
(📞 0530 967 2724; İskele Caddesi 41; ⏱ 9am-2am mid-May–Sep; 📶) Painted in the island's signature blue and white, this quirky cafe-bar on the road linking the *iskele* (dock) and the main square is one of the island's main meeting places in summer, and is always packed on sultry nights. Its cocktails, made with anything in season (cherries, mulberries, grapes), are inspired.

Bakkal BAR
(📞 0543 210 9410; Lale Sokak 22; ⏱ noon-2am May-Sep) As hipster as Bozcaada gets, this friendly place opposite the museum serves espresso coffee, local wine, cocktails, smoothies and sandwiches. Seating is on cushion-covered

BOZCAADA'S FINE WINE

Bozcaada has been one of Turkey's great wine-growing regions since ancient times, when enormous quantities of wine were used to fuel the debauchery at festivals for the wine god Dionysus. Nobody is quite sure why, but some magical alchemy of the island's climate, topography and soil make-up perfectly suits the growing of grapes. Among the island's best-known winemakers are Corvus, Talay, Amadeus and Yunatçılar, which markets its wines under the Çamlıbağ label.

The four major indigenous grape varietals are Vasilaki and Cavus for the production of white wine and Kuntra and Karalahana for red. Generally speaking, the cabernet sauvignon and cabernet shiraz wines produced here are the most impressive.

The annual Bozcaada Wine Festival takes place over the first weekend of September, during the grape harvest.

Corvus Vineyard (Map p178; 📞 0286-697 8181; www.corvus.com.tr) The island's best-known winery, owned by Turkish architect Reşit Soley, is a short drive from Merkez, on the road to Akvaryum Beach. A stylish on-site cafeteria sells food such as cheese plates and mezes, along with glasses and bottles of award-winning drops such as Corpus Reserve and Corvus Blend Number 5 (wine by glass from ₺20).

Amadeus Vineyard (Map p178; 📞 0533 371 0470; info@amadeuswine.com; ⏱ May-Sep) Austrian winemaker Oliver Gareis is the driving force behind the Gareis family's vineyard and winery on Bozcaada, and his vintages are winning fans across the country. Pop into the winery for a paid tasting (mini glass/glass ₺5/10), or to purchase bottles from the cellar door. His cabernets are particularly impressive.

Çamlıbağ Saraplari (📞 0286-697 8055; Emniyet Sokak 24; ⏱ 8am-7pm) The first Turkish-owned winery to be founded on the island (in 1925), Yunatçılar markets its wines under the Çamlıbağ label. Its quaffable vintages of local varietals, including Kuntra and Karalahna, can be tasted at this showroom near Cumhuriyet Meydanı (multiple taste ₺12).

Corvus (📞 0286-697 8181; Çinarlı Çarşı Caddesi 53; ⏱ 10am-6pm, to 9.30pm mid-Jun–mid-Sep) The island's best-known winery has a retail outlet just off Cumhuriyet Caddesi in Merkez.

Talay (📞 0533 370 3030; www.talay.com.tr; Lale Sokak 3; ⏱ 8am-6pm) There are no tastings at the Talay showroom, alas, but it's possible to purchase bottles of wine. If the store isn't open, ring the bell at its *şarapçılık* (wine cellar) opposite – there's a barrel in the street between the two.

benches and chairs on the lane, or among the corner-store products for sale inside.

ⓘ Information

There's a row of ATMs near the PTT on Çınar Çeşme Caddesi in Merkez.

There's a small wooden **information booth** (www.gobozcaada.com; İskele Caddesi; ⊘9am-6pm Jun–mid-Sep) near the *iskele*.

ⓘ Getting There & Away

BUS

In summer Metro, Truva, Pammukale and other companies run services between İstanbul's Büyük Otogar and Geyikli's Yükyeri İskelesi (₺60–₺70, 8¾ hours), from where ferries travel to the island. Make sure that your bus will connect with a ferry – it's usually best to travel overnight and connect with the morning ferry.

Outside summer, buses usually only travel as far as Ezine, from where you'll need to take a taxi or dolmuş (minibus that stops anywhere along its prescribed route) to the *iskele*; it's a 20km (₺6) trip.

BOAT

Gestaş (☑ 444 0752; www.gdu.com.tr) ferries run daily to Bozcaada from Yükyeri İskelesi (35 minutes; return per person/car ₺7/70), 4km west of Geyikli, south of Troy. Out of the high season, they operate three to four times daily. In the high season, there are many more services. Check the Gestaş website for the most up-to-date timetable, as these change frequently.

In the high season, Gestaş hydrofoils sail from Çanakkale (one way ₺10) every day except Monday. Make sure you double-check departure times. The same company also offers limited services between Gökçeada and Bozcaada (one way ₺10).

ⓘ Getting Around

Mountain bikes can be rented from **Akyüz** (☑ 0545 541 9515; Cınarlı Çarşı Caddesi; ⊘mid-Jun–mid-Sep), located around the corner from the Cumhuriyet Meydanı.

DOLMUŞ

Hourly dolmuşes leave from near the *iskele* in Bozcaada town and travel to Ayazma Beach (₺3). In summer more frequent dolmuşes also serve Ayazma via Sulubahçe Beach, and there's a service to Polente Feneri (Polente Lighthouse) on the westernmost point for watching sunsets.

TAXI

A taxi from Bozcaada town to Ayazma costs about ₺30.

Behramkale & Assos

☑0286

The hilltop *köyü* (village) of Behramkale is home to the ancient remains of the Greek settlement of Assos. These include a spectacularly sited Temple of Athena, a theatre and a necropolis. Below the village is a *liman* with a small pebble beach; the locals call this part of the village the İskele Mevkii (Wharf Area). Here, the old stone buildings and warehouses have been transformed into hotels and fish restaurants.

Try to avoid visiting on weekends and public holidays from the beginning of April to the end of August, when tourists pour in by the coachload. And definitely avoid coming here between December and February, when temperatures plummet and the wind chill is merciless.

There are few facilities other than an ATM and pharmacy in the upper village.

History

The Mysian city of Assos was founded in the 8th century BC by colonists from Lesbos, who built its great temple to Athena in 540 BC. The city enjoyed considerable prosperity under the rule of Hermeias, a former student of Plato who encouraged philosophers to live in Assos. Aristotle himself lived here from 348 to 345 BC and ended up marrying Hermeias' niece, Pythia. Assos' glory days came to an abrupt end with the arrival of the Persians, who crucified Hermeias and forced Plato to flee.

Alexander the Great drove the Persians out, but Assos' importance was challenged by the ascendancy of Alexandria Troas to the north. From 241 to 133 BC the city was ruled by the kings of Pergamum.

St Paul visited Assos briefly during his third missionary journey, walking here from Alexandria Troas to meet St Luke before boarding a boat for Lesbos. In late Byzantine times the city dwindled to a village, a state that it retains today.

◉ Sights

Temple of Athena RUINS
(₺10; ⊘8am-5pm, to 7pm Apr-Sep) Built in 540 BC on top of an 238m-high hill overlooking the Gulf of Edremit, this temple with its squat Doric columns has undergone a reconstruction that hurts more than helps. However, the setting with its view out to the Greek island of Lesbos is spectacular and

well worth the admission fee. Erected by settlers from Lesbos, the temple once boasted a decorative frieze that is now part of the collection of the İstanbul Archaeology Museum.

Theatre RUINS
(entry incl in ₺10 archaeological site ticket) **FREE** A heavily restored theatre and the remains of the ancient city walls can be seen below the agora; the theatre is accessed via a gate on the winding road leading down to the harbour. The surrounding fields are scattered with sarcophagi (from the Greek, 'flesh-eaters') from the ancient necropolis. According to Pliny the Elder, the sarcophagi were carved from stone that was caustic and that 'ate' the flesh off the deceased in 40 days. The theatre site opens intermittently.

Hüdavendigâr Mosque MOSQUE
Next to the entrance to the Temple of Athena, this poorly maintained 14th-century mosque is a simple structure – a dome on squinches set on top of a square room – that was constructed with materials from a 6th-century-AD church and is one of just two remaining Ottoman mosques of its kind in Turkey (the other is in Bursa, and Hüdavendigar is in fact a poetic name for that city).

🛌 Sleeping

Boutique options are in Behramkale, and resort-style places are down by the water. In high season, virtually all the hotels around the harbour insist on *yarım pansiyon* (half board).

🛌 Village

⭐ **Assosyal Otel** BOUTIQUE HOTEL $
(☎ 0286-721 7046; www.assosyalotel.com; Alan Meydanı 8, Behramkale; s/d/f €80/90/200; ❄ 📶) Why stay in a pension when there is a budget option like this on offer? This 16-room hotel is full of contemporary art, serves a lavish and delicious breakfast and has a series of terraces with mountain views. Occupying a vine-clad stone house that has been given a modern makeover, its rooms are cramped but comfortable nonetheless.

The lovely owner doesn't speak much English but goes out of her way to assist guests. There's a bar and restaurant on site, too.

Tekin Pansiyon PENSION $
(☎ 0286-721 7099; Behramkale; s/d €15/30; ❄ 📶) This simple but clean place in the upper village fulfills the basic pension requirements,

and even though the eight rooms face away from Behramkale's panoramic views, the little tables in the open verandah overlook village goings-on. No English is spoken.

⭐ **Assos Alarga** BOUTIQUE HOTEL $$
(☎ 0286-721 7260; www.assosalarga.com; Behramkale; r €100-130, ste €140-190; 🅿 ❄ 📶 ♨ 🏊) Located in the quiet end of the village just below the Temple of Athena, this lovely hotel has just five rooms, guaranteeing stellar service from Ece, the affable owner. The setting is wonderful, with plenty of trees, an attractive pool area and panoramic views over the mountains from all rooms. Note that the least expensive room, Vıya, doesn't have wi-fi.

The comfortable rooms are filled with art and bright kilims but it's the two suites that impress most: Orsa has attractive traditional decor, and sleek modern Ancora has a kitchenette and swish bathroom with tub. Ece can organise dinner at the hotel (₺40–₺75 depending on the menu) if given 24 hours' notice.

⭐ **Nar Konak** BOUTIQUE HOTEL $$
(☎ 0533 480 9393; www.assosnarkonak.com; Behramkale Köyü 62, Behramkale; r €90-120; ⊙ Mar-Dec; ❄ 📶) There can't be too many hotels in the world where St Paul preached, but Gizem and Juan's charming guesthouse has a huge rock in its flower-filled garden that apparently served as the apostle's pulpit. Five pretty rooms feature crocheted bedspreads and colourful rugs; the best (Daphne) has a terrace with Acropolis views. There a terrace bar and a comfortable lounge.

🛌 Harbour

Yıldız Otel PENSION $
(☎ 0286-721 7025; muzafferozden17@gmail.com; İskele Mevkii; s/d €36/53; ❄) The Star offers rooms with brightly coloured walls, small double beds with clean white linen, fridge and decent bathrooms. Those off the welcoming terrace restaurant and lounge aren't ideal – request one of the front rooms with a harbour view instead.

Dr No Antik Pansiyon PENSION $
(☎ 0286-721 7397; www.assosdrnoantikpansiyon.com; İskele Mevkii; s €15-22, d €30-43; ❄ 📶) No sign of an evil conspiracy at this very basic but friendly pension, which offers six cramped rooms over the restaurant of the same name. It's the best budget option down at the harbour.

WORTH A TRIP

BIGA PENINSULA

Postcard-perfect Aegean scenery and deserted ancient ruins make this coastal route between Bozcaada and Behramkale (Assos) one of the most enjoyable drives in the region. There are also some relatively isolated beaches along the route which, while not entirely off the beaten track, are seldom as crowded as others further south.

Ten kilometres southeast of Geyikli lie the ruins of Alexandria Troas (Dalyan) FREE, scattered around the village of Dalyan. After the death of Alexander the Great in 323 BC, his general Antigonus took control of this land, founding the city of Antigoneia in 311 BC.

Some 32km south is Gülpınar (pop 1333), a small farming village once the ancient city of Chryse (or Krysa), famous for its 2nd-century-BC Ionic temple to Apollo. Known as the Apollon Smintheion (Apollon Smintheus; ☑ 0286-742 8822; www.smintheion.com; ₺5; ☉ 8am-5pm, to 7.30pm mid-Jun–mid-Sep), the ruins are signposted 300m down a side road to the right as you enter the village.

From Gülpınar, a road heads 9km west past an enormous and unsightly residential development to Babakale (ancient Lekton), the westernmost point of mainland Turkey. It's a sleepy place that seems almost overawed by its 18th-century fortress, the last Ottoman castle built in present-day Turkey.

Travelling through the peninsula by public transport is difficult; you're much better off exploring by car, motorcycle or bicycle. There are six daily dolmuş (minibus that stops anywhere along its prescribed route) services between Gülpınar/Babakale (₺10/11) and Ayvacık but few others.

Assos Kervansaray Hotel   HOTEL $$

(☑ 0286-721 7093; www.assoskervansaray.com; İskele Mevkii; s €60-90, d €80-120, tr €110-170; P ❄ ☎ ≋) Housed in a 19th-century acorn warehouse that has been subjected to an endearingly eccentric renovation, the Kervansaray offers 40 rooms; 16 have a sea view. This is a great choice for families as there's an on-site fish restaurant on the waterside terrace, a small pebble beach, a pool table and two outdoor pools (one for children).

Assos Nazlıhan Hotel   RESORT $$

(☑ 0286-721 7385; www.assosnazlihanspahotel.com; İskele Mevkii; standard s/d €56/115, standard half board s/d €80/150, spa s/d €65/130; P ❄ ☎ ≋) Recently remodelled as a spa resort (a hamam, sauna and massage treatments are available), the Nazlıhan occupies three buildings at the western end of the harbour. Rooms in the new spa building are best. Five of these have sea views (opt for Leb-ı derya or Kaptan Deryaı; all have Jacuzzis. In summer standard rooms are available on half-board basis only.

✗ Eating & Drinking

Don't expect to eat well here. The fish restaurants on the harbour are unpleasantly crowded and barely acceptable in quality. They're expensive, too – be sure to check the cost of fish and bottles of wine before ordering. Other options are cheaper but no better. We suggest eating in your hotel if possible.

Uzun Ev   SEAFOOD $$

(☑ 0286-721 7007; İskele Mevkii; mezes ₺8-25, mains from ₺30; ☉ 8am-3am) The 'Long House' is the pick of the seafront restaurants and garners the most lively crowd, especially on weekends in high season. Blue wooden chairs line the terrace, while inside it feels like a warm Turkish pub. Try the succulent speciality, sea bass à l'Aristotle (steamed in a special stock) or the varied seafood meze.

Aile Çay Bahçesi   TEA GARDEN

(Family Tea Garden; Behram Köyü Yolu; ☎) For a coffee or Coke on the main square in the upper village, this place has a pleasant shaded terrace offering attractive views and good company.

❶ Getting There & Away

AIR

BoraJet (www.borajet.com.tr) flies between İstanbul (Sabiha Gökçen) and Koca Seyit airport in Edremit. Shuttle buses then travel to Küçükkuyu (₺20), from where you can take a taxi (₺40).

DOLMUŞ

There are two daily dolmuşes to/from Çanakkale (₺18, 1½ hours). Alternatively, regular dolmuşes travel between Çanakkale and Ayvacık (₺12, half-hourly), from where dolmuşes travel to/from Behramkale (₺6, five to seven daily). Services operate between 8am and 7pm.

To get to Küçükkuyu, Gülpınar or Babakale by dolmuş, you'll need to travel via Ayvacık.

TAXI
A taxi costs ₺30 to/from Ayvacık and ₺70 to/from Küçükkuyu.

❶ Getting Around

CAR & MOTORCYCLE
There is little to no parking at the harbour, and the road ends in a bottleneck that can be extremely stressful for drivers should they get trapped in it. There is a large paid car park on the winding road leading downhill – park there rather than risking getting stuck further down.

DOLMUŞ
From May to mid-October, a dolmuş links the harbour and village every 30 minutes during the day (₺2.50). A taxi costs ₺10. The steep walk takes around 30 minutes. The dolmuş stand at the harbour is next to the Rıhtım Büfe on the main road.

Ayvacık
☑ 0286 / POP 8480
Ayvacık's major attraction is its huge Friday market, which is held in the streets around the otogar (bus station) and Kültür Park. Farmers head here from surrounding villages to sell fresh produce, and the variety and quality of their offerings is quite astounding. Those villagers in long satiny overcoats or brightly coloured headscarves are the descendants of Turkmen nomads (Yörüks) who settled in this area in the 15th century. The town is also known for its diminutive carpets; some 20 villages and Turkmen communities in the region still produce them.

The otogar is on Edremit Caddesi in the centre of town.

Set up to help village women make a decent living from weaving carpets from naturally dyed hand-spun wool, the **Dobag Project** (Dobag Projesi; www.dobag-teppiche.de; İzmir-Çanakkale Yolu; ⊙9am-6pm) carpet salesroom is housed in an ugly modern building a kilometre outside Ayvacık, opposite the Total garage on the main road to Çanakkale. The retail outlet is upstairs, and may be empty out of season.

Bay of Edremit
If you're travelling down the E87 from Çanakkale to İzmir, or from Behramkale (Assos) to Ayvalık, you will follow the coastal route (aka the 550 Hwy) along the shore of this bay, which is very close to the Greek island of Lesbos. The coastal towns along its edge are popular holiday destinations and are full of ugly modern hotels and shopping malls, but the once-Greek villages in the hinterland – including Yeşilyurt and Adatepe – are relatively unspoiled, filled with pretty stone houses and surrounded by dense pine forest and ancient olive groves.

Olives are the region's most famous industry and olive products, including oil and soap, are available at the many farmers markets that are held in the major centres; the best are in Edremit (Friday) and in Altınoluk (Tuesday and Saturday).

◉ Sights & Activities
The area around the pretty village of Adatepe is great for walking, with waterfalls, plunge pools for swimming and a Roman bridge near the waterfalls at Başdeğirmen.

Adatepe Olive-Oil Museum   MUSEUM
(Adatepe Zeytinyağı Müzesi; ☑ 0286-752 1303; www.adatepedukkan.com; İzmir-Çanakkale Yolu, Küçükkuyu; ⊙9am-6pm) FREE Housed in an old olive-oil factory, this unassuming but interesting museum explains the process of making olive oil and illustrates the product's many uses. There's a cafe downstairs, as well as an excellent shop selling every olive-oil product imaginable.

Antandros   ARCHAEOLOGICAL SITE
(☑ 0266-395 0493; www.antandros.ege.edu.tr; Altınoluk; ⊙10am-4pm) FREE Located on the coastal slope of Mt Ida, the Greek city of Antandros was established in the 7th century BC and was famous for its dockyards and harbours. The city lost its strategic importance over the centuries and eventually disappeared

İZMIR & THE NORTH AEGEAN AYVACIK

SERVICES TO/FROM AYVACIK OTOGAR

DESTINATION	FARE (₺)	FREQUENCY	DEPARTURES
Babakale	11	6 daily	8.30am-6.45pm
Behramkale (Assos)	6	5-7 daily	8am-7pm
Çanakkal	12	half-hourly	8am-7pm
Gülpınar	10	6 daily	8.30am-6.45pm
Küçükkuyu	6	5-7 daily	8am-7pm

altogether, only to be partially rediscovered in recent times. This Roman-era villa is one of the sites that is being excavated by archaeologists from İzmir's Ege Universitesi (Aegean University), and its rooms adorned with frescoes and mosaic floors are open to visitors.

The villa is in a forested glade just off the main coastal highway just east of Altınoluk. Signage isn't all that clear, so you'll need to keep your eyes peeled. There's a small car park next to the site, and a caretaker who is responsible for security.

Alibey Kudar Etnografya Galerisi　MUSEUM (Alibey Kudar Ethnographic Gallery; ☑0266-387 3340; www.etnografya-galerisi.com; Tahtakuşlar; adult/student & child ₺4/2; ⊘8am-7pm) The jumble of objects at this privately operated museum below the village of Tahtakuşlar provides an insight into the history of the local Turkmen population – many Alevi – whose descendants moved to this part of Turkey in the 15th century. There's everything from a yurt to textiles, with strange exhibits on Shamanistic culture around the world also thrown into the mix.

🛏 Sleeping & Eating

The villages of Adatepe and Yeşilyurt are full of country-house hotels, and there are also a few in the village of Çamlıbel.

There are plenty of simple eateries on and behind the seafront in Akçay and also on Süleyman Sakallı Caddesi, Küçükkuyu's main market and shopping street.

★Zeytin Bağı　AEGEAN $$$ (☑0266-387 3761; www.zeytinbagi.com; Çamlıbel; starters ₺12-25, mains ₺20-45, s/d/f ₺200/270/350; ⊘8am-midnight) Owner/chef Erhan Şeker is rightly proud of his hybrid restaurant, hotel and cookery school overlooking the Bay of Edremit, and he loves to introduce guests from around the globe to the joys of local Aegean produce. You'll dine on local specialities in an elegant indoor dining space or panoramic garden terrace, and can stay overnight in simple but pretty guestrooms.

Staying overnight is highly recommended because the Zeytin Bağı organic breakfast spread (included in room price, ₺30 otherwise) is famous throughout the country for its freshness, variety and deliciousness. If you sign up for the full-day cooking class in spring and autumn (US$50 including meal), you may even be able to emulate it at home.

ⓘ Getting There & Away

AIR

BoraJet (www.borajet.com.tr) flies between İstanbul (Sabiha Gökçen) and Koca Seyit airport in Edremit. Shuttle buses then travel to Küçükkuyu (₺20) and Altınoluk (₺15).

BUS

Buses stop at Küçükkuyu's otogar on the main highway every hour en route to Çanakkale (₺20), İzmir (₺25–₺30) and İstanbul (₺65–₺85).

DOLMUŞ

Dolmuşes travel between Ayvacık and Küçükkuyu six times daily between 8.45am and 6.30pm (₺6); a taxi between the two towns costs ₺50.

TAXI

From Küçükkuyu, taxis cost ₺15 to Yeşilyurt, ₺20 to Adatepe and ₺70 to Behramkale (Assos).

Ayvalık

☑0266 / POP 39,100 INCL CUNDA

On first glance, Ayvalık may seem unremarkable, a port town similar to many others in this region. But wander a few streets back from the waterfront and you'll discover an old Greek village in spirited abandon. Colourful shuttered doors conceal boutique hotels in restored stone houses, mosques converted from Greek Orthodox churches welcome the faithful to prayer and historic cafes full of locals line hidden squares. Put simply, it's got Aegean ambience in spades.

The region's olive-oil production is centred on Ayvalık, and there are plenty of shops selling the end product. The broken chimneys in the town centre belonged to now-abandoned olive-oil factories; these days local production occurs on the edge of town.

⊙ Sights

There are a number of good sandy beaches a few kilometres south of the city. The oddly named **Sarımsaklı Plaj** (Garlic Beach) is the most popular and is almost always crowded in summer. **Badavut Plaj** (Badavut Beach) to the west is quieter.

★Old Town　HISTORIC SITE (Map p186) Ayvalık's old town is a joy to explore. A maze of cobbled streets east of the *liman*, it is full of market squares, atmospheric cafes, Greek Orthodox churches and pretty stone houses built by Greek residents during the Ottoman era. Be sure to wander along Barbaros Caddesi, home to historic businesses such as the **Karamanlar Unlu Mamülleri** bakery, and also visit the atmosphere-drenched Şeytan Kahvesı (p187), aka 'the Devil's Coffeehouse', on Alibey Cami Caddesi.

Taksiyarhis Memorial Museum CHURCH
(Taksiyarhis Anıt Müzesi; Map p186; ☑ 0266-327 2734; Mareşal Fevzi Çakmak Caddesi; ₺5; ⊘ 9am-5pm Tue-Sun) This erstwhile Greek Orthodox cathedral, built in 1844 but never used as a place of worship, was completely renovated in 2013 and positively shimmers in the noonday sun. Note the *catedra* (bishop's seat) decorated with pelicans and a crown, the wonderful pulpit and the 18th-century icons in the apse. The cathedral is huge, with three naves and a free-standing belfry.

Çınarlı Cami MOSQUE
(Map p186; Yeni Hamam Sokak) Built in 1790 as the Greek Orthodox church of Ayios Yorgis and converted to a mosque in 1923, this lovely building has three naves and three apses and retains the soaring stone iconostasis that separated the nave from the chancel. Sadly, its icons have long since been removed. The mosque is also known as the Alibey Cami.

Köy Pazarı MARKET
(Map p186) On Thursdays, a 'village market' is held in this square next to the main *pazar yeri* (marketplace), which is also filled with market stalls.

🏃 Activities

The waters around Ayvalık are famed among divers for their rare deep-sea red coral at sites including **Deli Mehmet** and **Kerbela**. Another boon for the industry was the discovery of a wrecked jet in 2009. Dive companies in Ayvalık can organise trips to see these places and their attendant marine life, including moray eels, grouper, octopus and sea horses.

In addition to the dive sites and summer ferries to Lesbos, **cruising boats** head around the bay's islands, including Alibey (Cunda), stopping here and there for swimming, sunbathing and walking. These generally depart at 11am and return by 6.30pm and cost around €30 per person, including lunch.

🛏 Sleeping

★Taksiyarhis Pansiyon PENSION, HOSTEL $
(Map p186; ☑ 0266-312 1494; www.taksiyarhis pension.com; Mareşal Çakmak Caddesi 71; dm ₺60, s/d without bathroom ₺80/150; ✿ 🛜) This 200-year-old Greek house behind the eponymous former cathedral is full of old Turkish textiles and objets d'art. Facilities include a communal kitchen and a vine-shaded terrace with sweeping views. Rooms are rustic chic and the small dormitory sleeping up to six is quite charming. Bathrooms are clean and plentiful, though wi-fi is on the ground floor only and breakfast costs ₺15.

İZMIR & THE NORTH AEGEAN AYVALIK

GHOSTS FROM THE PAST

The early 1920s hold mixed memories for Ayvalık. Pride over its role in the Turkish War of Independence – it was here that the first shots were fired – is tempered by what happened afterwards. The Ottoman Greeks, who made up the majority of the population in Ayvalık, were forced to abandon the land of their ancestors and relocate to the Greek island of Lesbos, while some Turks from that island were, in turn, forced to start new lives in Ayvalık. Despite the enormous distress this must have caused, the Ayvalık–Lesvos exchange is nonetheless regarded as one of the least damaging episodes of the period because of the proximity of the two communities, which enabled people from both sides to continue visiting their former homes – mixed though their emotions must have been during those trips. Furthermore, both communities were involved in the production of olive oil, and so would have found much that was familiar in the other.

Today, whispers from the past are everywhere here. Some elderly locals can speak Greek and many of the town's former Greek Orthodox churches remain standing, though converted into mosques. In 1923 the former Ayios Yannis (St John's) church became the **Saatlı Camii** (Clock Mosque; Map p186; Çarşi Sokak), named for its clock tower and now minaret. The former Ayios Yioryios (St George's) is today the **Çınarlı Camii**, named after the *çınar* (plane trees) that grew here. The grand Greek cathedral was never converted but has now been turned into the **Taksiyarhis Memorial Museum**.

Ayvalık

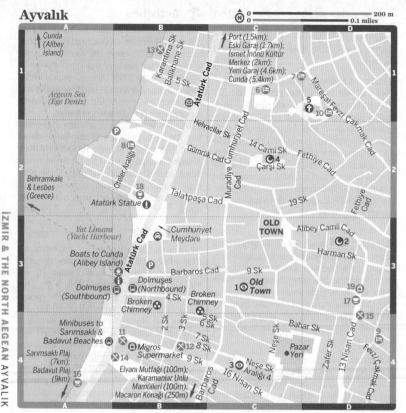

Madra House   PENSION **$$**
(Map p186; 📞0533 545 1620; www.madrahouse.
com; 13 Nisan Caddesi, Aralığı 29; per person ₺150;
❄@🛜) Australian-Turkish couple Diana
and Genghis opened this charming pen-
sion in 2016, offering seven rooms (one a
two-bedroom suite) and a large terraced gar-
den. The house itself is a lovely example of
the Greek houses built here in the late 19th
century, with original features galore.

Bonjour Pansiyon   PENSION **$$**
(Map p186; 📞0535 783 2663; www.bonjourpan
siyon.com; Mareşal Fevzi Çakmak Çeşme Sokak 5;
s/d without bathroom ₺75/150; ❄🛜) Amid the
faded grandeur of this fine-looking mansion
that once belonged to an ambassador to the
sultan are 11 clean rooms and two shared
bathrooms. Two cramped and dark rooms
with bathroom are in a modern annexe off
the tiled rear courtyard. The elderly owners
Yalçin and Hatice are very welcoming.

Macaron Konağı   BOUTIQUE HOTEL **$$**
(📞0266-312 7741; 18 Sokak 54; s/d ₺175/250;
☀Jun-Sep; ❄@🛜) The 'Marjoram Guest-
house' offers 13 rooms in the heart of the Old
City. The building, which dates from 1880 and
was originally the residence of a Greek priest,
has a stone staircase and a lovely inner court-
yard garden where breakfast and afternoon
tea are enjoyed. Rooms are very pretty, but
some are small.

Hotel Ayvalık Palas   HOTEL **$$**
(Map p186; 📞0266-312 1064; www.ayvalikpalas
hotel.com; Gümrük Meydanı Oteler Aralığı 1; s ₺80-
120, d ₺140-240; 🅿❄🛜) Desperately in need
of a facelift, this hotel is only notable for its
sea-fronting upstairs terrace and huge car
park (₺10-₺15 per night); the latter is a luxury in Ayvalık. The 33 poky rooms have basic
bathrooms; some have sea views. There's a
pub on the ground floor.

Ayvalık

Çeşmeli Han   B&B $$$

(Map p186; ☑0266 312 8084; www.cesmeli han.com; Mareşal Fevzi Çakmak Caddesi 87; d/tr ₺210/260; ⊗May-Oct; ☻❊�) The gorgeous courtyard garden and upstairs terrace with panoramic view are the major draw at this family-run B&B, which has seven cramped rooms with exposed-brick walls, tiled floors and spotless bathrooms. Guests rave about the lavish home-cooked breakfast.

✗ Eating

There are plenty of good cheap eats to be enjoyed in Ayvalık, but there are no restaurants of note – head to Cunda to eat in the evening. There are markets on Thursday (town centre) and Sunday (on Atatürk Bulvarı next to the İsmet İnönü Kültür Merkez building).

Hatipoğlu Pastaneleri   SWEETS, ICE CREAM $

(Map p186; ☑0266-312 2913; Atatürk Bulvarı 110; ⊗6am-1am, to 3am summer; ❊) With a great selection of traditional Turkish pastries and cakes, this friendly patisserie on the main street makes a terrific mid-morning or -afternoon stop. Try the local speciality of *lok* (sponge oozing honey) and consider adding a scoop of *sakızlı dondurma* (mastic ice cream) on the side.

Pino   CAFE $$

(Map p186; 13 Nisan Caddesi; mains ₺15-30; ⊗8am-9pm, closed Mon winter) Named after its English-speaking owner Pinar (Pino to her friends), this friendly cafe in an old stone house opened in 2016 and is a good choice for a coffee or light lunch. There's banquette seating inside and a few tables on the street. The menu includes burgers, bruschetta, pastas and quiche. No alcohol, but freshly squeezed juice is on offer.

Deniz Yıldızı Restorant   SEAFOOD $$

(Map p186; ☑0266-312 6666; www.ayvalikdeniz yildizi.com; Karantina Sokak 5a; mezes ₺7-20, fish price per kg; ⊗noon-midnight) Its food won't win any culinary awards, but this stylish indoor-outdoor affair right on the waterfront does command great views of Cunda's twinkling lights.

Café Caramel   CAFE

(Map p186; ☑0266-312 8520; Barbaros Caddesi 9 Sokak; ⊗9am-8pm Mon-Sat) This eccentrically decorated and very popular cafe in the old town offers a nostalgic jazz soundtrack, extensive dessert menu (cakes, soufflés, tiramisu), homemade soda and simple meals like *mantı* (Turkish ravioli) and *menemem* (scrambled eggs with peppers and tomatoes). There's indoor and outdoor seating.

Elvanı Mutfağı   TURKISH

(cnr Barbaros Caddesi & 16 Sokak; portions from ₺6; ⊗9am-4pm Mon-Sat) Local women work the stoves at this simple *mutfak* (kitchen) in the old town. Simple choices such as *menemen* and a range of daily dishes in the bain-marie feed a predominantly local clientele. Tea is supplied by the next-door cafe. The premium seating is outside under the wisteria vine.

🍸 Drinking & Nightlife

★ Şeytan Kahvesi   CAFE

(Palabahçe Kahvehanesi; Map p186; Alibey Cami Caddesi; ⊗6am-8pm, to 11pm Jun-Sep) One of the town's best-loved and most historic cafes, Şeytan Kahvesi (the Devil's Coffeehouse) was named after the current owner's grandfather, who certainly had an interesting name to live up to. Its streetside terrace is a hugely atmospheric people-watching spot – order a Turkish coffee or glass of

AYVALIK'S FAST FOOD

Ayvalık may have made its name as an olive-oil producer, but these days it's better known throughout Turkey for a rather less-refined culinary offering: Ayvalık *tost* (Ayvalık toast). The town's take on fast food is essentially a toasted white-bread sandwich crammed with all manner of ingredients, including cheese, *sucuk* (spicy veal or beef sausage), salami, pickles and tomatoes. These fillings are then lathered in ketchup and mayonnaise (unless you specifically request otherwise). The faint-hearted can opt just for one or two ingredients, but this is most decidedly frowned upon.

The *tostu* are available at cafes and stalls throughout town; **Avşar Büfe** (Map p186; Atatürk Caddesi; dishes ₺4-8; ☉24hr May-Sep, 7am-3am Oct-Apr) and the surrounding eateries with communal tables and benches are good places to try it.

koruk suyu (freshly pressed unfermented fresh grape juice available from June to November).

Açelya Cafe
CAFE

(Map p186; ☑0266-312 4141; www.ayvalikacela cafe.com; Atatürk Caddesi; ☉7am-2am Jun-Sep, 9am-midnight Oct-May) The outdoor terrace right at the water's edge makes this a popular local haunt, particularly at sunset, and the indoor dining space with its large TVs is always packed when *Süper Lig* (Super League) matches are telecast. Food choices include waffles, ice cream, *kumpir* (stuffed potatoes), pizzas and Ayvalık *tost* (the local version of a toasted sandwich).

White Knight Café
PUB

(Map p186; ☑0266-312 3682; Cumhuriyet Meydanı 13; ☉10am-2am; 🛜) This pub-cafe behind the Atatürk statue is a mellow place for a libation, except when major football matches are shown. It's popular with Ayvalık's small expat community.

🛍 Shopping

★Çöp(m)adam
ARTS & CRAFTS

(Map p186; ☑0266-312 1360; www.copmadam. com; off 13 Nisan Caddesi; ☉8.30am-5.30pm Mon-Sat winter, 9.30am-6.30pm Mon-Sat summer) 🌿 A social enterprise helping unemployed women earn a living by creating fashionable items from throwaway materials, the 'Garbage Lady' saves at least six tons of waste from going to landfill annually, and sells over 4000 items. Its workshop and retail outlet is near Şeytan Kahvesi (p187) in the old town and stocks cards, aprons, bags, toys and tea towels.

❶ Information

A **tourist information kiosk** (Map p186; ☑0266-312 4449; Yat Limanı; ☉9am-noon & 1-5pm Mon-Fri plus 9am-1pm Sat Jun-Sep) on the waterfront south of Cumhuriyet Meydanı provides maps and tourist information.

❶ Getting There & Away

BOAT

Boats to Mytilini (Midilli in Turkish) in Lesbos, Greece depart from the port building at the northern end of Atatürk Bulvarı. Look for the 'TC Ayvalık Deniz Hudut Kapısı' sign.

There are at least three weekly services (one way/return €20/30); the trip takes 1½ hours. From June to August, boats sail daily.

Note that times do change and you must make a reservation (in person or by telephone) 24 hours before departure. When you pick up your tickets, bring your passport.

For information and tickets, contact **Jale Tour** (☑0266-331 3170; www.jaletour.com; Gümrük Binası Karşısı, Atatürk Bulvarı; ☉10am-7pm Mon-Sat) or **Turyol** (☑0266-331 6700; www.turyol online.com; Güzide İş Karşısı, Atatürk Bulvarı 296/2; ☉10am-7pm Mon-Sat); both have offices on Atatürk Bulvarı opposite the port building.

BUS

There are two bus stations in Ayvalık: the Yeni Garaj (New Garage) on the main Çanakkale to İzmir Hwy and the Eski Garaj (Old Garage) on Atatürk Bulvarı in the centre of town. The following services leave from/arrive at the Yeni Garaj:

Çanakkale Regular services (₺25–₺35, 3½ hours, 170km), sometimes on İstanbul-bound buses.

İstanbul (₺65–₺80, 9½ hours, 560km) Usually via Çanakkale.

İzmir Regular services (₺20–₺25, two hours, 160km).

CAR

The inland route to Bergama, via Kozak, is much more scenic and only marginally slower than the coast road, winding through idyllic pine-clad hills. Backtrack north for 10km towards Edremit, then turn east.

DOLMUŞ

Bergama Hourly services to Bergama's otogar pick up passengers from outside the Garaj Büfe opposite the Eski Garaj and also from stops along Atatürk Bulvarı (₺10).

Cunda Frequent dolmuşes (₺2.50) travel two routes between Ayvalık and Cunda: the Yeni Yol (New Road) service goes to/from Cunda's harbour and the Eski Yol (Old Road) goes to Cunda from the beaches. The main stop in Ayvalık is in front of the Tourist Information booth on Atatürk Bulvarı.

Edremit Frequent services travel to/from the Eski Garaj between 7am and 8.15pm (₺8.50).

❶ Getting Around

CAR

Navigating Ayvalık old town's fiendishly narrow lanes can be an extremely stressful experience. You're much better off parking at one of the car parks along the waterfront. These generally charge ₺10–₺15 per day.

DOLMUŞ

Dolmuşes service the town centre, stopping to put down and pick up passengers along a series of short set routes. You can catch most of them at the stops near the Migros Supermarket and tourist information kiosk south of Cumhuriyet Meydanı. Fares are typically ₺2.50.

Regular domuşes run between the Yeni Garaj and Cumhuriyet Meydanı (₺2.50). They also pick up regularly from Cumhuriyet Meydanı and from the stop opposite the tourist information kiosk before continuing to the beaches around Sarımsaklı.

TAXI

A taxi from the Yeni Garaj to the town centre costs around ₺30. Taxis between the town centre and Cunda can cost as much as ₺40.

Cunda (Alibey Island)

☑ 0266

Named after a hero of the Turkish War of Independence, Alibey Island (Alibey Adası), known to locals as Cunda Island (Cunda Adası) or just Cunda, faces Ayvalık across the water. Linked to the mainland by a causeway (it can be reached by car, ferry or dolmuş), it's generally regarded as a quieter extension of Ayvalık itself, with residents of both communities regularly shuttling back and forth between the two.

The ferry docks at a small quay lined with fish restaurants. Behind these sits a small, distinguished-looking town made up of old (and in parts rather dilapidated) Greek stone houses. As with Ayvalık, the people here were compelled into a population exchange in the early 1920s, in this instance with Muslims from Giritli (Crete).

Just to the east of the ferry pier is the town's main square. Behind the square is a small tourist market with stalls selling jewellery and other trinkets.

◉ Sights & Activities

The prettiest parts of the island are to the west, where there are good beaches for sunbathing and swimming, and north, much of which is taken up by the **Pateriça Nature Reserve**. This has good walking routes and, on the north shore, the ruins of the Greek **Ayışığı Manastırı** (Moonlight Monastery).

Rahmi M Koç Museum   MUSEUM
(☑ 0266-327 2734; www.rmk-museum.org.tr/taksiyarhis/en/; Şeref Sokak 6a; ₺5; ◷ 10am-5pm Tue-Sun Oct-Mar, to 7pm Apr-Sep) Housed in the magnificently restored Taksiyarhis Church (Church of the Archangels), a Greek Orthodox church built in 1873 and now painted in a distinctive shade of yellow, this is a sibling museum to İstanbul's excellent Rahmi M Koç Museum and has a collection that is similarly strong on exhibits concerned with transportation and engineering.

🛏 Sleeping

Tutku Pansiyon   PENSION $$
(☑ 0266-327 1965; www.tutkupansiyon.com; Çarşı Sokak 3; s/d ₺75/150; ❄ 🛜) One of cheapest pensions, 'Passion' is centrally located, opposite a popular wine house and a few streets back from the water. It has five small, simple rooms with red tiled floors, small TVs and fridges. Owners Şevket and Abidin are relaxed and hospitable.

Taş Bahçe   BOUTIQUE HOTEL $$$
(☑ 0266-327 2290; www.tasbahcebutikotel.com; 15 Eylül Caddesi 33; s/d ₺250/400, deluxe s/d ₺350/400; 🅿 ❄ 🛜) The lovely 'Stone Garden' occupies two newly built townhouses that look centuries old. It's on the main road into town about 100m from the seafront, but the windows in the 10 rooms have double glazing, ensuring island tranquillity. There's a lounge-library and a lovely garden where breakfast is served. Deluxe rooms have views.

Cunda Fora   BOUTIQUE HOTEL $$$
(☑ 0266-327 3031; www.cundafora.com; 1 Sokak 7, off Mevlana Caddesi; r ₺520; 🅿 ❄ 🛜) Hugely popular with honeymooning couples, this relatively new hotel is located just off the main road back from the harbour, so it's quieter

than most of the places near the waterfront. There's a charming rear verandah with water views, an in-house hamam (complimentary for guests) and comfortable rooms with attractive decor and top-quality amenities. Breakfast is a highlight.

✗ Eating & Drinking

★ Lǎl Girit Mutfağı　　　GREEK $$

(Ruby Cretan Cuisine; ☑0266-327 2834; Altay Pansiyon Yanı 20; mezes ₺8-25, main ₺38; ⊘noon-midnight Sep-Jun, 7pm-1am Jul & Aug) Owner and chef Emine was taught to cook Girit (Cretan) dishes by her grandmother, and the results are simply inspired. Expect her to emerge from the kitchen to explain what's in the meze selection. You can be sure that your choice will be fresh, unusual and delectable. Slow-cooked lamb is the only main dish on offer.

★ Ayna　　　AEGEAN $$

(☑0266-327 2725; www.aynacunda.net; Çarşı Caddesi 22; soup ₺9, starters ₺20-30, mains ₺29-36; ⊘10am-midnight Tue-Sun Feb-Dec; ❋🛜) We love everything about this welcoming and extremely chic eatery behind Taş Kahve at the *liman*. Owned by the Kürsat olive-oil mill, it offers a delicious seasonal menu featuring *börek* (filled pastry) stuffed with wild herbs, vegetables cooked in olive oil and home-style soups and mains. The cakes, pastries and desserts are delicious, too. Pop in for lunch; book for dinner.

★ Taş Kahve　　　BAR

(☑0266-327 1166; www.taskahve.com.tr; Sahil Boyu 20; tea ₺1.50, beer ₺8; ⊘7am-midnight) It's worth the trip to the island just to sip tea and talk fishing in this cavernous venue adorned with stained-glass windows and period black-and-white photos. Its front terrace positively heaves with people in summer.

Vino Şarap Evi　　　WINE BAR

(Wine House; ☑0535-737 3384; www.vinosarapevi cunda.com; Cumhuriyet Caddesi 8) Lingering over a glass of wine at one of the laneway tables at this convivial wine bar close to the harbour is a popular local pastime. Choose from local and international drops, including a quaffable house-made one. Many patrons stay for a simple pasta dinner.

ℹ Getting There & Away

BOAT

Between late May and October ferries travel between Ayvalık and Cunda's *liman* every 30 minutes between 10.10am and 12.30am (₺5).

CAR

Parking on the waterfront is charged between 8am and midnight (₺5) and you will be fined if you don't have a ticket.

DOLMUŞ

Frequent dolmuşes (₺2.50) travel two routes between Cunda and Ayvalık: the Yeni Yol (New Road) service goes to/from Cunda's harbour and the Eski Yol (Old Road) goes to/from the beaches.

TAXI

A taxi between the island and central Ayvalık will cost around ₺40.

Bergama (Pergamum)

☑0232 / POP 63,825

The laid-back market town of Bergama is the modern successor to the once-powerful ancient city of Pergamum. Unlike Ephesus, which heaves with tourists year-round, Pergamum is for the most part a site of quiet classical splendour. Its ruins – especially the Asklepion and Acropolis – are so extraordinary that they were inscribed on Unesco's World Heritage List in June 2014, the 999th site in the world (and the 14th in Turkey) to be so honoured.

History

Pergamum owed its prosperity to Lysimachus, one of Alexander the Great's generals, who took control of much of the Aegean region when Alexander's far-flung empire fell apart after his death in 323 BC. In the battles over the spoils, Lysimachus captured a great treasure, estimated at over 9000 gold talents, which he entrusted to his commander in Pergamum, Philetaerus, before going off to fight Seleucus for control of Asia Minor. But Lysimachus lost the battle and was killed in 281 BC. Philetaerus then set himself up as governor.

Philetaerus, a eunuch, was succeeded by his nephew and heir Eumenes I (r 263–241 BC), who was in turn followed by his adopted son, Attalus I (r 241–197 BC). Attalus declared himself king, expanding his power and forging an alliance with Rome.

During the reign of Attalus' son, Eumenes II (r 197–159 BC), Pergamum reached its golden age. He founded a library that would in time rival that of Alexandria, Egypt, then the world's greatest repository of knowledge. This was partly due to the large-scale production here of *pergamena* (parchment), the writing

Bergama (Pergamum)

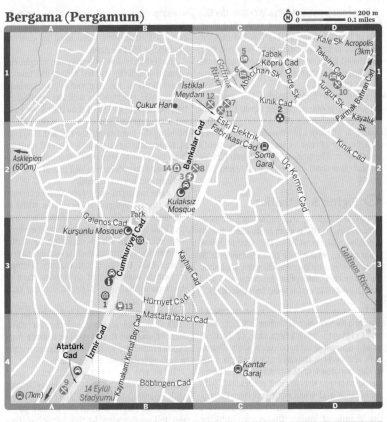

Bergama (Pergamum)

◎ Sights
1 Bergama Archaeology Museum	B3
2 Red Hall	C1

✪ Activities, Courses & Tours
3 Hacı Hekim Hamamı	B2

🛏 Sleeping
4 Aristonicus Boutique Hotel	D1
5 Hera Hotel	C1
6 Odyssey Guesthouse	C1

✗ Eating
7 Arzu	C1
8 Bergama Sofrası	C2
9 Kervan	A4
10 Kybele	D1
11 Paksoy Pide	C1
12 Sarmaşık Lokantası	C1

🍷 Drinking & Nightlife
13 Zıkkım Birahanesi	B3

🛍 Shopping
14 Şen Naoe Ev Tekstil	B2

material made from stretched animal skin and more durable than papyrus.

Eumenes also added the Altar of Zeus to the buildings already crowning the acropolis, built the 'middle city' on terraces halfway down the hill, and expanded and beautified the Asklepion. Much of what he

and the other kings built hasn't survived the ravages of the centuries (or the acquisitive enthusiasm of Western museums, notably the Pergamon Museum in Berlin), but what remains is impressive, dramatically sited and well worth visiting.

Eumenes' brother Attalus II (r 160–138 BC) kept up the good work, but under the short rule of his son, Attalus III (r 138–133 BC), the kingdom began to fall apart. With no heir, Attalus III bequeathed his kingdom to Rome, and Pergamum became the Roman province of Asia in 129 BC.

Along with İzmir, Sardis and Ephesus, Pergamum is one of the the Seven Churches of the Revelation (or Apocalypse), the major churches of early Christianity mentioned by St John the Divine in the New Testament's last chapter. The phrase 'where Satan has his throne' (Rev 2:13) may refer to the Red Hall (p193).

◉ Sights & Activities

If you are visiting museums and archaeological sites in the region, it makes sense to purchase a Museum Pass: The Aegean (www.muze.gov.tr), which will give entrance to 31 museums and archaeological sites, including the Acropolis, Asklepion, Museum and Red Hall. It costs ₺75 and is valid for seven days.

★ Bergama Acropolis   ARCHAEOLOGICAL SITE
(Bergama Akropol; Akropol Caddesi 2; ₺25; ⊙ 8am-5pm Oct-Mar, to 7pm Apr-Sep) One of Turkey's most impressive archaeological sites, Bergama's acropolis is dramatically sited on a hill to the northeast of the town centre. There's plenty to see in this ancient settlement, with ruins large and small scattered over the upper and lower cities. Chief among these are the Temple of Trajan; the vertigo-inducing 10,000-seat Hellenistic theatre, the Altar of Zeus (sadly denuded of its magnificent frieze, which now resides in Berlin) and the whimsical mosaic floors in Building Z.

There are two ways to access the site. You can drive to the upper car park (parking ₺5) or instead follow the signposts along Akropol Caddesi to the lower station of the Bergama Acropolis Cable Car (Bergama Akropolis Teleferik; ☑ 0232-631 0805; www.akropolisteleferik.com.tr; Akropol Caddesi; return ₺15; ⊙ 8am-5pm Apr-Sep, to 7pm Oct-Mar). There's a paid car park here, too (again ₺5). The cable-car ride takes five minutes.

From the Upper City, a line of rather faded blue dots marks a suggested route around the main structures – you might instead consider hiring the audio guide for ₺10. These structures include the library that helped put Pergamum on the map and the colossal marble-columned Temple of Trajan (or Trajaneum), built during the reigns of the emperors Trajan and Hadrian and used to

worship them as well as Zeus. It's the only Roman structure surviving on the Acropolis, and its foundations were used as cisterns during the Middle Ages.

Immediately downhill from the temple, descend through the vaulted tunnel-like temple foundations to the impressive and unusual Hellenistic theatre. Its builders decided to take advantage of the spectacular view (and conserve precious space on top of the hill) by building the theatre into the hillside. In general, Hellenistic theatres are wider and rounder than this, but at Pergamum the hillside location made rounding impossible and so it was increased in height instead.

At the northern end of the theatre terrace is the ruined Temple of Dionysus, while to the south is the Altar of Zeus (also known as the Great Altar), which was originally covered with magnificent friezes depicting the battle between the Olympian gods and their subterranean foes. However, 19th-century German excavators were allowed to remove most of this famous building to Berlin, leaving only the base behind.

Piles of rubble on top of the acropolis are marked as five separate palaces, including that of Eumenes II, and you can also see fragments of the once-magnificent defensive walls as well as barracks and arsenal.

To escape the crowds and get a good view of the theatre and Temple of Trajan, walk downhill behind the Altar of Zeus, or turn left at the bottom of the theatre steps, and follow the sign to the antik yol (ancient street) past the Upper Agora and the bath-gymnasium. Within what was once a sprawling residential area of the Middle City is modern Building Z (2004), protecting part of a peristyle court and some fantastic floor mosaics. Look for the grotesque masks with wild animals, the child Dionysus with Silenus supping from a cup and the remnants of tinted stucco on the walls. You'll then pass more baths, gymnasia and the sumptuous Palace of Attalus I before reaching the Lower Agora.

Asklepion   RUINS
(Prof Dr Frieldhelm Korte Caddesi 1; ₺20; ⊙ 8am-4.45pm Oct-Mar, to 6.45pm Apr-Sep) The Asklepion may not be as dramatic as the Acropolis, but in some ways it is even more extraordinary. One of the most important healing centres of the Roman world, it had baths, temples, a theatre, library, treatment centres and latrines in its heyday. Remnants of many of these structures have been preserved on site, and what

we see now is quite similar to how the centre would have appeared in the time of the Emperor Hadrian (117–138 BC).

Said to have been founded by Archias, a local who had been cured at the Asklepion of Epidaurus (Greece), Pergamum's Asklepion offered many different treatments, including mud baths, the use of herbs and ointments, enemas and sunbathing. Diagnosis was often by dream analysis.

The centre came to the fore under Galen (AD 129–216), who was born here and studied in Alexandria, Greece and Asia Minor before setting up shop as physician to Pergamum's gladiators. Recognised as perhaps the greatest early physician, Galen added considerably to the knowledge of the circulatory and nervous systems, and also systematised medical theory. Under his influence, the medical school at Pergamum became renowned throughout the ancient world. His work was the basis for Western medicine well into the 16th century.

The Roman Via Tecta, a colonnaded sacred way, leads from the entrance to the sanctuary, where you'll see the base of a column carved with snakes, the symbol of Asclepios, the god of medicine. Just as the snake sheds its skin and gains a 'new life', so the patients at the Asclepion were supposed to 'shed' their illnesses. Signs mark a circular Temple of Asklepios, a library and, beyond it, a heavily restored Roman theatre.

There are latrines over a channel in the southwest corner of the main courtyard and you can take a drink from the sacred well in the centre. From here pass along the vaulted tunnel to the treatment centre, a temple to another god of medicine called Telesphorus. Patients slept in the round temple hoping that Telesphorus would send a cure or diagnosis in a dream. The names of Telesphorus' two daughters, Hygeia and Panacea, have passed into medical terminology.

Soft drinks and snacks are available from an on-site snack bar.

To get here, turn into Galenos Caddesi between the small park and the Kurşunlu Mosque on Cumhuriyet Caddesi (look for a street sign pointing the way to Tiyelti, Çakırlar and the Asklepion), and head 2km uphill.

Bergama Archaeology Museum   MUSEUM
(Bergama Müze Müdürlüğü; Map p191; ☏ 0232-483 5117; Cumhuriyet Caddesi 6; ₺5; ⊗8am-5pm Tue-Sun Nov-Mar, to 5pm Apr-Oct) Boasting a small but impressive collection of artefacts, Bergama's museum is well worth a visit. On exhibit are reliefs from the Acropolis, includ-

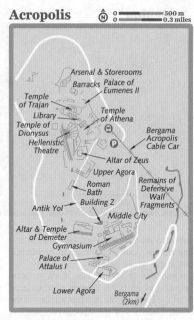

Acropolis   Ⓝ   0 — 500 m / 0 — 0.3 miles

Arsenal & Storerooms

Barracks — Palace of Eumenes II

Temple of Trajan

Library

Temple of Dionysus

Temple of Athena

Hellenistic Theatre

Bergama Acropolis Cable Car

Altar of Zeus

Upper Agora

Roman Bath

Remains of Defensive Wall Fragments

Antik Yol — Building Z

Middle City

Altar & Temple of Demeter

Gymnasium

Palace of Attalus I

Lower Agora

Bergama (2km)

ing a wonderful Roman-era relief from the Demeter Terrace, and a Hellenistic frieze and architrave from the Athena Terrace. Also impressive are the many statues from the Asklepion and a mosaic floor featuring Medusa's head that was originally in the Lower Agora. The ethnography gallery focuses on the crafts, costumes and customs of the Ottoman period.

Look out, too, for the scale replica of the Altar of Zeus (the original is in the Pergamon Museum in Berlin) and the many objects (ceramic, glazed terracotta, iron, marble and glass) salvaged from the excavations in both the Acropolis and Asklepion. Of the exhibits in the ethnography gallery, the extraordinary collection of dresses of the Bergama region – influenced by the nomadic Yürük (Turkomen) peoples – is most impressive.

Red Hall   RUINS
(Kızıl Avlu; Map p191; Kınık Caddesi; ₺5; ⊗8am-7pm Apr-Sep, to 5pm Oct-Mar) The cathedral-sized Red Hall, sometimes called the Red Basilica, is thought to have been built by the Romans as a temple to the Egyptian gods Serapis and Isis in the 2nd century AD. It's an imposing-looking structure with two domed rotundas; visitors can enter the southern rotunda but not the main temple (currently being restored) or the northern rotunda. The

Asklepion

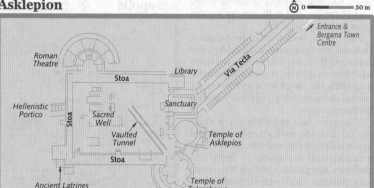

N 0 ————— 50 m

southern rotunda was used for religious and cult rituals – look for the huge niche where a cult statue would have sat.

Originally, this must have been an awe-inspiring place. In his Book of Revelation, St John the Divine wrote that this was one of the Seven Churches of the Apocalypse, singling it out as the 'throne of the devil'. In fact, the building is so big that the early Christians didn't convert it into a church, but in the 5th century AD built a basilica inside it instead.

Hacı Hekim Hamamı   HAMAM

(Map p191; ☑ 0232-631 0102; Bankalar Caddesi 42; hamam ₺25, scrub & massage ₺40; ⊗ men 6am-11pm, women 8.30am-7pm) This 16th-century hamam just north of the Kulaksız Mosque has separate entrances for men and women and charges ₺40 for the full works. The women's entrance is around the side.

🛌 Sleeping

The old town at the northern end of Cumhuriyet Caddesi is the quietest and most atmospheric area to stay.

Odyssey Guesthouse   PENSION $

(Map p191; ☑ 0232-631 3501; www.odyssey guesthouse.com; Abacıhan Sokak 13; dm/s/d/tr ₺25/65/85/120, s/d without bathroom ₺40/70; ⊗ closed Jan–mid-Feb; ※ @ 🛜) A superb views of all three archaeological sites from the upstairs terrace lounge is one of many enticements at this friendly and well-run pension. There are nine simple rooms spread over two buildings, a book exchange and a communal kitchen; the copy of Homer's *Odyssey* in every room is a nice touch. Breakfast costs ₺10.

★Aristonicus Boutique Hotel   BOUTIQUE HOTEL $$

(Map p191; ☑ 0232-632 4141; www.aristonicus. com; Taksim Caddesi 37; s/d/ste ₺85/165/215; P ※ 🛜) Offering extraordinarily good value, this new operation has converted two old stone houses into an attractive hotel offering six immaculately presented rooms with satellite TV, kettle and minibar. The singles are tiny and some of the doubles have slightly cramped bathrooms, but the comfort levels are generally more than acceptable. Breakfast is served in a small courtyard.

Hera Hotel   BOUTIQUE HOTEL $$$

(Map p191; ☑ 0232-631 0634; www.hotelhera. com; Tabak Köprü Caddesi 38; s/d/tr ₺310/410/425; P ※ 🛜) Here at the Hera, a pair of 200-year-old Greek houses have been cobbled into most sophisticated accommodation. Each of the 10 rooms, which are named after mythological Greek deities, feature timber ceilings, parquet floors and kilims. The best rooms are Zeus and Hera; both have views and Zeus' bathroom is particularly large. There's a garden and panoramic breakfast terrace.

🍽 Eating & Drinking

Bergama's bustling Monday market is in the streets near the hospital. It's great for fresh fruit and veg.

On warm nights, locals flock to the tea- and coffeehouses around the Ottoman Bazaar to meet up with friends. A party atmosphere with plenty of music prevails.

★Arzu   PIDE, KEBAP $

(Map p191; ☑ 0232-612 8700; İstiklal Meydanı 35; pides ₺10-12, İskender kebap ₺13; ⊗ 6am-1am)

Map labels: Roman Theatre; Stoa; Library; Via Tecta; Entrance & Bergama Town Centre; Hellenistic Portico; Stoa; Sacred Well; Sanctuary; Vaulted Tunnel; Temple of Asklepios; Stoa; Ancient Latrines & Baths; Temple of Telesphorus

Located on a busy corner, this ultrafriendly *pideci* (pide place) is probably the most popular eatery in town, The pides (Turkish-style pizzas) are excellent – try the unusual *biberli maydanozlu* (green pepper and parsley) topping – and there are also soups and kebaps on offer, including İskender kebap (or Bursa kebap; döner kebab on fresh pide and topped with tomato sauce and browned butter).

Bergama Sofrası   TURKISH $
(Map p191; ☑0232-631 5131; Bankalar Caddesi 44; portions ₺8-14; ◷7.30am-10pm) One of a number of *lokantas* (eateries serving ready-made food) that can be found on the town's main drag, Bergama Sofrası has indoor and outdoor seating, clean surfaces and an open kitchen under bright lights. The spicy *köfte* (meatball) is the speciality. The usual *lokanta* rule applies – eat here at lunch when the food is still fresh.

Paksoy Pide   PIDE $
(Map p191; ☑0232-633 1722; İstiklal Meydani 39; pide ₺9-12; ◷6.30am-10.30pm Sun-Fri) Pint-sized Paksoy is clean, but is most definitely outclassed in the pide and friendliness stakes by nearby Arzu.

Sarmaşık Lokantası   TURKISH $
(Map p191; ☑0232-632 2745; İstiklal Meydani 9; portions ₺9-12; ◷8am-11pm Mon-Sat) One of the more dependable local restaurants on the main street, the 'Ivy' has a heavy rotation of ready-made stews, soups and rice dishes.

Kervan   PIDE, KEBAP $
(Map p191; ☑0232-633 2632; Atatürk Caddesi 16; soups ₺5-7.50, pides ₺7-13, kebaps ₺12-32; ◷8am-11pm; ✤) Kervan is popular among locals for its cheap and tasty dishes. The menu features a good range of kebaps, pide, *çorba* (soup) and, for dessert, *künefe* (syrup-soaked dough and sweet cheese sprinkled with pistachios).

Kybele   TURKISH $$
(Map p191; ☑0232-632 3935; http://tr.lesper gamon.com; Les Pergamon Hotel, Taksim Caddesi 35; starters ₺10-20, mains ₺25-50; ◷7-10pm) The only fine-dining establishment in Bergama, this restaurant serves refined Turkish dishes in its elegant dining room and atmospheric courtyard garden. Desserts are particularly good – the ice cream–filled profiteroles have a legion of fans.

Zıkkım Birahanesi   PUB
(Map p191; Cumhuriyet Caddesi; ◷10.30am-1am) With shady garden seating just off the main road, this cool beer garden makes a welcome midtown pit stop. It's one of three dishevelled *birahanesi* (beer houses) in this stretch of Cumhuriyet Caddesi.

🛍 Shopping

Şen Naoe Ev Tekstil   ARTS & CRAFTS
(Map p191; ☑0232-633 4488; Kapalı Çarşı 9; ◷8am-9pm Jun-Sep, 10am-5pm Oct-May) This Japanese-run shop in the old Bedesten (Covered Bazaar) sells lovely *peştemals* (bath wraps), shawls and tablecloths that have been woven and embroidered by hand.

ℹ Information

Tourist Office (Map p191; ☑0232-631 2851; bergamaturizm@kultur.gov.tr; Cumhuriyet Caddesi 11; ◷8.30am-noon & 1-5.30pm) This helpful office is on the ground floor of the Hükümet Konağı (Provincial Government) building just north of the museum.

ℹ Getting There & Away

BUS

Bergama's *yeni* (new) otogar lies 7km from the centre, at the junction of the İzmir–Çanakkale highway and the main road into town. From the otogar, half-hourly dolmuşes head to the **Soma Garaj** (Map p191) near the Red Hall (₺2). Bus services include the following:

Ankara (₺85, 8½ hours, 480km, nightly)
Çanakkale (₺30–₺35, 220km, 4½ hours)
İzmir (₺10, two hours, 110km, every 45 minutes)

DOLMUŞ

Regular dolmuşes to Ayvalık (₺10) and Çandarlı (₺5) leave from the **Kantar Garaj** (Map p191); at other times, they leave from the *yeni* otogar.

TRAIN

İzmir's efficient İzban rail travels to Aliağa (₺2.40 on a Kent Kart), from where buses and dolmuşes continue to Bergama (₺5).

ℹ Getting Around

Modern Bergama lies spread out on either side of one long main street, which changes names, and along which almost everything you'll need can be found, including hotels, the tourist office, restaurants, banks and the PTT.

Bergama's sights are so spread out that it's hard to walk round them all in one day. The Red Hall is about a kilometre from the tourist office, the Asklepion is 2km away and the Acropolis is over 5km away.

DOLMUŞ

Between 6am and 10pm, half-hourly dolmuşes do a loop through town (₺2).

TAXI

A 'city tour' from the centre to the Asklepion, Red Hall and the Acropolis, with 30 minutes at the first two sights and an hour at the latter, will cost around ₺100. Taxis wait near the Archaeology Museum, Kulaksız Mosque and at the otogar. Individual fares from the taxi rank next to the park are ₺20 to the Asklepion and ₺25 to the Acropolis.

Çandarlı

📞 0232 / POP 6159

The small resort town of Çandarlı (ancient Pitane) sits on a peninsula jutting into the Aegean, 33km southwest of Bergama. It's dominated by the small but stately 15th-century restored Venetian Çandarlı Castle and has a small and slender sandy beach.

Local tourism fills most of the pensions in high summer. Out of season, Çandarlı is pretty much a ghost town.

Shops, internet cafes and the PTT are in the centre, 200m behind the seafront. The castle, pensions and restaurants line the seashore. Market day is Friday.

Çandarlı Castle   CASTLE
(Çandarlı Kilesi; ⊘ 24hr) FREE This 15th-century Ottoman castle was built by order of the Grand Vizier Çandarlı Halil Pasha the Younger.

🛏 Sleeping & Eating

Most of the hotels and pensions lie west of the castle, facing a thin strip of coarse sand.

Decent eating options are few and far between, so you'll probably need to rely on fast food. There are ice-cream stalls on the seafront east of the castle.

Kaffe Pansiyon   PENSION $$
(📱 0545 689 8789, 0232-673 3122; Sahil Plaj Caddesi 1; s/d ₺60/120; 🛜) This pretty basic pension above a cafe opposite the beach has 15 small and very basic rooms; wi-fi is in the lounge only. But the price is right, and some rooms face the sea.

Otel Samyeli   HOTEL $$
(📱 0232-673 3428; www.otelsamyeli.com; Sahil Plaj Caddesi; s/d/tr ₺100/180/240; 🅿 ✳ 🛜) A location facing the beach is the main draw here, as the rooms are ugly and pretty basic; some are cramped, too. Fortunately, the staff members are very welcoming.

❶ Getting There & Away

Frequent buses run between Çandarlı and İzmir (₺12, 1½ hours) via Dikili (₺3, 20 minutes). At least six dolmuşes run daily to/from Bergama (₺5, 30 minutes).

Eski Foça

📞 0232 / POP 26,036

Called Eski Foça (Old Foça) to distinguish it from its newer (and rather dull) neighbour, Yeni Foça, this happy-go-lucky holiday town straddles both the Büyük Deniz (Big Sea) and the picturesque Küçük Deniz (Small Sea). The Ottoman-Greek houses fronting the Küçük Deniz are among the finest on the Aegean coast, with doors that open onto a storybook esplanade where locals and visitors play, promenade and dine al fresco. The ruined structure on the small promontory between the Büyük Deniz and Küçük Deniz bays has been built and rebuilt over millennia, and traces of ancient shrines to Cybele and a Temple to Athena are being slowly excavated.

Once the site of ancient Phocaea, more recently Foça was an Ottoman-Greek fishing and trading port. It's now a prosperous, middle-class resort, with holiday villas gathered on the outskirts and a thin, dusty beach with some swimming platforms. There are some better beaches to the north heading towards Yeni Foça.

The otogar is just inland from the Büyük Deniz. Heading north from here, with the Büyük Deniz and its accompanying tour boats on your left, takes you through the centre of town to the Küçük Deniz. You'll pass the tourist office, the PTT, *belediye* (town hall) and banks, before reaching the harbour after around 350m. Continue north along the Küçük Deniz's shore for most of the pensions.

History

Foça was the site of ancient Phocaea, which takes its name from the seals (*phoce* in Greek) basking offshore at Siren Rocks. It was founded in the 8th century BC. During their golden age (5th century BC), the Phocaeans were great mariners, sending swift vessels, powered by up to 50 oars, into the Aegean, Mediterranean and Black Seas. They also founded Samsun on the Black Sea, as well as towns in Italy, Corsica, France and Spain.

⊙ Sights

A ruined theatre, the remains of an aqueduct near the otogar and traces of two shrines to the goddess Cybele on the promontory are all that remains of the ancient settlement. Some 7km east of town on the way to the İzmir highway and on the left-hand side of the road lies an *anıt mezarı* (monumental tomb) from the 4th century BC.

Beşkapılar   FORTRESS
(Five Gates) If you head west past the outdoor sanctuary of Cybele, you'll come to the city walls and the partially rebuilt Beşkapılar, effectively the docking area of a castle, built by the Byzantines, repaired by the Genoese and the Ottomans in 1539, and clearly much restored since. Sadly, it's often filled with rubbish.

Dış Kale   FORTRESS
Guarding the town's southwestern approaches, the late 17th-century 'Outer Castle' can only be seen from the water (on a boat trip) as it's inside a military zone.

🏃 Activities

Between May and late September, boats leave daily at about 11am from both the Küçük Deniz and Büyük Deniz for day trips around the outlying islands. Trips include various swim stops en route and return about 5pm. Most drop anchor at Siren Rocks and typically cost ₺45, including lunch.

Valinor: the Lord of the Boats   BOATING
(☑ 0532 798 6317; www.valinortour.com; Büyük Deniz; boat trip incl lunch ₺45) A long-established boat-trip operator, Valinor: the Lord of the Boats is based in front of the *jandarma* (police) station on the Büyük Deniz.

Belediye Hamamı   HAMAM
(☑ 0232-812 1959; 115 Sokak 22; hamam ₺20, scrub & massage ₺50; ⊙ 8am-midnight) The full works costs a mere ₺50 at this tourist-friendly mixed hamam above the Büyük Deniz.

🛌 Sleeping

Siren Pansiyon   PENSION $$
(☑ 0232-812 2660, 0532 287 6127; www.sirenpan siyon.com; 161 Sokak 13; s/d/tr ₺100/180/220; 🛜) This friendly family-run pension is very popular with budget travellers. Located in a quiet pocket just off the seafront promenade, it has 13 rooms, the best of which are upstairs (opt for the rear double with garden view or the terrace triple). Owner Remzi is extremely

hospitable, and the rooftop terrace with sea view is a great spot to relax.

İyon Pansiyon   PENSION $$
(☑ 0232-812 1415; www.iyonpansion.com; 198 Sokak 8; d/tr/q ₺160/200/210; ❄🛜) İyon's pretty garden is planted with mandarin, plum and almond trees, and is a tranquil retreat from the waterside mayhem in summer. The 10 rooms are simple and could do with new beds, but the Tutar family's welcome is so warm that the saggy mattresses are soon forgiven. Their boat trips with lunch (₺45) are very popular.

Lola 38 Hotel   BOUTIQUE HOTEL $$$
(☑ 0232-812 3826; www.lola38hotel.com; Reha Midilli Caddesi 140; r ₺400-500, ste ₺600; 🅿❄🛜) First, the warning: Lola's deluxe rooms with their lurid colour scheme and generally over-the-top decor won't be to all tastes. But now the good news: the garden rooms behind this converted Greek stone house at the quiet end of the Küçük Deniz are comfortable, attractive and beautifully maintained. No child guests under 10.

Bülbül Yuvası Hotel   BOUTIQUE HOTEL $$$
(Nightingale's Nest; ☑ 0232-812 5152; www.bulbul yuvasi.com.tr; 121 Sokak 20; s/d ₺300/320, deluxe d ₺420-520; ❄🛜) The 'Nightingale's Nest' is a slightly overdecorated but generally pleasing small hotel with 11 well-appointed rooms featuring oodles of brocade. Some of the standard rooms are cramped, so it's worth considering an upgrade to the larger sea-view variety. It's down a dead-end lane, so is quieter than many of its competitors.

🍴 Eating & Drinking

Foça's dining scene is mostly Turkish pescatarian. A market spreads through the back streets of the old town on Tuesdays.

Nazmi Usta Girit Dondurmaları   ICE CREAM $
(Reha Midilli Caddesi 82; ⊙ 9am-1am) Ice cream and the seaside go together like Fred and Ginger or Posh and Becks, and this is the best place in Foça to order a cone. Nazmi Usta is an acclaimed *dondurma* (ice cream) maker, and his fruit and nut flavours go down a treat with locals and visitors of every age.

Harika Köfte Evi   KÖFTE $
(☑ 0232-812 5409; 91 Sokak 2; soups ₺8, köfte ₺14, piyaz ₺4; ⊙ 8am-midnight) In addition to four types of *köfte* – reputedly the best in town – the 'Wonderful Köfte House' serves various

İZMIR & THE NORTH AEGEAN ESKİ FOÇA

types of *çorba* and *tavuk şiş* (roast skewered chicken kebap).

Çarşı Lokantası
TURKISH $

(☑0232-812 2377; 210 Sokak 18; portion ₺8-25; ☺8am-11pm) This *lokanta* is a great lunch choice. Make your choice of meat, vegetable and rice dishes from the bain-marie (the friendly Mesut and Fatoş will help).

Letafet
TURKISH $$

(☑0232-812 1191; 197 Sokak 3; mezes ₺6-28, mains ₺22-35; ☺noon-1am) This popular *meyhane* (tavern) and *şarap evi* (wine house) is hidden behind a stone wall in the old town, but the giveaway is the loud music and the clink of cutlery. Diners enjoy classic Turkish cuisine at reasonable prices, and are serenaded by live musicians every night except Monday.

Foça Restaurant
SEAFOOD $$

(☑0232-812 2446; Sahil Caddesi 56; mezes ₺8-30, mains ₺20-35; ☺9am-midnight) Highly recommended by locals, this seafood restaurant enjoys a prominent position on the quay just opposite the sanctuary of Cybele. The mezes are particularly good.

★ Kavala Cafe
CAFE, BAR

(☑0530 939 9975; www.kavalacafe.com; Reha Mıdıllı Caddesi 47) Enjoying a sunset drink on the waterside terrace of this beautifully restored stone house at the very end of Reha Midilli Caddesi is a Foça highlight, and a mid-morning coffee under the shade of an umbrella is enjoyable too. There's a decent selection of bottled beer, an even better one of rakı (aniseed brandy), and decent espresso coffee.

ℹ Information

Tourist Office (☑0232-812 1222; kocogluha run@hotmail.com; Foça Girişi 1; ☺8.30am-noon & 1-5.30pm Mon-Fri, 10am-7pm Sat Jun-Sep) Only open during the major summer holiday period, this small office can supply maps and advice.

ℹ Getting There & Around

BICYCLE

Rent bicycles from **Göçmen** (☑0232-812 3743; 119 Sokak 2; per day ₺40; ☺9am-8pm), near the hamam.

BUS

Between 6.30am and 9.15pm (11pm in summer), half-hourly buses run to İzmir (₺10, 1½ hours, 86km), passing through Menemen (₺5), where there are connections to Manisa.

Three to five city buses run daily to/from Yeni Foça (₺5, 30 minutes, 22km). They pass pretty little coves, beaches and camping grounds along the way.

İzmir

☑0232 / POP 2.89 MILLION

Turkey's third-largest city is proudly liberal and deeply cultured. Garlanded around the azure-blue Bay of İzmir, it has been an important Aegean port since ancient times, when it was the Greek city of Smyrna, and its seafront *kordon* (promenade) is as fetching and lively as any in the world.

The city's rich and fascinating heritage reflects the fact that it has been the home of Greeks, Armenians, Jews, Levantines and Turks over the centuries. While not as multicultural these days, it still has resident Jewish and Levantine communities and its unique and delicious cuisine attests to this.

Foreign visitors here are largely limited to business travellers and tourists en route to Ephesus. The reason for this is a mystery to us, as the city is home to compelling attractions including one of Turkey's most fascinating bazaars, an impressive museum of history and art, and a local lifestyle as laid-back as it is welcoming.

History

İzmir was once Smyrna, a city founded by colonists from Greece some time in the early part of the 1st millennium BC. Over the next 1000 years it would grow in importance as it came under the influence of successive regional powers: first Lydia, then Greece and finally Rome. By the 2nd century AD it was, along with Ephesus and Pergamum, one of the three most important cities in the Roman province of Asia. Its fortunes declined under Byzantine rule, as the focus of government turned north to Constantinople. Things only began to look up again when the Ottomans took control in 1415, after which Smyrna rapidly became Turkey's most sophisticated and successful commercial city.

After the collapse of the Ottoman Empire at the end of WWI, the Greeks invaded. They were eventually expelled following fierce fighting, which, along with a devastating fire, destroyed most of the Greek and Armenian neighbourhoods in the city – tens of thousands of residents perished. The day that Atatürk and his troops recaptured Smyrna (9 September 1922) marked the moment of victory in the Turkish War of Independence.

◉ Sights

İzmir is best explored on foot. Between the 17th and early 20th centuries, the city had one of the Ottoman Empire's most multi-cultural populations, with large Levantine, Greek and Armenian communities. Although the appalling events of September 1922 largely destroyed the historic Greek and Armenian sectors of the city, some of the original buildings remain on the *kordon*, in Alsancak and in Bornova, northeast of the centre. The city's Muslim heritage is showcased in and around the Kemeraltı Market and its Jewish heritage in Basmane, in the streets around Havra Sokağı in Kemeraltı and in Karataş, south of Konak Sq.

If you are visiting a few museums and archaeological sites in the region, it makes sense to purchase a Museum Pass: The Aegean (www.muze.gov.tr), which will give you entrance to 31 museums and archaeological sites. It costs ₺75 and is valid for seven days.

★**Kemeraltı Market**   MARKET
(Kemeraltı Çarşısı; Map p200; ⊘8am-7pm Mon-Sat; Ⓜ Çankaya, Konak) A labyrinthine bazaar stretching from Konak Sq through to the ancient Agora, Kemeraltı dates back to the 17th century and is home to shops, eateries, artisans' workshops, mosques, coffeehouses, tea gardens and synagogues. Those who spend a day exploring its crowded and colourful streets, historic places of worship, hidden courtyards and grand caravanseries will see the real İzmir – this is a local institution that is accurately described as the city's true heart and soul.

The bazaar's main drag is Anafartalar Caddesi – use this and the historic Hisar, **Şadırvan** (Map p200; off 892 Sokak, Kemeraltı Market; Ⓜ Çankaya, Konak) and **Kestanepazarı** (Map p200; off 873 Sokak, Kemeraltı Market; Ⓜ Çankaya, Konak) Mosques as navigational aids. You're bound to get lost – even locals do – but losing your way and coming across unexpected treasures is part of the attraction. Look out for the **Kızlarağası Hanı** (Cevahir Bedesteni; Map p200; off 895 Sokak, Kemeraltı Market; ⊘8am-5pm; Ⓜ Çankaya, Konak), built in 1744, an Ottoman *bedesten* (warehouse) and *kervansaray* (caravanserai) similar to the İç (Inner) Bedesten in İstanbul's famous Grand Bazaar. Other highlights include the cafes in Kahveciler Sokak between the Hisar Mosque and the Kızlarağası Han, which serve the city's famous *fincanda pişen Türk kahvesi* (Turkish coffee boiled in the cup); and the produce market in Havra (Synagogue) Sokak within the city's historic Jewish enclave. To spend a food-focused day within and around the bazaar, consider signing up for the Only in İzmir guided culinary walk (p203) operated by the well-regarded Culinary Backstreets outfit.

Note that it is not safe to wander through Kemeraltı at night, particularly in the area around Havra Sokağı.

Hisar Mosque   MOSQUE
(Fortress Mosque; Map p200; off 904 Sokak, Kemeraltı Market; Ⓜ Çankaya, Konak) Surrounded by popular coffeehouses, this mosque in the Kemeraltı Market is the largest in the city and dates from 1597. The interior is quintessentially İzmiri, with blue-and-gold motifs on the domed ceiling that are simpler and less Oriental than classic Ottoman designs. Also of note are the roses and grapes carved along the bottom of the women's gallery.

★**Kordon**   WATERFRONT
(Map p200; ☐12, 253, 811, Ⓜ Konak) It's difficult to imagine life in İzmir without its iconic seafront *kordon* (promenade), which stretches north from Cumhuriyet Meydanı to Alsancak and south from Konak Pier to Konak Meydanı. A triumph of urban renewal, these two stretches are grassed, have bicycle and walking paths, and are lined on their eastern edge with bars, cafes and restaurants. Locals flock here at the end of the day to meet with friends, relax on the grass and watch the picture-perfect sunsets.

A number of museums and attractions are located on the *kordon*, including the **Zübeyde Hanım Museum Ship** (Zübeyde Hanım Müze Gemisi; Map p200; Pasaport Pier, Konak; ⊘8am-4pm Tue-Sun; 🚻; Ⓜ Konak) FREE, the **Arkas Art Centre** (Arkas Sanat Merkezi; Map p200; ☎0232-464 6600; www.arkassanatmerkezi.com; 1380 Sk 1, Alsancak; ⊘10am-6pm Tue, Wed & Fri-Sun, to 8pm Thu; ☐12, 253) FREE and the **Atatürk Museum** (Atatürk Müzesi; Map p200; ☎0232-464 8085; Atatürk Caddesi 248, Alsancak; ⊘8.30am-5pm Tue-Sun; ☐12, 253, 811) FREE. There are also bicycles (p212) for hire and **horse-drawn carriages** (Map p200) offering short tours.

★**İzmir Museum of History & Art**   MUSEUM
(İzmir Tarih ve Sanat Müzesi; Map p200; ☎0232-445 6818; near Montrö Meydanı entrance, Kültürpark; ₺5; ⊘8am-4.45pm; ☐12, 253, Ⓜ Basmane) This museum is overlooked by many visitors to the city, who do themselves a great disservice in the process. Spread over three pavilions, it is one of the richest repositories of ancient artefacts in the country and its Sculpture pavilion –

İzmir

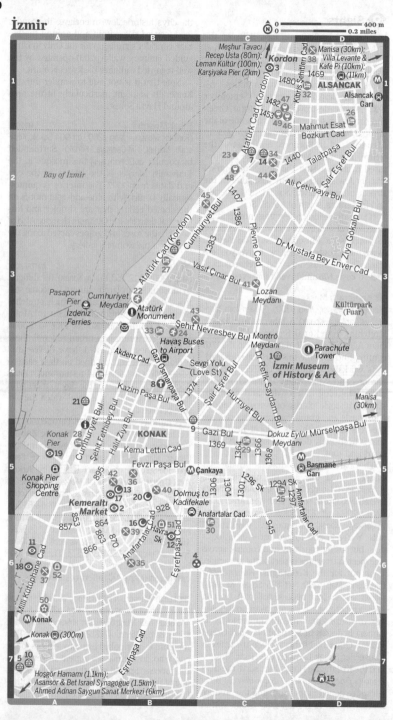

İZMIR & THE NORTH AEGEAN İZMIR

0 — 400 m
0 — 0.2 miles

Bay of İzmir

Meşhur Tavacı
Recep Usta (80m);
Leman Kültür (100m);
Karşiyaka Pier (2km)

Kordon

Manisa (30km);
Villa Levante &
Kafe Pi (10km);
(11km)

ALSANCAK

Alsancak
Garı

Mahmut Esat
Bozkürt Cad

Talatpaşa

Şair Eşref Bul

Ali Çetinkaya Bul

Dr Mustafa Bey Enver Cad

Ziya Gökalp Bul

Kültürpark
(Fuar)

Lozan
Meydanı

Pasaport
Pier
İzdeniz
Ferries

Cumhuriyet
Meydanı
Atatürk
Monument

Şehit Nevresbey Bul

Montrö
Meydanı

Parachute
Tower

İzmir Museum
of History & Art

Havaş Buses
to Airport

Akdenz Cad

Sevgi Yolu
(Love St)

Şair Eşref Bul

Hürriyet Bul

Dr Refik Saydam Bul

Manisa
(30km)

Gazi Osmanpaşa Bul

Kazım Paşa Bul

KONAK

Gazi Bul

Dokuz Eylül
Meydanı

Mürselpaşa Bul

Konak
Pier

Konak Pier
Shopping
Centre

Cumhuriyet Bul

Şehit Fethibey Bul

Halit Ziya Bul

Kema Lettin Cad

Fevzi Paşa Bul

Çankaya

Basmane
Garı

Kemeraltı
Market

Dolmuş to
Kadifekale

Anafartalar Cad

Anafartalar Cad

Havra
Sk

Eşrefpaşa Cad

Millî Kütüphane Cad

Konak

Konak (300m)

Eşrefpaşa Cad

Hoşgör Hamamı (1.1km);
Asansör & Bet Israel Synagogue (1.5km);
Ahmed Adnan Saygun Sanat Merkezi (6km)

İzmir

crammed with masterpieces from ancient Smyrna, Teos, Miletos and Pergamon – is simply sensational. The Precious Objects and Ceramics pavilions contain jewellery, coins and pots, all displayed in a somewhat dated fashion but with informative labelling in English.

Highlights include the coin collection in the **Precious Objects pavilion**, which includes some of the coins minted at Sardis during the reign of King Croesus. These date from the very early 7th century BC and were made of electrum, an alloy of gold and silver with traces of other elements. The jewellery in this pavilion is also impressive.

The **Sculpture pavilion** is so full of treasures that it is hard to single out only a few. Don't miss the friezes from the Temple of Dionysos at Teos and from the theatres and other buildings at Miletos – the frieze from the theatre at Miletos is particularly stunning. Also upstairs and of particular note are the sculptural

fragments from the Belevi Mausoleum near Ephesus, which date from the 3rd century BC.

Downstairs, look out for the Roman-era statue of the river god Kaistros (2nd century AD), the amazingly lifelike Hellenistic three-figure stele from Tralleis (Aydın) and the high reliefs of Demeter and Poseidon from İzmir's Agora.

Agora RUINS

(Map p200; Agora Caddesi; ₺10; ☺8am-4.30pm; Ⓜ Çankaya) Dating from the end of the 4th century BC, Smyrna's ancient agora was ruined in an earthquake in AD 178 but soon rebuilt by order of the Roman emperor Marcus Aurelius. The reconstructed Corinthian colonnade and Faustina Gate are eye-catching, but the vaulted chambers and cisterns in the basements of the two stoas (basilicas) are even more interesting, giving visitors a good idea of how this rectangular-shaped, multilevel marketplace

İZMIR'S SEPHARDIC SYNAGOGUES

When the Jews were expelled from Spain and Portugal by King Ferdinand and Queen Isabella in 1492, many settled in cities of the Ottoman Empire, in particular Constantinople (İstanbul), Salonika (now Thessaloniki in Greece) and Smyrna (today's İzmir). For several centuries they were the predominant power in commerce and trade; indeed, the sultan is said to have commented that Ferdinand's action made his own land poorer and the empire richer. Jews, who followed the Sephardic tradition and spoke a medieval Spanish language called Ladino, enjoyed a tolerance under the Muslim Ottomans unknown in Christian Europe. For instance, unlike in the West, there were no restrictions on the professions Jews could practice.

In Ottoman times, Jews were concentrated in the **Mezarlıkbaşı** quarter or around **Havra Sokağı** (Synagogue Street, 929 Sokak; Map p200; M Çankaya), both of which are located in or around **Kemeraltı Market** (p199). Here they built some three dozen synagogues in traditional Spanish style, eight of which remain in varying conditions. The Izmir Project, which runs **Jewish Heritage Tours** (p203), is a locally driven initiative trying to save these synagogues and create a living cultural monument to the city's rich Sephardic Jewish heritage; four of the synagogues – the **Şalom**, **Algazi**, **La Sinyora (The Lady)** and **Bikur Holim** – date from the 17th and 18th centuries and still function; one, the **Bet Hillel**, was the former house of a well-known rabbi and has recently been restored; and another, the 13th-century **Etz Hayim (Tree of Life)**, is in the process of being restored. All of the synagogues have an unusual 'triple arrangement' of the Torah ark. In Mezarlıkbaşı, there are four remaining *cortijos* (*yahudhane* in Turkish), distinctive Sephardic Jewish family compounds with a courtyard and fountain.

Also worth visiting is **Karataş**, an area about 3km south of the centre of town, where many members of the city's Jewish community once lived. Here you'll find **Bet Israel** (0232-421 4709; Mihat Paşa Caddesi 265; 10, 21), the city's largest synagogue, built in 1907, and the **Asansör** (off Mithatpaşa Caddesi, Karataş; 10, 21) FREE, a lift (elevator) built in the same year by a Jewish banker to facilitate trade between Karataş and the coastline – the alternative is 155 steps. At the foot of the lift, a plaque marks a typical old İzmir house where Darío Moreno (1921–68), the late Jewish singer of 'Canım İzmir' (My Dear İzmir), lived. Sadly, the city's Jewish community now has only 1500 members.

It is possible to visit the synagogues on a self-guided tour (₺20 per person) or on a fully guided half-/full-day tour of the city's Jewish sites (€45/75 per person). Both options can be organised through the **ÇİT-TUR Travel Agency** (0232-446 4400; www.cittur.com; Gazi Osmanpaşa Bulvarı 10/1-b, Pasaport; M Çankaya), which works with the Izmir Project to introduce this important heritage to peoples of all faiths. Bookings must be made in advance for security reasons. For more information about the synagogues see www.izmirjewishheritage.com and www.wmf.org/project/central-izmir-synagogues.

would have looked in its heyday. Archaeological investigations are still underway.

A Muslim cemetery was later built on the agora and many of the old tombstones remain on site. The ticket office is located on the south side, just off Gazi Osmanpaşa Bulvarı.

Konak Meydanı SQUARE
(Map p200; off Mustafa Kemal Sahil/Atatürk Bulvari, Konak; M Konak) On a pedestrianised stretch of Cumhuriyet Bulvarı, this wide plaza, named after the prominent Ottoman-era **Government House** (Hükümet Konağı; Map p200; Konak Sq; M Konak), built in 1872, to the east, marks the heart of the city. It's the

site of the late Ottoman **Konak Clock Tower** (Konak Saat Kulesi; Map p200; Konak Meydanı, Konak; M Konak) and the lovely **Yalı Mosque** (Waterside Mosque, Konak Mosque; Map p200; Konak Meydanı; M Konak), built in 1755, which is covered in Kütahya tiles.

Jutting into the sea to the north is the 1890 **Konak Pier** (Konak İskelesi; Map p200; Cumhuriyet Caddesi, Konak; M Konak), which was designed by Gustave Eiffel and was recently converted into a shopping mall.

Church of St Polycarp CHURCH
(Sen Polikarp Kilisesi; Map p200; 0232-484 8436; Necati Bey Bulvarı 2, İsmet Kaptan; 3-5pm

Mon-Sat; Ⓜ Çankaya) Built in the early 17th century, this Catholic church is the oldest still-functioning Christian house of worship in the city. Its survival during the 1922 fire, which razed all neighbouring buildings to the ground, was nothing short of miraculous. Inside, the walls are covered in frescoes that were restored and added to in the 19th century by local architect Raymond Charles Père, who depicted himself in the fresco of St Polycarp's martyrdom (he's the mustachioed chap with the bound hands).

Archaeology Museum MUSEUM
(Arkeoloji Müzesi; Map p200; ☏ 0232-489 0796; www.izmirmuzesi.gov.tr; Halil Rifat Paşa Caddesi 4, Bahri Baba Parkı; ₺10; ☺ 8am-7pm Tue-Sun mid-Apr–Sep, to 6.30pm Oct, to 5pm Nov–mid-Apr; Ⓜ Konak) The city's Archaeology Museum isn't as impressive as the İzmir Museum of History and Art, but it has some gems in its collection. These include a late-Hellenistic-period bronze statue of a runner from Kyme, near Aliağa, and the head of a gigantic statue of Domitian that once stood at Ephesus. The museum is a short walk up the hill from Konak Sq.

Ethnography Museum MUSEUM
(Etnografya Müzesi; Map p200; ☏ 0232-489 0796; Halil Rifat Paşa Caddesi 3, Bahri Baba Parkı; ☺ 8.30am-5.30pm Tue-Sun; Ⓜ Konak) **FREE** Housed in a splendid stone building that once functioned as a hospital, this museum showcases the arts, crafts and customs of İzmir. Dioramas, displays, photos and information panels focus on local traditions and though the dioramas are undeniably naff, many of the objects are fascinating. Subjects include everything from camel wrestling, pottery and tin-plating to felt-making, embroidery and weaponry.

City Museum & Archive MUSEUM
(Ahmet Piriştina Kent Arşivi ve Müzesi, Apikam; Map p200; ☏ 0232-293 3900; www.apikam.org.tr; Şair Eşref Bulvarı 1, Çankaya; ☺ 9.30am-4.30pm Mon-Sat; Ⓜ Çankaya) **FREE** Housed in a fire station built by the British in 1923, this small museum mounts changing displays on İzmir's history. It is named after Ahmet Piriştina, a former mayor of the city who spearheaded the urban redevelopment of the port and *kordon*, the construction of İzmir's metro and the creation of many new parks.

Kadifekale FORTRESS
(Velvet Castle; Map p200; Rakım Elkutlu Caddesi) Legend has it that in the 4th century Alexander the Great chose this site on Mt Pagos as

the location for Smyrna's acropolis. Nothing remains of the Greek settlement, but parts of the fortifications date back to the Roman era, as do the yet-to-be-excavated remains of a hillside theatre. These days there's not much to see on site, but the view of the Gulf of İzmir is pretty good. To get here take a **dolmuş** (Map p200; Anafartalar Caddesi; one way ₺2.50).

When here, you'll see women from Turkey's southeast baking bread in makeshift ovens and weaving colourful textiles that they happily sell to visitors. There is some talk of excavating the Roman theatre and extending the site all the way down to the Agora, but no concrete project or timeline has been announced.

İzmir Mask Museum MUSEUM
(İzmir Mask Müzesi; Map p200; ☏ 0232-465 3107; www.izmirmaskmuzesi.com; 1448/Cumbalı Sokak 22, Alsancak; ☺ 10am-7pm Tue-Sun; 🚌 12, 253) **FREE** Tucked away in an old house on a street filled with bars, this little museum spread over three floors has an esoteric collection of ceremonial and decorative masks from around the world as well as masks of notable Turks including Atatürk; his successor as president, İsmet İnönü; and poet Nâzım Hikmet.

🏃 Activities

⭐ Only in İzmir Culinary Walk WALKING TOUR
(http://culinarybackstreets.com/culinary-walks/izmir; per person US$125) The many unusual and delicious culinary treats of İzmir are investigated on this 5½-hour guided walk in and around the Kemeraltı district, which offers fascinating information about the city's history and culture as well as giving all participants the opportunity to eat and drink to their fullest capacity (and then some). Wear sensible shoes and skip breakfast on the day.

⭐ Jewish Heritage Tours TOURS
(☏ 0232-446 4400; www.izmirjewishheritage.com; per person €45; ☺ Mon-Fri & Sun) Operated by the İzmir Project, an initiative of the local Jewish community, working in association with the ÇİT-TUR Travel Agency (p202), these half-day guided tours of the synagogues around Havra Sokağı in the Kemeraltı Market visit four still-functioning places of worship: the Şalom, Algazi, La Sinyora (The Lady) and Bikur Holim synagogues, all of which date from the 17th and 18th centuries.

Pürovel Spa & Sport SPA
(Map p200; ☏ 0232-414 0000; www.swissotel.com/hotels/izmir; Swissôtel Büyük Efes, Gazi Osmanpaşa

IZZET KERIBAR / GETTY IMAGES ©

1. Northern shore, Bozcaada (p177) 2. Old house, Cunda (Alibey Island; p189) 3. Roman theatre seats, Asklepion (p192), Bergama 4. Plates of meze

OZAN MALKOCER/GETTY IMAGES ©

İzmir & the North Aegean Highlights

Travellers are spoiled for choice in this region and, at the risk of sounding cliché, there really is something for everyone here. Its ancient cities bring history alive, the beaches are seldom as frenetic as elsewhere, the food and wine are among the country's best and the ghosts of times past are ever present.

Ruins

The ancient city of Pergamum (now Bergama) is at the top of everyone's list of places to visit, and Assos in Behramkale is as dramatically situated as you'll find anywhere. But don't miss the wealth of ruins at lesser-known sites such as Teos on the Biga Peninsula or Sardis east of İzmir.

Beaches

The beaches at Bozcaada are rightfully celebrated and easily accessible. But go the extra kilometre to take the plunge at Badavut Plaj, south of Ayvalık. And if you prefer to be on rather than in the water, head for Alaçatı Surf Paradise, the centre for windsurfing in Turkey.

Memories

The north Aegean has been colonised for millennia and is one of the most ethnically diverse regions in Turkey. Reminders of the region's multilayered past are seen, felt and sometimes even heard – especially in places such as Ayvalık, where many Greeks made their home before independence, and in İzmir with its community of Sephardic Jews.

Food & Drink

Those rich, multi-ethnic influences are especially palpable in the region's cuisine, which has taken much from the Greek, Cretan and Jewish styles of cooking. There are well-regarded wineries on Bozcaada and southwest of İzmir.

Bulvarı 1; daily pool & gym pass ₺125; ☉6am-11pm; ⓂÇankaya) One of the best spa and fitness centers in the country, this facility in the up-market Swissôtel Büyük Efes offers a gym, tennis court, indoor and outdoor swimming pools, pilates and yoga studio, jacuzzi, hamam, sauna and steam bath. It also offers beauty and relaxation treatments including massage (₺200–₺350).

✸✸✶ Festivals & Events

İzmir European Jazz Festival   JAZZ
(☑0232-482 0090; www.iksev.org/en/caz-festivali) Held in March each year, this popular festival is organised by the İzmir Foundation for Culture, Arts and Education (İKSEV), and hosts a high-profile lineup of European and local jazz performers. Venues include the İKSEV Salonu and the Ahmed Adnan Saygun Sanat Merkezi (AASSM).

International İzmir Festival   FESTIVAL
(Uluslararası İzmir Festivali; ☑0232-482 0090; www.iksev.org/en) Usually held in early summer, this annual festival is organised by the İzmir Foundation for Culture, Arts and Education (İKSEV) and focuses on classical music. Venues include the Ahmed Adnan Saygun Sanat Merkezi (AASSM) in İzmir, as well as at the Celsus Kütüphanesi and Büyük Tiyatro at Ephesus.

🛏 Sleeping

İzmir's waterfront is dominated by large high-end business hotels, while most midrange and budget options are located in Alsancak or Basmane. All accommodation prices skyrocket during the trade fairs that are regularly held in the city; the most popular of these is the Marble Fair held in March. Because of these fairs, it's always sensible to book accommodation in advance of your stay.

Note that most of the city's hotels allow smoking in rooms. Fortunately, the larger establishments usually have dedicated smoke-free floors.

🛏 Bazaar & Basmane

Just southwest of Basmane train station, 1296 Sokak is known as 'Oteller Sokak' (Hotel Street) due to its plethora of budget and mid-range hotels, most of which are in restored Ottoman houses. Think twice before staying in any of the Anafartalar Caddesi or Kemeraltı hotels, as these locations are not particularly safe or pleasant at night.

Hotel Baylan Basmane   HOTEL $
(Map p200; ☑0232-483 0152; www.hotelbaylan.com; 1299 Sokak 8, Basmane; standard s/d/tr €30/40/46, deluxe s/d €34/46; P❄@☎; ⓂBasmane) A sound three-star choice, the Baylan has a loyal business clientele so you'll need to book in advance to snaffle a room. One of the cleanest and most professionally run hotels in the city, it has free on-site parking and a variety of room types, including deluxe rooms with private terraces, cramped twins and some singles with light well windows only.

Otel Antik Han   HOTEL $
(Map p200; ☑0232-489 2750; www.otelantikhan.com; Anafartalar Caddesi 600, Çankaya; s/d/tr €35/45/55; ❄@☎; ⓂÇankaya, Basmane) Though its glory days were long ago, this hotel in an 1857 building on Anafartalar Caddesi continues to offer cigarette-scented rooms of various type and standard. Its main drawcard is the central courtyard garden and restaurant. Request a renovated room in the front section and avoid the mezzanine 'suites' around the courtyard. Note that the location isn't for the faint-hearted.

Met Boutique Hotel   BOUTIQUE HOTEL $$
(Map p200; ☑0232-483 0111; www.metotel.com; Gazi Bulvarı 124; s/d/ste €100/125/200; ❄☎; ⓂBasmane) It certainly doesn't deliver on its claim to boutique status, being more of a business hotel, but the Met is worth considering nonetheless. Offering 38 well-presented rooms with kettles, satellite TVs and good beds, its most compelling draws are the central location and stylish foyer cafe. Front rooms can be noisy, as they overlook busy Gazi Bulvarı.

🛏 Alsancak & Seafront

The city's best hostels are in the eating and entertainment hot spot of Alsancak. Most midrange and top-end choices are on or close to the *kordon*, with the best being near Cumhuriyet Meydanı.

InHouse Hostel   HOSTEL $
(Map p200; ☑0232-404 0014; www.inhousehostel.com; 1460 Sokak 75, Alsancak; dm₺36-42, d₺120, s/d without bathroom ₺75/110; ❄@☎; 🚌12, 253, 🚉Alsancak) Opened in 2015, this hostel offers 56 beds in private rooms and in dorms sleeping between four and 10. Dorms have under-bed lockers, hard bunk beds and clean but limited shared bathrooms. There's 24-hour reception, a kitchen for common use, a small foyer lounge and an entertainment program pre-

dominantly consisting of nightly pub crawls. The Alsancak location is excellent.

Otel Kilim
HOTEL $

(Map p200; ☑ 0232-484 5340; www.kilimotel. com.tr; Atatürk Caddesi; s/d €50/75, deluxe r €90; [P][✻][@][✿]; [M]Çankaya) The decor at this multi-storey hotel in the Pasaport section of the *kordon* is old-fashioned (sometimes hilariously so) but rooms are well priced, comfortable, clean and well-equipped with kettle, work desk and reading lights. Deluxe rooms face the sea but none have balconies. There's a cafe and fish restaurant on the ground floor, and plenty of free parking is available.

Shantihome
HOSTEL $

(Map p200; ☑ 0546 235 0805; www.shantihome. org; 1464 Sokak 15, Alsancak; dm ₺30-35, s/d without bathroom ₺60/70; [✿]; [🖵] 12, 253, [🖵] Alsancak) You'll feel as if you've teleported to Rishikesh c 1968 when staying in this hostel run by chilled-out, English-speaking host Veli. Located in an at-mospheric street in Alsancak, it offers small dorms with power points and reading lights but no lockers (Veli told us that the world needs more love and trust). Bathroom facili-ties are stretched. Guests love the daily vege-tarian breakfasts (donation requested).

★ Swissôtel Büyük Efes
HOTEL $$

(Map p200; ☑ 0232-414 0000; www.swissotel. com/hotels/izmir; Gazi Osmanpaşa Bulvarı 1; s/d €140/150, executive s/d €190/200; [P][✻][@] [✿][✖][✿]; [M]Çankaya) Guests here have been known not to leave the premises at all dur-ing their city stay. Frankly, we're not at all surprised. Rooms are comfortable and well appointed, but it's the hotel's gorgeous gar-den and impressive facilities that are the real attraction. These include indoor and outdoor swimming pools, tennis court, spa, gym and rooftop bar with panoramic bay views.

The garden is filled with important works of art including pieces by Antony Gormley and Fernando Botero, and eating and drinking op-tions include the rooftop Equinox Restaurant and the Aquarium Restaurant in the garden. The breakfast buffet (€10) served in Cafe Swiss on the ground floor is both lavish and delicious.

Key Hotel
HOTEL $$

(Map p200; ☑ 0232-482 1111; www.keyhotel.com; Mimar Kemalettin Caddesi 1, Konak; r €145-200, ste €320-500; [P][✻][@][✿]; [M]Çankaya) This sleek offering near Konak Pier occupies a former bank building; the original vault is now a glass-topped atrium. Popular with visiting dignitaries and as a conference and wedding

venue, it offers 31 luxe rooms with high-tech fitout, work desks, rain showers and king-size beds. The huge top-floor grand suite with panoramic terrace is to die for.

İzmir Palas Oteli
HOTEL $$

(Map p200; ☑ 0232-465 0030; www.izmirpalas. com.tr; Vasif Çınar Bulvarı 2; s/d €65/90, with sea view €70/100, ste ₺130; [✻][@][✿]; [🖵] 12, 253) Estab-lished in 1927, this well-priced 138-room hotel on the *kordon* has enjoyed wonderful water views for decades. Sadly, many of these have been blocked by the huge new development opposite. Generously sized, well-maintained but slightly dowdy rooms have big beds, work desks and double-glazed windows. There's a top-floor bar and a ground-floor fish restau-rant (mains from ₺35).

🛏 Bornova

Villa Levante
BOUTIQUE HOTEL $$

(☑ 0232-343 1888; www.hotelvillalevante.com; 80 Sokak 25; standard r €140, ste €200; [P][✻][✿]; [M]Bornova) Located in leafy Bornova, 9km outside the city centre, this is İzmir's only boutique hotel. An 1831 Levantine villa that has been tastefully renovated, it offers six standard rooms and five suites, all with chan-delier, wooden floor, lofty ceiling, comforta-ble bed, satellite TV and work desk. There's also a popular restaurant in the rear garden (mains ₺25–₺55).

🍴 Eating

Most restaurants on the *kordon* specialise in seafood and have terraces overlooking the bay. The best cheap eats are available in and around the Kemeraltı Market, and the best cafes are in Alsancak.

★ Ayşa
LOKANTA $

(Map p200; ☑ 0232-489 8485; www.bosnakborek cisiaysa.com; Abacıoğlu Han, Anafartalar Caddesi 228, Kemeraltı Market; meze plates ₺8-9, portions from ₺10; ⊙ 8am-6pm Mon-Sat; [✻][✐]; [M]Konak, Çankaya) Serving Bosnian food that is remark-ably similar to Turkish home cooking, this stylish *lokanta* in the pretty Abacıoğlu Han of-fers both indoor and outdoor seating. Choose from the DIY meze display (yum!) and be sure to snaffle a piece of *börek* if it's on offer. Main dishes are displayed in the bain-marie and include both meat and vegetable choices.

★ Léone
CAFE $

(Map p200; ☑ 0232-464 3400; www.leone-tr.com; Vasıf Çınar Bulvarı 29a; croissants ₺4, cakes ₺7-12.50,

İZMIRI FAST FOOD

Culinary tourism is big business these days, and Turkey is a popular destination for foodies wanting to knock some big-ticket items off their culinary bucket list – baklava in Gaziantep, *hamsi* (anchovies) on the Black Sea etc etc. In recent years, a growing number of these enthusiasts have been heading to İzmir, lured by reports of its fascinating Sephardic-influenced fast food. When in the city, be sure to try the following:

Boyo (pl: *boyoz*) A fried pastry made with flour, sunflower oil and a small amount of tahini; traditionally enjoyed with hard-boiled eggs and a glass of *sübye* (drink made from melon seeds and sugar water). Try one at **Dostlar Fırını** (Map p200; ☎0232-421 9202; www.alsancakdostlarfirini.com; Kıbrıs Şehitleri Caddesi 120, Alsancak; boyoz ₺1.25-1.50, hard-boiled egg ₺1.25; ⊙6.30am-7pm; ☐12, 253, 811) in Alsancak.

Gevrek The local version of a *simit* (chewy bread ring dipped in water and molasses syrup and encrusted with sesame seeds), made with fewer sesame seeds and less salt. Sold by street vendors across the city.

Kumru Sandwiches made with soft bread, aged *kaşar* cheese from Kars, sausage from Urfa and local tomato paste; the name means 'collared dove', and derives from the shape of the sandwich. Note that the version with white cheese, fresh tomato and green pepper sold by some street vendors is not authentic; instead, head to **Kumrucu Apo** (Map p200; 1318 Sokak 12, Kemeraltı; sandwiches from ₺5; Ⓜ Konak, Çankaya) in the Kemeraltı Market.

Şambali A cake made with almond-studded semolina, yoghurt and sugar. After being cooked it's doused with sweet syrup and lathered with *kaymak* (clotted cream). The best place to try one of these is **Meşhur Hisarönü Şambalicisi** (Map p200; 901 Sokak, Kemeraltı Market; şambali ₺2.50; ⊙9am-7pm Mon-Sat; ☑; Ⓜ Konak, Çankaya) in the Kemeraltı Market.

Söğüş Poached tongue, cheek and brain served cold in bread with chopped onion, parsley, mint, tomato, cumin and hot chilli flakes. Not for the faint-hearted.

tartines ₺7-10, croque monsieurs ₺13; ⊙8am-8.30pm Mon-Sat, 10am-4pm Sun; ☐12, 253) A Parisian-style *divertissement* in the heart of the city, this stylish cafe on Lozan Meydanı is wildly popular with Alsancak's ladies-who-lunch, who congregate at the tables on the streetside terrace. Coffee is excellent and the croissants and gateaux are simply sensational. At lunch, *tartines* (filled baguettes) and *croque monsieurs* (baked ham, cheese and béchamel sandwiches) are the popular choices.

Bizim Mütfak
LOKANTA $

(Map p200; ☎0232-484 9917; www.bzmmutfak.com; 914 Sokak 12, Kemeraltı Market; soup ₺15, portion ₺10-20; ⊙7.30am-4.30pm Mon-Sat; Ⓜ Konak, Çankaya) The blue-and-white checked tablecloths give this popular *lokanta* in the courtyard of the Mirkelam Han near the Hisar Mosque a Greek-island vibe, but the food is resolutely İzmiri, with a focus on unusual soups (trotter, rabbit, duck or fish) and local specialities inclusing İzmir *köfte* (baked spicy meatballs). It opened in 1950 and has a passionately devoted clientele.

Sevinç
CAFE $

(Map p200; ☎0232-421 7590; www.sevincpasta nesi.com.tr; Ali Çetinkaya Bulvarı 31, Alsancak; cakes ₺11, pastries ₺3-7.50; ⊙7am-midnight; ☐12, 253) Romantic rendezvous, reunions and regular catch-ups – the terrace at this long-established cafe has been hosting all three for six decades. It's an excellent spot to relax after a saunter along the *kordon*.

Köfteci Salih Arslan
KÖFTE $

(Map p200; ☎0232-446 4296; 879 Sokak 16a, Kemeraltı Market; portions köfte ₺15, piyaz ₺4; ⊙11am-4pm Mon-Sat; Ⓜ Konak, Çankaya) In the Kestane Pazarı (Chestnut Market) section of Kemeraltı, this simple place has been serving tender and tasty Macedonian/Albanian–style *köfte* with *piyaz* (white-bean salad) since 1970 and has built a devoted local following in the process. Beware the fiendishly hot sun-dried chillies served on the side!

Can Döner
KEBAP $$

(Map p200; ☎0232-484 1313; www.candoner.com; Millıküpüphane Caddesi 6b, Kemeraltı; İskender kebap ₺22; ⊙11am-6.30pm; ❄; Ⓜ Konak) Kemeraltı's best-loved *kebapçı* (kebab eatery) is located near Konak Sq and serves an excellent İskender kebap. Eat inside or at one of the streetside tables.

Altın Kapı KEBAP **$$**
(Map p200; ☑0232-422 2709; www.altinkapi.com; 1444 Sokak 9, Alsancak; döner kebap ₺25; ⊙11am-11pm; ⊞12, 253) Thought by many to serve the best döner kebap in the city, clean and cheerful Altın Kapı is located in a side street off pedestrianised Kıbrıs Şehitleri Caddesi.

Meşhur Tavacı Recep Usta ANATOLIAN **$$$**
(☑0232-463 8797; http://tavacirecepusta.com; Atatürk Caddesi 364, Alsancak; kebaps ₺33-44; ⊙noon-10.30pm Mon-Thu, from 10am Fri-Sun; ⊞12, 253) Serving tasty dishes harking from Diyarbakır in the country's southeast, this is a popular venue for celebratory and family dinners, and is also known for its set weekend brunch (₺35 per person). Order a main course and you'll receive complimentary mezes, salad, *lavaş* bread and dessert. The house speciality is *lık kaburga dolma* (stuffed lamb ribs, ₺98 for two people).

Veli Usta Balık Pişiricisi SEAFOOD **$$$**
(Map p200; ☑0232-464 2705; www.balikpisiriciseveliusta.com; Atatürk Caddesi 212a, Alsancak; mezes ₺5-30, mains from ₺30; ⊙noon-11pm; ⊞12, 253) In İzmir, three ingredients make for the perfect meal: *balık* (fish), *roca* (rocket) and rakı. This friendly terrace restaurant on the *kordon* is a great spot to sample all three, and is hugely popular with locals. Be sure to order the rolled sole, grouper or dory (described as *şiş* on the menu), which is the signature dish,

Sakız MODERN TURKISH **$$$**
(Map p200; ☑0232-464 1103; www.sakizalsancak.com; Şehit Nevresbey Bulvarı 9a; mezes ₺7-38, mains ₺24-50; ⊙10am-11.45pm Mon-Sat; ❋⚲; Ⓜ Çankaya, Basmane) Specialising in Aegean and Cretan cuisine, this upmarket restaurant behind the Swissôtel serves fresh mezes and seafood mains replete with Aegean herbs. The restaurant is named after the aromatic gum mastic, a native tree of the Aegean region, which features in many of the desserts on the menu. Live traditional music sets the scene on Wednesday, Friday and Saturday.

Deniz Restaurant SEAFOOD **$$$**
(Map p200; ☑464 4499; Atatürk Caddesi 188b; mezes ₺17-34, mains from ₺35; ⊙11am-11pm; ❋⚲; ⊞12, 253) This long-established fish restaurant on the *kordon* is attached to the İzmir Palas hotel and is widely acknowledged as one of the best eateries in the city. The prime seating is on the terrace – book ahead to ensure you sit here rather than inside.

🍷 Drinking & Entertainment

Alsancak is the city's nightlife hub, particularly in the clubs and bars on the side streets running between Kıbrıs Şehitleri Caddesi and Cumhuriyet Caddesi – head to 1452, 1453 and 1482 Sokaks.

To enjoy a traditional Turkish coffee, make your way to Kahveciler Sokak (Coffeemaker's Street) behind the Hisar Mosque in the Kemeraltı Market. The cafes here all serve the local speciality of *fincanda pişen Türk kahvesi* (Turkish coffee cooked in the cup rather than in the usual long-handled copper coffee pan).

Kovan BAR
(Map p200; ☑0232-463 2393; 1482 Muzaffer İzgü/Sokak 6, Alsancak; ⊙8am-2am; ⊞12, 253) Those who are young and fond of partying in İzmir tend to be regulars here. A barnlike space with an open-air courtyard at the rear, it literally heaves with patrons on Friday and Saturday nights. The draws are an inclusive vibe, cheap beer, bar food (pizza, fries, samosas) and loud music supplied by in-house DJs.

Sunset Cafe BAR
(Map p200; ☑0232-463 6549; Ali Çetinkaya Bulvari 2a; ⊙7am-2am; ⊞12, 253) On the edge of the boulevard, the Sunset makes a great end-of-day watering hole, with tables on the pavement and a relaxed, youthful crowd.

Leman Kültür BAR, CAFE
(☑0232-463 0133; www.lmk.com.tr; Kıbrıs Şehitleri Caddesi 179, Alsancak; ⊙10am-midnight; ⚲; ⊞12, 253) This colourfully decorated bar-cafe at the northern end of Alsancak's main pedestrian mall is hugely popular with the city's 20-somethings.

Kahveci Ömer Usta COFFEE
(Map p200; ☑0232-425 4706; www.kahveciomerusta.com; 905 Sokak 15, Kemeraltı; ⊙9am-8pm; Ⓜ Çankaya, Konak) One of the popular cafes behind the Hisar Mosque in the Kemeraltı Market, Kahveci Ömer Usta specialises in *fincanda pişen Türk kahvesi*, Turkish coffee cooked in the cup.

Jackson's CLUB
(Map p200; ☑0232-422 6045; 1453 Sokak 17, Alsancak; ⊙10pm-4am; ⊞12, 253) One of the most popular clubs in Alsancak, Jackson's is

housed in what was once the British consul's residence. It has an in-house DJ, small dance floor and reasonably inclusive vibe.

Tren CLUB
(Map p200; ✆ 0544 463 8736; www.trenfoodmusic.com; 1453 Sokak 13, Alsancak; ⊙ 5pm-4am; 🚋 12, 253) Probably the most popular club in Alsancak, Tren (Train) is jam-packed on Friday and Saturday nights.

İzmir Milli Kütüphane PERFORMING ARTS
(Map p200; ✆ 0232-484 2002; www.izmirmilli kutuphane.com; Millikütüphane Caddesi 39, Konak; Ⓜ Konak) This handsome 1912 Ottoman Revival building is the home base of the İzmir Devlet Opera Ve Balesi (İzmir State Opera and Ballet Company).

Shopping

Şekercibaşı Ali Galip FOOD & DRINKS
(Map p200; ✆ 0232-483 7778; www.aligalip.com; Anafartalar Caddesi 10, Konak; ⊙ 8.30am-7pm Mon-Sat; Ⓜ Konak) It first opened for business in 1901, and this much-loved sweet shop is still the first port of call for many shoppers when visiting Kemeraltı. It sells *lokum* (Turkish delight), chocolate and *helva* (sweet made from sesame seeds) that are made at the shop's İzmir factory.

Altan Manisalı FOOD & DRINKS
(Map p200; ✆ 0232-425 5346; www.manisali.com; Havra/929 Sokağı 13, Kemeraltı Market; ⊙ 8.30am-7pm; Ⓜ Çankaya) Selling particularly delicious *helva,* tahini and *pekmez* (syrup made from grape juice) since 1885, this is one of the most famous food stores in the market. Members of the same family operate next-door Beşe, which sells the same produce and is equally historic and loved.

ⓘ Information

Tourist Office (Map p200; ✆ 483 5117; 1344 Sokak 2, Konak; ⊙ 8.30am-7.30pm May-Sep, 8am-5pm Oct-Apr; Ⓜ Konak) Housed on the ground floor of the ornate art nouveau İzmir Valiliği İl Turizm Müdürlüğü (Culture and Tourism Directorate) building near Konak Pier, this office can provide a city map and a few brochures. Staff don't always speak English, so getting advice can sometimes be a challenge.

ⓘ Getting There & Away

AIR

Many domestic and European flights arrive at İzmir's modern and efficient **Adnan Menderes Airport** (✆ 0232-455 0000; www.adnanmen deresairport.com). Some of the airlines offer

shuttle-bus services from the airport to regional destinations.

Anadolu Jet (www.anadolujet.com) Flies between İzmir and Ankara.

AtlasGlobal (Atlasjet; www.atlasglb.com) Flies between İzmir and İstanbul (Atatürk), and also between İzmir and North Cyprus (Ercan).

Borajet (www.borajet.com.tr) Flies between İzmir and İstanbul (Sabiha Gökçen).

Onur Air (www.onurair.com.tr) Flies between İzmir and İstanbul (Atatürk).

Pegasus Airlines (www.flypgs.com) Flies between İzmir and İstanbul (Atatürk and Sabiha Gökçen), Ankara, Kayseri, Antalya, Şanlıurfa Samsun, Adana and Mardin, as well as to Northern Cyprus (Ercan) and the Netherlands (Amsterdam).

Sun Express (www.sunexpress.com) Flies between İzmir and Van, Kars, Antalya, Diyarbekir, Erzurum, Malatya, as well as Austria (Vienna) and a number of destinations across Germany.

Turkish Airlines (✆ 484 1220; www.thy.com; Halit Ziya Bulvarı 65) Flies between İzmir and İstanbul (Atatürk and Sabiha Gökçen) and Germany (Berlin).

BUS

İzmir's mammoth but efficient otogar lies 6.5km northeast of the city centre. For travel on Friday or Saturday to coastal towns located north of İzmir, buy your ticket a day in advance; in high season, two days in advance. Tickets can also be purchased from the bus companies' offices in the city centre; most of these are located in Dokuz Eylül Meydanı in Basmane.

Inter-regional buses and their ticket offices are found on the lower level of the otogar; regional buses (eg Selçuk, Bergama, Manisa and Sardis) leave from the upper level (buy tickets on the bus). City buses and dolmuşes leave from a courtyard in front of the lower level.

Short-distance buses (eg the Çeşme Peninsula) leave from a smaller local bus terminal in Üçkuyular, 6.5km southwest of Konak, but pick up and drop off at the otogar as well.

TRAIN

Most intercity services arrive at/depart from **Alsancak Train Station** (Alsancak Garı; ✆ 0232-464 7795), but the Selçuk service pulls into the Basmane station. For northern or eastern Turkey, change at Ankara or Konya.

Ankara

There is one daily train to Ankara (₺44, 14 hours), leaving Alsancak at 6.35pm and travelling via Eskişehir (₺40.50, 12 hours).

Bergama

İzmir's efficient İzban rail travels to Aliağa (₺2.40 on a Kent Kart (p212)), from where buses and dolmuşes continue to Bergama (₺5).

Konya

There is one daily train to Konya (₺45.50, 14 hours), leaving Alsancak at 9.10pm.

Manisa

There are six daily trains between Alsancak and Manisa (₺5.50 to ₺7, 1¾ hours).

Selçuk

Six daily trains travel to Selçuk from Basmane station (₺6, 1½ hours) between 7.45am and 6.25pm.

BOAT

İzdeniz (Map p200; ☎ 0232-330 8922; www.izdeniz.com.tr; ☺ 7.15am-11.30pm) ferries sometimes sail between İzmir and Foça from June to September (₺10). A ferry service linking İzmir and the Greek island of Lesbos had just been announced at the time of research, with a projected launch in May 2017.

TO/FROM THE AIRPORT

İzmir's Adnan Menderes Airport is 15km south of the city centre on the way to Ephesus and Kuşadası.

Havaş Bus

This is the easiest way to travel between the airport and the city centre. **Havaş** (Map p200; www.havas.net; 1 way ₺10) buses (one hour) leave hourly from Gazi Osmanpaşa Bulvarı outside the Swissôtel Büyük Efes between 3.30am and 11.30pm; and from domestic arrivals to the same hotel between 8.40am and 3.30am.

Havaş Buses also travel from the airport to Çeşme, Kuşadası and Aydın.

Local Bus

Local bus 202 runs between both arrivals terminals and Cumhuriyet Meydanı via Üçkuyular bus station; the trip costs ₺4.80 on a Kent Kart. The buses leave from outside the Swissôtel Büyük Efes at 2am, 4am and then on the hour until midnight. From the airport, they leave at 1am, 4am and then on the hour until midnight.

Bus 204 (₺4.80 on a Kent Kart) travels between the airport terminals and the Bornova metro hourly between 5.40am and 3.40am.

Taxi

A taxi between the airport and Cumhuriyet Meydanı costs around ₺55.

Train

The city's commuter rail system **İzban** (www.izban.com.tr) has a stop at the airport and one at Alsancak in the city centre (₺2.40 on a Kent Kart).

TO/FROM THE BUS STATIONS

Passengers on intercity buses operated by the larger bus companies can usually take advantage of the free *servis* (shuttle bus) between the otogar and bus company offices in Dokuz Eylül Meydanı in the city centre. Alternatively, use local bus 302, which travels between the otogar and Konak, which is ₺2.40 on a Kent Kart.

A taxi between the city centre and the otogar costs around ₺35.

To get to Üçkuyular bus station, take the metro (Fahrettin Altay stop, ₺2.40 on a Kent Kart). Alternatively, use local bus 302, which travels between

SERVICES FROM İZMİR'S OTOGAR

DESTINATION	FARE (₺)	DURATION (HR)	DISTANCE (KM)	FREQUENCY	VIA
Ankara	75	8	550	hourly	Afyon
Antalya	65	7	450	hourly	Aydın
Bergama	10	2	110	half-hourly	Menemen
Bodrum	30	3	286	hourly	Milas
Bursa	40	5	300	hourly	Balıkesir
Çanakkale	40	6	340	hourly	Ayvalık
Çeşme	17	1¾	116	hourly	Alaçatı
Denizli	33	3	250	half-hourly	Aydın
Eski Foça	10	1½	86	half-hourly	Menemen
İstanbul	80	8	575	hourly	Bursa
Konya	45	10½	575	6 daily	Afyon
Kuşadası	15	1¼	95	hourly	Selçuk
Manisa	9	1	45	frequent	Sarnıç
Marmaris	40	4	320	hourly	Aydın
Salihli	14	1½	90	half-hourly	Sardis
Selçuk	10	1	80	frequent	Belevi

the otogar and Konak; the trip costs ₺2.40 on a Kent Kart.

❶ Getting Around

İzmir has two travel cards, which cover bus, metro, İzban and ferry trips. These are available and can be recharged at stations, piers and shops with the Kent Kart sign.

Kent Kart (City Card) You pay a ₺7 deposit when you buy the card and then top it up with credit. When you use the card, ₺2.40 is debited from it, then every journey you make for the next 90 minutes is free.

Üç-Beş (Three-Five) This card with two/three/five credits, each valid for a single journey, costs ₺5.50/7.75/12.25. It can be hard to access.

BICYCLE

İzmir has a cycle-share hiring scheme called **Bisim** (Map p200; ☑ 0232-433 5155; www.bisim.com.tr; per hr ₺2.40; ◷ 6am-11pm; 🚌169), with a couple of dozen docking stations, most along the seafront and *kordon*.

BOAT

İzdeniz (p211) operates regular ferry services (tickets ₺3, or ₺2.40 on a Kent Kart) from Konak to Karşıyaka and Bostanlı on the opposite side of the bay, and less frequent services to the same destinations from Pasaport and Alsancak.

BUS

Buses are operated by **ESHOT** (☑ 3200 320; www.eshot.gov.tr/en/Home). Check its website for route information. The city's main local **bus terminal** is at Konak, close to the metro.

CAR

Large international car-hire franchises have 24-hour desks at the airport, and some have offices in town.

You'll pay to park your car in the city. There are convenient car parks in front of Konak Pier, at the Kültürpark and at the Alsancak Municipal Carpark. These charge around ₺6 for one to three hours and ₺22 for 12 to 24 hours.

METRO

İzmir Metro (www.izmirmetro.com.tr; fare ₺2.40; ◷ 6am-0.20am) is clean, quick and cheap. There are currently 17 stations running from Fahrettin Altay to Evka-3 via Konak, Çankaya, Basmane and Ege Üniversitesi (Aegean University). Trips cost ₺2.40 on a Kent Kart.

TAXI

You can hail a taxi on the street or pick up one from a taxi stand or outside one of the big hotels. Fares start at ₺3 then cost ₺2.45 per kilometre.

TRAIN

The city's commuter rail system is called **İzban** (p211). The northern line runs from Aliağa, near

Bergama, to Alsancak; the southern line runs from Alsancak to Cumaovası, south of the city. The latter stops at the airport en route. Trips cost ₺2.40 on a Kent Kart (p212). There are plans to extend the service north to Bergama and Manisa, and south to Selçuk.

Manisa

☑ 0236 / POP 380,000

In ancient times, Manisa was known as Magnesia ad Sipylum and was a strategically important city. It prospered during the Byzantine period but reached its apogee under the Ottomans, when it became the place where the *şehzades* (crown princes) were trained for their imperial destinies. Many of the buildings in the historic centre date from the nine-year period when Süleyman the Magnificent and his mother Ayşe Hafsa Sultan lived here. The main reasons to visit are to see the exquisite Muradiye Mosque and attend the annual Mesir Macunu Festivalı, which is inscribed on Unesco's list of intangible cultural heritage.

◉ Sights & Activities

★ Muradiye Mosque   MOSQUE
(Murat Caddesi) The architectural genius of Mimar Sinan is well and truly on show at this exquisite mosque, which was commissioned by Sultan Murat III and constructed between 1583 and 1585. After admiring its twin minarets and front portico, enter through the ornately decorated door – a triumph of inlaid wood and marble – and you'll be confronted by one of the most beautiful of all Ottoman mosque interiors, with a profusion of İznik tiling and delicate stained glass.

The interior owes much to the work of Sedefkar Mehmed Aga, architect of İstanbul's Blue Mosque, who was one of the two architects who supervised the mosque's completion – its tiled *mihrab* (niche indicating the direction of Mecca) is particularly beautiful.

There's a pleasant garden courtyard in front of the mosque with clean public toilets (₺1).

Medical History Museum   MUSEUM
(Hafsa Sultan Şifahanesi Tıp Tarihi Müzesi; ☑ 0236-201 1070; www.cbu.edu.tr; ◷ 10am-10pm) **FREE** Tracing the history of medicine across the globe, this ambitious museum in the grounds of the Sultan Mosque occupies a handsome *bimarhane* (mental hospital) that was commissioned by Süleyman the Magnificent in 1539

SARDIS

Sardis was once the capital of the powerful Lydian kingdom that dominated much of the Aegean before the Persians arrived. It is also the site of one of the Seven Churches of Revelation (or Apocalypse) mentioned in the New Testament. From 560 BC to 546/7 BC the city was ruled by king Croesus. During his reign, local metallurgists discovered the secret of separating gold from silver, and produced both gold and silver coins of a hitherto unknown purity. This made Sardis rich and Croesus' name became synonymous with wealth itself. For this reason, Sardis is often described as the place where modern currency was invented.

Scattered around the village of Sartmustafa (or Sart), the **Ruins of Sardis** (₺10; ⊙ 8am-5pm, to 7pm Apr-Sep) make for a rewarding day trip from İzmir (80km away). It and Manisa can easily be visited on the same day. The ruins lie at the eastern end of the village, immediately north of the road, and include Byzantine shops, a synagogue, *palestra* (an open expanse where athletes trained and where the gymnasium and baths once stood), Roman villa, Temple to Artemis and 4th-century church.

Entry is via an 18m-long paved Roman road, past a well-preserved Byzantine latrine and a row of almost 30 Byzantine shops that belonged to Jewish merchants and artisans in the 4th century AD (Jews settled here as early as 547 BC). Turn left at the end of the Roman road to enter the **synagogue** (*havra*), impressive because of its size and beautiful decoration. The southern shrine housed the Torah.

Next to the synagogue is the **palestra**, which was probably built in the early 3rd century AD and abandoned after a Sassanian invasion in 616.

Right at the end is a striking two-storey building called the **Marble Court of the Hall of the Imperial Cult**, which, though heavily restored, gives an idea of the former grandeur of the building.

Continuing excavations on the way to the village to the south have uncovered a stretch of the Lydian city wall and a Roman villa with painted walls right on top of an earlier Lydian residence.

A sign points south to the **Temple of Artemis**, just over 1km away. Today only a few columns of the once-magnificent but never-completed building still stand. Nevertheless, the temple's plan is clearly visible and very impressive. Nearby is an early Christian **church** dating from the 4th century AD.

Getting There & Away

Half-hourly buses to Salihli (₺14, 1½ hours, 90km) leave from İzmir's otogar every 30 minutes and pass Sartmustafa en route. You can also catch dolmuşes (minibuses that stop anywhere along their prescribed route to Sartmustafa (₺2.5, 15 minutes, 9km) from behind the Salihli otogar.

Buses travelling between Salihli and Manisa (₺11, one hour) can be hailed along the highway, making it possible – just – to visit both Manisa and Sardis in the same day.

İZMIR & THE NORTH AEGEAN MANISA

as part of the *külliye* (mosque complex). Run by Celal Bayar Üniversitesi, its exhibitions are fascinating but sometimes quite gruesome. There's a pleasant cafe in the courtyard.

Tarihi Sultan Hamam　　　　　　　HAMAM
(☑ 0236-231 2051; www.sultanhamammanisa.com; 2505 Sokak 1; DIY bath ₺30, bath service ₺100-150; ⊙ men 7am-11pm, women 11am-6pm) This 16th-century hamam is part of the original *külliye* of the Sultan Mosque. It has separate baths for men and women; women should call ahead to make an appointment.

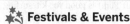 **Festivals & Events**

Mesir Macunu Festivalı　　　　　　CULTURAL
(Mesir Festival; www.manisakulturturizm.gov.tr) Those visiting Manisa in spring may be lucky enough to catch the Mesir Macunu Festivalı, a week-long festival in celebration of *Mesir macunu* (Mesir paste), a sugar-and-spice confection that has passionate fans and equally passionate detractors throughout the country. The festival usually occurs in late March or April.

🍴 Eating

Gülcemal KEBAPS $
(☑ 0236-231 5342; www.gulcemalkebap.com; 1603 Sokak, off Cumhuriyet Meydanı; Manisa kebap ₺14; ⊘ 8am-7pm) This is the best place to sample the town's speciality of Manisa kebap (cylindrical *köfte* served on pide and topped with tomato sauce and yoghurt).

❶ Getting There & Away

The easiest way to get here from İzmir is by bus (₺9, one hour, every 15 minutes). Don't alight at the first (blue) otogar – known as the Eski (Old) Garaj – as to get to the old section of town you must go to the Yeni (New) Garaj and then take a dolmuş. These leave from the western side of the otogar next to the fast-food stands. Dolmuş 1 (₺2.50) will take you to the Vilayet or Valiligi (Town Hall) on Mustafa Kemal Paşa Caddesi. From here, the mosques and museums are only a short walk away.

From the Yeni Garaj, buses to Salihli pass Sardis (₺11, one hour, every half-hour).

Çeşme

☑ 0232 / POP 25,340

Unlike many resort towns in this region, Çeşme has retained a local population and flavour. Only 8km from the Greek island of Chios (Sakız), the town has a long seafront perfect for promenading, a magnificent castle built by the Genoese and a bustling *merkez* (commercial centre) with plenty of shops and cheap eateries. Popular with weekending İzmiris and with those who balk at the high prices and style overload at nearby Alaçatı, it's an excellent base for exploring the region.

◉ Sights & Activities

Çeşme is surrounded by beaches. **Diamond Beach** (Pırlantı Plajı) is good for kitesurfing and windsurfing, and ultrapopular **Altınkum** has sandy coves and is good for swimming. Both are south of the city centre and can be easily accessed by dolmuş.

From late May to September, *gülets* (traditional Turkish wooden yachts) operated by companies including **Simay** (Map p215; ☑ 0532 151 2835; www.simayturizm.com; 1015 Sokak/Hulusi Öztin Çarşısı Caddesi 3) and **Çeşme Lady Bente** (☑ 0536 310 0560; www.cesme ladybente.com; cruise incl buffet lunch ₺40-50) offer boat trips to nearby **Donkey Island**, **Green Bay**, **Blue Bay**, **Paradise Island** and **Aquarium Bay**, where you can swim and snorkel.

The cruises usually cost ₺40-₺50 per passenger, including lunch, and involve plenty of partying on board. Boats depart 10am to 10.30am and return in the late afternoon.

Çeşme Museum FORTRESS
(Çeşme Müzesi, Çeşme Kalesi; Map p215; 1015 Sokak; ₺8; ⊘ 8.30am-5.30pm) Çeşme's majestic Genoese-built fortress dates from 1508 and was later repaired by order of Sultan Beyazıt II, son of Sultan Mehmet the Conqueror, in order to defend the coast from attack by pirates. Impressively restored, it now houses the town's museum. Rooms in the Umur Bey tower and around the bailey (inner enclosure) house archaeological and historical exhibits, and the terraced bailey is filled with historic gravestones and stelae. The battlements offer excellent views of the town and harbour.

Statue of Cezayirli Gazi
Hasan Paşa MONUMENT
(Map p215; 1015 Sokak) Facing the sea, with its back to the fortress, this statue shows the great Ottoman admiral (1713–90), who was sold into slavery but became a grand vizier and was fleet commander during the Battle of Çeşme against the Russians. He is shown accompanied by his pet lion, which he supposedly brought back from Africa.

Ayios Haralambos Church CHURCH
(Ayios Haralambos Kilisesi; Map p215; İnkılap Caddesi) North of Çeşme Fortress, this imposing but decommissioned 19th-century Greek Orthodox church, fully restored in 2012, is used for temporary exhibitions.

🛏 Sleeping

★ Yalçın Otel HOTEL $$
(Map p215; ☑ 0232-712 6981; www.yalcinotel. com; 1002 Sokak 14; s/d/tr ₺85/200/270; ☑ ✳ 🐭) Ebullient Bülent Ulucan runs this great little hotel on the hillside overlooking the marina. Its 18 rooms are clean and reasonably comfortable (some with recently renovated bathrooms), but the major draws here are the extremely friendly atmosphere, two harbour-facing terraces, lounge (free tea), small garden and Saturday night fish BBQ with live music (₺35). Excellent value.

Antik Rıdvan Otel HOTEL $$
(Map p215; ☑ 0232-712 9772; www.antikridvan otel.com; 1015 Sokak 10; economy s/d ₺80/160, s/d ₺200/300; ⊘ Apr-Nov; ☑ ✳ 🐭) A 120-year-old mansion near the marina, this old-fashioned place offers 12 rooms with dowdy decor, basic

Çeşme

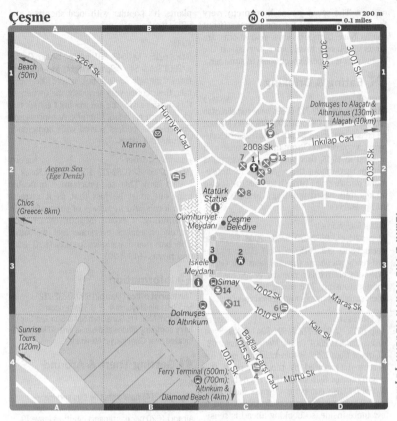

Çeşme

⊙ Sights

1 Ayios Haralambos Church	C2
2 Çeşme Museum	C3
3 Statue of Cezayirli Gazi Hasan Paşa	C3

🛏 Sleeping

4 Antik Rıdvan Otel	C4
5 Dantela Butik Otel	B2
6 Yalçın Otel	C3

🍴 Eating

7 Horasan	C2

8 İmren Lokantası	C2
9 Rumeli	C2
10 Tikos Meyhanesi	C2
11 Tokmak Hasan'ın Yeri	C3

🍷 Drinking & Nightlife

12 Friendly Corner	C2
13 Kaffé	C2

ℹ Transport

Ege Bırlık	(see 14)
14 Erturk	C3

bathroom, fridge and satellite TV. They're spacious, though, and two top-floor rooms (a double and triple) have marina views. Breakfast is served in a tiled open-air courtyard. The basement 'economy' rooms don't have air-con and are dark.

Dantela Butik Otel   B&B $$$
(Map p215; ☎0232-712 0389; www.dantelabutik otel.com; 3054 Sokak 4; r ₺300-400; ✳🛜) Right on the waterfront and close to the entertainment action, this B&B above the Penguen Restaurant is run by the same ultrafriendly

owners. The seven rooms have pretty, very feminine decor – opt for one upstairs (front rooms have harbour views, rear rooms are larger). A lavish breakfast is served on the restaurant terrace. Expect noise in summer.

✗ Eating & Drinking

Rumeli
BAKERY $

(Map p215; ☑0232-712 6759; www.rumelipastanesi.com.tr; İnkılap Caddesi/2001 Sokak 46, Merkez; ice creams per scoop ₺2.50; ☺8am-2am) Occupying a converted Ottoman stone house and opened in 1945, this *pastane* (patisserie) is known throughout the region for its housemade *dondurma* (Turkish ice cream). It also makes milk-based puddings, biscuits, jams and preserves.

Tikos Meyhanesi
TURKISH $

(Map p215; ☑0532 170 9730; 2008 Sokak 8a; mezes ₺8-10, grills ₺15; ☺24hr) This rough-and-ready *meyhane* (tavern) near the Greek Orthodox church is a popular venue for late-night carousing. The menu includes soups, stock-standard mezes and grilled meats.

★Horasan
SEAFOOD $$

(Map p215; ☑0232-712 7469; 3047 Sokak 8, off İnkılap Caddesi/2001 Sokak, Merkez; mezes ₺8-30, mains from ₺25; ☺4pm-midnight, closed Tue off-season) Operated by the owners of the neighbouring fish shop, this friendly *balık pişiricisi* (fish eatery) is Çeşme's foodie hot spot. There are six streetside tables and a few more inside, so booking ahead is sensible. Mezes are fresh and delicious and mains include grilled fish and a peppery seafood tagliatelle. Desserts are excellent, too – ask for a selection. No credit cards.

Tokmak Hasan'ın Yeri
LOKANTA $$

(Map p215; ☑0232-712 0519; 1015 Sokak/Çarşı Caddesi 11; soups ₺8-10, portions ₺9-17, döners ₺6-24; ☺7am-4.30pm; ❋) Winning the prize for the biggest and best döner in town (order an İskender), this long-established and friendly *lokanta* is hugely popular with locals, who flock here at lunchtime. Enter through the passage lined with souvenir shops, and arrive early to snaffle your choice from the huge and uniformly tasty spread displayed in the bain-maries. Also does *paket* (takeaway).

İmren Lokantası
TURKISH $$

(Map p215; ☑0232-712 7620; İnkılap Caddesi/2001 Sokak 6, Merkez; portions ₺15-22, grills ₺18-39; ☺noon-10pm) Çeşme's first restaurant, which opened back in 1953, is set in a bamboo-roofed atrium with a fountain and plants. It's popular with local shoppers and office workers at lunch.

Kaffé
COFFEE

(Map p215; ☑0543 931 5455; İnkılap Caddesi/2001 Sokak 54; ☺9am-midnight) Moving here from Cihangir in İstanbul, where the locals take their coffee very seriously, the owners of this hipster-style cafe are wooing Çeşme's residents with espresso, Chemex, Aeropress and French-press coffees served with homemade biscuits and cakes.

Friendly Corner
PUB, CAFE

(Map p215; ☑0232-712 1751; 3025 Sokak 2; ☺9am-3am) This self-proclaimed amicable hang-out must be just that as it attracts both locals and members of the wafer-thin community of expats. Münür, owner-chef-bartender, makes everyone feel welcome. The bar menu includes pastas (₺20–₺23) and pizzas (₺18–₺20)

ⓘ Information

The **tourist office** (Map p215; ☑0232-712 6653; İskele Meydanı 4; ☺8.30am-noon & 1-5.30pm Mon-Fri, 9am-5pm Sat & Sun Jun-Sep), ferry company offices and banks with ATMs are all located near Cumhuriyet Meydanı.

ⓘ Getting There & Around

AIR

Simay (p214) runs a shuttle-bus service between Çeşme and İzmir's Adnan Menderes Airport (€20 per passenger). Shuttles leave 10 times per day between 5am and midnight.

BUS

You'll need to change in İzmir if travelling between Çeşme and major destinations. Çeşme's otogar is a kilometre south of Cumhuriyet Meydanı, and bus companies have offices there. Most dolmuşes leave from the otogar and stop at various points in town (look for the signs with a large 'D').

Ankara

Metro offers two daily services to Ankara (₺70, nine hours).

İstanbul

There are morning and evening services to İstanbul (10 hours) with Metro (₺80) and Ulusoy (₺80); in summer other companies offer additional services.

İzmir

Çeşme Seyahat runs services every 15 to 40 minutes to both İzmir's main otogar (₺17, 1¾ hours) and the city's smaller Üçkuyular bus station (₺15, 1½ hours).

DOLMUŞ

Alaçatı & Altınyunus

Dolmuşeş to Alaçatı (₺4) depart from the otogar every 10 minutes from 7.30am to 7.30pm, then every 30 minutes from 7.30pm to 9pm, and at 10pm and at 11pm. These also pick up passengers at a stop at the eastern end of İnkılap Caddesi (1015 Sokak) and travel via Altınyunus (₺3).

Altınkum

Dolmuşes to Altınkum (Map p215; ₺4) leave half-hourly from Çeşme's otogar, and pick up on the main street 20m south of the tourist office.

FERRY

Erturk (Map p215; ☑ 0232-712 6768; www.erturk.com.tr; 1015 Sokak/Hulusi Öztin Çarşısı Caddesi 6-7; slow/fast ferry to Chios per person €26/32, car €90; ◷ 9am-8pm), **Ege Bırlık** (Map p215; ☑ 0232-712 3040; www.egebirlik.eu; 1015 Sokak/Hulusi Öztin Çarşısı Caddesi 3; per person/car €26/70) and **Sunrise Tours** (☑ 0232-712 9797; www.chiossunrisetours.com.tr; Atadağ Caddesi 2, Çeşme Liman) all offer services to Chios in Greece; slow ferries (50 minutes) take both passengers and cars; fast catamarans (20 minutes) take passengers only. Same-day return fares hover around €26 on the slow ferry and €32 for the fast ferry and ticket prices include a €2 port tax. Cars cost around €100.

The ferries sail at least twice a day between July and September and three times per week from October to June (usually Wednesday or Friday, and Saturday and Sunday). It's not necessary to purchase your ticket in advance unless you have a car. You'll need a passport.

TAXI

A taxi to Alaçatı costs around ₺50.

Alaçatı

☑ 0232 / POP 9954

A mere two decades ago this rather unassuming erstwhile Greek village some 10km southeast of Çeşme was known predominantly for its excellent olive oil and world-class windsurfing. But thanks to some forward-thinking hoteliers, who transformed many of its dilapidated *taş evleri* (stone houses) into high-end boutique accommodation, Alaçatı has become one of Turkey's hottest destinations for the free-spending middle class. A walk along Kemalpaşa Caddesi in Merkez (the centre) showcases the town's main attractions: world-class boutique hotels, restaurants specialising in Aegean cuisine, sleek cafes and high-end boutiques catering to glamour pusses of

both sexes. In the high season (May to September), it's a crowded, often-chaotic and always-chic place to spend a few days.

⭐ Festivals & Events

Alaçatı Herb Festival FESTIVAL
(Alaçatı Ot Festivalı; www.alacatiotfestivali.com) Turkey's major foodie festival celebrates *ot* (wild greens), an Aegean favourite, in late March or early April. There are seminars, special dinners and a huge number of street stalls on Uğur Mumcur Sokak near the *belediye* (town hall).

🛏 Sleeping

Prices drop sharply in the off season, but some hotels and restaurants only open from mid-May to mid-October and for Christmas and the New Year. Reservations are essential in the high season.

Çiprika Pansiyon PENSION $
(☑ 0232-716 7303; www.ciprika.com; 3045 Sokak 1; r ₺60; ▣🛜) This humble pension is one of a few budget options in the town, offering seven decently sized but frayed stone rooms. The main drawcard is the huge shaded corner garden.

İncirli Ev BOUTIQUE HOTEL $$
(Fig Tree House; ☑ 0232-716 0353; www.incirliev.com; cnr 3076 & 3074 Sokaks; r €160-200; ▣🛜) The quiet but still central location isn't the only draw at this boutique option. The eight rooms in the century-old property are attractive and comfortable, and owners Sabahat and Osman are extremely welcoming. Guests love the lavish breakfast and complimentary afternoon tea served under the old *incir* (fig) in the garden, which gives the hotel its name.

Yucca HOSTEL $$
(☑ 0232-716 7871; www.yuccaalacati.com; 18000 Sokak 35, Liman Mevkii; s/d €90/110; 🛜) Fancy staying in a carefully styled getaway designed around a lush garden near Alaçatı's main surf beach? Well, here you can do so on a budget. This designer hostel offers 12 simple rooms and a garden with hammocks, sun lounges, bar and restaurant. There's a party vibe (especially on weekends) and helpful hosts.

⭐ **Taş Otel** BOUTIQUE HOTEL $$$
(Stone Hotel; ☑ 0232-716 7772; www.tasotel.com; Kemalpaşa Caddesi 132, Merkez; s €150, d €185-220, villas €250-330; ▣@🛜🐾🐾) This is Alaçatı's first – and probably still best – boutique hotel. Owner Zeynep, assisted by manager Salih,

WINDSURFING IN ALAÇATI

Alaçatı was 'discovered' as a windsurfer's paradise in the 1970s by a handful of intrepid German campers. Its strong, consistent northerly winds – blowing at up to 25 knots – make it a big hit with the surfing community. The main windsurfing beach is Alaçatı Surf Paradise (Alaçatı Sörf Cenneti).

Sadly, the windsurfing beach has suffered here in recent years. The construction of a marina cannibalised 1km of the beach, reducing it to 2km and leading to fears for the surfers' safety with boats motoring past. The road there is now lined with large houses, which are part of the ongoing Port Alaçati residential development, but for now windsurfing continues largely unhindered.

The main season windsurfing season runs from mid-May to the beginning of November (outside which many operators close). ASPC and Myga Surf Company are the largest operators. English-speaking instructors are normally available, as are kitesurf boards. Hiring boards for longer periods lowers daily rates.

Active Alaçatı Windsurf Centre (☏ 0232-716 6383; www.active-surf.com; Liman Mevkii) Active charges between ₺120 and ₺180 per day for windsurfer hire depending on the board, and ₺180 for a one-hour beginner's course. A three-level, nine-hour kitesurfing course costs ₺900.

ASPC (Alaçatı Surf Paradise Club; ☏ 0232-716 6611; www.alacati.info; Liman Mevkii) This Turkish-German operation offers well-regarded windsurfing courses and hires high-quality equipment, charging €110 to €170 for a three-day package (board, wetsuit, harness and shoes). Basic, sport and pro boards are available. A starter course consisting of five hours (10 hours for three students or more) across three days costs €230. Sea-kayak and mountain-bike hire is also available.

Myga Surf Company (☏ 0232-716 6468; www.myga.com.tr; Liman Mevkii) This outfit has a range of equipment, charging ₺130 to ₺230 for a one-day package. A five-hour starter course (7½ hours for two students, 10 hours for three or more), which can be spread across a few days, costs ₺590.

has created a tranquil oasis comprising seven simple but charming rooms in the main building, two rear villas sleeping up to six that are perfect for families, a gorgeous library/lounge and a walled garden with large pool. Breakfast and afternoon tea (complimentary) are delicious.

Bey Evi   BOUTIQUE HOTEL $$$
(☏ 0232-716 8085; http://beyevi.com.tr/en; Kemalpaşa Caddesi 126, Merkez; standard/deluxe r €215/250, ste €275; ❄ 🛜 🏊) It's difficult to tag this popular hotel. The decor, size and personal service place it in the boutique category, but the variety of accommodation and the swish pool area with bar and pizzeria are reminiscent of a resort. Rooms are attractive and well equipped – opt for a spacious deluxe room or suite if possible.

🍴 Eating

Alaçatı has a well-deserved reputation as a foodie destination, so you'll eat well here. Most restaurants target the smart set, so those on a tight budget will need to rely on fast food.

Many restaurants close for lunch, when everyone heads to the beach, and many also close during the low season. The Alaçatı Pazarı (Produce Market) is held every Saturday on Şehitlik Caddesi (3000 Sokak).

Gözleme Stands & Cafes   ANATOLIAN $
(Merkez; gözleme ₺10, mantı ₺20) The lanes surrounding the Pazaryeri Mosque in the town centre are dotted with simple cafes and eateries serving *gözleme* (savoury pancakes) and *mantı* (Turkish ravioli). Most have outdoor seating only, so are only open in the high season.

★ **Asma Yaprağı**   AEGEAN $$
(☏ 0538 912 1290; www.asmayapragi.com.tr; 1005 Sokak 50; mezes ₺10-15, mains ₺55; ⏰ breakfast from 9.30am, lunch from 1pm, dinner from 8pm) A meal at the 'Vine Leaf' is an essential experience for gastronomes. Seating is in an atmospheric courtyard between April and November, and inside between December and March. Once seated, you'll wait in turn to visit the kitchen and choose from the sensational and ultra-fresh mezes and mains. Sadly, the wine list is

limited and service is shambolic. Reservations essential.

Roka Bahçe AEGEAN $$
(☑ 0232-716 9659; Kemalpaşa Caddesi 107, Merkez; mezes ₺13-26, mains ₺25-48; ⊙ 4pm-3am) A relative newcomer to the local dining scene, this stylish courtyard restaurant on the main eating and shopping strip offers unusual Aegean dishes including braised goat with chard and thistles, *tire köfte* (small meatballs in a casserole) and calamari stuffed with Aegean greens. Bookings essential.

Su'dan AEGEAN $$$
(☑ 0232-716 0737; www.sudan.com.tr; 1200 Sokak 23, Merkez; brunch ₺40, mezes ₺20-38, mains ₺49-54; ⊙ brunch 9am-3pm late Apr–mid-Oct, dinner Thu-Sun from mid-May) Known throughout the country for its brunch, Leyla Tabrizi's cafe is an ultrapopular destination during the high season. Housed in an elegant stone house with courtyard, it is a stylish spot to enjoy dishes featuring fresh Aegean produce. Leyla also offers dinners for up to 20 guests on high-season weekends, and has a few B&B rooms (double €150, three-/four-person apartment €200/270) above the restaurant.

Agrilia MEDITERRANEAN $$$
(☑ 0232-716 8594; Kemalpaşa Caddesi 86, Merkez; starters ₺14-36, pastas ₺32-34, mains ₺34-68; ⊙ 7pm-midnight Jul-Sep, 7pm-midnight Fri, 1pm-midnight Sat & Sun Oct-Jun) This long-running alternative to traditional Turkish fare recently moved into new and very swish digs within the Alavya hotel compound. Chef-owner Melih Tekşen creates Mod Med dishes but relies heavily on local Aegean produce to produce his seasonally driven flavours. Regulars love the steaks and art-directed cocktails.

Ferdi Baba SEAFOOD $$$
(☑ 0232-568 6034; www.ferdibababalik.com; Liman Caddesi, Yat Limanı; fish price per kg; ⊙ 10am-midnight) This is without doubt the best restaurant down on the Alaçatı marina. It serves all of the standards, and is known for the freshness of its mezes and the quality of its fish. There's another branch on Kemalpaşa Caddesi in Merkez.

Barbun MODERN TURKISH $$$
(☑ 0232-716 8308; www.alacatibarbun.com; 1001 Sokak 5, Merkez; mezes ₺10-32, pastas ₺26-35, mains ₺35-58; ⊙ 7pm-late May-Oct, noon-3pm & 7pm-midnight Nov-Apr) Using locally sourced and foraged produce to create its delicious Aegean dishes, Barbun's young and enthusiastic chefs create a daily menu featuring colourful and flavoursome mezes, handmade pastas and simple but well-executed mains. You'll dine in a stylish space with an open kitchen.

Drinking & Nightlife

Traktör BAR, CAFE
(☑ 0232-716 0679; cnr 11005 & 11011 Sokaks, Merkez) Hip staff, a courtyard garden, good coffee, cold beer and live jazz music – the recipe for a perfect bar-cafe! Traktör is one of the best watering holes in town, and is blessedly free of the attitude overload at many nearby establishments. It's near the Pazaryeri Mosque.

Dutlu Kahve CAFE
(0232-716 0597; 2001 Sokak 85, Merkez) Afternoons spent sipping good Turkish coffee at this cafe's outdoor tables are well spent; at night, mezes and rakı are the popular choices.

Getting There & Around

BICYCLE
ASPC (p218) and **Işıltı** (☑ 0232-716 8514; www.isiltirentacar.com; Atatürk Bulvarı 55a; mountain bike/scooter/car per day from ₺30/60/140) hire mountain bikes.

BUS
To get to İzmir and other major destinations, you'll need to transit through Çeşme.

CAR & MOTORCYCLE
You can hire cars and scooters at Işıltı.

DOLMUŞ
Dolmuşes run between Alacatı and Çeşme's otogar (₺4, 10 minutes, 10km) every 10 minutes between 7.30am and 7.30pm and less frequently from 7.30pm to 11pm. Between mid-May and September, dolmuşes run to/from Alaçatı Surf Paradise (₺3), which is 4km south of town on the western side of the *liman* (harbour).

Sığacık
☑ 0232

Sığacık is a small village clustered around a crumbling 16th-century Genoese castle and an ugly marina. There's little to do here except stroll the waterfront, watch the fishers returning with their famous catch of *kalamar* (squid) and *barbunya* (red mullet), head to nearby beaches or explore the ruins at Teos, 2km north.

🛏 Sleeping & Eating

Teos Lodge
HOTEL $

(☑ 0232-745 7463; 126 Sokak 26; s ₺120 d ₺250-300; 🅿 ❋ 🛜) Upgraded from a pension in recent years, this friendly hotel near the marina has simple rooms equipped with a kettle; some have sea views. Its main drawcard is an in-house restaurant with a lovely terrace overlooking the water.

Beyaz Ev
PENSION $$

(☑ 0532-598 1760; www.sigacikpansiyon.net; 162 Sokak 19; s/d/ste ₺130/170/200; ❋ 🛜) The three-room 'White House' is a popular and friendly pension located slightly inland but with a huge terrace overlooking the seafront. Rooms are spacious and bright, and the suite has a sitting area and kitchenette.

Liman
SEAFOOD $$

(☑ 0232-745 7011; www.sigaciklimanrestaurant. com; off Liman Caddesi; mezes ₺8-35, mains ₺20-40; ☉ 9am-midnight) Right on the marina, Liman (Harbour) is known throughout the region for its fresh fish and mezes. Seating is on the terrace or in the huge dining room, which overlooks the marina through large plate-glass windows.

ℹ Getting There & Away

ÇEŞME

For direct services, you must travel via İzmir. Alternatively, take the bus from Çeşme to İzmir as far as Güzelbahçe (where the university campus is) and change there to bus 730, which travels between İzmir and Seferihisar every half-hour.

İZMİR

Bus 730 travels between Seferihisar and İzmir's Üçkuyular bus station between 6am and 11.25pm (₺6, 70 minutes, half-hourly).

SEFERIHISAR

From Seferihisar, blue-and-yellow dolmuşes run half-hourly to Akkum (₺2.50) and Sığacık (₺2.50).

Akkum & Teos

☑ 0232

This waterfront settlement is popular with domestic tourists, who come here to swim or windsurf at the two sandy beaches and live it up in swish beach resorts. Büyük Akkum is the main beach and has the best facilities. Küçük Akkum is usually quieter.

The archaeological site at Teos is a 3km drive or walk away.

◉ Sights

★ Teos
ARCHAEOLOGICAL SITE

(☑ 0232-745 1413; www.teosarkeoloji.com; ₺5; ☉ 7am-7pm) The evocative ruins of this ancient city, which was one of the 12 cities of the Ionian League, are spread over a low hilly isthmus now used as farmland. A flourishing seaport with two fine harbours in Greek and Roman times, Teos was known for its wines, theatre and Temple of Dionysis; the ruins of the latter two can be explored on site and other features are being unearthed in ongoing excavations being conducted by the University of Ankara.

There are five major sites here, all of which can be reached via recently constructed paths: the rectangular **bouleuterion** (assembly or senate house), **agora temple**, **theatre**, columned **Temple of Dionysis** (the largest temple of Dionysis erected in the ancient world) and **ancient harbour**. Informative interpretative panels in Turkish and English are provided.

There are no eating or drinking options at the site, but Teos Park, a forestry department picnic grove, is located 1km away, on the road to Akkum. A shady restaurant operates here in summer, and there's a year-round shop where you can buy snacks and cold drinks to enjoy beneath the pine trees overlooking the Aegean.

ℹ Getting There & Away

DOLMUŞ

Blue-and-yellow dolmuşes travel between the Büyük Plaj (Main or Big Beach) and Seferihisar (₺2.50, 20 minutes), stopping at Sığacık (₺2.50) en route.

TAXI

A taxi from Sığacık to Akkum will cost about ₺15; a return trip to Teos (including waiting time) will cost around ₺50.

Ephesus, Bodrum & the South Aegean

Why Go?

Civilisation on Turkey's sparkling Aegean coast looks back thousands of years. Indeed, cave paintings discovered in the Beşparmak Mountains above Lake Bafa date to 6000 BC, the earliest evidence of human settlement in Turkey. Among the region's embarrassment of ruins is Ephesus, the celebrated capital of Roman Asia Minor. Nearby, the ancient ports of Priene and Miletus, and the temples at Euromos and Didyma, offer an evocative picture of the ancient past.

In summer the population swells as millions of tourists descend on Marmaris, Kuşadası and, especially, Bodrum, Turkey's most chichi seaside getaway. This whitewashed town beneath a 15th-century castle somehow maintains an air of refinement through the nonstop partying, while new boutique hotels and elegant eateries spring up, both here and in the sophisticated coastal villages of the Bodrum Peninsula. On the remote Bozburun and Datça Peninsulas, more elemental pleasures wait in the rugged terrain and fishing villages.

Best Places to Eat

➜ Orfoz (p266)

➜ Kaplan Dağ Restoran (p239)

➜ Culinarium (p281)

➜ Limon (p271)

➜ Ney (p278)

Best Places to Sleep

➜ Nişanyan Hotel (p242)

➜ Mr Happy's Liman Hotel (p245)

➜ El Vino Hotel (p265)

➜ Sabrinas Haus (p284)

➜ Big Blue Otel (p286)

When to Go
Selçuk

May & Jun Tour ancient sites while it's sunny but not oppressively hot or crowded.

Jul & Aug Party with Turks and foreigners till dawn in Bodrum and Marmaris.

Sep Enjoy the coast's beaches while the sea is still warm and costs are lower.

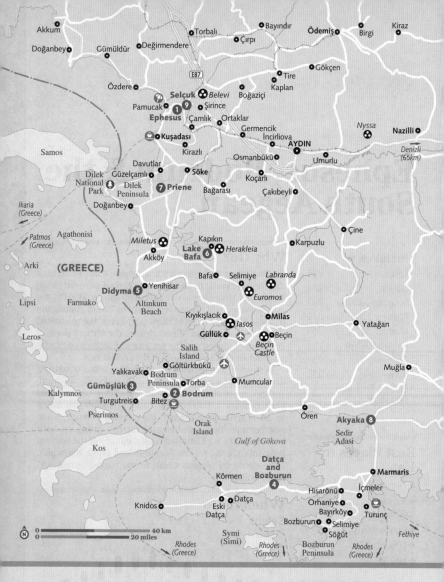

Ephesus, Bodrum & the South Aegean Highlights

1 Ephesus (p226) Walking the marble streets of Europe's best-preserved ancient city.

2 Bodrum (p257) Indulging in this resort town's dining and nightlife.

3 Gümüşlük (p270) Enjoying sea views over fresh fish in Bodrum Peninsula villages like this one.

4 Datça & Bozburun (p279) Feeling miles from anywhere on these rugged peninsulas.

5 Didyma (p252) Gaping in wonder at this ancient settlement's Temple of Apollo.

6 Lake Bafa (p253) Toasting sunset from a hilltop littered with Byzantine ruins.

7 Priene (p249) Surveying rolling fields where the sea once lay from this ancient port.

8 Akyaka (p285) Escaping the Aegean crowds at this river-mouth beach town among pine-clad mountains.

9 Selçuk (p234) Trying seasonal produce at this regional centre's markets.

History

Understanding the south Aegean coast's history requires visualising bays and peninsulas where they no longer exist – otherwise, the stories of the key ancient cities Ephesus, Priene and Miletus, all now several kilometres inland, make no sense. Before the lazy Büyük Menderes River silted up, these were economically and strategically significant port cities, fully integrated into the wider Greco-Roman world back when the Mediterranean Sea was dubbed the 'Roman lake'. Geographical changes, however, saw the coast's centres of power and commerce move to accommodate the subcontinent's evolving contours.

Mycenaeans and Hittites were among the region's earliest recorded peoples (from 1200 BC). More important, however, were the later Ionians, who fled here from Greece; they founded Ephesus, Priene and Miletus. South of Ionia was mountainous Caria – site of the great King Mausolus' tomb, the Mausoleum of Halicarnassus (now Bodrum). Along with Ephesus' Temple of Artemis, it was one of the Seven Wonders of the Ancient World.

Under the Romans, Ephesus prospered, becoming the capital of Asia Minor, while the Temple of Artemis and Didyma's Temple of Apollo were spectacular pagan pilgrimage sites. As Christianity spread, pagans, Jews and Christians coexisted peacefully in the big towns. Most famously, St John reputedly brought Mary, the mother of Jesus, to Ephesus, where tradition attests part of his gospel was written.

During subsequent Byzantine rule, the coastal communities maintained their traditional social, cultural and economic links with the nearby Greek islands. While the precise territorial divisions changed frequently, the general division of the Byzantine military regions (known as themes) here was between Thracesion (in the north and central coastal region) and Kibyrrhaeoton (in the south). The latter included some Aegean islands and was an important base for the Byzantine navy, especially when Arab fleets threatened attack.

In the late 11th and 12th centuries, overland Seljuk expansion coincided with Crusaders on the move to the Holy Land – along with the decline of the Byzantine navy, which allowed Italian fleets to eventually rule the Mediterranean. In 1402 the Knights Hospitaller (who then owned much of the Greek Dodecanese islands) built a grand castle in Halicarnassus with stones from the ancient mausoleum and renamed the town Petronium. After Süleyman the Magnificent's 1522 conquest of Rhodes, Petronium was ceded to the Ottomans (thus the Turkicised name 'Bodrum'). Although the coast would be Turkish-controlled thereafter, it remained significantly populated by Greeks called Rum; their traditional knowledge of sailing, shipping and shipbuilding would prove crucial to the empire's maritime commerce and naval success.

After Turkey's War of Independence, the 1923 Treaty of Lausanne decreed the tumultuous Greek-Turkish population exchanges – terminating three millennia of Greek coastal civilisation with one stroke of the pen. Although Turkey was officially neutral in WWII, the Aegean coast's curving bays provided cover for Greek resistance ships harassing the Germans.

Despite the peaceful holiday atmosphere here today, this frontier's strategic significance remains as vital now as always – Greek and Turkish fighter pilots regularly engage in mock dogfights over the coast. The two countries' long-standing 'Aegean Dispute' over territorial waters, sovereign territory and airspace almost caused a war in January 1996, when Turkish commandos briefly stormed the uninhabited Greek islet of Imia (Kardak in Turkish), causing frantic diplomatic activity in Western capitals. Today, you can gaze at this distant, hazy and very much off-limits speck of rock from the beachfront cafes of laid-back Gümüşlük, on the Bodrum Peninsula, and wonder what all the fuss was about.

EPHESUS & AROUND

Ephesus

The Greco-Roman world comes alive at Ephesus more than anywhere else. After more than a century and a half of excavation, the city's recovered and renovated structures have made Ephesus Europe's most complete classical metropolis – and that's with 80% of the city yet to be unearthed!

As capital of Roman Asia Minor, Ephesus was a vibrant city of over 250,000 inhabitants, the fourth largest in the empire after Rome, Alexandria and Antioch. Adding in traders, sailors and pilgrims to the Temple of Artemis, these numbers were even higher, meaning that in Ephesus one could encounter the full diversity of the

Ephesus

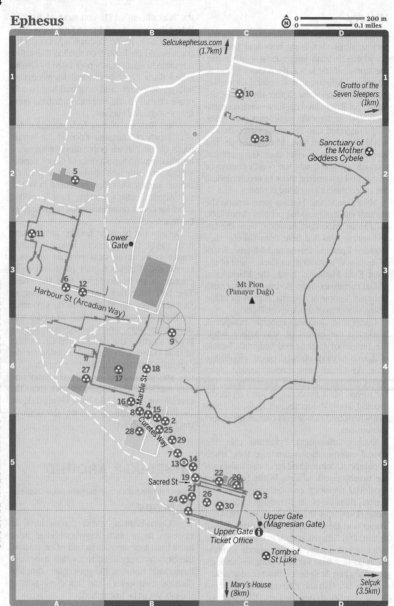

Selcukephesus.com
(1.7km)

Grotto of the
Seven Sleepers
(1km)

Sanctuary of
the Mother
Goddess Cybele

Lower
Gate

Harbour St (Arcadian Way)

Mt Pion
(Panayır Dağı)

Marble St

Curetes Way

Sacred St

Upper Gate
(Magnesian Gate)

Upper Gate
Ticket Office

Tomb of
St Luke

Mary's House
(8km)

Selçuk
(3.5km)

Mediterranean world and its peoples. So important and wealthy was Ephesus that its Temple of Artemis, on the western edge of present-day Selçuk, was the biggest on earth, and one of the Seven Wonders of the Ancient World.

History

Early Legend

According to legend, 10th-century-BC Dorian incursions forced Androclus, Ionian prince of Athens, to seek a safer settlement. First, however, he consulted the famed Delphic oracle,

Ephesus

⊚ Sights

which foresaw 'the fish, the fire and the boar' as markers of the new Ionian city.

After crossing the Aegean, Androclus and his crew rested on the Anatolian shore and cooked a freshly caught fish – so fresh, in fact, that it jumped out of the pan. The toppled coals set the nearby forest ablaze, smoking out a wild boar that Androclus chased down and killed; on that very spot, he resolved to build Ephesus. Other sources say Ephesus was founded by a tribe of Amazons. Parts of both legends are depicted on a frieze on the Temple of Hadrian (p230).

Worship of Artemis

Androclus and his Ionian followers had been preceded on the coast by the Lelegians, one of the aboriginal peoples of the Aegean littoral who worshipped the Anatolian maternal fertility goddess Cybele. The Ionians fused local ritual with their own, making their Artemis, the beautiful twin sister of Apollo, a unique fertility goddess here. Despite the 7th-century-BC flood that damaged the temple, and the Cimmerian invaders who razed the entire city around 650 BC, the Artemis cult continued, and the determined population rebuilt their temple after each setback.

Croesus & the Persians

Ephesus' massive wealth, accumulated from maritime trade and the pilgrims to the Temple of Artemis (or Artemision), aroused the envy of Croesus, King of Lydia, who attacked in around 560 BC. The autocratic king relocated the populace inland, where the new Ephesus was built (near the temple's southern edge). However, Croesus also respected the cult, funding the temple's reconstruction over the next decade to 550 BC.

Everyday life continued as the Ephesians paid tribute to Lydia and, later, to Persian invaders under Cyrus. Ephesus revolted in 498 BC, sparking the Greco-Persian War, which briefly drove out the eastern invaders, and Ephesus joined Athens and Sparta in the Delian League. However, in the later Ionian War, Ephesus picked the losing side and was again ruled by Persia.

In 356 BC, the year Alexander the Great was born, a young notoriety seeker, Herostratus, burned down the Temple of Artemis, to ensure his name would live on forever. The disgusted Ephesian elders executed Herostratus and declared that anyone who mentioned his name would also be killed. A new temple, bigger and better than anything before, was immediately envisioned. In 334 BC an admiring Alexander the Great offered to pay for the construction provided the temple was dedicated to him. But the Ephesians, who were fiercely protective of their goddess, declined, cunningly pointing out that it was unfitting for one divinity to erect a temple in honour of another. When completed, the Artemision was recognised as one of the Seven Wonders of the Ancient World.

Lysimachus & the Romans

Upon Alexander's death, one of his generals named Lysimachus took Ionia. However, by then silt from the River Cayster (Küçük Menderes in Turkish, which translates as 'Little Meander') had already started to block Ephesus' harbour, and Lysimachus moved the population eastward to today's site, strategically set between two hills and protected by walls 10km long and 5.6m thick. When the Ephesians revolted again, Lysimachus' Seleucid rivals invaded, leading to a messy period of conquest and reconquest that only ended when Ephesus was handed to the Romans in 133 BC.

Augustus' decision to make Ephesus capital of Asia Minor in 27 BC proved a windfall for the city; its population grew to around 250,000, drawing immigrants, merchants and imperial patronage. The annual festival of Artemis (now Diana to the Romans) became a month-long spring party drawing thousands from across the empire. Yet Ephesus also attracted Christian settlers, including St John, who supposedly settled here with the Virgin Mary after the death of Jesus and wrote his gospel here. St Paul also lived in Ephesus for three years (probably in the AD 60s) during three visits.

Decline & Fall

Despite Attalus II of Pergamum's rebuilding the harbour and Nero's proconsul's dredging it in AD 54, the harbour continued to silt up. A century later, Emperor Hadrian tried diverting the Cayster, but silt eventually pushed the sea back as far as today's Pamucak. Malarial swamps developed, the port was lost, and Ephesus' increasingly Christian population meant diminished funds for the Artemis/Diana cult. In 263 Germanic Goths sacked Ephesus, burning the temple yet again. Sackings by the Arabs in the 7th century hastened the decline.

Nevertheless, Ephesus' association with two disciples of Christ (not to mention his mother), and its status as one of the Seven Churches of Asia mentioned in the Book of Revelation, inspired pious Byzantine emperors to hold on to what they could. The 4th-century emperor Constantine the Great rebuilt many public buildings, with additional works overseen by Flavius Arcadius (r 395–408). And 6th-century Emperor Justinian I built a basilica dedicated to St John on Ayasuluk Hill in today's Selçuk.

The fortress settlement there later became known as Agios Theologos ('Divine Theologian' in Greek) – hence the later Turkicised name, Ayasuluk. Amusingly, medieval Crusaders versed in the classics were surprised to find a forlorn village here, rather than the epic ancient city they had anticipated.

Modern archaeological research in Ephesus dates to 1863, when British architect John Turtle Wood, sponsored by the British Museum, began to search for the Artemision, parts of which he uncovered six years later. The story continues to unfold more than a century and a half later.

◉ Sights

Ephesus (www.ephesus.us; main site adult/child ₺40/free, Terraced Houses ₺20, parking ₺7.50; ⊙ 8am-7pm Apr-Oct, to 5pm Nov-Mar, last entry 1hr before close) takes at least two hours (add 30 minutes if visiting the Terraced Houses). Visit in the early morning or late afternoon to avoid crowds and the bright midday sun (between 9.30am and 1.30pm is busiest). The softer morning light is best for photographing the ruins, but the site is generally quietest after 3pm, when the tour groups depart. If you can, avoid public holidays altogether. Take a hat, sunglasses, sunscreen and plenty of water, or you will have to pick them up in the overpriced shops and cafes at the entrances.

Ephesus' two gates are 3km apart. The most popular entrance is the Upper Gate (also known as the Magnesian Gate), which allows you to walk down the Curetes Way with the Library of Celsius below you and exit through the Lower Gate. However, the Lower Gate is quieter, as it receives fewer crowds from the cruise ships and tour buses, and is easier to reach by public transport. Either way, if you end up entering and exiting through the same gate, retracing your steps is not a huge hardship and you will get to see the site twice.

◉ Lower Ephesus

Church of St Mary   RUIN
(Double Church; Map p224; car park) The Ephesus Lower Gate car park is ringed with çay bahçeleri (teahouses), restaurants and souvenir shops, and to the west of the road are the ruins of the Church of St Mary, also called the Double Church. The original building was a Hall of the Muses, a place for lectures, teaching and debates. Destroyed by fire, it was rebuilt as a church in the 4th century – the first one named after the Virgin Mary.

Later it served as the site of the Council of Ephesus (AD 431), which condemned the Nestorian heresy which refused to refer to Mary as the 'Mother of God'. Over the centuries several other churches were built here, somewhat obscuring the original layout. The pile of rubble at the exit from the church area is a pile of milestones that once indicated distances to and from Ephesus.

Gymnasium of Vedius   RUIN
(Map p224) On a side road between the Lower Gate car park and the Selçuk road, this ruined 2nd-century-AD structure has exercise fields, baths, lavatory, covered exercise rooms, a swimming pool and a ceremonial hall. Unfortunately, it cannot be visited.

Stadium RUIN

(Map p224) Outside the Lower Gate, the stadium dates from the 2nd century AD. The Byzantines removed most of its finely cut stones to build the fortress and the Church of St John on Ayasuluk Hill. This 'quarrying' of precut building stone from older, often earthquake-ruined structures was a constant feature of Ephesian history. The stadium is not open to the public.

Harbour Street RUIN

(Arcadian Way; Map p224) The 530m-long Harbour St was built by Byzantine Emperor Arcadius (r 395-408) to link the Great Theatre and the Middle Harbour Gate in a late attempt to revive the fading city. At the time, it was Ephesus' most lavish thoroughfare, with the poshest shops of imported goods and illuminated at night by 50 lamps on its colonnades – the only city outside Rome and Antioch to have street lighting.

Look for the high column of the propylon (entry gate) at the end of the street to see how far inland the sea reached in ancient times.

Columns of the Evangelists RUIN

(Map p224) The middle of Harbour St (Arcadian Way) is marked by the shafts of Corinthian columns that once supported statues of the four Evangelists erected in the 6th century AD.

Harbour Baths RUIN

(Map p224) These baths, part of a complex that included a gymnasium and a sports area, were erected at the end of the 1st century AD but badly damaged by an earthquake in 262 and not completed until the 4th century.

Great Theatre RUIN

(Map p224) Originally built under Hellenistic King Lysimachus, the Great Theatre was reconstructed by the Romans between AD 41 and 117 and it is thought St Paul preached here. However, they incorporated original design elements, including the ingenious shape of the *cavea* (seating area), part of which was under cover. Seating rows are pitched slightly steeper as they ascend, meaning that upper-row spectators still enjoyed good views and acoustics – useful, considering that the theatre could hold an estimated 25,000 people.

Indeed, Ephesus' estimated peak population (250,000) is supported by the archaeologists' method of estimation: simply multiply theatre capacity by 10. Although rock concerts stopped taking place here in the 1990s, the theatre is still used for other events and has a seating capacity of 8000.

Marble Street RUIN

(Map p224) This street, paved with marble slabs slightly raised to aid drainage, formed part of the Sacred Way linking the city centre with the Temple of Artemis. Ruts indicate that vehicles used the thoroughfare frequently; manholes provided access to drains. The holes in the walls on either side of the street were caused by Crusaders who ripped out lamps for the metal.

Look for the footprint, the head of a woman and the rectangular shape (cheque? credit card?) etched in one of the pavement slabs. It indicates the way to the brothel.

Lower Agora RUIN

(Commercial Agora; Map p224) This 110-sq-metre market had a massive colonnade. The shops in the colonnades traded in food and textiles; the agora's proximity to the harbour suggest that the goods were imported.

Temple of Serapis RUIN

(Map p224) This massive structure, reached by a flight of marble steps in the southwest corner of the Lower Agora, may have contained a temple to the Greco-Egyptian god of grain. Egypt was one of the granaries of ancient Rome and Alexandria and Ephesus had close commercial links.

Library of Celsus RUIN

(Map p224) This magnificent library dating from the early 2nd century AD, the best-known monument in Ephesus, has been extensively restored. Originally built as part of a complex, the library looks bigger than it actually is: the convex facade base heightens the central elements, while the middle columns and capitals are larger than those at the ends. Facade niches hold replica statues of the Four Virtues. From left to right, they are: Sophia (Wisdom), Arete (Goodness), Ennoia (Thought) and Episteme (Knowledge).

The originals are in Vienna's Ephesus Museum; the Austrian Archaeological Foundation restored the Library of Celsus in the 1970s.

As a Greek and Latin inscription on the front staircase attests, Consul Gaius Julius Aquila built the library in AD 110 to honour his deceased father, Gaius Julius Celsus Polemaeanus, the governor of Asia Minor from 105 to 107, who was buried under the building's western side. Capable of holding 12,000

Ephesus

A DAY IN THE LIFE OF THE ANCIENT CITY

Visiting Ephesus might seem disorienting, but meandering through the city that was once the fourth largest in the Roman Empire is a highlight of any trip to Turkey. The illustration shows Ephesus in its heyday – but since barely 20% of Ephesus has been excavated, there's much more lurking underfoot than is possible to depict here. Keep an eye out for archaeologists digging away – exciting new discoveries continue to be made every year.

A typical Ephesian day might begin with a municipal debate at the **Odeon** ❶. These deliberations could then be pondered further while strolling the **Curetes Way** ❷ to the **Latrines** ❸, perhaps marvelling on the way at imperial greatness in the sculpted form of Emperor Trajan standing atop a globe, by the Trajan fountain. The Ephesian might then have a look at the merchandise on offer down at the Lower Agora, before heading back to the **Terraced Houses** ❹ for a leisurely lunch at home. Afterwards, they might read the classics at the **Library of Celsus** ❺, or engage in other sorts of activities at the **Brothel** ❻. The good citizen might then worship the gods at the **Temple of Hadrian** ❼, before settling in for a dramatic performance at Ephesus' magnificent **Great Theatre** ❻.

FACT FILE

» Ephesus was famous for its female artists, such as Timarata, who painted images of the city's patron goddess, Artemis.

» The Great Theatre could hold up to 25,000 spectators.

» According to ancient Greek legend, Ephesus was founded by Amazons, the mythical female warriors.

» Among Ephesus' 'native sons' was the great pre-Socratic philosopher, Heraclitus.

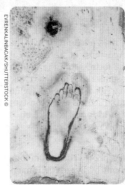

Brothel
As in other places in the ancient world, a visit to the brothel was considered rather normal for men. Visitors would undertake progressive stages of cleansing after entering, and finally arrive in the marble interior, which was decorated with statues of Venus, the goddess of love. A foot imprint on the pavement in Marble St indicates the way.

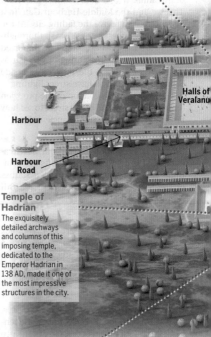

Halls of Veralanu

Harbour

Harbour Road

Temple of Hadrian
The exquisitely detailed archways and columns of this imposing temple, dedicated to the Emperor Hadrian in 138 AD, made it one of the most impressive structures in the city.

Library of Celsus
Generations of great thinkers studied at this architecturally advanced library, built in the 2nd century AD. The third-largest library in the ancient world (after Alexandria and Pergamum), it was designed to protect its 12,000 scrolls from extremes of temperature and moisture.

Great Theatre

Built into what is today known as Mt Pion, the Great Theatre was where Ephesians went to enjoy works of classical drama and comedy. Its three storeys of seating, decorated with ornate sculpture, were often packed with crowds.

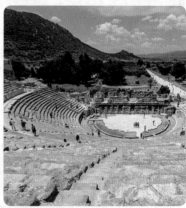

Latrines

A fixture of any ancient Greco-Roman city, the latrines employed a complex drainage system. Some wealthier Ephesians possessed a 'membership', which allowed them to reserve their own seat.

Odeon

The 1400-seat Odeon, with its great acoustics, was used for concerts and municipal meetings. Here, debates and deliberations were carried out by masters of oratory – a skill much prized by ancient Greeks and Romans.

Lower/Commerical Agora

Trajan Fountain

Hercules Gate

Upper/State Agora

Terraced Houses

These homes of wealthy locals provide the most intimate glimpse into the everyday lives of ancient Ephesians. Hewn of marble and adorned with mosaics and frescoes, they were places of luxury and comfort.

Curetes Way

Ephesus' grandest street, the long marble length of the Curetes Way, was once lined with buzzing shops and statues of local luminaries, emperors and deities.

scrolls in its wall niches, the Celsus was the third-largest library in the ancient world after those at Alexandria and Pergamum. The valuable texts were protected from temperature and humidity extremes by a 1m gap between the inner and outer walls.

◉ Curetes Way

Named for the demigods who helped Lena give birth to Artemis and Apollo, the Curetes Way (Map p224) was Ephesus' main thoroughfare, 210m long and lined with statuary, religious and civic buildings, and shops selling incense, silk and other goods, workshops and even restaurants. Walking this street is the best way to understand Ephesian daily life.

Circular depressions and linear grooves are sporadically gouged into the marble to keep pedestrians from slipping on the slick surface. This was important not only during winter rains, but also during the searing summer heat; shopkeepers would regularly douse the slippery marble street with water from the fountains to cool them down.

Flowering trees once shaded the street and shops which also lowered the temperature. Right under where they stood, there are occasional stone abutments adorned with 12 circular depressions – boards for games of chance that ancient Ephesians would play for fun and even bet on: the contest was known in Latin as Ludus Duodecim Scriptorum (Game of 12 Markings), the predecessor of backgammon.

There's a rather patchwork look to the street's marble blocks – many are not in their original places, due to ancient and modern retrofitting. An intriguing element in some blocks are the tiny, carved Greek-language initials; they denoted the name of the specific builder responsible for the relevant section. This helped labourers collect their pay, as it proved they had been put into place.

Several structures along the way have occasional oval depressions in the walls – these held the oil lamps that lent a magical glow to the city's main thoroughfare by night. The larger holes in the marble were for torches.

Gate of Hadrian   RUIN
(Map p224) This monumental arch, which links Curetes Way with Marble St, is thought to have been dedicated to Hadrian when he visited Ephesus.

Brothel   RUIN
(Map p224) This site, demurely called the 'Love House' on signboards, is eagerly anticipated by visitors, but its rather dishevelled state makes envisioning licentious goings-on a challenge. Indeed, some experts believe that visiting sailors and merchants simply used it as a guesthouse and bath, which of course would not necessarily exclude prostitution services on demand. The phallic statue of Priapus in the Ephesus Museum (p234) in Selçuk was found in a well here.

Whatever the brothel's fundamental purpose, its administrators reputedly required visitors to this windowless structure to undergo various degrees of cleansing before entering the inner areas, which were adorned with little statues of Venus and mosaics of the four seasons (Winter and Autumn still visible). Rumours also abound about the possible existence of a secret underground tunnel connecting the brothel to the Library of Celsus opposite

Terraced Houses   RUIN
(Map p224; ₺20) The roofed complex here contains (at present) seven well-preserved Roman homes, which are well worth the extra fee. As you ascend the snaking stairs through the enclosure, detailed signs explain each structure's evolving use during different periods. Even if you aren't a history buff, the colourful mosaics, painted frescoes and marbles provide breathtaking insight into the lost world of Ephesus and its aristocracy.

In dwelling 2, keep an eye out for handwritten wall graffiti including everything from pictures of gladiators and animals to love poems and shopping lists. Dwelling 3 has depictions of the Nine Muses, Sappho and Apollo and, in the spacious inner courtyard, renowned philosophers of the period. Dwelling 6 contains a huge 185-sq-metre marble hall as well as remarkable hot and cold baths, dating from the 3rd century AD.

The whole residential area was originally a graveyard – the Romans built the terraces for their homes over this and other Hellenistic structures.

Temple of Hadrian   RUIN
(Map p224) One of Ephesus' star attractions and second only to the Library of Celsus, this ornate, Corinthian-style temple honours Trajan's successor and originally had a wooden roof when completed in AD 138. Note its main arch; supported by a central keystone, this architectural marvel remains perfectly balanced, with no need for mortar. The temple's designers also covered it with intricate decorative details and patterns: Tyche, goddess of

chance, adorns the first arch, while Medusa wards off evil spirits on the second.

Sailors and traders in particular invoked Tyche, also the patroness of Ephesus, to protect them on their journeys. After the first arch, in the upper-left corner is a relief of a man on a horse chasing a boar – a representation of Ephesus' legendary founder Androclus. On the right-hand arch are a band of Amazons, other possible founders. At shoulder height are Greek 'key' designs that represent the nearby Büyük Menderes River.

Latrines   RUIN
(Map p224) This square structure has toilet 'seats' along the back walls with a roof above. Although some wealthy citizens had private home bathrooms, they also used the public toilets; some even paid a membership fee to claim a specific seat. Turning into the structure's entrance, you'll note a small aperture; here stood the clerk, who collected fees from visitors. While the whole experience was indeed a public one, the flowing Roman toga would have provided a modicum of privacy.

The rest of the room was open to the sky, with a floor covered in mosaics (visible though the wooden boards you walk on). 'Toilet paper' in ancient times was a natural sponge in a stick soaked in a vinegar solution.

Trajan Fountain   RUIN
(Map p224) This honorary fountain from the early 2nd century AD was once dominated by a huge statue of the great soldier-emperor Trajan (r AD 98–117), grasping a pennant and standing on a globe; the inscription reads, 'I have conquered it all, and it's now under my foot.' Today, only the globe and a single foot nearby survive. The fountain's water flowed under the statue, spilling onto and cleaning the Curetes Way. Note the superb mosaics on the opposite side.

Baths of Scholasticia   RUIN
(Map p224) Marble steps behind the Trajan Fountain lead up Bath St to this large hamam. In one niche is a headless statue of Scholasticia, who repaired the baths in the 4th century AD.

Hercules Gate   GATE
(Map p224) Marking the upper boundary of Curetes Way, this two-storey gate with reliefs of Hercules on both main pillars was constructed in the 4th century AD. One of its functions was to stop wagons from entering the pedestrian thoroughfare.

⊙ Upper Ephesus

Hydreion   RUIN
(Map p224) This rectangular fountain with four columns sits next to the Memmius Monument.

Memmius Monument   RUIN
(Map p224) This monument from the 1st century AD is dedicated to Caius Memmius, nephew of the dictator Sulla who sacked Ephesus in 84 BC. Pillars with dancing figures rest on a colossal square base.

Pollio Fountain   RUIN
(Map p224) Backing onto the state agora, this fountain honouring the builder of a nearby aqueduct hints at the lavish nature of ancient Ephesus' fountains, most of which were Roman and filled the city with the relaxing sound of rushing water.

Temple of Domitian   RUIN
(Map p224) This ruined temple recalls Domitian (r AD 81–96), the tyrant as evil as Nero who banished St John to Patmos, where the evangelist wrote the Book of Revelation, and executed his own nephew for showing interest in Christianity. The temple, which the unpopular ruler demanded be raised in his honour, and its statue was promptly demolished when news of his assassination reached Ephesus. The head of the statue is now in the Ephesus Museum (p234) in Selçuk.

Asclepion   RUIN
(Map p224) A side road called Sacred St running along the western edge of the state agora led to the Asclepion, the medical centre of Ephesus. Protected by the god Asclepius and his daughter Hygieia, doctors used the Rod of Asclepius snake symbol to indicate their presence; look nearby for the block of marble with such a symbol as well as a pharmaceutical cup.

The serpent was used as a medical symbol because of the snake's ability to shed its skin and renew itself. At the same time the ancients also knew that snake venom had curative powers. Ephesus was famous for its medical school.

Prytaneum   RUIN
(City Hall; Map p224) Two of six original Doric columns mark the entrance to the ruined Prytaneum, one of the most important civic structures in Ephesus. Within and dedicated to the goddess of the hearth, the Temple of Hestia contained the sacred flame of the city

LOCAL KNOWLEDGE

VISITING EPHESUS & SELÇUK

Tips for getting the most out of your visit.

➡ Enter Ephesus from the Lower Gate. This way you avoid a lot of the crowds from the cruise ships and tour buses that start from the Upper Gate.

➡ In the hot summer months take an umbrella with you, as there is no shade at all.

➡ Toilets are located at the entry gates only – there are no toilets once you are inside the site.

➡ Terraced Houses are a must-see (though they cost extra)!

➡ Mary's House is best seen in the afternoon, when it's quieter and the weather is cooler up there.

➡ Stay in Selçuk at least two nights as there is much to see in the area besides Ephesus, including the lively Saturday Market.

that was never allowed to go out. This is also where religious and civil officials received official guests.

Here and elsewhere in Ephesus, note the differences between the Ionian Greeks' heavily ornamented, spiralling **columns**, and their smooth, unadorned Roman counterparts. Both coexist in tandem across the site, due to ancient recycling and modern relocations. A similar difference is notable in **arches**: the genius of single-material, harmoniously balanced Ionian Greek arches, and the pragmatic use of mortar by the Romans.

Temple of Hestia   RUIN

(Map p224) The Prytaneum hosted this shrine, where the city's eternal flame was tended by vestal virgins, and was fronted by a giant statue of Artemis, now in the Ephesus Museum (p234) in Selçuk. The fertility goddess was portrayed with huge breasts and arms extended in welcome, though her hands (probably crafted from gold) are long gone.

Many of the statues of deities, emperors and other luminaries here originally had precious gemstones for eyes – another indicator of Ephesian wealth.

Odeon   RUIN

(Map p224) Built around AD 150, this once-lavish 1400-seat theatre boasts marble seats with lions' paws and other carved ornamentation. It was used primarily for lectures and musical performances but, given its location next to the state agora, it almost certainly also functioned as a 450-seat **bouleuterion** (council chamber) for matters concerning city government.

Ephesus had one of the ancient world's most advanced aqueduct systems, and there

are signs of this in **terracotta piping** for water along the way to the building. The holes that appear intermittently at the top were used to unblock the pipes.

Upper Agora   RUIN

(State Agora; Map p224) This large square measuring 58m by 170m, and used for legislation and local political talk, was flanked by grand columns and filled with polished marble. More or less in the middle was a small **Temple of Isis** (Map p224) – testament to the cultural and trade connections between Ephesus and Alexandria in Egypt.

The agora's columns would later be reused for a Christian **basilica** on the agora's northeastern edge, which was a typically Byzantine three-nave structure with a wooden roof. From here, there are several archways in the distance, once food-storage houses.

Baths of Varius   RUIN

(Map p224) Baths were situated at the main entrances to ancient cities so that visitors could be disinfected and wash before entering. These 2nd-century ones stand at the entrance to Upper Ephesus beside the Magnesian Gate erected under Emperor Vespasian in the 1st century AD. Greco-Roman baths also served a social function as a meeting and massage destination. This is one of four bath complexes at Ephesus.

☞ Tours

If signing up for a tour, make sure your guide is licensed and well informed, and understand exactly how much time you'll get on-site, compared to how much time will be spent on detours to carpet and other shops.

Random guides lurk at the entrances, asking about ₺200 for two hours (the official rate is now just over ₺300). The garbled and uninformative multilingual audio guides (₺20) available at the gates are not recommended. Many of the ruins in Ephesus have good English-language signage.

Selçuk-based operators such as Enchanting Tours (p237) and No Frills Ephesus Tours (p235) offer recommended tours.

SCENIC FLIGHTS
(☑0530 884 0854; www.selcukephesus.com; 20/60min flight ₺300/500) For a totally different take on Ephesus, see it from above in a two-seater microlight out of Selçuk Ephesus Airport, just 5km north of the archaeological site. Your journey will take you over the main sights of Selçuk and the archaeological site, before looping over the Kuşadası coast for sea views. Book online.

❶ Getting There & Away

Unless they hold a travel agent's license, hotels are not allowed to take guests to Ephesus, so take a taxi or a car or join a tour. Selçuk is roughly a 3.5km walk from both entrances, with the Temple of Artemis and shade provided by mulberry trees en route to the Lower Gate. Cycling is possible but much of the way is along a busy road.

Dolmuşes (minibuses that stop anywhere along their prescribed route) serve the Lower Gate (₺2.5) every half-hour in summer, hourly in winter. Alternatively, dolmuşes between Selçuk and Kuşadası drop off and pick up at the turn-off for the Lower Gate, about a 20-minute walk from the site.

A taxi to/from either gate costs about ₺20.

Around Ephesus

You should not miss the opportunity to visit what purports to be the residence of the Virgin Mary after the death of Christ. And the Grotto of the Seven Sleepers harbours a fascinating story.

Most Ephesus tours also visit nearby sites, though make sure you ask in advance.

Meryemana, the site of Mary's House, is 8km from Ephesus' Upper Gate and 9.5km from the Lower Gate. Dolmuşes don't go there; taxis from Selçuk's bus station are ₺40/70 single/return (including a 30-minute wait). The Grotto of the Seven Sleepers is a couples of kilometres northeast of the Lower Gate and best visited *after* touring Meryemana and Ephesus. Frequent dolmuşes link Selçuk with Çamlık (₺5, 20 minutes), which is 8.5km to the southeast.

◉ Sights

CHRISTIAN
(Meryem Ana Evi; ☑0232-894 1012; Meryemana; ₺20, parking ₺10; ⊙8am-6pm, mass 10.30am Sun, 6pm Sun-Fri Apr-Oct, 5pm daily Nov-Mar) Atop the foundations of a ruined house on the slopes of Bülbül Dağı (Mt Coressos), thought to be where the Virgin Mary lived, a chapel now receives busloads of pilgrims and tourists. There may not be space to see much inside the tiny chapel because of all the visitors lighting candles in front of the altar but note the small fresco on exiting and the larger orange bricks at the base of the exterior wall, which indicates the original foundation.

A 'wishing wall' below the chapel is covered in bits of white cloth, paper, plastic or anything else at hand that the faithful have tied to a frame while making a wish. Taps here dispense potable spring water.

The house foundations, discovered in 1881 by French priest Julien Gouyet, are from the 6th century AD (though certain elements are older). Although legend had long attested that the Apostle John brought the Virgin Mary to Ephesus near the end of her life (AD 37–48), it took until the 19th century for the site to become a place of pilgrimage. Gouyet claimed to have found Mary's house based on the visions of a bedridden German nun, Anne Catherine Emmerich (1774–1824), and four popes have visited since then (most recently, Benedict XVI in 2006). Although the Vatican has not taken an official position on the case, the late John Paul II beatified Emmerich in 2004.

Multilingual information panels line the walkway leading to the house, and brochures and booklets are available. *The Holy Virgin's House: The True Story of Its Discovery* (₺6) by P Eugene Poulin is available from the bookshop opposite the cafe.

Appropriate dress and behaviour is required when visiting this site, which many of the Christian faithful consider sacred.

RUIN
(Yedi Uyuyanlar Mağarası) FREE The road to/from Ephesus' Lower Gate passes this cave tomb on Panayır Dağı (Mt Pion), where seven young legendary Christians, persecuted by Emperor Decius in AD 250, are thought to be buried. Walk 200m south from the car park to see the ruins, following the hill path to the right. The grotto is clearly visible through a wire fence, though much must be left to the imagination.

The story goes that, having refused to recant their Christian beliefs, the seven young

DON'T MISS

EPHESUS MUSEUM

Ephesus Museum (Map p236; www.ephesus.us/ephesus/ephesusmuseum.htm; Uğur Mumcu Sevgi Yolu Caddesi; ₺10; ⊘8am-6.30pm Apr-Oct, to 4.30pm Nov-Mar) This fine museum, which reopened in 2014 with nine reorganised galleries after a massive renovation, contains artefacts from Ephesus' Terraced Houses (p230) and the Temple of Artemis (p235), including scales, jewellery and cosmetic boxes as well as coins, funerary goods and ancient statuary. The famous terracotta effigy of phallic god Priapus is in gallery 2 and most of gallery 4 is given over to Eros in sculpted form. The two multibreasted marble statues of Artemis in gallery 8 are very fine works.

Finds from a gladiators' cemetery are displayed here too, with commentary on their weaponry, training regimes and occupational hazards. Also worth seeing is the frieze from the Temple of Hadrian in gallery 9, which is devoted to the Imperial Cult. This shows four heroic Amazons with their breasts cut off – early Greek writers attributed Ephesus' founding to them.

The Ephesus Museum should be visited after touring Ephesus itself to see where the finds actually come from. Try to visit in the morning when it is less crowded.

men gave their possessions to the poor and went to pray in this hilltop cave. They soon fell asleep, and Decius had the cave sealed. When the men were awoken centuries later by a landowner seeking to use the cave, they felt they had slept but a day, and warily sent someone into pagan Ephesus. The dazed young emissary was just as surprised to find Christian churches there as the Ephesians were to find someone presenting 200-year-old coins. The local bishop, Stephen, met the Seven Sleepers, who later died and were buried in their cave around 450.

The bishop quickly proclaimed the miracle, immediately creating a Byzantine place of pilgrimage that would last for over 1000 years. The legend became famous as far away as France and England, and there's even a Koranic variation attracting Muslim pilgrims.

Excavation, begun in 1927, has unearthed hundreds of 4th- and 5th-century terracotta oil lamps, decorated with Christian and, in some cases, pagan symbols. They indicate that the scores of rock-carved graves in this necropolis were important to many people for many centuries.

Selçuk

☑ 0232 / POP 29,190

Were it not for nearby Ephesus, Selçuk might be just another Turkish farming town, with its lively weekly markets and ploughs rusting away on side streets. That said, the gateway to Ephesus does have plenty of its own attractions – many topped with a picture-perfect stork's nest: Roman/Byzantine aqueduct arches, a lone pillar

remaining from one of the Seven Wonders of the Ancient World, and hilltop Byzantine ruins of the Basilica of St John and Ayasuluk Fortress.

Like all small places catering to short-term visitors, there is plenty of competition in the local tourism trade, which can result in both good deals for visitors and less-than-welcome pressure. Yet all in all, Selçuk remains a likeable, down-to-earth place, mixing a traditional country feel with a tourist buzz and family-run pensions offering a taste of Turkish hospitality and home cooking. It's a relaxing place to cool your heels for a spell.

⊙ Sights

Basilica of St John   CHURCH
(Aziz Yahya Kilisesi; Map p236; St Jean Caddesi; incl Ayasuluk Fortress ₺10; ⊘8am-6.30pm Apr-Oct, to 4.30pm Nov-Mar) Despite a century of restoration, the once-great basilica built by Byzantine Emperor Justinian (r 527–65) remains a skeleton of its former self. Nonetheless, it is an atmospheric site with excellent hilltop views, and the best place in the area for a sunset photo. The information panels and scale model highlight the building's original grandeur, as do the marble steps and monumental gate.

Over time, earthquakes and attackers ruined Justinian's splendid church dedicated to the Apostle John, who reportedly visited Ephesus twice. His first visit (AD 37–48) was with the Virgin Mary; the second (AD 95) was when he is thought to have written his gospel on this very hill. These legends, and the existence of a 4th-century tomb supposedly containing the saint's relics, inspired Justinian to build the basilica here and it drew thousands of pilgrims until the late Byzantine period. The **tomb of St John**, marked by a marble slab in the sanctuary, is surrounded by the cruciform outlines of Justinian's basilica. Note the 12 **pillars** that supported the dome with Christian symbols etched onto them and a full-immersion **baptistery** which dates from the 4th century.

Ayasuluk Fortress
FORTRESS

(Ayasuluk Kalesi; St Jean Caddesi; incl Basilica of St John ₺10; ⊘8am-6.30pm Apr-Oct, to 4.30pm Nov-Mar) Selçuk's crowning achievement is accessed on the same ticket as the Basilica of St John, the citadel's principal structure. Earlier and extensive excavations here, concluded in 1998 after a quarter century, proved that there were castles on Ayasuluk Hill going back beyond the original Ephesian settlement to the Neolithic age. The fortress' partially restored remains, about 350m north of the church, date from Byzantine, Seljuk and Ottoman times and are well worth a visit.

Enter via the so-called **Gate of Persecution** and walk uphill beyond the church to the fortress. Well-signposted ruins through the West Gate include a **hamam**, several **cisterns** and the reconstructed **Castle Mosque**, with a discernible *mihrab* (prayer niche facing toward Mecca). Since 2010, more than 100m of the western **walls** and **towers** have been restored using original materials.

One section of the fortress, the partially restored **Castle Palace** (or Inner Fortress) made headlines when excavated in 2009 as it had last been mentioned by British traveller John Covell in 1670. Built for a ruling Ottoman family, the structure was probably created by the same architects as the nearby İsa Bey Camii.

Recent excavations of the palace have also uncovered the remains of three houses south of the mosque, an area comprised of 15 bedrooms now dubbed the **Southern Terrace Houses**. There is written record that the great Ottoman traveller Evliya Çelebi stayed here in the late 17th century.

Roman & Byzantine Aqueduct
RUIN

(Map p236) Running eastward from the southern base of Ayasuluk Hill, the remains of this long and quite tall Roman and Byzantine aqueduct are festively adorned with the huge nests of migrating storks, who stand guard from March through September.

İsa Bey Camii
MOSQUE

(Map p236; St Jean Caddesi) At the southern base of Ayasuluk Hill, this imposing mosque was built in a post-Seljuk/pre-Ottoman transitional style, when Selçuk was capital of the Aydın Emirate. An inscription in Arabic above the main entrance states that it was built in 1375. It is open to visitors (except at prayer times).

Temple of Artemis
RUIN

(Temple of Artemision, Artemis Tapınağı; Map p236; off Dr Sabri Yayla Bulvarı; ⊘8am-7pm Apr-Oct, 8.30am-6pm Nov-Mar) **FREE** In an empty field to the west of the centre, this lone reconstructed pillar is all that remains of the massive Temple of Artemis (or Artemision), one of the Seven Wonders of the Ancient World. At its zenith, the temple counted 127 columns; today, the only way to get any sense of its grandeur is to visit Didyma's better-preserved Temple of Apollo (which had a 'mere' 122 columns).

The temple was damaged by flooding – the surrounds are still frequently covered with water in spring – and various invaders during its 1000-year lifespan, but it was always rebuilt – a sign of the great love and attachment Ephesians felt for their fertility goddess (Diana to the Romans), whose cult brought tremendous wealth to the city from pilgrims and benefactors who included the greatest kings and emperors of their day.

From the south, there is a good view of the stork's-nest-topped pillar with İsa Bey Camii and Ayasuluk Hill beyond. Careful investigation of the area will reveal the ruins of an ancient **sanctuary** and the remains of the Artemision's **great altar**.

Saturday Market
MARKET

(Map p236; Şahabettin Dede Caddesi; ⊘9am-5pm Sat winter, 8am-7pm summer) Both sightseers and self-caterers will enjoy this lively weekend market east of the bus station. Like the smaller **Wednesday market** (Map p236; 3018 Sokak; ⊘9am-5pm Wed winter, 8am-7pm summer) to the northeast, it offer fruits, veg and cheeses from village farms in the surrounding area.

⮕ Tours

★No Frills Ephesus Tours
TOUR

(Map p236; ☑0232-892 8828, 0545 892 8828; www.nofrillsephesustours.com; St Jean Caddesi 3/A; half-/full-day tour from €40/55; ⊘9am Apr-Oct) Noticing how carpet-selling tactics were irritating time-poor independent travellers, Mehmet Esenkaya and his Australian wife Christine launched these small-group tours led by entertaining, well-informed guides, without any shopping side trips. Half-day tours include the Temple of Artemis and Ephesus;

Selçuk

200 m
0.1 miles

Villa Dreams (350m)

3005 Sk
3018 Sk
3004 Sk
26
3008 Sk
18
Akıncılar Cad
3006 Sk
Roman Aqueduct
İnönü Cad
Şehit er Yuksel Özülkü Cad
3007 Sk
3002 Sk

Bozkır Cad

Abuhayat Cad
Argenta Cad

Hotel Kalehan (300m)

Train Station
2001 Sk
25
2002 Sk
20
21
1010 Sk
9
1015 Sk
1006 Sk
1007 Sk
1016 Sk
1017 Sk
2006 Sk
Tabak Cad
29
1014 Sk
2003 Sk
4
22
Siegburg Cad
Lienz Cad
Tahsin Başaran Cad
Şahabettin Dede Cad
15
S.P. Metin Tavasılıoğlu Cad
Fevzi Paşa Cad
19
23
1003 Sk
Kızılay Cad
5
Atatürk Bul
7
Roman Aqueduct
2020 Sk
1013 Sk
Kublay Cad
14, 16
1038 Sk
24
Ahmet Ferahlı Parkı
1046 Sk
St Jean Cad
1049 Sk
1045 Sk
27
1
Ayasuluk Fortress (150m); Ayasuluk Hill (150m)
17
13
11
1050 Sk
1051 Sk
2
Uğur Mumcu Sevgi Yolu Cad
10
1054 Sk
1056 Sk
1065 Sk
1066 Sk
Dr Sabrı Yayla Bul
Ephesus Upper Gate
Atatürk Bul
8
3
28
1058 Sk
1059 Sk
12
1062 Sk
1063 Sk
Prof Anton Kallinger Cad
2040 Sk
1055 Sk
1080 Sk
1081 Sk
Ephesus Upper Gate (3.5km)
Entrance to Temple of Artemis
6
Atilla's Getaway (3km); Ephesus Lower Gate (3km)

Selçuk

full-day ones add the Ephesus Museum and Mary's House. The Basilica of St John, Terraced Houses and Şirince cost €10 extra each.

Enchanting Tours TOUR
(Map p236; ☑ 0232-892 6654, 0535 245 3548; www.enchantingtoursturkey.com; St John Caddesi 3/B, Hotel Bella) Based at the Hotel Bella in Selçuk, this outfit offers full-day tours of Ephesus as well as Mary's House, the temple of Artemis, Basilica of St John or Şirince. Half-day four-hour private tours of just Ephesus with a licensed guide cost ₺350; it's double that for a full day, including the Terraced Houses.

🛏 Sleeping

Selçuk offers a surfeit of good-value, family-run pensions, with more upscale hotels also available. With all of the attentive service, free extras, bus station pick-ups, airport transfers and eager assistance, though, there can be pressure to buy (carpets, etc). Be vigilant.

Atilla's Getaway RESORT $
(☑ 0232-892 3847; www.atillasgetaway.com; Acarlar Köyü; camping €8, dm/s/d/tr €13/22/36/54; ✳@🛜🏊) This 'travellers' resort', named after its affable Turkish-Australian owner, is all about relaxation, with a classically themed chill-out area gazing out at the hills, a garden filled with fruit trees and a bar with pool table and nightly fires. Twice-weekly barbecues (₺20) and six kinds of breakfast are offered and the volleyball court and table tennis add to the fun.

The roadside complex is 3km south of Selçuk, linked by free shuttles and a dolmuş every 20 minutes (₺2); it's a 50-minute walk through the hills to/from Ephesus' Upper Gate. The seven bungalows with shared facilities are fairly basic, but there are 20 comfortable, modern en-suite rooms on offer and two dorms with nine beds each.

Artemis Guesthouse GUESTHOUSE $
(Map p236; ☑ 0539 450 0187, 0232-892 6191; www.artemisguesthouse.net; 1012 Sokak 2; dm/s/d/tr ₺55/55/80/120; ✳🛜🏊) This spotless budget option, centrally located and just minutes from the bus station, comes highly recommended by readers. The walled garden with its pool and directional arrows telling visitors how far they are from home (BTW it's 14,938km to Sydney) is a delight and staff are well-informed and welcoming. Among the 20 rooms is a mixed dorm with four beds.

Nur Pension PENSION $
(Map p236; ☑ 0232-892 6595; info@nurpension. com; 3004 Sokak 20; dm/s/d/tr €10/20/27/33; ✳🛜) In a quiet residential area way off the beaten track but just over the tracks from the train station, the Turkish-Japanese Nur has seven basic but clean and bright rooms with renovated bathrooms on two floors. There's a dorm each for men and women with three beds and shared bathrooms. The rooftop terrace has a bar and kitchen.

★ Hotel Bella
HOTEL $$

(Map p236; ☑0232-892 3944; www.hotelbella.com; St Jean Caddesi 7; s ₺120-160, d & tw ₺130-175, tr/f ₺200/220; ❉ ❀) This posh hotel on a sloping street opposite the start of the aqueduct has 11 well-designed rooms with Ottoman flourishes in the decor, and a carpet, tile and porcelain shop on the ground floor. Even the economy rooms have a certain grandeur in their carpets and pictures of the harem, while antiques and artefacts decorate the rooftop lounge and restaurant.

Larger rooms are the triple No 6 and the family room No 12. Bella provides transport for guests to Ephesus daily at 9.30am and 1.30pm, having opened a travel agency in order to get the licence to do so. Return is three hours later.

★ Boomerang Guesthouse
GUESTHOUSE $$

(Map p236; ☑0534 055 4761, 0232-892 4879; www.boomerangguesthouse.com; 1047 Sokak 10; dm/s/d/tr/f from €10/30/40/60/70; ❉ @ ❀) People keep coming back to this welcoming Turkish/Australian-Chinese operation to spend chilled-out evenings among the trees in the stone courtyard with its excellent bar-restaurant. Some of the 10 rooms have balconies (ie Nos 11 and 14) and No 4 has its own courtyard; all have fridges. Bathroom-sharing budget options are also available (single/double/triple €20/30/45).

The dorm has 12 beds and shares two bathrooms. Affable host Hüseyin is a font of local information and rents bikes (₺15 a day).

★ Homeros Pension
PENSION $$

(Map p236; ☑0232-892 3995, 0535 310 7859; www.homerospension.com; 1048 Sokak 3; s/d ₺60/120; ❉ @ ❀) This long-time favourite offers 10 rooms in two buildings, with colourful hanging textiles and handcrafted furniture made by owner Derviş, a carpenter, antiques collector and ultrawelcoming host. Enjoy dinner and some of the best views in town on the roof terraces. The four rooms in the older building are more romantic but the six in the newer one offer better views.

Three of the rooms are economy ones with shared bathroom.

Nazar Hotel
HOTEL $$

(Map p236; ☑0232-892 2222; www.nazarhotel.com; Şehit Polis Metin Tavaslıoğlu Caddesi 34; s/d/tr/f from €38/55/60/80; ❉ @ ❀ ❀) In a residential neighbourhood beneath Ayasuluk Fortress, the Turkish/French-run Nazar stands out for its excellent service. Nothing is too much trouble for host İlker and the breakfasts and dinners (€10) on the roof terrace are home-cooked feasts with views of the fortress. The 13 rooms are plain (fauxwood lino) with decent bathrooms; four have balconies (eg No 301). We love the walled garden with swimming pool and caged birds and the computer for guests' use resting on an antique sewing machine.

Akay Hotel
HOTEL $$

(Map p236; ☑0232-892 3172; www.hotelakay.com; 1054 Sokak 7; s/d from €35/50; ❉ ❀ ❀) This smart hotel, hard by the İsa Bey Camii, has 24 well-appointed rooms in an older and a renovated building overlooking an inviting turquoise pool and bar. Dinners, a snip at €7, are served on the relaxing roof terrace. The pricier poolside rooms with small bathrooms are not worth the extra expense.

Wallabies Aquaduct Hotel
HOTEL $$

(Map p236; ☑0232-892 3204, 0535 669 0037; www.wallabiesaquaducthotel.com; Cengiz Topel Caddesi 2; s/d ₺75/120; ❉ ❀) Almost incorporating part of the ancient aqueduct, Wallabies has 24 smart rooms with rustic furnishings and views from the upper floors into the stork's nest atop the ruins or, for example from room 205, across town to the fortress. It lacks atmosphere, but is pleasant enough with a small lift, buffet breakfast and double-glazed windows to keep noise at bay.

Barım Pension
PENSION $$

(Map p236; ☑0232-892 6923; http://barimpension.com; 1045 Sokak 42; s/d ₺50/90; ❉ ❀) This long-running pension stands out for its unusual wrought-iron furnishings, crafted by two friendly metalworking brothers who run Barım with their wives. The pension occupies a characterful 140-year-old stone house, with a leafy back garden for breakfast. The 10 rooms are reasonably modern with good bathrooms; Nos 2 and 5 are good doubles (the latter up its own private staircase).

Owners Adnan and Recep are keen cyclists and can organise bike rental and suggest local routes.

Tuncay Pension
PENSION $$

(Map p236; ☑0232-892 6260, 0536 433 8685; info@tuncaypension.com.tr; Şehit Polis Metin Tavaslıoğlu Caddesi 13; s/d/tr ₺65/90/120; ❉ ❀) Tuncay's 11 wooden-and-whitewashed rooms are relatively spacious, have new beds and folksy furnishings. There's a lovely terrace for chilling with castle views and a courtyard decorated with knick-knacks.

TIRE & KAPLAN
....

The farming town of Tire, 40km northeast of Selçuk, lies on the fields beneath the Bozdağlar Mountains. Its popular Tuesday market provides a slice-of-life view of rural Turkey, sprawling across the town centre and filling streets with the aroma of fresh herbs and grilling *kokoreç* (season lamb or mutton intestines). A smaller market takes place on Friday.

Tire clings on to its traditional felt-making industry, with several *keçeci* (felt makers), still working on blends of teased wool on Lütfü Paşa Caddesi, the cobbled lane running uphill from the small **Leyse Camii** (1543).

To reach here from the main square/roundabout, walk south along Atatürk Caddesi and turn left (east) into Akyol Caddesi opposite Ziraat Bankası. Lütfü Paşa Caddesi is on the right-hand (north) side.

Up a steep and winding 5km road from Tire, the mountain village with the über-cool name of Kaplan (Tiger) attracts visitors as much with its wonderful Kaplan Dağ Restoran as its stunning scenery.

One of our favourite restaurants in provincial Turkey, **Kaplan Dağ Restoran** (Tiger Mountain; ☑ 0232-512 6652, 0507 745 7372; www.kaplandag.com; mezes ₺7, mains ₺16-25; ⏱ 12.30-9.30pm Tue-Sun; ☑) offers superbly prepared local dishes with lashings of olive oil and wild herbs. Seasonal mezes like fish in soya oil and stuffed zucchini flowers are offered, and mains include Tire-style *köfte* (meatballs) and *şiş* kebaps (roast skewered meat). Book ahead on Tuesdays and weekends.

Dolmuşes serve Tire from Selçuk (₺10, 45 minutes) every 40 minutes. A taxi costs about ₺70.

A taxi to Kaplan from Tire and back – the only way to get here – will cost ₺50. Ring driver **Mehmet Yıldırımer** (☑ 0531 883 2655) who is available 24/7.

Casa Callinos
BOUTIQUE HOTEL **$$**

(Map p236; ☑ 0232-892 4030; www.casacallinos.com; 1062 Sokak 2/A; d/tr from €50/60; ❋ 🛜) This new boutique hotel opposite the Temple of Artemis offers excellent value for its standard and location. Cobbled together from three buildings, it counts eight rooms, two of which look to the street and the rest to a tranquil courtyard. Furnishings veer towards the fussy but the use of brick and wood in the guestrooms is a plus. Good-sized bathrooms.

Nilya Hotel
BOUTIQUE HOTEL **$$$**

(Map p236; ☑ 0232-892 9081; www.nilya.com; 1051 Sokak 7; s/d/tr/ste ₺180/200/240/260; ❋ 🛜) Under the same ownership as nearby Hotel Bella, Nilya shows similar artistic flourishes in the hand-carved walnut headboards and ceiling roses, Kütahya tiles, Ottoman miniatures and travertine bathrooms adjoining the 12 rooms. The renovated stone house has a balcony gazing across the flats at the Aegean and a pleasant courtyard. The seven rooms on the 1st floor are nicer.

Villa Dreams
PENSION **$$$**

(☑ 0232-892 3514, 0545 379 5210; http://ephesusvilladreams.com; 3046 Sokak 15; s/d/f ₺50/65/80; ❋ 🛜 🏊) Villa Dreams offers great views, an outdoor swimming pool and communal kitchen. It has 10 modern standard rooms and two big family rooms with shiny wood floors and balconies. The rooftop terrace affords fantastic castle views. VD is a bit of a ways out of town en route to Şirince but there's a free shuttle six times a day.

Each room has a balcony, with eight looking to the Ayasuluk Fortress and three to the garden (where some 15 turtles lounge around their own pool). Ask the staff to point out the three castles visible from the bar of the roof terrace.

Nazhan
BOUTIQUE HOTEL **$$$**

(Map p236; ☑ 0532 214 2509, 0232-892 8731; www.nazhan.net; 1044 Sokak 2; s/d €60/70; ❋ 🛜) Nazhan occupies a century-old Greek house, its courtyard and lounge tastefully decorated with artefacts and antiques, and 12 small rooms juxtaposing whitewashed walls and carpets. There's also a cramped roof terrace with views, and home-cooked dinners and breakfasts featuring local products including olives from Nazhan's own grove.

Hotel Kalehan
HOTEL **$$$**

(☑ 0532 272 6584, 0232-892 6154; www.kalehan.com; Atatürk Caddesi 57; s/d €50/75/100; ❋ 🛜 🏊) On Selçuk's northern outskirts about 600m from the centre, the 'Castle Caravanserai' has flowery gardens leading to rooms mixing all the mod cons with a vintage feel created by scattered antiques and black-and-white photos. The bar-restaurant is a pleasant spot to relax after a day of ruins.

Eating

Selçuk's restaurants offer dependable and reasonably priced Turkish fare, although many pensions and hotels serve tastier home cooking. The outdoor restaurants and tea gardens beside the illuminated Byzantine aqueduct arches make for atmospheric dining in summer.

Boomerang Garden Restaurant CHINESE $
(Map p236; ☑0232-892 4879, 0534 055 4761; 1047 Sokak 10; mains ₺10-28; ☺8am-midnight; ☑) If you really can't last another day without a fix of rice and noodle and sweet-and-sour whatever, head for this delightful courtyard restaurant (and bar) that boasts its own Chinese cook. But don't limit yourself, if you want Turkish – from kebaps to cheese *köfte* – or even vegetarian fare, Candy (Çağıran) can oblige. Always a warm welcome.

Seçkin & Firuze TURKISH $
(Map p236; ☑0232-892 1184; Cengiz Topel Caddesi 20; mezes ₺6-10, mains ₺15-25; ☺8am-11pm) This lovely family-run eatery on Selçuk's 'restaurant row', with rattan tables and chairs outside on the pavement, serves grills and seafood dishes that taste just like *ana* (mum) makes because that's just who's preparing them in the kitchen. Excellent mezes too.

Sişçi Yaşar'ın Yeri KÖFTE $
(Map p236; ☑0232-892 3487; Atatürk Caddesi; mains from ₺10; ☺10am-10pm) Under vines next to a 14th-century mosque, 'Yaşar's Place' is good for a simple lunch of *izgara* (grills): *köfte* and *çöp şiş* (*şiş* kebap served rolled in a thin pita with onions and parsley).

★Wallabies Aquaduct Restaurant TURKISH $$
(Map p236; ☑0232-892 3204, 0535 669 0037; www.wallabiesaquaductrestaurant.com; Cengiz Topel Caddesi 2; mezes ₺10-14, mains ₺15-35; ☺11am-midnight) This hotel-restaurant spills out onto the square beneath the aqueduct, guaranteeing atmospheric summer dining at almost 36 tables. The traditional Anatolian fare is complemented by more international offerings, including vegie dishes and fish. Try the house speciality, *tavuklu krep sarması* (₺20), a seasoned chicken dish, baked under a ridge of mashed potatoes and dolloped with bechamel sauce.

St John's Café MEDITERRANEAN $$
(Map p236; ☑0232-892 4005, 0533 415 3434; http://stjohn-cafe-ephesus.com; Uğur Mumcu Sevgi Yolu Caddesi 4/C; dishes ₺10-25; ☺8am-11pm; ☎) Despite, or perhaps because of, it being Selçuk's most touristy cafe-shop, St John's has the town's widest coffee selection, various toasts, cakes, ice cream and other international snacks. There's a play area for restless youngsters, too.

Ejder Restaurant TURKISH $$
(Map p236; ☑0232-892 3296, 0542 892 3296; Cengiz Topel Caddesi 9/E; mezes ₺6-10, mains ₺10-25; ☺10am-midnight) Next to the aqueduct, this outdoor restaurant on a pedestrianised walkway is good for lunch on a sunny day, with lots of choices including the generous *tavuk şiş* (roast skewered chicken). The kind owners, Mehmet, Rahime and their son Akan, are proud to show off their guestbook, which include photos from the Clinton family's visit in 1999.

🍷 Drinking & Nightlife

While seaside Kuşadası offers an unbridled nightlife, Selçuk's desultory bar/cafe scene exists mainly to get local males out of their homes to watch televised football matches. Drinking with your hosts and fellow guests at your accommodation is generally more worthwhile.

Selçuk's liveliest bars are found on the cobbled pedestrian streets south of the Byzantine aqueduct, with a few mellow spots along Prof Anton Kallinger Caddesi just east of the Temple of Artemis.

Destina BAR
(Map p236; ☑0532 423 8223; Prof Anton Kallinger Caddesi 26; ☺9am-1am) Destina's little front garden overlooking the greenery around the Temple of Artemis is perfect for a late-afternoon çay or sunset beer.

Çadır Lounge CAFE
(Map p236; Uğur Mumcu Sevgi Yolu Caddesi; snacks ₺8-15; ☺8.30am-1am, to 7pm winter) The delightful 'Tent' with the canvas roof is more of a cafe than lounge, with good coffee, juices and sandwiches. It's the perfect place to cool your heels after a morning (or afternoon) in the Ephesus Museum.

Pink Bistro Cafe LIVE MUSIC
(Map p236; ☑0232-892 0205; Siegburg Caddesi 26; ☺10am-2am Sun-Thu, to 3am Fri & Sat) The oldest drinking establishment in Selçuk, Pink calls itself a bistro-cafe, looks like a pub, but

functions as a bar-cum-nightclub. Live music at 8pm on Friday and Saturday.

❶ Information

Tourist Office (Map p236; ☎ 0232-892 6945; www.selcuk.gov.tr; Uğur Mumcu Sevgi Yolu; ⊙ 8.30am-noon & 1-5.30pm daily May-Sep, Mon-Fri Oct-Apr) Just opposite the landmark Ephesus Museum.

DANGERS & ANNOYANCES

Look out for conniving 'coin-men': although savvy travellers won't fall for it, there are apparently still enough naive tourists willing to part with a couple hundred euros or dollars to make it worthwhile for locals to tinker with coin molds, base metals and household chemicals to create pieces of supposedly ancient numismatic treasure. Besides the illegality of purchasing antiquities in Turkey, it's a total waste of your money. The fraudsters are most often found around Ayasuluk Fortress, the Temple of Artemis and the gates of Ephesus.

❶ Getting There & Around

TO/FROM İZMIR ADNAN MENDERES AIRPORT

There are a number of options for getting to or from İzmir Adnan Menderes Airport

Shuttle Atlasjet shuttles their passengers to Selçuk for free. Going back, they depart from outside the hospital. Havas runs its shuttle hourly from the otogar (bus station) as does **No Frills** (p235); both cost ₺25.

Taxi Expect to pay around ₺120.

Train The simplest and cheapest public-transport option to the airport is the one-hour train journey (₺5). There are eight daily departures but as services are not punctual, you should aim to catch a train leaving Selçuk at least two hours before you are due to check in. Passengers are not assigned a seat and you may have to stand. Also note that the train's airport stop is a 15- to 20-minute walk from the departures terminal.

BUS & DOLMUŞ

Buses depart from the **otogar** (Map p236; Atatürk Caddesi).

Bodrum (₺35, three hours) Metro has a daily departure in summer. In winter, you must change in Kuşadası and Aydın.

Denizli (₺35, three hours) For Pamukkale and coastal destinations such as Fethiye and Antalya. Metro has a morning (11.45am) and afternoon (4.30pm) departure year-round, with additional Pamukkale services in summer.

Fethiye (₺50, four hours) Fethiye-based **Tribe Travel Bus** (☎ 0252-614 4627, 0543 779 4732; www.fethiyeselcukbus.com; 1-way ₺50) offers direct bus service from Fethiye to Selçuk at 9am on Tuesday, Thursday and Saturday, arriving

at 1.30pm. The return trip from Selçuk back to Fethiye departs on the same days at 2.30pm, arriving in at 6.30pm. Call to arrange hotel pick-up or meet at **No Frills** (p235).

İstanbul (₺85, 10 hours) Metro has two daily departures at 11am and 8.50pm year-round, with three additional Pamukkale services (10.40am, 2.15pm and 10.30pm) in summer.

İzmir (₺10, one hour) Every 40 minutes from 6.30am to 8.30pm (to 6pm in winter).

Kuşadası (₺6, 25 minutes) Every 30 minutes from 6.30am to midnight (to 7pm in winter). Via Pamucak (₺3.50, 10 minutes).

Pamukkale (₺35, 3¼ hours) Direct Pamukkale bus at 9.30am and 4.30pm in winter, with additional departures in summer. Otherwise, change in Denizli.

TRAIN

There are eight trains a day to İzmir (₺6.50, 1½ hours), via the airport, and to Denizli (₺16.50, three hours).

TAXI

A taxi across town costs about ₺10.

Şirince

☎ 0232 / POP 600

Nine kilometres southeast of the springboard town of Selçuk, and at the end of a long narrow road that wends its way up into the hills passing grapevines and peach and apple orchards, sits Şirince, a perfect collection of stone-and-stucco houses with red-tiled roofs. Şirince's bucolic wooded setting and long winemaking tradition have made it popular with Turkish and foreign tourists alike and it gets very busy at weekends. While this deluge has affected the village's original charms, it remains a beautiful place. It's much more tranquil by night, and a handful of tasteful boutique hotels offer overnight accommodation.

History

Şirince was originally settled when Ephesus was abandoned but what you see today mostly dates from the 19th century. The story goes that a group of freed Greek slaves settled here in the 15th century and called the village Çirkince (Foulness) to deter others from following them. This altered to Kirkinje by the 19th century, and, following the exodus of the Greeks in the population exchange of the 1920s, its name was changed to the more honest Şirince (Pleasantness).

Şirince was repopulated by Turks from northern Greece; they built a mosque, but retained the local alcohol trade, and today you can sample their unique fruit wines (made from raspberry, strawberry, peach, black mulberry and apple) in local restaurants and cafes. Sadly, you'll look high and low for grape-based *şarap* (wine).

◉ Sights

Late morning to mid-afternoon is the busiest time in Şirince but crowds dissipate by evening. There's a long gauntlet of souvenir stands and tourist restaurants, which eventually disperses near the Church of St John the Baptist (p242), allowing you to enjoy the cool, crisp air and lovely old houses from the cobbled lanes higher up.

Church of St Demetrius   CHURCH
This 18th-century church, at the northern end of the village, is up the steps to the right as you enter Şirince along the Selçuk road. It served as a mosque after 1923 but is now abandoned and open to the elements. Have a look at what remains of its frescoed vaulted ceiling and choir loft, iconostasis and marble floor.

Church of St John the Baptist   CHURCH
FREE The more important of Şirince's two churches dating back to 1805 takes pride of place at the southern end of the village. Neglected for decades by modern Turkey and held together (just barely) by an American charitable society, the church and its faded Byzantine wall frescoes are getting a much needed renovation and will remain closed for the time being.

🛏 Sleeping

Kırkınca Pansiyon   BOUTIQUE HOTEL $$
(📋 0232-898 3133, 0232-898 3069; www.kirkinca. com; s ₺140-200, d ₺180-350; ✳) At the northern end of Şirince, Kırkınca constitutes a trio of restored 250-year-old houses with 24 elegantly appointed rooms with flowery names. Some have four-poster beds and fireplaces, and Lale (Tulip) even has a mini-hamam. The main building's shaded roof terrace offers great views.

★ Nişanyan Hotel   BOUTIQUE HOTEL $$$
(📋 0232-898 3208, 0533 304 0933; www.nisanyan. com; d €100-170; 🛜 ✱) This stunner of a boutique hotel in the hills to the south offers a number of choices. The main inn, set in a 19th-century renovated stone house, counts five rooms individually decorated with antiques and frescoes, and there's a library, an excellent restaurant and real hamam. On

the extended grounds above are cottages, stone houses and a 12m-high tower folly.

Güllü Konak   BOUTIQUE HOTEL $$$
(Rosy Mansion; 📋 0232-898 3131; www.gullukonak. com; r €125-245; ✳ 🛜) This refined collection of 12 individually decorated rooms, all named after a different type of *gül* (rose), occupies two sturdy wood and stone mansions surrounded by olive groves and an exquisite flower garden. Our favourite is the Gülistan (Rose Garden), a suite in the lower house measuring a full 35 sq metres with fireplace and great views.

🍴 Eating & Drinking

Most restaurants here are outdoor affairs and most offer all-day *köy kahvaltısı* (village breakfast), which typically costs ₺15 and features numerous honeys, cheeses, hard-boiled eggs, endless cups of *çay* and so on. *Kuru fasülye* (dried bean stew) often but not always *etli* (with meat) is another popular local dish.

Licensed tourist restaurants are found around the mosque.

Pervin Teyze   TURKISH $
(📋 0232-898 3083, 0532 284 2831; gözleme ₺8, mezes & mains ₺10-15; ⊙ 8am-10pm) Signposted above the Church of St John the Baptist, this ramshackle terrace restaurant serves simple dishes made by village ladies, with choices changing according to the season and availability. Enjoy sweeping views while tucking into *gözleme* (stuffed savoury crepe), *dolmas* (rice or meat wrapped in grape leaves or chard), *mantı* (Turkish ravioli) and of course *kahvaltı* (breakfast).

Şirincem Restaurant   ANATOLIAN $$
(📋 0232-898 3180, 0537 831 8297; www.sirincem pansiyon.com; mezes ₺5-10, mains ₺10-35; ⊙ 8am-midnight; 🍴) This rustic restaurant under shady foliage up the steps from the main road into town and owned by a friendly fruit-farming family offers a good range of mezes, meat dishes and Anatolian wines as well as *kahvaltı*. There's a good choice of vegetarian dishes as well.

Yorgo Şarapevi   WINE BAR
(📋 0555 824 2684; www.sirinceyorgo.com; ⊙ 9am-11pm, to 7pm winter) It's not much more than a shack but 'George' has one of the best collections of wine on offer for tasting, with everything from fruit wines ranging in strength from 8% to 13% (₺25 to ₺30 a bottle) and real red and white grape *şarap* or from ₺40 a bottle.

ⓘ Getting There & Away

Dolmuşes (₺3) leave Selçuk for Şirince every 20 minutes (15 minutes at the weekend) in summer, half-hourly in winter. Parking at the village entrance costs ₺10.

Kuşadası

☑ 0256 / POP 77,860

Kuşadası is a popular package-tour destination and, as the coastal gateway to Ephesus, Turkey's busiest cruise port. Lacking the sights and ambience of Bodrum and the mix of Marmaris, Kuşadası remains a runner-up on the Aegean party scene, but the Irish pubs, discos and multilingual touts certainly create a memorably ribald atmosphere. If you prefer to mix your Ephesus visit with nightlife and sea views rather than the rural ambience of Selçuk then Kuşadası could be the right choice, offering some good hotels and restaurants, a surprisingly nontraditional bazaar and two quieter old quarters.

◉ Sights & Activities

Local travel agencies such as Barel Travel (p249) and Meander Travel (p249) offer trips to Ephesus (half-/full day €35/60), Priene, Miletus and Didyma (€45) and more distant destinations like Pamukkale (€50), all including lunch.

Kaleiçi Camii   MOSQUE
(Map p244; off Barbaros Bulavarı) The 'Old Town Mosque', built by Grand Vizier Öküz Mehmed Paşa in the 17th century, is the most impressive mosque in Kuşadası and can accommodate 550 worshippers.

Kuşadası Castle   FORTRESS
(Map p244; Güvercin Adası) Kuşadası's small, picturesque Byzantine fortress, standing on the causeway-connected **Güvercin Adası** (Pigeon Island), is attractively spotlit at night. A path leads around the island's eastern side with views of Kuşadası – popular with strolling couples, fishers and cats. The castle is getting a total makeover and a museum is set to open inside.

Kadınlar Denizi   BEACH
(Ladies Beach) Kuşadası's most famous beach is Kadınlar Denizi (literally 'Ladies Sea'), south of town and served by dolmuşes running along the coastal road. Kadınlar Denizi is small and crowded with big hotels, but beachgoers love it for its hustle and bustle. The coast further south of Kadınlar Denizi has several small beaches, each backed by big hotels.

Kuşadası Town Beach   BEACH
Kuşadası town's small artificial beach is eclipsed by Kadınlar Denizi, or 'Ladies Sea', some 2.5km south and served by regular dolmuşes down Güvercinada Caddesi. It's nice, but gets very crowded in summer with package tourists from the big nearby hotels.

Ottoman Turkish Bath   HAMAM
(Osmanlı Türk Hamamı; ☑ 0256-622 1050, 0535 864 3700; www.kusadasiottomanturkishbath.com; 3 Sokak 5, Hüseyin Can Bulvarı; admission incl body wash & bubble massage €25; ◔ 8am-11pm) Kuşadası has four hamams, but this one near Kadınlar Denizi is said to be the best on the Aegean coast. It offers male, female and mixed sections, plus female attendants and free transport to/from the centre.

◉ Boat Trips

Boats moored at the causeway leading to Kuşadası Castle or at the marina offer one-hour sunset cruises for about ₺10 and, between April and October, day trips around scenic local areas (₺40 including lunch and soft drinks). Operators, including **Ali Kaptan 2** (Map p244; ☑ 0535 438 0801, 0535 515 6821; www.kusadasitekneturu.com), **Matador** (Map p244; ☑ 0532 461 3889; https://www.facebook.com/matadorboattrip) and **Aydın Kaptan 53** (Map p244; ☑ 0532 206 4545, 0534 317 2623; https://www.facebook.com/aydinkaptan53boattrip/), depart daily at 9.30am and return at 4.30pm.

Stops usually include such places as Soğuksu Bay, Klaros Island and Baradan Beach. Call in advance for a pick-up from your accommodation.

🛏 Sleeping

Kuşadası centre has pensions and business hotels, while package-tour resorts and luxury hotels are generally on the outlying coasts.

Anzac Golden Bed Pension   PENSION $
(Map p244; ☑ 0256-614 8708; www.anzacgoldenbed.com; Uğurlu Sokak 1, Cıkmazı 4; r from ₺90, tr & f ₺130; ❋ @ 🗢) Perched in the hilltop old quarter, this pension owned by affable Australian Sandra Galloway has nine rooms decorated with antique furnishings and a superb rooftop garden terrace, where the view can be enjoyed over breakfast, afternoon tea or a barbecue. Four rooms have balconies and all have renovated bathrooms. It's been a favourite on the circuit since 1990.

EPHESUS, BODRUM & THE SOUTH AEGEAN KUŞADASI

Kuşadası

Samos, Patmos & Ikaria

Kadınlar Denizi (2km);
Ottoman Turkish
Bath (2km)

Kuşadası Town
Beach (100m);
Setur Marina (400m);
Adaland (8km);
Aqua Fantasy (10km)

Atatürk Bul

İstiklal Cad

Gençlik Cad.

Ülgen Sk

Toplanı Sk

Sevgi Sk

Dolmuşes for Selçuk
via Pamucak

Candan Tarhan Bul

Adnan Menderes Bul

Demiroğlu Sk

Dolmuşes for
Söke & Dilek
National Park

Süleyman Demirel Bul

Bus
Company
Offices

Tavası Sk

Bahçesaray Sk

50 Yıl Cad

İsmet İnönü Bul

İsmet İnönü Bul

Kemal Arıkan cad

Öge Sk

Sağlık Cad

Emek Sk

Atatürk Bul

Kışla Sk

Sevgi Sk

Cephane Sk

Bahar Sk

KALEİÇİ

Kahramanlar Cad

Bar St (Barlar Sk)

Zafer Sk

Hacı
İbrahim
Camii

Yıldırım Cad

Barbaros
Hayrettin Bul

Deniz Monumental
Arch

Deniz Monumental
Sk

Arslanlar Cad

Anıt Sk

Kıbrıs Cad

Bezirgan Sk

Aydınlık Sk

Sultu İmam Sk

Kuşadası
Cruise
Terminal

Scala
Nuova

Ferry to
Samos

Güvercinada Cad

Atatürk
Monument

Bazaar

N

0   400 m
0   0.2 miles

Kuşadası

The reception area has the feel of a private living/dining room. Rooms 304 and 305 have lovely views of the sea but our favourite is room 202.

Sezgin Hotel Guest House GUESTHOUSE **$**
(Map p244; ☎0256-614 4225; www.sezginhotel.com; Arslanlar Caddesi 68; dm/s/d/tr €15/25/35/50; ❋@🌐❄) Uphill from the action on Bar St, Sezgin has 20 bright and spacious rooms with modern bathroom, faux wood lino, satellite TV, fridge and hairdryer. The reception and corridors are less appealing, but the rear courtyard has a chill-out area and pool overlooked by orange trees. There are two dorm rooms with five and six beds.

The friendly and very well-travelled owner Sezgin dispenses information and offers free pick-ups from the otogar. Airport transfers are €60 for two people.

Ephesian Hotel Guesthouse GUESTHOUSE **$**
(Map p244; ☎0553 428 4335, 0256-614 6084; http://ephesianhotel.com; Aslanlar Caddesi 9; s/d/tr/f €18/30/36/44; ❋@🌐) There's a lot to like about this family-run budget pension in an old Greek house within spitting distance of Bar St. The 16 rooms are smallish but tastefully decorated and all have balconies (some with sea views), there's a stunning roof terrace with chill-out board games available and the helpful and very well-travelled owner Ceyhan will happily dispense travel information.

★**Mr Happy's Liman Hotel** HOTEL **$$**
(Map p244; ☎0256-614 7770, 0532 775 8186; www.limanhotel.com; cnr Kıbrıs & Güvercinada Caddesis; s/d/tr €35/55/65; ❋@🌐) Run by seasoned traveller Hasan 'Mr Happy' Değirmenci, the 'Harbour' Hotel is in full view of just that and is a welcoming haven for travellers. The 14 rooms (accessed by lift!) are more than comfortable, with balconies (half facing the sea) and renovated bathrooms. The real pleasure of staying here is the general vibe of holiday camaraderie.

There's a lobby lounge and a help desk offering assistance with everything from hamam visits to bus tickets and local excursions. Breakfast is served on the roof terrace, as the cruise liners glint in the docks below. The terrace is also the venue for drinks and nightly barbecues from mid-April to October, often accompanied by Hasan's brother Ömer singing Turkish pop songs. Just sit back, enjoy and pretend all the high-rises on the hills above you are on the other side of the sea. A couple of interior budget rooms rent at €35 per night.

Villa Konak BOUTIQUE HOTEL **$$**
(Map p244; ☎0256-614 6318; www.villakonakhotel.com; Yıldırım Caddesi 55; r €55-70, f €120; ❋🌐❄) Far above the coast in the quieter old quarter, Villa Konak occupies a restored 160-year-old stone house, with pictures of old Kuşadası and Ottoman knick-knacks scattered around the 17 rooms. The comfy deckchairs in the poolside garden and bookcases of paperbacks create the feel of a relaxing haven, completed by the homemade cookies served at complimentary afternoon tea.

Vila Konak is cobbled together from seven houses of varying ages so some bathrooms and other features are newer than others. Children under six are not allowed.

EPHESUS, BODRUM & THE SOUTH AEGEAN KUŞADASI

GETTING WET IN KUŞADASI

Aqua Fantasy (☑0232-850 8500; www.aquafantasy.com; Ephesus Beach, Sultaniye Köyü; adult/child/under 3 €24/17/free, online €21/15; ☺10am-6.30pm May-Oct) claims to be Turkey's top water park, while Adaland (☑0256-618 1252; www.adaland.com; Çamlimanı Mevkii; adult/child/under 3 €24/17/free; ☺10am-6pm May-Sep) says it's Europe's best. Both are about 10km north of Kuşadası near Pamucak, and have myriad pools, slides and so on. Kids under three enter for free at both. Aqua Fantasy offers a discount if booking online and has an adjoining hotel with restaurants, a hamam and spa.

Aquaventure Diving Center (Map p244; ☑0256-612 7845, 0542 434 7642; www.aqua venture.com.tr; Sağlık Caddesi, Miracle Beach Club; ☺8am-6pm) offers show/reef dives (from €25/30) and Professional Association of Diving Instructors (PADI) Open Water courses (€250), although other places like Kaş are better dive spots. It has an office in town but the diving is located by Kadınlar Denizi (p243). Free transfers from most hotels provided.

Hotel Stella
HOTEL $$

(Map p244; ☑0533 425 5666, 0256-614 1632; www.hotelstellakusadasi.com; Bezirgan Sokak 44; dm €10, s €35-40, d €50-60; ❄☏❆) Accessed from the seafront via a lift up the cliff, Stella spills down the hillside with good views of the castle and bay from its western end. Its 20 rooms are a little samey and the corridors gloomy, but pluses include superb balconies, a comfortable breakfast room, fridges in the rooms, and help with booking transport and tours from the English-speaking owner.

The dormitory on the top floor, with a shower and toilet on the corridor, costs €10 per person without breakfast.

Efe Boutique Hotel
HOTEL $$$

(Map p244; ☑0256-614 3660; www.efeboutique hotel.com; Güvercinada Caddesi 37; s/d/tr ₺200/300/450; ❄☏) Sleek lights and mirrors abound in this hotel's 40 airy rooms and suites, which are coloured black, white, chocolate and turquoise and contain transparent chairs, round beds and mirror-mounted plasma-screen TVs. All rooms have sea-facing balconies, but because of the hotel's pyramid shape, the upper rooms get more view and less space.

Choose enormous deluxe room 101 or room 301 for a bathroom with views.

Ilayda Avant Garde
HOTEL $$$

(Map p244; ☑0256-614 7608; www.ilaydaavant garde.com; Atatürk Bulvarı 42; r/ste from €65/140; ❄☏❆) Jet-setting beach bums will feel at home in this minimalist-on-holiday aesthetic with art deco touches. The 85 cool, neat rooms are slightly small but restful with parquet floors and multicoloured furnishings behind double glazing. Amenities include a lobby bar on the 2nd floor and rooftop pool and bar-restaurant.

✖ Eating

Waterfront dining is atmospheric but can be expensive. Fish is sold by weight so verify seafood prices before ordering. Watch out out for waiters sneaking extra lira onto the bill, used on cruise-liner passengers who don't notice. If ambience isn't important, head inland for cheaper kebap shops. Kaleiçi, Kuşadası's old quarter, offers backstreet eateries with character and some fun, more Turkish, cafes. A popular street food is *midye dolması* (mussels stuffed with rice).

Holiday Inn
KEBAP $

(Map p244; ☑0256-612 8940; 40 Kahramanlar Caddesi 61; pide ₺12, kebabs ₺18; ☺8am-midnight) Locals rate the pide (Turkish-style pizza), *lahmacun* (Arabic-style pizza, ₺5) and kebaps highly at this eatery, where the house special, *vali kebabı* (₺35), is an overstuffed kebap of chicken, lamb, beef and tomato. Sit on the pedestrianised street at the bottom of Bar St and, if you're not full, finish with some dessert from the adjoining *baklavacı* (baklava shop).

Avlu
LOKANTA $

(Map p244; ☑0256-614 7995; Cephane Sokak 15; mezes from ₺5, mains from ₺7-14; ☺10am-11pm) The great and the good regularly make their way to the glass-fronted 'Courtyard' eatery to feast on the traditional Turkish dishes on display in its open kitchen – though we found the staff less than welcoming. Choose a kebap from the menu or point and pick daily specials and mezes. Outside seating area.

Fish Market
SEAFOOD $

(Balık Halı; Map p244; Atatürk Bulvarı; fish sandwiches ₺6-10; ☺9am-midnight) Eateries around the fountain in the modern square at the fish market do *balık ekmeği* (fish bread), consisting of fish or calamari in sliced bread with salad. You can also buy fish here and ask nearby restaurants to cook it; restaurants should charge about ₺10 per kilo for the service, but ask beforehand or you could end up paying more.

Yuvam   LOKANTA $

(Map p244; ☑0256-614 9460, 0256-614 2928; 7 Eylül Sokak 4; mains ₺10-20; ⊙10am-6pm) This friendly, daytime only *lokanta* (eatery serving ready-made food) in the heart of the Old Town serves up some deliciously prepared home-cooked dishes in full view by the kitchen. The house speciality is *bulamaç çorbası*, a soup made with flour and semolina.

Hasan Kolcuoğlu Kebap   KEBAB $$

(Map p244; ☑0256-614 9979; Güvercinada Caddesi 37, Efe Boutique Hotel; kebaps ₺18-36; ⊙7am-11pm) This wonderful upscale kebap house below the Efe Boutique Hotel has great seating on a sprawling terrace with front-row views of the castle. Breakfast (₺22.50) is good value here but one of the best deals in Kuşadası is the ₺50 fixed menu offering five different mezes, a kebap, dessert and a soft drink.

Black & White   SEAFOOD $$

(Map p244; ☑0256-614 1881; Belediye Çarsısı 35; mezes ₺8, mains from ₺25; ⊙9am-midnight) If trying to decide which of the dozen or so restaurants in and around the *balık halı* (fish market) is deserving of your custom, try this one. The fish is cooked to perfection, the prices are right and the staff couldn't be more helpful and friendly.

Ferah   SEAFOOD $$

(Map p244; ☑0256-614 1281, 0536 321 2547; İskele Yanı Güvercin Parkı İçi; mezes ₺8, seafood portions ₺20-35; ⊙8.30am-2am) Next to the little park and city tea garden, this is one of Kuşadası's more popular waterfront fish eateries, with great sunset sea views and good-quality seafood and mezes.

★Kazım Usta   SEAFOOD $$$

(Map p244; ☑0256-614 1226; Liman Caddesi 4; mezes ₺10-30, mains ₺28-50; ⊙7am-1am) Still going strong after well over 60 years, Kazım Usta is Kuşadası's top (and priciest) fish restaurant, serving dishes ranging from swordfish kebap to farmed bream and meat options. Order fish by the kilo (1kg is ₺80 to ₺120) and book well ahead to bag a waterfront table in summer. Warm welcome.

Saray   INTERNATIONAL $$$

(Map p244; ☑0544 921 6224, 0256-612 7088; www.sarayrestaurant.com; Bozkurt Sokak 25; mains

₺17-45; ⊙11am-3am; ☑) The enormous 'Palace' in the Kaleiçi tries to be everything to everyone, serving mixed international fare – from Chinese to Mexican – and decent Turkish fare as well as a few vegetarian options. There's live music most nights, a kitschy 'Turkish Night' on Wednesday and a cabaret on Friday. Cruise folk seem to like it.

They'll also come to fetch you and bring you back home (before 2am).

🍷 Drinking & Entertainment

Head up Atatürk Bulvarı for seafront tea gardens and cafes. Bar St (p247) and Kaleiçi are where to head after dark.

On the atmospheric warren of streets in Kuşadası's Old Town, look out for Türkü bars, where locals knock back *rakı* (aniseed spirit) and dance to Turkish folk music. Also known as *meyhane* (taverns), the characterful, stone-walled bars are found on streets including Cephane, Bahar, Tuna and Kışla Sokaks.

Bar St   PUBS

(Map p244; Barlar Sokak) On this cacophonous strip, tattoo and piercing parlours line up alongside shamrocks, sex shops and gaudy bars, soundtracked by karaoke, televised football and loquacious touts. At the northern end, the long-standing **Jimmy's Irish Bar** and, opposite, **Kitty O'Shea** fulfil just a third of the leprechaun quota; halfway down, **Kuşadası Club & Bar** is a popular hang-out for young locals.

Orient Bar   LIVE MUSIC

(Map p244; ☑0256-612 8838; www.orientbar.com; Kışla Sokak 14; ⊙11am-4am) On a narrow street in the Kaleiçi, this perennial favourite in an atmospheric old stone house is the perfect escape from Bar St, where you can listen to the nightly acoustic guitarist or settle in for a cosy chat beneath the vine trellis.

Adı Meyhane   LIVE MUSIC

(Map p244; ☑0256-614 3496; Bahar Sokak 18; ⊙noon-3am) This characterful and slightly eccentric place in Kaleiçi, marked by low beams, stone walls and hung instruments, is popular with Turks and foreign tourists. They do good live Turkish music here.

ℹ Information

Özel Kuşadası Hastanesi (☑0256-613 1616; www.kusadasihastanesi.com; Ant Sokak) is an excellent, English-speaking private hospital 3km north of the centre (Selçuk road).

DILEK PENINSULA

The 277-sq-km mountainous reserve on the Dilek Peninsula-Büyük Menderes National Park (Dilek Yarımadası-Büyük Menderes Deltası Milli Parkı; www.dilekyarimadasi.com; per person/car ₺4.50/14; ⊙ 7am-7pm Jun-Sep, 8am-5pm Oct-May, last entry 1hr before close) has walking trails, stunning vistas, azure coves for swimming, and deep-green forests inhabited by wild boar and fallow deer and more than 250 species of bird, including cormorants, ospreys and flamingos.

Beyond the entrance, four semicircular bays with sand or pebble beaches lie below the road, which has great views from designated pullover points. The road tapers off at a high-security military compound covering the peninsula's end, from which soldiers can train their binoculars on the tourists frolicking on Samos.

The first cove, İçmeler Köyü (1km from the entrance), has a sandy beach, but it is the busiest and somewhat dirty with views of Kuşadası's urban sprawl. About 4km further on, Aydınlık Köyü is a quieter, 800m-long pebble strand backed by pines, and is busy enough to warrant a lifeguard station, though it is not always staffed.

About 1km further along, after the *jandarma* (provincial police) station turn-off, the signposted kanyon (canyon) appears on the left. Boards here give information and maps of the park. A 15km walk down a forest path, Doğanbey village has beautiful seaside stone houses, restored by affluent newcomers, as well as the park visitors centre. A few kilometres west of Doğanbey, the fishing village and ancient Hellenistic port of Karine has a waterfront fish restaurant. The path's first 6km are open to all, but after that you need a permit or to be led by a licensed guide. There is also a 25km cycle track to Doğanbey from Güzelçamlı, just east of the park entrance.

Dilek's third bay, Kavaklı Burun Köyü (1km past the canyon entrance), has a half-moon-shaped pebble beach. The final beach open to the public, pebbly Karasu Köyü (11km from the entrance), is the most placid, and enjoys delightful views of mountainous Samos rising from the sea. If you're lucky, you might see a dolphin or even a rare Mediterranean monk seal.

All four beaches have free wood-slatted chairs, which are quickly taken, and umbrellas and fold-out chairs to rent.

About 200m southeast of the park entrance a brown sign points to Zeus Mağarası (Zeus Cave), a show cave with azure-blue water that is refreshingly cold in summer and warm in winter.

In summer, dolmuşes (minibuses that stop anywhere along their prescribed route) run every 20 minutes from Kuşadası to the national park (₺7, 45 minutes), but only as far as the third bay (Kavaklı Burun Köyü). Off season, if your dolmuş is empty, the driver may just stop at the park gate. The park entrance fee is paid on the bus. Regular dolmuşes also run from Söke to Doğanbey (via Priene) in summer. With your own wheels, you can drive to Doğanbey, 30km southwest of Söke; look for the turn-off on the road from Priene to Miletus.

From June to October a ferry (₺6) links Kuşadası with Güzelçamlı, just east of the park entrance, three times a day at 8.30am, 1pm and midnight, returning at 7am, 11am and 6pm.

The **Tourist Office** (Map p244; ☎ 0256-614 1103; Liman Caddesi; ⊙ 8am-noon & 1.30-5.30pm Mon-Fri) Near the cruise-ship dock, staff speak a little English and give out maps and brochures.

❶ Getting There & Around

TO/FROM İZMIR ADNAN MENDERES AIRPORT

There are a number of ways to get to or from İzmir Adnan Menderes Airport:

Bus The best option at the moment is to take a dolmuş to Selçuk and change there though there is talk that the train line will be extended as far as Kuşadası.

Shuttle A number of companies, including **Last Minute Travel** (☎ 0256-614 6332; www.kusa dasihavalimaniservis.com/en/faq.asp; Otogar), run a shuttle from Kuşadası otogar (₺20), departing roughly every two hours. Atlasjet shuttles its passengers for free to/from Jappa garage, opposite the otogar, departing Kuşadası 2¾ hours before every flight. Havas (₺15) runs its shuttle hourly from the otogar. **Sözgen Turizm**

(☑0256-612 4949; www.izmirhavalimaniservisi. com; Otogar) offers a similar service.

Taxi About ₺170.

BOAT

Meander Travel (☑0256-612 8888; www. meandertravel.com; Mahmut Esat Bozkurt Caddesi 14/B; ☉7am-11pm Apr-Oct, 9am-6pm Mon-Sat Nov-Mar) operates a **ferry** (Map p244) to the Greek island of Samos. The daily service operates from April to October, with boats departing Kuşadası at 9am and Samos at 5pm. Tickets for the 1½-hour crossing cost €35 for a single, €40 for a same-day return and €55 for an open return, including the €10 port tax. Arrive one hour before departure for immigration formalities. If you are returning to Kuşadası, check your Turkish visa is multiple-entry.

Barel Travel (☑0256-614 4463, 0545 768 8932; www.bareltravel.com; Guvercinada Caddesi, Scala Nuova Shopping Center; ☉7.30am-10pm Apr-Oct, 9am-5pm Nov-Mar) runs faster high-speed ferries to Samos (single/same-day return/open-return €40/45/60) that take just 45 minutes and allow you to make connections to other islands. Boats depart Kuşadası at 9am, returning at 7pm or 8pm from April to October. There are also sailings to Patmos on Tuesday and Wednesday and Ikaria on Saturday and Sunday (both €50/55/60).

BUS & DOLMUŞ

Kuşadası's otogar is at the southern end of Süleyman Demirel Bul, on the bypass highway, with *servises* (free shuttles) running to/from the **bus companies' offices** (Map p244), which are (mostly) on İsmet İnönü Bulvarı. Dolmuşes depart from centrally located Candan Tarhan Bulvarı and from the otogar.

Şehiriçi minibuses (No 5, ₺2) run every few minutes in summer (every 15 to 20 in winter) from the otogar to the centre and along the coast to Kadınlar Denizi.

Bodrum (₺34, 2½ hours) Pamukkale has morning, afternoon and evening departures in summer; otherwise take a dolmuş to Söke, from where they run half-hourly.

İzmir (₺17, one hour) Half-hourly buses in summer, hourly in winter.

Pamukkale (₺36, 3½ hours) Departures twice a day via Selçuk and Aydın.

Selçuk (Map p244) (₺6, 20 minutes) Dolmuşes from the roundabout at the southern end of Candan Tarhan Bulvarı every 20 to 30 minutes via Pamucak and the turn-off for Ephesus Lower Gate.

Söke (Map p244) (₺6, 30 minutes) Dolmuşes from the same roundabout every 20 to 30 minutes.

CAR

Budget, Europcar, Avis and others rent out cars, and you can get good deals through Economy Car Rentals (www.economycarrentals.com).

TAXI

There are taxi ranks all over town, including on **Güvercinada Caddesi** (Map p244), **Adnan Menderes Bulvarı** (Map p244) and **İsmet İnönü Bulvarı** (Map p244), generally with their prices for longer journeys on display. Fares include €60 return to Ephesus, €80 including Mary's House. Other long-haul trips include the Dilek Peninsula (€50), Priene (€80) and Pamukkale (€160). For shorter journeys, meters start at ₺4 and charge ₺4 per kilometre.

PRIENE, MILETUS, DIDYMA & AROUND

Visiting the ancient settlements of Priene, Miletus and Didyma, which run more or less in a line 80km south of Kuşadası, is easily done in a nine-hour day by car or guided tour. A tour is worth considering – the sites are not as excavated or well signposted as Ephesus, so having a professional guide will help bring them to life. Travel agencies in Selçuk and Kuşadası offer the 'PMD' (Priene, Miletus and Didyma) tour for between €45 and €60, including transport, lunch, an hour at each site and possibly one or two add-ons such as Söke market and/or the beach at Altınkum. Tours usually require at least four participants. Ascertain in advance where you'll go and for how long; make sure the tour includes Miletus Museum (p251), which is sometimes forgotten but definitely worthwhile.

Visiting Priene, Miletus and Didyma all in a day by public transport is tricky. Regular dolmuşes connect Söke with all three, but they can be infrequent off-season and you might have to return to Söke between two of them. Nonetheless, with luck and a few changes in Söke, it may be possible to visit all three in summer.

Priene

Priene   RUIN
(₺5; ☉8.30am-7pm Apr-Oct, to 5pm Nov-Mar) Like Ephesus, Priene was once a sophisticated port city with two harbours. But all that went pear-shaped when the changing course of the Büyük Menderes River silted them both up. Although its relative lack of spectacular ruins leaves more to the imagination, Priene

EPHESUS, BODRUM & THE SOUTH AEGEAN PRIENE

Priene

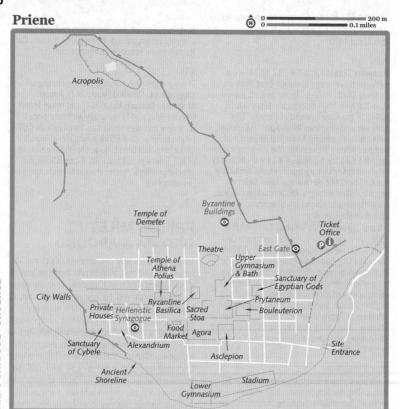

N   0 ————————— 200 m
     0 ————————— 0.1 miles

Acropolis

Byzantine Buildings

Temple of Demeter

Ticket Office

Theatre

East Gate

Temple of Athena Polias

Upper Gymnasium & Bath

Sanctuary of Egyptian Gods

City Walls

Byzantine Basilica

Prytaneum

Private Houses

Hellenistic Synagogue

Sacred Stoa

Bouleuterion

Food Market

Agora

Sanctuary of Cybele

Alexandrium

Asclepion

Site Entrance

Ancient Shoreline

Stadium

Lower Gymnasium

enjoys a commanding position just below Mt Mykale, giving it a certain natural grandeur missing at Ephesus. The site also offers plenty of shady trees, less crowds and views across the patchwork fields.

Priene was important by 300 BC (when the League of Ionian Cities held congresses and festivals here), peaking between then and 45 BC. Still, it was smaller than nearby Miletus, and the Romans made fewer modifications to its Hellenistic buildings, which has preserved its unique 'Greek' look. By the 2nd century AD, however, the silt had won the battle in this port city once famed for its shipbuilding industry and sailing tradition, and most of the population relocated to Miletus. Amid the rubble, a tiny Greek village called Samson existed until 1923, when the Greeks were expelled and the remaining Turks moved to the neighbouring village of Güllübahçe.

Digging, led by British and German archaeologists, only started here in the late 19th century. Plenty of marble statues and other antiquities ended up in their museums – in some cases, traded by sultans for such things as trains and modern farming equipment.

Beyond the ticket booth (ask for a copy of the free *Priene Visitor Information and Tour* map), walk along the paved pathway and turn right up the steep stone steps. Note that Priene's streets meet at right angles – a system invented by the Miletus architect Hippodamus (498–408 BC). Creator of the 'grid system' of urban planning, Hippodamus became influential, and his system was used not only in here and in Priene, but also in Rhodes, Piraeus (the port of Athens) and even ancient Greek Thurii, in southern Italy. As at Ephesus, Priene's marble streets also have gouged lines and notches to prevent slipping.

On a high bluff backed by stark mountain and overlooking what was once the sea (see the information panels to comprehend the extent of the silting) stands the ruined

Temple of Athena Polias, dating from the 4th century BC. Priene's biggest and most influential structure (it became the model for Ionic architecture), it was designed by Pytheos of Priene, who also designed the Mausoleum of Halicarnassus (now Bodrum). An original inscription, now in the British Museum, states that Alexander the Great funded the temple.

Unlike Hippodamus, whom Aristotle recalled as being rather the free spirit (he never cut his hair and wore the same clothes year-round), Pytheos was a stickler for detail. He saw his Classical Ionian temple design as solving the imperfections he perceived in preceding Doric design. Today's five re-erected columns give some sense of the temple's original look, though many others lie in unruly heaps around it.

Priene's theatre (capacity 6500) is among the best-preserved Hellenistic theatres anywhere. Whistle to test the acoustics, and slip your fingers between the lion's-paw indentations on the finely carved *prohedria* (marble seats for VIPs) in the front row.

Nearby lie the ruins of a Byzantine basilica from the 5th century AD; note the fine stone pulpit and steps to the apse. Also see the nearby bouleuterion, which could seat up to 640 interlocutors; from here a narrow path leads down to the ruined medical centre, the Asclepion (once thought to be a temple to Zeus Olympios). To the west are remains of private houses (some with two storeys) and a Hellenistic synagogue; to the south are the gymnasium, stadium and agora.

You can follow the remains of the city wall, once 2.5km long and 6m high with 16 towers, back to the car park via the main East Gate.

There are toilets in the car park and in the village of Güllübahçe below that abut a ruined Byzantine aqueduct.

Dolmuşes run from Söke to Güllübahçe (₺4, 20 minutes) every 20 minutes, stopping 250m from Priene, by the Byzantine aqueduct cafes. They run hourly in winter.

Miletus

Miletus   RUIN
(Milet; ₺10, parking ₺4, audio guide ₺10; ⊙8.30am-7pm Apr-Oct, to 5pm Nov-Mar) Ancient Miletus in the valley of the Büyük Menderes River was once a great port city. Though badly signposted, its mixed Hellenistic-Roman ruins are impressive, and the fascinating Miletus Museum (Milet Müzesi; ₺5; ⊙8.30am-7pm Apr-Oct, to 5pm Nov-Mar) exhibits findings not just from Miletus but from nearby Priene and explains the relationship between the two cities. Make the museum your first port of call in order to pick up the informative (and free) *Miletus Circular Tour* map. Skip the audio guide – it's confusing and overly detailed.

Although Miletus' distant origins remain unclear, it's likely that Minoan Cretans came in the Bronze Age (the word Miletus is of Cretan origin). Ionian Greeks consolidated themselves from 1000 BC, and Miletus became a leading centre of Greek thought and culture over the following centuries; most significantly, the Milesian School of Philosophy (from the 6th century BC) featured such great thinkers as Thales, Anaximander and Anaximenes. Their observations of nature emphasised rational answers rather than recourse to mythical explanations, putting them among the world's first scientists.

Like the other coastal cities in the region, Miletus was fought over by Athens and Persia, and finally taken in 334 BC by Alexander the Great, who ushered in the city's golden age. Rome took over exactly two centuries later, and a small Christian congregation developed after St Paul's visits at the end of his third missionary journey around AD 57. In Byzantine times Miletus was an archbishopric. Unlike other coastal cities, enough of its port was free from silt build-ups for the Seljuks to use it for maritime trade through the 14th century. The Ottomans abandoned the city when its harbour finally silted up, and the Büyük Menderes River has since pushed Miletus 10km inland.

You'll notice almost immediately that the streets of Miletus have a right-angle grid plan – the brainchild of local architect Hippodamus. Approaching the site from the car park, the Great Theatre dominates. Miletus' commercial and administrative centre from 700 BC to AD 700, the 5000-seat Hellenistic theatre had majestic sea views. The Romans reconstructed it in the 1st century AD to seat 15,000 spectators.

Exit the theatre through the *vomitorium* (an exit tunnel) on the right to reach the rest of the site. Above the theatre, Byzantine castle ramparts provide views to the east of the former port called Lion Harbour after the leonine statues that guarded its entrance. South of the harbour are the northern and southern agoras, and between them, the bouleuterion.

Miletus (Milet)

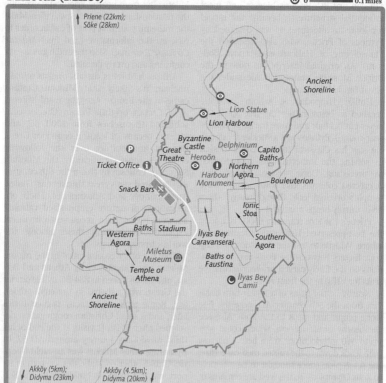

EPHESUS, BODRUM & THE SOUTH AEGEAN DIDYMA (DIDIM)

Adjoining the northern agora to the east is the **Delphinium** dedicated to Apollo; it's the oldest shrine in Miletus. It marked the start of a 15km-long processional way to the temple and oracle at Didyma. As if by magic, the laurel trees that Greeks considered sacred to Apollo still cast their shade near the Milesian temple ruins.

Southwest of the southern agora, the **Baths of Faustina**, constructed for Marcus Aurelius' wife, are worth visiting; the massive walls and inner floors of the two spacious structures still survive. The designers' ingenious plan used *hypocausts* (an underfloor system of hot-water pipes) and *tubuli* (terracotta wall flues), which kept the interior of the *caldarium* very hot. Next to it was a refreshing *frigidarium* (cold bath).

Southwest of the baths is the **stadium** for 15,000 spectators and the Miletus Museum. To the southeast is the post-Seljuk İlyas Bey

Camii (1404), renovated in 2012 with an intricate doorway.

There are cafes near the entrance, including one flanking a 14th-century caravanserai. You'll also find public toilets here.

Dolmuşes linking Söke (₺8, 40 minutes) with Didyma (₺5, 20 minutes) via Miletus run hourly in summer and every two hours in winter.

Didyma (Didim)

☑ 0256 / POP 59,865

◎ Sights

Temple of Apollo   RUIN
(₺10, audio guide ₺10; ⊙ 8.30am-7pm mid-May–mid-Sep, to 5pm mid-Sep–mid-May) Didyma (now Didim) was not a city in ancient times but a religious centre, and its astonishing Temple of Apollo was the ancient world's second largest; with its 122 original columns it had only five

fewer than Ephesus' Temple of Artemis. Since the latter has only one column standing today, visiting Didyma really helps travellers visualise the lost grandeur of Artemis' temple, too.

In Greek, Didyma means 'twin' (here, referring to the twin siblings Apollo and Artemis). Didyma's oracle of Apollo had an importance second only to the Oracle of Delphi. Although destroyed by Persians in the early 5th century BC, Alexander the Great revitalised it in 334 BC and, about 30 years later, Seleucid rulers planned to make it the world's largest temple. However, it was never completed and Ephesus' Temple of Artemis took first prize instead.

In AD 303 the oracle allegedly supported Emperor Diocletian's harsh persecution of Christians – the last such crackdown, since Constantine the Great soon thereafter made Christianity the state church of the Roman Empire. Oops. The now-unpopular oracle was silenced by Emperor Theodosius I (r 379–395), who closed other pagan temples such as the Delphic Oracle.

Entering from the ticket booth, clamber up the temple's 13 wide steps to marvel at the massively thick and towering columns.

Behind the temple porch, in a room called the chresmographeion, oracular poems were inscribed on a great doorway and presented to petitioners. Covered ramps by the porch lead down to an interior building called the cella (or naos in Greek), where the oracle prophesied after drinking from the sacred spring; reach it by way of two vaulted and sloped passages.

Just east of the temple is the purification well and circular altar where clients of the oracle offered their sacrifices. You can't miss the huge Medusa head nearby that once took pride of place in the frieze of the architrave over the outer row of columns. Further east is the sacred way lined with ornate statues (relocated to the British Museum in 1858) that led to Miletus.

🛏 Sleeping & Eating

Didyma has basic accommodation offering a tranquil evening with fantastic temple views. Overnighting here allows you to visit the temple early or late and dodge the coach parties.

★ **Medusa House**   PENSION **$$**
(☑ 0536 767 6734, 0256-811 0063; www.medusa house.com; Hisar Mahallesi 246; s/d €40/60; 🛜)
A short walk from the Temple of Apollo entrance, this lovingly restored 150-year-old Greek stone home, and a more recently built annexe, offer 10 pleasant rooms in a flowery garden to the back and the front. The six rooms in the old house have wooden ceilings and fireplaces but those in the out-building are larger and more modern.

Poseidon Sofrası   TURKISH **$$**
(☑ 0543 677 1813, 0256-813 3353; www.face book.com/pages/Table-of-Poseidon-Poseidon-Sof rası/841607029239988; Hisar Mahallesi 26/A; snacks ₺8-14, mains ₺25-45; ⊙ 10am-2am) Perched on a wide terrace overlooking the village's main square and the Temple of Apollo beyond it, 'Poseidon's Table' offers snacks like burgers and *börek* (filled pastry) as well as more substantial meat and fish main dishes. It's the restaurant of choice among locals.

Kamacı   BUFFET **$$**
(☑ 0256-811 0033; Hisar Mahallesi 96/A; mezes ₺5, mains ₺18-25; ⊙ 10am-midnight) Facing the temple's two sturdiest columns, Kamacı serves kebaps, *köfte*, fresh fish and better-value mezes to locals and tourists alike. Try the divine octopus *güveç* (stew) or the perfectly cooked grilled sea bass. And don't confuse this restaurant with the tour-group buffet hall of the same name by the town car park.

❶ Getting There & Away

Frequent dolmuşes run from Söke to Didyma (₺7, 40 minutes) and Altınkum (₺8, 1¼ hours). Services are less frequent in winter.

Lake Bafa

☑ 0252 / POP 1570 (BAFA)

Landlocked, but 50% saltwater, 70-sq-km Lake Bafa constitutes the last trace of the Aegean's former inland reach. It's a peaceful place, ringed by traditional villages such as Kapıkırı on the lake's far eastern shore. Bygone Byzantine hermitages and churches abound in the Bafa hills, and the region is a rich natural habitat boasting sights from orchids (up to 20 species) to owls, butterflies and chameleons. In particular, some 350 avian species are represented, including eagles, pink flamingos, pelicans and spoonbills.

The ruins of Herakleia (p254) are found throughout Kapıkırı, which is populated by roving chickens, donkeys and old women hawking trinkets and crafts. The ruins leave much to the imagination; it's the rustic 'other-worldly' scene and the lakeside setting that comprise most of the experience.

The upper village, where most of the ruins are, is called 'town side' and lower Kapıkırı is 'island side'.

◎ Sights & Activities

Pension owners organise boat and fishing trips (from ₺150) and half-day hikes to 6000-year-old Neolithic caves (from €150), with the possibility of spending a night camping in the hills. Many can also help with birdwatching, botany and photography tours; contact **Latmos Travel** (☑ 0252-543 5445, 0532 416 3996; www.latmos-travel.com; Agora Pansiyon, Kapıkırı) for details.

Herakleia
RUINS

(Kapıkırı) FREE The ruins of the ancient Carian port city Herakleia are scattered throughout Kapıkırı. In the upper village, the large **Temple of Athena**, just west of the central **agora**, occupies a promontory overlooking the lake. Only three of its walls remain, but the perfectly cut blocks (no mortar) are impressive. Other signposted paths lead eastwards to the **bouleuterion** in a private garden, a uniquely Roman **bathhouse** and the unrestored **theatre**, with barely a few seating rows remaining (it once sat up to 4000 spectators).

The Hellenistic **city walls** (circa 300 BC) extend for 6.5km. For sublime lake views, follow the road down past the rock-hewn **Temple of Endymion** and the ruined **Byzantine castle**, which overlooks the rock tombs from the **necropolis**. From the beach and its ruined **Byzantine church**, note the island just opposite – its base conceals ancient building foundations. Once joined to the mainland, the island is only accessible by boat nowadays, even at low tide.

🛏 Sleeping & Eating

The lake is popular with German tourists, and many pension owners speak German better than English. Staying in idyllic Kapıkırı commands high prices, but you can usually get discounts for longer stays.

Most pension restaurants are open to nonguests. Lake Bafa's unusual saltwater/freshwater composition – it's as salty as the Black Sea – means they serve both sea and lake fish caught in the same waters. A local speciality is smoked eel. Market day down in Bafa village is Friday.

Karia Pansiyon
PENSION $$

(☑ 0543 846 5400, 0252-543 5490; www.kariapen sion.com; Kapıkırı; s/d incl half board €55/70, campsites per person €4; ❄🛜) Little Karia and its friendly owner Emin offers some of the best lake views in town from its large terrace restaurant and four homely rooms climbing the rocky hillside. There's a bungalow (€90) for

up to four people. Camping is in the pension garden with hammocks and picnic table.

Kaya Pansiyon
PENSION $$

(☑ 0252-543 5579, 0542 723 4214; info@kaya pansiyon.com; Kapıkırı; s/d incl half board €45/75; ❄🛜) The closest accommodation to the beach, 'Rock Pension' offers accommodation in wooden cabins and a stone bungalow perched on boulders in a secluded valley. The six rooms are rustic and not generously sized, but breakfast and dinner on the terrace are farm-fresh feasts accompanied by the free lake breeze and island views.

★ Agora Pansiyon
PENSION $$$

(☑ 0532 416 3996, 0252-543 5445; www.agorapan siyon.com; Kapıkırı; s/d B&B €50/65, incl half board €65/100, apt €35-48; ❄🛜) Nestled between gardens and a shaded terrace with hammocks and an olive tree, this delightful pension, now in its third decade, has 10 rooms and cabins decorated with folk art and kilims (pileless woven rugs), plus a real hamam. The two brothers who run the place, Mithat and Oktay Serçin, are affable hosts and fonts of information. Mum's cooking is legendary.

Selene's Pension
PENSION $$$

(☑ 0542 316 4550, 0252-543 5221; www.selenes pansion.com; Kapıkırı; d/tr incl half board €90/120; ❄🛜) Kapıkırı's largest pension with 15 rooms and wooden cabins is like a mini village on the road down to the beach. Double 101 and triple 102 have sweeping views of the lake as does the enclosed terrace restaurant. The gardens below the Temple of Athena are a delight.

ℹ Getting There & Away

Buses and dolmuşes will drop you on the highway in Bafa village (formerly called Çamıçı) at the turn-off for Kapıkırı. It's 10km north from there to Kapıkırı; two dolmuşes (₺5) serve the route in the morning and two in the afternoon and a taxi costs ₺20. If you stay for a few days, your pension may provide a free pick-up.

Milas & Around

☑ 0252 / POP 58,390 (MILAS)

Mylasa (now Milas) was ancient Caria's royal capital, except for during the reign of Mausolus from Halicarnassus (present-day Bodrum). While this agricultural town is most interesting for its Tuesday farmers market, the surrounding area conceals several unique archaeological sites.

⊙ Sights

Milas' best sights are within a 25km radius. Ruins in town include **Baltalı Kapı** (Axe Gate), a well-preserved Roman gate with a carving of a *labrys* (Greek-style double-bitted axe) on the north side. It is also called Zeus Gate. Up a steep path from Gümüşkesen Caddesi is the 2nd-century-AD chambered Roman tomb called **Gümüşkesen** (Silver Purse), possibly modelled on the Mausoleum of Halicarnassus.

Euromos   RUIN
(₺5; ⊙ 8am-7pm May-Sep, to 5pm Oct-Apr) Founded in the 6th century BC, Euromos peaked between 200 BC and AD 200 under Hellenistic and then Roman rule. Its indigenous deity had earlier been synthesised with Zeus, and indeed the partially restored Corinthian **Temple of Zeus Lepsynus** is testimony to that. Inscriptions on the west columns record donations by prominent citizens; look to the south side for a **carving of a labrys**, Zeus' symbol, flanked by two ears, suggesting that an oracle was in residence.

The temple is between Bafa (formerly Çamıçı) and Milas, signposted from the highway just south of Selimiye village. To get here, take a bus or dolmuş running between Milas and Söke and ask to get off at the ruins, which lie about 200m north of the highway.

Labranda   RUIN
(⊙ 8am-7pm May-Sep, to 5pm Oct-Apr) **FREE** This remote hillside site occupies the area that supplied drinking water to Mylasa (Milas) and is one of the most interesting sites in Caria. Never a city but a religious centre linked by a **sacred way** with Mylasa, Labranda worshipped a local deity since at least the 6th century BC, subsequently becoming a sanctuary dedicated to Zeus. The great **Temple of Zeus Labrayndus** honours the god's warlike, 'Axe-Bearing' aspect. Festivals and athletic games occurred at Labranda, which possibly possessed an oracle.

To reach the temple, walk west from the guardians kiosk at the main entrance, past the distinctive **Doric House** and up a magnificent **stairway** with 24 steps. The **temple** and other religious buildings stand on a series of steep artificial terraces.

The Labranda turn-off is marked on the highway a short distance northwest of Milas. It's 14km from there; unless you're driving, take a Milas taxi (₺40 including an hour of waiting).

CARIAN TRAIL
The longest of Turkey's 20-odd long-distance hiking trails, the **Carian Trail** (Karia Yolu; www.cariantrail.com) meanders 820km from the Milas area south to the Datça and Bozburun Peninsulas, crossing through much of the ancient kingdom of Caria. It passes by many of the most important archaeological sites and offers an opportunity to see the emerald hills and azure coves of the Aegean at a slow pace, hiking beyond the tourist trail to secret corners such as Lake Bafa's Neolithic **cave paintings**. You can walk short sections of the route; find the *Carian Trail* guidebook (€19), 1:100,000-scale map and more information on the trail's website as well as at **Culture Routes in Turkey** (www.cultureroutesinturkey.com).

Beçin Castle   RUIN
(Beçin Kalesi; ₺5; ⊙ 8am-7pm mid-Apr–Oct, to 5pm Nov–mid-Apr) At the beginning of Beçin village, about 6km south of Milas on the road to Ören, a steep signposted road climbs to Beçin Castle. Originally a Byzantine fortress, it was remodelled by the short-lived Menteşe *beylik* (principality) in the 14th century. The castle, crowning a 210m-high rocky outcropping, offers great views of Milas below from its walls.

The ruins of more Menteşe-era structures can be seen across the valley and up another hill, including the **Kızılhan** (Red Caravanserai), **Bey Konağı** (Bey's Residence), **Orhan Mosque**, the **Büyük Haman** (Great Bathhouse) and the wonderfully restored **Ahmet Gazi Madrasah**. You can borrow an English-language guidebook from the ticket booth. Half-hourly dolmuşes run between Milas and Beçin village (₺3).

Iasos   RUIN
FREE The seaside village of Kıyıkışlacık is surrounded by ancient Iasos, a Carian city that was once an island and prospered from its excellent harbour, rich fishing grounds and red-tinted marble quarried in the nearby hills. A member of the ancient Delian League, Iasos participated in the Peloponnesian Wars, but later weakened and was sacked by the Spartans. Nevertheless, it was definitely a Byzantine bishopric from the 5th to the 9th centuries, before being finally abandoned in the 15th century.

❶ Getting There & Away

Milas' otogar is a kilometre north of the centre, on the highway near the Labranda turn-off, and well connected to the central **köy garaj** (Köy Tabakhane Garaji; Milas) (village otogar), from where dolmuşes serve local destinations.

BODRUM PENINSULA

The Bodrum Peninsula, named after the summer hot spot somewhere in the centre, offers a mix of exclusive resorts and laid-back coastal villages where you can enjoy good swimming and and upmarket restaurants. Despite the glaringly visible inroads of modern tourism, tradition and tranquillity are partially preserved by local open-air vegetable markets and the rugged coastline, overlooked by scarcely populated hills in the peninsula's centre. The area has an efficient and inexpensive dolmuş network, making it easy to hop between Bodrum and the outlying coves, where, with some advance planning, you can find quality beach accommodation at still-reasonable rates.

❶ Getting There & Around

AIR

Milas-Bodrum Airport (BJV; www.bodrumair port.com), 39km northeast from Bodrum town, receives flights from all over Europe, mostly with charters and budget airlines such as EasyJet and Sun Express in summer. Anadolu Jet, AtlasJet, Onur Air, Pegasus Airlines, Thomas Cook and Turkish Airlines all serve İstanbul (both airports) and/or Ankara, while Bora Jet flies to Adana and Mykonos (Greece).

Havaş (www.havas.net/en) and **Muttaş** (☑ 0252-212 4850; ttp://muttas.com.tr/hiz metlerimiz/havaalani-yolcu-tasimacilig) shuttle between the airport and Bodrum otogar (bus station; ₺10, 45 minutes), leaving the latter two hours before every Anadolu Jet, Pegasus Airlines, Sun Express and Turkish Airlines domestic departure. Atlasjet provides a free shuttle, leaving Turgutreis three hours before departures and stopping in Bitez, Gümbet, Bodrum otogar and Konacık en route to the airport. Both services also meet arrivals. Otherwise, an expensive taxi (₺120) is your only option.

BOAT

Visit operators' offices or phone to check their website departure info, which isn't always reliable. Check, too, if your ferry is departing from Bodrum's old port near the castle or the newer cruise port south of town. Drivers in particular should book in advance; this can often be done online. **Bodrum Ferryboat Association** (Bodrum Feribot İşletmeciliği; Map p258; ☑ 0252-316 0882; www.bodrumferryboat.com; Kale Caddesi 22; ⊕ 8am-7pm May-Sep, to 6pm Oct-Apr) and **Bodrum Express Lines** (Map p258; ☑ 0252-316 1087; www.bodrumexpresslines.com; Kale Caddesi 18; ⊕ 8am-11pm May-Sep, to 8pm Oct-Apr) serve Datça and the following Greek islands:

Datça (single/return/car/bicycle ₺35/60/105/10; 1½ hours) Two to four times daily June to October. The ferry docks at Körmen on the peninsula's northern coast, and the fare includes the 15-minute shuttle to Datça.

Kalymnos (one way/same-day return/open return €25/32/50; one hour) From Turgutreis Saturday at 10am, returning 5pm, early June to late September.

Kos (one way/same-day return/open return €17/19/30; 45 minutes) Daily year-round at 9.30am, returning at 4.30pm (4pm in winter, weather permitting). Also Turgutreis–Kos daily May to mid-October at 9.30am, returning at 5.30pm. From mid-June to October, **Yeşil Marmaris** (☑ 0252-313 5045; www.kosferry. com; Cruise Port) offers fast daily Bodrum–Kos catamarans one way (one way €20, same-day return €24, open return €35; 20 minutes) from the cruise port.

Rhodes (one way/same-day return/open return €50/60/75; two hours) Saturday and Sunday from early July to late September. Yeşil Marmaris also operates services to Rhodes (one way/same-day return €65, open return €78).

Symi Services suspended at the time of research.

BUS

All the major bus companies serve **Bodrum otogar** (Map p258). Some also serve Turgutreis and Yalıkavak. Metro links Bodrum with most destinations; heading east along the coast, Pamukkale is a better option, with at least one morning and one night bus to Antalya (₺60, seven hours) via Milas, Muğla, Dalaman and Fethiye. Has Turizm has several daily buses to Marmaris (₺25, three hours) via Muğla.

CAR & MOTORCYCLE

Numerous companies in Bodrum and at the airport rent out cars, motorbikes and scooters, including **Avis** (☑ 0252-316 2333; www.avis. com; Neyzen Tevfik Caddesi 66/A; ⊕ 9am-7pm), which is also in Turgutreis; Economy Car Rentals (www.economycarrentals.com); and Bodrum-based **Neyzen Travel** (☑ 0252-316 7204, car rental 0252-313 3330; www.neyzen.com.tr; Kıbrıs Şehitler Caddesi 34).

DOLMUŞ

Bodrum's dolmuşes whiz around the peninsula every 10 minutes (half-hourly in winter) and display their destinations in their windows. You can

Bodrum Peninsula

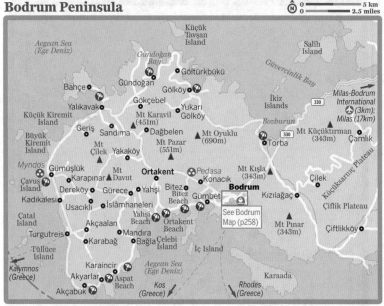

get to most villages for ₺6 or less, with services running from 8am to 11pm (round the clock June to September). From Bodrum to Yalıkavak on the far side of the peninsula takes about 30 minutes.

There are also services between Turgutreis and Akyarlar, Gümüşlük, Yalıkavak, Gündoğan and Göltürkbükü, and between Yalıkavak and Gümüşlük. To travel between the villages, you have to transit in Bodrum otogar or try your luck flagging down a passing dolmuş on the road.

Bodrum

☑ 0252 / POP 37,815

Although more than a million tourists flock to its beaches, boutique hotels, trendy restaurants and clubs each summer, Bodrum (ancient Halicarnassus) never seems to lose its cool. More than any other Turkish seaside getaway, it has an enigmatic elegance that pervades it, from the town's crowning castle and glittering marina to its flower-filled cafes and white-plastered backstreets. Even in the most hectic days of high summer, you can still find little corners of serenity in the town.

Urban planners have sought to preserve Bodrum's essential Aegean character, which was influenced by the Cretans who moved here during the population exchange of the 1920s. Today, laws restrict buildings' heights, and the whitewashed houses with bright-blue

trim evoke a lost era. The evocative castle and the ancient ruins around town also help keep Bodrum a discerning step above the rest.

Only in the past few decades has Bodrum come to be associated with paradisaical beaches and glittering summertime opulence. Previously, it was a simple fishing and sponging village, and old-timers can still remember when everything was in a different place or didn't exist at all. Long before the palmed promenades and upmarket seafood restaurants, Bodrum wasn't even desirable. Indeed, for a while it was the place where dissidents against the new Turkish republic were sent into exile.

All that started to change after one of the inmates took over the prison. Writer Cevat Şakir Kabaağaçlı (aka the 'Fisherman of Halicarnassus') was exiled to sleepy Bodrum in 1925, and quickly fell in love with the place. After serving his sentence, he proceeded to introduce a whole generation of Turkish intellectuals, writers and artists to Bodrum's charms in the mid-1940s.

From then on, there was no going back: by the mid-1980s, well-heeled foreigners started to arrive and today Bodrum is a favourite getaway for everyone from European package tourists to Turkey's prime movers and shakers. But it was Kabaağaçlı's early influence,

Bodrum

400 m
0.2 miles

Marmara Bodrum (500m)

Neyzon Travel & Yachting (300m)

Cevat Şakir Cad

Yaka Sk

Pamili Sk

Derviş Görgün Cad

Yıllıkçı Sk

Üçkuyular Cad

Hüseyin Nafiz Özsoy Cad

Cemil Uyar Cad

Kılcı Sk

Marsmabedi Cad

Türkkuyusu Camii

Türkkuyusu Cad

Göktepe Sk

Gerence Sk

Davut Sk

Turgutreis Cad

İmbat Çık

Menekşe Sk

Hamam Sk

1205 Sk

Saray Sk

Adnan Toker Sk

Frkateyn Sk

Mat smabedi Cad

Araplar Sk

TEPECİK

Tepecik Camii

Salmakis Bay

Marina

ESKİÇEŞME

Şafak Sk

Kıbrıs Şehitler Cad

Myndos Gate (200m)

Neyzen Tevfik Cad

1201 Sk

Yangı Sk

Neyzen Tevfik Cad

Belediye

Merkez Adliye Camii

Kale Cad

Dr Alim Bey

Ancient Harbour

Bodrum Ferryboat Association

Bodrum Express Lines

Ferry

Atatürk Cad

Ceviz Şakir Cad

Bazaar

Heilacılar Sk

Bahçe S k

Atatürk Cad

Taşlık Sk

Uslu Sk

Adliye Sk

Dere Sk

Cumhuriyet Cad

Kambahçe Bay

Artemis Cad

Kule Sk

Fabrika Sk

2430 Sk

Sevenceler Sk

Mandalin Sk

Uslu Sk

İlqın Sk

Çilek Sk

Tarla Sk

Zeki Müren Cad

Aegean Gate (700m)

Cumba Suites (100m); Cruise Port (1.5km)

Atatürk Cad

Bodrum

giving the town its arty identity, that saved it from the ignominious fate of other Turkish fishing-villages-turned-resorts.

◉ Sights

Bodrum Castle   CASTLE
(Bodrum Kalesi; Map p258; ☑ 0252-316 2516; www.bodrum-museum.com; İskele Meydanı; ₺30, audio guide ₺15; ⊙8.30am-6.30pm Apr-Oct, to 4.30pm Nov-Mar) There are splendid views from the battlements of Bodrum's magnificent castle, built by the Knights Hospitaller in the early 15th century and dedicated to St Peter. Today it houses the **Museum of Underwater Archaeology** (Sualtı Arkeoloji Müzesi), arguably the most important museum of its type in the world and a veritable lesson in how to bring ancient exhibits to life. Items are creatively displayed and well lit, and information panels, maps, models, drawings, murals, dioramas and videos all help to animate them.

Based on Rhodes, the Knights Hospitaller built the castle during Tamerlane's Mongol invasion of Anatolia in 1402, which weakened the Ottomans and gave the order an opportunity to establish a foothold here. They used marble and stones from Mausolus' famed Mausoleum, which had collapsed in an earthquake, and changed the city's name

from Halicarnassus to Petronium, recalling St Peter. By 1437 they had finished building, although they added new defensive features (moats, walls, cisterns etc) right up until 1522, when Süleyman the Magnificent captured Rhodes. The Knights were forced to cede the castle, and the victorious Muslim sultan promptly turned the chapel into a mosque, complete with new minaret. For centuries, the castle was never tested, but French shelling in WWI toppled the minaret (re-erected in 1997).

Spread around the castle, the attractively lit and informative museum has reconstructions and multimedia displays to complement the antiquities, and takes about two hours to see. It gets very busy and claustrophobic in the museum's small rooms, so try to arrive early. Look to the ground for green/red mosaic arrows indicating a short/long tour route. You'll see peacocks strolling, strutting and calling to prospective mates throughout the castle grounds.

➡ **Main Court**

Beyond the ticket booth, you'll pass carved marble **Crusader coats of arms** – just some of the 250-odd here. At the top of a flight of steps and through a gate is the castle's main courtyard, centred on an ancient (and heavily pruned) mulberry tree. Here is a massive amphorae collection, with pieces from the 14th century BC to modern times, all recovered from southern-coast waters.

On the east side of the courtyard is the chapel (1406) containing a full-sized reconstruction of a late-Roman ship's stern that sank off Yassıada in AD 626. Walk the decks, take the helm and inspect the galley and amphorae below.

Climbing towards the towers to the east, you next come to the Glass Wreck Hall on the left. It houses a 15m-long, 5m-wide ship that sank near Marmaris in AD 1025, while carrying 30 tonnes of glass between Fatimid Syria and a Byzantine glass factory on the Black Sea or the Danube. Archaeologists and historians were excited not only by what the find revealed about 11th-century ship construction – some 20% of it is on display – but also for what it indicated about Fatimid glass.

Next, the small Glass Hall exhibits finds from the 15th century BC to the 14th century AD, and includes Mycenaean beads, Roman glass bottles and Islamic weights.

➡ French Tower & Carian Princess Hall

A slight distance to the north, the French Tower has finds from the Tektaş Burnu, the world's only fully excavated classical Greek shipwreck (dating from 480 BC to 400 BC). Amphorae, talismanic discs and kitchen utensils from the vessel are displayed, plus 2001 excavation photos taken at the Çeşme Peninsula site. Ancient coins (including from Croesus' Caria) and jewellery are also on display.

The neighbouring Carian Princess Hall is a must-see, exhibiting a gold crown, necklace, bracelets, rings and an exquisite wreath of golden myrtle leaves. Popularly associated with the last Carian queen, Ada (Mausolus' sister who was reinstated by Alexander the Great after annexing Halicarnassus in 334 BC), they belonged to an unknown woman of status whose skeleton was found in the heavy terracotta sarcophagus on display here.

➡ English Tower

Guarding the castle's southeast corner, the three-storey English Tower, also known as the Lion Tower, was built during the reign of King Henry IV of England (1399–1413). In 1401 Henry became the first (and only) English monarch to host a Byzantine emperor, Manuel II Palaeologos, and he took seriously Manuel's warning about the Muslim threat posed by the Turks to Christian Europe. The tower was thus a symbol of support for their common cause.

Today, the interior is fitted out as a slightly kitsch medieval refectory, with a long dining table surrounded by suits of armour, stag horns, lions' heads and the standards of the Knights Hospitaller and their Turkish adversaries. Most interesting is the model of the *Sovereign of the Seven Seas,* a ship built on Charles I's orders in 1637, and the graffiti in Latin carved into much of the walls 500 years ago by the Knights Hospitaller.

➡ Bronze Age Shipwrecks Hall

Just opposite the English Tower is this hall containing three Bronze Age shipwrecks, including the world's oldest excavated wreck, the 14th-century BC *Uluburun,* which sank 8km off the coast near Kaş. Full-size replicas of the booty-laden hold and the wreck site on the sea floor are in place. The adjoining Treasure Room displays Canaanite gold jewellery, bronze daggers, ivory cosmetic boxes, wooden writing boards and Egyptian Queen Nefertiti's golden scarab found on a wreck and already several hundred years old by then.

➡ Gatineau Tower & Snake Tower

Turn left out of the hall to follow the battlements around the castle to the dungeons at Gatineau Tower, where the Knights imprisoned, and sometimes tortured, their enemies from 1513 to 1523. The inner gate's chilling inscription sums up the dungeon as being *Inde Deus abest* (Where God does not exist). Hold children's hands and mind your head – the 24 steps down are steep and narrow. En route you'll pass three uncomfortable-looking garderobes – outdoor medieval toilets.

On the way back to the exit, the Snake Tower displays more artefacts and statuary. Named after a snake carved in the stone, it was used as a hospital both by the Knights and later the Ottomans.

Bodrum Maritime Museum   MUSEUM
(Bodrum Deniz Müzesi; Map p258; ☑0252-316 3310; www.bodrumdenizmuzesi.org; Esiki Besdesten Binası; adult/reduced ₺5/2.50; ⊙11am-10pm Tue-Sun Jun-Oct, to 6pm Nov-May) This small but well-formed museum spread over two floors examines Bodrum's maritime past through finely crafted scale models of boats and an excellent video on traditional 'Bodrum-type' boat building. Much is made of Bodrum's role as a sponge-diving centre and local writer Cevat Şakir Kabaağaçlı – the much-loved 'Fisherman of Halicarnassus'.

Mausoleum   RUIN
(Mausoleion; Map p258; Turgutreis Caddesi; ₺10; ⊙8am-7pm Apr-Oct, to 5pm Nov-Mar) One of the

Seven Wonders of the Ancient World, the Mausoleum was the greatest achievement of Carian King Mausolus (r 376–353 BC), who moved his capital from Mylasa (today's Milas) to Halicarnassus. The only ancient elements to survive are the pre-Mausolean stairways and tomb chambers, the narrow entry to Mausolus' tomb chamber and a huge green stone that blocked it, the Mausolean drainage system, precinct wall bits and some large fluted marble column drums.

Before his death, the king planned his own tomb, to be designed by Pytheos, the architect of Priene's Temple of Athena. When he died, his wife (and sister), Artemisia, oversaw the completion of the enormous, white-marble colonnaded tomb topped by a 24-step pyramid and a quadriga, a four-horse chariot carrying Mausolus. In the late 15th century the Knights Hospitaller found the Mausoleum in ruins, perhaps destroyed by an earthquake, and between 1494 and 1522, almost all of it was reused as building blocks for the castle or burned for the lime content to strengthen the walls. Luckily, the more impressive ancient friezes were incorporated into the castle walls, while original statues of Mausolus and Artemisia were sent to the British Museum.

The site has relaxing **gardens**, with excavations to the west and a **covered arcade** to the east – the latter contains a copy of the famous frieze now in the British Museum. Four original fragments displayed were discovered more recently. Models, drawings and documents indicate the grand dimensions of the original Mausoleum. A **scale model** of Mausolus' Halicarnassus is also on display.

Ottoman Shipyard RUIN

(Osmanlı Tersanesi; Map p258; Şafak Sokak; ⊙9am-6pm Tue-Sun) FREE The restored Ottoman shipyard stands just above the marina. In 1770 Russia destroyed the entire Ottoman fleet at Çeşme; rebuilding it took place in boatyards such as this one. It was fortified against pirate attacks in the 18th and 19th centuries with a watchtower; today it occasionally hosts art exhibitions. Old tombstones, dating from the period when the Latin alphabet was replacing Arabic-based *eski yazı* (old-style writing) are kept above. Excellent views.

Ancient Theatre RUIN

(Antik Teatro; Map p258; Kıbrıs Şehitler Caddesi) On the main road to Turgutreis, ancient Halicarnassus' theatre was built in the hillside rock in the 4th century BC to seat 5000 spectators but that capacity was increased to 13,000 for gladiatorial contests in the 3rd century AD. It hosts concerts and other events in summer.

Myndos Gate GATE

(Myndos Kapısı; Cafer Paşa Caddesi) These are the restored remains of the only surviving gate from what were originally 7km-long walls probably built by King Mausolus in the 4th century BC. In front of the twin-towered gate are the remains of a moat in which many of Alexander the Great's soldiers drowned in 334 BC.

🏃 Activities

Travel agents all over town offer tours and activities, including a few on or just off Dere Sokak heading inland from Cumhuriyet Caddesi. Tours will take you to Ephesus, 2½ hours' drive away, for about €50 (€65 including one or two stops en route such as Euromos and/or Miletus); taxis charge from about €135 for up to five people.

Excursion boats moored in both bays offer day trips (usually 11am to 5pm) around the peninsula's beaches and bays, typically charging about ₺45 including five or so stops and lunch. **Karaada** (Black Island), with hot-spring waters gushing from a cave, is a popular destination where you can swim and loll in supposedly healthful orange mud.

Book through your hotel or direct with operators – **Bodex Travel & Yachting Agency** (📱0252-313 2843, 0533 638 1264; www.bodextravel. com; Atatürk Caddesi 74), **Ezgi Boats** (Map p258; 📱0542 345 4392; Cumhuriyet Caddesi; ⊙11am-6pm) or **Yağmur** (Map p258; 📱0533 341 1450; Cumhuriyet Caddesi) – ideally a day ahead.

Tarihi Bardakçı Hamamı HAMAM

(Map p258; 📱0536 687 3743; Dere Sokak 32; hamam ₺35, oil massage ₺35; ⊙8am-11pm) Going since 1749, Bodrum's oldest hamam offers mixed bathing. It has a Facebook page you can search for.

Neyzen Travel & Yachting BOATING

(📱0252-316 7204; www.neyzen.com.tr; Kıbrıs Şehitleri Caddesi 34) *Gület* (traditional Turkish wooden yacht) trips – it has four – with four to eight cabins. Trips include a week-long tour from Bodrum to Knidos, Datça, Bozburun and Selimiye and back for €700 per person, including all meals and drinks.

🛏 Sleeping

In high summer accommodation fills up fast in Bodrum, so be prepared to pound the pave-

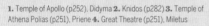

1. Temple of Apollo (p252), Didyma 2. Knidos (p282) 3. Temple of Athena Polias (p251), Priene 4. Great Theatre (p251), Miletus

DENIZ UNLUSUS / GETTY IMAGES ©

Ruins of the South Aegean

The Romans, Carians, Ionian Greeks and Byzantines were just a few of the ancient civilisations that left their mark on this ruin-strewn stretch of coastline, where the very contours of the land have changed but weathered theatres and temples still stand.

Ephesus

On the marble paving stones of this great Roman provincial capital, you can tread in the footsteps of such historical notables as Alexander the Great and St Paul.

Priene

Refreshingly quiet after a visit to Ephesus, Priene was, like its busier neighbour to the north, a port city. Silted up by the Meander River, the Aegean coast receded west to its current location, stranding these ports inland and accelerating their decline.

Miletus

Miletus suffered the same fate as nearby Ephesus and Pirene. Its most impressive ruin is the 15,000-seat Great Theatre, while the Delphinium dedicated to Apollo marked the start of a sacred road to Didyma and its oracle.

Didyma

With its towering columns, Didyma's Temple of Apollo is one of Turkey's most evocative classical ruins. It also helps to visualise the lost grandeur of Ephesus' Temple of Artemis, one of the Seven Wonders of the Ancient World.

Mausoleum of Halicarnassus

The tomb of the Carian King Mausolus was also one of the Seven Wonders of the Ancient World. Displays at the site in today's Bodrum recreate the white-marble mausoleum topped by a stepped pyramid and a quadriga.

Knidos

This Dorian port city, straddling two bays on the Datça Peninsula, is a stunning example of how ruins are given extra poetry by their lyrical settings at sites throughout Aegean and Mediterranean Turkey.

ℹ BODRUM BEDS

It's more expensive than other coastal areas, but if you're keen on a Bodrum-area base, try to plan in advance: many hotels offer discounted rates for early bookings. Those that stay open in winter also drop their rates considerably compared with the sky-high prices in August and, to a lesser extent, July. Many hoteliers close their doors and disappear from October to May; even in mid-May, resort towns such as Göltürkbükü sometimes resemble building sites as preparations are made for the approaching season.

ment if you haven't booked ahead. Hotels near the marina and Bar St get the most noise from the clubs and bars. If arriving by bus, you may be harassed by touts offering 'budget accommodation'. It's your call but we ignore them.

★ Kaya Pansiyon PENSION $

(Map p258; ☎0252-316 5745, 0535 737 7060; www.kayapansiyon.com.tr; Eski Hükümet Sokak 10; s/d ₺180/250; ☺Apr-Oct; ❋🛜) One of Bodrum's better pensions, the very central Kaya has 12 clean, simple rooms plus a studio apartment with hairdryer, safe and TV; six rooms count a balcony as well. There is a roof terrace with a castle view for breakfast, a flowering courtyard with a bar for lounging, and helpful owners Mustafa and Selda can arrange activities.

Albatros Otel HOTEL $

(Map p258; ☎0252-316 7117; www.albatrosotelbodrum.com; Neyzen Tevfik Çıkmazı 6; s/d ₺200/250; ❋🛜) A thorough upgrade had given this erstwhile low-key 20-room hotel a fresh and modern look. Rooms have an unusual purple and turquoise colour scheme (it works) and wooden ceilings. It's down a quiet lane just off the marina. Its friendly service and a location on the western bay make it a good pick for independent travellers and small families.

Hotel Güleç HOTEL $

(Map p258; ☎0252-316 5222, 0532 433 1847; www.hotelgulec.com; Üçkuyular Caddesi 22; r €40-65; ❋🛜) This good-value 18-room hotel has a central location and simple but bright and clean rooms (the white linoleum tends to lighten things up here). The tiny bathrooms leave a little to be desired, but there is a sunny garden for breakfast, a stunning marble staircase and assorted brothers and cousins to help find parking and so on.

Su Otel BOUTIQUE HOTEL $$

(Map p258; ☎0252-316 6906; www.bodrumsuhotel.com; Turgutreis Caddesi, Sokak 1201; s/d/ste from €65/95/135; ❋@🛜≋) Epitomising Bodrum's white-and-sky-blue aesthetic from the outside, the relaxing 'Water Hotel' has 25 rooms and suites, most with balconies giving on to a courtyard pool, an Ottoman restaurant open to the skies and a bar. The colour scheme within (think blue and red and yellow) and artwork decorating the premises is just this side of kitsch but it works.

The suites have kitchenettes and hamam-style bathrooms. Can't find the place? Follow the blue tiles set in the pavement leading from Turgutreis Caddesi.

Marina Vista RESORT $$

(Map p258; ☎0252-313 0356, 0549 792 9613; www.hotelmarinavista.com; Neyzen Tevfik Caddesi 168; s/d ₺280/375; ❋🛜≋) From the impressive woodcarving in the reception and enormous pool in the courtyard to the terrace restaurant overlooking the marina and bar with leather stools, this mini-chain hotel with 92 rooms is a relaxing waterfront option in Bodrum. A spa and children's activities are also on offer.

Antique Theatre Hotel BOUTIQUE HOTEL $$

(Atik Tiyatro Oteli; Map p258; ☎0252-316 6053; www.antiquetheatrehotel.com; Kıbrıs Şehitler Caddesi 169; r €120-140, ste €160-180; ❋🛜≋) Taking its name from the ancient theatre across the road, this lovely place enjoys great castle and sea views, and has a big outdoor pool and pretty gardens. Original artwork and antiques adorn the 18 bright rooms, which each have an individual character and offer better value than the suites. Alas, it's on a very busy road.

Aegean Gate BOUTIQUE HOTEL $$

(☎0532 223 5089, 0252-316 7853; www.aegeangatehotel.com; Guvercin Sokak 2; s/d/tr €105/140/175; ❋🛜≋) About 2.5km southeast of the castle on a quiet hill above the cruise port, the Aegean Gate has six sparkling suites and a relaxing pool with bar. It may seem a bit out of the way, but it's just 50m from a 24-hour taxi rank, five minutes' walk from a dolmuş connection, and a 20-minute walk from Bodrum's main party strip.

Note that a minimum two-night stay is required.

Artunç Hotel PENSION $$

(Map p258; ☎0532 236 3541, 0252-316 1550; www.artuncotel.com; Fabrika Sokak 32; s/d €50/90; ❋🛜≋) A complete renovation in 2015 has turned a somewhat rundown former family home into a lovely little blue-and-white hotel, with blond-wood floors in the 12 rooms, rich blue carpet in the hallways, and hammocks swinging poolside under the lemon trees. We'll come back for the young owner's collection of bright-red model Ferraris under glass in the reception area.

Atrium Otel
HOTEL $$
(Map p258; ☑0252-316 2181; www.atriumbodrum. com; Fabrika Sokak 21; s/d ₺100/120; P❄️🛜🏊) One of Bodrum's oldest hotels and one that seems to go on forever, the Atrium has 57 plain but spacious rooms that are decent value for families and independent travellers. There's a pool (with separate kid's section), a poolside bar, two restaurants and table tennis. It's meant to look like an old Roman villa but we can't see that somehow.

Cumba Suites
HOTEL $$
(☑0532 336 2193, 0252-313 0517; www.cumasuites. com; Kumbahçe Pasatarlası; ste ₺150-200; ❄️🛜) Should you be looking to get away from it all on a budget but still be close to the water, choose this little place with three suites above a popular cafe and bistro. It's just up from the cruise port and well served by public transport. The suites are comfortable but basic. Two of them have balconies facing the sea.

★El Vino Hotel
BOUTIQUE HOTEL $$$
(Map p258; ☑0252-313 8770; www.elvinobod rum.com; Pamili Sokak; r/ste €185/235; ❄️🛜🏊) This beautiful 'urban resort' with 31 rooms is contained in several stone buildings spread over an enormous garden in the backstreets of Bodrum that you'd never know was there. Try for a room with views of both the pool/garden and the sea (eg room 303). The rooftop restaurant is one of the best hotel ones in Bodrum.

Try some of the vintner-owners' own wine (H6). There are two pools (including a shallow rooftop one), an outdoor jacuzzi and a daily shuttle at 11am to El Vino's private beach at Göltürkbükü on the peninsula.

Marmara Bodrum
LUXURY HOTEL $$$
(☑0252-999 1010; www.themarmara-bodrum-hotel.aspx; Suluhasan Caddesi 18; s/d from €270/290; ❄️@🛜🏊) The upmarket Marmara, high on a bluff, has spectacular views and 97 swish rooms – make sure you get one facing the right way! It's part of a five-star chain, and facilities include tennis, spa, gym and two pools. We love the photo portraits of Turkish country people adorning the corridors and the antique locks and keys on display.

A free shuttle accesses a private beach at Göltürkbükü on the peninsula. The rooftop has a big jacuzzi, two balconies and a private roof terrace for throwing your own all-nighter. Note that children under 12 are not allowed.

✖ Eating

Like all harbourside resorts, Bodrum's waterfront has pricey restaurants with multilingual menus (not always bad), but also discreet backstreet contenders, fast-food stalls and some excellent fish-market restaurants. Generally, eateries on the western bay are more upscale, while the eastern bay has more informal fare marketed to the patrons of the adjacent bars and nightclubs. Kebap stands are also found in the market hall, where the Friday fruit and veg market (Map p258; Külcü Sokak; ⊙7am-2pm Fri) takes place.

★Nazik Ana
LOKANTA $
(Map p258; ☑0252-313 1891; www.nazikana restaurant.com; Eski Hükümet Sokak 5; mezes ₺7-10, kebaps ₺11-20; ⊙8.30am-11pm) This simple back-alley place with the folksy, rustic decor offers hot and cold prepared dishes, viewable *lokanta*-style at the front counter, allowing you to sample different Turkish traditional dishes at shared tables. You can also order kebaps and *köfte*. It gets busy with workers at lunchtime, offering one of Bodrum's most authentic eating experiences.

Tepecik Döner
KEBAP $
(Map p258; ☑0252-313 3737; Neyzen Tevfik Caddesi 13; kebaps from ₺6-18; ⊙11am-1am) Across from the eponymous mosque, this favourite hole-in-the-wall does tasty kebaps on homemade bread, including the İskender (döner lamb on a bed of pide, topped with hot tomato sauce, melted butter and yoghurt) variety.

Bodrum Denizciler Derneği
CAFE $
(Bodrum Mariners Association; Map p258; ☑0252-316 1490, 0542 316 4835; www.bodrumdenizciler dernegi.com; İskele Meydanı 44; snacks & mains ₺5-13; ⊙7am-midnight) This mariners' club cafe attracts locals from *çay*-drinking sea dogs to young landlubbers nursing bottles of Efes Malt. Burgers, sausage and chips, *tost* (toasted sandwiches) and *kahvaltı* (breakfast) are served with a front-row view of the yachts and tour boats. Very friendly.

Gayıkcı KEBAP $

(Map p258; 0252-313 2842, 0532 271 8295; Cevat Şakir Caddesi 15/D; kebaps ₺8-22; 9am-2am) Clean and relatively cheap, this open-fronted *kebapçı* near the entrance to the fish market serves meat feasts including İskender kebaps.

★**Kalamare** SEAFOOD $$

(Map p258; 0544 316 7076, 0252-316 7076; www.facebook.com/kalamare48; Sanat Okulu Sokak 9; mezes ₺10-15, mains ₺18-35; noon-1am) Though a bit cramped and inland, this distressed-looking place, with whitewashed tables and pastel-coloured walls, is one of our favourite seafood restaurants in Bodrum. Serving octopus, calamari, sea bass et al (as well as meat dishes for ichthyophobes), Kalamare attracts a cool young crowd, who hold court beneath the extravagant, Gaudí-style chimney.

Red Dragon CHINESE $$

(Map p258; 0533 954 8334, 0252-316 8537; www.reddragon.com.tr; Neyzen Tevzik Caddesi 150; mains ₺18.50-40; 10am-midnight) Don't expect to be bowled over by the authenticity of the Chinese dishes here but if you're desperate for a fix of rice and/or noodles, Red Dragon can oblige. It has a huge terrace facing the marina.

Avlu MODERN TURKISH $$

(Map p258; 0252-316 3694, 0535 328 8441; www.avlubistrobar.com; Sanat Okulu Sokak 14; mains ₺25-48; 2pm-midnight) The 'Courtyard' is a bistro in an old stone house on a cobbled lane that offers seating in its eponymous courtyard or in an intimate dining room spread over two minute floors. It has a good wine selection and serves mostly updated Turkish dishes with some international ones thrown in to keep everybody happy.

Le Man Kültür CAFE $$

(Map p258; 0252-316 5316; www.lmk.com.tr; Cumhuriyet Caddesi 161; mains ₺21-38; 8am-midnight) Decorated with comic-book and street art, this cool Turkish chain – originally a refuge for artists and writers in İstanbul – is popular with students for its smoothies, coffees, cocktails and huge sea-facing terrace. It does snacks and meals including sandwiches, burgers, pizza (₺12.50 to ₺21) and *kahvaltı* (₺7 to ₺22)

Gemibaşı SEAFOOD $$

(Map p258; 0252-316 1220; Neyzen Tevfik Caddesi 132; mezes from ₺8.50, mains ₺28-35; noon-1am) A popular fish restaurant, the 'Ship's Captain' has open-air seating backed by an at-mospheric old stone wall. It faces the marina and gets very busy at night.

Fish Market SEAFOOD $$

(Map p258; off Cevat Şakir Caddesi; 10am-midnight) Bodrum's fish market (sometimes called *manavlar* for the fruit stands at the entrance to this small network of back alleys) offers a unique sort of direct dining: you choose between myriad fresh fish and seafood on ice at fishmongers' tables and, having paid there, bring them to any adjoining restaurant to have it all cooked for ₺15.

If in doubt, waiters can help you decide – options run from top-end catches to cheaper farmed fish. It should cost about ₺10 for enough farmed sea bass or bream for one, but few fishmongers will go that low and many will try to sell you a whole kilo (₺25). Sea fish costs from about ₺80 per kilo, so here and in all seafood restaurants, if you pay less than about ₺25 for a portion then you may be eating something that is not fresh or is from a farm.

The plain restaurants spill across the small streets, which get incredibly crowded and have little atmosphere, save maybe for the people-watching. If you can't decide which one, pick the busiest-looking place – locals are fiercely loyal to their favourites.

★**Orfoz** SEAFOOD $$$

(Map p258; 0544 316 4285, 0252-316 4285; www.orfoz.net; Zeki Müren Caddesi 13; set menus from ₺120, incl wine from ₺200; 7pm-1am mid-Jun–mid-Sep, 6pm-midnight Tue-Sun mid-Sep–mid-Jun) Often cited as one of Turkey's best fish restaurants, this restaurant next door to the landmark Zeki Müren Art Museum, named after one of Turkey's greatest singers, serves delectable seafood such as oysters with parmesan, smoked eel, baby calamari with onions and garlic, scallops, sea urchins and blue crab. Reservations are essential. Excellent selection of Turkish wines.

La Pasión SPANISH $$$

(Restaurante Español; Map p258; 0530 643 8444, 0252-313 4594; www.lapasionbodrum.com; Uslu Sokak 8; tapas ₺12-30, mains ₺30-60; 9am-midnight) For something different, head for this refined Spanish tapas bar and restaurant down a cobbled side street for tapas, excellent paella (₺80 to ₺100 for two) or pasta. The restaurant occupies an old Greek stone house, with tables among fig trees in a flowering courtyard and Spanish music wafting through the breeze.

Set three-course lunch menus (₺25), which change weekly and feature intricate mains and desserts, are available off season.

Musto INTERNATIONAL **$$$**
(Map p258; ☑0252-313 3394; www.mustobistro. com; Neyzen Tevfik Caddesi 130; mains ₺18-45; ⊙8am-midnight) This bar-restaurant does draught Guinness and pub food in arty surrounds, with its packed tables creating a busy bistro atmosphere. Dishes include pasta (₺17 to ₺35), burgers and cheese plates. Breakfast too.

🍸 Drinking & Entertainment

Bodrum's varied nightlife scene caters to its diverse clientele. The Turkish jet set fills the clubs on the harbour, while the foreign visitors frequent the loud waterfront bars and clubs of Bar St (Dr Alim Bey Caddesi and Cumhuriyet Caddesi). In high summer Bodrum becomes a 24/7 town, with many nightspots partying until dawn, and more bars and clubs pop up on the peninsula's beaches and coves.

Both the castle and ancient theatre host opera, ballet and rock performances; for upcoming event schedules and tickets, visit Biletix Ticketmaster (www.biletix.com).

White House CLUB
(Map p258; ☑0536 889 2066; www.facebook. com/WhiteHouseBodrum; Cumhuriyet Caddesi 147; ⊙9am-5am) This doyenne of Bodrum's party scene, approaching its third decade, has beachfront chill-out rattan sofas, a dance floor pumping with house music and blissed-out tourists.

Helva CLUB
(Map p258; ☑0533 652 7766, 0252-313 2274; www.facebook.com/helvabar; Neyzen Tevfik Caddesi 54; ⊙8pm-4am) Just a bit less snobby than nearby Küba, marine-themed Helva is also less frenetic but attracts a similarly slick Turkish crowd, lounging on the big glass-fronted terrace.

Moonlight BAR
(Map p258; ☑0536 860 7150, 0252-313 2085; www.moonlightbodrum.com; Cumhuriyet Caddesi 60/B; ⊙10am-2am) Opening right onto the beach, chilled-out Moonlight is a friendly hang-out off Bar St – great to meet people or just enjoy the castle views.

Körfez BAR
(Map p258; ☑0252-316 5966; Uslu Sokak 2) Not to be confused with a similarly named sea-food restaurant dating back to 1927, this un-pretentious old favourite with its face to the sea and back to town does rock, with a dark-wood atmosphere to match and alleyway seating. Happy-hour deals are offered.

Marina Yacht Club BAR
(Map p258; http://english.marinayachtclub.com; Neyzen Tevfik Caddesi 5; ⊙10am-2am) This big, breezy waterfront nightspot has four bars and offers live music most nights year-round. Merrymakers congregate at the tables dotting the water-facing deck; in winter the inside section by the port gates is more popular.

Küba CLUB
(Map p258; ☑0252-313 4450; www.kubabar.com; Neyzen Tevfik Caddesi 50; ⊙7pm-4am) Bodrum's poshest and most popular address for Turk-ish clubbers, Küba has all the plasma screens, disaffected DJs and laser beams one would expect. Its terrace bar-restaurant is a cool spot for a waterfront drink.

Kule Rock City LIVE MUSIC
(Map p258; ☑0555 824 8834, 0252-313 2850; www.kulebar.com; Dr Alim Bey Caddesi 55/B; ⊙11am-6am) This rock bar and club is grungy by Bodrum's standards, although there are still plenty of beautiful people on the outside decking. Two-for-one drink promotions are sometimes offered. There are great old motor-bikes on the walls and if anyone cares to shoot some hoops, there's a basketball net.

Halikarnas CLUB
(Map p258; ☑0252-316 8000, 0530 372 2985; www.halikarnas.com.tr; Cumhuriyet Caddesi 132) Touching the laser since 1979, this baccha-nalian party temple, complete with faux clas-sical columns and balconies, hosts DJs and carnival-like shows in its half-dozen lounges and outdoor stage. Jade Jagger designed its Secret Garden restaurant. Entry is typically ₺60 including a drink; book a table for ₺900.

Marine Club Catamaran CLUB
(Map p258; ☑0252-313 3600; www.clubcat amaran.com; Dr Alim Bey Caddesi 10; from ₺75; ⊙10pm-4.30am Jun-Sep) Europe's biggest floating disco, this party boat sails at 1.30am, keeping the licentiousness offshore for a good three hours. Its transparent dance floor can pack in 2000 clubbers plus attendant DJs. A free shuttle operates every 10 minutes to the eastern bay.

Mavi Bar LIVE MUSIC
(Map p258; ☑0252-316 3932; www.facebook. com/pages/Bodrum-Mavi-Bar/241401119308343; Cumhuriyet Caddesi 175) This tiny white-and-

EPHESUS, BODRUM & THE SOUTH AEGEAN BODRUM

blue venue stages live music most nights. It's busiest after 1am.

Shopping

Bodrum Market MARKET
(Map p258; Külcü Sokak; ⊙7am-2pm Fri) This dumpy white building hosts Bodrum's Tuesday clothes market, a treasure trove of fake T-shirts, textiles, watches and Atatürk paraphernalia, as well as the Friday fruit and veg market.

ℹ Information

Bodrum State Hospital (☑0252-313 1420; http://bodrumdh.saglik.gov.tr; Elmadağ Caddesi 33)

Tourist Office (Map p258; ☑0252-316 1091; Kale Meydanı 48; ⊙8am-noon & 1-5pm Mon-Fri, daily Jun-Oct)

ℹ Getting There & Around

There's an intracity dolmuş service (₺3), which frequently gets stuck in traffic. Central Bodrum's roads are busy, slow and mostly follow a one-way clockwise system – missing your turn means repeating the whole process.

Taxis start with ₺4 on the meter and charge ₺4.50 per kilometre, with no night rate. It costs about ₺12 to cross town. **Köşem Taxi** (☑0542 326 3312; Atatürk Caddesi) is honest and reliable. There are taxi stands at **Cevat Şakir Caddesi** (Map p258), **Türkkuyusu Caddesi** (Map p258) and at the **centre** (Map p258) and **west** (Map p258) ends of Neyzen Tevfik Caddesi.

Otoparks (car parks) around town cost from ₺5 for one hour, ₺30 for a day; there's an otopark in the east of town. Your hotel may be able to organise a free space nearby.

Bitez

☑0252 / POP 9725

Less hectic than Gümbet just east, Bitez (the closest resort town to Bodrum) is still a major centre of coastal nightlife in summer, and draws as many foreigners as Turks. However, it's an actual village, framed by lovely orchards, so it doesn't go into total hibernation in winter. The fine sandy beach, 2km below the village centre, is good for swimming and packed with umbrellas and loungers, satellites of the restaurants and cafes behind them.

In summer, Siesta Daily Boat Cruises (☑0535 920 5242; www.bitezbeach.com/siesta.htm; trips incl lunch & tea ₺50-70) offers day trips from the beach departing at 10am and returning around 6pm.

For some cultural edification, visit the ruins of Pedasa, signposted just before the turnoff to Bitez village on the D330 linking Bodrum with Turgutreis. A relic of the lost Lelegian civilisation that predated the Carians, this small site features defensive wall foundations and a number of chamber graves.

Sleeping

★ **Ambrosia** RESORT $$
(☑0252-363 792; www.hotelambrosia.com.tr; Yalı Caddesi; s/d incl half board from ₺220/300; ❀❧⊛) This E-shaped resort hotel hard by the beach impresses from the outset with its domed lobby and enormous crystal chandelier. The large pool set in a landscaped garden is a delight; the bar-library just off the lobby is an oasis out of the sun. The 106 rooms, done up in blue and light pine, are quite large, most with sea views.

BUS SERVICES FROM BODRUM OTOGAR

DESTINATION	FARE (₺)	DURATION (HR)	DISTANCE (KM)	FREQUENCY (PER DAY)
Ankara	75	12	689	3
Antalya	60	78	496	1 morning, 1 night
Denizli	35	5	250	3
İstanbul	90	12	851	4
İzmir	25	3½	286	hourly
Konya	70	12	626	1 morning, 1 afternoon
Kuşadası	25	3	151	1 evening
Marmaris (via Muğla)	36	31	160	hourly
Muğla	17	2	110	hourly
Söke	19	2½	125	hourly

There's a fully loaded spa with hamam. Best of all, the Ambrosia is open year-round. The brunch buffet from 10am to 2pm at the weekend is very popular locally.

Garden Life   RESORT $$
(☑0252-363   9870;   www.bitezgardenlife.com; Bergamut Caddesi 52; s/d incl full board & drinks €90/120; ❄🐾🌊) In the orchards surrounding Bitez on the coast road from Gümbet, various pools (a total of four), bars, a private beach and 176 pleasant rooms in cool whites and blues are all set in Garden Life's eponymous greenery.

3S Beach Club   RESORT $$
(☑0532 321 5005, 0252-363 8001; www.3sbeach club.com; Yalı Caddesi 112; s/d incl half board from ₺250/350; ❄🐾🌊) Overlooking Bitez from the western end of the beach, 3S has a poolside bar, private beach, hamam, sauna and fitness centre. Its 62 rooms are not particularly attractive but are reasonably spacious with TV, minibar and balcony.

🍴 Eating

Bitez has a few good eateries working year-round. On weekends, seafront restaurants' brunch buffets have become a local tradition.

Bitez Mantıcı   TURKISH $
(☑0252-363 0440; Atatürk Bulvarı 60; mains ₺10-15; ⊙10am-10pm) On a roadside terrace in the village, this unassuming place does excellent versions of Turkey's extended carbohydrates family, from *mantı* (Turkish ravioli) and *börek* to *gözleme*.

Black Cat   TURKISH $$
(☑0252-363 7969; Şah Caddesi 8/7; mezes ₺10, mains ₺23-33; ⊙8am-11pm) The amiable Ferhan's whimsical restaurant, decorated with holidaying children's pictures of cats, serves light meals by day and heartier fare at night. House specials are *özel* (special) kebap, featuring aubergine piled with meat and yoghurt, and *kadayıf* dessert (dough soaked in syrup and topped with a layer of clotted cream). Find it one block up from the beach.

Lemon Tree   MEDITERRANEAN $$$
(☑0252-363 9543; Sahil Yolu 28, Mart Kedileri; mains ₺27-40; ⊙8am-late) Right on the beach promenade next to the small Yalı Mosque, this hugely popular place marked by breezy white-and-green decor lets you eat, drink and enjoy at shaded tables or on its lounge chairs on the sand. There's an appetising blend of Turkish and Mediterranean fare (try the house 'Lemon Tree chicken' – a light take on sweet-and-sour chicken).

Even locals come for the ridiculously massive and varied buffet brunch (₺35, from 9.30am to 3.30pm on Sunday), while set three-course meals are a good deal at ₺42. It's a lively watering hole by night, too.

Ortakent

☑0252 / POP 8530

Ortakent is becoming more popular as the relentless wave of summer-home building continues to carve out the peninsula hillside with alarmingly uniform giant white cubes. For now, the view at sea level of Ortakent's broad blue bay remains largely unblighted by development. Its 3km-long **Fink Beach**, the peninsula's longest strand, is mostly the domain of packed lounge chairs by summer, but the water here is nevertheless among the peninsula's cleanest (and coldest), due to wave action. The eastern **Stone Beach** is quieter.

🛏️ Sleeping & Eating

Yilmaz Hotel   HOTEL $
(☑0252-358 5508; www.yilmazhotel.com; Zümrüt Sokak; d B&B/half board €75/90; ⊙Jun-Oct; ❄🐾🌊) Oceanfront Yilmaz offers 30 rooms with sea or garden view and aims to appeal to families, independent travellers and active holidaymakers, with surfing and sailing schools and boat tours nearby. Meals feature organic vegetables from the hotel garden and afternoon tea is served. A two-bedroom apartment is also available for longer stays.

Satsuma Suites   APARTMENT $$
(☑0252-348 4249, 5437 282 925; www.satsuma suites.com; Eren Sokak 17; s/d from €80/130; ❄🐾🌊) For those looking to escape the noise of Bodrum, these 10 luxe suites with elegantly appointed baths and fully equipped kitchens set around flowering trees and a welcoming pool near Fink Beach are ideal. And the breakfast is solid as well.

Ayana   SEAFOOD $$
(☑0252-358 6290, 0532 666 9277; www.ayana bodrum.com; Fink Beach; mezes ₺10-15, fish from ₺30; ⊙8am-11pm) This popular fish restaurant follows the peninsula custom of dining right on the sand, with a delicious range of home-cooked mezes and fish dishes to complement the local wine.

Kefi TURKISH $$$
(☑ 0252-348 3145; http://kefibodrum.com; Yalı Caddesi 38; snacks ₺12-15, mains ₺30-50) This fledgling resort's beachfront bar-restaurant serves a range of dishes, including *köfte, güveç*, burgers, seafood and local speciality *çökertme* (meat fried with thin french fries and slathered with garlicky yoghurt). A live Greek band plays two nights a week.

Turgutreis

☑ 0252 / POP 22,190

Once an important sponge-diving centre, Turgutreis has turned its sights on tourism, particularly longer-term villa and apartment rentals, and it offers 5km of sandy beaches, more than a dozen tiny islets just offshore and some logistical advantages. As the peninsula's largest town after Bodrum, Turgutreis has more services, shops, ferry and dolmuş links than its neighbours, and more concrete – the Saturday market resembles dusty middle Anatolia more than an Aegean retreat. Indeed, the waterfront statue of a colourful blue and green woman holding an olive branch is meant to represent the peacefulness and diversity of the Aegean region. It is one of the peninsula's more workaday places, and for short stays the prettier neighbouring villages are a better option.

In 1972 the village, then called Karatoprak, was renamed after Ottoman Admiral Turgut Reis, who was born here in 1485 and led many maritime battles before dying in the 1565 siege of Malta.

Gümüşlük

☑ 0252 / POP 4700

Accessed from the main Bodrum–Turgutreis road via a lovely side road through the hills, Gümüşlük has an escapist feel. It's good for a swim and a drink or meal of fresh fish at simple yet stylish eateries on the beach. Its authenticity has, however, made it more than a little precious, with local accommodation and restaurant prices rising to match the village's increasingly upscale visitors.

It's said that famed Carian King Mausolus built Myndos (which largely awaits excavation) due to its strategic position and harbour – indeed, the sea just north of Rabbit Island is very deep. Look straight across these waters beyond Sergeant Island (Çavuş Adası) to see two specks of rock, Kardak Islands (Imia in Greek), the ownership of which almost sparked a war between Greece and Turkey in January 1996, following gratuitous flag-planting exchanges and a more serious but brief Turkish commando occupation. Today, the area is strictly off limits.

A car park (₺5 per day) and ATMs are close to the main beach.

◎ Sights & Activities

Unlike the many fishing villages hijacked by modern tourism, Gümüşlük has thankfully been spared a lot of development because it lies around the ruins of ancient Carian Myndos. As a protected archaeological zone, the village legally cannot be built upon – at least not on the waterfront where the ruins disappear into the sea, continuing out to the facing Rabbit Island (Tavşan Adası), which can be reached on foot at low tide.

Victoria's offers horse riding (from ₺50 per hour), 15-minute pony rides (₺25) and lessons from an English-speaking coach.

🛏 Sleeping

Gümüşlük is relatively expensive, but family-run pensions still exist, as do vacation rentals. In all cases, book ahead.

Victoria's FARMSTAY $
(☑ 0532 137 0111, 0252-394 3264; www.victorias club.net; 1396 Sokak 4, Çukurbük; s/d from €60/90; ❄ 🤙 🐾) Making a refreshingly rustic change from Bodrum bling, this pastoral hideaway nestles between a farmyard and a private beach. Accommodation is in five well-equipped stilted cabins overlooking the stables, and packages including horse riding are available. The speciality of the restaurant (mains ₺25 to ₺40) is *levrek buğulama* (steamed sea bass stew).

Club Hotel Zemda RESORT $$
(☑ 0252-394 3151; www.clubhotelzemda.com; s/d from €80/110; ❄ 🤙 🐾) At the bay's southern end, this getaway with 30 rooms and suites in a Mediterranean mix of colours and sun-bleached white is good for activities, with sailing and windsurfing on offer. The bar-restaurant is sandwiched between the pool and beach.

Otel Gümüşlük HOTEL $$
(☑ 0252-394 4828, 0544 645 2661; www.otel gumusluk.com; Yalı Mevkii 28; s/d €100/120; ❄ 🤙 🐾) Away from the water, this two-storey, ranch-style hotel open year-round has 36 airy, minimalist rooms around a pool. It's a three-minute walk to the dolmuş stop and

the hotel offers two- to four-bedroom villa and apartment rental in Gümüşlük, Yalıkavak and Bitez.

✖ Eating & Drinking

Gümüşlük's atmospheric little beach restaurants and cafes are excellent for eating, drinking or just whiling away the time. At the beach's northern end, a line of waterfront fish restaurants has fantastic views of the glittering waves and Rabbit Island.

Self-caterers can greet the incoming fisherfolk on the docks (8am to 10am) to relieve them of some of their burden, otherwise destined for local restaurants (cash only).

Limon Aile Lokantası   SEAFOOD $
(☑0252-394 4010, 0554 740 6265; www.limon gumusluk.com; Gümüşlük Köyü; mains ₺15-20; ☺8.30am-8.30pm Oct-May) The 'Lemon Family Restaurant' brings a little of its hilltop associate's magic to town, offering a changing menu of open-tray meat and seafood dishes in casual, family-friendly surrounds.

Leleg   SEAFOOD $$
(☑0533 283 0679, 0252-394 4747; Gümüşlük Yalısı; mezes ₺10, mains ₺25-30; ☺9am-midnight) A seafront fish restaurant like so many others in Gümüşlük, but Leleg stands out in particular for the quality of its mezes and the friendliness of the proprietor. Always a warm welcome here. Try the sweetened *irmek* (semolina) for dessert.

Siesta   TURKISH $$
(☑0532 326 6521, 0252-394 3627; Gümüşlük Yalısı; mezes ₺10, mains ₺25-30; ☺9am-2am) Commanding pride of place at the start of the restaurant parade along Gümüşlük Yalısı, Siesta serves fish and meat dishes in similar proportions and ample portions. Friendly staff too.

★ Limon   SEAFOOD $$$
(☑0544 740 6260, 0252-394 4044; www.limon gumusluk.com; Kardak Sokak 7; mezes ₺10, mains ₺30-50; ☺9.30am-2am Apr–mid-Oct; ⁄) In the hills above Gümüşlük, Limon sprawls across a series of garden terraces around a whitewashed farmhouse, overlooking a Roman bath and Byzantine chapel ruins. Dishes include seafood and carpaccios, while vegetarians will love the unique, olive oil–soaked mezes such as stuffed zucchini flowers and the house take on *sigara böreği* (deep-fried cigar-shaped pastries).

Ali Riza'nin Yeri   SEAFOOD $$$
(☑0505 652 8987, 0252-394 3047; www.balikcial irizaninyeri.com/; Gümüşlük Yalısı; mains from ₺8, mains ₺25-45; ☺8am-midnight) Serving expertly prepared fresh fish since 1972, this waterfront classic is run by a local fishing clan whose boats floats nearby. With eight different types of rakı to choose from, the business of feasting on fish is taken extremely seriously here.

Mimoza   SEAFOOD $$$
(☑0252-394 3139; www.mimoza-bodrum.com; Gümüşlük Yalı; mezes from ₺15-40, mains ₺30-50; ☺9am-2am Apr-Oct) Posh Mimoza, on the beach's north end, has cheery white tables perched above the sea, with boats bobbing in the secluded bay opposite. It does a good variety of seafood mains and mezes, including house specials calamari *köfte* and green mussels with cheese. It's popular with well-heeled Turkish visitors. Book ahead for evening dining.

Jazz Cafe   BAR
(☑0252-394 3977; http://gumusluk.com/en/r/ jazz-cafe; Çayıraltı Halk Plajı 21) This come-as-you-are beach bar, founded by jazz greats Cengiz Sanli and Mete Gurman in 2008, hosts live jazz and blues on weekend nights.

Yalıkavak

☑0252 / POP 14,160

A former fishing and sponge-diving village, Yalıkavak has played up its relative remoteness from Bodrum to attract a more exclusive Turkish clientele. However, it hasn't escaped the holiday-home-construction craze, and is known too for its upmarket private beaches, including popular Xuma Beach Club and Dodo Beach Club. Its marina keeps the village relatively lively out of season.

In mid-September the recently relocated Sunsplash Festival (http://sunsplash-festival. com) offers an eclectic mix of electronic, world and jazz DJs and musicians on Xuma Beach.

◉ Sights

Dibeklihan Culture & Art Village   GALLERY
(Dibeklihan Kültür ve Sanat Köyü; ☑0532 527 7649; www.dibeklihan.com; Çilek Caddesi 46/2, Yakaköy; ☺May-Oct) In the all-but abandoned village of Yakaköy just off the road between Yalıkavak and Ortakent, this complex contains an art gallery, cinema, shops, the Dibek Sofrası restaurant and an exhibition with Ottoman antiques such as jewelled daggers, antique fountain pens and ornate

coffee cups collected by the owners. Don't miss it.

🛏 Sleeping

4 Reasons Hotel BOUTIQUE HOTEL $$
(📞 0252-385 3212; www.4reasonshotel.com; Bakan Caddesi 2; s/d/tr/q from €170/190/255/300; ❄@🛜🏊) This friendly hillside retreat features 20 self-described 'nu-bohemian' rooms with lots of little designer touches and fine locally sourced marble fixtures. The garden is a venue for bocce, massage, yoga and Pilates, and the poolside bistro serves Aegean flavours with views of Yalıkavak Bay and what are arguably the best sunsets in Aegean Turkey.

Sandima 37 APARTMENT $$$
(📞 0252-385 5337, 0530 330 0637; www.sandima37suites.com; Atatürk Caddesi 37; ste €235-395; ❄🛜🏊) On the hillside road into town, Sandima 37's seven stylish suites are set around a lush garden with sweeping views of the marina and surrounding headlands. The restored stone cottage by the pool with its own spa bath has the most ambience. The staff are welcoming and full of restaurant recommendations and advice.

🍴 Eating

Yalıkavak runs pretty much year-round and day trippers will always find at least a few restaurants open. Geriş Altı, the western district towards Gümüşlük, is the place for the day's fishing catch. Yalıkavak's market, the most colourful on the peninsula, takes place on Thursday at Çınaraltı, 10 minutes' walk inland from the seafront.

Le Café ITALIAN, INDIAN $$
(📞 0532 362 3909, 0252-385 5305; www.lecafebodrum.com; İskele Caddesi 33; mains ₺20-30; ⊙ noon-midnight Mon-Fri, 10am-12.30am Sat, 10am-midnight Sun) This Indian-owned Italian/Indian restaurant is everything to everyone, serving up pizza, pasta and the house speciality, chicken parmigiana, with as much aplomb as it does pakoras, samosas and tikka masala. Ask nicely and they'll make you Turkish too. Davendra is both an expert chef and a charming host. The waterfront location is sublime.

Özmasa ANATOLIAN $$
(📞 0532 221 9099, 0252-385 3107; www.ozmasabodrum.com; İskele Meydanı; mains ₺19-35; ⊙ 9am-11pm) Run by a family from Gaziantep, Özmasa specialises in Anatolian dishes such as *testi kebabı* (lamb with onions and mushrooms cooked in a sealed terracotta pot) and *halep*

işi kebap (spicy minced beef with yoghurt and hot tomato sauce). Homemade pide, *tuzda balık* (fish baked in salt), lamb shank and organic *köy kahvaltısı* (village breakfast) are also offered.

Yalı Kıyı SEAFOOD $$
(📞 0530 920 1113, 0252-385 4143; İskele Meydanı 37/A; mezes ₺10, mains ₺25-35; ⊙ 8am-11pm) This seafood restaurant is as popular for its waterfront location with its incomparable views westward as its fresh fish dishes and mezes.

Gündoğan

📞 0252 / POP 7565

Placid Gündoğan Bay, deepest on the the Bodrum Peninsula, offers a sandy beach with good swimming right in the centre and stays relatively sedate at night. Most of its part- or full-time occupants in the villas climbing halfway up the hills on both sides are well-off retirees from İstanbul or Ankara who, despite their secularist proclivities, have not been able to get the local imam to turn down the volume at the mosque – about the only noise that could jolt you out of bed here.

Settlement here probably began around AD 1100, though an earlier Roman town, Vara, had existed nearby. In 1961 the village's original Greek name (Farilya) was changed to Gündoğan.

Although Gündoğan gets little attention on the historical-tour circuit, its back hills contain **Lelegian rock tombs**. A 15-minute boat trip from town, **Apostol Island**, also called Little Rabbit Island (Kücük Tavşan Adası), is crowned by a fairly well-preserved 9th-century **Byzantine church** with frescoes. Ask locally to arrange trips.

🛏 Sleeping & Eating

Chichi new hotels are springing up on the western side of the bay, offering private beaches and decks.

Villa Joya APARTMENT $
(📞 0536 238 3819; www.villajoyabodrum.com; Kızılburun Caddesi 34/A; 4-person villas €90; ❄🛜) One of a few family-run businesses renting to self-caterers in Gündoğan, Villa Joya offers three apartments with kitchens and lovely gardens. While each apartment sleeps four, there's only one master bedroom (the other two beds are pull-out sleepers in the living room). Still, the kitchens are fully equipped and the price is hard to beat.

Costa Farilya
RESORT $$$

(☑0252-387 8487; www.costafarilya.com; Yalı Mevkii 62; r €105-335; ❄🅿🛜🏊) Making a change from the peninsula's ubiquitous white cubes, the 70 rooms in this self-proclaimed 'special class hotel' are in ubermodern grey blocks, some formed of crushed stone behind metal grilling. Rooms are muted, with hardwood floors, a grey-and-white colour scheme, low-slung beds and dramatic views across the bay from those with balconies.

Facilities include a spa, stunning infinity pool and bar, fitness centre, various restaurants and biweekly yoga.

★Plaj Cafe Restoran
SEAFOOD $$

(Terzi Mustafa'nin Yeri; ☑0252-387 7089, 0535 925 0912; www.terzimustafaninyeri.com; Atatürk Caddesi 10; mezes from ₺8-10, mains from ₺25; ⊗8am-midnight) Just opposite the central waterfront, this local favourite run by a fishing family serves a good range of mezes and mains, marine and otherwise. There's no noise save for the wind, the waves and the caged birds chirping – ideal for those seeking great food and quiet conversation, whether they call it the 'Beach Cafe' or 'Tailor Mustafa's Place'.

Fish prices starts around ₺20 for marinated sea bass, a cold meze, but grilled fish mains are the house speciality.

Göltürkbükü

☑0252 / POP 4800

The reputation of Göltürkbükü – an amalgam of neighbouring villages Türkbükü and Gölköy – as Aegean Turkey's poshest beach getaway is kept alive by the celebrities, politicians and business moguls who flock here from İstanbul and Ankara each summer. Better beaches may exist elsewhere on the peninsula, but Göltürkbükü offers an opportunity for a meal and cocktail in style.

Even in a place where women go to the beach in high heels, sporting diamond-encrusted sunglasses, tongue-in-cheek reminders of social divisions remain; the tiny wooden bridge between the two halves of the main beach is jokingly said to divide the 'European side' from the 'Asian side' – a reference to İstanbul, and an insinuation of the wealth gap between the ultraposh homes and hotels on the western shores, and the ever-so-slightly less-expensive ones to the east. These days, in the words of one local hotelier, with the chi-chi resort town's increasing beautification, it's more a case of 'Europe' and 'Eastern Europe'.

---

❶ HOLIDAY RENTALS

Villa rentals can be great value, particularly for longer stays on the peninsula, with fully furnished apartments available by the day, week and month. Rentals are available in villages including Gümüşlük, Turgutreis and Gündoğan. For villa rentals, check out such websites as www.bodrum-exclusiveholidayrentals.com, www.bodrumresidence.com.tr and www.bodrumvillarentals.com.

🛏 Sleeping

Göltürkbükü's accommodation is unsurprisingly pricey, but you'll certainly have some interesting neighbours. Note that the summer clubs keep things loud until late.

Villa Kılıç Hotel
HOTEL $$

(☑0252-357 8118; www.villakilic.com; 36 Sokak, Gölköy; s/d from €120/180; ❄🛜🏊) Just 1km south from the centre of Türkbükü, Villa Kılıç Hotel in Gölköy offers 33 lavishly designed rooms with hardwood floors and marble accents. There's a big pool and good restaurant, or you can recline on Gölköy's largest bathing platform (300 sq metres), where DJs play and beach parties take place in summer.

Maçakızı
LUXURY HOTEL $$$

(☑0533 642 5976, 0252-311 2400; www.macakizi.com; Narçiçeği Sokak, Türkbükü; r incl half board from €495; ❄🛜🏊) Ground zero for Göltürkbükü's chic summer crowd and the last hotel on the inner bay, this luxurious Australian-owned place with 74 rooms combines a resort feel with boutique trimmings and minimalist decor. Rooms, all with balcony or terrace, are huge and some have glassed-in showers with sea views. There's a sociable restaurant, a lively bar and huge hamam and spa.

No:81 Hotel
BOUTIQUE HOTEL $$$

(☑0530 266 8490, 0252-377 6105; http://no81hotel.com; Mimoza Sokak 10, Türkbükü; r from €280; ⊗mid-May–Oct; ❄🛜🏊) Popular with İstanbul's movers and shakers, the family-run No:81 is an ongoing party during summer, with a big wooden deck for lounging on throw pillows; pool and beach bars; and a club extending over the water. The 49 rooms and suites have arty elements such as Plexiglas chairs and original paintings on the walls. Warm welcome, friendly service.

EPHESUS, BODRUM & THE SOUTH AEGEAN GÖLTÜRKBÜKÜ

LifeCo
RESORT $$$

(☑ 0543 819 2084, 0252-377 6310; www.thelifeco.com; Bağarası Caddesil 136, Türkbükü; s/d incl detox from €235/420; ✳ @ 🤖 ≋) The Göltürkbükü branch of LifeCo Well-being Centres offers a cleansing environment for detox programs, with 30 rooms and orange and mandarin trees lining its cool walkways. One- to 21-day packages are available, as is a one-day program without accommodation (€135). There's a 14-room LifeCo Beach charging the same prices on the waterfront.

Kuum
LUXURY HOTEL $$$

(☑ 0533 688 8233, 0252-311 0060; www.kuumhotel.com; Atatürk Caddesi 150, Türkbükü; r incl half-board from €600; ✳ 🤖 ≋) A hit with the Turkish elite, this stylish haven offers accommodation in brown cubes on grassy terraces, creating the dreamy feel of a 1960s science-fiction film. This impression continues in the 64 suites measuring 40 to 80 sq metres, where modern green wire-woven chairs mix with the luxury of glass-walled bathrooms and astonishing sea views.

Facilities include a private beach, spa, classical domed hamam and waterside restaurant.

Divan
HOTEL $$$

(☑ 0252-377 5601, 0530 405 9218; www.divan.com.tr; Keleşharim Caddesi 22, Türkbükü; r from €250; ✳ 🤖 ≋) This 60-room hotel on a hillside above the beachfront hotels is set in a large garden with pool, spa and treatment centre. About a dozen rooms have balconies facing the sea. The strange wooden atrium linking the reception lobby and guestrooms is unique.

5 Oda
BOUTIQUE HOTEL $$$

(Beş Oda; ☑ 0252-377 6219; www.otel5oda.com; İnönü Caddesi 161, Türkbükü; r €250-300; ⊙ May-Oct; ✳ 🤖) 'Five Rooms' offers exactly that, and its small size ensures personal service. The eclectic boutique spot has breezy, sea-facing rooms and a striking natural stone-and-wood design. The in-house Mediterranean restaurant is very popular.

✕ Eating & Drinking

Deluxe hotels have excellent (and exorbitantly priced) restaurants, while others are clustered by the waterfront. Book ahead.

Miam
INTERNATIONAL $$$

(☑ 0252-377 5612; Atatürk Caddesi 51/A, Türkbükü; mezes ₺10-25, mains ₺34-52; ⊙ 8.30am-midnight) Recommended locally, this small restaurant with waterfront tables is a good place to take a break from seafood. Options include deli and cheese plates, lamb chops and filet mignon with gorgonzola, cream or pepper sauce.

Garo's
SEAFOOD $$$

(☑ 0252-377 6171; www.garosturkbuku.com; 83 Sokak 9, Türkbükü; mezes ₺15, mains ₺30-50; ⊙ 9am-midnight) Local favourite Garo's is pricey but popular for its mezes in particular. The owner-chef serves seafood and meat dishes such as bonfile (sirloin steak) at white-and-blue tablecloths under dangling lights and open Aegean skies.

Ship Ahoy
COCKTAIL BAR

(☑ 0252-377 5070; Yalı Mevkii, Türkbükü; ⊙ 11am-2am May-Oct) Nothing says power and prestige like understated Ship Ahoy: essentially just a wide dock extending over the water, it's the antithesis of the lavish nightclub concept of entertainment, and the first port of call for Türkbükü's richest and most famous summer guests. Visit just for the experience.

Torba
☑ 0252 / POP 2500

Despite being just 6km northeast of Bodrum, Torba has stayed quieter and more family-oriented than most other places on the peninsula. It has a nice beach, but lacks the seclusion of places on the peninsula's more distant corners and has a more workaday feel.

🛏 Sleeping

Izer Hotel & Beach Club
RESORT $$

(☑ 0549 367 1755, 0252-367 1910; www.izerhotel.com; İsmet İnönü Caddesi 87; per person incl full board, drinks & activities from €75; ⊙ May-Oct; ✳ 🤖 ≋) Popular with package tourists, this well-run resort has a waterfront pool and one with giant slides and and a bar almost as long as the Bodrum Peninsula. Choose between 120 smaller rooms in the family-oriented club area, where numerous activities are offered and children are well taken care of, and the 70 larger and quieter rooms in the garden villas.

This is a cheery, colourful place to bring the family, and also boasts tennis courts and its own amphitheatre complete with shows.

★ Casa Dell'Arte Residence
BOUTIQUE HOTEL $$$

(☑ 0252-367 1848; www.casadellartebodrum.com; İsmet İnönü Caddesi 64-66; ste €450-950; ✳ 🤖 ≋) Staying at this exquisite 'house of art and leisure' with a dozen different suites, owned by an art-collecting Turkish family, is like visiting the home of an eminent curator. Modern art and antiques decorate the flowing interior and sculptures stand around the pool – the artistic environment even includes the odd installation, a library of art books and gallery tours.

Luxuries such as an outdoor jacuzzi in the garden, a spa complete with treatments, and tennis courts have not been overlooked and you can upgrade to a three-bedroom stone villa (€1600) or yacht (from €2000).

Casa Dell'Arte Village　　　RESORT $$$
(📋0252-367 1848; www.casadellartebodrum. com; İsmet İnönü Caddesi 64-66; ste incl half board €300-550; ✴🏵📶🏊) As children under 12 are not allowed at the Casa Dell'Arte Residence, families are catered for at this 36-suite resort, with such features such as a children's pool and an atelier to get kids' creative juices flowing. Children under six stay free and those under 12 for €40.

Eating

The resorts are awash in eateries though you'll find kebap houses in the village and fish restaurant on the beach.

Gonca Balık　　　SEAFOOD $$
(📋0252-367 1796; www.goncabalik.com; Mutlu Sokak 15; mezes ₺12-15, fish from ₺30; ⊗9am-11pm) With cheery orange and blue tables strung along the sand and looking to the ebbing waves, this friendly place is Torba's spot for a meal of mezes and fresh fish.

Eastern Peninsula
📋0252
The bays southeast of Bodrum are less well known than those to the west, in some cases because hotels have swallowed them whole. Inland, the villages and lanes are quiet and rustic, but the area lacks the overall atmosphere and appeal of the peninsula proper.

🛏 Sleeping

Hapimag Sea Garden Resort　　　RESORT $$
(📋0252-311 1280; www.hapimag-seagarden.com; Yalıçiftlik; per person incl full board & drinks €150; ⊗May-Oct; ✴@🏵📶🏊) The sprawling 19-hectare Hapimag Sea Garden is both a 285-room hotel open to the public and a time-share resort with lots of Swiss guests. It offers everything you could desire between three turquoise bays: two beaches, a fully loaded wellness centre, restaurants serving food from Italian to Turkish, a nightclub with huge

golden Buddha, and lots of watery fun for children.

Kempinski Barbaros Bay　　LUXURY HOTEL $$$
(📋0252-311 0303; www.kempinski-bodrum.com; Kızılağaç Köyü; s/d from €400/450; ⊗Apr-Sep; ✴🏵📶🏊) Bodrum's branch of the famed German hotel chain is cradled within a sea-facing cliff, isolated from any outside disturbances, with its own private beach and docks. The 173 ubermodern rooms have all of the expected amenities (as well as balconies with sea views), and there are five restaurants in season, three bars, a complete spa centre and hamam.

The real marvel here is the massive infinity pool, possibly Turkey's largest, with minaret-like lamps thrusting upward and an adjacent all-wood chill-out area featuring hanging greenery and lounge beds. The hotel is popular with families, offering daily children's activities and a kids club in summer.

MARMARIS & AROUND

Marmaris
📋0252 / POP 33,760
A popular resort town that swells to over a quarter-million people during summer, Marmaris is loud, brash and in your face all over town all of the time. It's one of the few places along the coast where you might leave feeling more stressed out than when you arrived.

That said, if it's a last night out, a *gület* cruise along the coast or a ferry to Greece you're after, then this tourist haven is pretty much the full Monty. Bar St offers unparalleled decadence, while from the *kordon* (promenade), charter-boat touts will happily whisk you eastward to Fethiye and beyond. Marmaris boasts a pretty harbour, crowned by a castle and lined with wood-hulled yachts and the vessels of visiting sailors. And it even has history. It was from here that Britain's Admiral Horatio Nelson organised his fleet for the attack on the French at Abukir in northern Egypt in 1798.

◉ Sights & Activities

Marmaris Castle & Museum　　　CASTLE
(Marmaris Kalesi ve Müzesi; Map p276; ₺8; ⊗8am-7pm Apr-Oct, to 5pm Nov-Mar) Marmaris' hilltop castle (1522) was Süleyman the Magnificent's rallying point for 200,000 troops, used to recapture Rhodes from the Knights Hospitaller.

Marmaris

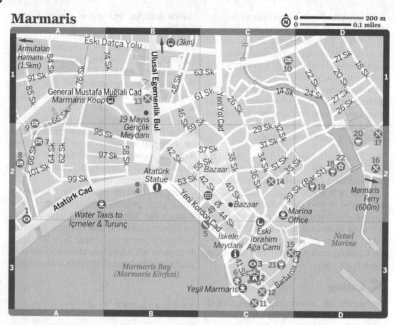

N
0 — 200 m
0 — 0.1 miles

Marmaris

◎ Sights

1 Jinan Garden	A2
2 Marmaris Castle & Museum	C3
3 Old Town	C3

◉ Activities, Courses & Tours

4 Black Pearl	B2
5 Professional Diving Centre	C3
6 Yeşil Marmaris	C3

⊜ Sleeping

7 Barış Motel	A2
8 Halıcı Hotel	A2
9 Maltepe Pansiyon	A2
10 Marina Apart Otel	C1

⊗ Eating

11 Aquarium Kitchen Cafe	C3

12 Fellini	C3
13 Köfteci Ramiz	B1
14 Meryemana Mantı Evi	C2
15 Ney	C3
16 Pineapple	D2
17 Rota	D2

⊜ Drinking & Nightlife

18 B52	D2
19 Bar St	D2
20 Kahve Dünyası	D2
21 Panorama Restaurant & Bar	C3

⊛ Entertainment

22 Davy Jones's Locker	D2

The castle hosts small **Marmaris Museum**, which exhibits amphorae, tombstones, figurines, oil lamps and other finds from surrounding archaeological sites, including from Knidos and Datça. Saunter along the castle's **walls** and **ramparts** and gaze down on the bustling marina.

Old Town HISTORIC SITE
(Map p276) The hilly streets around Marmaris Castle, atmospheric lanes that feel far removed from the yacht-filled marina, contain the city's last remaining traditional buildings.

Jinan Garden GARDENS
(Map p276; Atatürk Caddesi) This Zen-style garden, complete with a pagoda and soothing water, commemorates Marmaris' Chinese twin city, Jinan in Shandong province. There's also a restaurant here.

Armutalan Hamamı HAMAM
(☑0252-417 5374; www.armutalanturkishbath.com;
515 Sokak, off Yeni Datça Yolu/D400; bath & scrub
₺50, with oil massage ₺80; ☉9am-7pm Apr-Oct)
The enormous, full-serve 'Pear Field Bath'
is west of the big government hospital and
near a Kipa supermarket (2km west of the
centre). The complex boasts four hamams,
swimming pool, sauna and massage rooms.
It's quietest in late afternoon as the tour
groups are gone.

Call for a free pick-up; blue number 4 dolmuşes also get there from 19 Mayıs Gençlik
Meydanı (₺3).

Beaches
Marmaris' narrow, pebbly town beaches
allow decent swimming, but much better
are İçmeler and Turunç (10km and 20km
southwest, respectively). From late April
to October, water taxis (Map p276) serve
İçmeler (₺12.50, 30 minutes, half-hourly)
and Turunç (₺15, hourly, 50 minutes).

Dolmuşes by 19 Mayıs Gençlik Meydanı
also access İçmeler (₺3), Turunç (₺7) and
the beach at Günlücek Park, a forest park
reserve 3.5km southeast of Marmaris.

Boat Trips
Marmaris Bay day trips (₺35 to ₺40 including lunch, soft drinks and pick-up) offer
eye-opening views and inviting swimming
holes. Boats offering these trips (usually
from 10.30am to 4.30pm May to October) are
practically bumping into one another on the
docks, but Black Pearl (Map p276; ☑0535 549
2605, 0538 633 0863; Atatürk Caddesi) is reliable.
Before signing up, confirm all details (exact
boat, itinerary, lunch etc). 'All-inclusive' (including beer) costs ₺50 to ₺60.

Hiring a yacht, together with a group of
friends or with random new ones, offers the
pleasure of a blue cruise down the coast.
Cruises offered by Yeşil Marmaris (Map
p276; ☑0252-412 6486; www.bluevoyageyachts.
com; Barbaros Caddesi 13; 8- & 12-berth per day
€1500, 16-berth €1900, half/full board per person
€30/45) are recommended; as for the rest,
compare prices, ask around and negotiate.
Yeşil offers seven- to 10-day itineraries taking
in the Turquoise Coast or the Datça Peninsula
and Rhodes. Dalyan is a popular destination
for shorter trips.

Diving
Several dive boats moored opposite Ziraat
Bank on Yeni Kordon Caddesi offer excursions
and courses from April through October.

As with the numerous cruises, many boats
operate, so choose carefully; equipment,
insurance, lunch and pick-up are normally
included. Since diving is potentially more
life-endangering than lounging on a yacht,
ask whether the company is licensed by the
Turkish Underwater Sports Federation. Also,
ask whether your dive leader will be a certified instructor or 'assistant instructor' – the
latter often being a simple deckhand in scuba
gear, not ideal for safety. And be sure to report
any medical conditions beforehand.

Professional Diving Centre DIVING
(Map p276; ☑0533 456 5888; www.prodivingcen
tre.com; Yeni Kordon Caddesi) Offers excursions
(₺100 including two dives and lunch) and a
four-day Professional Association of Diving
Instructors (PADI) Open Water course (€300).

🛏 Sleeping
The preponderance of package tourists, who
usually stay in large beach hotels out of town,
means that good central options are limited.

Barış Motel PENSION $
(Map p276; ☑0534 650 7374, 0252-413 0652;
www.barismotel.com; 66 Sokak 16; s/d excl breakfast €20/26; ❋ 🛜) The sleepy 'Peace' has nine
spartan but clean rooms and a front patio.
Breakfast is €3. It's on the east side of the
canal running down to Atatürk Caddesi. Not
to be confused with Barış Hotel & Apart, located in a different part of town.

Maltepe Pansiyon PENSION $$
(Map p276; ☑0252-412 1629; www.maltepepansi
yon.com; 66 Sokak 9; s/d/tr/q ₺50/100/150/200;
❋🛜) The shady garden where guests can
drink *elma çay* (apple tea) under a grape
arbour is just one of the attractions of this
22-room pension, a backpacker's favourite
for decades. Rooms are small but spotless,
and the friendly manager Mehemt (Memo)
goes out of his way to help. A self-catering
kitchen is available, as are cheaper rooms
with shared bathroom.

Marina Apart Otel APARTMENT, HOTEL $$
(Map p276; ☑0252-412 2030; www.marinaapar
totel.com; Mustafa Kemal Paşa Sokak 24; d/q
€35/40; ❋@🛜▨) The 10 hotel rooms and 40
self-catering apartments for up to four people are bare but quite good value, each with
the full complement of cooking implements,
cutlery, sofa and balcony. There's a cafe-bar
in reception and a neighbouring bakery for
provisions. Rates include breakfast, and hotel

services such as Dalaman Airport transfers (€50) are available.

Halıcı Hotel
HOTEL $$$

(Map p276; ☑0252-412 3626; www.halicihotel. com; Çam Sokak 1; s/d from €60/120; ☺Apr-Oct; ❄❂❀) The bread and butter of the 'Carpet Seller Hotel' is package tours so expect to find every possible facility – from pools and bars to a landscaped tropical garden – at this enormous, 174-room facility. To find it, follow the canal up from the sea. Judging by the notices from management, they do their best to keep the volume at sociable levels.

✖ Eating

Beware of the few unscrupulous harbourside restaurants that offer a free bottle of wine with meals, and then recoup their outlay by charging for bread, service and so on.

Meryemana Mantı Evi
TURKISH $

(Virgin Mary Mantı House; Map p276; ☑0542 662 4863, 0252-412 7855; 35 Sokak 5/B; mains ₺6-15; ☺7.30am-11pm) In addition to *mantı*, the bizarrely named 'Virgin Mary Mantı House' serves *gözleme* as well as ready-made prepared *etli yemek* (meat dishes) and *sebzeli yemek* (vegetable dishes). It's a good place to try some Turkish classics.

★ Ney
TURKISH $$$

(Map p276; ☑0252-412 0217; 39 Sokak 324; mezes ₺10, mains ₺21-32; ☺noon-midnight) Tucked away up some steps from the western end of the marina is this tiny but delightful restaurant in a 250-year-old Greek stone house with Bugül at the stove. Decorated with seashells and wind chimes, it offers delicious home cooking such as *tavuklu mantı* (Turkish ravioli with chicken), *et güveç* (meat casserole) and wonderful mezes.

Köfteci Ramiz
KÖFTE $$$

(Map p276; ☑0532 441 3651; www.kofteciramiz. com; General Mustafa Muğlalı Caddesi 5/A; mains ₺15-40; ☺9am-midnight) At lunchtime, local suits queue for this long-established *köfte* chain's salad bar (₺7.50), not to mention the award-winning *köfte*, kebaps and other grills. Meal deals abound. Founded by two brothers from Macedonia, it's been here since 1928.

Pineapple
INTERNATIONAL $$$

(Map p276; ☑0252-412 0976; www.pineapple.com. tr; Netsel Marina; mains ₺28-45; ☺8am-midnight) As close as you'll get to the marine without falling in. Pineapple is a two-storey restaurant with an enormous upstairs balcony and equally large front terrace. Pizzas, pastas and salads (₺16–₺32) take the lion's share of the menu but there are more substantial seafood dishes and grills.

Rota
KEBAP $$$

(Map p276; ☑0252-413 0584, 0555 374 6585; Netsel Marina; mains ₺12.50-45; ☺7am-11pm) Safely removed from Bar St, at the far end of the shopping centre across the bridge, 'Ship's Course' serves meat dishes, pides and salads in a covered outdoor setting.

Aquarium Kitchen Cafe
INTERNATIONAL $$$

(Map p276; ☑0252-413 1522; Barbaros Caddesi 55; mains ₺28-48; ☺9.30am-2am) One of the cooler and more creative eateries on the waterfront, Aquarium has an eponymous fish tank behind the bar, women's shoes on the tables, a chess set made of piping, and salsa music. Large grills and steaks are offered, while the lunch menu features lighter meals including fish and chips, wraps and pizzas.

Fellini
ITALIAN $$$

(Map p276; ☑0252-413 0826; Barbaros Caddesi 71; mains ₺25-45; ☺8am-1am) With cheery yellow chairs and faux flower arrangements, this popular waterfront restaurant now in its 25th year serves great thin-crust pizzas, pasta, seafood, steaks and kebaps.

▯ Drinking & Entertainment

Marmaris by night offers more neon than Vegas, and almost as many drunks certain they're just one shot away from the big score. Away from the infamous debauchery of Bar St, there are quieter spots for drinks and harbour views, including the the more tranquil waterfront bar-restaurants lining Barbaros Caddesi and the marina.

Bar St
STREET

(Map p276; 39 Sokak) This raucous stretch of licentiousness is dominated by big, bold and brassy bar-club complexes that spill out onto the street. If you like laser beams, dance music, liquored-up louts, tequilas by the half-dozen and tattoo parlours, this is for you. The major action takes place between Eski İbrahim Ağa Cami and the Netsel Marina footbridge. Most bars open from 7pm to 4am.

As the night wears on, the street becomes a veritable cacophony, as each place tries to drown out its neighbours by cranking up the volume. Beers cost ₺15, shooters ₺5 to ₺10 and cocktails ₺15 to ₺20. Happy hours, free shots and buy-one-get-one-free incentives are offered, but there's no guarantee that 'name-brand' spirits will be authentic.

Heading east from the Eski İbrahim Ağa Cami, you first come to a strip of Türkü Bars and *meyhanes* (taverns), playing live Turkish folk and *fasıl* (Ottoman classical music); worth a stop to see how Turks unwind over a few milky glasses of *rakı*. These peter out around the marina office and the Ibiza beats and fluorescent shooters begin.

B52   CLUB
(Map p276; ☑ 0252-413 5292; 39 Sokak 120) The split personality B-52 comes in two parts: a boisterous club on one side and a chilled cocktail bar with outside seating on the other.

Kahve Dünyası   CAFE
(Map p276; ☑ 0252-412 9600; www.kahvedunyasi.com; Günücek Yolu, Netsel Marina; ⊙ 8am-midnight) This chain cafe, resembling the Left Bank of the Seine in comparison with tacky Bar St across the bridge, is a relaxed spot for coffee and cake.

Panorama Restaurant & Bar   BAR
(Map p276; ☑ 0252-412 8961; Hacı İmam Sokağı 40; mains ₺25-35; ⊙ 9am-1am) The marina-view terrace in this spot just off 26 Sokak is more famous than the food, but it's still a nice place for sunset drinks and nibbles.

Davy Jones's Locker   LIVE MUSIC
(Map p276; ☑ 0252-412 1510; 39 Sokak 156) This two-floor place on the far side of Bar St is Marmaris' only rock bar, with '90s American and Brit music especially well-represented. Live bands in summer.

❶ Information

Tourist Office (Map p276; ☑ 0252-412 1035; İskele Meydanı 2; ⊙ 8am-noon & 1-5pm Mon-Fri mid-Sep–May, daily Jun–mid-Sep) Exceptionally helpful tourist offices dispenses maps and solid information.

❶ Getting There & Around

AIR
The closest aiports are Dalaman (95km southeast) and Milas-Bodrum (130km northwest). Havaş (www.havas.net/en) runs a shuttle bus to/from Dalaman International Airport (₺15, 1½ hours). Otherwise, **Marmaris Koop** (Map p276; ☑ 0252-413 5542; www.marmariskoop.com; General Mustafa Muğlalı Caddesi) has hourly buses to Dalaman town (₺15, 1½ hours), from where you can catch an expensive taxi to the airport.

BOAT
From late April to October, daily catamarans serve Rhodes (one way/same-day return/open return including port tax €42/42/68, one hour) from the pier 1km southeast of Marmaris, departing in both directions at 9.15am and 5pm. There are also sporadic departures between March and May. Greek catamaran companies also serve this route, but are generally 10% more expensive.

Travel agencies, including **Yeşil Marmaris** (Map p276; ☑ 0252-412 1033, 0533 430 7179; www.rhodesferry.com; Barbaros Caddesi 13; ⊙ 9am-11.30pm) in town and **Marmaris Ferry** (☑ 0252-413 0230; www.marmarisferry.com; Mustafa Munir Elgin Bulvarı, Marmaris Cruise Port) at the Marmaris Cruise Port a couple of kilometres to the southeast, sell tickets. Book ahead at least one day and bring your passport. Be at the ferry dock one hour before departure for immigration formalities. Some agencies provide free hotel pick-up for same-day return passengers.

BUS
Marmaris' small otogar is 3km north of the centre. Dolmuşes serve it along Ulusal Egemenlik Bulvarı frequently in summer. Bus-company offices line General Mustafa Muğlalı Caddesi (between 19 Mayıs Gençlik Meydanı and 84 Sokak) in the city centre; some companies provide a *servis* between here and the otogar. Destinations include:

Antalya (₺60, 6¼ hours) Daily with Kamil Koç and Pamukkale.

Bodrum Catch a dolmuş to Muğla (₺15, one hour) and then the bus to Bodrum (₺20, two hours).

Fethiye (₺25, 3¼ hours) Hourly Marmaris Koop buses via Dalaman town and Göcek.

İstanbul (13 hours) A few daily year-round with Metro (₺90) and Pamukkale (₺100) among others.

İzmir (4¼ hours) Hourly with Metro (₺30) and Pamukkale (₺40) among others.

DOLMUŞ
Regular dolmuşes run down to the bay from near the northern end of 19 Mayıs Gençlik Meydanı opposite Migros.

Datça & Bozburun Peninsulas

If it is a less frenetic experience you're after, head for the rugged peninsulas that jut out from Marmaris and stretch for over 100km into the Aegean Sea. The western arm is called the Datça (sometimes called Reşadiye) Peninsula; its southern branch is called the Bozburun (or Loryma) Peninsula.

This is spectacular, raw Turkish coastline, seen from a bus, bike, boat or even a scooter.

Aside from the joy of sailing near the peninsula's pine-clad coasts and anchoring in some of its hundreds of secluded coves, visitors come to explore fishing villages, mountain towns, wee hamlets and epic ruins such as Knidos at the tip of the Datça Peninsula.

Datça

🗩 0252 / POP 13,000

Some 70km from the regional centre of Marmaris, down a winding road dotted with both traditional windmills and 21st-century wind turbines, Datça is the peninsula's major harbour town. Given its seaside location, it's surprisingly workaday but that lends it a certain laid-back authenticity.

Datça makes a pleasant base for seeing the area, with a string of waterside restaurants that spill onto the beach once the weather turns warm. You might prefer nearby Eski Datça (Old Datça; p282), which has preserved the traditional feel that Datça has lost. Off season, however, Datça is a better choice, as many businesses in the neighbouring village shut their doors.

Datça has three small but lovely beaches: Kumluk Plajı (Sandy Beach), tucked behind the main street, Atatürk Caddesi; Hastanealtı Plajı (literally 'Below the Hospital Beach'), the bigger strand hugging the northern shore; and Taşlık Plajı (Stony Beach) at harbour's end to the south. Behind it is is a large natural pool fed by underground hot springs.

Excursions boats and travel agencies including Karnea Travel Agency (p281) and Bora Es Tour (🗩 0252-712 2040, 0532 311 3274; www.boraestour.com; Yat Limanı) offer day trips from Datça harbour (from ₺50, including lunch and soft drinks), which often take in the ruins at Knidos (p282).

🛏 Sleeping

Budget pensions are available on or just off Atatürk Caddesi and above the harbour near Cumhuriyet Meydanı, the main square. Renting villas and apartments in Datça or nearby villages can be good value; check locally.

Tunç Pansiyon   PENSION $$
(🗩 0252-712 3036; www.tuncpansiyon.com; İskele Mahallesi; s/d/apt ₺100/150/200; ❋ @ 🛜) This terrific in-town pension is down a street off the roundabout; look for the Öğür taxi stand and Vestel shop. It's basic but spotless, featuring 22 sunny rooms with balconies and a fabulous rooftop deck. The friendly owner

Metin offers a free laundry service and car excursions for up to three to Knidos – you're charged just for the petrol (about ₺60).

⭐ Villa Tokur   BOUTIQUE HOTEL $$$
(🗩 0252-712 8728; www.hoteltokur.com; Koru Mevkii; d/ste €85/115; ❋ 🛜 ⊠) This Turkish-German-owned hilltop hotel with well-groomed grounds overlooking the sea and a large swimming pool offers 15 nicely furnished rooms. It's a 10-minute walk uphill from Taşlık Plajı and feels more like a home than a hotel.

Ulrikes Haus   PENSION $$$
(🗩 0539 970 1207, 0252-712 2931; www.ulrikeshaus.com; Akkaraca Sokak 20; s/d €60/85; ❋ 🛜) This small but perfectly formed pension just minutes from both the centre of the town and the beach has but three guestrooms, two with balconies facing the sea. The well-informed Turkish-German owners also operate the Culinarium restaurant (p281) on the way to the harbour so half-board options are available.

Konak Tuncel Efe   HOTEL $$$
(🗩 0252-712   4488;   www.konaktuncelefe.com; Atatürk Caddesi 55; s/d from €65/85; ❋ @ 🛜) İznik tiles and exposed walls abound in this purpose-built building, with a feeling of age created in the 20 rooms by a mix of modern and vintage furniture. The cool and shadowy lobby has a bar, scattered sofas and tables piled with books, while the penthouse family mansard rooms have skylights in their sloping ceilings.

Kumluk Otel   HOTEL $$$
(🗩 0252-712 2880; www.kumlukotel.com; Atatürk Caddesi 39; s ₺130-150, d ₺250-300; ❋ 🛜) Behind the harbourside cafe-bar of the same name, the Kumluk has 25 surprisingly modern rooms with long mirrors, glass-fronted fridges and flat-screen TVs. The decor attractively mixes white with flashes of primary colours and there's a glassed-in terrace to have breakfast in.

🍴 Eating

Away from fish dishes in all their guises, a speciality enjoyed in the region includes *keşkek* (lamb mince and coarse-ground wheat).

Zekeriya Sofrası   TURKISH $$
(🗩 0532 468 9997, 0252-712 4303; Atatürk Caddesi 70; dishes from ₺10; ⏱ 8am-11pm; 🍽) The pre-prepared and made-to-order dishes in this bright eatery on the main drag allow a great-value sampling of Turkish home cooking. The steam trays contain all sorts

of meat and vegetable creations from as far afield as Şanlıurfa, where the owner's family hails from, including the house speciality *borani* (lamb with yoghurt and chickpeas) from Antakya.

★ **Culinarium**   MEDITERRANEAN $$$
(✑ 0252-712 9770, 0539 970 1207; www.culinarium-datca.com; Yat Limanı Mevkii; mains ₺40-60; ☺ 10am-midnight Mar-Nov) The three-course menu (₺65) is a gourmet experience at this Turkish-German restaurant, its wraparound bar gazing at Bozburun and Symi. Favourite dishes are zucchini flowers stuffed with fish and prawns and a boneless fillet of fish (three or four types brought in daily) with light dressing. Desserts are largely based on Datça's famous almonds; the semifredo with almonds and chocolate being one example.

★ **Café Inn**   CAFE $$$
(✑ 0534 1169, 0252-712 9408; http://cafeinn datca.com; Atatürk Caddesi 51; mains ₺18-30; ☺ 9am-midnight) With its nose poking into the surf from Kumluk Plajı, this breezy and chilled hang-out with beach-house furniture serves a decent cappuccino and dishes from a full range of *dolmades* (stuffed grape leaves) to *börek* and pizzas (₺18 to ₺25). The talented chef can prepare just about anything; try the *keşkek* speciality or breakfast (₺16) with four preserves and fruit plate.

Küçük Ev   SEAFOOD $$$
(✑ 0533 550 0578, 0252-712 3266; www.kucukevres taurant.com; Yat Limanı; mezes from ₺8, mains ₺30-50; ☺ 8am-11pm) This decades-old and stylish harbourside eatery called the 'Little House' serves Mediterranean and seafood dishes including yellowtail or swordfish *şiş* (skewers) and such exotics as goat (order in advance).

Mayistra   ITALIAN $$$
(✑ 0252-712 2822; www.facebook.com/Mayistra Datca; Kumluk Yolu Sokak 14; mains ₺15-35; ☺ 8.30am-midnight; ⌁) This welcome Italian eatery on the seafront serves a wide range of pizza, pasta, antipasti and salads. It also offers a good wine selection.

🍺 **Drinking & Nightlife**

Roll Coffee House   BAR
(✑ 0252-712 2266; Atatürk Caddesi 94/A; ☺ 9.30am-3.30pm) A very welcome addition to Datça's night scene is this misnamed beer house with 90 different types of brew from around the world. Perched in a tiny shop high above the marina, Roll is in the hands of

owner Hüseyin, as welcoming a host as you'll find anywhere in Turkey.

Eclipse Music Bar   BAR, CLUB
(✑ 0532 424 2896, 0252-712 8321; www.facebook.com/Eclipse-Music-Bar-137610333066079; Atatürk Caddesi 89; ☺ 3pm-3am May-Oct) Offering happy-hour discounts from 3pm to 11pm, Eclipse's outside deck is a great spot for a sunset beer. Inside, beneath exposed beams, pop-art superheroes overlook the dancefloor. Live music on Saturday evening.

🛍 **Shopping**

Many shops along Atatürk Caddesi sell local produce and products such as figs, *lokum* (Turkish delight), honey and honeycomb, *helva* (a sweet made from sesame seeds), many types of prepared olives and herbs.

Özlü Datça   FOOD & DRINKS
(✑ 0252-712 3335; www.datcabalbadem.com; Atatürk Caddesi 72/H; ☺ 9am-11pm) Datça's three main products – almonds, honey and olive oil – are sold here in copious quantities.

ℹ **Information**

Karnea Travel Agency (✑ 0252-712 8842; www.karneaturizm.com; Atatürk Caddesi 54/B) Run by the helpful Beycan Uğur, Karnea provides local info, books Turkish Airlines flights, organises transfers, rents out cars and scooters, and runs local trips.

ℹ **Getting There & Away**

BUS

Hourly summer dolmuşes serve Marmaris (₺15, 1¾ hours, every two hours in low season) from the **Pamukkale office** (✑ 0252-712 3101; Atatürk Caddesi). The bus from Marmaris drops you on the main street, 500m before the square and harbourside pensions. Turkey's major bus companies, such as **Metro** (✑ 0252-712 9087; Atatürk Caddesi, Datça) and **Ulusoy** (✑ 0252-712 8292; Atatürk Caddesi 25; ☺ 8am-10pm), all have offices on Atatürk Caddesi, and offer daily departures to cities throughout western Turkey, but Marmaris bus station offers many more.

BOAT

Bodrum Ferries link Datça with Bodrum four times a day between June and September (twice a day in October). Buy tickets (one way/return ₺35/60, car/bicycle one way ₺105/10) and confirm times at the **Bodrum Ferryboat Association** (✑ 0252-316 0882, 0252-712 2323; www.bodrumferryboat.com; Turgut Özal Meydanı; ☺ 9am-8pm) in central Datça. Arrive at the office 30 minutes before departure for the *servis*

KNIDOS

What remains of **Knidos** (kuh-nee-dos; ₺10; h8am-7pm Apr-Oct, to 5pm Nov-Mar), a once-prosperous Dorian port city dating to 400 BC, lies scattered across 3km of the Datça Peninsula's tip. Steep hillsides, terraced and planted with groves of olive, almond and fruit trees, rise above two idyllic bays where yachts drop anchor and a lighthouse perches dramatically on a headland.

The peninsula's unpredictable winds meant that ancient ships often had to wait for favourable winds at Knidos (also known by the Latinised name, Cnidus); this boosted the ship-repairs business, hospitality and general trade. St Paul, en route to Rome for trial in AD 50 or 60, was one of many maritime passengers forced to wait out the storm here.

Although few of the ancient buildings are easily recognisable, the city paths are well-preserved. Don't miss the round **temple of Aphrodite Euploia**, which once contained the world's first free-standing statue of a woman. The 8000-seat Hellenistic **lower theatre** and the **sundial** from the 4th century BC comprise other ancient attractions, as do the remnants of a Doric **stoa** with a cross-stone balancing precariously on top and some fine carvings in what was once a **Byzantine church**.

The on-site **restaurant** at Knidos is only open in summer – it's worth a stop more for the great views than the overpriced food.

Knidos is a one-hour drive from Datça, along a winding and scenic road. Hiring a car or scooter allows you to detour onto the back roads on the peninsula's southern coast. Datça Koop ([icon]0252-712 3101; near Cumhuriyet Meydanı, Datça) will take up to three people to Knidos and back, with one hour's waiting time, for ₺150.

From June to August, Palamutbükü dolmuşes (₺10) leave from next to the **Metro bus office** (p281) for Knidos at 10.30am and noon, returning at 3.30pm and 5pm.

Datça harbour excursion boats also visit Knidos in summer, leaving around 9.30am and returning by 7pm and cost from ₺50 including lunch and soft drinks. Datça's **Karnea Travel Agency** (p281) offers this tour for ₺60 and a day trip by land for ₺85.

(shuttle bus) to Körmen harbour at Karaköy (5km northwest of Datça). If staying in Eski Datça, with prior notice the *servis* can pick you up on the main road.

Rhodes and Symi At the time of writing, regular ferries were not running from Datça. Greek ferries usually make day trips from the islands to Datça on summer Saturdays; Greece-bound passengers can return with them. In summer, operators such as **Seher Tour** ([icon]0252-712 2473, 0532 364 5178; www.sehertour.com; Atatürk Caddesi 88/E) offers day trips to Symi, charging about €75 to €100 per passenger with a minimum of six to eight passengers.

CAR & MOTORBIKE

Karnea Travel Agency (p281) Rents out cars (one day petrol/diesel ₺100/110) and scooters (one day ₺50).

Eski Datça

[icon]0252 / POP 8000

'Old Datça', capital of an Ottoman district stretching into what is now Greece, is much more atmospheric than its newer counterpart, Datça (p280). Its cobbled lanes wend beckoningly between whitewashed stone houses draped with bougainvillea, providing a blissful escape into the untroubled coast of yesteryear.

[icon] Sleeping & Eating

Olive Farm Guesthouse   INN **$$$**
([icon]0252-712 4151; http://guesthouse.olivefarm.com.tr; Güller Dağı Çiftliği, Reşadiye; s €60-75, d ₺80-120; ⊗May-Oct; [icons]) This stylish country retreat has 13 pastel-hued rooms and suites with bright bedding, rustic furnishings and its own branded olive-based toiletries. The mix of children's playroom, garden hammocks and artistic decoration creates the feel of a farm designed by Antoni Gaudí. Find it in Reşadiye, 2km north of Eski Datça.

Eski Datça Evleri   BUNGALOW **$$$**
(Old Datça Houses; [icon]0252-712 2129; www.eskidatcaevleri.com; s/d/tr from €80/120/160; [icon]) These purpose-built bungalows called Fig, Almond and Olive are built in traditional fashion, with thick stone walls keeping the heat from their white interiors. Inside are hamam-style bathrooms and small kitchens, while the courtyard cafe is a rustic hang-out.

Fig is closest to the centre; Almond and Olive 100m up the hill.

Datça Sofrası
TURKISH $$

(☑ 0252-712 4188; Eski Datça; mezes ₺8, mains ₺15-20; ⊙ 9am-midnight) This terrace restaurant beneath a vine-clad arbour serves good mezes and grilled-meat dishes, including house speciality *bademli köfte* (meatballs with local almonds).

🛍 Shopping

Olive Farm Mill Store
FOOD & DRINKS

(☑ 0252-712 8377; www.olivefarm.com.tr; Güller Dağı Çiftliği, Reşadiye; ⊙ 8.30am-9pm) Set amidst seemingly endless olive groves, this farm shop offers tastings of its olives and first-press oil, jams and vinegars distilled from anything you can think of – fig, orange, carob etc. It does an excellent line of olive oil–based toiletries and cosmetics. It's in Reşadiye, 2km north of Eski Datça.

ℹ Getting There & Away

In summer dolmuşes run hourly to/from Datça (₺2.50), 2.5km south. Eski Datça is just 100m from the main road, so you can get off the dolmuş from Marmaris at the turn-off and walk.

Selimiye
☑ 0252 / POP 1190

Popular with yachtspeople, this one-time traditional boat-building village is today little more than a lovely waterfront promenade of restaurants, pensions and bars on a calm bay. The price of land here is rising though, along with accommodation and restaurant charges, and the village is slowly starting to resemble the chichi Bodrum Peninsula.

Between June and September, boats offer **day cruises** around the bay, stopping at beaches for swimming, for about ₺55 including lunch and drinks.

The mountainous, deeply indented Bozburun Peninsula is the perfect place to escape the madness of Marmaris. For a real off-the-beaten-track adventure, kickstart a motorbike or scooter and roll down the winding country roads, into a natural paradise and villages that modernity forgot. From Marmaris, take the coast road to İçmeler and then wind through the hills to Turunç, Bayırköy, Söğüt and Bozburun, returning via Selimiye, Orhaniye, Hisarönü and the main Datça–Marmaris road – a circuit of about 120km.

🛏 Sleeping

★ Jenny's House
PENSION $$$

(☑ 0252-446 4289, 0507 667 8155; www.jennys house.co.uk; Selimiye Köyü Mahallesi; s ₺120-200, d ₺200-280; ❄ 🐾 🖵) Across the road from the harbour, this charming pension counts 14 different types of rooms surrounding a lush garden. A couple of rooms give on to the pool in the centre, but we prefer the two doubles on the 1st floor with a large shared balcony. Affable Briton Jenny and her Turkish brother-in-law Salih can also help with holiday rentals.

Two family rooms can accommodate four people.

Losta Sahil Ev
BOUTIQUE HOTEL $$$

(☑ 0252-446 4395, 0530 762 9740; www.losta sahilevi.com; Gemecit Mahallesi 9; s/d ₺200/400; ⊙ Apr-Nov; ❄ 🖵) This lovely boutique hotel is housed in two separate stone buildings on the waterfront about 100m apart. The 13 pastel-hued rooms are named after Greek and Lydian gods and goddesses, are ample-sized and some have small sea-facing balconies. We love the large sunny deck at the end of a short pier and the relaxing bar close at hand.

Sardunya Bungalows
BUNGALOW $$$

(☑ 0252-446 4003; www.sardunya.info; Selimiye Köyü Mahallesi; s/d ₺150/300; ❄ 🖵) Selimiye's anchor inn has 15 family-friendly rooms in stone 'bungalows' behind the beach, with a lovely garden and popular seafront restaurant. Rooms have dark, chunky furniture and up-to-date bathrooms. Some (eg room 16) are positively enormous.

🍴 Eating & Drinking

Paprika
DESSERTS $$

(☑ 0252-446 4369; Buruncuk Mevkii 80; desserts ₺10-16; ⊙ 8am-1am Apr-Oct) The name and the Julius Meinl shop sign outside this tiny gleaming-white cottage facing the marina might have some thinking they'd arrived in Macarıstan (Hungary). Not quite... This all-Turkish establishment focuses on desserts, with some 30 different calorific and inventive ones served up daily.

S.U.P.
TURKISH $$

(☑ 0555 363 2345, 0252-446 4048; www.facebook. com/supselimiye; Hanımpınar Mevkii 3; mezes ₺10-15, mains ₺23-40) This new waterfront restaurant-cafe serves locally sourced 'gourmet fast food' – *ızgara* (grilled) dishes like *köfte* and chicken *şiş* – village bread and homemade lemonade. But its real raison d'être is to rent out stand-up paddle boards (₺25 per hour) –

now you get the name – for use in the calm waters just in front.

Bülent'in Mutfağı
AEGEAN $$$

(Bülent's Kitchen; ☑ 0533 326 7575; Buruncuk Mevkii 103; mezes ₺8-12, mains ₺25-35; ☺ 9am-midnight May-Oct; ☑) From a tiny kitchen next to Migros supermarket at the marina, Bülent serves al fresco diners cuisine that combines the joys of home cooking with İstanbul-style mezes. Go for any of a dozen olive oil–drenched goodies including quince, celery, okra, broad bean, eggplant and zucchini, and don't miss the speciality: fish pie cooked with milk from İzmir.

Aurora
SEAFOOD $$$

(☑ 0252-446 4097; Buruncuk Mevkii 36; mezes ₺10-20, mains ₺20-40; ☺ 9am-midnight May-Oct) Set in an antique stone house on the seafront, Aurora is serious about mezes and seafood. Some 50 mezes are produced every day, along with a multitude of fish mains and charcoal-grilled steaks. Hosts Hüseyin and Suzanne are affable, helpful and multilingual.

Piano Jazz Bar
BAR

(☑ 0252-446 4086; www.facebook.com/pages/PIANO-JAZZ-BAR/430764627022582; Sahil Yolu; ☺ 7pm-2am Jun–mid-Sep) A pianist and singer perform in this cool blue-and-white 'dive bar' (their words, not ours) on the waterfront. It's jazz, Latin… Whatever takes their fancy.

ℹ Getting There & Away

Dolmuşes between Marmaris (₺12, one hour) and Bozburun stop in Selimiye every two hours on the main road at the village's northern end.

Bozburun

☑ 0252 / POP 2050

Bozburun (Grey Cape), a 30km drive down the Bozburun (or Loryma) Peninsula from the Marmaris–Datça road, retains its rustic farming, fishing and gület-building roots, though tourism (mostly from visiting yachts) has arrived too. It's an agreeable spot far from the masses, with some excellent accommodation, and you can swim in brilliantly blue waters just around the harbour to the west from the rocks (just watch out for sea urchins). Local charter boats venture into the idyllic surrounding bays. Market day is Tuesday.

🛏 Sleeping

Pensions line the waterfront south of the marina. Accommodation is snapped up by Turkish tourists in July and August, so book ahead.

Pembe Yunus
PENSION $$

(Pink Dolphin; ☑ 0536 250 2227, 0252-456 2154; www.bozburunpembeyunus.com; Cumhuriyet Caddesi 131; s/d incl half board from ₺120/240; ❄ 🛜) Located 700m southeast of the marina, the 13-room 'Pink Dolphin' is a friendly place, with white interiors, bleached wooden floors, mosquito nets and shared terraces (room 12) or little balconies (room 5) enjoying vast sea views. Dinner is enjoyed at the water's edge, and the hotel has a boat for trips to the Greek island of Symi across the bay.

Yilmaz Pansiyon & Apart
PENSION $$

(☑ 0537 046 2410, 0252-456 2167; www.yilmazpansion.com; İskele Mahallesi 391; s/d/apt from ₺120/150/230; ❄ 🛜) Around 500m southeast of the marina, this friendly pension offers six simple but cheerful rooms in an older building and 11 two-bedroom self-catering apartments – No 3 is a favourite – with kitchens and balconies in a newer one. All rates include breakfast served on a vine-covered terrace just metres from the sea. The Yilmaz also arranges local boat cruises.

★ Sabrinas Haus
LUXURY HOTEL $$$

(☑ 0252-456 2045; www.sabrinashaus.com; d incl half board €425-1170; ☺ May-Oct; ❄ 🛜 ☷) Reached by the sea – a skipper picks up guests in a speedboat – or on foot in a half-hour along the bay's eastern shore, Sabrinas Haus is the ultimate pamperific place. There are 17 individually designed rooms and suites (think lots of natural woods, shades of white, antiques and four-poster beds) in three buildings hidden in a beautiful mature garden.

The infinity pool, seafront deck and thatched bar at the end of a pier are all super; the spa offers myriad massages and treatments; and activities include cruises to Symi on the hotel's own 88ft gület Miss Austria and candle-lit picnic barbecues on a neighbouring island. Note that there is a minimum two-night stay (three nights June to September), and children under 14 aren't allowed.

✕ Eating

Papatya Lokantası
TURKISH $

(☑ 0537 384 9579; Cumhuriyet Caddesi; mains ₺6-8; ☺ 7.30am-11pm) Locals pile into this friendly little lokanta next to the mosque for çorba (soup), kebaps and unfussy, well-prepared Turkish favourites.

Kandil Restaurant
SEAFOOD $$

(☑ 0252-456 2227, 0532 626 2392; Kordon Caddesi 41; meze ₺7-10, mains ₺15-30; ☺ 7am-11pm Mar-Nov)

EPHESUS, BODRUM & THE SOUTH AEGEAN DATÇA & BOZBURUN PENINSULAS

This waterfront local favourite serves cheap mezes and various fish dishes and grills. Obviously aiming at water-starved sailors, the 'Oil Lamp' will even throw in a free shower.

Osman's Place/
Gordon Restaurant   STEAK $$$
(☑ 0252-456 2144, 0533 369 4988; www.gordon restaurant.com; Kordon Caddesi; mains ₺25-45; ☉ 7am-1am Mar-Nov) One of the more reasonably priced waterfront options, this double-moniker restaurant offers Lavazza coffee, shop-made cake and a range of Turkish and international mains. Steaks, the owner-chef's speciality, include T-bone, Mexican and pepper. The Turkish-Scottish owners are lovely hosts.

Bozburun Restaurant   SEAFOOD $$$
(☑ 0537 679 9451, 0252-456 2420; Kordon Caddesi; mezes ₺6-10, mains from ₺25; ☉ 8am-11pm Apr-Oct) A favourite of Bill Gates, who visited in 2006, this decades-old restaurant has a great harbourside location near the customs office and lighthouse, with outside seating to enjoy it. Dozens of different mezes are prepared every day and the house specials include grilled and fried calamari, grilled octopus and *saç kavurma* (stir-fried cubed meat dish).

Aperitif   SEAFOOD $$$
(☑ 0252-456 2616, 0532 211 9680; www.facebook. com/aperitif-bozburun-334850373221133/; Kordon Caddesi; mains ₺22-40; ☉ 8.30am-midnight) Arguably the most stylish eatery in Bozburun, Apertif is in the heart of the marina and serves excellent breakfast (₺12 to ₺16), pizza and Turkish dishes. The terrace facing the sea is the place to be seen.

ⓘ Getting There & Away

Six daily dolmuşes serve Marmaris (₺12, 1½ hours) via Selimiye, with a couple of extra services in summer.

Bozburun Transfer (☑ 0252-456 2603, 0535 749 0113; www.marmaristransfer.biz; Atatürk Caddesi 10; 1-3 people from ₺200) does transfers to/from Dalaman International Airport (2½ hours).

Akyaka
☑ 0252 / POP 2670

A refreshing change from boisterous Bodrum to the west and maddening Marmaris to the south, the laid-back village of Akyaka (White Shore) lies tucked between pine-clad mountains and a grey-sand beach at the far end of the Gulf of Gökova. It's especially popular with well-heeled Turkish tourists from İstanbul and İzmir.

At the mouth of the Azmak river, Akyaka was the second town in Turkey to join the Cittaslow (Slow City) movement and has resisted unsightly development, with half-timbered houses built and restored in 'Ula-Muğla' Ottoman style by the late architect Nail Çakırhan. Confusingly, Akyaka is sometimes also called Gökova, which is an older township located several kilometres inland.

The road from Muğla crosses the Sakar Pass (Sakar Geçidi; 670m), offering breathtaking views of the sea.

🏃 Activities

Blue Flag Akyaka Beach in the centre is good for swimming, and Çinar Beach, 2km to the northwest, has deep water for snorkelling. In summer the fishing cooperative offers boat tours (₺30 to ₺40 including lunch) to local beaches, bays and Cleopatra Island, which has bright golden sand and Hellenistic and Roman ruins. Year-round boat trips glide up the lovely Azmak (₺8, half-hour) over waving strands of green waterweed.

Orange Kiteboarding Center   KITESURFING
(☑ 0536 498 0317; www.orangekiteboarding.com; Gökova Kitesurf Beach; equipment hire half/full day €40/70, 8hr beginners' course €360) Akyaka gets steady summertime winds, making it ideal for windsurfing and kiteboarding and an excellent spot to learn either sport. Six operators offer equipment rental and tuition on Gökova Kitesurf Beach, a 25-minute walk over the Azmak and south of the village. Orange Kiteboarding Center is the major player here, offering kiteboarding instruction and full rental. Private lessons cost €70 per hour.

Free Wheelies   CYCLING
(☑ 0544 800 4011; www.gokova.com/profile/ free-wheelies; Karanfil Sokak 28/A; road bikes per hour/day from ₺5/20, mountain bikes ₺10/40; ☉ 9am-10pm) Hires out road and mountain bikes and recommends trails up the beach or into the hills.

Gökova Rüzgar Sports Center   WATER SPORTS
(☑ 0252-243 4217, 0252-243 5108; www.gokova ruzgar.com; Hamdi Yücel Gürsoy Sokak 4; kiteboard hire per day ₺180, 8-/12-hr course €350/550; ☉ 9am-7pm Apr-Oct) Hires out equipment and gives lessons for sea kayaking, canoeing and stand-up paddle boarding on Akyaka Beach in front of the landmark Yücelen Hotel.

ℹ️ **HOLIDAY APARTMENTS**

Numerous holiday apartments are available for rent in Akyaka. Contact Captain's Travel Agency (📞 0532 326 6094, 0252-243 5398; info@captains-travel.com; Negriz Sokak; ❄️🛜) or Tomsan Okaliptus (📞 0252-243 4370; www.tomsanokaliptus. com; Türkoğlu Sokak 8; ❄️🛜🏊).

🛏️ Sleeping

Akyaka Kamp CAMPGROUND $
(📞 0551 448 7034, 0252-243 5156; www.akyaka kamp.com; Akyaka Beach; campsites per tent/caravan ₺35/40, d/tr/q bungalow excl breakfast ₺150/200/225, stone cottage excl breakfast ₺350; ❄️🛜) At the western end of Akyaka Beach, this campground has tent pitches, bungalows and stone cottages accommodating up to five on a hill overlooking the beach as well as a lovely cafe-bar.

★ **Big Blue Otel** HOTEL $$
(📞 0252-243 4544; www.bigblueakyaka.com; Sanat Sokak 6; d/ste from €60/105; ❄️🛜) Six rooms hard by the sea with a 'Cape Cod' feel courtesy of white walls and stripy cushions... The ground-floor rooms are spacious and have terraces while three middle rooms have balconies and stunning sea views (choose No 5 with two windows). The penthouse King Studio has both sea and forest views, a huge balcony and a bonus rear window.

Holifera Hotel HOTEL $$
(📞 0532 742 3632, 0252-243 5863; www.holif erahotel.com; Cumhuriyet Caddesi 10; d/tr/q ₺250/300/350; ❄️🛜🏊) An Akyaka feature for decades, the Susam has metamorphosed as the Holifera tended by the next generation and has a new, fresher look, with wood parquet floors and balconies in all 10 rooms. Two of them look to the street, with the rest gazing at the pool and back garden, the perfect place to linger over the enormous breakfast spread.

Yücelen Hotel RESORT $$$
(📞 0252-243 5108; www.yucelen.com.tr; Hamdi Yücel Gürsoy Sokak 4; s/d from €65/95; ❄️🛜🏊) This enormous classic on the beach is a popular family resort and has one indoor and three outdoor pools, a fitness centre and a sauna. Accommodation is in Ottoman-style blocks, reached across bridges over a network of soothing streams. The 125 rooms have parquet or tile floors, stylish wooden furniture and all have balconies.

🍴 Eating & Drinking

Balık ekmeği (fish sandwiches) are sold all over town from ₺9. Fish restaurants line the north bank of the Azmak. It's a scenic, very peaceful locale, but the fare is much of a muchness.

Wednesday is market day in Akyaka, while on Saturday it's in Gökova village, 4km to the southeast.

The open terrace at Big Blue is a smart spot for a sundowner, serving cocktails and frozen milkshakes. One block inland, three popular bars on Nergiz Sokak and Lütfiye Sakıcı Caddesi draw a mixed crowd of tourists and local kitesurfers with ponytails. They were called The Bar, Kum Cafe and Poison Bar at the time of writing but tend to rebrand themselves according to the season

Big Blue Restaurant INTERNATIONAL $$$
(📞 0252-243 4544; www.bigblueakyaka.com; Sanat Sokak 6; meze ₺7-10, mains ₺25-40; ⊙ 8.30am-11pm) This breezy restaurant-cafe on a terrace that almost embraces the surf serves a potpourri of dishes – from pizzas and hamburgers to Thai red curries and beef enchiladas – and comes up trumps. For those who want to stay closer to home, there are half a dozen 'Turkish classics' on offer and an equal number of fish and seafood main courses.

Mev TURKISH $$$
(📞 0539 231 5673; www.facebook.com/pages/mev-restaurant-akyaka/367621696698253; Nilüfer Sokak 22; mains ₺22-48; ⊙ 11am-midnight) This restaurant, all wood and glass with a large covered terrace, is surprisingly meat-oriented given its location on the beach, though among the four or five fish dishes is an excellent fish *güveç* (a kind of stew). In season Mev is one of the buzziest bars on the beach.

ℹ️ Getting There & Away

Dolmuşes serve Muğla (₺4.50, 30 minutes) half-hourly (hourly in winter) and Marmaris (₺5, 45 minutes) twice daily (mid-May to mid-October). Otherwise, for points north and west (eg Muğla and Bodrum), walk to the highway junction 2km uphill from the beach. You can pick up frequent buses headed south from Gökova village, 4km to the southeast.

Western Anatolia

Best Places to Eat

➡ Kebapçı İskender (p299)

➡ Köfteci Yusuf (p291)

➡ Mezze (p304)

➡ Sagalassos Lodge & Spa (p322)

Best Places to Sleep

➡ Kitap Evi (p297)

➡ Fulya Pension (p317)

➡ Armistis Hotel (p302)

➡ Abacı Konak Otel (p304)

➡ Melrose House (p312)

Why Go?

Durable, diverse and down to earth, western Anatolia combines everything from ancient sites and spectacular mountain terrain to some of Turkey's heartiest food and friendliest people.

The region's diversity of ancient civilisations can be experienced directly: hike the rock-carved Phrygian Valley; pound marbled pavements in the ancient cities of Sagalassos and Afrodisias; or take a woodland pilgrimage on the St Paul Trail. Original Ottoman capital Bursa, meanwhile, is a cornerstone of Turkish identity, with mosques, imperial mausoleums and the İskender kebap. The shimmering travertine pools of Pamukkale, on the other hand, are just great for splashing in.

The region's lesser-known attractions constitute its secret weapon: escapist Eğirdir, set on a tranquil lake, is perfect for hiking, taking a jaunt in a local fisher's boat or for doing nothing at all; while vibrant Eskişehir, a student city with an atmospheric old town, offers river gondola rides and happening bars and restaurants.

When to Go
Bursa

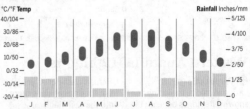

Jan–Feb Breathe in the alpine air while skiing on Uludağ, near Bursa.

May Fresh and sunny weather for hiking and exploring ruins around mountain-ringed Lake Eğirdir.

Sep Enjoy Pamukkale's crystal travertine pools, without the summer crowds.

Western Anatolia Highlights

❶ Pamukkale (p308)
Lazing in calcite travertines on snow-white ridges beneath the ruins of ancient Hierapolis.

❷ Eğirdir (p315) Finding B&B bliss by the idyllic lake and tackling the St Paul Trail through the Taurus Mountains.

❸ Afrodisias (p313) Channelling the exhilaration of a Roman gladiator as you gaze from the ancient site's tunnel onto the vast stadium.

❹ Sagalassos (p320) Ascending the lonely heights of this ruined mountain city with its magnificent rebuilt fountain.

❺ Uludağ (p301) Riding the world's longest cable car up the ski resort's leviathan slopes.

❻ Bursa (p291) Winding your way through bazaars and unwinding in a thermal hamam in the first Ottoman capital.

❼ Eskişehir (p302) Indulging in the nightlife, Ottoman quarter and all-around good vibes of inner Anatolia's most European city.

İznik

📙 0224 / POP 22,700

Turks are proud of İznik's Ottoman tile-making tradition, and the city's Byzantine incarnation as Nicaea once played a significant role through its church councils in shaping Christianity. Today, İznik is a somewhat dusty and run-down collection of tile shops, teahouses and handicraft stalls, though its ruined fortifications and lakeside setting make a visit worthwhile. Easily accessed from İstanbul via a ferry across the Sea of Marmara to Yalova, İznik is a good candidate for a rural break from the big city.

History

Founded around 1000 BC, İznik got its classical Greek name (Nikaea, Westernised to Nicaea) when one of Alexander the Great's generals, Lysimachus, captured it in 301 BC and named it after his wife, Nikaea.

In AD 325 Emperor Constantine the Great chose Nicaea for the first Ecumenical Council, which united ecclesiastical leaders from across Christendom and set a precedent for future councils. Huge differences then existed between different Christian sects, and the council (which considered Christ's divinity, the calculation of Easter and other issues) resulted in the Nicene Creed, enabling bishops and priests to speak in an authoritative and unified way – and thus, for the religion to expand. Four centuries later, the seventh Ecumenical Council was held in Nicaea's Aya Sofya (Hagia Sofia) church.

Under Justinian I (AD 527–65), Nicaea's buildings and defensive walls were renovated. In 1204, when Constantinople fell during the Fourth Crusade, Nicaea became a Byzantine empire-in-exile, one of three successor states (along with Trebizond/Trabzon on the Black Sea and Epiros in Greece).

In 1331 Sultan Orhan conquered the city, establishing İznik's first Ottoman *medrese* (seminary).

⊙ Sights & Activities

Aya Sofya HISTORIC BUILDING
(Orhanlı Camii; Map p290; cnr Kılıçaslan & Atatürk Caddesi) Originally a great Justinianic church, Aya Sofya (Church of the Divine Wisdom) is now a mosque surrounded by a rose garden. The building encompasses ruins of three different structures. A mosaic floor and a mural of Jesus, Mary and John the Baptist survive from the original church.

Destroyed by an earthquake in 1065, it was later rebuilt with the mosaics set into the walls. The Ottomans converted it to mosque, but a 16th-century fire again destroyed it. Reconstruction supervised by the great Ottoman architect Mimar Sinan (1489–1588) added İznik tiles to the decoration.

Yeşil Cami MOSQUE
(Green Mosque; Map p290; off Kılıçaslan Caddesi) Built between 1378 and 1387 under Sultan Murat I, Yeşil Cami has Seljuk Turkish proportions, influenced by Seljuk homeland Iran. The minaret's green-and-blue-glazed zigzag tiles foreshadowed the famous local tile-making industry. At the time of writing, the mosque was closed for significant restoration, but you could view the spectacular exterior of the minaret.

İznik Museum MUSEUM
(İznik Müzesi; Map p290; 📙 0224-757 1027; Müze Sokak; ₺5; ⊙9am-1pm & 2-6pm Tue-Sun) The city museum is housed in a soup kitchen that Sultan Murat I built for his mother, Nilüfer Hatun, in 1388. Born a Byzantine princess, Nilüfer was given to Sultan Orhan to cement a diplomatic alliance. The museum's grounds contain marble statuary, while its lofty halls display original İznik tiles of milky bluish-white and rich 'İznik red' hues. Other exhibits include 8000-year-old finds from a nearby tumulus (burial mound) at Ilıpınar, indicating links with Neolithic Balkan culture.

At the time of writing, the museum was scheduled to reopen mid-2017 following restoration.

City Walls & Gates RUIN
İznik's once-imposing Roman walls, renovated by the Byzantines, no longer dominate, but parts of their 5km circumference remain impressive. Four main gates still transect the walls, while remains of 12 minor gates and 114 towers also stand.

The most impressive walls, reaching 10m to 13m in height, stand between **Lefke Gate** (Map p290) and the southern **Yenişehir Gate** (Atatürk Caddesi). Lefke comprises three Byzantine gateways, and offers good views of the walls to the south.

The imposing northern **İstanbul Gate** (off Atatürk Caddesi) features huge stone carvings of heads facing outwards.

İznik

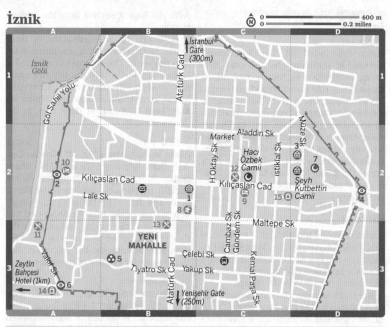

İznik

Göl (Lake) Gate (Map p290) has scant remains, as does the minor **Saray (Palace) Gate** (Map p290), named this because Sultan Orhan (r 1326–61) had a palace nearby. Just inside Saray is a ruined 15,000-seat **Roman theatre** (Map p290).

Il Murat Hamamı HAMAM

(Map p290; ☑0505 744 3259; Maltepe Sokak; hamam adult/child ₺14/10, scrubs ₺9, massages ₺10; ⊙men 6am-midnight, women 1-5pm Mon & Thu) Clean and kid-friendly, this 15th-century hamam was constructed during the reign of Sultan Murat II. The huge pile of wood outside will give you the confidence this is an authentic wood-fired affair. One of our favourite hamams in Turkey.

🛏 Sleeping

Most of İznik's better hotels overlook the lake, but there are also excellent inland options for midrange travellers.

Kaynarca Pansiyon PENSION $

(Map p290; ☑0224-757 1753; www.kaynarca. s5.com; Gündem Sokak 1; dm/s/d/tr excl breakfast ₺30/45/75/100; ☎) Guests receive a very warm welcome at this centrally located family-owned pension now under new management; repeat visitors will note there's not the same proficiency with English as previously. Rooms are simple but clean, and the property is near good shopping and eating options. Breakfast is available for ₺10.

Seyir Butik Pansiyon   PENSION $$

(Map p290; ✆0224-757 7799; www.seyirbutik.
com; Kılıçaslan Caddesi 5; s/d/f ₺80/120/200;
🅿🛜) Wrought-iron balconies, colourful
flower boxes and cosy wood-lined rooms
with spotless bathrooms all combine at
this recent opening a short walk from the
lake. The friendly family owners also run
a cafe downstairs, and there was plenty
of work going on to make the pension's
shaded garden even more inviting when
we dropped by. Good-value family rooms
for groups.

Zeytin Bahçesi Hotel   BOUTIQUE HOTEL $$$

(✆0224-757 2404; www.hotelzeytinbahcesi.com;
Oğlu Süleymanşah Caddesi 119; s/d ₺140/190;
🅿🛜🛏) İznik's newest accommodation is
also the town's most comfortable. Roughly
2.5km from İznik's main square, the Zeytin
Bahçesi (Olive Garden) is a low-slung, classy
and modern affair. Rooms are spacious and
enlivened by cool and classy decor, and the
pleasant garden is studded with fledgling
olive trees. Swim in the nearby lake or cool
off in the pool.

✕ Eating

★ Köfteci Yusuf   KÖFTE, GRILL $

(Map p290; Atatürk Caddesi 73; köfte portions
from ₺10; ⊗8am-10pm) This friendly local
chain is famous for its plump and juicy
köfte (meatballs); it even has its own brand
of *ayran* (yoghurt drink) and an on-site
butcher. Accompany your *köfte* with another meat such as *kuzu şiş* (roast skewered
lamb) or *tavuk* (chicken). It's also a top spot
for breakfast, serving a table-filling array of
cheeses, olives, bread and dips.

Çamlık Restaurant   SEAFOOD $

(Map p290; Göl Sahil Yolu; mezes ₺6, mains ₺12-
22; ⊗11.30am-11pm) The licensed restaurant
at the Çamlık Motel is a local favourite
for grilled lake fish enjoyed with views of
the water. When the weather's fine, enjoy
a meze and a drink in the lakeside garden, or angle for a table by the window
in the yawning interior. Either way, the
beer is cold and the rakı (aniseed brandy)
pleasantly robust.

Karadeniz   PIDE $

(Map p290; Kılıçaslan Caddesi 149; mains ₺10-15;
⊗11am-9pm) 'Black Sea' specialises in pide
(Turkish-style pizza), with toppings such as
sucuk (spicy veal sausage), and *lahmacun*
(Arabic-style pizza; ₺3).

ℹ Getting There & Away

From İznik's compact **otogar** (Map p290) (bus
station), there are daily departures to Ankara
(₺35, six hours) via Eskişehir. Half-hourly mi-
ni-buses shuttle from 6am to 9pm to Bursa (₺12,
1½ hours), and there are hourly departures to
Yalova (₺12, one hour), 62km northwest of İznik.
From Yalova, regular **İDO** (www.ido.com.tr) ferries
link to İstanbul Yenikapı (₺19, 1¼ hours), Pendik,
Kartal and Bostancı.

Bursa

✆0224 / POP 1,800,300

Modern, industrial Bursa is built around the
mosques, mausoleums and other sites from
its incarnation as first Ottoman capital. Despite being built-up and somewhat chaotic,
its durable Ottoman core and abundant parks
keep it remarkably placid in places. For some
fresh air after pounding the markets, the
soaring peaks of Mt Uludağ (Turkey's premier
ski resort) are nearby, with Çekirge's thermal
hamams en route.

Bursa was awarded Unesco World Heritage status in 2014 for being the birthplace
of the Ottoman Empire. The city's historic
contributions to Islamic development have
given it an austere reputation. Yet locals are
kind and welcoming, and you can take the
occasional photo inside historic religious
structures (just be respectful). You'll see a
majority of headscarved women here and
devout prayer in overflowing mosques.

History

Bursa was mentioned by both Aristotle and
ancient geographer Strabo as a Greek city,
called Kios. In 202 BC Macedonian king
Philip V bequeathed Kios to his Bithynian
counterpart, Prusias, who named it Prousa
after himself; this became the origin of the
modern name.

Under Byzantine rule, and especially
under Justinian I, Prousa grew in stature,
and Çekirge's thermal baths were developed.
However, tumultuous events such as the 1075
Seljuk occupation (which lasted 22 years until Crusaders rolled through) initiated a cycle
of conquest and reconquest. Prousa's proximity to Nicaea (today's İznik) cemented the
ties between the two cities, and they revolted
during a lurid 12th-century dynastic struggle.
In one of Byzantine history's more gruesome
scenes, the sadistic Emperor Andronikos I
Komnenos (r 1183-85) attacked Prousa, hanging rebellious Greeks from its lovely chestnut

trees, in a frenzy of mutilations, eye-gouging and impalement.

This instability made Prousa easy pickings for Seljuk conquerors. Small principalities arose around warlords such as Ertuğrul Gazi and, in 1317, Prousa was besieged by his son Osman, founder of the Ottoman line. The siege lasted years, but in 1326 Prousa was finally starved into submission, becoming Osman's capital. His successor, Orhan Gazi (r 1326–59), gradually expanded the empire towards Constantinople.

Sultan Orhan opened the first Ottoman mint, and eventually could dictate to Byzantine leaders. Although Edirne (then Hadrianople) became the capital in 1365, Bursa remained important. Both Osman and Orhan are buried here, and Muslim tourists flock to their tombs to pray and exalt their legacy. Throughout Ottoman times, Bursa's silk production was legendary and much sought-after by Turkish nobles.

Population changes began in the late 19th century, when Balkan Muslims arrived as the Ottoman Empire declined in that area. In a poignant twist, the city's Greek residents chose Kios as the name of their new village in Greece, following population exchanges in 1923. After the War of Independence, Bursa developed industrially and has been a major automotive producer since the 1960s.

◉ Sights

◉ Central Bursa (Osmangazi)

Central Cumhuriyet Alanı (Republic Sq) is also called Heykel (Statue), after its large Atatürk monument. Atatürk Caddesi runs west from Heykel through the commercial centre to Ulu Camii (Great Mosque). Further west, Zafer Plaza shopping centre's blue-glass pyramid is a landmark.

Bursa City Museum   MUSEUM
(Bursa Kent Müzesi; Map p294; ☑0224-220 2626; www.bursakentmuzesi.com; Heykel; ₺2; ☺9.30am-5pm Tue-Sun) Chronicling Bursa's history from the earliest sultans, their military campaigns and their ornate firearms to more recent characters such as Tarzan impersonator Ali Atay, this lively museum mixes cultural and ethnographic collections

---

İZNIK TILES

In 1514 Sultan Selim I captured Persian Tabriz, bringing its artisans to İznik. The Persian crafters were skilled tile-makers, and soon İznik's kilns were producing faience (tin-glazed earthenware) of a quality unequalled even today. Peaking in the 16th and 17th centuries, İznik's tile-making was a unique Ottoman artistic tradition.

However, the decreased demand for significant public works in post-Ottoman Turkey caused a rapid decline. To revive this craft, the **İznik Foundation** (İznik Vakıf Çinileri; Map p290; www.iznik.com/en; Vakıf Sokak; ☺8am-6pm Mon-Fri) has worked with historians, university laboratories and trained craftspeople from across Turkey.

All the İznik Foundation's designers are women, who you can watch at work. The results of their labours dot the garden and you can buy pieces in the showroom, starting from around ₺60 for an ashtray or a small tile. The patient craftswomen meticulously design the pristine white tiles – following tradition, only floral cross-sections are painted. It takes up to 70 days to complete larger works, such as tiles for İstanbul's metro system and the World Bank in Ankara.

Made of 85% quartz from local quarries, İznik tiles have unique thermal properties that keep buildings warm in winter and cool in summer. Their reflection of sound waves creates perfect acoustic qualities, a reason for their use in Ottoman mosques. When shopping, check if you are looking at quartz (preferable) or regular ceramic tiles, and if they are machine- or hand-painted.

Shops all over town sell multicoloured tiles, as well as other ceramics and handicrafts. Good places to start looking are the small workshops along Salim Demircan Sokak; the workshop belonging to the İznik Foundation; and shopping complexes such as **Nilüfer Haltun** (Map p290; Kılıçaslan Caddesi; ☺9am-7.30pm), which also has cafes and teahouses. Around Kılıçaslan Caddesi and Salim Demircan Sokak you'll find good studios. Shop around, and note there is room for bargaining at all. İznik tile-making has been undergoing a revival, and the fact that the town is proud of this is evident from the posters of tiles on display in many restaurants and hotels.

with multimedia wizardry. Displays, including a mock-up handicrafts bazaar, give a good understanding of local life and culture.

Ulu Camii MOSQUE

(Map p294; Atatürk Caddesi) This enormous Seljuk-style shrine (1399) is Bursa's most dominant and durable mosque. Sultan Beyazıt I built it in a monumental compromise – having pledged to build 20 mosques after defeating the Crusaders in the Battle of Nicopolis, he settled for one mosque, with 20 small domes. Two massive minarets augment the domes, while the giant square pillars and portals within are similarly impressive. The *mimber* (pulpit) boasts fine wood carvings, and the walls feature intricate calligraphy.

Bursa's Karagöz shadow-puppet theatre reportedly began with Ulu Camii's construction.

Kapalı Çarşı MARKET

(Covered Market; Map p294; Kapalı Çarşı Caddesi; ⊗8.30am-8pm Mon-Sat, 10.30am-6pm Sun) Bursa's sprawling Kapalı Çarşı (Covered Market) contains the 14th-century Bedesten, built by Sultan Beyazıt I (reconstructed after an 1855 earthquake), and the Eski Aynalı Çarşı, originally the Orhanbey Hamamı. Built in 1335, it features a domed ceiling with skylights. Karagöz shadow puppets and other traditional items are sold here.

Koza Han MARKET

(Cocoon Caravanserai; Map p294; Uzun Çarşı Caddesi) Just east of Eski Aynalı Çarşı is Koza Han, built in 1490. Expensive silk shops overlook the courtyard with its cafes and small mosque (1491) honouring Yıldırım Beyazıt.

Emir Han MARKET

(Map p294; Kapalı Çarşı Caddesi) Camel caravans travelling the Silk Road to Bursa once lodged at Emir Han, entered at the rear of Ulu Camii. Drovers and merchants slept and did business upstairs, with their precious cargo stored in the ground-floor rooms. The courtyard tea garden has a fine old fountain.

Bursa Citadel CASTLE

(Hisar; Map p294) Some ramparts and walls still survive on the steep cliff that is the site of Bursa's citadel and its oldest neighbourhood, Tophane. Walk up Orhan Gazi (Yiğitler) Caddesi to reach the Hisar (Fortress). On the summit, a park contains the Tombs of Sultans Osman and Orhan (Osman Gazi ve Orhan Gazi Türbeleri; Map p294; Timurtaş Paşa Park; by donation), the Ottoman Empire's founders.

Osman Gazi's tomb is the more richly decorated.

Although it was ruined in the 1855 earthquake, Sultan Abdül Aziz rebuilt the mausoleum in baroque style in 1863.

The six-storey **clock tower** (Map p294; Timurtaş Paşa Park), the last of four that also served as fire alarms, stands in a square with a cafe where families and couples gaze out over the valley and snap photos.

⊙ Muradiye

Muradiye Complex HISTORIC SITE

(Map p298; off Kaplıca Caddesi) This relaxing complex contains a shady park, a cemetery with historic tombs, and the 1426 **Sultan Murat II (Muradiye) Camii** (Map p298; off Kaplıca Caddesi). Imitating the painted decorations of Yeşil Camii, another of Bursa's great Ottoman mosques, the Muradiye features an intricate *mihrab* (niche in a minaret indicating the direction of Mecca).

The cemetery's 12 **tombs** (Map p298; off Kaplıca Caddesi) (15th to 16th century) include that of Sultan Murat II (r 1421–51). Although his son Mehmet II would capture Constantinople, Murat laid the groundwork by annexing territories from enemy states during his reign.

Like other Islamic dynasties, the Ottomans did not practice primogeniture – any royal son could claim power upon his father's death, which, unsurprisingly, resulted in numerous bloodbaths. The tombs preserve this macabre legacy: all the *şehzades* (imperial sons) interred here were killed by close relatives. While many tombs are ornate and trimmed with beautiful İznik tiles, others are simple and stark, like that of the ascetic and part-time dervish Murat II.

The 15th-century **Muradiye Medresesi** (Map p298) was a tuberculosis clinic in the 1950s and still houses a medical centre. The **Sultan Murat II Hamamı** (Map p298), which catered to the *medrese* (seminary) students, is now a government building.

Ulumay Museum of Ottoman Folk Costumes & Jewellery MUSEUM

(Osmanlı Halk Kıyafetleri ve Takıları Müzesi; Map p298; ☏0224-222 7575; off Kaplıca Caddesi; ₺5; ⊗8.30am-6.30pm Tue-Sun) Originally the Sair Ahmet Paşa *medrese* (1475), this museum exhibits around 70 costumes and more than 350 different pieces of jewellery.

Central Bursa & Yeşil

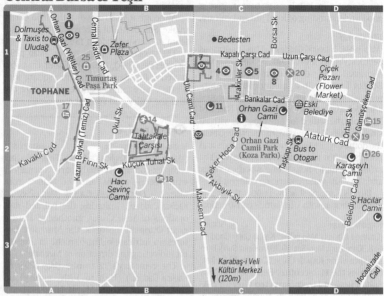

Central Bursa & Yeşil

Hüsnü Züber Evi   MUSEUM, HISTORIC BUILDING
(Map p298; Uzunyol Sokak 3; by donation; ⊙10am-noon & 1-5pm Tue-Sun) Knock to gain entry to this restored 19th-century Ottoman house, located uphill behind Sultan Murat II Hamamı. The collection inside includes ornate musical instruments and intricately carved and painted Anatolian wooden spoons. Beyond lie winding alleys, shops and crumbling Ottoman houses.

Ottoman House Museum   MUSEUM
(Osmanlı Evi Müzesi; Map p298; off Kaplıca Caddesi; ⊙8am-noon & 1-5pm Tue-Sun) **FREE** This restored 17th-century house has a beautiful exterior and a few Ottoman dioramas inside.

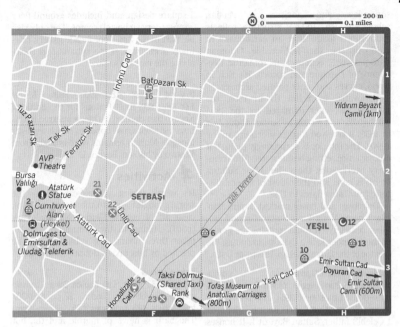

⊙ Kültür Parkı & Around

Kültür Parkı PARK

(Culture Park; Map p298) Leafy Kültür Parkı boasts fine lawns and flowers, tea gardens, restaurants, playgrounds and a lake where you can hire **bisikleti gezisi** (pedal boats; ⊘ per 20min ₺15). On the park grounds you will also find the **Archaeology Museum** (Arkeoloji Müzesi; Map p298; Kültür Parkı; ₺5; ⊘ 8am-noon & 1-5pm Tue-Sun). It's north and down the hill from the Muradiye complex.

⊙ Yıldırım

East of Heykel, Atatürk Caddesi crosses the Gök Deresi (Gök Stream), which tumbles through a gorge. Just after the bridge, Yeşil Caddesi veers left to Yeşil Camii and Yeşil Türbe, while Namazgah Caddesi leads straight on towards the Uludağ *teleferik* (cable car).

Yeşil Camii MOSQUE

(Green Mosque; Map p294; Yeşil Caddesi) Built for Mehmet I between 1412 and 1419, Yeşil Camii represents a departure from the previous, Persian-influenced Seljuk architecture. Exemplifying Ottoman stylings, it contains a harmonious facade and beautiful carved marble work around the central doorway.

The mosque was named for the interior wall's greenish-blue tiles.

Yeşil Türbe HISTORIC BUILDING

(Green Tomb; Map p294; Yeşil Caddesi; ⊘ 8am-noon & 1-5pm) **FREE** The mausoleum of 5th Ottoman sultan Mehmed I Çelebi (and several of his children) stands in a cypress-trimmed park opposite Yeşil Camii (Green Mosque). During his short rule (1413–21), he reunited a fractured empire following the Mongols' 1402 invasion. Despite its name, the *türbe* (tomb) is not green; it has blue Kütahya tiles outside that postdate the 1855 earthquake. The structure has a sublime, simple beauty, the original interior tiles exemplifying 15th-century decor. There is also an impressive tiled *mihrab*.

Turkish & Islamic Arts Museum MUSEUM

(Map p294; Yeşil Caddesi; ₺5; ⊘ 8.30am-noon & 1-7pm Tue-Sun) Housed in the former *medrese* of Yeşil Camii, this museum contains 14th- to 16th-century İznik ceramics, *mihrab* curtains, jewellery, embroidery, calligraphy, dervish artefacts and Karagöz puppets.

Emir Sultan Camii MOSQUE

(Emir Sultan Caddesi) An early Ottoman mosque, the 14th-century Emir Sultan Camii was named for Sultan Bayezit I's son-in-law and adviser, a Persian scholar-dervish. Today's structure reflects renovations made after an earthquake in 1766, in the then-fashionable Ottoman baroque style, echoing the romantic decadence of baroque and rococo; it's rich in wood, curves and outer painted arches.

Renovated by Selim III in 1805, the mosque was later damaged by the 1855 earthquake and rebuilt by Sultan Abdül Aziz in 1858; it received further touch-ups in the 1990s. The interior is surprisingly plain, but enjoys a nice setting beside a tree-filled cemetery overlooking the valley. Emir Sultan's tomb is here, and the oldest of several historic fountains dates to 1743.

Dolmuşes and buses marked 'Emirsultan' travel here. Along Emir Sultan Caddesi, another cemetery en route contains the graves of the İskender kebap dynasty, including the creator of the famous kebap, İskender Usta.

Yıldırım Beyazıt Camii   MOSQUE
(Mosque of Sultan Bayezit I; Yıldırım Cadessi) This twin-domed mosque (1395), also referred to as just Beyazıt Camii, was built by Mehmed I Çelebi's father, Sultan Bayezit I. It houses the tombs of Yıldırım Beyazıt (Thunderbolt Bayezit), as the sultan was known, and his other son, İsa. Its adjoining medrese is now a medical centre.

İrgandı Köprüsü   HISTORIC BUILDING
(İrgandı Bridge; Map p294; Gök Deresi) Spanning the gorge, north of the Setbaşı road bridge, this restored Ottoman structure houses shops, cafes and touristy artisan workshops.

Tofaş Museum of Anatolian Carriages   MUSEUM
(☑ 0224-329 3941; Kapıcı Caddesi; ⊙ 9am-5pm Tue-Sun) FREE Old cars and horse-drawn carts are housed in this former silk factory with gardens. It's a 550m walk uphill, signposted right after the Setbaşı road bridge.

⊙ Çekirge

Çekirge, Bursa's spa suburb, is 2km northwest of Kültür Parkı. Uludağ's warm mineralrich waters bubble up here and have been valued since ancient times for their curative powers. Hotels here usually have private mineral baths, and independent kaplıcalar (thermal baths) exist, too.

Murat I (Hüdavendigâr) Camii   MOSQUE
(İ Murat Caddesi, Çekirge) This unusual mosque from 1366 features a barrel-vaulted Ottoman

T-square design, and includes ground-floor zaviye (dervish hostel) rooms. The only visible part of the 2nd-floor facade gallery, originally a medrese, is the sultan's loge (box), above the mosque's rear.

Sarcophagus of Murat I   TOMB
(İ Murat Caddesi; ⊙ 8am-10pm) Sultan Murat I (r 1359–89), most famous for the Battle of Kosovo that claimed his life, is interred in this huge sarcophagus opposite Hudavendigar Mosque. Murat's remains were brought from Kosovo by his son, Bayezit I.

🏃 Activities

It's worth taking a cable-car ride – the world's longest – up to the views and cool, clear air of nearby Uludağ National Park (p301). Hiking to the summit of Uludağ takes three hours. The cable car can be reached by bus, taxi or dolmuş from Bursa.

Eski Kaplıca   HAMAM
(☑ 0224-233 9309; Eski Kaplıca Sokak; hamam men/women/children under 12yr ₺40/30/free, scrubs ₺25, massages ₺25; ⊙ 7am-10pm) The bath is hewn of marble and the hot rooms have plunge pools at this restored 14th-century hamam, run by the adjacent Kervansaray Termal Hotel on the eastern side of Çekirge. It also has a private section (two people ₺100).

Karagöz Travel Agency   TOUR
(Map p294; ☑ 0224-223 8583; www.karagoztravel.com; Eski Aynalı Çarşı) The English-speaking Uğur runs group tours every weekend that are popular with Bursa's Turkish and expat residents. Destinations range from Eskişehir to Turkey's Aegean islands; jump online for the program. Shorter local tours can also be arranged to destinations such as the village of Cumalikizik and mountain nomad villages on the slopes of Uludağ.

Yeni Kaplıca   HAMAM
(Map p298; ☑ 0224-236 6955; www.yenikaplica.com.tr; Mudanya Caddesi 10; hamam men/women ₺20/18, massages ₺25; ⊙ 5am-11pm) The 'new thermal bath' is actually the city's oldest, founded by 6th-century Emperor Justinian I, and renovated in 1522 by Süleyman the Magnificent's grand vizier, Rüstem Paşa. There are women-only kaynarca (boiling) baths here, and family-oriented baths at the neighbouring Karamustafa Hotel. Yeni Kaplıca is west of Kültür Parkı, signposted downhill from Çekirge Caddesi near Atatürk House.

Çakır Ağa Hamamı HAMAM
(Map p294; ☑0224-221 2580; Atatürk Caddesi; hamam ₺30, massages ₺20; ☻men 6am-midnight, women 10am-10pm) Çakır Ağa, a police chief under Murat II, built this oft-restored hamam in 1484.

✹ Festivals & Events

Uluslararası Bursa Festivali MUSIC, DANCE
(International Bursa Festival; www.bursafestivali.org; ☻mid-May) Bursa's music and dance festival features diverse regional and world music, plus an international 'star' headliner or two. Some performances are free, and tickets for top acts cost around ₺40. The festival runs for around 2½ weeks and usually begins mid-May.

**International Golden Karagöz
Folk Dance Competition** DANCE
(☻Jul) This dance event sees international groups perform at the open-air theatre in Kültür Parkı.

Karagöz Festival PERFORMING ARTS
(☻Nov) This week-long festival hosts performances by Karagöz shadow puppeteers, Western puppeteers and marionette performers each November in odd years.

⌂ Sleeping

Despite Bursa's historical sights, the city's hotels cater mainly to business travellers, leading to high prices. A few boutique options have opened in heritage buildings. Head to the streets east of Tahtakale Çarşısı for the best value in budget accommodation.

For R & R, try a *kaplıca* (thermal bath) hotel in Çekirge, 4.5km northwest of Ulu Camii. It's a quieter scene uphill in this spa suburb, and easily reached by regular dolmuşes.

⌂ Central Bursa

Otel Çamlıbel HOTEL $
(Map p294; ☑0224-221 2565; İnebey Caddesi 71; s/d ₺50/90; ☎) This blue-fronted central cheapie has seen better days but its en suite rooms have TVs and are clean and comfortable. Rooms with shared bathroom are basic with fan only, but usually have hot water. The English-speaking team at reception is warm and welcoming. Also contains triples and quadruples.

Hotel Çeşmeli HOTEL $$
(Map p294; ☑0224-224 1511; Gümüşçeken Caddesi 6; s/d ₺80/140; ❄☎) Run by women, the Çeşmeli remains a friendly central option,

near the market, and is a good spot for female travellers. Although the rooms are slightly dated, they are spacious and spotlessly clean; the lobby is a pleasant environment for watching Bursa bustle past.

Bursa City Hotel HOTEL $$
(Map p298; ☑0224-221 1875; www.bursacity hotel.com; Durak Caddesi 15; s/d ₺85/145; ❄☎) Good English is spoken at this friendly option right in the middle of the compelling commercial buzz of Bursa's rabbit warren of markets. Despite the central location, the recently redecorated rooms are quiet – especially after dark – and eating options abound within metres. The architectural splendour of Ulu Camii is a short stroll away through plenty of shopping opportunities.

★**Kitap Evi** BOUTIQUE HOTEL $$$
(Map p294; ☑0224-225 4160; www.kitapevi.com. tr; Burç Üstü 21; s/d €70/95, ste €145-175; ❄@) The 'Book House', a former Ottoman residence and book bazaar, is a peaceful haven, tucked inside the citadel battlements far above Bursa's minarets and domes. The 12 eclectic rooms each have their own style (one boasts a marble-lined hamam) and the city seems far away from the courtyard, which has a fountain and resident tortoise.

Well-polished wood fixtures and little touches such as artwork and stained glass complement the rows of bookshelves and vintage knick-knacks. Minibars and the à la carte restaurant make it a tempting place to while away an evening.

Ipek Yolu BOUTIQUE HOTEL $$$
(Map p294; ☑0224-222 5009; www.ipekyolubutik hotel.com; Batpazarı Sokak 12; s/d ₺180/280; ❄☎) In a quiet but central neighbourhood, several Ottoman-era buildings have been repurposed as a classy boutique hotel. The spacious inner courtyard is perfect for breakfast and for relaxing at the end of the day, and the antique-filled rooms are elegant and stylish. It's a short walk to streets lined with decent restaurants, and also to Bursa's main square and sights.

⌂ Çekirge

Kadi Konağı HOTEL $$
(☑0224-235 6030; www.kadikonagihotel.com; Çekirge; s/d €35/45; ❄☎) This small family-owned hotel is a great alternative to Çekirge's other larger spa hotels. Rooms are relatively compact but stylish and well kept, and there's an on-site hamam that can

Muradiye, Kültür Parkı & Around

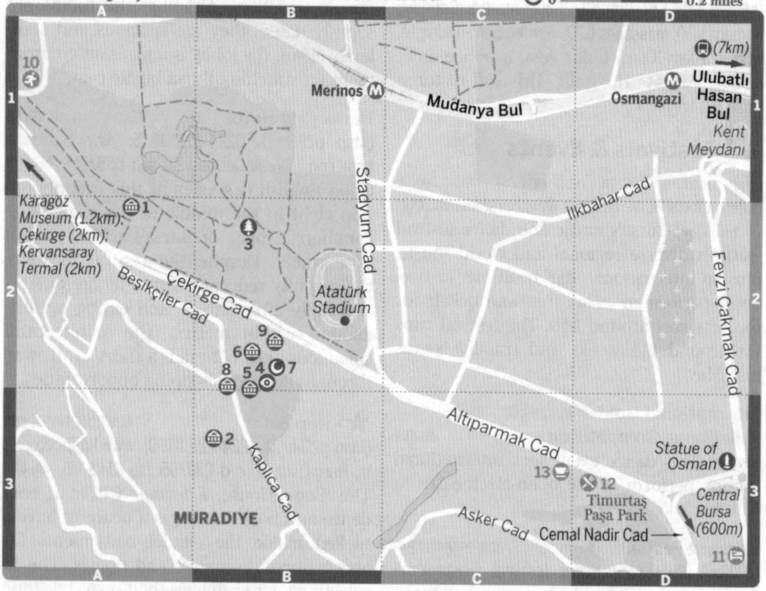

Muradiye, Kültür Parkı & Around

Sights

1 Archaeology Museum A2
2 Hüsnü Züber Evi B3
3 Kültür Parkı B2
4 Muradiye Complex B2
5 Muradiye Medresesi B2
Muradiye Tombs .... (see 4)
6 Ottoman House Museum B2
7 Sultan Murat II (Muradiye) Camii B2
8 Sultan Murat II (Muradiye) Hamamı B2
9 Ulumay Museum of Ottoman Folk Costumes & Jewellery B2

Activities, Courses & Tours

10 Yeni Kaplıca A1

Sleeping

11 Bursa City Hotel D3

Eating

12 Sakarya Caddesi Fish Restaurants D3

Drinking & Nightlife

13 Gren C3

be booked and used free of charge. Ask for a room with a balcony, and definitely make the short walk to nearby tea gardens for brilliant views of Bursa's impetuous sprawl.

Marigold Hotel LUXURY HOTEL, SPA **$$$**
(☎0224-234 6020; www.marigold.com.tr; I Murat Caddesi 47, Çekirge; s/d incl hamam from €90/120; ❄📶🏊) Beginning in the lobby, where cleansed-looking couples pad around in towelling robes, Marigold is all about relaxation. A traditional Ottoman hamam set is one of the items for sale in the rooms, and the spa features an 85-sq-metre thermal pool. The modern hotel is a comfortable and restful environment, with a restaurant, bar, patisserie and a four-storey atrium climbing to the rooms.

Gönlüferah 1890 LUXURY HOTEL, SPA **$$$**
(☎0224-232 1890; www.gonluferah.com; I Murat Caddesi, Cekirge; s/d incl 30min hamam from ₺200/270; ❄📶🏊) Dating from 1890, the hilltop Gönlüferah has been a hotel since the early 20th century, and in that time has hosted many a famous guest. It looks the part, with thick carpets and portraits of Bursa's Ottoman forefathers. Rooms range from standard with city or mountain views to 'Prince' and 'Sultan'.

Standard options are small, particularly the bathrooms, but continue the opulent tone through plush headboards, dangling lights and minibars featuring wine and spirits.

🍴 Eating & Drinking

Bursa is famous for its rich İskender kebap (döner lamb on fresh pide, topped with yoghurt, hot tomato sauce and browned butter), also known as the Bursa kebap; and for its *kestane şekeri* dessert, fashioned from candied chestnuts and also called *maron glacé*.

Mahfel CAFE, ICE CREAM $
(Map p294; Namazgah Caddesi 2; ice creams from ₺8; ⊙8am-11pm) With a nice shady ravine setting, Bursa's oldest cafe is known for its *dondurma* (ice cream). Order *bir porsiyon* (one portion) to dig into a veritable sundae. It's a handy refreshment stop if you're walking from Cumhuriyet Alanı (Republic Sq) up the (gentle) hill to Yeşil Camii and Yeşil Türbe in the Yıldırım neighbourhood.

Lalezar Türk Mutfağı TURKISH $
(Map p294; Ünlü Caddesi 14; mezes & soups ₺6-8, mains ₺15-20; ⊙7am-9pm) Snazzy wallpaper and waistcoated waitstaff raise Lalezar above the more simple fast-food joints and kebap places nearby. There's an ever-changing menu of meze, soup, and vegetable and meat dishes on offer in the gleaming bain-marie as you enter, and we can thoroughly recommend the liver and rice pilaf. Don't leave

without trying some of Bursa's best *fırın süt-lac* (rice pudding).

Karadeniz Pide & Kebap Salonu PIDE, KEBAP $$
(Selvi Sokak 2, Çekirge; mains ₺15-30; ⊙11am-10pm) With its photos of bygone Bursa and slick service from a friendly crew, this Çekirge favourite offers an impressive selection of pide plus İskender and myriad other kebaps, many available in *dürüm* form (wrapped in flatbread).

★Kebapçı İskender KEBAP $$
(Map p294; Ünlü Caddesi 7; İskender portions ₺26; ⊙11am-9pm) This refuge for serious carnivores is famous nationwide – it is where the legendary İskender kebap was created in 1867. The wood-panelled interior with tiled pillars and stained-glass windows is a refined environment in which to taste the renowned dish. There is no menu; simply order *bir* (one) or *bir buçuk* (1½) portions.

This is the main branch of a dozen eponymous eateries around Bursa; the **branch** (Map p294; İc koza Han; İskender kebap portions ₺26; ⊙11am-9pm) next to Koza Han market has an atmospheric vaulted setting.

İskender KEBAP $$
(Map p294; Atatürk Caddesi 60; İskender portions ₺27; ⊙11am-5pm) This central spot, which claims to have created the İskender kebap, does hearty versions of the local favourite at

---

SHADOW PUPPETS

Originally a Central Asian Turkic tradition, Karagöz shadow-puppet theatre developed in Bursa and spread throughout the Ottoman Empire. Puppets are made of camel hide, treated with oil to turn translucent and are then painted. They are manipulated by puppeteers behind a white cloth screen onto which their images are cast by backlighting.

Legend attests that Karagöz the Hunchback, foreman of Bursa's enormous mosque Ulu Camii, distracted the workforce with the humorous antics he carried out with 'straight man' Hacivat. An infuriated sultan executed the comic slackers, whose joking became immortalised in Bursa's Karagöz shadow puppetry. Director Ezel Akay revived this legend in 2006's comic film *Killing the Shadows* (original title *Hacivat Karagöz Neden Öldürüldü?*).

Puppeteer Şinasi Çelikkol has championed Karagöz puppetry. His **Karagöz Antique Shop** (Map p294; ☑0224-221 8727; www.karagozshop.net; Eski Aynalı Çarşı 12; ⊙9.30am-7pm) is a lively place to see the puppets and watch an impromptu performance. Ask about his ethnographic museum in the nearby village of Misi. He also founded Bursa's **Karagöz Museum** (Karagöz Müzesi; ☑0224-232 3360; Çekirge Caddesi 59; adult/child ₺6; ⊙9.30am-5.30pm, performances 11am Wed), opposite the Karagöz monument. The collection includes magnificent Turkish, Uzbek, Russian and Romanian puppets and puppet-making tools. Performances often take place at 11am on Wednesday mornings at the museum. Check with Şinasi Çelikkol at his shop for current show times.

very similar prices to rival claimant Kebapçı İskender.

Sakarya Caddesi
Fish Restaurants   SEAFOOD $$$
(Map p298; off Altıparmak Caddesi; mezes from ₺7, seafood ₺20-38; ⊙ 11am-11pm) In the former Jewish quarter, about a 10-minute walk from Ulu Camii, cobbled Sakarya Caddesi is a busy lane of fish restaurants. Crowds wander between the al fresco tables, joined by waiters carrying trays of rakı, and the occasional accordion-wielding *fasıl* (gypsy music) band.

★ Gren   CAFE
(Map p298; www.grencafe.com; Sakarya Caddesi 46; snacks & mains from ₺10; ⊙ 10am-midnight) Bursa's 'photography cafe' hosts exhibitions, workshops and other events matching its antique-camera decor and arty clientele. Relax on the deck with a good espresso or refreshing soda made from fresh fruit juice, or fill up on pasta, burgers and salads. A few surrounding buildings feature funky street art, and the area's burgeoning hipsterdom is also foreshadowed by nearby tattoo parlours.

La Bella   BAR
(Map p294; Hocaalizade Caddesi; ⊙ 4pm-late) This relaxed bar has a terrace overlooking the leafy Gök Deresi gorge. It is entered next to Simit Sarayı cafe; look for the sign to Yener Ocakbaşı. It's a top spot to watch a game featuring the city's beloved Bursaspor football team.

☆ Entertainment

Karabaş-i Veli Kültür Merkezi   CULTURAL
(Mevlâna Cultural Centre; ☑ 0224-222 0385; www. mevlana.org.tr; Çardak Sokak 2; entry free; ⊙ winter 8.30pm, summer 9.30pm) Sit in the tea garden and watch the *şeyh* (master dervish) lead his students through a *sema* (whirling dervish ceremony) for roughly an hour every evening in this 600-year-old *tekke* (dervish lodge). Saturday night is a major event, with various dervish groups participating.

🛍 Shopping

Bali Bey Han   ARTS & CRAFTS
(Map p294; Cemal Nadir Caddesi; ⊙ sunrisesunset) This 15th-century Ottoman caravanserai houses handicraft shops.

Kafkas   FOOD
(Map p294; www.kafkas.com; Atatürk Caddesi; ⊙ 7am-11.30pm) A good place to pick up *kestane şekeri* (candied chestnuts) and other sugary souvenirs.

ℹ Information

Bursa is heavily built up, crowded and, with its constant traffic, *tek yön* (one-way) roads and lack of street lights, can seem bewildering and difficult to navigate. Cross Atatürk Caddesi by the *alt geçidi* (pedestrian underpasses). People with disabilities can use the lift at Atatürk Alt Geçidi (the underpass nearest to Heykel); the nearby florist has the key.

Tourist Office (Map p294; ☑ 0224-220 1848; http://en.bursa.bel.tr/kategori/bursa/tourism; Atatürk Caddesi; ⊙ 8am-noon & 1-5pm Mon-Fri, 8am-12.30pm & 1.30-6pm Sat & Sun) Not particularly helpful as little English is spoken, but it does have maps and brochures. Around the city, Bursa has many excellent brown and white information signs that lead to historical buildings and other points of interest.

ℹ Getting There & Away

Travelling to/from İstanbul, a metro-bus-**ferry** (www.ido.com.tr) combo via Mudanya is fastest. Take the metro from Şehreküstü, the closest station to the city centre, to Emek station. Catch the 1/M bus from Emek metro station to Mudanya ferry terminal, from where regular BUDO ferries link Mudanya with İstanbul Kabataş (₺24, two hours).

İstanbul is linked to Yalova, 70km (one hour) northeast of Bursa, by ferry and by bus. *Karayolu ile* (by road) buses wind around the Bay of İzmit (four to five hours). Buses designated *feribot ile* (by ferry) are better; they take the ferry from Topçular, east of Yalova, across to Eskihişar; the ferry runs roughly every 20 minutes and the crossing takes 20 minutes.

AIR

Domestic flights with **Anadolu Jet** (www.anado lujet.com) link Bursa's **Yenişehir Airport** (www. yenisehir.dhmi.gov.tr) with Ankara, Erzurum, Diyarbakır, Samsun and Trabzon.

BUS

Bursa *terminal* (otogar; bus station) is 10km north of the centre on the Yalova road. Bus-company offices are found throughout the centre, including next to Çakır Ağa Hamamı on Atatürk Caddesi.

Frequent services from the Bursa otogar include the following:

Ayfon ₺35, five hours

Ankara ₺50, 6½ hours

Bandırma ₺15, two hours

Çanakkale ₺35, five hours

Denizli ₺65, nine hours

Eskişehir ₺25, 2½ hours

İstanbul ₺35, three hours

İzmir ₺40, 5½ hours

Kütahya ₺20, three hours

BURSA'S GREAT MOUNTAIN

Close to Bursa and İstanbul, Uludağ (Great Mountain; 2543m) is Turkey's favourite ski resort. The resort is 33km from Bursa, and the recently expanded *teleferik* (cable car) now transports visitors and snow-sports fans all the way to the mountain's hotel area and ski slopes.

At 8.2km, the **Uludağ Teleferik** (Uludağ Cable Car; www.teleferik.com.tr/bursa; adult/child ₺35/25; ⊙8am-8pm) took the mantle as the world's longest cable car when it reopened in mid-2016. The system begins at Teferrüç (236m) before travelling via Kadıyayla (1231m), and continuing to Sarıalan (1635m). At Sarıalan, passengers can disembark and explore teahouses, cook-your-own barbecue restaurants and wooded walking trails before continuing to the terminus station, Oteller (1810m), where Uludağ's hotels and snow-sports infrastructure are located. The entire ascent takes 22 minutes.

In summer come for the views and clean, cool air; the resort is dead outside the December-to-March ski season.

Getting There & Away

Dolmuşes (minibuses that stop anywhere along their prescribed route) and buses S/1 and S/2 run from Heykel to the Teferrüç **teleferik** (p301) station (₺2.50, 15 minutes), from where you can ascend by cable car. From the IDO ferry port at Mudanya, bus F/3 travels directly to Teferrüç (₺6, one hour).

Dolmuşes (₺14, one hour) run to the ski resort several times daily in summer (more frequently in winter) from Tophane in Bursa by road via Kadıyayla and Sarıalan.

Taxis from Tophane cost about ₺130; in winter you will likely find someone to share the ride with or be able to negotiate the price down. Motorists must pay ₺15 to enter the park at the **Uludağ National Park** (www.bursa.com.tr; per car ₺15) gate, 11km from the resort.

ⓘ Getting There & Around

Visit www.burulas.com.tr for more on transport in and around Bursa.

TO/FROM THE AIRPORT

Yenişehir Airport is around 50km east of Bursa. Public bus 80 (₺2.50, 45 minutes) runs from the Kent Meydanı shopping centre northeast of Kültür Parkı. A taxi to the airport costs around ₺50.

TO/FROM THE BUS STATION

Centre Bus 38 (₺3.90, one hour). Heading to the *otogar* (Map p294), wait at the stop on Atatürk Caddesi opposite the *eski belediye* (old town hall). Taxi ₺40.

Çekirge Bus 96 (₺2.50, one hour). Taxi ₺50.

BUS

City buses have their destinations and stops visible. A short journey costs ₺2, a long journey ₺2.50. The buses are prepay: buy single or multiuse tickets from kiosks or shops near most bus stops (look for the BuKART sign). Stops line Atatürk Caddesi opposite Koza Parkı and the *eski belediye*. Bus 1/C is useful, running around the city centre from Heykel to Çekirge via Atatürk Caddesi.

DOLMUŞ

Taksi dolmuşes (Map p294) (shared taxis), their destinations indicated by an illuminated rooftop sign, are the same price as buses (short journey ₺2, long ₺2.50), but faster and more frequent, especially to Çekirge. The most useful route around the city centre runs anticlockwise from Cumhuriyet Alanı (Heykel) up İnönü Caddesi to Kent Meydanı, Atatürk Stadium and along Çekirge Caddesi to Çekirge, returning via Altıparmak, Cemal Nadir and Atatürk Caddesi. Drivers pick up and drop off all along the route. There is also a rank on the eastern side of the Setbaşı road bridge, from where *taksi dolmuşes* follow a similar route to Çekirge.

Dolmuşes run from Heykel to the Teferrüç teleferik station (₺2.50, 15 minutes) to ascend **Uludağ** (Map p294). Dolmuşes (₺14, one hour) directly to the **ski resort** (Map p294) run via Kadıyayla and Sarıalan from Tophane in Bursa.

METRO

The metro (₺3) runs every eight to 12 minutes between 6am and midnight. The closest station to the city centre is Şehreküstü, near the Kapalı Çarşı, and around 500m north of Atatürk Caddesi.

TAXI

Taxis start with ₺3 on the meter and charge about ₺2 per kilometre. Heykel to Muradiye costs about ₺15, Çekirge ₺20.

TRAM

Red trams follow a similar route to *taksi dolmuşes*, from Heykel to Kent Meydanı, Atatürk Stadium and back. They are cheap (short journey ₺1.90, long ₺2.10) but slow. Buy tickets before boarding from BuKART kiosks near stations.

Mudanya

📞 0224 / POP 61,090

Mudanya is a lively seaside town most known for its İstanbul ferry. Strategically set on the Sea of Marmara, it is where the Armistice of Moudania was signed by Italy, France, Britain and Turkey on 11 October 1922 (Greece reluctantly signed three days later). Under it, all lands from Edirne eastward, including İstanbul and the Dardanelles, became Turkish. The whitewashed 19th-century house where the treaty was signed houses a museum (Mudanya Armistice House Museum; Mütareke Meydanı; ₺5; ⊘ 8am-5pm Tue-Sun) of historic Armistice-related photos.

🛏 Sleeping & Eating

Fish restaurants line the waterfront in the attractive Ottoman quarter west of the museum. Look forward to spying the local posse of cats mooching around.

★ **Armistis Hotel** BOUTIQUE HOTEL $$$
(📞 0224-544 6680; www.armistishotel.com.tr; Ünlü Sokak 7; r ₺170-200; ❄ 🛜) With a brilliant location one block from the waterfront, the Armistis is a charming boutique collection of 16 rooms in a restored Ottoman heritage building. Attention to detail in the rooms is excellent – look forward to superior bed linen and high-end bathroom products – and a cosmopolitan and international vibe is enhanced by the multilingual team at reception.

❶ Getting There & Away

Regular **BUDO** (www.burulas.com.tr) ferries link İstanbul Kabataş with Mudanya (₺24, two hours). BUDO also operates a summer Mudanya–Tekirdağ service. There is a helpful ticket and information booth near the ferry terminal for good advice on the best options to get to Bursa.

To Bursa, yellow bus 1/M runs from Mudanya ferry terminal to Bursa's Emek metro station

(₺3.50, half-hourly). From there you can continue to Şehreküstü metro station, the closest station to the city centre, just north of Kapalı Çarşı.

From Bursa, catch the 1/M bus from Emek metro station to Mudanya ferry terminal.

For other destinations, catch bus F/1 from the ferry terminal to Bursa *terminal* (otogar or bus station; ₺3.65, hourly).

Daily **İDO** (p291) ferries (more at weekends) link İstanbul Yenikapı and Kadıköy with Güzelyalı (₺32, 2¼ hours), 4km east of Mudanya ferry terminal. Bus 1/G links Güzelyalı to Bursa's Emek metro station, from where you can connect to central Bursa.

Eskişehir

📞 0222 / POP 685,130

Eskişehir may well be Turkey's happiest city – and with a massive university population, it is certainly among its liveliest. An oasis of liberalism in austere middle Anatolia, Eskişehir is increasingly popular with Turkish weekenders, and even boasts a small community of dedicated foreigners.

Eskişehir's progressive spirit is associated with mayor Yılmaz Büyükerşen, who realised the potential of the city's Porsuk River, adding walking bridges and a sand beach, while building pedestrian thoroughfares and a smoothly efficient tram system. In summer you can even explore the Porsuk by gondola or boat.

The cumulative result is Turkey's most liveable city, and a place where you can engage with the friendly and open-minded locals. With an atmospheric old quarter, roaring nightlife, cultivated cuisine, two parks and a fascinating science centre for kids, Eskişehir truly has much on offer.

◉ Sights

★ **Odunpazarı** HISTORIC SITE
(Ottoman Quarter) Eskişehir's protected heritage district is a real aesthetic treat. Elegant pastel-shaded traditional homes with distinctive overhanging stories and wood-framed shutters stand on narrow stone lanes, along with mosques and other historic structures. Many of the houses contain museums and cafes, while craftwork and vintage stalls dot the lanes. This was Eskişehir's first Turkish district, and it features Ottoman and even Seljuk structures. *Odun* means 'firewood' (the area was once a firewood bazaar).

★ **City Museum** MUSEUM
(Kent Müzesi; Türkmen Hoca Sokak 45, Odunpazarı; ⏱5; ⊙10am-5.30pm) Included in this collection is Eskişehir's Museum of Contemporary Glass Art, a unique display donated by about 70 Turkish and foreign artists. The tradition of melting and fusing glass dates to the Pharaohs, and a local Egyptologist (and university professor) revived the art and opened a studio in Eskişehir. The 1st floor details local history through informative panels and interactive screens.

★ **Eskişehir Science & Experiment Centre** SCIENCE CENTRE
(Eskişehir Bilim Deney Merkezi; ✆0222-444 8236; www.eskisehirbilimdeneymerkezi.com; Sazova Park, Kütahya Yolu; adult/student ⏱2/1; ⊙10am-5pm Tue-Sun) Like a cross between a science centre and a fairground, this colourful and hugely entertaining complex illustrates the many forces of nature through hands-on experiments. Interactive classics such as the oh-so-scary infinity bridge, the fountain-triggering xylophone and the counterweighted car get visitors pulling, pushing and pedalling. Free guided tours are available.

Kurşunlu Külliyesi Complex HISTORIC SITE
(Mücellit Sok, Odunpazarı; ⊙8am-10pm) This sublime old-town complex was built between 1517 and 1525 by a leading master of classical Ottoman architecture, Acem Ali, though internal structures were built and rebuilt in following centuries.

Behind the 1492 **Kurşunlu Mosque** with its *kurşunlu* (leaden) dome, the **medrese** houses the **Museum of Meerschaum** (⊙8am-5pm) FREE, which pays homage to the region's 'white gold', or meerschaum (luletaşı in Turkish), a light, porous white stone, in its artistically crafted form. There are some particularly elaborate pipes on display and a handicrafts bazaar.

Next to the *medrese,* the four-domed **tabhane** (guesthouse) may also have been a harem. The vaulted **imaret** (almshouse) and adjacent domed **aşevi** (kitchen), which respectively house glass-blowing and jewellery studios, were the culinary quarters. The dining hall, kitchen and alcoved oven partly remain. The Ottoman **caravansarai**, built after 1529, is a cultural centre used for weddings.

Atlıhan Complex MARKET, HISTORIC BUILDING
(Pazaroğlu Sokak 8, Odunpazarı; ⊙9am-8pm) Eskişehir is famous for its weird and wonderful white rock, mined locally and shaped into pipes and other objects. The Atlıhan Complex hosts two floors of local artisans' shops where you can browse objects made of this stone and see it being crafted. On the 1st floor, **Mavi Sanat Merkezi** (Atlıhan Complex 10; ⊙9am-8pm) has some unusual and beautiful ceramics and jewellery.

Archaeological Museum MUSEUM
(Atatürk Bulvarı; ⏱5; ⊙8am-6.30pm Tue-Sun) This modern museum showcases prehistoric artefacts, items from Hittite, Phyrygian and classical antiquity, including goddess figurines, floor mosaics and sarcophagi, plus many Greek, Byzantine and Ottoman coins. It has a good **cafe** (www.facebook.com/muzedecafe; off Atatürk Bulvarı; mains ⏱17-25; ⊙8am-midnight) overlooking the statuary dotting the garden.

🛏 Sleeping

Most recommended accommodation is found between the river and Anadolu University's Yunus Emre campus, walking distance from İsmet İnönü and Bağlar tram stops.

Book ahead if possible, especially at weekends, when Anatolian short-breakers hit town and some hotels hike prices.

Hosteleski HOSTEL $
(✆0505 204 8060; www.eskisehirhostel.com; Yıldırımer Sokak 27/1; dm/d/q €10/24/36; 🛜) Hosteleski offers all the backpacker essentials over three floors of a tall, narrow building: kitchen, terrace, lounge, laundry service, bike garage and movie nights. The friendly owners happily help with recommendations for sights, bars, restaurants and onward travel. The dorms and private rooms share bathrooms. Breakfast is an additional ⏱10; there is a bakery nearby on Cengiz Topel Caddesi. Some rooms have compact kitchenettes.

Arus Hotel HOTEL $$
(✆0222-233 0101; www.arusotel.com; Oğuz Sokak 1; s/d ⏱130/180; ❄🛜) Eskişehir's status as one of Anatolia's most vibrant cities is reflected in the opening of new hotels such as this. The central Arus offers modern and spacious rooms, a switched-on English-speaking team at reception and one of the city's best breakfast buffets. It's a short walk from here to bars, restaurants and Eskişehir's riverine charms.

Bulvar Hostel HOSTEL **$$**

(🖉 0222-335 0515; www.bulvarhostel.com; Porsuk Bulvarı 15; dm/d/f ₺38/110/155; 🌐🛜) Four-bed dorms (including a female-only option), comfy doubles and a four-person family room are combined at this excellent hostel with a central location just metres from the river. Bed linen and decor is bright and colourful, reflecting the city view just outside. There are on-site laundry facilities if you're down to your last shirt.

⭐ **Abacı Konak Otel** HISTORIC HOTEL **$$$**

(🖉 0222-333 0333; www.abaciotel.com; Türkmen Hoca Sokak 29; s/d ₺180/260; 🌐🛜) With its pastel heritage homes clustered around a flowering, fountain-filled courtyard, Abacı Konak is like your own personal Ottoman quarter. Its location in Odunpazarı, a protected heritage district, means the vintage furnishings, wood floors and ceilings are all original, and the tasteful, subdued decor matches.

Book ahead: the hotel is popular with Turkish groups, especially on weekends. The closest tram stop is Atatürk Lisesi.

🍴 Eating & Drinking

Eskişehir has a brilliant after-dark scene featuring great cafes, pubs, live venues and nightclubs fuelled by its student population, many of whom speak good English. Vural Sokak, known as Barlar Sokak (Bar Street), is a well-oiled lane where cocktail bars, shot bars, theme bars, DJ bars, *meyhanes* (Turkish taverns), clubs and venues jostle for attention, alongside the odd *kebapçı* (kebab eatery) to soak up the Efes beer.

⭐ **Avlu** TURKISH **$$**

(www.abaciotel.com/en/restaurants/avlu-restaurant; Abacı Konak Otel, Türkmen Hoca Sokak 29; mezes ₺10-12, mains ₺26-34) Avlu restaurant should be your go-to spot if you're only in town for a night. Its hotel location within a beautifully restored Ottoman mansion in Eskişehir's Odunpazarı historic district is elegant; the kitchen turns out classic Turkish cuisine; and there's live music from Tuesday to Saturday starting 8pm. In summer the dining action overflows to an outdoor pavilion.

⭐ **Mezze** SEAFOOD **$$**

(🖉 0222-230 3009; www.mezzebalik.com; Nazım Hikmet Sokak 2, Kızılcıklı Mahmut Pehlivan Caddesi; mezes ₺8-12, mains ₺20-40; 🕓4pm-1am) Aegean style comes to Anatolia at the excellent Mezze. Whitewashed decor brings to mind lazy lunches along Turkey's western coastline, and the shared meze plates and seafood are excellent. Sit back with river views from Mezze's terrace, and enjoy the beer, wine and rakı selection.

Ask up front the approximate cost of the various fish on offer to avoid surprises at the end of your meal.

Memphis INTERNATIONAL, PUB **$$**

(🖉 0222-320 3005; www.varunamemphis.com; İsmet İnönü Caddesi 102/C; mains ₺15-30; 🕓8am-midnight) Exposed brick, wine racks, ceiling-to-floor windows and cool artwork give Memphis the feel of a craft brewery; and its draught beer selection indeed extends beyond regular Efes to Efes Malt and ubercold Efes Şok Soğuk. The food is good too, a mix of Turkish flavours alongside international dishes from pizza and pasta to quesadillas and fajitas; the steak burger is recommended.

Cafe Del Mundo INTERNATIONAL, PUB **$$**

(www.delmundocafe.com; Siloönü Sokak 3; mains ₺14-35; 🕓11am-1am Mon-Fri, 8am-1am Sat & Sun) This cosy and colourful bar – created by travellers, for travellers – is the friendliest spot in town. The cheery yellow building near Barlar Sokak is splendidly decorated with assorted international memorabilia (licence plates, tickets, travel books and many billowing flags) and, continuing the global theme, serves dishes from pad Thai to pesto fusilli.

⭐ Entertainment

Peyote LIVE MUSIC

(www.peyote.com.tr; Vural Sokak; 🕓2pm-1am) This venue on Barlar Sokak hosts local acts from across the musical spectrum, including rock, metal, jazz, hip-hop and acoustic. Shows start around 11pm on Fridays and Saturdays and cost about ₺10; grab a drink beforehand in the adjoining courtyard. There are sometimes gigs on Wednesdays, too, so drop by if you're in town.

Eskişehir Municipal Symphony Orchestra LIVE MUSIC

(🖉 0222-211 5500; Büyükşehir Belediye Sanat ve Kültür Sarayı Opera Binası, İsmail Gaspıralı Caddesi 1) Eskişehir's symphony orchestra is one of Turkey's best, and offers weekly concerts for an enthusiastic local audience. It also provides backup for operas and ballets. Works performed here run the gamut from classical masterpieces to modern musicals, plus kids shows. The orchestra tours widely abroad and cooperates with visiting musicians, too.

❶ Information

At the **Tourist Office** (☎ 0222-230 1368; İki Eylül Caddesi; ⊙ 9am-5pm) little English is spoken, but helpful and maps and brochures are available. It's in the Valilik (regional government) building.

❶ Getting There & Away

The train station is northwest of the centre near İsmet İnönü tram stop. The otogar is 3km east.

Regular buses serve the following:

Afyon ₺28, three hours
Ankara ₺24, 3¼ hours
Bursa ₺23, 2½ hours
İstanbul ₺35, six hours
Kütahya ₺15, 1½ hours

Trains run to/from the following:

Ankara ₺30, 1½ hours, several daily
Konya ₺38.50, two hours, two daily
İzmir ₺40.50, 11 hours, nightly
İstanbul Pendik ₺45, 2½ hours, six daily

Car rental (☎ 0222-231 0182; www.europcar. com.tr; Kızılcıklı Mahmut Pehlivan Caddesi 22/B, Eskişehir; 1/3 days from ₺1130/400) is available from Europcar, handy for exploring the Phyrgian Valley on a day trip.

❶ Getting Around

The bus station is linked to central Eskişehir by trams and *servises* (free shuttles). A taxi from the centre costs around ₺15.

Prepaid tickets (₺2.40) are used for most public transport; buy from a booth or kiosk with the green-and-yellow circular Es Karti sign. Dolmuş journeys cost ₺2 and you pay the driver.

Trams on the ESTram network run between 6am and midnight; the normal waiting time is about seven minutes. Trams display their final destination at the front, but it can be confusing to identify which tram is which at certain crossover stops, so ask if unsure. Most accommodation, eating and drinking recommendations are between the İsmet İnönü and Bağlar tram stops.

Taxis are plentiful, and there are electronic signal buttons on some street-corner posts that you can press to hail one.

PHRYGIAN VALLEY

Anatolia's mysterious ancient Phrygians once inhabited this rock-hewn valley (Frig Vadisi), which runs haphazardly past Eskişehir, Kütahya and Afyon. Although an increasingly popular hiking destination, it is still relatively untouched and offers spectacular Phrygian relics. The rugged terrain is exhilarating and highly photogenic. The Afyon-area ruins are the best preserved, and the Eskişehir-area ruins also impress; Kütahya's are less abundant.

❂ Sights

Most sites are along dirt tracks and some can be very hard to find, even when you're right beside them. Navigation is slowly getting better, as local municipalities are collecting money to pave a 'Tourist Route' through the region.

❂ Eskişehir Ruins

As you travel from Seyitgazi to Afyon through Yazılıkaya Vadisi (Inscribed Rock Valley), turn south after 3km, down a road marked with a brown sign pointing to Midas Şehri. Further along this rough road a sign leads you right for 2km to the Doğankale (Falcon Castle) and Deveboyukale (Camel Height Castle), both riddled with formerly inhabited caves.

Further south, another rough track leads 1km to the Mezar Anıtı (Monumental Tomb), and a restored, rock-carved tomb. Continuing south again, you will find another temple-like tomb, Küçük Yazılıkaya (Little Inscribed Rock).

Midas Şehri (Midas City) is at Yazılıkaya village, several kilometres from Küçük Yazılıkaya and 32km south of Seyitgazi. The Midas Türbe (Midas Tomb) here is a 17m-high relief carved into volcanic tufa, and is covered in geometric patterns resembling a temple facade. During festivals, an effigy of Cybele would be displayed in the bottom niche. Phrygian-alphabet inscriptions – one bearing Midas' name – encircle the tomb.

A path behind the tomb leading to a tunnel passes a smaller tomb, unfinished and high in the rock. Continue upwards to the high mound, where an acropolis once stood. The stepped altar stone, possibly used for sacrifices, remains, along with traces of walls and roads. Interestingly, the first evidence of water collection comes from here – carved holes were found with slatted steps that trapped rainwater for the dry season.

❂ Afyon Ruins

Afyon-area ruins include examples from Phrygian to Turkish times. Start your

1. Tetrapylon (monumental gateway), Afrodisias (p313)
2. Roman theatre (p310), Hierapolis 3. Laodicea (p315) 4. Antonine Nymphaeum (p321), Sagalassos

Western Anatolia Highlights

Ancient ruins scatter this region where civilisations once prospered. On street corners and windblown plateaus, weathered inscriptions and chipped statues tell the stories of the Phrygians, Greeks, Romans, Ottomans and others. Wonderfully, because most of Western Anatolia's ruins are off the tourist circuit, at some sites it might be just you, the Anatolian wind and a ticket salesman who is keen to chat. Arrive early or late to have vast theatres and civic squares to yourself.

Hierapolis

The ruins of Hierapolis, a multicultural spa city in Roman and Byzantine times, stand in decaying splendour atop Pamukkale's famous snow-white mountain of travertine rock formations.

Afrodisias

Splendiferous Afrodisias boasts two of western Turkey's most photogenic relics. The tetrapylon (monumental gateway) welcomed travellers when Afrodisias was the provincial capital of Roman Caria, and the 30,000-seat stadium still echoes with the roars of gladiators and spectators.

Sagalassos

The Roman ruins of Sagalassos, which was also a major Pisidian city, are scattered in an unbeatably poetic location at an altitude of 1500m in the Taurus Mountains.

Laodicea

Entered along a colonnaded street, Laodicea was a prosperous city on two trade routes and home to one of the Seven Churches of Asia (mentioned in the Book of Revelation).

İznik

İznik's Roman walls and Byzantine churches recall its heyday when the first Ecumenical Council, which shaped Christianity, met here.

exploration in Doğer, around 50km north of Afyon. Head north on the D665 en route to Eskişehir, and turn left at Gazlıgöl after 22km. Doğer village's **han** (caravanserai) dates to 1434 (if it is locked, ask for the key at the municipal building opposite). From here, dirt tracks lead to lily-covered **Emre Gölü** (Lake Emre), which is overlooked by a small stone building once used by dervishes; and a rock formation with a rough staircase, the **Kırkmerdiven Kayalıkları** (Rocky Place with 40 Stairs). The track then continues 4km to **Bayramaliler** and Üçlerkayası, which feature rock formations called *peribacalar* (fairy chimneys), resembling Cappadocia's.

After Bayramaliler, **Göynüş Vadisi** (Göynüş Valley) is a 2km walk from the Eskişehir–Afyon road; it has fine Phrygian rock tombs decorated with lions.

At Ayazini village – turn right off the D665 around 9km north of Gazlıgöl – there once stood a rock settlement, **Metropolis**, also reminiscent of Cappadocia. The apse and dome of its Byzantine **church** are hewn from the rock face, and several rock-cut **tombs** have carvings of lions, suns and moons.

Around Alanyurt, east of Ayazini, more caves exist at **Selimiye**; and there are further fairy chimneys to discover at Kurtyurdu, Karakaya, Seydiler and İscehisar, including the bunker-like rock **Seydiler Kalesi** (Seydiler Castle).

☞ Tours

In Afyon and Eskişehir respectively, travel agents **Ceba Tour** (☑ 0506 437 6969, 0272-213 2715; cebaturizm@gmail.com; Ordu Bulvarı, Konak Apt Altı 20/B, Afyon; half-day tour 1/2/3 people €60/100/150) and **Ufuk Özkarabey** (☑ 0532 765 2540, 0222-220 0808; www.ufkunestur.com.tr; Cengiz Topel Caddesi 42/E, Eskişehir; ⊙ 10am-5pm Mon-Fri) offer day trips. Agencies in towns such as Pamukkale and Selçuk also offer excursions.

❶ Getting There & Away

The easiest way to explore the ruins is by rental car; try **Europcar** (p305) in Eskişehir. Between October and April, heavy rain sometimes renders the area's back roads impassable.

Visiting the ruins by public transport is difficult, but there are dolmuşes to the villages from Afyon otogar. Regular buses and dolmuşes on the main roads between Eskişehir, Kütahya and Afyon will also pick up from the roadside, so if you start early, it may be possible to visit a few sites in a day.

From Afyon, dolmuşes serve Ayazini (on the Afyon–Eskişehir road). From the church dropoff, walk 500m to find the Metropolis rock settlement. To continue to Doğer, take the dolmuş back towards Afyon, but disembark at Gazlıgöl and pick up a dolmuş heading northwest.

PAMUKKALE & AROUND

Pamukkale

☑ 0258 / POP 2630

Pamukkale has been made eternally famous by the gleaming white calcite travertines (terraces) overrunning with warm, mineral-rich waters on the mountain above the village – the so-called 'Cotton Castle' (*pamuk* means 'cotton' in Turkish). Just above the travertines lies Hierapolis, once a Roman and Byzantine spa city, which has considerable ruins and a museum.

Unesco World Heritage status has brought measures to protect the glistening bluffs, and put paid to the days of freely traipsing around, but the travertines remain one of Turkey's singular experiences.

While the photogenic travertines get busloads of day-trippers passing through for a quick soak and photo op, staying overnight allows you to visit the site at sunset and dodge some of the crowds. This also gives time for a day trip to the beautiful and little-visited ancient ruins of Afrodisias and Laodicea, and to appreciate the village of Pamukkale itself.

◉ Sights

Pamukkale is a dedicated tourist town around Cumhuriyet Meydanı, but in quieter parts of the village life is still soundtracked by bleating goats and birdsong. Pamukkale's double attractions – the shimmering white travertines/terraces and the adjacent ruins of ancient Hierapolis – are a package deal. Both are accessed on the same ticket and comprise their own national park, located on a whitewashed hill right above Pamukkale village.

Of the site's three entrances, the **south gate** (Map p310; ⊙ 6am-9pm) is most practical. It is about 2.5km from Pamukkale, on the hill near Hierapolis' main sights, meaning you see both Hierapolis and the travertines while walking downwards, exiting through the middle gate and finishing in the village. The **north gate** (⊙8am-8pm Apr-Oct, to 5pm Oct-Apr) is about 3km away, allowing you to enter Hierapolis via the necropolis and Frontinus St and, likewise, walk downhill to the village. Both gates are uphill from Pamukkale, best accessed by dolmuş, taxi or (in most cases) a free lift provided by your accommodation rather than walking; Hierapolis and the travertines comprise a large site, so save your energy.

The **middle gate** (Map p309; ⊙8am-8pm Apr-Oct, to 5pm Oct-Apr), on the edge of Pamukkale itself, is at the base of the terraced mountain, meaning you walk uphill over the travertines to Hierapolis and take the same route back to the village – not a logical route, but it does offer two looks at the travertines. If you are just after a little R & R in the pools, this is the quickest and easiest entrance.

Note the various opening times of the entrance gates; you can exit when you like. Tickets are only good for one entry, so you must see the site in one go. Nevertheless, you can stay inside as long as you like, and for most people a single visit is enough; pensions are generally happy to make a picnic lunch so you can take your time and enjoy an all-day visit. Additional fees apply for the Hierapolis Archaeology Museum and Antique Pool (though you can arguably get enough out of the experience without shelling out for these).

Travertines   NATURE RESERVE
(Map p310; ₺35; ⊙9am-7pm summer) The World Heritage–listed saucer-shaped travertines (or terraces, as they are also called) of Pamukkale wind sideways down the powder-white mountain above the village, providing a stunning contrast to the clear blue sky and green plains below. To protect the unique calcite surface that overruns with warm, mineral-rich waters, guards oblige you to go barefoot (or in socks or shower shoes), so if you're planning to walk down to the village via the travertines, be prepared to carry your shoes with you.

Although the ridges look rough, in reality the constant water flow keeps the ground mostly smooth, even gooey in places, and the risk of slipping is greater than that of cutting your feet. To walk straight down without stopping takes about 30 minutes. The constant downward motion can be hard on the knees.

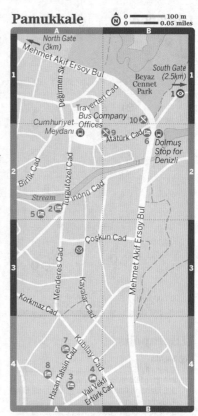

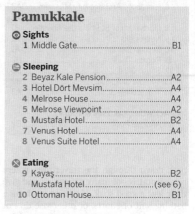

Pamukkale

◎ **Sights**
1 Middle Gate..B1

◎ **Sleeping**
2 Beyaz Kale Pension...........................A2
3 Hotel Dört Mevsim...........................A4
4 Melrose House..................................A4
5 Melrose Viewpoint............................A2
6 Mustafa Hotel..................................B2
7 Venus Hotel.....................................A4
8 Venus Suite Hotel.............................A4

◎ **Eating**
9 Kayaş...B2
  Mustafa Hotel...........................(see 6)
10 Ottoman House...............................B1

Although the terrace pools are not particularly deep, you can get fully submerged in the thermal water. There is a gushing channel of warm water at the top of the

Hierapolis

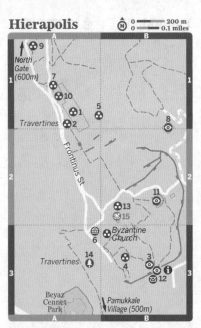

N 0 —— 200 m
0 —— 0.1 miles

The ruins of this Roman and Byzantine spa city evoke life in a bygone era, in which Greeks, Romans and Jews, pagans and Christians, and spa tourists peacefully co-existed. It became a curative centre when founded around 190 BC by Eumenes II of Pergamum, before prospering under the Romans and, even more so, the Byzantines, when large Jewish and Orthodox Christian communities comprised most of the population. Recurrent earthquakes brought disaster, and Hierapolis was finally abandoned after an AD 1334 tremor.

Hierapolis' location atop the tourist-magnet travertines above Pamukkale seems to have blessed it with a budget rather more ample than most Turkish archaeological sites. The orderly paved pathways, well-trimmed hedges, flower-filled expanses, slatted walkways and shady park benches make Hierapolis far more genteel than even the famous Ephesus. Wild and raw it is not, but for those wishing, or needing, to see an ancient site on well-maintained terrain, Hierapolis' curvaceous mountaintop home is ideal.

➡ **Byzantine Gate to the Roman Theatre**
Entering at the south gate, walk through the 5th-century Byzantine gate (Map p310), built of travertine blocks and marble among other materials, and pass the Doric columns of the 1st-century gymnasium (Map p310). An important building in health-oriented Hierapolis, it collapsed in a 7th-century earthquake. Continue straight on for the foundations of the Temple of Apollo (Map p310). As at Didyma and Delphi, eunuch priests tended the temple's oracle. Its alleged power derived from an adjoining spring, the Plutonium (named after the underworld god Pluto). Apparently only the priests understood the secret of holding one's breath around the toxic fumes that billowed up from Hades, immediately killing the small animals and birds they sacrificed.

The spectacular Roman theatre (Map p310), built in stages by emperors Hadrian and Septimius Severus, could seat more than 12,000 spectators. The stage mostly survives, along with some decorative panels and the front-row VIP 'box' seats.

➡ **Martyrium of St Philip the Apostle**
From the Roman theatre, tracks lead uphill and to the left towards the less-visited but fascinating Martyrium of St Philip the Apostle (Map p310), an intricate octagonal

Hierapolis

path down through the travertines, where representatives of many nations sit and give their legs a good soak. If you do not have a bathing suit or shorts, or otherwise do not wish to get too wet, there are plenty of dry sections leading down. Also note that going at midday means crowds and sharp sunlight reflecting off the dazzling white surface; later in the afternoon is better.

structure on terrain where St Philip was supposedly martyred. The arches of the eight individual chapels, marked with crosses, originally had heptagonal interiors.

Differing accounts from ancient sources have created confusion over precisely which Philip was commemorated here – if it really was Jesus's apostle, he was allegedly hung upside down from a tree after challenging the pagan snake-worshippers at their nearby temple. An apocryphal ancient source claims that at Philip's death, a yawning abyss opened in the earth, swallowing up the Roman proconsul, the snake-worshippers, their temple and about 7000 hapless bystanders.

Whichever Philip was martyred here, his body was reportedly found about 40m away, in a Byzantine structure excavated by Italian archaeologists. That sensational news of August 2011 revived interest in St Philip and Hierapolis. Considering that his martyrium clearly suffered fire damage in the 5th century, it is possible that the unearthed body was indeed relocated from the martyrium at that time.

➡ **Hellenistic Theatre to Frontinus Street**

From the Martyrium, a rough path that gives fantastic views of the site and the plains beyond leads west across the hillside to the completely ruined Hellenistic theatre (Map p310), above the 2nd-century agora (Map p310). One of the largest ever discovered, the agora was surrounded by marble porticoes with Ionic columns on three sides, and enclosed by a basilica on the fourth.

From the theatre, follow the steep overgrown diagonal path towards the poplars to reach the agora (alternatively, backtrack to the Martyrium of St Philip the Apostle for an easier path down). Walking downhill through the agora, you will reemerge on the ridgeline main path. Turn right on colonnaded Frontinus Street, where some original paving and columns remain. Monumental archways once bounded both ends of what was the city's main commercial thoroughfare. The ruined Arch of Domitian (Map p310), with its twin towers, is at the northern end; just before them, the large latrine (Map p310) building has two floor channels, for sewage and for fresh water.

➡ **Necropolis**

Beyond the Arch of Domitian are the ruined Roman baths (Map p310), and further past these, an Appian Way–style paved road leads to the north gate. An extraordinary necropolis (Cemetery; Map p310) extends several kilometres northwards. The clustered circular tombs here probably belonged to the many ancient spa tourists whom Hierapolitan healers failed to cure.

Hierapolis Archaeology Museum MUSEUM (Map p310; Roman Baths, Hierapolis; ₺5; ⊙8am-5pm) Housed in former Roman baths, this excellent museum exhibits spectacular sarcophagi from nearby archaeological site Laodicea and elsewhere; small finds include jewellery, oil lamps and stamp seals from Hierapolis and around; and in the third room, its entrance watched by a sphinx, there are friezes and Roman-era statuary from the nearby Roman theatre. Left of the entrance are impressive capitals from Hierapolis' agora and other parts of the site.

🏃 Activities

Ballooning and paragliding are growing in popularity in the skies over Pamukkale, and offer a bird's-eye view of Hierapolis and the travertines. Shop around; ask to see operators' credentials and check they are fully insured, for your personal safety as much as the good of your wallet. Ballooning in particular may only operate during the peak tourist season.

Antique Pool SWIMMING (Map p310; Hierapolis; adult/child under 6yr/7-12yr ₺32/free/13; ⊙8am-7.30pm summer, to 5.30pm winter) The sacred pool in this spa's courtyard has submerged sections of original fluted marble columns to lounge against. The water, which is abundant in minerals and is a more-than-balmy 36°C, was thought to have restorative powers in antiquity, and may well do still. In summer it is busiest from 11am to 4pm.

🛏 Sleeping

Pamukkale's numerous pensions and small hotels are split between the bustling centre, where travertine views and touristic businesses abound and Hierapolis' middle gate is a short walk away, and the rustic lanes on the village's south side. Stiff competition translates into good service. Most places offer free pick-ups from Pamukkale otogar and transport to the Hierapolis gates; a pool; laundry service; and tour-booking services.

Book ahead in high summer. Campers can usually pitch their tent on premises for a small fee.

Beyaz Kale Pension
PENSION **$**

(Map p309; ☑ 0258-272 2064; www.beyaz kalepension.com; Oguzkaan Caddesi 4; s/d/q/f ₺70/90/140/160; ❅ ☎ ☒) On a quiet street just outside the village centre, the cheery yellow White Castle has 10 spotless rooms on two floors, some more modern than others. The friendly lady of the house, Hacer, serves some of the best local pension fare (mains from ₺25 to ₺30) on the relaxing rooftop terrace, which has travertine views. A cot is available for junior travellers.

Hotel Dört Mevsim
PENSION **$**

(Map p309; ☑ 0258-272 2009; www.hoteldort mevsim.com; Hasan Tahsin Caddesi 27; s/d/tr/q €20/30/40/50; ❅ ☎ ☒) The 'Four Seasons' is run by a welcoming farming family on a quiet lane in the village. The cheaper rooms are basic, but the setting is a winner, with a shaded poolside terrace where you can dig into the home-cooked food. Recent renovations include a new roof above the welcoming restaurant.

Mustafa Hotel
PENSION **$**

(Map p309; ☑ 0258-272 2240; mustafamotel@ hotmail.com; Atatürk Caddesi 22; s/d ₺50/80; ❅ ☎) The 10 rooms here are basic but affordable options close to all the action in the village centre, and the excellent terrace has travertine views. There's a good restaurant downstairs.

★ Melrose House
HOTEL **$$**

(Map p309; ☑ 0258-272 2250; www.melrose househotel.com; Vali Vekfi Ertürk Caddesi 8; s €35-55, d €40-55; ❅ ☎ ☒) The closest thing to a boutique hotel in Pamukkale, Melrose House has 17 spacious, modern rooms, including a family room and suites with circular beds. Decor throughout mixes handmade Kütahya tiles and pillars, wallpaper and exposed stonework, and the poolside restaurant is an agreeable place to linger. A vegetarian menu is available

Venus Hotel
HOTEL **$$**

(Map p309; ☑ 0258-272 2152; www.venushotel. net; Hasan Tahsin Caddesi; r €38-45; ❅ @ ☎ ☒) The Venus is a comfortable hideaway with a traditional Turkish poolside restaurant, and quiet corners for reading or chatting with fellow travellers. Reached along corridors decorated with Ottoman tiles, the modern rooms at the rear are pleasant, with white and turquoise bedding. The owners also organise day trips to local sights.

Melrose Viewpoint
HOTEL **$$**

(Map p309; ☑ 0258-272 3120; www.melrose viewpoint.com; Çay Sokak 7; s/d/tr/f from €35/40/50/60; ❅ ☎ ☒) Resembling a turquoise cruise ship complete with porthole windows, this hotel has 17 rooms with king-size beds, full-length mirrors, small balconies and a tasteful smattering of curves and flourishes. Rooms on the 1st floor have travertine views, and the terrace restaurant enjoys sweeping vistas. When we last dropped by, the finishing touches were being made to a sun-trap rooftop restaurant.

Venus Suite Hotel
HOTEL **$$$**

(Map p309; ☑ 0258-272 2270; www.venushotel.net; Sümbül Sokak 7; r €50-55; ❅ ☎ ☒) Pamukkale's newest hotel is one of its best. Rooms are stylish and spacious – including compact, sunny balconies – and shared spaces are arrayed around a well-shaded pool. The breakfast buffet is one of the best we've seen in Turkey – literally spanning two long walls of the dining room – and there's usually a friendly welcome from the canine co-manager.

✕ Eating

Pamukkale's restaurants are mostly unremarkable and overpriced – your accommodation will likely offer better fare. A recent trend is restaurants offering Asian flavours – including Korean and Chinese – to cater to travellers from north Asia.

Ottoman House
TURKISH **$**

(Map p309; Atatürk Caddesi 29; gözleme ₺6; ☉ 11am-11pm) For a snack and a beer after visiting the travertines, this place opposite Hierapolis's middle gate does *gözleme* (savoury pancake), made by a woman at the entrance. Head through the Ottoman-style salon for a terrace overlooking the nearby water park and travertines. Prices for mains are less reasonable.

Kayaş
TURKISH, BAR **$$**

(Map p309; Atatürk Caddesi 3; mezes ₺8, mains ₺15-25; ☉ 11am-11pm) This central place with a long bar and big TV (for football matches, generally) is the best spot for a beer, but it also serves Turkish food at better prices than other eateries. *Sigara böreği* (deep-fried, cigar-shaped *börek* – filled pastry – filled with cheese) are among the tasty mezes, and mains include *güveç* (meat and vegetable stew) and *şiş* kebaps (roasted skewered meat).

Mustafa Hotel PIDE, INTERNATIONAL **$$**
(Map p309; Atatürk Caddesi 22; mains ₺10-24, set menu ₺15; ⊘10am-11pm; 𝄐) Wood-fired pide and pizza are the speciality, but kebaps, crepes, felafel, hummus and other mezes are also available.

❶ Information

Pensions offer advice, maps and assistance. As in any tourist town, most have their own favourite travel providers and disparage everyone else, so compare offers. The **tourist office** (Map p310; 𝄐0258-272 2077; ⊘8am-5.30pm summer, to 5pm winter) has Hierapolis maps.

DANGERS & ANNOYANCES

Pamukkale's travel agencies have a bad reputation; stories of poor service and fly-by-night operations abound. They are best avoided apart from booking a day trip to Afrodisias. Definitely do not book tours and activities in other parts of Turkey, such as Cappadocia. Many agencies share offices with the bus companies, so when buying bus tickets make sure you are dealing directly with the bus operator or their appointed agent.

Travellers are sometimes taken off the *servis* from Denizli and taken to a pension to receive the hard sell. Asian travellers in particular have been targeted with this and other scams. If this happens, leave and go to your first choice of accommodation.

❶ Getting There & Away

AIR

Turkish Airlines (p605) flies between **Denizli Çardak Airport** (www.cardak.dhmi.gov.tr) and İstanbul Atatürk, and Pegasus Airlines serves İstanbul Sabiha Gökçen. A shuttle to/from Pamukkale costs from ₺25. Make sure you will not have to change at Denizli otogar.

BUS

Most services to/from Pamukkale involve changing in Denizli. Buses and **dolmuşes** (Map p309) (₺4, 40 minutes) run frequently between Pamukkale and Denizl's modern new otogar. If you buy a ticket beginning or ending in Pamukkale, the bus company should provide a *servis* to/from the otogar.

Bus companies (Map p309) including Metro (www.metroturizm.com.tr), Kamil Koç (www.kamilkoc.com.tr) and Pamukkale (www.pamukkale.com.tr) have offices on and around Pamukkale's Cumhuriyet Meydanı, and most buses drop passengers here or on Mehmet Akif Ersoy Bulvarı, the main road into town. Eager

touts hawking accommodation sometimes lie in wait, but you can make up your own mind. Most accommodation will pick you up for free.

The following are frequent services from Denizli:

Afyon ₺40, four hours
Ankara ₺55, seven hours
Antalya ₺35, four hours
Aydın (for Selçuk) ₺15, two hours
Bodrum ₺30, five hours
Bursa ₺65, 10 hours
Eğirdir ₺30, four hours
Isparta ₺25, three hours
İstanbul ₺75, 12 hours
İzmir ₺20, four hours
Konya ₺50, six hours
Marmaris ₺30, four hours
Nevşehir (for Cappadocia) ₺50, nine hours

For direct services between Pamukkale and Fethiye, book online with **Selçuk-Fethiye Bus** (𝄐0543-779 4732; www.selcukfethiyebus.com; ₺40; ⊘departs Fethiye/Pamukkale 9am/4pm Mon, Wed, Fri & Sun). Pick-up from your accommodation is included in the price.

CAR

Operators including **Europcar** (𝄐0258-264 5354; www.europcar.com.tr; Denizli Cardak Airport; ⊘7.30am-7pm) are located at Denizli airport, and hotels and pensions in Pamukkale can also arrange cars. This is a good option if you wish to explore Afrodisias independently.

TAXI

Taxis to Hierapolis's south gate costs ₺25 from Pamukkale or ₺50 from Denizli. Some Pamukkale accommodation operators will also drop you there at no charge.

TRAIN

Daily trains run from nearby Denizli to Selçuk. Travel agencies in Pamukkale can arrange shuttles to/from Denizli train station for around ₺20.

Afrodisias

The remoteness of Afrodisias (admission ₺15, parking ₺10; ⊘8am-7pm Apr-Oct, to 5pm Nov-Mar, last entry 1hr before closing), out in the Anatolian hinterland among Roman poplars, green fields and warbling birds, safeguards its serenity from the masses. Afrodisias may not have fine individual ruins to match those of Turkey's famous archaeological site Ephesus, but it wins for sheer scale, and its on-site museum is impressive too, housing many of the site's treasures. The site is relatively untended, with some side paths disappearing into thickets and bramble, and with luck you could have it almost to yourself, creating the exotic sensation of discovering lost ruins.

History

Afrodisias' acropolis began around 5000 BC as a prehistoric mound. Its later temple was a pilgrimage site from the 6th century BC and, by the 1st century BC, the city had become large and prosperous, due to its rich marble quarry and imperial favour. In the 3rd century AD, the 150,000-strong city became provincial capital of Roman Caria.

Early Byzantine Afrodisias developed into an Orthodox city, with the Temple of Aphrodite being transformed into a church, while the stone from other buildings was reused for defensive walls (c AD 350). By the 7th century, Afrodisias had been renamed Stavroupolis (City of the Cross), and historical sources attest to the presence of Byzantine bishops here until the 10th century. Despite being abandoned in the 12th century, it remained a Byzantine titular bishopric until the 15th century.

Sometime after the city's abandonment, a Turkish village, Geyre, developed here. The village was ruined by a 1956 earthquake and relocated, allowing archaeologists to work on the site.

◉ Sights

From the car park, a tractor will tow you 500m to the entrance in a connected carriage. Take the circular site tour first, then dry your sweat over a drink, saving the cooler indoor museum for last. You have two route choices; the anticlockwise route is less affected by the occasional mid-morning package-tour groups.

Turn right beside the museum for the grand house with Ionic and Corinthian pillars on the left. Further on the left, the elaborate tetrapylon (monumental gateway) once greeted pilgrims coming to the Temple of Aphrodite. The impressive monument has been reconstructed using 85% of its original blocks.

The tomb of Professor Kenan T Erim is on the lawn here. A Turkish professor from New York University, the trailblazing archaeologist oversaw excavations here from 1961 to 1990.

Continue down the steps on the straight footpath, and turn right across the grassy field for the 270m-long stadium. One of the biggest and best-preserved classical stadiums, this massively long structure has 30,000 overgrown seats. Some were reserved for individuals or guilds, and the eastern end was a gladiatorial arena.

Afrodisias

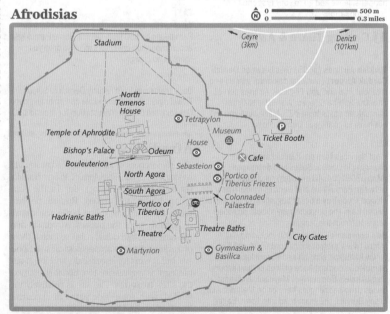

Standing in the dark and sloping tunnel and looking out onto the huge field, you can yourself imagine the fear, exhilaration and sheer adrenaline the ancient warriors would have felt, striding towards imminent death amid a raucous crowd demanding blood.

The erstwhile Temple of Aphrodite, once dedicated to the goddess of love, was converted to a basilica around AD 500. Its cella was removed, its columns shifted to form a nave, and an apse was added, making it hard to now visualise the original structure. Nearby, the Bishop's Palace is a grand house that previously accommodated Roman governors. Just beyond, the left fork in the path leads to the beautiful marble bouleuterion (council chamber of a Hellenistic city), preserved almost undamaged for 1000 years by mud.

Return to the fork and follow the sign to the *tiyatro* (theatre). The path leads past the north agora and through the early 2nd-century AD Hadrianic baths to the south agora, with a long, partially excavated pool, and the grand Portico of Tiberius.

Stone stairs up the earthen, prehistoric mound lead to the white marble theatre, a 7000-capacity auditorium complete with stage and individually labelled seats. Just southeast was the large theatre baths complex.

The path now leads downhill to the Sebasteion: originally a temple to the deified Roman emperors, it was visually spectacular, with a three-storey-high double colonnade decorated with friezes of Greek myths and imperial exploits. In the same area, the impressive many-faced friezes come from the Portico of Tiberius.

❶ Getting There & Away

Afrodisias is 55km southeast of Nazilli and 101km from Denizli. Visiting by public transport from Pamukkale is tricky, as you have to change dolmuş numerous times. A guided tour or transfer (transport only) is easier; book with travel agencies around Cumhuriyet Meydanı in Pamukkale. Transfers/guided tours cost about ₺50/150 per person, though this fluctuates depending on the number of participants and by operator. Generally, agencies will not undertake the journey for less than about ₺200 total; between May and October, there are normally enough travellers to guarantee departures. Most operators leave around 9.30am and return by 4pm, giving you 2½ hours on-site.

WORTH A TRIP

LAODICEA

Laodicea was once a prosperous commercial city straddling two major trade routes, famed for its black wool, banking and medicines. Cicero lived here for a time before Mark Antony had him liquidated, and large Jewish and Orthodox Christian populations coexisted here. Today, the columns standing in the long grass have good views of the travertines at Pamukkale.

Laodicea is 8km from Pamukkale. Pamukkale–Denizli dolmuşes (minibuses that stop anywhere along their prescribed route) pass the turn-off for Laodicea (₺3 from Pamukkale). From the signpost on the Pamukkale–Denizli road, it is a 1km walk to the ruins past the ticket office, cafe and toilets. Alternatively, pensions can arrange transport, and it may be possible to tag Laodicea onto a visit to the nearby mountaintop ruins of Afrodisias.

LAKE DISTRICT

Tucked away within the forested hills and mountains of inner Anatolia, the lake region has an escapist, even otherworldly feel. At its heart is Eğirdir (*ey*-eer-deer), a placid town overlooked by mountains including Sivri (1749m), Davraz (2653m) and Barla (2800m). It makes an excellent base for hiking, climbing and seeing regional sights – or for simply relaxing by the tranquil lake surrounding it.

In addition to the lake, its water activities and tasty fish, the Eğirdir area offers year-round action, including the rose harvest in May and June, apple harvest in autumn and skiing in winter. History-loving hikers can explore the St Paul Trail and ascend to the lofty ruins of Sagalassos, perched among the rocky peaks of the Taurus Mountains. But you may find it is the kind hospitality of the locals, unaffected by mass tourism, that makes visiting most worthwhile.

Eğirdir

☏ 0246 / POP 17,600

Surrounded by Eğirdir Gölü (Lake Eğirdir) and ringed by steep mountains, Eğirdir offers a relaxing respite from Anatolia's heat and dust. Highlights include a Byzantine fortress, Seljuk structures and an old quarter ringed by beaches and fishing boats. Good-value family-run pensions offer hearty home-cooked meals, adding to the attraction of Eğirdir as an excellent base for exploring regional sites and undertaking outdoor activities.

Like all lake towns, Eğirdir has much going on under the surface, and it attracts a varied population. Hills above the town host an army special-forces training base, while a distant western shore conceals its underwater equivalent. In summer Muslim devotees of the quasi-mystical Nur movement gather in nearby Barla village. At summer's end, Yörük mountain nomads descend to do business, while autumn's influx of apple wholesalers stimulates certain dens of iniquity on Yeşilada (Green Island), which was joined to the mainland and the rest of Eğirdir 55 years ago.

Sights

Hızır Bey Camii
MOSQUE

(Map p318) Originally a Seljuk warehouse (built 1237), this simple stone structure in the centre became a mosque in 1308 under Hamidoğulları emir Hızır Bey. It features a clerestory (an upper row of windows) above the central hall and new tiles around the *mihrab*. Note the finely carved wooden doors and stone portal, and the minaret's faded blue tile trim.

Pınar Pazarı
MARKET

On Sundays between August and October, you can buy apples, cheese, yoghurt or even a goat at this village market run by the Yörük Turks, who descend from their mountain redoubts to hawk their wares and stock up for winter. In the old days, wily Yörük mothers would use these public events to negotiate marriages for their children. Pınar is 7km southeast of Eğirdir, served by dolmuş (₺2.25).

Castle
RUIN

(Map p318) A few hundred metres down the peninsula from the centre stand the massive walls of the ruined castle of Akrotiri (the Byzantine name for Eğirdir), which allegedly dates back to 5th-century BC Lydian king Croesus.

Dündar Bey Medresesi
HISTORIC BUILDING

(Map p318) In 1281 Hamidoğulları emir Felekeddin Dündar Bey turned this grand stone structure in the centre – then a 67-year-old Seljuk caravanserai – into a *medrese*. The small on-site bazaar sells Galatasaray and Fenerbahçe (football team) strips, floppy hats and holiday gear.

Ayastafanos Church
CHURCH

(Map p318) Eğirdir's last remaining Orthodox church is on Yeşilada, near İskele Park. Thirteen other churches were torn down after the Greek community departed in the 1923 population exchange. The 12th-century Byzantine stone building originally had a roof made of a ship's hull. Unfortunately it is usually locked.

Activities & Events

★ Eğirdir Outdoor Centre
ADVENTURE SPORTS

(Map p318; ☑ 0246-311 6688; www.facebook.com/Egirdir-Outdoor-Centre-646795995451585; ⊙ 8am-7pm) Run by outdoor enthusiast İbrahim Ağartan and family, this activities centre offers free information and is the go-to place for everything from mountain-bike hire (per hour/half-day/day ₺4/25/35) to boat trips and transport for independent travellers to remote local sights and stops on the St Paul Trail. It also offers camping equipment hire (tent, sleeping bag, mat, rucksack and stove for ₺50) and tours from fishing to snowshoeing. On the left as you walk from the castle to Yeşilada.

The centre has loads of excellent recommendations and self-guided maps for biking and walking trails around the area, and popular guided excursions include day trips to the hilltop ruins of Sagalassos (per person ₺75) or to Lake Kovada National Park (Kovada Gölü Milli Parkı) and the Çandır Kanyon (per person ₺75). If you're a keen kayaker or windsurfer, ask here to borrow equipment from the local training centres for a nominal fee. Also has a laundry (₺20) and acts as a book exchange.

Sivri Dağı
HIKING

(Mt Sivri; Akpınar) Mt Sivri (1749m) on the St Paul Trail makes a good day walk from Eğirdir. The 6km return trek to the peak from the hill village of Akpınar takes about 3½ hours. Organise transport to/from Akpınar, 5km from Eğirdir, through your accommodation or Eğirdir Outdoor Centre.

If you have a car, Akpınar is worth a drive for its viewpoint and teahouse overlooking the lake and peninsula. A return taxi from Eğirdir costs around ₺20. Also ask the outdoor centre about local walks and mountain-biking opportunities in the area.

Eğirdir Hamam HAMAM
(Map p318; hamam ₺15, massages ₺30; ⏰7am–11pm, men Sat-Wed, women Thu & Fri) Renovated 13th-century hamam located behind the post office on Isparta Konay Yolu.

Dedegöl Dağcılık Şenliği HIKING
(Dedegöl Mountaineering Festival; ⏰May) Over a Friday and Saturday on or after 19 May, Eğirdir's mountaineering club organises this communal scramble up Mt Dedegöl (2998m). A night is spent at the Karagöl base camp (1600m), before a 4am start for a long day's trek to the peak and back down.

Participation is free, and transport and meals are arranged for 1000 hikers; you must register through Eğirdir Outdoor Centre and organise your own equipment.

🛏 Sleeping

Eğirdir's family-run pensions cluster around the castle ruins (a short walk from the centre) and at the peninsula's far end, on the road-accessible island of Yeşilada (1.5km from the centre). Make sure your bedroom windows have screens – Eğirdir's harmless but irritating little lake bugs will fly towards any lit area.

Şehsuvar Peace Pension PENSION $
(Map p318; ☎0246-311 2433; www.peacepension.com; Yeşilada; s/d ₺60/110; 🛜) Tucked away in the middle of the island, near Yeşilada's tranquil *meydan* (square), friendly Şehsuvar has a shaded terrace with grapevines and four bright, spotless rooms. The owners don't speak much English, but nonetheless try to help with information about local activities.

Çetin Pansiyon PENSION $
(Map p318; ☎0246-311 2154; 3 Sokak 12; s/d ₺40/70) Near the castle, Çetin has six basic rooms up a narrow staircase, some with views across the lake. The room at the top has a rudimentary kitchenette, and all the bathrooms have recently been refurbished. Breakfast is an additional ₺15.

★ Fulya Pension PENSION $$
(Map p318; ☎0543-486 4918; www.fulyapension.com; Camiyanı Sokak 5; s/d €40/50; 🌀🛜) Recent renovations have transformed the well-established Fulya into one of Eğirdir's best places to stay. Rooms are sunny and spacious – some have heritage stone walls and hand-crafted day beds – and the new rooftop restaurant provides lake and mountain views. The multilingual owner also runs the Eğirdir Outdoor Centre (p316),

DON'T MISS

ST PAUL TRAIL

Almost two millennia ago, the apostle Paul trekked northwards from Perge (near the coast and Antalya) through the Anatolian wilds to today's Yalvaç, near Eğirdir. The winding 500km route – from sea level to a 2200m peak – passes crumbling ancient ruins. Although some hikers today start the trail from the south, you will have more options and help available by starting in Eğirdir, which is a good base for both the northern and southern sections of the 500km trail.

Check out Culture Routes in Turkey (http://culturaeroutesinturkey.com), Trekking in Turkey (www.trekkingintur key.com) and Kate Clow's *St Paul Trail* guidebook, which is available along with much other information in **Eğirdir Outdoor Centre** (p316).

and can provide plenty of information about exploring the area.

Charly's Pension PENSION, HOSTEL $$
(Map p318; ☎0246-311 4611; www.charlyspension.com; 5 Sokak 2; s/d €30/40; 🌀🛜) In the heart of the old Greek quarter behind the castle, İbrahim Ağartan and family offer characterful accommodation in an Ottoman-era building with sweeping lake views. This is the place to linger over a generous buffet breakfast or a beer, chatting to other guests while the multilingual İbrahim organises activities and dispenses information to make the most of your time.

Nearby Lale Pension is part of the same operation, and guests enjoying Lale's laid-back vibe make the short walk to Charly's for breakfast.

Ali's Pension PENSION $$
(Map p318; ☎0246-311 2547; www.alispension.com; Yeşilada; s/d/tr/f from €28/40/55/70; 🌀🛜) At the far end of the island, Eğirdir's oldest pension is a great choice, with eight handsomely furnished and spotless rooms. English- and German-speaking Birsan and her fishing family offer excellent hospitality, and the home-cooked breakfasts and dishes such as crayfish are delicious and abundant.

Göl Pension PENSION $$
(Map p318; ☎0246-311 2370; www.golpension.com; Yeşilada; r ₺160; 🌀🛜) On the island,

Eğirdir

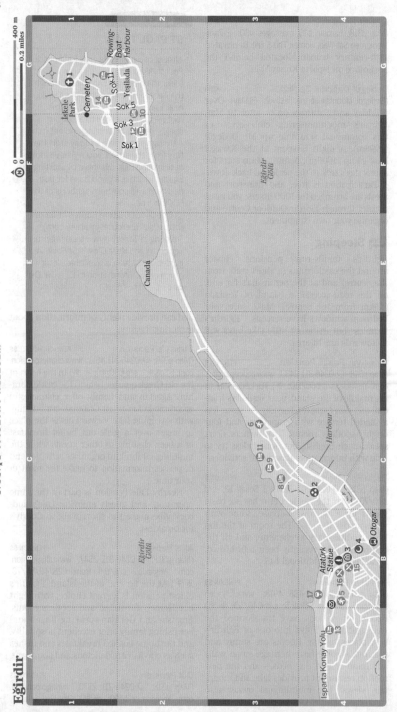

WESTERN ANATOLIA EĞİRDIR

0 0
0.2 miles
400 m

İskele Park
Cemetery
Rowing-Boat Harbour
Sok 11
Yeşilada
Sok 5
Sok 3
Sok 1
Eğirdir Gölü
Canada

Eğirdir Gölü

Harbour

Atatürk Statue
Isparta Konya Yolu
Otogar

Eğirdir

the family-run 'Lake' Pension has a pleasant breakfast room and great views from a roof terrace, where two rooms open onto a private section. At the top of the stairs is a cute attic-style room with sloped ceiling. It usually opens for the season from late April.

Choo Choo Pension PENSION $$
(Map p318; ☎0246-311 4926; www.choochoopension.com; Yeşilada; s/d/tr/f ₺100/140/180/240; ❄☎) This island pension is run by an old fishing clan, which also runs neighbouring Halikarnas restaurant on the lakefront. The nine rooms are rather pricey by local standards, but they are spacious and modern, recently renovated with new beds and mattresses. There is a roof terrace, and homemade *börek* features in the lakeside breakfast.

Nis Otel BOUTIQUE HOTEL $$$
(Eskiciler Konaği; Map p318; ☎0246-333 2016; www.eskicilerkonagi.com; Kaynak Sokak 19; s/d ₺140/210; ❄☎) This carefully restored wooden mansion is definitely raising the quality of accommodation in Eğirdir. Rooms are a subtle combination of heritage features and modern decor, and the beautiful shared public spaces are dotted with antiques and colourful Turkish rugs. In fine weather,

breakfast and meals are served on what is probably Eğirdir's most spacious al fresco deck. Lake-view rooms cost ₺20 more.

✖ Eating & Drinking

Pension dinners are tasty, convenient, and great for meeting fellow travellers. Local specialities include *istakoz* (crayfish), lake carp, bass and other fish. Between mid-March and mid-June, it is illegal to fish the lake, so catches served at this time are likely come from the freezer. Head to Yeşilada for fish restaurants with a view, and to the Hızır Bey Camii area for economic pide and kebap sandwiches. Eğirdir is famous for *elma* (apples).

Coşkun Döner KEBAP $
(Map p318; kebaps from ₺3; ⊙11am-3pm) With plastic tables on the pavement, 'Lively' Döner does kebaps in *dürüm* (that is, in sandwich form) or on a plate. For a postprandial cuppa, the neighbouring *çay ocağı* (tea stove) serves Eğirdir's best brew, according to locals. It's a short walk from the town's Atatürk statue.

Eğirdir Outdoor Centre CAFE $
(Map p318; mains ₺10-15; ⊙10am-8pm; ☑) This outdoor activity centre does home food and olive oil–soaked dishes including green beans and aubergine. *Gözleme* (₺5), cappucino and espresso are also on the menu. It's on the left as you walk from the castle to Yeşilada.

Günaylar PIDE, KEBAP $
(Map p318; mains ₺10-20; ⊙11am-10pm) One of two pide and kebap restaurants on the small, central square overlooking the Atatürk statue, Günaylar also serves *güveç* and *ızgara* (grill) dishes.

Eğirdir Elma Evi JUICE BAR
(Map p318; Kubbeli Mahallesi Mehmet Yiğitbaşı Caddesi; juices from ₺2; ⊙8am-7pm) The Eğirdir region is renowned for apples, and this compact red kiosk on the lakeside is a handy one-stop shop for crisp apples, freshly squeezed juices, apple *pekmez* (syrup made from juice) and even apple-infused soaps. Tasty snacks of sliced dried apple come with a side order of stunning lake views.

Akpınar Yörük Çadiri TEAHOUSE
(Akpınar Koyu; snacks ₺7; ⊙11am-10pm) Eğirdir's best views are from this mountain-top teahouse in the village of Akpınar, 5km uphill from Eğirdir. Grab a table in the cosy interior – designed to look like a nomad's yurt – or

WESTERN ANATOLIA EĞİRDİR

LOCAL KNOWLEDGE

BEACHES & BOAT TRIPS

From the peninsula's northern shore by the castle to its tip at Yeşilada, you'll find several relaxing small beaches, many with food stalls and *çay ocakları* (tea stoves). Out of town, at Yazla (less than 1km down the Isparta road) lies sandy **Belediye Beach**. Several kilometres further north is pebbly **Altınkum Beach**. In summer dolmuşes run every 15 minutes (₺2) from the otogar (bus station). Taxis cost around ₺15. Further north again, 11km towards Barla, is long, sandy **Bedre Beach**. Cycle or catch a taxi (₺30). **Eğirdir Outdoor Centre** (p316) offers mountain-bike rental.

Some of Eğirdir's best swimming spots are accessible only by **boat trips** (per person ₺75), which also allow you to relax, try some fishing, and generally bliss out on the lake's breezy blue waters and in its verdant lagoons.

Boat trips, which run from 15 June to 15 September, have traditionally provided a second income for fishers and pension owners. Arrange a trip through your pension or Eğirdir Outdoor Centre, which charges ₺75 per person for a six-hour excursion. The trip involves visiting hidden coves, swimming, sunbathing, a barbecue lunch of freshly caught fish, and you'll gain an insight into a local fisher's life.

Fishing trips (per person ₺25) can also be booked through the Eğirdir Outdoor Centre. Count on an early start (between 5am and 7am), two to three hours on the water, and a hands-on, sunrise experience helping a local fisher haul in the nets. It can be chilly on the lake so wrap up warmly. Fishing trips are not offered from March 15 to June 15, to allow the lake's fish to breed.

---

enjoy a *gözleme* crammed with cheese, potato and tahini on the huge deck. Akpınar is a bracing walk or a ₺20 taxi ride.

ℹ Information

The best sources of information are the **Eğirdir Outdoor Centre** (p316) and, if arriving by bus, the Kamil Koç office at the otogar.

ℹ Getting There & Around

From Eğirdir otogar, pensions near the castle are within walking distance; Yeşilada is 1.5km away (₺12 by taxi, ₺2 by dolmuş).

AIR

Turkish Airlines (p605) connects İstanbul Atatürk Airport with **Isparta Süleyman Demirel Airport** (www.suleymandemirel.dhmi.gov.tr). Travelling to Isparta Süleyman Demirel Airport, 66km west of Eğirdir, catch a dolmuş from Eğirdir to Isparta (₺5, 30 minutes). Get off at Migros supermarket in Isparta and either take a taxi from across the road (₺20, 30 minutes) or the free shuttle from outside Isparta *belediye* (town hall) or *köy garaj* (village otogar) to the airport (30 minutes).

Accommodations can organise airport transfers to Eğirdir (from ₺130).

BUS

A few buses per day (more in summer) run to the following:

Antalya ₺25, three hours
Aydın (for Selçuk) ₺45, six hours
Denizli (for Pamukkale) ₺35, 3½ hours
İstanbul ₺72, 10 hours
İzmir ₺52, eight hours

Buy tickets at least a day in advance, especially over summer weekends. Kamil Koç and Isparta Petrol offices at Eğirdir **otogar** (Map p318) also sell tickets for other bus companies.

Kamil Koç (www.kamilkoc.com.tr) runs some direct services to Göreme in Cappadocia (₺60, eight hours), but you'll have more options if you connect through Konya (₺40, four hours); if you leave Eğirdir early, you can spend a few hours sightseeing in Konya before continuing to Cappadocia.

The frequency of long-haul buses is greater from nearby Isparta, accessible by frequent buses and dolmuşes (₺5, 30 minutes) or taxi (₺100). In Isparta, intercity buses terminate at the main otogar and services from local destinations such as Eğirdir at the *köy garaj*, 5km away on the other side of the city centre. *Servises* connect the two.

Sagalassos

To visit the sprawling ruins of Sagalassos, high amid the jagged peaks of Ak Dağ (White Mountain), is to approach myth: the ancient ruined city set in stark mountains seems to illuminate the Sagalassian perception of a sacred harmony between nature, architecture and the great gods of antiquity.

Sagalassos is one of the Mediterranean's largest archaeological projects, but it is rarely troubled by tour buses or crowds; sometimes the visiting archaeologists or sheep wandering the slopes outnumber tourists. This is a place for getting perspective, for feeling the raw Anatolian wind on your face, and of course for seeing some very impressive ancient ruins. While you can rush through in about 90 minutes, take the time to linger and properly appreciate this mountaintop site.

Although repeatedly devastated by earthquakes, the ancient city was never pillaged, and reconstruction is slowly moving ahead.

History

Sagalassos was founded about 1200 BC by a warlike tribe of 'Peoples from the Sea' who were seeking defensive positioning. A large swamp (perhaps even a lake) probably covered part of the lowland where today's village stands. Ancient Sagalassos would thus have been protected on three sides by mountains, and on the other by water.

Sagalassos later became second only to Antiocheia-in-Pisidia in Pisidian society. The locals adopted Greek cultural, linguistic and religious mores. Alexander the Great claimed it in 333 BC, and its oldest ruins date from the Hellenistic period he opened. Although most surviving structures are Roman, inscriptions are in Greek (the ancient world's lingua franca).

Sagalassos prospered under the Romans, its grain export, mountain springs and iron ore making it economically important and self-sufficient. Despite the high elevation, Sagalassos was well integrated into Rome's Anatolian road system. In the 4th century AD, the city became a Christian, Byzantine outpost. However, plague and disasters such as the 590 earthquake damaged the city's sophisticated structures and dispersed its surviving population. After a massive 7th-century quake, Sagalassos was abandoned; survivors moved to villages or occupied fortified hamlets among the rubble.

Seljuk warriors defeated the last Byzantine defenders in the mid-13th century, but the remote and largely ruined city had little strategic value for the Ottomans. And so it slumbered for centuries, guarded by sheep and birds, until 1706, when a French traveller commissioned by King Louis XIV 'discovered' it. Yet it was not until 1824 that the ancient city's actual name was finally deciphered, by a British reverend and antiquarian, FVJ Arundell.

◉ Sights

At the **ticket booth** (www.tursaga.com; ₺10; ⊘ 7.30-6pm, to 7pm in summer), request the *anahtar* (key) to the oft-closed Neon Library. From the entrance you can turn up to the right, starting from the top and working your way downhill (a somewhat steeper approach), or proceed from the bottom and work your way up and around.

Following the latter, clockwise route, you'll see the marble **colonnaded street** that marked the city's southern entrance from the lowland valleys. The lack of wheel indentations suggests that is was mainly used by pedestrians. It is the spine and central axis of Sagalassos, stretching upwards through it.

From the bottom, it would have appeared that the city's terraced fountains were one triple-tiered tower of water – an impressive optical illusion. Passing through the **Tiberian gate**, see the **lower agora** and the massive reconstructed **Roman baths** complex to the right. At the agora's rear (back up the metal staircase), the **Hadrianic nymphaeum** stands flanked by the mountainside. The well-preserved former fountain here contains elaborate sculptures of mythic (and mostly headless) nereids and muses. A ruined **Odeon** sits just beyond.

The main path now winds up to the **upper agora**, once the main civic area and political centre. Thanks to restoration, it boasts Sagalassos's most impressive attraction: the **Antonine Nymphaeum**, a huge fountain complex some 9m high and 28m wide. Originally wrought from seven different kinds of stone, the fountain was ornately decorated with Medusa heads and fish motifs. Although it collapsed in an earthquake in AD 590, the rubble lay clustered, aiding modern restorers. The impressive result is a massive structure supported by rows of thick columns (including bright blue marble ones in the centre), through which huge sheets of water gush into a lengthy receptacle. The fountain is bedecked by statues, including a large marble Dionysus replica (the original is in nearby Burdur Museum).

The agora's western edge is flanked by the **bouleuterion**; some of its seating remains intact. Rising over the fountain in the northwest corner is a 14m-high **heroon** (hero's monument). In 333 BC Alexander the

ℹ VISITING SAGALASSOS

Since Sagalassos sprawls uphill across steep terrain, wear sturdy shoes. Even on hot and sunny days, the treeless and exposed site is often windy, and clouds can suddenly arrive (bring an extra shirt or sweater). In summer go early or late to avoid the midday sun.

It takes roughly 1½ to four hours to explore Sagalassos. Signage is excellent, with detailed and colourful representations of the various structures. A map at the entrance details various routes around the site (you may wish to photograph it, as it does not appear again). During the summer, archaeologists sometimes give free guided tours and answer questions. Out of season, it is basically all yours.

The site www.tursaga.com is an excellent resource. It has downloadable maps and guides covering the exploration of both Ağlasun and Sagalassos.

Great had a statue of himself erected here (now also in Burdur Museum). Peer over the agora's southern edge to spot the **macellon** (food market), dedicated to Emperor Marcus Aurelius, with its trademark Corinthian columns. Note the **tholos** in the middle; the deep fountain was used to sell live fish.

From here, turn right and up into the hills for the late-Hellenistic **Doric fountainhouse**, its piping now reattached to its original Roman-era source. Behind it is Sargalassos's only restored covered building, the **Neon Library**, which features a fine mosaic floor. In the darkness at the rear, an original Greek inscription commemorates Flavius Severianus Neon, a noble who funded the library in AD 120. The back podium contained curving and rectangular niches for storing reading material. The library was modified over the following centuries, with the striking mosaic of Achilles' departure for Troy commissioned during the brief reign of Emperor Julian (361–363), whose

unsuccessful attempt to restore paganism to the Orthodox empire augured his demise.

Finally, atop the hill is Sagalassos's 9000-seat **Roman theatre** – one of Turkey's most complete, despite earthquake damage to the seating rows. Just above its top steps, walk parallel with the theatre through its eerie tunnel, where performers and contestants once entered (note that it is dark, strewn with debris and has a very low exit point). The bluff east of here offers stunning panoramic views over the city, mountains and plains.

🛏 Sleeping & Eating

⭐ **Sagalassos Lodge & Spa**   HOTEL $$$
(📞 0248-731 3232; www.sagalassoslodge.com; Kıraç Mahallesi, Yaylakent 1 Sokak 1; s/d ₺130/190; ❄ 🛜 ⛲) Surrounded by pine trees, the new Sagalassos Lodge & Spa is located midway between Ağlasun and the hilltop ruins of Sagalassos. Modern and spacious rooms feature huge bathrooms; bikes are available for independent exploration; and other relaxing options include a sun-kissed pool, and a spa and wellness centre featuring a hamam. The excellent restaurant is also open to outside guests.

ℹ Getting There & Away

A return taxi from Eğirdir costs about ₺200 (minimum three passengers), with vehicles typically leaving at 9am and returning by 4pm. Organise through your pension or **Eğirdir Outdoor Centre** (p316), which links up independent travellers to reduce costs and runs trips for ₺75 per person.

Hourly dolmuşes run from Isparta's *köy garaj* to Ağlasun (₺6, one hour, from 6.30am). A few daily **Ağlasun Minibüs Kooperatifi** (www.aglasunkoop.com) minibuses link Ağlasun with Antalya (₺15, 2½ hours).

From Ağlasun, a steep and winding road climbs 7km to the Salagassos ticket office. There is also a 3km path. A return taxi costs ₺50 (including waiting time at Sagalassos of an hour or so); your dolmuş driver from Isparta may be persuaded to do the same for a similar fee.

Antalya & the Turquoise Coast

Best Places to Eat

➡ İzela Restaurant (p339)

➡ Kalamaki Restaurant (p350)

➡ Retro Bistro (p358)

➡ Fethiye Fish Market (p336)

➡ Yöruk Restaurant (p365)

Best Places to Sleep

➡ Hotel Unique (p335)

➡ Hotel Villa Mahal (p350)

➡ Hideaway Hotel (p356)

➡ Mehtap Pansiyon (p360)

➡ Myland Nature Hotel (p364)

Why Go?

The ancient Lycians were on to something when they based their empire on the stunning Teke Peninsula, the chunk of Mediterranean paradise between Antalya and Fethiye. This is Turkey at its most staggeringly beautiful: sandy sweeps of shore hug a coastline lapped by jade waters and backed by forest-blanketed slopes. The Turquoise Coast is prime sun-and-sea territory, but step off the beach and you'll find ancient cities such as Xanthos, Tlos and Arykanda perched precariously atop hills, and ornate tombs carved into cliffs at Pınara and Myra. Hike between ruins on a section of the 500km-long Lycian Way and you'll be richly rewarded with scenery worth the sweat.

If you just want the beach, though, you're in the right place. For starters there's Patara's knock-'em-dead stretch of sand, the beach linking Olympos and Çıralı, and photogenic Kaputaş. Of course there are ancient sites just around the corner from all three.

When to Go
Antalya

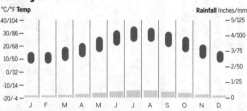

°C/°F **Temp**										Rainfall Inches/mm	

Mar–Apr Prime walking time. Stride across rugged hills alive with spring flowers.

May Sneak in before peak season and set sail on the Med. September's also good.

Jun–Aug Summer silly season: Antalya, Kaş, Fethiye and Dalyan are bustling and festive.

Antalya & the Turquoise Coast Highlights

1 Kekova Island (p361) Kayaking or cruising over the city of Simena, submerged by 2nd-century earthquakes.

2 Kayaköy (p339) Discovering the eerie and surreal Greek ghost town abandoned a century ago.

3 Patara (p346) Brushing up on classical history among the ruins before an afternoon on the 18km-long beach.

4 Lycian Way (p334) Hiking some of the famous trail, from holiday havens such as Kaş to blissful villages like Kaleköy.

5 Kaleiçi (p366) Wandering the labyrinthine streets of Antalya's historic district, before hopping on a tour boat at the Roman harbour.

6 Blue Voyages (p337) Setting sail from Fethiye, Göcek or Demre to experience this lush slice of the Med on a *gület* (Turkish yacht).

7 Chimaera (p364) Hiking up Mt Olympos at night, after a day of Olympos' beach and ruins, to see the eternal flame.

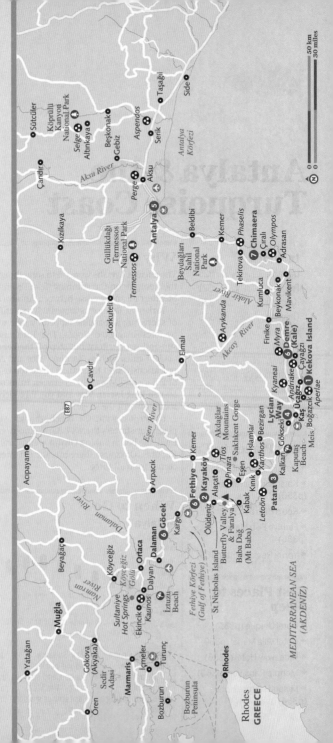

❶ Getting There & Away

Antalya is the region's transport hub, receiving numerous daily flights from all over Turkey and Europe in summer. Dalaman also has a busy international airport, while all the major Turkish bus companies serve the towns and cities from Antalya west to Dalyan.

If you catch a long-distance bus on the Teke Peninsula, you will likely follow the coast to Antalya or Fethiye before heading inland. It's normally possible to pick up an overnight bus to İstanbul from the major towns, with extra services laid on in summer.

Daily ferries link Kaş with the Greek island of Meis (Kastellorizo).

Dalyan

📞 0252 / POP 5094

Laid-back little Dalyan may be prime package-tour fodder, but away from the main street, lined cheek-to-jowl with restaurants and bars, it retains much of its original sleepy riverside character. Once a small farming community, today the atmospheric ruins of Kaunos and the hinterland of fertile, beautiful waterways bring an armada of excursion boats from Marmaris and Fethiye during summer.

As well as the ruins on its doorstep, Dalyan is an excellent base for exploring Köyceğiz Gölü (Lake Köyceğiz) and the turtle rehabilitation centre at nearby İztuzu Beach. Once you're done lapping up the sun on a boat trip or traversing ancient city ruins, pull up a pew riverside to admire Dalyan's most famous feature: the mighty Kings' Tombs of ancient Kaunos. Hewn into the cliffs, they take on a golden glow as the sun sets.

◎ Sights

★ Kaunos   ARCHAEOLOGICAL SITE

(Map p328; admission ₺10; ⊙ 9am-8pm Apr-Oct, 8am-5pm Nov-Mar) Founded in the 9th century BC, Kaunos (or Caunus) was an important Carian city by 400 BC. On the border with Lycia, its culture reflected aspects of both empires.

On the left as you enter, the theatre is well preserved; on the hill above are remnants of an acropolis and fabulous views over the surrounding countryside. Straight ahead when you enter are impressive ruins of a Roman bath and a 6th-century church, while down the slope is the port agora.

Kings' Tombs   TOMB

(Map p328) Dalyan's famous Lycian-style tombs are carved into cliffs across the Dalyan River, southwest of the centre. You can get good views of the house-like Carian tombs by walking south from town along Maraş Caddesi to the western end of Kaunos Sokak. Alternatively, board one of the private rowing boats moored next to Saki restaurant in Dalyan (₺5 return); it will take you across the river to the teensy settlement of Çandır, from where it's a five-minute walk to the tombs.

İztuzu Beach   BEACH

(İztuzu Kumsalı) An excellent swimming beach, İztuzu (Turtle) Beach is one of the Mediterranean nesting sites of the loggerhead turtle, and special rules to protect it are enforced. Although the beach is open to the public during the day, night-time visits (8pm to 8am) are prohibited from May to September. A line of wooden stakes on the beach indicates the nest sites, and visitors are asked to keep behind them to avoid disturbing the nests.

This 4.5km-long strip of sand is 10km south of Dalyan's centre and accessible via road and the Dalyan River. Minibuses (₺3.50, 20 minutes) run between the beach and Cumhuriyet Meydanı in the centre of Dalyan every half-hour in season (four services daily in winter).

Sea Turtle Research, Rescue & Rehabilitation Centre   WILDLIFE RESERVE

(Deniz Kaplumbağaları Araştırma, Kurtarma ve Rehabilitasyon Merkezi (DEKAMER); 📞 0252-289 0077; http://dekamer.org.tr; İztuzu Beach; donations welcome; ⊙ 10am-6pm) ⌖ At the southern end of İztuzu Beach is the headquarters of this turtle rescue centre, established in 2009 largely through the influence of June Haimoff (Kaptan June (p327)), whose reconstructed *baraka* (beach hut) now serves as a small museum to her life and work. The centre has saved many loggerhead and green turtles, and you'll see 30kg to 40kg turtles injured by fishing hooks, nets and boat propellers being treated.

🏃 Activities

Dalyan Kooperatifi   BOATING

(Map p328; 📞 0541 505 0777) You can save yourself a lot of hassle by taking boats run by the Dalyan Kooperatifi, whose members moor on the river southwest of Dalyan's main square. Boats leave the quayside at 10am or 10.30am heading to Lake Köyceğiz, Sultaniye Hot Springs and İztuzu Beach. The tours, including lunch, cost ₺35 per person.

The shorter four-hour afternoon tour, leaving at 2pm, costs ₺25.

Boats belonging to the cooperative also operate a river dolmuş service between Dalyan and İztuzu Beach, charging ₺10 for the return trip. In high summer boats head out every 20 minutes from 10am or 10.30am to 2pm and return between 1pm and 7pm (5pm or 6pm in shoulder season). Avoid any trips advertising themselves as 'turtle-spotting' tours, which inappropriately lure turtles out during daylight using bait. Only join tours on boats with propeller guards to protect the turtles; these can be identified by a flag bearing the Kaptan June Sea Turtle Conservation Foundation's logo.

If you can drum up a team of like-minded folk, you can hire a passenger boat that holds from eight to 12 people. A two-hour tour just to Kaunos costs ₺100 for the boat; if you want to visit the Sultaniye Hot Springs as well, count on three hours and ₺130. Clearly negotiate a price per boat or per person, as captains have been known to claim misunderstandings to drive the price up. Tours also cross the lake to Köyceğiz' Monday market (₺20, 10.30am to 4pm with three hours in Köyceğiz) and follow the coast west from İztuzu Beach to Ekincik beach and caves (₺50 including lunch, 10am to 4pm).

Sultaniye Hot Springs   HOT SPRINGS
(Sultaniye Kaplıcaları; ☑ 0507 853 8333; admission ₺8; ⊙ 8am-11pm) For some good (and dirty) fun, head for the Sultaniye Hot Springs, on the southwest shore of Lake Köyceğiz, which are accessible from both Köyceğiz and Dalyan. These bubbling hot mud pools (temperatures can reach 39°C) contain mildly radioactive mineral waters that are rich in chloride, sodium, hydrogen sulphide and bromide.

To get here from Dalyan, take a boat tour or a dolmuş boat (₺10, 30 minutes), which leave when full (every half-hour or so in summer, every hour otherwise) from the riverfront. You can also cross the river on a rowboat to Çandır (₺5 return) and walk 17km from there.

From Köyceğiz, take the bus headed for Ekincik (₺10) at 9am, which will drop you at the springs. The bus runs daily between June and September, returning at 6pm. Alternatively you can hire a taxi (₺70 return) or visit on a boat tour.

Kaunos Tours   ADVENTURE SPORTS
(Map p328; ☑ 0252-284 2816; www.kaunostours. com; Sarısu Sokak 1/A) At the eastern end of the main square, opposite the landmark sea-turtles statue, Kaunos Tours offers any number of organised activities, both on and off the water. These include canyoning (₺120), sea kayaking (₺120), jeep safaris (₺100), guided treks (₺112) and a luxury *gület* (Turkish yacht) cruise around a dozen islands in the Göcek area (₺144). Prices include lunch.

Ethos Dalyan Dive Centre   DIVING
(Map p328; ☑ 0555 412 5438, 0252-284 2332; www.dalyandive.com; Yalı Sokak 5) This professional outfit offers snorkelling and diving trips. Day-long excursions, including two dives and lunch, are offered, leaving at 10am and returning by 4.45pm.

🛌 Sleeping

Dalyan Camping   CAMPGROUND $
(Map p328; ☑ 0252-284 5316, 0506 882 9173; www.dalyancamping.net; Kaunos Sokak 4; campsites per person ₺20, caravans ₺50, bungalows incl breakfast ₺80-120, without bathroom ₺60-90; P ⊛ ❄ ⚛) This well-shaded site offers rustic bungalows in three sizes, with stone floors and basic furniture, as well as space to park the caravan or set up your tent. Smaller bungalows don't have en suites or air-conditioning. There's a kitchen and washing machines for guest use, and the spa jetty-terrace attached to the barbecue restaurant looks over to the Kings' Tombs.

Bahaus Resort Dalyan   HOSTEL $$
(☑ 0533 688 2988, 0252-284 5050; www.bahaus resort.com; İztuzu Yolu 25; dm €20, r/tr/q/ste from €65/85/95/110; P ⊜ ❄ ⊛ ⚛) Originally a 'hostel resort' and now more family oriented, this southern sister of İstanbul's Bahaus Hostel is spread over an enormous farm-like property with 17 boutiquey rooms, including a dorm. Food at breakfast is locally sourced, barbecues regularly take place, free bikes are offered to guests and a raft of activities can be arranged. The complex even has a gym.

Midas Pension   PENSION $$
(Map p328; ☑ 0252-284 2195; www.midasdalyan. com; Kaunos Sokak 32; s/d ₺120/150; P ⊜ ❄ ⚛) Selçuk and Saadet Nur are the welcoming hosts at this family-friendly riverside pension complete with waterside deck-cum-dock shaded by trees. The 10 whitewashed rooms, five in the main house and five in the garden, are cosy and clean with towel-art swans laid out to welcome you. The adjoining Likya Pension charges the same prices, but is less pleasant.

LOCAL KNOWLEDGE

KAPTAN JUNE, MARINE ENVIRONMENTALIST

Sea turtles were the last thing on Briton June Haimoff's mind when she sailed into Dalyan on her boat *Bouboulina* in 1975. But after 'Kaptan June', as the locals affectionately dubbed her, set up house in a *baraka* (hut) on İztuzu Beach, got to observe the *caretta caretta* (loggerhead turtles) at ground level, and fended off, with the help of a number of Turkish and foreign environmentalists, plans to develop the beach into a 1800-bed Marmaris-style hotel resort, they became her life's work. June set up the Kaptan June Sea Turtle Conservation Foundation (www.dalyanturtles.com) and was awarded an MBE in 2011 at age 89.

What is the greatest threat to the sea turtles?

Humans. The proliferation of dams and roads has devastated lots of the Mediterranean coast. The turtles' habitats are being destroyed for the sake of tourist development. As for injuries to the turtles, more than 90% are human-inflicted and come from fishing hooks and nets and, most commonly, boat propellers.

What steps has the foundation taken to reduce these?

Our first project was to give away locally manufactured propeller guards to excursion boats on the Dalyan River. We are now looking into sourcing and distributing biodegradable fishing line that won't harm the turtles if they happen to ingest it. It has not been easy to persuade local boat operators to fit propeller guards, but interest is growing. We maintain our promise to supply and fit these guards to boats without charge to the boat owners.

How can visitors to İztuzu Beach reduce their impact?

The urge to see a turtle in nature is not easily satisfied; they only come out at night during mating season and the beach is closed then. Some boat companies offer 'turtle-spotting' tours by day and attract the turtles by feeding them their favourite crab or chicken, which is not suitable for them. I recommend travellers join tours run by boats with propeller guards; these can be identified by a flag bearing the foundation's logo. The boat cooperative, especially the younger captains, is becoming more supportive. Once visitors use the services of these captains exclusively, others will follow suit. We hope that one day local legislation will be introduced to stop the unsuitable feeding of turtles and support the fitting of propeller guards, but in the meantime we continue to work towards these aims.

★ **Kilim Hotel**　BOUTIQUE HOTEL **$$$**
(Map p328; 0532 573 9577, 0252-284 2253; www.kilimhotel.com; Kaunos Sokak 11; s/d/f €52/66/79; P ⊕ ✴ 🛜 🌊) With its 15 huge, airy rooms, you can't go wrong at this peaceful home away from home. Turkish-British owners Becky and Emrah have created a relaxing retreat where guests really do feel like friends. From the rugs adorning the walls to the rooftop physiotherapy, massages, shiatsu and holistic treatments, a feeling of culture pervades the tranquil getaway.

★ **Happy Caretta**　HOTEL **$$$**
(Map p328; 0532 645 8400, 0252-284 2109; www.happycaretta.com; Kaunos Sokak 26; s/d/tr from €55/75/105; P ⊕ ✴ 🛜) Amid a magical garden of cypress trees and palms, the 14 rooms here are simple and rather small, but comfortable and stylishly decorated with natural materials. The lovely terrace-dock waiting for you to take the plunge is a plus,

and the view of the illuminated Kings' Tombs by night is priceless.

Dalyan Resort　RESORT **$$$**
(Map p328; 0533 683 4466, 0252-284 5499; www.dalyanresort.com; 114 Sokak 12; s €90-102, d €120-136; P ⊕ ✴ 🛜 🌊) This 100-room spa resort is on its own little peninsula jutting into the river about 1.2km from the town centre, with boat shuttles to İztuzu Beach. The service is discreet and there are views of the Kings' Tombs from the skittle-shaped pool, which is overlooked by the rooms and restaurant.

Kamarca House Hotel　BOUTIQUE HOTEL **$$$**
(0252-284 4517; www.kamarcahotel.com; Tepearası Köyü; r €220; P ⊕ ✴ 🛜 🌊) If you're seeking luxury amid absolute tranquillity, head for this 'gourmet hotel' in Tepearası village, 8km from Dalyan en route to Köyceğiz. The rooms and suites are wonderfully decorated in a tactile mix of natural wood and stone, antique furnishings and original

Dalyan

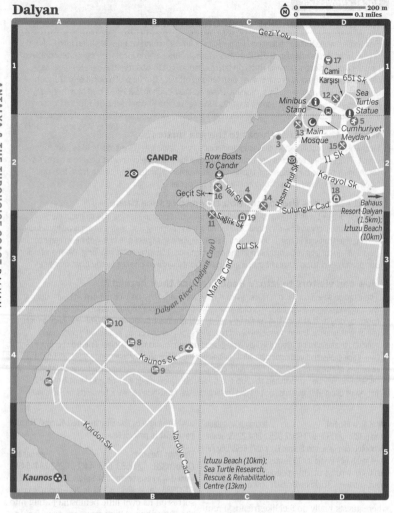

There is a host of cafes, bars and nightspots along Maraş Caddesi.

artwork. Hostess Kamer's cooking is legendary; she ran a restaurant in the USA. Full-board accommodation is available.

🍴 Eating & Drinking

Dalyan's restaurant scene swings between good quality and tourist-oriented places making generally poor versions of international staples, with most eateries found on Cumhuriyet Caddesi and Maraş Caddesi. For local eateries, head to the warren of side streets between Cumhuriyet Caddesi and Karayol Sokak to the south. Saturday is market day – great for fresh local produce.

Dalyan İz CAFE $
(Map p328; ☎ 0542 451 5451; www.dalyaniz.com; Özalp Sokak 1; cakes ₺5-9; ☺ 9.30am-7pm Fri-Wed) This sweet garden cafe is hugely popular with Dalyan expats due to the ever-changing array of homemade baking and good filter coffee. It's also home to a shop selling interesting hand-painted ceramics and tiles, and the friendly Turkish-British owners are a great source of local information.

Dalyan

Metin Pide PIDE $
(Map p328; ☎ 0252-284 2877; Sulunger Sokak; pide/pizza ₺10/15; ☺ 11am-10pm) This garden restaurant is popular locally for its pizza and pide (Turkish-style pizza), with all the classic toppings on offer, but the other dishes are not as good.

Dostlar Cafe TURKISH $
(Map p328; ☎ 0252-284 2156; Camı Karşısı 10; mains ₺15; ☺ 11am-10pm) Attached to a honey shop, 'Friends' Cafe has a rustic feel with its chequered tablecloths. It does *börek* (filled pastry) and all-day *kahvaltı* (Turkish breakfast) as well as Dalyan's usual burgers and international staples.

★ **Kordon** SEAFOOD $$
(Map p328; ☎ 0252-284 2261; Çarşı İçi 2; mezes ₺8, mains ₺22-35; ☺ 11am-10pm; ☞ ☑ ⛟) Dalyan's long-established (since 1987) fish restaurant, Kordon has a riverside garden with a commanding position near where the excursion boats moor. Ichthyophobes can choose from a large selection of steaks and grills, with hand-cut chips on the side and plenty for vegetarians.

Casa Nova MODERN TURKISH, INTERNATIONAL $$
(Map p328; ☎ 0530 223 5505, 0252-284 5057; www.casanovadalyan.com; Sağlik Sokak 5; mains ₺30; ☺ 8am-1am; ☑) The former Dalyan La Vie has metamorphosed into the town's most appealing new restaurant, serving snacks and mains from nachos to noodles on its gorgeous riverside deck.

Mai Steakhouse INTERNATIONAL $$
(Map p328; ☎ 0252-284 2642; Sulungur Caddesi 1; mains ₺25-35; ☺ 11am-10pm) This relaxed restaurant, with a nifty blue-and-white decoration theme going on, whips up a decent steak, some Mediterranean flavours and a few other international dishes.

Saki TURKISH $$
(Map p328; ☎ 0252-284 5212; Geçit Sokak; mains ₺17-30; ☑) With a breezy location right on the riverfront, this authentic eatery serves some of the most wholesome Turkish food in Dalyan. There's no menu; choose from the glass cabinet of homemade mezes (₺8 to ₺13) as well as meat, vegetarian and fish dishes.

Jazz Bar Dalyan BAR
(Map p328; ☎ 0507 063 4614; www.jazzbardalyan.com; Gülpinar Caddesi; ☺ 9pm-late) With a fine array of cocktails on offer, this cool neon-lit place has a garden for enjoying the river views and live music nightly (Friday and Saturday only from mid-October to mid-April).

🛍 Shopping

Dalyan İz ART
(Map p328; ☎ 0542 451 5451; www.dalyaniz.com; Özalp Sokak 1; ☺ 9.30am-7pm Fri-Wed) Aiming to introduce customers to Turkish culture, Dalyan İz has a wonderful assortment of Turkish artwork as well as a minigallery with information on the artists. With rooms themed around dervishes, hamams and ceramics, it sells pieces including paintings, sculptures, miniatures and hand-painted tiles.

Unique Art JEWELLERY
(Map p328; ☎ 0546 545 1719; www.theuniqueart.com; Maraş Caddesi 42; ☺ 8.30am-midnight Apr-Nov) For 10 years jeweller Kenan has sold his pieces and gifts from across Turkey in

his shop-cum-gallery. Choose between coral earrings from İstanbul, rings from İzmir, textiles, ceramics, and soap made with olive oil and cinnamon from eastern Anatolia. Kenan's work has a vintage style with Ottoman motifs, and the jewellery comes with a lifetime guarantee.

ℹ Information

Tourist Office (Map p328; ☎ 0252-284 4235; Cumhuriyet Medanı; ⏱ 9am-noon & 1-5.30pm Mon-Fri) Stocks a few brochures and maps in a modern glass-walled kiosk on Dalyan's main square.

ℹ Getting There & Away

Dolmuşes (minibuses that stop anywhere along their prescribed route) stop in Cumhuriyet Meydanı, near the main mosque. There are no direct minibuses from here to Dalaman. First take a minibus to Ortaca (₺4, every 25 minutes in high season, every hour in low season, 14km) and change there. From Ortaca otogar (bus station), regular buses go to Köyceğiz (₺6, 25 minutes, 22km), Dalaman (₺4, 15 minutes, 9km) and Fethiye (₺10, 1¼ hours, 75km). A taxi to Dalaman International Airport costs around ₺80.

From May to September there are daily dolmuşes from Dalyan to Köyceğiz, Marmaris and Fethiye at 10am.

Travel agencies, including **Kaunos Tours** (p326), offer car rental.

Dalaman

☎ 0252 / POP 25,313

Little has changed for this agricultural town since the ever-expanding Dalaman International Airport (p604) was built on the neighbouring river delta, with most arrivals moving on immediately.

It's just over 5km from Dalaman International Airport (p604) to Dalaman town, and another 5km to the D400 coastal highway. Besides the summer flights to/from many European cities, Turkish Airlines (p605), Pegasus Airlines (p605) and Atlasglobal (p605) operate several daily flights to/from both İstanbul airports year-round, while AnadoluJet (www.anadolujet.com) flies to/from Ankara.

From the airport, **Havaş Airport Bus** (☎ 0555 985 1165; www.havas.net/en) has a schedule that meets all incoming domestic flights. The fare to Fethiye otogar (one hour, via Göcek) is ₺10, and to Marmaris otogar (1½ hours, via Ortaca and Köyceğiz) is ₺15. Returning to the airport, there are five to eight services daily throughout the year.

A taxi into Dalaman town is around ₺35; to Dalyan will be around ₺80 and Fethiye, ₺120.

From Dalaman's otogar, near the junction of Kenan Evren Bulvarı and Atatürk Caddesi, you can catch buses to Antalya (₺35, four hours, 335km), Köyceğiz (₺8, 30 minutes, 26km) and Marmaris (₺15, 1½ hours, 90km). All routes north and east pass through either Muğla (₺20, two hours, 87km) or Fethiye (₺15, one hour, 46km).

Car-hire agencies line the main road from the airport through Dalaman to the highway. You can get good deals through Economy Car Rentals (www.economycarrentals.com).

Göcek

☎ 0252 / POP 4285

Göcek (*geuh*-jek) is the western Mediterranean's high-end yacht spot and the attractive bay makes a relaxing alternative to Fethiye, despite all the building going on in the hills surrounding town. There's a small but clean swimming beach at the western end of the quay, and boat-charter companies throughout town offer '12 island' day tours around this end of Fethiye Körfezi (Gulf of Fethiye). These tours are mostly private, so you have to hire the whole boat and they are more suitable for groups than individuals or couples.

🛏 Sleeping

Although Göcek is geared towards yachties, there is accommodation for all budgets. Most pensions are found in the centre and just to the west, along Turgut Özal Caddesi. As some streets are pedestrianised and parking is limited, you may find it easier to park on the edge of the centre and walk to your accommodation. Many budget pensions offer rooms without breakfast.

Göcek Dim Hotel HOTEL **$$**
(☎ 0532 796 2798, 0252-645 1294; www.gocek dimhotel.com/eng; Günlük Sokak 13; s/d ₺80/100; ⓟ❄✳🛜🐾) With 15 plain but well-furnished rooms and a pleasant terrace, medium-sized pool and a location just opposite the beach, this hotel to the west of the centre offers good value. All rooms have a fridge and TV. With an neighbouring old-timers' cafe, Dim is conveniently located straight down Turgut Özal Caddesi from the dolmuş stop at the PO garage.

Efe Hotel LUXURY HOTEL **$$$**
(☎ 0252-645 2646; www.efehotelgocek.com; Likya Caddesi 1; s ₺189-208, d ₺220-230; ⓟ❄✳🛜🐾)

Hidden in a lush garden about 200m north of the Skopea Marina, Göcek's most ambitious central hotel has 20 bright and modern rooms and a half-Olympic-sized pool. It feels like a country retreat from the delightful garden bar to the mountain views.

Villa Danlin HOTEL $$$
(☑0252-645 1521; www.villadanlin.com; Çarşı Yolu Caddesi 36a; s/d €65/75; ❀❄☎☒) You'll find homely, light-filled rooms and friendly service at this lovely hotel on Göcek's main street. The charming little building at the front contains the lobby and three rooms, while the other 10 are in a modern extension at the back overlooking a generous-sized pool.

🍴 Eating & Drinking

Fish restaurants, cafes, bars and eateries of all stripes cluster around Skopea Marina and line the waterfront promenade İskele Meydanı heading east.

Kebab Hospital Antep Sofrası KEBAP, PIDE $
(☑0252-645 1873; İskele Meydanı; mains ₺20; ☺8am-midnight) It may have a joke name and not look like much, but this is Göcek's top spot for chargrilled meat feasting. Grab a table on the marina side for kebap dining with a view. It also does *lahmacun* (Arabic-style pizza) and pide, including the recommended *kıymalı* (with ground meat), which comes with a plate of salad and onion.

★West Cafe & Bistro INTERNATIONAL $$
(☑0252-645 2794; www.westcafegocek.com; İskele Meydanı; mains ₺30; ☎☒) Göcek's most appealing hang-out has a contemporary-country feel with an olive-oil shop attached and a menu ranging from crêpes to quesadillas. There is an impressive attention to detail, from the cookie and glass of strawberry-flavoured water accompanying the excellent coffee to the faux-leather-bound novel bill-holders.

With international beers such as Peroni, Hoegaarden and Guinness, it offers a menu of 'beer-friendly' and 'rakı-friendly' snacks.

Blue Lounge Bar BAR
(Skopea Marina; ☺8am-2am) This relaxed and friendly bar is great for a sundowner after a day on the sea. Happy hour (5pm to 7pm) offers two-for-one cocktails, the beer (₺10 to ₺12) is cold and the margaritas and daiquiris are frozen. Snacks (₺15) come in the form of nachos and burgers, as well as the usual mezes such as cigar *börek* (filled pastry).

ⓘ Getting There & Away

The bus and dolmuş stops for Fethiye and Dalaman are at the PO garage on the main road, 1km west of the centre (towards Dalaman). Dolmuşes depart hourly for Fethiye (₺7, 45 minutes, 30km) and Dalaman (₺5, 30 minutes, 17km). For Dalyan, change at Ortaca (₺5.50, 35 minutes, 19km). Bus-company offices are found on the main square with its requisite bust of Atatürk.

Fethiye

☑0252 / POP 82,000

In 1958 an earthquake levelled the seaside city of Fethiye (feh-*tee*-yeh), sparing only the remains of the ancient city of Telmessos. More than half a century on, it is once again a prosperous hub of the western Mediterranean, and a major base for *gület* cruises. Despite its booming growth, Fethiye is low-key for its size, due mostly to restrictions on high-rise buildings and the transitory nature of the *gület* business, which brings travellers flocking here between April and October.

Fethiye's natural harbour is perhaps the region's finest, tucked away in the southern reaches of a broad bay scattered with pretty islands, including Şövalye Adası, glimpsed briefly in the James Bond film *Skyfall*. Fethiye also makes a good base for visiting Ölüdeniz, one of Turkey's seaside hot-spots, and many interesting sites in the surrounding countryside, including the ghost town of Kayaköy (or Karmylassos) just over the hill.

ⓞ Sights

There isn't much left to see of ancient Telmessos. Dotted around town are Lycian stone sarcophagi dating from around 450 BC and broken into by tomb robbers centuries ago. One excellent **Lycian sarcophagus** (Map p332) is just east of the *belediye* (city hall). Another good example is the **sarcophagus** (Map p332) in the middle of Kaya Caddesi; on the neighbouring patch of waste ground are more tombs in a worse state of repair.

Fethiye Museum MUSEUM
(Map p332; ☑0252-614 1150; www.lycianturkey.com/fethiye-museum.htm; 505 Sokak; admission ₺5; ☺8am-7pm mid-Apr–mid-Oct, to 5pm mid-Oct–mid-Apr) Focusing on Lycian finds from Telmessos as well as the ancient settlements of Tlos and Kaunos, this museum exhibits pottery, jewellery, small statuary and votive stones (including the important Grave Stelae and the Stelae of Promise). Its most prized significant possession, however, is the so-called

Fethiye

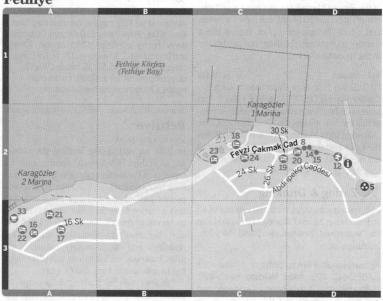

Fethiye

Trilingual Stele from Letoön, dating from 338 BC, which was used partly to decipher the Lycian language with the help of ancient Greek and Aramaic.

Tomb of Amyntas　　　　　　　TOMB
(Map p332; ⊗8am-7pm) **FREE** Fethiye's most recognisable sight is the mammoth Tomb of Amyntas, an Ionic temple facade carved into a sheer rock face in 350 BC, in honour of

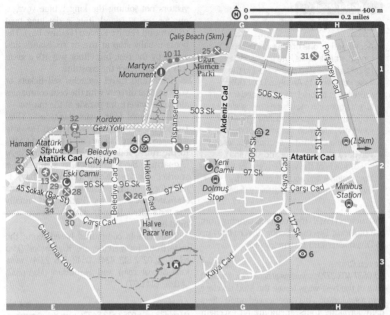

'Amyntas son of Hermapias'. Located south of the centre, it is best visited at sunset. Other, smaller rock tombs lie about 500m to the east.

Roman Theatre
RUIN

(Map p332) FREE In the centre of Fethiye, just behind the harbour, is Telmessos' 6000-seat Roman theatre dating from the 2nd century BC. Neglected for years, it was undergoing serious restoration when we passed through.

Çalış Beach
BEACH

About 5km northeast of Fethiye's centre is Çalış, a narrow stretch of gravel beach lined with mass-produced hotels as well as pubs and chip shops patronised by British expats. Part of the James Bond film *Skyfall* was shot here. Dolmuşes depart for Çalış (₺2, 10 minutes) from the minibus station beside the mosque every five to 10 minutes.

Crusader Fortress
FORTRESS

(Map p332) On the hillside above (and south of) Fethiye and along the road to Kayaköy, you can't miss the ruined tower of a Crusader fortress, built by the Knights of St John at the start of the 15th century on earlier (perhaps Lycian, Greek and Roman) foundations.

🏃 Activities

Ocean Yachting Travel Agency
OUTDOORS

(Map p332; ☎0252-612 4807; www.gofethiye. com; Fevzi Çakmak Caddesi) Ocean Yachting sells blue voyages and local tours and activities, including paragliding (₺170), day-long rafting trips (₺100), jeep safaris to Saklıkent and Tlos (₺60), Dalyan tours (₺75), the 12-island boat trip (₺40 to ₺60) and cruises to Butterfly Valley (by bus to Ölüdeniz; ₺50). It also has a swag of three- and seven-night cruise choices (€180 to €300).

Old Turkish Bath
HAMAM

(Tarihi Fethiye Hamamı; Map p332; ☎0252-614 9318; www.oldturkishbath.com; Hamam Sokak 4, Paspatur; bath & scrub ₺50, massage ₺35-80; ⊙7am-midnight) Low-key and small, the Old Turkish Bath in Paspatur, the oldest section of Fethiye, dates to the 16th century. There are separate sections for men and women (and a mixed section for couples). Extra services include aromatherapy massages (₺80) and face masks (₺10).

European Diving Centre
DIVING

(Map p332; ☎0252-614 9771; www.europeandiv ingcentre.com; 2nd fl, Demirci İş Hanı 26, Dispanser Caddesi 27) Daily diving trips and the full gamut of Professional Association of Diving

DON'T MISS

LYCIAN WAY

Acclaimed as one of the world's top-10 long-distance walks, the **Lycian Way** follows signposted paths around the Teke Peninsula to Antalya. The 500km route leads through pine and cedar forests beneath mountains rising almost 3000m, past villages, stunning coastal views and an embarrassment of ruins at Lycian cities. Walk it in sections (unless you have plenty of time and stamina).

Fethiye is at the western end of the trail, which leads south from nearby Ovacık to Faralya and Butterfly Valley.

Instructors (PADI) dive courses, ranging from the day-long Discover Scuba Diver (€50) up to Divemaster and Instructor level.

Seven Capes OUTDOORS
(☎0537 403 3779; www.sevencapes.com; Kayaköy) One of the best ways to see the Med up close is in a sea kayak. This experienced outfit offers daily kayaking tours, including an excellent one between Ölüdeniz and Butterfly Valley and a 'night paddling' tour (€60) between the stars and the watery bioluminescence below.

It also offers stand-up paddle boarding (SUP), Turkish cooking courses in Kaş and walking tours in the south Aegean.

☞ Tours

Fethiye is a major base for travellers wanting to explore the surrounding countryside and coastline.

Some boat tours are little more than booze cruises that cram passengers aboard and blast out loud music for the entire time on the water. If this isn't your scene, make sure you check beforehand. In general the busier double-decker boats usually charge ₺30 to ₺35 for a day-long boat trip, while tours on less-crowded sailboats cost around ₺50.

Day tours also visit Butterfly Valley (per person ₺50), with a shuttle to Ölüdeniz; Dalyan (per person ₺75), including a shuttle and a tour of the lake, mud baths at Sultaniye, Dalyan town, tombs at Kaunos and beach at İztuzu; and Saklıkent Gorge (per person ₺60), including the ruins at Tlos and a trout lunch.

12-Island Tour Excursion Boats BOATING
(Map p332; per person incl lunch ₺30-35, on sailboat ₺50; ◷10.30am-6.30pm mid-Apr–Oct) Many

visitors not joining the longer blue voyages opt for the 12-Island Tour, a day-long boat trip around Fethiye Körfezi (Fethiye Bay). The boats usually stop at five or six islands and cruise by the rest, but either way it's a great way to experience the coastline.

Hotels and travel agencies sell tickets or you can deal directly with the boat companies along the waterfront parade at the marina.

The normal tour visits **Yassıcalar** (Flat Island) for a stop and a swim, then **Tersane Adası** (Shipyard Island) for a dip and a visit to the ruins, followed by **Akvaryum Koyu** (Aquarium Bay) for lunch, a swim and a snorkel. **Cennet Koyu** (Paradise Bay) is next for a plunge, followed by **Kleopatra Hamamı** (Cleopatra's Bath) and finally **Kızılada** (Red Island) with its beach and mud baths.

Two reliable companies based along the waterfront promenade are **Kardeşler** (Map p332; ☎0252-612 4241, 0542 326 2314; www.kardeslerboats.com) and **Hanedan** (Map p332; ☎0252-614 1937).

Alaturka BOATING
(Map p332; ☎0252-612 5423; www.alaturkacruises.com; Fevzi Çakmak Caddesi 21A; 3-night cruise per person €220) Recommended by readers, Alaturka offers blue voyages to or from Olympos. Also bus tours to Pamukkale, Ephesus, Cappadocia and southeastern Anatolia.

🛏 Sleeping

The bulk of accommodation options are up the hill behind the Karagözler 1 marina, or further west behind the Karagözler 2 marina. Many pensions will organise transport from the otogar, but there are also frequent dolmuşes to/from Karagözler 2.

If you're a family looking for self-catering accommodation, most holiday villas and apartments are at Çalış Beach, in the nearby resorts of Hisarönü and Ovacık, and in the village of Kayaköy.

★**Duygu Pension** PENSION $
(Map p332; ☎0252-614 3563, 0535 796 6701; www.duygupension.com; Ordu Caddesi 54; s/d/tr ₺60/80/120; P🐾❄@🛜❄) Cute as a button, this warm and welcoming family-run pension near the Karagözler 2 marina has 10 homely rooms brightened by colourful wall stencils and frilly touches, while the rooftop terrace has blinding sea views. Birol is your man and a great source of information.

Tan Pansiyon
PENSION $

(Map p332; ☑0546 711 4559, 0252-614 1584; www.tanpansiyon.com; 30 Sokak 41; s ₺50-60, d ₺80-100, f ₺120-150; ❄❋📶) If the backpacker grind wears thin, try this pension run by the charming Öztürk family. The nine small and spartan rooms (their bathrooms even smaller) contrast with the large roof terrace overlooking the bay. It's all sparkling clean and quiet, with a kitchen for guests' use on the stunning terrace.

Ferah Pension
PENSION $

(Map p332; ☑0532 265 0772, 0252-614 2816; www.ferahpension.com; 16 Sokak 23; dm/s/d/tr/q €14/30/35/50/70; ❄❋❋📶✎) The characterful 'Lighthouse' has an inner terrace dripping in vines and bedecked by flowerpots, with a teensy pool. The basic rooms are kept spick and span; grab one atop the spiral staircase for harbour views to die for. Owner Tuna, daughter Sevtap and wife Monica (try her home cooking) offer advice about taxi deals, Fethiye nightlife and Turkish men respectively.

Villa Daffodil
HOTEL $

(Map p332; ☑0252-614 9595; www.villadaffodil. com; Fevzi Çakmak Caddesi 139; s/d from €35/50; ❄❋❋📶✎) A fairly plain but decent-value option, with views of the sea or forested hills from its rooms and suites. The rooms opening onto the walkway to the pool are better, as a low-ceilinged and worn staircase leads to some internal rooms (eg 304 to 307). The rear pool area is perfect for glamour-puss lounging after a day's sightseeing.

Half board is an extra €10 per person.

V-Go's Hotel & Guesthouse
HOSTEL $

(Map p332; ☑0252-612 5409; www.v-gohotel.com; Fevzi Çakmak Caddesi 109; dm/r €17/58; ❄❋❋@📶✎) This hostel near the Karagözler 2 marina is a firm favourite with budget travellers looking to party. The 26 decent-sized rooms and good-sized dorms are spread over two buildings between a large terrace with bar, chill-out chairs and pool. If you're looking for action, this is your place. Those after something more sedate, look elsewhere.

Yıldırım Guest House
PENSION $$

(Map p332; ☑0252-614 4627; www.yildirimguest house.com; Fevzi Çakmak Caddesi 53; dm/tw/d/tr ₺40/110/120/180; ❄❋❋📶) In a strip of four pensions, 'Lightning' is popular with Japanese travellers and distinguishes itself through its services rather than its infrastructure. There are six-bed female and mixed dorms, a four-bed male dorm and simple, spotless rooms. Host Ömer Yapış is a mine of local information; he also manages Tribe Travel (p338), so pick-ups and excursions are easily arranged.

★Hotel Unique
BOUTIQUE HOTEL $$$

(Map p332; ☑0252-612 1145; www.hotelunique turkey.com; 30 Sokak 43a; r €130-260; P❄❋ 📶✎) Opened in 2014, this stone building with colourful shutters seems considerably older, offering a contemporary seaside take on Ottoman-village chic. The service and attention to detail are impressive, with wooden beams, floors and hand-carved doors from Black Sea houses in the rooms and pebbles from the beach in the bathroom floors.

Yacht Classic Hotel
BOUTIQUE HOTEL $$$

(Map p332; ☑0252-612 5067; www.yachtclassic hotel.com; Fevzi Çakmak Caddesi 1; s €90-160, d €120-200, ste/villas €250/350; P❄❋📶✎) This boutique hotel is a symphony in soothing pastels and cream with luxurious bathrooms and a tasteful contemporary ambience. Guests get to enjoy the large pool terrace overlooking the harbour and what could be the most stylish hotel hamam on the Med.

Hotel Doruk
HOTEL $$$

(Map p332; ☑0252-614 9860; www.hoteldoruk. com; Yat Limanı; s €69-84, d €74-89; P❄❋❋📶✎) Not to be confused with the neighbouring, fortresslike Hotel Status, this stalwart of the Fethiye scene remains a good choice with a poolside breakfast room overlooking the Karagözler 1 marina. Touches like the local olive oil on sale in reception save it from business blandness, and half the 30 rooms have balconies surveying the bay.

✗ Eating

Weekly Market
MARKET $

(Map p332; ✗) Fethiye's enormous market takes place on Tuesday along the canal between Atatürk Caddesi and Pürşabey Caddesi, next to the stadium.

Fish Kebap Boats
FISH $

(Map p332; Kordon Gezi Yolu; fish kebaps ₺8; ⏱11am-10pm) A few small boats moored off Uğur Mumcu Parkı offer *balık ekmek* (fish in bread) and fish and chips (₺15), with seating on their bobbing decks. They offer a cheap way to sample the local fish, but are better for lunch, as their small kitchens may not exactly be squeaky clean after a busy day.

★ **Meğri Lokantasi** LOKANTA $$

(Map p332; ☑0252-614 4047; www.megrirestaurant.com; Çarşı Caddesi 26; plates ₺7-14; ⊙11am-10pm; ☑) Looking for us at lunchtime in Fethiye? We're usually here. Packed with locals who spill onto the streets, this *lokanta* (eatery serving ready-made food) offers excellent and hearty homestyle cooking at very palatable prices. Mix and match your meal by choosing from the huge glass display window of vegetable (₺7) and meat (₺14) dishes. It's pretty much all delicious.

★ **Hilmi** SEAFOOD $$

(Map p332; ☑0252-614 2232; www.hilmi.com.tr; Hal ve Pazar Yeri; mezes from ₺7, mains ₺30; ⊙11am-10pm) This stylish little eatery with blue and red chairs at white tables allows you to experience the buzz of the Fish Market without purchasing from the fishmongers. The delightful mezes and mains include calamari, octopus, prawns with garlic butter and chilli, and dramatic-looking fried organic mushrooms.

★ **Paşa Kebab** TURKISH $$

(Map p332; ☑0252-614 9807; www.pasakebap.com; Çarşı Caddesi 42; pides ₺12-19.50, kebaps ₺17.50-30; ⊙11am-late) Nearly always bustling, and with a menu that's something of a novella, Paşa does a fine line in Turkish staples. If you're hungry, try the Paşa Special, a gigantic and delicious kebap concoction of beef, tomato, bulgur wheat and cheese.

İskele Ocakbaşı KEBAP $$

(Map p332; ☑0252-614 9423; Şehit Feti Bey Parkı; mezes from ₺6, mains ₺20-45; ⊙9am-1am) Head to İskele for kebaps and steaks in style. The grilled dishes from its *ocakbaşı* (grill house, or 'fireside') are excellent and the super-friendly service really makes this place shine. The shady outdoor patio overlooking bobbing boats on the harbour is a bonus, too.

★ **Fish Market** SEAFOOD $$$

(Balık Pazarı, Balık Halı; Map p332; Hal ve Pazar Yeri; ⊙11am-10pm) This circle of fishmongers ringed by restaurants is Fethiye's most atmospheric eating experience: buy fresh fish (per kilo ₺10 to ₺35) and calamari (₺45), take it to a restaurant to have them cook it, and watch the fishmongers competing for attention with the waiter-touts, flower sellers and roaming *fasıl* (gypsy music) buskers.

The fishmongers are much of a piscatory muchness, but you could try Pehlivan Baş. They may try to steer you towards a restaurant they work with, but you are, of course,

under no obligation. There is also little to distinguish the restaurants, which typically charge ₺8 for mezes and ₺6 per head to cook the fish, with an olive oil and garlic sauce, lemon, rocket and çay thrown in. Make sure they don't place unordered mezes on the table and charge you for it. **Reis Balık** (Map p332; ☑0532 472 5989, 0252-612 5368; www.reisrestaurant.com; Hal ve Pazar Yeri; ⊙11am-10pm) and **Cem & Can** (Map p332; Hal ve Pazar Yeri; ⊙11am-10pm) are both good choices. A small vegetable market and produce shops selling cheese and honey adjoin the market's central covered courtyard.

Meğri Restaurant INTERNATIONAL $$$

(Map p332; ☑0252-614 4046; www.megrirestaurant.com; 40 Sokak 10; mezes & salads ₺9-20, mains ₺22-50; ☑) If you want a change from the tomato-cucumber-parsley Turkish salad combo, Meğri Restaurant (not to be confused with nearby Meğri Lokantasi) is a great choice. We really like its broccoli and chicken salad, its huge meze selection and the seating under awnings on the Paspatur walkway. Mains range from pasta to steaks, kebap and a whole section for vegetarians.

🍷 Drinking & Nightlife

Bars, clubs, *meyhanes* (taverns) and everything in between spill onto the pedestrianised 45 Sokak in the old town. Known as Barlar Sokak (Bar St), this debauched strip is a smaller version of its counterparts in Marmaris and Bodrum. On Kordon Gezi Yolu, near the Atatürk statue, several bars and restaurants are ideal for a waterfront sundowner.

Flow BAR

(Map p332; ☑0506 389 8220; 45 Sokak 11; ⊙4pm-late) This 'art lounge bar' is a cut above the raucous rest on Bar St, with eclectic beach furniture spilling onto the walkway and a cocktail menu featuring both White and Black Russians. Live music sparks up from 9pm until late on Wednesday, Friday and Saturday.

Deniz Kafe CAFE

(Map p332; 2 Karagözler Kürek Yarışları; ⊙9am-11pm) This little makeshift cafe-bar has tables nudging the boats at Karagözler 2 marina and even one or two on a small wooden platform over the water. It's a great place to while away a lazy afternoon with a cold beer or çay.

Address BAR, CAFE

(Map p332; ☑0252-614 4453; Kordon Gezi Yolu; ⊙4pm-late) The name says it all: Address' roomy waterfront garden is kilometre zero for everyone from çay-sipping locals to beer-drinking expats watching the football on two big screens. Fit in with both groups by ordering an Efes beer and a nargile (water pipe; ₺11).

 Shopping

Old Orient Carpet & Kilim Bazaar CARPETS (Map p332; ☑ 0532 510 6108; c.c_since.1993@ hotmail.com; 45 Sokak 5; ☺ 9am-midnight mid-Apr–Oct, to 6pm Nov–mid-Apr) As solid as Gibraltar and reliable as rain, this shop is where the

---

BLUE VOYAGES

For many travellers, a four-day, three-night cruise on a *gület* (traditional wooden Turkish yacht) along the Turquoise Coast – known locally as a 'blue voyage' *(mavi yolculuk)* – is the highlight of their trip to Turkey. Although advertised as a voyage between Fethiye and Olympos, the boats usually start (or stop) at Demre and the trip to/from Olympos (1¼ hours) is by bus. From Fethiye boats usually call in at Ölüdeniz and Butterfly Valley and stop at Kaş, Kalkan and/or Kekova, with the final night at Gökkaya Bay, opposite the eastern end of Kekova. A less common (but some say prettier) route is between Marmaris on the Aegean Sea and Fethiye.

Food is usually included in the price, but you sometimes have to pay for water and soft drinks and always for alcohol. All boats are equipped with showers, toilets and smallish but comfortable double and triple cabins (usually between six and eight of them). Most people sleep on mattresses on deck as the boats are not air-conditioned.

Blue voyage prices vary by season, but are generally not cheap – in summer prices typically range from around €200 to €300 – so it makes sense to shop around. We also receive feedback from travellers who have had disappointing experiences with badly organised or dishonest operators. Here are some suggestions to avoid getting fleeced:

➡ Ask for recommendations from other travellers.

➡ Avoid touts at the bus stations and go straight to agencies (especially those listed here).

➡ Bargain, but don't necessarily go for the cheapest option, because the crew might skimp on food and services.

➡ Check out your boat if you are on site and ask to see the guest list.

➡ Ask whether your captain and crew speak English.

➡ Ask for details of the itinerary and whether the weather and sailing conditions will allow you to stick to it.

➡ Don't go for gimmicks such as free water sports; they often prove to be empty promises and boats rarely have insurance for them in case of accidents.

➡ Confirm whether the boat ever actually uses the sails (though most don't, in any case) rather than relying on a diesel engine.

➡ Avoid buying your ticket in İstanbul, as pensions, travel agents and tour operators there take a healthy cut.

➡ Book well ahead – both in high season (July and August), when spaces are in great demand, and low season, when far fewer boats take to the water.

The following Fethiye-based, owner-operated outfits have a good reputation. Boats depart at least daily between late April and October.

Alaturka (p334) Recommended by readers, Alaturka offers blue voyages to/from Olympos.

Before Lunch Cruises (☑ 0535 636 0076; www.beforelunch.com; 3-night cruise per person €275-350) Run by a reputable company that follows its own unique itinerary, incorporating Göcek Bay and covering the highlights according to weather and sailing conditions. The ecofriendly tours include two optional morning walks. More expensive than most, but garners high praise from guests.

Ocean Yachting (p333) Highly professional outfit with a swag of three- and seven-night cruise choices.

discerning buy their carpets and kilims, following the sage advice of carpet seller Celal Coşkun. Hoping to preserve the dying art of carpet making, Celal also offers classes in making and repairing carpets.

ℹ️ Information

Tourist Office (Map p332; ☑ 0252-614 1527; İskele Meydanı; ⊙ 8am-noon & 1-5pm) Not terribly helpful, but stocks a few glossy brochures and a free town map.

ℹ️ Getting There & Away

Fethiye's busy otogar is 2.5km east of the town centre, with a separate **station** (Map p332) for minibuses 1km east of the centre near the petrol station. You can also catch dolmuşes to Ölüdeniz, Faralya and Kabak on the main road outside the otogar, in front of the Carrefour supermarket.

Buses and dolmuşes to Antalya (₺35, six hours, 300km) head east along the coast at least every hour in high season, stopping at Kalkan (₺16, 1½ hours, 83km), Kaş (₺20, two hours, 107km) and the Olympos turn-off (₺33, 4¾ hours, 228km). The inland road to Antalya (₺30, 3½ hours, 200km) is much quicker.

Between May and August, **Tribe Travel** (Map p332; ☑ 0252-612 2936; www.tribetravel-tours.com; Fevzi Çakmak Caddesi 25a) operates shuttles most days to Pamukkale (₺40, four hours, 240km) and Selçuk (₺50, 4½ hours, 285km), picking up from Fethiye accommodation at 8.30am and returning at 3.30pm from both.

Minibuses heading for destinations in the local vicinity depart from the handy **dolmuş stop** (Map p332) in the town centre, near the new mosque and opposite the TTNet shop. Destinations include Ovacık (₺4), Hisarönü (₺4), Kayaköy (₺4.50), Ölüdeniz (₺5.50; change for Faralya and Kabak), Göcek (₺5.50) and Saklıkent (₺11).

Catamarans sail daily to Rhodes in Greece (one way/same-day return/open return €50/60/75, 1½ hours) from Fethiye pier, opposite the tourist office. They run from April to mid-October, generally departing from Fethiye at 9am Monday, Wednesday, Thursday and Friday, and returning from Rhodes at 4.30pm. Tickets are available near the pier from **Ocean Yachting Travel Agency** (p333) and **Yeşil Dalyan** (Map p332; ☑ 0252-612 8686; www.yesildalyantravel.com).

ℹ️ Getting Around

Minibuses (₺2) ply the one-way system along Atatürk Caddesi and up Çarşı Caddesi to the otogar, as well as along Fevzi Çakmak Caddesi to/from the Karagözler 2 pensions and hotels,

west of the centre. There are also minibuses to Çalış Beach. A taxi from the otogar to Karagözler 2 costs about ₺22, and to Dalaman International Airport, between ₺100 and ₺120.

Head to the Karagözler 1 section of Fevzi Çakmak Caddesi for travel agencies and car-rental outfits, including **Levent Rent a Car** (☑ 0252-614 8096; www.leventrentacar. net; Fevzi Çakmak Caddesi 37b). Companies hire out scooters from ₺30 per day, and cars from ₺70.

Kayaköy

☑ 0252 / POP 2200

About 9km south of Fethiye by road is Kayaköy (ancient Karmylassos), an eerie ghost town of 4000-odd abandoned stone houses and other structures that once made up the Greek town of Levissi. Today this timeless village, set in a lush valley with some vineyards nearby, forms a memorial to Turkish-Greek peace and cooperation. In the evening, when the ruined village's churches are spotlit, Kayaköy is truly surreal.

History

Levissi was deserted by its mostly Greek inhabitants in the general exchange of populations supervised by the League of Nations in 1923 after the Turkish War of Independence. Most Greek Muslims came to Turkey and most Ottoman Christians moved from coastal Turkey to Greece. The abandoned town was the inspiration for Eskibahçe, the setting of Louis de Bernières' 2004 novel, *Birds Without Wings*.

As there were far more Ottoman Christians than Greek Muslims, many Turkish towns were left unoccupied after the population exchange. Greeks did come to Kayaköy from Thessaloniki, but they were settled in the modern village in the valley below, where the accommodation and restaurants are now. The original Kayaköy, or Kaya as it is known locally, was later damaged by an earthquake in 1957.

With the tourism boom of the 1980s, a development company wanted to restore Kayaköy's stone houses and turn the town into a holiday village. Scenting money, the local inhabitants were delighted, but Turkish artists and architects were alarmed and saw to it that the Ministry of Culture declared Kayaköy a historic monument, safe from unregulated development.

⊙ Sights

★ Kayaköy (Levissi) Abandoned Village
RUINS

(admission ₺5, free after closing; ⊙ 9am-8pm Apr-Oct, 8am-5pm Nov-Mar) The tumbledown ruins of Levissi are highly atmospheric. The roofless, dilapidated stone houses sit on the slopes like sentinels over the modern village below.

Not much is intact except the two churches. The 17th-century **Kataponagia Church**, with an ossuary containing the mouldering remains of the long-dead in its churchyard, is on the lower part of the slope, while the **Taxiarkis Church** is near the top of the hill. Both retain some of their painted decoration and black-and-white pebble mosaic floors.

Near the latter is a ruined **castle**, while the hilltop **tower** above Kataponagia Church has commanding views of the valley.

🛏 Sleeping

There are numerous pensions in the modern village in the valley beneath the hillside ruins. Self-catering apartments also abound, making Kayaköy a beautiful holiday base for families or groups of friends to explore the region.

Selçuk Pension
PENSION $

(☑ 0252-618 0075, 0535 275 6706; istanbulrestaurant@hotmail.com; r ₺100; 🅿 ⊖ ❄) Set amid flower and vegetable gardens at the back of the affiliated İstanbul Restaurant, the Selçuk has six rooms and apartments (up to four people ₺150), which are slightly worn but spotless, quite spacious and homely. Some have small balconies with lovely views of the abandoned village.

★ Villa Rhapsody
GUESTHOUSE $$

(☑ 0532 337 8285, 0252-618 0042; www.villarhapsody.com; s/d/tr €43/59/78; 🅿 ⊖ ❄ 🛜 🛝) This welcoming place has 16 comfortable rooms with balconies overlooking a delightful walled garden and poolside bar. Atilla and Jeanne, the Turkish and Dutch owners, are full of advice about local hikes, activities and restaurants, and breakfast is a feast. It's 200m west of the village, at the beginning of the 7km road to Gemiler Beach and St Nicholas Island.

★ Günay's Garden
RESORT $$$

(☑ 0534 360 6545, 0252-618 0073; www.gunaysgarden.com; 2-/3-bed villas per week €1020/1118; 🅿 ⊖ ❄ @ 🛜 🛝) A top choice for families or groups of friends who want to use Kayaköy as their base, this positively scrumptious boutique resort consists of six self-catering villas hidden within lush gardens and set around a shimmering pool. Some of the villas have both front and back balconies, and the views of the abandoned village are evocative.

🍴 Eating

In addition to a few excellent restaurants, cafes in the modern village beneath the hillside ruins serve *gözleme* (savoury pancake) and *börek* for around ₺5. There is also a small shop and bakery.

Cin Bal Kebap Salonu
BARBECUE $$

(☑ 0252-618 0066; www.cinbal.com; mains ₺20, meat per kg ₺65; ⊙ 11am-10pm) Arguably the region's most celebrated grill restaurant, Cin Bal specialises in lamb *tandir* (clay oven) dishes and kebaps, with seating inside and in its grapevine-covered garden courtyard. If you fancy trying your hand at grilling, staff will bring one to your table; otherwise, choose from the choice cuts and leave it to the experts. It's just off the Hisarönü road.

★ İzela Restaurant
MEDITERRANEAN $$$

(☑ 0534 360 6545, 0252-618 0073; www.gunaysgarden.com; mezes/mains ₺20/45; ⊙ 7.30am-10pm; 🛜 ☑) This lovely restaurant is located in the lush grounds of Günay's Garden, with its poolside bar for aperitifs. It specialises in Mediterranean cuisine, with more than a tip of the hat to modern Turkish, and serves generous dishes from seafood and steaks to a meze selection offering tastes of southwest Turkey (₺32 for two).

The kitchen's inventiveness comes into its own on the İzela Classics menu, with dishes ranging from the memorably flavoursome oven-baked lamb shank to *imam bayıldı*

LOCAL KNOWLEDGE

HIKING FROM KAYAKÖY

The Kayaköy to Ölüdeniz extension of the **Lycian Way** (p334) trek takes in serene forest scenery and jaw-droppingly beautiful coastal panoramas. For keen walkers who don't have time for a longer trek, it's a fantastic half-day hike. The signposted trailhead starts within Kayaköy's abandoned village ruins and is waymarked the entire length. The 8km walk takes two to 2½ hours.

You can also walk over the hill and through the forestry to Fethiye (5km, 1½ hours), or west to Gemiler Beach and St Nicholas Island (7km, two hours).

(imam fainted; famous aubergine dish). Almost everything is sourced locally (as in the farm next door), from olive oil and vegetables to chickens, ducks and turkeys.

İstanbul Restaurant
TURKISH $$$

(☑ 0252-618 0148; www.kayakoy.co.uk; mains ₺30-70; ☺ 8am-midnight Apr-Oct; ☞ ☑) Friendly and fun, this central eatery serves up excellent homestyle grills and mezes made from the produce of the surrounding vegetable gardens and orchards. It's a delightful dinner spot near the ruins, offering both delicious traditional Turkish dishes and a new menu of international dishes devised by a chef recruited from Berlin. It offers free pick-up/drop-off from Fethiye and Ölüdeniz.

Owner Engin also has three one- and two-bedroom poolside stone cottages (from ₺1600 per week) at the rear. They're well equipped for self-catering and have a spa and cedar floors and beams.

Levissi Garden
MEDITERRANEAN $$$

(☑ 0252-618 0173, 0532 354 4038; www.levissigarden.com; mains ₺40; ☺ 11am-10pm; ☑) This 400-year-old stone building houses a stunning wine house and restaurant, with a cellar containing hundreds of bottles of Turkey's finest. From its stone oven, the Levissi produces Mediterranean specialities such as *klevtiko* (leg of lamb cooked in red wine, garlic and herbs) with a wonderful meze selection. Book to avoid disappointment. It's near the ruins on the Hisarönü road.

❶ Getting There & Away

Dolmuşes run to Fethiye (₺4.50, 20 minutes, 9km) every half-hour or so from May to October and every couple of hours in low season. A taxi from Fethiye costs ₺50, a little less from Ölüdeniz. All dolmuşes on their way to/from Kayaköy pass through Hisarönü, from where dolmuşes leave every 10 minutes for Ölüdeniz. It's about a half-hour walk downhill through pine forest from Hisarönü to Kayaköy.

Ölüdeniz

☑ 0252 / POP 4708

With its sheltered (and protected) lagoon beside a lush national park, a long spit of sandy beach and Baba Dağ (Mt Baba) casting its shadow across the sea, Ölüdeniz (*eu*-leu-den-eez), 15km south of Fethiye, is a dream sprung from a glossy brochure. Problem is, like most beautiful destinations, it has become a victim of its own package-tourism success – in high summer the motionless charms of the 'Dead

Sea' are swamped by the Paradise Lost of the tacky adjoining town.

If you're looking for an easygoing day on the beach, though, you can't really go wrong here. Similarly, if you've always wanted to throw yourself off a mountain, Ölüdeniz is one of Turkey's top destinations for tandem paragliding. Nearby is the starting point for the wonderful Lycian Way (p334) walking trail, which runs high above the fun and frolics.

◉ Sights & Activities

A string of beach clubs running north of town, including Sugar Beach (p341) and Seahorse (☑ 0252-617 0888; www.seahorsebeachclub.com; Ölüdeniz Caddesi; caravan s/d from €68/75, r €110-160, q €280; 🅿 ☺ ❄ ☞), offer access to their beaches and use of their facilities, including sun-loungers, parasols, showers, canoes and paddle boats, for varying charges. Some offer all-inclusive day entry, also including lunch, drinks and snacks, for around €40 per person.

Ölüdeniz Beach & Lagoon
BEACH

(Ölüdeniz Caddesi; lagoon admission adult/child ₺7/3.50, bicycle/car parking ₺7/25) The beach is why most people visit Ölüdeniz. While the decent strip of shore edging the village is free, the famed lagoon beach is a protected national park (Ölüdeniz Tabiat Parkı) that you pay to enter. Both the public beach and lagoon get heavily crowded in summer, but, with the mountains soaring above you, it's still a lovely place to while away a few hours. There are showers, toilets and cafes, and sunshades, loungers and paddle boats can be rented.

Boat Excursions
BOATING

(tour per person incl lunch ₺40-50; ☺ 11am-6pm) Throughout summer, boats set out from Ölüdeniz beach to explore the surrounding coast. The day-long boat tours typically include the Blue Cave, Butterfly Valley, St Nicholas Island, Camel Beach, Akvaryum Koyu (Aquarium Bay, also covered by the 12-Island Tour (p334) from Fethiye) and a cold-water spring, with time for swimming included. Ask the tourist office for more information.

🛏 Sleeping

Sultan Motel
HOTEL $$

(☑ 0252-616 6139; www.sultanmotel.com; Ölüdeniz Yolu; s/d/tr from ₺75/100/165; 🅿 ☺ ❄ ☞ ☲) Just off the main road on the left as you descend from Hisarönü into Ölüdeniz, the Sultan is at the trailhead of the Lycian Way and is a favourite of hikers. There are excellent views down to Ölüdeniz from the pool terrace and 20 rooms and studios. The latter are well equipped and recently renovated with kitchens for self-catering.

Oyster Residences
BOUTIQUE HOTEL $$$

(☑ 0252-617 0765; www.oysterresidences.com; 224 Sokak 1; s/d/tr from €140/150/200; ☉ May-Oct; P ☕ ✿ ☎ ≋) This delightful boutique hotel, inspired by old Fethiye-style houses, was built in 2004 but looks at least a century older. It has 26 bright and airy rooms done up in a kind of neotropical style that will have most mortals swooning. Rooms open on to lush gardens that creep all the way to the beach. Stunning stuff.

Sugar Beach Club
RESORT $$$

(☑ 0252-617 0048; www.thesugarbeachclub.com; Ölüdeniz Caddesi 63; bungalow s ₺220-250, d ₺250-300, tr ₺300-330, q ₺330; P ☕ ✿ ☎) This ultra-chilled spot is the pick of the crop in Ölüdeniz. The design is first class – a strip of beach shaded by palms and lounging areas, with a waterfront bar and restaurant and backed by two-dozen colourful bungalows with bathrooms and air-conditioning. It's 500m north of the lagoon entrance.

✖ Eating & Drinking

Restaurants and bars lining the beachfront serve cold beer and international dishes with a sea view. Most close outside the summer season of mid-April to October.

İnci Restaurant
TURKISH $$

(☑ 0536 967 6716; Jandarma Sokak; mains ₺30; ☉ 11am-10pm; ☎) One of Ölüdeniz' more authentic eateries, 'Pearl' Restaurant serves Turkish classics, *ev yemekleri* (home cooking), international dishes and daily specials. Choose between the Turkish set dinner for two (₺82), the daily set menu (₺67), pasta, kebaps, and lighter lunch fare (₺12) such as *gözleme* and burgers. Find it a short stroll inland from the tourist office.

Cloud 9
INTERNATIONAL $$

(☑ 0252-617 0391; Belcekız 1 Sokak; mains ₺20-30; ☉ 11am-10pm; ☎ ♿) This popular hang-out has a menu that meanders through pizza, pide, steaks, seafood, burgers, omelettes and salads, with a more limited menu in low season. Sipping a mojito or draught beer at the shaded outdoor tables, soundtracked by cool tunes, is a great end to a beach day. The nearby play park makes it a family-friendly lunch spot.

Buzz Beach Bar
INTERNATIONAL $$$

(☑ 0252-617 0526; www.buzzbeachbar.com; Belcekız 1 Sokak; mains ₺20-65; ☉ 8am-2am; ☎) With a commanding position on the waterfront, this two-level place offers a wide menu, from burgers and pasta (₺21 to ₺30) to fillet steak and seafood. The roof terrace is the beachfront's top spot for a sunset cocktail or beer.

ⓘ Information

Tourist Office (☑ 0252-617 0438; www.oludeniz.com.tr; Ölüdeniz Caddesi 32; ☉ 8.30am-11pm May-Oct, to 5pm Mon-Sat Nov-Apr) Helpful information booth and booking service in the centre near the beach. There are ATMs and an *otopark* (car park) nearby.

ⓘ Getting There & Away

In high season dolmuşes leave Fethiye (₺5, 25 minutes, 16km) for Ölüdeniz roughly every 10 minutes, passing through Ovacık and Hisarönü. In low season they go every 20 minutes by day and hourly at night. You can reach Faralya and Kabak on hourly minibuses in summer (four daily in spring and three in winter). A taxi to Kayaköy costs around ₺35; to Fethiye, ₺50.

Butterfly Valley & Faralya

Tucked away on the Yedi Burun (Seven Capes) coast 12km from Ölüdeniz is the village of Faralya, also called Uzunyurt. Below it is the paradise-found of Butterfly Valley, with a fine beach and some lovely walks through a lush gorge. It is home to the unique Jersey tiger butterfly, from which it takes its name.

There are two ways to reach Butterfly Valley: by boat from Ölüdeniz, or on foot via a very steep path that wends its way down a cliff from Faralya. If you choose the latter, be sure to wear proper shoes and keep to the marked trail (indicated with painted red dots). It usually takes 30 to 45 minutes to descend and an hour up. There are fixed ropes in the steepest or most dangerous parts. Take extra care after it rains, when the rock is slippery – walkers have fallen to their death.

Faralya is on a stage of the Lycian Way (p334) and is prime hiking territory. There is an excellent waymarked walk across the hill to Kabak from here.

🛏 Sleeping & Eating

There is a basic **campsite** (Kelebekler Vadisi; ☑ 0555 632 0237; http://thebutterflyvalley.blogspot.com.tr; incl half board tent or dm per person ₺35, bungalows ₺45; ☉ Mar-Oct) in Butterfly Valley,

PARAGLIDING

The descent from 1960m Baba Dağ (Mt Baba) can take up to 40 minutes, with amazing views over the Blue Lagoon, Butterfly Valley and, on a clear day, as far as Rhodes.

Operators include **Easy Riders** (☑0252-617 0148; www.easyriderstravel.8m.com; Ölüdeniz Caddesi), **Pegas Paragliding** (☑0252-617 0051; www.pegasparagliding.blogspot.com.tr; Çetin Motel, Ölüdeniz Caddesi) and **Gravity Tandem Paragliding** (☑0252-617 0379; www.flygravity.com; Denizpark Caddesi), who typically charge around ₺200, with discounts offered in the off season. Whichever company you choose, ensure it has insurance and the pilot has the appropriate qualifications. Parasailing on the beach is also possible.

and numerous pensions above the valley in Faralya.

Butterfly Guesthouse PENSION $$
(☑0533 140 8000, 0252-642 1042; www.butterfly guesthouse.com; s/d €50/60, without bathroom €30/45; P❀❄✿) At the Kabak end of Faralya, Önur, Gülser and daughter Eliz offer an experience of local life in a whitewashed house on a village lane, among the twittering birds and crowing cocks. There are five simple rooms in the main house, three sharing a bathroom, and a spacious and modern room in the garden of citrus and olives.

Melisa Pansiyon PENSION $$
(☑0252-642 1012, 0535 881 9051; www.melisa pension.com; s/d/tr/q/f ₺80/120/145/180/300, roof terrace s/d/tr ₺60/100/120; P❀✿) Offering as warm a welcome as you'll find anywhere along the Yedi Burun coast, this Turkish-Austrian pension has four well-maintained and cheerful rooms, a pretty garden, a fully stocked kitchen for guests who want to self-cater and a vine-bedecked terrace overlooking the valley. Owner Mehmet speaks English and is a good source of local information.

George House PENSION $$
(☑0535 793 2112, 0252-642 1102; www.george housefaralya.com; incl half board campsites per person ₺55, s/d/tr ₺120/170/255, without bathroom ₺80/140/210; P❀❄✿) With commanding valley views from its clifftop platform, this Faralya institution, atop the path down

to the beach, offers simple bungalows (some with air-conditioning and bathroom), pension rooms and campsites. There's also a four-person apartment with kitchenette (₺120).

Die Wassermühle LUXURY HOTEL $$$
(The Watermill; ☑0252-642 1245; www.natur-rei sen.de; r/ste incl half board from €111/119; ☀mid-Apr–Oct; P❀❄✿✿) This German-owned resort is hidden on a wooded slope to the left as you enter Faralya and is the coolest – in both senses – place around. Both the suites (with kitchenettes) and standard rooms are spacious and use all-natural materials. Views from the restaurant and spring-water pool terraces are commanding.

Gül Pansiyon CAFE $
(☑0252-642 1145; www.gulpensiyon.com; mains ₺17; ☀11am-10pm; ✿) On the main road, 'Rose' Pension serves *gözleme* (₺8), *çorba* (soup), *köfte* (meatballs), seafood and chicken dishes on a shaded terrace overlooking the valley.

ⓘ Getting There & Away

You can take a boat tour of Butterfly Valley from Fethiye or Ölüdeniz, or board the shuttle boat (₺20 return), which departs from Ölüdeniz daily between April and October at 11am, 2pm and 6pm, returning at 9.30am, 1pm and 5pm. In July and August there are two extra daily sailings in both directions.

Hourly minibuses (four daily in spring and three in winter) run to/from Fethiye (₺7, 40 minutes, 26km) via Ölüdeniz (₺6, 20 minutes, 11km). The road up here from Ölüdeniz is as memorable for its views as for its knuckle-whitening corners. A taxi from Fethiye should cost about ₺60.

Kabak
☑0252
Six kilometres south of Faralya – and worlds away from everywhere else – Kabak calls to camping and hiking enthusiasts, yoga devotees and all fans of untapped beauty. Once this region's best-kept secret and a haven for Turkish alternative lifestylers, the cat (not to mention the downward dog) is firmly out of the bag: the pine-tree-flanked valley above the beach now counts a dozen camps. Nonetheless, Kabak remains one of the Fethiye area's most tranquil spots and anyone craving a slice of back-to-nature bliss will adore a stay here. Whether you walk or take a high-suspension vehicle down the steep track to Kabak Valley (Gemile Beach), you'll be rewarded with a spectacular beach flanked by two long cliffs.

🛏 Sleeping & Eating

Accommodation down in Kabak Valley consists of camping or tented platforms and bungalows. Nearly all include half board in the price, as there are no stand-alone restaurants on Gemile Beach, only up in Kabak village, on the road to/from Faralya. Most camps open from mid-April to October and most can organise transport down if you phone, email or text ahead.

Reflections Camp — BUNGALOW $$
(📞 0252-642 1020; www.reflectionscamp.com; incl half board per person own/camp tent ₺50/60, bungalow r ₺240, without bathroom ₺110-180; 🛜)
🏄 American founder Chris, who built this place from scratch, has moved on, but the friendly new crew is sticking to the camp's ethos of simple, sustainable living. Reflections is a comfortable place with some of Kabak's best sea views from its inviting terrace, and bungalows constructed from compacted-earth bags, bamboo and wood.

★ Turan Hill Lounge — BUNGALOW $$$
(📞 0252-642 1227, 0532 710 1077; www.turancamping.com; incl half board per person own/deluxe tent ₺75/85, semiopen bungalows without bathroom s/d ₺170/200, balcony houses s ₺270-330, d ₺320-380, deluxe houses ₺420-440; P❄🛜♨)
The epitome of Turkish glamping, Turan Hill was the first accommodation to open in Kabak and, two decades later, Turan, Ece and Ahmet's place remains the trendsetter. It's long grown out of its hippyish roots to become a stylish luxe-camping getaway. There's a choice of tented platforms, rustic semiopen cabins and incredibly cute bungalows brimming with colourful character.

Olive Garden — BUNGALOW $$$
(📞 0536 439 8648, 0252-642 1083; www.olivegardenkabak.com; incl half board s/d ₺150/250; P🛜♨) Unlike Kabak's camps, the Olive Garden is not at the bottom of the valley, but conveniently down a side track just 100m from the village. Accommodation is in wooden bungalows surrounded by gorgeous views, with an infinity pool jutting into the void high above the aquamarine shallows. Owner Fatih is a former chef and the food here is superb.

Turan Hill Lounge — CAFE $
(📞 0252-642 1227; www.turancamping.com; mains ₺18; 🕐 noon-2.30pm) Among hanging lanterns and wooden fish on a terrace with sea views, Turan Hill serves an à la carte lunch menu of seafood, wraps, omelettes, pizza and pasta. The mushroom Alfredo pasta dish with parmesan is recommended.

ℹ Getting There & Around

The road from Faralya carries on for another 6km until it reaches tiny Kabak village. Between June and October hourly minibuses trundle to/from Hisarönü (₺7, 40 minutes, 20km) via Ölüdeniz and Faralya. There are three daily services in winter. A taxi from Fethiye should cost about ₺70.

From the dolmuş stop on the main road, next to Last Stop Cafe at the far end of the village, a 4WD vehicle or van is usually on hand to transfer people down to the camps (₺50 for one to eight people), or you can take the 20-minute walking path leading down into the valley. Phone 📞 0538 888 0298 to be picked up.

Tlos

On a rocky outcrop high above a pastoral plain, Tlos was one of the most important cities of ancient Lycia. So effective was its position that the well-guarded city remained inhabited until the early 19th century.

As you climb the winding path to the ruins, look for the **acropolis** topped with an **Ottoman fortress**. Beneath it, reached by a narrow path, are **rock tombs**, including that of the warrior Bellerophon, of Chimaera fame. It has a temple-like facade carved into the rock face and to the left a fine bas-relief of our hero riding Pegasus, the winged horse.

Next to the ticket kiosk are the ruins of the **stadium**, its central pool suggesting it was used for social and ritual activities as well as sports and games.

The **theatre** is 100m up the road from the ticket office. It's in excellent condition, with most of its marble seating intact, and the stage wall is being rebuilt. It was fenced off when we visited, but if you can access it, look among the rubble of the stage building for blocks carved with an eagle, a player's mask and garlands. Just across the road are ruins of the ancient **baths** (note the apothecary symbol – snake and staff – carved on an outer wall on the south side) and **basilica**.

The site is open 9am to 7pm mid-April to October, and 8am to 5pm November to mid-April. Admission is ₺5.

🛏 Sleeping & Eating

A small cafe at the site serves *gözleme* (₺8) and freshly squeezed orange juice. Mountain Lodge, midway between Güneşli and Tlos, offers a half-board accommodation option.

Mountain Lodge   LODGE $$$

(☎0252-638 2515; www.tlosmountainlodge.com; per person €40-60; ✹@☎✹) Set in a pretty garden full of birdsong, with lots of shady seating areas and a spring-fed pool, Mountain Lodge is a peaceful gem of a place. The homely cabin-style rooms look like old stone houses and each has a verandah. The lodge is halfway between Güneşli and Tlos; walk the 2km from Güneşli or call beforehand for a pick-up.

For walkers and nature lovers, it's a wonderful place to stay. Dinner is an extra €15 per person.

ℹ Getting There & Away

From Fethiye, minibuses travel to Saklıkent via Tlos (₺8.50, 45 minutes) every 20 minutes. Some services travel directly to Saklıkent, in which case you can get off at the junction in the village of Güneşli, from where the site is a 4.5km hike (uphill all the way).

Saklıkent Gorge

☎0252

Some 12km after the turn-off to Tlos heading south, this spectacular **gorge** (adult/student ₺6/3; ◷8.30am-7.30pm) is really just a fissure in the Akdağlar, the mountains towering to the northeast. Some 18km long, and up to 200m high, the gorge is too narrow in places for even sunlight to squeeze through. Luckily *you* can, but prepare yourself for some very cold water year-round – even in summer.

You approach the gorge along a wooden boardwalk towering above the river. On wooden platforms suspended above the water, you can relax, drink tea and eat fresh trout while watching other tourists slip and slide their way across the river, hanging onto a rope and then dropping into the gorge proper. Good footwear is essential, though plastic shoes and helmets can be rented (₺5).

Across the river from the Saklıkent Gorge car park is **Saklıkent Gorge Club** (☎0252-659 0074, 0533 438 4101; www.gorgeclub.com.tr; camp sites ₺30, riverside platform dm ₺50, tree house dm ₺70, tree houses s/d ₺110/140, cabins s ₺100-125, d ₺125-250; P✜✹☎✹), a rustic, backpacker-oriented camp with basic but very real tree houses, campsites and snazzier cabins for those who don't want to rough it. It's well set up with a pool, bar and restaurant. With the exception of camping, rates include half board.

Saklıkent Gorge Club can organise various activities including rafting (₺40/60/100 for one/1½/three hours), canyoning (₺70 for one hour), zip lining through the trees and over the river (₺40), guided hikes (from two hours in the gorge to one or two days in the Akdağlar), fishing, 4WD safaris and tours of Tlos and Patara.

ℹ Getting There & Away

Minibuses run every 20 minutes between Fethiye and Saklıkent (₺11, one hour). The last one back is at 10pm between May and October, and 7pm from November to April. In summer a daily minibus runs from Patara to Saklıkent (₺13, one hour) at 11am, returning at 4pm.

Pınara

Some 46km southeast of Fethiye along the D400 is the turn-off for Pınara and its spectacular ruins. Pınara was one of the six highest-ranking cities in ancient Lycia, but although the site is vast, the actual ruins are not the region's most impressive. Instead it's the sheer splendour and isolation that makes it worth visiting.

Rising high above the site is a sheer column of rock honeycombed with **rock tombs**; archaeologists are still debating as to how and why they were cut here. Other tombs are within the ruined city itself. The one to the southeast, called the **Royal Tomb**, has fine reliefs, including several showing walled Lycian cities. With its photogenic mountain backdrop, Pınara's **theatre** is in good condition, but its **odeion** and **temple** to Aphrodite (with heart-shaped columns) are ruined. On the latter's steps, note the graffiti carved by its builders: an enormous (and anatomically correct) phallus.

The site is open 9am to 7pm mid-April to October, and 8am to 5pm November to mid-April. Admission is ₺5.

ℹ Getting There & Away

From the Pınara turn-off, the road winds through citrus orchards and across irrigation channels for 3.5km to the village of Minare, then takes a sharp left turn to climb a steep slope for another 2km. The final approach to the ruins is rocky but doable in a car.

Half-hourly dolmuşes from Fethiye (₺5, one hour) drop you at the Pınara turn-off, from where you can walk to the site. In summer taxis wait at the turn-off, charging ₺15 to ₺20 to ferry you to the site, wait and bring you back.

Xanthos

Up on a rock outcrop at Kınık, 63km southeast of Fethiye, are the ruins of ancient Xanthos (☑0242-871 6001; admission ₺10; ☺9am-7pm mid-Apr–Oct, 8am-5pm Nov–mid-Apr, ticket office shuts 30min before closure), once the capital and grandest city of Lycia, with a fine Roman theatre and pillar tombs.

From Kınık, it's a short walk uphill to the site past the city gates and the plinth where the fabulous Nereid Monument (now in London's British Museum) once stood. For all its grandeur, Xanthos had a chequered history of wars and destruction. At least twice, when besieged by clearly superior enemy forces, the city's population committed mass suicide.

You'll see the Roman theatre with the agora opposite the open car park, but the acropolis is badly ruined. As many of the finest sculptures (eg the Harpies Monument) and inscriptions were carted off to London by Charles Fellows in 1842, most of the inscriptions and decorations you see today are copies of the originals.

Follow the path in front of the ticket office and cafe along the colonnaded street (uphill towards the highway) to find some excellent mosaics, the attractive Dancers' Sarcophagus and Lion Sarcophagus and some excellent rock tombs.

ⓘ Getting There & Away

Any of the regular (about every hour) minibuses between Fethiye and Kaş can drop you at the Xanthos turn-off on the highway (₺8, one hour, 63km), from where it's a 1.5km walk to the site, or in the village of Kınık, which is closer.

Letoön

Sharing a place with the Lycian capital Xanthos on Unesco's World Heritage list since 1988, Letoön is home to some of the finest ruins (admission ₺8; ☺9am-7pm mid-Apr–Oct, 8am-5pm Nov–mid-Apr) on the Lycian Way. Located about 17km south of the Pınara turn-off, this former religious centre is often considered a double site with Xanthos, but Letoön has its own romantic charm.

Letoön takes its name and importance from a large shrine to Leto, who, according to legend, was Zeus' lover and bore him Apollo and Artemis. Unimpressed, Zeus' wife Hera commanded that Leto spend eternity wandering from country to country. According to local folklore she passed much time in Lycia

WALKING BETWEEN LETOÖN & XANTHOS

The road between Letoön and Xanthos is an easy 5km section of the Lycian Way (p334) walking trail. Head out of Letoön and turn right at the turn-off to Kumluova village. Head straight up this road for about 1km until you get to Lycian Way signposted crossroads. Take the road signed for Xanthos and follow it until you reach Kınık village and the entrance road for the ruins.

and became the national deity. The federation of Lycian cities then built this very impressive religious sanctuary to house her statue.

ⓘ Getting There & Away

Minibuses run from Fethiye via Eşen to Kumluova (₺8, one hour, 60km) every half-hour or so. They can drop you off at the (signposted) Letoön turn-off, from where it's an easy 1km walk to the site.

If driving from Fethiye and the north, turn right off the highway at the 'Letoön/Kumluova/Karadere' signpost. Go 4km, bear right, turn left after another 3.5km at the T-junction then right after 100m and proceed 1km – all signposted – to the site through fertile fields, orchards and hectares of polytunnels full of tomato plants.

Patara

☑0242 / POP 950

Patara, on the coast 8km south of Xanthos, can claim Turkey's longest uninterrupted beach as well as a swag of atmospheric Lycian ruins. Just inland, 1.5km from the beach and ruins, is the laid-back village of Gelemiş. This is the perfect spot to mix ruin rambling with some dedicated sun worship. Once a stop on the hippy trail (visitors now mostly arrive on the Lycian Way), Gelemiş remains refreshingly unspoiled – a miracle given its obvious charms – and traditional village life goes on.

◉ Sights & Activities

Patara is on the Lycian Way (p334) and two-day walks lead to Patara Aqueduct, either along the coast (12km, 4½ hours) or inland (10km, four hours). You can catch a bus back to Gelemiş from the aqueduct (₺5). A shorter 7km circuit leads through the village (turn right at the Golden Pension) to the forest, over the dunes to the beach and back past the ruins.

Ancient Patara ARCHAEOLOGICAL SITE
(admission incl Patara Beach ₺15; ⊙9am-7pm mid-Apr–Oct, 8am-5pm Nov–mid-Apr) Patara's grand monuments lie scattered along the road to the beach. The main section of ruins is dominated by the dilapidated 5000-seat **theatre**. Next door is the **bouleuterion**, ancient Patara's 'parliament', where it is believed members of the Lycian League met. It has been thoroughly restored, following a two-year, ₺8.5-million reconstruction. The **colonnaded street**, with re-erected columns, runs north from here. This would have been Patara's grandest boulevard, lined by shops and with the agora at its southern end.

Away from the main ruins there are plenty more remnants of Patara's long history to fossick through. From the ticket booth, along the Gelemiş–Patara Beach road, you first pass the 2nd-century triple-arched triumphal **Arch of Modestus**, with a **necropolis** containing a number of Lycian tombs nearby. As you head along the road, next is a **Harbour Baths** complex and the remains of a **Byzantine basilica** before you arrive at the central section of ruins.

From the colonnaded street a dirt track leads to a **lighthouse** built by Emperor Nero that lays claim to being one of the three oldest lighthouses in the world. This is the area of the **ancient harbour**, once on a par with Ephesus and now a reedy wetland. It is also home to the enormous **Granary of Hadrian**, used to store cereals and olive oil, and a Corinthian-style **temple tomb**.

Patara's place in history is well documented. It was the birthplace of St Nicholas, the 4th-century Byzantine bishop of Myra who later passed into legend as Santa Claus. Before that, Patara was celebrated for its temple and oracle of Apollo, of which little remains. It was Lycia's major port – which explains the large storage granary still standing – and boasted three churches and five bathhouses in Roman times. According to Acts 21:1–2, Saints Paul and Luke changed boats here while on their third mission from Rhodes to Phoenicia. The **inscribed tablets** flanking the entrance to the bouleuterion give fascinating insights into daily life here in millennia past.

ANCIENT LYCIA 101

The Lycian kingdom stretched roughly from Antalya to Dalyan, encompassing the bump of coastal terrain known as the Teke Peninsula. The enigmatic people who inhabited this area, the Lycians, date back to at least the 12th century BC, but first appear in writing when Homer's *Iliad* records their presence during an attack on Troy. It is thought they may have been descended from the Lukkans, a tribe allied with the ancient Hittites.

By the 6th century BC the Lycians had come under the control of the Persian Empire. Thus began a changing of the guard that occurred as regularly as today's ritual at Buckingham Palace. The Persians gave in to the Athenians, who were defeated in turn by Alexander the Great, the Ptolemaic Kingdom in Egypt and then Rhodes.

Lycia was granted independence by Rome in 168 BC and it immediately established the Lycian League, a loose confederation of 23 fiercely independent city states. Six of the largest – Xanthos, Patara, Pınara, Tlos, Myra and Olympos – held three votes each; the others just one or two. The Lycian League is often cited as the first protodemocratic union in history, and the *bouleuterion* (council chamber) among the ruins of Ancient Patara has been dubbed the world's first parliament.

Partly as a result of this union, peace held for over a century, but in 42 BC the league made the unwise decision not to pay tribute to Brutus, the murderer of Caesar, whom Lycia had supported during the civil war. Brutus' forces besieged Xanthos and the city state's outnumbered population, determined not to surrender, committed mass suicide.

Lycia recovered under the Roman Empire, but in AD 43 all of Lycia was amalgamated into the neighbouring province of Pamphylia, a union that lasted until the 4th century, when Pamphylia became part of Byzantium.

Lycia left behind very little in the way of material culture or written documents. A matrilineal people, they spoke their own unique language – which has still not been fully decoded. What Lycia did bequeath to posterity, however, were some of the most stunning funerary monuments from ancient times. Cliff tombs, 'house' tombs, sepulchres and sarcophagi – the Teke Peninsula's mountains and valleys are littered with them, and most are easily accessible on foot or by car.

If you plan to visit a few times, you will save money by buying a long-stay ticket allowing 10 entries over 10 days.

Patara Beach
BEACH

(admission incl Patara ruins ₺15) Backed by large sand dunes, this splendid, 18km-long sandy beach is one of Turkey's best. Due to its length, you can find a quiet spot even in the height of summer. Sunshades (small ₺7.50, large ₺10) and loungers (₺7.50) can be rented and there's a cafe for when you get peckish. Depending on the season, parts of the beach are off limits as it is an important nesting ground for sea turtles. It closes at dusk and camping is prohibited.

You can get here either by following the road for 1km past the Patara ruins, or by turning right at the Golden Pension in Gelemiş and following the road through the village, which heads for the sand-dunes area along the western side of the archaeological section. Between May and October, half-hourly minibuses (₺3) run from the highway through the village to the beach. If you plan to visit a few times, you will save money by buying a long-stay ticket allowing 10 entries over 10 days. In summer ask your pension owner about accompanying the students who count the turtles' eggs at night.

Kirca Travel
CANOEING, HORSE RIDING

(✆0242-843 5298; www.kircatravel.com) Kirca specialises in six-hour canoeing trips on the Xanthos River (₺70 including lunch), but also offers horse riding, day hikes and 4WD safaris to Xanthos and Saklıkent Gorge.

🛏 Sleeping

As you come into Gelemiş, the main road and the hillside on your left contain hotels and pensions. A turn to the right at the Golden Pension takes you to the village centre, across the valley and up the other side to more accommodation. Outside of summer, most places offer decent discounts on rooms. Many also offer self-catering apartments, making Gelemiş a great base for families and long stays.

★ Akay Pension
PENSION $

(✆0532 410 2195, 0242-843 5055; www.pataraakaypension.com; s/d/tr/apt ₺70/100/130/180; P🐾❄🛜❄) Run by keen-to-please Kazım and his wife Ayşe, the Akay has a comfy Ottoman-style lounge to hang out in and meet other travellers, and 11 well-maintained, sweetly decorated rooms with new bathrooms and balconies overlooking citrus groves. There's a

pair of two-bedroom apartments for families, too. Ayşe's cooking is legendary; sample at least one set meal (from ₺26) while here.

★ Flower Pension
PENSION $$

(✆0242-843 5164, 0530 511 0206; www.pataraflowerpension.com; s/d/tr/studio €30/40/50/50, apt €60-85; P🐾❄@🛜❄) The Flower has 15 bright and airy rooms with balconies overlooking the garden, including two self-catering studios and two apartments with well-equipped kitchens and two bedrooms. In the garden itself are four refreshingly cool new rooms. Knowledgable manager Bekir's mum Ayşe presides over the kitchen, producing Turkish food at its best (dinner ₺25 to ₺30), with biweekly barbecues in summer.

Golden Pension
PENSION $$

(✆0242-843 5162; www.pataragoldenpension.com; s/d/tr €30/35/40; P🐾❄🛜) Patara's original pension, run by ex-mayor Arif and family, is peaceful despite its central location on the main crossroads. There are 16 homely rooms (all with balconies) and a popular restaurant with a pretty shaded terrace. Choose a room with a garden view. Half board is an extra €7 per person.

Patara View Point Hotel
HOTEL $$

(✆0242-843 5184; www.pataraviewpoint.com; s/d with fan ₺140/170, apt per week ₺1800; P🐾❄@🛜❄) This country-chic hotel has a lovely pool, 27 sea- or mountain-facing rooms, a cosy library and an Ottoman-style terrace with a cedar fire to banish mosquitoes. Owner Muzaffer is a history buff and you'll find 350-plus antiques here and old farm implements outside, including a 2000-year-old olive press, an ancient beehive and a replica Lycian tomb (for his dog).

🍴 Eating

With a little notice, most pensions prepare excellent home-cooked meals for both guests and nonguests. In the village centre, just downhill from Golden Pension, three rudimentary cafes serve savoury and sweet *gözleme* pancakes (₺5 to ₺8), which you can take away or eat on the floor.

Tlos Restaurant
TURKISH $

(✆0242-843 5135; mains ₺12-20; ⊙8am-midnight; ✆) Run by the moustached and smiling chef Osman, the popular Tlos serves tasty pide (₺6 to ₺15), *guveç* (casserole) and mezes (₺3 to ₺8), including a garlicky and delicious oven-baked mushroom dish.

Lazy Frog INTERNATIONAL $

(☑0242-843 5160; mains ₺15-25; ⊗8am-1am)
With its very own kitchen garden, this central,
popular place offers steaks as well as various
vegetarian options and *gözleme* on its relaxing terrace.

❶ Getting There & Away

Any bus heading between Kaş and Fethiye can
drop you on the highway, 3.5km from the village.
Between May and October, local dolmuşes run
to the village every 30 to 40 minutes from the
highway drop-off point (₺3). If you're arriving early
or late in the year, ring your pension in Gelemiş
to check.

Gelemiş has hourly dolmuşes in summer to/
from Kalkan (₺6, 20 minutes, 15km) and Kaş (₺8,
45 minutes, 40km) and a daily departure to Saklıkent Gorge (₺10, one hour, 52km) at 11am. Year-
round, you can catch minibuses at the turn-off on
the main road to Fethiye (₺12, 1½ hours, 73km)
and Antalya (₺30, 3¾ hours, 230km).

Kalkan

☑0242 / POP 3349

Kalkan is a well-to-do harbourside town
built largely on hills that look down on an
almost-perfect bay. It's as justly popular for
its excellent restaurants as its small but central beach. Just be aware that Kalkan is pricier and more dominated by British expats
and tourists than most other coastal spots,
including nearby Kaş.

A thriving Greek fishing village called Kalamaki until the 1920s, Kalkan is now largely
devoted to high-end tourism. Development
continues up the hills, with scores of new
villas appearing each season. But look for
Kalkan's charms in the compact old town.

🏃 Activities

Most people use Kalkan as a base to visit the
Lycian ruins, or engage in the many local activities. Apart from the beach (Map p349; Yat
Limanı) near the marina, and Kaputaş, a perfect little sandy cove about 7km east of Kalkan
en route to Kaş, watery activities include the
beach clubs and swimming platforms at
hotels such as the Caretta, open to the public
for a nominal fee.

Boat Trips BOATING

(Map p349; ⊗daily mid-Apr–Oct) Kalkan is an
excellent place for a day-long boat trip. Operators such as Anıl Boat (Map p349; ☑0533
351 7520; Kalkan harbour) line up at the harbour,
charging from ₺50 per person (€180 for the

boat) for a day on the water with swimming
stops, sometimes at Kaputaş Beach, and
lunch included.

Aristos Watersports WATER SPORTS

(Map p349; ☑0537 600 9827; www.kalkanwater
sports.com; İskele Sokak) This decade-old Turkish-Australian operation offers adrenaline-
pumping watery fun, including speedboat
trips, waterskiing, jet skiing, inflatable rides,
SUP, wakeboarding and mono-skiing.

Dolphin Scuba Team DIVING

(Map p349; ☑0542 627 97 57; www.dolphinscuba
team.com; İskele Sokak; day €52, PADI discover
scuba €60) Kaş may have a better reputation
for diving, but there are a couple of wrecks
and a fair amount of sea life to the west of
Kalkan harbour. Dolphin Scuba offers rec-
reational diving and the full gamut of PADI
and CMAS courses. Any nondiving friends
and family who want some snorkelling action are welcome along while you dive (€13).

🛏 Sleeping

Most of Kalkan's accommodation is made up
of private villas and apartment rentals. Between May and October the majority of rooms
in town are block-booked by travel agencies
and wholesalers, so it pays to book in advance.
Kalkan is geared towards top-end and, to a
lesser degree, midrange accommodation. You
will find much better budget options in other
destinations such as Kaş.

Gül Pansiyon PENSION $

(Map p349; ☑0242-844 3099; www.kalkangul
pansiyon.com; 7 Nolu Sokak 10; s/d/apt €30/35/45;
🅿☕✳🛜) The 'Rose' has a rooftop with million-dollar views, small but tidy rooms with
balconies, and three apartments with kitchenettes and washing machines. Try to bag one
of the rooms on the 3rd floor for the views
and the light. There are discounts outside of
peak summer, when it's a popular pit stop for
hikers.

Caretta Hotel HOTEL $$

(☑0505 269 0753, 0242-844 3435; www.caret
tahotelkalkan.com; İskele Sokak 6; s/d ₺110/180;
🅿☕✳🛜🏊) This boutique-hotel-cum-
pension is a perennial favourite for its swimming platforms, homestyle cooking, warm
welcome and away-from-it-all appeal. The 14
bright, sunny rooms have excellent terraces
and modern Ottoman decorative touches. A
private beach, boat trips and sea taxi from
Kalkan harbour are offered.

Kalkan

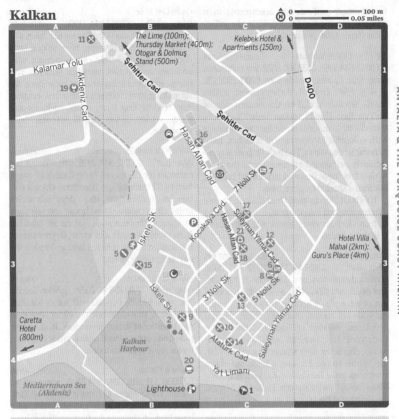

Kalkan

⊙ Sights
1 Public Beach..C4

✪ Activities, Courses & Tours
2 Anıl Boat...B4
3 Aristos Watersports.............................B3
4 Boat Trips...B4
5 Dolphin Scuba Team............................B3

⌂ Sleeping
6 Courtyard Hotel....................................C3
7 Gül Pansiyon...C2
8 White House Pension...........................C3

✗ Eating
9 Aubergine..B4
10 Cafe Del Mar...C4

11 Hünkar Ocakbaşı..................................A1
12 Iso's Kitchen Restaurant.....................C3
13 Kalamaki Restaurant...........................C3
14 Korsan Fish Terrace.............................C4
15 Marina Restaurant...............................B3
16 Mussakka...C2
17 Salonika...C2
18 Zeytinlik...C3

🍷 Drinking & Nightlife
19 Blue Turtle...A1
20 Fener Cafe & Brasserie........................B4

🛍 Shopping
21 Just Silver..C3

Kelebek Hotel & Apartments APARTMENT **$$**
(📞0242-844 3770; www.butterflyholidays.co.uk;
Karayolları Sokak 4; apt/r from €32/36; 🅿🈂❄
📶🏊) North of the centre, just off the D400,
this family-run hotel offers good value for
self-caterers. The rooms, fronted by a large
swimming pool, are clean, if slightly frayed
around the edges, but the eight one- and

two-bedroom self-catering apartments in a separate block are a great deal. It also offers villas (from €520 per week).

★ **Hotel Villa Mahal** LUXURY HOTEL $$$
(☎ 0242-844 3268, 0533 766 8622; www.villamahal.com; Kışla Caddesi; s/d/tr from €200/250/325; P ➛ ✿ 🛜 ☎) One of Turkey's most stylish hotels lies atop a cliff on the eastern side of Kalkan Bay. The 13 rooms, individually designed in whiter-than-white minimalism with colourful Mediterranean splashes, have panoramic sea views. The infinity pool is spectacularly suspended on the edge of the void, while stone steps descend to seafront bathing platforms shaded by olive trees.

It's about 2km by road from Kalkan. There's a free water taxi into the centre; a normal taxi to/from Kalkan costs about ₺15. Minimum stay three nights.

Courtyard Hotel BOUTIQUE HOTEL $$$
(Map p349; ☎ 0242-844 3738, 0532 443 0012; www.courtyardkalkan.com; Süleyman Yilmaz Caddesi 24-26; s/d ₺240/420; P ➛ ✿ 🛜 ☎) Cobbled out of a couple of 19th-century village houses, with six rooms retaining their original fireplaces, wooden ceilings and floors, the Courtyard has lashings of Ottoman old-world character and shares a garden with the White House Pension. Check out room 1 with its 'cave bathroom' converted from a 400-year-old water cistern. Halıl and Marion are delightful hosts.

White House Pension PENSION $$$
(Map p349; ☎ 0532 443 0012, 0242-844 3738; www.kalkanwhitehouse.co.uk; 5 Nolu Sokak 19; s/d ₺160/240; P ➛ ✿ 🛜) Situated on a quiet corner at the top of the old-town hill, this attentively run pension has 10 compact, breezy rooms – four with balconies – in a spotless family home. The real winner here, though, is the view from the terrace and friendly owners Halıl and Marion.

✕ Eating

While the restaurants and bars on the harbour have considerable appeal, there are also interesting options inland. Running through the old town, Süleyman Yilmaz Caddesi has taken off in recent years with its little restaurants, bars and *meyhanes*. In season, book ahead no matter where you plan to eat.

Kalkan's main market day is Thursday, though there is a smaller Sunday market in the Akbel district to the northwest.

Cafe Del Mar CAFE $
(Map p349; ☎ 0242-844 1068; www.cafedel markalkan.com; Hasan Altan Caddesi 61a; cakes ₺12; ⊙ 11am-10pm; 🛜) Inviting blue saloon-style doors lead to this little cafe brimming with antiques and curios, hanging lanterns and curvy metalwork furniture. Come here for something sweet: coffee in flavoured, cappuccino (₺8) or iced form, cakes, cocktails and nargiles (₺30). Up top is a grill restaurant with sea views.

Iso's Kitchen Restaurant TURKISH $$
(Map p349; ☎ 0242-844 2415; http://isoskitchen restaurant.com; Süleyman Yilmaz Caddesi 17; mezes from ₺9.50, mains ₺30; ⊙ 11am-11pm) Once a cottage on an olive farm, these days Iso's serves grills, *güveç*, seafood and house specials such as spicy *köfte* on a stick. Taking its moniker from owner Ismael's nickname, the restaurant has seating on the cobbled lane and inside the old stone Greek house.

Hünkar Ocakbaşı KEBAP $$
(Map p349; ☎ 0242-844 2077; Şehitler Caddesi 38e; mains ₺10-35) Popular with locals for Sunday lunch, this authentic *ocakbaşı* serves all the traditional kebap favourites. It also does pide and pizzas as well as five kinds of *guveç*, including a vegetarian one.

Guru's Place ANATOLIAN $$
(☎ 0536 331 1016, 0242-844 3848; www.kalkangu ru.com; D400; mezes ₺12, mains ₺15-35; ⊙ 8am-11pm; ✐) Affable Hüseyin and his family, who have been in the area for four centuries, have been running this scenically located seaside restaurant for 20 years. Food is authentic and fresh, coming from their own garden. The small menu is mostly focused on daily specials and Turkish classics such as *mantı* (Turkish ravioli).

It's on the coastal highway to Kaş. If driving, look out for it on the corner as you crest the brow, opposite Gümüşün Yeri restaurant. Two-hour morning cooking classes are offered.

★ **Kalamaki Restaurant** MODERN TURKISH $$$
(Map p349; ☎ 0242-844 1555; www.kalkankalama ki.com; Hasan Altan Caddesi 47a; mains ₺45; ⊙ 11am-10pm; ✐) A modern venue with a very stylish minimalist pub on the terrace and restaurant upstairs, serving superb Turkish dishes with a European twist. Try the scrumptious lamb with prunes and almonds or the vegetarian *şiş* kebap (roasted on a skewer). Host Tayfur takes it all in his stride – even when celebs like Gordon Ramsay come a-calling.

★ **Mussakka** TURKISH $$$

(Map p349; ☑0242-844 1576, 0537 493 2290; www.mussakkarestaurant.com; Hasan Altan Caddesi; mains ₺25-65; ⊗9am-2am; ☑🚼) With its pink theme and wood burner, this casually elegant eatery offers sea views, good service and dishes from champagne and scampi risotto to the recommended house moussaka, cooked *saç kavurma* (stir-fried) style and brought sizzling to the table. Also on offer are six meatless mains (₺25 to ₺36), curry nights in winter and *digestif* nargile (₺25).

Aubergine MODERN TURKISH $$$

(Patlıcan; Map p349; ☑0242-844 3332; www.kalkanaubergine.com; İskele Sokak; mains ₺19-65; ⊗8am-3am; 🛜☑) With a shaded terrace bang on the marina, as well as cosy seats inside, this stylish restaurant is a magnet for its location alone. House specialities include slow-roasted wild boar, Ottoman lamb ragout and the succulent dish that inspired Aubergine's name, *imam bayıldı*.

Salonika MEYHANE $$$

(Map p349; ☑0242-844 2422; www.salonika.co; Süleyman Yılmaz Caddesi; mains ₺40; ⊗11am-11pm; ☑🚼) With tables on the lane and exposed stone walls inside, this white building with blue trim calls itself a *meyhane,* but the atmosphere is romantic rather than ribald. Occasional live music accompanies the mezes (from ₺9; platter for two ₺30), Turkish dishes such as *kuzu güveç* (lamb stew), grills and fish.

Marina Restaurant TURKISH $$$

(Map p349; ☑0536 487 2163; İskele Sokak; mains ₺30-60; ⊗8am-1am) Just below the landmark Pirat Hotel, this dependable grill restaurant has a good menu of Turkish and international dishes, including kebaps, moussaka, pasta, steaks, seafood and chicken. Its white-and-turquoise decor and wood burner make it a pleasant waterside venue for some mezes (₺9; platter for two ₺26).

Zeytinlik MODERN TURKISH $$$

(Olive Garden; Map p349; ☑0242-844 3408; 1st fl, Hasan Altan Caddesi 17; mains ₺25-40; ☑) This British-Turkish restaurant above Merkez Cafe serves some of the most adventurous Turkish food around. Try the fish *dolmas,* the samosa-like minced lamb in filo pastry triangles, or any of the several vegetarian options.

Korsan Fish Terrace SEAFOOD $$$

(Map p349; ☑0242-844 3076; www.korsankalkan.com; Atatürk Caddesi; mains ₺30-45; ⊗10am-midnight) On the roof of the 19th-century Patara Stone House, this restaurant is among the finest seafood experiences in Kalkan. Its homemade lemonade is legendary and there's regular live jazz on summer evenings. Ichthyophobes will be consoled by the alternative, fishless menu of modern Turkish and international dishes.

Drinking & Nightlife

Blue Turtle BAR

(Map p349; ☑0242-844 1614; www.blueturtle.club; Akdeniz Caddesi; ⊗11am-3am) On summer evenings, live music regularly strikes up in the trellis-shaded courtyard of this cool hangout above the waterfront throng. The small library entertains in winter. Given the steep climb up here from the sea, perhaps come before that harbourside dinner, rather than afterwards.

The Lime BAR

(☑0242-844 1144; Şehitler Caddesi 36; ⊗8am-1am) Previously called the Lemon Garden, this garden bar-restaurant is the watering hole of choice for expats to mourn the old country over cocktails, pizza and table tennis. Check Facebook for details of upcoming quiz nights and live music.

Fener Cafe & Brasserie CAFE

(The Lighthouse; Map p349; ☑0242-844 3752; Yat Limanı; ⊗8am-1am) The closest thing Kalkan has to a tea garden, the square at the tiny *fener* (lighthouse) is popular with locals, expats and visitors alike. Looking for someone in Kalkan during the day? Try here.

Shopping

Just Silver JEWELLERY

(Map p349; ☑0242-844 3136; www.justlivingkalkan.com; Hasan Altan Caddesi 28) Designing and selling ear, nose, neck, finger and toe baubles for 30 years, Kalkan's best-known shop offers silver and gold-plated jewellery in traditional and modern styles.

Getting There & Away

Hourly dolmuşes and small buses run to/from Patara (₺6, 25 minutes, 15km), Fethiye (₺16, 1½ hours, 83km) and Kaş (₺6, 35 minutes, 29km) via the beach at Kaputaş (₺3, 15 minutes, 7km).

Pamukkale buses depart for İstanbul (₺110, 11 hours, 840km) at 7.15pm and İzmir (₺63, 5½ hours, 440km) at 10.30pm. Ulusoy, Varan and Kamil Koç also serve Kalkan.

GSO IMAGES / GETTY IMAGES ©

1. Üçağız harbour, near Kekova (p359) 2. Fethiye Körfezi (Fethiye Bay: p331) 3. Ölüdeniz Beach & Lagoon (p340) 4. Kaş (p354)

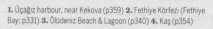

STUART BLACK / GETTY IMAGES ©

The Blue Cruise

A blue cruise is sightseeing with swags of style. Board a *gület* (Turkish yacht) to experience the Turquoise Coast's scenery in all its glory, from lazy days filled with swimming and sunbathing to sunset toasts in one of the prettiest corners of the Mediterranean.

Casting Off

Fethiye is the most popular departure point for average landlubbers who want a taste of on-the-sea life. More experienced yachties (and those chartering an entire boat rather than a cabin) often head for Göcek or Kaş.

Day One

Gülets head out from Fethiye and skim the lush green coastline to Ölüdeniz before cruising on to the cliff-hemmed beach at Butterfly Valley. The first day usually ends at St Nicholas Island, where there's plenty of time for swimming, snorkelling and – if you want your land legs back – exploring the island's ancient ruins.

Day Two

A full day of soaking up some sun on-board, with opportunities aplenty for swimming. On day two you usually cruise by the dinky harbour towns of Kalkan and Kaş and moor near the Liman Ağzı peninsula.

Day Three

Mixing history into the sunshine and salt spray, day three sails past tiny Üçağız to Kekova Island's famous sunken-city remnants, before visiting Kaleköy to clamber up the hilltop to the fortress ruins of ancient Simena.

Day Four

On this day you head east along the coast, with plentiful swimming stops to savour the scenery. Çayağzı (the ancient harbour of Andriake), just south of Demre, is the usual disembarking point.

İslamlar

This alpine former Greek village is a favourite escape from Kalkan, 6.5km south. The attractions here are a temperature that is 5°C cooler than the coast in summer, and the dozen-or-so trout restaurants making use of icy mountain streams to fill their tanks. In the village square, have a look at one of two working mills that still use water power and a great millstone to turn local residents' grain into flour.

🛏 Sleeping & Eating

Seven or so roadside restaurants serve the local trout and other dishes, accompanied by views of the distant Med. A small village shop sells basic supplies and alcohol.

Grapevine Cottage   COTTAGE **$$**
(📱0534 744 9255; www.grapevinecottage.hosted.me/index.htm; İslamlar; cottage d per week €450; P🅿👻🛜) Set among citrus groves and vineyards, this charming two-bedroom, self-catering cottage is an arty, rustic retreat run by a Briton Deborah. The views down to the sea from the breakfast terrace are priceless and the garden full of wandering ducks and chickens adds bags of appeal for those seeking an escape-to-the-country setting.

Değirmen   FISH, TURKISH **$$**
(📱0242-838 6295, 0532 586 2734; İslamlar; mains ₺11-35; ⏱11am-10pm; 🅿) You walk past a trout farm on the way into this authentic restaurant, which makes its own tahini from sesame picked from the fields and ground in the basement. The upstairs terrace has an unbeatable view and the menu features mezes, sea fish and meat dishes as well as the obligatory trout.

❶ Getting There & Away

There is no regular dolmuş service from Kalkan, 6.5km south. A taxi from Kalkan costs about ₺40.

Bezirgan

In an elevated valley 17km northeast of Kalkan by road sits the beautiful village of Bezirgan, a timeless example of Turkish rural life. Towering some 725m above the fruit orchards and fields of wheat, barley, chickpeas, almonds and sticky sesame are the ruins of the Lycian hilltop citadel of Pirha. In the colder months there is a distant backdrop of snowcapped peaks.

A 9km (three-hour) section of the Lycian Way climbs from Kalkan, emerging at the distinctive grain stores at the western end of the village. You can also walk from here to İslamlar (about 10km), either by road or over the mountain on the old mill track, once used by locals taking their corn to İslamlar's mills.

Accommodation is available at Owlsland (Erol's Pansiyon; 📱0242-837 5214; www.owlsland. com; Bezirgan; per person €45, incl half board €65; P🅿❄🛜), a 150-year-old farmhouse idyllically surrounded by fruit trees and run by a charming Turkish-Scottish couple, Erol and Pauline. The three cosy rooms, previously a kitchen, a stable and Erol's grandparents' bedroom, contain most of their original features and are decorated with old farm implements. The upstairs room with balcony, traditional decor and wood burner is especially nice.

❶ Getting There & Away

Hourly 'yayla' (mountain pasture) minibuses from Kalkan to Antalya via Elmalı stop by both mosques in Bezirgan (₺4, 30 minutes).

If you're under your own steam, head north from Kalkan, cross over the D400 linking Fethiye and Kaş and follow the signs for Elmalı. The road climbs steadily, with stunning views across the sea, and heads further up the mountain. Once the road crests the pass, you can see Bezirgan below on the left.

To find Owlsland, take the signposted turn-off to Bezirgan at the far end of the village, just before the road begins climbing towards İslamlar. Turn right after 1km and Owlsland is on the right after another 1km.

Kaş

📱0242 / POP 7558

It may not sport the region's finest beaches but its central Teke Peninsula location, mellow atmosphere and menu of adventure activities have made Kaş – pronounced (roughly) 'cash' – an ideal base for forays into the surrounding area. For divers this is Turkey's hub for underwater exploits, with excellent wreck diving just offshore. A plethora of boat trips, kayaking tours and hikes are also easily arranged from here.

The 6km-long Çukurbağ Peninsula extends west of the pretty old town, town square and harbour. At the start of it, you'll find a well-preserved ancient theatre, which is about all that's left of ancient Antiphellos, the original Lycian town. Above Kaş, several Lycian rock tombs in the mountain wall can be seen even at night, when they're illuminated.

Lying just offshore, dominating the harbour view, is the geopolitical oddity of the Greek island of Meis (Kastellorizo), which can be visited on a day trip.

◎ Sights

Antiphellos Ruins
RUIN

FREE Antiphellos was a small settlement and the port for Phellos, the much larger Lycian town further north in the hills. Its small Hellenistic theatre (Map p356; Hastane Caddesi), 500m west of the main square, could seat 4000 spectators and is in very good condition. You can also walk to the rock tombs (Map p356; Likya Caddesi) cut into the sheer cliffs above town, which are illuminated at night. The walk is strenuous so go at a cool time of day.

Walk up hilly Uzun Çarşı Sokak, the Roman-era road that locals call Slippery St, to the east of the main square to reach the King's Tomb (Map p356; Uzun Çarşı Sokak), a superb example of a 4th-century BC Lycian sarcophagus. It's mounted on a high base and has two lions' heads on the lid.

Büyük Çakıl Plajı
BEACH

(Big Pebble Beach; Hükümet Caddesi) For swimming, head for 'Big Pebble Beach', a relatively clean beach 1.3km from Kaş' town centre. Although it's largely pebble-based, there's a few metres of sand at one end. There are shaded cafes for refreshments, which also rent out sunloungers and sunshades.

Liman Ağzı
BEACH

If you're after a full day on the beach, the best idea is to hop on one of the water taxis (Map p356) in Kaş harbour and head for one of three beaches on the peninsula opposite at Liman Ağzı. All three have cafes, you can rent sunloungers and sunshades, and the cove has calm water. You can also hike here (3km) on a pleasant section of the Lycian Way footpath, which begins at Büyük Çakıl Plajı.

🏃 Activities

Kaş is the centre for diving in the Mediterranean, with wrecks and a lot more underwater life than you'd expect below the surface. It's also an excellent base for exploring the region further, and local travel agencies offer a huge range of day tours and adventure activities. Most companies offer more or less the same tours, but you can always tailor your own for a negotiated price.

Among the stalwarts, the various boat trips to Kekova (from €25) are a fine day out and include swimming stops as well as time to see several ruins. There are also popular kayaking tours to Kekova, and longer trips to the area incorporating the Lycian ruins of Aperlae. A great idea is to charter a boat from the marina. A whole day spent around the islands of Kaş should cost from ₺200 to ₺250 for the entire boat, accommodating up to eight people.

Dragoman
OUTDOORS

(Map p356; ☑0242-836 3614; www.dragoman-turkey.com; Uzun Çarşı Sokak 15) This dynamic outdoor activities centre has built a reputation for its diving, offering underwater packages from PADI and CMAS courses to snorkelling with a marine biologist. Its outdoor activities include many interesting and unique options, such as 'mermaid' tours, SUP, botanical excursions, horse riding and coasteering. It also offers excellent day and multi-day sea kayaking, hiking and mountain-biking routes.

Bougainville Travel
OUTDOORS

(Map p356; ☑0242-836 3737; www.bougainville-turkey.com; İbrahim Serin Caddesi 10, Kaş) This reputable English-Turkish tour operator has much experience in organising any number of activities and tours, including Kekova island boat tours (€30), canyoning (€50), mountain biking (€40), tandem paragliding (€80 for flight lasting 20 to 30 minutes), scuba diving (€23 for one dive including equipment, €30 for a sample dive and €300 for a PADI course) and sea kayaking (€35).

Xanthos Travel
OUTDOORS

(Map p356; ☑0242-836 3292; www.xanthostravel.com; İbrahim Serin Caddesi 5/A) Xanthos runs popular boat day tours in the Kekova area (€30), sea-kayaking tours that get you up close with the sunken city ruins (€35 to €45) and diving trips. For landlubbers there are jeep safaris to the mountain village of Gömbe and Yeşil Gölü (Green Lake) in the Akdağlar range (€30), mountain biking, trekking, canyoning, abseiling and paragliding.

🛏 Sleeping

Kaş Camping
CAMPGROUND $

(☑0242-836 1050; www.kaskamping.com; Hastane Caddesi 3; campsites 1/2 people €12/16, chalets incl breakfast s/d €57/80, bungalows without bathroom & breakfast s/d €21/32; ℗❄🛜) Located on an attractive rocky outcropping at the start of the peninsula 800m west of Kaş, this popular site is 100m from the sea and features a terrace bar. There's space to pitch your tent or pull up in your motorhome, as well as cute en-suite

ANTALYA & THE TURQUOISE COAST KAŞ

Kaş

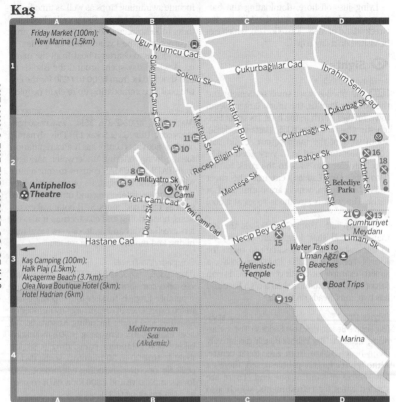

Friday Market (100m);
New Marina (1.5km)

Uğur Mumcu Cad

Süleyman Çavuş Cad

Sokollu Sk

Çukurbağlılar Cad

İbrahim Serin Cad

1 Çukurbağ Sk

Meltem Sk

Atatürk Bul

Çukurbağlı Sk

Bahçe Sk

Öztürk Sk

Recep Bilgin Sk

Amfitiyatro Sk

Menteşe Sk

Ortaokul Sk

Belediye
Parkı

Antiphellos
Theatre

Yeni
Camii

Yeni Cami Cad

Yeni Cami Cad

Deniz Sk

Cumhuriyet
Meydanı

Hastane Cad

Necip Bey Cad

Water Taxis to
Liman Ağzı
Beaches

Liman Sk

Kaş Camping (100m);
Halk Plajı (1.5km);
Akçagerme Beach (3.7km);
Olea Nova Boutique Hotel (5km);
Hotel Hadrian (6km)

Hellenistic
Temple

Boat Trips

Mediterranean
Sea
(Akdeniz)

Marina

chalets and more basic bungalows. Nonguests can use the beach for €5 per day.

Scuba-diving tours, PADI courses and holiday packages are offered through **Sundiving** (☑0242-836 2637; www.sundiving.com; Kaş Camping, Hastane Caddesi 3).

Anı Pension
PENSION $

(Map p356; ☑0242-836 1791, 0533 326 4201; www.motelani.com; Süleyman Çavuş Caddesi 12; dm/s/d ₺35/50/90; P ⊜ ❈ @ 🛜) With a seven-bed dorm and kitchen for guest use, the Anı leads the way for budget digs in Kaş, having recently been renovated by hosts Ömer and brother Ahmet. The decent-sized rooms all have balconies and the roof terrace is a hub where you can kick back, cool off with a beer and swap travel stories with fellow guests.

★ Hideaway Hotel
HOTEL $$

(Map p356; ☑0242-836 1887; www.hotelhideaway.com; Anfitiyatro Sokak 7; s €45, d €55-65, ste €80; P ⊜ ❈ @ 🛜 ⊠) Run by the unstoppable Ahmet, a fount of local information, this lovely hotel has large, airy rooms (some with sea views) with a fresh white-on-white minimalist feel and gleaming modern bathrooms. There's a pool for cooling off and a chilled-out roof terrace that's the venue for morning yoga and sundowners at the bar with Meis views.

★ Ateş Pension
PENSION $$

(Map p356; ☑0532 492 0680, 0242-836 1393; www.atespension.com; Anfitiyatro Sokak 3; dm/s/d/tr/f ₺50/130/145/185/210; P ⊜ ❈ 🛜) Offering four-bed dorms and private rooms in two buildings, 'Hot Pension' is a cut above Kaş' other pensions, with snugly duvets and modern bathrooms. Owners Recep and Ayşe are superfriendly hosts and serve Turkish feasts (₺30) and breakfasts of 55 items on the partly covered roof terrace, which is a relaxing lounge with a book exchange and partial sea views.

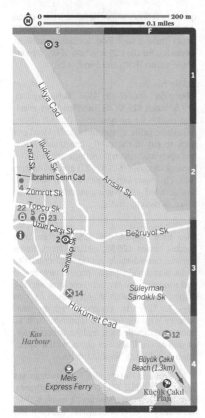

Meltem Pension   PENSION **$$**
(Map p356; ☎0242-836 1855; www.meltem
pansiyon.com; Meltem Sokak; s ₺80, d ₺150-
160; P❄✳❄) The simple rooms at this
friendly, family-run place are bright and
airy with modern bathrooms and most
have balconies. The shady roof terrace is
a fine spot for hanging out in the evening,
and during summer barbecues are organ-
ised there.

Hilal Pansiyon   PENSION **$$**
(Map p356; ☎0532 615 1061, 0242-836 1207;
www.hilalpension.com; Süleyman Çavuş Caddesi
8; s/d/tr ₺60/100/140; P❄✳@❄) Run by
friendly Süleyman, 'Crescent Pension' offers
18 simple but spotless rooms and a leafy roof
terrace with great views and a fridge of Efes
beer. There are daily barbecues (₺25 to ₺30)
in summer, bikes are free for guests and you
also get a 10% discount on activities and
tours.

★**Olea Nova**
Boutique Hotel   BOUTIQUE HOTEL **$$$**
(☎0242-836 2660; www.oleanova.com.tr; Demokra-
si Caddesi 43; r/f/ste from €120/220/310; P❄
✳@❄✷) Set amid olive groves and villas,
6km from Kaş' centre, with panoramic views
across the water to the Greek island of Meis,
this swish boutique hotel is just the ticket for
those seeking a peaceful break. The 20 rooms
and suites are all pristine white minimal-
ism, while the kidney-shaped pool, adjoining
bar-restaurant and private beach are slothing
central.

★**Nur Beach Hotel**   BOUTIQUE HOTEL **$$$**
(Map p356; ☎0242-836 1828; www.nurbeach
hotel.com; Hükümet Caddesi; r ₺300-400;
P❄✳❄) There's a contemporary beachy
feel to these 20 rooms, including 13 with sea
view and five with small private pool. We
love the broken-glass effect, cage lampshades

and mammoth marbled showers in the deluxe rooms, while one standard room has a spa, and 502 is a loft-style standard with killer views. Breakfast is served on the beach in summer.

Hotel Hadrian
HOTEL $$$

(🖉 0242-836 2856; www.hotel-hadrian.de; Doğan Kaşaroğlu Sokak 10; r incl half board from €150; 🅿 🌀 ❄ 🛜 🌊) About halfway out on the Kaş peninsula, the German-owned Hadrian is a tropical oasis with bougainvillea climbing the white balconies of some 20 rooms and family suites (from €200). The 250-sq-metre seawater pool and private swimming platform are excellent, and the restaurant and bar nestle in an 850-sq-metre garden with wow-factor views.

🍴 Eating

Kaş has a burgeoning dining scene, with the old town packed full of restaurants, little bars and *meyhanes*. You'll find some excellent eateries to the southeast of the main square, Cumhuriyet Meydanı, especially around Sandıkçı Sokak.

The Friday market (Ugar Mumcu Caddesi; ⊙ 7am-7pm Fri) takes place near the otogar.

Havana Balık Evi
SEAFOOD $

(Map p356; 🖉 0242-836 4111; Öztürk Sokak 7; mains ₺8-20; ⊙ 9am-midnight; 🍴) Head to the 'Atmospheric Fish House' for cheap and cheerful *balık ekmek* (₺8 to ₺10), the simple fish sandwich that is a staple in coastal Turkey. Keeping up with the fishy theme, there are also hearty bowls of *balık guveç* (fish casserole; ₺20) and *hamsı tava* (pan-fried Turkish anchovies; ₺15).

★ Hünkâr Ocakbaşı
TURKISH $$

(Map p356; 🖉 0242-836 3660; Çukurbağlı Sokak 7e; pides ₺10-16, mains ₺18-30; ⊙ 11am-10pm) For a quick but quality lunch, local foodies recommend this clean and friendly eatery serving everything from light lunches (the bijou ₺2 *lahmacun* might be the smallest pizza you ever see) to kebabs, mixed grills and *güveç*. A great place to try Turkish classics and local adaptations of international dishes such as deep-pan pizza topped with *sucuk* (spicy sausage).

Bi Lokma
ANATOLIAN $$

(Map p356; 🖉 0242-836 3942; www.bilokma.com.tr; Hükümet Caddesi 2; mains ₺20-28; ⊙ 9am-midnight; 🍴) Also known as 'Mama's Kitchen', this place has green tables in a terraced garden high above the harbour. The 'mama' in question is Sabo, whose daughters have taken the culinary baton, turning out great traditional Turkish soul food, including excellent mezes (go for the ₺25 selection of 10), famous house *mantı* (₺20) and *börek* (₺18).

Enişte'nin Yeri
TURKISH $$

(Map p356; 🖉 0242-836 4404; Necip Bey Caddesi 5; mains ₺15-32; ⊙ 11am-10pm) An excellent choice for no-nonsense Turkish dishes of kebaps, grills, soups and salads. Head out back to eat in the pretty courtyard, which has open and covered sections and an oven turning out pide (₺15 to ₺22) and *lahmacun* (₺5). The *beyti* kebap, wrapped in flatbread and drizzled with yogurt, tomato and butter sauce, is recommended.

★ Retro Bistro
INTERNATIONAL $$$

(Map p356; 🖉 0242-836 4282; İbrahim Serin Caddesi; mains ₺26-52; ⊙ 11am-10pm) Retro devotes considerable energy and creativity to its homemade pasta, pizza bases, bread and *sous vide* (water bath) cooking, serving dishes such as lamb shank cooked for two days. Its inventive creations include great burgers with all sorts of toppings, such as homemade garlic aioli and barbecue sauce, as well as the Black Sea pizza, with a squid-ink-infused black Napolitana base.

Bella Vita and Ratatouille
INTERNATIONAL $$$

(Map p356; 🖉 0531 724 5846; erkalmavis@yahoo. com; 1st fl, Cumhuriyet Meydanı 10; mezes ₺20-46, mains ₺22-60) Overlooking the main square, two of Kaş' most popular international bistros have joined pasta- and burger-slinging forces, offering a diverse menu that includes steaks, pizzas and seafood dishes from classic to gourmet. The three-course Turkish tasting menu (₺110), featuring Mediterranean produce such as Saklıkent honey, and boutique Turkish wines add a local flavour.

🍷 Drinking & Nightlife

Head to the old town for atmospheric little bars and *meyhanes*, and to the main square, Cumhuriyet Meydanı, for bars with al fresco seating.

Echo Cafe & Bar
BAR

(Map p356; 🖉 0242-836 2047; www.echocafebar. com; Limanı Sokak; ⊙ 4pm-4am) Hip and stylish, this lounge near an ancient (5 BC, anyone?) cistern on the harbour has Kaş high society sipping fruit daiquiris to both live and canned jazz. A bonfire glows in the garden, and the historic building has an airy upstairs gallery with little balconies overlooking the water.

Asmaltı BAR
(Map p356; off Limanı Sokak; ⊙4pm-late) With its fairy lights and wooden decks right on on the water, this bar 'under the grape tree' is a top spot for a sunset beer (₺12) or cocktail with Meis views.

Hideaway Bar & Cafe BAR
(Map p356; ☑0242-836 3369; Cumhuriyet Meydanı 16/A; ⊙4pm-3am) We adore this enchanting garden cafe and bar, accessed by a nondescript doorway on the main square. This is our favourite spot for a restorative mid-afternoon coffee and for relaxed evening drinks, only a stone's throw from the hustle and yet a world away.

🛍 Shopping

Turqueria ANTIQUES, ART
(Map p356; ☑0242-836 1631; nauticakas@super online.com; Uzun Çarşı Sokak 21; ⊙9am-midnight mid-Mar–mid-Nov, by appointment mid-Nov–mid-Mar) Run by Orhan and Martina, a charming Turkish-German couple long resident in Kaş, Turqueria is an Aladdin's cave of treasures that include old advertisements, camel-skin Karagöz shadow puppets, and jewellery by celebrated İstanbul designer Hüseyin Sağtan.

Seyahan Jewellery JEWELLERY
(Map p356; ☑0242-836 1618; www.seyahan.com; Uzun Çarşı Sokak 10; ⊙9am-2pm & 6pm-midnight) This branch of the İstanbullu jeweller sells collections of fine silver jewellery from throughout Anatolia, selected by owners Matthias and Laura on their visits to craftspeople and collectives. Prices start at ₺50 for simple pieces and rise to ₺1000 for more exclusive items.

ℹ Information

Tourist Office (Map p356; ☑0242-836 1238; Cumhuriyet Meydanı; ⊙9am-6pm mid-Apr–Oct, 8am-5pm Mon-Fri Nov–mid-Apr) Marginally helpful office on the main square with town maps, a few brochures and a list of hotels.

ℹ Getting There & Away

Bus From the **otogar** (Map p356; Atatürk Bulvarı), 350m north of the centre, there are daily Kamil Koç buses to İstanbul (₺110, 15 hours, 985km) at 6.30pm and İzmir (₺63, 8½ hours, 440km) via Pamukkale at 9.45pm. Metro and Pamukkale provide additional services in summer. Kamil Koç serves Ankara (₺95, nine hours, 690km) at 8.30pm in summer; otherwise, you must change at Fethiye. Batı Antalya serves Fethiye (₺20, 2½ hours, 107km) every two hours.

Dolmuş Every 20 minutes to Kalkan (₺7, 35 minutes, 29km) and half-hourly to Antalya (₺30, 3½ hours, 188km) via Demre (₺7, one hour, 45km) and the Olympos turnoff (₺15, 2½ hours, 109km). Services to Patara (₺10, 45 minutes, 40km) run every hour at least. Öz Kaş leaves for Saklıkent Gorge (₺10, one hour, 52km) at 10am daily.

Servis To the centre from the otogar and back every 20 minutes (₺3).

Meis Express Ferry (Map p356; ☑0242-836 1725; www.meisexpress.com; adult €25, child 3-6 €12.50, child 0-2 free) The Meis Express ferry sails throughout the year at 10am and returns at 4pm (3pm in winter). The voyage takes 20 minutes. The ticket office is on Cumhuriyet Meydanı.

Üçağız & Kekova

☑0242 / POP 400

Declared off limits to development, Üçağız (ooch-eye-iz) is a quaint fishing and farming village in an idyllic setting on a bay amid islands and peninsulas. Little has changed here over the years and the teensy squiggle of lanes behind the harbour remains a watercolour-worthy scene of rustic cottages. Üçağız is a regular stop on the *gület* yacht circuit and the jumping-off point for visiting the sunken city at Kekova and the secluded settlement of Kaleköy. Tour buses descend on the car park daily during summer, groups are rushed onto the waiting boats and then shuffled back onto the buses at the end of the day, when Üçağız snaps back into snooze mode for the evening. Staying overnight, with little to do except appreciate the glorious silence, is a delight.

To the west, on the Sıcak Peninsula, is **Aperlae**, an isolated and evocative ancient Lycian city on the Lycian Way.

🛏 Sleeping & Eating

Üçağız' pensions all offer free boat services to the beaches and swimming platforms on and around Kekova island. They are also excellent bases for hiking sections of the Lycian Way (p334). Apart from Likya Pension, most pensions are on the waterfront.

You will find good seafood restaurants at the western end of the waterfront and casual cafes serving snacks such as *gözleme* at the eastern end. Most pensions offer dinners of local catches and home cooking, while some will prepare picnics for hikers.

★ Onur Pension
PENSION $$

(☑0242-874 2071, 0532 762 9319; www.onur pension.com; s/d/tr from €35/45/60; ☺Feb-Oct; P⊜❄☎) With a picturesque setting right on the harbour, this well-maintained pension has eight small, simple and tidy rooms, including four with full sea views and cute attic rooms with beds under the eaves. Helpful owner Onur, a trekking guide, marked local hiking routes and offers pointers.

★ Cennet Pension
PENSION $$

(☑0242-874 2250, 0533 462 8554; kekoval4@ mynet.com; s/d/tr/f €40/50/60/60; P⊜❄☎) 'Paradise' indeed: gregarious Mehmet and friendly wife Zuhra have eight large, bright and spotlessly clean rooms right on the waterfront, with a self-catering kitchen and killer views across the harbour from the terrace. We love the garden full of fruit trees (mulberry, plum, orange, lemon, banana, apricot and more) and Zuhra's home cooking (fish dinner ₺50).

Likya Pension
PENSION $$

(☑0242-874 2251, 0531 596 8408; likyapansiyon@ outlook.com; s/d/tr €25/45/55, dinner ₺25-30; P⊜❄☎) This peaceful oasis snuggles in a lush garden of fruit trees, on an alleyway just up from the harbour, with sea views from the breakfast terrace. Eight cosy rooms in three buildings brim with rustic charm. Guests can use the kitchen and laundry, and owner Halil can organise canoeing, diving, car rental and boat transfers for hikers.

Apollonia Lodge
PENSION $$

(☑0535 592 1236; www.apollonialodge.com; Boğazcık; s/d/tr/f ₺120/150/180/180) Saffet and family from Mehtap Pansiyon (p360) in Kaleköy set up this pension to accommodate Lycian Way hikers on the stretch from Kaş, 18km (five hours) from here, to Kaleköy (16km from here) via Aperlae and Üçağız. The pension occupies a sturdy stone house on a smallholding, with views of Boğazcık village tumbling through a valley around its glinting mosque.

İbrahim Restaurant
TURKISH $$

(☑0533 363 9206, 0242-874 2062; mains ₺18-35; ☺11am-10pm) Going for 35 years, the village's first restaurant is perennially popular for its decent kebap and seafood mains, as well as *köfte, güveç* and a great selection of mezes (₺7.50). The harbour-front location is another plus.

❶ Getting There & Away

There is no bus service from Kaş, but tour companies in Kaş will let you hitch a lift on their daily boat-tour transfers to Üçağız if they have a spare seat (₺20). These generally leave Kaş around 10am. If there are a few of you, you can arrange a boat transfer from Kaş to Üçağız or Kaleköy for ₺35 each.

One dolmuş leaves Antalya for Üçağız daily at 2.45pm (₺24, four hours). It stops in Demre en route at 5.30pm (₺7, 30 minutes). From Üçağız, the dolmuş leaves at 8am. Pensions can organise transfers from Antalya International Airport (€90), Dalaman International Airport (€90), Demre (₺50) and Kaş (₺80). If you take a taxi, do not let the driver use the meter or these fares will double.

Kaleköy
☑0242 / POP 150

The watery paradise of Kaleköy is one of the western Mediterranean's truly delightful spots, home to the ruins of ancient **Simena** and an impressive **Crusader fortress** (admission ₺10; ☺8am-7pm mid-Apr–Oct, to 5pm Nov–mid-Apr) perched above the hamlet looking out to sea. Within the fortress, the ancient world's tiniest **theatre** is cut into the rock, and nearby you'll find ruins of several temples and public baths. From the top you can look down upon a field of **Lycian tombs**, and the old **city walls** are visible on the outskirts.

🛏 Sleeping

★ Mehtap Pansiyon
PENSION $$$

(☑0242-874 2146, 0535 592 1236; www.mehta ppansiyon.com; s/d/tr €80/90/100; ⊜❄☎) The 10-room Mehtap has million-dollar views over the harbour and submerged Lycian tombs from its bougainvillea-draped terraces. Four rooms are in a 200-year-old stone house so quiet and tranquil you may start snoozing as you check in. Another four are in a Lycian building dating back over two millennia. The other two occupy a pair of purpose-built wood cottages.

Paradise Teras
PENSION $$$

(☑0535 794 9186; r ₺200; ⊜❄☎) Three of Osman and family's rooms are worthy of Cappadocia, being organically built into the cliff with the toilet slotted into a crevice in one. The remaining two rooms in a stone house and the panoramic terrace gaze down on Kaleköy's stunning bay, where a Lycian tomb rises from the shallows.

The restaurant does pizza, Turkish food and homemade goat's-milk ice cream.

Simena Pansiyon
PENSION $$$

(☑ 0532 779 0476, 0242-874 2025; www.simena pansiyon.com; r €80; ☒ ❋ ☎) Set slightly back from Kaleköy harbour near Hassan Deniz Restaurant, this gorgeous 150-year-old Greek stone house (look out for the lovely mosaic on the verandah) has four rooms brimming with colourful character and antiques. All share a wide verandah where you could happily sloth away the day staring out to sea.

Hassan Deniz Restaurant
SEAFOOD $$

(☑ 0242-874 2101; mains ₺25; ☎) Not to be confused with neighbouring Hasan's Roma, Hassan Deniz is much favoured by yachties and their crews for its fresh fish and great mezes. Its long pier has a single table for scenic dining on calm evenings.

❶ Getting There & Away

Kaleköy is accessible from Üçağız by boat (10 minutes; ₺30 or free with accommodation) or on foot (45 minutes) on a 4km section of the Lycian Way trail, which takes you through a boatyard and up to the fortress. Cars can navigate most of this footpath; park at the far end of the boatyard.

Demre
☑ 0242 / POP 16,200

Officially 'Kale' but called by its old name 'Demre' by just about everyone, this sprawling, dusty town was once the Lycian (and later Roman) city of Myra. By the 4th century it was important enough to have its own bishop – most notably St Nicholas, who went on to catch the Western world's imagination in his starring role as Santa Claus. In AD 60 St Paul put Myra on the liturgical map by changing boats at its port, Andriake, while on his way to Rome (or so Acts 27: 4-6 tells us).

Once situated on the sea, Demre moved inland as precious alluvium – deposits of clay, silt, sand and gravel – flowed from the Demre stream. The resultant fertile soil is the foundation of the town's wealth, and it remains a major centre for the growing and distribution of fruit and vegetables.

◉ Sights

Myra
ARCHAEOLOGICAL SITE

(admission ₺20; ⊙ 9am-7pm mid-Apr–Oct, 8am-5pm Nov–mid-Apr) If you only have time to see one striking honeycomb of Lycian rock tombs, choose the memorable ruins of ancient Myra.

EXPLORING THE KEKOVA AREA

Arriving in the Kekova area, the fishing village you enter from the coast road is Üçağız (p359). Across the water on the peninsula to the southeast is Kaleköy (called Kale locally), a protected village on the site of the ancient city of Simena. South of the villages and the entrance to the bay is the long island of Kekova with its famous underwater ruins; local people generally use this name to refer to the whole area.

Given the difficulty of getting to the Kekova area by public transport, most people end up taking a boat tour from Kaş or Kalkan, which starts with a bus ride to Üçağız, where you'll board the boat.

Along the northern shore of Kekova island are ruins, partly submerged 6m below the sea and referred to as the **Batık Şehir** (Sunken City). These ruins are the result of a series of severe earthquakes in the 2nd century AD; most of what you can still see is a residential part of ancient Simena. Foundations of buildings, staircases, moorings and smashed amphorae are visible. It is forbidden to anchor or swim around or near the Sunken City.

After the visit to Kekova you'll have lunch on the boat and then head on to Kaleköy, passing a couple of submerged (and very photo-worthy) Lycian tombs just offshore. There's usually about an hour to explore Kaleköy and climb up to the hilltop fortress.

Tours from Kaş, which cost €25 per person, generally leave at 10am and return around 6pm. Tours that include the nearby ruins of Aperlae usually cost €5 extra. You can also organise a tour by negotiating with boat captains at Üçağız harbour or your pension owner there. A private boat tour costs from ₺120 (1½ hours) to ₺300 (3½ hours). Hikers can pick up a boat ride from Üçağız to Aperlae (₺100) and walk back.

The closest you can get to the Kekova sunken city ruins is on the sea-kayaking tours (€30 per person, or €50 with Aperlae, including transfers and lunch) run by Kaş operators such as **Bougainville Travel** (p355) and **Dragoman** (p355). Some Kaleköy pensions lend kayaks to guests.

Located about 2km inland from Demre's main square, they are among the finest in Lycia. There's a well-preserved Roman theatre here, which includes several theatrical masks carved on stones lying in the nearby area. The so-called Painted Tomb near the river necropolis portrays a man and his family in relief both inside and out.

Alakent Caddesi leads 2km north from the square (3km from the highway) to the tombs; it's a 20-minute walk or ₺10 taxi ride.

Church of St Nicholas
CHURCH

(Noel Baba; Müze Caddesi; admission ₺15; ⊙9am-7pm mid-Apr-Oct, 8am-5pm Nov-mid-Apr) It may not be vast like Aya Sofya, or brilliant with mosaics like İstanbul's Chora Church (Kariye Museum), but Demre's Church of St Nicholas, where the eponymous saint was laid upon his death in AD 343, is nonetheless a star attraction for pilgrims and tourists alike. Although St Nicholas is no longer in situ (Italian merchants smashed open the sarcophagus in 1087 and supposedly carted his bones to Bari), the church features interesting Byzantine frescoes and mosaic floors.

Andriake
RUIN

FREE About 5km southwest of Demre's centre is the seafront settlement of Çayağzı, called Andriake by the Romans at a time when it was an important entrepôt for grain on the sea route between the eastern Mediterranean and Rome.

The ruins of ancient Andriake are strewn over a wide area to the north and south of the access road approaching Çayağzı. The great granary built by Hadrian and completed in AD 139 lies in the southern section.

🛏 Sleeping & Eating

★ Hoyran Wedre
Country House
BOUTIQUE HOTEL $$$

(☑0532 291 5762, 0242-875 1125; www.hoyran.com; s/d from €100/120; ⊙Apr-Oct; P❄✿⊛🛋🐕) A destination hotel if ever there was one, this complex of stone buildings is a rural oasis up in the Taurus Mountains, with astounding views across the countryside down to the Kekova area. There are 20 rooms and suites done in traditional fashion (wattle-and-daub plastered walls) with antique furniture and wooden balcony or stone terrace.

İpek Restaurant
PIDE, KEBAP $

(☑0242-871 5150; Müze Caddesi; pides/mains ₺8/15; ⊙11am-10pm) With jolly green tablecloths covering its tables on pedestrianised

Müze Caddesi, 'Silk' Restaurant is great for a quick lunch of pide, *lahmacun*, kebap or grill. Find it opposite Türkiye Bankası.

ℹ Getting There & Away

Buses and dolmuşes travel half-hourly to/from Kaş (₺8, one hour, 45km) and Antalya (₺22, 2½ hours) via the Olympos and Çıralı turn-offs (₺18, 1½ hours).

The otogar is 200m southwest of the main square. Eynihal Caddesi, the street running south from the Church of St Nicholas, passes it.

Olympos & Çıralı

✎ 0242

About 65km northeast of Demre, past Finike and Kumluca, a road leads southeast from the main highway (veer to the right then follow the signs for 11km) to ancient Olympos with its tumble of beachside ruins and backpacker camp community. On the other side of the mountain, and over the narrow Ulupınar Stream, is Çıralı, a holiday hamlet with dozens of hotels and pensions that may look like it was born yesterday but contains that most enigmatic of classical icons: the eternal flame of the Chimaera. A 7.5km section of the Lycian Way (p334) winds through the wild Mediterranean hills between the two villages.

Olympos

An important Lycian city in the 2nd century BC, Olympos is more famous these days for being the beach resort of choice for backpackers. Staying in an Olympos 'tree house' at one of the dozen-or-so camps that line the 1.5km-long track along the valley down to the ruins and beach has long been the stuff of travel legend. The former hippy-trail hot-spot has gentrified considerably in past years and during summer can be pretty overcrowded and institutionalised.

Love it or hate it, Olympos still offers good value and an up-for-it party atmosphere in a lovely setting. Just remember that 'tree house' is a misnomer; most huts are very firmly on the ground. If you plan on staying, don't forget to bring enough cash to last your visit, as there is no ATM or bank in Olympos.

◉ Sights & Activities

Most people come to loll about and swim at the beach that fronts the ruins, but there are also numerous activities available from agencies and camps in Olympos, including boat cruises (full day with lunch €20 to €25), canyoning (full-day trip €30), sea kayaking (half-day trip €18), paragliding (€75), diving (try dive €25, two dives with equipment included €46), mountain-biking trips and rock climbing. Some of the best and most difficult rock climbing is at Hörguc, a wall opposite Olympos.

All camps organise nightly transport to view the Chimaera (₺30).

Olympos Beach
BEACH

For most visitors, the sand-and-shale beach is the main attraction. Entrance is free from the Çıralı end, whereas at the Olympos end you have to access it from the Olympos ruins and thus pay.

Olympos Ruins
ARCHAEOLOGICAL SITE

(☑0242-238 5688; www.muze.gov.tr; admission incl Olympos Beach ₺20, parking ₺4; ☉9am-7pm Apr-Oct, 8am-5pm Nov-Mar) The rambling ruins of ancient Olympos are scattered beside the trickling Ulupınar Stream and set inside a deep, shaded valley that runs directly to the sea. If you plan to visit a few times, you will save money by buying a long-stay ticket allowing 10 entries over 10 days.

🛏 Sleeping & Eating

Accommodation prices at Olympos' treehouse camps generally include half board (breakfast and dinner). Outside peak summer months expect good discounts. Per-person bungalow rates are based on two people sharing; a single supplement is often expected.

While many tree houses (small, rustic bungalows, sometimes slightly raised off the ground) have shared bathrooms, most camps now boast bungalows with en suite and air-conditioning. Not all tree houses have reliable locks, so store valuables at reception.

Be extra attentive to personal hygiene while staying at Olympos. In summer, particularly, the huge numbers of visitors can stretch the camps' capacity for proper waste disposal to the limit, so be vigilant about where and what you eat. Every year some travellers wind up ill.

★ Şaban Pension
BUNGALOW $

(☑0242-892 1265; www.sabanpansion.com; Yazırköyü; dm ₺45, bungalows s/d/tr ₺100/140/180, tree houses without bathroom s/d ₺75/100; P✿❄❝) Our personal favourite, this is the place to lounge in a hammock in the orchard or on a wooden platform by the stream enjoying sociable owner Meral's home cooking. Şaban isn't a party spot; it's a tranquil getaway where relaxed conversations strike up around the bonfire at night. Accommodation is in charming cabins and tree houses. Rates include half board.

Kadır's Tree Houses
CAMPING GROUND, PENSION $

(☑0242-892 1250, 0532 347 7242; www.kadirstreehouses.com; Yazırköyü; dm ₺40-45, s/d/tr with air-con ₺90/120/180, without air-con ₺75/100/150; ✸❝) The place that put Olympos on the map looks like a Wild West boom town that just kept a-growin' and not the Japanese POW camp that some others resemble. Accommodation includes four-bed dorms with private bathroom, five-bed tree houses without, and bungalows. Its bars are the valley's liveliest and the **Olympos Adventure Center** (☑0532 686 1799; www.olymposadventurecenter.com) is here. Rates include half board.

Orange Pension
BUNGALOW $

(☑0242-892 1317; www.olymposorangepension.com; Yazırköyü; dm/r ₺45/150; P✿✸❝) Orange's pine-clad bungalows have a touch of Swiss Family Robinson and are reasonably spacious compared to some camps. Some even have TVs. On the downside they're more crammed together; seen from the walkway to the 1st-floor rooms, the corrugated roofs resemble a backpacker shanty town. The bar-restaurant in the front courtyard has hammocks and shady seating. Rates include half board.

Pehlivan Pansiyon
CAFE $

(☑0242-892 1113; www.olympospehlivan.com; mains ₺10; ☉11am-10pm; ❝) Locals recommend 'Hero' pension's *gözleme* (savoury pancakes), which are rolled and cooked by headscarf-clad ladies and are certainly preferable to the chewy pancakes offered by neighbouring eateries. Alcohol and, in summer, sandwiches and grills are served, with cushions on wooden platforms for reclining. Find it just before the inland entrance to the Olympos ruins.

Çıralı

Çıralı (cher-*ah*-luh) is a relaxed, family-friendly hamlet of mostly upscale pensions and hotels leading down to and along the beach. It's a quieter alternative to the

ℹ ATMS

Çıralı has an ATM; Olympos does not, but there is an ATM at the Olympos junction on the highway.

ARYKANDA

Built over five terraces, **Arykanda** (admission ₺5; ⊙9am-7pm mid-Apr–mid-Oct, 8am-5pm mid-Oct–mid-Apr) is one of the most dramatically situated ruins in Turkey. The city's most outstanding feature is its 10m-tall two-storey baths complex, standing next to the gymnasium on the lowest terrace. Following a path to the next terrace you'll come to a large colonnaded agora. Its northern arches lead into an odeon. Above is a fine 2nd-century theatre and stadium. Another agora, a *bouleuterion* (council chamber) and cistern are found on the upper terraces.

One of the oldest sites on the Teke Peninsula, Arykanda was part of the Lycian League from its inception in the 2nd century BC, but was never a member of the 'Big Six' group of cities that commanded three votes each. This may have been due to its profligate and freewheeling ways as much as anything else. Arykanda was apparently the party town of Lycia and forever deeply in debt. Along with the rest of Lycia, it was annexed by Rome in AD 43 and survived as a Byzantine settlement until the 9th century, when it was abandoned.

If you're driving from the coast, there's an exit off the D400 at the unremarkable provincial centre of Finike, leading north for another 30km to Arykanda.

Dolmuşes headed for Elmalı (₺13) from Finike will drop you off at the foot of the hill leading to the site entrance, from where it's a steep 3km walk to the ruins. A taxi will cost about ₺125 from Demre, 29km southwest of Finike.

backpackers' haunt 1km down the beach at Olympos. And it's close to the magical and mystical Chimaera.

Chimaera
HISTORIC SITE

(admission ₺6; ⊙24hr) Known in Turkish as Yanartaş, or 'Burning Rock', the Chimaera is a cluster of flames that naturally blaze on the rocky slopes of Mt Olympos. At night it looks like hell itself has come to pay a visit, and it's not difficult to see why ancient peoples attributed these extraordinary flames to the breath of a monster – part lion, part goat and part snake – that had terrorised Lycia.

The mythical hero Bellerophon supposedly killed the Chimaera by mounting the winged horse Pegasus and pouring molten lead into the monster's mouth. Today, gas still seeps from the earth and bursts into flame upon contact with the air. The exact composition of the gas is unknown, though it is thought to contain methane. Although a flame can be extinguished by covering it, it will reignite close by into a new and separate flame. At night the 20 or 30 flames in the main area are visible at sea.

The best time to visit is after dinner. From Çıralı, follow the Chimaera signs 3.5km on the main road along the hillside until you reach a valley and walk up to a car park. From there it's another 20- to 30-minute climb up a stepped path to the site; bring or rent a torch. From Olympos, most camps organise transport every night after dinner.

🛏 Sleeping & Eating

Sima Peace Pension
BUNGALOW $$

(☑0532 238 1177, 0242-825 7245; www.simapeace.com; off Yanartaş Yolu; s/d €30/50; 🅿😊❄🛜) With its hammocks, swing chairs, rocking horse and views across the fields from its 1st-floor balconies, this Çıralı stalwart is about 750m up from the beach, with rustic bungalows surrounded by fruit trees. The quaint rooms have basic bathrooms, and those upstairs are nearing a tree-house-style experience. Assisted by Coco the parrot, eccentric owner Aynur's cooking is legendary (dinner €10).

Hotel Canada
HOTEL $$

(☑0242-825 7233, 0538 647 9522; www.canadahotel.net; s/d from €30/40, 4-person bungalows from €80; 🅿😊❄🛜🏊) This is a beautiful place, offering the quintessential Çıralı experience: warmth, friendliness and homemade honey. The main house rooms are comfortable and the garden is filled with hammocks, citrus trees and 11 bungalows. Canadian Carrie and foodie husband Şaban also offer excellent set meals. It's 750m from the beach; grab a free bike and pedal on down.

★ Myland Nature Hotel
BUNGALOW $$$

(☑0242-825 7044, 0532 407 9656; www.mylandnature.com; Sahil Yolu; s/d €70/95; 🅿😊❄🛜) 🌿 This is an artsy, holistic and very green place that is sure to make you sing like its wind chimes. It offers free yoga and meditation, bikes and umbrellas on the neighbouring beach. The spotless and spacious wooden bungalows are set around a pretty garden with hammocks strung between the orange trees. Breakfast includes organic fruit from the 4.5-hectare garden.

★**Odile Hotel**　　　　　　　HOTEL $$$
(📞0242-825 7163; www.hotelodile.com; Sahil Yolu; s/d €70/80, bungalows with kitchenette s/d/tr/q €100/120/150/180; 🅿🚭❄🛜🏊) On this country-estate-like property, spacious and modern bungalows are set around a curvy pool with terraces looking at the mountains. Just behind the main complex, surrounding another pool and child's pool, are larger 'luxe' bungalows made of lovely scented cedar. They are an excellent option for families wanting to self-cater. Rates include afternoon tea.

★**Orange Motel**　　　　　PENSION $$$
(📞0242-825 7328; www.orangemotel.net; Yanartaş Yolu; s/d €50/70, 2-bedroom bungalows €105; 🅿🚭❄🛜) In the middle of an orange grove, the Orange feels like a farm despite its central location. Come here in spring and you'll never forget the overwhelming scent and buzz of bees. The garden is hung with hammocks, rooms are veritable wooden suites and there's a house travel agency. Breakfast features homemade orange and lemon marmalades and orange-blossom honey.

Olympos Lodge　　　　　RESORT $$$
(📞0242-825 7171; www.olymposlodge.com.tr; s €195, d €225-540; 🅿🚭❄🛜) The poshest place in Çıralı, Olympos Lodge is situated right on the beach within a private 1.5-hectare paradise of citrus orchards, manicured gardens and strutting peacocks. The 14 rooms are gorgeously attired in a style that oozes bohemian glamour; two have sea views. There's a sauna and a lovely winter garden open in the cooler months.

★**Yörük Restaurant**　　　TURKISH $$
(📞0536 864 8648; Köprü Başı Mevkii; gözlemes ₺7-9, pides ₺9-14, mains ₺15-28; ⏱11am-10pm; 🅿🛜🍴♿) Just after the bridge into Çıralı, the village's best restaurant feels like a Yörük nomad camp with its central fire and tented section. Behind a counter heaving with mezes and seafood, the open kitchen turns out elongated pide, light and fluffy *gözleme, mantı,* kebaps and grills. Well priced and welcoming, with space for children to roam.

ℹ Getting There & Away

Virtually any bus taking the coastal road between Fethiye and Antalya can drop you off or pick you up at the Olympos and Çıralı junctions. Just make sure you specify which one you want, as they are 500m apart. From there, minibuses (₺6) leave for both destinations.

For Olympos (10km from the D400), minibuses depart every half-hour between 8am and 8pm from May to October. Returning, minibuses leave Olympos at 9am then every hour until 7pm. From October to April they generally run two-hourly, with the last minibus usually departing Olympos at 6pm.

Transport to Çıralı (7km) is considerably less regular; minibuses often don't depart until they are full, so you may wait some time. On average, there are departures every hour or so in summer, and one morning and one afternoon service in winter. When they reach Çıralı, minibuses usually head along the beach road then turn inland and pass the Chimaera turn-off, before returning to the village along the edge of the hillside.

If you book in advance, many accommodation options will pick you up from the highway, either for free if you are staying for a while, or for about ₺25; from Antalya International Airport is around ₺250. Taxis waiting at the junctions charge roughly ₺30 to Çıralı and ₺35 to Olympos.

Local travel agencies, including **Dark Travel** (📞0242-892 1311, 0507 007 6600; www.darktravel.com; Yazırköyü) and **Yanartaş** (📞0242-825 7188; www.yanartas.net; Sahil Yolu; boat tour incl lunch ₺60), hire cars.

Antalya

📞0242 / POP 1,027,500

Once seen simply as the gateway to the Turkish Riviera, Antalya today is very much a destination in its own right. Situated right on the Gulf of Antalya (Antalya Körfezi), the largest city on Turkey's western Mediterranean coastline is both classically beautiful and stylishly modern. At its core is the wonderfully preserved old-city district of Kaleiçi (literally 'within the castle'), which offers atmospheric accommodation in the finely restored Ottoman houses on its winding lanes. The old city wraps around a splendid Roman-era harbour with clifftop views of hazy-blue mountain silhouettes that are worth raising a toast to. Just outside of the central city are two beaches and one of Turkey's finest museums.

History

Antalya was originally named Attaleia, after its 2nd-century founder, Attalus II of

Pergamum. His nephew, Attalus III, ceded the town to Rome in 133 BC. When the Roman Emperor Hadrian visited the city more than two centuries later, in AD 130, he entered the city through a triumphal arch (now known as Hadrian's Gate) built in his honour.

There followed a succession of new 'landlords': the Byzantines took over from the Romans, followed by the Seljuk Turks in the early 13th century. The latter gave Antalya both a new name and an icon – the Yivli Minare (Fluted Minaret).

The city became part of the Ottoman Empire in 1391. After WWI the empire collapsed and Antalya was ceded to Italy. In 1921 it was liberated by Atatürk's army and made the capital of Antalya Province.

◉ Sights & Activities

Kaleiçi   HISTORIC SITE
(Map p368) Antalya's historic district begins at the main square, Kale Kapısı (Fortress Gate; Map p368), which is marked by the old stone Saat Kulesi (Clock Tower; Map p368) and statue of Attalus II, the city's founder. To the north is the İki Kapılar Hanı, a sprawling covered bazaar dating to the late 15th century.

Walk south along Uzun Çarşi Sokak, the street that starts opposite the clock tower. Immediately on the left is the 18th-century Tekeli Mehmet Paşa Camii (Map p368; Paşa Camii Sokak), a mosque built by the Beylerbey (Governor of Governors), Tekeli Mehmet Paşa, and repaired extensively in 1886 and 1926. Note the beautiful Arabic calligraphy in the coloured tiles above the windows and along the base of the dome.

Wander further into this protected zone, where many of the gracious old Ottoman houses have been restored and converted into pensions, boutique hotels and shops. To the east, at the top of Hesapçi Sokak, is the monumental Hadrian's Gate (Hadriyanüs Kapısı; Map p368; Atatürk Caddesi), also known as Üçkapılar or the 'Three Gates', erected for the Roman emperor's visit to Antalya in 130 AD.

The Roman Harbour (p367) at the base of the slope was Antalya's lifeline from the 2nd century BC until late in the 20th century, when a new port was constructed about 12km to the west, at the far end of Konyaaltı Plajı. The harbour was restored during the 1980s and is now a marina for yachts and excursion boats. An elevator (asansör; Map p367) descends the cliff to the harbour from the western end of Cumhuriyet Meydanı.

At the southwestern edge of Kaleiçi, on the corner of Karaalioğlu Parkı (Map p368; Atatürk Caddesi) (a large, attractive, flower-filled park with panoramic sea views) rises Hıdırlık Kalesi (Map p368; Karaalioğlu Parkı), a 14m-high tower dating to the 1st or 2nd century AD. It was built as a mausoleum and later, due to its excellent position above the bay, played an important role in the city's defences as a watchtower and lighthouse.

★ **Antalya Museum**   MUSEUM
(Map p367; ☑0242-238 5688; www.antalyamuzesi.gov.tr/en; Konyaaltı Caddesi; admission ₺20; ◉9am-7pm Apr-Oct, 8am-5pm Nov-Mar, ticket office shuts 30min before closure) Do not miss this comprehensive museum with exhibitions covering everything from the Stone and Bronze Ages to Byzantium. The Hall of Regional Excavations exhibits finds from ancient cities in Lycia (such as Patara and Xanthos) and Phrygia, while the Hall of Gods displays beautiful and evocative statues of 15 Olympian gods, many in excellent condition. Most of the statues were found at Perge, including the sublime Three Graces and the towering Dancing Woman dominating the first room.

Yivli Minare   HISTORIC SITE
(Fluted Minaret; Map p368; Cumhuriyet Caddesi) This handsome and distinctive 'fluted' minaret, erected by Seljuk Sultan Aladdin Keykubad I in the early 13th century, is Antalya's symbol. The adjacent mosque (1373) is still in use.

Suna & İnan Kıraç Kaleiçi Museum   MUSEUM
(Map p368; ☑0242-243 4274; www.kaleicimuzesi.org; Kocatepe Sokak 25; adult/child ₺3/1.50; ◉9am-noon & 1-5pm Thu-Tue) This small ethnography museum is housed in a lovingly restored Antalya mansion. The 2nd floor contains a series of life-size dioramas depicting some of the most important rituals and customs of Ottoman Antalya. More impressive is the collection of Çanakkale ceramics housed in the former Greek Orthodox church of Aya Yorgi (St George), just behind the main house, which has been fully restored and is worth a look in itself.

Sultan Alaadın Camii   MOSQUE
(Map p368; Seferoğlu Sokak) This gem of a mosque is squirreled away in the back alleys of Kaleiçi. It began life as the Greek Orthodox Panhagia Church in 1834 and was converted to a mosque in 1958. Uniquely in Antalya, the prayer hall's original painted ceiling, with its intricate star motifs, has been preserved.

Antalya

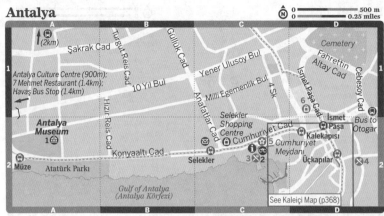

Yenikapı Greek Church CHURCH
(Hagios Alypios; Map p368; ☎0242-244 6894; www.spcturkey.com; Yeni Kapı Sokak) This small 19th-century church, renovated in 2007, has a beautiful interior with frescoes and hand-carved decorations. Orthodox services still take place here.

Kesik Minare HISTORIC SITE
(Truncated Minaret; Map p368; Hesapçı Sokak) This stump of a tower marks the ruins of a substantial building that played a major role in Antalya's religious life over the centuries. Built as a 2nd-century Roman temple, it was converted into the Byzantine Church of the Virgin Mary in the 6th century and then a mosque three centuries later. It became a church again in 1361 but fire destroyed most of it in the 19th century.

Konyaaltı Plajı BEACH
For a good dose of beach culture, head west from the centre to Konyaaltı, accessed by taking the tram to its final stop (Müze) and then walking further west and down the snaking road.

Lara Plajı BEACH
South of the centre, Lara is sandier than Konyaaltı to the west. Dolmuşes run here down Atatürk and Fevzi Çakmak Caddesis.

Sefa Hamamı HAMAM
(Map p368; ☎0532 526 9407, 0242-241 2321; www.sefahamam.com; Kocatepe Sokak 32; ⊙11am-8pm Mon-Sat) This atmospheric hamam retains much of its 13th-century Seljuk architecture. A bath costs ₺30 and the full works with soap massage and scrub costs ₺55. Oil massages

Antalya

◎ **Top Sights**
1 Antalya Museum.................................A2

◎ **Sights**
2 Elevator...C2

✖ **Eating**
3 Arma Restaurant...............................C2
4 Can Can Pide ve Kebap Salonu..........D2

✦ **Entertainment**
5 Antalya State Opera & Ballet
   Ticket Booth....................................C2

🛍 **Shopping**
6 İki Kapılar Hanı..................................D1

are an extra ₺30. Men and women bathe separately, with mixed bathing also available.

Balık Pazarı Hamamı HAMAM
(Fish Market Bath; Map p368; ☎0242-243 6175; Balık Pazarı Sokak; ⊙8am-11pm Apr-Oct, to 8pm Nov-Mar) This 700-year-old hamam offers Turkish bath packages of soak, scrub and soap for ₺80. There are separate sections for men and women, with mixed bathing also available.

⬅ Tours

Excursion boats tie up in Kaleiçi's **Roman Harbour** (Map p368; İskele Caddesi). One-, two- and six-hour trips are offered (€10/15/30 at the top end; your accommodation can likely get you a better deal). The latter includes lunch and stops such as Kemer, the Gulf of Antalya islands and some beaches for a swim. Additionally, ferries (₺10) run three times daily in either

Kaleiçi

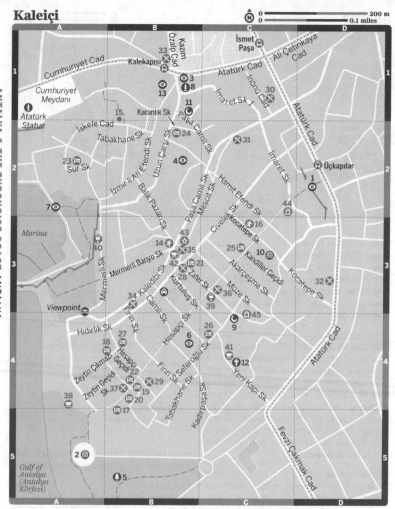

ANTALYA & THE TURQUOISE COAST ANTALYA

direction (less frequently in winter) between the harbour and Kemer marina.

For ferry times and information, visit www.antalyaulasim.com.tr.

Antalya is an excellent base for excursions to the ancient sites of Phaselis, Termessos, Perge, Aspendos and Selge, as well as to Köprülü Kanyon's white-water rafting and the town of Side. There's a huge array of travel agencies in Antalya's Kaleiçi area offering tours.

Nirvana Travel Service TOURS
(Map p368; ☎ 0532 521 6053, 0242-244 3893; www.nirvanatour.com; İskele Caddesi 38/4) Offers a huge range of excursions, including full-day tours to Termessos, with a stop at the Düden Şelalesi (Düden Falls), Perge and Aspendos with a waterfall side trip, and Pamukkale. A three-day tour to Cappadocia is also offered. Trips can run with or without a guide, and a minimum of four people is required for day tours.

Kaleiçi

Sleeping

Sabah Pansiyon PENSION $
(Map p368; ☑0555 365 8376, 0242-247 5345; www.sabahpansiyon.com; Hesapçı Sokak 60; s/d/tr €25/30/45, 2-bedroom self-catering apt €75-100; ❀❄🖥🛜♨) The Sabah has long been the first port of call for travellers watching their kuruş, thanks to the Sabah brothers who run the show and organise transport and tours aplenty. Rooms vary in size but all are sweet, simple and superclean. The shaded courtyard is prime territory for meeting other travellers, and breakfast takes place across the lane in Yemenli (p371).

Lazer Pension PENSION $
(Map p368; ☑0242-242 7194; www.lazerpansiyon.com; Hesapçı Sokak 61; s/d/tr €19/35/50; ❀❄🛜♨) Recommended by Antalya regulars, this excellent no-frills option has spacious rooms with modern bathrooms, an upstairs terrace and a courtyard decorated with pot plants. Much care has been taken to ensure the rooms are shipshape, giving this old-town pension the edge on its competitors.

★White Garden Pansion PENSION $$
(Map p368; ☑0242-241 9115; www.whitegardenpansion.com; Hesapçı Geçidi 9; s/d €40/60, self-catering apt €95-140; ❀❄🖥🛜♨) A positively delightful place to stay, combining quirky Ottoman character, modern rooms with an old-world veneer, and excellent service from Metin and team. The building itself is a fine restoration and the courtyard is particularly charming with its large pool. The breakfast also gets top marks.

Mediterra Art Hotel BOUTIQUE HOTEL $$
(Map p368; ☑0242-244 8624; www.mediterraarthotel.com; Zafer Sokak 5; s/d €35/55; ❀❄🛜♨) This upscale masterpiece of wood and stone once housed a Greek tavern, with 19th-century frescoes and graffiti to prove it. It offers sanctuary by the courtyard pool, summer and winter restaurants and 33 small, though modestly luxurious, rooms in four buildings. Lovely touches include headboards carved with stars, and wall paintings of Ottoman characters on the landing.

Villa Verde
PENSION **$$**

(Map p368; ☑ 0242-248 2559; www.pension villaverde.com; Seferoğlu Sokak 8; s/d from €40/50; ☺ ❋ 🛈) All the rooms here are named after fruit and have a fresh, minimalist appeal with liberal use of white-on-white decor with wood accents. Grab 'Greyfurt' (Grapefruit) or 'Dut' (Mulberry) to wake up with views over the ruins of Kesik Minare; avoid 'Portakal' (Orange), which has a substandard shower. The rear courtyard bar is a suave hang-out.

At the front, right next to Kesik Minare, the trellis-shaded restaurant (mains ₺20) offers appealing open-air dining, serving Turkish dishes and pizza as the strain of a busker drifts down the lanes.

Hotel Blue Sea Garden
HOTEL **$$**

(Map p368; ☑ 0242-248 8213, 0537 691 4164; www.hotelblueseagarden.com; Hesapçı Sokak 65; s/d/tr/ste €30/50/65/75; ☺ ❋ 🛈 🛈) The main event here is the pool and decidedly lovely outdoor area, overlooked by two floors of recently renovated rooms. The in-house restaurant is an appealing place to while away an evening, and the hotel organises car rental and tours.

The 'boutique' annexe around the corner has a poky economy room and pleasant standard rooms with exposed stone and brick walls. Guests have breakfast at Blue Sea Garden and can use the pool.

Hotel Hadrianus
HOTEL **$$**

(Map p368; ☑ 0242-244 0030; www.hadrianus hotel.com; Zeytin Çıkmazı 4; s/d/tr €40/50/70; ☺ ❋ 🛈) Named after the Roman emperor who visited in AD 130 (the city's first bona fide tourist), this 11-room hotel is set in a 750-sq-metre garden: a veritable oasis in Kaleiçi, and the setting for breakfast under the trees where hammocks hang. Rooms contain faux antique and Ottoman-style furnishings; rooms at the top are larger.

Mavi & Anı Pansiyon
PENSION **$$**

(Map p368; ☑ 0242-247 0056; www.maviani.com; Tabakhane Sokak 13-23; s/d €30/45; ☺ ❋ 🛈) This restored Ottoman house has a fabulously peaceful garden, common areas decorated with old Anatolian furniture and bric-a-brac, and rooms brimming with old-world character. Some rooms are Turkish style (beds on a low platform). The only let-down is the basic showers. If you want something more contemporary, it also has four apartments, all with kitchen facilities, nearby.

★ Tuvana Hotel
BOUTIQUE HOTEL **$$$**

(Map p368; ☑ 0242-247 6015; www.tuvanahotel.com; Karanlık Sokak 18; s/d from ₺250/270; P ☺ ❋ @ 🛈 🛈) This discreet compound of six Ottoman houses has been stylishly converted into a refined city hotel with 47 rooms and suites. The plush rooms have a historic feel, with varnished floorboards, rugs and wall hangings, plus mod-cons such as DVD players and safes. The swimming pool is a bonus and there are three on-site restaurants: Seraser (p373), Il Vicino and Pio.

Tekeli Konakları
BOUTIQUE HOTEL **$$$**

(Map p368; ☑ 0242-244 5465, 0545 662 2117; www.tekeli.com.tr; Dizdar Hasan Sokak; s/d €60/85; ☺ ❋ 🛈) An unfussy sense of history pervades this beautiful property, comprising eight rooms in a complex of lemon-yellow Ottoman buildings. Rooms feature stained glass, bathrooms with all-over İznik tiles, beds on raised platforms in Ottoman style and even a display cabinet with Ottoman porcelain and tapestries.

Villa Perla
BOUTIQUE HOTEL **$$$**

(Map p368; ☑ 0242-248 4341; www.villaperla.com; Hesapçı Sokak 26; s/d €70/90; ☺ ❋ 🛈 🛈) This authentic Ottoman place, snuggled around a courtyard complete with orange trees, pool, tortoises, and a fire on cold nights, feels like the ramshackle home of an exiled sultan. Its seven comfortable rooms, reached up a staircase starting with a 12th-century stone step, have features such as wooden ceilings, four-poster beds and folk-painted cupboards.

Mod cons include shower with foot massager. The in-house restaurant (mains ₺25) wins plaudits from readers for its meze platters (six/12 mezes ₺17/30) and the romantic setting of the courtyard or stone-walled dining room with fireplace.

✖ Eating

A nearly endless assortment of cafes and restaurants is tucked in and around the Kaleiçi area, many colonising the cobbled lanes with their outdoor tables. For cheap eating, walk east to the **Dönerciler Çarşısı** (Market of Döner Makers; Map p368; İnönü Caddesi), or north to the rooftop kebap places across the main drag from Kale Kapısı (p366). Snack bars and Starbucks-aping cafes line the western side of Atatürk Caddesi north of Yeni Kapı Sokak, fuelling the promenading students.

WORTH A TRIP

PHASELIS & AROUND

About 16km north of the exits for Olympos and Çıralı from the D400 is the romantically sited ancient Lycian port of Phaselis. Shaded by pines, the ruins (admission ₺20; ⊗ 8am-7pm Apr-Oct, to 5pm Nov-Mar, ticket office shuts 30min before closure) of Phaselis are arranged around three small, perfectly formed bays. Some 9km inland, a cable car called the Olympos Teleferik (☑ 0242-242 2252; www.olymposteleferik.com; adult/child 7-16yr one way €16/8, return €32/16; ⊗ 9.30am-6pm May & Jun, 9am-7pm Jul-Sep, to 6pm Oct, 10am-4.30pm Nov-Mar, to 5pm Apr) climbs almost to the top of 2365m-high Tahtalı Dağ (Wooded Mountain), the centrepiece of Olympos Beydağları National Park (Olimpos Beydağları Sahil Milli Parkı).

Frequent buses on the highway from Antalya (₺9, 45 minutes, 58km) and Kemer (₺6, 20 minutes, 15km) pass both the exits for Phaselis and the Olympos Teleferik.

The cable-car company runs hourly shuttle buses from the highway exit to the *teleferik* station between 10am and 5pm. On Wednesday and Saturday it provides a direct bus service to/from Antalya (adult/child €15/7.50) and Kemer (€10/5), which you must book in advance.

★ **ÇaY-Tea's** CAFE $
(Map p368; ☑ 0542 732 7000; www.cayteas.com; Hıdırlık Sokak 3; mains ₺20; ⊗ 9am-midnight mid-Apr–mid-Oct, 2-10pm Mon-Fri, 9am-midnight Sat & Sun mid-Oct–mid-Apr) Çay comes with lemons, fake flower garnish and a biscuit in a heart-shaped dish at this eclectic Dutch-Turkish cafe, where vintage furniture spills into the street and a wine cellar houses an inviting country-kitchen-style space. The menu includes sandwiches (₺12), omelettes, pancakes, homemade cakes, high tea and more substantial dishes.

★ **Can Can Pide ve Kebap Salonu** TURKISH $
(Map p367; ☑ 0242-243 2548; Arık Caddesi 4; pides & dürüm ₺8; ⊗ 7am-midnight Mon-Sat) Can Can (jan jan) certainly has lots of *can* (soul), and is worth the walk for a neighbourhood experience, with street tables and locals buying *güveç* (stews) from its bains-marie well into the evening. Choose between *çorba*, thin and crispy *kıymalı* pide and Adana *dürüm* (beef kebap rolled in pitta) and *mantı*.

Tarihı Balık Pazarı Unlu Mamülleri BAKERY $
(Map p368; Balık Pazarı Sokak; pastries ₺3-5) This excellent little bakery churns out a mind-boggling array of sweet and savoury baked goods. We're partial to the *kıymalı* (meat) and *sosis* (sausage) *börek* pastry cigars, the spinach *gözleme* (stuffed savoury crepe) and the sugar-dusted treats with fillings such as fig and walnut or apple. Accompany with *ayran* (yoghurt drink) from the fridge and grab a stool outside.

Cunda Meze TURKISH $$
(Map p368; ☑ 0242-243 8060; www.castlebou tiquehotel.com; Tabakhane Geçidi 7; mezes ₺6-11,

mains ₺25-30; ⊗ 11am-10pm; ⊘) True to its namesake (the Greek-influenced Aegean island off Ayvalık, the first thing you see in the Castle Boutique Hotel's courtyard is a fridge loaded with olive-oil-soaked mezes. Begin a Kaleiçi evening here, between attractively lit pools, orange trees and fairy lights, with a platter (₺25 for one) of classic Turkish mezes.

Hasanağa Restaurant TURKISH $$
(Map p368; ☑ 0242-247 1313; Mescit Sokak 15; mains ₺25-30; ⊗ 11am-10pm) Expect to find the garden at this restaurant and *şarap odası* (wine room) chock-a-block on the nights when traditional Turkish musicians and folk dancers entertain from 8pm onwards. Dishes are predictable Turkish fare – *köfte*, mixed grills and the like – although the kitchen does produce seasonal salads (around ₺8).

7 Mehmet Restaurant TURKISH $$
(☑ 0242-238 5200; www.7mehmet.com; Atatürk Kültür Parkı 201; mezes ₺8, mains ₺20-40; ⊗ 11am-10pm) Antalya's most famous eatery is a couple of kilometres west of the centre, with its spacious indoor and outdoor dining areas occupying a hill overlooking Konyaaltı Beach and the city. Yedi Mehmet's menu of grilled mains, fish and mezes is unsurprising but of high quality, attracting businesspeople and other discerning diners.

Yemenli TURKISH $$
(Map p368; ☑ 0242-247 5345; Zeytin Sokak 16; mains ₺20, set menu ₺15) Tried-and-true Turkish favourites are served up at this lovely restaurant with dining either in the leafy garden courtyard or inside the charmingly renovated stone house. It's run by the team behind Sabah Pansiyon (and named after

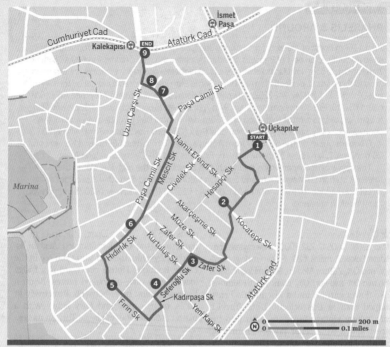

🏃 City Walk
Kaleiçi's Architecture Through the Ages

START HADRIAN'S GATE
END KALE KAPISI
LENGTH 1.5KM; TWO HOURS

Begin by strolling through the arches of **❶ Hadrian's Gate** (p366) and taking the first narrow alley to your left into Kaleiçi's quiet residential district. You'll see some good examples of Ottoman mansions. Note the characteristic protruding shuttered oriel (*cumba* in Turkish) windows, where the women of the house would host guests – being able to see out but not be seen themselves.

Turn right onto Kocatepe Sokak to visit the **❷ Suna & Inan Kıraç Kaleiçi Museum** (p366). Backtrack and continue along the lane until you arrive at a square with a trickling fountain. Turn right here onto Zafer Sokak then left onto Seferoğlu Sokak to reach **❸ Sultan Alaadın Camii** (p366). At the far end of the ruined **❹ Kesik Minare** (p367), turn left again onto Kadırpaşa Sokak, noting the finely restored Ottoman mansion with a stone-pebble entrance. Until recently this housed

the Antalya Kültür Evi, which covered Antalya's architectural history and may reopen.

You'll notice that nearly all of the houses are built of stone – a fire in 1895 destroyed much of the original timber housing. Turn right onto pretty **❺ Fırın Sokak** with its mix of restored mansions now used as pensions and dilapidated houses awaiting restoration, and then right onto Hıdırlık Sokak.

As you walk up the road you'll see the crumbling remains of the **❻ Roman- and Byzantine-era walls** that once encircled the town. Follow the road up until you come to a lonely, incisor-like wall chunk marking a split in the road. Take the left-hand road and follow tourist-shop-lined Mescit and Paşa Camii Sokaks; look out for another large chunk of the **❼ old city walls** with derelict examples of complete timber-framed Ottoman houses incorporated.

End your walk by visiting 17th-century **❽ Tekeli Mehmet Paşa Camii** (p366) before exiting the old town at **❾ Kale Kapısı** (p366), marked by an old stone *saat kulesi* (clock tower) and a statue of Attalus II, the city's founder.

their Yemen-born grandfather), so service is friendly and on the ball.

LeMan Kültür
CAFE $$
(Map p368; ☑0242-243 7474; www.lmk.com.tr; Atatürk Caddesi 44; mains ₺15-25; ☺9am-midnight) If you want to catch a bit of Antalya's hip young vibe, this garden cafe south of Hadrian's Gate is the place to come. The chain cafe takes as its theme cartoons and caricatures, and is vastly popular with students.

Parlak Restaurant
ANATOLIAN $$
(Map p368; ☑0242-241 6553; www.parlakres taurant.com; Kazım Özalp Caddesi 7; mains ₺20; ☺11am-10pm) Just off pedestrian Kazım Özalp Caddesi, this sprawling open-air patio restaurant in an old caravanserai is favoured by locals. It's famous for its charcoal-grilled chicken (one-half ₺13), which you'll see roasting over coals, and excellent mezes.

Sim Restaurant
TURKISH $$
(Map p368; ☑0242-248 0107; Kaledibi Sokak 7; mains ₺16-30; ☺11am-10pm) Honest, homestyle Turkish favourites are served at this simple but charming restaurant run by a friendly family. When the weather's fine, dine underneath the canopy in the narrow passageway at the front, wedged against ancient Byzantine walls. The peaceful setting perfectly complements kebaps, *köfte*, a choice of six mezes and *börek* (₺8.50).

★ Vanilla
INTERNATIONAL $$$
(Map p368; ☑0242-247 6013; www.vanillaan talya.com; Hesapçı Sokak 33; mains ₺30-50; ☺11.30am-midnight) This outstanding, ultramodern restaurant, led by British chef Wayne, has a streamlined and unfussy atmosphere with its banquettes, glass surfaces and pleasant outside area dotted with cane-backed chairs. On the menu are Mediterranean-inspired international dishes, including a good pizza selection (₺25).

Seraser
MEDITERRANEAN $$$
(Map p368; ☑0242-247 6015; www.seraserres taurant.com; Karanlık Sokak 18; mains ₺25-55; ☺noon-midnight) Tuvana Hotel's signature restaurant offers international dishes with an emphasis on Italian in especially fine Ottoman surrounds, featuring pasha-style chairs, a glass-bead chandelier and lovely outdoor seating. The Turkish coffee crème brûlée is legendary. The lunch menu is more casual, and Seraser stages lives jazz on Wednesday, Friday and Saturday from 8pm to 11pm.

Also at the hotel are pizzeria Il Vicino and Latin restaurant and cocktail bar Pio.

Arma Restaurant
SEAFOOD $$$
(Map p367; ☑0242-244 9710; www.clubarma. com.tr; İskele Caddesi 75; mezes/mains ₺35/40; ☺11am-10pm; ☑) Housed in a former oil depot on the rocks overlooking the harbour, this upmarket *balık evi* (fish restaurant) specialises in mezes and seafood from sea bass to shrimp. On a balmy evening, the fabulous terrace with its five-star view is one of the city's most romantic dining experiences. The myriad mezes include novel choices such as mushroom and parmesan risotto.

🍷 Drinking & Nightlife

Buzzy beer gardens with million-dollar views, live-music venues with everything from rock to *türkü* (Turkish folk music): Kaleiçi has much to offer after dark. The old town is wonderfully atmospheric at night, with *meyhanes*, bars and cafes filling the cobbled streets with tables and the strains of live music. Yeni Kapı Sokak has a strip of *meyhanes*, while bars line Hesapçı Sokak south of the Kesik Minare.

★ Castle Café
CAFE, BAR
(Map p368; ☑0242-248 6594; Hıdırlık Sokak 48/1; ☺8am-11pm) This lively hang-out along the cliff edge is a local favourite, attracting a crowd of young Turks with its affordable drinks (300mL beer ₺11). Service can be slow, but the terrace's jaw-dropping views of the beaches and mountains west of town more than compensate, as do generous bar snacks such as fish and chips and burgers (₺24).

Dem-Lik
BAR
(Map p368; ☑0242-247 1930; Zafer Sokak 6; ☺noon-midnight) This chilled-out garden bar-cafe, with tables scattered along stone walls and beneath shady fruit trees, is where Antalya's university crowd reshapes the world over ice-cold beers, while listening to Turkish troubadours perform live jazz, reggae, blues and more (on Wednesday, Friday and Saturday evenings). There's a menu of cheap pasta and other international dishes (₺10 to ₺15) as well.

Paul's Place
CAFE
(Map p368; ☑0242-244 6894; www.spccturkey. com; Yeni Kapı Sokak 24; ☺9.30am-6pm Mon-Fri; ☎) The good word comes in a cup at this informal cafe in the St Paul Cultural Center. Regardless of your faith, you'll enjoy the filter coffee (₺5) and scrumptious baked goods (₺6).

Çorba (₺4) and light lunches (₺11) are offered and there's a well-stocked lending library and small craft shop.

Kale Bar
BAR

(Map p368; ☑0242-248 6591; Mermerli Sokak 2; ⏰11am-midnight) This patio bar attached to the CH Hotels Türkevi may very well command the most spectacular harbour and sea view in all of Antalya. Cocktails are accordingly priced north of ₺20.

Pupa Cafe
CAFE

(Map p368; Paşa Camii Sokak; ⏰4pm-late) Next to a slab of Byzantine wall, this casual garden cafe is a relaxed and friendly place scattered with pot plants and hanging lamps. Whether you opt for çay (₺2) or rakı (aniseed brandy; ₺15), 'Ship's Stern' is a good choice for a quiet evening of chatting. There's a good-value menu of seafood and Turkish staples (₺20).

☆ Entertainment

Filika Cafe-Bar
LIVE MUSIC

(Map p368; ☑0242-244 8266; Paşa Camii Sokak; ⏰8pm-5am) This venue with live pop and rock music in the centre of Kaleiçi attracts Antalya's hipster-alternative crowd. Sit outside, enjoying the balmy Mediterranean evening, and listen to the music drifting out.

Antalya Cultural Centre
THEATRE

(Antalya Kültür Merkezi; ☑0242-249 5326; 100 Yıl Bulvarı, Atatürk Kültür Parkı) West of the city centre, near 7 Mehmet Restaurant (p371), this theatre has an interesting program of cultural events, from opera and ballet to folk dancing and performances by the university choir.

Antalya State Opera & Ballet Ticket Booth
PERFORMING ARTS

(Map p367; www.biletiva.com; Cumhuriyet Caddesi; ⏰9am-7pm Mon-Sat) Sells tickets for performances from Carmen to Çanakkale (a Turkish production about the Gallipoli campaign).

🛍 Shopping

Yaz
JEWELLERY, FASHION

(Map p368; ☑0533 556 3339; Zafer Sokak 31; ⏰10am-8pm Mon-Sat) Graphic designer Ebru's concept store sells Turkish design, coffee and cakes. Pick up perfume, cushions, jewellery (from about ₺20 to ₺500) and T-shirts (₺50 to ₺120) featuring amusing designs such as a selfie-taking Ottoman horseman.

Osmanlı Sultan Çarık
SHOES

(Map p368; ☑0242-247 1540, 0532 677 0642; info@osmanlicarik.com; Hesapçı Sokak 3; ⏰9am-

6pm) The 'Ottoman Sultan Slipper' shop will whip you up a pair of hand-stitched, pointy-toed slippers in dyed ox and buffalo leather. Sandals, boots and bags are also available.

İki Kapılar Hanı
MARKET

(Old Bazaar; Map p367) This sprawling covered bazaar, dating to the late 15th century, is centred between Kazım Özalp Caddesi and İsmet Paşa Caddesi, just north of the Kaleiçi district. There are plenty of jewellers, metalwork merchants and textiles to be found here, among the sundry nargiles, Ottoman-patterned tiles, spices and Spiderman suits.

ℹ Information

Antalya Guide (www.antalyaguide.org) A comprehensive website with info on everything Antalya-related, from climate to cultural events.

Tourist Office (Map p367; ☑0242-241 1747; Cumhuriyet Caddesi 55; ⏰8am-6pm) This tiny office with city maps and a few brochures is just off Cumhuriyet Caddesi at the western end of the tea gardens around Cumhuriyet Meydanı. A little English is spoken.

ℹ Getting There & Away

AIR

Antalya's busy **international airport** (p604) is 10km east of the city centre on the D400 highway. There's a tourist information desk, and a number of car-hire agencies have counters here as well. It is well connected to Turkey and Europe by the Turkish airlines and summer flights operated by European carriers. **Turkish Airlines** (p605) and **Pegasus Airlines** (p605) have several flights daily to/from İstanbul, while **Sun Express** (p605) serves useful destinations, including Kayseri (for Cappadocia).

BUS

Antalya's otogar, about 4km north of the city centre on highway D650, consists of two large terminals fronted by a park. Looking at the otogar from the main highway or its parking lot, the Şehirlerarası Terminalı (Intercity Terminal), which serves long-distance destinations, is on the right. The İlçeler Terminalı (Domestic Terminal), serving nearby destinations such as Side and Alanya, is on the left.

ℹ Getting Around

TO/FROM THE AIRPORT

The AntRay tram is extending east to the airport; İsmet Paşa is the closest stop to Kaleiçi. If that hasn't happened when you visit, take the tram

one stop to Murat Paşa (₺1.80) and catch bus 600 (₺4.20, half hourly).

To ride any public transport, you must buy an Antalyakart (rechargeable transport card) from a newsagent or on the bus. It costs ₺10, including ₺5 credit.

A taxi will cost ₺40 to ₺50.

There is also an hourly **Havaş** (☏ 0242-330 3800; www.havas.net; ₺10; ☉ 4am-10pm) shuttle, which runs from the 5M Migros shopping centre near Konyaaltı Plajı (about 45 minutes). Coming into the city, it meets every domestic flight and stops at the otogar (bus station) before following the ring road to 5M Migros.

TO/FROM THE BUS STATION

The AntRay tram is the quickest way into town. Follow the signs from the bus station to the underpass which brings you to Otogar tram stop. Note that the underpass is long and dimly lit, so solo women should avoid it at quiet times.

You will have to buy an Antalyakart (rechargeable transport card) at the tram-stop ticket office. It costs ₺10, including ₺5 credit, and is valid for both tram (₺1.80) and bus (₺2.10) journeys. It's a 20-minute ride (eight stops) to the central İsmet Paşa stop just outside Kaleiçi.

Bus 40 heads for Atatürk Caddesi in the town centre every 20 minutes or so from the bus shelter near the airport taxi stand and takes about an hour. To the otogar from Kaleiçi, dolmuşes and buses, including 93, head up Fahrettin Altay/Cebesoy Caddesi; look out for 'otogar' or 'terminal' on the front of the vehicle.

A taxi between the otogar and Kaleiçi should cost ₺25.

CAR & MOTORCYCLE

There are plenty of car-rental agencies, including **Gaye Rent a Car** (☏ 0242-247 1000; www.gaye rentacar.com; İmaret Sokak), and most accommodation places can also arrange rental.

PUBLIC TRANSPORT

To ride any public transport, you must buy an Antalyakart (rechargeable transport card) from a newsagent or on the bus. It costs ₺10, including ₺5 credit. Tram journeys cost ₺1.80 and bus journeys ₺2.10.

Antalya's original 6km-long single-track *antik* or *nostalji tramvay* (tram) has 10 stops and provides the simplest way of crossing town. It runs every half-hour between 7am and 11pm. The tram stops at Kale Kapısı at 12 and 42 minutes past the hour, and heads along Cumhuriyet and Konyaaltı Caddesis to Antalya Museum (Müze stop).

A sleek, double-track tram line with 16 stations called AntRay links northern areas of the city to the centre and the east. It is mainly helpful for

ANTALYA & THE TURQUOISE COAST ANTALYA

SERVICES FROM ANTALYA'S OTOGAR

DESTINATION	FARE (₺)	DURATION (HR)	DISTANCE (KM)	FREQUENCY (PER DAY)
Adana	60	11	565	every 2hr
Alanya	22	3	135	every 20min
Ankara	60	8	555	frequent
Çanakkale	80	12	770	9am; 2 overnight
Denizli (Pamukkale)	40	4	225	several
Eğirdir	24	3½	195	hourly to Isparta (transfer there)
Fethiye (coastal)	35	6	300	hourly
Fethiye (inland)	30	3½	200	several
Göreme/Ürgüp	55	9	485	2 overnight
İstanbul	80	11½	785	frequent
İzmir	55	8	470	several
Kaş	30	3½	188	every 30min
Kemer	12	45min	55	every 15min
Konya	49	5	305	several
Marmaris	50	6	365	several
Olympos/Çıralı	14	1½	80	every 30min
Side/Manavgat	15	1½	75	every 20min in season

travelling to/from the otogar, although it is being extended east from Meydan to the airport and Aksu (for Perge).

The two tram lines are not linked, but the İsmet Paşa stop on the AntRay is a short walk from the central Kale Kapısı stop on the *antik tramvay*.

Bus 8 links the centre with both Konyaaltı and Lara beaches. For bus and tram times and information, visit www.antalya-ulasim.com.

Taxis around the centre cost around ₺10, while it's ₺40 to ₺50 from Kaleiçi to the airport, and ₺25 to the otogar.

Around Antalya

Antalya is an excellent base for excursions to the ancient sites of Termessos, Perge and Aspendos. The latter two sites are east of the city, just off the D400, and can also easily be visited from the town of Side. Termessos is in the mountains northwest of Antalya, off the inland road to Fethiye.

◉ Sights

Aspendos   ARCHAEOLOGICAL SITE
(admission ₺25, parking ₺5; ⊙9am-7pm mid-Apr–mid-Oct, 8am-5pm mid-Oct–mid-Apr) People come in droves to this ancient site near the modern-day village of Belkıs for one reason: to view the awesome **theatre**, considered the best-preserved Roman theatre of the ancient

world. It was built during Aspendos' golden age in the reign of Emperor Marcus Aurelius (AD 161–80), and was used as a caravanserai by the Seljuks during the 13th century. The history of the city, though, goes all the way back to the Hittite Empire (800 BC).

After touring the area in the early 1930s, Atatürk declared Aspendos too fine an example of classical architecture to stay unused. Following a restoration that didn't please many historians, the 15,000-seat theatre became a venue once again. Operas, concerts and events, including the **Aspendos Opera & Ballet Festival** (Aspendos Opera ve Bale Festivalı; www.aspendosfestival.gov.tr) and **Golden Orange Film Festival** (Altın Portakal Film Festivalı; www.altinportakal.org.tr; ⊙Nov-Dec), are staged here. The acoustics are excellent and the atmosphere at night is sublime.

Apart from the theatre, the ancient city ruins are extensive and include a **stadium**, **agora** and 3rd-century **basilica**, although there is little left intact. To reach them follow the trail to the right of the theatre entrance. Further on are the remains of the city's **aqueduct**.

Aspendos lies 47km east of Antalya and 3km north of Belkıs. If driving, immediately on your right as you exit the D400 for Aspendos is a restored Seljuk-era switchback **bridge** with seven arches spanning the Köprü River. It dates from the 13th century but was built on an earlier Roman bridge.

From Antalya, minibuses (₺15) heading along the D400 to Manavgat and beyond will drop you at the Aspendos turn-off, from where you can walk (45 minutes) or hitch the remaining 4km to the site. Taxis waiting at the highway junction will take you to the theatre for an outrageous ₺20. Another option is to catch a dolmuş to Serik (₺15), from where you can walk 9km or pick up another dolmuş to Belkıs.

Alternatively, you can join an excursion from Antalya, stopping at Perge along the way. A taxi tour will cost about ₺150.

Perge   ARCHAEOLOGICAL SITE
(admission ₺25; ⊙9am-7pm mid-Apr–mid-Oct, 8am-5pm mid-Oct–mid-Apr) Some 17km east of Antalya and 2km north of Aksu on highway D400, Perge was one of the most important towns of ancient Pamphylia. Inside the site, walk through the massive **Roman Gate** with its four arches. To the left is the southern **nymphaeum** and well-preserved **baths**, and to the right, the large square-shaped **agora**. Beyond the **Hellenistic Gate**, with its two huge towers, is the fine **colonnaded street**,

Perge

0 — 200 m
0 — 0.1 miles

Acropolis

Northern Nymphaeum

Palaestra

◉ Northern Baths

Northern Basilica

◉

Ancient Shop Houses

Water Canal

City Wall

City Wall

Colonnaded Street

Hellenistic Gate

Propylaeum & Southern Baths

Agora

Southern Nymphaeum

Eastern Basilica

Later Southern City Wall

Roman Gate

Cafe ⊗

Theatre

Stadium

Ticket Booth

Ⓟ

Ⓟ

Aksu (2km);
Highway (2km)

where an impressive collection of columns still stands.

The water source for the narrow concave channel running down the centre of the colonnaded street was the northern **nymphaeum**, which dates to the 2nd century AD. From here it's possible to follow a path to the ridge of the hill with the **acropolis**.

Perge experienced two golden ages: during the Hellenistic period in the 2nd and 3rd centuries BC and under the Romans in the 2nd and 3rd centuries AD (from which most of the ruins here date). Turkish archaeologists first began excavations here in 1946 and a selection of the statues discovered – many in magnificent condition – can be seen at the Antalya Museum (p366).

Excavations and restoration work continue on-site. At the time of writing Perge's 12,000-seat **theatre** was closed, but the equally massive **stadium** had reopened. Both are located along the access road before you reach the site entrance.

Antalya's AntRay tram is extending east to Aksu. If that hasn't happened when you visit, take the tram to Meydan and catch bus AC03 from there to Aksu (₺3, 30 minutes, 15km). You can easily walk the 2km north from Aksu to the ruins. Many Antalya travel agencies run combined excursions to Perge and Aspendos. A taxi tour will be about ₺100; ₺150 including Aspendos.

Termessos ARCHAEOLOGICAL SITE
(admission ₺5; ⊙9am-7pm mid-Apr–mid-Oct, 8am-5pm mid-Oct–mid-Apr) Hidden high in a rugged mountain valley, 34km northwest of Antalya, lies the ruined but still massive ancient city of Termessos. Neither Greek nor Lycian, the inhabitants were Pisidian, fierce and prone to warring. They successfully fought off Alexander the Great in 333 BC, and the Romans (perhaps wisely) accepted Termessos' wishes to remain independent and an ally in 70 BC.

In the car park, at the end of the Termessos access road (King's Rd), you come across the **lower city ruins**. The portal on the hillock to the west was once the entrance to the **Artemis-Hadrian Temple** and **Hadrian Propylaeum**. From here follow the steep path south; you'll see remains of the **lower city walls** on both sides and pass through the **city gate** before reaching, in about 20 minutes, the lower **gymnasium** and **baths** on your left.

A short distance uphill from the lower city ruins are the remnants of Termessos' **upper**

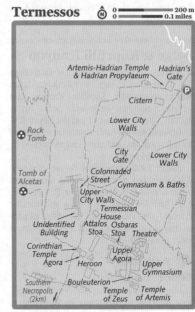

Termessos ⓝ 0 —— 200 m / 0 —— 0.1 miles

Artemis-Hadrian Temple & Hadrian Propylaeum
Hadrian's Gate
Cistern
Lower City Walls
Rock Tomb
City Gate
Lower City Walls
Tomb of Alcetas
Colonnaded Street
Gymnasium & Baths
Upper City Walls
Termessian House
Unidentified Building
Attalos Stoa
Osbaras Stoa
Theatre
Corinthian Temple
Upper Agora
Agora
Heroon
Upper Gymnasium
Southern Necropolis (2km)
Bouleuterion
Temple of Zeus
Temple of Artemis

city walls and a **colonnaded street**. Just above is the upper **agora** and its five large cisterns, an ideal spot to explore slowly and to catch some shade.

On the eastern side of the upper agora is the **theatre**, which enjoys a positively jaw-dropping position atop a peak, surrounded by a mountain range; you can see Antalya on a clear day. Walk southwest from the theatre to view the cut-limestone **bouleuterion**, but use caution when scrambling across the crumbled **Temple of Artemis** and **Temple of Zeus** to the south.

Termessos' southern **necropolis** is at the very top of the valley, 3km (one hour's walk) up from the car park at the site entrance.

The site is spread out and requires much scrambling over loose rocks and up steep, though well-marked, paths. Allow a minimum of two hours to explore and bring plenty of drinking water.

Taxi tours from Antalya cost around ₺170, or you could take an organised or group excursion for about ₺50 less. A cheaper option is to catch a bus from Antalya otogar bound for Korkuteli (₺12) and alight at the entrance to **Güllükdağı Termessos National Park** (Termessos Milli Parkı). Taxis waiting here in the warmer months will run you up the 9km-long King's Rd to the ruins and back. The fare should be about ₺25, but you will have to negotiate.

Selge & Köprülü Kanyon

The ruins of ancient Selge are strewn about the Taurus-top village of Altınkaya, 12km above spectacular Köprülü Kanyon and within a national park with peaks up to 2500m. The road climbs from the Köprü River through increasingly dramatic scenery of rock formations and olive groves backed by snowcapped peaks.

About 350m of ancient Selge's city wall still exists, but its most striking monument is its theatre, restored in the 3rd century AD. Close by is the agora. As you wander through the village and its ruins, consider that Selge once counted a population of more than 20,000.

🏃 Activities

Rafting

There are more than two-dozen companies offering rafting trips in the canyon, including Antalya Rafting (☏ 0532 604 0092, 0242-311 4845; www.antalya-rafting.net), Gökcesu Rafting (☏ 0242-765 3384, 0533 522 3205; www.gokcesu.net) and independent local guides such as Adem Bahar (☏ 0535 762 8116). Antalya Rafting offers day-long trips on the excellent intermediate rapids, starting from €23, including pick-up from hotel in Antalya, a lesson, a two- to three-hour trip and lunch.

Hiking

Around the Oluk Bridge, you'll find villagers keen to guide you on hikes up from Köprülü Kanyon along the original Roman road for about ₺60. It's about two hours up and 1½ hours down. An excellent qualified guide who knows the area inside out is Adem Bahar.

You can arrange guided mountain treks for groups to Mt Bozburun (2504m) and other points in the Kuyucak Dağları (Kuyucak Range) for about ₺60 per group per day. There is a three-day walk through the Köprülü Kanyon on the St Paul's Trail.

🛏 Sleeping

There are a few waterfront pensions with restaurants on the west side of the Köprü River, about 4km past the modern Karabük Bridge en route to the Bürüm Bridge. Most offer rafting trips and packages, including accommodation, food and rafting.

Selge Pansiyon PENSION $
(☏ 0535 577 9475, 0242-765 3244; www.selgepans iyon.com; s/d ₺60/100; ▣ ➔ 🛜) Right on the river, this good-value budget option offers little wooden cabins with pine-clad interiors and hand-held en-suite showers.

Perge Pansiyon PENSION $$
(☏ 0242-765 3074, 0533 475 8108; info@pergepansi yon.com; s/d/tr/q ₺100/140/210/280; ▣ ➔ ❄ 🛜) This sprawling, modern option has timber bungalows with your front door just one stride from the water's edge, and surrounded by beautifully tended gardens, orchards, weirs and wooden platforms for taking it all in.

In this sylvan setting, Perge's restaurant (set menu ₺20 to ₺30) serves meals of fish, lamb, chicken or *köfte* with chips, rice, salad and a drink.

ℹ Getting There & Away

Many travel agencies in Antalya include Köprülü Kanyon Milli Parkı and Selge in their tours. Unless you have your own transport, this is your best option.

If you do have a vehicle, however, you can visit in half a day, though it deserves a lot more time. The turn-off to Selge and Köprülü Kanyon is about 5km east of the Aspendos road (51km from Antalya) along highway D400. Another 30km up into the mountains, the road divides, with the left fork marked for Karabük and the right for Beşkonak. If you take the Karabük road along the river's west bank, you'll pass most of the rafting companies and the three pensions. About 11km from the turn-off is the graceful old Oluk Bridge, from where the paved road marked for Altınkaya climbs 12km to the village and the Selge ruins.

If you follow the river's east bank via Beşkonak, it is 6.5km from the fork in the road to the canyon and the narrow Oluk Bridge, which you can just squeeze a car over.

Side

☏ 0242 / POP 11,933
Down at Side harbour, the re-created colonnade of the Temple of Athena marches towards the blue sea, while at the top of Side old town's gentle hill, the 2nd-century theatre still lords it up over the surrounding countryside. Between these two ancient relics, the lanes of this once-docile fishing village have long since given themselves over to souvenir peddlers and restaurant touts hustling for business. Despite the constant stream of visitors, the liberal scattering of glorious Roman and Hellenistic ruins sitting incongruously between shops means you can

Side

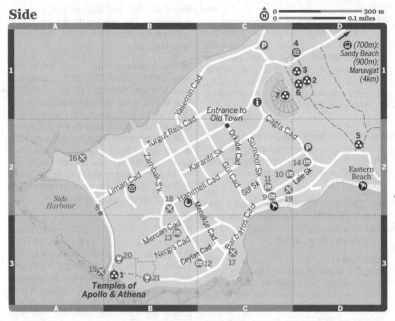

Side

just about imagine (if you scrunch up your eyes) the tourists picking over togas rather than T-shirts.

◎ Sights & Activities

Not only is the whole town an archaeological site, but the approach from Side otogar through a field of ruins is seriously impressive. Driving or strolling down this road to the theatre and car park is a little like walking through Ephesus. A roadside boardwalk leads past ruined walls and pillars stretching away on both sides of the tarmac.

★**Temples of Apollo & Athena** RUIN, TEMPLE
(Map p379) This compact site is one of the most romantic on the Mediterranean coast. Apollo and Athena were Side's deities, although Apollo eventually became more important. The Temple of Athena dates from the 2nd century BC, and a half-dozen columns have been placed upright in their original spots with a frieze of Medusa heads.

Theatre
RUIN

(Map p379; admission ₺20; ⊙8am-7pm late Apr-late Oct, to 5pm late Oct-late Apr) Built in the 2nd century AD, Side's spectacular theatre could seat up to 20,000 spectators and rivals the nearby theatre of Aspendos for sheer drama. Look at the wall of the *skene* (stage building) for reliefs of figures and faces, including those of Comedy and Tragedy.

Side Museum
MUSEUM

(Map p379; admission ₺10; ⊙8am-5pm) Contained within a 5th-century bathhouse, Side's museum has an impressive (if small) collection of statues, sarcophagi, reliefs and coins.

Agora
RUIN

(Map p379) Just east of Side Theatre and across the road from Side museum are these agora remains, which once functioned as the ancient town's slave market.

State Agora
RUIN

(Map p379) These remnants of the state agora sit dramatically beside Side's eastern beach. An interpretive panel shows the two storeys of statues that once decorated the structure.

Temple of Tyche
RUIN

(Map p379) The ruined, circular-shaped Temple of Tyche is dedicated to the goddess of fortune.

Right next door is an arresting **ancient latrine** (Map p379) with two-dozen marble seats.

Sandy Beach
BEACH

Side's main beach is north of the centre, and backed by rows of resort hotels. Follow the main road out of town (Side Caddesi) and turn left at Şarmaşık Sokak opposite the otogar. There is regular dolmuş transport to the beach from near Side Theatre.

Boat Tours
BOATING

(Map p379; tours €15-20) Day tours departing from the harbour include beaches, dolphin sightings, Manavgat waterfall and market and a look at the Temples of Apollo and Athena from the water.

🛏 Sleeping

Sempati Motel
PENSION $

(Map p379; ☑0242-753 3935; sempatimotel side@gmail.com; Mercan Caddesi 74; s/d/tr from €20/28/34; ❋❋🛜) The pros of the family-run 'Sympathy' are the simple and peaceful rooms with artfully arranged origami towels and plastic flowers on the bed, the roof terrace with views of the temple and sea beyond

the village roofs, and the ramshackle garden at breakfast. The cons are the devilishly poky bathrooms, compounded in the attic rooms by sloping eaves.

★ Beach House Hotel
HOTEL $$

(Map p379; ☑0242-753 1607; www.beach house-hotel.com; Barbaros Caddesi; s/d €25/50; ❋❋@🛜🏊) Once the celebrated Pamphylia Hotel, which was a magnet for celebrities in the 1960s, the Beach House's prime seafront location and welcoming Turkish-Australian owners lure a loyal band of regulars. Most rooms face the sea and all have balconies. We love the roof terrace (with teensy pool), the library full of beach-reads and the garden that's complete with Byzantine ruins.

Hotel Poseidon
MOTEL $$

(Map p379; ☑0242-753 2687; www.poseidon motel.com; Lale Sokak 11; s/d €37.50/50; ❋❋🛜) Offering 20 small, motel-style rooms around a garden, the English- and German-speaking hotel veteran Cem distinguishes his property through the service offered, organising boat and rafting tours through his travel agency. Rooms are white and appealing with tiled floors, TV and fridge; those downstairs are more spacious.

Hotel Sevil
HOTEL $$

(Map p379; ☑0242-753 2041; www.hotelsevil. com; Ceylan Caddesi; s/d €40/50; ❋❋🛜) Set around a courtyard with mulberry trees and palms, this midrange option has a smart little outdoor bar within earshot of the ocean roar, and a chilled vibe with friendly management. The rooms all have balconies (some with sea views) and feature wood panelling and classical neutral tones.

Hotel Lale Park
HOTEL $$

(Map p379; ☑0242-753 1131; www.hotellalepark. com; Lale Sokak 7; s/d/apt €50/55/110; ❋❋🛜🏊) One of Side's nicest small hotels, the 'Tulip Park' has simple, decent-sized rooms set around a manicured garden with pretty pool and al fresco bar. Management are friendly and keep everything sparkling clean. Dinner (₺25) is a good-value alternative to Side's other restaurants, and is open to outside guests. You'll need to book by noon.

Side Doğa Pansiyon
PENSION $$

(Map p379; ☑0242-753 6246; www.sidedoga.com; Lale Sokak 8; r/tr €50/55; ❋❋🛜) Colourful wall decorations give the large rooms in this lovely stone house a fresh, breezy feel, while the flower-festooned courtyard is a chilled-out, shady spot to relax. All up, it's a great Side choice.

Eating

Balık & Köfte Ekmek SANDWICHES $

(Map p379; Harbour; sandwiches ₺10; ⏲11am-10pm) Bobbing away gently in Side's sheltered harbour, this converted fishing boat serves up good-value fish and *köfte* sandwiches. Meze platters and fish soup of the day are also available. In a tourist town with uniformly expensive restaurants, it's a thrifty haven for travellers watching their lira.

★Ocakbaşı TURKISH $$

(Map p379; ☎0242-753 1810; Zambak Sokak 46; mains ₺25-45; ⏲11am-10pm; ✎) With excellent service and a huge menu of tasty Turkish grills, mezes, seafood, stews and vegetarian dishes, Ocakbaşı has been a popular dinner spot since 1986. The restaurant atmospherically overlooks a spotlit 2nd-century Roman bath. In summer it can get noisy and crowded, so dine early (before 7.30pm) if you don't fancy being squeezed between tables of large tour groups.

Soundwaves Restaurant INTERNATIONAL $$

(Map p379; ☎0242-753 1059; Barbaros Caddesi; mains ₺25-35; ⏲11am-10pm) This long-running Side eatery has a friendly and relaxed vibe. A small, focused menu is delivered by an experienced chef and there are regular seafood specials. Ask if the swordfish kebaps are available, and kick off with a few mezes and a cold beer. Owned by the Beach House Hotel, its beachfront terrace is perfect for watching the moon rise.

Moonlight Restaurant SEAFOOD $$

(Map p379; ☎0242-753 1400; Barbaros Caddesi 49; mains ₺20-35) In business since 1983, this long-stayer of the Side scene offers solid Turkish cooking, an extensive local wine list and professional yet unstuffy service. Seafood is the mainstay of the menu and is superfresh. For romantic dining, head to the back terrace on the water.

Karma INTERNATIONAL $$$

(Map p379; Turgut Reis Caddesi; mains ₺32-68; ⏲11am-10pm) This slick, cosmopolitan bar-restaurant has an unbeatable garden fronting iridescent blue ocean (lit by submerged turquoise lights). The emphasis here is on meat, and the international menu jumps between Cajun chicken and chateaubriand.

Drinking & Nightlife

Atmospheric watering holes are scattered across Side old town, ranging from glamorous places near the harbour to the hang-outs around Barbaros Caddesi.

Apollonik's BAR

(Map p379; ☎0242-753 1070; Liman Yolu; ⏲4pm-late) Right beside the Temples of Apollo and Athena, Side's oldest bar remains its most popular local hang-out, deriving much character from its Bavarian-cottage-like appearance. It does decent food (burgers ₺15) and classically themed cocktails (₺19), named after the likes of Zeus and Dionysus. Sit on the terrace overlooking the harbour, or inside snuggled up on the cushion-strewn *sedir* (bench) seating.

Stones Bar BAR

(Map p379; Barbaros Caddesi 119; ⏲4pm-late) The biker theme here extends beyond the *Easy Rider* posters, old bikes and mopeds to an outdoor fireplace and empty Jack Daniel's bottles used as candlesticks. The spectacular waterfront views from the outside terrace are perfect fodder for sunset drinks, and live music is staged most nights in summer.

Information

Tourist Office (Map p379; ☎0242-753 1367; ⏲8am-10pm Mon-Sat late Apr-late Oct, to 5pm late Oct-late Apr) German- and English-speaking office next to the theatre. Wheelchairs are available here for touring the ruins.

Getting There & Away

Vehicular entrance to the old town is restricted: you can only enter and exit between midnight and 10am. Parking at the entrance to the old town costs ₺10 for up to six hours, or ₺20 for six to 24 hours.

Side's otogar is east of the ancient city. In summer a shuttle (₺1) transports visitors between the otogar and the old-town gate.

Frequent minibuses connect Side otogar with the Manavgat otogar (₺3), 4km to the northeast, from where buses go to Antalya (₺15, 1½ hours, 75km), Alanya (₺15, 1½ hours, 60km) and Konya (₺30, four hours, 230km). Coming into Side, most buses drop you at either the Manavgat otogar or the petrol station at the Side *kavşağı* (junction) on the highway, from where a free *servis* will transfer you to Side. Minibuses from Manavgat to Side run to the old-town gate until 10am, but thereafter only to the otogar.

A taxi from Side to Manavgat otogar should cost about ₺15; taxi drivers at the old-town gate will initially ask for more.

Eastern Mediterranean

Best Places to Eat

➡ Hatay Sultan Sofrası (p408)

➡ Deniz Kizi (p391)

➡ Öz Asmaaltı (p402)

➡ Çağlayan Restaurant (p408)

Best Places to Sleep

➡ Hotel Bosnalı (p402)

➡ Centauera (p385)

➡ Liwan Hotel (p406)

➡ Hotel Esya (p389)

Why Go?

This is Turkey's non-airbrushed slice of Mediterranean coastline. A handful of distinctly local-style beach resorts lie between the industrial port cities. Crumbling ruins sit among acres of intensely farmed countryside with nary a tourist in sight. In the ancient towns of Tarsus and Antakya, atmospheric old-town fragments cling on amid the modern hubbub.

Southern Hatay Province's fascinating melding of religions, languages and foods is reason enough for many to linger. For others, the wealth of important early Christian sites is the eastern Med's ace up its sleeve. The area's historical riches encompass a dizzying timeline of kings and conquerors that stretches from Karatepe's late-Hittite remnants, through Roman Anemurium, to the clifftop castles of once-mighty Cilicia. The stretch of the Mediterranean that most people miss is full of surprises for those that make the trip.

When to Go
Antakya

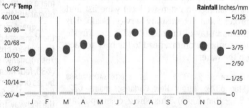

Apr & May Munch on Anamur's bananas and strawberries during the spring harvest glut.

Jul & Aug Thermometers shoot sky-high and Turkish families hit Kızkalesi beach.

Oct Autumn is ideal for exploring Antakya's old town in between cafe stops for syrupy *künefe*.

Eastern Mediterranean Highlights

1 Hatay Archaeology Museum (p405) Marvelling at Roman and Byzantine artistry while surrounded by some of the world's finest mosaics.

2 Kızkalesi Castle (p393) Swimming to this perfect island castle.

3 Anemurium (p388) Exploring the beautiful, lonely remnants of an ancient city.

with grazing cows and sheep your only company.

4 Caves of Heaven & Hell (p395) Descending into the massive Chasm of Heaven and then test out your vertigo.

5 Narlıkuyu (p395) Eating freshly grilled fish while turtles swim by your feet.

6 Karatepe (p404) Learning about Hittite history amid stone reliefs and statuary.

7 Tarsus (p399) Soaking up the ramshackle atmosphere of bygone days in the compact old town centre.

Alanya

0242 / POP 109,656

A former seaside bastion for a succession of Mediterranean powers, Alanya has boomed in recent decades and is a densely populated tourist haven for predominantly Dutch and Scandinavian sunseekers. At night, the downtown area can resemble 'Vegas by the Sea' – aside from taking a boat cruise or a stroll along the waterfront, many visitors only shuffle between their hotel's pool and all-inclusive buffet restaurant, perhaps dropping into a raucous nightclub after dark.

But look up from the bars and tattoo parlours for a minute, and you'll find Alanya has abundant charms. Looming high above the promontory, to the south of the modern centre, is an impressive fortress complex with the remains of a fine Seljuk castle, some atmospheric ruins and a sprinkling of traditional red-tile-roofed houses rimming the alleys that climb up the hillside. Alanya is a tale of two cities if ever we saw it.

◎ Sights

★ Alanya Castle
FORTRESS

(Alanya Kalesi; Map p386; Kaleyolu Caddesi) FREE Surmounting Alanya's rocky peninsula is its awesome Seljuk-era castle, wrapped in 6.5km of walls and tentatively awaiting Unesco World Heritage listing. Climb to it through the steep streets of the Tophane district to get a sense of its scale, and wonderful views across the city and Cilician mountains. Right at the top is the İç Kale (Inner Fortress; Map p386; admission ₺15; ◎8am-7.30pm Apr-Oct, to 5pm Nov-Mar), while elsewhere within are plentiful (though poorly preserved) ruins, including a half-dozen cisterns and the shell of an 11th-century Byzantine church.

If you're not up to the steep 3.5km climb, catch bus 4 from the dolmuş (minibus that stops anywhere along its prescribed route) station behind the Grand Bazaar (₺2.50, hourly from 9am to 7pm, half-hourly in summer) or opposite the tourist office (10 minutes past the hour and, in summer, also 15 minutes before the hour). Taxis are around ₺15.

Tersane
HISTORIC BUILDING

(Map p386; admission ₺5, combined ticket with Red Tower & guard house ₺10) A wooden walkway runs south along the old harbour walls from the Red Tower to the Tersane, the only Seljuk-built shipyard remaining in Turkey.

Antique ceramic shards litter the stones, indicating the succession of civilisations that have built here – with the waves sloshing through its restored stone arches, it's highly atmospheric. From here the walkway continues further along the shoreline to a small guard house (Map p386; admission ₺5, combined ticket with Red Tower & Tersane ₺10), which would have served as a coastal watchtower during the Seljuk era.

Ehmedek
AREA

(Map p386) As you walk up towards Alanya Castle, the road passes a turn-off for the village of Ehmedek, which was the Turkish quarter during Ottoman and Seljuk times. Today a number of old wooden houses still cluster around the fine 16th-century Süleymaniye Camii (Map p386; Ehmedek Sokak), the oldest mosque in Alanya. Also here is a former Ottoman bedesten (Map p386) (vaulted covered market) and the Akşebe Türbesi (Map p386), a distinctive 13th-century mausoleum. There's also a Kültür Evi (Ömürlü Kemal Atli Culture House; Map p386; Kocabas Sokak; ◎9.30am-12.30pm & 2-6.30pm Tue-Sun) FREE (Culture House), re-creating comfortable life in Ottoman times.

Red Tower
HISTORIC BUILDING

(Kızılkule; Map p386; İskele Caddesi; admission ₺5, combined ticket with Tersane & guard house ₺10; ◎9am-7pm) This five-storey octagonal defence tower, measuring nearly 30m in diameter, more than 30m in height and with a central cistern within for water storage, looms over the harbour at the lower end of İskele Caddesi. Constructed in 1226 by Seljuk Sultan Alaeddin Keykubad I (who also built Alanya Castle), it was the first structure erected after the Armenian-controlled town surrendered to the sultan, and is now symbolic of the city. It's worth visiting, not least for the interesting museum within.

Alanya Museum
MUSEUM

(Map p386; İsmet Hilmi Balcı Caddesi; admission ₺5; ◎9am-7.30pm Tue-Sun summer, 8am-5pm winter) Refurbished in 2012, Alanya's small museum is worth a visit to see artefacts, including tools, jugs, jewellery, letters and coins, from the succession of cultures that has called the surrounding area home. Its prize piece is a fine 52cm bronze of Hercules from the 2nd century AD.

Alanya Aqua Park
AMUSEMENT PARK

(Map p386; 0242-519 3674; www.alanyaaquapark.net; İsmet Hilmi Balcı Caddesi 62; adult/child

₺25/15; ⊙9am-6pm; 🏊) Kids had enough of castles and ruins? This large water park, near Alanya's centre, has plenty of wet and wild fun with pools and 15 slides appropriate for both little ones and their minders. There's a nice area with sunloungers for wiped-out parents, too.

🏃 Activities & Tours

Many local operators organise tours to the ruins along the coast west of Alanya and to Anamur. A typical tour to Aspendos, Side and Manavgat will cost around €22 per person, while trips to Anamur and ancient Anemurium will cost about €35 per person. Tours to Sapadere Canyon (p388) are usually €25 per person.

Excursion Boats   BOATING
(Map p386; per person incl lunch ₺70) Every day at around 10.30am, boats leave from near Rıhtım Caddesi for a six-hour voyage around the promontory, visiting several caves, as well as Cleopatra's Beach. Other cruises include sunset jaunts around the harbour (from ₺20). Some boats, made up to look like pirate ships, are essentially floating parties – foam-filled dance floors and everything.

🛏 Sleeping

Alanya has hundreds of hotels and pensions, although almost all of them are designed for groups. İskele Caddesi and near the otogar (bus station) are the best places to look for budget offerings, while the Tophane district under the castle is now home to a scattering of boutique hotels set in beautifully restored Ottoman houses.

Tayfun Pansiyon   PENSION **$**
(Map p386; ☑0242-513 2916; Tolupaşa Sokak 17a; s/d excl breakfast ₺30/40) With a lovely landlady who speaks no English (or Dutch) and basic, clean rooms tucked away in a central residential neighbourhood, the Tayfun is a nice (if not luxurious) alternative to Alanya's bling. Adjacent, there's a leafy garden for end-of-day relaxing, and plenty of cafes on nearby Damlataş Caddesi for breakfast.

Temiz Otel   HOTEL **$$**
(Map p386; ☑0242-513 1016; www.temizotel. com.tr; İskele Caddesi 12; s/d ₺80/120; 🏊🛜) If you want to be slam in the centre of the city action, the Temiz has 32 decently sized, if bland, rooms. Those at the front have balconies, but light sleepers should ask for a room at the back as the thumping noise from the bars goes on into the wee hours.

★ Centauera   BOUTIQUE HOTEL **$$$**
(Map p386; ☑0242-519 0016; www.centauera. com; Andızlı Camii Sokak 4, Tophane; r €60-120; P🏊🛜) A 10-minute stroll from the harbour, the blissful Centauera is a world away from central Alanya, with views across the elegant sweep of bay and only birdsong to disturb your mornings. This restored Ottoman house is packed full of old-world elegance and ably run by friendly owner Koray. With just five rooms, it's an intimate choice.

We love the roll-top baths in the deluxe rooms and little touches such as coffee makers in all rooms. Dinner is also available on request if you preorder.

Lemon Villa   BOUTIQUE HOTEL **$$$**
(Map p386; ☑0242-513 4461; www.lemonvilla. com; Tophane Caddesi 20; r/ste from €65/150; 🏊🛜) The stone-walled rooms at this restored Ottoman house are full of authentic details, with ornate wooden ceiling panels, hanging lamps and original fireplaces. The two suites at the top are particularly sumptuous, with suitably grand sea views to top it off.

Villa Turka   BOUTIQUE HOTEL **$$$**
(Map p386; ☑0242-513 7999; www.hotelvillatur ka.com; Kargı Sokak 7, Tophane; r/ste €84/130; 🏊🛜) This 200-year-old Ottoman mansion has been lovingly restored to showcase its original wooden ceilings and tiled floors. There are 10 rooms here featuring quality bed linen, honey-toned cedar decor and antiques, while views take in the Taurus mountains and the nearby Red Tower. Breakfast often incorporates organic goodies from farms surrounding Alanya.

🍴 Eating

★ İskele Sofrası   TURKISH **$$**
(Map p386; Tophane Caddesi 2b; mezes ₺9, mains ₺20-50; ⊙9.30am-1am; 🥗) Three generations of the friendly Öz family run this restaurant, uphill from the harbour. There are never less than 10 mezes on at once – perhaps *girit ezmesi,* an unforgettable mash of feta, walnuts and olive oil. All the usual grills and loads of seafood headline the menu, but special lamb hotpots can be cooked, with a day's notice.

The terrace with harbour views is a delight, and perfect with a cold beer.

EASTERN MEDITERRANEAN ALANYA

Alanya

EASTERN MEDITERRANEAN ALANYA

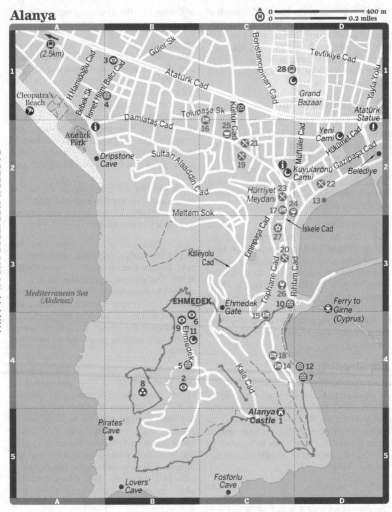

0 ——— 400 m
0 ——— 0.2 miles

Mediterranean Sea
(Akdeniz)

Sofra

ANATOLIAN **$$**

(Map p386; ☑0242-513 1016; İskele Caddesi 10; mains ₺15-28; ⊙8am-4pm, from 9am in low season) Sofra is a rare and refreshing thing in central Alanya: a traditional Turkish *lokanta* (eatery serving ready-made food) with unfussy, home-cooked food made by people who make you feel genuinely welcome. Ottoman veal kebabs, slow-cooked white beans, cabbage rolls, aubergine fritters...it wouldn't raise an eyebrow in many parts of Turkey, but here it's a godsend.

Bistro Floyd

EUROPEAN **$$$**

(Map p386; ☑0242-511 4444; www.echt-hol lands.com; Damlataş Caddesi 19; mains ₺35-45; ⊙10am-midnight, from 5pm in winter; ☎) This Turkish-Dutch operation occupies possibly the most handsome of Damlataş Caddesi's few remaining Ottoman houses. It's beautifully restored inside, while outside a spacious terrace allows tables of merrymakers to tuck into good Turkish, Dutch and European food without getting in each other's way.

Alanya

Lokanta Su
MEDITERRANEAN $$$

(Map p386; ☑ 0242-512 1500; Damlataş Caddesi 16; mains ₺43-52; ◷ 10am-11pm) One of the most prominent and clearly upmarket places on touristy Damlataş Caddesi (the house was originally the governor's but, although restored, only the facade is original), this is a lovely courtyard restaurant, with one of the best wine lists in town. The food's good and it has a kids menu, and even a kids cocktail list.

Mahperi Restaurant
INTERNATIONAL $$$

(Map p386; ☑ 0242-512 5491; www.mahperi.net; Rihtim Caddesi; mains ₺27-41; ◷ 8.30am-1am) This classy waterfront fish and steak restaurant has been in operation since 1947 – quite a feat in fly-by-night Alanya – and offers a good selection of homestyle Turkish dishes, too. In this part of town, it stands out – in a good way.

 Drinking & Entertainment

Alanya features some of the most bawdy, bright and banging nightclubs in all of Turkey. It's all good fun if that's what you're looking for, though solo female travellers may find some of the late-night scene a little on the sleazy side. For the non-party animals there are also more restrained nightlife options.

Ehl-i-Keyf
CAFE

(Map p386; ☑ 0555-227 4957; www.ehlikeyfnarg ile.com; Damlataş Caddesi 32; ◷ 10am-3am) The shaded garden of this restored Ottoman residence is a trendy hang-out for Alanya's bright young things, and a great antidote to the more touristy bars and cafes around town. Enjoy a relaxing combo of tea, nargile (water pipe) and backgammon, or a freshly squeezed juice. Note that only alcohol-free beer is available.

Club Zapfhahn
CLUB

(Map p386; Rihtim Caddesi 34; ◷ 10pm-3am May-Oct) One of Alanya's most popular clubs gets packed with a fun, young and up-for-it crowd of both local and holidaying revellers. There's usually a different DJ every night during the height of summer, plus go-go dancers, if that's your thing.

Tudors Pub
BAR

(Map p386; ☑ 0546-532 1160; www.tudorsan talya.com; İskele Caddesi 80; ◷ 2pm-3am) Live music and decent beer are the draws at this slick, multistorey venue by the harbour. There's not too much about it that's reminiscent of a certain 16th-century royal house from Wales, but it can provide a regal night of fun.

Çello Türkü Bar
LIVE MUSIC

(Map p386; ☑ 0242-511 4290; İskele Caddesi 36; ◷ 2pm-3am) This rollicking, friendly Turkish bar features live 'protest and folk music' and is a top spot for an acoustic-fuelled night of rakı (aniseed brandy) and beers. Locals crowd in before the bands start (at 10pm), escaping the booming manufactured beats in the superclubs down by the harbour.

ℹ Information

Tourist Office (Map p386; Damlataş Caddesi; ☺9am-5pm Mon-Fri) Small branch near the corner of Damlataş and Iskele Caddesis.

ℹ Getting There & Away

The otogar is on the coastal highway (Atatürk Caddesi), 3km west of the centre. Most services are less frequent in the off season, but buses generally leave hourly for Antalya (₺22, 2½ hours, 115km) and eight times daily to Adana (₺60, nine hours, 440km). Buses to Konya (₺50, 5½ hours, 320km) take the Akseki–Beyşehir route.

If you're travelling down the coast from Side, most buses from Manavgat otogar conveniently drop you off at the central dolmuş station behind the Grand Bazaar.

ℹ Getting Around

Dolmuşes to the otogar (₺2) can be picked up at the **dolmuş station** (Map p386) near the mosque behind the Grand Bazaar, north of Atatürk Caddesi. From the otogar, walk out towards the coast road and the dolmuş stand is on the right.

Buses 101 and 102 run the same route (₺2.50). A taxi to the otogar from the centre costs ₺15.

Around Alanya

There are several notable attractions on or just north of the D400 as you travel east from Alanya, including the seldom-visited ancient sites of **Laertes** and **Syedra**. A turn-off near the 11km marker leads northward for 6km to **Dim Cave** (Dim Mağarası; ☑0242-518 2275; www.dimcave.com.tr; adult/child ₺10/4; ☺9am-7pm), a subterranean fairyland of spectacular stalactite and stalagmite formations with a crystal-clear pool at the deepest depth. A 360m-long walkway leads you through the entire length of the cave. From a turning at 27km, another road leads 18km northeast to beautiful **Sapadere Canyon** (Sapadera Kanyonu; adult/child ₺4/2; ☺9am-7pm). Access for walkers through the gorge is along a 750m-long path.

Around 30km west towards Antalya, and just after Incekum beach, is a turning for a road leading north for 9km to **Alarahan**, a 13th-century *han* (caravanserai), which can be explored with a torch. At the head of the valley nearby are the 13th-century ruins of **Alara Castle** (Alara Kalesi).

Southeast from Alanya, the twisting clifftop road occasionally descends to the ocean to pass through the fertile delta of a stream, planted with bananas or crowded with greenhouses. It's a long drive to Anamur, but it's a beautiful procession of sea views and cool pine forests. This region was ancient Cilicia Tracheia (Rugged Cilicia), a somewhat forbidding part of the world because of the mountains and the fearsome pirates who preyed on ships from the hidden coves.

Anamur

☑0324 / POP 36,401

Surrounded by fertile banana plantations and mammoth polytunnels hiding strawberry crops, Anamur is a prosperous farming town with a laid-back resort as an adjunct. The waterfront İskele district, with its pleasant strip of sand, springs into action on summer weekends when locals head to the coast to cool off. The beach's eastern end is capped by the storybook bulk of Mamure Castle, while just to the west of town is the massive Byzantine city of Anemurium, with tumbledown ruins galore.

Whether it's the ruins or relaxed beach life that brings you here, don't leave town without sampling the local *muzler* (bananas). Piles of the bananas, which are shorter and sweeter than imported varieties, are on sale everywhere. Do as the holidaying Turks do and buy them by the bagful to munch on the sand.

Anamur lies north of highway D400. About 2.5km southeast of the main roundabout is the İskele beachfront area. Anemurium is 8.5km west, while Mamure Castle is 7km east.

⊙ Sights

★ **Anemurium**
Ancient City   ARCHAEOLOGICAL SITE
(Anemurium Antik Kenti; admission ₺5; ☺9am-7pm) Anemurium's sprawling and eerily quiet ruins stretch for 500m down to a pebble beach, with mammoth city walls scaling the mountainside above. From the huge **necropolis** area (which itself looks like a city), walk southeast past a **4th-century basilica**; look behind it for a mosaic pathway of tiles leading to the sea. Above the church is one of two **aqueducts**. The best-preserved structure in Anemurium is the **baths complex** with coloured mosaic tiles that still decorate portions of the floor.

Also worth seeking out is the **theatre** dating from the 2nd century AD and, opposite, the more complete **odeon**, with 900 seats and a tiled floor.

Although founded by the Phoenicians in the 4th century BC, Anemurium suffered a number of devastating setbacks, including an attack in AD 52 by a vicious Cilician tribe, and most of the visible ruins date from the late Roman and Byzantine periods onward. Archaeologists have also uncovered evidence that an earthquake destroyed the city in about 580.

Approaching Anamur from the west, or down from the Cilician mountains, a sign points south towards the ruins of Anemurium Antik Kenti. The road then bumps along for 2km to the *gişe* (ticket kiosk); it's another 500m to the car park.

🛏 Sleeping

The popular İskele district is where most visitors to Anamur end up. Pensions and hotels run along Fevzi Çakmak Caddesi (or İskele Yolu) down to the harbour and around İnönü Caddesi, the main street running along the waterfront. Town buses stop at the beachfront intersection.

★ Hotel Esya HOTEL $$
(☑ 0324-816 6595; www.anamur.gen.tr/hotel esya; İnönü Caddesi 55; s/d ₺50/100; ❀ 🛜) Somehow managing to be both multistorey

beachside hotel and family home, this is surely Anamur's friendliest accommodation option. The rooms are simple but very comfortable, and breakfast usually includes freshly cooked *sigara böreği* (fried filo and cheese pastries). Often the family's English-speaking son is on hand, but French, Turkish or smiles are also understood.

Hotel Luna Piena HOTEL $$
(☑ 0324-814 9045; www.hotellunapiena.com; Süleyman Bal Sokak 14; s/d ₺80/140; ❀ 🛜) Just paces from the beach, this block-shaped beige hotel offers 32 rooms with parquet floors, balconies with full sea views, spacious showers and a preference for sparkling white decor.

Yan Hotel HOTEL $$
(☑ 0324-814 2123; www.yanhotel.com; Adnan Menderes Caddesi; s/d ₺80/120; ❀ 🛜) On a quiet side street, the Yan has good sea views and a lovely leafy garden, just 30m from the beachfront. The downstairs bar is good for a beer, too. Rooms are basic but very light and airy.

🍴 Eating & Drinking

İskele Sofrası TURKISH $
(Sokak 1909; mains ₺15; ⏱ 10am-midnight) Just one block back from the beach, this popular, marine-coloured family eatery turns out top-notch mezes and generous grills – order the *beyti* kebap (minced lamb with garlic). Good fish dishes and Anamur's best pide

---

TURTLES AT RISK!

The beach at Anamur is one of a dozen nesting sites of the loggerhead turtle (Turkish: *deniz kaplumbağası*) – a large, flat-headed turtle that spends most of its life in the water – along Turkey's Mediterranean coast.

Between May and September, females come ashore at night to lay their eggs in the sand. Using their back flippers, they scoop out a nest about 40cm deep, lay between 70 and 120 soft-shelled white eggs the size of ping-pong balls, then cover them over. If disturbed the turtles may abandon the nests and return to the sea.

The eggs incubate in the sand for around 60 days and the temperature at which they do determines the gender of the hatchlings: below 30°C and all the young will be male; above 30°C and they will be female. At a steady 30°C a mix is assured.

As soon as they're born (at night, when it's cool and fewer predators are about), the young turtles make their way towards the sea, drawn by the reflected light. If hotels and restaurants are built too close to the beach (as is often the case in the western Mediterranean), their lights can confuse the youngsters, leading them to move up the beach towards danger – in Anamur's case, the D400 highway. Plenty of young can be seen in the waterway next to Marmure Castle, a short waddle from the road.

Loggerhead turtles also nest on the beaches at Demirtaş and Gazipaşa, both southeast of Alanya, and in the Göksu Delta. In the western Mediterranean, important nesting grounds are at Dalyan, Fethiye, Patara, Demre (Kale), Kumluca and Tekirova (both northeast of Demre), and Belek (east of Antalya).

(Turkish-style pizza) round out the menu, and cold beer is also available.

Mare Vista Restaurant INTERNATIONAL $$
(☑0324-814 2001; İnönü Caddesi 28; mains ₺15-25; ⊙11am-midnight) Directly opposite the beach, the 'Sea View' strays beyond the Turkish playbook, with pizzas, salads and sandwiches. It's a very relaxed place (part of its charm), so count on ordering a second beer. There's also occasional live music, especially in summer.

Masalim TEA GARDEN
(İnönü Caddesi; ⊙7am-2am Mar-Dec) We really like this sand-between-your-toes tea garden smack-dab on the seafront. Run by a couple of friendly sisters, its highlights include cheap eats and a couple of kilim-bedecked day beds. Fire up a nargile session, or order a cold beer and listen to the bouncy Turkish pop music cascading over nearby waves.

❶ Information

Tourist Office (☑0324-814 5058; ⊙8am-noon & 1-5pm Mon-Fri) In the otogar complex behind the police station, this office is very helpful, and some English is spoken.

❶ Getting There & Away

Anamur's otogar is on the intersection of the D400 highway and 19 Mayıs Caddesi. Frequent buses depart daily to Alanya (₺30, three hours, 130km), Taşucu/Silifke (₺30, three hours, 140km) and Adana (₺45, six hours, 305km).

❶ Getting Around

Town buses to İskele depart from a small stand behind the otogar (₺1.50, every 30 minutes). You have to buy a ticket before boarding the bus: the small *bakkal* (grocery shop) across the road from the bus stand sells them, or the driver will stop at a shop that does. A taxi between İskele and the otogar costs around ₺12.

If you're heading to Anemurium, flag down a dolmuş to Ören (₺2, half-hourly) from outside the Yağmur Market, opposite the mosque in front of the otogar. Let the driver know and he can drop you off at the Anemurium turn-off on the main highway, from where it's a 2.5km walk. Expect to pay ₺70 for a taxi to Anemurium and back, with an hour's waiting time.

Frequent dolmuşes headed for Bozyazı (₺2) will drop you off outside Mamure Castle, or it's about a 3.5km walk along the beach from İskele. Walk east to the end of İnönü Caddesi and across the bridge where the fishing boats dock in the river, then take the dirt track down to the beach and walk towards the battlements.

Taşucu

☑0324 / POP 9035

It may be the working port of nearby Silifke, but a lovely strip of beach and well-maintained seafront promenade make Taşucu (tah-shoo-joo) a destination in its own right. This is an extremely low-key holiday resort that's a favourite stop for birdwatchers who want to combine some swimming and sunbathing with visits to the nearby wetlands of the Göksu Delta.

Taşucu is also an important transport hub, with ferries for both walk-on passengers and cars travelling to/from Girne in Northern Cyprus. The beach is fronted by Sahil Caddesi, which stretches east from the ferry pier and has several good pensions. Around the harbour, excursion boats depart for day trips (per person ₺40) along the coastline and to nearby islands.

🛏 Sleeping

Outside of summer there are excellent discounts on room prices at all of the hotels.

Taşucu Motel PENSION $$
(☑0324-741 2417; www.tasucumotel.com; Sahil Caddesi 25; d/tr ₺150/200; ❄️📶) Recently spruced up, the Taşucu has big, airy rooms with great seafront views and a chilled-out roof terrace for end-of-day relaxing. It's directly opposite the harbour promenade, on the main beach road.

Meltem Pansiyon PENSION $$
(☑0324-741 4391; www.meltempansiyon.net; Sahil Caddesi 75; s/d/tr excl breakfast ₺80/100/120; ❄️📶) Superfriendly and smack on the beach, this family-run pension is a homely choice. Eight of the 20 modest rooms face the sea. The rest of the rooms have balconies facing the street. Breakfast (₺7.50 extra) is served on the delightful seafront back patio.

Lades Motel HOTEL $$
(☑0324-741 4008; İsmet İnönü Caddesi 45; s/d ₺90/180; ❄️📶🏊) Behind this hotel's (slightly faded) classic '70s-motel facade, the rooms, with balconies overlooking the pool and harbour, are looking good – with new beds and modern bathrooms. It's a favourite with birdwatchers, and the downstairs bar is prime territory for comparing twitching notes with fellow birders. It's on the road down to the harbour.

Holmi Hotel
HOTEL $$

(☑ 0324-741 5378; www.holmihotel.com; Sahil Caddesi 23; d ₺100; ❄️🛜) The rooftop terrace at this 15-room pension on the main harbour-front road is particularly nice on a hot day. Around half the rooms have sea views, and a shared guest kitchen is also available. All the rooms have benefited from renovation and now boast shiny modern bathrooms.

✕ Eating

For a good-value seafood fix, head to one of the excursion boats lining the harbour. They also double as restaurants with fish sandwiches (₺6) and grilled seafood.

Alo Dürüm
TURKISH $

(☑ 0324-741 5657; İsmet İnönü Caddesi 17; mains ₺15-16) Ebullient host Ahmet runs this cheerful open-air kebap place right in the middle of the main drag along the seafront. His hearty portions of döner (spit-roasted lamb slices) and *dürüm* (döner sandwiches) are popular with locals and travellers alike. Don't miss the *tantuni dürüm* (sandwich of beef, peppers, garlic and onion; ₺7).

★ Deniz Kizi
SEAFOOD $$

(☑ 0324-741 4194; İsmet İnönü Caddesi 62c; mains ₺20-35; ⊘ noon-11pm Tue-Fri, from 2pm Sat, from 7pm Mon) The kind of fish restaurant you hope for when visiting the Med, the 'Mermaid' does superfresh fish, simply and with real generosity of spirit. Housed in a lovely, solid stone building by the waterfront, with a rooftop deck strung with shells, it does a wonderful *balık buğulama* – fish stewed with tomatoes, peppercorn and pasrley. The pastries are top-notch, too.

Baba Restaurant
SEAFOOD $$

(☑ 0324-741 5991; İsmet İnönü Caddesi 43; mains ₺20-30) Regarded as the area's best eatery, the Baba's terrace is a beautiful place to sip a cold beer or slurp imported Italian gelato (₺4 to ₺6). It's the excellent food that really lures diners though, especially the tempting cart of mezes (₺3 to ₺5).

⊕ Getting There & Away

BOAT

Akgünler Denizcilik (☑ 0324-741 4033; www. akgunlerdenizcilik.com; İsmet İnönü Caddesi, Galeria İş Merkezi 12) runs *feribotlar* (car ferries) from Taşucu to Girne in Northern Cyprus on Sunday, Tuesday and Thursday (passenger one way/return ₺75/130, with car one way/return ₺175/330). Boats are boarded at midnight and depart from the harbour at 2am, arriving in Girne at 8am. You must be at the harbour to clear immigration at 10.30pm. For the return leg, ferries leave Girne every Monday, Wednesday and Friday, also at midnight. Not included in the fare is the harbour tax: ₺20 out of Taşucu and ₺30 from Girne.

The same company also runs a fast boat on the same route, leaving Taşucu at midday on Wednesday and Friday, and Girne the same time on Thursday and Sunday. It's ₺115/195 per adult one way/return.

BUS

Buses heading south to Silifke can drop you (if you let them know) on the main highway just past the turn-off for the road down to the harbour. It's an easy five-minute walk to the waterfront and the hotels.

There are dolmuşes every half-hour between Taşucu and Silifke otogar (₺2), where you can make long-distance bus connections. The dolmuş route trundles the full length of the waterfront, and they can be flagged down anywhere along Sahil Caddesi and İsmet İnönü Caddesi.

Silifke
☑ 0324 / POP 57,427

Silifke is a riverside country town with a long history. A striking castle towers above the mineral-rich blue-green Göksu River, dubbed the Calycadnus in ancient times. In the vicinity are other archaeological and natural sights that deserve a visit.

Seleucia ad Calycadnum, as Silifke was once known, was founded by Seleucus I Nicator in the 3rd century BC. He was one of Alexander the Great's most able generals and founder of the Seleucid dynasty that ruled Syria after Alexander's death.

The town's other claim to fame is that Emperor Frederick Barbarossa (r 1152–90) drowned in the river near here while leading his troops on the Third Crusade. It was apparently the weight of his armour that brought him down.

⊙ Sights

Silifke Castle
CASTLE

(Silifke Kalesi) **FREE** This Byzantine hilltop fortress, with its moat, two dozen towers and vaulted underground chambers, was once Silifke's command centre. The walls are its most impressive feature, as the interior is still undergoing excavation. At the time of writing, archaeological and restoration work meant the entire castle was off limits. Hopefully by the time you visit, it will be open again.

Tekir Ambarı
CISTERN

(Su Sarnıcı; Eğitim Sokak) FREE The Tekir Ambarı is an ancient cistern carved from rock that can be entered via a spiral staircase. To reach the cistern, head to the junction of İnönü Bulvarı and Menderes Caddesi, then walk up the alleyway (348 Sokak) to the left of the Küçük Hacı Kaşaplar butcher shop. Turn left onto Eğitim Sokak, just before the school. The cistern is hidden in a mound just behind a basketball court.

Silifke Museum
MUSEUM

(Taşucu Caddesi 29; ⊙8am-5pm) FREE To the east of Silifke's centre, on the main road heading to Taşucu, this local museum showcases Roman figurines and busts, and Hellenistic black-on-red ceramics. The four-room collection also includes ancient coins and jewellery, amphorae and pottery, and tools and weapons from the Roman and Byzantine eras.

Merkez Camii
MOSQUE

(Central Mosque; Fevzi Çakmak Caddesi) Also called the Alaeddin Camii (Aladdin's Mosque), the Seljuk-era Merkez Camii dates from 1228, although it's seen many renovations over the centuries.

Church of St Thekla
CHURCH

(Aya Tekla; Aya Tekla Sokak; admission ₺5; ⊙9am-5pm) This Christian site is dedicated to St Thekla, one of St Paul's early devotees. Thekla is said to have spent her later years here, trying to convert the locals of Seleucia to Paul's teachings. She ruffled the feathers of local healers, who decided to kill her, but on their arrival at her cave she vanished into thin air. The very atmospheric (though modest) church carved out of the cave where she lived is an important pilgrimage site.

In the 5th century a large basilica was built on the grassy knoll above the cave, but only an incisor-like chunk of the apse is still standing.

The church is signposted off the D400 highway, 3km southwest of Silifke. Any dolmuş travelling between Taşucu and Silifke can drop you at the turn-off, from where it's a 1km walk to the site.

🛏 Sleeping & Eating

Try the Silifke *yoğurdu*, a local yoghurt famous throughout Turkey.

Göksu Otel
HOTEL $$

(☑0324-712 1021; Atatürk Bulvarı 20; s/d ₺80/120; 🖲) Right in the heart of things, between the town centre and the river, the Göksu is a good choice if you're overnighting in Silifke. In sight of the bridge and castle, its pea-green and orange lobby furnishings and scuffed wine-coloured carpets give the impression it's dated, but the rooms are perfectly comfortable.

Tekin Ali Usta
TURKISH $

(☑0324-714 3370; Seyhan Caddesi 4a; mains ₺15-20; ⊙8am-10pm) Just what you want from a classic *lokanta* and *kebap salonu:* friendly owners, bang-on renditions of *lahmacun* (Arabic-style pizza), *mercimek çorbasi* (lentil soup served with bread, herbs, pickled chilies, lemon and olive oil) and other favourites, fans for the hot weather and plenty of room to spread out.

Gözde Restaurant
KEBAP $

(☑0324-714 2764; Özlem İş Hanı 7; mains ₺14-18; ⊙10am-11pm) This kebab and *lahmacun* joint also serves up delicious soups, mezes and grills in a shaded outdoor dining area down a small street.

🛈 Information

Tourist Office (☑0324-714 1151; Veli Gürten Bozbey Caddesi 6; ⊙8am-noon & 1-5pm) Just north of Atatürk Caddesi, you'll find lots of literature and dedicated staff here.

🛈 Getting There & Away

Buses from Silifke otogar depart hourly for Adana (₺30, three hours, 165km). Other frequent services include Mersin (₺15, two hours, 95km), Alanya (₺45, six hours, 265km) and Antalya (₺55, eight hours, 395km).

Dolmuşes to Taşucu (₺2) depart every 20 minutes from a stand on the south bank of the Göksu, near the stone bridge; they pass by the otogar on their way out of town. A taxi to Taşucu costs ₺25.

Around Silifke

Just southeast of Silifke are the lush salt marshes, lakes and sand dunes of the Göksu Delta, an important wetland area that's home to around 330 bird species. To the north and northeast, the slopes of the *maquis*-covered Olba Plateau stretch along the coast for about 60km before the Cilician plain opens into an ever-widening swathe of fertile land. It is one of Turkey's richest areas for archaeological sites and includes many destinations more easily accessed from Kızkalesi.

Uzuncaburç

The **ruins** (admission ₺3; ☉ 8am-7pm) of Roman Diocaesarea sit within the village of Uzuncaburç, 30km northeast of Silifke. Originally this was the Hellenistic city of Olba, home to a zealous cult that worshipped Zeus Olbius.

The impressive **Temple of Zeus Olbius**, with two dozen erect columns, lies to the left of the **colonnaded street**. Beside the temple are various sarcophagi bearing reliefs. Important Roman structures include a **nymphaeum** (2nd century AD), an arched **city gate** and the **Temple of Tyche** (1st century AD).

Just before the entrance to the main site is a small **Roman theatre**. To view a Hellenistic structure built before the Romans sacked Olba, head north through the village, where you'll pass a massive, five-storey **watch tower** with a **Roman road** behind it. Another 600m down into the valley leads to a long, roadside necropolis of rock-cut tombs and more sarcophagi.

On the road to Uzuncaburç, 8km out of Silifke at Demircili – ancient Imbriogon – you'll pass several superb examples of Roman **monumental tombs** that resemble houses.

Hamza, who mans the information stall under the old mulberry tree in Uzuncaburç's colonnaded street, can take individuals on his scooter to the equally impressive nearby ruins at **Olba** FREE. Tip him well: he's worth it.

❶ Getting There & Away

Minibuses to Uzuncaburç (₺8) leave from Celal Bayar Caddesi, diagonally opposite the Silifke tourist office, at 10am on weekdays and noon on weekends. From Uzuncaburç there's one daily service to Silifke, at 3pm.

Hiring a taxi costs about ₺150 return, usually incorporating a visit to the tombs at Demircili.

Kızkalesi

☏ 0324 / POP 1709

The coastal village of Kızkalesi boasts a lovely swathe of beach bookended by two perfect castles: one on the mainland, the other perching photogenically on an island just offshore. Unfortunately the town itself is a grid of rather grim-looking concrete-slab apartment blocks that look like they were slapped up in five minutes. Kızkalesi really springs into action from June to September when locals make a beeline for the beach on steaming-hot weekends. For archaeology and history buffs, though, the village is a popular base as a springboard for the virtual open-air museum of ruins scattered across the Olba Plateau.

◉ Sights

Kızkalesi Castle CASTLE
(Maiden's Castle; ☉ 9am-5pm) FREE Rising from an island 300m offshore, Kızkalesi Castle is like a suspended dream. Check out the **mosaics** in the central courtyard and the vaulted **gallery**, and climb one of the four **towers** (the one at the southeast corner has the best views). It's possible to swim to the castle, but most people catch the boat (₺10) from the beach pier near Corycus Castle. Another option is to rent a dolphin-themed pedalo (around ₺25) and pedal on over.

Corycus Castle CASTLE
(Korykos Kalesi; admission ₺5; ☉ 8am-8pm) At the northern end of Kızkalesi beach, Corycus Castle was either built or rebuilt by the Byzantines, briefly occupied by the Armenian kingdom of Cilicia and once connected to Kızkalesi by a causeway. Walk carefully up the worn stairway to the east, where a ruined tower affords a fine view of Kızkalesi Castle.

Across the highway is a **necropolis**, once the burial ground for tradespeople. Tombs and rock carvings include a 5th-century relief of a warrior with a raised sword.

Elaiussa-Sebaste ARCHAEOLOGICAL SITE
FREE Some 4km northeast of Kızkalesi at Ayaş are the extensive remains of ancient Elaiussa-Sebaste, a city dating back to the early Roman period and perhaps even to the Hittite era. Important structures on the left (west) side include a 2300-seat hilltop **theatre**, the remains of a **Byzantine basilica**, a **Roman temple** with floor mosaics of fish and dolphins, and a total-immersion cruciform **baptistery**. The ruins of a **Byzantine palace** are on the eastern side of the highway.

⌇ Sleeping

Yaka Hotel HOTEL $$
(☏ 0324-523 2444; www.yakahotel.com.tr; s/d ₺80/120; ✳ 🛜) Yakup Kahveci, the Yaka's multilingual and quick-witted owner, runs the most welcoming hotel in Kızkalesi. The 17 rooms are impeccably tidy, breakfast (or specially ordered dinner) is eaten in the attractive garden and there's nothing in the area Yakup doesn't know and/or can't

OFF THE BEATEN TRACK

ALAHAN MONASTERY

Tentatively listed for World Heritage status, Alahan Monastery (admission ₺5; ⊙ 9am-5pm) is a remarkable monastery that perches on a terraced slope high above the Göksu Valley. Above the entrance is a cave-church chiselled into the cliff face. A grand entry adorned with richly carved reliefs of angels and demons leads into the ruins of the west basilica with its re-erected Corinthian columns. More ruins dot the path up to the mammoth, well-preserved 5th-century east basilica, thought to be one of most ambitious early examples of domed-basilica architecture.

Although today the location amid the pine-forested slopes of the Taurus Mountains has a middle-of-nowhere feel, during the Byzantine age the monastery sat near a vital trade and communications route, and archaeologists believe Alahan was probably one of Turkey's most important religious centres during the 5th and 6th centuries.

To get here, take the inland (D715) highway from Silifke to Mut (1½ hours, 76km) and then continue north for another 24km to the village of Geçimli, where a signposted turn-off to the monastery leads for 3km up a steep incline.

organise. The Yaka is also a great place to meet other travellers, especially those interested in archaeology.

Hotel Hantur HOTEL $$
(☑ 0324-523 2367; www.hotelhantur.com; s/d/f €40/50/60; ❋ 🛜) The Hantur has a front-row seat on the sea, and the 20 colourful rooms are cool and comfortable. Only the back rooms have balconies, but for a true seaside experience forgo the balcony and grab a room facing the sea (such as 301). The breezy front garden is another bonus, as is the helpful and friendly family running the hotel.

Rain Hotel HOTEL $$$
(☑ 0324-523 2782; www.rainhotel.com; s/d/tr/f €50/70/80/90; ❋ 🛜) With a warm and friendly vibe, the Rain is a perennially popular choice, with 18 spotless and spacious rooms, a few with tiny balconies. The homely downstairs lounge is a good place to kick back and meet other travellers, and the on-site travel agency (English and German spoken) can organise pretty much any activity or tour for guests.

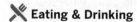 **Eating & Drinking**

A lovely dining option is the 10-minute bus ride (₺2.50, every 30 minutes during the day) to the seafood restaurants at Narlıkuyu.

Zeugma KEBAB $
(Silifke Mersin Bulvari; mains ₺14-20; ⊙ 9am-4pm) The best in a row of welcoming *mangal* (barbecue)/pide places on the main strip, Zeugma does spot-on *mercimek çorbası*, *lahmacun* and kebaps. Tending his wood-fired oven, the perspiring *fırıncı* (baker) is the reason the bread's so good.

Paşa Restaurant KEBAB $
(☑ 0850-602 4757; Plaj Yolu 5; mains ₺14-20; ⊙ 8am-midnight May-Sep) Just off central Cumhuriyet Meydanı, this large, open spot has grills and mezes at better prices than the beachfront restaurants. The staff are super-attentive.

Villa Nur CAFE $$
(☑ 0324-523 2340; Avcılar Sokak 30; mains ₺20) If you're craving something non-Turkish, then this seafront pension, owned by a Turkish-German couple, may be able to help you out. The European-style cakes are very good.

Albatros BAR
(www.albatrosbeachclub.com; ⊙ 9pm-4am) One of the biggest clubs/bars on the Kızkalesi beach, the Albatros is perfect for sundowners around the outdoor bar, with full views of the sea castle. In season things get younger and noisier as the night progresses.

ⓘ **Getting There & Away**

Frequent buses link Kızkalesi with Silifke (₺15, 30 minutes, 24km) and Mersin (₺18, 1½ hours, 60km).

Around Kızkalesi

There are several places to the southwest and northeast of Kızkalesi that are of genuine historical interest and importance. They include everything from an idyllic seaside village with an important mosaic to a descent into the very bowels of the earth.

Frequent dolmuşes link Narlıkuyu and Kızkalesi. You'll need a taxi or to be willing to walk to get to Adamkayalar or the Caves of Heaven and Hell.

Narlıkuyu

Lovely little Narlıkuyu, on a cove 5km southwest of Kızkalesi, is renowned for its fish restaurants, but the other-worldly mountain caves nearby also can't be overlooked.

There's a more-than-worthwhile **Mosaic Museum** (Mozaik Müzesi) `FREE` here, and the town is wrapped around a delightful Mediterranean cove that's a favourite of loggerhead turtles.

Spanning a lovely terrace on one arm of the little cove, **Narlıkuyu** (☑ 0324-723 3286; seafood priced by weight, meals ₺40-70; ☺ 8am-11pm) seafood restaurant of the same name is a delight. Seafood meals come complete with huge piles of salads and scrumptious meze, including pickled *kaya koruğu*, a wild plant growing on rocks by the shore. There's no menu, but a fish meal with all the extras is about ₺50.

Caves of Heaven & Hell

Near Narlıkuyu, a road winds north for 1.5km to several the **Caves of Heaven and Hell** (admission ₺15; ☺ 8am-7pm) – sinkholes carved out by a subterranean river and places of great mythological significance. The walk from Narlıkuyu junction to the main entrance gate is quite steep. Enterprising locals usually offer taxi services up the hill for ₺5 (one way).

The mammoth underground **Chasm of Heaven** (Cennet Mağarası) – 200m long, 90m wide and 70m deep – is reached by 450-odd steps to the left of the ticket booth. Right in front of the cave mouth are the tiny but beautiful remains of the 5th-century Byzantine **Chapel of the Virgin Mary**, used for a short time in the 19th century as a mosque. Once inside the cave, the stairs can be very wet and slippery and there are no handrails, so wear decent shoes and walk carefully. At the furthest end of the colossal grotto is the **Cave of Typhon** (Tayfun Mağarası), a damp, jagged-edged, devilish theatre. Locals believe this to be a gateway to the eternal furnace and Strabo mentions it in his *Geography*. According to legend, the cave's underground river connects with the hellish River Styx – this seems plausible

when you hear the underground current thundering away below.

Follow the path from the ticket office further up the hill to the **Gorge of Hell** (Cehennem Mağarası) with its almost vertical walls that you view by stepping out onto a heart-stopping platform extending over the 120m-deep pit. This charred hole is supposedly where Zeus imprisoned the 100-headed, fire-breathing monster Typhon after defeating him in battle.

Around 600m west of the main entrance is the **Asthma Cave** (Astım Mağarası), which supposedly relieves sufferers of the affliction. It's worth the extra ₺5 to explore these other-worldly grottoes, with their staggering limestone formations.

Adamkayalar

Tricky to get to, but well worth the effort, is **Adamkayalar** (Men Rock Cliff), 17 Roman-era reliefs carved on a cliff face about 8km north of Kızkalesi. They are part of a 1st-century-AD necropolis and immortalise warriors wielding axes, swords and lances, and citizens, sometimes accompanied by their wives and children. High up on a cliff face overlooking a breathtaking gorge, it's a slightly difficult (and dangerous) scramble to get there.

From the inland side of the coastal road through Kızkalesi, a sign points west (uphill) to the site. Follow the road uphill for 5km and, at another sign, turn left; the car park is around 2km down this road. Follow the painted blue and brown arrows down a rather tricky incline into the gorge for about 750m and don't go alone: you might fall and be stranded.

Kanlıdivane

About 8.5km northeast of Kızkalesi at Kumkuyu is the road leading 3km to the ruins of **Kanlıdivane** (admission ₺5; ☺ 8am-7pm), the ancient city of Kanytelis.

Central to Kanlıdivane (Bloody Place of Madness) is a 60m-deep chasm where criminals were tossed to wild animals. Peering down, you'll see reliefs on the cliff walls of a six-member family (southwest) and a Roman soldier (northwest). Ruins ring the pit, including four **Byzantine churches** and a **necropolis** to the northeast with a 2nd-century **temple tomb**.

EASTERN MEDITERRANEAN AROUND KIZKALESI

1. Hittite pottery, Karatepe (p404) 2. Alahan Monastery (p394) 3. Mosaic, Anemurium Ancient City (p388)

Antiquities of the Eastern Med

Want to explore rugged crumbling ruins without the crowds? The eastern Mediterranean is chock-a-block full of vast archaeological sites, important early Christian sites and craggy clifftop castles that are all the more fun to explore because of their half-forgotten ambience.

Anemurium Ancient City

This swath of rickety ruins tumbles down the cliffside to the beach. Soak up the heady atmosphere of long-lost grandeur while surveying the city from high on the citadel walls, or clambering through the once lavish Roman baths.

Caves of Heaven & Hell

The underworld has come a-calling. Stand over Hell's abyss and inside the wide, yawning mouth of Heaven and check visiting the abode of gods off your list.

Yılankale

If you only see one castle in the eastern Mediterranean, pick this wondrous pile of ramparts and towers clinging onto a hilltop south of Adana. It's a sweat-inducing scramble to get up to the highest tower, but the views are worth it.

Karatepe

Giant slabs of inscribed reliefs guarded by glaring-eye sphinxes and lions are all that are left of the 8th-century-BC Hittite town of Azatiwataya.

Uzuncaburç

Roman and Hellenistic ruins, including the columns of the Temple of Zeus Olbius, are found in this village in the Mediterranean hinterland.

THE BEST CHRISTIAN SITES

➡ Church of St Peter (p406)
➡ Tarsus (p399)
➡ Alahan Monastery (p394)
➡ Church of St Thekla (p392)

Mersin (İçel)

☑ 0324 / POP 898,813

Mersin was earmarked a half-century ago as the seaside outlet for Adana and its rich agricultural hinterland. Today it is the largest port in Turkey, and for the most part a sprawling, workaday place that most travellers don't explore. But Mersin, with an official new name of İçel (also the name of the province of which it is capital), does have some attractions, despite the neglect: museums and food are but two of them. If you scrunch up your eyes, some of the streets near the sea almost have a Marseilles feel to them, and there are definitely worse ways to while away an afternoon than a lazy seafood lunch on the excursion boats lining the harbour.

◉ Sights

Mersin Museum　　　　　　　　　　MUSEUM
(Atatürk Caddesi Kültür Merkezi; ⊙ 8am-noon & 1-4.45pm) **FREE** Mersin's archaeology museum has finds from nearby tumuli (burial mounds) and sites (including Elaiussa-Sebaste near Kızkalesi), a great statue of Dionysus and curious odds and ends, such as a Roman-era glass theatre 'token', Hellenistic figurines and Hittite artefacts around 3500 years old.

Greek Orthodox Church　　　　　　CHURCH
(Atatürk Caddesi Kültür Merkezi; ⊙ divine liturgy 9-11.15am Sun) Next to Mersin Museum, this walled 1852 church is still in use and has a lovely iconostasis. To gain entry go to the left side of the church facing 4302 Sokak and ring the bell.

Atatürk Evi　　　　　　　　　　　MUSEUM
(Atatürk House; Atatürk Caddesi 36; ⊙ 8am-5pm Tue-Sun) **FREE** Along the pedestrianised section of Atatürk Caddesi is a museum in a beautiful seven-room villa where Atatürk once stayed. It's full of photographs, clothes and other artefacts from his life, and has a pleasant garden.

🛌 Sleeping

Budget and midrange hotels huddle around the otogar.

Tahtalı Hotel　　　　　　　　　　HOTEL $
(☑ 0324-238 8853; www.hoteltahtali.com; Mersinli Ahmet Caddesi 21; s/d ₺50/100; ❈ 🛜) Despite its less-than-pretty bus-station location – it's right across the road from Mersin's otogar –

the Tahtalı is a decent budget sleep. The rooms are nothing to write home about, but it's clean, safe and friendly. The train station is close, too.

Nobel Oteli　　　　　　　BUSINESS HOTEL $$
(☑ 0324-237 2210; www.nobeloteli.com; İstiklal Caddesi 73; s/d ₺130/180; ❈ 🛜) Behind the big, brash and very yellow exterior, the Nobel is a smart choice in the heart of the city, with 74 big, comfortable rooms that come with some deft design touches and satellite TV. The foyer is a hive of business activity, and the adjoining restaurant is popular at lunch.

🍴 Eating & Drinking

Mersin's local speciality is *tantuni* kebap – chopped beef sautéed with onions, garlic and peppers, wrapped in pitta-like *lavaş ekmek*. To be honest, *tantuni*, often accompanied by *şalgam suyu*, a crimson-coloured juice made by boiling turnips and adding vinegar, is not the highest point of Turkish gastronomy.

For something sweet try *cezerye*, a semigelatinous confection made from carrots and packed with walnuts. For a cheap seafood fix, try the floating fish restaurants around the harbour. Fish sandwiches (*balik ekmek*) can be had for around ₺6.

Hacıbaba　　　　　　　　　　　TURKISH $$
(☑ 0324-238 0023; İstiklal Caddesi 82; mains ₺15-22; ⊙ 24hr; 🍴) Claiming that it never closes, the very popular Hacıbaba does excellent *zeytinyağli biber dolması* (stuffed peppers) and other homestyle Turkish dishes. There are also kebaps and pide, if you'd prefer.

Erden　　　　　　　　　　　　SEAFOOD $$
(☑ 0324-237 6314; 4701 Sokak 10b; mains ₺18-25; ⊙ 11am-midnight) There's a row of fish restaurants between Silifke Caddesi and Atatürk Caddesi, in the centre of town. Erden seems to be the best of them.

ⓘ Information

Tourist Office (☑ 0324-238 3271; İsmet İnönü Bulvarı; ⊙ 8am-noon & 1-5pm Mon-Fri) Near the harbour at the eastern end of town.

ⓘ Getting There & Away

BUS

Mersin's otogar is on the city's eastern outskirts. To get to the centre, leave by the main exit, turn right and walk up to the main road

(Gazi Mustafa Kemal Bulvarı). Cross to the far side and catch a city bus travelling west (₺2). Buses from the otogar leave from outside the train station, as well as from a stop opposite the Mersin Oteli.

From the otogar, frequent buses run to Adana (₺15, one hour, 75km), Silifke (₺25, two hours, 85km, three an hour) via Kızkalesi (₺10, one hour), and Alanya (₺55, 8½ hours, 375km). There are also dolmuşes every 30 minutes to Tarsus (₺5).

TRAIN
There are frequent rail services to Tarsus (₺4, 20 minutes) and Adana (₺5, 45 minutes) between 6am and 10.30pm.

Tarsus

📞 0324 / POP 252,649

Should Tarsus' most famous son, St Paul, return two millennia after his birth, he would hardly recognise the place through the sprawl of concrete apartment blocks. For pilgrims and history buffs, the scattering of early Christian sites here is reason enough to linger, but stroll through the historic city core, with its twisting narrow lanes rimmed by houses slouching in various states of dilapidation, and you'll really find this town's timeless appeal.

◉ Sights

Old City　　　　HISTORIC SITE

(Antik Şehir) The compact Old City lies between Adana Bulvarı and Hal Caddesi. It includes a wonderful 60m-long stretch of **Roman road** and a labyrinth of alleyways hemmed by **historical Tarsus houses**, many crumbling, but one now housing the Konak Efsus boutique hotel.

Just southeast are several historic mosques, including the **Eski Cami** (Old Mosque), a medieval structure that was originally a church dedicated to St Paul. Adjacent looms the barely recognisable brickwork of a huge old **Roman bath**.

Across Atatürk Caddesi is the late-19th-century **Makam Camii** (Official Mosque), and to the east is believed to be the tomb of the Prophet Daniel. To the west is the 16th-century **Ulu Cami** (Great Mosque), sporting a curious 19th-century minaret moonlighting as a clock tower. Next door is the 19th-century **Kırkkaşık Bedesten** (Forty Spoons Market), still used as a covered bazaar.

A PLACE OF PILGRIMAGE
Jewish by birth, Paul (born Saul) was one of early Christianity's most zealous proselytisers and during his lifetime converted hundreds of pagans and Jews to the new religion throughout the ancient world. After his death in Rome about AD 67, the location of his birthplace became sacred to his followers. Today pilgrims still flock to the site of his ruined house in Tarsus to take a drink from the 30m-deep well on the grounds.

St Paul's Well　　　　HISTORIC SITE

(St Paul Kuyusu; Hal Caddesi; admission ₺5; ⊘8am-7pm) Just on the edge of the Old City (signs point the way from Atatürk Bulvarı) are the ruins of St Paul's house and supposed birthplace, which can be viewed underneath sheets of plexiglass. The well stands just beyond the traces of the house.

Church of St Paul　　　　CHURCH

(St Paul Kilisesi; Abdı İpekçi Caddesi; ⊘8am-8pm) FREE South of the Old City, this Orthodox church was originally built in the 1850s to commemorate St Paul. It was utilised as a storage depot (among other uses) up until the mid-1990s, when the Ministry of Culture began a restoration. It was opened up for services again in 2011. There are simple frescoes on the interior ceiling.

Cleopatra's Gate　　　　GATE

Walk 1km southwest of the Old City along İsmetpaşa Bulvarı to get to the Roman Kancık Kapısı, literally the 'Gate of the Bitch', but better known as Cleopatra's Gate. Despite the name it has nothing to do with the Egyptian queen, although she is thought to have had a rendezvous with Mark Antony here in 41 BC.

Tarsus Museum　　　　MUSEUM

(Muvaffak Uygur Caddesi 75; ⊘8am-5pm) FREE About 750m southwest of the Old City, this museum showcases a small but interesting trove of ancient statuary, coins and other artefacts dating back to the Hellenistic period and beyond.

🛏 Sleeping & Eating

★**Konak Efsus**　　　　BOUTIQUE HOTEL $$

(📞0324-614 0807; www.konakefsus.com; Tarihi Evler Sokak 31-33; s/d €40/60; ❄🔊) Tarsus' best accommodation is this delightful boutique hotel converted from a traditional Ottoman house. The eight rooms, with stone walls, antique furniture and 21st-century plumbing, are all unique and bear different names. The Cleopatra Suite is especially fine, as is the lovely patio. It's very popular, especially at weekends, so booking ahead is recommended. The courtyard restaurant is also great.

Cafe Maça
CAFE $

(Tarihi Evler Sokak; mantı ₺7, cakes ₺4-7; ⊙9am-11pm) We're big fans of this funky cafe snuggled inside a creaky 200-year-old house just up the road from the Konak Efsus hotel. Run by a superfriendly, arty couple, this is a top spot for delicious homemade *mantı* (Turkish ravioli) as well as a good coffee and cake stop.

⊕ Getting There & Away

Tarsus' otogar is 3km east of the centre. A taxi is ₺10 and a city bus is ₺1.50. Frequent small buses and dolmuşes connect Tarsus with Mersin (₺6, 29km) and Adana (₺6, 42km). They always pick up and drop off passengers from just beside Cleopatra's Gate and also along Adana Bulvarı.

The train station, with regular services to Mersin (₺4) and Adana (₺5), is northwest of the tourist office at the end of Hilmi Seçkin Caddesi.

Adana

📳 0322 / POP 1.66 MILLION

Despite a pedigree stretching to the ancient Hittites and beyond, Adana is an energetic, modern place with just a handful of sights, some pretty good cafes and bars and excellent transport links. Turkey's fourth-largest city makes a good base for exploring the little-visited historic sites and ruins to the southwest, and if you've been travelling lazily along the Med, the urban buzz may be just the city-slicker injection you need.

The city is more or less cut in two by the D400 highway. North of the road (called Turan Cemal Beriker Bulvarı in town and running west to east and over Kennedy Bridge) are leafy and well-heeled districts. South of the trendy high-rise apartments and pavement bars and cafes, things get more cluttered and housing starts to sprawl. The Seyhan River delimits the city centre to the east.

⊙ Sights & Activities

Unfortunately, Adana's two excellent museums, the **Archaeology Museum** (Fuzuli Caddesi 10) and **Ethnography Museum** (Ziyapaşa Bulvarı 143), are closed pending the relocation of their collections to the New Adana Museum. Planned to occupy nearly 70 acres on the site of a former textile factory, the new complex will incorporate museums of industry, agriculture, children and the city, alongside archaeology and ethnography. There is no reliable completion date yet; check with the tourist office for updates.

★ Sabancı Merkez Camii
MOSQUE

(Sabancı Central Mosque; Map p401; Turan Cemal Beriker Bulvarı) The most imposing mosque in Adana is the six-minaret Sabancı Merkez Camii, rising gracefully from the left bank of the Seyhan River. The largest mosque between İstanbul and Saudi Arabia, it was built by the late industrial magnate Sakıp Sabancı (1933–2004), a philanthropist and founder of the second-richest family dynasty in Turkey, and is covered top to tail in marble and gold leaf. With a 54m-high central dome, it can accommodate an estimated 28,500 worshippers.

Ulu Cami
MOSQUE

(Great Mosque; Map p401; Kızılay Caddesi) The beautiful 16th-century Ulu Cami is reminiscent of the Mamluk mosques of Cairo, with black-and-white banded marble and elaborate window surrounds. It includes a *medrese* (school) and a *türbe* (mausoleum) housing remains of the Ramazanid Beys. The tiles in the *mihrab* (niche indicating the direction of Mecca) came from Kütahya and İznik.

Roman Bridge
BRIDGE

(Taşköprü; Map p401; Abidin Paşa Caddesi) This Roman-era stone bridge over the Seyhan at the eastern end of Abidin Paşa Caddesi was probably built under Hadrian (r AD 117–138) and repaired in the 6th century. Taşköprü to the Turks, its 300m-long span had 21 arches – seven of which are now underwater – and carried vehicles up until 2007.

Yağ Camii
MOSQUE

(Oil Mosque; Map p401; Ali Münif Caddesi) The Yağ Camii (1501), with its imposing portal and typical Seljuk-style architecture, started life as the Church of St Jacques.

St Paul's Catholic Church
CHURCH

(Bebekli Kilise; Map p401; 10 Sokak) Built in 1870 by the Armenian community, this

Adana

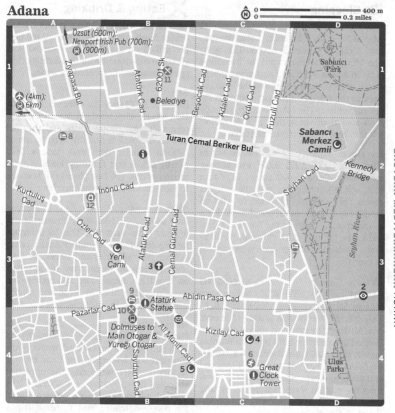

Adana

◎ Top Sights
1 Sabancı Merkez Camii D2

◎ Sights
2 Roman Bridge D3
3 St Paul's Catholic Church.................... B3
4 Ulu Cami.. C4
5 Yağ Camii B4

✦ Activities, Courses & Tours
6 Çarşi Hamamı...................................... C4
Mestan Hamamı............................(see 10)

⊜ Sleeping
7 Hotel Bosnalı.......................................D3
8 Ibis Hotel.. A2
9 Otel Mercan...B3

✗ Eating
10 Öz Asmaaltı.. B4
11 Şen B1

⊜ Shopping
12 Tourist Office & Craft Shop A2

church is still in service today as a Roman Catholic place of worship.

Mestan Hamamı　　　　　　　HAMAM
(Merry Hamam; Map p401; Pazarlar Caddesi 3; soak & scrub ₺15; ⊘6am-11pm) The Mestan Hamamı, right in the centre of town, is a great place to experience a soak and scrub.

Çarşi Hamamı　　　　　　　HAMAM
(Market Hamam; Map p401; Ali Münif Caddesi 145; ⊘men 5-9am & 3.30-10.30pm, women 9am-3.30pm) This atmospheric local hamam is a good place to enjoy a traditional Turkish bath.

🛏 Sleeping

Otel Mercan   HOTEL **$$**
(Map p401; ☑0322-351 2603; www.otelmercan.
com; Küçüksaat Meydanı 5; s/d ₺80/130; ❈🖸)
The Mercan wins our award for friendliest
hotel in Adana. Both staff and management
go out of their way to help, and the location,
right in the middle of the city centre, is su-
per convenient. The lobby is more recently
renovated than the rather prosaic rooms,
but they're still perfectly comfortable.

Ibis Hotel   BUSINESS HOTEL **$$**
(Map p401; ☑0322-355 9500; www.ibishotel.
com; Turhan Cemal Beriker Bulvari 49; r from
₺115; 🌐❈🖸) In true Ibis style, the compact
rooms here are chic and modern with all
mod cons, and we also applaud its decision
to incorporate nonsmoking floors. It's central to the buzzing CBD, although the location – on the main highway – won't appeal
to everyone.

★**Hotel Bosnalı**   BOUTIQUE HOTEL **$$$**
(Map p401; ☑0322-359 8000; www.hotelbos
nali.com; Seyhan Caddesi 29; s/d €99/130; ❈🖸)
This splurge-worthy treat is one of the east-
ern Mediterranean's best places to stay.
Housed in a mansion built by a rich Bosnian
immigrant in 1889, the 'Bosnian' is all stone-
tile floors, hand-carved wooden ceilings and
antique Ottoman furnishings. The city views
from the rooftop restaurant are lovely, and
the staff are uniformly friendly and profes-
sional. Top stuff.

🍴 Eating & Drinking

Famous worldwide is Adana kebap: minced
beef or lamb mixed with powdered red pep-
per grilled on a skewer. It is served with
sliced onions dusted with the slightly acidic
spice sumac and barbecued tomatoes.

Şen   TURKISH **$**
(Map p401; 62001 Sokak 16a; mains ₺15-18; ⏲11am-
11pm; ☑) Heading north on Atatürk Caddesi,
turn right into 62002 Sokak and then left
into 62001 Sokak to find this neighbourhood
lokanta popular with desk jockeys from
nearby offices and featuring loads of vege-
tarian options. The best place to sit is on the
terrace shaded by a spreading arbour.

★**Öz Asmaaltı**   KEBAP **$$**
(Map p401; ☑0322-351 4028; Pazarlar Caddesi
9; Adana kebap meals ₺20) This local favourite may look like just another Adana *kebap
salonu*, but the mains and mezes are a cut
above. This is *the* place to try Adana kebap,
and you'll get mezes, salad and perhaps *kadayıf* (dough soaked in syrup and topped
with clotted cream) with your meal.

Newport Irish Pub   IRISH PUB
(Şinasi Efendi Caddesi 23; ⏲8am-1am; 🖸) An
Irish pub in name (and some decor) only, the
Newport is a pleasant option for an evening
restorative after wandering the upmarket
shopping streets north of Atatürk Parkı. The
open-plan layout and corner siting are good
for people-watching, and there's a happy
'hour' between 3pm and 6pm every day.

SERVICES FROM ADANA'S OTOGAR

DESTINATION	FARE (₺)	DURATION (HR)	DISTANCE (KM)	FREQUENCY (PER DAY)
Adıyaman (for Nemrut Dağı)	35	6	335	frequent
Alanya	55	10	440	frequent
Ankara	55	8	475	hourly
Antakya	20	3½	190	hourly
Antalya	67	11½	565	frequent
Diyarbakır	45	8	535	frequent
Gaziantep	25	3	220	hourly
İstanbul	75	14	920	frequent
Kayseri	40	5½	355	frequent
Konya	40	5	335	frequent
Şanlıurfa	35	5½	360	frequent
Silifke	30	2½	165	frequent
Van	70	14	910	up to 8

Shopping

★ **Tourist Office & Craft Shop** GIFTS & SOUVENIRS
(Map p401; ☑ 0322-359 5070; İnönü Caddesi 71; ◷ 8.30am-5.30pm Mon-Sat) Adana's new tourist office has an adjoining, government-controlled shop selling handicrafts, jewellery, ceramics, musical instruments and more. Made in the surrounding villages, there are many stunning examples of dwindling skills: the finely painted ceramics are particularly beautiful, and very reasonably priced.

ⓘ Information

Tourist Office (Map p401; ☑ 0322-363 1448; Atatürk Caddesi 7; ◷ 8.30am-5.30pm Mon-Sat)

ⓘ Getting There & Away

Adana's airport (Şakirpaşa Havaalanı) is 4km west of the centre on the D400. The otogar is 2km further west on the north side of the D400. The train station is at the northern end of Ziyapaşa Bulvarı, 1.5km north of İnönü Caddesi.

BUS & DOLMUŞ

Adana's large otogar has direct bus and/or dolmuş services to just about everywhere in Turkey. Note that dolmuşes to Kadirli (₺15, two hours, 108km) and Kozan (₺10, one hour, 72km) leave from the Yüreği otogar, on the right bank of the Seyhan River.

TRAIN

The *Çukurova Ekspresi* sleeper train links the ornate *gar* (station) at the northern end of Ziyapaşa Bulvarı with Ankara (7.30pm, ₺35, 12 hours). Both the *Toros Ekspresi* (7am, ₺25, 6½ hours) and the *İçanadolu Mavi* (3.45pm, ₺25, 6½ hours) head to Konya daily. There are trains almost twice an hour between 6am and 11.15pm to Mersin (₺5) via Tarsus (₺4).

ⓘ Getting Around

A taxi from the airport into town costs ₺20, and from the otogar into town it's about ₺25. A taxi from the city centre to the Yüreği otogar will cost ₺7.50.

Around Adana

Adana is the natural base for forays to some of the Eastern Med's most fascinating ancient sites. Inland from the Bay of İskenderun (İskenderun Körfezi) are the little-visited remains of castles and settlements connected with the Armenian kingdom of Cilicia, including its capital, Sis, at Kozan. Some, such as Anazarbus, date back to Roman times or earlier.

WORTH A TRIP

YILANKALE

Built in the mid-13th century, when this area was part of the Armenian kingdom of Cilicia, Yılankale (Snake Castle) took its name from a serpent once entwined in the coat of arms above the entrance. From the car park there's a well-laid path for 100m then a rough trail. Reaching the castle's highest point requires a steep climb over the rocks, past gatehouse, cisterns and vaulted chambers. Standing high above the wheat fields, though, you'll feel on top of the world.

Yılankale is 38km east of Adana and just over 3km south of the D400 highway.

Kozan

This large market town and district seat, 72km northeast of Adana, was once Sis, the capital of the kingdom of Cilicia and the linchpin of a cavalcade of castles overlooking the expansive (and hard-to-defend) Çukurova plain. Towering above the plain is stunning **Kozan Castle** (Kozan Kalesi) FREE, built by Leo II (r 1187–1219), stretching some 900m along a narrow ridge.

Along the 1km-long road to the castle are the ruins of a church, locally called the *manastır* (monastery). From 1293 until 1921 this was the seat of the Katholikos (Patriarchate) of Sis, one of the two senior patriarchs of the Armenian Church.

Inside the castle is a mess of ruined buildings, overgrown with weeds, but continue up to the many-towered keep on the right. On the left is a massive tower, which once held the royal apartments. In all there are 44 towers and lookouts and the remains of a *bedesten* (covered market).

Kozan has some lovely old houses and makes a good day trip by minibus along the D815 from Adana.

Quirky **Yaver'in Konaği** (Yaver's Mansion; ☑ 0322-515 0999; Manastır Sokak 5; s/d ₺80/100; ❄@🛜) inn is at the bottom of the ascent to the castle. It is housed in an old mansion dating from 1890 and features rustic but comfortable rooms over three storeys in the original building, with two newer outbuildings as well. There's a good restaurant here, serving superb *lahmacun* baked in an open-air stone oven.

Only a few buses per day run to Kozan from Adana (₺18, 1¼ hours).

Anazarbus

When the Romans moved into this area in 19 BC, when there was already an Assyrian settlement, they built this fortress city on top of a hill dominating the fertile plain and called it Caesarea ad Anazarbus. Later, when Cilicia was divided in two, Tarsus remained the capital of the west and Anazarbus the main seat in the east. It changed hands at least 10 times over the centuries, falling to the Persians, Arabs, Byzantines, the Hamdanid princes of Aleppo, the Crusaders, a local Armenian king, the Byzantines again, the Turks and the Mamluks. When that last group finally swept away the Armenian kingdom of Cilicia in 1375, the city was abandoned.

Some 5km after leaving the highway, you reach a T-junction and a large gateway set in the city walls; beyond this was the fortress city, now just fields strewn with ancient stones. Turn right and you'll soon reach the house of the *bekçi* (watchman); look for the blue gate. His own property contains Roman sarcophagi (one with the face of the 3rd-century emperor Septimius Severus) and pools with glorious mosaics of Titus and dolphins, fish and seabirds. A guided walk (be generous) will showcase the stadium, theatre and baths. Make sure you see the dedication stone of the ruined 6th-century Church of the Apostles in the field, with a carved cross and the alpha and omega symbols, the very rare Roman vaulted stables south of the castle, and the main aqueduct, with several arches still standing.

The hilltop castle looms above the ruins and village. If you are hiking to the castle (up 400 steps), make sure to wear good walking shoes. The furthest portion of the extensive fortress remnants that trail across the ridge are extremely precarious and shouldn't be entered; at least one traveller has died in recent years trying to climb through to the castle's outermost keep.

ⓘ Getting There & Away

If driving from Yılankale, return to the D400 highway and take the D817 (Kozan/Kadirli) north for 27km to the village of Ayşehoca, where a road on the right is marked for Anavarza/Anazarbus, 5km to the east. If you're in a dolmuş or minibus you can get out here and hitch a ride. From Kozan follow the D817 south for 28km and turn left at Ayşehoca.

Karatepe-Aslantaş Open-Air Museum

Archaeology buffs should make a beeline for the Karatepe-Aslantaş Open-Air Museum (Karatepe-Aslantaş Acık Hava Müzesi; admission ₺5; ☉10am-7pm), within the national park of the same name. The ruins date from the 8th century BC, when this was an important town for the late-Hittite kings of Cilicia, the greatest of whom was named Azitawatas. Today the remains on display consist of statuary, stone reliefs and inscribed tablets –

ARMENIAN KINGDOM OF CILICIA

During the early 11th century, the Seljuk Turks swept westwards from Iran, wresting control of much of Anatolia from a weakened Byzantium and pushing into the Armenian highlands. Thousands of Armenians fled south, taking refuge in the rugged Taurus Mountains and along the Mediterranean coast, where in 1080 they founded the kingdom of Cilicia (or Lesser Armenia) under the young Prince Reuben.

While Greater Armenia struggled against foreign invaders and the subsequent loss of its statehood, the Cilician Armenians lived in wealth and prosperity. Geographically, they were in the ideal place for trade and they quickly embraced European ideas, including its feudal class structure. Cilicia became a country of barons, knights and serfs, with the court at Sis (today's Kozan) even adopting Western-style clothing. Latin and French became the national languages. During the Crusades the Christian armies used the kingdom's castles as safe havens on their way to the Holy Land.

This period of Armenian history is regarded as the most exciting for science and culture, as schools and monasteries flourished, teaching theology, philosophy, medicine and mathematics. It was also the golden age of Armenian ecclesiastical manuscript painting, noted for its lavish decoration and Western influences.

The Cilician kingdom thrived for nearly 300 years before it fell to the Mamluks of Egypt. The last Armenian ruler, Leo V, spent his final years wandering Europe trying to raise support to recapture his kingdom before dying in Paris in 1393.

some of which have played a critical role in helping archaeologists decipher the hieroglyphic Luwian language.

Karatepe's small but excellent **museum**, beside the entrance gate, displays items unearthed by excavations here and has plenty of information panels explaining the site's significance. There is also a scale model of the site, which helps put everything into perspective.

The first group of Karatepe's statuary is displayed at the **Palace Gate**, with views across the forested hilltop overlooking Lake Ceyhan (Ceyhan Gölü), an artificial lake used for hydroelectric power and recreation. From here, traces of the 1km-long walls that defended the town are still evident. Under the protective shelter are statue representations of lions and sphinxes and rows of fine stone reliefs, including one showing a relaxed feast at Azitawatas' court, complete with sacrificial bull, musicians and chariots.

The northeast **Lower Gate** is home to Karatepe's best stone carvings, including reliefs of a galley with oarsmen, warriors doing battle with lions, a woman suckling a child under a tree, and the Hittite sun god. The sphinx statues guarding the reliefs are extremely well preserved.

Antakya (Hatay) & Around

At the time of writing, government advisories including the British Foreign and Commonwealth Office advised against all but essential travel to Antakya (Hatay), İskenderun and the surrounding areas. They further advised against all travel to within 10 km of the border with Syria. We visited Antakya on our last trip to the region, but travellers are advised to check out the situation on the ground before coming to this area.

Antakya (Hatay)

📞 0326 / POP 218,568

Built on the site of ancient Antiocheia ad Orontem, Antakya, officially known as Hatay, is a prosperous and modern city near the Syrian border. Under the Romans, Antioch's important Christian community developed out of the already large Jewish population that was at one time led by St Paul. Today Antakya is home to a mixture of faiths – Sunni, Alevi and Orthodox Christian – and has a cosmopolitan and civilised air. Locals call their hometown Barış Şehri (City of Peace),

and that's just what it is. In the ecumenical city of Antakya you'll find at least five different religions and sects represented within a couple of blocks of one another.

The Arab influence permeates local life, food and language; indeed, the city only became part of Turkey in 1939 after centuries conjoined in some form or another to Syria. Most visitors come to Antakya for its archaeology museum or as pilgrims to the Church of St Peter. Be sure to take time to stroll along the Orontes (Asi) River and through the bazaars and back lanes of a city we rate as an underrated jewel of the Turkish Mediterranean.

⊙ Sights

★**Hatay Archaeology Museum**   MUSEUM
(Hatay Arkeoloji Müzesi; 📞0326-225 1060; www.hatayarkeolojimuzesi.gov.tr; Atatürk Caddesi 64; admission ₺8; ⊙9am-6.30pm Tue-Sun, 8am-4.30pm in winter) This museum contains one of the world's finest collections of Roman and Byzantine mosaics, covering a period from the 1st century AD to the 5th century. Many were recovered almost intact from Tarsus or Harbiye (Daphne in ancient times), 9km to the south.

At the time of writing, the museum was in the final stages of a long-awaited move to purpose-built premises on the main road to Reyhanlı, about 1km past the Church of St Peter.

The new museum is set to provide a brilliant modern canvas on which to display the dazzling collection, much of which has never been put on show before, due to a lack of room at the old museum.

Among the museum's highlight pieces are the full-body mosaic of **Oceanus & Thetis** (2nd century) and the **Buffet Mosaic** (3rd century), with its depictions of dishes of chicken, fish and eggs. **Thalassa & the Nude Fishermen** shows children riding whales and dolphins, while the fabulous 3rd-century mosaics of **Narcissus** and **Orpheus** depict stories from mythology. Other mosaics in the collection have quirkier subjects: three of the museum's most famous are the happy hunchback with an oversized phallus; the black fisherman; and the mysterious portrayal of a raven, a scorpion, a dog and a pitchfork attacking an 'evil eye'.

As well as the mosaics, the museum also showcases artefacts recovered from various mounds and tumuli in the area, including a Hittite mound near Dörtyol, 16km north of

İskenderun. Taking pride of place in the collection is the so-called **Antakya Sarcophagus** (Antakya Lahdı), an impossibly ornate tomb with an unfinished reclining figure on the lid.

Church of St Peter   CHURCH
(St Pierre Kilisesi; admission ₺15; ◷ 9am-noon & 1-6pm) This early Christian church cut into the slopes of Mt Staurin (Mountain of the Cross) is thought to be the earliest place where the newly converted met and prayed secretly. Both Peter and Paul lived in Antioch for a few years and they almost certainly preached here. Tradition has it that this cave was the property of St Luke the Evangelist, who was born in Antioch, and that he donated it to the burgeoning Christian congregation.

When the First Crusaders took Antioch in 1098, they constructed the wall at the front and the narthex, the narrow vestibule along the west side of the church. To the right of the altar faint traces of an early fresco can be seen, and some of the simple mosaic floor survives. The water dripping in the corner is said to cure disease.

Just 2.5km northeast of town, the church is accessible on foot in about half an hour along Kurtuluş Caddesi.

Old Town   HISTORIC SITE
(Map p407) The squiggle of lanes between Kurtuluş Caddesi and Hurriyet Caddesi is an atmospheric huddle of Antakya's remaining old houses, with carved lintels, wooden overhangs and courtyards within the compounds. Slightly north, around the 7th-century **Habibi Neccar Camii** (Map p407; Kurtuluş Caddesi), you'll find more preserved examples of Antakya architecture. The priests at the Catholic church believe St Peter would have lived in this area between AD 42 and 48, as it was then the Jewish neighbourhood.

Orthodox Church   CHURCH
(Map p407; Hürriyet Caddesi 53; ◷ divine liturgy 8.30am & 6pm) Most of the city's 1200-strong Christian population worships at the fine Orthodox church. Rebuilt with Russian assistance after a devastating earthquake in 1900, the church is fronted by a lovely courtyard up some steps from the street, and contains some beautiful icons, an ancient stone lectern and valuable church plate.

Roman Catholic Church   CHURCH
(Map p407; Prof Atman Sokak; ◷ 10am-noon & 3-5pm, mass 8.30am daily & 6pm Sun) The Italian-ministered Roman Catholic Church was built in 1852 and occupies two houses in the city's old quarter, with the chapel in the former living room of one house.

Sermaye Camii   MOSQUE
(Capital Mosque; Map p407; Kurtuluş Caddesi 56) The Sermaye Camii has a wonderfully ornate şerefe (balcony) on its minaret (you'll see it on posters of Antakya).

Bazaar   BAZAAR
(Map p407) A sprawling market fills the back streets north of Kemal Paşa Caddesi. The easier way to see it is to follow Uzunçarşı Caddesi, the main shopping street.

🛏 Sleeping

Antakya Catholic Church Guesthouse   GUESTHOUSE $
(Map p407; ☎ 0326-215 6703; www.anadoluka tolikkilisesi.org/antakya; Prof Atman Sokak; per person ₺40; ❄) A positively delightful place to stay (if you can get in), this guesthouse run by the local Catholic church has nine tidy double rooms wrapped around a leafy (and suitably reflective) courtyard. Guests are invited (though not required) to attend daily Mass in the church opposite.

Mozaik Otel   HOTEL $$
(Map p407; ☎ 0326-215 5020; www.mozaikotel. com; İstiklal Caddesi 18; s/d ₺85/150; ❄🛜) The rooms at this midrange choice are surprisingly peaceful, despite its great central position near the bazaar. Service lets the side down slightly, being rather haphazard, but the 24 rooms are decorated with folksy bedspreads and mosaic reproductions, and the excellent Hatay Sultan Sofrası (p408) restaurant is just next door.

Antik Beyazıt Hotel   BOUTIQUE HOTEL $$
(Map p407; ☎ 0326-216 2900; www.antikbeyazit oteli.com; Hükümet Caddesi 4; s/d/tr ₺110/150/ 200; ❄🛜) Housed in a pretty French Levantine colonial house (1903), Antakya's first boutique hotel is looking a bit frayed, though it's as friendly as ever and the antique furnishings, oriental carpets and ornate chandelier in the lobby still evoke a more elegant past. The 27 rooms are fairly basic; the ones on the 1st floor have the most character.

★ Liwan Hotel   BOUTIQUE HOTEL $$$
(Map p407; ☎ 0326-215 7777; www.theliwanhotel. com; Silahlı Kuvvetler Caddesi 5; s/d ₺150/220; ❄🛜) This 1920s eclectic building was once

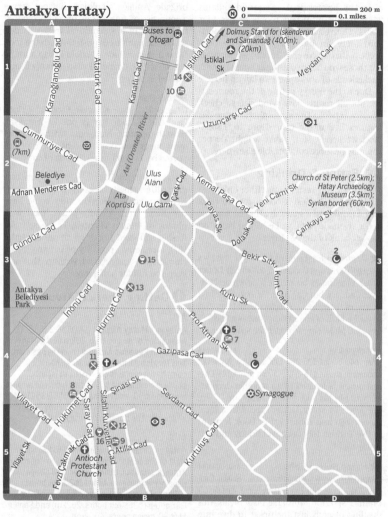

Antakya (Hatay)

0 — 200 m
0 — 0.1 miles

Antakya (Hatay)

◎ Sights
1 Bazaar	D2
2 Habibi Neccar Camii	D3
3 Old Town	B5
4 Orthodox Church	B4
5 Roman Catholic Church	C4
6 Sermaye Camii	C4

⌂ Sleeping
7 Antakya Catholic Church Guesthouse	C4
8 Antik Beyazıt Hotel	A4
9 Liwan Hotel	B5
10 Mozaik Otel	B1

✕ Eating
11 Anadolu Restaurant	A4
12 Antakya Evi	B5
13 Çağlayan Restaurant	B3
14 Hatay Sultan Sofrası	B1

◉ Drinking & Nightlife
15 Antakya Vitamin Bar	B3
16 Barudi Bar	B5

owned by the president of Syria and contains 24 tastefully furnished rooms across four floors. The restaurant is in an open courtyard (once an internal garden with ogee arches) that is covered in chillier months. For those who adore old-timer hotels, there's bucketloads of atmosphere to lap up here.

Due to the quirky nature of the room set-up, not all rooms have windows, so check when you book. The atmospheric stone bar features live music from 11pm to 2.30am most weekends, so if you're a light sleeper you may be more comfortable elsewhere.

✕ Eating & Drinking

There are many restaurants either on or just off Hürriyet Caddesi. Good places to relax over a drink and a snack are the tea gardens in the riverside Antakya Belediyesi Parkı, on the left bank of the Asi River.

★ Çağlayan Restaurant   KEBAP $
(Map p407; Hürriyet Caddesi 17; dürüm ₺8) Döner kebap places may be a dime a dozen on Hürriyet Caddesi, but Çağlayan's *dürüm* are in a league of their own – spectacularly tasty and so packed full of goodies that one is a feast all by itself. Make sure to order the spicy sauce.

Antakya Evi   ANATOLIAN $
(Map p407; ☑ 0326-214 1350; Silahlı Kuvvetler Caddesi 3; mains ₺15-20; ☺10am-midnight) This restaurant is located in an old villa decorated with photos and antique furniture. There are loads of spicy Hatay specialities, local mezes (₺9) and robust grills. Look forward to live Turkish folk music on Friday and Saturday night.

★ Hatay Sultan Sofrası   ANATOLIAN $$
(Map p407; www.sultansofrasi.com; İstiklal Caddesi 20a; mains ₺15-25; ☺9am-9pm) Antakya's premier spot for affordable tasty meals, this bustling place is just the ticket to dive into Hatay's fusion of Middle Eastern and Turkish cuisine. The articulate manager loves to guide diners through the menu, and will help you pick from the diverse array of mezes and spicy local kebap options. Leave room to order *künefe* for dessert.

Anadolu Restaurant   TURKISH $$
(Map p407; ☑ 0326-215 3335; www.anadolu restaurant.com; Hürriyet Caddesi 30a; mains ₺20-30; ☺11am-midnight) Popular with families, the local glitterati and the expense-account

brigade, Antakya's culinary hotspot serves a long list of fine mezes on gold-coloured tablecloths in a splendid al fresco garden where the palm trees push through the roof. Meat dishes include Anadolu kebap and the special *kağıt* ('paper' kebap, wrapped and cooked in paper).

Barudi Bar   BAR
(Map p407; Silahlı Kuvvetler Caddesi; ☺1pm-2am) The Barudi Bar is one of Antakya's most happening hang-outs, with its hideaway inner courtyard, decent range of imported beers and impressive list of cocktails.

Antakya Vitamin Bar   JUICE BAR
(Map p407; Hürriyet Caddesi 7; ☺10am-midnight) Need a vitamin injection after some hard travelling? This friendly place, lined with photos of famous clientele, is the spot for freshly squeezed juices or an 'atom shake' (₺7), a regional speciality of banana, pistachio, honey, apricot and yoghurt that will keep you full for half a day.

❶ Getting There & Around

AIR
Antakya's **Hatay Airport** (☑ 0326-235 1300; www.hatay.dhmi.gov.tr) is 20km north of the city. Both **Pegasus Airlines** (www.flypgs.com) and **Turkish Airlines** (www.turkishairlines. com) have regular flights to/from İstanbul starting from about ₺70. A taxi from the airport is around ₺30, and **Havaş** (☑ 0555 985 1101; www.havas.net; per person ₺10) runs a regular airport shuttle bus into central Antakya.

BUS
Antakya's intercity otogar is 7km to the northwest of the centre. Direct buses go to Ankara, Antalya, İstanbul, İzmir, Kayseri and Konya, usually travelling via Adana (₺20, 3½ hours, 190km). There are also frequent services to Gaziantep (₺25, four hours, 262km) and Şanlıurfa (₺30, seven hours, 400km).

Minibuses and dolmuşes for İskenderun (₺6, one hour, 58km) and Samandağ (₺5, 40 minutes, 28km) leave from near the Shell petrol station along Yavuz Sultan Selim Caddesi, at the top of İstiklal Caddesi.

A taxi to/from the centre from the otogar will cost ₺15. Many of the big bus companies run free *serviş* (shuttle bus) transfers into central Antakya. Ask on arrival. Buses 5, 9, 16 and 17 (₺1.50) run from just outside the otogar to the western bank of the Asi (Orontes) River, central to hotels.

Ankara & Central Anatolia

Best Places to Eat

➜ Atış Cafe (p426)

➜ Somatçi (p448)

➜ Sema Hanımın Yeri (p442)

➜ Balıkçıköy (p418)

Best Places to Sleep

➜ Kahveciler Konağı (p426)

➜ Teşup Konak (p436)

➜ Hich Hotel (p447)

➜ Deeps Hostel (p417)

➜ Derviş Otel (p447)

Why Go?

Somewhere between the cracks in the Hittite ruins, the fissures in the Phyrgian burial mounds and the scratches in the Seljuk caravanserais, the mythical, mighty Turks raced across this highland steppe with big ideas and bigger swords. Alexander the Great cut that eponymous knot in Gordian where King Midas displayed his deft golden touch. Julius Caesar came, saw and conquered, and in Konya, the whirling dervishes first spun. This central sweep of Turkey was also where Atatürk forged his secular revolution along dusty Roman roads that all lead to Ankara; an underrated capital city and geopolitical centre. Further north through the nation's fruit bowl, in Safranbolu and Amasya, 'Ottomania' is still in full swing; here wealthy weekenders come to capture a glimmer of a bygone age amid bendy-beamed mansions. Central Anatolia is the meeting point between the fabled past and the present – a sojourn here will enlighten and enchant.

When to Go

Ankara

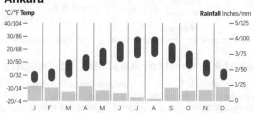

May–Jun Fruit harvest: cherries the size of a baby's fist, apricots sweeter than a baby's face.

Jul–Aug Join summer's crowds of Turkish tourists in the Ottoman towns of Safranbolu and Amasya.

Dec Konya's Mevlâna Festival is a Sufi spectacular of extraordinary human spirit.

Ankara & Central Anatolia Highlights

❶ Safranbolu (p423)
Turning back the clocks among Çarşı's cobblestones and timber-framed houses.

❷ Museum of Anatolian Civilisations (p411) Brushing up on Turkey's roots at the country's premier museum in Ankara.

❸ Konya (p442) Paying homage to Rumi at the Mevlâna Museum then exploring the city's glut of Seljuk and Ottoman architecture.

❹ Hattuşa (p428) Hitting the hills in the heartland of Anatolia's first great empire.

❺ Divriği (p438) Marvelling at doorways of sublime artistry on the Ulu Cami & Darüşşifası in this out-of-the-way town.

❻ Amasya (p433)
Pondering tombs that poke out from cliffs above a rim of restored mansions.

❼ Tokat (p437) Meandering crooked alleys to search out *medreses* (seminaries), mosques and museums.

Ankara

☑ 0312 / POP 4.7 MILLION

Turkey's 'other' city may not have any showy Ottoman palaces or regal facades, but Ankara thrums to a vivacious, youthful beat unmarred by the tug of history. Drawing comparisons with İstanbul is pointless – the flat, modest surroundings are hardly the stuff of national poetry – but the civic success of this dynamic city is assured thanks to student panache and foreign-embassy intrigue.

The country's capital has made remarkable progress from a dusty Anatolian backwater to today's sophisticated arena for international affairs. Turkey's economic success is reflected in the booming restaurant scene around Kavaklıdere and the ripped-jean politik of Kızılay's sidewalk cafes, frequented by hip students, old-timers and businessmen alike. And while the vibrant street life is enough of a reason to visit, Ankara also boasts two extraordinary monuments central to the Turkish story – the beautifully conceived Museum of Anatolian Civilisations and the Anıt Kabir, a colossal tribute to Atatürk, modern Turkey's founder.

History

Although Hittite remains dating back to before 1200 BC have been found in Ankara, the town really prospered as a Phrygian settlement on the north–south and east–west trade routes. Later it was taken by Alexander the Great, claimed by the Seleucids and finally occupied by the Galatians around 250 BC. Augustus Caesar annexed it to Rome as Ankyra.

The Byzantines held the town for centuries, with intermittent raids by the Persians and Arabs. When the Seljuk Turks came to Anatolia, they grabbed the city, but held it with difficulty. Later, the Ottoman sultan Yıldırım Beyazıt was captured near here by Central Asian conqueror Tamerlane and subsequently died in captivity. Spurned as a jinxed endeavour, the city slowly slumped into a backwater, prized for nothing but its goats.

That all changed when Atatürk chose Angora, as the city was known until 1930, to be his base in the struggle for independence. When he set up his provisional government here in 1920, the city was just a small, dusty settlement of some 30,000 people. After his victory in the War of Independence, Atatürk declared it the new Turkish capital, and set about developing it. From 1919 to 1927, Atatürk never set foot in İstanbul, preferring to work at making Ankara top dog.

⊙ Sights

★ **Museum of Anatolian Civilisations**   MUSEUM
(Anadolu Medeniyetleri Müzesi; Map p415; ☑ 0312-324 3160; www.anadolumedeniyetlerimuzesi.gov.tr; Gözcü Sokak 2; ₺20; ⊙ 8.30am-6.45pm; Ⓜ Ulus) The superb Museum of Anatolian Civilisations is the perfect introduction to the complex weave of Turkey's ancient past, with beautifully curated exhibits housing artefacts cherry-picked from just about every significant archaeological site in Anatolia.

ANKARA BOMBINGS

Turkey's capital has found itself hitting international headlines for all the wrong reasons of late. In October 2015 suicide bombers targeted a peace rally, demonstrating against ongoing violence between the Turkish authorities and the PKK (Kurdistan Workers Party) in the country's southeast, which had gathered outside Ankara's train station. The twin explosions, carried out by Isis cell members, left 103 dead and 250 injured.

Then 2016 began badly with Ankara rocked by two more attacks. The first, in February, claimed 28 lives and left 60 injured when a car bomb exploded near a convoy carrying security forces personnel. The second attack, in March, took place right in the heart of the central city; outside a bustling bus transport hub on Atatürk Bulvarı in Kızılay, leaving 37 dead and 125 injured. Both attacks were claimed by Kurdish militant group TAK (Kurdistan Freedom Falcons).

In the aftermath of the bombings, security in the capital has been tightened up considerably. Security forces are a visible presence throughout the city, including at entrance gates to metro lines and at historical sites; bag-scanners are in place at major transport hubs; and checkpoints have been set up at all major road arteries into Ankara to check IDs (if you're arriving by bus, make sure to keep your passport in your hand luggage at all times).

Ankara

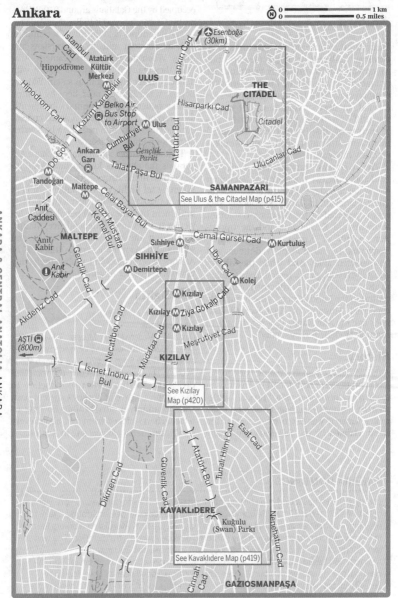

The central hall houses reliefs and statuary, while the surrounding halls take you on a journey of staggering history from Palaeolithic, Neolithic, Chalcolithic, Bronze Age, Assyrian, Hittite, Phrygian, Urartian and Lydian periods. Downstairs is a collection of Roman artefacts unearthed at excavations in and around Ankara.

The exhibits are chronologically arranged starting with the Palaeolithic and Neolithic displays to the right of the entrance, then continue in an anticlockwise direction. Do the full loop before visiting the central hall and then backtrack to see the Roman exhibits downstairs.

Items unearthed from one of the most important Neolithic sites in the world – Çatalhöyük, southeast of Konya – are displayed here including the most famous mother goddess sculptures and the wall mural thought by some experts to be the world's first town map.

Also on show are many finds from the Assyrian trading colony Kültepe, one of the world's oldest and wealthiest bazaars. These include baked-clay tablets found at the site, which dates to the beginning of the 2nd millennium BC.

The hall devoted to Hittite artefacts is where the museum really shines, with fascinating displays of Hattuşa's haul of cuneiform tablets and striking figures of bulls and stags. The Hittites were known for their relief work, and some mighty slabs representing the best pieces found in the country, generally from around Hattuşa, are on display in the museum's central room.

Most of the finds from the Phrygian capital Gordion, including incredible inlaid wooden furniture, are on display in the last hall. The exhibits also include limestone blocks with still-indecipherable inscriptions resembling the Greek alphabet, and lion- and ram-head ritual vessels that show the high quality of Phrygian metalwork.

Urartian artifacts are also on display here. Spurred by rich metal deposits, the Urartians were Anatolia's foremost metalworkers, as the knives, horse-bits, votive plates and shields on display demonstrate. This last hall also contains neo-Hittite artefacts and terracotta figures of gods in human form, some revealing their divine powers by growing scorpion tails.

★ **Anıt Kabir** MONUMENT
(Atatürk Mausoleum & Museum; Map p412; www.anitkabir.org; Gençlik Caddesi; audioguide ₺10; ⊙9am-5pm; Ⓜ Tandoğan) FREE The monumental mausoleum of Mustafa Kemal Atatürk (1881–1938), the founder of modern Turkey, sits high above the city with its abundance of marble and air of veneration. The tomb itself actually makes up only a small part of this fascinating complex, which consists of museums and a ceremonial courtyard. For many Turks a visit is virtually a pilgrimage, and it's not unusual to

see people visibly moved. Allow at least two hours in order to visit the whole site.

The main entrance to the complex is via the Lion Road, a 262m walkway lined with 24 lion statues – Hittite symbols of power used to represent the strength of the Turkish nation. The path leads to a massive courtyard, framed by colonnaded walkways, with steps leading up to the huge tomb on the left.

To the right of the tomb, the extensive museum displays Atatürk memorabilia, personal effects, gifts from famous admirers, and recreations of his childhood home and school. Just as revealing as all the rich artefacts are his simple rowing machine and huge multilingual library, which includes tomes he wrote.

Downstairs, extensive exhibits about the War of Independence and the formation of the republic move from battlefield murals with sound effects to over-detailed explanations of post-1923 reforms. At the end, a gift shop sells Atatürk items of all shapes and sizes.

As you approach the tomb itself, look left and right at the gilded inscriptions, which are quotations from Atatürk's speech celebrating the republic's 10th anniversary in 1932. Remove your hat as you enter, and bend your neck to view the ceiling of the lofty hall, lined in marble and sparingly decorated with 15th- and 16th-century Ottoman mosaics. At the northern end stands an immense marble cenotaph, cut from a single piece of stone weighing 40 tonnes. The actual tomb is in a chamber beneath it.

The memorial straddles a hill in a park about 2km west of Kızılay and 1.2km south of Tandoğan, the closest Ankaray-line metro station to the entrance. A free shuttle regularly zips up and down the hill from the entrance; alternatively, it's a pleasant walk to the mausoleum (about 15 minutes). Note that security checks, including a bag scan, are carried out on entry.

Citadel AREA
(Ankara Kalesi; Map p415; Gözcü Sokak; Ⓜ Ulus) The imposing *hisar* is the most interesting part of Ankara to poke about in. This well-preserved quarter of thick walls and intriguing winding streets took its present shape in the 9th century AD, when the Byzantine emperor Michael II constructed the outer ramparts. The inner walls date from the 7th century.

After you've entered Parmak Kapısı (Finger Gate), the main gate, and passed through a gate to your left, you'll see Alaettin Camii on the left. The citadel mosque dates from the 12th century, but has been extensively rebuilt. To your right a steep road leads to a flight of stairs that leads to the Şark Kulesi (Eastern Tower), with panoramic city views. Although it's much harder to find, a tower to the north, Ak Kale (White Fort), also offers fine views.

Some local families still live inside the citadel walls and the houses here often incorporate broken column drums, bits of marble statuary and inscribed lintels into their walls. For a long time the neighbourhood here was extremely run-down but the past few years have seen the area gentrified somewhat although once you duck off the main route there are still many narrow, ramshackle alleys to explore.

Erimtan Archaeology & Arts Museum   MUSEUM

(Map p415; ☑ 0312-311 0401; www.erimtan museum.org; Gözcü Sokak 10; ₺10; ⊙ 10am-6pm Tue-Sun; M Ulus) Ankara's newest museum houses the astounding collection of mostly Roman (but also Bronze Age, Hittite and Byzantine) artefacts collected over the years by Turkish businessman and archaeology enthusiast Yüksel Erimtan. Exhibits are creatively curated with an eye for storytelling and feature state-of-the-art multimedia displays. There are some fabulously beautiful ceramic and jewellery pieces here as well as a vast coin collection, cuneiform tablets from Kültepe and an ornate Urartian belt.

The cafe downstairs has a tranquil garden setting and serves excellent coffee.

The basement floor hosts temporary exhibitions and also a program of cultural events. Check the website to see what's on while you're in town.

Rahmi M Koç Industrial Museum   MUSEUM

(Map p415; ☑ 0312-309 6800; www.rmk-museum.org.tr; Depo Sokak 1; adult/student ₺8/4; ⊙ 10am-5pm Tue-Fri, to 7pm Sat & Sun; M Ulus) The surprisingly absorbing Rahmi M Koç Industrial Museum, which is located inside the beautifully restored Çengelhan building (which is also home to a posh hotel and restaurant), has three floors covering subjects as diverse as transport, science, music, computing, Atatürk and carpets; some displays have interactive features.

Vakıf Eserleri Müzesi   MUSEUM

(Ankara Museum of Religious Foundation Works; Map p415; Atatürk Bulvarı; ⊙ 9am-5pm Tue-Sun; M Ulus) FREE The tradition of carpets being gifted to mosques has helped preserve many of Turkey's finest specimens. This extensive collection – which once graced the floors of mosques throughout the country – was put on display to the public in 2007. A must for anyone interested in Turkish textiles, the exhibits also include a fascinating Ottoman manuscript collection, tile-work, metalwork and intricately carved wood panels.

Ethnography Museum   MUSEUM

(Etnografya Müzesi; Map p415; Türkocağı Sokak, Samanpazarı; ₺10; ⊙ 8.30am-7pm; M Sıhhiye) The Ethnography Museum is housed inside a white marble post-Ottoman building (1927) that served as Atatürk's mausoleum until 1953. Past the equestrian statue out the front, the mausoleum is preserved in the entrance hall. Around the walls are photographs of Atatürk's funeral.

The ethnography collection here is superb, with displays covering henna ceremonies, Anatolian jewellery, rug-making, Seljuk ceramics, early-15th-century doors, and (opposite the anxious-looking mannequins in the circumcision display) coffee.

Painting and Sculpture Museum   MUSEUM

(Resim ve Heykel Müzesi; Map p415; Türkocağı Sokak, Samanpazarı; ⊙ 9am-6pm Tue-Sun; M Sıhhiye) FREE The Painting and Sculpture Museum showcases the cream of Turkish artists. Ranging from angular war scenes to society portraits, the pieces demonstrate that 19th- and 20th-century artistic developments in Turkey paralleled those in Europe, with increasingly abstract form.

Hacı Bayram Camii   MOSQUE

(Map p415; Hacı Bayram Veli Caddesi; M Ulus) Ankara's most revered mosque is Hacı Bayram Camii. Hacı Bayram Veli was a Muslim 'saint' who founded the Bayramiye dervish order around 1400. Ankara was the order's centre and Hacı Bayram Veli is still revered by pious Muslims. The mosque was built in the 15th century, with tiling added in the 18th century. Surrounding shops sell religious paraphernalia (including wooden toothbrushes as used, supposedly, by the Prophet Mohammed).

Kocatepe Camii   MOSQUE

(Map p420; Bankacı Sokak; M Kızılay) The huge outline of Kocatepe Camii is the symbol

Ulus & the Citadel

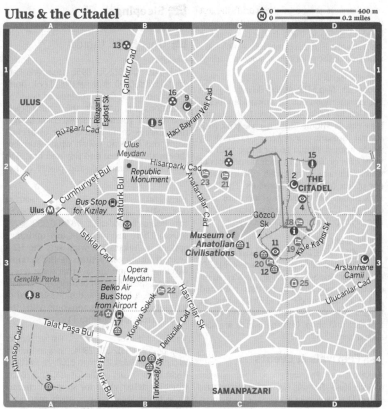

ANKARA & CENTRAL ANATOLIA ANKARA

Ulus & the Citadel

of Ankara. It is one of the world's largest mosques, but it is also very new (it was built between 1967 and 1987). In the basement of the mosque is a supermarket, which says much about the priorities of modern Turkey!

Gençlik Parkı
PARK

(Youth Park; Map p415; Atatürk Bulvarı; 🚻) The biggest afternoon out for Ankara families is the Gençlik Parkı, in the heart of the city. It's a classic Middle Eastern–style park with several pleasant *çay bahçesi* (tea gardens; single women should go for those with the word *aile*, or 'family', in their name), lots of water fountains lit in garish colours, and a few plastic (obviously) dinosaurs. The Luna Park funfair provides amusement for children and, thanks to a few terrifying-looking rides, cheap thrills for teenagers.

Cer Modern
GALLERY

(Map p415; 🖉0312-310 0000; www.cermodern. org; Altınsoy Caddesi 3; adult/student ₺15/10; ⏰10am-8pm Tue-Sun; Ⓜ Sıhhiye) Located in an old train depot, this huge artists' park and gallery exhibits modern and challenging art from across Europe, plus there's an excellent cafe and shop. Cultural events are also staged here.

⭐ Festivals & Events

Ankara Music Festival
MUSIC

(Ankara Müsik Festivalı; www.ankarafestival.com; ⏰Apr) Three weeks of classical performances held in a variety of venues across Ankara.

Ankara Film Festival
FILM

(www.filmfestankara.org.tr/en; ⏰Apr-May) The city's film festival is held over two weeks in spring and hosts a selection of both local and foreign cinema.

🛏 Sleeping

🛏 Ulus & the Citadel

Otel Pınar
HOTEL €

(Map p415; 🖉0312-311 8951; Hisarparkı Caddesi 14; s/d ₺50/90; ❄ 🛜; Ⓜ Ulus) Look, don't expect anything fancy. As long as your expectations are in check, the Pınar's selection of small rooms are an excellent budget find. Rooms come with a dose of peeling paint and have no polish whatsoever but they're all kept neat and tidy and have TVs (no English channels), and plenty of hot water for showers.

Hitit Otel
HOTEL €€

(Map p415; 🖉0312-311 4102; www.otelhitit. com; Hisarparkı Caddesi 12; s/d ₺100/150; ❄ 🛜; Ⓜ Ulus) There are plenty of low midrange options in Ankara but what sets the Hitit apart from its competitors is the genuine welcome here and the fact that some reception staff speak English (a rarity in the city). Rooms are a bit twee and old fashioned in style but all are spotless and come with little seating areas and satellite TV.

And Butik Hotel
HISTORIC HOTEL €€

(Map p415; 🖉0312-310 2304; www.andbutikho tel.com; İstek Sokak 2; r from ₺100; 🛜; Ⓜ Ulus) Right in the heart of the Citadel, this place, which is stellar value for so much character, is housed inside a pleasingly renovated Ottoman-era building. The small rooms exude buckets of traditional flavour, there's a warm welcome from your hosts, and there's a little courtyard garden. The only small niggle is that wi-fi doesn't generally reach the rooms.

ROMAN RUINS
··

Roman Baths (Roma Hamaları; Map p415; Çankırı Caddesi; ₺5; ⏰8.30am-5pm; Ⓜ Ulus) At the sprawling 3rd-century Roman Baths ruins, the layout is still clearly visible; look for the standard Roman *apoditerium* (dressing room), *frigidarium* (cold room), *tepidarium* (warm room) and *caldarium* (hot room). A Byzantine tomb and Phrygian remains have also been found here.

Temple of Augustus & Rome (Map p415; Hacı Bayram Veli Caddesi; ₺5; ⏰8.30am-5pm Tue-Sun; Ⓜ Ulus) Except for a couple of imposing, inscribed walls, not much remains of this temple (AD 25) built to honour the Roman Emperor Augustus.

Column of Julian (Jülyanus Sütunu; Map p415; Çam Sokak; Ⓜ Ulus) Erected in honour of Roman Emperor Julian the Apostate's visit to Ankara, the Column of Julian sits proudly in a square ringed by government buildings, it is usually topped by a stork's nest.

Roman Theatre (Map p415; Hisarparkı Caddesi; Ⓜ Ulus) From Hisarparkı Caddesi, you can view the sparse remains of a Roman theatre from around 200 to 100 BC.

Otel Mithat
HOTEL €€

(Map p415; ☑0312-311 5410; www.otelmithat.com.tr; Tavus Sokak 2; s/d/tr €30/43/54; ☺✳☎; Ⓜ Ulus) With groovy carpeting and sleek neutral bed linen, the Mithat's rooms are fresh and modern. The teensy bathrooms do let the side down somewhat, but this is a minor complaint about what is, overall, an excellent choice. Nonsmokers will be pleased that unlike most Ankara hotels in this price range, the Mithat takes its no-smoking policy seriously.

★Angora House Hotel
HISTORIC HOTEL €€€

(Map p415; ☑0312-309 8380; www.angorahouse.com.tr; Kale Kapısı Sokak 16; s/d/tr €44/60/75; ☺☎; Ⓜ Ulus) Be utterly charmed by this restored Ottoman house, which oozes subtle elegance at every turn. The six spacious rooms are infused with loads of old-world atmosphere, featuring dark wood accents, creamy 19th-century design textiles and colourful Turkish carpets, while the walled courtyard garden is the perfect retreat from the citadel streets. Delightfully helpful staff add to the appeal.

Divan Çukurhan
HISTORIC HOTEL €€€

(Map p415; ☑0312-306 6400; www.divan.com.tr; Depo Sokak 3, Ankara Kalesi; r from €120, ste €180-400; ✳; Ⓜ Ulus) This fabulous upmarket hotel offers guests a chance to soak up the historic ambience of staying in the 16th-century Çukurhan caravanserai. Set around a dramatic glass-ceilinged interior courtyard, each individually themed room blends ornate decadence with sassy contemporary style. Ankara's best bet for those who want to be dazzled by oodles of sumptuous luxury and sleek service.

Booking through the website often results in healthy discounts.

🛏 Kızılay & Kavaklıdere

★Deeps Hostel
HOSTEL €

(Map p420; ☑0312-213 6338; www.deepshostelankara.com; Ataç 2 Sokak 46; dm/s/d without breakfast ₺30/55/90; ☺☎; ⓂKızılay) At Ankara's best budget choice, friendly owner Şeyda has created a colourful, light-filled hostel with spacious dorms and small private rooms with squeaky-clean, modern shared bathrooms. It's all topped off by masses of advice and information, a fully equipped kitchen and a cute communal area downstairs where you can swap your Turkish travel tales.

Hotel Kayra
HOTEL €€

(Map p420; ☑0312-419 7575; www.hotelkayra.com; Bayındır 2 Sokak 46; s/d ₺100/120; ✳☎) Popular with Turkish travellers for good reason, this place is one of Kızılay's cheapest deals. Rooms are small and lacking in character but come with good beds, reliable hot water and satellite TV. Being next door to a school and steps away from the Kızılay cafe scene it's probably not the best choice for light sleepers.

Gordion Hotel
HISTORIC HOTEL €€€

(Map p419; ☑0312-427 8080; www.gordionhotel.com; Büklüm Sokak 59; s/d from ₺170/200; ✳☎) This independent hotel in the middle of the Kavaklıdere neighbourhood is a fabulously cultured inner-city residence with grand and stately rooms, a basement swimming pool, Vakko textiles in the lobby, centuries-old art engravings, a conservatory restaurant, beautiful beds and an extensive DVD library. At current rates it's an out-and-out bargain.

🍴 Eating

Most downtown Ulus options are basic.

In Kızılay it's all about street-side eating and cafe-hopping. Much of the food on offer though is a fairly identikit mix of snacky or fast-food type meals and finding a decent restaurant can be harder than it might first appear.

In Kavaklıdere the scene is European and sophisticated, catering primarily to the embassy set.

🍴 Citadel

Kınacızade Konağı
TURKISH €

(Map p415; ☑0312-324 5714; Kale Kapısı Sokak 28; mains ₺8-23; ☺9am-9pm Mon-Sat; ☑; Ⓜ Ulus) This Ottoman house serves up a range of typical Turkish kebap dishes alongside cheaper pide and delicious gözleme (savoury pancake). The shady courtyard, enclosed by picturesque timber-framed facades in various states of higgledy-piggledy disrepair, is a delightful place to while away time over a lazy lunch.

🍴 Kızılay

Ata İskender
KEBAP €

(Map p420; ☑0312-419 9027; Karanfil Sokak 19/1; mains ₺10-22; ☺10am-10pm; ⓂKızılay) If we're in the mood for Urfa kebap or İskender kebap (or Bursa kebap; döner kebap on fresh pide and topped with tomato sauce and browned butter) in Ankara, this is where we head. It's nothing fancy, just a typical Turkish grill restaurant with solid service, great complimentary salads and some seriously well-cooked meat.

Big Baker
BURGERS €

(Map p420; ☑ 0312-419 3777; www.bigbaker.com.tr; Yüksel Caddesi 17a; mains ₺16-22; ⊗ 8am-10pm; ⟨⟩☑; ⓂKızılay) Gourmet burgers have hit Ankara and this place is one of the best in town to sink your teeth into one. There are Mexican-style, goat's cheese, and BBQ burger options or for a truly Turkish take on the humble burger try the Köz Patlıcanlı, which comes with roasted aubergine and peppers.

Masabaşi Kebapçisi
KEBAP €€

(Map p420; ☑ 0312-417 0781; www.masabasi.com.tr; Mithat Paşa Caddesi; mains ₺18-25; ⊗ 11am-11pm; ⓂKizilay) At seemingly any time of the day there's a mass of people here tucking into an impressive selection of different kebaps and other grilled meats and many people will tell you it's the best such place in the neighbourhood to eat.

✖ Kavaklıdere

Mangal
TURKISH €

(Map p419; ☑ 0312-466 2460; www.mangalkebap.com; Bestekar Sokak 78; mains ₺15-25; ⊗ 9am-10pm) For over 20 years this neighbourhood star has been churning out perfectly prepared pide and every kind of kebap or grilled meat you can think of as well as many you can't. It's fairly smart, which makes the decent prices an unexpected surprise.

Leman Kültür
INTERNATIONAL €

(Map p419; ☑ 0312-310 8617; www.lmk.com.tr; Bestekar Sokak 80; mains ₺10-25; ⊗ 11am-midnight; ⟨⟩) Named after a cult Turkish comic strip – and decorated accordingly – this is the pre-party pick for a substantial feed and for spotting beautiful young educated things. The food is generally of the meatballs, burgers, pizza and grilled meats variety. Drinks are reasonably priced and the speakers crank everything from indie-electro to Türk pop.

Elizinn
DESSERTS €

(Map p419; www.elizinn.com.tr; Tunali Hilmi Caddesi 81; cakes ₺7-9; ⊗ 7.30am-10pm; ⟨⟩) You like sweet and naughty things? Then you, alongside zillions of locals who pour in here every afternoon, will love Elizinn and its irresistible range of pastries, cakes and other

sugar-coated treats. It also does meals but with sandwiches starting at ₺18, do like the locals and come just for a çay and a sugar hit.

★ Balıkçıköy
SEAFOOD €€

(Map p419; ☑ 0312-466 0450; Kırlangıç Sokak 3; mains ₺18-25; ⊗ noon-midnight) Ankara's favourite seafood restaurant. Take the waiter's recommendations for the cold meze, then take your pick of the fried and grilled fish – the fried whitebait is a favourite – all perfectly cooked and quick to the table. Book ahead to avoid disappointment.

Marmaris Balikçisi
SEAFOOD €€

(Map p419; ☑ 0312-427 2212; Bestekar Sokak 88/14a; mains ₺17-30; ⊗ 11am-11pm) At this well-regarded, and very fairly priced, seafood restaurant, with its suitably blue-and-white oceanic theme, you can pluck your creature of the deep off its bed of ice and have it quickly grilled or fried up and doused in olive oil and lemon ready for your taste buds to enjoy.

Although the menu is very long, they normally only have a fraction of what is listed, indicating that everything is freshly caught and in season.

Mezzaluna
ITALIAN €€

(Map p419; ☑ 0312-467 5818; Turan Emeksiz Sokak 1; mains ₺22-40; ⊗ noon-11pm) The capital's classiest Italian restaurant is busy busy busy, with chefs crafting some of Ankara's best pasta and slapping pizzas on the counter for apron-clad waiters to deliver. The choices include antipasti, risotto, wood-fired pizzas and seafood (a better bet than the steaks).

Günaydın
STEAK €€

(Map p419; ☑ 0312-466 7666; www.gunaydin.com; Arjantin Caddesi 6; mains ₺20-30; ⊗ 10am-11.30pm) This popular *izgara* (grill) restaurant seriously knows its meat. This carnivore heaven pumps out mountains of kebaps as well as steaks and ribs to the masses daily with snappy, professional service.

La Gioia
INTERNATIONAL €€€

(Map p419; www.lagioia.com.tr; Tahran Caddesi 2; mains ₺20-40; ⊗ 10am-11.45pm; ⟨⟩☑) This ever-so swanky cafe-bistro at the heart of the embassy district looks seriously Parisian – as do much of the clientele. If you're in need of a break from the endless kebaps of central Turkey then you'll enjoy the exciting salads here: black rice salad, grilled sea bream salad and goats cheese salad are just some of those on offer.

The main dining room is a giant conservatory-style affair, but when it's fine you can also eat at the outdoor tables.

Drinking & Nightlife

Kızılay is ripe for a night out with Ankara's student population – try Bayındır Sokak, between Sakarya and Tuna Caddesis. The tall, thin buildings pack in up to five floors of bars, cafes and *gazinos* (nightclubs). Many of the clubs offer live Turkish pop music, and women travellers should feel OK in most of them.

Aylak Madam CAFE
(Map p420; ☑ 0312-419 7412; Karanfıl Sokak 2; ⊙ 10am-late; Ⓜ Kızılay) A super-cool French bistro-cafe with a mean weekend brunch (from 10am to 2.30pm), plus sandwiches, head-kicking cappuccinos, and a jazz-fusion soundtrack. Postgraduates and writers hang out here, hunched over their laptops or with pens tapping against half-finished manuscripts.

Hayyami WINE BAR
(Map p419; ☑ 0312-466 1052; Bestekar Sokak 82b; ⊙ noon-late) Named after the renowned Sufi philosopher, this thriving wine house–restaurant attracts a hobnobbing crowd to its lowered courtyard. It boasts a long and diverse wine selection, which you can savour with a tapas-like array of dishes including *salçalı sosis* (barbecued sausage) and devilishly large cheese platters (mains ₺14 to ₺25).

Café des Cafés CAFE
(Map p419; ☑ 0312-428 0176; Tunalı Hilmi Caddesi 83; ⊙ 8.30am-11pm) Quirky vintage styling and comfy sofas make Café des Cafés a popular Kavaklıdere haunt. Pull up a chair on the tiny streetside terrace and sharpen up your people-watching skills. The orange-and-cinnamon hot chocolate is bliss in a glass.

Cafemiz CAFE
(Map p419; www.cafemiz.com.tr; Arjantin Caddesi 19; ⊙ 9am-10pm) A favourite with the embassy set, this cafe with its garden setting is a tranquil spot to recharge your batteries after exploring Ankara's bustle. Sit back with a glass of wine or coffee (drinks from ₺9) and enjoy the (relative) quiet. There's also an extensive menu of salads, sandwiches and desserts.

Kavaklıdere

Kavaklıdere

🛏 **Sleeping**
1 Gordion Hotel B1

🍴 **Eating**
2 Balıkçıköy B3
3 Elizinn B1
4 Günaydın B3
5 La Gioia B3
6 Leman Kültür A1
7 Mangal A1
8 Marmaris Balıkçısı A2
9 Mezzaluna B3

🍷 **Drinking & Nightlife**
Café des Cafés .... (see 3)
10 Cafemiz B3
11 Hayyami A1

Biber BAR
(Map p420; Inkılap Sokak 19; ⊙ 4pm-late; Ⓜ Kızılay) Biber attracts everyone from pale-faced student goths to alternative rockers and people who just want to boogie. The music can be as mixed as the crowd on the right night. There are dozens of other rowdy, beer-swilling bars with big outdoor terraces on the same road.

☆ Entertainment

Ankara State Opera House PERFORMING ARTS
(Opera Sahnesi; Map p415; ☎0312-324 6801; www.dobgm.gov.tr; Atatürk Bulvarı 20; Ⓜ Sıhhiye) This venue plays host to all the large productions staged by the Ankara State Opera

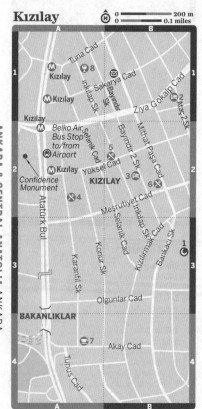

Kızılay

◉ Sights
1 Kocatepe Camii.....................................B3

🛏 Sleeping
2 Deeps Hostel.. B1
3 Hotel Kayra..B2

✕ Eating
4 Ata İskender...A2
5 Big Baker..B2
6 Masabaşı Kebapçisi.............................B2

◉ Drinking & Nightlife
7 Aylak Madam..A4
8 Biber..A1

and Ballet. The season generally runs from September to June and it's worthwhile trying to catch a performance if you're in town at that time.

🛍 Shopping

To see what fashionable Turkey spends its money on, head south along Tunalı Hilmi Caddesi in Kavaklıdere where lots of local stores stand alongside more familiar names such as Mango and British department store Marks & Spencer. There are several massive malls outside of the central city including the **AnkaMall**, easily accessed by alighting at Akköprü metro station.

Hisar Area ARTS & CRAFTS
(Map p415; Ⓜ Ulus) The alleyways southeast of the Parmak Kapısı entrance to the citadel were traditionally the centre for trading in angora wool. Walk downhill from the dried-fruit stalls in front of the gate, and you'll come across copper-beaters, as well as plenty of carpet and antique stores, small galleries and craft shops that are good for a rummage.

ℹ Information

MEDICAL SERVICES

Pharmacists take it in turns to open around the clock; look out for the *nobetçi* (open 24 hours) sign.

Bayındır Hospital (☎0312-428 0808; www.bayindirhastanesi.com.tr; Atatürk Bulvarı 201, Çankaya) An up-to-date private hospital.

MONEY

There are lots of banks with ATMs in Ulus, Kızılay and Kavaklıdere. To change money, *döviz bürosu* (currency-exchange offices) generally offer the best rates, often without commission.

TOURIST INFORMATION

Tourist Office (Map p415; ☎0312-310 3044; Kale Kapısı Sokak; ⊙10am-5pm; Ⓜ Ulus) Ankara's main tourist office is inside the Citadel. There are also (usually unstaffed) branches at the AŞTİ otogar and at the train station.

ℹ Getting There & Away

AIR

Although domestic and international carriers serve Ankara's **Esenboğa airport** (p604), İstanbul's airports offer more choice and usually better prices.

Turkish domestic carriers have direct flights from Esenboğa to Adana, Dalaman, İstanbul, İzmir and Malatya. For international destinations,

Mahan Air (www.mahan.aero/en/) flies to Tehran; Royal Jordanian (www.rj.com) has connections to Amman; Pegasus Airlines (www.flypgs.com) flies direct to north Cyprus; Sun Express (www.sunexpress.com.tr) has departures to various German cities; and Qatar Airways (www.qatarairways.com), flies to Doha.

BUS

Every Turkish city or town of any size has direct buses to Ankara. The gigantic otogar (bus station), also referred to as AŞTİ (Ankara Şehirlerarası Terminali İşletmesi; Mevlâna Bulvarı), is at the western end of the Ankaray underground train line, 4.5km west of Kızılay.

Buses to/from İstanbul (₺40 to ₺45, six hours), Antalya (₺60, nine hours), İzmir (₺60, eight hours) and other major destinations leave numerous times daily. Buses to Cappadocia (₺40, 4½ hours) often terminate in Nevşehir. Be sure your ticket states your *final* destination (eg Göreme, Ürgüp) so you qualify for the bus company's free *servis* (shuttle bus) onward from Nevşehir.

Because there are so many buses to many parts of the country, you can often turn up, buy a ticket and be on your way in less than an hour. Don't try this during public holidays, though.

The *emanet* (left-luggage room) on the lower level charges ₺4 per item stored; you'll need to show your passport.

TRAIN

A high-speed train line links **Ankara Train Station** (Ankara Garı; Talat Paşa Bulvarı) with İstanbul Pendik (a suburb 25km east of İstanbul). There are six trains a day and the journey takes just four hours. Economy class tickets cost ₺70. Get to the station at least 15 minutes before departure as there are a number of security checks to pass through.

High-speed train services run to Eskişehir (economy/business class ₺30/43, 1½ hours, five daily) and Konya (economy/business class

₺30/43, two hours, seven daily) and are comfortable, fast and efficient.

ⓘ Getting Around

If you're going to be kicking around the city for a couple of days it's worth investing ₺1 to get an **Ankara Kart** travel card (available at all metro station ticket counters and many kiosks around town) which gives you discounted fares of ₺2.35 on both the metro and bus system.

TO/FROM THE AIRPORT

Esenboğa airport is 33km north of the city.

Belko Air airport buses (☏ 444 9312; www.belkoair.com; arrivals floor, AŞTİ Otogar; ₺10) link the airport with the AŞTİ otogar (main bus station; 45 minutes), Kızılay (one hour), and Ulus (1¼ hours). Departures to/from the airport are every 30 minutes between 5am and midnight daily. After midnight buses leave hourly.

From the airport, buses leave from in front of the passenger arrivals gate H (domestic arrivals); international arrivals should walk left on leaving the airport terminal. Heading to the airport, buses depart from the AŞTİ (on the ground-floor arrivals terminal) and then pick up passengers at their **Kızılay** (Map p420; Atatürk Bulvarı, Gama İş Merkezi Bldg) and **Ulus** (Map p412; 19 Mayıs Stadyumu, door B, off Kazım Karabekir Caddesi) stops on the way to the airport. Coming from the airport the Ulus drop-off point is at **Opera Meydanı** (Map p415; Atatürk Bulvarı).

A taxi between the airport and the city should cost around ₺70. From Belko Air's Ulus stop to the hotels in the *hisar* (citadel) area it costs about ₺10.

TO/FROM THE BUS STATION

The easiest way to get into town is on the Ankaray metro line, which has a station at the AŞTİ otogar. Get off at Maltepe for the train station (a

LONG-DISTANCE SERVICES FROM ANKARA TRAIN STATION

DESTINATION	VIA (MAJOR STOPS)	TRAIN NAME	TIME (HOURS)	DEPARTURE TIME
Adana	Kayseri	Çukurova Mavi Tren	11	8.07pm daily
Diyarbakır	Kayseri, Sivas, Malatya	Güney Kurtalan Ekspresi	22¼	11.15am Mon, Wed, Thu, Fri & Sat
İzmir	Eskişehir	İzmir Mavi Tren	13¼	6.05pm daily
Kars	Kayseri, Sivas, Erzurum	Doğu Ekspresi	27¾	6pm daily
Malatya	Kayseri, Sivas	Eylül Mavi Tren	14½	7pm daily
Tatvan (for ferry to Van)	Kayseri, Sivas, Malatya	Vangölü Ekspresi	36	11.15am Tue & Sun

ANGORA WOOL

Can you tell the difference between a goat and a rabbit? It's not as easy as you think – or at least not if all you have to go on is the wool. One of the most popular misconceptions about Ankara's famous angora wool is that it comes from angora goats, a hardy breed believed to be descended from wild Himalayan goats. Not so: the soft, fluffy wool produced from these goats is correctly known as mohair. Angora wool in the strictest sense comes from angora rabbits, also local but much cuter and whose fur, weight for weight, was once worth as much as gold.

10-minute walk), or go to Kızılay for midrange hotels. Change at Kızılay (to the Metro line) for Ulus and cheaper hotels.

A taxi costs about ₺30 to the city centre.

TO/FROM THE TRAIN STATION

Ankara Train Station is about 1km southwest of Ulus Meydanı and 2km northwest of Kızılay. Many dolmuşes (minibuses) head northeast along Cumhuriyet Bulvarı to Ulus, and east on Talat Paşa Bulvarı to Kızılay.

It's just over 1km from the station to Opera Meydanı; any bus heading east along Talat Paşa Bulvarı will drop you within a few hundred metres if you ask for Gazi Lisesi.

BUS

Ankara has a good bus, dolmuş and minibus network. Signs on the front and side of the vehicles are better guides than route numbers. Buses marked 'Ulus' and 'Çankaya' run the length of Atatürk Bulvarı. Those marked 'Gar' go to the train station, those marked 'AŞTİ' to the otogar.

Standard ₺4 tickets are available anywhere displaying an EGO Bilet sign (easiest purchased from metro station ticket booths), or buy an Ankara Kart (p421).

CAR

Driving within Ankara is chaotic and signs are inadequate; it's easier to ditch your car and use public transport.

If you plan to hire a car to drive out of Ankara, there are many small local companies alongside the major international firms; most have offices in Kavaklıdere along Tunus Caddesi, and/or at Esenboğa airport. For your sanity it's probably easier to get a bus out to the airport and hire a car there, thus hopefully avoiding driving in Ankara.

METRO

Ankara's underground train network is the easiest way to get between Ulus and Kızılay and the otogar. There are currently two lines: the Ankaray line running between AŞTİ otogar in the west through Maltepe and Kızılay to Dikimevi in the east; and the Metro line running from Kızılay northwest via Sıhhiye and Ulus to Batıkent. The two lines interconnect at Kızılay. Trains run from 6.15am to 11.45pm daily.

A one-way fare costs ₺4. Tickets are available at all stations, or ₺2.35 with the Ankara Kart (p421).

TAXI

Taxis are everywhere and they all have meters (normally built into the mirror), with a ₺2.70 base rate. It costs about ₺12 to cross the centre; charges rise at night and the same trip will cost well over ₺15.

Around Ankara

Gordion

The capital of ancient Phrygia, with some 3000 years of settlement behind it, Gordion lies 106km southwest of Ankara in the village of Yassıhöyük.

Gordion was occupied by the Phrygians as early as the 9th century BC, and soon afterwards became their capital. Although destroyed during the Cimmerian invasion, it was rebuilt before being conquered by the Lydians and then the Persians. Alexander the Great came through here and famously cut the Gordian knot in 333 BC, but by 278 BC the Galatian occupation had effectively destroyed the city.

The moonscape-like terrain around Yassıhöyük is dotted with tumuli (burial mounds) that mark the graves of the Phrygian kings. Of some 90 identified tumuli, 35 have been excavated; you can enter the largest tomb, and also view the site of the Gordion acropolis, where digs revealed five main levels of civilisation from the Bronze Age to Galatian times.

⊙ Sights

Midas Tumulus　　　　　　　　　RUINS
(incl Gordion Museum ₺5; ⊙8.30am-7pm) In 1957 Austrian archaeologist Alfred Koerte discovered Gordion, and with it the intact tomb of a Phrygian king, probably buried some time between 740 and 718 BC. The tomb is actually a gabled 'cottage' of cedar surrounded by juniper logs, buried inside a

tumulus 53m high and 300m in diameter. It's the oldest wooden structure ever found in Anatolia, and perhaps even in the world. The tunnel leading into the depths of the tumulus is a modern addition.

Inside the tomb archaeologists found the body of a man between 61 and 65 years of age, 1.59m tall, surrounded by burial objects, including tables, bronze situlas (containers) and bowls said to be part of the funerary burial feast. The occupant's name remains unknown (although Gordius and Midas were popular names for Phrygian kings).

Gordion Museum   MUSEUM
(incl Midas Tumulus ₺5; ⊙8.30am-7pm) In the museum opposite the Midas Tumulus, Macedonian and Babylonian coins show Gordion's position at the centre of Anatolian trade, communications and military activities, as do the bronze figurines and glass-bead jewellery from the Syro-Levantine region of Mesopotamia.

Acropolis   RUINS
FREE Just beyond Yassıhöyük village is the weatherbeaten 8th-century-BC acropolis. Excavations here have yielded a wealth of data on Gordion's many civilisations. The site is a mass of jumbled, half-buried walls and, thanks to the scarcity of other visitors, feels remote and forgotten.

🛈 Getting There & Away

Baysal Turizm buses connect Ankara's otogar with Polatlı every half hour (₺8, one hour). Dolmuşes also go direct to Polatlı from a small bus station (more of a parking lot really) on the edge of Ulus. Once in Polatlı, you can travel the last 18km to Yassıhöyük in a minibus (₺5), but this involves a 1.5km walk across town to the minibus stand, and services depart very sporadically. You'd be lucky to get a taxi from Polatlı for less than ₺100 return with waiting time. You could also try and hitch from Polatlı. The road to Gordion is signed just 50m from the otogar. However, even if you get a lift from here you'll probably be dropped off at the junction 7km from Yassıhöyük from where you may well have to walk (and then walk back to the junction again).

Safranbolu

📞 0370 / POP 44,000
Safranbolu's old town, known as Çarşı, is a vision of red-tiled roofs and meandering alleys chock-a-block full of candy stores and cobblers. Having first found fame with traders as an isolated source of the precious spice saffron, Safranbolu now attracts people seeking to recapture the heady scent of yesteryear within the muddle of timber-framed mansions now converted into quirky boutique hotels. Spending the night here is all about soaking up the enchanting Ottoman scene – all creaky wooden floors, exuberantly carved ceilings and traditional cupboard-bathrooms. A day at the old hamam or browsing the market shops and revelling in the cobblestone quaintness is about as strenuous as it gets, but if history begins to feel a bit like old news, then hiking in the wondrous Yenice Forest nearby, remapped and rediscovered, will show you exactly why Unesco stamped this region as a World Heritage site in 1994.

History

During the 17th century, the main Ottoman trade route between Gerede and the Black Sea coast passed through Safranbolu, bringing commerce, prominence and money to the town. During the 18th and 19th centuries, Safranbolu's wealthy inhabitants built mansions of sun-dried mudbricks, wood and stucco, while the larger population of prosperous artisans built less impressive but similarly sturdy homes. Safranbolu owes its fame to the large numbers of these dwellings that have survived.

The most prosperous Safranbolulus maintained two households. In winter they occupied town houses in the Çarşı (market) district, which is situated at the meeting point of three valleys and protected from winter winds. During the warm months they moved to summer houses in the garden suburb of Bağlar (vineyards). When the iron- and steelworks at Karabük were established in 1938, modern factory houses started to encroach on Bağlar, but Çarşı has remained virtually untouched.

During the 19th century about 20% of Safranbolu's inhabitants were Ottoman Greeks, but most of their descendants moved to Greece during the population exchange after WWI. Their principal church, dedicated to St Stephen, was converted into Kıranköy's Ulu Camii (Great Mosque).

◉ Sights & Activities

★**Çarşı**   ARCHITECTURE
(Map p424) The real joy of Safranbolu is simply wandering the cobblestone alleys. Everywhere you look in Çarşı is a feast for the eyes. Virtually every house in the

Safranbolu - Çarşı

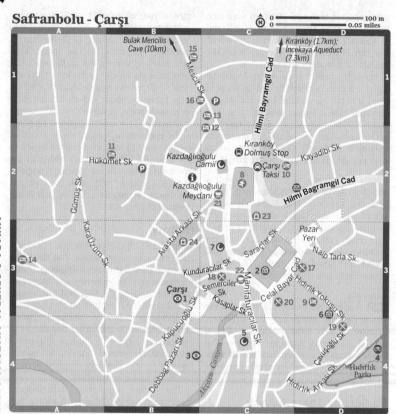

neighbourhood is an original, and what little modern development there is has been held in check. Many of the finest historic houses have been restored, and as time goes on, more and more are being saved from deterioration and turned into hotels, shops or museums.

Kaymakamlar Müze Evi
MUSEUM

(Map p424; Hıdırlık Yokuşu Sokak; adult/student ₺4/3; ⊙9am-5.30pm) This typical Safranbolu home has all the classic features of Ottoman houses. Once owned by a lieutenant colonel, it still feels like an address of note as you climb the stairs looking up to the wooden ceiling decoration. Tableaux (featuring some rather weary mannequins) recreate scenes such as bathing in a cupboard and a wedding feast.

There's a peaceful cafe in the garden outside.

Cinci Hanı
HISTORIC BUILDING

(Map p424; Saraçlar Sokak; ₺2; ⊙9am-9pm) Çarşı's most famous and imposing structure is this brooding 17th-century caravanserai that's now a hotel. Nonguests are welcome to come and explore: climb up to the rooftop for panoramas over the town. On Saturdays a market takes place in the square behind it.

Demirciler Arastası
MARKET

(Metalworker's Bazaar; Map p424; Debbag Pazarı Sokak) You'll hear the clang of hammers before you get here. This fascinating area is where the traditional metalworkers of Safranbolu still ply their trade and you can see them at work shaping farm implements and household goods.

Towards the back of the bazaar you'll also find shops selling antiques and metalworkers making intricately engraved handcrafted trays and plates.

Safranbolu - Çarşı

İzzet Paşa Camii MOSQUE
(Map p424; Manifaturacılar Sokak) This is one of the largest mosques constructed during the Ottoman Empire. It was built by the grand vizier in 1796 and restored in 1903. Its design was influenced by European architecture.

Köprülü Mehmet Paşa Camii MOSQUE
(Map p424; Manifaturacılar Sokak) This beefy, helmet-roofed building beside the Yemeniciler Arastası dates to 1661. The metal sundial in the courtyard was added in the mid-19th century.

Hıdırlık Tepe VIEWPOINT
(Map p424; Hıdırlık Yokusu Sokak; ₺1) For the best vantage point over town head up to the top of Hıdırlık *tepe* (hill) where you'll find a park and cafe as well as excellent views.

Cinci Hamam HAMAM
(Map p424; ☎0370-712 2103; Kazdağlıoğulu Meydanı; full treatment ₺35; ⊙men 6am-11pm, women 9am-10pm) One of the most renowned bathhouses in all of Turkey, with separate baths for men and women. If you're going to get scrubbed down to rosy-pink skin just once on your Turkey travels, this is the place to do it.

Festivals & Events

International Golden Saffron Documentary Film Festival FILM
(Altınsafran Belgesel Film Festivali; www.altinsafran.org; ⊙Oct) This three-day festival of both Turkish and foreign documentary films sees the Cinci Hanı, and other historical buildings, turned into sites for film screenings and talks. A slew of other cultural events, including photography exhibitions, usually run in conjunction to the actual film competition.

Sleeping

Safranbolu is very popular with Turkish tourists during weekends and holidays. Prices may rise at busy times, and it can be worth booking ahead. Splashing out a bit is virtually an obligation, as you may never get another chance to sleep anywhere so authentically restored. If you'd rather stay in a family home than a hotel, the tourist office (p427) has a list of basic pensions (the *Safranbolu'daki Ev Pansiyonları Listesi*).

Bastoncu Pansiyon PENSION €
(Map p424; ☎0370-712 3411; www.bastoncupension.com; Hıdırlık Yokuşu Sokak 4; dm/s/d ₺30/70/100; 📶) In a 350-year-old building, Bastoncu is a Safranbolu institution with a superb higgledy-piggledy feel. Connected by a labyrinth of staircases, rooms and dorms have all their original wood panelling, jars of dried flowers and some (slightly pongy) cupboard bathrooms. It's run by a friendly couple who speak English and Japanese and appreciate travellers' needs.

Efe Guesthouse PENSION €
(Map p424; ☎0370-725 2688; www.efeguesthouse.com; Kayadibi Sokak 8; dm/s/d ₺25/70/90; 📶) This place dishes up all of Safranbolu's Ottoman charm at a smidgen of the cost of other hotels. There's a basic dorm for those

really saving their lira and the snug private rooms are packed full of local character.

★ **Kahveciler Konağı** BOUTIQUE HOTEL €€
(Map p424; ☎0370-725 5453; www.kahvecilerkonagi.com; Mescit Sokak 7; s/d ₺90/150; 📶) The eight large rooms here have whitewashed walls, glorious wood-panel ceilings and lovely views of red-tiled roofs. Amiable host Erşan has transformed his grandfather's house into a comfortable home away from home topped off by a genuine welcoming vibe. As a bonus for those less agile, the bathrooms are big by Safranbolu standards and require no climbing into cupboards.

Selvili Köşk BOUTIQUE HOTEL €€
(Map p424; ☎0370-712 8646; www.selvilikosk.com; Mescit Sokak 23; s/d ₺100/160; 📶) From the engraved banisters to the carved ceilings, this wonderful restoration job offers a regal-feeling, romantic retreat. Dazzling carpets cover every inch of floor and are layered over the *sedirs* (bench seating that runs along the walls), and local embroidered linens grace the beds in sun-drenched rooms.

Ingeniously hidden bathrooms are found through opening cupboard doors (for those who cannot, or will not, climb into a cupboard to use the bathroom, it might pay to look elsewhere).

Mehveş Hanım Konağı BOUTIQUE HOTEL €€
(Map p424; ☎0370-712 8787; www.mehveshanimkonagi.com.tr; Mescit Sokak 30; s ₺120, d ₺150-180; 📶) With every nook and cranny crammed with curios and Ottoman paraphernalia, the Mehveş brims with authentic character. It's run with cheerful competency; the spacious rooms have intricately carved wooden ceilings, *sedir* (bench) seating, teensy cupboard bathrooms (some rooms share much larger and more modern bathrooms) and Ottoman princess nets around the beds. There's also a lovely hidden garden.

Gülevi BOUTIQUE HOTEL €€€
(Map p424; ☎0370-725 4645; www.canbulat.com.tr; Hükümet Sokak 46; s €75-100, d €90-120, ste from €150; 📶) Architect-design couple İbrahim and Gül have crafted what might be Safranbolu's most striking reinterpretation of the Ottoman aesthetic. 'Rose House' is an affordable masterpiece where urban luxury mingles seamlessly with traditional Ottoman design. Amid a shaded, grassy garden, the rooms (spread over three houses) are all soft colours, wood panelling and Turkman carpets, set off by flamboyant artistic touches.

Guests lucky enough to stay here can enjoy a drink in the tiny underground cave bar (once the treasury of the house) or dine at the private restaurant where the pick of local produce is on the menu.

Imren Lokum Konak BOUTIQUE HOTEL €€€
(Map p424; ☎0370-725 2324; www.imrenkonak.com; Kayyim Ali Sokak; s/d ₺160/220; 📶) This old Ottoman building houses a fine hotel with rooms that, though keeping all their old Safranbolu flavour, have enough modern touches to make them truly user friendly. There's a large open courtyard and restaurant that attracts many an overnighting tourist from Ankara at weekends and this ensures a holiday vibe.

Leyla Hanım Konağı HISTORIC HOTEL €€€
(Map p424; ☎0370-725 1272; www.leylahanimkonagi.com; Çeşme Mahallesi Hükümet Sokak 25; s/d ₺150/250; 📶) This place was once a barracks for soldiers, but if those men could see it today they'd probably never guess that this now wonderful boutique hotel was once their, no-doubt, rather grimy home. Today its all ye-olde elegance mixed with flashes of modernity such as deep-purple theatre curtains draped over exposed stone walls.

Eating & Drinking

Safranbolu's dining scene is on the up and many places offer menus dishing up Safranbolu's local cuisine (much of which hails from the Black Sea region). *Erişte* (pasta with walnuts) is one of the town's specialities. Also be sure to try all flavours of the locally produced soft drink, Bağlar Gazozu, an institution since 1936.

★ **Atış Cafe** ANATOLIAN €
(Map p424; Celal Bayer Caddesi; mains ₺10-15; ⏲10am-10pm; 📶🌶) Safranbolu has cute cafes dishing up regional cuisine aplenty but Atış is our favourite for its genuinely friendly management and solid home-style cooking. Dig into local dishes of *peruhi* (pasta parcels drenched in a butter sauce) and *Rum mantı* (Turkish ravioli served in a soy sauce broth) on the itsy terrace or inside in the delightfully cosy floral-styled salon.

Zencefil ANATOLIAN €
(Map p424; ☎0370-712 5120; Celal Bayer Sokak; mains ₺10-20; ⏲9am-9pm; 📶🌶) Run by a foodie couple, this place dishes up plenty of local dishes like *etli keşkek* (a meat and wheat dish) and *kuymak* (Turkish-style

cheese fondue). All the food is cooked up right in front of you and service is friendly.

Bizım Cafe   TURKISH €
(Map p424; Çeşme Mahallesi; mains ₺5-12; ⊙10.30am-6pm) Deep in the old shopping district is this welcoming little family-run restaurant that serves whatever's on the stove, which luckily is always pretty good, including dolmades rolled on the street and deliciously spicy soups. Locals love it.

Taşev   MODERN TURKISH €€
(Map p424; ☑0370-725 5300; www.tasevsanat vesarapevi.com; Hıdırlık Yokuşu Sokak 14; mains ₺17-30; ⊙10am-11pm Tue-Sun; 🐾🍴) This is Safranbolu's bona fide contemporary dining option and it delivers with thick steaks and creamy pasta dishes. The Turkish cheese platter is a must for cheese lovers. Service is warm and they'll helpfully explain menu items and help you choose from the extensive wine list.

Saraçoğlu Kahve Evi   CAFE
(Map p424; Manıfaturacılar Sokak; Türk kahve ₺7.50; ⊙10.30am-10pm) This is the place to head for a properly made *Türk kahve* (Turkish coffee) served with some serious panache – on a silver tray with a dish of *lokum* (Turkish delight) and a glass of local *şerbet* (sweet fruit drink) to wash it down.

Çızgi Cafe   NARGILE CAFE
(Map p424; ☑0370-717 7840; Arasta Arkası Sokak; mains ₺7-15) The prime people-watching territory is the cushioned benches out in the alleyway or head inside to cosy up in one of the intimate cubby-hole dining areas. There's a small menu of local dishes such as *cevizli yayım* (macaroni topped with walnuts) but most people are here to waste hours talking over tea, coffee and *nargile* (water pipe).

🛍 Shopping

Yemeniciler Arastası   MARKET
(Shoe-Maker's Bazaar; Map p424; Arasta Arkası Sokak; ⊙9.30am-7pm) The restored Yemenicil-er Arastası is the best place to start looking for crafts, although the makers of the light, flat-heeled shoes who used to work here have long since moved out. The cubbyhole stores here are mostly home to textile shops. Be aware that prices tend to be high.

Safranbolu Tasarım Design   ARTS & CRAFTS
(Map p424; Sadrı Artunç Caddesi; ⊙10am-7pm) For something completely different, this shop sponsored by the *belediye* (local council) supports local craftspeople and artisans.

There's a small but interesting collection of items (mostly art prints and ceramics) which take a contemporary approach to traditional Turkish motifs in their design.

ℹ Information

Çarşı has a bank with an ATM on Kazdağlıoğulu Meydanı.
Tourist Office (Map p424; ☑0370-712 3863; www.safranboluturizmdanismaburosu.gov.tr; Kazdağlıoğulu Meydanı; ⊙9am-5.30pm) One of Turkey's most helpful tourist information offices. Informed, multilingual staff can provide loads of tips and advice, and will even help with booking bus tickets.

ℹ Getting There & Away

Most buses stop in Karabük first and then finish at Kıranköy otogar (actually called 'Safranbolu otogar' but in upper Safranbolu). From the otogar most bus companies provide a *servis* (free shuttle bus) which will deposit you in central Kıranköy, near the dolmuş stand for Çarşı.

There are several bus-company offices in central Kıranköy. Take the small side street with the sign 'Şehirlerarası Otobüs Bilet Satış Büroları', three blocks down Sadrı Artunç Caddesi, to find them. You can buy onward bus tickets here and all provide a *servis* to Kıranköy otogar. Destinations with regular bus departures include Ankara (₺30, three hours), İstanbul (₺55, seven hours) and Kastamonu (₺20, two hours).

For Amasra take a bus to Bartın (₺20, 1½ hours) and change there. Buses to Bartın go every hour at the quarter past.

If you're driving, exit the Ankara–İstanbul highway at Gerede and head north, following the signs for Karabük/Safranbolu.

The Karabük to Ankara train is currently out of service.

ℹ Getting Around

Dolmuşes (₺1.25) ply the route from **Çarşı's main square** (Map p424), over the hills, and into central Kıranköy every 15 minutes. From the last stop you can catch another minibus to Karabük. You only have to pay the bus fare once if you're going all the way. A **taxi** (Map p424; ☑0370-725 2595; Hilmi Bayramgil Caddesi) from Çarşı to Kıranköy will cost you ₺10 to ₺12.

Boğazkale, Hattuşa & Yazılıkaya

Out in the centre of the Anatolian plains, two Unesco World Heritage sites evoke a vital historical moment at the height of Hittite civilisation. Hattuşa was the Hittite capital, while Yazılıkaya was a religious sanctuary with fine rock carvings.

The best base for visiting the sites around here is Boğazkale, a farming village 200km east of Ankara. Boğazkale has simple traveller services; if you want or need something fancier you'll need to stay in Çorum or, if you get going early enough in the morning, Ankara.

Transport to the area is via Sungurlu, which is serviced by plenty of buses doing the Ankara to Samsun route (₺25, 2½ hours from Ankara).

Boğazkale

✔ 0364 / POP 1300

The village of Boğazkale has geese, cows and wheelbarrow-racing children wandering its cobbled streets; farmyards with Hittite and Byzantine gates; and a constant sense that a once-great city is just over the brow. Most visitors come solely to visit Hattuşa and Yazılıkaya, which can be accessed on foot if it's not too hot, but there is more to explore. Surrounded by valleys with Hittite caves, eagles' nests, butterflies and a neolithic fort, the area around Hattuşa is ripe for hiking. Head 4km east of Yazılıkaya and climb Yazılıkaya Dağı to watch the sun set, or head to the swimming hole (locally known as *hoşur*) on the Budaközü river to cool off after Hittite rambles.

Late in the day, the silence in Boğazkale is broken only by the occasional car kicking up dust on the main street, and the rural solitude may tempt you to stay an extra night. There is a bank with an ATM.

Boğazkale Museum   MUSEUM
(Map p429; Sungurlu Asfalt Caddesi; ₺5; ⊙ 8am-7pm) Unsurprisingly, Hittite artefacts dominate the small Boğazkale Museum which does a good job of explaining the history and culture of the Hittite empire with plenty of information boards in English. The pride of the collection are the two sphinx statues that once stood guard at Hattuşa's Yer Kapı gate. They were only returned to Boğazkale in 2011, having previously been on display in Berlin and İstanbul. Free audioguides are available.

🛏 Sleeping & Eating

The village's hotels all have restaurants. For snacking needs, there's a very well-stocked *bakkal* (grocery store) in the village centre, opposite the bank.

Aşıkoğlu Hotel & Pension   GUESTHOUSE €€
(Map p429; ✔ 0364-452 2004; www.hattusas.com; Sungurlu Asfalt Caddesi; s ₺25-80, d ₺40-120, tr ₺150, campsite & caravan for 2 people ₺30; P ❀ 🕏) The friendly service sets this place apart, and the simple, spick-and-span rooms in both budget and midrange styles are just the ticket for resting your head after visiting Hattuşa, although in winter the unheated rooms get very cold. There's a shady apple garden for campers, a cosy Ottoman-style cafe-restaurant and Hittite documentaries are shown on a cinevision screen in the evening.

Set menus at the restaurant cost ₺30 and there's decent wood-fired pide for ₺10 to ₺15. If you ring ahead the hotel can organise taxi transfers from Sungurlu otogar.

Hittite Houses   GUESTHOUSE €€
(Map p429; ✔ 0364-452 2004; www.hattusas.com; Sungurlu Asfalt Caddesi; s/d/f ₺60/100/120; P ❀ 🕏) Behind a mocked-up Hittite wall-facade, this hotel's large, light-filled rooms (some with balconies) are a bargain while the tranquil garden out front is a great place to wind down after a day's exploring. It's run by the knowledgeable owners of the Aşıkoğlu Hotel opposite, so guests have access to all the facilities and services there.

❶ Getting There & Away

To get to Boğazkale by public transport, you'll need to go via Sungurlu. From Sungurlu otogar your bus should provide a *servis* to the Boğazkale dolmuş stand (Map p429), 1km from the otogar near the football stadium and park. From Sungurlu there are five dolmuşes daily (₺5) Monday to Friday between 7.30am and 5.30pm. Taking a taxi may be your only resort at the weekend. The going rate is ₺50. Be aware that some taxi drivers at Sungurlu otogar will try to insist on using their meter for the journey (resulting in a fare of over ₺150). If you are having problems, ring your hotel in Boğazkale.

Travellers coming from Cappadocia should note that there are no dolmuşes between Boğazkale and Yozgat, 41km southeast. You're better off going via Sungurlu.

Hattuşa

The mountainous, isolated site of Hattuşa (Map p429; incl Yazılıkaya ₺8; ⊙ 8am-7pm) was once the capital of the Hittite kingdom, which stretched from Syria to Europe. At its zenith this was a busy and impressive city of 15,000 inhabitants with defensive walls over

6km in length, some of the thickest in the ancient world, studded with watchtowers and secret tunnels.

As you climb out of the village to the **site** (Map p429), an evocative reconstruction of a section of city wall comes into view. Imagine the sense of purpose that drove the Hittites to haul stone to this remote spot, far from oceans and trade routes, and build an engineering masterpiece that launched a mighty empire.

◉ Sights

Büyük Mabet   TEMPLE

(Great Temple; Map p429) The vast complex of the Büyük Mabet, dating from the 14th century BC and destroyed around 1200 BC, is the closest archaeological site to the entrance gate and the best preserved of Hattuşa's Hittite temple ruins, but even so you'll still need plenty of imagination.

As you walk down the wide processional street, the administrative quarters of the temple are to your left. The well-worn cube of green nephrite rock here is thought to have played a significant role in the Hittite religion.

The main temple, to your right, was surrounded by storerooms thought to be three storeys high. In the early 20th century, huge clay storage jars and thousands of cuneiform tablets were found in these rooms. Look for the threshold stones at the base of some of the doorways to see the hole for the hinge-post and the arc worn by the door's movement. The temple is believed to have been a ritual altar for the deities Teshub and Hepatu; the large stone base of one of their statues remains.

Sarı Kale   RUINS

(Yellow Fortress; Map p429) About 250m south of the Büyük Mabet, the road forks; take the right fork and follow the winding road up the hillside. On your left in the midst of the old city you can see several ruined structures. The rock-top ruins of the Sarı Kale may be a Phrygian fort on Hittite foundations.

Yenice Kale   RUINS

(Map p429) Upon the top of this rock outcrop are the remains of the Yenice Kale, which may have been a royal residence or small temple. You can climb to the summit from the east side.

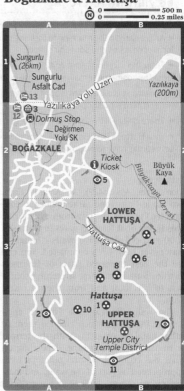

Boğazkale & Hattuşa

◎ Top Sights

◎ Sights

⬤ Sleeping

ANKARA & CENTRAL ANATOLIA BOĞAZKALE, HATTUŞA & YAZILIKAYA

ⓘ VISITING HATTUŞA

➡ The ruins are an easy, and extremely pretty, walk from Boğazkale.

➡ Arrive early in the morning to tour the ruins before the 21st century intrudes in the form of coaches and souvenir sellers.

➡ Enter the Büyük Mabet (p429) temple ruins from the trail uphill of Hattuşa's ticket kiosk, opposite the remains of a house on the slope.

➡ The circuit is a hilly 5km loop; if you want to walk, wear sturdy shoes and take enough water (there is no shop on site).

➡ There is very little shade so don't forget a hat and sunblock.

➡ Your Hattuşa ticket is also valid for Yazılıkaya, but staff at the ticket office in Hattuşa sometimes have to be prompted to give a ticket, so make sure you do get one.

Aslanlı Kapı · GATE

(Lion's Gate; Map p429) At Aslanlı Kapı, two stone lions (one rather poorly reconstructed) protect the city from evil spirits. This is one of at least six gates in Hattuşa's 4000-year-old defensive walls, though it may never have been completed. You can see the best-preserved parts of Hattuşa's fortifications from here, stretching southeast to Yer Kapı and from there to Kral Kapı.

The walls illustrate the Hittites' engineering ingenuity, which enabled them to either build in sympathy with the terrain or transform the landscape, depending on what was required. Natural outcrops were appropriated as part of the walls, and massive ramparts were built to create artificial fortresses.

Yer Kapı · GATE

(Earth Gate; Map p429) The Yer Kapı is Hattuşa's most impressive gate, with an artificial mound pierced by a 70m-long tunnel. The Hittites built the tunnel using a corbelled arch (two flat faces of stones leaning towards one another), as the 'true' arch was not invented until later.

Primitive or not, the arch of Yer Kapı has done its job for millennia, and you can still pass down the stony tunnel as Hittite soldiers did, emerging from the postern. Afterwards, re-enter the city via one of the monumental stairways up the wide stone glacis and pass through the Sphinx Gate, once defended by four great sphinxes. Of the original statues, one is still in situ, two are in the Boğazkale museum and the other has been lost. The two replica sphinxes gracing the inner gate here used to call the Boğazkale museum home before the originals were returned in 2011.

There are wonderful views over the upper city temple district from here.

Kral Kapı · GATE

(King's Gate; Map p429) Kral Kapı is named after the regal-looking figure in the relief carving. The kingly character, a Hittite warrior god protecting the city, is (quite obviously) a copy; the original was removed to Ankara's Museum of Anatolian Civilisations for safekeeping.

Nişantaş · RUINS

(Map p429) At Nişantaş a rock with a faintly visible Hittite inscription cut into it narrates the deeds of Suppiluliuma II (1215–1200 BC), the final Hittite king.

Güney Kale · RUINS

(Southern Fortress; Map p429) Immediately opposite Nişantaş, a path leads up to the excavated Güney Kale with a fine (fenced-off) hieroglyphics chamber with human figure reliefs.

Büyük Kale · RUINS

(Great Fortress; Map p429) Although most of the Büyük Kale site has been excavated, many of the older layers of development have been re-covered to protect them, so what you see today can be hard to decipher. This fortress held the royal palace and the Hittite state archives.

☞ Tours

Hattuşas Taxi · CULTURAL

(📱 0535 389 1089; www.hattusastaxi.com) Murat Bektaş is a mine of Hittite information and runs excellent tours in Hattuşa and around the surrounding area. For those with little time, his full-day Hittite tour of Hattuşa, Yazılıkaya and Alacahöyük (₺100 to ₺110 per person) is highly recommended.

❶ Getting There & Around

The Hattuşa entry gate is 1km from the Aşıkoğlu Hotel and Boğazkale Museum at the start of the village.

To get around Hattuşa and Yazılıkaya without your own transport you'll need to walk or hire a taxi. From the site entrance and ticket kiosk, the road looping around the site is 5km (not including Yazılıkaya which is a further 2km away). The walk itself takes at least an hour and a half, plus time spent exploring the ruins, so figure on spending a good three hours here.

Yazılıkaya

Yazılıkaya (Yazılıkaya Yolu Üzeri; incl Hattuşa ₺8; ◷8am-7pm) means 'Inscribed Rock', and that's exactly what you'll find in these outdoor rock galleries, around 2km from Hattuşa. There are two galleries: the larger one, to the left, was the Hittite empire's holiest religious sanctuary; the narrower one, to the right, has the best-preserved carvings. Together they form the largest known Hittite rock sanctuary, sufficiently preserved to make you wish you could have seen the carvings when they were new.

In the larger gallery, **Chamber A**, there are the faded reliefs of numerous goddesses and pointy-hatted gods marching in procession. Heads and feet are shown in profile, but the torso is shown front on, a common feature of Hittite relief art. The lines of men and women lead to some large reliefs depicting a godly meeting. Teshub stands on two deified mountains (depicted as men) alongside his wife Hepatu, who is standing on the back of a panther. Behind her, their son and (possibly) two daughters are respectively carried by a smaller panther and a double-headed eagle. The largest relief, on the opposite wall, depicts the complex's bearded founder, King Tudhaliya IV, standing on two mountains. The rock ledges were probably used for offerings or sacrifices and the basins for libations.

On the way into **Chamber B**, you should supposedly ask permission of the winged, lion-headed guard depicted by the entrance before entering. The narrow gallery is thought to be a memorial chapel for Tudhaliya IV, dedicated by his son Suppiluliuma II. The large limestone block could have been the base of a statue of the king. Buried until a century ago and better protected from the elements, the carvings include a procession of 12 scimitar-wielding underworld gods. On the opposite wall, the detailed relief of Nergal depicts the underworld deity as a sword; the four lion heads on the handle (two pointing towards the blade, one to the left and the other to the right) double as the deity's knees and shoulders.

THE HITTITES OF HATTUŞA

While the name may evoke images of skin-clad barbarians, the Hittites were a sophisticated people who commanded a vast Middle Eastern empire, conquered Babylon and challenged the Egyptian pharaohs more than 3000 years ago. Apart from a few written references in the Bible and Babylonian tablets, there were few clues to their existence until 1834 when a French traveller, Charles Texier, stumbled upon the ruins of the Hittite capital of Hattuşa.

In 1905 excavations turned up notable works of art and the Hittite state archives, written in cuneiform on thousands of clay tablets. From these tablets, historians and archaeologists were able to construct a history of the Hittite empire.

The original Indo-European Hittites swept into Anatolia around 2000 BC, conquering the local Hatti, from whom they borrowed their culture and name. They established themselves at Hattuşa, the Hatti capital, and in the course of a millennium enlarged and beautified the city. From 1660 to 1190 BC Hattuşa was the capital of first a Hittite kingdom and then empire that, at its height, shared Syria with Egypt and extended as far as Europe.

The Hittites worshipped over a thousand different deities; the most important were Teshub, the storm or weather god, and Hepatu, the sun goddess. The cuneiform tablets revealed a well-ordered society with more than 200 laws. The death sentence was prescribed for bestiality, while thieves got off more lightly provided they paid their victims compensation.

Although it defeated Egypt in 1298 BC, the empire declined in the following centuries, undone by internal squabbles and new threats such as the invasion into Anatolia of the 'sea peoples'. Hattuşa was torched and its inhabitants dispersed. Only a few outlying city states survived until they, too, were swallowed by the Assyrians.

Alacahöyük

The tiny farming hamlet of Alacahöyük is 36km north of Boğazkale and 52km south of Çorum. The site is very old, but the excavation area is small and most of the movable monuments are now in Ankara's Museum of Anatolian Civilisations (p411), so it's really only worth the effort if you've got some spare time after visiting Hattuşa.

◉ Sights

Alacahöyük Museum   MUSEUM
(incl excavation area ₺5; ⊗8am-7pm) Alacahöyük's museum is beside the excavation area and displays artists' impressions of the site at various points in its history, as well as finds dating back to the Chalcolithic and Old Bronze ages.

Monumental Gate   ARCHAEOLOGICAL SITE
The site entry is marked by a monumental gate with two eyeless sphinxes guarding the door. The detailed reliefs (copies; the originals are in Ankara) show musicians, a sword swallower, animals for sacrifice and the Hittite king and queen – all part of festivities and ceremonies dedicated to Teshub, shown here as a bull. Once through the gate, the main excavations on the right-hand side are of a Hittite palace/temple complex.

Royal Shaft Graves   ARCHAEOLOGICAL SITE
To the left of the monumental gate, protected under plastic covers, are the pre-Hittite royal shaft graves. Dating to 2300 to 2100 BC, each skeleton was buried individually along with a variety of personal belongings and several oxen skulls, which archaeologists presume to be the leftovers of a funereal meal.

Tunnel   ARCHAEOLOGICAL SITE
On the far left of the back of the excavation area is an underground tunnel. Walk through it and look down at the fields to see how the Alacahöyük site was built up over the millennia.

❶ Getting There & Away

There's no public transport between Alacahöyük and Boğazkale, so the best way to reach the site is by taxi or with your own transport. If you're really keen, you could take a bus or dolmuş from Çorum to Alaca and another from Alaca to Alacahöyük (one or two services per day, none at weekends).

Çorum

📞 0364 / POP 243,700

Set on an alluvial plain on a branch of the Çorum River, Çorum is a prosperous but unremarkable provincial capital, resting on its modest fame as the chickpea capital of Turkey. The town is full of *leblebiciler* (chickpea roasters) and sacks upon sacks of the chalky little pulses, sorted according to fine distinctions obvious only to a chickpea dealer.

The main reason to stop here is the Çorum Museum; an excellent preparation for Hattuşa. Although it can serve as a base for exploring the region's Hittite and pre-Hittite ruins, the town itself is a rather humdrum affair so unless you want to sample a taste of provincial town life it's usually a better bet to head on to the village of Boğazkale to overnight.

Çorum Museum   MUSEUM
(Cengiz Topel Caddesi; ₺8; ⊗8am-7pm) By the time a traveller reaches Çorum, there's a good chance they'll have seen more than enough small-town museums, but Çorum's is well worth a stop if you're interested in Turkey's pre-Hittite and Hittite past. The museum's centrepiece is a reconstruction of Alacahöyük's royal tomb, with bull skulls and a crumpled skeleton clad in a crown, while other interesting artefacts include a Hittite ceremonial jug with water-spouting bulls around its rim, and the stunning sword of Hittite king Tudhaliya.

🛏 Sleeping & Eating

Anitta Otel   BUSINESS HOTEL €€
(📞0364-213 8515, 0364-666 0999; www.anitta hotel.com; İnönü Caddesi 80; s/d from ₺140/180; ❄🛜🏊) The town's snazziest offering probably doesn't deserve the five stars it's been awarded, but nevertheless this is a genuinely comfortable place to stay. There are numerous facilities and a rooftop restaurant that produces excellent Turkish and international dishes. There are two types of room on offer, with only size and desk space differing between them. Two rooms have disabled access.

Grand Park Hotel   HOTEL €€
(📞0364-225 4131; www.grandpark.com.tr; İnönü Caddesi 60; s/d ₺70/120; ❄🛜) This smart hotel has good-sized rooms with light modern decor and shipshape bathrooms. The friendly

staff and lightning-bolt-fast wi-fi are an extra bonus.

ⓘ Getting There & Away

Being on the main Ankara–Samsun highway, Çorum has good bus connections. Regular buses go to Alaca (₺5, 45 minutes), Ankara (₺25, four hours) via Sungurlu (₺8, 1¼ hours) and Samsun (₺20, three hours). There are also a couple of services daily to Amasya (₺15, two hours) and Kayseri (₺35, 4¾ hours).

The otogar is 3km out of the centre. Nearly all bus companies provide a *servis* into town. A taxi costs around ₺13.

Amasya

☑ 0358 / POP 98,900

Amasya is a tale of two shores. On the north of the Yeşilırmak River, rows of half-timbered Ottoman houses sit squeezed together like chocolate cakes in a patisserie window. To the south, the newer, more modern Turkey tries to get on with things in an outward-looking ode to the succession of empires that reigned in this narrow, rocky valley. Towering above the minarets and the *medreses* (seminaries) are pockmarks of Pontic tombs, etched into the highrise bluff and guarded by a lofty citadel. Amasya's setting may evoke high drama, but life here unfolds as slowly as the train takes apples out of town via a mountain tunnel. In local folklore, these tunnels were dug by Ferhat, a tragic star-crossed figure who was in love with Sirin, the sister of a sultan queen.

History

Called Hakmış by the Hittites, the Amasya area has been inhabited continuously since around 5500 BC. Alexander the Great conquered Amasya in the 4th century BC, then it became the capital of a successor kingdom ruled by a family of Persian *satraps* (provincial governors). By the time of King Mithridates II (281 BC), the kingdom of Pontus entered a golden age and dominated a large part of Anatolia from its Amasya HQ. During the latter part of Pontus' flowering, Amasya was the birthplace of Strabo (c 63 BC to AD 25), the world's first geographer.

Amasya's golden age continued under the Romans, who named it a 'first city' and used it as an administrative centre for rulers such as Pompey. It was Julius Caesar's conquest of a local town that prompted his

immortal words *Veni, vidi, vici* – 'I came, I saw, I conquered'.

After the Romans came the Byzantines, the Danışmend Turks, the Seljuks, the Mongols and the national republic of Abazhistan. In Ottoman times, Amasya was an important military base and testing ground for the sultans' heirs; it also became a centre of Islamic study, with as many as 18 *medreses* and 2000 theological students by the 19th century.

After WWI, Atatürk met his supporters here and hammered out the basic principles of the Turkish struggle for independence, which were published in the Amasya Circular.

◉ Sights

◉ North of the River

The Hatuniye Mahallesi is Amasya's wonderful neighbourhood of restored Ottoman houses, interspersed with good modern reproductions, which lines the north bank of the river. After dark the riverfront buildings, and the castle and rock tombs on the hill behind are lit up like an architectural Christmas tree with rather unsubtle blue and red up-lighting.

★**Tombs of the Pontic Kings** TOMB
(Kral Kaya Mezarları; Map p434; ₺10; ⊙8.30am-6.30pm) Looming above the northern bank of the river is a sheer rock face with the conspicuous cut-rock Tombs of the Pontic Kings. The tombs, cut deep into the limestone as early as the 4th century BC, were used for cult worship of the deified rulers. Up close, the tombs aren't that impressive and some are covered in graffiti. They're much more striking when viewed, as a whole, from the southern bank of the river.

There are more than 20 (empty) tombs in the valley but there are four that you can walk up to. Climb the steps from the souvenir stalls to the ticket office. Just past the office the path divides: turn right to view the most impressive tombs (Map p434), with good panoramas of Amasya. Turn left to find the remnants of the Baths of the Maidens Palace (Map p434), built in the 14th century, and, through a rock-hewn tunnel, a couple more tombs (Map p434).

Hazeranlar Konağı HISTORIC BUILDING
(Map p434; Hazeranlar Sokak; ₺5; ⊙8.30am-5pm Tue-Sun) The Hazeranlar Konağı, constructed in 1865 and restored in 1979, was built by Hasan Talat, the accountant of governor-poet

Amasya

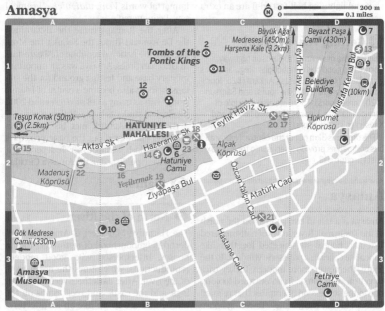

Amasya

◎ Top Sights

◎ Sights

⦿ Activities, Courses & Tours

🛏 Sleeping

🍴 Eating

◉ Drinking & Nightlife

Ziya Paşa, for his sister, Hazeran Hanım. The restored rooms are beautifully furnished in period style, with a refined feel to their chandeliers and carved wood. The **Directorate of Fine Arts gallery** in the basement has changing exhibitions.

Harşena Kale CASTLE
(Kale; ₺5; ⊙8am-7pm) Perched precariously atop rocky Mt Harşena, the *kale* offers magnificent views down the valley. The much-repaired walls date from Pontic times, perhaps around King Mithridates' reign, but a fort stood here from the early Bronze Age. Destroyed and rebuilt by several empires, it once had eight defensive layers descending 300m to the Yeşilırmak River, and a tunnel with 150 steps cut into the mountain.

To reach the castle turn left when you get to the Büyük Ağa Medresesi and follow the road for about 1km to a street on the left marked 'Kale'. It's 1.7km up the mountainside to the entrance.

If you're travelling with little ones in tow, keep a close eye on them; there are plenty of sheer drops and very few safety barriers. Although the castle is exceedingly popular with families during the day, travellers of either sex are advised not to go up unaccompanied on foot during the evening.

Büyük Ağa Medresesi
MEDRESE

(Teyfik Havız Sokak) The impressive Büyük Ağa Medresesi (1488) has an octagonal layout, rarely seen in Ottoman *medrese* architecture. It was built by Sultan Beyazıt II's chief white eunuch Hüseyin Ağa, also known as Grandagha. It still serves as a seminary for boys who are training to be *hafız* (theologians who have memorised the entire Koran) and is not open to the public.

Just before the *medrese* is a small, and not totally natural, waterfall that's a hit with local families.

◉ South of the River

★ Amasya Museum
MUSEUM

(Map p434; ☑ 0358-218 4513; Atatürk Caddesi; ₺5; ◷ 8.30am-5pm) This superb museum packs in beautifully laid out treasures from the Bronze Age and the Hittite, Pontic and Roman eras. Look out for the famous Statuette of Amasya, a bronze figure of the Hittite storm god Teshub. The highlight though is a collection of mummies dating from the 14th-century İlkhan period. The bodies, mummified without removing the organs, were discovered beneath the Burmalı Minare Camii. They're not very suitable for squeamish or young eyes.

There's also a wealth of manuscripts, Ottoman artefacts, an armoury of flintlock guns and the original wooden doors from Amasya's Gök Medrese Camii. All the displays have detailed information panels in English.

Sabuncuoğlu History of Medicine Museum
MUSEUM

(Darüşşifa; Map p434; Mustafa Kemal Bulvarı; adult/child ₺4/2; ◷ 8.30am-5pm Tue-Sun) Built as a mental hospital in 1309 by Ilduş Hatun, wife of the İlkhanid Sultan Olcaytu, the Darüşşifa (or Bimarhane) may have been the first place to try to treat psychiatric disorders with music. It was used as a hospital until the 18th century. One of the most important

physicians who worked here was Serefedin Sabuncuoğlu; today the hospital is a museum to his work and includes surgical equipment and some fascinating (and rather graphic) illustrations of treatments.

Sultan Beyazıt II Camii
MOSQUE

(Map p434; Ziyapaşa Bulvarı) The graceful Sultan Beyazıt II Camii (1486) is Amasya's largest *külliye* (mosque complex), with a *medrese*, fountain, *imaret* (soup kitchen) and library. The main door, *mihrab* (niche in a minaret indicating the direction of Mecca) and pulpit are made of white marble, and its windows feature *kündekari* (interlocking wooden carvings). It's surrounded by manicured lawns which are a popular hang-out place with locals.

In the mosque grounds is the small and rather eccentric Minyatür Amasya Müzesi (Map p434; Ziyapaşa Bulvarı, Sultan Beyazıt II Camii; ₺2; ◷ 9am-noon & 1-7pm), which is a near perfect recreation of Amasya in miniature.

Burmalı Minare Camii
MOSQUE

(Twisted Minaret Mosque; Map p434; Özkan Yalçın Caddesi) This Seljuk-era mosque was built between 1237 and 1247. Inside, the plain white, domed interior is offset by a gold-coloured *mihrab* framed by blue tiles. Outside, the single minaret with its spiral stone design is a later addition, having been added in the 17th century.

Gök Medrese Camii
MOSQUE

(Mosque of the Sky-Blue Seminary; Atatürk Caddesi) The Gök Medrese Camii was built from 1266 to 1267 for Seyfettin Torumtay, the Seljuk governor of Amasya. The *eyvan* (vaulted recess) serving as its main portal is unique in Anatolia, while the *kümbet* (domed tomb) was once covered in *gök* (sky-blue) tiles, hence the name.

Mehmet Paşa Camii
MOSQUE

(Map p434; Mustafa Kemal Bulvarı) The pretty Mehmet Paşa Camii was built in 1486 by Lala Mehmet Paşa, tutor to Şehzade Ahmet, the son of Sultan Beyazıt II. Don't miss the beautiful marble *minber* (pulpit). The complex originally included the builder's tomb, an *imaret*, *tabhane* (hospital), hamam and *handan* (inn).

Gümüşlü Cami
MOSQUE

(Silvery Mosque; Map p434; Meydanı, Atatürk Caddesi) The Gümüşlü Cami (1326) is the earliest Ottoman mosque in Amasya, but has been rebuilt several times: in 1491 after an earthquake, in 1612 after a fire, and again in 1688. It was added to in 1903 and restored again in 1988.

🏃 Activities

Yıldız Hamamı
HAMAM

(Star Hamam; Map p434; Hazeranlar Sokak; wash & massage ₺12; ⊗ men 6-10am & 4-11pm, women 10am-4pm) Built by a Seljuk commander in the 13th century and restored in the 16th century, the Yıldız is a good hamam option on Amasya's north bank of the river.

Mustafa Bey Hamamı
HAMAM

(Map p434; Mustafa Kemal Bulvarı; wash & massage ₺12; ⊗ men 6-10am & 4-11pm, women 10am-4pm) Built in 1436, the Ottoman Mustafa Bey Hamamı is a suitably historic building to have a scrub-down in.

🛏 Sleeping

★ Teşup Konak
BOUTIQUE HOTEL €€

(☑0358-218 6200; www.tesupkonak.com; Yalıboyu Sokak 10; s/d ₺130/180; ❈ 🕸) Teşup is a gem of a place, presided over by English- and German-speaking owner Levent, who goes out of his way to help. In the rooms (two with balconies over the river), everything is kept refined and simple with the dark-wood ceilings and beams offset by gorgeous white linens while bathrooms are large and contemporary (a rarity in Amasya).

Gönül Sefası
GUESTHOUSE €€

(Map p434; ☑0358-212 9461; www.gonul sefasi.com; Yalıboyu Sokak 24; s/d ₺80/150; 🕸) Antique farming equipment decorates the courtyard while Ottoman curios fill every nook in the little restaurant, adding lots of local character to this family-run hotel. The large rooms are kept elegantly simple with comfy beds. Grab one of the two hosting teensy balconies over the Yeşilırmak River to make the most of this delightfully dinky place.

Şükrübey Konağı
GUESTHOUSE €€

(Map p434; ☑0358-212 6285; www. sukrubeykonagi.com.tr; Hazeranlar Sokak 55; s/d ₺70/140; 🕸) A sweet family choice with simple, cosy rooms set around a courtyard, Şükrübey is a winner for its genuinely warm and welcoming atmosphere. Rooms lead out to narrow balconies with views of either the courtyard or the Yeşilırmak River.

The hotel is quite discreet, with only a very small sign.

Uluhan Otel
BOUTIQUE HOTEL €€

(Map p434; ☑0358-212 7575; www.oteluluhan. com; Teyfik Haviz Sokak 15; r ₺150-180; ❈ 🕸) Location, location, location; next door to the main bridge over the Yeşilırmak, the Uluhan is in prime position. Service here is superb and the two restored Ottoman buildings host spacious rooms with classically European-style furniture, carved wood ceilings and shiny modern bathrooms. You'll want to bag a room in the riverfront building for the views.

🍴 Eating & Drinking

Amasya's best eating is found in its hotels, but there are a few reasonable cafes and restaurants in Hatuniye Mahallesi and plenty of basic options in the town centre. Amasya is famed for its apples, which give autumn visitors one more thing to sink their teeth into.

Amaseia Mutfağı
TURKISH €

(Map p434; Hazeranlar Sokak; mains ₺9.50-22; ⊗11.30am-11pm; 🍴) Head up the creaky stairs to the dining room of this old Ottoman house and munch on mantı (Turkish ravioli), scoff down dolmades or get your meat fix with one of their grills. Amaseia has solid food, superb service and, if you're lucky to get one of the tables on the tiny balcony, excellent riverfront views.

Sehzade Balık Ekmek
TURKISH €

(Map p434; Ziyapaşa Bulvarı; sandwich ₺6-8; ⊗11am-11pm) Balık ekmek (fish sandwich) and köfte ekmek (meatball sandwich) served up on a boat moored on the Yeşilırmak. Skip it for dinner – when they woo in the students by blasting incredibly loud Turkish rock music – but this is great stuff for a cheap lunch.

Strabon Restaurant
MODERN TURKISH €€

(Map p434; ☑0358-212 4012; Teyfik Haviz Sokak; mains ₺17-25; ⊗10am-11pm) Our favourite riverside deck in Amasya. The hot or cold mezes (₺6 to ₺12) are tasty and fresh, the meat grills are low on oil, and the grilled balık (fish) is so perfectly cooked it literally falls off the bone. If you're not hungry, Strabon doubles as a fun venue for a few beers.

Taşhan Restaurant
TURKISH €€

(Map p434; ☑0358-212 9900; 11 Özan Yalçın Caddesi; mains ₺16-35; ⊗11am-midnight) Built in 1758 as a caravanserai, and now fully restored and remade as a hotel and restaurant, the beautiful Taşhan is Amasya's top ticket for fine dining. The menu is thoroughly traditional Turkish and the ambience, eating in the vast courtyard where travelling merchants once traded, can't be beaten.

Sehr-i Zade Konağı Hotel Cafe CAFE
(Map p434; Teyfik Haviz Sokak; beer ₺10; ⊘10.30am-11pm) Park yourself up on the riverfront terrace here and enjoy a few beers. Popular with locals and tourists alike for a late afternoon çay or sundowner beer. If you can't be bothered moving on for dinner, it also has a small menu of light meals such as *gözleme* (₺6).

On Cafe CAFE
(Map p434; Şifre Sokak 4; drinks ₺5-13; ⊘11am-midnight) There may be no view but this cafe, with courtyard seating and more tables within the old *konak* rooms and on the rickety wooden balcony, is a relaxing place to kick back with a fruit juice, coffee, or one of a very large menu of frappes. There's also sweet treats such as tiramisu and savoury snacks.

❶ Information

Tourist Office (Map p434; Alçak Köprüsü; ⊘8am-5pm Mon-Sat) Can dole out a couple of leaflets, but that's about the limit of things.

❶ Getting There & Away

BUS
The **otogar** (Boğazköy) is inconveniently 10km northeast of Amasya centre, on the main highway. All bus companies provide free *servis* shuttles from their respective booking offices in the centre. Taxis cost between ₺20 and ₺25.

From the otogar there are regular services to Samsun (₺15, 2½ hours), and Tokat (₺15, two hours); and four to five departures daily to Ankara (₺35, five hours), Çorum (₺15, two hours), İstanbul (₺60, 11 hours) and Kayseri (₺40, six hours).

TRAIN
Amasya **train station** (🖰0358-218 1239; İstasyon Caddesi; ⊘4am-10pm) is served by daily local trains to Samsun and Sivas.

Tokat
🖰0356 / POP 137,800
Locals claim you can hear the steps of civilisations creeping up behind you in Tokat, where history buffs gorge themselves on the mosques, mansions, hamams and *hans* (caravanserais) in this ancient town at the heart of Anatolia.

The town's history features an inevitable roll-call of Anatolian conquerors. The Hittites and Phrygians, the Medes and the Persians, the empire of Alexander the Great, the kingdom of Pontus, the Romans, the Byzantines, the Danışmend Turks, the Seljuks and the Mongol İlkhanids all once marched through this trading entrepôt.

Physically on the rise due to seven centuries of sodden silt, Tokat's architectural treats guarantee the town won't sink into obscurity any time soon. You can easily spend a day here exploring the mazy riddle of back alleys, visiting the excellent museum and getting knuckled by Tokat's notorious masseurs.

◉ Sights

The neighbourhood of squiggling lanes lined with old half-timbered Ottoman houses, behind the Taş Han and running west to Tokat Museum, is fun to explore.

★Tokat Museum MUSEUM
(Sulusokak Caddesi; ⊘8am-5pm Tue-Sun) **FREE**
Tokat's impressive museum is housed within the beautifully restored Arastalı Bedesten (covered market). The collection packs in intricately decorated Bronze Age and Hittite artefacts, Phrygian ceramics, Hellenic jewellery, Roman tombs, and icons and relics from Tokat's churches (including a Greek Orthodox representation of John the Baptist with his head on a platter), all with plenty of English information to help you make sense of the vast amount of history on display here. It's easily one of central Anatolia's best museums.

Gök Medrese MEDRESE
(Blue Seminary; GOP Bulvarı) Constructed after the fall of the Seljuks and the coming of the Mongols by local potentate Pervane Muhinedin Süleyman, the 13th-century Gök Medrese has also served as a hospital and a school.

Very few of the building's *gök* (sky-blue) tiles are left on the facade, but there are enough on the interior courtyard walls to give an idea of what it must have looked like in its glory days.

At the time of writing the *medrese* was closed for renovations.

Mevlevihane MUSEUM
(Bey Sokağı; ⊘8am-6pm Mon-Fri, from 9am Sat & Sun) **FREE** Turn left on GOP Bulvarı just before Latifoğlu Konağı and cross the canal

DON'T MISS

DIVINE DOORS OF DIVRIĞI

The quadruplet of 780-year-old stone doorways on Divriği's Ulu Cami and Darüşşifası complex are so intricately carved that some say their craftmanship proves the existence of god.

Although the sleepy settlement of Divriği seems an obscure place for one of Turkey's finest old religious structures, this was once the capital of a Seljuk *beylik* (principality), ruled over by the local emir Ahmet Şah and his wife, Melike Turan Melik, who founded the adjoining institutions in 1228.

The entrances to both the **Ulu Cami and the Darüşşifası** (Grand Mosque & Hospital; ⊙ 8am-5pm) FREE are truly stupendous, their reliefs densely carved in such minute detail that it's hard to imagine the stone started out flat. It's the tasteful Seljuk equivalent of having a cinema in your house, the sort of thing only a provincial emir with more money than sense could have dreamt of building.

Entered through the 14m-high **Darüşşifa Gate**, the hospital (one of the oldest in Anatolia) is pervaded by an air of serenity. The vast domed inner courtyard is centred on an octagonal pool with a spiral run-off, which allowed the tinkle of running water to break the silence of the room and soothe patients' nerves. A platform raised above the main floor may have been for musicians who likewise soothed the patients. The building was used as a *medrese* (seminary) from the 18th century.

Next door to the Darüşşifası, the **West Gate** of the mosque is a riot of kilim motifs, rosettes and textured effects. Note the carvings of the two-headed eagles on the far sides of the gate. Inside the mosque is very simple with an intricately carved wooden *minber* (a pulpit in a mosque) and unique *mihrab* (niche in a minaret indicating the direction of Mecca).

On the northern side of the mosque is the spectacular **North Gate**, a dizzying cornucopia of floral designs, Arabic inscriptions and a wealth of geometric patterns and medallions. Climb the stairs to the eastern side to view the smaller **Shah's Gate**.

You could easily lose an hour or so wandering Divriği's old neighbourhood of dilapidated Ottoman houses, across the highway from the Ulu Cami. Of particular note, check out the once extremely grand **Shevkut Efendi Evi** with its octagonal tower still protruding from the roof although the entire building looks like it's about to keel over at any minute.

Dolmuş services from Sivas leave from the terminal beside Sivas otogar at 9am, noon, 3pm and 5pm (₺20, 2½ hours), and from Divriği back to Sivas at 8.30am, noon and 4.30pm. All stop in Kangal.

A return taxi from Sivas costs about ₺200. Take ID as there is sometimes a police checkpoint after Kangal.

There are three (very slow) train services daily between Sivas and Divriği.

Drivers should note that there's no through road to Erzincan from Divriği, forcing you to head northwest to Zara and the highway before you can start driving east.

to get to this restored dervish lodge with its museum to all things dervish, built in 1613 by Muslu Ağa, vizier to Sultan Ahmet I (r 1603–17). One of the most tranquil corners of Tokat, the building is set inside a small garden compound of cobbled streets and Ottoman houses buckling under the weight of years.

The exhibits inside include metalwork, illustrated Korans and prayer carpets gathered from mosques throughout the region. The *semahane* (where whirling ceremonies were held) is upstairs. The room contains an interesting collection of dervish paraphernalia, but the effect is unfortunately tarnished by the tacky mannequins illustrating the *sema* (whirling ceremony).

Follow the garden path round to the back of the building to get to **Muslu Ağa Köşkü**, which the vizier used as his family residence.

Just outside, back across the canal, is Tokat's **Ottoman Clock Tower**; the numbers on its faces are in Arabic.

Sulusokak Caddesi
ARCHITECTURE

Many of Tokat's old buildings still survive, though in ruins, along Sulusokak Caddesi, which was the main thoroughfare before the perpendicular Samsun–Sivas road was improved in the 1960s. With its ancient buildings and dusty side-streets it's an interesting area to poke about.

Sulusokak Caddesi runs west from the north side of Cumhuriyet Meydanı on GOP Bulvarı, past Ali Paşa Camii (1572), which has classical Ottoman features on its grand central dome. Continue along the road and on the right you'll see the tiny Ali Tusi Türbesi (1233), a brick Seljuk work that incorporates some fine blue tiles.

Further on, on the same side of the road, the brick-and-wood Sulu Han is still in use, with its interior painted turquoise and white. This 17th-century Ottoman caravanserai provided accommodation for merchants visiting the Arastalı Bedesten (covered market) next door, which has been superbly reconstructed and now houses the Tokat Museum (p437). Right after the *bedesten* is the 16th-century Takyeciler Camii, displaying the nine-domed style of great Ottoman mosques.

Across the road from the *bedesten* are two spectacular buildings that are currently being restored: the Yağıbasan Medresisi (1152), one of Anatolia's first open-domed medreses, and beside it the enormous bulk of the 16th-century Ottoman Deveciler Hanı, one of Tokat's finest caravanserais.

Carry on up the road and you'll come to the tiny 14th-century Kadı Hasan Camii and the Ottoman Paşa Hamamı (1434).

Taş Han　　　　　　HISTORIC BUILDING
(GOP Bulvarı; ⊙8am-8pm; `FREE`) The 17th-century Taş Han is an Ottoman caravanserai and workshop with a cafe in the courtyard which makes a good pit-stop while exploring. The shops within its arched arcades sell a mixture of hand-painted *yazmas* (headscarves) and other textiles, copperware and knick-knacks.

Sümbül Baba Türbesi　　　　TOMB
(GOP Bulvarı) This octagonal Seljuk tomb dates from 1291 and is a few hundred metres north of the Taş Han.

Tokat Castle　　　　　　CASTLE
(Tokat Kalesi) Tokat's 5th-century castle was restored during the Seljuk and Ottoman eras but little remains today except the fine view. To get here, take the road beside the Sümbül Baba Türbesi; it's about a 1km walk uphill. Solo female travellers should not go up alone.

Latifoğlu Konağı　　HISTORIC BUILDING
(GOP Bulvarı; ⊙8am-noon & 1-5pm; `FREE`) Two blocks south of Cumhuriyet Meydanı, the splendid 19th-century Latifoğlu Konağı is a fine example of baroque architecture in the Ottoman style. The rooms have been restored to their former finery with elaborately carved wood ceilings and intricately embellished plasterwork detail.

🏃 Activities

Ali Paşa Hamam　　　　　　HAMAM
(GOP Bulvarı; ⊙men 5am-11pm, women 9am-5pm) These baths, under domes studded with glass bulbs to admit natural light, were built in 1572 for Ali Paşa, one of the sons of Süleyman the Magnificent. They have separate bathing areas for men and women, and the full works should cost around ₺15.

🛏 Sleeping

Çamlıca Otel　　　　　　HOTEL €€
(☑0356-214 1269; 79 GOP Bulvarı; s/d ₺60/100; 🛜) Look, don't expect anything flashy because then the small beige rooms are bound to disappoint, but this central cheapie is a comfortable, friendly and safe place to bed down for the night.

Çavuşoğlu Tower Hotel　BUSINESS HOTEL €€€
(☑0356-212 3570; www.cavusoglutowerhotel. com; GOP Blvd 172a; r from ₺180; 🅿🛜🛗) The smartest address in town has large rooms with floor-to-ceiling windows (which from the upper levels will make a vertigo sufferer wobble). There's a decent breakfast spread, a pool and a gym. No, it's not worth the four stars it's awarded itself but hey, this is Tokat.

🍴 Eating & Drinking

Restaurants are clustered all along GOP Bulvarı. While in town try a Tokat kebap (lamb cubes grilled with potato, tomato, aubergine and garlic).

★Ocakbaşı Mis Kebap　　　　KEBAP €
(Hükümet Caddesi; mains ₺13-23; ⊙10am-11pm) Ask a local where the best Tokat kebaps (and pretty much any other kind of kebap) can be found and there's a good chance they will send you to this bustling, upmarket restaurant with smartly turned-out waiters and on-the-ball service. The monster-sized Tokat kebap (₺40) is a must if you're not dining solo.

Chef Un's Çi Börek – Mantı　　TURKISH €
(Mihatpaşa Caddesi; mantı ₺10; ⊙8am-8pm; 🛜) With its flowerpot-covered entrance, blue-and-white decor and tattooed wait staff, Chef Un's has a vibe more Turkish Med than

Anatolian heartland. And you know the *mantı* (Turkish ravioli) has got to be good when Turks are crammed in at lunch time slurping down bowls of the stuff. They do *börek* as well, and good soup. But you're here for the *mantı*.

Cadde CAFE €

(GOP Bulvarı; mains ₺8-18; ⊙8am-midnight; 🖥) This modern cafe hums with students and young professionals who come here to slouch on the comfy sofas and gossip over umpteen glasses of çay or grab a cheap lunch or dinner. There's always set menu specials such as *çorba* (soup) and *İskander kebap* for ₺16 and the Tokat kebap here is one of the cheapest in town.

Konak Café NARGILE CAFE

(☏0356-214 4146; GOP Bulvarı; mains ₺7-15; ⊙9am-11pm) This friendly cafe has multilevel outdoor shaded seating to lounge on after stomping all those historic streets. The menu does the usual *köftes* and kebaps, but it's a great place to just chill out with a juice or çay and puff on a nargile. It's located at the rear of the Latifoğlu Konağı.

❶ Getting There & Away

Tokat's small **otogar** (Gültekin Topçam Bulvarı) is about 1.7km northeast of the main square. Bus companies should provide a *servis* (shuttle) to ferry you to/from town but they can take a while to turn up; if you don't want to wait a taxi will cost about ₺14.

Several bus companies have ticket offices around Cumhuriyet Meydanı. It's worthwhile confirming departure times and booking tickets beforehand as Tokat doesn't have all that many bus departures. Bus-company offices in the centre will also provide a *servis* to the otogar.

There are semi-regular services to Amasya (₺15, two hours), Ankara (₺50, 7½ hours), İstanbul (₺70, 12 hours), Samsun (₺30, three hours) and Sivas (₺15, 1½ hours).

Local minibuses leave from the separate **İlçe ve Köy terminal** (Meydan Caddesi), one block east from the Taş Han.

Sivas

☏0346 / POP 319,500

With a colourful, sometimes tragic history and some of the finest Seljuk buildings ever erected, Sivas is a good stopover en route to the wild east. The city lies at the heart of Turkey politically as well as geographically, thanks to its role in the run-up to the War of Independence. The Congress building resounded with plans, strategies and principles as Atatürk and his adherents discussed their great goal of liberation. At night, as the red flags on the *meydan* (town square) compete for attention with the spotlit minarets nearby, İnönü Bulvarı might be central Anatolia's slickest thoroughfare outside Ankara. The occasional horse and cart gallops down the boulevard, past the neon lights, like a ghost of Anatolia's past.

◉ Sights & Activities

★ **Şifaiye Medresesi** MEDRESE

(Map p441; Hükümet Meydanı) **FREE** Dating to 1218, this was one of the most important medical schools built by the Seljuks and was once Anatolia's foremost hospital. But it wasn't just built to help the sick. It was built to look good, and 800 years later it still impresses.

The decoration features stylised sun/lion and moon/bull motifs, blue Azeri tile work and a poem in Arabic composed by the sultan. Today the courtyard is chock-a-block with teahouse tables while the surrounding *eyvans* (vaulted halls) are home to souvenir stalls.

★ **Çifte Minare Medrese** MEDRESE

(Seminary of the Twin Minarets; Map p441; Hükümet Meydanı) **FREE** Commissioned by the Mongol-İlkhanid vizier Şemsettin Güveyni after defeating the Seljuks at the battle of Kosedağ, the Çifte Minare Medrese (1271) has a *çifte* (pair) of mighty minarets. In fact, that's about all that is left, along with the elaborate portal and facade. Stand on the path between the Çifte and Şifaiye *medreses* (seminaries) to see the difference made by half a century and a shift in power.

Bürüciye Medresesi MEDRESE

(Map p441; Hükümet Meydanı) **FREE** The Bürüciye Medresesi's monumental Seljuk gateway is a fitting entry to this *medrese*, built to teach 'positive sciences' in 1271. Inside, in a modest salon to the left of the entrance, is the tiled tomb of the building's sponsor, Iranian businessman Muzaffer Bürücerdi. The courtyard interior is often used for exhibitions and during the summer months it's used as a tea garden. During the evening, when spotlights illuminate the building, it's a good place to sit back with a çay.

Sivas

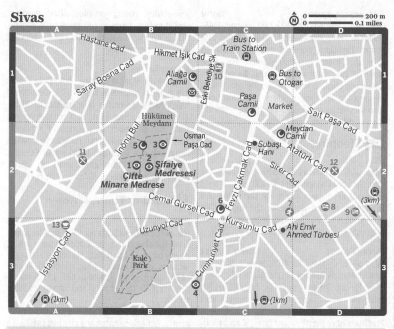

Kale Camii   MOSQUE

(Map p441; Hükümet Meydanı) The squat Ottoman Kale Camii (1580) was constructed by Sultan Murat III's grand vizier Mahmut Paşa.

Gök Medrese   MEDRESE

(Sky-blue Seminary; Map p441; Cumhuriyet Caddesi) Although it's currently undergoing a restoration project that will see it closed for some years to come, you can still view the twin minarets and (scaffolding-covered) facade of the Gök Medrese from outside. It was built in 1271 at the behest of Sahib-i Ata, the grand vizier of Sultan Gıyasettin Keyhüsrev III, who funded Konya's Sahib-i Ata mosque complex. The facade is exuberantly decorated with tiles, brickwork designs and carvings.

Ulu Cami   MOSQUE

(Great Mosque; Map p441; Cemal Gürsel Caddesi) The Ulu Cami (1197) is Sivas' oldest significant building, and one of Anatolia's oldest mosques. Built by the Danışmends, it's a large, low room with a forest of 50 columns. The super-fat brick minaret was added in 1213 and if you look at it from the southern side of the road you'll notice it has a very distinct tilt. Inside, 11 handmade stone bands surround the main praying area and the ornate *mihrab* was discovered during renovations in 1955.

Kuṛşunlu Hamam
HAMAM

(Map p441; ☑men 0346-222 1378, women 0346-221 4790; Kuṛşunlu Caddesi; soak & scrub ₺15; ⊙men 7am-11pm, women 9am-6pm) Built in 1576 this huge, multiple-domed structure had the indignity of being put to work as a salt warehouse for 30 years before it was restored to its former glory and put back into service as a hamam. There are separate men's and women's sections.

🛏 Sleeping

Otel Çakır
HOTEL €

(Map p441; ☑0346-222 4526; www.cakiroteli.com; Kuṛşunlu Caddesi; s/d ₺70/100; 🤶) As long as you don't expect any frills, the Çakır is a fine place to bed down for the night. The poky rooms are clean and tidy and the friendly manager speaks a smattering of English.

Revag Palace
BUSINESS HOTEL €€

(Map p441; ☑0346-223 4105; www.revagpalace.com.tr; Atatürk Caddesi 91; s/d ₺120/160; ❄🤶) The Revag knows how to keep Turkish businessmen happy; with large rooms and a minibar stocked with decent-priced beer. Facilities here (kettles, satellite TV and modern bathrooms) are great and the staff are super-friendly.

★ Sultan Otel
HOTEL €€€

(Map p441; ☑0346-221 2986; www.sultanotel.com.tr; Eski Belediye Sokak 18; s/d ₺120/200; ☷❄🤶) This boutique-style hotel has 27 rooms brushed up with swanky fixtures and furnishings in soft sage and neutral tones, while the bathrooms are sparkling and modern. It's all squeaky-clean and professionally run, with a rooftop bar-restaurant and extensive breakfast buffet to add to the mix. It also seems to be the only hotel in Sivas with a strict no-smoking policy.

🍴 Eating & Drinking

★ Sema Hanımın Yeri
ANATOLIAN €

(Map p441; ☑0346-223 9496; Reşat Şemsettin Sokak; mains ₺6-12; ⊙8am-11pm) The welcoming Madame Sema serves home-cooked food such as *içli köfte* (meatballs stuffed with spices and nuts) to a packed audience of young locals in this small restaurant snaffled down a backstreet off İnönü Caddesi. If you've never eaten in a Turkish home before then this is the next best thing.

Sultan Sofrasi
KEBAP €

(Map p441; Atatürk Caddesi 67; mains ₺8-15; ⊙11am-11pm) Attracting an eclectic mix of love-struck young couples, tired workers and domino-slapping old guys in flat caps, this is an ever-bustling kebap place serving hearty, meaty meals.

Kahve Sarayı
CAFE

(Map p441; Istasyon Caddesi; hot drinks ₺6-10, milkshakes & smoothies ₺11-14; ⊙9.30am-10pm) European-style coffee has landed in Sivas. This place is always bustling with everyone from businessmen to gaggles of students and loved-up couples popping in to down a cappuccino or a frappe. There's also a decent menu (mains ₺13 to ₺23) of grills and Turkified versions of *quesadillas* and burgers.

❶ Getting There & Away

BUS

Bus services from Sivas aren't all that frequent. From the **otogar** (Kayseri Caddesi) there are hourly buses to Tokat (₺15, 1½ hours) and regular services to Amasya (₺30, 3½ hours), Ankara (₺35, seven hours), İstanbul (₺70, 13 hours), Kayseri (₺25, three hours) and Samsun (₺35, six hours).

Buses should provide a *servis* into the city centre. Otherwise catch any city bus (₺1.75, but you'll also need to purchase Sivas' Kentkart transport card, ₺3) heading to the **city centre** (Map p441) from their terminal, next to the otogar. Buses head up Atatürk Caddesi and end their run just uphill from the Paşa Camii. Taxis cost ₺13 from the otogar to the centre.

TRAIN

Sivas **train station** (☑0346-221 7000; İstasyon Caddesi) is a major rail junction for both east–west and north–south lines. The main daily express services are the *Doğu Ekspresi* between Ankara and Kars and the *4 Eylül Mavi Tren* between Ankara and Malatya. There are also local services to Kangal, Divriği and Amasya.

A bus runs to the train station from **Hikmet İşik Caddesi** (Map p441).

Konya

☑0332 / POP 1.2 MILLION

An economic powerhouse that is religiously inspired and a busy university city that's as conservative as they come: Konya treads a delicate path between its historical significance as the home town of the whirling dervish orders and a bastion of Seljuk culture, and its modern importance as an economic boom town. The city derives considerable charm from this juxtaposition of old and

WATCHING THE WHIRLING DERVISHES

The Mevlevi worship ceremony, or *sema,* is a ritual dance representing union with the divine; it's what gives the dervishes their famous whirl, and appears on Unesco's third Proclamation of Masterpieces of the Oral and Intangible Heritage of Humanity. Watching a *sema* can be an evocative, romantic, unforgettable experience. There are many dervish orders worldwide that perform similar rituals, but the original Turkish version is the smoothest and purest, more of an elegant, trancelike dance than the raw energy seen elsewhere.

The dervishes dress in long white robes with full skirts that represent their shrouds. Their voluminous black cloaks symbolise their worldly tombs, their conical felt hats their tombstones.

The ceremony begins when the *hafız,* a scholar who has committed the entire Koran to memory, intones a prayer for Mevlâna and a verse from the Koran. A kettledrum booms out, followed by the plaintive sound of the *ney* (reed flute). Then the şeyh (master) bows and leads the dervishes in a circle around the hall. After three circuits, the dervishes drop their black cloaks to symbolise their deliverance from worldly attachments. Then one by one, arms folded on their breasts, they spin out onto the floor as they relinquish the earthly life to be reborn in mystical union with the divine.

By holding their right arms up, they receive the blessings of heaven, which are communicated to earth by holding their left arms turned down. As they whirl, they form a 'constellation' of revolving bodies, which itself slowly rotates. The şeyh walks among them to check that each dervish is performing the ritual properly.

The dance is repeated over and over again. Finally, the *hafız* again chants passages from the Koran, thus sealing the mystical union with the divine.

It's worthwhile planning your Konya trip to be here on a Saturday when the *sema* ceremony is performed at the Mevlâna Culture Centre (Whirling Dervish Performance; www.emav.org; Aslanlı Kışla Caddesi; ⊙7pm Sat; 🚇 Mevlâna Kültür Merkezi) FREE. There's usually no need to book but you should arrive by 6.40pm to guarantee your seat.

new. Ancient mosques and the maze-like market district rub up against contemporary Konya around Alaaddin Tepesi, where hip-looking university students talk religion and politics in the tea gardens. If you are passing through this region, say from the coast to Cappadocia, then make time to explore one of Turkey's most compelling cities.

History

Almost 4000 years ago the Hittites called this city 'Kuwanna'. It was Kowania to the Phrygians, Iconium to the Romans and then Konya to the Turks. Iconium was an important provincial town visited several times by Saints Paul and Barnabas.

From about 1150 to 1300, Konya was the capital of the Seljuk Sultanate of Rum, which encompassed most of Anatolia. The Seljuk sultans endowed Konya with dozens of fine buildings in an architectural style that was decidedly Turkish, but had its roots in Persia and Byzantium. Traditionally Konya lay at the heart of Turkey's rich farming 'bread basket', but these days

light industry and pilgrimage tourism are at least as important.

◉ Sights

★ Mevlâna Museum   MUSEUM
(Map p444; ☎0332-351 1215; Asanlı Kışla Caddesi; audioguide ₺10; ⊙10am-6.30pm Mon, 9am-6.30pm Tue-Sun; 🚇 Mevlâna) FREE For Muslims and non-Muslims alike, the main reason to come to Konya is to visit the Mevlâna Museum, the former lodge of the whirling dervishes. It's Celaleddin Rumi (later known as Mevlâna) that we have to thank for giving the world the whirling dervishes and, indirectly, the Mevlâna Museum. Calling it a mere museum, however, makes it sound dead and stale, but the truth couldn't be more different. As one of the biggest pilgrimage centres in Turkey, the museum constantly buzzes with energy.

For Muslims, this is a very holy place, and more than 1.5 million people visit it a year, most of them Turkish. You will see many people praying for Rumi's help. When entering, women should cover their head

Konya

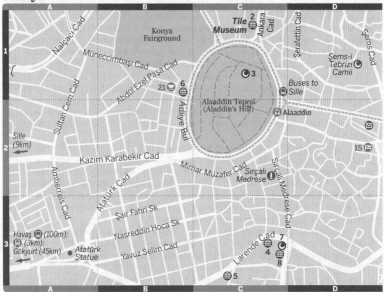

and shoulders, and no one should wear shorts.

The lodge is visible from some distance, its fluted dome of turquoise tiles one of Turkey's most distinctive sights. After walking through a pretty garden you pass through the **Dervişan Kapısı** (Gate of the Dervishes) and enter a courtyard with an ablutions fountain in the centre.

At the entrance to the mausoleum, the Ottoman silver door bears the inscription, 'Those who enter here incomplete will come out perfect'. Remove your shoes before entering. Once inside the mausoleum, look out for the big bronze **Nisan tası** (April bowl) on the left. April rainwater, vital to the farmers of this region, is still considered sacred and was collected in this 13th-century bowl. The tip of Mevlâna's turban was dipped in the water and offered to those in need of healing. Also on the left are six sarcophagi belonging to Bahaeddin Veled's supporters who followed him from Afghanistan.

Continue through to the part of the room directly under the fluted dome. Here you can see **Mevlâna's Tomb** (the largest), flanked by that of his son Sultan Veled and those of other eminent dervishes. They are all covered in velvet shrouds heavy with gold embroidery, but those of Mevlâna and Veled

bear huge turbans, symbols of spiritual authority; the number of wraps denotes the level of spiritual importance. Bahaeddin Veled's wooden tomb stands on one end, leading devotees to say Mevlâna was so holy that even his father stands to show respect. There are 66 sarcophagi on the platform, not all visible.

Mevlâna's tomb dates from Seljuk times. The mosque and *semahane*, where whirling ceremonies were held, were added later by Ottoman sultans (Mehmet the Conqueror was a Mevlevi adherent and Süleyman the Magnificent made charitable donations to the order). Selim I, conqueror of Egypt, donated the Mamluk crystal lamps.

The small **mosque and semahane** to the left of the sepulchral chamber contain exhibits such as musical instruments, the original copy of the Mathnawi, Mevlâna's prayer rug, and a 9th-century gazelle-skin Christian manuscript. There is a casket containing strands of Mohammed's beard, and a copy of the Koran so tiny that its author went blind writing it. Look to the left of the *mihrab* for a *seccade* (prayer carpet) bearing a picture of the Kaaba at Mecca. Made in Iran of silk and wool, it's extremely fine, with some three million knots (144 per square centimetre).

The **matbah** (kitchen) of the lodge is in the southwest corner of the courtyard. It is decorated as it would have been in Mevlâna's day, with mannequins dressed as dervishes. Look out for the wooden practise board, used by novice dervishes to learn to whirl. The dervish cells (where the dervishes lived) run along the northern and western sides of the courtyard. Inside are a host of ethnographical displays relating to dervish life.

The complex can get oppressively busy, and seeing any of the contents of the museum display cases can be a pushing and shoving, head-ducking affair. Come early on a weekday if you want to see all the items in peace. On the other hand, the atmosphere on busy days is almost addictive and more than makes up for not being able to properly examine the museum pieces.

Beside the museum is the **Selimiye Camii** (Map p444; Mevlâna Caddesi).

★**Tile Museum**   MUSEUM
(Karatay Medresesi Çini Müzesi; Map p444; ☑0332-351 1914; Alaaddin Meydanı; ₺5; ⊙9am-6.40pm) Gorgeously restored, the interior central dome and walls of this former Seljuk theological school (1251) showcase some finely preserved blue-and-white Seljuk tilework. There is also an outstanding collection of ceramics on display including exhibits of the octagonal Seljuk tiles unearthed during excavations at Kubad Abad Palace on Lake Beyşehir. Emir Celaleddin Karatay, a Seljuk general, vizier and statesman who built the *medrese,* is buried in one of the corner rooms.

**Museum of Wooden Artefacts
& Stone Carving**   MUSEUM
(Tas ve Ahsap Eserler Müzesi; Map p444; ☑0332-351 3204; Adliye Bulvarı; ₺5; ⊙9am-6.40pm) The İnce Minare Medresesi (Seminary of the Slender Minaret), now the Museum of Wooden Artefacts & Stone Carving, was built in 1264 for Seljuk vizier Sahip Ata. Inside, many of the carvings feature motifs similar to those used in tiles and ceramics. The Seljuks didn't heed Islam's traditional prohibition against human and animal images: there are images of birds (the Seljuk double-headed eagle, for example), humans, lions and leopards.

The octagonal minaret in turquoise relief outside is over 600 years old and gave the seminary its popular name. If it looks short, this is because the top was sliced off by lightning.

Alaaddin Camii
MOSQUE

(Map p444) Konya's most important religious building after the Mevlâna shrine, this Seljuk mosque bestrides Alaaddin Tepesi. Built for Alaeddin Keykubad I, Sultan of Rum from 1219 to 1231, the rambling 13th-century building was designed by a Damascene architect in Arab style. Over the centuries it was embellished, refurbished, ruined and restored. The grand original entrance on the northern side incorporates decoration from earlier Byzantine and Roman buildings.

Surrounding the mosque is the Alaaddin Tepesi, the town's favourite flower garden and park. It is at its sweetest in the spring when its summit is a glowing carpet of tulips.

There are several pleasant tea shops and cafes here.

The mosque and some of the surrounding area on Alaaddin Tepesi was undergoing a huge restoration during our last visit.

Sahib-i Ata Külliyesi
MOSQUE

(Map p444; Larende Caddesi; ⊙ 9am-noon & 1-5pm) Behind its requisite grand entrance with built-in minaret is the Sahib-i Ata Külliyesi, originally constructed during the reign of Alaaddin Keykavus. Destroyed by fire in 1871, it was rebuilt in 13th-century style. The *mihrab* is a fine example of blue Seljuk tile work.

Sahib-i Ata Vakıf Müzesi
MUSEUM

(Map p444; Sırçalı Medrese Caddesi; ⊙ 9am-5pm) FREE This old dervish lodge, with its redbrick and blue-tiled interior is home to the Sahib-i Ata Vakıf Müzesi, with an interesting collection of religious artefacts.

RUMI – THE MAN WHO MADE THE DERVISHES WHIRL

Celaleddin Rumi, the Seljuk Sultanate of Rum, was one of the world's great mystic philosophers. His poetry and religious writings, mostly in Persian, the literary language of the day, are among the most beloved and respected in the Islamic world. Rumi later became known as Mevlâna (Our Guide) to his followers.

Rumi was born in 1207 in Balkh (Afghanistan). His family fled the impending Mongol invasion by moving to Mecca and then to the Sultanate of Rum, reaching Konya by 1228. His father, Bahaeddin Veled, was a noted preacher, known as the Sultan of Scholars, and Rumi became a brilliant student of Islamic theology. After his father's death in 1231, he studied in Aleppo and Damascus, returning to live in Konya by 1240.

In 1244 he met Mehmet Şemseddin Tebrizi (Şemsi Tebrizi or Şems of Tabriz), one of his father's Sufi (Muslim mystic) disciples. Tebrizi had a profound influence on Rumi but, jealous of his overwhelming influence on their master, an angry crowd of Rumi's disciples put Tebrizi to death in 1247. Stunned by the loss, Rumi withdrew from the world to meditate, and wrote his greatest poetic work, the 25,000-verse Mathnawi (Mesnevi in Turkish). He also wrote many aphorisms, ruba'i and ghazal poems, collected into his 'Great Opus', the *Divan-i Kebir*.

Tolerance is central to Mevlâna's teachings, as in this famous verse:

Come, whoever you may be. Even if you may be an infidel, a pagan, or a fire-worshipper, come. Ours is not a brotherhood of despair. Even if you have broken your vows of repentance a hundred times, come.

Rumi died on 17 December 1273, the date now known as his 'wedding night' with Allah. His son, Sultan Veled, organised his followers into the brotherhood called the Mevlevi, or whirling dervishes.

In the centuries following Mevlâna's death, over 100 dervish lodges were founded throughout the Ottoman domains. Dervish orders exerted considerable conservative influence on the country's political, social and economic life, and numerous Ottoman sultans were Mevlevi Sufis. Atatürk saw the dervishes as an obstacle to advancement for the Turkish people and banned them in 1925, but several orders survived on a technicality as religious fraternities. The Konya lodge was revived in 1957 as a 'cultural association' intended to preserve a historical tradition.

Archaeological Museum
MUSEUM

(Map p444; ☑0332-351 3207; Larende Caddesi; ₺5; ◷9am-6.30pm) The rather dusty Archaeological Museum houses interesting finds from Çatalhöyük, including the skeleton of a baby girl, clutching jewellery made of stone and bone. Other artefacts range across the millennia, from Chalcolithic terracotta jars to Hittite hieroglyphs, an Assyrian oil lamp shaped like a bunch of grapes, and bronze and stone Roman sarcophagi, one narrating the labours of Hercules in high-relief carvings.

Ethnographic Museum
MUSEUM

(Map p444; Larende Caddesi; ₺5; ◷8.30am-12.30pm & 1.30-5pm Tue-Sun) The little-visited Ethnographic Museum has a good collection of Ottoman craftwork although some of the exhibits do look a little dusty and unloved.

Koyunoğlu Museum
MUSEUM

(Kerimler Caddesi 25; ◷8am-12.30pm & 1.30-5pm Tue-Sun) **FREE** This curious museum contains the legacy of railway inspector Izzet Koyunoğlu who built up his esoteric collection of rare, er, collectables on his travels through Turkey. Our heart goes out to the tired-looking stuffed pelican, but there is a wonderful variety of exhibits, encompassing prehistoric bones, rhinoceros-horn rosaries, mammoth bones, boxwood spoons bearing words of wisdom about food, 19th-century carriage clocks, and old photos of Konya.

⭐ Festivals & Events

Mevlâna Festival
RELIGIOUS

(Mevlâna Culture Centre; ◷Dec) The annual Mevlâna Festival runs for a fortnight, culminating on 17 December, the anniversary of Mevlâna's 'wedding night' with Allah. Tickets (and accommodation) should be booked well in advance; contact the tourist office (p448) for assistance. If you can't get a ticket, other venues around town host dancers during the festival, although they are not of the same quality.

🛏 Sleeping

There's certainly no shortage of hotels in Konya. Be aware though that during the Mevlâna Festival, room rates go up and you'll need to book well in advance.

Ulusan Otel
HOTEL €

(Map p444; ☑0332-351 5004, 0532 488 2333; ulusanhotel@hotmail.com; Çarşi PTT Arkasi 4; s/d ₺40/80; ◉🛜) This is the pick of the Konya cheapies. The rooms may be totally basic, but they're bright and spotlessly clean. Shared bathrooms are immaculately kept (some rooms have private bathrooms) and the communal area is full of homey knick-knacks.

Hotel Yasin
HOTEL €

(Map p444; ☑0332-351 1624; www.otelyasin.com; Yusuf Ağa Sokak 21; s/d ₺50/100; 🛜) In the heart of the souk, this place has more than just price going for it. Backpackers will find amply proportioned, light-filled rooms that are well looked after, and friendly management.

⭐ Derviş Otel
BOUTIQUE HOTEL €€

(Map p444; ☑0332-350 0842; www.dervishotel.com; Güngör Sokak 7; r €50-75, f €100; ◉❄🛜) This airy, light-filled, 200-year-old house has been converted into a rather wonderful boutique hotel. All of the seven spacious rooms have lovely soft colour schemes with local carpets covering the wooden floors, comfortable beds and modern bathrooms to boot. With enthusiastic management providing truly personal service this is a top-notch alternative to Konya's more anonymous hotels.

Hotel Rumi
HOTEL €€

(Map p444; ☑0332-353 1121; www.rumihotel.com; Durakfakih Sokak 5; s/d/tr €35/55/70; ❄🛜) Rooms at the Rumi (with home comforts such as kettles) are a tad on the small side and styled plainly in beige but staff seem to delight in offering genuine service and the top-level breakfast room has killer views over to the Mevlâna Museum. It's an oasis of calm in central Konya.

Bera Mevlâna
BUSINESS HOTEL €€

(Map p444; ☑0332-350 4242; www.bera.com.tr; Mevlâna Caddesi; s/d ₺100/150; ❄🛜) With its spacious rooms and snazzy modern bathrooms, this mid-size Turkish business-style hotel seriously punches above its weight when it comes to value. Staff are friendly and the central location can't be beaten.

⭐ Hich Hotel
BOUTIQUE HOTEL €€€

(Map p444; ☑0332-353 4424; www.hichhotel.com; Celal Sokak 6; r €80-150; ◉❄🛜) This design hotel mixes contemporary furnishings and luxurious touches such as espresso coffee machines in the rooms with the elegant original structure of the two

150-year-old buildings it occupies. There are gorgeous floor tiles and stained-glass window features in abundance. Outside is a sunny garden terrace cafe and you can spin your way to the Mevlâna Museum in but a moment.

🍴 Eating & Drinking

Konya's speciality is *fırın kebap*, slices of (hopefully) tender, fairly greasy, oven-roasted mutton served on puffy bread. The city bakers also make excellent fresh pide topped with minced lamb, cheese or eggs, but in Konya pide is called *etli ekmek* (bread with meat).

★ Somatçı ANATOLIAN €
(Map p444; ☑ 0332-351 6696; www.somatci.com; Mengüç Sokak 36; dishes ₺6.50-25; ⏱ 9am-11pm; 🍴) Rekindling old recipes from the Seljuk and Ottoman age, this restaurant uses the finest ingredients and cooks everything with panache. Staff are happy to advise on dishes and the setting inside a carefully restored old building is spot on.

★ Konak Konya Mutfağı ANATOLIAN €
(Map p444; ☑ 0332-352 8547; Piriesat Caddesi 5; mains ₺10-22; ⏱ 11am-10pm; 🍴) This traditional restaurant is run by well-known food writer Nevin Halıcı, who puts her personal twist on Turkish classics. Grab an outside table and dine beside vine-draped pillars and a fragrant rose garden. The *tirit* (bread smothered in yoghurt and browned butter) and *fıran kebap* are both good here and sweet tooths should definitely save room to try the unusual desserts.

Deva 1 Restaurant KEBAP €
(Map p444; ☑ 0332-350 0519; Mevlâna Caddesi; mains ₺16-22; ⏱ 11.30am-10pm) Our favourite place in town for Konya's speciality *fırın kebap*. The meat here is always succulent and cooked to perfection.

Şifa Lokantası LOKANTA €
(Map p444; ☑ 0332-352 0519; Mevlâna Caddesi 29; mains ₺8-21; ⏱ 10am-9.30pm; 🍴) Super-fast service makes this cheap and cheerful restaurant a favourite with the lunchtime crowd. The pide is filling, fresh and tasty, the kebaps are decent and there's always a couple of veg dishes on offer.

HI Cafe CAFE
(Map p444; Mevlâna Caddesi; coffee ₺8-10; ⏱ 10.30am-8pm) In a serious sign of Konya moving with the times, this funky cafe serves up cappuccinos, French press and frappes a hop-skip-jump from the Mevlâna Museum entrance. Very contemporary presentation – all chunky wooden boards and icing sugar–dusted complimentary treats – and endearingly sweet service tops off the coffee experience.

Osmanlı Çarşısı CAFE
(Map p444; ☑ 0332-353 3257; İnce Minare Sokak 35a; ⏱ 11am-9pm) An atmospheric early-20th-century house with terraces, pavement seating and cushions galore where students talk politics while sucking on nargile and old-timers slapping dominoes down sit in the same chairs they've occupied for years and years.

🛍 Shopping

Bazaar MARKET
(Map p444) Konya's bazaar sprawls back from the post office building virtually all the way to the Mevlâna Museum, cramming the narrow streets with stalls, roving vendors and the occasional horse-drawn cart. There's a concentration of shops selling religious paraphernalia and tacky souvenirs at the Mevlâna Museum end.

ℹ Information

There is an exceedingly helpful **Tourist Office** (Map p444; ☑ 0332-353 4020; Aslanı Kışla Caddesi; ⏱ 9am-5pm Mon-Sat) with free city maps and bundles of brochures covering historic sites in and around Konya. It can also organise guides and has information on the weekly whirling dervish shows.

DANGERS & ANNOYANCES

Konya has a longstanding reputation for religious conservatism. Not that this should inconvenience you, but take special care not to upset the pious and make sure you're not an annoyance. If you visit during Ramadan, be aware that many restaurants will be closed during the daylight fasting hours; as a courtesy to those who are fasting, don't eat or drink in public during the day.

Non-Muslim women seem to encounter more hassle in this bastion of propriety than in many other Turkish cities, and dressing conservatively will help you avoid problems. Men can wander around in shorts without encountering any tension, but may prefer to wear something longer to fit in with local customs.

Male travellers have reported being propositioned in the Tarihi Mahkeme Hamamı.

SILLE

If you're looking for an easy excursion from Konya, head to the village of Sille, where a rock face full of cave dwellings overlooks a valley of bendy-beamed village houses dolled up with flowerpots overflowing with pansies.

Sille's domed Byzantine **St Helen's Church** (Ayaelena Kilisesi; Hükümet Caddesi; ⊙9am-6pm Tue-Sun), near the last bus stop, was reputedly founded by Empress Helena, mother of Constantine the Great, although the present-day structure dates to the late 19th century. Its interior wall and pillar frescoes – including a scene showing Christ's baptism, and depictions of the apostles – have been fully restored.

On the hill to the north of Sille stands the tiny **Küçük Kilese** (⊙9am-6pm Tue-Sun). The chapel has been fully renovated and is now home to the **Zaman Müzesi** (Time Museum) with a small collection of time-keeping implements from across history. The collection itself isn't particularly inspiring but the view over the village from the terrace is worth the walk up the hill.

Apart from the town's churches, you can search out a whole series of **cave dwellings** and chapels running behind the village, carved into the soft rock. None are in very good condition, but they're fun to explore.

Getting There & Away

Bus 64 from Mevlâna Caddesi (opposite Alaaddin Tepesi) in **Konya** (Map p444) leaves roughly every half-hour for Sille (₺3.20, 25 minutes). Heading back, the bus leaves from the bus stop opposite St Helen's Church.

You'll need a Konya ELKart travelcard (₺1, available in Sille and Konya) to travel on the bus.

❶ Getting There & Away

AIR

Both **Turkish Airlines** (☑ 0332-321 2100; Ferit Paşa Caddesi; ⊙ 8.30am-5.30pm Mon-Fri, to 1.30pm Sat) and **Pegasus Airlines** (www.flypgs.com) operate several flights daily to and from İstanbul.

The airport is about 13km northeast of the city centre; expect to pay ₺40 to ₺50 by taxi.

Havaş (☑ 0332-239 0105; www.havas.net; Turkish Airlines Office, Ferit Paşa Caddesi; ₺10) runs an airport shuttle-bus service (30 minutes, bus schedule according to flight arrival/departure times) between the airport and central Konya. Buses leave from outside the Turkish Airlines office near Anıt Meydanı.

BUS

Konya's **otogar** (İstanbul Caddesi) is about 7km north of Alaaddin Tepesi, accessible by tram from town. Regular buses serve all major destinations, including Ankara (₺30, 3½ hours); Antalya (₺40, five hours); İstanbul (₺70, 11½ hours); Karaman (₺20, 1½ hours); Nevşehir (₺30, three hours); and Sivas (₺50, seven hours). There are bus company ticket offices on Mevlâna Caddesi and around Alaaddin Tepesi.

The **Karatay Terminal** (Eski Garaj; Map p444; Pırıeasat Caddesi), 1km southwest of the Mevlâna Museum, has bus and dolmuş services to local villages.

TRAIN

The **train station** (Alay Caddesi) is about 3km southwest of the centre. There are seven high-speed train links between Konya and Ankara daily (economy/business class ₺30/43, two hours).

❶ Getting Around

In order to use Konya's city buses, trams and minibuses you need to have a Konya ElKart travel card (₺1), which can be bought from booths, kiosks and many small grocery shops near any of the larger transport stops.

To get to the city centre from the otogar take any tram from the east side of the station to Alaaddin Tepesi (30 minutes); fares, which cover two journeys, are ₺3.20. Trams run 24 hours a day, with one per hour after midnight. A taxi costs around ₺25.

There are half-hourly minibuses from the train station to the centre. A taxi from the station to the Mevlâna Museum costs about ₺15.

Innumerable minibuses and city buses ply Mevlâna Caddesi. The main bus stop (for buses heading towards the otogar and into the suburbs) is at the intersection of Mevlâna Caddesi and Adliye Bulvarı.

Around Konya

Çatalhöyük

No, this isn't a hallucination brought on by the parched Konya plain. Rising 20m above the flatlands, the East Mound at Çatalhöyük (⊙8am-5pm) **FREE** is left over from one of the largest neolithic settlements on earth. About 9500 years ago, up to 8000 people lived here, and the mound comprises 13 levels of buildings, each containing around 1000 structures. Little remains of the ancient centre other than the excavation areas, which draw archaeologists from all over the world.

If you visit between June and September, when the digs mostly take place, you might find an expert to chat to. At other times, the museum does a good job of explaining the site and the excavations, which began in 1961 under British archaeologist James Mellaart and have continued with the involvement of the local community. Mellaart's controversial theories about mother-goddess worship here caused the Turkish government to close the site for 30 years.

Near the museum entrance stands the experimental house, a reconstructed mud-brick hut used to test various theories about neolithic culture. People at Çatalhöyük lived in tightly packed dwellings that were connected by ladders between the roofs instead of streets, and were filled in and built over when they started to wear out. Skeletons were found buried under the floors and most of the houses may have doubled as shrines. The settlement was highly organised, but there are no obvious signs of any central government system.

From the museum you can walk across the mound to the dome-covered north shelter where excavation work has uncovered the remains of several buildings with their outlines still visible. A short trail then leads to the south area. With 21m of archaeological deposits, many of the site's most famous discoveries were made here. The lowest level of excavation, begun by Mellaart, is the deepest at Çatalhöyük and holds deposits left more than 9000 years ago. There are information panels on the viewing platforms of both excavation areas which help you decipher the site.

ⓘ Getting There & Away

To get here by public transport from Konya, 33km northwest, get the Karkın minibus, which leaves the Karatay Terminal (also called Eski Garaj) at 7am, 9.30am and 4.50pm on weekdays. Get off at Kük Koy (₺7.50, 45 minutes) and walk 1km to the site, or you may be able to persuade the driver to take you the whole way. Going back, minibuses leave Kük Koy at 7.15am, 3pm and 7pm. Getting there by bus at the weekend is much harder: there are buses at 9am and midday on Saturdays and none on Sundays.

A taxi from Konya to the site and back will cost about ₺50.

Gökyurt

A little piece of Cappadocia to the southwest of Konya, the landscape at Gökyurt (ancient Kilistra) is reminiscent of what you'll see in Cappadocia's Ihlara Valley: a gorge with dwellings and medieval churches cut into the rock face, but without the crowds. A trip out here makes a lovely half-day excursion.

St Paul is thought to have stayed here on his three Anatolian expeditions and the area has long been a Christian pilgrimage site.

There's one particularly fine church cut completely out of the rock, but no frescoes. The village the cave dwellings are found in is full of ever-smiling farming folk who will literally take you by the hand and lead you to the best of the caves. After you've finished exploring here set out to create your own adventures by taking a walk through the stunning surrounding landscape and looking for more cave dwellings.

ⓘ Getting There & Away

The only way to get here directly from Konya, 45km away, is by car or taxi; the latter will charge ₺150 to ₺200 return (including waiting time). There are several daily buses from Konya's Karatay Terminal to Hatunsaray, 18km from Gökyurt, but from there you'll still have to get a taxi and Hatunsaray's taxi drivers are known for making the most of their captive audience by charging fares more expensive than those from Konya.

Driving, you should take the Antalya road, then follow signs to Akören. After about 34km, and a few kilometres before Hatunsaray, look for a tiny brown-and-white sign on the right (marked 'Kilistra-Gökyurt, 16km'). Cyclists need to watch out for sheepdogs roaming about.

Cappadocia

Best Places to Eat

➡ Cappadocia Home Cooking (p483)

➡ Ziggy Cafe (p479)

➡ Saklı Konak (p465)

➡ Topdeck Cave Restaurant (p462)

Alamet-i Farika (p495)

Best Places to Sleep

➡ Hezen Cave Hotel (p475)

➡ Koza Cave Hotel (p461)

➡ Kelebek Hotel (p460)

➡ Sota Cappadocia (p477)

➡ Esbelli Evi (p477)

Why Go?

As if plucked from a whimsical fairytale and set down upon the stark Anatolian plains, Cappadocia is a geological oddity of honeycombed hills and towering boulders of otherworldly beauty. The fantastical topography is matched by the human history here. People have long utilised the region's soft stone, seeking shelter underground and leaving the countryside scattered with fascinating cavern architecture. The fresco-adorned rock-cut churches of Göreme Open-Air Museum and the subterranean refuges of Derinkuyu and Kaymaklı are the most famous sights, while simply bedding down in one of Cappadocia's cave hotels is an experience in 21st-century cave living.

Whether you're wooed here by the hiking potential, the history or the bragging rights of becoming a modern troglodyte for a night, it's the lunarscape panoramas that you'll remember. This region's accordion-ridged valleys, shaded in a palette of dusky orange and cream, are an epiphany of a landscape – the stuff of psychedelic daydreams.

When to Go
Kayseri

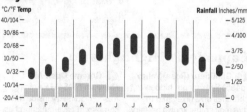

May A shake-up of art, music and yoga descends on the valley moonscapes with the Cappadox Festival.

Jul Pull on your hiking boots. This is the prime time to tackle the Ala Dağlar.

Dec–Feb Join the snow bunnies at Erciyes Dağı (Mt Erciyes) ski resort.

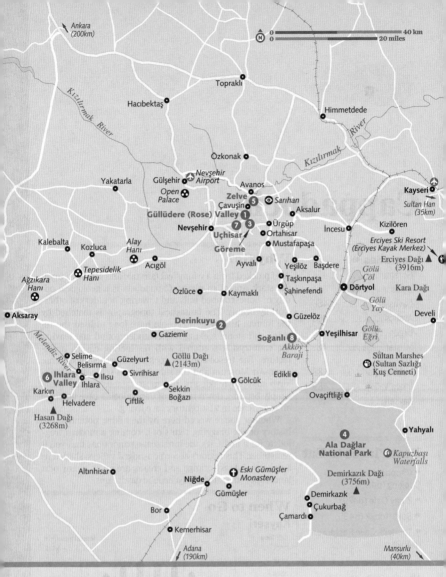

Cappadocia Highlights

1 Güllüdere (Rose) Valley
(p455) Seeking out hidden
churches on a hike amid the
thin rock spires known as 'fairy
chimneys'.

2 Derinkuyu (p473)
Delving into the Byzantine
tunnels below the surface
at Cappadocia's deepest
underground city.

**3 Göreme Open-Air
Museum** (p454) Examining
fresco-clad finery inside this
complex of cave-cut churches.

4 Ala Dağlar National Park
(p488) Hitting the lonely
trails to experience the Taurus
Mountains' stark beauty.

5 Zelve (p467) Imagining
cave-cut life amid knobbly
cliffs of abandoned caverns.

6 Ihlara Valley (p489)
Strolling between verdant fields
and soaring cliffs speckled with
rock-cut chapels.

7 Uçhisar Castle (p464)
Gazing out over a panorama of
rippling rock from the summit.

8 Soğanlı (p483)
Exploring this monastic clutch
of churches hewn out of
conical rocks.

History

The Hittites settled Cappadocia (Kapadokya) from 1800 BC to 1200 BC, after which smaller kingdoms held power. Then came the Persians, followed by the Romans, who established the capital of Caesarea (today's Kayseri). During the Roman and Byzantine periods, Cappadocia became a refuge for early Christians and, from the 4th to the 11th century, Christianity flourished here; most churches, monasteries and underground cities date from this period. Later, under Seljuk and Ottoman rule, Christians were treated with tolerance.

Cappadocia progressively lost its importance in Anatolia. Its rich past was all but forgotten until a French priest rediscovered the rock-hewn churches in 1907. The tourist boom in the 1980s kick-started a new era, and now Cappadocia is one of Turkey's most famous and popular destinations.

👉 Tours

Tour companies abound in Cappadocia. Prices are usually determined by all operators at the beginning of each season. Make your decision based on the quality of the guide and the extent of the itinerary.

Most tour companies offer two standard full-day tours referred to locally as the Red Tour and the Green Tour.

The Red Tour usually includes visits to Göreme Open-Air Museum, Uçhisar rock castle, Paşabağı and Devrent Valleys and Avanos. The Green Tour generally includes a hike in Ihlara Valley and a trip to an underground city. Most companies charge between ₺100 and ₺110 for the Red Tour and ₺120 for the Green Tour.

Most itineraries finish at a carpet shop, onyx factory or pottery workshop, but it is still worth taking a tour. It is interesting to see traditional Cappadocian craftspeople at work, but make it clear before the trip begins if you are not interested. Most of the hotels work with one or two of the travel agencies. Itineraries do differ slightly between agencies, so it pays to look around.

Guided day hikes, usually in the Güllüdere (Rose), Kızılçukur (Red) or Meskendir Valleys, are also offered by most operators. Costs vary according to destination, degree of difficulty and length.

Other popular tour destinations are Soğanlı Valley (including stops at Keşlik Monastery and Sobesos) and multi-day trips to Nemrut Dağı (Mt Nemrut).

We strongly advise you to avoid booking an expensive Cappadocia tour package upon arrival in İstanbul. If your time is limited and you want to take a tour in Cappadocia, you're better off booking directly from an agent in Cappadocia itself.

ℹ Dangers & Annoyances

Most buses arriving in Cappadocia from the west terminate in Nevşehir, from where a free *servis* (shuttle bus) will ferry you to your final destination. Make sure that your ticket states that it is for Göreme, Ürgüp etc, not just 'Cappadocia'. Be aware that tour companies based at Nevşehir otogar (bus station) have a bad reputation for attempting to get tourists onto their private shuttle buses and then proceeding to hard-sell them tours and accommodation in Nevşehir. We suggest that you avoid any dealings with the tour agents here. The official bus-company *servises* usually meet your bus as it arrives and are clearly marked with the bus-company logo.

If you do find yourself without a *servis* or taxi and you have booked a hotel, it is worth phoning it for assistance; Nevşehir's otogar has long been problematic for travellers and the tourist industry in the rest of Cappadocia is well aware of it.

Walking in central Cappadocia's valleys is a wonderful experience and should not be missed, but solo travellers who do not want to hire a guide should buddy up before venturing into the more isolated areas as there have been several attacks on female tourists in the valleys in recent years. It's also advisable to avoid the valleys and the unlit roads between villages in the evenings.

That said, compared to many other popular traveller destinations across the world, Cappadocia remains an incredibly safe place for solo female travellers. As with any destination, common sense should prevail. Solo travellers should be wary of accepting invitations to go out into the valleys with new acquaintances and all hikers with mobile phones should program their hotel's number into it and take it while walking as a sensible precaution in case they get lost or have an accident.

ℹ Getting There & Away

AIR

Two airports serve central Cappadocia: **Kayseri Airport** (Kayseri Erkilet Havalimanı; ☏0352-337 5494; www.kayseri.dhmi.gov.tr; Kayseri Caddesi) and **Nevşehir Airport** (Nevşehir Kapadokya Havalimanı; ☏0384-421 4451; www.kapadokya.dhmi.gov.tr; Nevşehir Kapadokya Havaalanı Yolu, Gülşehir). Both have several flights daily to/from İstanbul. The main operators are **Turkish Airlines** (www.turkishairlines.com) and **Pegasus Airlines** (www.flypgs.com).

Nevşehir Airport was closed for an indefinite time as of mid-2016 so flights may only be heading to/from Kayseri.

BUS

Most buses from İstanbul and other western Turkey destinations travel to Cappadocia overnight and bring you to Nevşehir, where (if the bus is terminating there) a bus-company *servis* will take you on to Uçhisar, Göreme, Avanos or Ürgüp. From Ankara there are several services throughout the day.

TRAIN

The nearest train stations are at Niğde and Kayseri.

🛈 Getting Around

TO/FROM THE AIRPORT

Very reasonably priced airport shuttle-bus services operate between both Cappadocia airports and the various villages. They must be pre-booked. If you have booked your accommodation the easiest solution is to ask your hotel to arrange an airport-shuttle pick-up for you, though be aware that some hotels beef up the price of shuttle transfers ridiculously. You can also book directly with the shuttle-bus services.

There are a few companies to choose from but **Helios Transfer** (Map p456; ☑ 0384 271 2257; www.heliostransfer.com; Adnan Menderes Caddesi 24/A, Göreme; per passenger to/from either airport €10) and **Cappadocia Express** (Map p456; ☑ 0384-271 3070; www.cappadocia transport.com; Iceridere Sokak 3, Göreme; per passenger to/from Nevşehir Airport ₺20, to/from Kayseri Airport ₺25) seem to be the pick of the bunch, with services operating for all flights coming into and going out of both airports. Both will pick up and drop off to hotels in Avanos, Çavuşin, Göreme, Nevşehir, Ortahisar, Uçhisar and Ürgüp.

CAR & MOTORCYCLE

Cappadocia is great for self-drive visits. Roads are often empty and their condition is reasonable. There is ample parking space, but pulling up outside some cave hotels can be tricky.

LOCAL TRANSPORT

Dolmuşes (minibuses; ₺2 to ₺4 depending on where you get on and off) travel between Ürgüp and Avanos via Ortahisar, the Göreme Open-Air Museum, Göreme, Çavuşin, Paşabağı and Zelve. The services leave Ürgüp otogar hourly between 8am and 7pm. Going in the opposite direction, starting from Avanos, the dolmuşes operate hourly between 8am and 8pm. You can hop on and off anywhere along the route.

There are several other dolmuş services between villages.

The Ihlara Valley in southwest Cappadocia can be visited on a day tour from Göreme. If you want to visit it independently plan to spend the night, as bus changes in Nevşehir and Aksaray prolong travelling time.

TAXI

Taxis are a good option for moving between villages, particularly during the evening when public transport stops. Meters operate but for longer trips including waiting time – eg to Soğanlı or Ihlara – a quoted flat rate is the norm.

Göreme

📶 0384 / POP 2200

Surrounded by epic sweeps of golden, moonscape valley, this remarkable honey-coloured village hollowed out of the hills has long since grown beyond its farming-hamlet roots. Although the central 'downtown' strip has suffered what can only be described as 'un-beautification' recently from a flurry of roadworks, which have partially concreted over the old canal, in the back alleys Göreme's charm has not diminished. Sure, new boutique cave hotels are constantly popping up everywhere, but tourists still have to stop for tractors trundling up narrow, winding streets where elderly ladies knit on sunny stoops. Nearby, the Göreme Open-Air Museum is an all-in-one testament to Byzantine life, while if you wander out of town you'll find storybook landscapes and little-visited rock-cut churches at every turn. With its easygoing allure and stunning setting, it's no wonder Göreme continues to send travellers giddy.

⊙ Sights

★ **Göreme Open-Air Museum** HISTORIC SITE (Göreme Açık Hava Müzesi; ☑ 0384-271 2167; Müze Caddesi; ₺30; ☉ 8.30am-6.45pm Apr-Nov, to 4.45pm Dec-Mar) One of Turkey's Unesco World Heritage Sites, the Göreme Open-Air Museum is an essential stop on any Cappadocian itinerary and deserves a two-hour visit. First an important Byzantine monastic settlement that housed some 20 monks, then a pilgrimage site from the 17th century, this splendid cluster of monastic Byzantine artistry with its rock-cut churches, chapels and monasteries is 1km uphill from Göreme's centre.

Note that the museum's highlight – the Karanlık Kilise – has an additional ₺10 entrance fee.

From the museum ticket booth, follow the cobbled path until you reach the **Aziz**

Basil Şapeli (Chapel of St Basil), dedicated to Kayseri-born St Basil, one of Cappadocia's most important saints. In the main room, St Basil is pictured on the left; a Maltese cross is on the right, along with St George and St Theodore slaying a (faded) dragon, symbolising paganism. On the right of the apse, Mary holds baby Jesus with a cross in his halo.

Just above, bow down to enter the 12th-century Elmalı Kilise (Apple Church), overlooking a valley of poplars. Relatively well preserved, it contains both simple, red-ochre daubs and professionally painted frescoes of biblical scenes. The Ascension is pictured above the door. The church's name is thought to derive from an apple tree that grew nearby or from a misinterpretation of the globe held by the Archangel Gabriel, in the third dome.

Byzantine soldiers carved the 11th-century Azize Barbara Şapeli (Chapel of St Barbara), dedicated to their patron saint, who is depicted on the left as you enter. They also painted the mysterious red ochre scenes on the roof – the middle one could represent the Ascension; above the St George representation on the far wall, the strange creature could be a dragon, and the two crosses the beast's usual slayers.

Uphill is the Yılanlı Kilise (Snake Church), also called the Church of St Onuphrius, where St George's ubiquitous dragon-foe is still having a bad day. To add insult to fatal injury, the church got its current moniker when locals mistook the pictured dragon for a snake. The hermetic hermaphrodite St Onuphrius is depicted on the right, holding a genitalia-covering palm leaf. Straight ahead, the small figure next to Jesus is one of the church's financiers.

The stunning, fresco-filled Karanlık Kilise (Dark Church; admission ₺10) is the most famous of the museum's churches. It takes its name from the fact that it originally had very few windows. Luckily, this lack of light preserved the vivid colour of the frescoes, which show, among other things, Christ as Pantocrator, Christ on the cross and the Betrayal by Judas. The church was restored at great expense and the entrance fee is intended to limit visitor numbers to further preserve the frescoes.

Just past the Karanlık Kilise, the small Azize Katarina Şapeli (Chapel of St Catherine) has frescoes of St George, St Catherine and the Deesis (a seated Christ flanked by the Virgin and John the Baptist).

ℹ **VISITING THE MUSEUM**

➡ Arrive early in the morning or near closing to bypass tour groups.

➡ Avoid weekends if possible, when the museum is at its busiest.

➡ Don't skimp on Karanlık Kilise – it's worth the extra ₺10.

➡ The museum is an easy, though uphill, 1km walk from town.

➡ Beware the sun – this is an 'open-air' museum.

The 13th-century Çarıklı Kilise (Sandal Church) is named for the footprints marked in the floor, representing the last imprints left by Jesus before he ascended to heaven. The four gospel writers are depicted below the central dome; in the arch over the door to the left is the Betrayal by Judas.

Downhill, the Rahibeler Manastırı (Nunnery) was originally several storeys high. All that remain are a large plain dining hall and, up some steps, a small chapel with unremarkable frescoes, but the entire craggy structure is cordoned off due to rock falls now.

When you exit the Open-Air Museum, don't forget to cross the road to visit the Tokalı Kilise (Buckle Church), 50m down the hill towards Göreme and covered by the same ticket. This is one of Göreme's biggest and finest churches, with an underground chapel and fabulous, recently restored frescoes painted in a narrative (rather than liturgical) cycle. Entry is via the barrel-vaulted chamber of the 10th-century 'old' Tokalı Kilise, with frescoes portraying the life of Christ. Upstairs, the 'new' church, built less than a hundred years later, is also alive with frescoes on a similar theme. The holes in the floor once contained tombs, taken by departing Greek Christians during Turkey's population exchange.

Güllüdere (Rose) Valley   OUTDOORS

FREE The trails that loop around Güllüdere Vadısı (Rose Valley) are easily accessible to all levels of walkers and provide some of the finest fairy chimney–strewn vistas in Cappadocia. As well as this, though, they hide fabulous, little-visited rock-cut churches boasting vibrant fresco fragments and intricate carvings hewn into the stone.

If you only have time to hike through one valley in Cappadocia, this is the one to choose.

Göreme

200 m
0.1 miles

Tokalı Kilise (600m);
Göreme Open-Air
Museum (700m);
Aziz Basil Şapeli (780m);
Elmalı Kilise (830m);
Azize Barbara Şapeli (850m);
Rahibeler Manastırı (880m);
Yılanlı Kilise (890m);
Aynalı Kilise (1.5km);
Meskendir Valley
Trail Head (1.5km);
Ürgüp (7km)

Saklı Kilise
(250m)

Zemi Valley
Trailhead

Güllüdere (Rose) and
Kızılçukur (Red) Valley
Trailheads (50m)

Dolmuş Stop for
Çavuşin; Zelve
& Avanos

Müze Cad (Open-Air Museum Rd)

Sunset
View Hill

Royal Balloon
(270m);
Çavuşin (3km);
Avanos (8km)

Ragıp Üner
Cad

Posta Sk

Dolmuş Stop
for Ürgüp

Müze Cad

Fatih Sk

Sağlık Sk

Kale Cad

Hafız Şükrü Sk

Direk

Park Sk

İlkokul Sk

Bus Stand for
Uçhisar &
Nevşehir

Otogar

Mudür Sk

Ünlü Sk

Cappadocia
Express

Kazım Yolu

Helios
Transfer

Adnan Menderes Cad

Uçhisar (4km);
Nevşehir (12km)

Uzundere Cad

Karşıbucak Cad

Harım Sk

Cami Sk

İçerdere Sk

İsali Cad

Konak Sk

Aslan Sk

Hafız
Abdullah
Efendi Sk

Kazım Eren Sk

Güngör Sk

Aydınlı Sk

Çakmaklı Sk

Çakmaklı Sk

Adnan

Güvercinlik
(Pigeon) Valley
Trailhead

1
2
4
5
6
7
8
9
10
11
12
13
14
15
16
17
18
19
20
21
22
23
24
25
26
27
28
29
30
31
32
33
34
35
36
37
38
39
40
41
42

Göreme

Follow the signs from the Güllüdere Valley trailhead to the **Kolonlu Kilise** (Columned Church), chiselled out of a nondescript rock facade. Take the trail through the orchard and then cross the tiny bridge over the gully to enter the church's gloomy lower chamber. Climb up the staircase and you'll find a white stone nave studded with sturdy columns carved out of the rock.

From there, backtrack through the orchard and follow the main trail to the **Haçlı Kilise** (Church of the Cross), where the shady cave cafe at the entrance is the perfect pit stop. The church, accessed by a rickety wooden staircase, has frescoes dating to the 9th century on its apse and a spectacular large cross carved into its ceiling.

Head north from the Haçlı Kilise and, when the trail branches, take the right-hand path to reach the **Üç Haçlı Kilise** (Church of the Three Crosses), with its stunning ceiling relief and damaged frescoes featuring an enthroned Jesus.

El Nazar Kilise CHURCH
(Church of the Evil Eye; Map p456; admission ₺5; ⊙8am-5pm) Carved from a ubiquitous cone-like rock formation, the 10th-century El Nazar Kilise has been well restored with its snug interior a riot of colourful frescoes. To find it, take the signposted Zemi Valley trailhead off Müze Caddesi.

Saklı Kilise CHURCH
(Hidden Church) A yellow sign points the way off Müze Caddesi to the Saklı Kilise, only rediscovered in 1956. When you reach the top of the hill, follow the track to the left and look out for steps leading downhill to the right.

Aynalı Kilise CHURCH
(Mirror Church; admission ₺5) From the Open-Air Museum entrance, a 1km walk uphill along Müze Caddesi brings you to the signposted trail leading down to the little-visited Aynalı Kilise. The main chapel is adorned only with simple red ochre geometric decorations, but the real highlight here is shimmying through the network of narrow tunnels interconnecting a series of rooms within the rock face. Ahmet, the on-site guardian, provides torches for visitors.

🏃 Activities

Mehmet Güngör HIKING
(☑0532 382 2069; www.walkingmehmet.net; 3/5/7hr €60/80/100) Mehmet Güngör's nickname, 'Walking Mehmet', says it all.

Göreme's most experienced local walking guide has an encyclopaedic knowledge of the surrounding valley trails and can put together itineraries to suit all interests and levels of fitness. Highly recommended.

Cappadocia Bike
MOUNTAIN BIKING

(☑0505 656 1064; www.cappadociabike.com; bike tours per person €20-40 incl transport to/from hotel) This little start-up showcases Cappadocia's weird and wacky landscape by bike. The full-day tour does a loop from Göreme through Güllüdere and Meskendir Valleys via Zelve Open-Air Museum and Ürgup. Shorter morning and sunset tours also capture the fairy-chimney views on rides through Güvercinlik and Görkündere Valleys. Bikes are BTWIN 24-speed mountain bikes, and helmets are provided.

Dalton Brothers
HORSE RIDING

(Map p456; ☑0532 275 6869; www.cappadocia horseriding.com; Müze Caddesi; 2/4hr €45/85) Ekrem Ilhan – Göreme's resident horse whisperer – trains Cappadocia's wild horses from Erciyes Dağı (Mt Erciyes) and runs this trekking stable from where you can set out to explore Cappadocia from the saddle.

Many of the horses are not suitable for first-time riders. If you're not an experienced rider please make sure you specify this.

Fatma's Turkish Cooking Class
COOKING

(Map p456; ☑0536 965 2040, 0384-271 2597; www.cafesafak.weebly.com; per person ₺100) These cooking classes – operated out of the Çingitaş family's home – will have you rustling up the hearty dishes of the Anatolian plains like a pro. Classes run from 9am to 1pm and take you through the Turkish staples of lentil soup, stuffed vine leaves, stuffed aubergines (eggplants) and the Cappadocian *aside* (dough and *pekmez*) pudding. Book through Cafe Şafak (28 Müze Caddesi).

Elis Kapadokya Hamam
HAMAM

(Map p456; ☑0384-271 2974; Adnan Menderes Caddesi; soak, scrub & massage ₺85; ☺10am-10pm) This hamam provides a typical soak-and-scrub experience with mixed and women-only areas. Be aware that the included 'massage' is a blink-of-the-eye effort. You need to pay extra (₺2 per minute) for a proper oil massage.

Kelebek Turkish Bath Spa
HAMAM

(Map p456; ☑0384-271 2531; Kelebek Hotel, Yavuz Sokak; soak & scrub €35, 30min massage €35) Unwind after the chimney-spotting and treat yourself to Cappadocia's most luxurious hamam experience with a full range of spa-style added extras.

Tours

Heritage Travel
TOURS

(Map p456; ☑0384-271 2687; www.turkishheritage travel.com; Uzundere Caddesi; day tours per person cash/credit card €45/55) This highly recommended local agency offers different day-tour itineraries to most operators in Cappadocia, including an 'Undiscovered Cappadocia' trip which visits Soğanlı, Mustafapaşa, Keslik Monastery and Derinkuyu Underground City. There's a range of more off-beat activities as well including jeep safaris, cooking classes in King's Valley, and grape harvesting and *pekmez* (syrup made from grape juice) making day trips during harvest season (September to October).

Private day trips to Hacıbektaş, and a fresco trip exploring Cappadocia's Byzantine heritage, are also offered and they also specialise in tailor-made Turkey itineraries.

Middle Earth Travel
ADVENTURE

(Map p456; ☑0384-271 2559; www.middleearth travel.com; Adnan Menderes Caddesi; per person day hike €50-90, bike ride €90-180) This adventure travel specialist offers a range of day hikes and daily bike tours, as well as multi-day biking itineraries and treks through Ala Dağlar National Park, along the Lycian Way or St Paul's Trail, through the Kaçkar Mountains or up Mt Ararat. Prices depend on number of people and the itinerary.

Nomad Travel
TOURS

(Map p456; ☑0384-271 2767; www.nomadtravel. com.tr; Belediye Caddesi 9; group day tours ₺100-150) Nomad's 'Red' group day tour heads to the major sights around Göreme, while its 'Green' tour takes in a valley walk and Kaymaklı Underground City (p473). It also offers an excellent Soğanlı tour and their three-day Nemrut Dağı (Mt Nemrut, €250) trip, which leaves on Monday, is a worthwhile though whirlwind-fast option if you're short on time to explore further east.

Metis Travel
TOURS

(Map p456; ☑0384-271 2188; www.metistravel. com; Müdür Sokak 9; group day tours per person from ₺100) This boutique travel agency is run by the folk behind Koza Cave Hotel (p461), so attention to detail is on top form. They run Cappadocia's classic 'Red' and 'Green' group day tours as well as smaller group tours exploring Cappadocia highlights. Private itinerary options include trips to

WALKING IN THE VALLEYS AROUND GÖREME

Göreme village is surrounded by the magnificent Göreme National Park. The valleys are easily explored on foot; each needs about one to three hours. Most are interconnected, so you could easily combine several in a day, especially with the help of the area's many dolmuşes (minibuses). Don't forget a bottle of water and sunscreen.

Some of the most interesting and accessible valleys:

Bağlıdere Vadısı (White Valley) From Uçhisar to Göreme.

Görkündere Vadısı (Love Valley) Trailheads off Zemi Valley and from Sunset View Hill in Göreme; particularly spectacular rock formations.

Güllüdere Vadısı (Rose Valley) Trailheads just north of Göreme, at Çavuşin, and Kızılçukur viewpoint (opposite the Ortahisar turn-off); superb churches and panoramic views.

Güvercinlik Vadısı (Pigeon Valley) Connecting Göreme and Uçhisar; colourful dovecotes.

İçeridere Vadısı Running south from İçeridere Sokak in Göreme.

Kılıçlar Vadısı (Swords Valley) Running north off Müze Caddesi on the way to the Göreme Open-Air Museum.

Kızılçukur Vadısı (Red Valley) Running between the Güllüdere and Meskendir Valleys; great views and vibrant dovecotes.

Meskendir Vadısı Trailhead next to Kaya Camping, running north off Müze Caddesi past the Göreme Open-Air Museum; tunnels and dovecotes.

Zemi Vadısı Trailhead running south off Müze Caddesi.

A word of warning: Although many of the valleys now have trailhead signposts and signage has been put up at strategic points along the paths of Güllüdere and Kızılçukur Valleys, many of the trails remain only basically marked and there's no detailed map of the area available. It's quite easy to get lost if you don't stick to the trails.

Hattuşa and a 'Monasteries of Cappadocia' trip that visits lesser-seen Byzantine remnants in the region.

Yama Tours TOURS
(Map p456; ☎0384-271 2508; www.yamatours.com; Müze Caddesi 2; group day tours ₺110-120) This popular backpacker-friendly travel agency runs daily Cappadocia North (Göreme Open-Air Museum, Paşabağı and Avanos) and South (Ihlara Valley and Derinkuyu Underground City) tours and can organise a bag full of other Cappadocia adventures and activities for you. It also runs tours to Hacıbektaş and Soğanlı that take in plenty of sights along the way.

Festivals & Events

Klasik Keyifler CLASSICAL MUSIC
(☎0532 614 4955; www.klasikkeyifler.org; ☉Aug) Klasik Keyifler is an innovative organisation that holds chamber-music concerts by Turkey's brightest stars in intimate natural settings. The summer series hits Cappadocia in August, when you can hear the sounds of

Schumann bouncing off the valley walls in Zelve and Mustafapaşa. Workshops run in conjunction with the performances.

Sleeping

Most Göreme hotels open all year round and offer excellent discounts during quiet periods. If arriving by bus, many are happy to pick you up from Göreme's otogar when you arrive if you've booked ahead. Due to the overly complicated and rather undecipherable blue hotel signposts put up by the *belediye* (town council), this can be a good idea on arrival.

Köse Pension PENSION $
(Map p456; ☎0384-271 2294; www.kosepension.com; Ragıp Üner Caddesi; dm ₺20, rooftop hut per person ₺35, d/tr ₺120/135; ☀☎☀) It may have no cave character, but traveller favourite Köse is still the pick of Göreme's budget digs. Ably managed by Sabina, this friendly place provides a range of spotless rooms featuring brilliant bathrooms, bright linens and comfortable beds, more basic rooms

and a spacious rooftop dorm. The swimming pool is a bonus after a long, hot hike.

There are a swag of options for breakfast (₺5 to ₺8) including proper coffee, while evening meals are ₺25 and there's always cold beer in the fridge.

Shoestring Cave Pension HOSTEL $

(Map p456; ☑ 0384-271 2450; www.shoestringcave. com; Kazım Eren Sokak; dm ₺40, d/ste ₺130/210; ☺ 🛜 🏊) The private rooms at this old-school backpacker paradise have been jazzed up significantly – though we're personally not keen on the disco-light bed headboard in the suite – but the funky cave-dorm means those counting their kuruş still have a dependable place to crash. The swimming-pool terrace, with bar, provides a proper communal feel to pull up a pew and swap Turkish travel tales.

Ali's Guest House HOSTEL $

(Map p456; ☑ 0384-271 2434; www.alisguest house.com; Harım Sokak 13; dm/d/tr €7/20/30; ☺ 🛜) We've whinged about Göreme's backpacker digs trussing themselves up to cater for the boutique crowd, so a big thumbs up to Ali's as it's aimed squarely at the budget end of the market. There are two snug cave-dorms (one female-only) sharing small, clean bathrooms, and three cosy private rooms upstairs. The outdoor courtyard is a pot plant–strewn communal haven.

Dorm Cave HOSTEL $

(Map p456; ☑ 0384-271 2770; www.travellers cave.com; Hafız Abdullah Efendi Sokak 4; dm/d €10/€30, ste from €45; ☺ 🛜) Who needs to pay wads of cash to stay in a Cappadocian cave? This hostel offers three spacious cave-dorms that share small bathrooms across the courtyard and three petite private rooms upstairs. Next door, they've branched out with new comfortable suite-style rooms but if you're in that price range you're better off heading further up the hill for terrace views.

★ Kelebek Hotel BOUTIQUE HOTEL $$

(Map p456; ☑ 0384-271 2531; www.kelebekhotel. com; Yavuz Sokak 31; fairy-chimney s/d €44/55, deluxe €56/70, ste from €68/85; 🅿 ☺ ❄ 🛜 🏊) Local guru Ali Yavuz leads a charming team at one of Göreme's original boutique hotels, which has seen a travel industry virtually spring from beneath its stunning terraces. Exuding Anatolian inspiration at every turn, the rooms are spread over a labyrinth of stairs and balconies interconnecting two gorgeous stone houses, each with a fairy chimney protruding skyward.

With an in-house hamam, a swimming-pool deck complete with bar and hammocks, and a village-garden project offering guests a slice of the Cappadocia of old – with cooking classes and complimentary valley breakfasts – Kelebek continues to innovate. It's no wonder people leave smitten.

Taşkonak GUESTHOUSE $$

(Map p456; ☑ 0384-270 2680; www.taskonak. com; Güngör Sokak 23; s/d/ste/f €35/40/80/120; ☺ 🛜) Angela and Yılmaz provide huge helpings of hospitality at this hideaway. Standard rooms are snug but sweet, while spacious cave-suites with snazzy contemporary bathrooms (bag Room 3 for the roll-top bath and double shower), are the best-value deal in town. Killer views from the terrace and breakfast feasts of freshly baked delights and proper coffee leave you grinning at your good fortune.

ErenBey Cave Hotel BOUTIQUE HOTEL $$

(Map p456; ☑ 0384-271 2131; www.erenbeycave hotel.com; Kazım Eren Sokak 19; d/ste €60/125; ☺ 🛜) This rather lush boutique-style hotel plays up its quirky shaped cave rooms with aplomb. The Eren family have converted their generations-old homestead into nine exceedingly spacious and rather swish rooms that all have bucket loads of idiosyncratic design. Room 9, with its rock-carved four-pillared bed and bathtub-with-a-view, is the stuff of romantic getaway dreams.

Hanzade Suites BOUTIQUE HOTEL $$

(Map p456; ☑ 0384-271 3536; www.hanzade suites.com; Ali Çavuş Sokak 7; d €60, ste €80-100; ☺ ❄ 🛜) Good things definitely do come in small packages. This once-typical village dwelling has been transformed by owner Mustafa into a haven of just seven generously proportioned rooms that effortlessly blend local craftwork with modern elegance and a hat-tip to minimalism. We're particularly enamoured with the drop-dead-gorgeous onyx-and-travertine flooring and the glamorously high beds. Superb stuff.

Vista Cave Hotel BOUTIQUE HOTEL $$

(Map p456; ☑ 0384-271 3088; www.vistacavehotel. com; Aydınlı Sokak 15/1; r €40-65, ste €70-90; ☺ ❄ 🛜) Vista by name, vista by nature; the panoramic views from the top terrace make breakfast an occasion. Stone-cut rooms, with balconies, are elegant and bright while cave-cut suites come with carved ceiling motifs and bags of traditional Ottoman styling. Hosts Şenol and Yvette dish out plenty of

WHICH CAPPADOCIAN BASE TO CHOOSE

Göreme The pretty village at the epicentre of Cappadocia's tourism industry has plenty of accommodation for budget, midrange and high-end travellers; a good restaurant and cafe scene; easy on-foot access into the main valley; and Göreme Open-Air Museum. It also has excellent transport links to other villages and sights.

Ürgüp This is the main town for the outlying villages. Accommodation is mostly high-end; there's a decent variety of restaurants and cafes, and excellent transport links to villages and sights.

Ortahisar Traditional, sleepy agricultural village huddled around a rock-citadel. Midrange and high-end sleeping options are available; only a handful of dining choices; on-foot access to lesser-seen valleys and, for enthusiastic walkers, to main valleys. There are decent transport links.

Çavuşin Tiny village in the shadow of a carved-out cliff face. Both midrange and high-end hotels are available; only a few eating options; easy on-foot access into the main valleys and to Göreme.

Uçhisar Village wrapped around Cappadocia's largest rock-citadel. Accommodation is mostly larger upmarket hotels with a scatter of boutique options; small dining scene; on-foot access to some main valleys; decent transport links.

Avanos Small, riverside provincial town famed for its pottery. Hotel scene of mostly small midrange boutique offerings; good choice of restaurants and cafes; excellent transport links to villages and sights.

Mustafapaşa Little village known for its glut of old Greek house architecture. A handful of small midrange and high-end hotels; a couple of restaurants and cafes; on-foot access to lesser-visited valleys; excellent transport links to Ürgüp.

local advice, and complimentary home-baked goodies are a winner with peckish guests.

Kismet Cave House
GUESTHOUSE $$

(Map p456; ☑ 0384-271 2416; www.kismetcave house.com; Kağnı Yolu 9; s €42, d €50-80, f €120; ☻ 🛜) Kismet's fate is assured. Guests consistently rave about the intimate experience here, created by welcoming, well-travelled host Faruk. Rooms (some in actual fairy chimneys) are full of local antiques, carved wood features, colourful rugs and quirky artwork, while communal areas are home to cosy cushion-scattered nooks. This honest-to-impending-greatness Anatolian cave house is delightfully homey in every way.

A new cave-annexe, with suite-style rooms and a hamam, was being built across the road in mid-2016.

Kemal's Guest House
GUESTHOUSE $$

(Map p456; ☑ 0384-271 2234; www.kemals guesthouse.com; Ayzazefedi Sokak 4; s/d/tr ₺130/160/225; ☻ ❄ 🛜) This old timer has brand-spanking new stone rooms but still delivers old-fashioned hospitality in spades. Kemal is a terrific cook (dinner feasts €15), and Dutch wife Barbara leads guests out to

hike Cappadocia's trails. Pull up a seat in the sun-dappled garden, or on the roof terrace, with views across to Uçhisar, and thumb your nose at your 'boutique' friends.

★ Koza Cave Hotel
BOUTIQUE HOTEL $$$

(Map p456; ☑ 0384-271 2466; www.kozacave hotel.com; Çakmaklı Sokak 49; d €80-90, ste €110-175; ☻ ❄ 🛜) 🖋 Bringing a new level of eco-inspired chic to Göreme, Koza Cave is a masterclass in stylish sustainable tourism. Passionate owner Derviş spent decades living in Holland and has incorporated Dutch eco-sensibility into every cave crevice of the 10 stunning rooms. Grey water is reused, and recycled materials and local handcrafted furniture are utilised in abundance to create sophisticated spaces. Highly recommended.

Aydınlı Cave House
BOUTIQUE HOTEL $$$

(Map p456; ☑ 0384-271 2263; www.thecave hotel.com; Aydınlı Sokak 12; r €60-70, f €140, ste from €100; ☻ ❄ 🛜) Proprietor Mustafa has masterfully converted his family home into a haven for honeymooners and those requiring swags of swanky rock-cut style. Leading off terraces scattered with old farming utensils, salons once used for drying fruit and making wine are now swoon-worthy cave rooms while a secret tunnel under the road leads to a hamam and new garden-house annexe.

✖ Eating

The local specialty is *testi kebap* ('pottery kebap'; meat, chicken or vegetables cooked in a terracotta pot) which you'll find on nearly every menu in town.

Pick up fresh produce, locally made cheese and all sorts of other foodie delights at Göreme's weekly Wednesday **market** (Map p456; ⊙ 9am-4pm Wed).

Nazar Börek   TURKISH $
(Map p456; ☑ 0384-271 2441; Müze Caddesi; gözleme & börek ₺7-9; ⊙ 10.30am-10pm; 🕿🍴) Head here for *gözleme* (savoury pancake) and *sosyete böregi* (stuffed spiral pastries served with yoghurt and tomato sauce) served by friendly Rafik and his team. Dessert fans should also pull in to taste Turkey's wacky, sweet-cheese *künefe*. In summer, when the ice-cream stand is outside, order the *künefe* with a luscious portion of cherry or lemon Kahramanmaraş ice cream. Yum.

Fırın Express   PIDE $
(Map p456; ☑ 0384-271 2266; Camı Sokak; pide ₺7-13; ⊙ 10am-10pm; 🕿🍴) Simply the best pide (Turkish-style pizza) in town is found in this local haunt. The cavernous wood oven fires up meat and vegetarian options and anything doused with egg. We suggest the *patlıcanı* (aubergine) pide or *ıspınaklı kaşarlı* (spinach and cheese) pide and adding an *ayran* (yoghurt drink) to wash it down with, for a bargain feed.

Keyif Cafe   TURKISH $
(Map p456; Karşıbucak Caddesi; meze ₺7, mains ₺7-23; ⊙ 10.30am-10pm; 🍴) One of our favourite new places to kick back with a beer (₺10) while grazing on meze at the end of the day. The small menu offers decent salads as well as *gözleme* (savoury pancake) and Turkish kebap classics, and the large selection of local wines is a winner.

Nostalji Restaurant   ANATOLIAN $$
(Map p456; ☑ 0384-271 2906; Kale Sokak 4; mains ₺12-15, testi kebap ₺35-45; ⊙ 11am-10pm) Bring your appetite and prepare to feast on the soul food that fuelled Cappadocian farmers for centuries. Nostalji has brought the homespun flavours of village dishes into a fine dining environment. It gets major brownie points for

complimentary meze and salad with meals, and for the free pick-up and drop-off service (reserve in advance); perfect if you're feeling too lazy to walk up the hill.

Peking Chinese Restaurant   CHINESE $$
(Map p456; ☑ 0384-271 2128; Bilal Eroğlu Caddesi 5; mains ₺16-25; ⊙ 11am-10pm; 🕿🍴) A few years ago we'd never have thought we'd see wontons on a menu in Göreme. Peking, complete with red Chinese lanterns dangling outside, brings noodles, dumplings, sizzling Sichuan dishes and tofu to town. A good option for that night when you need a bit of a break from menus heavy on *testi kebap* (meat, chicken or vegetables cooked in a terracotta pot).

★ Topdeck Cave Restaurant   ANATOLIAN $$$
(Map p456; ☑ 0384-271 2474; Hafız Abdullah Efendi Sokak 15; mains ₺21-43; ⊙ 6-10pm Wed-Mon) If it feels as though you're dining in a family home, it's because you are. Talented chef Mustafa (aka Topdeck) and his gracious clan have transformed an atmospheric cave room in their house into a cosy restaurant where the kids pitch in with the serving and diners dig into hearty helpings of Anatolian favourites with a spicy twist.

Choose the mixed meze plate (₺32) for a flavour-packed blowout your stomach will thank you for. Reservations are recommended.

★ Seten Restaurant   MODERN TURKISH $$$
(Map p456; ☑ 0384-271 3025; www.setenrestaurant.com; Aydınlı Sokak; mains ₺16-45; ⊙ 11am-11pm; 🍴) Brimming with an artful Anatolian aesthetic, Seten is a feast for the eye as well as for the stomach. Named after the old millstones used to grind bulgur wheat, this restaurant is an education for newcomers to Turkish cuisine and a treat for well-travelled palates. Attentive service complements classic main dishes and luscious and unusual meze.

Try the *hünkar beğendi* (beef cubes on a bed of pureed aubergine) or *çiçek dolması* (stuffed squash blossoms) to see why this is by far Göreme's most sophisticated dining experience.

Pumpkin Cafe   ANATOLIAN $$$
(Map p456; ☑ 0542 808 5050; İçeridere Sokak 7; set menu incl soft drinks, tea & coffee ₺60, vegetarian ₺50; ⊙ 6-11pm; 🍴) With its dinky balcony decorated with whimsically carved-out pumpkins (what else), this cute-as-a-button cafe is one of the cosiest dining picks in Göreme. The daily-changing four-course set menu (with a choice of main) is a fresh

feast of home-style dishes, all presented with delightful flourishes and topped off by some of the friendliest service in town.

Orient Restaurant
INTERNATIONAL $$$
(Map p456; ☑ 0384-271 2346; Adnan Menderes Caddesi; meze ₺10-15, mains ₺15-50; ⊘ 11am-10.30pm) Orient's impressively meaty menu romps from traditional Turkish to more continental-style options with ease. Most people are here for a steak fix (₺45) which is the speciality, but we prefer coming here for a long lazy lunch of multiple meze on the terrace festooned with blooming roses.

Dibek
ANATOLIAN $$$
(Map p456; ☑ 0384-271 2209; Hakkı Paşa Meydanı 1; mains ₺23-45; ⊘ 11am-11pm Mon-Sat; ☑) Diners sprawl on cushions and feast on traditional dishes at this family restaurant, set inside a 475-year-old building. After dinner make sure to order the homemade sour cherry liqueur for a lush digestif. Owner Mehmet is a wine buff and also runs wine-tasting sessions (five tastings plus a bottle to take home from €25, reservations essential) in the cave cellar downstairs.

🍸 Drinking & Nightlife

Fat Boys
BAR, RESTAURANT
(Map p456; ☑ 0535 386 4484; Belediye Caddesi; 500ml Efes ₺11, mains ₺12-32; ⊘ noon-late; 🛜) This bar-restaurant is a winner. We love kicking back on the terrace's fat cushions, munching on hummus and watching the world go by with an Efes in hand. The menu stars good-value Turkish staples alongside global pub grub offerings of burgers and Aussie-style pies, and a moreish aubergine soup (yes, really). Hands-down, this is Göreme's best evening hang-out with friendly staff and a well-stocked bar.

Cafe Şafak
CAFE
(Map p456; Müze Caddesi; coffee ₺6-8, smoothies ₺10; ⊘ 10am-10pm; 🛜) Fellow coffee lovers, this is, hands down, Göreme's best caffeine fix. Owner Ali trained as a barista in coffee-hipster Melbourne, and Fatma (his mum) serves up great cappuccinos, espressos and flat whites. They also do sandwiches and *gözleme* (savoury pancakes) – including a banana and chocolate one – and whip up picnic packs (₺15) for hikers heading into the valleys.

M&M Cafe
CAFE
(Map p456; Isalı Caddesi; drinks ₺4-10, snacks ₺7-10; ⊘ 10am-10pm) Any place that serves you an iced coffee with a hilarious palm-tree

swizzle stick and complimentary smarties gets a big tick in our book. The hot coffees are nothing to write home about but the multiple cold coffee confections hit the spot on a Cappadocian summer day. Plus there's *gözleme* (savoury pancake) and chicken döners for a cheap lunch.

🛍 Shopping

Tribal Collections
CARPETS
(Map p456; ☑ 0384-271 2760; www.tribalcollections.net; Köşe Cikmazı Sokak 1; ⊘ 9am-9pm) As well as being the proprietor of this mighty fine rug shop, owner Ruth is well known for her highly recommended carpet educationals (think of it as a carpets 101), which explain the history and artistry of these coveted textiles.

Naile Art Gallery
ARTS & CRAFTS
(Map p456; ☑ 0544 477 3144; www.nailesanat.com; Gül Sokak 6/1; ⊘ 10am-7pm) Cappadocian artist Naile Bozkurt displays and sells her *ebru* (paper marbling) work in this gallery with a fine selection of both traditional and contemporary artworks, as well as her highly abstract, modern *ebru* work on ceramic tiles and silk scarves.

Argos
CERAMICS
(Map p456; ☑ 0384-271 2750; Cevizler Sokak 22; ⊘ 10am-8pm) A classy selection of handmade ceramics, both modern and traditionally inspired, with a lot of unusual pieces that you won't see at Cappadocia's other ceramic shops, as well as unusual stone pieces.

ℹ Information

There are standalone clusters of ATM booths on and around Belediye Caddesi and Uzundere Caddesi. Some of the town's travel agencies will exchange money, although you're probably better off going to the **post office** (PTT; Map p456; Posta Sokak; ⊘ 9am-12.30pm & 1.30-5pm Mon-Fri) or **Deniz Bank** (Müze Caddesi 3; ⊘ 9am-12.30pm & 1.30-5pm Mon-Fri).

The **Accommodation information booth** (Map p456; ☑ 0384-271 2558; www.goreme.org) at the otogar (open when most long-distance buses arrive) is not an official tourist office; instead it's run by the Göreme Turizmciler Derneği, a coalition of local hotel and restaurant owners, and is solely aimed at directing travellers to accommodation in the village. Staff can't supply any meaningful information but they do give out free maps.

ℹ Getting There & Away

There are daily long-distance buses to all over Turkey from Göreme's **otogar** (Bus Station; Map p456), although for most services heading west, you're ferried to Nevşehir's otogar by a free *servis* first to pick up the main service. Note that the morning bus to İstanbul goes via Ankara and so takes an hour longer than the overnight bus. For Aksaray, change in Nevşehir.

ℹ Getting Around

BUS

Göreme has good connections to the other Cappadocian villages. The Ürgüp–Avanos dolmuş (₺2 to ₺3.50 depending on where you get off) picks up and drops off passengers on its way through town in both directions. To Ürgüp it stops in Göreme at 20 to 25 minutes past the hour between 8am and 7pm and to Avanos (via Zelve Open-Air Museum) at 10 to 15 minutes past the hour between 8am and 6pm.

The Göreme Belediye Bus Corp has a regular bus service from Göreme otogar to Nevşehir (₺2.50) via Uçhisar (₺2) every 30 minutes between 8am and 6.30pm. To get to Derinkuyu and Kaymaklı Underground Cities by public transport take this bus and change at Nevşehir's central dolmuş stand.

CAR & MOTORCYCLE

Hitchhiker (Map p456; ☑ 0384-271 2169; www.cappadociahitchhiker.com; Uzundere Caddesi) One of several places in town to hire mountain bikes, scooters, cars and quads.

Since there are no petrol stations in Göreme and your rental car comes with a near-empty tank, head to one of the garages on the main road near Ortahisar to fill up.

TAXI

A taxi to Ürgüp costs around ₺30.

Uçhisar

☑ 0384 / POP 3900

Pretty little Uçhisar has undergone rapid development since its heady Club Med days. The French love affair with the clifftop village continues each summer as Gallic tourists unpack their *joie de vivre* in trendy hotels at the foot of Uçhisar Castle. The royal rectangular crag, visible from nearby Göreme, is the dramatic centrepiece of a stylish Cappadocian aesthetic, albeit at times a touch manufactured. Unfortunately, some ill-judged large hotel construction has spoilt some of the village's dreamlike fairy-chimney vistas, which somewhat disrupts Uçhisar's famously surreal setting. Despite this, it remains a quiet alternative as a base for exploring the region.

◉ Sights & Activities

There are some excellent hiking possibilities around Uçhisar, with trailheads to both Bağlıdere Vadısı (White Valley) and Güvercinlik Vadısı (Pigeon Valley) on the outskirts of town.

Uçhisar Castle   FORTRESS
(Uçhisar Kalesi; ₺6.50; ⊙8am-7pm) This tall volcanic-rock outcrop is one of Cappadocia's most prominent landmarks and visible for miles around. Riddled with tunnels, it was used for centuries by villagers as a place of refuge when enemy armies overtook the surrounding plains. Winding your way up the stairs to the panoramic vantage point of

---

CAPPADOCIA UÇHISAR

SERVICES FROM GÖREME'S OTOGAR

DESTINATION	FARE (₺)	DURATION (HR)	FREQUENCY (PER DAY)
Adana	40	5	2 morning, 3 afternoon & 1 evening
Ankara	40	4½	4 morning, 6 afternoon & 1 evening
Antalya	55	9	2 morning & 5 evening
Çanakkale	70	16	1 evening
Denizli (for Pamukkale)	55	11	6 evening
Fethiye	65	14	3 evening
İstanbul	65	11-12	1 morning, 1 afternoon & 5 evening
İzmir	60	11½	3 evening
Kayseri	15	1	1 morning, 3 afternoon & 1 evening
Konya	35	3	3 morning, 1 afternoon & 7 evening
Marmaris/Bodrum	70	13	2 evening
Şanlıurfa	65	11	1 afternoon & 1 evening
Selçuk	65	11½	2 evening

its peak is a sublime way to watch the sun set over the rock valleys of the Cappadocian countryside.

✴ Festivals & Events

Cappadox Festival   CULTURAL

(www.cappadox.com/en; ⊙ May) Sunrise *pranayama* sessions, electro-funk and experimental rock concerts held in ambient ancient cave-buildings; it may be a newbie on the Turkish festival scene but Cappadox sure has ambition. The program merges music, nature walks, art exhibitions, yoga and gastronomy events into a three-day extravaganza fusing Turkish contemporary culture and Cappadocia's natural beauty together.

⌶ Sleeping

Kilim Pension   GUESTHOUSE $$

(☑ 0384-219 2774; www.sisik.com; Göreme Caddesi; d €60; 🛜) The pride of fun-loving, multilingual 'Şişik', Kilim Pension is an unpretentious home away from home with a glorious vine-draped terrace and a cosy restaurant that dishes up first-class local fare. Spacious rooms are smartly simple, light and airy, with swish bathrooms as a bonus. The complimentary chaperoned hikes into the valleys are highly recommended.

Uçhisar Pension   PENSION $$

(☑ 0384-219 2662; Göreme Caddesi; s/d ₺80/100, cave r €50-80; 🛜) Mustafa and Gül dispense lashings of old-fashioned Turkish hospitality in their cosy pension. Simple rooms are spick and span with white-washed walls and small but squeaky-clean bathrooms. Downstairs, the roomy cave suites are decorated traditionally. In summer, swing from the rooftop hammock and pinch yourself for your luck on finding million-dollar views for budget prices.

★ Kale Konak   BOUTIQUE HOTEL $$$

(☑ 0384-219 2828; www.kalekonak.com; Kale Sokak 9; s €100, d €120, ste €135-150; 🛜) Take a handful of minimalist retreat-chic, blend it with touches of artistic flair and balance it all out with wads of Ottoman style and you get this effortlessly elegant hotel. Spacious rooms lead out through underground passageways to comfortable reading corners, communal areas strewn with fat cushions, and shady terraces in the shadow of Uçhisar's craggy *kale* (fortress).

The marble hamam tops off what has to be Uçhisar's most super sophisticated place to stay; the epitome of casual luxury.

Şira Hotel   HOTEL $$$

(☑ 0384-219 3037; www.hotelsira.com; Göreme Caddesi 87; d/ste from €100/120; 🛜) Multilingual Filiz and her family have created a beautiful retreat where modern comfort and traditional architecture sit in harmony side by side. The panoramic views from the terrace may be enough to tempt you never to leave, but the real bonus is the management's appreciation for wine, food and nature – all on show in the restaurant's flavourful feasts.

Argos   LUXURY HOTEL $$$

(☑ 0384-219 3130; www.argosincappadocia.com; Kayabaşi Sokak; r/ste from €165/680; ❄🛜) Designer luxury meets caveman chic head on at this offering from the Istanbul advertising firm with its feet in the hotel game. The hotel spills over the hillside in a cluster of 'mansions' and cave warrens connected by alleyways and manicured lawns. The original hotel area, sporting renowned architect Turgut Cansever's sympathetic restorative edge, has the most authentic atmosphere.

✗ Eating

Kapadokya Peri Cave   CAFE $

(Uçhisar Valley; gözleme ₺6-10; ⊙ 10am-6pm) Follow the signs down into the valley, from the ridge in front of Uçhisar Castle (p464) to find the sweetest cafe in town on a terrace right in front of a fairy chimney. Sit back on the battered old sofas with a tea or coffee while the friendly, local family who own it rustle you up some excellent *gözleme* (savoury pancake).

★ Saklı Konak   ANATOLIAN $$

(☑ 0384-219 3066; www.saklikonakhotel.com; 2 Karlık Sokak 3; mains ₺20-40; ⊙ 10am-10pm Tue-Sun) We can think of no better place for a tastebud tour of village food than this cosy restaurant, where owner Rıza takes time to explain the small menu to you, dishes are cooked by local ladies traditionally in the *tandır* (clay oven), and ingredients are sourced from the neighbour's gardens. Thoroughly local flavours, contemporary presentation, complimentary meze and charming personal service – we love it.

Center Café & Restaurant   TURKISH $$

(☑ 0384-219 3117; Belediye Meydanı; mains ₺10-35; ⊙ 11am-10pm) A former top-notch Club Med chef presides over this humble town-square cafe-restaurant with a menu of tasty meze, kebap plates, steaks and flavourful tagines. The verdant garden setting is a shady haven in summer months, perfect for lazy lunches

CAPPADOCIA UÇHISAR

watching the hum of village life. We almost wish this place was still a secret.

House of Memories TURKISH $$
(Göreme Caddesi; mains ₺18-25; ☉10.30am-10pm) Bags of homespun rustic appeal and kooky service are why we like this little restaurant serving up traditional Turkish favourites. It's behind Üçhisar Castle (p464) on the main hotel road.

🔒 Shopping

Kocabağ Winery Shop WINE
(www.kocabag.com; Adnan Menderes Caddesi; ☉10am-7pm) This rather swish outlet for Cappadocia's Kocabağ Winery is the best place in town for a spot of wine tasting. Just outside, a small selection of vines displays the different grape varieties for interested connoisseurs, while the shop stocks all of Kocabağ's wines and offers free tastings. It's on the main road off Uçhisar's town square.

ℹ Getting There & Away

The Nevşehir–Avanos bus and the Nevşehir–Göreme dolmuş both pass through Uçhisar and will drop off and pick up passengers on the main highway at the bottom of the village.

Dolmuşes to Nevşehir (₺2) leave from opposite the *belediye* (town hall) on the main square every half-hour between 7am and 7pm.

A taxi to Göreme costs ₺18.

ℹ **MUSEUM PASS**
....

If you're keen on cramming in as many of Cappadocia's historical sites as possible, this new pass (www.muze.gov.tr/en/museum-card) provides an excellent discount on entry fees. It costs ₺45 and is valid for three days, allowing entry to Çavuşin Kilisesi (p466); Derinkuyu Underground City (p473); Göreme Open-Air Museum (p454), including the Karanlık Kilise (p455); Ihlara Valley (p489); Kaymaklı Underground City (p473); Özkonak Underground City (p471); and Zelve Open-Air Museum (p467). Purchased individually, visiting all these sites would cost ₺143, representing a whopping saving of ₺98. Even with a visit to only one of the underground cities included in the pass, there is still a significant saving to be made.

The pass is available to buy at all the participating sites.

Çavuşin

Midway between Göreme and Avanos is little Çavuşin, dominated by a cliff where a cluster of abandoned houses spills down the slope in a crumbling stone jumble. The main hive of activity is the clutch of souvenir stands at the cliff base, which spring into action when the midday tour buses roll into town. When the last bus has left for the day, Çavuşin hits the snooze button and resumes its slumber.

◉ Sights & Activities

Çavuşin is a starting point for scenic hikes through Güllüdere Vadısı (Rose Valley), Kızılçukur Vadısı (Red Valley) and Meskendir Vadısı. You can even go as far as the Kızılçukur viewpoint (6.5km), then walk out to the Ürgüp–Ortahisar road and catch a dolmuş back to your base.

Çavuşin Kilisesi CHURCH
(Nicephorus Phocas Church; Göreme-Avanos Hwy; ₺8; ☉8am-5pm) Just off the highway on the northern edge of Çavuşin you'll find this church, accessed via a steep and rickety iron stairway. Cappadocia's first post-iconoclastic church, it served as a pigeon house for many years and is home to some fine frescoes.

Çavuşin Old Village Ruins RUINS
FREE Walk up the hill through the new part of Çavuşin and continue past the main square to find the old village ruins. Carved into the steep cliff face here is a labyrinthine complex of abandoned houses that you can wander through by climbing up the cliff path. The timeless ambience has been lost somewhat due to the hotel that has been slapped right in the middle of the ruins, but there's still plenty to explore.

Church of St John the Baptist CHURCH
FREE Right at the top of Çavuşin's village-ruins rock outcrop is the Church of St John the Baptist, one of the oldest churches in Cappadocia. While the interior frescoes are severely damaged and faded, the still-standing columns inside the cavern are impressive and the views across the countryside from the church entry are sublime.

☞ Tours

Mephisto Voyage ADVENTURE
(☎0384-532 7070; www.mephistovoyage.com; Mehmet Yılmaz Caddesi) Based at the İn Pension (p467), this group has a good reputation. It's been operating for over 15 years

and offers multi-day trekking, horse-riding and biking packages in Cappadocia and the Taurus Mountains. It also gets big kudos for being the only operator in Cappadocia that offers tours specifically designed for mobility-impaired people using the Joëlette system.

🛏 Sleeping & Eating

İn Pension
PENSION $

(📞 0384-532 7070; www.pensionincappadocia.com; Mehmet Yılmaz Caddesi; old wing d €30, new wing d/tr €40/50, ste €70-100; 🛜) This little pension by the main square comes with built-in travel advice courtesy of owner Mephisto Voyage. There are a couple of simple and small budget rooms, while the new wing has a range of spruced-up, bright doubles with little bathrooms. Downstairs the deluxe rooms come with loads of traditional stone features and lovely decorative touches.

★ Azure Cave Suites
BOUTIQUE HOTEL $$$

(📞 0384-532 7111; www.azurecavesuites.com; r/ste from €60/100; 🛜) This gorgeous warren of caves, at the top of Çavuşin hill, is a romantic refuge with incredible views and a Mediterranean-inspired decorative touch, which gives a distinctly fresh approach to Cappadocia's cave aesthetic. We're particularly enamoured with the new garden-house annexe with its cosy communal lounge, and Room 11 for its hot tub with millionaire views.

Kavi Cafe
CAFE $

(gözleme ₺5; 🕙10am-6pm) Right at the top of the trail on Çavuşin's old village ruins, just before St John the Baptist Church, you'll find this modest place with battered old sofas on a shaded, rickety terrace. The charming local family who run it rustle up good *gözleme* (savoury pancake) and serve tea (₺1) and coffee (₺3) to hikers in need of a refreshment break.

Seyyah Han
TURKISH $$

(📞 0384-532 7214; Maltepi Sokağı; mains ₺15-30; 🕙10am-10pm) Lots of meaty mains head up the menu here with the usual *şiş kebap* (roast skewered meat) suspects alongside dishes such as slow-cooked *kuzu gerdan* (lamb neck). The outdoor terrace is the place to be for sunset dining in Çavuşin.

ℹ Getting There & Away

Çavuşin is on the route of both the hourly Nevşehir–Avanos bus and the Ürgüp–Avanos dolmuş service. Walk down to the highway and flag them down as they go by.

Paşabağı

This valley, halfway along the turn-off road to Zelve, next to a fairy-chimney *jandarma* (police station), has a three-headed rock formation and some of Cappadocia's best examples of mushroom-shaped fairy chimneys. Monks once inhabited the valley and you can climb up inside one chimney to a monk's quarters, decorated with Hellenic crosses. Wooden steps lead to a chapel where three iconoclastic paintings escaped the vandals; the central one depicts the Virgin holding baby Jesus.

ℹ Getting There & Away

Paşabağı is on the Ürgüp–Avanos dolmuş route. Going to Avanos, it reaches the valley at around 25 minutes past the hour. Heading in the opposite direction for Göreme and Ürgüp, you can flag it down on the road when it trundles past at approximately 10 to 15 minutes past the hour,

Zelve

The road between Çavuşin and Avanos passes a turn-off to the **Zelve Open-Air Museum** (Zelve Açık Hava Müzesi; admission ₺10; 🕙8am-7pm), where three valleys of abandoned homes and churches converge. Zelve was a monastic retreat from the 9th to the 13th century and although it doesn't have as many impressive painted churches as the Göreme Open-Air Museum, its sinewy valley walls with rock antennae are a wonderfully picturesque place for poking around.

The valleys were inhabited until 1952, when they were deemed too dangerous to live in and the villagers were resettled a few kilometres away in Aktepe, also known as Yeni Zelve (New Zelve).

An excellent walking trail loops around the valleys allowing access to the various caverns, although erosion continues to eat into the valley structures and certain areas are cordoned off due to rockfalls.

There are cafes with simple menus of *gözleme* (savoury pancake) and *menemen* (scrambled eggs with peppers, tomatoes, and sometimes cheese) in the car park beside Zelve's site entrance.

ℹ Getting There & Away

The Ürgüp–Avanos dolmuş stops at Zelve. If you're heading onward to Avanos after your visit, the dolmuş swings by Zelve car park at roughly 30 minutes past the hour; going the other way, towards Göreme and Ürgüp, it passes at around 10 to 15 minutes past the hour.

It's an easy 1.5km flat walk along the road from Zelve to Paşabağı.

Devrent Valley

Look: it's a camel! Nicknamed 'Imagination Valley' locally, Devrent Valley's rock formations are some of the best formed and most thickly clustered in Cappadocia, and looking at their fantastic shapes is like gazing at the clouds as a child. See if you can spot the dolphin, seals, Napoleon's hat, kissing birds, Virgin Mary and various reptilian forms.

Most of the rosy rock cones are topped by flattish, darker stones of harder rock that sheltered the cones from the rain until all the surrounding rock was eaten away. This process is known to geologists as differential erosion but you can just call it kooky.

Devrent Valley lies on the direct (east) road between Avanos and Ürgüp. There's no public transport along this route but if it's not too hot and you don't mind a roadside walk, it's easy enough to get here on foot from Zelve. From the Zelve site entrance, go about 200m back down the access road to where the road forks and take the right-hand road marked for Ürgüp. After about 2km you'll come to the village of Aktepe (Yeni Zelve). Bear right and follow the Ürgüp road uphill for less than 2km.

To cut down on walking time, the Ürgüp-Avanos dolmuş can drop you off at Aktepe. You can get çay and cold drinks from the souvenir stand at Devrent Valley but you'll have to head on to Zelve, Ürgüp or Avanos for lunch.

Avanos

📱 0384 / POP 13,500 / ELEV 910M

The Kızılırmak (Red River) is the slow-paced pulse of this provincial town and the unusual source of its livelihood, the distinctive red clay that, mixed with a white, mountain mud variety, is spun to produce the region's famed pottery. Typically painted in turquoise or the earthy browns and yellows favoured by the Hittites, the beautiful pieces are traditionally thrown by men and painted by women. Aside from the regulation tour groups (who, quicker than an eye blink, get bussed into the pottery workshops and then bussed out again), Avanos is relatively devoid of foreign visitors, leaving you alone

to meander the alleys that snake up the hillside, lined with gently decaying grand Greek-Ottoman houses. Occasional (and slightly incongruous) Venetian-style gondolas now ply the river, but riverside is still the place to ponder the sunset as you sip your umpteenth çay.

⊙ Sights

Most visitors come to Avanos to see the pottery artisans at work. Tour groups are shuffled into the pottery warehouses lining the main roads outside of town. The smaller, independent pottery workshops in the centre are more relaxed and offer better prices, and most will happily show you how to throw a pot.

Chez Galip Hair Museum   MUSEUM
(110 Sokak 24; ⊙ 8.30am-6pm) **FREE** This pottery gallery, in the alley opposite the post office, is home to Cappadocia's infamous hair museum. Yes, that's right: it's a museum dedicated to locks of hair that past female visitors have left here for posterity – roughly 16,000 samples of hair hang down from the walls and ceiling of the back caves here. You'll find it either kookily hilarious or kind of (okay, a lot) creepy. Feel free to add your own contribution. Scissors are provided. Snip. Snip.

Güray Ceramic Museum   MUSEUM
(Dereyamanlı Caddesi; admission ₺3; ⊙ 9am-7pm) This rather snazzy museum sits in a mammoth series of newly tunnelled-out caves underneath the Güray Ceramic showroom. It displays its private collection of ceramic art amassed over the years, with the ancient ceramics hall featuring pieces from as far back as the Chalcolithic era.

To get here from Avanos centre, cross the river at Taş Köprü bridge (at Atatürk Caddesi's western end), take the first right-hand turn onto Kapadokya Caddesi and follow the signs.

⛵ Tours

Kirkit Voyage   TOURS
(📱 0384-511 3259; www.kirkit.com; Atatürk Caddesi 50, Avanos) This company has an excellent reputation and friendly multilingual staff. As well as the usual guided tours, it can arrange walking, biking, canoeing, horse-riding and snowshoeing trips and can arrange airport transfers (reservation essential). The highly recommended guided horse-riding treks range from €40 for two hours to €80 for a

CAPPADOCIA FROM ABOVE

If you've never taken a flight in a hot-air balloon, Cappadocia is one of the best places in the world to try it. Flight conditions are especially favourable here, with balloons operating most mornings throughout the year. Seeing this area's remarkable landscape from above is a truly magical experience and many travellers judge it to be the highlight of their trip. Transport between your hotel and the balloon launch site is included in the hefty price, as is a sparkling-wine toast.

Flights take place just after dawn. Unfortunately, due to demand, even most of the reputable companies now offer a second, later-morning flight as well. Winds can become unreliable and potentially dangerous later in the morning, so you should always book the dawn flight.

You'll quickly realise that there's a fair amount of hot air among the operators about who is and isn't inexperienced, ill equipped and under insured. Be aware that, despite the aura of luxury that surrounds the hot-air ballooning industry, this is an adventure activity and is not without its risks. There have been three fatal ballooning accidents here over the past several years. It's your responsibility to check the credentials of your chosen operator carefully and make sure that your pilot is experienced and savvy – even if it means asking to see their licences and logbooks. And don't pick the cheapest operator if it means they might be taking short cuts with safety or overfilling the balloon baskets (which, if nothing else, will mean you won't be able to see the views you've paid a princely sum for).

It's important to note that the balloons travel with the wind, and that the companies can't ensure a particular flight path on a particular day. All companies try to fly over the fairy chimneys, but sometimes – albeit rarely – the wind doesn't allow this. Occasionally, unfavourable weather means that the pilot will cancel the flight for safety reasons; if this happens you'll be offered a flight on the next day or will have your payment refunded. Although this may be an inconvenience, it is preferable to flying in dangerous conditions.

All passengers should take a warm jumper or jacket and should wear trousers and flat shoes. Children under six will not be taken up by reputable companies.

The following agencies have good credentials.

Butterfly Balloons (Map p456; ☑0384-271 3010; www.butterflyballoons.com; Uzundere Caddesi 29) This seamless operation has an excellent reputation, with highly skilled and professional pilots including Englishman Mike, who has vast international experience and is a fellowship member of the Royal Meteorological Society. Standard flights (one hour, up to 20 passengers) cost €175.

Royal Balloon (☑0384-271 3300; www.royalballoon.com; Dutlu Sokak 9) Seasoned pilot Suat Ulusoy heads up this reputable balloon operation. Standard flights (one hour, up to 20 passengers) cost €175.

Turkiye Balloons (Map p456; ☑0384-271 3222; www.turkiyeballoons.com; Mezar Sokak 8) Most of Turkiye's balloon pilots have over 10 years' experience flying for various companies. Standard flights (one hour, up to 20 passengers) cost €160.

Voyager Balloon (Map p456; ☑0384-271 3030; www.voyagerballoons.com; Müze Caddesi 36/1) Recommended for its multilingual pilots and professional service. Standard flights (one hour, up to 24 passengers) cost €160.

full day including proper riding equipment and lunch.

🛏 Sleeping

Ada Camping CAMPGROUND $
(☑0384-511 2429; www.avanosadacamping.com; Jan Zakari Caddesi 20; campsites per person ₺15;

☎) This large, family-run camping ground is in a superb setting near the Kızılırmak River. The toilet block could be cleaner, but there's lots of shade and grass, a restaurant and a cold but inviting large swimming pool. It's on the southern bank of the river, west of the main bridge.

★ **Kirkit Hotel** BOUTIQUE HOTEL **$$**
(☑ 0384-511 3148; www.kirkithotel.com; Genç Ağa Sokak; s/d/tr/f €40/55/70/90; 🛜) This Avanos institution, right in the centre of town, is a rambling stone house with rooms full of kilims (pileless woven rugs), old black-and-white photographs, intricately carved cupboards and *suzanis* (Uzbek bedspreads), all set around a courtyard brimming with plants and quirky antiques. Looked after by incredibly knowledgeable and helpful management, Kirkit is the perfect base for trips around Cappadocia.

Venessa Pansiyon PENSION **$$**
(☑ 0384-511 3840; www.venessapension.com; 800 Sokak 20; r ₺120-150; 🛜) Owned by enthusiastic local history expert Mükremin Tokmak, the Venessa is a homey Avanos option with simple, bright rooms full of local kilims and traditional *yastık* (cushions), and a cosy rooftop terrace with great views and bundles of local character. The pension also has its own small Cappadocian art exhibition and museum, which nonguests are welcome to visit.

Sofa Hotel BOUTIQUE HOTEL **$$**
(☑ 0384-511 5186; www.sofahotel.com; Gedik Sokak 9; d €40-70; 🛜) A higgledy-piggledy wonderland for adults struck by wanderlust, Sofa is the creation of artist Hoja, who has spent a fair chunk of his life redesigning the Ottoman houses that make up the hotel. Rooms merge eclectic-chic and traditional decoration with plenty of wood-beam accents and colourful textiles.

✗ Eating

Avanos' huge Friday **market** (⊙ 9am-5pm Fri) is the best in the region. It's held on the south bank of the Kızılırmak River, near Taş Köprü bridge.

★ **Hanım Eli** ANATOLIAN **$**
(Atatürk Caddesi; mains ₺8-15; ⊙ 11am-9pm) This modest diner serves wholesome local dishes packed full of fresh, local flavour. This is home-style cooking executed brilliantly and without any pretentious flourish. The *mantı* (Turkish ravioli) we had here was the best in Cappadocia. Wily diners looking for Anatolian soul food without the price tag of Göreme and Ürgüp's restaurants would do well to lunch here.

Kapadokya Urfa Sofrası KEBAP **$**
(Atatürk Caddesi; pide & dürüm ₺6-7, mains ₺12-20; ⊙ 10.30am-10pm) Our pick of Avanos'

multitude of kebap joints is this welcoming place right near the main square with cheerful service and excellent-value meals. Looking for a cheap, tasty lunch? We recommend ordering a couple of *lahmacun* (Arabic-style pizza; ₺3). Want something more substantial? The *beyti sarma* (spicy ground meat baked in a thin layer of bread) here is superb.

Dayının Yeri KEBAP **$$**
(☑ 0384-511 6840; Atatürk Caddesi; mains ₺17-30; ⊙ 10.30am-11pm) Locals grumble that it's not as cheap as it used to be, but this modern grill restaurant is one of Cappadocia's best. Steer clear of the meze and it's still decent value, too. Don't leave without sampling the *künefe* – layers of *kadayıf* dough cemented together with sweet cheese, doused in syrup and served hot with a sprinkling of pistachio.

It's right beside Taş Köprü (the town's main bridge).

Bizim Ev INTERNATIONAL **$$$**
(☑ 0384-511 5525; Baklacı Sokak 1; mains ₺20-55; ⊙ 11am-11pm) The cave cellar could easily tempt you into a few lost hours, but if you can make it upstairs the terrace is the place for atmospheric dining. Service is sleekly unobtrusive and the menu ranges from steaks to kebaps to house trout and roasted lamb specialities.

🛍 Shopping

Avanos' many small ceramic workshops are located in the alleyways around the main square and in the group of shops opposite the post office.

Le Palais du Urdu CERAMICS
(⊙ 10am-6pm) Our favourite Avanos artisan haunt, this unique drum-making and pottery studio is just off the main square, to your right if you're facing the hill.

ℹ Information

Avanos Tourist Office (☑ 0384-511 4360; Atatürk Caddesi; ⊙ 8.30am-5pm) gives out free town maps, although it doesn't always stick to its opening hours.

ℹ Getting There & Away

You can book long-distance buses at Avanos' small **otogar** (Kapadokya Caddesi), a 10-minute walk across the Kızılırmak river from the centre. The bus companies here all provide a *servis* to Nevşehir.

Dolmuşes from Avanos to Nevşehir (₺4) leave every 20 minutes between 7am and 7pm. Services departing on the hour travel via Çavuşin, Göreme and Uçhisar (₺3); other departures take the direct route.

Dolmuşes to Ürgüp (₺4) leave hourly between 7am and 8pm, travelling via Zelve, Paşabağı, Çavuşin, Göreme and Göreme Open-Air Museum.

Both of these dolmuş services drop off and pick up passengers along Atatürk Caddesi.

Around Avanos

The countryside immediately around Avanos is home to a couple of sights that can easily be tacked onto a day spent exploring the town. Özkonak Underground City is the most interesting, particularly if you want to explore one of Cappadocia's famed subterranean dwellings without the crowds.

Özkonak Underground City

About 15km north of Avanos, the village of Özkonak hosts a smaller version of the underground cities of Kaymaklı and Derinkuyu, with the same wine reservoirs and rolling stone doors. Although **Özkonak Underground City** (Özkonak Yeraltı Şehri; ₺10; ⊙8am-7pm) is neither as dramatic nor as impressive as the larger ones, it is much less crowded.

The easiest way to get here is by dolmuş from Avanos (₺2, 30 minutes, hourly between 8.30am and 5.30pm). Be aware that services can be erratic due to lack of customers so it's best to check times locally for the current schedule. There are no services on the weekend. Ask to be let off for the *yeraltı şehri* (underground city); the bus stops at the petrol station, a 500m stroll from the entrance.

Sarıhan

Built in 1249, the **Sarıhan** (Yellow Caravanserai; ⊋0384-511 3795; www.sarihan1249.com; Kayseri Yolu; ₺3; ⊙9am-midnight) has an elaborate gateway with a small mosque above it. Having been restored in the late 1980s, it's one of the best remaining Seljuk caravanserais. Gunning down the highway towards it makes you feel like a 13th-century trader, ready to rest his camels and catch up with his fellow dealers.

Inside, in the bare stone courtyard, you'll have to use your imagination to capture a sense of the building's history.

The main reason to come to the Sarıhan is for the nightly 45-minute **whirling dervish ceremony** (Sema; ⊋0384-511 3795; admission €25; ⊙9pm). Getting to the Sarıhan, 6km east of Avanos, without your own transport is difficult, as there are no dolmuşes and few vehicles with which to hitch a ride. An Avanos taxi driver will probably want around ₺30 to take you there and back, including waiting time.

Nevşehir

⊋0384 / POPULATION 98,800 / ELEV 1260M

Poor old Nevşehir. Surrounded by the stunning countryside of Cappadocia, this provincial capital of bland apartment buildings has never offered travellers an incentive to linger. Things may be looking up though; an underground city was discovered when the town council began clearing away the old neighbourhood around Nevşehir castle. Continuing excavations have since revealed a vast tunnel network and a frescoed church that may date back to as early as the 5th century. The site is partially pegged to be open for visitors by 2018 but check locally for confirmation.

Nevşehir Museum   MUSEUM

(⊋0384-213 1447; Türbe Sokak 1; ⊙8am-5pm) **FREE** This tiny museum is housed in an ugly building 1km from the centre. The collection includes a surprisingly good archaeological room with Phrygian, Hittite and Bronze Age pots and implements, as well as Roman, Byzantine and Ottoman articles. Upstairs, the dusty ethnographic section is less interesting.

To get here by dolmuş from the Cappadocian villages, get off at Migros supermarket just as you enter central Nevşehir, cross the road and you'll see the Müze sign on the next intersection.

ⓘ Getting There & Around

Nevşehir is the main regional transport hub for the nearby Cappadocian villages.

A taxi to Göreme should cost around ₺35.

AIR

Nevşehir Airport (p453) is 30km northwest of town, past Gülşehir.

Airport shuttle buses (p454) run between the airport and the villages of central Cappadocia. They must be pre-booked.

BUS

Nevşehir **otogar** (Aksaray Nevşehir Yolu) is 2.5km southwest of the city. Most bus services from İstanbul and other towns in western Turkey

GOING UNDERGROUND

Thought to have been first carved out by the Hittites, the vast network of underground cities in this region was first mentioned by the ancient Greek historian Xenophon in his *Anabasis* (written in the 4th century BC).

During the 6th and 7th centuries, Byzantine Christians extended the cities and used them as a means by which to escape persecution. If Persian or Arab armies were approaching, a series of beacons would be lit in warning – the message could travel from Jerusalem to Constantinople in hours. When it reached Cappadocia, the Christians would relocate to the underground cities, hiding in the subterranean vaults for months at a time.

One of the defense mechanisms developed by the cities' inhabitants was to disguise the air shafts as wells. Attackers might throw poison into these 'wells', thinking they were contaminating the water supply. Smoke from residents' fires was absorbed by the soft tuff rock and dispersed in the shafts – leaving the prowling attackers none the wiser.

The shafts, which descend almost 100m in some of the cities, also served another purpose. As new rooms were constructed, debris would be excavated into the shafts, which would then be cleared and deepened so work could begin on the next floor. Some of the cities are remarkable in scale – it is thought that Derinkuyu and Kaymaklı housed about 10,000 and 3000 people respectively.

Around 37 underground cities have already been opened. There are at least 100 more, though the full extent of these subterranean refuges may never be known. A newly discovered one, currently being excavated in Nevşehir (p471), may be about to flip the commonly accepted theory of how the cities were used on its head, as archaeologists say there is evidence that city was used as a permanent habitation rather than a temporary shelter.

Touring the cities is like tackling an assault course for history buffs. Narrow walkways lead you into the depths of the earth, through stables with handles used to tether animals, churches with altars and baptism pools, granaries with grindstones, and blackened kitchens with ovens. While it's a fascinating experience, be prepared for unpleasantly crowded and sometimes claustrophobic passages. Avoid visiting on weekends, when busloads of domestic tourists descend.

---

terminate in Nevşehir but then provide a free *servis* bus service to Göreme, Ürgüp, Ortahisar, Avanos and Uçhisar.

Nevşehir has excellent transport links to the surrounding Cappadocian villages from its dolmuş stand on Osmanlı Caddesi in the city centre. From here local dolmuşes run Monday to Saturday to Göreme (₺2.50, every 30 minutes from 7.30am to 7.30pm); Uçhisar (₺2, every 30 minutes from 7.30am to 7.30pm); Ürgüp (₺3.50, every 15 minutes from 7am to 8pm); Avanos (₺4, every 20 minutes from 7am to 7pm); Ortahisar (₺3.50, hourly from 8am to 5pm); Kaymaklı and Derinkuyu Underground Cities (₺5, every 30 minutes between 9am and 7pm); and Niğde (₺12, hourly between 9am and 7pm). Many village dolmuşes have fewer services on Sundays. Buses to Hacıbektaş leave from the Has Hacıbektaş office, just around the corner.

Gülşehir

☑ 0384 / POP 12,300

This small town has two rocky attractions on its outskirts that are worth visiting if you're passing through. It's 19km north of Nevşehir.

◉ Sights

Church of St Jean
CHURCH

(Karşı Kilise; Kırşehir-Nevşehir Yolu; ₺5; ⊙8am-5pm) On the main highway into Gülşehir, just before the turn-off to the centre (another 500m further) is a signposted trail leading to the incredible 13th-century Church of St Jean. This two-levelled, rock-cut church is home to marvellous frescoes, including scenes depicting the Annunciation, the Descent from the Cross, the Last Supper, the Betrayal by Judas and the Last Judgement (rarely depicted in Cappadocian churches), which were all painstakingly restored to their original glory in 1995.

Open Palace
MONASTERY

(Açık Saray; Kırşehir-Nevşehir Yolu; ⊙8am-5pm) **FREE** This fine rock-cut monastery complex has a cluster of churches, refectories, dormitories and a kitchen, all carved out of fairy chimneys and dating from the 6th and 7th centuries. It's signposted off the main Gülşehir–Nevşehir road, about 4km before Gülşehir's town centre.

Below are four of the most interesting to visit but there are others, including the underground cities in the village of Güzelyurt (p491), and at Özkonak (p471) near Avanos.

Kaymaklı Underground City (admission ₺30; ⊙8am-7pm) Kaymaklı underground city features a maze of tunnels and rooms carved eight levels deep into the earth (only four are open). As this is the most popular of the underground cities, you should aim to get here early in July and August to beat the tour groups, or from about 12.30pm to 1.30pm, when they tend to be having lunch.

Derinkuyu Underground City (admission ₺25; ⊙8am-7pm) Located 10km south of Kaymaklı, this underground city has large, cavernous rooms arrayed on seven levels. When you get all the way to the bottom, look up the ventilation shaft to see just how far down you are – claustrophobics, beware!

Gaziemir Underground City (admission ₺10; ⊙8am-6pm) Some 18km east of Güzelyurt, just off the road to Derinkuyu, is Gaziemir underground city. Churches, a winery with wine barrels, food depots, hamams and *tandır* (clay-oven) fireplaces can be seen. Camel bones and loopholes in the rock for tethering animals suggest that it also served as a subterranean caravanserai.

Özlüce Underground City (⊙9am-6.30pm) **FREE** Turn right as you enter Kaymaklı village from the north and you'll be heading for the small village of Özlüce, 7km further away. More modest than the caves of Kaymaklı or Derinkuyu, this underground city is also much less developed and less crowded.

Getting There & Away

Although you can visit one of the cities as part of a day tour, it's also easy to see them on your own. From Nevşehir, Derinkuyu Koop runs dolmuşes to Derinkuyu (₺5, 45 minutes, every 30 minutes between 9am and 6.30pm), which also stop in Kaymaklı (₺3, 30 minutes). Dolmuşes leave from the central bus stand on Osmanlı Caddesi.

You'll need a taxi or a hire car to take you to Özlüce from Kaymaklı or to visit Gaziemir.

CAPPADOCIA HACIBEKTAŞ

❶ Getting There & Away

Dolmuşes to Gülşehir (₺3.50, 25 minutes, every 30 minutes) from Nevşehir depart from a dolmuş stand on Lale Caddesi, just north of the Alibey Cami. Ask to be let off at the Açık Saray or Karşı Kilise to save a walk back from town. Returning, just flag the bus down from the side of the highway. You can also flag down dolmuşes heading onward to Hacıbektaş from the highway.

Hacıbektaş

☑ 0384 / POP 5200

Hacıbektaş could be any unremarkable, small Anatolian town if it weren't for the beautiful dervish *dergah* (lodge) and museum set right in the main square. A visit here is a glimpse at the history and culture of the Bektaşi Alevi religious sect. The annual **Hacı Bektaş Veli pilgrimage and festival** (⊙16-18 Aug) is a fascinating experience if you're here at that time.

Born in Nishapur in Iran in the 13th century, Hacı Bektaş Veli inspired a religious and political following that blended aspects of Islam (both Sunni and Shi'ite) with Orthodox Christianity. During his life he is known to have travelled around Anatolia and to have lived in Kayseri, Sivas and Kırşehir, but eventually he settled in the hamlet that is now the small town of Hacıbektaş.

Although not much is known about Hacı Bektaş, the book he wrote, the *Makalât,* describes a mystical philosophy less austere than mainstream Islam. In it he laid out a four-stage path to enlightenment (the Four Doors). Though often scorned by mainstream Islamic clerics, Bektaşi dervishes attained considerable influence in Ottoman times. Along with all the other dervishes, they were outlawed by Atatürk in 1925.

The annual pilgrimage of Bektaşi dervishes is an extremely important event for the modern Alevi community. Politicians tend to hijack the first day's proceedings, but days two and three are given over to music and dance.

Hacıbektaş Veli Museum MUSEUM
(Hacıbektaş Veli Müzesi; Atatürk Caddesi; ⊙8am-7pm) **FREE** Right in Hacıbektaş' centre is this tranquil dervish *dergah* (lodge), now a

museum as well as a place of pilgrimage for those of the Bektaşı faith. Several rooms are arranged as they might have been when the Bektaşı order lived here, with dioramas of dervish life and beautiful exhibits of clothing, musical instruments and jewellery. The **Meydan Evi** (meeting house), where initiation ceremonies were performed, has an intricate wooden dove-tailed ceiling, its crossbeams symbolising the nine levels of heaven.

Amid the rose gardens of the museum's inner courtyard is the **Pir Evi** (House of the Masters), which contains the **Mausoleum of Haci Bektaş Veli**. Walk down the stairs, passing the tiny cell where dervishes would retreat to pray, to enter the Kırklar Meydanı (where dervish ceremonies took place), its walls decorated with colourful floral and geometric motifs. Haci Bektaş Veli's tomb is in a separate room to the right.

Across the rose gardens from the Pir Evi is the **Mausoleum of Balım Sultan** (another important religious leader), with a 700-year-old mulberry tree – its aged branches propped up by wooden posts – just outside.

❶ Getting There & Away

From Nevşehir, two dolmuş companies, both on Lale Caddesi, service Hacıbektaş (₺5, 40 minutes). The Has Hacıbektaş office, near the Alibey Camii, has hourly departures between 8am and 2pm. The Hacıbektaş office, two blocks north up the road, has services at 7.30am, 8.45am, 10.30am, 11.30am, 12.30pm, 1.30pm, 2.45pm, 5pm and 6pm.

Catch a returning dolmuş from Hacıbektaş otogar (hourly between 8am and 5pm). There are also seven daily departures for Ankara.

Ortahisar

🌙 0384 / POP 3600

Known for the jagged castle that gives the town its name, Ortahisar is the epitome of Cappadocia's agricultural soul. Wander downwards from the central square and you'll discover cobbled streets rimmed by gorgeously worn stone-house ruins leading out to a gorge of pigeon house–speckled rock. Head upwards (towards the highway) and you'll see the cave complexes where Turkey's citrus-fruit supply is still stashed. Overlooked for years by travellers, the secret is now firmly out. The past couple of years have seen a flurry of boutique and larger luxury-hotel openings here as visitors searching for the Cappadocia-of-old begin to discover Ortahisar's beguiling, arcadian beauty. Despite the sudden influx, Ortahisar's

rustic nature is still very much in place. Donkey carts rattle down the lanes regularly, elderly men mooch all day outside teashops and, if you're here in April when the citrus storage caves are thrown open, the scent of lemons permeates the town.

◉ Sights & Activities

Pigeon house–studded **Ortahisar Valley** is easiest accessed from the bottom of Tahir Bey Sokak. There's also easy access into the **Uzengi Valley** (home to some incredible pigeon-house views) from the southeast end of the village.

Ortahisar Castle   CASTLE

(Cami Sokak; ₺2; ⊙9am-6pm) Slap in the middle of Ortahisar's town centre, this 18m-high rock outcrop was used as a fortress in Byzantine times. It was reopened after a restoration project stabilised the crumbling edifice, and you can now climb the precarious metal ladders and stairways to the viewing terrace halfway up and admire the glorious view. Head up in late afternoon for the best photography light.

Pancarlı Kilise   CHURCH

(Beetroot Church; ₺5; ⊙9am-4.30pm Apr-Oct) This rarely visited 11th-century church is snuggled amid a particularly photogenic vista of orange-hued rock. The small nave has a dazzling interior of well-preserved frescoes, while the surrounding cliff face is pockmarked with a warren of rooms that once served as living areas for hermit monks. To find it, head southeast from Ortahisar Castle, following Hacı Telegraf Sokak down the hill. Cross the bridge across the gully and take the eastern (signposted) farm track for 3km.

Culture Folk Museum   MUSEUM

(Kültür Müzesi; Cami Sokak 15; ₺5; ⊙9am-5pm) On the main square, near Ortahisar's castle, the Culture Folk Museum is a good place to get to grips with the basics of local culture. In the dioramas, with multilingual interpretive panels, mannequins in headscarves and old men's şapkas (hats) make yufka (thinly rolled, unleavened bread), pekmez (syrup made from grape juice) and kilims (pileless woven rug).

Hallacdere Monastery   MONASTERY

FREE The columned church of this rock-cut monastery complex contains unusual features. Look for the animal heads on the column capitals and the human figure sculpted onto the wall. It's just off the main road into town, 1km northeast of Ortahisar centre.

Cemal Ranch
HORSE RIDING

(☑ 0532 291 0211; www.cemalranch.com; İsak Kale; incl transport to/from hotel 1/2hr ₺75/150, 4/6hr incl dinner afterwards ₺300/400) Set amid stunning valley views, Cemal Ranch offers riding excursions in the surrounding countryside. Shorter tours head through Ortahisar Valley and visit the Hallacdere Monastery. Four- and six-hour treks give you enough time to explore the secluded Üzengi Valley and to sample some slap-up Turkish home cooking afterwards. The ranch is 1km east of (and well signposted from) Ortahisar centre.

🛏 Sleeping

Castle Inn
BOUTIQUE HOTEL $$

(☑ 0384-343 3022; www.castleinn.com.tr; Bahçe Sokak 5; r €55-95; 🛜) With just five rooms, this old Greek house a stone's throw from the village square is a snug choice, with friendly advice and historical titbits dished out by personable host Suat. Each of the stone-arch rooms (and one cave suite) is scattered with mementos picked up on Suat's travels, while the terrace has sweeping village views.

Elaa Cave Hotel
BOUTIQUE HOTEL $$

(☑ 0384-343 2650; www.elaacavehotel.com; Tahir Bey Sokak 4; r €40-50; ❄🛜) Chickens wander the alley outside but through Elaa Cave's gate that rural Anatolian aesthetic gets a Turkish-modern shake-up. Vibrant colours sit alongside intricately carved wood panels, fine carpets and quirky art in six snug cave rooms. There's proper espresso on offer with breakfast, and the chic contemporary vibe of the roof terrace is perfect for sundowners loomed over by Otahisar's rock castle.

★ Hezen Cave Hotel
BOUTIQUE HOTEL $$$

(☑ 0384-343 3005; www.hezenhotel.com; Tahir Bey Sokak 87; s/d €125/145, ste from €220; ☑ Mar-Nov; ❄✳🛜) We think we've fallen in love. From the foyer's statement-piece ceiling of recycled *hezen* (telegraph poles) to the gourmet breakfasts on the terrace with 360-degree village views, every detail at this gorgeous design hotel has been thought through. A riot of colours enlivens doors, window frames and fixtures, adding a shot of contemporary chic to cave rooms that exude effortless cool.

Queen's Cave
BOUTIQUE HOTEL $$$

(☑ 0384-343 3040; www.queenshotelcappadocia. com; Dere Sokak 24-26; d €60-80, f €140-180; ❄🛜) Snuggled at the bottom of Ortahisar is this hideaway, amid gardens of lavender and pansies. Cave and traditional stone-cut rooms merge modern comforts and lashings of wood and stone to emerge with a distinctively stylish cave-house vibe. There's a guest-use kitchen, and the interconnecting suites are great for families or groups of friends. For troglodyte whimsy, reserve the fairy-chimney room.

The House Hotel
LUXURY HOTEL $$$

(☑ 0384-343 2425; www.thehousehotel.com; Hacı Telgraf Caddesi 3/1; r €109-229; ❄✳🛜) City-slicker style lands in Ortahisar as İstanbul's House Hotel branches out to bring some contemporary edge to village life. Generously proportioned rooms are home to huge flat-screen TVs and marble-clad bathrooms complete with double showers, while decoration is kept deliberately stark allowing original cave-wall features to shine in the suites.

Muti Restaurant
(☑ 0384-341 5858; Hacı Telgraf Caddesi No 3/1, The House Hotel; ₺28-46; ⊙ 11.30am-11pm) offers formal Turkish dining on the first floor and rooftop terrace.

🍽 Eating

Hisar Teras Cafe
TURKISH $

(Cami Sokak; gözleme from ₺8; ⊙ 10am-9pm) A couple of doors down from Ortahisar's central mosque, you'll find this unassuming place. Walk straight out back to the balcony for comfy old sofas and a stunning village view. The menu is as modest as the decor but that's OK because you're here for the *gözleme* (savoury pancake). These are the fattest, juiciest, most soaked-in-butter moreish *gözleme* we've ever had.

Kapadokya Cafe
LOKANTA $

(Cami Sokak; döner & dürum ₺2.50-3.50, dishes from ₺8; ⊙ 10.30am-10pm) Our pick of central Ortahisar's cheap and cheerful diners is this little place with just a couple of tables and rustic, hearty Turkish staples.

Tandır Restaurant
ANATOLIAN $$

(☑ 0384-477 8575; Manzara ve Kültür Park, Esentepe Mahallesi; mains ₺15-30; ⊙ 11am-10pm; 🅿) Ortahisar's top dining spot has plenty of homespun local flavours and gorgeous views out to the town's rock castle. The menu offers up traditional dishes such as *kabak çiçeği dolması* (stuffed courgette flowers) and *tandır kuzu* (lamb tandoor) all served with gracious aplomb. It's up the hill from the centre, in Ortahisar's Manzara ve Kültür Park.

ℹ Getting There & Away

Dolmuşes leave from the main square to Ürgüp (₺2.50, every 30 minutes from 8am to 5pm Monday to Saturday) and Nevşehir (₺3.50, hourly from 8am to 6pm Monday to Saturday). Heading to Göreme, you have to walk 1km uphill to the Ortahisar turn-off on the main highway, where you can catch the Ürgüp–Avanos dolmuş as it goes by.

You can book onward travel to other destinations in Turkey at the **Nevşehir Seyahat** (☑ 0384-343 3383; www.nevsehirlilerseyahat. com.tr; Tepebası Meydanı) bus company office in the centre.

Ürgüp

☑ 0384 / POP 20,700

When Ürgüp's Greek population was evicted in 1923 the town's wealth of fine stone-cut houses was left teetering into gentle dilapidation until tourism began to take off. Now, more than 90 years later, these remnants of another era have found a new lease of life as some of Cappadocia's most luxurious boutique hotels. Ürgüp is the rural retreat for those who don't fancy being too rural, with its bustling, modern downtown area a direct foil to the old village back lanes still clinging to the hillside rim. There's not a lot to do in town itself. Instead, Ürgüp has cleverly positioned itself as the connoisseur's base for exploring the geographical heart of Cappadocia, with boutique-hotel frippery at your fingertips.

◎ Sights & Activities

Three Graces Fairy Chimneys   LANDMARK
(Üç Güzeller; Nevşehir-Ürgüp Yolu) These three black-capped fairy-chimney formations (also known as 'the three beauties') are Ürgüp's best-known landmark. Overlooking the rolling countryside just outside of town, it's a prime spot to capture a sunset photo. The site is 1km along the main road, heading towards Ortahisar, from the roundabout at the top of Tevfik Fikret Caddesi.

★ **Old Village**   AREA
(Map p478) The back alleys of Ürgüp are home to many fine examples of the traditional stone architecture of this region, and are well worth a stroll.

Temenni Wishing Hill   VIEWPOINT
(Map p478; Cami Kebir Sokak) Home to a saint's tomb and a cafe, this viewpoint has 360-degree views over Ürgüp.

Turasan Winery   WINERY
(Map p478; ☑ 0384-341 4961; Tevfik Fikret Caddesi; wine tasting ₺20; ◎ 8.30am-6pm) The abundant sunshine and fertile volcanic soil of Cappadocia produce delicious sweet grapes, and several wineries carry on the Ottoman Greek winemaking tradition. You can sample some of the local produce here.

Tarihi Şehir Hamamı   HAMAM
(Map p478; ☑ 0384-341 2241; İstiklal Caddesi; soak, scrub & massage ₺45; ◎ 7am-10pm) Partly housed in what was once a small church, Ürgüp's hamam offers mixed but respectable bathing.

☞ Tours

Several Ürgüp-based travel agents run tours around Cappadocia.

Argeus Tourism & Travel   TOURS
(Map p478; ☑ 0384-341 4688; www.argeus.com. tr; İstiklal Caddesi 47) Offers two- to 15-day packages across Turkey, including a nine-day Cappadocia mountain-biking option, as well as private Cappadocia day tours, flights and car hire. It's Ürgüp's Turkish Airlines representative and it runs a reputable airport shuttle service for Turkish Airlines flights arriving in Kayseri (₺25) and Nevşehir (₺20). Book in advance.

Peerless Travel Services   TOURS
(Map p478; ☑ 0384-341 6970; www.peerless excursions.com; İstiklal Caddesi 41) A range of private tours and package trips in the Cappadocia region including more off-beat options such as a one-day tour of the sights around Niğde, two-day jeep safaris that visit Soğanlı and Sultan Marshes, and four-day winter ski packages to Erciyes Dağı (Mt Erciyes). Also can arrange tours across Turkey.

🛏 Sleeping

Ürgüp has a glut of luxury boutique hotels. Most are snuggled amid the old village district, up the hill from the modern town centre. If you're looking for a good selection of mid-range and budget options, you're better off in nearby Göreme. Some hotels close between November and March, when Ürgüp's weather keeps locals indoors and travellers elsewhere.

Hotel Elvan   PENSION $
(Map p478; ☑ 0384-341 4191; www.hotelelvan. com; Barbaros Hayrettin Sokak 11; s/d/f ₺60/80/150, deluxe r ₺120; 🐾) Bah – who needs boutique style when you have pensions like the Elvan, where Hasan and

family dish out oodles of homespun hospitality. Set around an internal courtyard brimming with colourful pot plants, the 22 neat rooms feature daisy bedspreads and sparkling-clean bathrooms. On the ground floor, newly fitted-out stone-arch deluxe rooms come with snazzy onyx travertine bathrooms and TVs.

Canyon Cave Hotel BOUTIQUE HOTEL $$

(Map p478; ☑ 0384-341 4113; www.canyoncave hotel.com; Sair Mahfi Baba 3 Sokak 9; r €63-95, ste €130; ☺🛜) Host Murat İşnel creates a fun and sociable atmosphere at his nine-room hilltop pad with its rooftop bar overlooking the entire sweep of Ürgüp and the majestic peak of Erciyes Dağı (Mt Erciyes) beyond. Rooms (both half and full cave) are generously sized and simply furnished, and breakfast is a slap-up feast featuring cafetiere coffee and banana bread.

Cappadocia Palace HOTEL $$

(Map p478; ☑ 0384-341 2510; www.hotel-cappa docia.com; Mektep Sokak 2; s/d/tr ₺80/140/170, cave r ₺220; 🛜) This Ürgüp old-timer has helpful management and a choice of either enormous cave rooms hosting bathrooms big enough to boogie in or plainer (and smaller) motel-style rooms for those who aspire to the boutique scene but don't have the budget to match.

★Sota Cappadocia BOUTIQUE HOTEL $$$

(Map p478; ☑ 0384-341 5885; www.sotacappa docia.com; Burhan Kale Sokak 12; r/ste from €130/180; ☺🛜) 🍃 Ürgüp's hippest new opening. Nil Tuncer, with help from acclaimed interior decorator Oytun Berktan, has stamped the eight rooms with a minimalist design as much at home in New York as within the swirling natural colours of the cave walls. Dramatic black accenting, re-purposed *gözleme*-pans as statement wall art, hanging lamps salvaged from a Russian tanker – Sota's swaggering style shakes up the Cappadocia scene.

This place has serious substance, with exceptional attention paid to all the little details. Guests can borrow iPads and stacks of books, and chill out on the sun-lounger-scattered terraces, there's a well-stocked bar, and breakfast includes espresso and artisan breads. Even better, this little hotel has got sustainability credentials with grey water reuse in place and eco-pellets (rather than coal) being used for the central heating.

★Esbelli Evi BOUTIQUE HOTEL $$$

(Map p478; ☑ 0384-341 3395; www.esbelli.com; Esbelli Sokak 8; r €80-270; ☺Mar-Oct; ☺❄🛜) Jazz in the bathroom, whisky by the tub, secret tunnels to secluded walled gardens draped in vines – this is one of Cappadocia's most individual boutique hotels. A lawyer who never practised, Süha Ersöz instead (thank God!) purchased the 12 surrounding properties over two decades and created a highly cultured yet decidedly unpretentious hotel that stands out on exclusive Esbelli Hill.

The detailed rooms feel more like first-class holiday apartments for visiting dignitaries, from the state-of-the-art family room with fully decked-out kids' room to the raised beds and provincial kitchens in the enormous cave suites. The breakfast spread is organic and delicious, while an enchanting evening on the terrace is an education in local history, humility and grace.

Serinn House BOUTIQUE HOTEL $$$

(Map p478; ☑ 0384-341 6076; www.serinnhouse. com; Esbelli Sokak 36; d from €80; ☺🛜) Charming hostess Eren Serpen has truly set a new standard for hotel design in Cappadocia with this contemporary effort that seamlessly merges İstanbul's European aesthetic with Turkish provincial life. The six minimally furnished rooms employ dashes of colour and feature Archimedes lamps, signature chairs, hip floor rugs and tables too cool for coffee.

Yunak Evleri LUXURY HOTEL $$$

(Map p478; ☑ 0384-341 6920; www.yunak.com; Yunak Sokak; d €180, ste from €200; 🛜) Yunak is a labyrinth of good taste cut into the cliffside. The hotel's mazy structure – in some parts dating back to the 5th century – unfurls itself through flower-filled patios and up stone steps to elegant carved-stone chambers. This is a hotel for connoisseurs of exceptional travel.

Melekler Evi BOUTIQUE HOTEL $$$

(Map p478; ☑ 0384-341 7131; www.meleklerevi. com.tr; Dere Sokak 59; d from €85; ☺🛜) This sweet little hideaway brims with inspired artistic flourishes. Each room is a piece of interior-design heaven (unsurprisingly, owner Arzu is an interior decorator by trade) where hi-fi music and high-tech shower systems merge with smatterings of winged sculpture, grand old stone fireplaces and touches of homespun whimsy.

Ürgüp

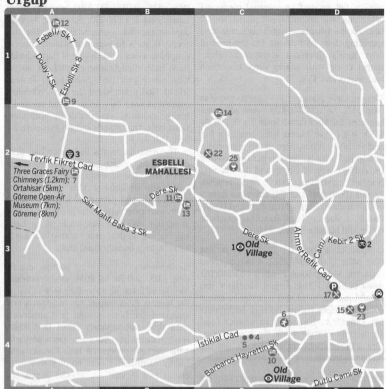

✕ Eating

Ürgüp's mammoth Saturday **market** (Fabrika Caddesi; ⏰9am-4pm) is a buzzing hive of activity and full of local produce. It's held in the Migros supermarket car park.

Zeytin Cafe
LOKANTA $

(Map p478; ☎0384-341 7399; Atatürk Bulvarı; dishes ₺6-15; ⏰10am-10pm; ✐) Our top lunchtime spot in Ürgüp is this thoroughly welcoming, modern *lokanta* (eatery serving ready-made food) dishing up wholesome homemade stews, *mantı* (Turkish ravioli) and Turkish staples. Head inside to the counter and choose from the daily-changing selection.

Develili Deringöller Pide
ve Kebap Salonu
PIDE $

(Map p478; Dumlupınar Caddesi; pide ₺6-13; ⏰10am-10pm; ✐) Shh... We're going to tell you a secret the locals have been trying to hide for years: this is, hands down, the best pide in Cappadocia.

Merkez Pastaneleri
BAKERY $

(Map p478; Güllüce Caddesi; baked goods from ₺1, ice-cream scoop ₺2; ⏰9.30am-8pm) In business since 1975, this *pastane* (patisserie) is still churning out some of Cappadocia's best baked goods including cheap, filling *börek* (filled pastries) and tempting, sticky baklava. On a summer day Cappadocian locals have been known to drive to Ürgüp just to buy a *dondurma* (ice cream) here. Check out the honey-and-almond flavour and you'll see why.

Yeni Lokanta
LOKANTA $$

(Map p478; ☎0384-341 6880; Postane Sokak 3; mains ₺10-32; ⏰10.30am-10pm) This new-wave *lokanta* (eatery serving ready-made food) is a roaring success. Yeni Lokanta drags the traditional working-man canteen into the 21st century with smart-attired waiters, a contemporary dining room and some impressive dish presentation. Prices, though, remain lokanta-style with meze and small

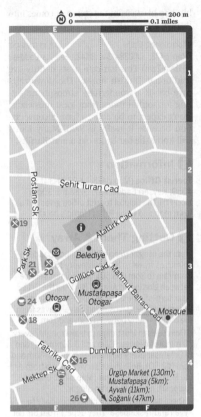

dishes like *börek* (filled pastries) between ₺4 and ₺8, and grills beginning at ₺16. The *izgara köfte* (grilled meatballs) here is lush.

Osmanlı Konağı　　　　ANATOLIAN $$
(Map p478; ☑0384-341 5441; Sağırmescit Sokak; meals ₺30/25 per person for group of 2/4; ⊙6-11pm) With just four tables and mum in the kitchen doing the cooking, this cosy family-run restaurant does excellent-value village food. There's no menu as such; instead a volley of dishes (six meze and five mains), all made to share, arrive at your table – containing whatever they've decided to cook that day. It's a tasty romp through the Anatolian heartland.

Han Çirağan Restaurant　　RESTAURANT, BAR $$
(Map p478; ☑0384-341 2566; Cumhuriyet Meydanı; mains ₺15-35; ⊙10am-1am; ☑) The menu here is a meander through Turkish favourites with a modern twist and service is super friendly. After dinner, retire to the very cool

bar downstairs, under the vine trellis, that has a city atmosphere and an excellent wine list, and serves up a mean martini.

Cappadocia Restaurant　　　TURKISH $$
(Map p478; Cumhuriyet Meydanı; meals ₺20-25; ⊙10am-9pm) Savvy travellers join the locals packing out the pavement tables here to sample generous helpings of Cappadocian flavour.

★Ziggy Cafe　　　MODERN TURKISH $$$
(Map p478; ☑0384-341 7107; www.ziggycafe.com; Tevfik Fikret Caddesi 24; meze set menus ₺60-65, mains ₺20-45; ⊙11.30am-11pm; ☑) This tribute to the adored pet dog of charismatic hosts Nuray and Selim is a luscious success. The two-tiered terrace fills day and night with a hip clientele enjoying strong cocktails and feasting on the finest meze

menu in Cappadocia, created by chef Ali Ozkan. Ziggy's has nailed the essence of casual-yet-classy Cappadocian dining.

 Drinking & Nightlife

Ürgüp's main square (Cumhuriyet Meydanı) is the best place to grab a drink at an outside table and watch Cappadocia cruise by. By far the most convivial and relaxed place is the bar in Han Çirağan Restaurant (p479) but if you want to go exploring, a few other places pass muster.

Efendi Şarap Evi   WINE BAR
(Map p478; ☎0384-341 4024; Tevfik Fikret Caddesi 12; wine tasting ₺15, glass/bottle of wine ₺10/from ₺25; ☒11am-8pm) The shady terrace here is one of the nicest places in Cappadocia to partake in a spot of wine tasting. Tastings consist of seven wines plus a cheese plate to munch on and afterwards, plus you can buy your favourites by the bottle or glass and keep kicking back on the terrace watching the world go by.

Cafe In   CAFE
(Map p478; Cumhuriyet Meydanı; ☒10.30am-10pm) This dinky cafe does the best coffee in town and the street-side tables make a great beer pit-stop after a meander through the centre. There's also decent pasta and some inventive salads.

Angel Café Bistro   BAR
(Map p478; ☎0384-341 6894; Cumhuriyet Meydanı; ☒11am-late) Ürgüp's bright young things lounge around on the sofas out the front and

hip-hop blasts from the stereo. It comes into its own after dark.

Moonlight Cafe   BAR, RESTAURANT
(Map p478; ☎0384-341 8442; Fabrika Caddesi; ☒11am-2am) This bar-cafe hosts nightly live traditional Turkish music. The downstairs cave bar is a wonderfully atmospheric setting for soulful tunes from local musicians. Don't expect to be able to have a conversation because it really is loud. Many locals still know the bar by its old name 'Barfiks'.

ⓘ Information

Tourist Office (Map p478; ☎0384-341 4059; Kayseri Caddesi 37; ☒8am-5.30pm Mon-Fri) The helpful tourist office gives out a town map and has a list of Ürgüp's hotels.

ⓘ Getting There & Away

From the **otogar** (Map p478; Güllüce Caddesi) dolmuşes travel to Nevşehir every 15 minutes from 7am to 8pm (₺3.50). The dolmuş service between Ürgüp and Avanos (₺4), via the Ortahisar turn-off, the Göreme Open-Air Museum, Göreme village, Çavuşin and Zelve, leaves from the otogar hourly between 8am and 7pm.

Dolmuşes to Mustafapaşa leave roughly every 30 minutes between 8am and 8.30pm (₺2) and to Ortahisar every 30 minutes between 8am and 7pm (₺2.50). Both these services leave from the **Mustafapaşa otogar** (Map p478; Güllüce Caddesi), next to the main otogar.

There are also a couple of services daily to Ayvalı and Taşkınpaşa. They depart from the car park that connects Dumlupınar Caddesi to the main otogar.

SERVICES FROM ÜRGÜP'S OTOGAR

DESTINATION	FARE (₺)	DURATION (HR)	FREQUENCY (PER DAY)
Adana	40	5	2 morning, 3 afternoon & 1 evening
Ankara	40	5	3 morning, 3 afternoon & 1 evening
Antalya	50	10	1 morning & 1 evening
Çanakkale	80	17	1 evening
İstanbul	65	11	1 morning & 2 evening
İzmir & Selçuk	65	11½	1 evening
Kayseri	10	1¼	hourly 7am-4pm, 5.30pm & 6.30pm
Konya	30	4	2 morning, 1 afternoon & 3 evening
Marmaris/Bodrum/Pamukkale	55-70	11-15	1 evening
Mersin	40	5	1 morning & 1 afternoon
Trabzon	80	12	1 evening

HOW TO MAKE A FAIRY CHIMNEY LANDSCAPE

The *peribacalar* (fairy chimneys) that have made Cappadocia so famous began their life when a series of megalithic volcanic eruptions was unleashed over this region about 12 million years ago. A common misconception is that the culprits for this reign of fire were the now-dormant volcanic peaks of Erciyes Dağı (Mt Erciyes) and Hasan Dağı (Mt Hasan) that still lord it over Cappadocia's landscape. These volcanoes were formed much later, however. The true perpetrators have long since been levelled by erosion, leaving only slight evidence of their once mighty power.

During this active volcanic period – which lasted several million years – violent eruptions occurred across the region, spewing volcanic ash that hardened into multiple layers of rock geologically known as tuff (consolidated volcanic ash). These layers were then slowly but surely whittled away by the grinding effects of wind, water and ice.

This natural erosion is the sculptor responsible for the weird and wacky Cappadocian landscape. Where areas of a harder rock layer sit above a softer rock layer, the soft rock directly underneath is protected while the rest gets winnowed away, creating the bizarre isolated pinnacles nicknamed 'fairy chimneys'. Depending on your perspective, they look like giant phalluses or outsized mushrooms. The villagers call them simply *kalelar* (castles).

ⓘ Getting Around

If you don't fancy the steep walk from the centre of town up to Esbelli Mahallesi you can catch a **taxi** (Map p478) from the rank on the main square.

Ürgüp is a good base for hiring a car, with most agencies located on the main square or İstiklal Caddesi. Rates hover around ₺90 to ₺100 per day for a small manual sedan such as a Fiat Palio and climb to ₺120 to ₺140 for a larger automatic.

Europcar (☑ 0384-341 8855; www.europcar. com; İstiklal Caddesi 10; ⊙ 8.30am-7pm)

Avis (☑ 0384-341 2177; www.avis.com.tr; İstiklal Caddesi 19; ⊙ 8.30am-6.30pm)

Acar (☑ 0384-341 5576; www.acarrentacar. com.tr; Belediye Pasajı 26, İstiklal Caddesi)

Several outlets rent mopeds and motorcycles from ₺50 a day, and bicycles from ₺25.

Mustafapaşa

☑ 0384 / POP 1600

This beautiful Cappadocian village is shifting slowly from yesteryear but remains well beneath the tourist radar. Still known widely by its pre-WWI Greek name of Sinasos, Mustafapaşa is home to some of the region's loveliest examples of typical Greek stone carved–mansion architecture, serving as a reminder of its prosperous past when wealthy Greek-Ottoman merchants made up a sizeable portion of the community. When you've finished admiring the faded grandeur of the facades, the minor rock-cut churches amid the outlying valleys allow a decent dose of natural scenery.

You enter Mustafapaşa at an enlarged intersection, the Sinasos Meydanı, where a signboard indicating the whereabouts of the local rock-cut churches is located. Follow the road downhill and you'll come to Cumhuriyet Meydanı, the centre of the village, which sports the ubiquitous bust of Atatürk and several tea houses.

⊙ Sights & Activities

To the west of Mustafapaşa there are 4km to 8km walks in **Gomeda Valley**. Local guide Niyazi, who charges €25 for individuals and groups, can be contacted through Old Greek House (p482) hotel.

Ayios Kostantinos-Eleni Kilise   CHURCH
(Church of SS Constantine & Helena; Cumhuriyet Meydanı; ₺5; ⊙ 8.30am-5.30pm) Right on Mustafapaşa's main square is the imposing Ayios Kostantinos-Eleni Kilise, erected in 1729 and restored in 1850. A fine stone grapevine runs around the door, while the ruined domed interior with faded 19th-century frescoes has a picturesquely shabby ambience and is home to a series of information boards explaining Mustafapaşa's history and the story of the Greece-Turkey population exchange in the early 20th century.

Ayios Vasilios Kilise   CHURCH
(St Basil Church; ₺5; ⊙ 9am-6pm) A sign pointing off Sinasos Meydanı leads 1km to the 12th-century Ayios Vasilios Kilise, perched near the top of a ravine. Its interior features unimpressive 20th-century frescoes. There

CAPPADOCIA MUSTAFAPAŞA

should be someone there with a key; if not, enquire at the *belediye* (town hall).

Medrese
MEDRESE

FREE Between Sinasos Meydanı and Cumhuriyet Meydanı is a 19th-century *medrese* (seminary) with a finely carved portal. The stone columns on either side of the doorway are supposed to swivel when there's movement in the foundations, thus warning of earthquake damage. The door is usually open so you can enter the courtyard.

Monastery Valley
PARK

Follow Zafer Caddesi to the old bridge at the end of the village to head out into this small valley studded with fairy chimneys. There are four rock-carved chapels and one monastery here, though most are kept locked and are disappointing in comparison to other Cappadocian churches – still, it makes for a lovely walk.

🛏 Sleeping & Eating

Both Old Greek House and Pacha Hotel double as restaurants.

Old Greek House
HISTORIC HOTEL $$

(☑0384-353 5306; www.oldgreekhouse.com; Şahin Caddesi; d ₺150; 🕏) If this 250-year-old Greek mansion is good enough for the ex-mayor to sleep in, it's good enough for us. Although it's best known for its Ottoman-flavoured set menus (from ₺50), enjoyed in the atmospheric grand halls, this place also has 14 generously sized, spotlessly clean rooms with an antique vibe.

Pacha Hotel
PENSION $$

(☑0384-353 5331; www.pachahotel.com; Sinasos Meydanı; s/d/tr €30/50/60; 🕏) This sprawling Ottoman-Greek house boasts neat-as-a-pin rooms and a tasty upstairs restaurant (meals €10) full of local bric-a-brac. The vine-covered courtyard provides sunseeker bliss on lazy summer afternoons.

Upper Greek House
HOTEL $$$

(☑0384-353 5352; www.uppergreekhouse.com; Zafer Sokak; d ₺200; 🕏) Right at the top of Mustafapaşa's hill, this quiet retreat has big and airy stone-arch rooms – decorated with simple elegance and a bit of sparkly bedspread pizazz – opening onto large terraces or the shady courtyard downstairs.

Perimasali Cave Hotel
HOTEL $$$

(☑0384-353 5090; www.perimasalihotel.com; Sehit Aslan Yakar Sokak 6; d €120-150, ste €200-250;

🕏) Over-the-top sculpture, gilded accents and spotlight features; this opulent Cappadocian hideaway has rooms that do nothing by half. The attention to detail befits a five-star hotel, though the decor won't be to everyone's taste. Service is charming and the terrace provides killer above-ground views.

Hanımeli Kapadokya Restaurant
ANATOLIAN $$$

(Yılmaz Sokak 14; set menu per person ₺40; ⊗11am-10pm) Set on the Karagöz family's rooftop, this friendly place rustles up hearty home-cooking feasts. Local mezes are followed by your choice of wholesome mains – have the *testi kebap* (meat, chicken or vegetables cooked in a terracotta pot); it's particularly good here. If you manage to demolish that lot, you're doing better than we did and there's still dessert to go.

❶ Getting There & Away

Dolmuşes to Ürgüp leave from the main square (₺2, every 30 minutes between 8am and 8pm). A taxi costs ₺25.

Ayvalı
☑0384 / POP 500

This lovely little village in a valley south of Ürgüp is a snapshot of the Cappadocia of old. It's a sleepy place surrounded by farming plots with a meander of cobbled alleyways rimmed by wonky stone houses. Tourists are virtually unsighted…for now.

If you don't have your own transport, getting to Ayvalı is a bit tricky. From Ürgüp's Mustafapaşa otogar, dolmuşes depart for Ayvalı at 8.30am, 2pm and 5pm (₺2, 20 minutes). Returning from Ayvalı to Ürgüp the dolmuses leave at 8am, 9.30am and 3pm.

🛏 Sleeping & Eating

Aravan Evi
GUESTHOUSE $$$

(☑0384-354 5838; www.aravan.com; Ayvalı; s/d/tr €70/90/125; 🕏) Looking for a slice of the simple life without sacrificing modern comforts? This charming guesthouse has just three lovely stone-arch rooms elegantly decorated in traditional fashion. A stay here is a welcoming time-out from the bustle of life. The gorgeous terrace restaurant (open to nonguests, reservations essential) is a flavourful trip through Cappadocian dishes and specialises in *tandır* (clay oven) cooking.

★**Cappadocia Home Cooking** ANATOLIAN $$$
(🖉 0384-354 5907; www.cappadociahomecooking.
com; Ayvalı; cooking class & meal per person €50)
Tolga and his family have swung open the
doors to their home – surrounded by their
organic garden and overlooking Ayvalı's
deep gorge – to offer a taste of true home-
style Cappadocian cooking. They offer meals
and highly recommended cooking classes
with hands-on appeal, guided by Tolga's
tiny dynamo of a mother, Hava. It's a foodie
haven. Reservations are essential.

It's on the Ayvalı main road. Tolga can
arrange transport to/from Ayvalı from your
base in Cappadocia. They also have a couple
of rooms for guests who want a homestay-
style experience.

Soğanlı

📞 0352 / POP 500

Let's get one thing straight: despite its
science-fiction setting, no scene in *Star
Wars* was ever filmed near **Soğanlı** (admis-
sion ₺5; ⏱ 8am-6.45pm), or anywhere else in
Turkey. But don't despair Chewbacca fans,
there's still ample reason to travel to this
tiny village 36km south of Mustafapaşa;
namely, a reverential series of rock-cut
churches hidden amid the two dramatic,
secluded valleys of Aşağı (Lower) Soğanlı
and Yukarı (Upper) Soğanlı. An afternoon
exploring at the foot of these sheer faces
may inspire you to write your own script.

To reach Soğanlı turn off the main road
from Mustafapaşa to Yeşilhisar and proceed
4km to the village. The ticket office for the
site is next to Hidden Apple Garden (p484)
restaurant. At stalls in the site car park, lo-
cal women sell the dolls for which Soğanlı is
supposedly famous.

◉ Sights

Soğanlı's valleys were first used by the Ro-
mans as necropolises and later by the Byz-
antines for monastic purposes.

The most interesting churches are in the
Yukarı Soğanlı (the right-hand turn on en-
tering the site) and the entire site can be eas-
ily circuited on foot in about two hours. All
the churches are signposted, but be careful
and wear decent walking shoes as the crum-
bly tuff slopes you walk up to access them
can be slippery.

The **Aşağı Soğanlı** is accessed by taking
the left-hand road from the entrance.

Tokalı Kilise CHURCH
(Buckle Church) On the main road into So-
ğanlı, about 800m before the ticket office,
signs point to the Tokalı Kilise on the right,
reached by a steep flight of worn steps.

Gök Kilise CHURCH
(Sky Church) The Gök Kilise is just to the left
of the Tokalı Kilise. It has twin naves sepa-
rated by columns and ending in apses. The
double frieze of saints is badly worn.

Karabaş Kilisesi CHURCH
(Black Hat Church) In Soğanlı's Yukarı Valley
the first church on your right is the Kara-
baş Kilisesi, which is covered in paintings
showing the life of Christ, with Gabriel and
various saints. A pigeon in the fresco reflects
the importance of pigeons to the monks,
who wooed them with dovecotes cut into
the rock.

Yılanlı Kilise CHURCH
(Church of St George, Snake Church) The Yılan-
lı Kilise sits in the furthest corner of the
Yukarı Valley, its frescoes deliberately paint-
ed over with black paint, probably to protect
them. The hole in the roof of one chamber,
surrounded by blackened rock, shows that
fires were lit there.

Kubbeli Kilise CHURCH
(Domed Church) Turn left at the Yılanlı
Kilise, cross the Yukarı Valley floor and
climb the far hillside to find the Kubbeli
Kilise. The Kubbeli is unusual because of
its Eastern-style cupola cut clean out of the
rock.

Saklı Kilise CHURCH
(Hidden Church) Nestling in the Yukarı Valley
hillside, very near the Kubbeli Kilise, is the
Saklı Kilise (Hidden Church), which as its
name suggests is indeed completely obscured
from view until you get close.

Geyikli Kilise CHURCH
(Deer Church) In the Aşağı Valley, the Geyik-
li Kilise has a monks' refectory and a still-
visible fresco on the wall of St Eustace with
a deer (from where the church's name is
derived).

Tahtalı Kilise CHURCH
(Church of St Barbara) The Tahtalı Kilise sits
at the furthest end of the Aşağı Valley. It
has well-preserved Byzantine and Seljuk
decorative patterns.

SOĞANLI ROAD TRIP

If you only rent a car/taxi once on your trip, the day you visit Soğanlı could be the time to do it. Not only is Soğanlı impossible to reach by public transport but also the drive there is beautiful. The open countryside makes a change from central Cappadocia's canyons and you can stop in sleepy country villages that give an idea of what Göreme was like 30 years ago. Here are our top stops along the way.

Cemil Church (☑ to reach the guardian 0535 045 1160) **FREE** Signposted from the main Soğanlı road, some 6km south of Mustafapaşa, is the town of **Cemil**, where chickens rule the cobblestone paths, overlooked by abandoned Greek mansions on the hillside that are teetering into disrepair. Follow the signposted alleyway through the village to the picturesque blue-columned Cemil Church with its fresco fragments (all extremely defaced). To make sure the church is open (they tend to keep the door locked these days), ring the guardian before you arrive.

Keşlik Monastery (admission ₺5; ⊗ 9am-6.30pm Apr-Nov) This rock-cut Byzantine complex, 10km south of Mustafapaşa, is a labyrinth of a place where hundreds of monks lived. The main 13th-century monastery **chapel** has blackened frescoes, which friendly site guardian Cabir Coşkuner will explain to you. The maze of monk living quarters underneath include a **refectory** and **kitchen**. Next door is the rock cone harbouring the 9th-century **Stephanos Church** with a vibrant, well-preserved cross-form ceiling fresco which extends all along the vault.

Taşkınpaşa Mosque **FREE** Some 7km south of Keşlik Monastery, tractors bounce along hilly, cobbled streets in **Taşkınpaşa**, which is named after its 600-year-old **Seljuk mosque**. The original, 14th-century pulpit is now in Ankara's Ethnographical Museum. Outside, Taşkın Paşa himself is buried in one of the two **Seljuk tombs**; traders stayed under the arches during the caravanserai days. On the way back to the main road you will see a *medrese* (seminary) with an ornate door frame.

Sobesos (Şahinefendi village; ⊗ 8.30am-5.30pm) **FREE** At the ancient city of Sobesos, signposted from Şahinefendi village, the various sections of the **Roman baths** can easily be distinguished. The late 4th-century **Byzantine Church** ruins behind hold some fine Roman and Byzantine mosaics and graves. Sobesos is undergoing a restoration of its mosaics which is likely to continue until at least 2018. The site is currently closed to visitors. Check locally for up-to-date information on its status.

🛏 Sleeping & Eating

Soğanlı has a couple of simple restaurants clustered around the car park area before you enter its valleys. There's also a handy cafe at the far end of the Yukarı Soğanlı valley.

Hidden Apple Garden TURKISH $
(Soğanlı Kapadokya Restaurant; ☑ 0352-653 1045; 3-course set lunch menu ₺20; ⊗ 8.30am-7.30pm) Head down the stairs beside Soğanlı (p483) ticket office to find this tranquil garden where Yılmaz Ablak and his family serve hearty meals full of rustic flavour. We could spend all day eating his wife's *acılı ezme* (spicy tomato and onion paste) but leave room for tasty mains such as *güveç* and the simple, but lush, yoghurt and honey dessert.

Campers can pitch their tent in the garden for free. There are clean toilets and a shower onsite. Yılmaz also offers accommodation

in his family's house (per person, including half-board, ₺100).

ℹ Getting There & Away

It's impossible to get to Soğanlı by public transport. From Kayseri you can get as far as Yeşilhisar (₺3.50, every 30 minutes from 7am to 9pm) but you'd then have to negotiate for a taxi to take you the last 15km. From Ürgüp, there are four dolmuşes daily to Taşkınpaşa but no onward transport options. It's easier to hire a car/taxi or sign up for a day tour.

Niğde

☑ 0388 / POP 128,000

Backed by the snow-capped Ala Dağlar mountain range, Niğde, 85km south of Nevşehir, is a busy agricultural centre with a small clutch of historic buildings dating back to its foundation by the Seljuks. Unless you have a soft spot for provincial towns, you most likely won't want to stay, but may have to if you want to visit the fabulous Eski Gümüşler Monastery, 10km northeast. You may also pass through en route to the basecamp villages for trekking in the Ala Dağlar National Park.

⊙ Sights

Central Niğde is spotted with fine Seljuk tombs such as the **Hüdavend Hatun Türbesi** (Hatun Caddesi) dated to 1312.

Eski Gümüşler Monastery　　MONASTERY
(Gümüşler; ₺5; ⊙8.30am-5pm) Some of Cappadocia's best-preserved and most captivating frescoes are hidden within this rarely-visited ancient rock-hewn monastery that was only rediscovered in 1963.

The lofty main church is covered with colourful Byzantine frescoes, painted between the 7th and 11th centuries. Of particular interest is the striking Virgin and Child to the left of the apse which depicts the elongated Mary giving a Mona Lisa smile – it's said to be the only smiling Mary in existence.

Although the frescoes are the monastery's most famous feature, the warren of rooms here are fun to explore too. You enter the complex via a rock-cut passage, which opens onto a large courtyard with reservoirs for wine and oil, and rock-cut dwellings, crypts, a kitchen and a refectory. A small hole in the ground acts as a vent for a 9m-deep shaft leading to two levels of subterranean rooms. You can descend through the chambers or climb to an upstairs bedroom.

Eski Gümüşler Monastery sprawls along the base of a cliff about 10km northeast of Niğde. To get there, Gümüşler Belediyesi dolmuşes (₺2, 20 minutes) depart every hour from Niğde's eski otogar. As you enter Gümüşler, don't worry when the bus passes a couple of signs pointing to the monastery – it eventually passes right by it. To catch a bus back to Niğde, wait at the bus stand across the road from the monastery entrance. The bus back to Niğde comes past at roughly 10 minutes to the hour and 20 minutes past the hour.

Niğde Museum　　MUSEUM
(Niğde Müzesi; ☎0388-232 3397; Dışarı Caddesi; ₺5; ⊙8am-5pm) Niğde Museum houses a well-presented selection of finds from the Assyrian city of Acemhöyük near Aksaray, through the Hittite and Phrygian Ages to sculptures from Tyana (now Kemerhisar), the former Roman centre and Hittite capital 19km southwest of Niğde. There's also a collection of 10th-century mummies (four baby mummies, and the mummy of a blonde nun discovered in the 1960s in the Ihlara Valley).

🛏 Sleeping & Eating

Hotel Şahiner　　HOTEL $$
(☎0388-232 2121; www.hotelsahiner.com; Giray Sokak 4; s/d ₺80/120; ❄☎) Sure, it doesn't have much character, but professional staff and decent-sized, clean rooms with comfortable beds make the Şahiner a solid and safe choice if you need to stay the night in Niğde. It's in an alleyway off Bankalar Caddesi, right in the centre of town.

Konyalı Hanedan　　LOKANTA $
(İsmail Hakkı Altan Caddesi; mains ₺7-18; ⊙10.30am-10pm) On Niğde's bustling pedestrian strip (one block down from the Atatürk statue), this *lokanta* (eatery serving ready-made food) dishes up huge plates of pide and sizzling kebaps, all served with mountains of complimentary bread and salad.

ℹ Getting There & Away

BUS

Niğde's otogar (Adana Yolu) is 4km out of town on the main highway. There are hourly buses run by Derinkuyu Koop to Nevşehir (₺12, 1½ hours), via Derinkuyu and Kaymaklı and their underground city sites (p473). The otogar also has buses to Ankara (₺35, 4½ hours, five daily), Aksaray (₺15, 1½ hours, hourly between 7am and 9pm), İstanbul (₺70, 11 hours, five daily), Kayseri (₺15, 1½ hours, hourly between 7am and 9pm) and Konya (₺35, 3½ hours, 10 daily).

The **eski otogar** (Old Bus Station; Emin Erişingil Bulvarı) is right in the centre of town. It has dolmuşes to Gümüşler Monastery (₺2, 20 minutes, half hourly) and Çamardı (₺5, 1½ hours, hourly) as well as frequent services to other outlying villages.

Niğde city buses (₺2.25) trundle between the otogar and the centre of town – passing right beside the *eski* otogar – every 20 minutes during the day. Buy a travel pass (₺4.50, valid for two journeys) before hopping on. You can also usually buy them on the buses when you board.

TRAIN

Niğde's **train station** (İstasyon Caddesi), on the Ankara–Adana train line, is at the end of İstasyon Caddesi in the town centre. The *Çukurova Mavi Ekspresi* to Ankara pulls into town daily at 11.21pm (₺27.50, 9½ hours).

CAPPADOCIA NİĞDE

Cappadocian Frescoes 101

The frescoes of Cappadocia's rock-cut churches are, to be exact, *seccos* (whereby tempera paints are applied to dry plaster). Most of the frescoes here date from the 10th to the 12th centuries.

Christ Pantocrator

Christ 'the All-Powerful: typically painted on the church dome, depicting Jesus holding a book in one hand and giving a blessing with his other.

Nativity

Jesus' birth in Bethlehem. The Nativity in Eski Gümüşler Monastery is particularly striking.

Transfiguration

Portrayal of the miracle of Christ's metamorphosis in front of his disciples. A good depiction of this scene is in the Tokalı Kilise.

Anastasis

The 'Resurrection': Christ pictured with prophets, freeing souls from hell. The Karanlık Kilise has a superb example.

Deesis

Similar to 'Christ Pantocrator', Deesis scenes show a seated Christ flanked by the Virgin Mary and St John the Baptist.

Last Judgement

'Judgement Day': when righteous souls will ascend to heaven. The depiction in the Church of St Jean in Gülşehir is vividly well preserved.

Know Your Fresco Saints

St George Legend says this epic dragon slaughter took place upon Erciyes Dağı.

St Basil the Great Archbishop of Caesarea, credited with beginning monasticism in Cappadocia.

St Gregory the Theologian Friend of St Basil and Archbishop of Constantinople.

St Barbara Early Syrian Christian convert, martyred by being beheaded by her father.

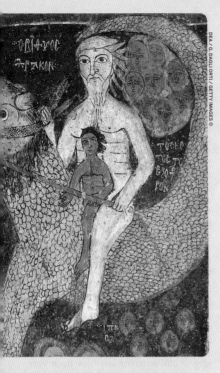

DEA / G. DAGLI ORTI / GETTY IMAGES ©

1. Last Judgement fresco, Church of St Jean (Karşı Kilise; p472), Gülşehir
2. Nativity fresco, Eski Gümüşler Monastery (p485) 3. Christ Pantocrator fresco, Karanlık Kilise (p455), Göreme

Ala Dağlar National Park

The Ala Dağlar National Park (Ala Dağlar Milli Parkı) protects the rugged middle range of the Taurus Mountains between Kayseri, Niğde and Adana. It's famous throughout the country for its extraordinary trekking routes, which snake through craggy limestone ranges and across a high plateau dotted with lakes. For bird enthusiasts a trip to the Ala Dağlar is all about spotting the elusive Caspian snowcock, which makes its home in the high reaches of the Taurus.

The most popular walks start at the small settlements of Çukurbağ and Demirkazık, 40km east of Niğde. Çukurbağ is also the best base from which to plan any Ala Dağlar adventures thanks to clued-up pension owners who can organise a range of activities.

You can also reach the mountains via Yahyalı, 80km due south of Kayseri. From here it's another 60km to the impressive Kapuzbaşı waterfalls (best seen between March and May) on the Zamantı River.

It's best to trek between June and late September; at other times weather conditions can be particularly hazardous, especially since there are few villages and little support other than some mountaineers' huts. Bring warm gear and prepare for extreme conditions.

There are a variety of walks in the mountains. The most famous is the five-day trek across the Ala Dağlar range beginning in Demirkazık, traversing the Karayalak Valley and the beautiful Yedigöller (Seven Lakes Plateau, 3500m), and ending at the Kapuzbaşı waterfalls. There are plenty of shorter options and day-hike opportunities as well.

Although solo trekkers do sometimes venture into the mountains, unless you're experienced and prepared you should consider paying for a guide or joining a tour. All trekking arrangements, including guide and equipment hire, can be made through the guesthouses in Çukurbağ. Costs depend on number of hikers/days; a five-day hike for three people including guide, mules (to carry luggage), muleteer, food and all equipment hire costs around €500 per person. If you prefer to trek as part of an organised tour, Middle Earth Travel (p458) is a good first port of call in Göreme. The agency offers both a three-day and a five-day program in the Ala Dağlar, with prices starting at €320 per person for a minimum of four people on the three-day option. Other agencies such as Sobek Travel

(☑ 0388-232 1507; www.trekkinginturkeys.com; Avanoğlu Apt 70/17, Bor Caddesi), based in Niğde, and Terra Anatolia (☑ 0242-244 8945; www. terra-anatolia.com; 1312 Sokak, Suer Apt 12/3, Gençlik Mahalle, Antalya), based in Antalya, can also organise Ala Dağlar trekking tours.

🛏 Sleeping

Ala Dağlar Camping   CAMPGROUND $
(☑ 0534 201 8995; www.aladaglarcamping.com; Çukurbağ Köyü Martı Mahallesi; campsites per person ₺20, cabin s/d/tr without bathroom ₺65/80/100, bungalow s/d/tr/q from ₺100/120/150/180) Run by climbing couple Zeynep and Recep, this alpine hideaway has an ample camping area and basic mountain-log-cabin accommodation. Shared amenities (including kitchen) are good and there's a cafe if you're not in the cooking mood. Trekking and climbing guides as well as a host of activities can be arranged. It's a 2km walk from Çukurbağ junction and village.

Özşafak Pension   PENSION $$
(☑ 0536 230 3120; www.ozsafak.net; Çukurbağ; r per person incl half board €30, campsites per person €10) This delightfully homey pension is run by enthusiastic English-speaking local guide Başar, who can organise all your trekking or bird-watching activities. Rooms are super simple but clean, with beds piled high with snugly thick duvets. There are majestic mountain views from the pension's balcony and both breakfast and dinner are feasts of fresh, hearty local fare.

It's right on the main road's intersection to Çukurbağ village. All the dolmuş drivers can drop you off here if you let them know.

Şafak Pension & Camping   PENSION $$
(☑ 0388-724 7039; www.safaktravel.com; Çurkurbağ Village; r per person incl half board €30, campsites per person €10) Run by friendly, multilingual local guide Hasan, who can organise pretty much any activity, Şafak offers simple, clean rooms with hot water, heating and comfortable beds. Campsites have electricity and their own bathroom facilities, and the terrace and garden command magnificent views of Mt Demirkazık. It's on the main-road intersection with the Çurkurbağ village turn-off.

ℹ Getting There & Away

From Niğde's otogar take a Çamardı-bound dolmuş (₺5, 1½ hours, hourly between 7am and 5pm from Monday to Saturday, fewer services on Sunday) and ask to be let off at Çukurbağ junction and village (it's 5km before Çamardı).

SULTAN MARSHES

An afternoon ploughing the Sultan Marshes (Sultansazlığı) in your gumboots might not sound like your cup of birdseed, but there's something undeniably fascinating about observing a flock of flamingos at a waterhole or an eagle swooping to snap the neck of a curious baby squirrel. This giant patch of Ramsar-listed wetland in between Soğanlı and Ala Dağlar incorporates marshes, wet-meadow and steppe fields and is world famous among the twitching fraternity, which descends here year-round to spot the 300-odd species that breed or overwinter here. At Ovaciftliği there's an information centre and an impressive boardwalk and wildlife viewing tower, and it's easy and free to drive yourself on the lanes through the steppe. To get completely amidst the wetlands though, you're going to need a boat.

The affable owners at **Sultan Pansion** (✉ 0352-658 5549; www.sultanbirding.com; Ovaçiftliği, Sultansazlığı; s/d/tr €30/50/65, boat trips €30 per person, per hour; P ✱ @ 🛜) operate well-regarded boat trips from their hotel, which backs onto the marshes themselves. If you want to overnight, this is your only accommodation option. The spick and span rooms here are simple but comfortable.

From Çamardı there are 10 services to Niğde between 6am and 5.30pm from Monday to Saturday and three services on Sunday.

Ihlara Valley

✆ 0382

Southeast of Aksaray, the Ihlara Valley scythes through the stubbly fields and today is home to one of the prettiest strolls in the world. Once called Peristrema, the valley was a favourite retreat of Byzantine monks, who cut churches into the base of its towering cliffs.

Following the Melendiz River – hemmed in by jagged cliffs – as it snakes between painted churches, piles of boulders and a sea of greenery ringing with birdsong and croaking frogs, is an unforgettable experience. The best times to visit are midweek in May (when spring blossoms abound) or September, when fewer people are about.

◉ Sights

Hiking the full **Ihlara Valley** (Ihlara Vadısı; admission incl Selime Monastery, Güzelyurt's Monastery Valley & Aksaray Museum ₺20; ⊙8am-6.30pm) trail between Ihlara village and Selime is a wonderfully bucolic day out. Most visitors come on a tour and only walk the short stretch with most of the churches, entering via the 360 steps of the **Ihlara Vadısı Turistik Tesisleri** (Ihlara Valley Tourist Facility) ticket booth and exiting at Belisırma. This means the rest of the path is blissfully serene, with farmers tilling their fields and shepherds grazing their flocks the only people you're likely to meet.

Other entrances are at **Ihlara village**, **Belisırma** and **Selime**. Including stops to visit the churches along the way, it takes about an hour to walk from Ihlara village to the Ihlara Vadısı Turistik Tesisleri stairs, 1½ hours to walk from there to Belisırma, and another hour to walk from Belisırma to Selime.

If you're planning to walk the entire trail, it's best to start early in the day, particularly in summer, when you'll need to take shelter from the fierce sun. Along the valley floor, signs mark the different churches.

Travel agencies in Göreme, Avanos and Ürgüp offer tours incorporating Ihlara for about ₺120 per person.

Kokar Kilise CHURCH
(Fragrant Church) This church has some fabulous frescoes dating from the 9th and 11th centuries.

Pürenli Seki Kilisesi CHURCH
This double-nave church has a wealth of 10th- and 12th-century frescoes depicting stories from the Gospels.

Ağaçaltı Kilise CHURCH
(Daniel Pantonassa Church) This cruciform-plan church is most famous for its well-preserved fresco ceiling depicting the Ascension.

Sümbüllü Kilise CHURCH
(Hyacinth Church) Some frescoes remain, but this church is mostly noteworthy for its simple but elegant facade.

Yılanlı Kilise CHURCH
(Snake Church) Many of the frescoes are damaged, but it's possible to make out the one outlining the punishments for sinners,

Ihlara Valley

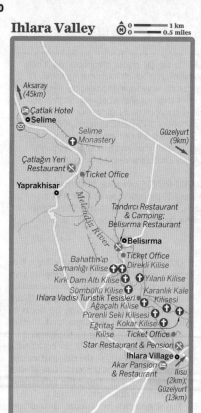

Ⓝ 0 ▬▬ 1 km
0 ▬▬ 0.5 miles

Aksaray
(45km)

🏨 Çatlak Hotel
○ Selime
Selime
Monastery
Güzelyurt
(9km)
Çatlağın Yeri
Restaurant 🍴
● Ticket Office
Yaprakhisar ○

Melendiz River

Tandırcı Restaurant
& Camping;
Belisırma Restaurant

● Belisırma

Bahattın'ın ● Ticket Office
Samanlığı Kilise 🟢🟢 Direkli Kilise
Kırk Dam Altı Kilise 🟢 🟢 Yılanlı Kilise
Sümbüllü Kilise 🟢 Karanlık Kale
Ihlara Vadısı Turistik Tesisleri 🟢 Kilisesi
Ağaçaltı Kilise 🟢 🟢 🟢
Pürenli Seki Kilisesi 🟢
Eğritaş Kokar Kilise 🟢
Kilise Ticket Office ●
Star Restaurant & Pension 🍴
Ihlara Village ○
Akar Pansion 🏨
& Restaurant
Ilısu
(2km);
Güzelyurt
(13km)

especially the three-headed snake with a sinner in each mouth and the nipple-clamped women (ouch) who didn't breastfeed their young.

Kırk Dam Altı Kilise
CHURCH

(St George's Church) Although badly graffitied, the frescoes are still gloriously vibrant, and above the entrance you can see St George on a white horse, slaying a three-headed snake.

Direkli Kilise
CHURCH

(Belisırma village) This cross-shaped church has four columns, with lovely partially preserved frescoes of saints. The large adjoining chamber originally had two storeys, as you can see from what's left of the steps and the holes in the walls from the supporting beams. It's in Belisırma village, off the main Ihlara Valley trail; a sign near the Belisırma trailhead ticket booth points the way to the entry.

Bahattın'ın Samanlığı Kilise
CHURCH

(Bahattın's Granary; Belisırma village) Sitting on Belisırma village's cliff face, next door to the Direkli Kilise (p490), this tiny church contains defaced but still vivid frescoes depicting scenes from the life of Christ. It's named after a local who used to store grain here.

Selime Monastery
MONASTERY

(Selime village; admission incl Ihlara Valley, Güzelyurt's Monastery Valley & Aksaray Museum ₺20; ⊘8am-6pm) The monastery at Selime is an astonishing rock-cut structure incorporating a vast kitchen with a soaring chimney, three churches, stables with rock-carved feed troughs and other evidence of the troglodyte lifestyle.

🛏️ Sleeping & Eating

If you want to walk all of the gorge and don't have your own transport you'll have to stay overnight. There are modest accommodation options handily placed at both ends of the gorge (in Ihlara village and Selime). Note that most accommodation is closed from December to March.

Both Selime and Ihlara village have riverside restaurants and midway along the gorge, below Belisırma village, a cluster of low-key restaurants feed hungry hikers, with dining on platforms right upon the river. Trout is the local specialty here.

🛏️ Ihlara Village

Akar Pansion & Restaurant
PENSION $

(☎0382-453 7018; www.ihlara-akarmotel.com; Ihlara village; s/d/tr ₺50/90/120; 🛜) One of the best options in Ihlara Valley, Akar's large rooms have cheerfully bright linen and are kept spotlessly clean. Grab one of the rooms in the new building with private balconies. Helpful English-speaking staff can fill you in on any Ihlara queries, the restaurant serves tasty local dishes (₺10 to ₺20) and the attached shop sells picnic ingredients.

Star Restaurant & Pension
TURKISH $

(☎0382-453 7020; Ihlara village; mains ₺15-20; ⊘10am-9pm; 🛜⏣) Right beside the river, this friendly, family-run place has a wonderful shady terrace and is just the spot for lunch and chilling out with a beer after a hike. Local trout is the specialty, but there are also meaty casseroles and vegetarian options. It also has 10 simple rooms upstairs (s/d ₺50/100) and a small, grassy camping area (campsites ₺30).

Selime

Çatlak Hotel HOTEL $$
(☎0382-454 5006; www.catlakturizm.com.tr; Selime village; s/d ₺80/100; 📶) Despite the gaudy 1970s-style decor, Çatlak has good-sized rooms and smiley staff.

Çatlağın Yeri Restaurant TURKISH $
(☎0382-454 5006; Selime village; mains ₺15-25; ⏲10.30am-10pm) Across the road from Selime's Ihlara Valley trailhead, this large riverside restaurant with friendly staff dishes up plenty of *köfte* (meatball), fresh local trout and *güveç* options. Camping is available on the grounds.

Belisırma

Tandırcı Restaurant & Camping TURKISH $
(☎0382-457 3110; Belisırma village; mains ₺15-20; ⏲11am-8pm) Tour groups often bypass this restaurant, leaving a mellow, shady spot and a chance of scoring a river platform for a lunch of local trout (₺15) or hiking fuel-up of meat *güveç* (₺20). Campsites are free.

Belisırma Restaurant TURKISH $
(☎0382-457 3057; Belisırma village; mains ₺15-20; ⏲11am-8pm) Popular with tour groups, this place serves up standard trout and *güveç* (stewed meat) mains with friendly service. They also have free campsites.

Getting There & Away

On weekdays six dolmuşes per day make the run between Aksaray and Ihlara village, travelling down the valley via Selime and Belisırma. Dolmuşes leave Aksaray at 7.30am, 10am, noon, 2pm, 4pm and 6pm. They leave Ihlara village for the return run at 6.45am, 8am, 9am, 11am, 1pm and 4pm (₺5, 45 minutes). On weekends there are fewer services. To get to Güzelyurt ask the driver to drop you at the Selime T-junction, where you can wait for a Güzelyurt dolmuş.

Güzelyurt

☎0382 / POP 2600 / ELEV 1485M

This hillside tumble of crumbling stone houses, with back alleys presided over by strutting cockerels and the odd stray cow, leads down to a valley studded with the remnants of rock-cut churches. Surrounded by rolling hills, a lakeside monastery, and with the silhouette of Hasan Dağı (Mt Hasan) glowering over the horizon, the gentle-paced rhythm of life here is a refreshing glimpse of rural Cappadocia.

Known as Karballa (Gelveri) in Ottoman times, up until the population exchanges of 1924 the town was inhabited by 1000 Ottoman Greek families and 50 Turkish Muslim families. Afterwards the Greeks of Gelveri went to Nea Karvali in Greece, while Turkish families from Kozan and Kastoria in Greece moved here. The relationship between the two countries is now celebrated in an annual **Turks & Greeks Friendship Festival** in July.

Sights

Monastery Valley HISTORIC SITE
(₺5 or incl in Ihlara Valley ticket; ⏲8am-6.30pm) The 4.5km Monastery Valley is full of rock-cut churches and dwellings cut into the cliff walls. It's a lovely place for a stroll and panoramic viewpoints abound. From Güzelyurt's main square, take the signposted right-hand turn and follow the street down about 400m to the ticket booth.

Right beside the ticket office is **Güzelyurt Underground City**. The restored complex ranges across several levels and includes one hair-raising section where you descend through a hole in the floor.

The impressive facade of the **Büyük Kilise Camii** (Mosque of the Great Church) is the first major building after the ticket office. Built as the Church of St Gregory of Nazianzus in AD 385, it was restored in 1835 and turned into a mosque following the population exchange in 1924. St Gregory (330–90) grew up locally and became a theologian, patriarch and one of the four Fathers of the Greek Church. Check out the wooden sermon desk that was reputedly a gift from a Russian tsar.

Opposite the Büyük Kilise Camii, a set of stairs leads up to the tranquil **Sivişli Kilisesi** (Church of the Panagia), with damaged but still colourful frescoes decorating the apse and domed ceiling. There are fantastic views over Güzelyurt if you climb up to the ridge.

Some 2km after the ticket office you enter a gorge hemmed by high cliffs. The **Kalburlu Kilisesi** (Church with a Screen) with its superb chiselled entrance is the first rock-outcrop building in the group. Almost adjoining it is the **Kömürlü Kilisesi** (Coal Church), which has carvings including an elaborate lintel above the entrance and some Maltese crosses.

Yüksek Kilise & Manastır MONASTERY
(High Church & Monastery) This religious complex is perched high on a rock overlooking Güzelyurt lake, some 2km south of a signposted turn-off on the Ihlara road 1km west of Güzelyurt. The walled compound

containing the plain church and monastery is graffitied inside and looks more impressive from afar but has sweeping views of the lake and mountains.

Kızıl Kilise
CHURCH

(Red Church) Against a backdrop of stark, sweeping fields, the red masonry of the Kızıl Kilise stands out for miles. One of Cappadocia's oldest churches, it was built in the 5th or 6th century and dedicated to St Gregory of Nazianzus. It's 8km out of Güzelyurt on the Niğde road, just past the village of Sivrihisar.

🛏️ Sleeping & Eating

There are a couple of *lokantas* (eateries serving ready-made food) on the main street, near the main square, serving dishes such as kebaps and pide.

Osmanoğlu Hotel
GUESTHOUSE $$

(📱 0533 736 3165, 0382-451 2767; osmanoglu konak@hotmail.com; Necdet Sağlam Caddesi; cave r from ₺80, s/d/f ₺100/150/200) Mother and son duo, Nuriye and Semih, provide lashings of Cappadocian hospitality at this charming guesthouse on Güzelyurt's main road. Large stone-arched rooms brim with local character with rustic textiles and traditional *sedir* seating rimming the windows. Downstairs there are cosy cave rooms but claustrophobes should beware: these are proper caves with no windows.

Ailem Restaurant
LOKANTA $

(Necdet Sağlam Caddesi; mains ₺8-18; ⏰ 11am-9pm) This *lokanta* (eatery serving ready-made food) in the centre of town is a solid bet for filling meals of various *güveç* (stewed meat), beans and simple meat dishes.

❶ Getting There & Away

From Aksaray, dolmuşes leave from the bus stop across the road from the Eski Garaj for Güzelyurt (₺5, one hour) at 7.30am, 9.45am, 11.30am, 1.30pm, 3.30pm, 5.30pm and 6.30pm. Returning dolmuşes travel from Güzelyurt to Aksaray at 6.30am, 7.30am and then every two hours, with the last at 5.30pm. On weekends there are fewer services. Going either way, dolmuşes can drop you at the T-junction near Selime, from where you can wait for an Ihlara Valley–bound dolmuş.

Aksaray

📱 0382 / POP 196,000

Sitting in the shadow of Hasan Dağı (Mt Hasan), Aksaray is symptomatic of Turkey's economic rise: quietly prospering, with high consumer confidence. With a bland, modern town centre, the city doesn't have much to hold your interest, but as it's a jumping-off point for the Ihlara Valley you may find yourself snared here for a couple of hours. If so, the Ulu Cami is a reminder of the beauty of Seljuk architecture while a mooch through the throng in the town centre, where the odd horse and cart still rattles down the main road holding up traffic, is an unequivocally Anatolian experience.

◎ Sights

Aksaray Museum
MUSEUM

(Aksaray Müzesi; Atatürk Bulvarı; ⏰ 8.30am-5.30pm Tue-Sun) **FREE** Well, you certainly won't have problems finding this massive museum en route from the otogar (bus station) along the main road to Aksaray centre. The recently revamped displays covering early Cappadocian human history have excellent English information boards, but the prize exhibit is the small collection of mummies unearthed in the Ihlara Valley.

Ulu Cami
MOSQUE

(Bankalar Caddesi) The Ulu Cami has decoration characteristic of the post–Seljuk Beylik period. A little of the original yellow stone remains in the grand doorway.

Eğri Minare
MONUMENT

(Crooked Minaret; Nevşehir Caddesi) Built in 1236 and leaning at an angle of 27 degrees, the curious Eğri Minare in the older part of Aksaray is, inevitably, known to locals as the 'Turkish Tower of Pisa'.

🛏️ Sleeping & Eating

Ahsaray Otel
BUSINESS HOTEL $$

(📱 0382-216 1600; www.otelahsaray.com; Karayolu Caddesi 1; s/d ₺100/150; 🅿️❄️📶) By far Aksaray's best choice, even if its location – near the otogar, a 2km walk into the centre – is a bit annoying. The friendly English-speaking manager here goes out of his way to help travellers while the spacious business-style rooms come with kettles, flat-screen TVs, big comfy beds, and bathrooms decked out with hilarious gold-coloured fittings.

Harman
TURKISH $

(📱 0382-212 3311; Bankalar Caddesi 16a; mains ₺9-22) Adorned with photos of visiting Turkish celebrities posing with the star-struck waiters, Harman offers a great selection of *ızgara* (grills), döner kebaps (spit-roasted lamb slices), pide (Turkish-style pizza) and soups.

❶ Getting There & Away

From Aksaray's **otogar** (Konya Caddesi/Atatürk Bulvarı), buses go to Ankara (₺25, 4½ hours); Göreme (₺15, 1½ hours) via Nevşehir (₺15, one hour); Konya (₺20, two hours) via Sultanhanı (₺5, 45 minutes); and Niğde (₺20, 1½ hours). City buses make the regular trundle from the otogar into the centre of town. A taxi to the centre will cost around ₺16.

Dolmuşes run between the **Eski Garaj** (Old Otogar; Atatürk Bulvarı), little more than a group of bus stands in a car park opposite the Migros supermarket in the centre, to Güzelyurt (₺5, one hour), the Ihlara Valley (₺5, 45 minutes) and Sultanhanı (₺5, 45 minutes). The Eski Garaj was undergoing a major revamp in mid-2016 and dolmuşes were all leaving from the roadside in front of it and across the road (in front of Migros supermarket).

Around Aksaray

The road between Aksaray and Nevşehir follows one of the oldest trade routes in the world, the Uzun Yol (Long Road). The route linked Konya, the Seljuk capital, with its other great cities (Kayseri, Sivas and Erzurum) and ultimately with Persia (Iran).

The Long Road was formerly dotted with *hans* (caravanserais) where the traders would stop for accommodation and business. The remains of three of these can be visited from Aksaray, the best preserved being the impressive **Ağzıkara Hanı** (admission ₺3; ☺8am-6pm), 16km northeast of Aksaray, which was built between 1231 and 1239.

Further towards Nevşehir you'll pass the scant remains of the 13th-century **Tepesidelik Hanı**, 23km northeast of Aksaray, and the 12th-century **Alay Hanı**, another 10km on.

❶ Getting There & Away

From Aksaray a taxi will charge about ₺50 for the run to the Ağzıkara Hanı and back. You can also catch any bus heading to Nevşehir and jump off at the *han* (caravanserai).

Kayseri

📞0352 / POP 1.3 MILLION / ELEV 1067M

Mixing Seljuk tombs, mosques and modern developments, Kayseri is both Turkey's most Islamic city after Konya and one of the economic powerhouses nicknamed the 'Anatolian tigers'. Most travellers whizz through town on their way from the airport to Cappadocia's villages, only seeing the shabby high-rises and ugly industrial factories on Kayseri's outskirts. The city centre of this Turkish boom town, though, is full of surprises. An afternoon pottering within the narrow bazaar streets and poking about the Seljuk and Ottoman monuments – all loomed over by mighty Erciyes Dağı (Mt Erciyes) – is an interesting contrast to exploring the more famous fairy-chimney vistas to the city's west.

◉ Sights

A 'cultural route' has been established in central Kayseri complete with information boards and route-plan maps outside strategic heritage buildings.

★**Museum of Seljuk Civilisation** MUSEUM (Selçuklu Uygarlığı Müzesi; Map p494; Mimar Sinan Parkı; ₺2; ☺9am-5pm Tue-Sun) This excellent museum is set in the restored Çifte Medrese, a 13th-century twin hospital and seminary built at the bequest of Seljuk sultan Keyhüsrev I and his sister Gevher Nesibe Sultan and thought to be one of the world's first medical training schools. The strikingly serene architecture is offset by beautiful exhibits of Seljuk artistry, culture and history, complemented by up-to-the-minute multimedia displays. Our one grumble is that not enough of the information panels have English translations.

Güpgüpoğlu Konağı MUSEUM (Ethnography Museum; Map p494; Tennuri Sokak; ☺8am-5pm Tue-Sun) FREE Ignore the scruffy mannequin-inhabited dioramas and instead feast your eyes on the glorious interior of painted wooden wall-panels and ceilings. The building dates from the 15th century and Mamluk architectural influence is obvious in its black-and-white stone facade. During the 19th century the house, with its multicoloured beams and intricately carved woodwork, was home to composer and lyricist Ahmet Mithat Güpgüpoğlu.

The building was closed for a much-needed restoration when we last pulled into town but it's pegged to open again by 2018.

Mahperi Hunat Hatun Complex HISTORIC BUILDING (Map p494; Seyyid Burhaneddin (Talas) Caddesi) FREE The austere and stately Mahperi Hunat Hatun complex is one of Kayseri's finest Seljuk monuments, built in the 13th century during the reign of Sultan Alaattin Keykubat. It comprises the **Hunat Hatun Medresesi**, with its shady courtyard now

Kayseri

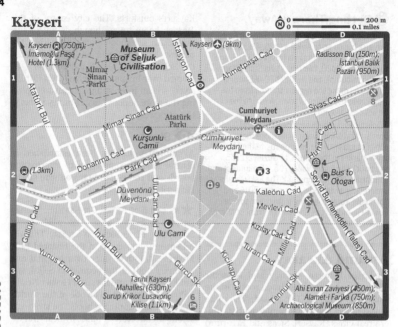

used as a cafe with the surrounding student cells home to various artisan shops, the **Mahperi Hunat Hatun Camii** (mosque) and a still-functioning **hamam**.

Kayseri Castle   CASTLE
(Kayseri Kalesi; Map p494; Cumhuriyet Meydanı) The monumental black-basalt walls of Kayseri castle were first constructed under the Roman emperor Gordian III and rebuilt by the Byzantine emperor Justinian 300

years later. The imposing edifice you see today though is mostly the work of 13th-century Seljuk sultan Alaattin Keykubat. The castle is undergoing a mammoth restoration project, now in its final phase. Once finished (estimated for 2018) the interior will become the new home of Kayseri's Archaeological Museum as well as providing space for an art centre.

Sahabiye Medresesi   MEDRESE
(Map p494; Ahmetpaşa Caddesi) This Seljuk theological school dates from 1268. Today its courtyard is a cafe with the surrounding rooms used as bookshops. Its richly decorated doorway with stalactite detailing is particularly notable.

Archaeological Museum   MUSEUM
(Hoca Ahmet Yesevi Bulvarı; ₺5; ⊗8am-5.30pm Tue-Sun) Kayseri's small archaeological museum is a minor magpie's nest, featuring finds from nearby Kültepe (ancient Kanesh, chief city of the Hatti people and the first Hittite capital). Other exhibits include a stunning sarcophagus illustrating Hercules' labours, and a fascinatingly creepy exhibit of child mummies. It's a 1.5km stroll from Cumhuriyet Meydani. To find it walk down Talas Caddesi until you get to the cemetery. Turn left, walk behind the cemetery and

you'll see the museum on the far right-hand corner.

Note that the museum is set to move location into Kayseri Kale when restoration work on the kale is completed.

Ahi Evran Zaviyesi   MUSEUM
(Esnaf ve Sanatkarlar Müzesi; Seyyid Burhaneddin (Talas) Caddesi; ⊙9am-5pm) **FREE** The gloomy interior of this 13th-century technical school for artisans and craftspeople is great to poke about in. It's crammed with a jumble sale–style delight of dusty exhibits from calligraphy to metalwork, and agricultural implements to carpet looms. It's 1km down Talas Caddesi, opposite the cemetery.

Surup Krikor Lusavoriç Kilise   CHURCH
(Church of St Gregory the Illuminator; Necip Fazıl Bulvarı; donation appreciated) **FREE** The 19th-century Surup Krikor Lusavoriç Kilise is one of Anatolia's few remaining Armenian churches. Its domed interior, complete with dilapidated frescoes and three gilded altars, provides a glimpse of the prominence of Kayseri's once vibrant Armenian community. For entry, head around the back wall of the church, ring the doorbell and the guardian – one of the five Armenians left in the city – will let you in. The church is located 2km straight down Necip Fazıl Bulvarı, off Osman Kavuncu Bulvarı.

Tarihi Kayseri Mahallesi   ARCHITECTURE
(historic Kayseri neighbourhood; between Bayram Sokak & Şiremenli Caddesi) Kayseri spent years bulldozing away the dilapidated old neighbourhoods in the central city so that shiny, modern towers could rise up in their place but this project is an example of the major U-turn in thinking that has occurred in recent years. On this one city block, a row of traditional **Kayseri evleri** (houses) has been restored to finery and will, when finished, house a cafe, restaurant, boutique hotel, hamam, and various boutiques selling local foodstuffs.

🛌 Sleeping

★İmamoğlu Paşa Hotel   HOTEL **$$**
(☑0352-336 9090; www.imamoglupasaotel.com.tr; Kocasinan Bulvarı 24; s/d ₺90/140; ❋⚡) Kayseri's stand-out midranger is a pleasant shock. Contemporary rooms come complete with wide-screen satellite TVs, rainfallshowers, kettles, probably the most comfortable beds in town, and minibars (yes, there's beer). You want a room on the fifth

floor or higher for views of Erciyes Dağı (Mt Erciyes). It's on the road opposite the train station, and next door to the police station.

Hotel Büyük   HOTEL **$$**
(Map p494; ☑0352-232 2892; www.kayseribuyuk otel.com; İnönü Bulvarı 55; s/d/tr ₺85/135/200) The facade may not inspire confidence but the small rooms here are modern, come with flat-screen TVs and kettles, and are kept scrupulously clean. The bathrooms are a bit of a squeeze though.

Radisson Blu   BUSINESS HOTEL **$$$**
(☑0352-315 5050; www.radissonblu.com; Sivas Caddesi 24; r from €103) A sign of Kayseri's rise in stock, the Radisson is a very cool, contemporary customer with huge rooms, accented by soft greys and funky acid-yellows, complete with all mod-cons and floor-to-ceiling windows with great city views. The rooftop bar and restaurant (open to nonguests) is the best spot in town for a sundowner while contemplating stunning Erciyes Dağı (Mt Erciyes) vistas.

🍴 Eating

Kayseri boasts a few special dishes, among them *pastırma* (pressed beef preserved in spices), the original pastrami.

★Alamet-i Farika   ANATOLIAN **$**
(☑0532 232 1080; Deliklitaş Caddesi 8; mains ₺10-24; ⊙10am-10pm) The interior is all European-style elegance, but the food is top-notch Anatolian. Tuck into the *mantı* (Turkish ravioli), devour the meaty specialty *çentik kebap* (grilled meat served atop potatoes with a yoghurt and tomato sauce) and save room for the naughtily sweet desserts. Finish up with Turkish coffee, served in dainty teacups with a shot glass of lemonade on the side.

Elmacıoğlu İskander Merkez   KEBAP **$**
(Map p494; ☑0352-222 6965; 1st & 2nd fl, Millet Caddesi 5; mains ₺10-22; ⊙10.30am-10pm) Bring on the calories. Skip the diet for the day and ascend the lift to the top-floor dining hall, with views over the citadel, to order the İskender kebap (döner kebap on fresh pide and topped with tomato sauce and browned butter) house specialty. Your waistline won't thank us, but your tastebuds will.

İstanbul Balık Pazarı   SEAFOOD **$**
(Map p494; ☑0352-231 8973; Sivas Caddesi 12; fish sandwich ₺6, mains ₺15-20; ⊙10am-10pm) You can choose your fish from the glistening

catches in the fishmongers by the door then dig into seafood flavours in the dining room, but we come here to grab a *balık ekmek* (fish sandwich). The fish is grilled in front of you with a choice of four or five fish-fillings – a cheap, delicious lunch.

Shopping

Kapalı Çarşı　　　　　　　　　　　MARKET
(Vaulted Bazaar; Map p494; Cumhuriyet Meydanı; ☉10am-8pm) Set at the intersection of age-old trade routes, Kayseri has long been an important commercial centre. Its Kapalı Çarşı was one of the largest bazaars built by the Ottomans. Restored in the 1870s and again in the 1980s, it remains the heart of the city and is well worth a wander.

❶ Information

Tourist Office (Map p494; ☎ 0352-222 3903; Cumhuriyet Meydanı; ☉10am-12.30pm & 1.30-5pm Mon-Fri) Gives out maps and various brochures.

❶ Getting There & Away

AIR

Kayseri Airport (p453) is 9km north of the centre. A taxi from the central city to the airport costs around ₺15, or hop on a city bus for ₺1.25.

If you're heading straight to one of the Cappadocian villages, **shuttle bus services** (p454) pick up and drop off passengers at the airport. They must be pre-booked.

BUS

Kayseri's massive **otogar** (☎ 0352-336 4373; Osman Kavuncu Bulvarı) is 9km west of the centre. Nearly all bus companies provide a free *servis* into the central city. If there's no *servis*, grab a taxi (₺15), catch a local bus (₺1.25) from the main road or take the tram (₺1.85).

Dolmuşes to Ürgüp (₺8, one hour, 11 services between 8am and 7.30pm) leave from the smaller building across the car park from the main otogar. There is no direct dolmuş service

to Göreme, but you can take the Ürgüp service and change there or hop on any of the big bus-company services travelling to Nevşehir. Most will drop you in Nevşehir, where you can get a *servis*. Some, though, will drop off passengers in Göreme along the way. The 7pm service run by Nevşehir Seyahat is your best bet though both Süha and Metro bus companies are worth asking too.

TRAIN

Kayseri Train Station (Kayseri Garı; Kocasinan Bulvarı) is served by the daily *4 Eylül Mavi* train (between Ankara and Malatya), the *Doğu Ekspresi* (between Ankara and Kars) and the *Çukurova Mavi* Train (between Ankara and Adana). The daily *Erciyes Ekspresi* between Kayseri and Adana is currently not working due to track works.

To reach the centre from the train station, walk out of the station, cross the big avenue and board any bus heading down Atatürk Bulvarı towards Cumhuriyet Meydanı. Alternatively, you could walk along Altan Caddesi, which isn't as busy as Atatürk Bulvarı.

Erciyes Dağı

On the northeastern side of ruggedly beautiful Erciyes Dağı, **Erciyes Dağı Ski Resort** (Erciyes Kayak Merkez; www.kayserierciyes.com.tr; Erciyes Dağı; 1-day ski pass ₺45), has, over the past few years, been undergoing a multi-million-lira revamp intended to establish the mountain as a rival to European ski destinations. The ski runs themselves, and the modern gondola ski-lift system connecting them, are fantastic, with pistes to suit both beginners and hardcore snow-bunnies looking for empty slopes.

❶ Getting There & Away

Erciyes resort is around 80km from the Cappadocian villages (1½ hours' drive) and 25km (30 minutes) from central Kayseri. During the ski season there are shuttle buses to and from central Kayseri.

Black Sea Coast

Best Places to Eat

➡ Okyanus Balık Evi (p503)

➡ Sofra Osmanli Mutfagi (p506)

➡ Vosporos (p512)

➡ Kayadibi Saklıbahçe (p515)

Best Places to Sleep

➡ Sebile Hanım Konağı (p506)

➡ Denizci Otel (p503)

➡ Hotel İkizevler (p508)

➡ Adelante (p511)

Why Go?

While many visitors flock south to the Mediterranean or west to the Aegean, Turks know the Black Sea (Karadeniz) is equally deserving. Surprisingly lush and subtropical, its ancient Greek coastal cities are backed by terraced tea plantations fading into a stunning mountainous hinterland. After Amasra's seaside-holiday vibe and Trabzon's big-city buzz, you can relax in pint-size fishing villages, or head inland to alpine *yaylalar* (mountain pastures). The spectacular coastline also makes for a scenic route across Turkey to other parts of Anatolia.

This is a historic region, scattered with the legacies of civilisations and empires that ebbed and flowed like Black Sea waves. Castles, churches, monasteries and architecturally important mosques recall the days of the kings of Pontus, the Genoese and the Ottomans. Queen Hippolyte and her tribe of female Amazon warriors supposedly lived here, and the seafront chapel at Yason Burnu (Cape Jason) marks the spot where Jason and his Argonauts passed by.

When to Go
Trabzon

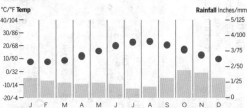

| **May** Springtime revelry kicks off at the traditional International Giresun Aksu Festival. | **Jun–Aug** Black Sea beaches beckon; Trabzon buzzes with summer festivals. | **Apr & Sep** Time to soak up the lazy-day off-season charms of Amasra and Sinop. |

Black Sea Coast Highlights

1 Sumela Monastery (p514) Climbing through pine forests to this cliff-hugging wonder.

2 Sinop (p501) Enjoying the cosmopolitan hum of this historic port.

3 D010 coastal highway (p500) Counting the vertigo-inducing curves on the scenic road from Amasra to Sinop.

4 Amasra (p499) Swimming beneath this beautiful town's Byzantine walls.

5 Trabzon (p508) Cruising big-city streets then soaking off the dust at a hamam.

6 Uzungöl (p515) Discovering mountain plateaus and alpine hamlets on a day trip to villages such as this one.

7 Bakırcılar Sokak (p506) Stepping back in time along Ünye's rat-a-tat-tat Street of Coppersmiths.

8 Ordu (p507) Hopping on the cable car and enjoying a picnic high above town.

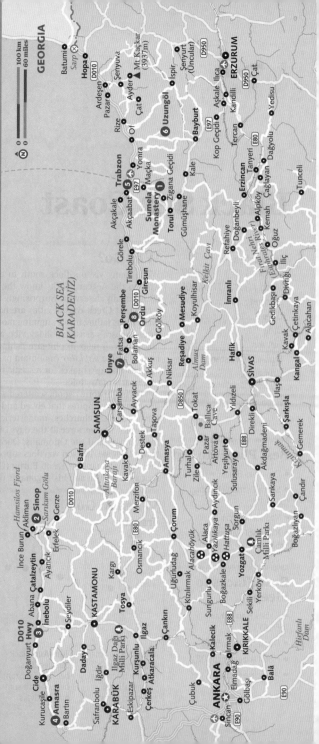

Amasra

☑ 0378 / POP 6800

Straddling a peninsula with two bays and a rocky island reached by a Roman bridge, Amasra is the Black Sea's prettiest port. With a long history of settlement and strategic importance, it's nonetheless relatively isolated from Turkey's main tourist beats, and all the better for it. While regarded with longing affection by Turkish holidaymakers, it's low-key in comparison with many Aegean and Mediterranean resorts.

A Greek colony called Sesamos Amastris (mentioned by Homer) was established here by the 6th century BC, and perhaps earlier. The Byzantines held Amasra as part of the Pontic kingdom, but rented the port to the Genoese as a trading station from 1270 until 1460, when Mehmet the Conqueror took it without a fight. Under Ottoman rule, Amasra lost its commercial importance to other Black Sea ports, and today it's a laid-back and very attractive spot to relax.

Restaurants and bars can be found on both Büyük Liman (Big Harbour) to the east and prettier Küçük Liman (Little Harbour) to the west; most accommodation is closer to the former. The statue in the square overlooking Küçük Liman is of Turkish rock star Barış Akarsu, a much-loved local boy who died in a car accident at age 28 in 2007.

◎ Sights & Activities

Amasra Castle   CASTLE

(Amasra Kalesi) **FREE** A mixed Roman/ Byzantine/Genoese effort, Amasra's citadel occupies the two districts straddling the promontory that commands access to the harbour: Boztepe and Zindan. Reached through three massive gateways from Küçük Liman, or on steps from Büyük Liman, and linked by a Roman bridge, the area is now mostly residential. The impressive original walls survive, however, as do relics such as the restored 9th-century Byzantine **Church Mosque** (Kilese Camii), and the **Dereağzı Tunnel**, which leads under the castle to a freshwater pool.

Amasra Museum   MUSEUM

(Amasra Müzesi; ☑ 0378-315 1006; http://amasra muzesi.com; Çamlık Sokak 4; ₺5; ⊙ 8am-5pm) This excellent museum occupies a 19th-century naval school at the southern end of Küçük Liman. Four rooms of exhibits – from coins to carpets across the Roman, Byzantine, Hellenistic and Otto-

man periods – showcase Amasra's multi-layered history.

Boat Trips   BOATING

(Büyük Liman) Amasra's charms are best viewed from the sea. Head to Büyük Liman (Big Harbour), where several operators offer boat trips around both harbours and the nearby island (from ₺15 for a 45-minute tour to ₺70 for six hours, including swimming stops and lunch on the island). Boats mostly run on summer weekends, but a few operate year-round.

⌁ Sleeping

Rates on busy summer weekends from mid-June to mid-September are up to 50% higher than during other periods, and many places will charge solo travellers the cost of a double room. Most hotels open only at the weekend from November to April.

Kuşna Pansiyon   PENSION **$$**

(☑ 0378-315 1033; www.kusnapansiyon.com; Kurşuna Sokak 36a; s/d ₺70/140; ❈ @ 🛜) The friendly Doğu family has really thought of travellers' requirements at this pension in the castle precincts. Nine bright, modern rooms, including a cute attic room, overlook a verdant garden and rocky cove. Breakfast features homemade jam and unlimited tea and coffee. It's near the Church Mosque; access via the steps near the Büyük Liman tour boats.

Balkaya Pansiyon   PENSION **$$**

(☑ 0378-315 1434; www.balkayapansiyon.com; General Mithat Ceylan Caddesi 35; s/d without breakfast ₺70/130; 🛜) This is one of Amasra's cheaper pensions, offering 15 neat, whitewashed rooms on a side street inland from the Büyük Liman tourist office, and beside some Roman ruins. Choose room 104 for a view.

Timur Otel   HOTEL **$$**

(☑ 0378-315 2589; www.timurotel.com; Çekiciler Çarşısı 53; s/d ₺78/180; ❈ 🛜) This very friendly hotel has 25 spotless (though somewhat dark) rooms overlooking a square with a fountain, just off Büyük Liman. Double glazing ensures a good night's sleep despite the nearby mosque. Some rooms have views to the Big Harbour and the hills beyond.

✗ Eating

Lining both seafronts you'll find mostly licensed restaurants serving fresh fish by the *porsiyon* (portion). In between are *lokantas* (eateries serving ready-made food) focusing on meat- and vegetable-based food.

Amasra Sofrası
TURKISH $

(☑0378-315 1994; İskele Sokak 25; mains ₺14-20; ⊙7am-midnight; 🏃) On a quiet square just west of Büyük Liman, this friendly grill house and *lokanta* has al fresco tables with good views of the street life. Come dinner time it's usually bustling with locals enjoying the many vegetable dishes, pide, kebaps and fish.

Balıkçının Yeri
SEAFOOD $$

(☑0378-315 2683; Büyük Liman Caddesi 57a; fish portion ₺15-25; ⊙8am-midnight) An inviting open facade trimmed with world-flag bunting makes 'Fisherman's Place' stand out from a row of cheaper seafood restaurants lining the northern edge of Büyük Liman. *Barbun* (red mullet), *levrek* (sea bass) and *solmon* (sea trout) are usually available, or you can grab a *balık ekmek* (fish sandwich, ₺6) and eat by the water.

Hamam Cafe
CAFE $$

(☑0378-315 3878; www.hamamcafe.com; Büyük Liman; village breakfast ₺20; ⊙8.30am-11.30pm; 🛜) In what was an Ottoman-era hamam on the big harbour, this easy-going cafe is perfect for sipping tea and playing backgammon among colourful lights on the disused *göbek taşı* (heated central 'navel stone'). The *peynirli gözleme* (stuffed savoury crepes with cheese) are moreish and the Amasra *mantısı* (Turkish ravioli; ₺15) is a speciality.

★Mustafa Amca'nin Yeri
SEAFOOD $$$

(☑0378-315 2606; www.amasracanlibalik.com; Küçük Liman Caddesi 8; fish portion ₺25-45, meze ₺7; ⊙8am-midnight) In situ here since 1945, 'Uncle Mustafa's Place' is unmissable – a pebble-and-timber 'chalet' facade giving way to a marine theme, complete with squawking parrot, within. Locals recommend it for its excellent *canlı balık* (fresh fish), switched-on service and terrace with sweeping views of Little Harbour.

🍷 Drinking & Nightlife

★Lutfiye
CAFE

(☑0378-315 3222; www.lutfiye.com; Küçük Liman Caddesi 20a; ⊙9am-midnight) The flashy central chandelier initially makes it appear over the top, but this classy little cafe serves decent coffee, snacks and breakfast to a chilled-out soundtrack. It also sells marmalade, nut-studded *lokum* (Turkish delight) and *helva* (sesame-seed sweet), a nice alternative to the garish souvenirs of the bazaar outside.

Çınar
BAR

(☑0378-315 1018; www.amasracinarbalik.com; Küçük Liman Caddesi 1; ⊙9am-midnight) The west-facing 'Plane Tree' is a winner for Amasra sunsets and sweeping harbour views. Twinned with the fish restaurant next door, it serves crisply chilled draught beer, a wide range of cocktail-ready spirits and meze.

Ağlayan Ağaç Çay Bahçesi
TEA GARDEN

(☑0378-315 2930; Nöbethane Sokak; tea ₺1; ⊙8am-10pm) To find the whimsically named 'Weeping Tree Tea Garden', follow the signs up through the castle precincts into Boztepe. Once there, take your time sipping çay on the clifftop overlooking 'Rabbit Island' and its population of swirling, squawking gulls.

ℹ️ Getting There & Away

If you're heading east along the coast, get an early start. Dolmuşes (minibuses) become increasingly scarce later in the day.

Intercity bus companies don't travel to Amasra. Instead, minibuses to Bartın (₺4, 30 minutes) leave every 30 minutes from near the PTT (post office). From Bartın there are buses to Safranbolu (₺18, two hours), Ankara (₺35, 4½ hours) and İstanbul (₺45, seven hours). For Sinop you will need to change in Karabük (₺18, two hours) and/or Kastamonu (₺25, four hours).

Metro and Kamil Koç have offices in Amasra's main square, next to the Atatürk statue.

Amasra to Sinop

Winding sinuously around rugged hills hugging the sea, the D010 highway from Amasra to Sinop (320km) is breathtakingly scenic. Expect minimal traffic and stunning views at every turn, with glistening turquoise waters, lush forested headlands and rugged cliffs of marla, a distinctive, slate-like volcanic rock used for roofing. Though the condition of these sealed roads is good, the average driving speed is about 45km/h, which means that it takes more than seven hours to reach Sinop. By public transport, you'll need to use local services between the small towns and villages along the way. Get going at daybreak and don't expect to complete the journey in a day.

A few villages have camping grounds, including Çakraz, just west of Bozköy Beach. Kurucaşile, 45km east of Amasra, has some pensions and modest hotels, and you can see boats being built in the village. Other spots within day-trip distance of Amasra are the picturesque two-beach village of Kapısuyu and, 10km further east, the tiny harbour at

Gideros, the idyllic cove of your dreams. There are a couple of restaurants here where you can feast on local seafood and watch the sunset, including **Günbatımı** (☑0366-871 8140; Gideros Koyu; fish ₺25-40; ⊗9am-11.30pm). From here the road descends to **Kalafat** and **Kumluca**, a sand-and-pebble beach stretching 8km. Many dolmuşes terminate in **Cide**, 3km east of Kumluca. Seafront pensions, mostly only open from June to September, and fish restaurants huddle at the western end of town, around 2km from the central otogar (bus station).

The road beyond Cide is particularly bendy and hilly. Around 12km east, a signpost points to **Kuscu Köyü**, a small village with access to the **Aydos Canyon**, a steep river ravine. **Doğanyurt**, 31km before İnebolu and about 4½ hours from Amasra, is yet another pleasant harbour town, with a Friday market, a big pier and a few little cafes and *lokantas* (eateries serving ready-made food).

About 150km (three hours) west of Sinop, **İnebolu** is a possible stopping point; onward transport may be hard to find by late afternoon. The **Yakamoz Tatıl Köyü** (Phosphorescence Holiday Village; ☑0366-811 3100; www.yakamoztatilkoyu.com.tr; İsmetpaşa Caddesi; bungalow s/d ₺70/100, r s/d ₺80/120; ⊞🛜⊠) is a beachside resort 800m west of the centre, with a cafe and licensed restaurant (mains ₺20); book ahead in summer. In the town centre are old Ottoman houses painted a distinctive ox-blood red and a relatively lively seafront promenade; eat at the **İne Balık & Et** (☑0366-811 4123; Hacı Mehmet Aydın Caddesi 9; mains ₺18-35; ⊗8am-11pm).

Abana, 24km east of İnebolu, has a decent beach and, about 23km further on, near **Çatalzeytin**, is a long pebble beach surrounded by beautiful scenery. Not far east, about 4km before reaching Türkeli, is the delightful **Güllüsu Aile Balık Lokantası** (Güllüsu Family Fish Restaurant; ☑0535-487 7241; Oymayaka Köyü; mains ₺15-30; ⊗9am-midnight) for another fish feast. At **Ayancık** the road divides, with the northern route offering the more scenic journey to Sinop (58km). To get onto this route, cross the bridge and continue through Ayancık.

Sinop

☑0368 / POP 39,200

Wrapped around a rocky promontory, delightful Sinop is a town of superlatives. It is the most northerly point in Anatolia and the only southern-facing spot on the coast. According to an old-salty saying, 'the Black Sea has three harbours – July, August and Sinop'. The naturally sheltered harbour here is safe even in the roughest winter weather, when it can be dangerous for ships to enter other ports.

Sinop is today a holiday town with a cosmopolitan air. Its heritage as a trading port for nigh on three millennia is reflected in model ships on sale in shops all over town.

Colonised from Miletus on Anatolia's Aegean coast in the 8th century BC, Sinop's trade grew, and successive rulers, including the Pontic kings (who made it their capital), Romans and Byzantines, turned it into a busy trading centre. The Seljuks took Sinop in 1214 and used it as a port, but the Ottomans preferred to develop nearby Samsun, which had better land communications. On 30 November 1853, a Russian armada attacked Sinop without warning, overwhelming the local garrison and killing or wounding about 3000 people. The battle brought on the Crimean War, in which the Ottomans allied themselves with the British and French to fight Russian ambitions to expand westward and southward.

◉ Sights

★**Tarihi Sinop Cezaevi** HISTORIC BUILDING
(Historical Sinop Prison; Map p502; www.sinop ale.org/historical-sinop-prison; Sakarya Caddesi; ₺5; ⊗9am-7pm Apr-Sep, to 5pm Oct-Mar) The cells, empty corridors, exercise yards and children's reform school of this hulking former prison within the fortress are haunting and unforgettable. Founded in 1887, it 'did time' as a prison until 1997, when inmates were moved to a more modern facility nearby. That it's been left largely as it was when decommissioned, with minimal explanatory signage, only enhances its grim fascination. Also fascinating is the jumble of stonework: some of the walls clearly reuse ancient columns and lapidary work.

Sinop Fortress FORTRESS
(Sinop Kalesi; Map p502) **FREE** Open to attack from the sea, Sinop was first fortified by the Hittites around 2000 BC. The existing walls are additions made by the Romans, Byzantines, Seljuks and Ottomans to those erected in 72 BC by Pontic king Mithridates VI. Some 3m thick, the walls were once more than 2km long, with 25m-high towers and seven gates. The tower by the harbour, which can be climbed and has a relaxed cafe/bar (p503) on top, remains the most impressive.

Sinop

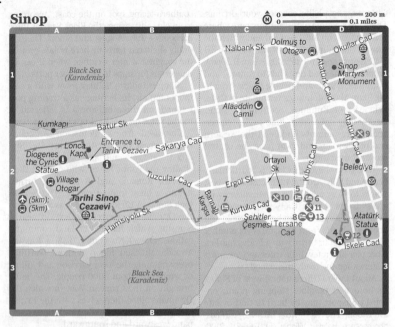

Sinop

◎ Top Sights

◎ Sights

⬛ Sleeping

✖ Eating

🍷 Drinking & Nightlife

🛍 Shopping

Sinop Archaeological Museum   MUSEUM
(Sinop Arkeoloji Müzesi; Map p502; www.sinop
muzesi.gov.tr; Okullar Caddesi 2; ₺5; ◎8am-7pm
Tue-Sun) Highlights of this excellent museum
include the fabulous Meydankapı mosaic
from the 4th century AD, depicting the four
seasons and seven muses; a marble statue of
lions savaging a deer from the 4th century
BC; various coin hoards, including the celebrated one from Gelincik; and an excellent
collection of Byzantine religious objects, including icons from local churches. The garden contains funerary steles, mosaics and
the remains of a Temple of Serapis from the
4th century BC.

Pervane Medresesi   HISTORIC BUILDING
(Map p502; Batur Sokak; ◎8am-10pm) The
powerful Seljuk grand vizier Süleyman Pervane built this seminary in 1262 to commemorate the conquest of Sinop a half-century
earlier. Pleasingly geometrical, with a marble
entry and octagonal central fountain, it now
houses a cafe and shops selling local crafts,
including lovely embroidered linen, a Sinop
specialty.

🛏 Sleeping

Yılmaz Aile Pansiyonu   PENSION $
(Map p502; ☎0368-261 5752; Tersane Çarşısı, Tersane Caddesı; s/d ₺50/100; ⊛⊛) Tucked away

down a narrow lane, this friendly, family-run pension a few steps from the waterfront has 12 simple but renovated rooms. Room 47 has its own bathroom and a sea view.

★**Denizci Otel**   HOTEL $$
(Map p502; ☑0368-260 5934; www.denizciotel.com.tr; Kurtuluş Caddesi 13; s/d ₺100/150; ❄🕸) The waterfront 'Sailor' is a superb option, with orientalist artefacts and reproductions of slightly erotic Lawrence Alma-Tadema paintings decorating the walls and 27 large rooms with big plasma-screen TVs and window alcoves. Room 503 should be your first choice.

Otel 57   HOTEL $$
(Elli Yedi; Map p502; ☑0368-261 5462; www.otel57.com; Kurtuluş Caddesi 29; s/d ₺80/150; ❄🕸) At this friendly place, spick-and-span leatherette chairs in reception give way to 20 comfortable (though smallish) rooms. There's a plentiful breakfast buffet and the clientele is a mix of Turkish businessmen and tourists. If you must know, '57' is the number of Sinop province and appears on local license plates.

Otel Mola   HOTEL $$$
(Map p502; ☑0368-261 1814; www.sinopmolaotel.com.tr; Barınağı Karşısı 34; s/d ₺170/240; ❄🕸) Overlooking the harbour, 'Hotel Rest' has two dozen rooms, many of them (including rooms 201 and 202) facing the sea. Real wooden parquet floors, carpets, balconies and a back garden with ancient walls complete the picture. High marks also go to the friendly staff.

✖ Eating

Sinop's waterfront is lined with licensed open-air seafood restaurants. Inland are places to try Sinop-style *mantı* (Turkish ravioli) with lashings of yoghurt.

Mangal   TURKISH $
(Map p502; Kurtuluş Caddesi 15; mains ₺15-20; ⊙8am-9pm) With walls decorated with fishing photos and guns, this homely grill house serves *mantı* (Turkish ravioli) and grilled fish, chicken and *köfte*.

Antep Sofrası   KEBAP, PIDE $
(Map p502; ☑0368-260 3434; Atatürk Caddesi 3a; mains ₺16-20; ⊙8am-midnight) Locals head to Antep's split-level, avocado-painted dining rooms for kebaps, from *patlıcan* (aubergine) to İskender (döner kebap on fresh pide topped with savoury tomato sauce and browned butter). A welcoming place that's good for female travellers, it's not far from the museum.

★**Okyanus Balık Evi**   SEAFOOD $$
(Ocean Fish House; Map p502; ☑0368-261 3950; www.mevsimbalikcilik.com; Kurtuluş Caddesi; mains ₺25-45; ⊙11am-11pm) Possibly the best fish restaurant on the Black Sea coast, the 'Ocean Fish House' is run by Mert Kanal, whose grandfather founded the fishmonger on the ground floor. Expect fresher than fresh and only in season, plus excellent and unusual meze. The rooftop terrace is a lovely place for rakı at sundown, followed by a lip-smacking fish meal.

Öz Diyarbakır Mangal Sofrası   TURKISH $$
(Map p502; ☑0368-261 1909; Kurtuluş Caddesi 18; mains ₺18-25; ⊙10am-midnight; 🖪) 🍷 Close to the seafront bars and hotels, this large but simple placc serves good *lahmacun* (Arabic-style pizza), soup, pide and a range of kebaps. *Paket servis* (takeaway) is available.

🍷 Drinking & Nightlife

Tea gardens line the seafront, offering backgammon and other board games. Pubs and bars cluster behind the harbour, towards the fortress.

Burç Café   BAR
(Map p502; Tersane Caddesi, Sinop Kalesi; ⊙8am-6pm Oct-Mar, to midnight Apr-Sep) In a tower of the fortress, this atmospheric spot attracts a young crowd for live music (in

BLACK SEA COAST SINOP

SERVICES FROM SINOP'S OTOGAR

DESTINATION	FARE (₺)	DURATION (HR)	DISTANCE (KM)	FREQUENCY (PER DAY)
Ankara	50	7	443	2
İstanbul	70	11	700	2
Karabük (for Safranbolu & Amasra)	35	4	340	1
Kastamonu	25	3	170	5
Samsun (for Trabzon)	25	3	168	hourly

season) and ocean views. Bring something warm to wear as it can get chilly even in the summer. A beer will set you back ₺13.

Nihavent PUB
(Map p502; ☑ 0368-261 6633; Balıkçı Yolu Aralığı 3; ⊙ 6pm-2am) In many ways a restaurant, but more fun when treated as a pub, this friendly place down a narrow alley towards the harbour has several beers on tap and live music in summer.

🛍 Shopping

Yöresel El Sanatları Satış Mağazası ARTS & CRAFTS
(Regional Handicrafts Shop; Map p502; Batur Sokak, Pervane Medresesi; ⊙ 9am-5pm Mon-Sat) This lovely shop in the restored Pervane Medresesi sells both new and antique embroidered linen tablecloths, scarves and decorative items. The charming and helpful English-speaking staff can provide tourist information.

ℹ Information

The most helpful source of information in English is the **Yöresel El Sanatları Satış Mağazası** shop. The **tourist office** (Map p502; İskele Caddesi; ⊙ 8am-7pm mid-Jun–mid-Sep, 9am-5pm May–mid-Jun & mid-Sep–Oct) and **booth** (Map p502; Sakarya Caddesi, Tarihi Cezaevi; ⊙ 8am-7pm Apr-Sep, to 5pm Oct-Mar) are less so.

ℹ Getting There & Away

Turkish Airlines flies to/from İstanbul only. A taxi to the airport, 5km west of the centre, costs ₺25.

Sinop's otogar is 5km southwest of town on the main road to Kastamonu. Dolmuşes run there from next to the museum (₺2) on Okullar Caddesi.

Dolmuşes run to villages such as Akliman and Gerze from the **village otogar** (Map p502; Sakarya Caddesi).

Samsun

☑ 0362 / POP 541,300
Few travellers stop in the sprawling port city of Samsun for more than a change of bus. Indeed, even the enterprising Genoese only paused long enough to burn the city to the ground in the 15th century. But with accommodation and eateries handily located around Cumhuriyet Meydanı (Republic Sq) and some of the Black Sea coast's best museums, Samsun makes a worthwhile stop on your journey east or west. From Cumhuriyet Meydanı, Cumhuriyet Caddesi runs eastwards, along the south side of Atatürk

Park, which is bordered to the north by Atatürk Bulvarı (the coastal highway). The main thoroughfare heading west from the square is Gazi Caddesi.

◉ Sights

Archaeology & Ethnography Museum MUSEUM
(Arkeoloji ve Etnoğrafya Müzesi; www.samsunkent muzesi.com; Cumhuriyet Caddesi 35; ₺5; ⊙ 8am-5pm) The most striking item in this museum is the huge Romano-Byzantine mosaic found at nearby Kara Samsun (Amisos). It depicts Thetis and Achilles from the Trojan War and the four seasons alongside sea monsters and nymphs. Other highlights include elegant gold jewellery dating from the 1st century BC – the time of the legendary Pontic King Mithridates VI.

Amisos Antik Kenti ARCHAEOLOGICAL SITE
(Amisos Ancient City; Amisos Tepesi) FREE The Amisos treasure in Samsun's Archaeology and Ethnography Museum was found at this hilltop site in 1995. The south tumulus has a rock-hewn tomb with two chambers; the north one contains a tomb with three linked chambers. There's a boardwalk running around both, with some explanatory signs. To get here take the SHRS (Samsun Hafif Raylı Sistem; www.samulas.com.tr) tram to Batıpark (stop: Baruthane) then board the Samsun Amisos Hill Cable Car (Samsun Amisos Tepesi Teleferik Hattı; Batıpark & Amisos Tepesi; admission ₺2.50; ⊙ 9am-10pm), which takes you up in just four minutes.

🛏 Sleeping

Explore the Tarihi Bedesten Çarşısı (Old Bazaar Market) area west of the main square, Cumhuriyet Meydanı, for good-value accommodation options.

Otel Necmi HOTEL $
(☑ 0362-432 7164; www.otelnecmi.com.tr; Tarihi Bedestan Sokak 6; s/d/tr without bathroom ₺60/95/145; ❄ 🛜) This character-filled budget choice at the beginning of the clothes bazaar west of the main square, Cumhuriyet Meydanı, feels like your eccentric uncle's house, with pot plants, mirrors and big old chairs in reception. The 20 rooms aren't gleaming or palatial, but the staff are helpful, speaking a little English and offering maps and advice.

Samsun Park Otel BUSINESS HOTEL $$
(☑ 0362-435 0095; www.samsunparkotel.com; Cumhuriyet Caddesi 38; s/d/tr ₺70/100/130; ❄ @ 🛜) Book ahead to bag a compact but

comfortable room at the all-white Samsun Park. It's 200m east of the main square and has 37 rooms; our favourite is room 601.

Yıldızoğlu Hotel BUSINESS HOTEL $$$
(☑0362-333 3400; www.yildizogluhotel.com; Talimhane Caddesi 13; s/d ₺130/200; 🅿🛜) This stylish option, east of the central square and opposite the police station, offers 46 rooms with turquoise trimmings, little black lampshades, minibar and walk-in shower. Facilities include a free fitness centre and sauna, and a bar in the blue-lit reception area. The generous breakfast stretches to soup, *börek* (filled pastry) and *dolmas* (vegetables stuffed with rice or meat).

✖ Eating

Gaziantep Kebap Salonu KEBAP, TURKISH $
(☑0362-432 0227; Osmaniye Caddesi 7; mains ₺8-12; ☺8am-11pm) This slice of southeast Turkey is a relaxed neighbourhood *kebapçı*, where couples and male groups snack on *lahmacun* (Arabic-style pizza) and local *ayran* (yoghurt drink) from nearby Tokat. Heading east on Cumhuriyet Caddesi, turn right after the Hotel Amisos.

Sıla Restaurant KÖFTE, KEBAP $
(Cumhuriyet Caddesi 36; mains ₺16-18; ☺8am-8pm) Sıla, 100m east of the main square, is popular for a meaty lunch; try the chicken *şiş* kebap, served with fiery charred peppers. Everything is slick and switched on at this place, not least the darting waiters – artistes of hustle-bustle, even by Turkish standards.

**★Pamuk Kardeşler
Balık Restaurant** SEAFOOD $$
(☑0362-445 0433; www.pamukkardesler.com; Batıpark; mains ₺25-45; ☺11.30am-midnight) A trinity of seafood restaurants line the marina near the cable car in Batıpark and this licensed one is far and away the best. Try the

hamsi sis (barbecued anchovy), followed by the *barbun* (red mullet). Reach it on foot along the Sahil Yürüyüş Yolu (Coastal Walking Path) or the Samulaş tram (stop: Fener).

ℹ Information

Tourist Office (☑0362-431 1228; Atatürk Bulvarı, Atatürk Kültür Merkezi; ☺9am-5pm Mon-Fri, to 6pm Sat & Sun Jun-Sep) Helpful office with limited handouts between the Büyük Samsun Otel and the Atatürk Kültür Merkezi (Atatürk Cultural Centre).

ℹ Getting There & Around

AIR
Regular shuttle buses link the city with Samsun Çarşamba Airport (₺10, 30 minutes). **Havaş** (☑0362-444 0487; www.havas.net) also connects the airport and Ordu (₺20, two hours) via Ünye and Fatsa (₺15).

Anadolu Jet (www.anadolujet.com) Flies to Ankara and Istanbul.

Onur Air (www.onurair.com) Flies to İstanbul.

Pegasus Airlines (www.flypgs.com) Flies to İstanbul and İzmir.

Sun Express (www.sunexpress.com) Flies to Antalya and İzmir.

Turkish Airlines (www.turkishairlines.com) Flies to Ankara and İstanbul and several cities in Germany and Austria.

BUS
Bus companies have offices at the Cumhuriyet Meydanı end of Cumhuriyet Caddesi. *Servises* (shuttle buses) run between there and the otogar, 3km inland. There are also frequent dolmuşes (₺2.50) from the otogar to Cumhuriyet Meydanı. The otogar has left-luggage facilities.

CAR & MOTORCYCLE
You can hire a car in the city or at Samsun Çarşamba Airport through a number of agencies, including Avis and Budget.

SERVICES FROM SAMSUN'S OTOGAR

DESTINATION	FARE (₺)	DURATION (HR)	DISTANCE (KM)	FREQUENCY (PER DAY)
Amasya	15	2½	130	frequent
Ankara	50	6-7	420	frequent
Giresun	30	3½	220	frequent
Hopa	50	9½	520	frequent
İstanbul	80	11	750	frequent
Kayseri	60	7	530	frequent
Sinop	25	3½	168	hourly
Trabzon	35	5½	355	frequent
Ünye	12	1½	95	half-hourly

Ünye

🔊 0452 / POP 82,500

This seaside town, 90km east of Samsun, has one of Anatolia's longest settlement histories. There is evidence the Hittites and even Stone Age people were here, and Ünye was an important junction between the Silk Road and the coastal highway during the Ottoman period. Smaller and more conservative than Samsun and as pretty as Ordu, with some lovely Ottoman and Greek architecture, Ünye is worth a stop for its coastal promenade and labyrinth of well-kept winding streets and lanes. These fan out from the main square (Cumhuriyet Meydanı) across the coastal road from the seafront.

◉ Sights

Bakırcılar Sokak STREET

(Street of Coppersmiths) Just near Orta Camii (Middle Mosque), this street of bygone times is home to a handful of coppersmiths, including **Bizim Bakırcı** (Our Coppersmith; Bakırcılar Sokak 13; ⊘ 8am-5pm), who still hammer and shape items for the home, as their forebears did for centuries.

Tozkoparan Rock Tomb TOMB

(Tozkoparan Mağara Mezarı) FREE This ancient cave tomb, one of a few in the area, is off the D010 coastal road 5km east of the town centre. Carved bull figures flank the entrance to the tomb, which is thought to date to between 7000 BC and 5000 BC. Eastbound minibuses can drop you by the cement factory at the turn for the tomb (₺2). A taxi will cost ₺30 (or ₺40 waiting and return).

Ünye Müze Evi MUSEUM

(Ünye Museum House; 🔊 0452-324 0209; Hacı Emin Caddesi 24; ⊘ 9am-6pm Tue-Sun) FREE This tiny but ambitious museum occupies a handsome, breezy, 250-year old Ottoman house, with displays bringing to life the history, lifestyles and folklore of the different ethnic groups who have made Ünye their home over the centuries. It's up the hill west of the main square, Cumhuriyet Meydanı.

Eski Hamam HAMAM

(Old Hamam; Cumhuriyet Meydanı 8a; ₺16; ⊘ men 5am-midnight Mon, Wed, Thu & Sun, women 11am-5pm Tue & Sat, to 9pm Fri) The Old Hamam occupies a former church on the southeast corner of the main square.

🛏 Sleeping

Gülen Plaj Camping CAMPGROUND $

(🔊 0452-324 6686; Devlet Sahil Yolu, Uzunkum; campsites per person ₺20, bungalow ₺200) Overlooking a pleasant sweep of beach 2.5km west of the centre, Gülen's wooden bungalows among the trees have balconies and kitchenettes, and sleep up to four.

★ Sebile Hanım Konağı BOUTIQUE HOTEL $$

(🔊 0452-323 7474; www.sebilehanimkonagi.com; Çubukçu Arif Sokak 10; s/d/ste ₺110/175/230; ❋ 🕸 🛜) In the former Armenian district, this gloriously restored hilltop property dating to 1877 has 14 cosy wood-lined rooms with private baths, fridges and lovely fabrics on the walls. The cheapest rooms are mansard ones on the top floor; choose instead room 201, with its carved stone fireplace and sauna, or one of the two suites (105 or 205).

There's also an excellent licensed **restaurant** (mains ₺15 to ₺25) open 10am to 11pm daily with courtyard seating in the warmer months. From the central square, Cumhuriyet Meydanı, follow the signs uphill from the western edge of the old city walls.

Otel Güney HOTEL $$

(🔊 0452-323 8406; www.otelguney.com; Belediye Caddesi 14; s/d ₺60/100; ❋ 🛜) An excellent choice south of the main square, this hotel is spotless and has 17 rooms with modern bathrooms and a pleasant rooftop cafe on the 4th floor. It's possibly Ünye's best value.

🍴 Eating

Kaptan Balıkçılık SEAFOOD $

(Captain Fishery; 🔊 0452-323 2333; Kasaplar Sokak 11; mains ₺15; ⊘ 10am-11pm) Hidden in the market, next to a fishmonger, is this excellent budget fish eatery, a gleaming white contrast to the bustle outside. Try the *karides güvec* (prawn stew, ₺15), or the *balik ekmek* (fish sandwich, ₺5).

★ Sofra Osmanli Mutfagi TURKISH $$

(🔊 0452-323 2691; Belediye Caddesi 25a; mains ₺18-22; ⊘ 7am-10pm) Sofra occupies a lovely stone house with a terrace facing the coast road, just a couple of blocks east of the main square. Wildly popular at lunch, it's presided over by briskly efficient, bow-tied waiters serving pide, kebaps and *Osmanlı mutfağı* (Ottoman cuisine). The lamb fillet on charred eggplant is sensational.

Kahve Durağı CAFE

(🔊 0452-310 2020; www.kahveduragi.com.tr; Cumhuriyet Meydanı 3; ⊘ 7.30am-midnight; 🛜) Set

THE OLD COAST ROAD

At Bolaman, 30km east of Ünye, the D010 runs inland and doesn't touch the coast again until 7km short of Ordu. It's a spectacular stretch, through one of Turkey's longest road tunnels (3.82km), and the diversion inland has created a lovely alternative route – the old coast road.

A winding few kilometres northeast from Bolaman, a small brown sign points 500m left to rugged **Yason Burnu** (Cape Jason), where a tiny chapel (1868) has replaced an ancient temple erected by sailors marking the spot where Jason and his Argonauts braved the waters around the cape en route to Colchis (now in Georgia) in search of the golden fleece. A nearby cafe serves fish and *köfte* (meatballs). To the east is lovely **Çaka**, a 400m-long strip of white sand regarded as the Black Sea's best beach. There's a leafy picnic area here, too.

Some 15km west of Ordu, the fishing port of **Perşembe** is an attractive, slow-paced Black Sea village. At night locals fish from the slender pier and fish restaurants prepare the day's 'catch', presumably collected from the dozens of fish farms visible from shore. Across the main road from the seafront fish restaurants, peaceful **Otel Dede Evi** (📞 0452-517 3802; Atatürk Bulvarı 266; s/d ₺100/150; 🅿 🛜) has shipshape rooms with TV and fridge.

This meandering detour is best attempted with your own transport, but there are dolmuşes (₺2.75) to Perşembe from Fatsa to the west and Ordu to the east.

---

in a restored villa-style town house on the southwest edge of Ünye's main square, this local branch of a national franchise is a popular, relaxed terrace cafe with a predominantly young clientele. If you're hungry, there's a menu of simple things such as *tost* (toasted sandwiches) and *köfte*.

ℹ Information

Tourist Office (📞 0452-323 4952; Hukumet Binası, Cumhuriyet Meydanı; ⊗8.30am-5.30pm Mon-Fri) In a kiosk on the southeast side of the main square.

ℹ Getting There & Away

Bus companies have offices on the coast road. Buses travel to Samsun (₺25, 1½ hours) and Ordu (₺25, 1½ hours). Go to Fatsa (₺5) to catch a bus along the old coast road to Perşembe (₺10).

Ordu

📞 0452 / POP 154,900

A Greek-founded trading port that's passed through the hands of Romans, Byzantines and many others, Ordu is a prosperous, attractive place unmatched as the hazelnut capital of the world. Geographically blessed, central Ordu sits between Kiraz Limani (Cherry Port) and the handsome green slopes of Boztepe (550m). While the city sprawls in both directions, the winding narrow lanes give the old centre a village-like feel, while the palm-lined seaside boulevard comes into its own in the warmer months. There's a good stretch of sand beaches 5km west of town.

◉ Sights

Paşaoğlu Mansion & Ethnography Museum MUSEUM
(Paşaoğlu Konağı ve Etnoğrafya Müzesi; www.ordukulturturizm.gov.tr; Taşocak Caddesi; ⊗8am-5pm) FREE Occupying a handsome stone mansion built for a wealthy local in 1896, this ethnographic museum provides a glimpse into the life of upper-class Ottoman society, before it all came to an end in the early 20th century. The beautiful high-ceilinged interior contains displays of weapons, costumes and a sand-needle embroidery of Atatürk, who visited in 1924. It's 500m northwest (and uphill) from the main square, Cumhuriyet Meydanı, past a bazaar; look for signs reading 'Müze – Museum'.

Ordu Boztepe Cable Car CABLE CAR
(Ordu Boztepe Teleferik Hattı; Mon-Fri ₺6, Sat & Sun ₺8; ⊗9am-11pm) Take a seven-minute *teleferik* (cable-car) ride from the seafront promenade to the gondola station (498m) on Boztepe for breathtaking views of the bay, city and mountains behind. There's a restaurant and cafe up top, plus a number of *dondurma* (Turkish ice-cream) carts and a shady wooded area for picnics.

Taşbaşı Cultural Centre HISTORIC BUILDING
(Taşbaşı Kültür Merkezi; Menekşe Sokak; ⊗8am-noon & 1-5pm) FREE Standing in a hilltop garden littered with (sadly defaced) statuary and overlooking the sea, this former Greek church (1853) is now a cultural centre. It's largely empty when nothing cultural has been scheduled, but is worth visiting for its austere

BLACK SEA COAST ORDU

beauty and its situation – the surrounding old Greek quarter, 500m west of central Ordu, is an attractive neighbourhood of tumbledown houses and a couple of lovely boutique hotels.

🛏 Sleeping & Eating

Taşbaşı Butik Otel   BOUTIQUE HOTEL $$
(📞 0452-223 3530; www.tasbasihotels.com; Kesim Evi Sokak 1; s/d ₺120/180; 🅿❄🛜) The decor occasionally strays into chintz territory, but the Black Sea views are terrific from this restored hilltop mansion, a short walk up the hill that dominates Ordu's old Greek neighbourhood. Each of the six rooms is named after an Ordu district; our absolute favourite is Zaferi Milli.

Atlıhan Hotel   HOTEL $$
(📞 0452-212 0565; www.atlihanhotel.com.tr; Kazım Karabekir Caddesi 9; s/d ₺100/150; ❄🛜) Right in the centre of Ordu, one block back from the seafront behind the town hall, this welcoming hotel has sea views and a top-floor jazz club (🕐4pm-2am). The 39 rooms are a very good size and the bathrooms are up to date – choose room 304 for a double-window sea view.

★ Hotel İkizevler   BOUTIQUE HOTEL $$$
(Twins Hotel; 📞 0452-225 0081; www.ikizevler hotel.com.tr; Sıtkıcan Caddesi 44-46; r ₺200; ❄🛜) 'Twins' is a delightful boutique hotel delivering 12 rooms of gracious Ottoman style. The property was originally two stately homes, and it now dominates a hilltop in the old Greek district just inland from the Taşbaşı Cultural Centre (p507). Wooden floors, antique rugs and huge bathrooms all contribute to the relaxed heritage ambience.

Ordu Kervansaray Lokantası   TURKISH $
(📞 0452-214 9518; Kazım Karabekir Caddesi 1; mains ₺15; 🕐6am-9pm; 🍴) Below the hotel of the same name (but unrelated) this bustling eatery serves a good range of kebaps, rice dishes and desserts on place mats bearing pictures of old Ordu. Mouthwatering *hazır yemek* (ready-to-eat food) also awaits in the steaming bains-maries, including stuffed peppers, stewed greens and plenty of other veggie options.

Grand Mıdı Restaurant   SEAFOOD $$
(📞 0452-214 0340; Atatürk Bulvari 121a; mains ₺20; 🕐10am-1am) On its own 60m pier striking out from the boulevard, this wooden seafood restaurant-on-the-waves is as atmospheric as any place in Ordu to take your evening meal. Naturally the seafood is recommended: try the *balık buğulama* – fish stewed with tomato – or one of the various aubergine dishes.

ℹ Information

Tourist Office (📞 0452-223 1444; www.ordu. gov.tr; Atatürk Bulvarı; 🕐10am-6pm Mon-Thu, to 8pm Fri & Sat, to 2pm Sun) This helpful tourist office is housed in a kiosk on the inland side of the coast road, about 250m west of the town hall.

ℹ Getting There & Around

Ordu's otogar is 5km east of the town centre, on the coast road. Buses depart regularly to Giresun (₺20, one hour), Ünye (₺25, one hour) and Perşembe (₺2.75, 20 minutes). You can also usually flag down buses along the coast road.

From Ordu's central square, local dolmuşes run uphill to Taşbaşı Cultural Centre in one direction, and near the otogar in the other (₺2).

Trabzon

📞 0462 / POP 244,100

Founded by Greek traders from Miletus in the 8th century BC, Trabzon has been handballed down the years between Cimmerians, Medes, Hellenes, Byzantines and a succession of other peoples. Once an important stop on the Silk Road, it remains the Black Sea's busiest port. Somewhat louche, it's not the largest, but is certainly the most sophisticated city in the region, too caught up in its own whirl of activity to worry about what's happening in far-off İstanbul or Ankara.

Contrasting with the gracious, medieval church (now mosque) of Aya Sofya, and the one-time Byzantine monastery at nearby Sumela, the modern world shines through on Atatürk Alanı, Trabzon's busy main square in the eastern section of the city centre. Indeed, the exotic city Rose Macaulay described in *The Towers of Trebizond* (1956) is very much a distant memory now.

East of Atatürk Alanı (also known as Meydan Parkı) and down a steep hill is the port. West of the centre, past the bazaar, is Ortahisar, a picturesque old neighbourhood straddling a ravine.

History

Trabzon's recorded history begins in the middle of the 8th century BC, when Miletan colonists came from Sinop and founded a settlement, Trapezus, with an acropolis on the *trapezi* (Greek for 'table') of land above the harbour.

The port town did well for 2000 years, until the Christian soldiers of the Fourth Crusade seized and sacked Constantinople in 1204, forcing its noble families to seek refuge in Anatolia. The Comnenus imperial family subsequently established an empire along the Black Sea coast in 1204, with Alexius Comnenus I reigning as the emperor of Trebizond.

Over the next two centuries the Trapezuntine emperors and empresses skilfully balanced alliances with the Seljuks, Mongols and Genoese. Prospering through trade with eastern Anatolia and Persia, the empire peaked under Alexius II (1297–1330), before declining in factional disputes. The empire of Trebizond survived until the Ottoman conquest in 1461, eight years longer than Constantinople.

⊙ Sights

Pedestrianised Kunduracılar Caddesi leads from Atatürk Alanı to Trabzon's bazaar, located in the Çarşı (Market) quarter. Near the restored **Çarşı Camii** (Market Mosque; Map p510; Çarşı (Market) Quarter), central Trabzon's largest mosque, are the **Taş Han** (Map p510) and **Alaca Han** (Map p510; Çarşı (Market) Quarter) caravanserais and the **Bedesten** (Covered Bazaar; Map p510), Trabzon's oldest marketplace, now full of workshops, stores and cafes.

★ Aya Sofya Mosque & Museum
MOSQUE, MUSEUM

(Aya Sofya Müzesi ve Camii; ☑0462-223 3043; Ayasofya Caddesi; ⊙9am-7pm Jun-Aug, to 6pm Apr, May, Sep & Oct, 8am-5pm Nov-Mar) **FREE** Originally called Hagia Sophia (Church of Divine Wisdom), Aya Sofya sits 4km west of Trabzon's centre on a terrace close to the sea. Built between 1238 and 1263, it was influenced by Georgian and Seljuk design, although the wall paintings and mosaic floors follow the prevailing Constantinople style of the time. It was converted to a mosque after Ottoman conquest in 1461, and later used as an ammunition-storage depot and hospital by the Russians, before restoration in the 1960s.

In 2013 local religious authorities gained control of the building and converted it into a mosque again. A local judge has ruled the transformation of the former church to be illegal and ordered it to be maintained as a museum. For the moment it is both, though some of the ceiling frescoes and floor mosaics have been covered.

The church has a cross-in-square plan, topped by a single dome, showing Georgian influence. A stone frieze on the south porch depicts the expulsion of Adam and Eve from the Garden of Eden. On the western side of the building, the vaulted narthex has the best-preserved frescoes of various biblical themes, and the facade has a relief of an eagle, symbol of the church's founders, the Comnenus family. Unfortunately, most of the frescoes within arm's reach have been heavily defaced. The best frescoes (Annunciation, Visitation, Doubting Thomas etc) are in the main apse. The astonishing Christ Pantocrator on the ceiling dome is now covered with a tarpaulin, but can be glimpsed from the eastern transept.

The museum stands in gardens with a square bell tower erected in 1427, and the marble remains of a 2nd-century Roman temple unearthed in 1997. The garden cafe here is reputed to serve the best *kuymak* and *kaygana* (local herb omelette) in Trabzon.

Signposted uphill from the coastal highway, Aya Sofya can be reached by dolmuş (₺1.75) from near the southeastern end of Atatürk Alanı. A taxi costs about ₺15.

Trabzon Museum
MUSEUM

(Trabzon Müzesi; Map p510; Zeytinlik Caddesi 10; ₺5; ⊙9.15am-5.45pm Tue-Sun) The Kostaki Mansion (1917), built for a Greek banker in the Ottoman Black Sea style, briefly hosted Atatürk in 1924. One of provincial Turkey's most comely museums – with ornate rooms, painted ceilings, carved wooden doors and original furnishings – it displays interesting ethnographic and Ottoman artefacts. The basement 'archaeological opus' has more significant pieces, including a flattened bronze statue of Hermes unearthed at Tabakhane in 1997, plus icons, coins and jewellery from the Roman, Byzantine and Comnenos periods.

Atatürk Mansion
HISTORIC BUILDING

(Atatürk Köşkü; ☑0462-231 0028; Köşk Caddesi; ₺2; ⊙8am-7pm Apr-Sep, to 5pm Oct-Mar) Nestled in leafy Soğuksu, 5km southwest of Atatürk Alanı, this three-storey, blindingly white late-19th-century mansion has fine views and lovely formal gardens. Built for a wealthy Greek banking family in the Black Sea style popular in the Crimea, it was bequeathed to Atatürk in 1924, and it's believed he wrote part of his will here. See photos and mementos of the great man, including a map of the WWI Dardanelles campaign scratched into the table in the study.

City buses labelled 'Köşk' leave from opposite the post office on Kahramanmaraş Caddesi and drop you outside the mansion (₺2). A taxi will cost about ₺20.

BLACK SEA COAST TRABZON

Trabzon

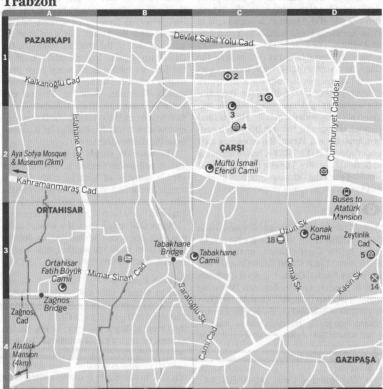

Trabzon

🏃 Activities

There are numerous local tour companies around Atatürk Alanı that organise day trips to places of interest around Trabzon, including Sumela, Uzungöl, Ayder and Batumi (Georgia).

Meydan Hamamı　　　　　　　　　　HAMAM

(Map p510; www.meydanhamami.com; Kahramanmaraş Caddesi 3; hamam ₺20, scrub ₺10, massage ₺10; ⊙ men 6am-11pm, women 8am-8pm) Clean and well run, the 'Hamam on the Square' offers saunas, scrubs, bubble washes

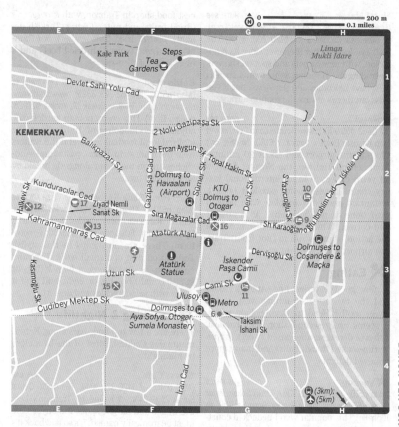

N 0 ⎯⎯⎯⎯⎯⎯ 200 m
0 ⎯⎯⎯⎯⎯⎯ 0.1 miles

Liman Mukli İdare

Kale Park

Steps

Tea Gardens

Devlet Sahil Yolu Cad

KEMERKAYA

2 Nolu Gazipaşa Sk

Balıkpazarı Sk

Sh Ercan Aygün Sk

Topal Hakim Sk

Kunduracılar Cad

Ziyad Nemli Sanat Sk

Gazipaşa Cad

Dolmuş to Havaalanı (Airport)

Sümer Sk

KTÜ Dolmuş to Otogar

Deniz Sk

S Yazıcıoğlu Sk

İskele Cad

10

Halkevi Sk

12

17

Kahramanmaraş Cad

Sıra Mağazalar Cad

16

Sh Karaoğlano Blu İbrahim Cad

9

13

Atatürk Alanı

Dervişoğlu Sk

Dolmuşes to Coşandere & Maçka

Kasımoğlu Sk

7

Atatürk Statue

İskender Paşa Camii

Uzun Sk

15

Cami Sk

11

Cudibey Mektep Sk

Ulusoy

Metro

Dolmuşes to Aya Sofya, Otogar, Sumela Monastery

6

Taksim İshani Sk

İran Cad

(3km); (5km)

BLACK SEA COAST TRABZON

and massages. There are separate areas for men and women; the women's entrance is around the corner.

🛏 Sleeping

Many of the hotels along Güzelhisar Caddesi are popular with business travellers, so book ahead during the week and ask for a discount at weekends. Many places book out in high season (July and August).

★ Adelante
HOSTEL **$**

(Map p510; ☏ 0462-544 4344; www.trabzon hostel.com; Saray Atik Cami Sokak 5; s/d €15/30; 🛜) Within the old city, this very decent new hostel provides some of Trabzon's cheapest and best accommodation. Rooms have either single, bunk or double beds, and Elif, the English-speaking hostess, is very friendly. *Kuymak*, *kaygana* (a thin herb omelette) and other local specialities feature in the optional breakfast.

Hotel Efe
HOTEL **$**

(Map p510; ☏ 0462-326 8281; Güzelhisar Caddesi 2; s/d ₺50/80; ❄🛜) You won't find too many central-Trabzon hotels as cheap as the Efe, and the staff are friendly, too. Aside from this, there isn't much difference between this tall, narrow 18-room hotel and some of its pricier neighbours. Late risers will be happy to know the breakfast buffet runs to 11am.

★ Hotel Nur
HOTEL **$$$**

(Map p510; ☏ 0462-323 0445; Cami Sokak 15; s/d ₺120/240; ❄🛜) A long-standing travellers' favourite, with a fabulous lounge/bar on the rooftop and very helpful staff, the Nur has 20 rooms with bathrooms and five with shared facilities. Some rooms are pint-sized but the views across Atatürk Alanı make up for the squeeze. The nearby mosque doesn't skimp on the 5am call to prayer. Lower prices for longer stays.

Hotel Nazar
HOTEL $$$

(Map p510; ☑0462-323 0081; www.nazarotel.com.tr; Güzelhisar Caddesi 5; s/d ₺120/200; ❋🛜) The 'Evil Eye' looks better then ever since its renovation, with new carpets and spot-on showers upgrading the 41 rooms. Some rooms, such as 404, have balconies and sea views, but if you miss out there's always the rooftop terrace.

Novotel
HOTEL $$$

(☑0462-455 9000; www.novotel.com; Cumhuriyet Mah Kasustu Beldesi, Yomra; r €180; ❋@🛜🏊) Close to the airport and about 20 minutes from central Trabzon, the Novotel delivers all you'd expect from an international luxury chain. Fitness room, excellent beds, a restaurant and bar (complete with tasteful saxophone-shaped beer tap) – all is present and correct. While it's a fair distance from the action, shuttles run to (not from) Trabzon airport and the Forum mall.

✖ Eating

A few good eateries line Atatürk Alanı and the two streets running west. Got a sweet tooth? Head to Uzun Sokak, where it seems every second shop sells baklava, *helva* (a dense, sesame-based sweet), *lokma* (syrup-soaked dough balls) and many more honeyed delights.

★ Vosporos
TURKISH $

(Map p510; ☑0462-321 7067; Uzun Sokak, Zafer Çarşısı 53; mains ₺15; ⊙noon-9pm Sat-Thu, to 10pm Fri) This popular wood-bedecked courtyard cafe – two floors up a shopping centre off Uzun Sokak and plastered with murals of Sumela, the Atatürk Mansion and other local sights – has very good food. Try the pencil-thin stuffed vine leaves, or the local speciality, *kuymak*.

★ Kalender
TURKISH $

(Map p510; ☑0462-323 1011; Zeytinlik Caddesi 16b; mains ₺15, salads ₺6-10; ⊙8.30am-9pm Mon-Sat; ❋) This welcoming cafe-restaurant, just south of the museum, has a cosmopolitan vibe. It's perfect for a post-museum coffee and brunch of *menemen* (scrambled eggs with peppers and tomatoes) or *kuymak* (Trabzon 'polenta'). Front tables overlook a side street and, on weekdays, you can choose a mixed plate of three or four of the seven or eight hot and cold dishes.

Yeşil Mandıra
DELI $

(Green Dairy; Map p510; ☑0462-321 2243; www.yesilmandiratrabzon.com; Sıra Mağazalar Caddesi 13a; ⊙8am-10pm) The Green Dairy is the best food shop in Trabzon, with *kuruyemiş* (dried fruits and nuts), *lokum* (Turkish delight), *pestil* (dried fruit leather), *bal* (honey), *pastırma* (spiced air-dried beef) and a huge array of cheeses.

Bordo Mavi
INTERNATIONAL $$

(Map p510; ☑0462-323 3325; www.bordomavirestaurant.com; Halkevi Sokak 12; mains ₺20-28; ⊙8am-11pm) This cosmopolitan garden-cafe adjoins the clubhouse of Trabzonspor, the idolised local football team, and the waiters wear the team strip. Pizzas, pastas and sandwiches are on the menu alongside breakfast and Turkish meals.

Fevzi Hoca Balık-Köfte
FISH, KÖFTE $$

(Map p510; ☑0462-326 5444; www.fevzihoca.com.tr; Kahramanmaraş Caddesi 8, İpekyolu İş Merkezi, 2nd fl; fish/köfte meal ₺35/30; ⊙noon-10pm) There are no menus in this stylish Trabzon outpost of a small *balık* (fish) and *köfte* empire. Just choose a *büyük* (big) or *küçük* (small) beastie, or *köfte,* and wolf it down with salad, pickles and dessert.

Drinking & Nightlife

There are a few top-floor bars along Kahramanmaraş Caddesi. Most of the bars close by midnight.

Stress Cafe
CAFE, BAR

(Map p510; ☑0426-321 3044; Nemlioğlu Cemal Sokak 2; ⊙24hr; 🛜) One of Trabzon's best live-music and nargile spots, the Stress Cafe must be ironically named: it's so laid back it's almost horizontal. The Ottomans-R-Us decor is slightly naff (especially the Egyptian-statue 'door staff'), but this really is a good place to kick back. Live music starts on the top floor at 7.30pm most nights, and plays on til 11.

Koza Caffe
CAFE

(Map p510; ☑0462-321 0225; 1st fl, Ziyad Nemli Sanat Sokağı 1; ⊙11am-11pm; 🛜) Diagonally opposite Şekerbank, 'Cocoon Cafe' has an eccentric interior: something like a spray-concreted 'cave' with a mishmash of fish tanks and faux medieval decor. Grab a seat on one of the tiny outdoor balconies and settle in for coffee and snacks.

❶ Information

Tourist Office (Map p510; ☑0462-326 4760; Atatürk Alanı; ⊙8am-5.30pm Jun-Sep, to 5pm Mon-Fri Oct-May) The tourist office sits on the ground floor of the refurbished municipal building on the northeastern corner of Atatürk Alanı. Staff are helpful and English-speaking, and some of the literature is in English, too. Rumour has it that it will be open 24/7 during high season.

ℹ Getting There & Away

AIR

Anadolu Jet (www.anadolujet.com) Flies to Ankara and İstanbul.

Onur Air (www.onurair.com.tr) Flies to İstanbul.

Pegasus Airlines (www.flypgs.com) Flies to Ankara and İstanbul.

SunExpress (www.sunexpress.com.tr) Flies to Antalya and İzmir.

Turkish Airlines (www.turkishairlines.com) Flies to Ankara and İstanbul.

BOAT

Due to tensions with Russia, the usual ferry service between Trabzon and Sochi has been suspended. Russia's Olympia Line (www.olympia-line.ru) runs a car ferry twice a week (₺380, five hours) but you'll need Russian to navigate the booking site.

BUS

Bus company offices, such as **Metro** (Map p510; www.metroturizm.com.tr) and **Ulusoy** (Map p510; www.ulusoy.com.tr), are scattered around Atatürk Alanı and serve destinations including Batumi and Tbilisi in Georgia.

For Ayder and the Kaçkar Mountains, catch a Hopa-bound bus and change at Ardeşen or, better, Pazar. If you miss the daily Kars bus, head to Hopa or Erzurum for more services. For Yerevan in Armenia, you must change at Tbilisi in Georgia.

There's also a Havaş bus to/from Giresun (₺22).

CAR

You can hire a car to pick up, or drop off, in Trabzon or at the airport through Economy Car Rentals. **Avis** (☑ 0462-325 5582; www.avis.

com.tr), **Dollar Rent A Car** (☑ 0462-444 1170; www.dollar.com.tr; Taksim Caddesi), **Europcar** (☑ 0462-444 1399; www.europcar.com.tr; Cikmaz Sokak 38/1A, off Kunduracılar Caddesi) and **National** (☑ 0462-325 3252; www.nationalcar.com.tr) also have offices in town or at the airport.

ℹ Getting Around

TO/FROM THE AIRPORT

Dolmuşes to the *havaalanı* (airport, ₺1.75), 5.5km east of the centre, leave from a side street on the northern side of Atatürk Alanı. They drop you on the opposite side of the coast road from the airport, 500m from the terminal entrance across a pedestrian bridge.

A taxi costs ₺25. Buses bearing 'Park' or 'Meydan' go to Atatürk Alanı from the airport.

Havaş (☑ 0462-325 9575; www.havas.net) operates shuttle buses to/from the airport (₺5), but they are inconvenient as they run along Yavuz Selim Bulvarı south of the centre. More useful are Havaş shuttles to/from Ardeşen (₺20) via Of and Rize (₺15).

BUS & DOLMUŞ

Trabzon's otogar is 3km east of the port, on the interior side of the coastal road. To reach Atatürk Alanı from the otogar, cross the shore road in front of the terminal, turn left, walk to the bus stop and catch any bus with 'Park' or 'Meydan' in its name. The dolmuş for Atatürk Alanı is marked 'Garajlar-Meydan'. A taxi between the otogar and Atatürk Alanı costs ₺10.

To get to the otogar, catch a dolmuş marked 'Garajlar' from near the southeastern end of Atatürk Alanı, or one marked 'KTÜ' from next to Otel Horon.

Dolmuşes (₺1.75) mainly leave from under the flyover near the southeastern end of Atatürk Alanı, although you can flag them down along their routes.

BLACK SEA COAST TRABZON

SERVICES FROM TRABZON'S OTOGAR

DESTINATION	FARE (₺)	DURATION (HR)	DISTANCE (KM)	FREQUENCY (PER DAY)
Ankara	60	12½	780	8
Erzurum	30	5	325	4
Hopa	20	2½	165	hourly
İstanbul	80	17½	1110	3
Kayseri	70	12	686	5
Rize	10	1½	75	hourly
Samsun	30	7	355	hourly
Sinop	50	9½	533	1
Tbilisi, Georgia (via Batumi)	50	9½	430	2

Sumela Monastery

The Greek Orthodox Monastery of the Virgin Mary, better known as **Sumela Monastery** (Sümela Manastırı; ☑ 0462-326 0748; www.sumela.com; Altındere Vadisi, Maçka; ₺25; ⊙ 9am-7pm Apr-Oct, 8am-4pm Nov-Mar), 46km south of Trabzon, is one of the Black Sea coast's historical highlights. Founded in the 4th century AD, it was abandoned in 1923 after the creation of the Turkish Republic and the 'exchange of populations'. Its highlight is the main church, with damaged but stunningly coloured frescoes both inside and out. Undergoing extensive renovation at the time of research, it was due to reopen in spring 2017.

Sumela (the name is derived from nearby Mt Melat) clings improbably to a sheer rock wall, high above evergreen forests and a rushing mountain stream. It's a mysterious place, especially when mists swirl in the tree-lined valley below (most of the time) and the call of a hidden mosque drifts ethereally through the forest.

Visit early or late to avoid the hordes of Turkish tourists. At the entrance to the **Altındere Vadisi Milli Parkı** (Altındere Valley National Park) there's a ₺10/5 charge for cars/motorbikes. About 2km further on is a shady riverside park with picnic tables and a restaurant.

The main trail to the monastery begins over the footbridge past the restaurant, and is steep but easy to follow. You'll ascend 300m in about 30 minutes, the air growing noticeably cooler as you climb through forests and alpine meadows. A second trail begins further up the valley. Follow the concreted road 1km uphill and across two bridges until you come to a wooden footbridge over the stream on the right. This trail cuts straight up through the trees, past the shell of the **Ayavarvara Chapel**. It's usually much quieter than the main route and takes the same amount of time.

You can drive almost to the monastery ticket office. The 3km drive is challenging at busy times, with cars coming the other way on the narrow mountain road. En route are **waterfalls** and a **lookout point**, from where you can see the monastery suspended on a cliff face high above the forest.

From the car park it's a 300m walk along a very rough and steep trail to the ticket office and monastery complex, sheltered underneath a hefty outcrop. On the way to the main church you'll pass the remains of a 19th-century aqueduct, a guards' room, a library with a fireplace, a kitchen, a bakery

BLACK SEA BITES

The local Black Sea cuisine provides quite a few tastes unique to the region (but increasingly popular throughout Turkey).

Not surprisingly fish reigns supreme in these parts and the *hamsi* (anchovy) is lord of them all. It's even used to make a dense cornbread peculiar to Rize, called *hamsikoli*. The damp coastal climate is perfect for things such as tea, hazelnuts and cherries, but bad for wheat, which is replaced by more accommodating corn (maize). Popular here is *muhlama* (or *kuymak*, as it's known in Trabzon), a polenta-like dish of cornmeal cooked with butter and cheese. Rib-stickingly filling, it's eaten as a staple, and if consumed at breakfast will set you up for a long day's trekking.

Despite what you may have read elsewhere, Tembel and Fadime – slang for a man and a woman from the region – do not have an obsession with cabbage. *Beyaz lahana* (white cabbage) is usually either pickled or cooked, while red cabbage (*kırmızı lahana*) is sliced finely in salads, but it certainly doesn't dominate Black Sea meals. What people eat in abundance here – in soups, stews, salads and *dolmas* – is *karalahana*: literally 'black cabbage' but actually a weedy-looking variety of collard. *Lahana sarması* (stuffed collard rolls) often contain corn or fish. *Karalahana çorbası* (collard soup with various other vegetables, including sweet green peppers, and cornmeal) is a speciality of Rize.

If your taste buds crave more saccharine stimulation, try *Laz böreği*, a delicious custard-soaked pastry devised by the Laz people, numerous in Rize province. The Hemshin, another minority of the region, are similarly famous for their skill with pastry. When you consider that many Black Sea pastry chefs are renowned throughout Turkey, you know it's going to be good.

Two great places to try Black Sea cuisine are **Kayadibi Saklıbahçe** (p515) in Maçka and **Vosporos** (p512) in Trabzon.

and a vaulted refectory. The two-part church, formed from a natural cave and also built in the shape of an extended apse, is covered both inside and out with colourful frescoes depicting everything from the Virgin Mary to the Last Judgement. The earliest examples date from the 9th century, but most are from the 19th century. Sadly, many have been defaced, some deliberately and in recent times.

The monastery has been substantially restored to showcase the various chapels and rooms used by pious types in earlier centuries. Continuing restoration in no way detracts from the experience, although on busy days views of the building will likely be more memorable than touring its cramped interiors.

Ulusoy and Metro run buses from Trabzon (₺25 return, one hour), leaving at 10am and departing from Sumela at 1pm/2pm in winter/summer. **Eyce Tours** (Map p510; ☑0462-326 7174; www.eycetours.com; Taksim İşhanı Sokak 11, 1st fl) in Trabzon runs organised tours.

Dolmuşes to Maçka (₺3, every 20 minutes) depart from the minibus ranks downhill from Atatürk Alanı, across the coast road from the port. Some carry on to Coşandere or even Sumela. A taxi to Maçka/Sumela costs ₺90/130; from Maçka to Sumela it's ₺40.

Driving from Trabzon, take the E97 highway south and turn left at Maçka, 29km from Trabzon. The monastery is also signposted as Meryemana (Virgin Mary), as it is known in the area.

🛏 Sleeping & Eating

Coşandere Tourist Resort   PENSION, MOTEL $$
(Coşandere Turistik Tesisleri; ☑0462-531 1190; www.cosandere.com; Sumela Yolu, Coşandere; r half/full board ₺125/150, bungalow half/full board ₺320/380; ⊛) Located in Coşandere, a stream-fed village 5km southeast of Maçka, this pension has converted, pine-clad *serenderler* (granaries) sleeping up to six, and a huge, wooden motel-like building favoured by groups. It's a handy way to get out and about in the mountains without your own transport, as various tours, treks and day trips are offered, including *yayla* (mountain) safaris.

The **restaurant** (☑0462-531 1190; www.cosandere.com; Sumela Yolu, Coşandere; mains ₺18), with outside tables, makes a cool and pleasant lunch stop for Akçaabat *köfte* or *saç kavurma* (cubed lamb or beef cooked in a heavy metal skillet).

★ **Kayadibi Saklıbahçe**   BLACK SEA $
(☑0462-512 2318; www.kayadibisaklibahce.com; Tünel Çıkışı, Maçka; mains ₺20; ⊙8am-11pm)

This 'Hidden Garden' restaurant with great views in Maçka wins hands down for offering the best Black Sea dishes in the region, including polenta-like cheesy *kuymak, etli karalahana sarması* (mince-stuffed collard leaves) and *mısır ekmeği* (cornbread). It's worth the trip in itself.

Uzungöl
☑0462 / POP 1600
With its lakeside mosque and forested mountains that recall Switzerland, the 'hidden valley' of Uzungöl (Long Lake) remains idyllic, but be prepared for more than a few tacky hotels. There are currently over 2000 rooms here, catering to a growing number of visitors from the Gulf States. A flurry of recent development, including a retaining wall against the lake, makes it feel a little artificial compared with much of the Kaçkars further east, but it makes a good base for hikes in the Soğanlı Mountains and to the tiny lakes around Demirkapı in the Haldizen Mountains. Summer weekends get very busy, so try to visit during the week.

Minibuses travel to/from Of (₺12), 43km north, and Trabzon (₺20).

Rize
☑0464 / POP 107,400
In the heart of Turkey's picturesque tea-growing area, Rize is a modern city centred on an attractive main square. The verdant slopes above town look almost southeast Asian, and are lavishly planted with çay, which is dried, blended and shipped throughout Turkey. Rizeans are equally proud of local-boy-turned-prime-minister Recep Tayyip Erdoğan, who grew up here and now has a university named after him.

The main square, with its inevitable Atatürk monument, beautifully reconstructed PTT and the Şeyh Camii (Sheik Mosque), is 200m inland from the coastal road. Principal thoroughfares Cumhuriyet Caddesi and Atatürk Caddesi run east from the square and parallel with the coast.

◉ Sights

Ziraat Tea Garden   GARDENS
(Narenciye Sokak 31) Rize's fragrant and floral tea garden is next to the Çaykur tea factory, 20 minutes' walk above town along the steep main road (Zihni Derin Caddesi) leading uphill behind the Şeyh Camii. Enjoy the superb

views with a fresh brew of local leaves, and see a scaled-down version of tea production. Taxis charge around ₺10 from the main square up to the garden.

Rize Castle — CASTLE

(Rize Kalesi; ⏰8am-11pm) FREE Built by the Byzantines on the steep hill at the back of town, Rize's ancient *kale* (castle) has both a lower castle and the so-called inner castle above it. The latter, which may date to the 6th century AD, contains a cafe with sweeping coastal views. To reach the castle, head west of the main square along Atatürk Caddesi and turn left up Kale Sokak; a taxi should cost about ₺10.

🛏 Sleeping & Eating

Green Hotel — HOTEL **$$**

(☑0464-236 0000; www.rizegreenotel.com; Cumhuriyet Caddesi 195; s/d ₺100/150; ❄🛜) With 72 well-appointed and clean rooms, just a little east of the town centre, the Green Hotel is a solid choice. The colour scheme can be a little hard on the eyes (picture mint green cosying up to flamingo pink and cherry red), but there's nothing to make your stay uncomfortable.

Sefam Iskender & Kebap — TURKISH **$**

(☑0464-201 0222; Deniz Caddesi 6a; mains ₺12-14; ⏰24hr) With a small terrace opening onto Deniz Caddesi's pedestrian strip, super-friendly Sefam is the place to go for local dishes such as *kuru fasulye* (white beans stewed with meat) and *laz böreği* (pastry with custard).

Evvel Zaman — TURKISH **$$**

(☑0464-212 2188; www.evvelzaman.com.tr; Harem Sokak 2; mains ₺18-25; ⏰9am-11pm; 🚗) This lovingly restored Ottoman house on the southeast edge of the main square is like a joyously jumbled museum, even displaying cases of swords and daggers. It's a great place to try traditional Black Sea dishes such as *hamsi pilavi* (anchovy pilaf) and a *köy kahvaltısı* (village breakfast) that makes use of produce from local villages.

ℹ Getting There & Away

Bus-company offices and travel agents front the main square.

Frequent minibuses run to Hopa (₺18, 1½ hours) and Trabzon (₺16, 1¼ hours). For the northern Kaçkars, take an east-bound minibus to Ardeşen (₺5) or, better, Pazar (₺5) and change.

The otogar is along the old coast road, 2km northwest of the main square. For Trabzon,

Pazar, Ardeşen and Hopa, it's easier to pick up a local minibus from the small otogar next to Halkbank, a few blocks northeast of the main square.

Hopa

📞0466 / POP 18,900

Just 37km southwest of the Georgian border, Hopa is the archetypal border town, with cheap hotels, traders markets and takeaway-food shops. On the shaded streets inland from the seafront highway are cafes clicking to backgammon counters, windowless bars, shoe shiners and a town going about its everyday business, seamlessly mixing old and new – headscarves and mobile-phone shops – in classic Turkish fashion. While it's perfectly pleasant, it's not worth overnighting here unless you arrive late en route to/from Georgia.

🛏 Sleeping & Eating

Eateries cluster around and behind the hotels on Sahil Caddesi.

Otel Heyamo — BUSINESS HOTEL **$$**

(☑0466-351 2315; www.hotelheyamo.com; Sahil Caddesi 44; s/d ₺90/120; ❄🛜) Behind the gushing-waterfall artwork of the lobby and the fluoro-lit corridors lie 40 garish but comfortable bedrooms, with flat-screen TVs, small desks and towels artfully folded into swan shapes. Half the rooms have balconies facing the sea and there's a large, bright breakfast room on the roof.

Green Garden Kebap — PIDE, KEBAP **$**

(☑0466-351 4277; Eski Hopa Artvin Yolu, Belediye Parkı; mains ₺15-20; ⏰11am-midnight) Named for the public garden onto which its tables spill, this friendly, well-run *lokanta* and *kebap salonu* does great pide, *lahmacun*, kebaps and salads. Little English is spoken, but a pictorial menu and plenty of goodwill make it an easy, tasty experience.

ℹ Getting There & Away

Hopa's otogar is on the old coastal road 1.5km west of town (₺1 by dolmuş). Seven buses a day leave for Erzurum (₺40, three hours) and there are plenty for Artvin (₺20, 1½ hours), Rize (₺10, 2½ hours) and Trabzon (₺25, 2½ hours).

For Georgia, **Metro** (www.metroturizm.com.tr) serves Tbilisi (₺40, eight hours) at 7am and 1am via Batumi (₺10, one hour, hourly). From Batumi take bus 16 to the border, then a waiting minibus to Hopa.

A taxi to the Georgian border from Hopa costs ₺35.

Eastern Anatolia

Best Places to Eat

➡ Sini Ev (p540)
➡ Emirşeyh Nedim (p522)
➡ Ocakbaşı Restoran (p539)
➡ Hanımeli Kars Mutfağı (p541)

Best Places to Sleep

➡ Hotel Katerina Sarayı (p539)
➡ Taşmektep Otel (p527)
➡ Otel Doğa (p527)
➡ Laşet Bungalov Tatil Evleri (p537)
➡ Karahan Pension (p534)

Why Go?

If you've a soft spot for far-flung outposts, make a beeline for Turkey's northeast. Despite its awe-inspiring landscapes and ruins such as Ani, you may have precipitous gorges, expansive steppe, soaring mountains and highland pastures to yourself. No wonder the region, especially the Kaçkar Mountains, is prime territory for trekking, skiing and white-water rafting.

Southeastern Anatolia is a unique part of Turkey, with a predominantly -Kurdish population that is extremely welcoming to visitors. Sadly, fighting between the PKK (Kurdistan Workers Party) and Turkish government forces, along with possible effects of the Syrian conflict in territory near the border, have rendered large areas risky for travellers. Check your government's travel advice before considering travelling here.

Nemrut Dağı National Park, a highlight of Turkish travel with its haunting 2000-year-old statues, is not, at the time of writing, considered risky.

When to Go
Erzurum

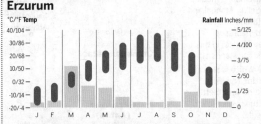

May Vivid hues and scents as the steppe blossoms and spring warmth awakens mountain pastures.

Jun–Sep Hike and raft around the Kaçkar Mountains, and visit Nemrut Dağı National Park.

Dec–Apr Cross-country ski in the Kaçkars and see Ani looking atmospheric in the snow.

Eastern Anatolia Highlights

❶ Ani (p543)
Losing yourself in the ruins of this medieval Armenian capital strewn across the windswept steppe.

❷ Kaçkar Mountains (p523)
Trekking across 3000m-plus passes or high-level *yaylalar* (mountain pastures), or enjoying day walks from quaint villages such as Barhal or Olgunlar.

❸ Georgian churches (p537)
Exploring the haunting remains of 1000-year-old churches such as Öşkvank.

❹ Kars (p538)
Hanging out in this distinctive Russian-influenced city with enjoyable restaurants and cafes, and a historic castle.

❺ Nemrut Dağı (p552) Soak up the eerie vibes while watching the sun set (or rise) from the 'thrones of gods'.

❻ Erzurum (p520) Discovering a fascinating medley of Seljuk, Mongol and Ottoman mosques and *medreses* (seminaries) in this bustling steppe city.

❼ White-water rafting (p526) Testing your mettle on the rivers around Yusufeli.

❽ Mt Ararat (p549) Making the (nontechnical) ascent of Turkey's majestic highest peak (5137m) when it is open to climbers.

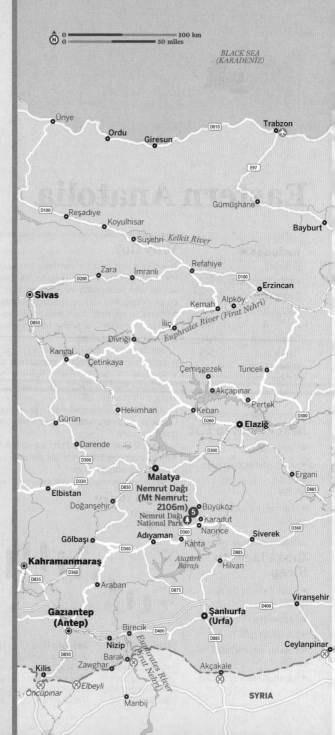

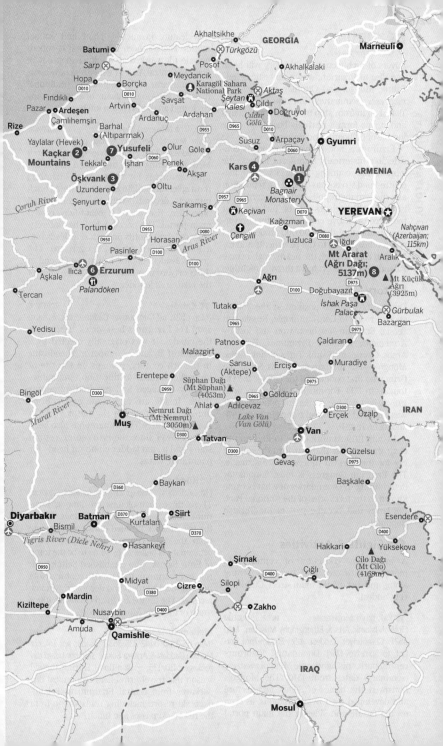

ERZURUM

📞 0442 / POP 386,000

Lovers of architecture and history will be in paradise in Erzurum, where fantastic Seljuk, Saltuk, Mongol and Ottoman mosques and *medreses* (seminaries) line the main drag. Take it all in from atop the citadel: mountains and steppe form a heavenly backdrop to the jumble of billboards and minarets.

Erzurum is not a city resting on its considerable historically significant laurels; the vibrant life coursing along its shopping-centre-lined streets has earned it a reputation as a modern metropolis and an eastern Turkish hub. Although it's one of Turkey's most pious, conservative cities, it has two universities with more than 100,000 students who add a relaxed buzz to the pavements and cafes. And come winter, the nearby high-octane Palandöken ski resort has a thriving nightlife.

History

Due to its strategic position at the confluence of roads to Constantinople, Russia and Persia, Erzurum has been won and lost by Armenians, Romans, Byzantines, Persians, Arabs, Georgians, Saltuk Turks, Seljuk Turks, Mongols and Turkomans. It was Selim the Grim who first conquered the city for the Ottomans in 1514. For much of its history until 1915 it had a large Armenian population. It was captured by Russian troops in 1829, 1878 and again in 1916.

In July 1919 Atatürk came to Erzurum to chair the congress that provided the rallying cry for the Turkish independence struggle. The Erzurum Congress is most famous for determining the boundaries of what became known as the territories of the National Pact, the lands that became part of the Turkish Republic.

◉ Sights & Activities

A marvellous collection of centuries-old mosques, *medreses* and tombs is strung along, and just off, the main street, Cumhuriyet Caddesi.

★ **Yakutiye Medresesi**　　MEDRESE, MUSEUM
(Turkish-Islamic Arts & Ethnography Museum; Map p521; Cumhuriyet Caddesi; ₺5; ⊙8am-7pm Apr-Oct, to 5pm Nov-Mar) Dominating Erzurum's central park, this handsome Mongol *medrese* (seminary) dates from 1310. The Mongols borrowed the basics of Seljuk architecture and developed their own variations, as seen on the facade and sides of the main portal

that feature geometric, plant and animal motifs. The southern minaret sports superb mosaic tile work that wouldn't look out of place in Central Asia. The *medrese* now houses a museum with exhibits on traditional regional crafts and tableaux of a Koran study circle and an old Erzurum kitchen.

★ **Çifte Minareli Medrese**　　MEDRESE
(Twin Minaret Seminary; Map p521; Cumhuriyet Caddesi) The Seljuk-style Çifte Minareli Medrese, dating from the second half of the 13th century, is for most people Erzurum's most splendid building. The twin fluted brick minarets, decorated with eye-catching small blue tiles, rise above a beautifully carved main portal. The portal, which has interestingly different motifs on each side, leads into a long, dignified porticoed courtyard. The grand 12-sided, domed hall at the far end of the courtyard may have served as the tomb of the *medrese*'s founder.

★ **Kalesi**　　FORTRESS
(Map p521; off Cumhuriyet Caddesi; ₺5; ⊙8am-5pm) For Erzurum's best views, head up to the citadel. It was originally erected by a general of Byzantine emperor Theodosius in the 5th century, perhaps on the site of an earlier Urartu fortification, and subsequently damaged and repaired numerous times. Inside are a mosque and a brick minaret constructed by the Saltuk Turks in the 12th century. The minaret has also been a clock tower since the 19th century: spiral stairs and a step ladder climb up inside for panoramic vistas.

Üç Kümbetler　　TOMB
(Three Tombs; Map p521; off Yenikapi Caddesi) These three mausoleums are among Erzurum's most perfect small buildings. While the two smaller 12-sided ones probably date from the 14th century, the largest one – octagonal – is believed by some to be the tomb of Emir Saltuk, who established Saltuk Turk rule in Erzurum in the late 11th century. Note the near-conical roofs and decorated window recesses. The tombs are in an enclosure 100m south of the Çifte Minareli Medrese.

Medam Turizm　　SKIING
(Map p521; 📞0442-235 3538; Esadaş apt 1/4, cnr Mumcu Caddesi & Ankara Sokak; ski/snowboard day package ₺110/135; ⊙8am-11pm) During the ski season this travel firm offers economical day packages from central Erzurum to Paland-öken ski resort, including transport to/from the resort, ski passes and lunch.

Erzurum

Erzurum

◎ Top Sights
1 Çifte Minareli Medrese	D3
2 Kalesi	C2
3 Yakutiye Medresesi	B3

◎ Sights
4 Üç Kümbetler	D3

✦ Activities, Courses & Tours
5 Medam Turizm	B2

⊜ Sleeping
6 Butik Rafo Otel	B1
7 Hekimoğlu Otel	B1
8 Hotel Grand Hitit	B1

⊗ Eating
9 Arzen	B3
10 Aspava	B3
11 Çagin Cağ Kebap Lokanta	C1
12 Emirşeyh Nedim	D3
13 Erzurum Evleri	C3
14 Güzelyurt Restaurant	B3
15 Kılıçoğlu	B3
16 Salon Asya	B3

⊝ Shopping
17 Rüstem Paşa Çarşısı	C2

🛏 Sleeping

Several dependable budget and midrange options cluster around Kazım Karabekir Caddesi, about 600m north of the main thoroughfare of Cumhuriyet Caddesi. For top-end accommodation, stay at the Palandöken ski resort, 5km south of central Erzurum.

Hekimoğlu Otel　　　　HOTEL **$$**
(Map p521; ☎0442-234 3049; hekimogluotel omer@hotmail.com; Kazım Karabekir Caddesi 66; s/d/tr ₺60/100/130; 🛜) With a jovial, welcoming team at reception, the Hekimoğlu is a good-value option in Erzurum's main hotel area. Rooms are simple and on the small side,

but are clean and the pink bedspreads add a touch of colour. There's a busy *lokanta* (eatery serving ready-made food) downstairs, so that's everything sorted after a long Anatolian bus ride.

Hotel Grand Hitit HOTEL $$

(Map p521; ☑0442-233 5001; www.grandhitit hotel.com.tr; Kazım Karabekir Caddesi 26; s/d/tr ₺110/170/240; ❀❂) The Hitit has pleasant, good-sized rooms with a modern feel to the light- or dark-wood decor. Well-sprung mattresses, sizeable bathrooms, minibars and safes. It's professionally run and a good choice for solo women travellers.

Butik Rafo Otel BOUTIQUE HOTEL $$$

(Map p521; ☑0442-235 0225; www.rafootel. com; Milletbahçe Sokak 25; s/d ₺130/210; ❀❂) Rooms with splashes of bright colour, panels of stone-cube tiling, light-wood decor, good wi-fi and a comfortable feel just about justify the 'Butik' label. Rooms and bathrooms are medium-sized, but you can relax in two large, bright lobby-lounges – one with a soothing fish tank.

✖ Eating & Drinking

Eateries on Cumhuriyet Caddesi serve everything from *çiğ köfte* (raw ground lamb mixed with pounded bulgur, onion, spices and salt) to *lokum* (Turkish delight). Head to **Arzen** (Map p521; Cumhuriyet Caddesi; snacks & light dishes ₺5-12; ❂7am-midnight; ❂) or **Kılıçoğlu** (Map p521; Cumhuriyet Caddesi 13; cakes & desserts ₺9-10; ❂6am-midnight; ❂) for baklava, ice cream and espresso coffee, or to **Aspava** (Map p521; Cumhuriyet Caddesi; mains ₺8-14; ❂24hr) or **Salon Asya** (Map p521; Cumhuriyet Caddesi 27; mains ₺8-14; ❂8am-midnight) for pide and kebaps at good prices.

★ Emirşeyh Nedim KEBAP, KÖFTE $

(Map p521; www.emirseyh.com.tr; Tebrizkapı Caddesi 172; mains ₺12-18; ❂9am-11pm; ❂) Erzurum's choice meat-eating experience is a lovely two-storey building with carved stone pillars and beautifully painted recessed ceilings. With very good food and efficient, friendly service, it's popular with everyone from families to couples and groups of friends. You won't go wrong with the Emirşeyh *köfte* (meatballs), any of the kebaps or a *karışık ızgara* (mixed grill), all prepared at open ranges.

Çagin Cağ Kebap Lokanta KEBAP $

(Map p521; Orhan Şerifsoy Caddesi; mains ₺7-20; ❂7am-10pm) A friendly place with bright,

modern decor, specialising in local favourite *cağ kebap* (mutton grilled on a horizontal spit). You can either use a fork to eat the wood-fired morsels or follow the lead of the locals and consume straight from the skewer. Each skewer is ₺7 and comes with flatbread and tasty salads and dips. The waiter will keep offering you more until you're full.

Erzurum Evleri ANATOLIAN $

(Map p521; www.tarihierzurumevleri.com; Yüzbaşı Sokak 5; mains ₺10-25; ❂9am-11pm) This cluster of three-centuries-old houses has been restored as an atmospheric restaurant-cafe. A warren of small rooms and alcoves are set with cushions at low tables; a couple of larger rooms have chairs and regular-height tables; and all are filled with Ottoman paraphernalia. The tasty fare, centred on local Erzurum dishes, includes soups, *böregi* (cheese-stuffed pastries) and a good *tandır kebap* (shredded lamb served here with rice, mashed potato and salad).

Güzelyurt Restaurant TURKISH, EUROPEAN $$

(Map p521; ☑0442-234 5001; www.guzelyurt restaurant.com.tr; Cumhuriyet Caddesi 42; mezes ₺5-14, mains ₺14-28; ❂noon-midnight; ❂❂) Erzurum's smartest restaurant, operating since 1928, is quaintly anachronistic, with shrouded windows and bow-tied waiters creating an old-fashioned charm. It's licensed, and a good place to splurge on a fine meal, though servings are not huge. The many meze offerings include plenty of vegetarian options, while main dishes are predominantly meaty, from the speciality *şiş tava* (tender beef chunks with tomato, capsicum and shallot) to Wienerschnitzel.

🛍 Shopping

Rüstem Paşa Çarşısı JEWELLERY

(Taşhan; Map p521; Adnan Menderes Caddesi; ❂8am-11pm) Erzurum is known for the manufacture of jewellery and other items from *oltutaşı*, the local black amber. Browse or buy it in this atmospheric *çarşı* (market), built as a caravanserai in the 16th century by Süleyman the Magnificent's grand vizier.

ℹ Information

Tourist Office (Map p521; www.facebook. com/erzurumtdb; Havuzbaşı; ❂10am-6pm) The very helpful, English-speaking staff here will go out of their way to assist tourists. Good maps and brochures available, too.

❶ Getting There & Away

AIR

Anadolu Jet (p605) To/from İstanbul, Ankara and Bursa.
Pegasus Airlines (p605) To/from İstanbul.
Sun Express (p605) To/from İzmir.
Turkish Airlines (p605) To/from İstanbul and Ankara.

BUS

The otogar (bus station) is 9km northwest of the centre along the airport road. Bus companies have offices on and near the western part of Cumhuriyet Caddesi. **Metro** (p606) serves many destinations.

For Kars, **Kars Vipturizm** (p542) runs midi-buses (₺25, three hours) every one or two hours from 7.30am to 6pm departing from an office on Yavuz Sultan Selim Bulvarı in the Yenişehir district 2km south of the centre. Tickets are sold at the **Kamilkoç office** (Cumhuriyet Caddesi; ⏰ 9am-10pm) and *servis* minibuses take you to the departure point from there.

Buses to Yusufeli, and most of those to Artvin and Hopa, are run by **Yeşil Artvin Ekspres** (www.yesilartvinekspres.com.tr). Tickets for these, and for buses to Diyarbakır, are sold at the **Has Bingöl office** (Çaykara Caddesi). Yeşil Artvin Ekspres buses start from the otogar and most of them stop at **Şükrüpaşa Semt Garajı** (off Necip Fazıl Kısakürek Caddesi), a small terminal about 3km north of the centre, about 15 to 20 minutes later. Dolmuşes (minibuses) to the Şükrüpaşa Semt Garajı (₺2) leave every few minutes from Hastaneler Caddesi (the first corner north of the Havuzbaşı roundabout).

For Doğubayazıt, most buses leave at pre-dawn hours but Ağrı Yavuz Turizm has a bus at 11.30am; buy tickets from the **Kanberoğlu office** (Çaykara Caddesi).

For Iran, take a bus to Doğubayazıt and connect from there.

TRAIN

The daily **Doğu Ekspresi** (http://en.tcdd.gov.tr/mainline-trains+m97) departs at 1.57pm to Kars (₺16.50, 4½ hours), and at 12.26pm to Ankara (₺41, 20 hours), via Sivas (₺23, 10 hours) and Kayseri (₺29, 13 hours).

CAR

The international car-rental firms Europcar, Avis and Enterprise have branches in Erzurum.

❶ Getting Around

A taxi to/from the airport, 13 km northwest of town, costs around ₺50. Buses meet planes and travel into central Erzurum for ₺2.50: going out to the airport, these are marked 'Havalimanı' and leave from a **bus stop** (Map p521) on Hastaneler Caddesi 80 minutes before flight departure times.

Some bus companies run *servis* minibuses between the otogar and the centre. City bus K4 (₺2.50) also connects the otogar and centre: going out to the otogar, catch the bus at the southbound stop on Hastaneler Caddesi just north of Havuzbaşı roundabout. A taxi should cost ₺35.

KAÇKAR MOUNTAINS

The Kaçkar Mountains (Kaçkar Dağları) are the easternmost and highest part of the Pontic Alps (in Turkish: Kuzey Anadolu Dağları, meaning North Anatolian Mountains), which stretch about 1000km west to east, inland from the Black Sea. The main line of 3000m-plus peaks stretches about

SERVICES FROM ERZURUM'S OTOGAR

DESTINATION	FARE (₺)	DURATION (HR)	DISTANCE (KM)	FREQUENCY (PER DAY)
Ankara	65-75	12-14	872	approx 20
Artvin	30	3	192	4
Diyarbakır	50	6	320	7
Doğubayazıt	30	4	275	4
Hopa	40	5	266	4
İstanbul	80-90	17-20	1290	approx 15
Kayseri	50-60	9-11	628	10
Rize	40	6	390	13
Trabzon	30-35	5	310	approx 20
Van	40	7	410	6
Yusufeli	25	2½	140	3

Kaçkar Mountains

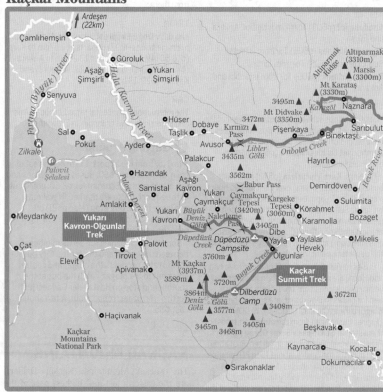

50km southwest to northeast, with craggy, snow-covered heights rising above mountain lakes and high-level *yaylalar* (mountain pastures) and dense forests clothing the valleys of rushing rivers down below.

It's well worth spending a few days to explore this stunning region. Hiking amid spectacular scenery is what pulls most visitors here. There are dozens of possible routes, from day hikes in the valleys and *yaylalar*, to multiday treks across the range or ascents (nontechnical) of the highest point, Mt Kaçkar (Kaçkar Dağı; 3937m). Other area attractions include white-water rafting, and experiencing the life of the local people, who occupy their high-altitude villages only during the summer months.

🏃 Activities

In addition to hiking, trekking and rafting, ski touring attracts some visitors in winter: you need to bring your own gear and make arrangements in advance. **Kardelen** (☑ 0537 243 1648, 0464-657 2107; www.ayderkardelen. com; s/d/tr/q ₺100/200/300/320; ☺mid-Mar– Dec; P ⊜ 🛜) in Ayder and Kaçkar Pansiyon (p534) in Olgunlar are among lodgings that host skiers, and **Türkü Tour** (☑ 0464-651 7230; www.turkutour.com; İnönü Caddesi 47) offers winter programs.

Hiking

The Kaçkars hiking season is short; the best time to tackle the higher mountain routes is between mid-July and the end of August, when the snowline is highest, though some routes can be possible from late June to mid-September, depending on weather conditions. From May to September or even October there are plenty of walks on the lower slopes (also weather permitting). Conditions are most dependably dry and clear in July and August, and the autumn colours in September and October are beautiful.

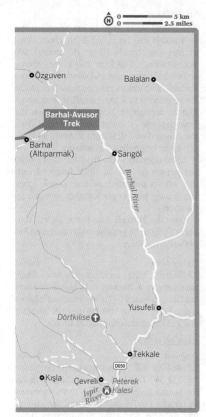

0 ————— 5 km
0 ————— 2.5 miles

Özgüven

Balalan

Barhal-Avusor Trek

Barhal (Altıparmak)

Sarıgöl

Barhal River

Yusufeli

Dörtkilise

Tekkale

D050

Kışla Çevreli Peterek
İspir Kalesi
River

Treks across the range can last from one day upwards. Week-long routes, including circular ones, taking in a number of different valleys and passes are possible. The easiest pass, and the only one where the trail is marked (by cairns), is the 3100m Babur Pass between Palakçur on the west side and Körahmet on the east. The most frequently used trans-Kaçkar route is the Naletleme Pass (3215m) between Yukarı Kavron (west) and Olgunlar (east); this route takes one (long) day.

Ascents to the summit of Mt Kaçkar normally start from the Dilberdüzü base camp (p534), which is 7.5km (about 3½ hours' walk) up from Olgunlar. You climb from the camp to the summit (1100m higher) and return to the camp in one long day. In season, Dilberdüzü has a cafeteria, tents, mats and sleeping bags for rent, and a mountain-guide service. If you're not up for a long trek, the hike from Olgunlar to Dilberdüzü and back is a good day's outing in itself.

A popular trekking option (minimum four days) is to combine the summit ascent with crossing the range once or twice. Other possible routes head across the Altıparmak range in the north (two or three days from Barhal to Avusor or vice versa), or make a four-to-six-day circuit from Olgunlar or Yaylalar to west-side villages such as Yukarı Kavron, Amlakit or Elevit via passes to the south or southwest of Mt Kaçkar.

There are pensions in several villages on the west side of the range, and in Barhal, Yaylalar and Olgunlar on the east side. But camping is necessary on some treks. A further option, if you are not desperate to cross the range, is to base yourself in a pension and take day walks from there. There is stunning scenery almost anywhere you go. On the west side, the Samistal area, accessible by road from Palovit, is one of the loveliest. On the east, English-language leaflets detailing six local day walks, published by Culture Routes in Turkey, are available at pensions in Barhal, Yaylalar and Olgunlar.

As a general rule, you have to climb above the treeline at about 1900m to get the most panoramic views, but walks at lower altitudes can also be stunning, with a scenery of rushing rivers, ancient Georgian churches and Ottoman bridges in the forests.

For anything more than day hikes, do as much preparatory homework about routes and arrangements as you can.

RESOURCES

The following are useful hiking and trekking resources:

➤ *The Kaçkar: Trekking in Turkey's Black Sea Mountains* is a highly recommended book detailing many Kaçkar routes and includes an excellent map plus good planning and background material; available from www.trekkinginturkey.com.

➤ *Culture Routes in Turkey* (www.cultureroutesinturkey.com) has accommodation listings and other Kaçkar information.

➤ *Kulindağ Dağevi* (www.kulindag.com) has information on village pensions and mountain lodges.

➤ The *Kaçkar* website (www.kackar.org) is in Turkish, but has useful maps and photos.

GUIDES

It's a good idea to hire a local who knows the trails if you plan to tackle high altitudes or multiday hikes. The walks are mostly unsigned, and misty weather can make orientation difficult at any time of year. Guides can also arrange mules to carry your luggage and camping equipment, and transport to/from trailheads. For the main trekking season (July and August) it's advisable to make enquiries in advance about guides and pack animals, as they can get heavily booked up.

Essential equipment includes good boots and waterproofs, clothes for both cold and hot weather, sunblock and head coverings. Guides can often provide camping, sleeping and cooking equipment, but it's cheaper if you bring your own. Meals may be included in your deal, but if you are bringing your own food, you are expected to feed the guide, too.

Cappadocia-based nationwide hiking specialist **Middle Earth Travel** (www.middleearthtravel. com) runs one-week group walking and trekking tours in the Kaçkars with English-speaking guides for around €760 per person, including Trabzon or Erzurum airport transfers. Local operator **Türkü Tour** (p524) does week-long group programs for around ₺1700 to ₺1900.

Pensions in villages including Ayder, Yukarı Kavron, Barhal, Yaylalar and Olgunlar can organise guided treks. **Barhal Pansiyon** (📞 0535 264 6765, Germany +49 89 818 981 619; www. barhalpansiyon.com; half-board per person mid-Jun–Sep ₺75, Oct–mid-Jun ₺65; 🅿 🛜) and **Karahan Pension** (p534) in Barhal and **Çamyuva Pension** (p534) in Yaylalar are especially recommended. Typical basic costs include ₺150 a day for a mule and guide, and ₺40 a day for a tent and two sleeping mats. A mule can carry bags for three people.

For fully guided treks for two people, including tents, mat, transport and food, expect to pay around US$200 to US$250 per day with a professional operation from Ayder.

Çoruh Outdoor (📞 0533 453 3179, 0466-811 3151; www.coruhoutdoor.com.tr; Ersis Caddesi, Yusufeli) This established firm offers rafting, hiking, trekking and sightseeing trips. The office is not always open, but you can contact director Sirali Aydin by phone: he speaks some English.

Rafting

The Çoruh River, and the Barhal and İspir Rivers which meet at Yusufeli to form the Çoruh, are among the world's best white-water rafting rivers, with superb rapids and brilliant play holes, and rafting options from grade II to grade V.

Sadly the construction of the Yusufeli dam, about 12km downstream of Yusufeli on the Çoruh, will put an end to most of the white water (and will also involve flooding the town). The dam may be completed by 2019.

Rafting is possible from May to October on the Fırtına (Büyük) River below Çamlıhemşin. The rapids are smaller than the more exciting waters near Yusufeli, but the Fırtına has arguably more impressive scenery.

YUSUFELI

The Barhal River from below Sarigöl down to Yusufeli can be rafted from about April to mid-June (grade III to IV, around two hours rafting). The İspir and Çoruh Rivers, respectively upstream and downstream from Yusufeli, with grades ranging from II (suitable for beginners) to V, can be rafted from about May to September. However, rafting on the İspir depends on water being released from the Arkun dam 34km from Yusufeli, and this can never be predicted in advance.

Local operators run trips for about ₺100 per person for two to three hours of rafting, with a minimum of four people (they can usually put people together to make up numbers).

Once the Yusufeli dam is completed, rafting is likely to be possible only on about 5km of the Barhal River.

Oktay Alkan   RAFTING
(📞 0466-811 3620; www.birolrafting.com; Greenpiece Camping & Pansiyon, Arıklı Mahallesi) Local lad Oktay is coach to Turkey's national slalom canoe team; he's in Yusufeli over the summer and guides rafting trips at that time.

ÇAMLIHEMŞIN

Dağ-Raft   RAFTING
(📞 0464-752 4070; www.dagraft.com; per person ₺60-120; 👣) Dag-Raft offers rafting trips on the Fırtına River for all levels from beginners up (grades I to IV; 3km to 13km), and also offers ziplining across the rushing river (₺15). It's 13km from Çamlıhemşin on the Ardeşen road.

Western Kaçkars

The western side of the Kaçkars, easily accessed from the Black Sea coast, comprises the valleys of the fast-flowing Hala (or Kavron) and Fırtına (or Büyük) Rivers, meeting at Çamlıhemşin, and their many tributaries. The area is a rainy one, and the steep valley sides are covered in wonderfully luxuriant forest. Above the treeline at about 1900m the upper valleys have much open *yaylalar* (mountain pastures) with a backdrop of craggy, snow-capped mountains. In season (roughly from June to September, depending on the weather) there is wonderful walking and trekking around the upland valleys and their seasonal *yayla* villages. The passes over to the southern and eastern sides of the Kaçkars can be crossed from about July to September.

April to June are the wettest months (typically more than 20 rainy days each). July and August are among the driest.

Çamlıhemşin & Around

☑ 0464

At an altitude of 300m, 20km off the D010 coast road, the tiny town of Çamlıhemşin is a climatic transition point. Mist and drizzle indicate that you've left the coastal zone, and once you continue further up the valleys, you experience increasing alpine influence in climate, terrain and vegetation. Çamlıhemşin is a functional, workaday spot, but has an appealing authenticity. The locals are mostly Hemşin.

At the top end of Çamlıhemşin the road forks: left up the Hala valley to Ayder (17km) or straight on up the Fırtına valley towards Çat. Both are beautiful routes up densely wooded valleys, passing several elegant Ottoman-era arched stone bridges across the rivers, frequently adorned with selfie-posing tourists.

Çamlıhemşin has a post office, supermarket, ATM and (2km down towards the coast) a petrol station. Stock up on provisions.

The **Tourist Office** (⊙ 8am-5pm Mon-Fri) is a welcoming place in the *belediye* (town hall) building by the main road at the north end of town. Some English spoken.

🛏 Sleeping & Eating

★**Otel Doğa**   GUESTHOUSE **$$**

(☑ 0464-651 7455; www.facebook.com/oteldoga; Şenyuva Yolu; r per person ₺50, half-board ₺75; ⊙ Apr-Oct; [P](⊕)(?)) Right beside the river on the beautiful Fırtına valley road, 4.5km south of Çamlıhemşin, this friendly, old-fashioned hotel is welcoming and well kept. Good home-cooked local meals are served in the riverside

dining room. Nearly all bedrooms have private bathrooms and many have balconies; go for a corner room.

★**Taşmektep Otel**   BOUTIQUE HOTEL **$$$**

(☑ 0464-651 7010; www.facebook.com/camlihem sintasmektepotel; Halil Şişman Caddesi, Konaklar Mahallesi; s/d/tr mid-May–Jul & Sep–mid-Nov €45/75/100, Aug €60/90/110; ⊙ mid-May–mid-Nov; [P](⊕)(?)) One kilometre south of Çamlıhemşin en route to the Fırtına Valley, a historic stone schoolhouse has been transformed by a local NGO into this excellent boutique hotel. It has a contemporary country feel, and plenty of photos and antiques to tell of the building's and local community's histories. Rooms are spacious, airy and pine furnished.

Ekodanitap   PENSION **$$$**

(☑ 0464-651 7787; www.ekodanitap.com; Aşağı Çamlıca Yolu; half-board bungalows s/d/tr/q ₺200/320/480/640, tree houses s/d ₺110/220; (?)) 🍽 Highly original Ekodanitap is hidden 1km up a winding road (signposted just before Çamlıhemşin when approaching from the coast) and then 400m along a forest footpath. Good meals featuring home-grown organic produce are served on a terrace overlooking the deep, green Fırtına valley. Accommodation is in four wooden bungalows with terraces (comfy enough, though not luxurious), or tiny 'tree houses' with shared bathrooms.

ℹ Getting There & Away

Dolmuşes (minibuses) run about hourly, 8am to 6pm, from Pazar on the coast to Çamlıhemşin (₺5, 45 minutes) and on to Ayder (₺7, 30 minutes) and vice versa. Those going down to Pazar stop at Ardeşen town en route, but those going up to Çamlıhemşin stop at the turn-off from the coast road, 3km west of Ardeşen.

HEMŞIN CULTURE

The northwestern side of the Kaçkars is the homeland of the Hemşin people, thought by many to be descended from medieval Armenian settlers, though they are now Turkish-speaking and Muslim. The Hemşin traditionally migrated with their herds from lowland homes to upland *yayla* (mountain pasture) villages in summer, but most Hemşin have now moved away to towns or further to other countries, and return to their *yayla* villages chiefly for summer holidays or seasonal tourism work.

In summer you may spot groups of Hemşin holidaymakers gathering in meadows to dance the *horon*, a cross between the conga and the hokey-pokey, set to the distinctive whining skirl of the *tulum*, a type of goat-skin bagpipe. You'll also see women all around the mountains wearing splendid headdresses, often incongruously matched with cardigans, long skirts and running shoes or woollen boots. Many Hemşin émigrés return from overseas for the **Çamlıhemşin Ayder Festival** (p531).

528

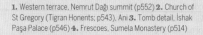

1. Western terrace, Nemrut Dağı summit (p552) 2. Church of St Gregory (Tigran Honents; p543), Ani 3. Tomb detail, İshak Paşa Palace (p546) 4. Frescoes, Sumela Monastery (p514)

IZZET KERIBAR / GETTY IMAGES ©

Historical Highlights

Across the rugged swath of northern and eastern Anatolia the historical ebb and flow of conquering, trading and colonising civilisations is revealed in a compelling roll call of ancient cities, grandiose monuments and hushed religious structures. Amid this sprawling region of deserts, mountains and steppe, look forward to being immersed in wildly scenic landscapes as you discover testaments to 12 millennia of history.

Sumela Monastery

From the silvery coastline of the Black Sea, ascend through misty forests to this Byzantine monastery. Founded in the 4th century it now seemingly defies gravity as it clings to sheer rocks.

Ani

On the desolate steppe bordering Armenia, consider the power, glory and eventual downfall of this once world-leading city that was a vital stop on the ancient Silk Road trade route.

Dörtkilise

Tracking down the northeast's romantically ruined medieval Georgian churches in their isolated locations is a fascinating adventure; none more so than the still-majestic 10th-century Dörtkilise in a green river valley 6km from Tekkale village.

İshak Paşa Palace

A wonderful reminder of eastern Anatolia's multiple cultures with its Seljuk, Ottoman, Persian, Armenian and other decorative styles. Enjoy its heavenly stone carving and heavenly panoramas of Turkey's highest mountain, Ararat.

Nemrut Dağı

Be astounded by one man's megalomania amid the giant stone heads on this peak rising from ancient lands. Spending sunrise or sunset atop the summit reinforces a sense of the march of time and the transience of all great empires.

Fırtına Valley

☑ 0464

This steep-sided, beautifully green river valley, used as a location in the Turkish film *Bal* (Honey), is a wonderful place to experience traditional Hemşin life. Along the 7km stretch from Çamlıhemşin to Şenyuva, winch wires, for hoisting goods up to remote mountain houses, criss-cross the thickly forested slopes above the road. Look for the hillside mansions built in the early 20th century by families enriched by their menfolk working as chefs and bakers in pre-revolutionary Russia.

Graceful arched stone bridges built in early Ottoman times cross the rushing Fırtına River 5km from Çamlıhemşin (just after Otel Doğa) and at Şenyuva. From the latter you'll get supreme bridge views from the cafe terrace 200m upstream.

The road up the valley is paved as far as Çat (1250m), a riverside hamlet that can be used as a trekking base, 27km from Çamlıhemşin.

◎ Sights

Zilkale CASTLE

(adult/child & senior ₺3/free; ☉ 8am-6pm or later; P) South from Şenyuva the road climbs into the hills to reach the restored 13th-century Zil Castle after 5.5km. A rectangular stone tower surrounded by sturdy walls on a rock pinnacle above the sheer gorge, this was a defensive outpost for both Byzantines and Ottomans. The hillside across the road is thick with rhododendrons.

Çat Yayla VILLAGE

The Çat summer village (1800m), where locals move to in the warmer months when the road is passable, lies 3.5km uphill from Çat. It's well worth the walk for the *yaylalar*, overlooked by snowy peaks and swathed in buttercups in spring. Turn left 700m after the Çılanç Köprüsü, an Ottoman-period arched bridge on the Elevit road.

⌊═⌋ Sleeping

A growing number of pensions and small hotels are dotted along and just off the valley road as far as Çat and there are other pensions higher up in Elevit, Palovit and Amlakit. Booking ahead is recommended in July and August. Pensions mostly close from about October to April.

Toşi Pansiyon PENSION $$

(☑ 0464-654 4002; www.tosipansiyon.com; Çat; half-board per person ₺90; ☉ approx Mar-Nov; ☏)

The first pension you come to arriving from the north on the outskirts of Çat, Toşi is clean and friendly, with a licensed riverside restaurant, and accommodation in wooden cabins and rooms in the main house. Trekking advice is available.

ℹ Getting There & Away

BUS & DOLMUŞ

During the summer months when the highland villages are inhabited, at least one daily dolmuş (minibus) heads up the Fırtına valley from Çamlıhemşin to Çat and villages beyond. Schedules are changeable, so check locally for the latest timings.

Daily in July and August, and most days in June and September, a dolmuş leaves Pazar (beside the Çamlıhemşin minibus stop) about 7.30am for Palovit (₺35, about 3½ hours), via Çamlıhemşin, Çat, Elevit and Tirovit; another leaves from the same place about the same time, a few days a week, for Verçenik (₺35, about three hours), about 20km south of Çat, via Çamlıhemşin and Çat. To board these at Çamlıhemşin (around 8.30am), ask your accommodation to call to get the driver to stop for you.

From July to about the end of September, a dolmuş leaves Çamlıhemşin (Dogum bakery) at 8am on Wednesday and Saturday for Amlakit (₺25, about 3½ hours) via Çat, Elevit, Tirovit and Palovit. It starts back from Amlakit at 2pm.

CAR

From Çat unpaved roads – drivable with care in an ordinary car in dry conditions from some time in May/June to September/October (depending on the weather) – head up east or southeast to Elevit, Haçivanak, Tirovit, Palovit and Amlakit, and south to Kaleköy, Başyayla and Verçenik. Amlakit and Palovit can also be reached by continuing up the road past the Palovit Şelalesi (waterfall) – shorter and quicker than going via Çat and Elevit, though the road is poorer.

TAXI

A taxi from Çamlıhemşin costs around ₺70 to ₺80 one way to Çat or about ₺100 to Elevit.

Ayder

☑ 0464

The tourism hub of the Kaçkars, this formerly bucolic *yayla* (mountain pasture) village has become a highly popular tour stop, welcoming coach-loads of Saudi Arabians, Iranians and Georgians as well as Turks; from spring to autumn it's not a place to escape from other travellers. That said, Ayder has a gorgeous setting at around 1300m altitude in a verdant, waterfall-ribboned valley, and the broadest

range of accommodation in the Kaçkars. The village straggles more than 2km from west to east up the valley, and the Kaçkar Dağları Milli Parkı (Kaçkar Mountains National Park) is nearby.

There's an ATM towards the lower (western) end of the village.

Activities

Good day walks in the area include up to Hüser and back (about 5km each way, with about 1000m of ascent), and along the panoramic ridge west of Ayder between Hazındak and Sal, via Pokut – this can be accessed by a steep walk up from Ayder to Hazındak or by using a vehicle to Sal.

Kaplıca SPA
(Hot Springs; ☑ 0464-657 2102; www.ayderkaplicalari.com; ₺13, private room ₺50; ⊙ 8am-7pm Sep-Jun, to 10pm Jul & Aug) Post-trek muscle relief is offered in marble environs at Ayder's spotless *kaplıca* (spa), where water temperatures reach 56°C.

Festivals

Çamlıhemşin Ayder Festival CULTURAL
(⊙ 1st or 2nd weekend Jun) This highly popular early-summer festival highlights Hemşin culture with folk dance and music, and also features northeast Turkey's bloodless form of *boğa güreşleri* (bullfighting), in which two bulls lock heads and push at each other until one gives up and backs off.

Sleeping & Eating

Older wooden pensions have been joined by many new alpine-style hotels and pensions of varying size (and tastefulness); new buildings must be built in traditional style (ie sheathed in wood). Those on the fairly steep hillside above the road are usually approached by flattish footpaths starting further up the road. Often your bags will be whisked up on nifty *'teleferik'* winch arrangements.

Accommodation gets heavily booked over weekends from June to August, and can be almost impossible to secure during the Çamlıhemşin Ayder Festival.

Some lodgings open year-round; others close from roughly December to March.

Fora Pansiyon PENSION **$$**
(☑ 0464-657 2153; www.turkutour.com; Aşağı Ambarlık; s/d ₺130/180; ❀✳🖵) This hillside pension provides small, rustic pine-clad bedrooms, some with private bathrooms and some with bunks as well as beds. Dinner (₺30) on the panoramic terrace is a good bet, and the laundry is a welcome feature if you've been on the road for a while. It's near the west end of the village, 200m to the left from the top of the steps opposite Hotel Yeşil Vadi.

Zirve Ahşap Pansiyon PENSION **$$**
(☑ 0464-657 2177; mirayzirve@hotmail.com; Aşağı Ambarlık; per person with/without breakfast ₺60/50; ⊙ Apr–mid-Nov; ❀🖵) This very good budget option above the road towards the west end of town has three floors of spick-and-span rooms, all with bathrooms, and some attractive kilims (pileless woven rugs) on the floors. Views are lacking, but the chairs in the reception area are great for sitting and chatting with the friendly owner.

Villa de Pelit BOUTIQUE HOTEL **$$$**
(☑ 0464-657 2111; www.villadepelit.com; s/d/tr Jul-Sep ₺262/350/525, Oct, Nov, Apr-Jun ₺135/180/270; ⊙ Apr-Nov; ❀✳🖵) Near the top of the meadow 600m east of the dolmuş/taxi stand, Villa de Pelit features soft furnishings, black faux-leather bedheads, toiletries, bathrooms of varying sizes, and coffee- and tea-making equipment. The restaurant, serving Turkish and international fare (mains ₺15 to ₺30), looks across the hubbub below to the white river tumbling down the green mountainside.

A 200m walking path leads to the hotel from beside Vesile Otel up the road.

Pilita TURKISH **$**
(mains ₺10-25; ⊙ 8am-11pm Apr-Oct; 🖵🍴) A quirky place where they may not have half of what's chalked on the blackboard, but you'll probably enjoy the carefully prepared dishes that are served – mezes such as *yoğurtlu patlıcan* (aubergine salad with yoghurt), and main dishes such as *sarma* (mincemeat-stuffed cabbage rolls), *bonfile* (steak) or even *tereyağı karides* (butter shrimp).

It's licensed, English is spoken, and you can sit in the cosy dining room on cushioned benches or out on the front terrace. It's 600m east from the dolmuş/taxi stand.

Getting There & Away

The dolmuş (minibus) and taxi stand is towards the lower (western) end of the village.

Hourly dolmuşes run to/from Pazar (₺11, 1¼ hours) via Çamlıhemşin (₺7, 30 minutes) from 8am to 6pm. Services are scarcer in winter (as few as two each way daily in January and February). A taxi from Çamlıhemşin to Ayder costs about ₺35.

Dolmuşes run up to some highland villages when the roads are passable (approximately June to

November/December). Services generally run from Çamlıhemşin via Ayder to Yukarı Kavron (₺20, 1½ hours; ₺10, one hour from Ayder), and vice versa, every hour or two from 7am or 8am to 6pm; and from Çamlıhemşin via Ayder to Avusor (₺25, 1½ hours; ₺15, one hour from Ayder) once daily at 8am, returning in the afternoon. The unpaved roads from Ayder to Yukarı Kavron, Yukarı Çaymakçur, Avusor and Huser are normally drivable with care in an ordinary car during the same period.

The entrance gate to Kaçkar Dağları Milli Parkı (Kaçkar Mountains National Park) is 4km before Ayder coming from Çamlıhemşin.

Eastern Kaçkars

The eastern side of the Kaçkars is generally drier than the western side, meaning better conditions for hiking but a less lush forest cover. The main access town, Yusufeli, is also a white-water rafting centre (until such time as it is flooded by a planned new reservoir), and has the added advantage of being a good base for exploring the Georgian valleys.

Yusufeli

📞 0466 / POP 7250 / ELEV 560M

This likeable valley town at the confluence of the Barhal and İspir Rivers (whose joint waters become the Çoruh River here) is sadly slated to vanish underwater. The Yusufeli dam, being built about 12km down the Çoruh, may be completed by 2019 and the resulting reservoir will submerge the town – and put an end to most of the white-water rafting for which it's famed. Construction of Yeni (New) Yusufeli on the hillside on the west side of the Barhal River has already started. For now, Yusufeli remains the gateway to the southern Kaçkars, a good base for the Georgian valleys, and a white-water rafting centre.

The town straddles the Barhal River, with three road bridges and three footbridges crossing this within 1km.

🛏 Sleeping & Eating

Greenpiece Camping & Pansiyon PENSION, CAMPING $

(📞 0466-811 3620; www.birolrafting.com; Arıklı Mahallesi; s/d/tr without breakfast ₺40/60/90, campsite tent/campervan per person ₺15/20, breakfast ₺15; 🅿 ❄ ✳ 📶) Birol Alkan and his family run this laid-back pension in a peaceful spot on the west side of the Barhal River 300m

upstream from the top bridge. There's a camping area with bathroom facilities, and guests can use the kitchen. Accommodation includes six good air-conditioned upstairs rooms, and six cosy singles in a wooden house behind.

Good English is spoken and rafting trips can be organised here.

Otel Almatur HOTEL $$

(📞 0466-811 4056; www.almatur.com.tr; Ersis Caddesi 53; s ₺70-85, d ₺120-140, ste s/d ₺140/200; ❄ ✳ 📶) Look forward to rooms with big beds and crisp linen, fridges and windows giving sweeping views, particularly from the 4th-floor corner rooms (405 and 406). The 5th-floor restaurant's tinted windows have more stunning views. Dishes (mains ₺10 to ₺15) include *köfte*, mezes and *sebzeli* (vegetable) kebap, and the included breakfast is an excellent spread.

İhtiyaroğlu PENSION $$

(📞 0466-824 4086; Sarıgöl Yolu; s/d/tr ₺60/120/150, bungalows ₺300, campsites ₺20; 🅿 📶) Thirteen kilometres from Yusufeli en route to Barhal, a winding track descends 500m to this blissful place set around a riverside garden. Chalet-like buildings have 19 impeccable, pine-clad rooms and there are four bungalows for up to six people. Even if you don't stay the night, it's well worth a stop for a meal of barbecued trout (₺15) in riverside gazebos; the restaurant is open from 7am to 11pm.

The pension is accessible by dolmuşes heading for Sarigol, Barhal or Yaylalar. Campers have access to toilets but no shower.

Yusufeli Kültür Evi CAFE $

(Yusufeli Culture House; İnönü Caddesi; dishes ₺3-5; ⏰ noon-11pm) This town-hall-run venture is a lovely place to enjoy tasty local dishes at excellent prices, or a game of backgammon or pool and a Turkish coffee with Turkish delight. You can sit in the spacious main room that has comfy seating or on the airy terrace above the river. It's up steps from the small square just south of the tourist office.

ℹ Information

Tourist Office (İnönü Caddesi; ⏰ 8am-9.30pm daily May-Oct, 8am-5.30pm Mon-Fri Nov-Apr) On the main street in the centre of town.

ℹ Getting There & Away

Yusufeli's otogar is between the main street and the river, 150m south of the tourist office.

Dolmuşes to Artvin (₺17, 1½ hours) leave 11 times daily, from 6am to 4.30pm. **Yeşil Artvin Ekspres** (www.yesilartvinekspres.com.tr) buses depart for Erzurum (₺25, 2½ hours) at 7am, 9am and 11am, and to Hopa (₺30, three hours) and Trabzon (₺45, six hours) at 9am. You can also change at Artvin for Hopa and Trabzon.

A bus to Kars (₺35, four hours), coming from Artvin, passes the Su Kavuşumu junction on the D950 Artvin–Erzurum road 10km east of Yusufeli around 1pm. You can reach Su Kavuşumu by an Artvin-bound dolmuş (₺5) or a taxi (around ₺35).

Driving into the Kaçkars from Yusufeli is a spectacular trip along the valleys (in parts, gorges) of the rushing Barhal and Hevek Rivers. The winding road is paved (though often single-track) as far as Barhal (29km). Thereafter it's unpaved, but with a good surface, as far as Yaylalar (21km from Barhal), and concreted in parts from there to Olgunlar (3.5km). The road can driven by careful, confident drivers in an ordinary car all the way to Olgunlar, but seek local advice about possible hazards (including rockfalls and landslides) in wet weather or when the snow is melting; springtime can be risky.

There's dolmuş service from Yusufeli to Barhal, Yaylalar and Olgunlar in the early afternoon, and vice versa in the early morning.

Tekkale & Dörtkilise

⭐**Dörtkilise**   CHURCH
The wonderful 10th-century Georgian church of Dörtkilise (in Georgian Otkhta Eklesia, meaning Church of the Four) stands 6km up a green river valley from Tekkale village, 7km southwest of Yusufeli. A large, domeless, three-nave basilica, similar to the church in nearby Barhal, it's almost hidden among the trees on its remote hillside. The structure, though abandoned and decaying, with weeds and vines springing picturesquely from mossy stones, is still to a large extent intact.

Tek Kale Kalesi   CASTLE
One kilometre before Tekkale village coming from Yusufeli, the ruined medieval Georgian castle Tek Kale Kalesi perches high above the road, complete with small church on its inaccessible rock pinnacle.

ℹ️ Getting There & Away

Dolmuşes to Tekkale (₺2) depart from the road outside **Otel Almatur** (p532) in Yusufeli at 11am, 3pm and 5pm. From Tekkale, you can walk up the road to Dörtkilise: it's 6km from the village (despite the sign saying 7km), among trees above a stretch of stone wall on the left, and almost invisible till you're about 150m past it at a

spring inscribed '*Mehmet Kaçmazın hayratısıdır yap 2007*'.

A taxi from Yusufeli to Dörtkilise and back (including one hour waiting time) costs ₺80.

If driving, note the narrow road from Tekkale is surfaced for only about the first 3km; take care in wet weather.

Barhal (Altıparmak)

📞 0466 / POP 1500 / ELEV 1300M
Barhal (today officially called Altıparmak) is an alluring base for forays into the Kaçkars. The village nestles in a verdant valley amid a beautiful mountainscape, with two rushing rivers meeting at its heart. Inviting pensions offer trekking guides and equipment, and advice on day walks and longer expeditions.

◉ Sights & Activities

Barhal is the main starting point for crossings of the Altıparmak range, to Avusor via the 3107m Kırmızı Pass – two or three days depending which route you choose. English-language leaflets detailing four good day walks, published by Culture Routes in Turkey, are available at pensions.

Barhal Church   CHURCH, MOSQUE
(Ⓟ) The majestic lines of this 10th-century Georgian church (Parkhali to Georgians) rise 1km from the centre. A domeless three-nave basilica, the structure lacks much ornamentation, but the soaring dignity of its form, with stately blind arcading on all sides, more than makes up for that. It has been used as a mosque for some considerable time and is well preserved. The imam lives in the building next door and will open it up for visitors.

Chapels Walk   WALKING
For views over the village and the jagged peaks beyond, you can walk up to two small ruined chapels across the valley from Barhal Church (from which the upper chapel is visible on a ridge). The walk of around 5km (90 minutes return) starts over a plank footbridge opposite the foot of the access road to the church and Karahan Pension.

Karagöl Lake Hike   WALKING
A very scenic but quite strenuous full-day hike runs from Naznara hamlet, 7km northwest of Barhal, up to Karagöl, one of the most beautiful lakes in the Kaçkars, and back via Sarıbulut hamlet.

🛏 Sleeping & Eating

There are a couple of food shops and cafes in the village centre.

★**Karahan Pension**   PENSION $$
(☑ 0539 559 5059, 0466-826 2071; www.karahan pension.com; per person incl breakfast/half-board ₺55/75; ☺Apr-Nov; 🅿🐾📶) Run by Mehmet and sons Ahmet and Bekir (who speak some English), cosy Karahan has an adorable and scenic hillside setting 1km above the village, and a terrace and sitting room that are perfect for unwinding. Rooms are simple but appealing, with either rugs or bare floorboards, and Mehmet's home-style meals and honey from his own hives are tasty.

ℹ Getting There & Away

Barhal is 29km northwest of Yusufeli. Two or three dolmuşes to Barhal (₺18, 1¼ hours) leave Yusufeli's otogar between about 2pm and 4pm when they have enough passengers, returning from Barhal about 6.30am or 7am. Outside those times, you will probably have to hire a taxi (around ₺150).

Yaylalar (Hevek)

☑ 0466 / POP 700

It's a winding and narrow ride up to Yaylalar (Hevek), 21km up the valley of the rushing Hevek River from Barhal, but you'll be rewarded with a wonderfully bucolic setting with plenty of traditional farmhouses and scenic *yaylalar* (mountain pastures) all around. You may well agree with the sign proclaiming Yaylalar 'heaven on earth'. It's an excellent base for day hikes and longer adventures including Kaçkar summit ascents and trans-Kaçkar treks via the Naleteme, Körahmet or Babur Passes.

Çamyuva Pansiyon   PENSION $$
(☑ 0466-832 2001, 0534 361 6959; www.facebook. com/camyuvapansiyon; half-board per person ₺100-110, without bathroom ₺80, r without bathroom ₺30; 📶) Çamyuva resembles a big Swiss chalet, with comfortable pine-clad rooms and balconies for watching the village go by. Across the street are wooden bungalows sleeping up to five, with a stream gurgling underneath – soothing in summer, chilly in winter. Another house nearby has shared bathrooms for tighter budgets.

ℹ Getting There & Away

Dolmuşes to Yaylalar (₺35, 1¾ hours, usually two daily) leave Yusufeli otogar between about 2pm and 4pm when they have enough passengers. They start back from Yaylalar about 6am. Taxis charge around ₺250 from Yusufeli to Yaylalar.

Olgunlar

☑ 0466 / POP 50

The quiet hamlet of Olgunlar (Meredet) really feels like the end of the line. Standing in splendid isolation at 2130m altitude, it's a bucolic spot with soaring peaks, soul-stirring vistas, babbling brooks and some of Turkey's purest air. Its pensions provide the closest beds to Mt Kaçkar and the Naletleme Pass (to Yukarı Kavron). Passes to the south and southwest are also accessible from here. Olgunlar is also starting to attract ski tourers in winter.

🛏 Sleeping & Eating

Aside from meals available in the pensions, there is a surprisingly well-appointed cafe.

Dilberdüzü Camp   CAMPING $
(per tent site/rental ₺5/20; ☺mid-Jul–mid-Sep) In 2016 the **Yusufeli Tourism Development Cooperative** (Yusufeli Turizm Geliştirme Kooperatifi; ☑ 0505 453 4151; www.facebook.com/Yusufeli-Turizm-Gelistirme-Kooperatifi-1102734493111759) inaugurated this camp for hikers and climbers at the spot called Dilberdüzü, a 7.5km walk (about 3½ hours) up the valley from Olgunlar. Tents, sleeping bags and mats are available to rent, and there's a cafeteria (dishes ₺7.50 to ₺15), plus a first-aid tent and a guide service for Mt Kaçkar summit treks (US$100 for one day).

Kaçkar Pansiyon   PENSION $$
(☑ 0538 306 4564, 0466-832 2047; www.kackar. net; half-board per person May-Dec €30, Jan-Apr €40; 🅿🐾📶) A top choice for walkers, this pine-clad haven of peace features superclean rooms, a kitchen for guests' use, a comfy and panoramic sitting area and delectable meals. Bag a room overlooking the stream. Friendly owner İsmail speaks French and some English. Likely to close December and the first half of January unless it has bookings.

ℹ Getting There & Away

Olgunlar is 3.5km beyond Yaylalar on a scenic road. Dolmuşes from Yusufeli to Yaylalar (leaving Yusufeli otogar roughly between 2pm and 4pm) continue to Olgunlar (₺35, two hours) if asked. For the return trip they can pick up on request at Olgunlar around 5.30am.

FAR NORTHEAST

Georgian Valleys

The spectacular, mountainous country southeast of Yusufeli was once, along with the territory to the north and northeast as far as the modern Turkey–Georgia border, part of medieval Georgia. Numerous churches and castles, mostly in romantically ruined states and isolated locations, survive from this bygone era, and tracking them down in this beautiful landscape is a fascinating adventure. From spring to autumn the valleys turn green with poplars and cherry and apricot trees, in stark contrast to the bare, rocky hillsides above.

History

The region stretching from around Tortum in the south up to the Turkey–Georgia border area in the north is known to Georgians as Tao-Klarjeti, after the two principal Georgian principalities that existed here in medieval times. From the last few centuries BC the region fell mostly within the ambit of the eastern Georgian kingdom of Iveria (or Kartli), but by the 8th century AD it was largely abandoned and deserted as a result of war and invasion. In the 9th century AD, with the Iverian capital Tbilisi now under Arab rule, Tao-Klarjeti was resettled and revived and, with Byzantine support, developed into the leading centre of Georgian Christian culture. Under the Bagrationi line of kings, who established a capital at Artanuji (now Ardanuç, east of Artvin), an intensive monastic and church-building movement was led by the monk Grigol Khandzteli (Gregory of Khandzta). By the year 1000 this rugged, isolated region just 150km or so long and 120km wide had an estimated 300 Georgian churches, monasteries and castles.

When Tao-Klarjeti and eastern Georgia were inherited by King Bagrat of Abkhazia (northwest Georgia) in the early 11th century,

EASTERN ANATOLIA GEORGIAN VALLEYS

Georgian Valleys & Around

ARDANUÇ & ŞAVŞAT

The area east of Artvin is a stunning tapestry of rivers, canyons, mountains, forests and *yaylalar* (mountain pastures), with the added appeal of a Caucasian flavour, courtesy of its proximity to Georgia. Among the off-the-beaten-track villages and towns, several medieval Georgian churches and castles stand in delightful settings.

A DIY approach with your own wheels is preferable, as public transport is infrequent. Seek local advice before attempting secondary roads, which may be in bad shape.

About 18km east of Artvin on the winding D010, a side-road signposted 'Dolişhane Kilisesi 3' climbs to the lovely little 10th-century Georgian Dolişhane Church (Hamamlı village). It's empty inside but has a few relief carvings, notably of its founder, King Sumbat II (holding a church), and the angels Gabriel and Michael, on the south facade. Back on the D010, you cross the Okçular River (at this point a reservoir) after a further 3km. At the far end of the bridge, turn right to Ardanuç (11km), and follow signs up to the dramatic ruined Ardanuç (Gevhernik) Kalesi, surrounded by sheer cliffs. Park beneath its east side and follow the path up to its north end, where a short ladder and iron steps form the only access to this near-impregnable fortress. It's no wonder Ashot I made Ardanuç his capital when establishing his Georgian kingdom in this region in the early 9th century.

Seventeen kilometres past Ardanuç (signposted from the town and again later) is the 10th- or 11th-century Georgian Yeni Rabat Church (near Bulanık). It's abandoned but still largely intact, and exquisitely sited on a grassy platform overlooking an emerald-green valley. The last 1.5km from Bulanık village are along an unpaved road with a precipitous drop at one point – dangerous in wet conditions.

Northeast from the Ardanuç turn-off, the D010 passes along the deep, lushly wooded valley of the Okçular (Berta) River. After 13km a brown sign points left to 'Porta Monastiri 2'. This is the start of a 2km walking track up to the ruined Porta Monastery, which is generally believed to be what Georgians know as Khandzta, the monastery founded in 782

most of the Georgian territory became officially united under one rule. Kutaisi in western Georgia was its capital until 1122 when the great Georgian king Davit IV ('David the Builder', 1089–1125) was finally able to retake Tbilisi and initiate Georgia's medieval 'golden age', which peaked during Queen Tamar's reign (1184–1213).

Tao-Klarjeti suffered Byzantine and Seljuk Turk invasions during the 11th century. Because of these and the northward shift in the centre of Georgian gravity, its importance declined. The Turks were driven out by David the Builder but continued to raid; then came the Mongols, who took over the region in 1235. In the later 13th century Tao-Klarjeti came under the sway of the south Georgian principality of Samtskhe (Meskheti), which managed to get along OK with the Mongols and kept the Seljuks at bay, though it couldn't stop the Central Asian conqueror Tamerlane (Timur) ravaging the region in 1394. Ottoman Turk attacks from the west began in the 1530s, and in 1555 the Treaty of Amasya divided Samtskhe between the Ottomans and Safavid Persia, with the western part (Tao-Klarjeti) becoming an Ottoman possession. Over the following centuries the great majority of the population converted to Islam and the churches were turned into mosques or abandoned. Many locals, however, retain a measure of Georgian heritage, and the Georgian language is still spoken in a few villages near the modern Turkey–Georgia border.

❶ Getting There & Away

Hiring a car in Erzurum, or even Artvin, is the easiest way to see the valleys. Hiring a taxi in Yusufeli costs about ₺100 to İşhan return (including waiting time) or ₺300 for a day.

Public transport mostly consists of dolmuşes (minibuses) that head from the villages to Yusufeli in the morning, returning in the afternoon. Bağbaşı is served by dolmuşes from Erzurum. It's also possible to take buses between Erzurum and Yusufeli or Artvin to the turn-offs for Bağbaşı or Öşkvank, and walk or hitch the 6km or 8km up to the churches.

İşhan Church of the Mother of God

İşhan's wonderful Church of the Mother of God reached more or less its final form as Tao-Klarjeti's most important cathedral in

from which the monk Grigol Khandzteli pioneered the monastic movement in Tao-Klarjeti. The walk up is steep but it's a wonderfully romantic spot in a thickly wooded canyon. About 17km further northeast on the D010, a tarred road leads north to Meydancık, a quintessential *yaylalar* settlement near the Georgian border.

As you enter the town of Şavşat on the D010, 10km east of the turn-off to Meydancık, the fairy-tale castle Şavşat Kalesi (ⓟ) stands sentinel. This was the ruling seat of Shavsheti, one of the Georgian princedoms within medieval Tao-Klarjeti. Detailed excavations have taken place and informative signboards identify features such as a wine cellar and an Ottoman hamam.

A road signposted to Karagöl Sahara Milli Parkı (Karagöl Sahara National Park) starts beside Şavşat Kalesi. Seven kilometres along it, a 'Cevizli Kilesesi 4' sign points left to the ruined 10th-century Georgian Tbeti Church (Cevizli village), standing in a peaceful *yaylalar* village with a couple of cafes next door. The south facade has handsome blind arcades and some detailed relief carving.

Laşet Motel (Laşet Tesisleri; ☑ 0466-571 2136; www.laset.com.tr; Şavşat-Ardahan Karayolu; s/d ₺100/170; ⓟ 🛜), beside a mountain stream 10km east of Şavşat on the D010, has eight cosy, wood-lined rooms, and its licensed restaurant serves good fish and kebaps. Owner Mete speaks some English. Mete also owns the excellent Laşet Bungalov Tatil Evleri (Laşet Bungalov Tatil Köyü; ☑ 0466-571 2157; www.laset.com.tr; Kocabey village; s/d/tr/q ₺150/200/300/400; ⓟ 🛜) 5km away, where comfortable, well-equipped pine bungalows look out over the village and the hills beyond, and a licensed restaurant has the same good menu.

Continuing east, the D010 leaves the wooded valleys and snakes over the Çam Pass (2470m) on to the high steppe lands around Ardahan.

1032. It was founded by an Armenian bishop in the 7th century and later rebuilt by Georgians several times. Later it served as a mosque, before its roof caved in the 1980s, at which time whole walls were still covered in frescoes, of which only traces remain today.

From outside you can admire the grand scale and proportions of the cruciform building with its near-conical dome, tall arcades and elaborate fretwork around the windows.

Inside, the four free-standing pillars supporting the dome are particularly impressive, and there's a superb arcade of horseshoe-shaped arches in the apse.

İşhan Church of the Mother of God has been under restoration by the Turkish government, meaning you may only be able to gaze at it from the perimeter fence. Hopefully it will be reopened to visitors in 2017.

From Yusufeli, head east to the D950 Artvin–Erzurum road (9km), turn right and head 7km to the junction with the D060. From here follow the brown 'İşhan Kilisesi' signposts for 13km. İşhan upper village, where the church stands, is spectacularly situated 7km up a steep, narrow road carved out of the mountainside. Drive slowly in wet weather, when the road gets slippery.

Tortum Gölü & Tortum Şelalesi

The impressive Tortum Şelalesi (Tortum Waterfalls) lies 16km south of the İşhan turn-off on the D950, 700m off the main road (signposted). It's overlooked by a tea garden.

South along D950 you can skirt the western shore of the 8km-long Tortum Gölü (Lake Tortum), which was formed by landslides about three centuries ago.

İskele Et & Balık Lokantası (☑ 0535 366 9052; mains ₺6-16; ⊙ variable; 🍽) is slightly scruffy but has a great location on a promontory in the Tortum Gölü (Lake Tortum). It serves *alabalık* (local trout) and assorted kebaps. Camping is possible here too, and you can rent rowing boats to head out on the lake.

Öşkvank Cathedral

Two kilometres south of the south end of Tortum Gölü (Lake Tortum), 'Öşkvank Kilesesi' signs point west off the D950 to the cathedral, which stands in the village of Çamlıyamaç, 8km up a pretty valley road.

The big mid-10th-century cathedral of Öşkvank (Oshki to Georgians) is one of the

ⓘ GETTING INTO GEORGIA

There are road border crossings into Georgia at **Türkgözü**, between Posof (north of Ardahan) and Vale (Georgia, west of Akhaltsikhe); and at **Aktaş**, between Çıldır (east of Ardahan and north of Kars) and Kartsakhi (Georgia, west of Akhalkalaki). There's little to choose between them in terms of travel time to most places inside Georgia: the choice depends chiefly on transport schedules (which are notoriously changeable, so check locally). The crossing at **Sarp**, on the Black Sea coast south of Batumi, is convenient from the northern part of the region. All these crossings are open 24 hours.

two grandest remaining medieval churches in the Georgian valleys, along with the İşhan Church of the Mother of God, 48km to its northeast. Unlike İşhan, Öşkvank remains in a semiruined state, which somehow enhances its evocative atmosphere. The cathedral was the centrepiece of one of Tao-Klarjeti's most important monasteries, a centre of learning and literature that remained active until at least the 15th century. It is one of the most impressive and evocative of all the old Georgian churches in the region, and served as the model for the Bagrati Cathedral built in Kutaisi in Georgia in the early 11th century.

A three-aisled cruciform structure still topped by a dome, the cathedral has a very impressive main facade on its south side, with tall blind arcades and reliefs of archangels and an eagle clutching a deer. The cathedral's relief carvings, outside and inside, are the finest on any of the churches in the region. The interior is jaw-dropping, with four massive pillars soaring upwards to high arches on which the 12-windowed drum and the dome rest.

Haho Church

Bağbaşı village is home to one of the larger and better preserved Georgian churches in the region. The late 10th-century Haho Church (also called Khakhuli by Georgians) was once part of a big monastery and centre of arts and learning, which remained active till the 16th century. Today it's in use as a mosque so is in a reasonable state of repair.

Thirteen kilometres south of the Öşkvank turn-off on the D950 (6km south of Uzundere,

80km north of Erzurum) a sign points west to Bağbaşı. Three kilometres up the pretty valley road, bear right at the 'Taş Camii Meryem Ana Kilisesi' sign. Haho Church is 3km up this road, on the right.

Oltu & Penek

The startling citadel of **Oltu Kalesi**, thought to have been originally built by Urartus around 1000 BC, rises above the centre of peaceful Oltu town. It has been closed for restoration but it's worth checking if it has reopened. The castle was of some importance during the Roman and Byzantine periods, and was later occupied by the Seljuks and Genoese colonists before being taken by the Ottomans in the 16th century.

The awesome 7th-century Armenian **Bana Cathedral** stands on a hillock 2.5km from Penek village amid bright green grasslands, with the surrounding mountains forming a fantastic backdrop. The building's ruined state makes it hard to appreciate how it must once have appeared: a three-tier, rotunda-shaped structure 30m high peaking in a conical dome, similar to Armenia's famous Zvartnots Cathedral of the same era.

The two medieval castles of **Kizkalesi** and **Erkek Kalesi**, visible from the D060 north of Yolboyu village, were evidently a pair (their names mean Girl Castle and Boy Castle), designed to command a valley where two rivers meet. Kizkalesi, 3.5km from Yolboyu, on a clifftop east of the road, is an eerie sight, in keeping with a surreal landscape where craggy gorges alternate with reddish bluffs. Erkek Kalesi, 500m further north, overlooks a poplar-lined river from a rocky mound.

Kars

📝 0474 / POP 79,300 / ELEV 1768M

With its pastel-coloured stone buildings dating from the 19th-century Russian occupation, and its well-organised grid plan, Kars looks like a slice of Russia teleported to northeastern Anatolia. And the city's mix of influences – Kurdish, Azeri, Turkmen, Turkish and Russian – adds to its distinct feel. No wonder it provided the setting for Turkish author Orhan Pamuk's acclaimed novel *Kar* (Snow).

Kars is usually regarded as a base for visiting the ruins at Ani, but it's worth spending time exploring its sights, soaking up the lively vibe (to which the large Kafkas University contributes significantly), and sampling some of the excellent local cuisine. It also makes a convenient base for exploring remote villages and sights in the surrounding steppe.

◎ Sights

Belle époque mansions and other examples of so-called Baltic (ie northern Russian) architecture are plentiful around Kars; externally it's a rather dour style but it's unusual for Turkey. Some of these buildings have been turned into boutique hotels and cafes. Along Ordu Caddesi look for the yellow-and-white **Old Governor's Mansion** (Map p540), built in 1883, where the Treaty of Kars was signed in 1921; the late-19th-century **Revenue Office** (Map p540), a three-storey building with a long, false-columned facade; and the **Gazi Kars Anatolian High School** (Map p540), occupying a late 19th-century winter mansion. The **Fethiye Camii** (Map p540; Cumhuriyet Caddesi), a 19th-century Russian church converted to a mosque, stands picturesquely south of the centre, now with twin minarets instead of its original onion domes.

Kars Culture & Art Association   MUSEUM
(Kars Kültür Sanat Derneği; Map p540; Bakırcılar Caddesi 39; ◎8am-5pm Mon-Sat) FREE Local historian Vedat Akçayöz's paint shop (its sign says *Yeni Akçay Kollektif Şirketi*) doubles as a small library and museum about the Molokan and Doukhobor Spiritual Christian sects (his grandmother was a Molokan). These peaceful Christian groups disagreed with the Russian Orthodox Church, and some Molokans settled in the Kars area during the Russian occupation more than a century ago (nearly all have now emigrated). Vedat speaks reasonable English and is also an authority on the 'underground city' below the main monumental area at Ani.

Kars Museum   MUSEUM
(Kars Müze; Cumhuriyet Caddesi; ◎8.30am-5pm) FREE Northeast of the centre, just off the road to Ani, the city museum has archaeological exhibits from the early Bronze Age (including some from the Ani area, showing how far back settlement there stretched), the Urartu and Roman periods, and the Seljuk and Ottoman eras. Upstairs are some fine old kilims (pileless woven rugs) and Ottoman kaftans.

🛏 Sleeping

Hotel Temel   HOTEL $
(Map p540; ☑0474-223 1376; Yenipazar Caddesi 9; s/d ₺60/80; 🛜) The rooms at 'Hotel Base' are a little frayed at the edges but they're neat, with immaculate sheets and soothing blue-and-yellow colour schemes. The best thing about the hotel is the lobby lounge with its regal blue-and-gold chairs. Nearby, the rooms at **Hotel Temel 2** (Map p540; ☑0474-223 1616; Yenipazar Caddesi; s/d/tr without breakfast ₺30/50/75) are small and old but clean.

★Hotel Katerina Sarayı   BOUTIQUE HOTEL $$
(☑0474-223 0636; www.katerinasarayi.com; Celalbaba Caddesi 52; s/d/tr ₺120/180/220; 🅿🛜) Opened in 2015 in a large 1879 Russian stone building (originally a military hospital), the Katerina Sarayı is all tsarist-style elegance and comfort with high ceilings, kilims and floral gilt bedheads and mirror frames. It has a lovely quiet location beside the Kars River, right beneath the castle, but is only 10 minutes' walk from the centre.

Kar's Otel   BOUTIQUE HOTEL $$$
(Map p540; ☑0474-212 1616; www.karsotel. com; Halitpaşa Caddesi 31; s/d €99/139; 🅻🛜) This seven-room boutique hotel in a 19th-century Russian mansion feels like a luxurious cocoon. The pastel-coloured rooms are very comfortable, with big beds and carpets, and there are good toiletries in the marble bathrooms. Snacks plus hot and cold drinks (including alcohol) are available all day in the dining room, courtyard and rooms.

🍴 Eating & Drinking

Kars has the northeast's best restaurant scene, with a couple of relatively classy restaurants and places specialising in home-style local dishes. The city is noted for several specialities including roast goose, honey and cheeses. There's a lively cafe scene as well.

★Ocakbaşı Restoran   TURKISH $
(Map p540; ☑0474-212 0056; www.kaygisizocak basi.com; Atatürk Caddesi; mains ₺13-22; ◎8am-11pm; 🛜✐) This classy 40-year-old favourite with a large upstairs dining room serves tasty and unusual regional and Turkish dishes, such as its speciality *alinazik* (strips of beef tenderloin with aubergine, tomato and capsicum; you can ask for *et siz* for a vegetarian version) and some good pide with unusual ingredient combinations (including vegetarian options).

Kars

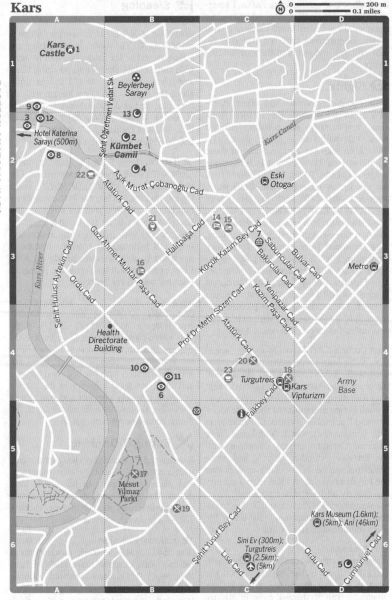

★ Sini Ev   ANATOLIAN $

(Borsa Sokak 71; mains ₺10-20; ⊙8am-9pm Mon-Sat; ☎✐) This unassuming and friendly establishment, slightly away from the centre, is more than worth the short trip for its delicious home-style local dishes. Options range from fresh daily soups (such as sorrel, lentil or a cool yoghurt-and-herbs creation) to stuffed vegetables (aubergines, capsicums or vine leaves) with or without meat; bean and chickpea dishes; aubergine-and-*köfte* kebaps; and baked or fried meat dishes. No grills here.

Kars

Hanımeli Kars Mutfağı   ANATOLIAN $
(Map p540; www.karshanimeli.com; Faikbey Caddesi 156; mains ₺10-15; ⊘9am-9pm; 🕾) With a rustic, country-kitchen vibe, Hanımeli specialises in home-style cooking influenced by the broader Caucasian region. Dishes include *Revan köfte* (Armenian-style steamed meatballs), a silky-smooth pasta soup called *erişte aşi* and the ravioli-like *hangel*. There's roast goose, delicious Kars honey for sale, and a refreshing local drink called *reyhane*, made from purple basil.

Anatolia Cafe   CAFE $
(Map p540; Mesut Yılmaz Parkı; mains ₺10-25, cakes & desserts ₺7.50-10; ⊘8am-10pm; 🕾) The Anatolia has a calm, relaxed, spacious atmosphere and a lovely location in a riverside park. It's great for everything from tempting cakes and desserts to cheese toasties, filter coffee, pizza, *köfte* and fajitas.

Han-I Hanedan   TURKISH $
(Map p540; Faikbey Caddesi; mains ₺15-25; ⊘8am-1pm; 🕾) The best place to head if you want beer or wine with your meal, Han-I Hanedan offers mainly meaty Turkish and international options, from *çoban kavurma* (lamb braised in its own fat with capsicum and tomato) to chicken Madras. There are also mezes and roast goose (₺70).

Pasha Cafe   CAFE
(Map p540; Gazi Ahmet Muhtar Paşa Caddesi; ⊘9am-midnight) The favoured spot of Kars' fashionable under-35s, Pasha has lively staff, a great glass-fronted upstairs gallery, and a buzzing atmosphere from morning till night, especially when there's live Turkish pop (from 7pm). The cakes, desserts and

coffee (₺5 to ₺10; including Colombian filter) are fine, the more substantial dishes less so (mains ₺10 to ₺25).

Barış Türkü Evi   PUB, CAFE
(Map p540; Atatürk Caddesi; ⊘9am-2.30am; 🕾) Housed in a historic mansion, this cafe-bar serves beer and attracts students and under-35s of both sexes, especially for the live Turkish/Caucasian/Kurdish music on Friday and Saturday evenings.

ⓘ Information

Tourist Office (Map p540; ✉0474-212 6865, 0474-212 2179; cnr Faikbey & Gazi Ahmet Muhtar Paşa Caddesis; ⊘8am-5pm Mon-Fri) Gives out useful booklets on Kars and Ani.

ⓘ Getting There & Around

Kars airport is 6km south of the city centre. A shuttle bus marked 'Servis Otobüs' (₺5) runs into town from outside the terminal building. Going out to the airport, it will pick up at airline ticket agencies about 1½ hours before departures. A taxi costs ₺20 to ₺25.

Without your own transport, the best way to see the countryside around Kars, including the ruins at Ani, is with **Celil Ersözoğlu** (✉0532 226 3966; celilani@hotmail.com), who acts as a private driver (guiding is extra) and speaks good English. Hiring a taxi and a cooperative driver is also an option.

AIR

The following airlines serve Kars:

Anadolu Jet (www.anadolujet.com) To/from İstanbul and Ankara.

Pegasus Airlines (www.flypgs.com) To/from İstanbul.

Sun Express To/from İzmir.

DON'T MISS

KARS CASTLE WALK

Rising above the curves of the Kars River, Kars Castle is well worth the climb for its excellent views over the town and the steppe in fine weather. Below it huddle assorted reminders of Kars' history, currently undergoing a refurbishment that will certainly add to its aesthetic appeal. The following 2km walk takes around 1¼ hours.

Turn right from Atatürk Caddesi just before the river to head to the 16th-century Ottoman **Evliya Camii** (Saint's Mosque; Map p540; Aşık Murat Çobanoğlu Caddesi), which features a domed tomb of the 11th-century Anatolian sufi saint Hasan-i Harakani in the area's yard. Above the Evliya Camii, the imposing, basalt **Kümbet Camii** (Map p540) was built as a church between 932 and 937 when Kars was (briefly) capital of the Bagratuni kingdom of Armenia. Reliefs of the 12 apostles adorn the drum beneath the conical dome. The church was converted to a mosque in 1064, when the Seljuks conquered Kars, then used as a church again in the 19th century by the Russians, who added the porches.

Above the Kümbet Camii, the 17th-century **Ulu Camii** (Grand Mosque; Map p540) is the city's largest Ottoman mosque. Past here the path curves upward to the gate of **Kars Castle** (Kars Kalesi; Map p540) FREE. Records show that Saltuk Turks built a fortress here in 1153. It was demolished by the Central Asian conqueror Tamerlane (Timur) in 1386 and rebuilt several times over the following centuries. The *kale* (fortress) was the scene of bitter fighting during and after WWI. When the Russians withdrew in 1920, Kars was left in control of Armenian forces, until Turkish republicans took the castle. Inside are a janissary barracks, arsenal, small mosque, the tomb of Celal Baba who died in a Mongol attack in 1239, and a cafe.

Returning down from the castle, head along the east side of the river to the attractive 16th-century basalt bridge, **Taş Köprü** (Map p540), which was destroyed by a flood and rebuilt by the Ottomans in 1719. The bridge is flanked by the abandoned Ottoman **Muradiye Hamam** (Map p540) and **Cuma Hamam** (Map p540). Head back towards the city past the rectangular 18th-century basalt **Mazlum Ağa Hamam** (Map p540) to the leafy riverside tea garden **İstihkam Aile Çay Bahçesi** (Map p540; Atatürk Caddesi; ⊙10am-midnight).

BUS

Kars' otogar for long-distance services is 4km northeast of the centre. *Servises* ferry passengers to/from the bus companies' city offices, which are mostly on and around Faikbey Caddesi. Destinations include Erzurum (₺25, three hours, eight buses between 11am and 4pm), Trabzon (₺60, seven hours, Kanberoğlu bus at 12.30pm) and Ankara (₺70, 17 hours, Doğu Kars bus at 4pm). **Metro** (Map p540; www.metroturizm.com.tr; Faikbey Caddesi) has a daily service to Amasya (₺90, 11 hours), and İstanbul (₺100, 22 hours) at 11am.

For Erzurum a more convenient midibus service (₺25, three hours, 12 daily, from 5am to 5.30pm) is run by **Kars Vipturizm** (Map p540; http://karsvip.com; Atatürk Caddesi 187) from its downtown office.

Turgutreis (Map p540; www.turgutreis.com.tr; cnr Faikbey & Atatürk Caddesi) shuttles passengers to its own otogar, 2km southeast of the centre. It has buses to Van (₺50, six hours) at 9am and Kayseri (₺70, 12 hours) at 11am.

Dolmuşes to local towns leave from the **Eski Otogar** (Map p540; Halitpaşa Caddesi) dolmuş terminal. Destinations include the following:

Ardahan (₺15, 1½ hours, hourly from 8am to 5pm)

Çıldır (₺20, 1¼ hours, noon or 1pm)

Iğdır (for Doğubayazıt and Azerbaijan; ₺20, 2½ hours, around hourly from 7am to 5pm)

Posof (₺30, two hours, one departure between noon and 1.30pm)

Sarıkamış (₺8, one hour, around hourly 7.30am to 6pm)

Also departing from the Eski Otogar, **Yeşil Artvin Ekspres** (www.yesilartvinekspres.com.tr) buses leave at 9.30am for Artvin (₺40, five hours) and Hopa (₺45, 6½ hours) on the Black Sea coast. For Yusufeli, ask to be dropped at the Su Kavuşumu junction on the Erzurum–Artvin road, from where dolmuşes travel the last 10km to Yusufeli.

CAR

Steer clear of the car-hire companies in central Kars, as they often don't provide proper insurance. It's better to hire in Erzurum.

TRAIN

The daily *Doğu Ekspresi* to Ankara (₺47, 24 hours) via Erzurum (₺16.50, four hours), Sivas

(₺29, 14 hours) and Kayseri (₺35, 17 hours) departs at 7.45am. It's a scenic ride, especially as far as Sivas. When the much-delayed new Kars–Tbilisi–Baku railway is finally in service (officially expected in 2017) there will also be trains to/from Akhalkalaki and Tbilisi in Georgia, and Baku in Azerbaijan.

Ani

Recognised as a World Heritage site by Unesco in 2016, the ruins of Ani (₺8; ⊙8am-7pm Apr-Oct, to 5pm Nov-Mar; ℗), 45km east of Kars, are an absolute must-see, even if you're not an architecture buff. Your first view is stunning: wrecks of great stone buildings adrift on a sea of undulating grass, landmarks in a ghost city that was once the stately Armenian capital and home to nearly 100,000 people, rivalling Constantinople in power and glory. The poignant ruins, the windswept plateau above the gorge of the Arpaçay river (Akhurian to Armenians) that forms the Turkish–Armenian border, and the total lack of crowds make for an eerie ambience that is unforgettable. In the silence broken only by the river gurgling along the border, ponder what went before: the thriving kingdom; the solemn ceremony of the Armenian liturgy; and the travellers, merchants and nobles bustling about their business in this Silk Road entrepôt.

History

Well served by its natural defences, Ani was selected by the Armenian Bagratid king Ashot III (r 952–77) as the site of his new capital in 961, when he moved here from Kars. Ashot's successors Smbat II (r 977–89) and Gagik I (r 990–1020) presided over Ani's continued prosperity. But internecine feuds and Byzantine encroachment weakened the Armenian state and the Byzantines took over Ani in 1045.

Then in 1064 came the Great Seljuks from Persia, followed by the Kingdom of Georgia and, for a time, local Kurdish emirs. The struggle for the city went on until the Mongols arrived in 1236 and decisively cleared everybody else out. The nomadic Mongols had no use for city life, so cared little when the great earthquake of 1319 toppled much of Ani. The depredations of Central Asian conquerer Tamerlane later that century hastened the decline; trade routes shifted, Ani lost what revenues it had managed to retain, and the city died. The earthquake-damaged hulks of its great buildings have been slowly crumbling away ever since.

⊙ Sights

Snow-topped Mt Aragats (4090m) in Armenia overlooks Ani from the east. In clear weather Mt Ararat is visible about 100km to the southeast from a rise in the road a couple of kilometres before you reach Ani. If you want to do some preparatory reading, Virtual Ani (www.virtualani.org) is a fine place to start.

The ticket office for the ruins is just inside the Arslan Kapısı gate. Allow at least 2½ hours to explore. Note that some parts are off limits: if you're thinking of visiting the İç Kale (Citadel), ask at the ticket office beforehand whether it's OK to do so.

Arslan Kapısı   GATE
(Map p544) Just inside the Ani ruins, the sturdy Arslan Kapısı (or Aslan Kapısı – Lion Gate) was supposedly named after Alp Arslan, the Seljuk sultan who conquered Ani in 1064, but was probably also after the *aslan* (lion) relief on the wall inside.

Church of the Redeemer   CHURCH
(Church of St Prkitch; Map p544) Ani's Church of the Redeemer (1034–36) was half-destroyed by lightning in 1957. It was supposedly built to house a portion of the True Cross, brought here from Constantinople; the facade's Armenian inscriptions relay the history. The facade also sports a superb *khatchkar* (cross stone) carved on an elaborate rectangular background, about 3m above ground. The church lies near the remains of a 12th-century Seljuk oil press (Map p544).

**★Church of St Gregory
(Tigran Honents)**   CHURCH
(Resimli Kilise; Map p544) The Church of St Gregory the Illuminator (in Turkish, Resimli Kilise – Church with Pictures) perches very photogenically above the gorge of the Arpaçay, below an 11th-century hamam (Map p544). Built in 1215 by a pious merchant, Tigran Honents, it's in better condition than most buildings at Ani. Look for the long Armenian inscription carved on the exterior, as well as the colourful and lively frescoes inside depicting scenes from the Bible and Armenian church history.

It also features well-preserved relief work, especially on the south wall, including animal motifs.

Convent of the Virgins CHURCH
(Kusanatz; Map p544) Dramatically set just above Arpaçay gorge, the Convent of the Virgins is unfortunately off limits. Probably built in the 11th century, its dainty, serrated-domed chapel is enclosed by a defensive wall. It's clearly visible from the nearby Manuçehr Camii (p545), but for a closer look, you can descend the path signed 'Silk Road' part-way down towards it. Scant ruins of a probably 9th-century **Silk Road bridge** (Map p544), also off limits and also visible from the Manuçehr Camii, stand a little way downriver.

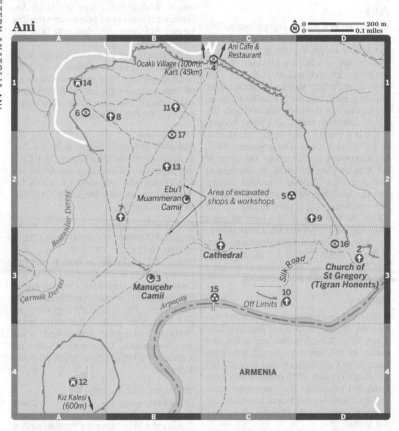

Ani

★ Cathedral
CATHEDRAL

(Map p544) The cathedral at Ani, completed in 1010 and renamed the Fethiye Camii (Victory Mosque) by the Seljuks, is the largest and most impressive building among the ruins. Ani was once the seat of the Armenian Orthodox Patriarchate; the cathedral's three doorways were separate entrances for the patriarch, the king and the people. The building was transformed into a mosque at points in history when Muslims held Ani, but reverted to a church under the Christians. The wide dome, once supported by four massive columns, fell down centuries ago.

Seen from a distance, the building looks quite featureless, but closer inspection reveals eye-catching decorative elements, including several port-hole windows, slender windows surrounded by elegant fretwork, several triangular niches, inscriptions in Armenian near the main entrance, and a blind arcade with slim columns running around the structure.

Heading west from the cathedral towards the site's Manuçehr Camii, you pass an excavated area of former shops and workshops lining a street leading north to the toppled minaret of the Ebu'l Muammeran Camii.

★ Manuçehr Camii
MOSQUE

(Map p544) With a tall octagonal, truncated minaret and six vaults, the Manuçehr Camii at Ani was built by the Seljuk Turks in 1072 and is considered to be the first Turkish mosque in Anatolia. The blend of Armenian and Seljuk design resulted from the Seljuks employing Armenian architects and artisans. Distinctive features are the red-and-black stonework and the polychrome stone inlays adorning the ceilings. The minaret sports the Arabic inscription *bismillah* ('in the name of Allah').

Climb the dingy spiral staircase (if it's not locked) for excellent views. There's no parapet, so take care. To the south is an excavated area, containing remains of houses, with ovens, a granary and bathrooms. The structure next to the mosque may have been a Seljuk *medrese* or palace.

İç Kale
FORTRESS

(Citadel; Map p544) On the rocky eminence at the southern point of the Ani plateau rises the İç Kale; its jumble of tumbled stone includes half of the Church of the Palace, the oldest church at Ani (dating from 622). In the past the İç Kale has been out of bounds, but this changed in 2016.

Also here are vestiges of the Bagratid kings' palace, walls that were probably constructed by the early Armenian Kamsarakan dynasty in the 5th or 6th century, and even walls that may go back to Urartu times (8th century BC). From here you can see the picturesquely perched but out-of-bounds little church known as the Kız Kalesi, on a rock pinnacle above the Arpaçay.

Church of St Gregory (Abughamrents)
CHURCH

(Map p544) This well-preserved, rotunda-shaped church, topped by a conical roof, dates from about 980. It was built at Ani for the wealthy Pahlavuni family by the same architect as Ani's Church of the Redeemer. On the 12-sided exterior, a series of deep niches are topped by scallop-shell carvings; above them, the windows of the drum are framed by double blind arcades. In contrast to the 12-faced exterior, the interior has a six-leaf clover plan.

Kervansaray
CHURCH

(Church of the Holy Apostles; Map p544) The Church of the Holy Apostles (Arak Elots Kilisesi) dates from 1031, but after the Seljuks took the city in 1064, they added a gateway with a fine dome and used the building as a caravanserai – hence its name.

It's fairly well preserved, with decorative carvings, port-hole windows, diagonally intersecting arches in the nave, and ceilings sporting geometric patterns of polychromatic stone inlays. Look also for the various Armenian inscriptions and the *khatchkar* carved on a rectangular background.

Zoroastrian Temple
TEMPLE

(Fire Temple; Map p544) This ruined temple is thought to have been built in the 4th century AD, during a period of Sassanian influence from Persia. It might have been converted into a Christian chapel afterwards. The remains consist of four squat circular columns.

Church of St Gregory (Gagik I) CHURCH

(Map p544) This once-enormous circular church was begun in 998 to plans by the same architect as Ani's cathedral. Its ambitious dome collapsed shortly after completion, and the rest of the building is now also ruined. You can still see the outer walls and a jumble of columns.

Cave Church CAVE, CHURCH

(Map p544) The most easily accessible of the dozens of churches carved out of the rock around the Ani plateau is this 10th-century example just south of the Seljuk Palace.

Seljuk Palace PALACE

(Map p544) At the western tip of the Ani plateau is a Seljuk palace built into the city's defensive walls. It's so painstakingly over-restored that it looks quite out of place, though the portal's star-motif red stonework is very handsome.

Georgian Church CHURCH

(Gürcü Kilisesi; Map p544) Just one wall survives of this Georgian church, probably erected in the 13th century. It used to be a large building, but most of the south wall collapsed around 1840. Of the three remaining arcades, two sport bas-reliefs, one representing the Annunciation, the other the Visitation.

❶ Getting There & Away

The easiest option for Ani is a round-trip taxi (car or minibus) trip from Kars organised by the knowledgeable, English-speaking driver-guide **Celil Ersözoğlu** (p541). He charges ₺150 for one or two people and ₺50 per person for three or more, which includes about three hours' waiting time and a rundown on Ani's history en route. The drive is 50 minutes each way. Celil can group travellers together to make up numbers. He also offers optional guiding services: ₺200 for either the main plateau site or the 'underground city'; ₺350 for both (five to six hours).

A round-trip taxi from Kars with a Turk-ish-speaking driver typically costs around ₺120 with about two hours at the site. Hotels can help organise this. For more time you'll probably have to pay more.

Doğubayazıt

📞 0472 / POP 77,000 / ELEV 1950M

Doğubayazıt's setting is superb. To the north, the talismanic Mt Ararat (Ağrı Dağı; 5137m), Turkey's highest mountain, lords it over the landscape. To the south, the beautiful İshak Paşa Palace surveys town from a rocky perch beneath jagged peaks. The town itself – nick-named 'doggy biscuit' by travellers on the hippie trail – doesn't have too much charm, but it's the obvious base for climbing Mt Ararat (when open to climbers) and exploring a few nearby sights, and its sense of bordertown wildness has a certain appeal. Coming from Erzurum or Kars, you'll quickly notice the distinct atmosphere in this predominantly Kurdish city.

◎ Sights & Activities

★ İshak Paşa Palace PALACE

(İshak Paşa Sarayı; ₺5; ⊙ 9am-6pm Apr-Oct, 8am-4pm Nov-Mar; 🅿) The splendid İshak Paşa Palace stands on a small plateau beneath stark cliffs 6km southeast of town. Combining Ottoman, Seljuk, Georgian, Persian and Armenian design, the palace was begun in 1685 and completed in 1784 by an Ottoman general, İshak Paşa. Dolmuşes (₺2) rattle to the palace until about 5pm from a stop behind the belediye (city hall), leaving when about half-full. Taxis charge ₺25 one way, or ₺30 return with a one-hour wait.

The protective glass roofing over several parts of the palace means you can visit on a rainy day.

Until the early 1930s the palace was surrounded by the town of Eski Bayazıt, but that was demolished by the Turkish army after a Kurdish uprising (you can see its ruins scattered around below the palace), leading to the founding of modern Doğubayazıt.

The palace's elaborate main portal leads into the first courtyard, which would have been open to merchants and guests. Check out the dungeons in the far right corner.

Only family and special guests would have been allowed into the second courtyard, which gives access to the palace's selamlık (men's quarters) and haremlik (women's quarters). A staircase down to the left as you pass into the courtyard leads to servants' quarters and granaries. Steps on the right of the courtyard lead up to the selamlık. Inside, guests would have been entertained in the ceremonial hall-courtyard to the right. The selamlık also has a lovely mosque, which has

Doğubayazıt

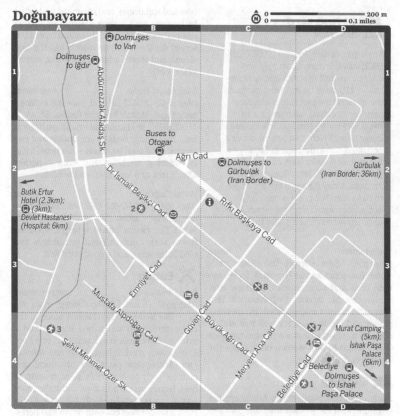

kept much of its original relief decoration (note the trees of life) and ceiling frescoes.

Outside the entrance to the *selamlık* an elaborate tomb, believed to be that of İshak Paşa, is richly decorated with a mix of Seljuk carvings and Persian relief styles.

The marvellously decorated portal of the *haremlık* rises at the far end of the courtyard. These women's quarters include a kitchen, hamam, (squat) toilet and rooms with carved-stone fireplaces and panoramic windows, but the highlight here is undoubtedly the beautiful ceremonial hall, a melange of styles with walls topped by Seljuk triangular stonework, Armenian floral-relief decoration, ornate column capitals that show Georgian influence, and black-and-white chequerboard stone wall sections.

Clinging to the cliffs east of the palace are the remains of the **Eski Kale** (Old Castle), probably founded in Urartian times c 800 BC, with Eski Bayazıt's still-stand-

Doğubayazıt

🔵 Activities, Courses & Tours

1 Sunrise Trekking	D4
2 Tamzara Turizm	B2
3 Yeni Hamam	A4

🛏 Sleeping

4 Hotel Doğus	D4
5 Star Apart Hotel	B4
6 Tehran Boutique Hotel	B3

🍴 Eating

7 Ergül'ün Mutfağı	D4
8 Evin Restaurant	C3

ing 16th-century mosque at its foot. To the castle's right stands the striped-stone **tomb of Ahmad Khani** (Ehmedê Xanî, a beloved 17th-century Kurdish poet and philosopher). The peaks above the car park here have excellent views of the palace, with Doğubayazıt and Mt Ararat beyond.

ℹ GETTING INTO AZERBAIJAN

From Iğdır, **Iğdırlı Turizm** (☏ 0476-228 6901; www.igdirliturizm.com.tr) has six daily buses east to Nahçıvan city (Azerbaijan; ₺10, three hours). Buy tickets at the office on the east side of Meydan: *servises* (shuttles) run from here to the out-of-centre terminal, from where buses depart. Note that you need a visa and must plan in advance to obtain one; the nearest **Azerbaijani consulate** (☏ 0474-223 6475; http://kars.mfa.gov. az; Ordu Caddesi 9, Kars) is in Kars. To get to Baku from Nahçıvan, which is in an enclave separated from the rest of Azerbaijan by Armenia, you'll have to fly.

Yeni Hamam   HAMAM
(Map p547; Şehit Mehmet Özer Sokak; ₺15; ⊙ men 6am-10pm, women 7am-6pm) To rejuvenate tired and sore muscles, perhaps after conquering Mt Ararat, Doğubayazıt's Yeni Hamam comes recommended by trekking guides and locals alike. It's well run and as clean as a whistle. Go for a private massage (short/long ₺10/30); women often enjoy the Turkish coffee massage.

🛏 Sleeping

Some of Doğubayazıt's cheap hotels are not recommended for women travellers, but fortunately there's a reasonable supply of decent midrange places.

Murat Camping   CAMPGROUND $
(☏ 0542 437 3699; www.facebook.com/murat-camping-395575547195635; İshakpaşa Yolu; sites per tent or campervan ₺15, dm/r ₺10/50; P 🖥) Located right beneath İshak Paşa Palace, Murat offers camping, campervan parking with electricity, and basic rooms and dorms. Trekking and mountaineering advice and expeditions are available. There's a licensed kebap restaurant with Ararat views, which is popular with nonguests, plus a mini-funfair, so don't expect a tranquil country retreat. Breakfast costs an extra ₺10.

⭐ **Tehran Boutique Hotel**   BOUTIQUE HOTEL $$
(Map p547; ☏ 0472-312 0195; www.tehranbou tiquehotel.com; Büyük Ağrı Caddesi 72; s ₺60-100; d ₺100-160; ⊜🖥) Super-comfortable and spacious rooms, some with Ararat views and balconies, have their own tea- and coffee-making equipment, minibars stocked with beer and soft drinks, and gleaming, up-to-date bathrooms with spacious rainhead shower compartments. A good breakfast spread is served on the top floor (which has the best views), and there's a bar and inviting seating in the lobby.

Star Apart Hotel   APARTMENT $$
(Map p547; ☏ 0472-312 6261; www.starhoteldogu-bayazit.com; Mustafa Alpdoğan Caddesi 57; s/d/tr ₺60/110/150; 🖥) Large and bright apartments have two double beds or one double and two singles, good tiled bathrooms, kitchens, fridges, washing machines and irons – perfect after a trek or a long spell on the road.

Hotel Doğus   HOTEL $$
(Map p547; ☏ 0472-312 6161; http://dogushotel. net; Belediye Caddesi 100; s/d/tr ₺60/100/130; ⊜🖥) The Doğus provides bright, spotlesss rooms with wood-surfaced furnishings and tiled bathrooms, and a good breakfast.

🍴 Eating

Evin Restaurant   TURKISH, KURDISH $
(Map p547; Dr İsmail Beşikçi Caddesi; mains ₺9-15; ⊙ 24hr Mon-Sat) The classiest place in the city centre, with uniformed waiters and a professional clientele at lunchtime, two-floor Evin serves good kebaps, pide and *lahmacun* (Arabic-style pizza) but also local specialities such as *bozbaş* (a stew or soup of beef, beans, herbs, tomatoes and aubergines served in a pot) and *abdigör köfte* (meatballs from a tender beef cut with onion and herbs, boiled not grilled). You can follow up with a tasty, sweet *aşure* (fruit pudding).

Ergül'ün Mutfağı   KURDISH, ANATOLIAN $
(Map p547; Dr İsmail Beşikçi Caddesi; mains ₺7-11; ⊙ 7am-8pm; 🍴) Clean, family-run Ergül'ün Mutfağı serves up a variety of Kurdish and Anatolian dishes with different specials each day of the week. It's good for soups and vegetarian dishes, and meat-eaters should try to be there on Monday, Thursday or Saturday when the local speciality *abdigör köfte* is prepared.

ℹ Information

Moneychangers here do not exchange Iranian rials. If you're heading into Iran, offload Turkish lira in the first town across the border, Bazargan: it can be hard to get rid of them elsewhere.

English is spoken at the **Tourist Information Office** (Map p547; Rıfkı Başkaya Caddesi; ⊙ 7.30am-noon & 12.30-4pm Mon-Fri) and there's a selection of maps and brochures, but this office only opens when it feels like it.

❶ Getting There & Around

AIR

The nearest airports are at Iğdır or Ağrı, both served by daily Anadolu Jet flights to/from Ankara and daily Turkish Airlines flights to/from İstanbul. The airlines run shuttles to/from Doğubayazıt for all flights:

Ağrı ₺15, 100km, 1½ hours
Iğdır ₺12, 70km, 1¼ hours

BUS & DOLMUŞ

The otogar (bus station) is 3km west of the centre on the D100 towards Ağrı. Buses to Erzurum (₺30, four hours) mostly leave between 10am and 3pm. 'Hastane' buses (₺1) run from the centre (Ağrı Caddesi) to the otogar, and 'Belediyesi' buses from the otogar to the centre; a taxi costs ₺15.

Dolmuşes to İshak Paşa Palace (₺2, till 5pm) depart from behind the belediye (city hall).

Dolmuşes to Iğdır, Van and Gürbulak (for Iran) leave from separate stops in central Doğubayazıt:

Iğdır (₺8, 45 minutes) From Abdürrezzak Aladaş Sokak, north of Ağrı Caddesi, once or twice an hour.

Kars Take a dolmuş to Iğdır and change.

Van (₺25, three hours) From just off Abdürrezzak Aladaş Sokak at 6.30am and about every two hours from 8am to 4pm.

Iran From Ağrı Caddesi in the centre to the border at Gürbulak (₺8, 30 minutes) from 6am to about 5pm. Get going before 10am; after that you'll have to wait longer for vehicles to fill up. On the Iranian side, pay ₺1 or ₺0.50 for a shared taxi to Bazargan (3km), where you can change money and find onward transport. The border is open 24 hours.

Mt Ararat

A highlight of any trip to eastern Turkey, the twin peaks of Mt Ararat (Ağrı Dağı) have figured in legends since time began, most notably as the supposed resting place of Noah's Ark. The western peak, Büyük Ağrı (Great Ararat), is 5137m high, while Küçük Ağrı (Little Ararat) rises to 3925m. Climbing Great Ararat is a fantastic and challenging (if nontechnical) experience. Sadly for climbers, in 2016 Ararat was declared a military restricted zone and climbers were banned from the mountain. It was hoped the ban would be lifted for the 2017 climbing season.

Climbing Mt Ararat

All climbers must have a permit and must go with a guide licensed by the Turkish Mountaineering Federation, the Ağrı province Culture & Tourism Department or the Doğubayazıt district governorship. A dependable guide is important for your safety. People have died on the mountain; in 2010, Scotsman Donald Mackenzie went missing while searching for Noah's Ark.

The permits procedure has changed from time to time but most recently permits (US$70) were issued by the district governor's office in Doğubayazıt. They can be issued to the individual climber (who can obtain the permit before organising a guide) or to the agency or guide taking the climber up the mountain. Processing normally takes two or three days. If you are climbing with a reputable travel firm it's normally easiest to let them get the permit for you.

Individuals can apply and pay online at http://dogubayazitrehberi.com, or in person at the Doğubayazıt tourist information office (p548). In either case you have to supply a copy of your passport, the dates of your climb and give a few personal details such as your blood group. The permit holder and guide must check in with the *jandarma* (police) in Doğubayazıt on the morning of departure for Ararat.

If unofficial guides, hotel staff or touts in Doğubayazıt tell you they can get the permit cheaper or immediately, be very sceptical. There may be corruption involved or, worse, they will let you think they have obtained the permit but in reality will be taking you up Ararat unofficially. This scam has landed hikers in prison. Follow the official procedure, and ask for evidence that the permit has been granted.

Prices vary between agency and package. Shop around; check what's included and consider joining a group. Some agencies offer fixed-date open-group ascents, which individuals can join at group prices. Typically, agencies charge about €400 per person to lead a four-person group on a four- to five-day trek from Doğubayazıt, including guides, transport, permit, packhorses, camping and food. Most reputable agencies recommend five-day treks to allow acclimatisation before tackling the summit. Some offer packages including a night's accommodation and dinner in Doğubayazıt at each end of the trek. Try to contact agencies a month or more in advance so you have time to sort out arrangements.

Despite the costs and effort involved (Ararat is relentlessly steep and can be very cold even in high summer), climbing Ararat is a fantastic experience. Expect stupendous views and stunning landscapes. The climbing season is from mid-June to mid-September; the warmest weather and best views are from about mid-July to the end of August. You'll need to be comfortable with snow-climbing techniques using crampons past 4800m, even in the height of summer.

The usual starting points are at about 2200m near the southern foothill villages of Eli Köyü and Çevirme. Routes from both villages head to a first camp site at 3200m, and the second one at 4200m. Five-day treks acclimatise on day two by climbing from 3200m to 4200m then returning to 3200m; on day three you camp at 4200m; on day four you start about 2am for the summit, then descend to 3200m for the night.

You can also do one- and two-day treks around the mountain. Provided you stay under 2500m you won't have to go through as much official process, but it's still best to go with a local guide; risks include ferocious shepherd dogs. Expect to pay around €100 per person for a day hike including transport and dinner afterwards. Another option is to hike the hills south of Doğubayazıt, on sections of the Silk Road between İshak Paşa Palace and Iran.

Guides

Tamzara Turizm TREKKING
(Map p547; ✏0472-312 5232, 0541 655 3582; www.mtararattour.com; Dr İsmail Beşikçi Caddesi 147C, Doğubayazıt) Tamzara's Doğubayazıt operation is run by English-speaking Mustafa Arsin, who has summited Ararat more than 200 times. The website is a useful source of information. Also offers Ararat ski tours. The office entrance is in the front yard of the Ahmedi Hani Camii.

Sunrise Trekking TREKKING
(Map p547; ✏0543 365 4249, 0543 564 7725; www.araratsunrises.com; Kat 3 No 22, Mertoğlu İş Merkezi, Belediye Caddesi, Doğubayazıt) This Kurdish-Polish team works chiefly with foreign groups but also has regular fixed-date open-group Ararat climbs, listed on the website. It gets good reports from clients.

Middle Earth Travel TREKKING
(www.middleearthtravel.com) Cappadocia-based nationwide hiking-tour specialist offering Mt Ararat climbing packages.

East Turkey Expeditions TREKKING
(✏0551 111 8998; zaferonay@hotmail.com) Local operator Zafer Onay is a recommended trip organiser for Mt Ararat climbs. He's knowledgeable and speaks English.

NEMRUT DAĞI NATIONAL PARK

No photos can do justice to the haunting reality of this bare, windy, isolated mountaintop with its strange, gravel-covered, 50m-high burial cone and the presence of those pitilessly staring statues with their partly mutilated, partly weathered features.

The spellbinding peak of Nemrut Dağı (*nehm*-root dah-uh) rises to a height of 2106m in the Anti-Taurus Range between Malatya to the north and Kahta to the south. It's set within the 138-sq-km **Nemrut Dağı Milli Parkı** (Nemrut Dağı National Park; www.milliparklar.gov.tr/mp/nemrutdagi; ₺12), which also encompasses other monuments from the ancient Commagene kingdom. (This Nemrut Dağı is not to be confused with the less visited Nemrut Dağı near Lake Van.)

It's relatively easy to get to the summit with your own vehicle, and it's also easy to take a tour from Kahta or Malatya. There are also several accommodation options a few kilometres from the summit; most are reachable by public transport and will drive guests up to the summit.

Try to visit Nemrut between May and September, when the roads to the summit should be snow-free. They may be passable as early as mid-March and as late as mid-November, but this can't be guaranteed. July and August are the warmest months, but even in high summer it will be chilly and windy on top of the mountain. This is especially true at sunrise, the coldest time of the day. Take warm clothing no matter when you go.

History

From 250 BC onwards, this region straddled the border between the Seleucid Empire (the Hellenistic successor to the empire of Alexander the Great) and the Persian-based Parthian Empire.

Under the Seleucid Empire, the governor of Commagene declared his kingdom's independence. In 80 BC, with the Seleucids in disarray and Roman power spreading into Anatolia, a Roman ally named Mithridates I Callinicus proclaimed himself king and set up his capital at Arsameia, near the modern village of Kocahisar.

Nemrut Dağı Area

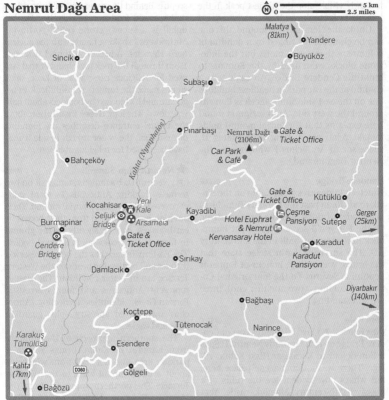

Mithridates was succeeded by his son Antiochus I Epiphanes, who ruled from about 70 to 38 BC and consolidated his kingdom's security by signing a nonaggression treaty with Rome, turning his kingdom into a Roman buffer against attack from the Parthians. His good relations with both sides allowed him to revel in delusions of grandeur, and it was Antiochus who ordered the building of Nemrut's fabulous temples and funerary mound. This megalomaniacal monarch had two platforms cut in the mountaintop, filled them with colossal statues of himself and the gods (his relatives – or so he thought), and ordered an artificial mountain peak of crushed rock 50m high to be piled between them. Antiochus' own tomb and those of three female relatives are reputed to lie beneath those tonnes of rock.

In the fourth decade of his reign, Antiochus sided with the Parthians in a squabble with Rome, and in 38 BC the Romans deposed him. The great days of Commagene were thus limited to the 32-year reign of Antiochus.

Before long Nemrut Dağı had been completely forgotten – until 1881, when a German engineer employed by the Ottomans to assess transport routes was astounded to come across the now-famous statues on this remote mountaintop. The American School of Oriental Research began archaeological work here in 1953.

◎ Sights

Karakuş Tümülüsü   RUINS
(ℙ) Eight kilometres north of Kahta on highway D360, a road forks left towards Sincik; 1.2km along here, a second fork left leads 700m to the Karakuş Tümülüsü, a large burial mound built in 36 BC. The small, loose stones covering the mound give it more than a passing similarity to the great cone-shaped mound atop Nemrut Dağı – which in good weather

is clearly visible atop the highest peak in the mountains far to the northeast.

Unlike the Nemrut Dağı mound, this one can be climbed. It's ringed by a handful of columns – there were more, but the limestone blocks were used by the Romans to build the Cendere Bridge. An eagle tops a column at the car park, a headless bull tops one on the east side, and a faceless lion sits around the west side. An inscription found here explains that the burial mound holds female relatives of King Mithridates II, successor to Antiochus I who created the Nemrut Dağı mound.

Cendere Bridge   BRIDGE

Nineteen kilometres from Kahta on the Sincik road (10km past the Karakuş Tümülüsü) is a modern bridge over the Cendere River. To the left you'll see a magnificent humpback Roman bridge built in the 2nd century AD. The surviving Latin stelae state that the bridge was built in honour of Emperor Septimius Severus. Of the four original Corinthian columns (two at either end), three are still standing.

Yeni Kale   CASTLE

(New Fortress; **P**) Five kilometres east of Cendere Bridge en route towards Nemrut Dağı is a 1km detour to Kocahisar (Eski Kahta) village. There was a Commagene palace here, but what's now evident are the ruins of a massive 13th-century Mamluk castle, Yeni Kale. The castle was being renovated at the time of writing and may reopen in 2017.

Seljuk Bridge   BRIDGE

Immediately east of the Kocahisar turn-off on the road towards Nemrut Dağı, an old road veers north off the modern one to cross the Kahta (Nymphaios) River on a graceful Seljuk bridge.

★ Arsameia   RUINS

(Eski Kale; **P**) **FREE** About 1.5km south of the Kocahisar turn-off, a turn to the east brings you to a national park gate and ticket office and, 1.5km past this, the ancient Commagene capital of Arsameia. Here a path leads 400m uphill from the road, past several intriguing monuments, to the jumbled-stone ruins of Mithridates I's palace on a hilltop with superb panoramas.

First up on the left after about 100m is a large stele depicting Mithras (or Apollo), the sun god. Further along are the bases of two steles depicting Mithridates I and Antiochus I, the latter (on the taller stele) holding a

sceptre. Behind them you can peer into a deep underground food-storage chamber. Further uphill is a superb **stone relief** portraying Mithridates I shaking hands with the ancient hero Heracles. Adjacent, a tunnel descends 158m through the rock to a chamber that was used for religious rites; a lot of loose small stones make the tunnel's steps difficult to negotiate and it's blocked by boulders about halfway down. The long **Greek inscription** above the tunnel entrance describes the founding of Arsameia; the water trough beside it may have been used for religious ablutions.

★ Nemrut Dağı Summit   RUINS

(**P**) Nemrut Dağı's famous statues sit on two terraces flanking Antiochus I's giant gravel-covered, mountaintop burial mound. Their 2m-high heads, toppled from their bodies by earthquakes, now sit silently on the ground in front of their colossal, bethroned bodies. The Eastern Terrace has the better-preserved thrones and bodies; the heads on the Western Terrace are in better condition. The statues represent Antiochus and four syncretistic Persian-Greek identities (reflecting Antiochus' own mixed ancestry), plus guardian lions and eagles.

The southern approach to the summit, from Karadut or Kahta, brings you to a parking area and tea stall from which it's about a 600m uphill walk to the Western Terrace. The northern approach, from the Malatya direction, brings you to within 250m of the Eastern Terrace. It's a 300m walk round either side of the mound from one terrace to the other.

The statues and heads are arranged in the same order on each side: from left to right, lion, eagle, Antiochus, the Commagene Tyche (goddess of fortune and fertility), Zeus-Oromasdes, Apollo-Mithras, Heracles-Artagnes, eagle, lion.

On the backs of the eastern statues are inscriptions in Greek. Low walls at the sides of each terrace once held carved reliefs showing processions of ancient Persian and Greek royalty, Antiochus' 'predecessors'. The site was to be approached by a ceremonial road to what Antiochus termed 'the thrones of the gods', which would be based 'on a foundation that will never be demolished'.

☞ Tours

The main tour centres are Kahta and Malatya, but there are also tours from Şanlıurfa and Cappadocia.

From Kahta

Historically Kahta has had a reputation as a rip-off town. Check exactly what you'll see during the tour, in addition to the summit, how long you'll be away for, whether park fees or food and drinks are included, and whether you'll have a proper guide or just a driver.

From Kahta, visitors to the mountain have the option of a long tour or a short tour. Most long tours are timed to capture a dramatic sunrise or sunset. If you opt for a sunrise tour you'll leave Kahta about 3am, arriving at Nemrut Dağı for sunrise. After an hour or so you'll go down again via Arsameia (p552), Kocahisar, Cendere Bridge (p552) and Karakuş Tümülüsü (p551). Expect to be back in Kahta about 10am. On a sunset tour you'll do the same loop but in the reverse order. You'll leave around 1pm or 2pm and start with the 'subsidiary sights', then go up to the summit, before returning to Kahta (getting back about 8pm or 9pm).

A short tour lasts about three hours and just zips you from Kahta to the summit and back again, allowing about an hour at the top and skipping the other interesting sights en route. Tour prices can vary from year to year and according to seasonal demand but a typical asking price for either long or short tours at research time was ₺150 for a minibus for up to 10 or 12 people. Kommagene Tours and the Zeus Hotel (☑0416-725 5694; www.zeus hotel.com.tr) are reliable tour providers.

Another option is to hire a taxi at the Kahta otogar. Otogar Taksi (☑0416-725 6264) asks around ₺100 for a short tour and ₺125 for a long tour. Don't expect any informed commentary, however.

From Malatya

Malatya offers an alternative way to approach Nemrut Dağı. However, visiting Nemrut from this northern side means you miss out on the other fascinating sights on the southern flanks (reached from Kahta), unless you make special arrangements – or traverse the top on foot and hitch a ride.

Hassle-free minibus tours to Nemrut Dağı are available from May to October (depending on weather) through English-speaking Ramazan Karataş (☑0536 873 0534; ramo4483@hotmail.com) or the Malatya tourist office (☑0422-323 4490). The tour starts from Malatya at noon and gets back around 10am the next day, giving you both sunset and sunrise at the Nemrut summit. You sleep at the simple but pleasant Güneş Motel Karapinar (p554) at Yandere village, 14km below the

summit on the north side, with dinner and breakfast (not lunch or park fees) included for a total price of ₺160 per person. Solo travellers or even pairs may have to pay more if there is no one else going.

From Cappadocia

Travel companies in Cappadocia offer minibus tours to Nemrut despite the distance of over 500km each way. Two-day tours cost about €200 per person and involve many hours of breakneck driving. If you have enough time, opt for a more leisurely three-day tour – these usually also include Harran and Şanlıurfa. Ask for details on night stops and driving times before committing.

Kahta's Kommagene Tours (☑0532 200 3856, 0416-725 5385; www.nemrutguide.com) offers a three-day, two-night package including accommodation, with pick-up in Cappadocia and drop off at Adiyaman airport or a local otogar for ₺775 per person.

🛏 Sleeping & Eating

There are several places to stay in Karadut, as well as between there and the summit. There is one pension at Yandere on the north side of the mountain. Village-house accommodation at Kayadibi on the southwest approach, run by Kahta's Kommagene Hotel (☑0532 200 3856, 0416-725 9726; www.kommagenehotel.com; Mustafa Kemal Caddesi; s/d/tr €20/35/45, camping per car/tent €10/6; P☀️🛜), was expected to open by 2017, with the possibility of horse rides from there to the summit.

Nemrut Kervansaray Hotel HOTEL **$$**
(☑0416-737 2190; osmanaydin.44@hotmail.com; Karadut; s/d half-board €44/64; P🛜🏊) One of Karadut's two larger hotels, the 22-room Kervansaray has small but attractive rooms with comfy beds, big glass-door showers and, in some, mountain views and private balconies. English is spoken, there is a decent onsite restaurant with wine and cold beer, and the swimming pool is a welcome feature on summer days.

Işık Pansion PENSION **$$**
(☑0416-737 2010; www.nemrutisikpansiyon.com; Karadut; s/d/tr without meals €9/19/19, campsite ₺20; P☀️🛜) In Karadut village centre, Işık has just five bright rooms with colourful bedding. It serves a generous breakfast (₺10), and dinner is also available (starting at ₺12).

Hotel Euphrat HOTEL **$$**
(☑0416-737 2175; Karadut; s/d half-board ₺120/180, without meals ₺60/110; P🛜🏊) The friendly

management at this relatively large (46 rooms) but low-rise hotel offers good-sized, clean rooms with writing desks and glassed-in showers, plus a pool and spectacular views from the restaurant terrace. It's popular with tour groups at peak seasons; offers good discounts when business is quiet.

Karadut Pansiyon
PENSION $$

(☏ 0416-737 2169, 0533 616 4564; karadutpan siyon@hotmail.com; Karadut; per person without meals ₺30-40, campsite ₺5; P ✴ ☏) This pension, 1km up the road from Karadut village centre, is run by two amiable brothers and has 14 neat, compact rooms (some with air-con), cleanish bathrooms and a shared kitchen. Good meals are available (breakfast/dinner ₺10/20), along with wine or beer, in the al fresco terrace bar.

Güneş Motel Karapinar
PENSION $$

(☏ 0536 972 1482; www.nemrutgunesmotel.com; Yandere; per person half-board ₺80; ☏) In Yandere village, 14km from the summit on the road from Malatya, Güneş Motel Karapinar is set by a tumbling mountain stream with ample airy sitting areas and half a dozen small but freshly painted rooms with bathrooms.

ℹ Getting There & Around

There are three ways of approaching the summit. From the southeastern side, a good, paved road leads 12km up from Karadut village to a car park 500m before the summit. From the southwestern side, another good, paved road goes up past Arsameia and climbs for 10km until it meets the road from Karadut, 3km before the summit car park.

From the northern side, 93km of good, paved road runs from Malatya, via the D300 and then the Kubbe Geçidi pass and Pazarcık, Tepehan and Yandere villages, to the old Güneş Motel (closed at the time of research). From the old motel, 2.5km of unpaved road (a bit rough in parts, but passable in an ordinary car) leads to a parking area 200m from the summit. It is not possible to cross the summit by car from the northern side to the southern side.

Entrance gates to **Nemrut Dağı Milli Parkı** (p550) are just past **Çeşme Pansiyon** (☏ 0416-737 2032; cesmepansion02@gmail.com; r without meals ₺50, campsite ₺20) above Karadut, at the turn-off to Arsameia if you're coming from the

southwest, and just past the old Güneş Motel on the north side.

CAR

From Kahta it's 46km to the south-side summit car park via **Karakuş Tümülüsü** (p551), **Cendere Bridge** (p552), Kocahisar and **Arsameia** (p552). The alternative route, staying on the D360 to Narince then approaching the summit through Karadut, is a few kilometres longer but takes a similar amount of time, around 1¼ hours at a careful pace, not counting stops. Both routes follow decent paved roads all the way. Remember that you'll be driving a good part of the way in low gear, which uses more fuel than normal highway driving.

From Malatya it's a good, paved road, albeit winding and steep in parts, as far as the old Güneş Motel (93km, about two hours; the motel was closed at the time of research), from which it's a further 2.5km to the summit car park (about 200m from the summit) on an unpaved road that is a bit rough in parts but OK with a normal car in dry weather.

There is no road at the summit linking the southern and the northern sides, but a reasonable (in dry weather) 20km road does skirt the west side of the mountain from Kocahisar in the southwest to Büyüköz, 13km north of the summit on the road from Malatya. The first 12km from Kocahisar, up to Subaşı village, are surfaced. The final 8km to Büyüköz are unpaved, with some sharp, steep bends, but OK for careful, confident drivers in dry weather. For anyone taking this road in a north–south direction, it's signposted (to Kahta) at the turn-off just north of Büyüköz.

TAXI & MINIBUS

Two or three minibuses leave Karadut for Kahta (₺6, 45 minutes) between 7am and 8am. For an extra few lira they will pick up at the hotels and pensions up the road towards the summit (₺10 from Çeşme Pansiyon to Kahta). There are also minibuses to Kahta every hour or two till about 5pm from the Karadut junction on the Gerger road, 2.5km down from Karadut.

Some Karadut pension owners will pick you up at Kahta's otogar for ₺40 to ₺60 per vehicle (similar to the taxi fare). Agree on the price beforehand.

All Karadut pensions and hotels can run you up to the summit and back, for anywhere between ₺50 to ₺110 per car or minibus, with an hour or so wait. Generally the cheaper the rooms, the cheaper the transport too.

Understand
Turkey

Turkey Today

After over a decade of strong economic growth, Turks have seen their standard of living rise significantly, but long-standing issues remain – including the Kurdish conflict and juggling Islamic and secular lifestyles – and a failed coup increased these tensions. The war in Syria has brought Islamic State of Iraq and the Levant (ISIL) suicide bombers to İstanbul while Turkey has become the refugees' route to Europe, prompting a deal for Turkey to take back refugees in exchange for EU privileges.

Best on Film

Mustang (2015) Turkish-French film about orphaned sisters in a remote village.

Innocence of Memories (2015) Documentary about Orhan Pamuk's Museum of Innocence.

Winter Sleep (2014) Poignant character study in snowy Anatolia.

The Cut (2014) Drama by Turkish-German director Fatih Akin, set during the Armenian tragedy of 1915.

Once Upon a Time in Anatolia (2011) Night-time search for a corpse on the steppe.

Best in Print

The Architect's Apprentice (Elif Şafak) The magical realist's tale of Ottoman architect Mimar Sinan.

A Strangeness in My Mind (Orhan Pamuk) 20th-century İstanbul through the eyes of an Anatolian street hawker.

Birds Without Wings (Louis de Bernières) *Captain Corelli's Mandolin* author covers the Turkish-Greek population exchange.

The Janissary Tree (Jason Goodwin) First in the Yashim series about a eunuch detective in 19th-century İstanbul.

Turkish Awakening (Alev Scott) Turkish-British writer's personal discovery of modern Turkey.

Political Turmoil

Turkey's troubled period of suicide bombings and conflict with Kurdish insurgents seemingly reached a nadir in July 2016, when a faction of the military instigated a coup against the ruling Justice and Development Party (AKP). The night of drama saw the Turkish parliament bombed and a military blockade of İstanbul's Bosphorus Bridge – subsequently renamed the 15th July Martyrs' Bridge for the civilian lives lost in the thwarted putsch. The AKP responded by dismissing or detaining over 100,000 suspected plotters from judges and generals to civil servants and teachers, and lobbied the US to extradite the accused coup mastermind, Turkish cleric Fetullah Gülen. Some 38,000 prisoners were released early to accommodate arrested plotters, and Amnesty International raised concerns about treatment of detainees.

Terrorist Attacks

The coup came against a background of increased violence in Turkey, largely due to the collapse of a two-year ceasefire with the Kurdistan Workers Party (PKK). The virtual civil war between the Turkish military and Kurdish insurgents in southeastern Anatolia is bleakly symbolised by Cizre, where the deserted, bullet-riddled houses reflect those found across the nearby Syrian border. PKK splinter group the Kurdistan Freedom Falcons (TAK) has also carried out bomb attacks in Ankara and İstanbul. Meanwhile, ISIL suicide bombers struck locations including İstanbul's Hippodrome, the city's main thoroughfare İstiklal Caddesi, and Atatürk International Airport.

Economic Progress

The 2016 coup was an unwelcome flashback for a country that once experienced a coup every decade, but has recently enjoyed the kind of golden age not seen since its 18th-century Tulip Era. When the AKP came to power in 2002, the Islamic party took a sure hand of the secular state and oversaw bullish economic growth and improvements to infrastructure and living standards. Indeed, many Turkish middle-class professionals enjoy a better lifestyle than their counterparts in Western nations. In affluent spots such as Bodrum and parts of İstanbul, the air of breezy prosperity seems a realisation of founding father Atatürk's modern, Europe-facing dream for Turkey. Equally, in the blue-collar boomtowns known as the Anatolian Tigers, economic gains have been made; many locals are also happy that the AKP is giving Islam a more dominant role in society. This conservative heartland far outweighs the liberal Turks in İstanbul and on the Mediterranean and Aegean coasts who are critical of the AKP's agenda.

Political Scene

With this support, Recep Tayyip Erdoğan has moved from two terms as prime minister to his current presidential term. The Turkish president is traditionally a figurehead with a largely ceremonial role, while the prime minister leads the government, but Erdoğan is the de facto political leader; as was seen when prime minister Ahmet Davutoğlu resigned over their political differences. The AKP juggernaut faltered in the June 2015 general election, which resulted in a hung parliament due to the 80 seats won by the pro-Kurdish Peoples' Democratic party (HDP). The AKP subsequently regained power in a snap election, but it was 13 seats short of the 330 needed to call a referendum to change the constitution – which would allow the creation of a presidential government headed by Erdoğan.

Press Freedom

With the next elections due in 2019, the AKP forges on despite controversies such as the Gezi Park protests in 2013, which turned central İstanbul into a virtual warzone following a heavy-handed police response to an environmental demonstration. In this autocratic environment, Turkey dropped to 151 out of 180 countries in the 2016 World Press Freedom Index. Government moves against press freedom included sentencing two *Cumhuriyet* editors to five years in prison for running a story about the Turkish secret services supplying arms to Islamic rebels in Syria.

European Relations

The European refugee crisis prompted a controversial deal for Turkey to take Syrian refugees back from the EU, adding to the two million already in camps on the Syrian border and elsewhere, and to close the people-smuggling routes from Turkey's Aegean coast to the Greek islands. In exchange, Turks will have easier access to the EU, and Turkey will receive financial aid and the acceleration of its EU membership application. However, relations between the AKP and Europe are often strained, for example when Germany became the latest country to recognise the 1915-17 Armenian genocide; Turkey continues to reject the 'genocide' label.

POPULATION: **79,414,269**

AREA: **783,562 SQ KM**

URBAN POPULATION: **73.4% OF TOTAL POPULATION**

UNEMPLOYMENT: **10.4%**

LIFE EXPECTANCY: **74.57 YEARS**

if Turkey were 100 people

75 would be Turkish
18 would be Kurdish
7 other minorities

belief systems
(% of population)

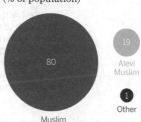

80 Muslim
19 Alevi Muslim
1 Other

population per sq km

TURKEY USA UK

= 30 people

History

Fate has put Turkey at the junction of two continents. A land bridge, meeting point and battleground, it has seen many people – mystics, merchants, nomads and conquerors – moving between Europe and Asia since time immemorial. Many have left their mark, so that the Turkish landscape is littered with Byzantine castles, Greek and Roman ruins, Seljuk caravanserais and Ottoman palaces, and the great book of Turkish history is full of remarkable and intriguing events, cultures and individuals.

> Archaeologist Ian Hodder's *Çatalhöyük: The Leopard's Tale* is an account of the excavation of the site and vividly portrays life as it was during the city's heyday.

Early Cultures, Cities & Clashes

Archaeological finds indicate that Anatolia (the Turkish landmass in Asia) was inhabited by hunter-gatherers during the Palaeolithic era. Neolithic people carved the stone pillars at Göbektepe around 9500 BC. By the 7th millennium BC some folk formed settlements; Çatalhöyük arose around 6500 BC. Perhaps the first-ever city, it was a centre of innovation, with locals creating distinctive pottery. Relics can be seen at Ankara's Museum of Anatolian Civilisations.

During the Chalcolithic age, communities in southeast Anatolia absorbed Mesopotamian influences, including the use of metal tools. Across Anatolia more and larger communities sprung up and interacted. By 3000 BC advances in metallurgy led to the creation of various Anatolian kingdoms. One such was at Alacahöyük, in the heart of Anatolia, yet even this place showed Caucasian influence – evidence of trade beyond the Anatolian plateau.

Trade was increasing on the western coast too, where Troy was trading with the Aegean islands and mainland Greece. Around 2000 BC, the Hatti established a capital at Kanesh near Kayseri, ruling over a web of trading communities. Here for the first time Anatolian history materialises and becomes 'real', with clay tablets providing written records of dates, events and names.

No singular Anatolian civilisation had yet emerged, but the tone was set for millennia to come: cultural interaction, trade and war would be recurring themes in Anatolian history.

TIMELINE	c 9500 BC	c 6500 BC	c 4000–3000 BC
	Neolithic man creates the circular array of megaliths at Göbekli Tepe. Previously thought to be a medieval cemetery, the site is now considered the world's oldest place of pilgrimage yet discovered.	Founding of Çatalhöyük, the world's first city. Over time 13 layers of houses are built, beehive style, interconnected and linked with ladders. At its peak the city houses around 8000.	Hattian culture develops at Alacahöyük in the early Bronze Age, though settlement here had been continuous since the Chalcolithic age. The Hatti develop jewellery, metalwork and weapons.

Ages of Bronze: The Hittites

The Hatti soon declined and the Hittites swallowed their territory. From Alacahöyük, the Hittites shifted their capital to Hattuşa (near present-day Boğazkale) around 1800 BC. The Hittites' legacy consisted of their capital, as well as their state archives and distinctive artistic styles. By 1450 BC the kingdom, having endured internal ructions, re-emerged as an empire. In creating the first Anatolian empire, the Hittites were warlike but displayed other imperial trappings, ruling over vassal states while also displaying a sense of ethics and a penchant for diplomacy. This didn't prevent them overrunning Ramses II of Egypt in 1298 BC, but did allow them to patch things up by marrying the crestfallen Ramses to a Hittite princess.

The Hittite empire was harassed in later years by subject principalities, including Troy. The final straw was the invasion of the iron-smelting Greeks, generally known as the 'sea peoples'. The landlocked Hittites were disadvantaged during an era of burgeoning sea trade and lacked the latest technology: iron.

Meanwhile, a new dynasty at Troy became a regional power. The Trojans, in turn, were harried by the Greeks, which led to the Trojan War in 1250 BC. This allowed the Hittites breathing space but later arrivals hastened their demise. Some pockets of Hittite culture persisted. Later city-states created a neo-Hittite culture, which became the conduit for Mesopotamian religion and arts to reach Greece.

> Until the rediscovery of the ruins at Boğazkale in the 19th century, the Hittites were known only through several obscure references in the Old Testament.

Classical Empires: Greece & Persia

Post-Hittite Anatolia was a patchwork of peoples, indigenous Anatolians and recent interlopers. In the east, the Urartians forged a kingdom near Lake Van. By the 8th century BC the Phrygians arrived in western Anatolia. Under King Gordius, of Gordian knot fame, the Phrygians created a capital at Gordion, their power peaking later under his son Midas. In 725 BC Gordion was put to the sword by horse-borne Cimmerians, a fate that even Midas' golden touch couldn't avert.

On the southwest coast, the Lycians established a confederation of city-states extending from modern-day Fethiye to Antalya. Inland, the Lydians dominated western Anatolia from their capital at Sardis and created the first-ever coinage.

Meanwhile, Greek colonies spread along the Mediterranean coast and Greek influence infiltrated Anatolia. Most of the Anatolian peoples were influenced by the Greeks: Phrygia's King Midas had a Greek wife, the Lycians borrowed the legend of the Chimera, and Lydian art was an amalgam of Greek and Persian art forms. The admiration was almost mutual: the Greeks were so impressed by the wealth of

> Homer, the Greek author of the *Iliad*, which told the story of the Trojan War, is believed to have been born in Smyrna (present-day İzmir) before 700 BC.

c 2000 BC	c 1200 BC	547 BC	333 BC
The Hittites, an Indo-European people, arrive in Anatolia and conquer the Hatti, claiming their capital at Hattuşa. The Hittites go on to create a kingdom extending to Babylon and Egypt.	The destruction of Troy, later immortalised in Homer's *Iliad*. For 10 years the Mycenaeans had besieged the city strategically placed above the Dardanelles and the key to Black Sea trade.	Cyrus of Persia overruns Anatolia, setting the scene for a long Greco-Persian rivalry. Later Darius I and Xerxes further Persian influence in Anatolia and forestall the expansion of Greek colonies.	Alexander the Great advances on the Persians and conquers most of Anatolia. Persian Emperor Darius abandons his wife, children and mother, who is so appalled she disowns him and 'adopts' Alexander.

the Lydian king Croesus that they coined the expression 'as rich as Croesus', but the Lycians were the only Anatolian people they didn't deride as 'barbarians'.

Heightened Hellenic influence didn't go unnoticed. Cyrus, the Persian emperor, would not countenance this in his backyard. He invaded in 547 BC, initially defeating the Lydians, then extending control to the Aegean. Under emperors Darius I and Xerxes, the Persians checked the expansion of coastal Greek colonies. They also subdued the interior, ending the era of home-grown Anatolian kingdoms.

Ruling Anatolia through local proxies, the Persians didn't have it all their own way. There was periodic resistance from feisty Anatolians, such as the revolt of the Ionian city of Miletus in 494 BC. Allegedly fomented from Athens, the revolt was abruptly put down. The Persians used the connivance of Athens as a pretext to invade mainland Greece, but were routed at Marathon.

> Tradition states that St John retired to Ephesus to write the fourth gospel, bringing Mary with him. The indefatigable St Paul roamed across Anatolia spreading the word, capitalising on the Roman road system.

Alexander & After

Persian control continued until 334 BC, when Alexander and his adventurers crossed the Dardanelles, intent on relieving Anatolia of the Persian yoke. Sweeping down the coast, they defeated the Persians near Troy then pushed down to Sardis, which willingly surrendered. Having later besieged Halicarnassus (modern-day Bodrum), Alexander ricocheted ever-eastwards, disposing of another Persian force on the Cilician plain.

Alexander was more a conqueror than a nation-builder. When he died leaving no successor, his empire was divided in a flurry of civil wars. However, in his mission to remove Persian influence and bring Anatolia within the Hellenic sphere, Alexander was entirely successful. In his armies' wake, steady Hellenisation occurred, the culmination of a process begun centuries earlier. A formidable network of municipal trading communities spread across Anatolia, the most notable of which

ALEXANDER & THE GORDIAN KNOT

In 333 BC in the former Phrygian capital of Gordion, Alexander encountered the Gordian knot. Tradition stated that whoever untied it would come to rule Asia. Frustrated in his attempts to untie it, Alexander dispatched it with a blow of his sword. He resumed his eastward advance, Asia lying before him, and thundered across Persia to the Indus, until all the known world was his dominion. However, the enormous empire Alexander created was to prove short-lived – perhaps he should have been more patient unravelling that pesky twine…

205 BC	133 BC	AD 45–60	330
The Lycian League is formed by a group of city-states along the Mediterranean coast, including Xanthos, Patara and Olympos. Later Phaselis joins, and the league persists after the imposition of Roman rule.	On his deathbed, Pergamene king Attalus III leaves his state to Rome. The Romans swiftly establish a capital at Ephesus, an already buzzing port, and capitalise on vigorous sea trade.	St Paul, originally from Antioch (modern Antakya), undertakes his long proselytising treks across Anatolia. St John and the Virgin Mary are thought to have ended up in Ephesus.	Constantine declares his 'New Rome', later called Constantinople, as the capital of the Eastern Roman Empire (Byzantium). A convert to Christianity, in 325 he hosted the First Council of Nicaea.

was Pergamum (now Bergama). The Pergamene kings were great warriors and patrons of the arts, and the most celebrated ruler was Eumenes II, who built much of what remains of Pergamum's acropolis. As notable as the building of Hellenic temples and aqueducts in Anatolia was the gradual spread of the Greek language, which eventually extinguished native Anatolian languages.

The cauldron of Anatolian cultures continued to produce various flavour-of-the-month kingdoms. In 279 BC the Celts romped in, establishing the kingdom of Galatia, centred on Ancyra (Ankara). To the northeast Mithridates carved out the kingdom of Pontus, centred on Amasya, and the Armenians (from the Lake Van region) reasserted themselves, having been granted autonomy under Alexander.

Meanwhile, the increasingly powerful Romans, based on the other side of the Aegean, eyed up Anatolia's rich trade networks.

Roman Rule

Roman legions defeated the Seleucid king Antiochus the Great at Magnesia (Manisa) in 190 BC. Later Pergamum, the greatest post-Alexandrian city, became the beachhead for the Roman embrace of Anatolia when King Attalus III died, bequeathing the city to Rome. By 129 BC, Ephesus was capital of the Roman province of Asia and within 60 years the Romans had extended their rule to the Persian border.

Over time, Roman might dissipated. In the late 3rd century AD Diocletian tried to steady the empire by splitting it into eastern and western administrative units, simultaneously attempting to wipe out Christianity. Both endeavours failed. The fledgling religion of Christianity spread, albeit clandestinely and subject to intermittent persecution.

Diocletian's reforms ultimately resulted in a civil war, which Constantine won. A convert to Christianity, Constantine was said to have been guided by angels to build a 'New Rome' on the ancient Greek town of Byzantium. The city came to be known as Constantinople (now İstanbul). On his deathbed, Constantine was baptised, and by the end of the 4th century Christianity was the official religion of the empire.

> Julius Caesar made his famous 'Veni, vidi, vici' ('I came, I saw, I conquered') speech about a military victory at Zile, near Tokat, in 47 BC.

Rome Falls, Byzantium Arises

Even with a new capital at Constantinople, the Roman Empire proved unwieldy. Once the steadying hand of Theodosius (379–95) was gone, the empire split. The western (Roman) half of the empire succumbed to decadence and 'barbarians'; the eastern half (Byzantium) prospered, adopting Christianity and the Greek language.

395	412	527–65	654–76
Under Theodosius the Roman Empire becomes Christian, with paganism forbidden and Greek influence pervasive. Upon his death, the empire is split into east and west, along the line Diocletian had set a century earlier.	Theodosius II builds the land walls of Constantinople to protect the riches of his capital. They prove effective, withstanding multiple sieges, and were only ever breached once: by Mehmet the Conqueror in 1453.	During the reign of Justinian, Byzantium enjoys a golden age. His military conquests include much of North Africa and Spain. He also pursues reform within the empire and embarks on building programs.	Muslim Arab armies capture Ankara and besiege Constantinople. Arab incursions in the west are temporary but the eastern and southern fringes (Syria and Egypt) of the Byzantine domain are lost forever.

BYZANTIUM: THE UNDERRATED EUROPEAN EMPIRE

Byzantium is often reduced to an afterthought in European history. As the Byzantines never accepted the authority of the popes in Rome, they were regarded as being outside Latin Christendom, hence barely a part of Europe. Nonetheless, Byzantium acted as a bulwark for Europe, protecting it for centuries against the expanding armies of Islam. On the periphery of Europe, with its combination of Greek learning and language and Orthodox Christianity, Byzantium forged a magnificent cultural and artistic legacy for 11 centuries, yet it is generally – and somewhat dismissively – remembered merely for the complexity of its politics.

After the fall of Constantinople in 1453, Europe largely forgot the Greeks. Only in the 19th century did Greece again became flavour of the month when the Romantic poets, such as Byron and Shelley, rallied to the cause of Greek liberation from the Ottoman Empire. But it was the glories of classical Greece that such Hellenophiles aspired to, the Greece of Plato, Aristotle and Sappho, rather than Byzantium.

Under Justinian (527–65), Byzantium took the mantle of imperialism from Rome. The emperor built the Aya Sofya, codified Roman law, and extended his empire's boundaries to envelop southern Spain, North Africa and Italy. It was then that Byzantium became a distinct entity from Rome, although sentimental attachment to the idea of Rome remained: the Greek-speaking Byzantines still called themselves Romans, and later the Turks would refer to them as 'Rum'. Justinian's ambition eventually overstretched the empire, and plague and encroaching Slavic tribes curtailed further expansion.

Later, a drawn-out struggle with age-old rivals, the Persians, further weakened the Byzantines, leaving eastern Anatolia easy prey for the Arab armies exploding out of Arabia. The Arabs took Ankara in 654 and by 669 had besieged Constantinople. Here was a new people, bringing a new language, civilisation and religion: Islam.

On the western front, Goths and Lombards advanced; by the 8th century Byzantium was pushed back into the Balkans and Anatolia. The empire hunkered down until Basil assumed the throne in 867 and boosted its fortunes, chalking up victories against Islamic Egypt, the Bulgars and Russia. Basil II (976–1025) earned the moniker the 'Bulgar Slayer' after allegedly putting out the eyes of 14,000 Bulgarian prisoners of war. When Basil died, the empire lacked anyone of his calibre – or ferocity, perhaps – and the era of Byzantine expansion comprehensively ended.

Byzantium: The Surprising Life of a Medieval Empire by Judith Herrin takes a thematic approach to life in the Byzantine realm and in doing so reveals the secrets of the little-understood empire.

867	976–1025	1071	1080
Basil I helps to restore Byzantium's fortunes, catalysing a resurgence in military power and a flourishing of the arts. He is known as the 'Macedonian' but is actually an Armenian from Thrace.	Under Basil II (the Bulgar Slayer), Byzantium reaches its high-tide mark. He overcomes internal crises, pushes the frontiers to Armenia in the east, retakes Italy and defeats the Bulgarians.	New arrivals the Seljuk Turks take on and defeat a large Byzantine force at Manzikert. The Seljuks don't immediately follow on their success but it is a body blow for the Byzantines.	The Armenians, fleeing the Seljuks in Anatolia, establish the Kingdom of Cilicia on the Mediterranean coast. The kingdom raises Armenian culture to new heights and lasts almost 300 years.

First Turkic Empire: The Seljuks

From about the 8th century, nomadic Turks had moved westward from Central Asia, encountering the Persians and converting to Islam. Vigorous and martial, the Turks swallowed up parts of the Abbasid empire, and built a kingdom of their own centred on Persia. Tuğrul, of the Turkish Seljuk clan, took the title of sultan in Baghdad, and from there the Seljuks began raiding Byzantine territory. In 1071 Tuğrul's son Alp Arslan faced down a Byzantine army at Manzikert. The nimble Turkish cavalry prevailed, laying Anatolia open to wandering Turkic bands and beginning the demise of the Byzantine Empire.

Not everything went the Seljuks' way, however. The 12th and 13th centuries saw incursions by Crusaders, who established short-lived statelets at Antioch (modern-day Antakya) and Edessa (now Şanlıurfa). In a sideshow to the Seljuks, an unruly Crusader army sacked Constantinople, the capital of the Byzantines, ostensibly the Crusaders' allies. Meanwhile the Seljuks succumbed to power struggles and their empire fragmented.

The Seljuk legacy persisted in Anatolia in the Sultanate of Rum, centred on Konya. Celaleddin Rumi, the Sufi mystic who founded the Mevlevi, or whirling dervish, order, was an exemplar of the cultural and artistic heights reached in Konya. Although ethnically Turkish, the Seljuks were purveyors of Persian culture and art. They introduced woollen rugs to Anatolia, as well as remarkable architecture – still visible at Erzurum, Divriği, Amasya, Konya and Sivas. These buildings were the first truly Islamic art forms in Anatolia, and were to become the prototypes for Ottoman art.

In the meantime, the Mongol descendants of Genghis Khan rumbled through Anatolia, defeating a Seljuk army at Köse Dağ in 1243. Anatolia fractured into a mosaic of Turkish *beyliks* (principalities), but by 1300 a single Turkish *bey* (tribal leader), Osman, established a dynasty that would eventually end the Byzantine line.

Fledgling Ottoman State

Osman's bands flitted around the borderlands between Byzantine and Seljuk territory. In an era marked by destruction and dissolution, they provided an ideal that attracted legions of followers and quickly established an administrative and military model which allowed them to expand. From the outset they embraced all the cultures of Anatolia – as many Anatolian civilisations before them had done – and their traditions became an amalgam of Greek and Turkish, Islamic and Christian elements.

In 1054, the line along which the Roman Empire had split in 395 became the dividing line between Catholicism and Orthodox Christianity; a line that persists to this day.

1204	1207–70	1243	1300
The rabble of the Fourth Crusade sack Constantinople, an indication of the contempt with which the Western Christians regard the Eastern Orthodox Church.	The lifetime of Celaleddin Rumi, known as Mevlâna, founder of the Mevlevi Sufi order of whirling dervishes. A great mystic poet and philosopher, Rumi lives in Konya after fleeing the Mongols.	The Mongols rumble out of Central Asia, taking Erzurum and defeating the Seljuks at Köse Dağ. The Seljuk empire limps on and the Mongols depart, leaving only some minor states.	Near Eskişehir on the marches between the moribund Byzantines and the shell-shocked Seljuks, Osman comes to prominence. He takes on the Byzantine army, slowly attracting followers and gaining momentum.

Seemingly invincible, the Ottomans forged westward, establishing a first capital at Bursa, then crossing into Europe and taking Adrianople (now Edirne) in 1362. By 1371 they had reached the Adriatic and in 1389 they met and vanquished the Serbs at Kosovo Polje, effectively taking control of the Balkans.

In the Balkans, the Ottomans encountered resolute Christian communities and absorbed them neatly into the state with the creation of the *millet* system, by which minority communities were officially recognised and allowed to govern their own affairs. However, neither Christian insolence nor military bravado were countenanced: Sultan Beyazıt trounced the armies of the last Crusade at Nicopolis in Bulgaria in 1396. Beyazıt perhaps took military victories for granted thereafter, taunting the Tatar warlord Tamerlane. Beyazıt was captured, his army defeated and the burgeoning Ottoman Empire abruptly halted as Tamerlane lurched through Anatolia.

Ottomans Ascendant: Constantinople & Beyond

The dust settled slowly after Tamerlane dragged Beyazıt away. Beyazıt's sons wrestled for control until Mehmet I emerged victorious in 1413, and the Ottomans returned to the job at hand: expansion. With renewed momentum they scooped up the rest of Anatolia, rolled through Greece, made a first attempt at Constantinople and beat the Serbs a second time.

The Ottomans had regained their mojo by the time Mehmet II became sultan in 1451. Constantinople, the last redoubt of the Byzantines, was now encircled by Ottoman territory. Mehmet, as an untested sultan, had no choice but to claim it. He built a fortress on the Bosphorus, imposed a naval blockade and amassed his army, while the Byzantines appealed forlornly to Europe for help. After seven weeks of siege the city fell on 29 May 1453. Christendom shuddered at the seemingly unstoppable Ottomans and fawning diplomats declared Mehmet – now known as Mehmet the Conqueror – a worthy successor to earlier Roman and Byzantine emperors.

The Ottoman machine rolled on, alternating campaigns between eastern and western fronts. The janissary system, where Christian youths were converted and trained for the military, gave the Ottomans Europe's only standing army – an agile and highly organised force. Successive sultans expanded the realm, with Selim the Grim capturing the Hejaz in 1517, and with it Mecca and Medina, thus claiming for the Ottomans the status of guardians of Islam's holiest places. It wasn't all mindless militarism, however: Beyazıt II demonstrated the multicultural nature

Defending Constatinople, Emperor Constantine XI placed a chain across the Golden Horn to prevent Ottoman ships entering. Mehmet II ordered his ships over land – rolled over oiled logs – to breach the blockade and demoralise the Byzantine defenders.

1324	1349	1396	1402
Osman dies while campaigning against the Byzantines at Bursa. The city becomes the first Ottoman capital, where Osman's son and successor, Orhan, rules over a rapidly expanding realm.	As allies of the Byzantines, the Ottomans, under Orhan, make their first military foray into Europe. Orhan has by now consolidated Islam as the religion of the Ottomans.	The Crusade of Nicopolis, a group of Eastern and Western European forces, aims to forestall the Turks marching into Europe with impunity. Ottoman forces abruptly defeat them; Europe is left unguarded.	Beyazıt, victor over the Crusade of Nicopolis, turns his focus to the ultimate prize: Constantinople. Ever cocky, he takes on the forces of Tatar warlord Tamerlane. His army is crushed and he is enslaved.

of the empire when he invited the Jews expelled by the Spanish Inquisition to İstanbul in 1492.

The Ottoman golden age came during Süleyman's 46-year reign (1520–66). A remarkable figure, Süleyman the Magnificent was lauded for codifying Ottoman law as well as military prowess. On the battlefield, the Ottomans enjoyed victories over the Hungarians and absorbed the Mediterranean coast of Algeria and Tunisia. Süleyman's legal code meanwhile was a visionary amalgam of secular and Islamic law, and his patronage saw the Ottomans reach their artistic zenith.

Süleyman was also notable as the first Ottoman sultan to marry. While previous sultans had enjoyed the comforts of concubines, Süleyman fell in love and married Roxelana. Sadly, monogamy did not make for domestic bliss. Palace intrigues brought about the death of his first two sons, and the period after Roxelana's ascension became known as the 'Sultanate of Women'. A wearied Süleyman died campaigning on the Danube in 1566.

> Painting portraits of the great port cities of Smyrna (modern İzmir), Beirut and Alexandria, *Levant: Splendour and Catastrophe on the Mediterranean* by Philip Mansel tells of the rise and fall of these centres of Ottoman wealth and culture.

Sick Man of Europe

Determining exactly when or why the Ottoman decline set in is tricky, but some historians pinpoint the death of Süleyman. The sultans following Süleyman were not up to the task. His son by Roxelana, Selim, known disparagingly as 'the Sot', lasted only briefly as sultan, overseeing the naval catastrophe at Lepanto, which spelled the end of Ottoman naval supremacy. Süleyman was the last sultan to lead his army into the field. Those who came after him were sequestered in the fineries of the palace, having minimal experience of everyday life and little inclination to administer the empire. This, coupled with the inertia that was inevitable after 250 years of expansion, meant that Ottoman military might, once famously referred to by Martin Luther as irresistible, was declining.

The siege of Vienna in 1683 was the Ottomans' last tilt at expansion. It failed. Thereafter it was a downward spiral. The empire remained vast and powerful, but was falling behind the West militarily and scientifically. Napoleon's 1799 Egypt campaign indicated that Europe was willing to take the battle to the Ottomans. Meanwhile, the Habsburgs in central Europe and the Russians were increasingly assertive. The Ottomans, for their part, remained inward-looking and unaware of the advances happening elsewhere.

> Roxelana, the wife of Süleyman, has inspired many artistic works, including paintings, Joseph Haydn's Symphony No 63 and novels in Ukrainian, English and French.

It was nationalism, an idea imported from the West, that sped the Ottoman demise. For centuries manifold ethnic groups had coexisted relatively harmoniously in the empire, but the creation of nation-states in Europe sparked a desire among subject peoples to throw off the Ottoman

1453	1480–1	1512–17	1520–66
Mehmet II lays siege to Constantinople, coinciding with a lunar eclipse. The Byzantines interpret this as a fatal omen, presaging the doom of Christendom. Sure enough, the Turks are victorious.	Mehmet II endeavours to establish himself as a true heir to Roman glory by invading Italy. He succeeds in capturing Otranto in Puglia, but he dies before he can march on Rome.	Selim the Grim defeats the Persians at Çaldiran. He proceeds to take Syria and Egypt, assuming the mantle of Caliph, then captures the holy cities of Mecca and Medina.	The reign of Süleyman the Magnificent is the zenith of the Ottoman Empire. Süleyman leads his forces to take Budapest, Belgrade and Rhodes, doubling the empire's size.

'yoke' and determine their own destinies. Soon, pieces of the Ottoman jigsaw came apart: Greece attained its freedom in 1830. In 1878 Romania, Montenegro, Serbia and Bosnia followed suit.

As the Ottoman Empire shrunk there were attempts at reform, but they were too little, too late. In 1876, Abdülhamid allowed the creation of an Ottoman constitution and the first-ever Ottoman parliament, but he used the events of 1878 as an excuse for overturning the constitution. His reign henceforth grew increasingly authoritarian.

It wasn't just subject peoples who were restless: educated Turks, too, looked for ways to improve their lot. In Macedonia the Committee for Union and Progress (CUP) was created. Reform-minded and influenced by the West, in 1908 the CUP, which came to be known as the 'Young Turks', forced Abdülhamid to abdicate and reinstate the constitution. However, any rejoicing by the Turks proved short-lived. The First Balkan War saw Bulgaria and Macedonia removed from the Ottoman map, with Bulgarian, Greek and Serbian troops advancing rapidly on İstanbul.

The Ottoman regime, once feared and respected, was now deemed the 'sick man of Europe'. European diplomats plotted how to cherry-pick the empire's choicest parts.

WWI & Its Aftermath

The military crisis saw three nationalistic CUP *paşas* (generals) take control of the ever-shrinking empire. They managed to push back the Balkan alliance and save İstanbul, before siding with the Central Powers in the looming world war. Consequently the Ottomans had to fend off the Western powers on multiple fronts: Greece in Thrace, Russia in northeast Anatolia, Britain in Arabia and a multinational force at Gallipoli. It was during this turmoil that the Armenian tragedy (p569) unfolded.

By the end of WWI the Turks were in disarray. The French, Italians, Greeks and Armenians, with Russian support, controlled parts of Anatolia. The Treaty of Sèvres in 1920 demanded the dismembering of the empire, with only a sliver of steppe left to the Turks. European triumphalism did not count on a Turkish backlash, but a Turkish nationalist movement developed, motivated by the humiliation of Sèvres. At the helm was Mustafa Kemal, the victorious commander at Gallipoli. He began organising resistance and established a national assembly in Ankara, far from opposing armies and meddling diplomats.

Meanwhile, a Greek force pushed out from İzmir. The Greeks saw an opportunity to realise their *megali idea* (great idea) of re-establishing the Byzantine Empire. They took Bursa and Edirne – just

Subjects of the Sultan: Culture and Daily Life in the Ottoman Empire, by Suraiya Faroqhi, portrays what life was like for everyday Ottoman folk, looking at townships, ceremonies, festivals, food and drink, and storytelling in the empire.

1553	1571	1595–1603	1683
Mustafa, Süleyman's first-born, is strangled upon his father's orders. Allegedly, Süleyman's wife Roxelana conspired to have Mustafa killed so her own son could succeed to the throne.	The Ottoman navy is destroyed at Lepanto by resurgent European powers who are in control of Atlantic and Indian Ocean trade routes, and who are experiencing the advances of the Renaissance.	Stay-at-home sultan, Mehmet III, has 19 brothers strangled to protect his throne. His successor Ahmed I institutes 'the Cage' to distract potential claimants to the throne with concubines and confections.	Sultan Mehmet IV besieges Vienna, ending in the rout of his army. By century's end, the Ottomans have sued for peace for the first time and have lost the Peloponnese, Hungary and Transylvania.

the provocation that Mustafa Kemal needed to galvanise Turkish support. After initial skirmishes, the Greeks pressed on for Ankara, but stubborn Turkish resistance stalled them at the Battle of Sakarya. The two armies faced off again at Dumlupınar. Here the Turks savaged the Greeks, sending them in retreat towards İzmir, where they were expelled from Anatolia amid pillage and looting.

Mustafa Kemal emerged as the hero of the Turkish people, realising the earlier dream of the 'Young Turks': to create a Turkish nation-state. The Treaty of Lausanne in 1923 undid the insult of Sèvres and saw foreign powers leave Turkey. The borders of the modern Turkish state were set.

In *Gallipoli*, historian Peter Hart takes a detailed look at the tragic WWI campaign, from its planning stages to the bloody disembarkations at Anzac Cove and the eventual retreat.

Atatürk & the Republic

The Turks consolidated Ankara as their capital and abolished the sultanate. Mustafa Kemal assumed the newly created presidency of the secular republic, later taking the name Atatürk – literally, 'Father Turk'. Thereupon the Turks set to work. Mustafa Kemal's energy was apparently limitless; his vision was to see Turkey take its place among the modern, developed countries of Europe.

At the time, the country was devastated after years of war, so a firm hand was needed. The Atatürk era was one of enlightened despotism; he established the institutions of democracy while never allowing any opposition to impede him. His ultimate motivation was the betterment of his people, but one aspect of the Kemalist vision was to have enduring consequences: the insistence that the nation be solely Turkish.

THE GALLIPOLI CAMPAIGN

Engaged on multiple fronts during WWI, the Ottomans held fast only at Gallipoli. This was due partially to inept British command but also to the brilliance of Turkish commander Mustafa Kemal. Iron-willed, he inspired his men to hold their lines, while also inflicting shocking casualties on the invading British and Anzac forces, who had landed on 25 April 1915.

Difficult territory, exposure to the elements and the nature of hand-to-hand trench warfare meant that the campaign was a bloody stalemate; however, there are reports of remarkable civility between invading and defensive forces. The Allies eventually withdrew after eight months.

Unbeknown to anyone at the time, two enduring legends of nationhood were born on the blood-spattered sands of Gallipoli. Australians see the episode as the birth of their national consciousness, while Turks regard the successful campaign to defend Gallipoli as the genesis of their independence.

1760–90s	1826	1839	1876
Despite attempts to modernise and military training from France, the Ottomans lose ground to the Russians under Catherine the Great, who anoints herself protector of the Ottomans' Orthodox subjects.	Major attempts at reform under Mahmut II. He centralises the administration and modernises the army, resulting in the 'Auspicious Event' where the unruly Janissaries are put to the sword.	Reform continues with the Tanzimat, a charter of legal and political rights, the underlying principle of which is the equality of the empire's Muslim and non-Muslim subjects.	Abdülhamid II takes the throne. The National Assembly meets for the first time and a constitution is created, but Serbia and Montenegro, emboldened by the pan-Slavic movement, fight for independence.

Encouraging national unity made sense, considering the nationalist separatist movements that had bedevilled the Ottoman Empire, but in doing so a cultural existence was denied the Kurds. Sure enough, within a few years a Kurdish revolt erupted, the first of several to recur throughout the 20th century.

The desire to create homogenous nation-states on the Aegean also prompted population exchanges: Greek-speaking communities from Anatolia were shipped to Greece, while Muslim residents of Greece were transferred to Turkey. These exchanges brought great disruption and the creation of ghost villages, such as Kayaköy (Karmylassos) near Fethiye. The intention was to forestall ethnic violence, but it was a melancholy episode that hobbled the development of the new state. Turkey found itself without the majority of the educated elites of Ottoman society, many of whom had not been Turkish speakers.

Atatürk's vision gave the Turkish state a comprehensive makeover. Everything from headgear to language was scrutinised and where necessary reformed. Turkey adopted the Gregorian calendar, reformed its alphabet (replacing Arabic with Roman script), standardised the language, outlawed the fez, instituted universal suffrage and decreed that Turks should take surnames, something they had previously not had. By the time of his death in November 1938, Atatürk had, to a large degree, lived up to his name, spearheading the creation of the nation-state and dragging it into the modern era.

Bruce Clark's *Twice a Stranger* is an investigation of the Greek–Turkish population exchanges of the 1920s. Analysing background events and interviewing those who were transported, Clark shines new light on the two countries' fraught relationship.

Working Towards Democratisation

Though reform proceeded apace, Turkey remained economically and militarily weak, and Atatürk's successor, İsmet İnönü, avoided involvement in WWII. The war over, Turkey found itself allied with the USA. A bulwark against the Soviets, Turkey was of strategic importance and received significant US aid. The new friendship was cemented when Turkish troops fought in Korea, and Turkey became a member of NATO.

Meanwhile, democratic reform gained momentum. In 1950 the Democratic Party swept to power. Ruling for a decade, the Democrats failed to live up to their name and became increasingly autocratic; the army intervened in 1960 and removed them. Army rule lasted briefly, and resulted in the liberalisation of the constitution, but it set the tone for future decades. The military considered themselves the guardians of Atatürk's vision and felt obliged to step in when necessary to ensure the republic maintained the right trajectory.

The 1960s and '70s saw the creation of political parties of all stripes, but profusion did not make for robust democracy. The late 1960s

1908	1912–13	1915–18	1919–20
The Young Turks of the Committee for Union and Progress (CUP), based in Salonika, demand the reintroduction of the constitution. In the ensuing elections the CUP wins a convincing majority.	The First and Second Balkan Wars. An alliance of Serbian, Greek and Bulgarian forces take Salonika, previously the second city of the Ottoman Empire, and Edirne. The alliance later turns on itself.	Turks fight in WWI on the side of the Central Powers. Defending four fronts, they repel invaders only at Gallipoli; at war's end, a British fleet is positioned off the coast of İstanbul.	The Turkish War of Independence begins. The Treaty of Sèvres (1920) reduces Turkey to a strip of Anatolian territory, but the Turks, led by Mustafa Kemal, rise to defend their homeland.

were characterised by left-wing activism and political violence, which prompted a move to the right by centrist parties. The army stepped in again in 1971, before handing power back in 1973.

ARMENIANS OF ANATOLIA

The twilight of the Ottoman Empire saw human misery on an epic scale, but nothing has proved as enduringly melancholic and controversial as the fate of Anatolia's Armenians. The tale begins with eyewitness accounts, in April 1915, of Ottoman army units marching Armenian populations towards the Syrian desert. It ends with an Anatolian hinterland virtually devoid of Armenians. What happened in between remains a subject of huge controversy.

Armenians maintain that they were subjected to the 20th century's first orchestrated genocide; that 1.5 million Armenians were summarily executed or killed on death marches and that Ottoman authorities intended to remove the Armenian presence from Anatolia. To this day, Armenians demand a Turkish acknowledgment that the episode was a genocide.

While several Western countries officially recognise the Armenian genocide, Turkey denies that it occurred. It admits that thousands of Armenians died, but claims the order had been to relocate Armenians without intending to eradicate them. The deaths, according to Turkish officials, were due to disease and starvation, consequences of the chaos of war. Some also claim that Turks were subjected to genocide by Armenian militias.

A century on, the issue remains unresolved. The murder of outspoken Turkish-Armenian journalist Hrant Dink in 2007 by Turkish ultranationalists appeared to confirm that antagonism was insurmountable, but apparently reconciliatory progress is being made: thousands of Turks, bearing placards saying 'We are all Armenians', marched in solidarity with the slain journalist.

There is also increasing contact between Turkish and Armenian artists, students, academics and civil-society groups. Political obstacles remain, however, with both sides finding it difficult to compromise, particularly as nationalistic voices tend to be loudest. The USA does not recognise the genocide, despite promises made by Barack Obama in his 2008 presidential campaign; in a statement released in 2014, he described the tragedy as 'one of the worst atrocities of the 20th century'. The issue frequently reignites, causing diplomatic arguments and accusations, and as long as the question remains officially unresolved between Turkish and Armenian governments, it will continue to resurface. A brief diplomatic thaw, which included the signing of protocols aimed at normalising relations, ended in 2010.

The Turkish–Armenian border has been closed since 1993, but brisk trade between the two countries continues. Turkish manufacturers send goods to Armenia via neighbouring Georgia, proof that Turks and Armenians have much to gain if they bury their mutual distrust.

1922	1923	1938	1945–50
The Turks push back the Greek expeditionary force, which has advanced into Anatolia, and eject them from Smyrna (İzmir). Turkey reasserts independence and the European powers accede.	The Treaty of Lausanne, signed by general and statesman İsmet İnönü, undoes the wrongs of Sèvres. The Republic of Turkey is unanimously supported by the members of the National Assembly.	Atatürk dies, at the age of 57, in the Dolmabahçe Palace in İstanbul on 10 November. All the clocks in the palace are stopped at the time that he died: 9.05am.	After WWII, which the Turks avoided, the Truman Doctrine brings aid to Turkey on the condition of democratisation. Democratic elections are held (1950) and the Democratic Party emerges victorious.

European observers referred to Anatolia as 'Turchia' as early as the 12th century. The Turks themselves didn't do this until the 1920s.

Political chaos reigned through the '70s, and the military seized power again to re-establish order in 1980. They did this through the creation of the highly feared National Security Council, but they allowed elections in 1983. Here, for the first time in decades, was a happy result. Turgut Özal, leader of the Motherland Party (ANAP), won a majority and was able to set Turkey back on course. An astute economist and pro-Islamic, Özal made vital economic and legal reforms that brought Turkey in line with the international community and sowed the seeds of its current vitality.

Turn of the Millennium

In 1991, Turkey supported the allied invasion of Iraq, with Özal allowing air strikes from bases in southern Anatolia. After decades in the wilderness, Turkey now affirmed its place in the international community and as an important US ally. At the end of the Gulf War millions of Iraqi Kurds fled into Anatolia. The exodus caught the attention of the international media, bringing the Kurdish issue into the spotlight, and resulting in the establishment of a Kurdish safe haven in northern Iraq. This, in turn, emboldened the Kurdistan Workers Party (PKK), who stepped up their violent campaign aimed at creating a Kurdish state. The Turkish military responded with an iron fist, such that the southeast effectively endured a civil war.

Meanwhile, Turgut Özal died suddenly in 1993, creating a power vacuum. Weak coalition governments followed throughout the 1990s, with a cast of figures flitting across the political stage. Tansu Çiller served for three years as Turkey's first female prime minister, but despite high expectations she did not solve the Kurdish issue or cure the ailing economy.

In December 1995 the religious Refah (Welfare) Party formed a government led by veteran politician Necmettin Erbakan. Heady with power, Refah politicians made Islamist statements that raised the ire of the military. In 1997 the military declared that Refah had flouted the constitutional ban on religion in politics. Faced with a so-called postmodern coup, the government resigned and Refah was disbanded.

Turkey: What Everyone Needs to Know, by İstanbul-based journalist Andrew Finkel, explores the ins and outs of Turkish culture, society and politics.

The capture of PKK leader Abdullah Öcalan in early 1999 seemed like a good omen for the state after the torrid '90s. His capture offered an opportunity to settle the Kurdish question, although a solution remains elusive with the recent conflict in southeastern Anatolia recalling the darkest days. In August 1999, disastrous earthquakes struck İzmit, ending any premillennial optimism. The government's handling of the crisis was inadequate; however, the global outpouring

1971	1980	1983	1985–99
Increasing political strife prompts the military to step in (again) to restore order. The military chief hands the prime minister a written ultimatum, thus this is known as a 'coup by memorandum'.	The third of Turkey's military coups, this time as the military moves to stop widespread street violence between left- and right-wing groups. The National Security Council is formed.	In elections after the 1980 coup, the Özal era begins. A pragmatic leader, Turgut Özal institutes economic reforms, encouraging foreign investment. Turkey opens to the West and tourism takes off.	Abdullah Öcalan establishes the Kurdistan Workers Party (PKK), an armed political group calling for a Kurdish state. There is a long, low-intensity war in southeast Anatolia until Öcalan's capture in 1999.

of aid and sympathy did much to reassure Turks they were valued members of the world community.

Rise of the AKP

A new political force arose in the new millennium: Recep Tayyip Erdoğan's Justice & Development Party (AKP) came to power in 2002, heralding an era of societal reforms, capitalising on improved economic conditions. With Islamist roots, the AKP sought to pursue Turkey's entry to the EU and to end military intervention in the political scene.

Much of the support for the AKP arose in the burgeoning cities nicknamed the Anatolian Tigers, such as Konya and Kayseri. These cities of the interior were experiencing an economic boom, proof that the modernising and economic development projects begun earlier were finally bearing fruit. The Turkish economy continues to grow, with GDP increasing from around US$500 billion in 2006 to US$800 billion in 2014, and many Turks are thus relieved not be in the EU, having avoided the economic perils that beset Greece.

FATHER OF THE MOTHERLAND

Many Western travellers remark on the Turks' devotion to Atatürk. In response, the Turks reply that the Turkish state is a result of his energy and vision: without him there would be no Turkey. From the era of Stalin, Hitler and Mussolini, Atatürk stands as a beacon of statesmanship and proves that radical reform, deftly handled, can be hugely successful.

The Turks' gratitude to Atatürk manifests itself throughout the land. He appears on stamps, banknotes and statues across the country. His name is affixed to innumerable bridges, airports and highways. And seemingly every house in which he spent a night, from the southern Aegean to the Black Sea, is now a museum; İzmir's is worth a visit.

Turkish schoolchildren learn by rote and can dutifully recite Atatürk's life story. But it may be that the history-book image of Atatürk is more simplistic than the reality. An avowed champion of Turkish culture, he preferred opera to Turkish music and was a Francophile. Though calling himself 'Father Turk', he had no offspring.

Years as a military man, reformer and public figure took their toll, and Atatürk died relatively young (aged 57) in 1938. His friend and successor as president, İsmet İnönü, ensured that Atatürk was lauded by his countrymen. The praise continues; any perceived insult to Atatürk is considered highly offensive and is illegal.

There are several outstanding Atatürk biographies: Patrick Kinross' *Ataturk: The Rebirth of a Nation* sticks closely to the official Turkish view; Andrew Mango's *Atatürk* is detached and detailed; while *Atatürk: An Intellectual Biography* by Şükrü Hanioğlu examines the intellectual currents that inspired him.

1997	2002	2005	2007–11
The coalition government headed by Necmettin Erbakan's Islamically inspired Refah (Welfare) Party is disbanded, apparently under military pressure, in what has been called a 'postmodern coup'.	Recep Tayyip Erdoğan's new Justice and Development Party (AKP) wins a landslide election victory, a reflection of the Turkish public's disgruntlement with the established parties. The economy recovers.	EU-accession talks begin, and economic and legal reforms begin to be implemented. Resistance to Turkish membership by some EU states leads to a decrease in approval by some Turks.	Further resounding election victories for the AKP, which increases its share of the vote, as well as winning two referenda in favour of amending the constitution.

The AKP pursued a new direction in foreign policy, attempting to restore relations with Turkey's near neighbours, a modestly successful policy until the Syrian civil war in 2012. Domestically, the AKP worked to curtail military intervention in Turkey's political sphere, while also initiating 'openings' to address long-term dilemmas such as minority rights, the Kurdish issue, acrimonious relations with Armenia and recognising the rights of the Alevis, an Anatolian Muslim minority. However, thus far these 'openings' have not produced long-term solutions. The AKP has also attracted criticism at home and abroad, particularly for curtailing press freedoms, including social media. Others contend that its Islamic political philosophy is eroding respect for women and long-held social freedoms such as drinking alcohol. Grandiose schemes put forward by Erdoğan, who swapped the prime minister's office for the presidency in 2014, include digging a canal between the Black and Marmara seas, and building one of the world's biggest mosques at Çamlıca in İstanbul.

Such controversies raise many eyebrows and elicit strong views: Turks are either entirely in support of, or entirely against, the AKP and its agenda, making for a polarised society. Whatever your position, however, it is clear that Turkey is on the move.

An appetiser for those wanting to know more, *Turkey: A Short History* by Norman Stone is a succinct and pacey wrap-up of the crucial events and personalities of Turkey's long history.

2013	2014	2015	2016
Criticism of the AKP mounts during the Gezi Park protests, when demonstrations against a shopping-mall project in İstanbul cause weeks of unrest, with eight civilians and two policemen killed.	Unrest continues during the Turkish government and Kurdish insurgents' short-lived 'solution process'. Riots erupt as a result of Turkey's lack of support for Kurds fighting the Islamic State (Isis) group in Syria.	The general election results in a hung parliament. In a snap election six months later, the AKP reasserts its dominance, but without the majority needed to call a referendum on rewriting the constitution.	As the Syrian war sends millions of refugees into Turkey, ISIL suicide bombers hit İstanbul's Hippodrome, İstiklal Caddesi and Atatürk International Airport. In July, factions of the military launch a failed coup attempt.

Architecture

Turkey's rich architectural heritage has been moulded by the rise and fall of countless civilisations who have settled here over millennia. From a neolithic temple-complex through to the imperial monuments of both the Byzantine and Ottoman eras, the dizzying array of architectural styles on display reveals how diverse cultural influences have inspired and shaped the human-built history stamped across this land.

Ancient (9500 BC–550 BC)

The earliest Anatolian architectural remnants, the carved megaliths of Göbekli Tepe, date back to approximately 10,000 BC. The mud-brick constructions of Çatalhöyük (p450), which were accessed through their roofs, were first constructed around 7500 BC. Alacahöyük (p432), dating from 4000 BC, was characterised by more complex buildings. By the time Troy (p170) was established (3000 BC), temple design began to advance while in the treeless southeast, a distinctive 'beehive' construction technique developed, which can still be seen at Harran).

Later, the remnants of hefty gates, walls and ramparts of Hattuşa (p428; Hittite capital from 1660 BC) reveal an increasing sophistication in working with the landscape.

The visually stunning *Constantinople: Istanbul's Historical Heritage,* by Stéphane Yerasimos, provides history and context to many of the city's magnificent buildings.

Greek & Roman (550 BC–AD 330)

The architects of ancient Greece displayed a heightened sense of planning and sophistication in design and construction, incorporating vaults and arches into their buildings. Later the Romans built upon the developments of the Greeks. The Romans were also accomplished road builders, establishing a comprehensive network linking trading communities.

Fine examples of classical Greco-Roman architecture can be seen today at the theatre of Aspendos (p376), the nymphaeum at Sagalassos (p321), Bergama's Acropolis (p192) area, and Letoön's (p345) fine temples. Other superb sites include Afrodisias (p313), Termessos (p377), Patara (p346) and Hierapolis (p310).

CAPITAL OF ROMAN ASIA

Ephesus (Efes; p226) is the pre-eminent example of Roman city construction in Turkey; its flagstoned streets, gymnasium, sewerage system, mosaics and theatre form a neat set-piece of Roman design and architecture.

A prosperous trading city, Ephesus was endowed with significant buildings. The Temple of Artemis, boasting a forest of mighty columns, was one of the Wonders of the Ancient World, but was later destroyed under orders of a Byzantine archbishop. The **Great Theatre** (p227), one of the biggest in the Roman world, is evidence of Roman expertise in theatre design and acoustics, while the **Library of Celsus** (p227) is ingeniously designed to appear larger than it actually is.

Byzantine (AD 330–1071)

For a scholarly investigation of the challenges faced by Byzantine architects see *The Master Builders of Byzantium* by Robert Ousterhout.

Ecclesiastical construction distinguishes Byzantine architecture from that of the pagan Greeks. The Byzantines developed church design while working in new media, such as brick and plaster, and displaying a genius for dome construction, as seen in the Aya Sofya (p66).

Mosaics were a principal Byzantine design feature; fine examples can be seen in the Hatay Archaeology Museum (p405) or in situ at the Chora Church (p92; now called the Kariye Museum) in İstanbul, which features a sumptuous array of mosaics. An example of the burgeoning skill of Byzantine civil engineers is the Basilica Cistern (p70), also in İstanbul.

In the east, Armenian stonemasons developed their own distinctive architectural style. The 10th-century church at Akdamar is a stunning example, while the site of Ani (p543) includes fascinating ruins and remnants.

Seljuk (1071–1300)

The architecture of the Seljuks reveals significant Persian influences in design and decorative flourishes, including Kufic lettering and intricate stonework. The Seljuks created cosmopolitan styles incorporating elements of nomadic Turkic design traditions with Persian know-how and the Mediterranean-influenced architecture of the Anatolian Greeks.

The Seljuks left a legacy of magnificent mosques and *medreses* (seminaries), distinguished by their elaborate entrances; you can see the best of them in Konya (p442), Sivas (p440) and Divriği (p438). As patrons of the Silk Road, the Seljuks also built a string of caravanserais through Anatolia; two of the best examples are Sultanhanı, and Sultan Han. The Anatolian countryside is also stippled with the grand conical *türbe* (tombs) of the Seljuks, such as those at Konya, Battalgazi and on both shores of Lake Van.

In the southeast, competitors to the Seljuks, the Artuklu Turks created the cityscapes of Mardin and Hasankeyf, featuring distinctive honey-toned stonework and brick tombs, while also embellishing and adding to the imposing black basalt walls of Diyarbakır.

Ottoman (1300–1750)

From the 14th century, as the Ottomans expanded across Anatolia, they became increasingly influenced by Byzantine styles, especially ecclesiastical architecture. Ottoman architects absorbed Byzantine influences, particularly the use of domes, and incorporated them into their existing Persian architectural repertoire to develop a completely new style: the T-shape plan. The Üç Şerefeli Mosque (p148) in Edirne became the

IMPERIAL MOSQUES

The rippling domes and piercing minarets of mosques are the quintessential image of Turkey for many travellers. The most impressive mosques, in size and grandness, are the imperial mosques commissioned by members of the royal households.

Each imperial mosque had a *külliye*, or collection of charitable institutions, clustered around it. These might include a hospital, asylum, orphanage, *imaret* (soup kitchen), hospice for travellers, *medrese* (seminary), library, baths and a cemetery in which the mosque's imperial patron and other notables could be buried. Over time, many of these buildings were demolished or altered, but İstanbul's **Süleymaniye Mosque** (p85) complex still has much of its *külliye* intact.

The design, perfected by the revered Ottoman architect Mimar Sinan during the reign of Süleyman the Magnificent, proved so durable that it is still being used, with variations, for mosque construction all over Turkey.

Rüstem Paşa Mosque (p89), İstanbul

model for other mosques. One of the first forays into the T-plan, it was the first Ottoman mosque to have a wide dome and a forecourt with an ablutions fountain.

Aside from mosques, the Ottomans also developed a distinctive style of domestic architecture, consisting of multistorey houses with a stone ground floor topped by protruding upper floors balanced on carved brackets. These houses featured separate women's and men's areas (*haremlik* and *selamlık* respectively), and often included woodwork detailing on ceilings and joinery, ornate fireplaces and expansive rooms lined with *sedirs* (low benches) ideal for the communal interaction that was a feature of Ottoman life. Cities including Amasya (p433), Safranbolu (p423), Muğla and Beypazarı still feature houses of this design.

Ottoman architectural styles spread beyond the boundaries of modern Turkey. There are still Ottoman constructions – mosques,fortresses, mansions and bridges – throughout the Balkans.

In later centuries in İstanbul, architects developed the *yalı* (grand seaside mansions constructed solely of wood) to which notable families would escape at the height of summer. Prime examples are still visible on the Bosphorus.

Turkish Baroque & Neoclassical (1750–1920)

From the mid-18th century, rococo and baroque influences hit Turkey, resulting in a pastiche of curves, frills, scrolls and murals, sometimes described as 'Turkish baroque'. The period's archetype is the extravagant Dolmabahçe Palace (p98). Although building mosques was passé, the later Ottomans still adored pavilions where they could enjoy the outdoors; the Küçüksu Kasrı (p102) in İstanbul is a good example.

In the 19th and early 20th centuries, foreign or foreign-trained architects began to concoct a neoclassical blend: European architecture mixed in with Turkish baroque and some concessions to classic Ottoman style. Vedat Tek, a Turkish architect educated in Paris, built the capital's central post office, a melange of Ottoman elements and European symmetry. His style is sometimes seen as part of the first nationalist architecture movement, part of the modernisation project of the early Turkish republic. This movement sought to create a 'national' style specific to Turkey by drawing on Ottoman design elements and melding them with modern European styles. Notable buildings in this style include the Ethnography Museum (p414) in Ankara and Bebek Mosque (p101) in İstanbul. Sirkeci Train Station, by the German architect Jachmund, is another example of this eclectic neoclassicism.

Modern (1920–present)

The rapid growth that Turkey has experienced since the 1940s has seen a profusion of bland, grey apartment blocks and office buildings pop up in Anatolian cities and towns. Yet even these, taken in context of the Turkish landscape, climate and bustle of convivial neighbourhood interaction, have a distinctive quality all their own.

Turkey: Modern Architectures in History, by Sibel Bozdoğan and Esra Akcan, examines the philosophy and impact of architecture in the new Turkey.

During the 1940s and '50s a new nationalist architecture movement developed as Turkish-trained architects working on government buildings sought to create a homegrown style reflecting Turkish tradition and aspirations of the new republic. This architecture tended to be sturdy and monumental; examples include the Anıt Kabir (p413) in Ankara and the Çanakkale Şehitleri Anıtı (p159) (Çanakkale Martyrs' Memorial) at Gallipoli.

Since the 1990s there has been more private-sector investment in architecture, leading to a diversification of building styles. The Levent business district in İstanbul has seen the mushrooming of shimmering office towers, and other futuristic buildings have arisen, such as the Esenboğa Airport in Ankara.

The most interesting development in recent decades is that Turks have begun to take more notice of their history, particularly the Ottoman era. This has meant reclaiming their architectural heritage, especially those parts of it that can be turned into dollars via the tourism industry. These days many restoration projects – in Sultanahmet and other parts of İstanbul, but also in cities across the country such as Antakya, Antalya and Tokat – are focused on classic Ottoman style.

Arts

Turkey's rich and diverse artistic traditions display influences of the many cultures and civilisations that have waxed and waned in Anatolia over the centuries. Internationally, it may still be best known for its textile and ceramic artisan heritage but the country's contemporary artists, writers, and filmmakers are making a name for themselves by finding inspiration in Turkey's long history and commenting in their work on the country's role in the world today.

Carpets

The art form that travellers are most likely to associate with Turkey is the carpet – there are few visitors who do not end up in a carpet shop at some time.

The carpets that travellers know and love are the culmination of an ages-old textile-making tradition. Long ago Turkic nomads weaved tents and saddle bags and established carpet-making techniques on the Central Asian steppes.

As in many aspects of their culture, the Turks adopted and adapted from other traditions. Moving ever-westward, the Turks eventually brought hand-woven carpets, into which they incorporated Persian designs and Chinese cloud patterns, to Anatolia in the 12th century.

Within Anatolia, distinctive regional designs evolved. Uşak carpets, with star and medallion motifs, were the first to attract attention in Europe: Renaissance artist Holbein included copies of them in his paintings. Thereafter, carpet-making gradually shifted from cottage industry to big business. Village women still weave carpets but usually work to fixed contracts, using a pattern and being paid for their final effort rather than for each hour of work.

Fearing the loss of old carpet-making methods, the Ministry of Culture has sponsored projects to revive weaving and dyeing methods. One scheme is the Natural Dye Research and Development Project (Doğal Boya Arıştırma ve Geliştirme Projesi). Some shops keep stocks of these 'project carpets', which are usually high quality.

One of the giants of Turkish literature was Evliya Çelebi, who travelled the Ottoman realm for 40 years and produced a 10-volume travelogue from 1630. A recent edition, *An Ottoman Traveller*, presents a selection of his quirky observations.

Literature

Only in the last century has Turkey developed a tradition of novel writing, but there is a wealth of writing by Turks and about Turkey that offers insight into the country and its people.

The Turkish literary canon is made up of warrior epics, mystical verses (including those of Rumi, founder of the Mevlevi order of whirling dervishes), and the elegies of wandering *aşık* (minstrels). Travellers may encounter tales of Nasreddin Hoca, a semi-legendary quasi-holy man noted for his quirky humour and left-of-centre 'wisdom'.

Yaşar Kemal was the first Turkish novelist to win international attention, writing gritty novels of rural life. His *Memed, My Hawk*, a tale of impoverished Anatolian villagers, won him nomination for the Nobel Prize in Literature.

ORHAN PAMUK: NOBEL LAUREATE

The biggest name in Turkish literature is Orhan Pamuk. Long feted in Turkey, Pamuk has built a worldwide audience since first being translated in the 1990s. He is an inventive prose stylist, creating elaborate plots and finely sketched characters while dealing with the issues confronting contemporary Turkey.

His *Black Book* is an existential whodunit told through a series of newspaper columns, while *My Name is Red* is a 16th-century murder mystery that also philosophises on conceptions of art. In his nonfiction *İstanbul: Memories and the City*, Pamuk ruminates on his complex relationship with the beguiling city. *Cevdet Bey and His Sons*, one of his earliest works, was translated into English for the first time in 2014.

His 2008 novel, *The Museum of Innocence*, details an affair between wealthy Kemal and shop girl Füsun in İstanbul. In 2012 Pamuk opened a **museum** (p96) in İstanbul based on that in the novel and displaying the ephemera of everyday life. His latest novel *A Strangeness in My Mind* again returns to the city to track the life of an İstanbul seller of *boza* (drink made from water, sugar and fermented grain) over four decades and illustrates Pamuk's uncanny ability to evoke the ambience of modern Turkey.

Pamuk was awarded the Nobel Prize in Literature in 2006, becoming the first Turk to have won a Nobel Prize.

Recently, the prolific Turkish-American writer and academic Elif Şafak has attracted an international following. Her controversial and acclaimed *The Bastard of Istanbul* centres on the Armenian tragedy while *The Forty Rules of Love* retells the story of Rumi and Shams of Tabriz. Both were bestsellers in Turkey. All her work, including her most recent novel *The Three Daughters of Eve*, deal with issues confronting modern Turkey as well as its historical richness.

Ayşe Kulin has a huge following and her novels have been translated widely. *Last Train to İstanbul* is her novel of Turkish diplomats' attempts to save Jewish families from the Nazis, while *Farewell* is set during the era of Allied occupation after WWI.

Irfan Orga's autobiographical *Portrait of a Turkish Family*, set during the late Ottoman/early Republican era, describes the collapse of his well-to-do İstanbullu family. In *The Caravan Moves On* Orga offers a glimpse of rural life in the 1950s as he travels with nomads in the Taurus Mountains.

Hakan Günday is one of the rising stars of Turkey's literary scene. His novel *More* is an unflinching look at the refugee crisis and human trafficking.

One of Turkey's biggest cultural exports in recent years has been *Muhteşem Yüzyıl* (literally 'Magnificent Century'), a sumptuous TV series detailing the life and loves of sultan Süleyman the Magnificent, which has attracted an enormous audience in Turkey and elsewhere.

Music

Even in the era of YouTube and pervasive Western cultural influences, Turkish musical traditions and styles have remained strong and homegrown stars continue to emerge.

Pop, Rock, Experimental

You'll hear Turkish pop everywhere: in taxis, bars and long-distance buses. With its skittish rhythms and strident vocals, it's undeniably energetic and distinctive.

Sezen Aksu is lauded as the queen of Turkish pop music, releasing a string of albums in diverse styles since the 1970s. However, it is Tarkan, the pretty-boy pop star, who has achieved most international recognition. His 1994 album, *A-acayipsin*, sold mightily in Turkey and Europe, establishing him as Turkey's biggest-selling pop sensation. 'Şımarık', released in 1999, became his first European number one. He continues to release albums and his metrosexual hip-swivelling ensures he remains a household name in Turkey.

Burhan Öçal is one of the country's finest percussionists. His seminal *New Dream* is a funky take on classical Turkish music, and his Trakya All-Stars albums are investigations of the music of his native Thrace.

Mercan Dede has released a string of albums incorporating traditional instruments and electronic beats. In a similar vein, BaBa ZuLa create a fusion of dub, *saz* (Turkish lute) and pop – accompanied by live belly dancing.

Notable rock bands include Duman and Mor ve Ötesi. maNga create an intriguing mix of metal, rock and Anatolian folk. Their 2012 album *e-akustik* is worth seeking out.

Arabesk

A favourite of taxi drivers across Turkey is arabesk, an Arabic-influenced blend of crooning backed by string choruses and rippling percussion.

The two biggest names in arabesk are the hugely successful Kurdish singer İbrahim Tatlıses, a burly, moustachioed, former construction worker who survived an assassination attempt in 2011, and Orhan Gencebay, a prolific artist and actor.

Cinema

Turkey has long been a favoured location for foreign filmmakers: the James Bond pic *Skyfall* (2012) and the Liam Neeson thriller *Taken 2* (2012) include scenes shot in İstanbul while Russell Crowe's *The Water Diviner* (2014) is both set and shot in Turkey.

The Turkish film industry itself came of age in the 1960s and '70s, when films with a political edge were being made alongside innumerable lightweight Bollywood-style movies, labelled *Yeşilçam* movies. During the 1980s, the film industry went into decline as TV siphoned off audiences, but during the 1990s Turkish cinema re-emerged.

Yılmaz Güney was the first Turkish filmmaker to attract international attention. Joint winner of the best film award at Cannes in 1982, his film *Yol* explored the dilemmas of men on weekend-release from prison, a tragic tale that Turks were forbidden to watch until 2000. Güney's uncompromising stance led to confrontations with authorities and several stints in prison. He died in exile in France in 1984.

Turkish directors have comedic flair, too. Yılmaz Erdoğan's *Vizontele* is a wry look at the arrival of the first TV in Hakkari, a remote town in

The biggest cinema event in the Turkish calendar, the International Antalya Film Festival (www.altinportakal.org.tr) brings together film industry figures, glitterati and a range of Turkish and international films, for a week in December.

ARTS CINEMA

A BEGINNERS' GUIDE TO TURKISH MUSIC

These are our picks to start your collection.

➡ *Turkish Groove* (compilation) Must-have introduction to Turkish music, with all the big names.

➡ *Crossing the Bridge: the Sound of İstanbul* (compilation) Soundtrack to a documentary about İstanbul's music scene.

➡ *Işık Doğdan Yükselir* – Sezen Aksu (contemporary folk) Stunning collection drawing on regional folk styles.

➡ *Nefes* – Mercan Dede (Sufi-electronic-techno fusion) Highly danceable synthesis of beats and Sufi mysticism.

➡ *Duble Oryantal* – Baba Zula (fusion) Baba Zula's classic, 'Belly Double', mixed by British dub master Mad Professor.

➡ *Gipsy Rum* – Burhan Öçal and İstanbul Oriental Ensemble (gypsy) A thigh-slapping introduction to Turkey's gypsy music.

A CINEMA AUTEUR IN ANATOLIA

Internationally, Nuri Bilge Ceylan has become the most widely recognised Turkish director. Since emerging in 2002 with *Uzak* (Distant), a meditation on the lives of migrants in Turkey, he has been a consistent favourite at international film festivals. *Uzak* won the Grand Prix at Cannes in 2003; he also won best director at Cannes in 2008 for *Üç Maymun* (Three Monkeys).

His 2011 release, *Once Upon a Time in Anatolia*, with brooding landscape shots and quirky dialogue, is an intriguing all-night search for a corpse in the Turkish backwoods. In 2014 he won the Palme d'Or at the Cannes Film Festival with *Winter Sleep*. He is the first Turkish director to win since Yılmaz Güney.

the southeast. *Düğün Dernek* is similarly quirky and entertaining. Ferzan Özpetek received international acclaim for *Hamam* (Turkish Bath), which follows a Turk living in Italy who reluctantly travels to İstanbul after he inherits a hamam.

Fatih Akin captured the spotlight after winning the Golden Bear award at the 2004 Berlin Film Festival with *Duvara Karşı* (Head On), a gripping telling of Turkish immigrant life in Germany. He followed this with *Edge of Heaven,* again pondering the Turkish experience in Germany. In 2010 Semih Kaplanoğlu won the Golden Bear award with *Bal* (Honey), a coming-of-age tale in the Black Sea region; while Reha Erdem's *Jîn* is an intriguing allegory.

In 2015 Turkish-French director Deniz Gamze Ergüven caused quite a stir with her critically acclaimed and controversial debut film *Mustang,* which tells the story of five sisters rebelling against their family's conservatism. The film went on to be nominated for the Academy Award for Best Foreign Language Film.

Visual Arts

Turkey does not have a long tradition of painting or portraiture. Turks channelled their artistic talents into textile- and carpet-making, as well as *ebru* (paper marbling), calligraphy and ceramics. İznik became a centre for tile production from the 16th century. The exuberant tiles that adorn İstanbul's Blue Mosque and other Ottoman-era mosques hail from İznik. You'll find examples of *ebru,* calligraphy and ceramics in bazaars across Turkey.

İstanbul is the place to see what modern Turkish artists are up to. İstanbul Modern (p99) is one of the country's best modern art galleries, but the small private art galleries along İstiklal Caddesi are worth seeing, too.

Ara Güler is one of Turkey's most respected photographers. For almost 60 years he has documented Turkish life; his *Ara Güler's İstanbul* is a poignant photographic record of the great city.

Belly dancing may not have originated in Turkey, but Turkish women have mastered the art, reputedly dancing with the least inhibition and the most revealing costumes.

Dance

Turkey boasts a range of folk dances, ranging from the frenetic to the hypnotic, and Turks tend to be enthusiastic and unselfconscious dancers, swivelling hips and shaking shoulders in ways entirely different from Western dance styles.

Folk dance can be divided into several broad categories. Originally a dance of central Anatolia, the *halay* is led by a dancer waving a handkerchief, and can be seen especially at weddings and in *meyhanes* (taverns) when everyone has downed plenty of rakı. The *horon,* from the Black Sea region, is most eye catching – it involves plenty of Cossack-style kicking.

The *sema* (dervish ceremony) of the whirling dervishes is not unique to Turkey, but it's here that you are most likely to see it performed.

People

Turkey has a population of almost 80 million, the great majority of whom are Muslim and Turkish. Kurds form the largest minority, but there is an assortment of other groups – both Muslim and non-Muslim – leading some to say Turkey is comprised of 40 nations. Whether Muslim or Christian, Turkish, Kurdish or otherwise, the peoples of Turkey tend to be family-focused, easy going, hospitable, gregarious and welcoming.

Turks

The first mentions of the Turks were in medieval Chinese sources, which record them as the Tujue in 6th-century Mongolia. The modern Turks descended from Central Asian tribes that moved westward through Eurasia over 1000 years ago. As such the Turks retain cultural links with various peoples through southern Russia, Azerbaijan, Iran, the nations of Central Asia and western China.

As they moved westward Turkic groups encountered the Persians and converted to Islam. The Seljuks established the Middle East's first Turkic empire. The Seljuks' defeat of the Byzantines in 1071 opened up Anatolia to wandering Turkish groups, accelerating the westward drift of the Turks. Over succeeding centuries, Anatolia became the core of the Ottoman Empire and of the modern Turkish Republic. During the Ottoman centuries, Turkish rule extended into southeast Europe so today there are people of Turkish descent in Cyprus, Iraq, Macedonia, Greece, Bulgaria and Ukraine.

Shared ancestry with peoples in Central Asia and the Balkans means that Turks can merrily chat to locals all the way from Novi Pazar in Serbia to Kashgar in China. Turkish is one of the Turkic languages, a family of languages spoken by over 150 million people across Eurasia.

A Modern History of the Kurds by David McDowall investigates the plight of Kurds in Turkey, Iraq and Iran, examining how they have fared over the last two centuries as modern states have arisen in the Middle East.

Kurds

Kurds have lived for millennia in the mountains where the modern borders of Turkey, Iran, Iraq and Syria meet. Turkey's Kurdish minority is estimated at over 15 million people. Sparsely populated southeastern Anatolia is home to perhaps eight million Kurds, while seven million

---

IN THE FAMILY WAY

Turks retain a strong sense of family and community. One endearing habit is to use familial titles to embrace friends, acquaintances and even strangers. A teacher may address his student as *çocuğum* (my child); passers-by call elderly men in the street *amca* (uncle); and elderly women are comfortable being called *teyze* (auntie) by strangers.

Males and females of all ages address older men and women as *abi* (older brother) and *abla* (older sister), which is charming in its simplicity. It's also common for children to call elder male family friends *dede* (grandfather).

These terms are a sign of respect but also of inclusiveness. Perhaps this intimacy explains how the sense of community persists amid the tower blocks of sprawling cities, where most Turks now live.

SEPARATISM OR THE 'BROTHERHOOD' OF PEOPLES?

In 1978 Abdullah Öcalan formed the Kurdistan Workers Party (PKK), which became the most enduring – and violent – Kurdish organisation that Turkey had seen. The PKK remains outlawed. Many Kurds, while not necessarily supporting the demands of the PKK for a separate Kurdish state, wanted to be able to read newspapers in their own language, teach their children their language and watch Kurdish TV. The Turkish government reacted to the PKK's violent tactics and territorial demands by branding calls for Kurdish rights as 'separatism'. Strife escalated until much of southeastern Anatolia was in a permanent state of emergency. After 15 years of fighting and suffering and the deaths of over 30,000 people, Öcalan was captured in Kenya in 1999.

In the early 2000s, following Öcalan's arrest, an increasingly reasoned approach by both the military and government went some way towards making progress on the 'Kurdish question'. In 2002 the Turkish government approved broadcasts in Kurdish and gave the go-ahead for Kurdish to be taught in language schools, and emergency rule was lifted in the southeast. The government's 2009 'Kurdish opening' was an attempt to address the social and political roots of the issue.The creation of TRT6, a government-funded Kurdish-language TV channel, was hailed as a positive initiative. In early 2013 the government entered into negotiations with Öcalan, which resulted in both sides announcing an end to the armed struggle.

But the ceasefire wouldn't hold. By mid-2015, with the war in Syria spilling over Turkey's border, violence between government forces and the PKK erupted again. By the end of the year tit-for-tat skirmishes had descended into drawn-out urban clashes in several cities in eastern Turkey. More than 200,000 people have been displaced by the current fighting, irreparable damage has been caused to historic city centres such as Diyarbakır, and the conflict reverberated through the entirety of Turkey in 2016 with a series of deadly bomb attacks on Ankara, Bursa and İstanbul claimed by TAK (Kurdistan Freedom Falcons; a PKK splinter group). In the current climate, the hope of finally resolving and ending the 40-year conflict seems a long way off.

more live elsewhere in the country, largely integrated into mainstream Turkish society. The majority of Turkish Kurds are Sunni Muslims.

Despite having lived side by side with Turks for centuries, the Kurds retain a distinct culture and folklore and speak a language related to Persian. Some Kurds claim descent from the Medes of ancient Persia. The Kurds have their own foundation myth which is associated with Nevruz, the Persian New Year (21 March).

Small numbers of Turkish Kurds profess the Yazidi faith, a complex mix of indigenous beliefs and Sufi tradition, in which *Melek Taus* – a peacock angel – is seen as an earthly guardian appointed by God.

The struggle between Kurds and Turks has been very well documented. Kurds fought alongside the Turks during the battle for independence in the 1920s, but they were not guaranteed rights as a minority under the 1923 Treaty of Lausanne. The Turkish state was decreed to be homogeneous – inhabited solely by Turks – hence the Kurds were denied a cultural existence. After the fragmentation, along ethnic lines, of the Ottoman Empire, such an approach may have seemed prudent, but as the Kurds were so numerous problems swiftly arose.

Until relatively recently the Turkish government refused to recognise the existence of the Kurds, insisting they were 'Mountain Turks'. Even today the census form and identity cards do not allow anyone to identify as Kurdish. However, this lack of recognition has begun to be addressed in recent years and there are now Kurdish newspapers, books and media outlets, and the Kurdish language is taught in some schools.

The results of the June 2015 elections, when the pro-Kurdish HDP (People's Democratic Party) led by Figen Yüksekdağ and Kurdish politician Selahattin Demirtaş won 13% of the vote, seemed indicative of a greater acceptance of Kurdish voices within Turkey as a whole.

These inroads have been dealt a blow though with the current upsurge in violence.

Muslim Minorities

Turkey is home to several other Muslim minorities, both indigenous and recent arrivals, most of whom are regarded as Turks, but who nonetheless retain aspects of their culture and native tongue.

Laz & Hemşin

The Black Sea region is home to the Laz and Hemşin peoples, two of the largest Muslim minorities after the Kurds.

The Laz mainly inhabit the valleys between Trabzon and Rize. East of Trabzon you can't miss the women in their maroon-striped shawls. Laz men were once among the most feared of Turkish warriors. Once Christian but now Muslim, the Laz are a Caucasian people speaking a language related to Georgian. They are renowned for their sense of humour and business acumen.

Like the Laz, the Hemşin were originally Christian. They mainly come from the far-eastern end of the Black Sea coast, although perhaps no more than 15,000 still live there; most have migrated to the cities where they earn a living as bread and pastry cooks. In and around Ayder, Hemşin women are easily identified by their leopard-print scarves coiled into elaborate headdresses.

Others

The last link to the wandering Turkic groups who arrived in Anatolia in the 11th century, the Yörük maintain a nomadic lifestyle around the Taurus Mountains. Named from the verb *yürümek* (to walk), the Yörük move herds of sheep between summer and winter pastures.

In Turkey's far southeast, along the Syrian border, there are communities of Arabic speakers. Throughout Turkey there are also various Muslim groups that arrived from the Caucasus and the Balkans during the later years of the Ottoman Empire. These include Circassians, Abkhazians, Crimean Tatars, Bosnians, and Uighurs from China.

Since the 1950s there has been a steady movement of people into urban areas, so today 70% of the population lives in cities. Cities such as İstanbul have turned into pervasive sprawls, their historic hearts encircled by rings of largely unplanned new neighbourhoods.

ISLAM IN TURKEY

For many travellers, Turkey is their first experience of Islam. While it may seem 'foreign', Islam actually shares much with Christianity and Judaism. Like Christians, Muslims believe that Allah (God) created the world, pretty much according to the biblical account. They also revere Adam, Noah, Abraham, Moses and Jesus as prophets, although they don't believe Jesus was divine. Muslims call Jews and Christians 'People of the Book', meaning those with a revealed religion (in the Torah and Bible) that preceded Islam.

Where Islam differs from Christianity and Judaism is in the belief that Islam is the 'perfection' of these earlier traditions. Although Moses and Jesus were prophets, Mohammed was the greatest and last, to whom Allah communicated his final revelation.

Islam has diversified into many versions over the centuries; however, the five 'pillars' of Islam – the profession of faith, daily prayers, alms giving, the fasting month of Ramazan, pilgrimage to Mecca – are shared by the entire Muslim community.

Islam is the most widely held belief in Turkey, however many Turks take a relaxed approach to religious duties and practices. Fasting during Ramazan is widespread and Islam's holy days and festivals are observed, but for many Turks Islamic holidays are the only times they'll visit a mosque. Turkish Muslims have also absorbed and adapted other traditions over the years, so it's not uncommon to see Muslims praying at Greek Orthodox shrines, while the Alevis, a heterodox Muslim minority, have developed a tradition combining elements of Anatolian folklore, Sufism and Shia Islam.

Non-Muslim Groups

The Ottoman Empire was notable for its large Christian and Jewish populations. These have diminished considerably in the last century.

There has been a Jewish presence in Anatolia for over 2000 years. A large influx of Jews arrived in the 16th century, fleeing the Spanish Inquisition. Today most of Turkey's Jews live in İstanbul, and some still speak Ladino, a Judaeo-Spanish language.

Armenians have lived in Anatolia for a very long time; a distinct Armenian people existed by the 4th century, when they became the first nation to collectively convert to Christianity. The Armenians created their own alphabet and established various kingdoms in the borderlands between Byzantine, Persian and Ottoman empires. Until 1915 there were significant communities throughout Anatolia. The controversy surrounding the Armenians in the final years of the Ottoman Empire (p569) means that relations between Turks and Armenians remain predominantly sour. About 70,000 Armenians still live in Turkey, mainly in İstanbul, and in pockets in Anatolia, particularly Diyarbakır.

Turkish-Armenian relations are tense, but there are signs of rapprochement. In the last decade Armenian churches on Akdamar Island and in Diyarbakır have been refurbished. There have been services held in the refurbished churches (annually on Akdamar) attracting Armenian worshippers from across the border.

The Greeks are Turkey's other significant Christian minority. Greek populations once lived throughout the Ottoman realm, but after the population exchanges of the early Republican era and acrimonious events in the 1950s, the Greeks were reduced to a small community in İstanbul. Recent years, however, have seen a warming of relations and the return of some young Greek professionals and students to İstanbul.

Rugged southeastern Anatolia is also home to ancient Christian communities. These include adherents of the Syriac Orthodox Church, who speak Aramaic and whose historical homeland is Tür Abdin, east of Mardin. There are also some Chaldean Catholics remaining in Diyarbakır.

Turkey hosts the largest refugee population in the world with an estimated 2.5 million refugees within its borders. Most are from Syria but there are also substantial communities from Afghanistan and Iraq.

Environment

Turkey has one foot in Europe and another in Asia, its two parts separated by İstanbul's famous Bosphorus, the Sea of Marmara and the Dardanelles. Given this position at the meeting of continents, Turkey has a rich environment with flora and fauna ranging from Kangal dogs to purple bougainvillea. Unfortunately, the country faces the unenviable challenge of balancing environmental management with rapid economic growth and urbanisation, and to date it's done a sloppy job.

The Land

Boasting 7200km of coastline, snowcapped mountains, rolling steppes, vast lakes and broad rivers, Turkey is stupendously diverse. Eastern Thrace (European Turkey) makes up a mere 3% of its 769,632 sq km land area; the remaining 97% is Anatolia (Asian Turkey).

The country's western edge is the Aegean coast, lined with coves and beaches and the Aegean islands, most belonging to Greece and within a few kilometres of mainland Turkey. Inland, western Anatolia has the vast Lake District and Uludağ (Great Mountain, 2543m), one of over 50 Turkish peaks above 2000m.

The Mediterranean coast is backed by the jagged Taurus Mountains. East of Antalya, it opens up into a fertile plain before the mountains close in again after Alanya.

Central Anatolia consists of a vast high plateau of rolling steppes, broken by mountain ranges and Cappadocia's fantastical valleys of fairy chimneys (rock formations).

The Black Sea is often hemmed in by mountains, and the coastline is frequently rugged and vertiginous. At the eastern end, Mt Kaçkar (Kaçkar Dağı; 3937m) is the highest point in the Kaçkar range, where peaks and glaciers ring mountain lakes and *yaylalar* (mountain pastures).

Mountainous and somewhat forbidding, the rest of northeastern Anatolia is also wildly beautiful, from Yusufeli's valleys via the steppes around Kars to snowcapped Mt Ararat (Ağrı Dağı; 5137m), dominating the area bordering Iran, Armenia and Azerbaijan. Southeastern Anatolia offers windswept rolling steppe, jagged outcrops of rock, and the extraordinary alkaline, mountain-ringed Lake Van (Van Gölü).

> The action of wind and water on *tuff* (rock composed of compressed volcanic ash, thrown for miles around by prehistoric eruptions) created Cappadocia's fairy chimneys.

Wildlife

Birds

Some 400 species of bird are found in Turkey, with about 250 of these passing through on migration from Africa to Europe. Spring and autumn are particularly good times to see the feathered commuters. Eager birdwatchers flock here to spot wallcreepers, masked shrike and Rüppell's warbler, and to tick the elusive Caspian snowcock off their list. There are several *kuş cennetleri* (bird sanctuaries) dotted about the country.

Endangered Species

Anatolia's lions, beavers and Caspian tigers are extinct, and its lynx, striped hyena and Anatolian leopard have all but disappeared. A leopard was shot in Diyarbakır province in 2013, following a dramatic clifftop battle with a shepherd; the only previous sightings were in Siirt province in 2010 and outside Beypazarı in 1974. Another feline, the beautiful, pure-white Van cat, often with one blue and one amber eye, has also become endangered in its native Turkey. In good news, a rebreeding program at Birecik's semi-wild colony of northern bald ibis has managed to raise population numbers of this critically endangered bird up to 205.

Rare loggerhead turtles nest on various Mediterranean beaches, including Anamur, Patara, İztuzu Beach at Dalyan, and the Göksu Delta. A few rare Mediterranean monk seals live around Foça, but you would be lucky to see them. Greenpeace has criticised Turkey for not following international fishing quotas relating to Mediterranean bluefin tuna, which is facing extinction.

Plants

Turkey is one of the world's most biodiverse temperate-zone countries. Not only does its fertile soil produce an incredible range of fruit and vegetables, it is blessed with an exceptionally rich flora: over 9000 species, over a third endemic and many found nowhere else on earth.

Common trees and plants are pine, cypress, myrtle, laurel, rosemary, lavender, thyme and, on the coast, purple bougainvillea, introduced from South America. Isparta is one of the world's leading producers of attar of roses, a valuable oil extracted from rose petals and used in perfumes and cosmetics.

National Parks & Reserves

In recent years, thanks to EU aspirations, Turkey has stepped up its environmental protection practices. It has 14 Ramsar sites (wetlands of international importance) and is a member of Cites, which covers international trade of endangered species. There are now almost 100 areas designated as *milli parkıs* (national parks), nature reserves and nature parks, where the environment is supposedly protected, and hunting controlled. Sometimes the regulations are carefully enforced, but in other cases problems such as litter-dropping picnickers persist.

Tourism is not well developed in the national parks, which are rarely well set up with facilities. It is not the norm for footpaths to be clearly marked, and camping spots are often unavailable. Most of the well-frequented national parks are as popular for their historic monuments as they are for the surrounding natural environment.

Environmental Issues

Inadequate enforcement of environmental laws, lack of finances and poor education have placed the environment a long way down Turkey's list of priorities. But there are glimmers of improvement, largely due to the country endeavouring to comply with EU environmental legislation.

Nuclear Turkey

The government's plan to build two nuclear power plants by 2023 is one of the biggest current issues for Turkey's environmentalists. Despite local protests, the initial construction phase for the site of the Akkuyu plant (on the eastern Mediterranean coast) has begun while the second site, at the Black Sea town of Sinop, remains in the proposal stage. The community-run organisation Sinop is Ours (www.sinopbizim.org) remains a vocal opponent to the project. The country's seismic vulnerabilities increase the risk posed by nuclear reactors, but more plants are set to follow.

The government says the plants will aid economic growth and and reduce dependency on natural gas supplies from Russia and Iran. Electricity consumption is increasing by about 6% a year in Turkey, which only has significant domestic supplies of coal.

Top Bird-watching Spots

Çıldır Gölü *(Çıldır Lake)* Important breeding ground, well off the beaten track.

Göksu Delta Over 330 species have been recorded here.

Sultan Marshes Vast wetland Ramsar site near Kayseri..

Kangal dogs were originally bred to protect sheep from wolves and bears on mountain pastures. People wandering off the beaten track, especially in eastern Turkey, are sometimes startled by these huge, yellow-coated, black-headed animals, with optional spiked collar to protect against wolves.

The Bosphorus

One of the biggest environmental challenges facing Turkey is the threat from maritime traffic along the Bosphorus. The 1936 Montreux Convention decreed that, although Turkey has sovereignty over the strait, it must permit the free passage of shipping through it. At that time, perhaps a few thousand ships a year passed through, but this has risen to over 45,000 vessels annually; around 10% are tankers, which carry over 100 million tonnes of hazardous substances through the strait every year.`

There have already been serious accidents, such as the 1979 *Independenta* collision with another vessel, which killed 43 people and spilt and burnt some 95,000 tonnes of oil (around 2½ times the amount spilt by the famous *Exxon Valdez* in Alaska). Following the Gulf of Mexico disaster in 2010, the Turkish government renewed its efforts to find alternative routes for oil transportation. Its ambitious plans include a US$12 billion canal to divert tankers, which would see the creation of two new cities by the Bosphorus and the world's largest airport. There is already an 1800km-long pipeline between Baku, Azerbaijan and the Turkish port of Ceyhan, and another pipeline is planned between Samsun and Ceyhan.

Construction

Rampant development is taking a terrible toll on the environment. Mega-construction projects, including İstanbul's recently completed Yavuz Sultan Selim Bridge and the ongoing construction of the city's third airport, are contributing to mass deforestation in the Bosphorus region. On the Aegean and Mediterranean coasts, spots such as Kuşadası and Marmaris (once pleasant fishing villages) have been overwhelmed by urban sprawl and are in danger of losing all appeal.

Dams

Short of water and electricity, Turkey is one of the world's major builders of dams. There are already more than 600 dams and many more on the way, with controversy surrounding new and proposed developments. The gigantic Southeastern Anatolia Project, known as GAP, is one of Turkey's major construction efforts. Harnessing the headwaters of the Tigris and Euphrates Rivers, it's creating a potential political time bomb, causing friction with the arid countries downstream that also depend on this water. Iraq, Syria and Georgia have all protested, and a UN report said the project is in danger of violating human rights.

Inside Turkey itself, one of the most controversial components of the GAP project is the İlisu Dam, which is scheduled to submerge the historic

Despite its environmental shortcomings, Turkey is doing well at beach cleanliness, with 444 beaches and 21 marinas qualifying for Blue Flag status; see www.blueflag.org. Dolphins survive in İstanbul's Bosphorus and the Anatolian wild sheep, unique to the Konya region, has protected status. Turkey also ratified the Kyoto protocol in 2009.

ENVIRONMENT ENVIRONMENTAL ISSUES

POPULAR PARKS

The following are among the most popular parks with foreign visitors to Turkey. Visit the Turkish Ministry of Culture and Tourism (www.turizm.gov.tr) for more information.

Gallipoli Historical National Park (p155) Historic battlefield sites on a gloriously unspoilt peninsula surrounded by coves.

Göreme National Park (p454) An extraordinary landscape of valleys speckled with fairy chimneys.

Kaçkar Dağları Milli Parkı (p523; Kaçkar Mountains National Park) Stunning mountain range with excellent trekking trails.

Köprülü Kanyon National Park (p378; Bridge Canyon National Park) Dramatic canyon with spectacular scenery and white-water rafting facilities.

Nemrut Dağı National Park (p550; Mt Nemrut National Park) Pre-Roman stone heads surmounting a man-made mound with wonderful views.

EARTHQUAKE DANGER

Turkey lies on at least three active earthquake fault lines: the North Anatolian, the East Anatolian and the Aegean. Most of Turkey lies south of the North Anatolian fault line, which runs roughly parallel with the Black Sea coast. As the Arabian and African plates to the south push northward, the Anatolian plate is shoved into the Eurasian plate and squeezed west towards Greece.

More than 25 major earthquakes, measuring up to 7.8 on the Richter scale, have been recorded since 1939. A 7.6-magnitude quake in 1999 hit İzmit (Kocaeli) and Adapazarı (Sakarya) in northwestern Anatolia, killing more than 18,000. A 7.1-magnitude earthquake shook Van in 2011, killing more than 600, injuring over 4000 and damaging over 11,000 buildings, with thousands left homeless.

If a major quake struck İstanbul, much of the city would be devastated, due to unlicensed, jerry-built construction. When a 4.4-magnitude earthquake hit in 2010, no deaths or damage were caused, but it highlighted how ill-prepared the city was, with many locals hitting the phone and social networking sites rather than evacuating their houses.

Turkey's 58 'nature monuments' are mostly protected trees, including 1500- to 2000-year-old cedars in Finike, southwest of Antalya; a 1000-year-old plane tree in İstanbul; and a 700-year-old juniper at 2100m near Gümüşhane, south of Trabzon.

town of Hasankeyf by 2019. Due to the project plans, the town featured on the World Monuments Watch list of the planet's 100 most endangered sites in 2008 (not the first or last time Turkey has appeared on the list). Despite both local and international opposition, work towards the dam completion continues to steamroll ahead. Although the town's major monuments – relics of a time it was a Silk Road commercial centre on the border of Anatolia and Mesapotamia – are now hidden under a layer of scaffolding, readying to be moved to higher ground, it's estimated that 80% of the town's ruins will vanish under the dam water, along with their atmospheric setting on the Tigris river and dozens of other villages. Up to 80,000 people will be displaced, many of them Kurds and minority groups.

In northeast Anatolia a separate dam project harnessing the Çorah River has already changed the face of the region's valley landscapes and signalled the end of the river's white-water rafting activities. The opening of the project's Yusefeli Dam (scheduled for 2019) will see the current town of Yusefeli disappear beneath the water.

The ruins of the world's oldest-known spa settlement, Allianoi, disappeared beneath the waters of the Yortanlı Dam in 2011. A last-ditch appeal from the tenor Plácido Domingo, president of the European cultural heritage federation Europa Nostra, failed to save the 2nd-century Roman spa near Bergama.

Other Issues

Turkey's environmental shortcomings are vast. Blue recycling bins are an increasingly common sight on the streets of İstanbul, but the government still has a long way to go in terms of educating its citizens and businesses.

The country's once-rich fishing waterways are in rapid decline due to commercial overfishing and water pollution. A recent seasonal fishing ban enforced during the summer months is seen by many as shutting the gate after the horse has bolted. Despite the potential for renewable energy in Turkey, 80 new coal-fired power plants are on the proposal table to keep up with the country's expanding development needs.

Issues for Turkey to address as part of its bid to join the EU include water treatment, waste-water disposal, food safety, soil erosion, deforestation, degradation of biodiversity, air quality, industrial pollution control and risk management, climate change and nature protection.

The documentary *Polluting Paradise* is a poignant comment on Turkey's environmental issues, telling the heartbreaking story of director Fatih Akın's father's village, which was wrecked by a waste landfill site.

Survival Guide

Directory A-Z

Accommodation

Turkey has accommodation options to suit all budgets, with concentrations of good, value-for-money hotels, pensions and hostels in places most visited by independent travellers, such as İstanbul and Cappadocia.

Rooms are discounted by around 20% to 50% during the low season (October to April; November to late March in İstanbul), but not during Christmas and Easter periods and major Islamic holidays. Places within easy reach of İstanbul and Ankara may hike their prices during summer weekends.

If you plan to stay a week or more in a coastal resort, check package-holiday deals. British, German and French tour companies in particular often offer money-saving flight-and-accommodation packages to the South Aegean and Mediterranean.

Accommodation options in more Westernised spots such as İstanbul often quote tariffs in euros as well as (or instead of) lira; establishments in less touristy locations generally quote in lira. Many places will accept euros (or even US dollars in İstanbul). We've used the currency quoted by the business being reviewed.

Sleeping options generally have a website where reservations can be made.

Price Ranges

Ranges are based on the cost of a double room. The rates we quote are for high season (June to August, apart from İstanbul, where high season is April, May, September, October, Christmas and Easter). Unless otherwise mentioned, rates include tax (KDV), an en suite bathroom and breakfast. Listings are ordered by price range, starting with budget, and within those groups by preference.

In tourist areas, hoteliers peg their room prices to the euro to insulate their businesses against fluctuations in the lira. Their rates in lira thus rise and fall according to the currency's value against the euro. In contrast, hoteliers in less touristy areas are more likely to simply set their rates in lira – a difference that compounds the already huge regional variations across Turkey. We have thus allowed some leeway in our price ranges. In some cases for example, a budget pension that has edged into the midrange bracket by the euro–lira exchange rate will still be marked as budget.

Conversely, in tourist areas such as Sultanahmet, İstanbul, many accommodation owners cut their inflated high-season prices in response to the crisis in the tourist industry following the suicide bombings in İstanbul in early 2016. While researching this content, Lonely Planet has tried to collect realistic high-season prices rather than bargain-basement discounts.

İstanbul & Bodrum Peninsula
€ less than €90
€€ €90 to €200
€€€ more than €200

Rest of Turkey
€ less than ₺90
€€ ₺90 to ₺180
€€€ more than ₺180

Apartments

➡ Good value for money, especially for families and small groups.

➡ Outside a few Aegean and Mediterranean locations, apartments for holiday rental are often thin on the ground.

➡ In coastal spots such as Kaş, Antalya and the Bodrum Peninsula, emlakçı (real-estate agents) hold lists of available holiday rentals.

- *Emlakçı* are used to dealing with foreigners.
- Also look out for *apart otels:* hotels containing self-catering units.

Camping

- Most camping facilities are along the coasts and are usually privately run.
- Camping facilities are fairly rare inland, with the exception of Cappadocia and Nemrut Dağı National Park.
- Best facilities inland are often on Orman Dinlenme Yeri (Forestry Department Land); you usually need your own transport to reach these.
- Pensions and hostels often let you camp on their grounds and use their facilities for a fee.
- Female travellers should stick to official sites and camp where there are plenty of people, especially out east.
- Camping outside official sites is often more hassle than it's worth. The police may drop by to check you out and possibly move you on, and out east there are wolves in the wild, so be wary and don't leave food and rubbish outside your tent. Also look out for Kangal dogs.

Hostels

- There are plenty of hostels with dormitories in popular destinations.
- Dorm beds are typically €10 to €20 per night.
- Hostelling International has accommodation in İstanbul, Cappadocia and the Aegean and Turquoise Coast areas.

Hotels

BUDGET

- Good, inexpensive beds are readily available in most cities and resort towns.
- Difficult places to find good cheap rooms include İstanbul, Ankara, İzmir and package-holiday resort towns such as Alanya and Çeşme.
- The cheapest hotels typically charge from around ₺40/50 for a single room without/with private bathroom, including breakfast.
- Outside tourist areas, solo travellers of both sexes should be cautious about staying in budget options and carefully suss out the staff and atmosphere in reception; theft and even sexual assaults have occurred in budget establishments (albeit very rarely).

MIDRANGE

- One- and two-star hotels are less oppressively masculine than budget hotels in atmosphere, even when clientele is mainly male.
- Such hotels typically charge around ₺100 to ₺150 for an en suite double, including breakfast.
- Hotels in more traditional towns normally offer only Turkish TV, Turkish breakfast and none of the 'extras' commonplace in pensions.
- In many midrange hotels, a maid will not make your bed and tidy your room unless you ask in reception or hang the sign on the handle.
- Prices should be displayed in reception.
- You should never pay more than the prices on display, and will often be charged less.
- Often you will be able to haggle.
- Unmarried foreign couples don't usually have problems sharing rooms.
- Out east, couples are often given a twin room, even if they ask for a double.
- Many establishments refuse to accept an unmarried couple when one of the parties is Turkish.
- The cheaper the hotel, and the more remote the location, the more conservative its management tends to be.

BOUTIQUE HOTELS

- These are old Ottoman mansions, caravanserais and other historic buildings refurbished, or completely rebuilt, as hotels.
- They're equipped with all mod-cons and bags of character.
- Most are in the midrange and top-end price brackets.
- Many are reviewed at Small Hotels (www.boutiquesmallhotels.com).

Pensions

In destinations popular with travellers you'll find *pansiyons* (pensions): family-run guesthouses where you can get a good, clean single/double from around ₺60/90. Many also have triple and quadruple rooms. At the top end, some pricier pensions are almost on a par with boutique hotels.

In touristy areas in particular, the advantages of staying in a pension, as opposed to a cheap hotel, include:

- A choice of simple meals
- Book exchange

> **NO VACANCY**
>
> Along the Aegean, Mediterranean and Black Sea coasts, the majority of hotels, pensions and camping grounds close roughly from mid-October to mid-April. Before visiting those regions in the low season, check accommodation is available.

➡ Laundry service

➡ Staff who speak at least one foreign language

EV PANSIYONU

In a few places, old-fashioned *ev pansiyonu* (pension in a private home) survive. These are simply rooms in a family house that are let to visitors at busy times of year. They do not normally advertise their existence in a formal way: ask locals where to find them and look out for *kıralık oda* (room for rent) signs. English is rarely spoken by the proprietors, so some knowledge of Turkish would be helpful.

Tree Houses

Olympos is famous for its 'tree houses': rough-and-ready shelters in forested settings near the beach. The success of these backpacker hang-outs has spawned imitators elsewhere in the western Mediterranean, for example in nearby Çıralı and Saklıkent Gorge.

Touts

In smaller tourist towns such as Selçuk, touts may approach you as you step from the bus and offer you accommodation. Some may string you a line about the pension you're looking for, in the hope of reeling you in and getting a commission from another pension. Taxi drivers also play this game.

It's generally best to politely decline these offers, but if you're on a budget, touts sometimes work for newly opened establishments

---

EATING PRICE RANGES

Price ranges reflect the cost of a standard main-course dish.

€ less than ₺20

€€ ₺20 to ₺35

€€€ more than ₺35

---

offering cheap rates. Before they take you to the pension, establish that you're only looking and are under no obligation to stay.

Many pensions operate in informal chains, referring travellers from one to another. If you've enjoyed staying in a place, you may enjoy its owner's recommendations, but stay firm and try not to sign up to anything sight unseen.

Booking Services

Lonely Planet (www.lonely planet.com/turkey/hotels) Recommendations and bookings.

Simpson Travel (www.exclusive escapes.co.uk) Stylish apartments, romantic boutique hotels and luxury villas.

Customs Regulations

Imports

Jewellery and items valued over US$15,000 should be declared, to ensure you can take it out when you leave. Goods including the following can be imported duty-free:

➡ 200 cigarettes

➡ 200g of tobacco

➡ 1kg each of coffee, instant coffee, chocolate and sugar products

➡ 500g of tea

➡ 1L bottle or two 750ml bottles of wine or spirits

➡ Five bottles of perfume (max 120ml each)

➡ Personal electronic devices, but only one of each type

➡ Unlimited currency

➡ Souvenirs/gifts worth up to €300 (€145 if aged under 15)

Exports

➡ Buying and exporting genuine antiquities is illegal.

➡ Carpet shops should be able to provide a form certifying that your purchase is not an antiquity.

➡ Ask for advice from vendors you buy from.

➡ Keep receipts and paperwork.

Discount Cards

The Ministry of Culture and Tourism offers various discount cards covering museums and sights. Visit www.muze.gov.tr/en/museum-card for more information.

Museum Pass: İstanbul (p135) The five-day card (₺85) offers a possible ₺175 saving on entry to the city's major sights, including Aya Sofya, and allows holders to skip admission queues.

Museum Pass: Cappadocia (p466) The three-day card (₺45) covers the major sights including Göreme Open-Air Museum, offering a possible ₺98 saving.

Museum Pass: The Aegean The seven-day card (₺75) covers 31 museums and sights from İzmir to Muğla, including Ephesus and Pergamum.

Museum Pass: The Mediterranean The seven-day card (₺60) covers 27 museums and sights from the Turquoise Coast east to Adana, including the Lycian sites on the Teke Peninsula.

Museum Pass: Turkey The 15-day card (₺185) covers some 300 museums and sights nationwide, from Topkapı Palace to Ani.

İstanbulkart (p137) The rechargeable travel card offers savings on İstanbul's public transport.

The following offer discounts on accommodation, eating, entertainment, transport and tours. They are available in Turkey but easier to get in your home country.

International Student Identity Card (www.isic.org)

International Youth Travel Card (www.isic.org)

International Teacher Identity Card (www.isic.org)

Electricity

➜ Electrical current is 230V AC, 50Hz.

➜ You can buy plug adaptors at most electrical shops.

➜ A universal AC adaptor is also a good investment.

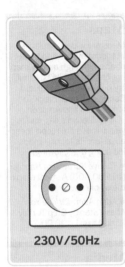

230V/50Hz

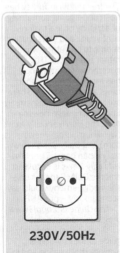

230V/50Hz

Embassies & Consulates

➜ Most embassies and consulates in Turkey open from 8am or 9am to noon Monday to Friday, then after lunch until 5pm or 6pm for people to pick up visas.

➜ Embassies of some Muslim countries may open Sunday to Thursday.

➜ To ask the way to an embassy, say: '[Country] başkonsolosluğu nerede?'

➜ Embassies are generally in Ankara.

➜ There are consulates in other Turkish cities.

Australian Embassy (☎0312-459 9500; www.turkey.embassy.gov.au; 7th fl, MNG Bldg, Uğur Mumcu Caddesi 88, Gaziosmanpaşa)

Azerbaijani Embassy (☎0312-491 1681; ankara.mfa.gov.az; Diplomatik Site, Bakü Sokak 1, Oran)

Bulgarian Embassy (☎0312-467 2071; www.mfa.bg/embassies/turkey; Atatürk Bulvarı 124, Kavaklıdere)

Canadian Embassy (☎0312-409 2700; turkey.gc.ca; Cinnah Caddesi 58, Çankaya)

Dutch Embassy (☎0312-409 1800; turkije.nlambassade.org; Hollanda Caddesi 5, off Turan Güneş Bulvarı)

French Embassy (☎0312-455 4545; www.ambafrance-tr.org; Paris Caddesi 70, Kavaklıdere)

Georgian Embassy (☎0312-491 8030; www.turkey.mfa.gov.ge; Diplomatik Site, Kılıç Ali Sokak 12, Oran)

German Embassy (☎0312-455 5100; www.ankara.diplo.de; Atatürk Bulvarı 114, Kavaklıdere)

Greek Embassy (☎0312-448 0647; www.mfa.gr/ankara; Zia Ür Rahman Caddesi 9-11, Gaziosmanpaşa)

Iranian Embassy (☎0312-468 2821; en.mfa.ir; Tahran Caddesi 10, Kavaklıdere)

Iraqi Embassy (☎0312-468 7421; www.mofamission.gov.iq; Turan Emeksiz Sokak 11, Gaziosmanpaşa)

Irish Embassy (☎0312-459 1000; www.embassyofireland.org.tr; 3rd fl, MNG Bldg, Uğur Mumcu Caddesi 88, Gaziosmanpaşa)

New Zealand Embassy (☎0312-446 3333; www.nzembassy.com/turkey; Kizkulesi Sokak 11, Gaziosmanpaşa)

Russian Embassy (☎0312-439 2122; www.turkey.mid.ru; Karyağdı Sokak 5, Çankaya)

UK Embassy (☎0312-455 3344; ukinturkey.fco.gov.uk; Şehit Ersan Caddesi 46a, Çankaya)

US Embassy (☎0312-455 5555; turkey.usembassy.gov; Atatürk Bulvarı 110, Kavaklıdere)

Insurance

➜ A travel insurance policy covering theft, loss and medical expenses is recommended.

➜ A huge variety of policies is available; check small print.

➜ Some policies exclude 'dangerous activities', which can include scuba diving, motorcycling and even trekking.

➜ Some policies may not cover you if you travel to regions of the country where your government warns against travel, such as areas near the Syrian border.

➜ If you cancel your trip on the advice of an official warning against travel, your insurer may not cover you.

➜ Look into whether your regular health insurance and motor insurance will cover you in Turkey.

➜ Worldwide travel insurance is available at www.lonelyplanet.com/travel-insurance. You can buy, extend and claim online anytime – even if you're already on the road.

Internet Access

➜ Throughout Turkey, the majority of accommodation options of all standards offer wi-fi.

➜ Wi-fi networks are also found at locations from cafes and carpet shops to otogars (bus stations) and ferry terminals.

➜ Our Turkey coverage uses the wi-fi access icon to indicate that a business offers a network.

➜ The internet access icon indicates that an establishment provides a computer with internet access for guest use.

Internet Cafes

➜ Internet cafes are common, although declining with the proliferation of wi-fi and hand-held devices.

➜ They are typically open from 9am until midnight, and charge around ₺2 an hour (İstanbul ₺3).

➜ Connection speeds vary, but are generally fast.

➜ Viruses are rife.

➜ The best cafes have English keyboards.

➜ Some cafes have Turkish keyboards, on which 'ı' occupies the position occupied by 'i' on English keyboards.

➜ On Turkish keyboards, create the @ symbol by holding down the 'q' and ALT keys at the same time.

Language Courses

İstanbul is the most popular place to learn Turkish, though there are also courses in Ankara, İzmir, Antalya and other places. Try to sit in on a class before you commit, as the quality of your experience definitely depends on the teacher and your classmates.

Private tuition is more expensive, but tutors advertise at http://istanbul.en.craigs list.com.tr and the expat

website www.mymerhaba. com. Many books and online resources are available; the books and CDs by David and Asuman Pollard in the 'Teach Yourself' series are recommended.

Schools include the following:

Dilmer (www.dilmer.com) İstanbul.

International House (www. turkishlesson.com) İstanbul.

Tömer (tomer.ankara.edu.tr) Ankara, İstanbul, İzmir, Antalya, Adana, Bursa and Samsun.

Turkish For Foreigners (www. spokenenglishtr.com) İstanbul.

Turkish Language Center (www. turkishlanguagecenter.com) İzmir.

Legal Matters

Technically, you should carry your passport at all times. In practice, you may prefer to carry a photocopy.

There are laws against lese-majesty, buying and smuggling antiquities, and illegal drugs. Turkish jails are not places where you want to spend any time.

LGBTQI Travellers

Homosexuality is not a criminal offence in Turkey, but prejudice remains strong and there are sporadic reports of violence towards gay people – the message is discretion.

İstanbul has a flourishing gay scene, as does Ankara. In other cities there may be a gay bar.

For more on the challenges facing LGBT people in Turkey, visit the websites iglhrc.org/region/turkey, www.ilga-europe.org and ilga. org/country/turkey.

BHN Mavi Tours (www.turkey-gay-travel.com) Gay-friendly İstanbul travel agent, with useful links on its website.

Kaos GL (www.kaosgl.com) Based in Ankara, the LGBT rights

organisation publishes a gay-and-lesbian magazine and its website has news and information in English.

Lambdaistanbul (www.lambda istanbul.org) The Turkish branch of the International Lesbian, Gay, Bisexual, Trans and Intersexual Association.

LGBTI News Turkey (lgbtinews turkey.com) News and links.

Maps

Maps are widely available at tourist offices and bookshops, although quality maps are hard to find. In İstanbul, try bookshops on İstiklal Caddesi; online, check Tu lumba.com and Amazon.

Mep Medya's city and regional maps are recommended, as are its touring maps including the following:

➜ *Türkiye Karayolları Haritası* (1:1,200,000) A sheet map of the whole country

➜ *Adım Adım Türkiye Yol Atlası* (Step by Step Turkey Road Atlas; 1:400,000)

Media

The free media in Turkey has been undergoing something of a trial by ordeal over recent years, and the situation seems to be getting worse rather than better. This government interference has made sourcing impartial news a real challenge. There are now only two mainstream English-language newspapers: the *Hürriyet Daily News* (www.hurriyetdailynews. com) and *Daily Sabah* (www. dailysabah.com). The *Hürriyet Daily News* is secularist and the *Daily Sabah* is unashamedly – many would say scandalously – pro-AKP.

The Guide İstanbul (www. theguideistanbul.com) is a listings-heavy bimonthly guide to the city that is available both online and in magazine format. Many of the city's hotels offer copies of it in guest rooms.

Money

Turkey's currency is the Türk Lirası (Turkish lira; ₺). The lira comes in notes of five, 10, 20, 50, 100 and 200, and coins of one, five, 10, 25 and 50 kuruş and one lira.

The Yeni Türk Lirası (new Turkish lira; YTL) was used between 2005 and 2008 as an anti-inflationary measure. Yeni Türk Lirası is no longer valid, but if you have some notes and coins left over from a previous visit to Turkey, branches of Ziraat bank will exchange your 'new' lira for the same value of today's lira.

Lack of change is a constant problem; try to keep a supply of coins and small notes for minor payments. Post offices have Western Union counters.

ATMs

ATMs dispense Turkish lira, and occasionally euros and US dollars, to Visa, Master-Card, Cirrus and Maestro card holders. Look for these logos on machines, which are found in most towns. Machines generally offer instructions in foreign languages including English.

It's possible to get around Turkey using only ATMs if you draw out money in the towns to tide you through the villages that don't have them. Also keep some cash in reserve for the inevitable day when the machine throws a wobbly. If your card is swallowed by a stand-alone ATM booth, it may be tricky to get it back. The booths are often run by franchisees rather than by the banks themselves.

Credit Cards

Visa and MasterCard are widely accepted by hotels, shops and restaurants, although often not by pensions and local restaurants outside the main tourist areas. You can also get cash advances on these cards. Amex is less commonly accepted outside top-end establishments. Inform your credit-card provider of your travel plans; otherwise transactions may be stopped, as credit-card fraud does happen in Turkey.

Foreign Currencies

Euros and US dollars are the most readily accepted foreign currencies. Shops, hotels and restaurants in many tourist areas accept foreign currencies, and taxi drivers will take them for big journeys.

Moneychangers

The Turkish lira is weak against Western currencies, and you will probably get a better exchange rate in Turkey than elsewhere. The lira

---

THE ART OF BARGAINING

Traditionally, when customers enter a Turkish shop to make a significant purchase, they're offered a comfortable seat and a drink (çay, coffee or a soft drink). There is some general chitchat, then discussion of the shop's goods in general, then of the customer's tastes, preferences and requirements. Finally, a number of items are displayed for the customer's inspection.

The customer asks the price; the shop owner gives it; the customer looks doubtful and makes a counter-offer 25% to 50% lower. This procedure goes back and forth several times before a price acceptable to both parties is arrived at. It's considered bad form to haggle over a price, come to an agreement, and then change your mind.

If you can't agree on a price, it's perfectly acceptable to say goodbye and walk out of the shop. In fact, walking out is one of the best ways to test the authenticity of the last offer. If shopkeepers know you can find the item elsewhere for less, they'll probably call after you and drop their price. Even if they don't stop you, there's nothing to prevent you from returning later and buying the item for what they quoted.

To bargain effectively you must be prepared to take your time, and you must know something about the items in question, including their market price. The best way to learn is to look at similar goods in several shops, asking prices but not making counter-offers. Always stay good-humoured and polite when you are bargaining – if you do this the shopkeeper will too. When bargaining, you can often get a discount by offering to buy several items at once, by paying in a strong major currency, or by paying in cash.

If you don't have sufficient time to shop around, follow the age-old rule: find something you like at a price you're willing to pay, buy it, enjoy it, and don't worry about whether or not you received the world's lowest price.

In general, you shouldn't bargain in food shops or over transport costs. Outside tourist areas, hotels may expect to 'negotiate' the room price with you. In tourist areas pension owners are usually fairly clear about their prices, although if you're travelling in winter or staying a long time, it's worth asking about *indirim* (discounts).

is virtually worthless outside Turkey, so make sure you spend it all before leaving.

US dollars and euros are the easiest currencies to change, although many exchange offices and banks will change other major currencies such as UK pounds and Japanese yen.

You'll get better rates at exchange offices, which often don't charge commission, than at banks. Exchange offices operate in tourist and market areas, with better rates often found in the latter, and some post offices (PTTs), shops and hotels. They generally keep longer hours than banks.

Banks are more likely to change minor currencies, although they tend to make heavy weather of it. Turkey has no black market.

Tipping

Turkey is fairly European in its approach to tipping and you won't be pestered for baksheesh. Tipping is customary in restaurants, hotels and taxis; optional elsewhere.

Restaurants A few coins in budget eateries; 10% to 15% of the bill in midrange and top-end establishments.

Hotel porter Give 3% of the room price in midrange and top-end hotels only.

Taxis Round up metered fares to the nearest 50 kuruş.

Travellers Cheques

Banks, shops and hotels usually see it as a burden to change travellers cheques, and will either try to persuade you to go elsewhere or charge you a premium for the service. If you do have to change them, try one of the major banks.

Opening Hours

Most museums close on Monday; from April to October, they shut 1½ to two hours later than usual. Other businesses with seasonal variations include bars, which are likely to stay open later in summer than in winter, and tourist offices in popular locations, which open for longer hours and at weekends during summer.

The working day shortens during the holy month of Ramazan, which currently falls during the early summer. More Islamic cities such as Konya and Kayseri virtually shut down during noon prayers on Friday (the Muslim sabbath); apart from that, Friday is a normal working day.

We've provided summer high-season opening hours in our coverage; hours will generally decrease in the shoulder and low seasons. The following are standard opening hours.

Information 8.30am-noon and 1.30-5pm Monday to Friday

Eating 11am-10pm

Drinking 4pm-late

Nightclubs 11pm-late

Shopping 9am-6pm Monday to Friday (longer in tourist areas and big cities – including weekend opening)

Government departments, offices and banks 8.30am-noon and 1.30-5pm Monday to Friday

Postal Services

Turkish *postanes* (post offices) are indicated by black-on-yellow 'PTT' signs. Most post offices open Monday to Friday from around 8.30am to noon and 1.30pm to 5pm, but a few offices in major cities have extended opening hours.

Letters take between one and several weeks to get to/from Turkey. Sending a postcard or letter (up to 20g weight) to Europe or the USA costs ₺2.80.

When posting letters, the *yurtdışı* slot is for mail to foreign countries, *yurtiçi* for mail to other Turkish cities, and *şehiriçi* for local mail. Visit www.ptt.gov.tr for more information.

Parcels

If you are shipping something from Turkey, don't close your parcel before it has been inspected by a customs official. Take packing and wrapping materials with you to the post office.

Airmail tariffs are typically about ₺40 for the first kilogram, with an additional charge for every extra kilogram (typically ₺5 to Europe).

Parcels take months to arrive.

International couriers including DHL also operate in Turkey.

MAJOR ISLAMIC HOLIDAYS

The rhythms of Islamic practice are tied to the lunar calendar, which is slightly shorter than its Gregorian equivalent, so the Muslim calendar begins around 11 days earlier each year. The following dates are approximate.

ISLAMIC YEAR	NEW YEAR	PROPHET'S BIRTHDAY	START OF RAMAZAN	ŞEKER BAYRAMI (END OF RAMAZAN)	KURBAN BAYRAMI
1438	3 Oct 2016	12 Dec 2016	27 May 2017	25 Jun 2017	3 Sep 2017
1439	22 Sep 2017	1 Dec 2017	16 May 2018	14 Jun 2018	23 Aug 2018
1440	11 Sep 2018	20 Nov 2018	5 May 2019	3 Jun 2019	12 Aug 2019

Public Holidays

New Year's Day (Yılbaşı) 1 January

National Sovereignty & Children's Day (Ulusal Egemenlik ve Çocuk Günü) 23 April

International Workers' Day (May Day) 1 May

Youth & Sports Day (Gençlik ve Spor Günü) 19 May

Şeker Bayramı (Sweets Holiday) See table

Democracy and Freedoms Day 15 July

Victory Day (Zafer Bayramı) 30 August

Kurban Bayramı (Festival of the Sacrifice) See table

Republic Day (Cumhuriyet Bayramı) 28 to 29 October

Safe Travel

Although Turkey is by no means a dangerous country to visit, it's always wise to be a little cautious.

➡ Despite the suicide bombings in central İstanbul in 2016, the likelihood of being caught in such incidents (p598) remains small. Coastal resorts have not been targeted to date, and, although attacks have hit airports in İstanbul and Ankara, the usual targets are government and military installations.

➡ Be aware of cultural differences, for example the lese-majesty rule about not insulting the Turkish Republic.

➡ In more conservative parts of the country, women should be aware of cultural differences in the way men and women interact – if in doubt, follow the lead of local women.

Assaults

Sexual assaults have occurred against travellers of both sexes in hotels in central and eastern Anatolia. Make enquiries, check forums and do a little research in advance if you are travelling alone or heading off the beaten track.

Demonstrations

Marches and demonstrations are a regular sight in Turkish cities, especially İstanbul. These are best avoided as they can lead to clashes with the police.

Flies & Mosquitoes

In high summer, mosquitoes are troublesome even in İstanbul; they can make a stay along the coast a nightmare. Some hotel rooms come equipped with nets and/or plug-in bugbusters, but it's a good idea to bring some insect repellent and mosquito coils.

Lese-Majesty

The laws against insulting, defaming or making light of Atatürk, the Turkish Republic, the Turkish flag, the Turkish government, the Turkish people and so on are taken very seriously. Making derogatory remarks, even in the heat of a quarrel, can be enough to get a foreigner carted off to jail.

Safety Standards

Turkey is not a safety-conscious country: holes in pavements go unmended; precipitous drops go unguarded; seat belts are not always worn; lifeguards on beaches are rare; and dolmuş (minibus) drivers negotiate bends while counting out change.

Scams & Druggings

Various scams operate in İstanbul. In the most notorious, normally targeted at single men, a pleasant local guy befriends you in the street and takes you to a bar. After a few drinks, and possibly the attention of some ladies, to whom you offer drinks, the bill arrives. The prices are astronomical and the proprietors can produce a menu showing the same prices. If you don't have enough cash, you'll be frogmarched to the nearest ATM. If this happens to you, report it to the tourist police; some travellers have taken the police back to the bar and received a refund.

A less common variation on this trick involves the traveller having their drink spiked and waking up in an unexpected place with their belongings, right down to their shoes, missing – or worse.

Single men should not accept invitations from unknown folk in large cities without sizing the situation up carefully. You could invite your new-found friends to a bar of *your* choice; if they're not keen to go, chances are they are shady characters.

The spiking scam has also been reported on overnight trains, with passengers getting robbed. Turks are often genuinely sociable and generous travelling companions, but be cautious about accepting food and drinks from people you are not 100% sure about.

ANTIQUITIES

Do not buy coins or other artefacts offered to you by touts at ancient sites such as Ephesus and Perge. It is a serious crime here, punishable by long prison terms, and the touts are likely in cahoots with the local police.

SHOE CLEANERS

In Sultanahmet, İstanbul, if a shoe cleaner walking in front of you drops his brush, don't pick it up. He will insist on giving you a 'free' clean in return, before demanding an extortionate fee.

Smoking

Turks love smoking and there's even a joke about the country's propensity for puffing: Who smokes more than a Turk? Two Turks.

➡ Smoking in enclosed public spaces is banned, and punishable by a fine. Hotels, restaurants and bars are generally smoke-free, although bars sometimes relax the rules as the evening wears on.

➡ Off the tourist trail in budget and midrange hotels, the ban is enforced in public areas but more leniently in rooms, which may have ashtrays.

➡ Public transport is meant to be smoke-free, although taxi and bus drivers sometimes smoke at the wheel.

Street Crime

Incidents on the street remain rare, but do happen in big cities such as İstanbul, İzmir and Ankara, often perpetrated by young men and even boys in busy areas such as bazaars and transport terminals. Risks include pickpocketing, bag-slashing, bag-snatching and, very rarely, mugging.

Terrorism

As the world tragically saw in January 2016, there is an increased danger of terrorist attacks in Turkey, with jihadis linked to the Islamic State (Isis) group entering the country from war-torn Syria and Iraq. The Isis suicide bomber targeted the heart of Sultanahmet, İstanbul's main tourist area, killing 10 and wounding 15 mostly German tourists. The terrorist group, often referred to as Daesh in Turkey, carried out the attack with the specific intention of harming Turkey's tourist industry, in retaliation for the country's active role in the US coalition against Isis.

A similar attack followed in March 2016, killing five and injuring 36, including tourists from across Europe and the Middle East, on main drag İstiklal Caddesi in Beyoğlu, İstanbul. Isis seemed to be upping the ante in June 2016, when it attacked İstanbul's Atatürk International Airport, killing over 40 and injuring well over 200 travellers from around the world.

The attacks followed two explosions in Ankara the previous October, which killed over 100 and injured many more people attending a pro-Kurdish peace rally. Both this incident and an attack in July 2015, which killed over 30 in Suruç on the border of southeastern Anatolia and Syria, are thought to have been carried out by suicide bombers linked to Isis. These are the highest profile incidents; there have been others, for example the Ankara attacks in February and March 2016 by the TAK (Kurdistan Freedom Falcons), a splinter group from the PKK (Kurdistan Workers Party).

There is ongoing fighting between the Turkish state and the PKK, after peace talks faltered and a two-year ceasefire ended in 2015. The PKK, considered a terrorist organisation by the USA and the EU, wants greater rights and autonomy for Turkey's Kurdish population. Despite TAK's bombs in Ankara and İstanbul, attacks by the PKK and splinter groups still generally happen far from travellers' routes in remote parts of mountainous southeastern Anatolia, and target the Turkish military and government. However, check the latest situation if visiting southeastern Anatolia, as fighting has been seen in urban areas such as Diyarbakır.

At the time of writing, the UK Foreign & Commonwealth Office and the US Department of State's Bureau of Consular Affairs both advised of a high threat from terrorism in Turkey. However, it is worth remembering that, as with the atrocities seen in Western cities, these attacks are random; the chance of being caught in an incident is statistically low, so keep things in perspective amid the media coverage. The terrorists want to create a climate of fear and uncertainty, so do not fall into their trap; instead, weigh up the situation cautiously but rationally when deciding whether to visit. Once in Turkey, always

---

GOVERNMENT TRAVEL ADVICE

For the latest travel information log on to the following websites:

Australian Department of Foreign Affairs and Trade (☏61 2 6261 3305; www.smartraveller.gov.au)

Dutch Ministry of Foreign Affairs (☏31 77 465 6767; www.minbuza.nl)

German Federal Foreign Office (☏49-3018-17-0; www.auswaertiges-amt.de)

Global Affairs Canada (☏1 613 996 8885; www.travel.gc.ca)

Japanese Ministry of Foreign Affairs (☏81-3-3580-3311; www.mofa.go.jp)

New Zealand Ministry of Foreign Affairs and Trade (☏64 4 439 8000; www.safetravel.govt.nz)

UK Foreign & Commonwealth Office (☏44 20 7008 1500; www.fco.gov.uk/travel)

US Department of State's Bureau of Consular Affairs (☏1 202-501-444;, www.travel.state.gov)

avoid political rallies and large gatherings of people.

Do not visit areas in close proximity to the Syrian border, which are the most dangerous parts of Turkey. Here, there is the risk of being caught in the Turkish-Kurdish conflict and of being kidnapped or harmed by terrorists from Syria.

Traffic

As a pedestrian, note that some Turks are aggressive, dangerous drivers; 'right of way' doesn't compute with many motorists, despite the little green man on traffic lights. Give way to vehicles in all situations, even if you have to jump out of the way.

Telephone

Türk Telekom (www.turktele kom.com.tr) has a monopoly on phone services, and service is efficient if costly. Within Turkey, numbers starting with ☑444 don't require area codes and, wherever you call from, are charged at the local rate.

Kontörlü Telefon

If you only want to make one quick call, it's easiest to look for a booth with a sign saying *kontörlü telefon* (metered telephone). You make your call and the owner reads the meter and charges you accordingly. In touristy areas you can get rates as low as ₺0.50 per minute to Europe, the UK, the US and Australia.

Mobile Phones

➡ Turks adore mobile (*cep;* pocket) phones.

➡ Reception is excellent across most of Turkey.

➡ Mobile phone numbers start with a four-figure number beginning with ☑05.

➡ Major networks are Turkcell (www.turkcell.com. tr), the most comprehensive, and Vodafone (www. vodafone.com.tr).

➡ The queue will likely be shorter in the Vodafone store, but Turkcell coverage is better, especially out east.

➡ A pay-as-you-go Turkcell SIM including ₺35 credit costs between ₺65 and ₺95; the cost varies between branches.

➡ You need to show your passport, and ensure the seller phones through or inputs your details to activate your account.

➡ SIM cards and *kontör* (credit) are widely available – at streetside booths and shops as well as mobile phone outlets.

➡ You can buy a local SIM and use it in your mobile from home, although the networks detect and bar foreign phones after 120 days.

➡ The minimum Turkcell credit you can buy is ₺15.

➡ The bigger the credit bundle, the better the rates you receive.

➡ Data bundles typically cost ₺20 to ₺25 for 1GB, with larger bundles also available.

➡ Buy 1GB for ₺19 by texting 'YILDIZ 1 GB' to ☑2222.

➡ Most shops charge a small commission on credit (eg ₺20 credit costs ₺22).

➡ The networks offer SMS bundles (for Turkey or abroad).

➡ Dial ☑*123# to check credit.

➡ For assistance and information in English, call ☑8088 on Turkcell.

➡ On Turkcell, reverse charges by dialling ☑*135*53, followed by the number, followed by #.

LONG STAYS

Staying in Turkey longer than 120 days? To avoid having your home phone banned, register it within a month of arrival.

➡ Take the device to a government tax office, show your passport and your

Turkish residence permit and fill in a form.

➡ You will need to know your device's unique 15-digit International Mobile Equipment Identity (IMEI) number.

➡ Foreigners without a Turkish identity number should write 0009151009 on the form.

➡ The registration costs ₺132 cash.

➡ Complete the process by taking your phone, passport, residence permit and registration receipt to a certified mobile-phone shop and buying a SIM card.

➡ You can pick up a second-hand mobile phone for about ₺50 to ₺70 – simpler and cheaper than the registration rigmarole.

Payphones & Phonecards

➡ Türk Telekom payphones can be found in most major public buildings, facilities and squares, and transport terminals.

➡ International calls can be made from payphones.

➡ All payphones require cards that can be bought at telephone centres or, for a small mark-up, at some shops. Some payphones accept credit cards.

➡ Two types of card are in use: floppy cards with a magnetic strip, and Smart cards, embedded with a chip.

➡ The cards typically cost ₺5 to ₺20.

➡ A ₺5 card should be sufficient for local and short intercity calls; ₺10 for intercity and short international conversations.

INTERNATIONAL PHONECARDS

➡ Phonecards are the cheapest way to make international calls.

➡ Cards can be used on landlines, payphones and mobiles.

➡ As in other countries, you call the access number, key in the PIN on the card and dial away.

➡ Stick to reputable phonecards such as IPC (www.ipccard.com).

➡ Cards are widely available in the tourist areas of major cities, but can be difficult to find elsewhere.

Time

➡ Eastern European Summer Time all year round (GMT/ UTC plus three hours).

➡ Turkish bus timetables and so on use the 24-hour clock, but Turks rarely use it when speaking.

Toilets

Most hotels have sit-down toilets, but hole-in-the-ground models – with a conventional flush, or a tap and jug – are common. Toilet paper is often unavailable, so keep some with you. Many taps are unmarked and reversed (cold on the left, hot on the right).

In most bathrooms you can flush paper down the toilet, but in some places this may flood the premises. This is the case in much of İstanbul's old city. If you're not sure, play it safe and dispose of the paper in the bin provided. Signs often advise patrons to use the bin. This may seem slightly gross to the uninitiated, but many Turks (as well as people from other Middle Eastern and Asian countries) use a jet spray of water to clean themselves after defecating, applying paper to pat dry. The used paper is thus just damp, rather than soiled.

Public toilets can usually be found at major attractions and transport hubs; most require a payment of around 50 kuruş. In an emergency it's worth remembering that mosques have basic toilets (for both men and women).

Tourist Information

Every Turkish town of any size has an official tourist office run by the Ministry of Culture and Tourism. Staff are often enthusiastic and helpful, particularly when it comes to supplying brochures, but may have sketchy knowledge of the area, and English speakers are rare. Tour operators, pension owners and so on are often better sources of information.

Ministry of Culture and Tourism (www.goturkey.com) Has details of Turkish tourist offices overseas.

Travellers with Disabilities

Improvements are being made, but Turkey is a challenging destination for disabled (özürlü) travellers. Ramps, wide doorways and properly equipped toilets are rare, as are Braille and audio information at sights. Crossing most streets is particularly challenging, as everyone does so at their peril.

Airlines and the top hotels and resorts have some provision for wheelchair (tekerlekli sandalye) access, and ramps are beginning to appear elsewhere. Dropped kerb edges are being introduced to cities, especially in western Turkey – in places such as Edirne, Bursa and İzmir they seem to have been sensibly designed. Selçuk, Bodrum and Fethiye have been identified as relatively user-friendly towns for people with mobility problems because their pavements and roads are fairly level. In İstanbul, the tram, metro, funicular railways and catamaran ferries are the most wheelchair-accessible forms of public transport. İstanbul Deniz Otobüsleri's (İDO) Sea Bus catamaran ferries, which cross the Sea of Marmara and head up the Bosphorus from İstanbul, are generally accessible. Urban and inter-city buses often accommodate wheelchairs, but fully accessible vehicles are uncommon. Ankara and İzmir's metros are also accessible. A breakdown of how the major cities are making their transport networks more accessible can be found at www. raillynews.com/2014/ accessibility-disabled -2015-target-turkey.

Turkish Airlines offers a 20% discount on most domestic flights, and 25% on international fares, to travellers with minimum 40% disability, and in some cases to their companions. Some Turkish trains have disabled-accessible lifts, toilets and other facilities, although many are still boarded by steps. The bigger bus and ferry companies also often offer discounts.

Organisations

Businesses and resources serving travellers with disabilities include the following:

Access-Able (www.access-able. com) Has a small list of accommodation and tour and transport operators in Turkey.

Apparleyzed (www.apparelyzed. com) Features info on facilities in İstanbul.

Hotel Rolli (www.hotel-rolli.de) Specially designed for wheelchair users.

Mephisto Voyages (www. mephistovoyage.com) Special tours for mobility-impaired people, utilising the Joëlette wheelchair system.

> ### ACCESSIBLE TRAVEL
>
> Download Lonely Planet's free Accessible Travel guide from http:// lptravel.to/Accessible Travel.

Physically Disabled Support Association (www.bedd.org.tr) Based in İstanbul.

SATH (www.sath.org) Society for Accessible Travel and Hospitality.

Visas

➡ Nationals of countries including Denmark, Finland, France, Germany, Israel, Italy, Japan, New Zealand, Sweden and Switzerland don't need a visa to visit Turkey for up to 90 days.

➡ Nationals of countries including Australia, Austria, Belgium, Canada, Ireland, the Netherlands, Norway, Portugal, Spain, the UK and USA need a visa, which should be purchased online at www.evisa.gov.tr before travelling.

➡ Most nationalities, including the above, are given a 90-day multiple-entry visa.

➡ You must enter details of your passport and date of arrival in Turkey, click on the link in the verification email and pay with a Mastercard or Visa credit or debit card.

➡ Having completed this process, the e-visa can be downloaded in Adobe PDF format; a link is also emailed so it can be printed out later.

➡ It is recommended that you print out the e-visa to show on arrival in Turkey; keep it while in the country.

➡ It is recommended that applications are made at least 48 hours before departure.

➡ Many Western nationals can obtain a visa on arrival in Turkey, but this is not recommended as travellers have reported extra charges and bad experiences with the customs officials.

➡ At the time of writing, the e-visa charge was US$20 for most nationalities, with a few exceptions including Australians and Canadians, who paid US$60, and South

Africans, who received one month free.

➡ In some cases, the 90-day visa stipulates 'per period 180 days'. This means you can spend three months in Turkey within a six-month period; when you leave after three months, you can't re-enter for three months.

➡ Check the Ministry of Foreign Affairs (www.mfa.gov.tr, www.evisa.gov.tr) for more information.

➡ No photos required.

Residency Permits

➡ There are various types of *ikamet tezkeresi* (residence permit).

➡ Visit e-ikamet.goc.gov.tr for more information.

➡ Apply through this website soon after arrival.

➡ If you don't have a Turkish employer or spouse to support your application, you can get a permit for touristic purposes.

➡ Touristic permits are typically valid for up to a year; the price varies according to the applicant's nationality and office of application, with charges starting at a few hundred lira including administrative charges.

➡ More details are available in Pat Yale's *A Handbook for Living in Turkey*.

➡ Expat websites and forums – including istanbul.angloinfo.com, www.mymerhaba.com, thisismyistanbul.wordpress.com/turkey-online and www.turkeycentral.com – are also sources of (anecdotal) information and advice.

Volunteering

Opportunities include everything from teaching to working on an organic farm.

Alternative Camp (www.ayder.org.tr) A volunteer-based organisation running camps for disabled people.

Culture Routes in Turkey (tinyurl.com/d6fld8l) Opportunities to help waymark and repair its hiking trails such as the Lycian Way. A project to renovate old buildings for use as trekking accommodation is coming up.

European Youth Portal (europa.eu/youth/evs_database) Database of European Union–accredited opportunities.

Gençlik Servisleri Merkezi (www.gsm.org.tr/en) GSM runs voluntary work camps for young people in Turkey.

Gençtur (genctur.com.tr) Organises voluntourism including farmstays, with offices in İstanbul and Berlin.

GoAbroad.com (www.volunteerabroad.com) A US-based company listing a range of opportunities in Turkey, mostly through international organisations.

Open Arms in Kayseri (www.oakcharity.org) Grassroots charity working to improve the living conditions of Kayseri's large refugee population.

Ta Tu Ta (www.tatuta.org) Turkey's branch of WWOOF (Worldwide Opportunities on Organic Farms) organises work on dozens of organic farms around the country, where you receive accommodation and board in exchange for labour.

Women Travellers

Travelling in Turkey is straightforward for women, provided you follow some simple guidelines.

Accommodation

Outside tourist areas, the cheapest hotels, as well as often being fleapits, are generally not suitable for lone women. Stick with family-oriented midrange hotels.

If conversation in the lobby grinds to a halt as you enter, the hotel is not likely to be a great place for a woman.

If there is a knock on your hotel door late at night, don't open it; in the morning, complain to the manager.

We recommend female travellers stick to official campsites and camp where there are plenty of people around – especially out east. If you do otherwise, you will be taking a risk.

Clothing

Tailor your behaviour and your clothing to your surrounds. Look at what local women are wearing. On the streets of Beyoğlu in İstanbul you'll see skimpy tops and tight jeans, but cleavage and short skirts without leggings are a no-no everywhere except nightclubs in İstanbul and heavily touristed destinations along the coast.

Bring a shawl to cover your head when visiting mosques.

On the street, you don't need to don a headscarf, but in eastern Anatolia long sleeves and baggy long pants should attract the least attention.

Eating & Drinking

Restaurants and tea gardens aiming to attract women and children usually set aside a special family (aile) room or area. Look for the term aile salonu (family dining room).

Holiday Romances

It is not unheard of, particularly in romantic spots such as Cappadocia, for women to have holiday romances with local men. As well as fuelling the common Middle Eastern misconception that Western women are more 'available', this has led to occasional cases of men exploiting such relationships. Some men, for example, develop close friendships with visiting women, then invent sob stories and ask them to help out financially.

Regional Differences

Having a banter with men in restaurants and shops in western Turkey can be fun, and many men won't necessarily think much of it.

Particularly out east, however, passing through some towns, you can count the number of women you see on one hand, and those you do see will be headscarved and wearing long coats. Life here for women is largely restricted to the home. Eastern Anatolia is not the place to practise your Turkish (or Kurdish) and expect men not to get the wrong idea; even just smiling at a man or catching his eye is considered an invitation. Keep your dealings with men formal and polite, not friendly.

Transport

When travelling by taxi and dolmuş, avoid getting into the seat beside the driver, as this can be misinterpeted as a come-on.

On the bus, lone women are often assigned seats at the front near the driver. There have been cases of male passengers or conductors on night buses harassing female travellers. If this happens to you, complain loudly, making sure that others on the bus hear, and repeat your complaint on arrival at your destination; you have a right to be treated with respect.

Work

Outside professional fields such as academia and the corporate sector, bagging a job in Turkey is tough. Most people teach English or nanny.

Check whether potential employers will help you get a work permit. Many employers, notably language schools, are happy to employ foreigners on an informal basis, but unwilling to organise work permits due to the time and money involved in the bureaucratic process. This necessitates working illegally on a tourist visa/residence permit. The '90 days within 180 days' regulation stipulated by some tourist visas (for more on this, see www.mfa.gov.tr/visa-information-for-foreigners.en.mfa) rules out the option of cross-border 'visa runs' to pick up a new visa on re-entry to Turkey.

Locals also occasionally report illegal workers, and there have even been cases of English teachers being deported.

Job hunters may pick up leads on the following expat and advertising websites:

➡ istanbul.angloinfo.com

➡ istanbul.craigslist.com.tr

➡ www.mymerhaba.com

➡ www.sahibinden.com

➡ thisismyistanbul.wordpress.com/turkey-online

➡ www.turkeycentral.com

Nannying

One of the most lucrative non-specialist jobs open to foreigners is nannying for the wealthy urban elite, or looking after their teenage children and helping them develop their language skills.

There are opportunities for English, French and German speakers, and openings for young men as well as women, all mostly in İstanbul.

You must be prepared for long hours, demanding employers and spoilt children.

Accommodation is normally included, and the digs will likely be luxurious. However, living with the family means you are always on call, and you may be based in the suburbs.

Teaching English

You can earn a decent living, mostly in İstanbul and the other major cities, as an English teacher at a university or a school. Good jobs require a university degree and TEFL (Teaching English as a Foreign Language) certificate or similar.

As well as the job-hunting resources listed in the introduction to this section, log onto www.eslcafe.com, which has a Turkey forum, and www.tefl.com.

If you want to proactively contact potential employers, Wikipedia has lists of universities and private schools in Turkey.

DERSHANE
There are lots of jobs at *dershane* (private schools), which pay good wages and offer attractions such as accommodation (although it may be on or near the school campus in the suburbs) and work permits. Some even pay for your flight to Turkey and/or flights home.

Jobs are available at all levels, from kindergarten to high school. Teachers who can't speak Turkish often find very young children challenging; many are spoilt and misbehave around foreign teachers. The best preschools pair a foreign teacher with a Turkish colleague.

You will often be required to commit to an unpaid trial period, lasting a week or two.

Unless a teacher has dropped out before the end of their contract, these jobs are mostly advertised around May and June, when employers are recruiting in preparation for the beginning of the academic year in September. Teachers are contracted until the end of the academic year in June.

LANGUAGE SCHOOLS
Teaching at a language school is not recommended. The majority are exploitative institutions untroubled by professional ethics; for example making false promises in job interviews. A few Turkish schools are 'blacklisted' at teflblacklist.blogspot.com.

At some schools you teach in a central classroom, but at business English schools you often have to schlep around the city between the clients' workplaces.

Schools often promise you a certain number of hours a week, but classes are then cancelled, normally at the last minute, making this a frustrating and difficult way to make a living in Turkey.

PRIVATE TUITION
The advantage of teaching privately is that you don't need a TEFL certificate or even a university degree. You can advertise your services on istanbul.craigslist.com.tr and www.sahibinden.com.

The disadvantage is that, unless you are willing to travel to clients' offices and homes (which is time-consuming, and potentially risky for women), they tend to cancel when they get busy and learning English suddenly becomes a low priority. As with business English schools, most teaching takes place on weekends and evenings, when the students have spare time.

UNIVERSITIES
University jobs command the best wages, with work permits and, often, flights thrown in. Universities also generally operate more professionally than many establishments in the previous sectors.

The teacher's job is often to prepare freshman students for courses that will largely be taught in English.

As with *dershane,* jobs are advertised around May and June, and run roughly from September until June.

Tourism
Travellers sometimes work illegally for room and board in pensions, bars and other businesses in tourist areas. These jobs are generally badly paid and only last a few weeks, but they are a fun way to stay in a place and get to know the locals.

Given that you will be in direct competition with unskilled locals for such employment, and working in the public eye, there is a danger of being reported to authorities and deported.

Working Visas
➡ Visit www.konsolosluk.gov.tr for information on obtaining a *çalışma izni* (work permit).

➡ Your Turkish employer should help you get the visa.

➡ If it's an employer such as a school or international company, they should be well versed in the process and can handle the majority of the paperwork.

➡ The visa can be obtained in Turkey or from a Turkish embassy or consulate.

➡ The government plans to introduce a 'turquoise card', which will be a points-based system based on the applicant's vocational qualifications, educational background and professional experience.

Transport

GETTING THERE & AWAY

Flights, cars and tours can be booked online at lonelyplanet.com/bookings.

Entering the Country

Most visitors need an e-visa (p601), purchased online before travelling.

Passport

Make sure your passport will still have at least six months' validity after you enter Turkey.

Air

It's a good idea to book flights months in advance if you plan to arrive in Turkey any time from April until late August. If you plan to visit a resort, check with travel agents for flight and accommodation deals. Sometimes you can find cheap flights with Turkish carriers and smaller airlines.

Airports

The main international airports are in western Turkey.

Atatürk International Airport (IST, Atatürk Havalimanı; Map p140; ☑+90 444 9828; www.ataturkairport.com) Istanbul's main airport, Atatürk International Airport, is in Yeşilköy, 23km west of Sultanahmet. The international terminal (Dış Hatlar) is polished and organised. Close by, the domestic terminal (İç Hatlar) is smaller but no less efficient.

Sabiha Gökçen International Airport (SAW, Sabiha Gökçen Havalimanı; ☑0216-588 8888; www.sgairport.com) This airport on İstanbul's Asian side is popular with low-cost European airlines, but is not as conveniently located as Atatürk.

Antalya International Airport (Antalya Havalimanı; ☑444 7423; www.aytport.com) Receives flights from across Turkey and Europe.

Adnan Menderes Airport (☑0232-455 0000; www.adnanmenderesairport.com) There are many flights to İzmir's Adnan Menderes Airport from European destinations.

Bodrum International Airport (BJV; www.bodrumairport.com) Receives flights from all over Europe, mostly with charters and budget airlines in summer, and from İstanbul and Ankara with the Turkish airlines. Also known as Milas-Bodrum Airport.

Dalaman International Airport (☑0252-792 5555; www.yda.aero/Dalaman_en/index.php) Seasonal flights from many European cities, and year-round from İstanbul.

Esenboğa Airport (☑0312-590 4000; www.esenbogaairport.com; Özal Bulvarı, Balıkhisar) Numerous international and domestic connections from Ankara, although İstanbul's airports offer more choice.

CLIMATE CHANGE & TRAVEL

Every form of transport that relies on carbon-based fuel generates CO_2, the main cause of human-induced climate change. Modern travel is dependent on aeroplanes, which might use less fuel per kilometre per person than most cars but travel much greater distances. The altitude at which aircraft emit gases (including CO_2) and particles also contributes to their climate change impact. Many websites offer 'carbon calculators' that allow people to estimate the carbon emissions generated by their journey and, for those who wish to do so, to offset the impact of the greenhouse gases emitted with contributions to portfolios of climate-friendly initiatives throughout the world. Lonely Planet offsets the carbon footprint of all staff and author travel.

Airlines

Turkish Airlines (☑0850-333 0849; www.turkishairlines. com), the national carrier, has extensive international and domestic networks, including budget subsidiaries **Sun Express** (☑444 0797; www. sunexpress.com) and **Anadolu Jet** (☑444 2538; www. anadolujet.com). It is generally considered a safe airline, and its operational safety is certified by the International Air Transport Association (IATA). Like many airlines, it has had accidents and incidents over the years – nine crashes since 1974, most recently at Amsterdam's Schiphol airport in 2009.

AUSTRALIA & NEW ZEALAND

You can fly from the main cities in Australia and New Zealand to İstanbul, normally via Dubai (or elsewhere in the Middle East), Kuala Lumpur or Singapore.

You can often get affordable flights with European airlines, if you're prepared to change flights again in Europe.

CONTINENTAL EUROPE

There's not much variation in fares from one European airport to another; with the exception of Germany, which has the biggest Turkish community outside Turkey, enabling some great deals.

Most European national carriers fly direct to İstanbul. Cheaper indirect flights can be found, for example changing in Frankfurt or Munich en route from Amsterdam to İstanbul.

Budget and charter airlines fly between several European cities and the major western Turkish airports.

Condor (www.condor.com)

Corendon Airlines (www. corendon-airlines.com)

Eurowings (www.eurowings.com)

Pegasus Airlines (☑0888-228 1212; www.pegasusairlines.com)

Sun Express (☑444 0797; www.sunexpress.com)

EASTERN EUROPE

Atlasglobal (☑0850-222 0000; www.atlasglb.com/ en) flies between İstanbul and Yerevan (Armenia) twice weekly. The flights don't appear on the airline's website but tickets can be purchased from agents in both cities.

MIDDLE EAST & ASIA

From Central Asia and the Middle East, you can usually pick up flights with Turkish Airlines or the country's national carrier.

Affordable flights from further afield normally travel to İstanbul via Dubai, Kuala Lumpur or Singapore.

Atlasglobal (☑0850-222 0000; www.atlasglb.com/en)

Azerbaijan Airlines (www. azal.az)

Correndon Airlines (www. corendonairlines.com)

Onur Air (☑0850-210 6687; www.onurair.com.tr)

Pegasus Airlines (☑0888-228 1212; www.pegasusairlines.com)

UK & IRELAND

In addition to the airlines listed, flights are available with European carriers via continental Europe. With major airlines such as British Airways and Turkish Airlines, the cheapest flights are normally in and out of London airports.

Charter flights are a good option, particularly at the beginning and end of the peak summer holiday season.

Atlasjet (www.atlasjet.com)

EasyJet (www.easyjet.com)

Pegasus Airlines (☑0888-228 1212; www.pegasusairlines.com)

Thomson (www.thomsonfly.com)

USA & CANADA

Most flights connect with İstanbul-bound flights in the UK or continental Europe, so it's worth looking at European and British airlines in addition to North American airlines.

Another option is to cross the Atlantic to, say, London or Paris, and continue on a separate ticket with a budget carrier.

Land

If you're travelling by train or bus, expect to be held up at the border for two to three hours – or even longer if your fellow passengers don't have their paperwork in order. You'll usually have to disembark and endure paperwork and baggage checks on both sides of the border. Security at the crossings to/from countries to the east and southeast (Georgia, Azerbaijan, Iran and Iraq) is tightest. The process is elongated by a trainload of passengers or the long lines of trucks and cars that build up at some crossings.

Turkey's relationships with most of its neighbours tend to be tense, which can affect when and where you can cross. Check for the most up-to-date information; sources of information include Lonely Planet's Thorn Tree forum, your embassy in Turkey and the Turkish embassy in your country.

Crossing the border into Turkey with your own vehicle should be fairly straightforward, providing your paperwork is in order.

Armenia

At the time of writing, the Turkey–Armenia border was closed.

BUS

Buses run to Tbilisi (Georgia), with connections to Armenia. There is also a Yerevan–İstanbul service once a week.

Crossing from Turkey to Georgia via the Türkgözü and Aktaş borders, the only minibus services onward to Armenia from the towns on the Georgian side are in the morning.

Azerbaijan

The remote Borualan–Sadarak crossing, east of Iğdır (Turkey), leads to the Azerbaijani enclave of Nahçıvan (Naxçıvan). Nahçıvan is separated from the rest of Azerbaijan by the disputed Nagorno-Karabakh region and the only way to get from Nahçıvan to the rest of Azerbaijan is to fly.

BUS

Buses run from İstanbul and Trabzon to Baku and to Tbilisi (Georgia), with onward connections to Baku. Many use İstanbul's Emniyet Garajı, rather than the main bus station. There are also daily buses from Iğdır to Nakhichevan. The following serve the İstanbul–Baku route:

Alpar (www.alparturizm.com.tr; Büyük İstanbul Otogarı)

Mahmut (www.mahmutturizm. com.tr; Emniyet Garajı)

Ortadoğu Turizm (ortadogutur. com.tr)

Öznuhoğlu (www.oznuho gluseyahat.com)

Perla Trans (perlatrans.com.ro)

TRAIN

The Kars–Tbilisi–Baku line is set to open in 2017.

Bulgaria & Eastern Europe

Bulgarian border guards only occasionally allow pedestrians to cross the frontier; take a bus or hitch a lift with a cooperative motorist. There are three border crossings:

Kapitan Andreevo–Kapıkule This 24-hour post is the main

crossing – and the world's second busiest land border crossing. Located 18km northwest of Edirne (Turkey) on the E80 and 9km from Svilengrad (Bulgaria).

Lesovo–Hamzabeyli Some 25km northeast of Edirne, this is favoured by big trucks and should be avoided.

Malko Tărnovo–Aziziye Some 70km northeast of Edirne via Kırklareli and 92km south of Burgas (Bulgaria), this is only useful for those heading to Bulgaria's Black Sea resorts.

BUS

Half a dozen companies have daily departures between İstanbul and eastern European destinations including Albania, Bulgaria, Kosovo, Macedonia and Romania. Many use İstanbul's Emniyet Garajı, rather than the main bus station.

Alpar (www.alparturizm.com.tr; Büyük İstanbul Otogarı)

Huntur (www.hunturturizm. com.tr)

Metro Turizm (☑0850-222 3455; www.metroturizm.com.tr)

Nişikli (www.nisikli.com.tr)

Varan (☑0850-811 1999; www. varan.com.tr)

Vardar (www.vardarturizm.com.tr)

TRAIN

The daily **Bosfor/Balkan Ekspresi** runs from İstanbul to Bucharest (Romania) and Sofia (Bulgaria), with onward connections. At the time of research, the İstanbul–Sofia leg of the journey was by bus, and the Sofia–Bucharest leg by train. It departs at 10pm daily (₺65 to Sofia, ₺125 to Bucharest).

Note that the Turkey–Bulgaria border crossing is in the early hours of the morning and you need to leave the train (or bus at the moment) to get your passport stamped. We've heard stories of harassment, especially of women, at the border, so lone women may be best taking an alternative route. For more information, see **The Man in**

Seat 61 (www.seat61.com/ turkey2) and **Turkish State Railways** (☑444 8233; www. tcdd.gov.tr).

Georgia

Sarp The main 24-hour crossing, on the Black Sea coast between Hopa (Turkey) and Batumi (Georgia).

Türkgözü Near Posof (Turkey), north of Kars and southwest of Akhaltsikhe (Georgia). The border should be open 24 hours.

Aktaş South of Türkgözü, this new crossing between Ardahan and Ahalkalaki (Georgia) reduces the driving time to Armenia. It should also be open 24 hours.

BUS

Several bus companies depart from İstanbul, Ankara and other cities to Batumi, Kutaisi and Tbilisi. Many use İstanbul's Emniyet Garajı, rather than the main bus station.

Closer to Georgia, buses and minibuses run from Trabzon via Rize, Pazar, Hopa and Sarp to Batumi (and vice versa).

There's one daily bus each way between Ardahan (Turkey) and Akhaltsikhe (Georgia) via Türkgözü. In theory it continues to/from Tbilisi, but it doesn't always do so.

Three daily minibuses connect Ardahan and Akhalkalaki (Georgia) via Aktaş, stopping at Çıldır between Ardahan and the border.

Crossing the border by bus or minibus normally takes about an hour, and the passengers generally walk across and wait for the vehicle. It is thus usually quicker to catch a bus to the border, walk through and pick up another on the far side.

Golden Turizm (goldenturizm. com.tr)

Mahmut (www.mahmut turizm.com.tr; Emniyet Garajı) İstanbul–Tbilisi daily

Metro Turizm (☑0850-222 3455; www.metroturizm. com.tr)

TRAIN
The Kars–Tbilisi–Baku line is set to open in 2017.

Greece & Western Europe
Greek and Turkish border guards allow you to cross the frontier on foot. The following are open 24 hours.

Kastanies–Pazarkule About 9km southwest of Edirne.

Kipi–İpsala Located 29km northeast of Alexandroupolis (Greece) and 35km west of Keşan (Turkey).

BUS
Germany, Austria and Greece have most direct buses to İstanbul, so if you're travelling from other European countries, you'll likely have to catch a connecting bus. Several companies have daily departures for Greece and beyond.

Derya Tur (www.deryatur.com.tr in Turkish) Serves Athens (Greece).

Metro Turizm (☑0850-222 3455; www.metroturizm.com.tr)

Ulusoy (☑0850-811 1888; www.ulusoy.com.tr) Serves Germany.

Varan (☑0850-811 1999; www.varan.com.tr) Serves Austria.

CAR & MOTORCYCLE
The E80 highway makes its way through the Balkans to Edirne and İstanbul, then on to Ankara. Using the car-ferries from Italy and Greece can shorten driving times from Western Europe, but at a price.

From Alexandroupolis, the main road leads to Kipi-İpsala, then to Keşan and east to İstanbul or south to Gallipoli, Çanakkale and the Aegean.

TRAIN
From Western Europe, you will come via Eastern Europe. A suggested route from London to İstanbul is the three-night journey via Paris,

Munich, Zagreb, Belgrade and Sofia (or four nights via Paris, Munich, Budapest and Bucharest); see www.seat61.com/turkey for more information.

Iran
Gürbulak–Bazargan This busy post, 35km southeast of Doğubayazıt (Turkey), is open 24 hours.

Esendere–Sero Southeast of Van, this road crossing is not currently recommended for security reasons.

BUS
There are regular buses from İstanbul and Ankara. Thor Tourism (www.thortourism.com) offers three buses a week from Ankara to Tabriz and Tehran.

From Doğubayazıt Catch a dolmuş to Gürbulak, then walk or catch a shared taxi across the border. It's Iran's busiest border crossing, and Turkey's second busiest. The crossing might take up to an hour, although tourists are normally waved through without much fuss. Change any unused Turkish lira in Bazargan, as it's harder to do so in Tabriz and Tehran. There are onward buses from Bazargan.

From Van There are direct buses to Orumiyeh (Iran).

TRAIN
For more information visit www.tcdd.gov.tr and www.seat61.com/iran.

Trans-Asya Ekspresi The İstanbul–Tehran service had been indefinitely suspended at the time of writing. An alternative is taking the train to Ankara and on to eastern Turkey, crossing the border with a guide and catching the train from Tabriz to Tehran. See www.orientbahn-reisen.de/de/aktuelles/#turkey-to-iran-train.

Van–Tabriz Also suspended at the time of writing.

Iraq
Between Silopi (Turkey) and Zahko (Kurdish Iraq), there's no town or village at

the Habur–Ibrahim al-Khalil crossing and you can't walk across it. Not recommended for security reasons at the time of writing, when Western governments advised against travelling in southeastern Anatolia and crossing the Iraqi border. This situation is unlikely to change in the near future.

BUS
There are direct daily buses from Diyarbakır to Dohuk (₺50, six hours) or Erbil (₺60, nine hours) in Kurdish Iraq, and from Cizre.

TAXI
More hassle than the bus, a taxi from Silopi to Zakho costs between US$50 and US$70. Your driver will manoeuvre through a maze of checkpoints and handle the paperwork. On the return journey, watch out for taxi drivers slipping contraband into your bag.

Syria
At the time of writing, advisories warned against all travel to Syria due to the civil war there. Advisories also warned against travel to the area of Turkey near the Syrian border. Check government travel advice and www.lonelyplanet.com/thorntree for updates.

Sea
Departure times change between seasons, with fewer ferries running in the winter. The routes available also change from year to year. A good starting point for information is Ferrylines (www.ferrylines.com).

Day trips on ferries to Greece are popular. Remember to take your passport, and check you have a multiple-entry Turkish visa so you can get back into the country at the end of the day. (Tourist visas issued on arrival in Turkey normally allow multiple entries.)

Routes

Ayvalık–Lesvos (Midilli), Greece (www.erturk.com.tr/en, www.jaletour.com)

Bodrum–Kalymnos, Kos, Rhodes and Symi, Greece (www.bodrumexpresslines.com, www.bodrumferryboat.com, www.erturk.com.tr/en, www.rhodesferry.com)

Çeşme–Chios, Greece (www.erturk.com.tr/en)

İstanbul–Illyichevsk (Odessa), Ukraine (www.sea-lines.net)

Kaş–Meis (Kastellorizo), Greece (www.erturk.com.tr/en, www.meisexpress.com)

Kuşadası–Samos, Patmos and Ikaria, Greece (www.bareltravel.com, www.erturk.com.tr/en, www.meandertravel.com)

Marmaris–Rhodes (www.erturk.com.tr/en, www.marmarisferry.com, www.rhodesferry.com)

Taşucu–Girne, Northern Cyprus (www.akgunlerdenizcilik.com)

Turgetreis–Kalymnos, Kos and Leros (İleriye) (www.bodrumexpresslines.com, www.bodrumferryboat.com)

Tours

Many international tour companies offer trips to Turkey.

Backroads (www.backroads.com) Offers a combined bike and sailing tour on the Mediterranean and Aegean.

Cultural Folk Tours (www.culturalfolktours.com) Cultural and historical tours.

Dragoman (www.dragoman.com) Overland itineraries starting in İstanbul and heading through Turkey and the Middle East to various far-flung destinations.

EWP (www.ewpnet.com) Mountaineering and trekking specialist covering the Kaçkars, Lycian Way, Cappadocia, Phrygian Valley and elsewhere.

Exodus (www.exodus.co.uk) Adventure company offering a range of tours covering walking, biking, kayaking, diving and history.

Imaginative Traveller (www.imaginative-traveller.com) Various trips with themes such as food.

Intrepid Travel (www.intrepidtravel.com) Offers a variety of small-group tours, covering Turkey, the Middle East and Eastern Europe, for travellers who like the philosophy of independent travel but prefer to travel with others.

Pacha Tours (www.pachatours.com) Long-running Turkey specialist offering general tours plus special-interest packages and itineraries incorporating Greece.

GETTING AROUND

Air

Turkey is well connected by air throughout the country, although many flights go via the hubs of İstanbul or Ankara. Domestic flights are a good option in such a large country, and competition between the following keeps tickets affordable.

Airlines in Turkey

Anadolu Jet (☑444 2538; www.anadolujet.com) The Turkish Airlines subsidiary serves a large network of some 40 airports.

Atlasglobal (☑0850-222 0000; www.atlasglb.com/en) A limited network including Adana, Antalya, Bodrum, Dalaman, İstanbul, İzmir, and Lefkoşa (Nicosia) in Northern Cyprus.

Onur Air (☑0850-210 6687; www.onurair.com.tr) Flies between İstanbul and a dozen locations from Adana to Trabzon.

Pegasus Airlines (☑0888-228 1212; www.pegasusairlines.com) A useful network of some 30 airports, including far-flung eastern spots such as Erzurum and Kars.

Sun Express (☑444 0797; www.sunexpress.com) The Turkish Airlines subsidiary has a useful network of about 20 airports, with most flights from Antalya and İzmir.

Turkish Airlines (☑0850-333 0849; www.turkishairlines.com) State-owned Turkish Airlines provides the main domestic network, covering airports from Çanakkale to Erzurum.

Bicycle

Turkish cycling highlights include spectacular scenery, easy access to archaeological sites – which you may have all to yourself in some obscure corners – and the curiosity and hospitality of locals, especially out east.

Bicycles and parts Good-quality spare parts are generally only available in İstanbul and Ankara. Bisan (www.bisan.com.tr) is the main bike manufacturer in Turkey, but you can buy international brands in shops such as Delta Bisiklet (www.deltabisiklet.com), which has branches in İstanbul, Ankara, İzmir, Antalya, Konya and Kayseri. Delta services bicycles and can send parts throughout the country.

Hazards These include Turkey's notorious road-hog drivers, rotten road edges and, out east, stone-throwing children, wolves and ferocious Kangal dogs. Avoid main roads between cities; secondary roads are safer and more scenic.

Hire You can hire bikes for short periods in tourist towns along the coast and in Cappadocia.

Maps The best map for touring by bike is the *Köy Köy Türkiye Yol Atlası*, available in bookshops in İstanbul.

Transport You can sometimes transport your bike by bus or ferry free of charge, although some will charge for the space it takes up. Trains generally do not accept bikes.

Boat

İstanbul Deniz Otobüsleri (İDO; ☑0850 222 4436; www.ido.com.tr) and **BUDO** (budo.burulas.com.tr) operate passenger and car ferries across the Sea of Marmara, with routes to/from İstanbul including:

➡ Kabataş–Princes' Islands

➡ Kabataş–Bursa

➡ Kadıköy–Bursa

➡ Yenikapı–Bandırma, Bursa and Yalova

Gestaş (www.gdu.com.tr) operates passenger and car ferries across the Dardanelles and to/from the Turkish Aegean islands of Bozcaada and Gökçeada.

Bus

Turkey's intercity bus system is as good as any you'll find, with modern, comfortable coaches crossing the country at all hours and for very reasonable prices. On the journey, you'll be treated to hot drinks and snacks, plus liberal sprinklings of the Turks' beloved *kolonya* (lemon cologne).

Companies

These are some of the best companies, with extensive route networks:

Kamil Koç (☑444 0562; www. kamilkoc.com.tr) Serves most major cities and towns throughout western and central Turkey and along the Black Sea coast.

Metro Turizm (☑0850-222 3455; www.metroturizm.com. tr) Serves most cities and towns throughout Turkey.

Ulusoy (☑0850-811 1888; www.ulusoy.com.tr) Serves most major cities and towns throughout western and central Turkey and along the Black Sea coast.

Varan (☑0850-811 1999; www. varan.com.tr) Mostly western Turkey, plus Ankara and the Black Sea coast.

Costs

Bus fares are subject to fierce competition between companies, and bargains such as student discounts may be offered. Prices reflect what the market will bear, so the fare from a big city to a

village is likely to be different to the fare in the opposite direction.

Tickets

Although you can usually walk into an otogar (bus station) and buy a ticket for the next bus, it's wise to plan ahead on public holidays, at weekends and during the school holidays from mid-June to mid-September. You can buy or reserve seats online with some companies.

At the otogar When you enter bigger otogars prepare for a few touts offering buses to the destination of your choice. It's usually a good idea to stick to the reputable big-name companies. You may pay a bit more, but you can be more confident the bus is well maintained, will run on time and will have a relief driver on really long hauls. For shorter trips, some companies have big regional networks.

Men and women Unmarried men and women are not supposed to sit together, but the bus companies rarely enforce this in the case of foreigners. You may be asked if you are married, without having to produce any proof of your wedlock, or both travellers may find their tickets marked with *bay* (man).

Refunds Getting a refund can be difficult; exchanging it for another ticket with the same company is easier.

Identification Take your passport/ID when booking tickets, as many bus companies now ask to see it. Also keep your passport with you on the journey for security checks.

All seats can be reserved, and your ticket will bear a specific seat number. The ticket agent will have a chart of the seats with those already sold crossed off. They will often assign you a seat, but if you ask to look at the chart and choose a place, you can avoid sitting in the following blackspots:

At the front On night buses you may want to avoid the front row of seats behind the driver, which

have little legroom, plus you may have to inhale his cigarette smoke and listen to him chatting to his conductor into the early hours.

Above the wheels Can get bumpy.

In front of the middle door Seats don't recline.

Behind the middle door Little legroom.

At the back Can get stuffy, and may have 'back of the cinema' connotations if you are a lone woman.

Otogars

Most Turkish cities and towns have a bus station, called the otogar, *garaj* or *terminal*, generally located on the outskirts. Besides intercity buses, otogars often handle dolmuşes (minibuses that follow prescribed routes) to outlying districts or villages. Most have an *emanetçi* (left luggage) room, which you can use for a nominal fee.

Don't believe taxi drivers at otogars who tell you there is no bus or dolmuş to your destination; they may be trying to trick you into taking their taxi. Check with the bus and dolmuş operators.

Cities where the otogar is out of the centre generally have a more central terminal for minibus services to nearby towns – often called Eski Otogar (Old Otogar), because it used to be the main bus station.

Servis

Because most bus stations are some distance from the town or city centre, the bus companies provide free *servis* shuttle minibuses. These take you to the bus company's office or another central location, possibly with stops en route to drop off other passengers. Ask *'Servis var mı?'* ('Is there a *servis*?'). Rare cities without such a service include Ankara and Konya.

Leaving town Ask about the *servis* when you buy your ticket at the bus company's central office; they will likely instruct you to arrive at the office an hour before the official departure time.

Drawbacks This service saves you a taxi or local bus fare to the otogar, but involves a lot of hanging around. If you only have limited time in a location, a taxi fare may be a good investment.

Scams Pension owners may try to convince you the private minibus to their pension is a *servis*. Taxi drivers may say the *servis* has left or isn't operating in the hope of convincing you that their cab is the only option. If you do miss a *servis*, inquire at the bus company office – they normally run regularly.

Car & Motorcycle

Driving around Turkey gives you unparalleled freedom to explore the marvellous countryside and coastline, and to follow back roads to hidden villages and obscure ruins.

Bear in mind that Turkey is a huge country and covering long distances by car will eat up your time and money. Consider planes, trains and buses for long journeys, and cars for localised travel.

Public transport is a much easier and less stressful way of getting around the traffic-clogged cities.

Automobile Associations

Turkey's main motoring organisation is the Türkiye Turing ve Otomobil Kurumu (Turkish Touring & Automobile Club; www.turing.org.tr).

Motorcyclist website Horizons Unlimited (www.horizonsunlimited.com/country/turkey) also has Turkey-related information and contacts.

Motorcyclists may want to check out One More Mile Riders Turkey (www.omm riders.com), a community resource for riding in Turkey.

Bring Your Own Vehicle

You can bring your vehicle into Turkey for six months without charge. Ensure you have your car's registration papers, tax number and insurance policy with you. The fact that you brought a vehicle to Turkey will be marked in your passport to ensure you take it back out again.

Checkpoints

Roadblocks are common in eastern Turkey, with police checking vehicles and paperwork are in order. In southeastern Anatolia you may encounter military roadblocks, and roads are sometimes closed completely if there is trouble ahead.

Driving Licences

Drivers must have a valid driving licence. Your own national licence should be sufficient, but an international driving permit (IDP) may be useful if your licence is from a country likely to seem obscure to a Turkish police officer.

Fines

You may be stopped by blue-uniformed *trafik polis*, who can fine you on the spot for speeding. If you know you have done nothing wrong and the police appear to be asking for money, play dumb. You'll probably have to pay up if they persist, but insisting on proof of payment may dissuade them from extracting a fine destined only for their pocket. If they don't ask for on-the-spot payment, contact your car-rental company (or mention the incident when you return the vehicle), as it can pay the fine and take the money from your card. Do the same in the case of fines for other offences, such as not paying a motorway toll.

Fuel & Spare Parts

Turkey has the world's second-highest petrol prices. Petrol/diesel cost about ₺5 per litre. Petrol stations are widespread in western Turkey, and many are mega enterprises. In the vast empty spaces of central and eastern Anatolia, it's a good idea to have a full tank when you start out in the morning.

Yedek parçaları (spare parts) are readily available in the major cities, especially for European models. Elsewhere, you may have to wait a day or two for parts to be ordered and delivered. Ingenious Turkish mechanics can contrive to keep some US models in service. The *sanayi bölgesi* (industrial zone) on the outskirts of every town generally has a repair shop; for tyre repairs find an *oto lastikçi* (tyre repairer).

Spare motorcycle parts may be hard to come by everywhere except major cities.

Hire

You need to be at least 21 years old, with a year's driving experience, to hire a car in Turkey. Most car-hire companies require a credit card. Most hire cars have standard (manual) transmission; you'll pay more for automatic. The majority of the big-name companies charge hefty one-way fees, starting at around TL150 and climbing to hundreds of euros for longer distances.

The big international companies – including Avis, Budget, Europcar, Hertz, National and Sixt – operate in the main cities and towns, and most airports. Particularly in eastern Anatolia, stick to the major companies, as the local agencies often do not have insurance. Even some of the major operations are actually franchises in the east, so check the contract carefully; particularly the section relating to insurance. Ask for a copy in English.

If your car incurs any accident damage, or if you cause any, do not move the car before finding a police officer and obtaining a *kaza raporu* (accident report). Contact your car-rental company as soon as possible. In the case of an accident, your hire-car insurance may be void if it can be shown you were operating under the influence of alcohol or drugs, were speeding, or if you did not submit the required accident report within 48 hours to the rental company.

Agencies generally deliver cars with virtually no fuel, unless you specifically request otherwise.

CarHireExpress.co.uk (www.carhireexpress.co.uk/turkey/) A booking engine.

Economy Car Hire (www.economycarhire.com) Gets good rates with other companies, including Avis and Thrifty.

Economy Car Rentals (www.economycarrentals.com) Gets good rates with other companies, including Budget and National.

Rentalcars.com (www.rentalcars.com) Good rates with other companies, including Alamo.

Insurance

You must have international insurance, covering third-party damage, if you are bringing your own car into the country (further information is available at www.turing.org.tr/eng/green_card.asp). Buying it at the border is a straightforward process (one month €80).

When hiring a car, 100%, no-excess insurance is increasingly the only option on offer. If this is not the only option, the basic, mandatory insurance package should cover damage to the vehicle and theft protection – with an excess, which you can reduce or waive for an extra payment.

As in other countries, insurance generally does not cover windows and tyres. You will likely be offered cover for an extra few euros a day.

Road Conditions

Road surfaces and signage are generally good – on the main roads, at least. There are good *otoyols* (motorways) from the Bulgarian border near Edirne to İstanbul and Ankara, and from İzmir around the coast to Antalya.

Elsewhere, roads are being steadily upgraded, although they still tend to be worst in the east, where severe winters play havoc with the surfaces. In northeastern Anatolia, road conditions change from year to year; seek local advice before setting off on secondary roads. There are frequent roadworks in the northeast; even on main roads traffic can crawl along at 30km/h. Dam building and associated road construction in the Artvin/Yusufeli area can cause waits of up to half an hour on some roads. Ask locally about the timing of your journey; on some roads, traffic flows according to a regular timetable, posted at the roadside.

In winter, be careful of icy roads. In bad winters, you will need chains on your wheels almost everywhere except along the Aegean and Mediterranean coasts. The police may stop you in more remote areas to check you're properly prepared for emergencies. In mountainous areas such as northeastern Anatolia, landslides and rockfalls are a danger, caused by wet weather and snow-melt in spring. Between İstanbul and Ankara, be aware of the fog belt around Bolu that can seriously reduce visibility, even in summer.

Road Rules

In theory, Turks drive on the right and yield to traffic approaching from the right. In practice, they often drive in the middle and yield to no one. Maximum speed limits, unless otherwise posted, are 50km/h in towns, 90km/h on highways and 120km/h on *otoyols*.

Safety

Turkey's roads are not particularly safe, and claim about 10,000 lives a year. Turkish drivers are impatient and incautious, rarely use their indicators and pay little attention to anyone else's, drive too fast both on the open road and through towns, and have an irrepressible urge to overtake – including on blind corners.

To survive on Turkey's roads:

➡ Drive cautiously and defensively.

➡ Do not expect your fellow motorists to obey road signs or behave in a manner you would generally expect at home.

➡ As there are only a few divided highways and many two-lane roads are serpentine, reconcile yourself to spending hours crawling along behind slow, overladen trucks.

➡ Avoid driving at night, when you won't be able to see potholes, animals, or even vehicles driving without lights, with lights missing, or stopped in the middle of the road. Drivers sometimes flash their lights to announce their approach.

➡ Rather than trying to tackle secondary, gravel roads when visiting remote sights, hire a taxi for the day. It's an extra expense, but the driver should know the terrain and the peace of mind is invaluable.

➡ The US embassy in Ankara has a page of safety tips for drivers at http://turkey.usembassy.gov/driver_safety_briefing.html.

Tolls

Turkey has a motorway toll system, known as HGS (Hızlı Geçiş Sistemi – 'fast transit system'). Paying tolls should be automatic if you hire a car in Turkey; the vehicle should be equipped with an electronic-chip sticker or a small plastic toll transponder. You simply pay the rental company a flat fee of about €10 for unlimited use of the *otoyols*. Confirm that the car is equipped with a device, which should be located in the top centre of the windscreen. If it is not, you will likely end up with a fine.

If you are driving your own car, you must register the vehicle and buy credit at the earliest opportunity in a branch of the PTT (post office).

Dolmuşes & Midibuses

As well as providing transport within cities and towns, dolmuşes (minibuses) run between places; you'll usually use them to travel between small towns and villages. Ask, '[Your destination] *dolmuş var mı?'* (Is there a dolmuş to [your destination]?). Some dolmuşes depart at set times, but they often wait until every seat is taken before leaving. To let the driver know that you want to hop out, say *'inecek var'* (someone wants to get out).

Midibuses generally operate on routes that are too long for dolmuşes, but not popular enough for full-size buses. They usually have narrow seats with rigid upright backs, which can be uncomfortable on long stretches.

Local Transport

Bus

For most city buses you must buy your *bilet* (ticket) in advance at a special ticket kiosk. Kiosks are found at major bus terminals and transfer points, and sometimes attached to shops near bus stops. The fare is normally around ₺2.

Private buses sometimes operate on the same routes as municipal buses; they are usually older, and accept either cash or tickets.

Local Dolmuş

Dolmuşes are minibuses or, occasionally, *taksi dolmuşes* (shared taxis) that operate on set routes within a city. They're usually faster, more comfortable and only slightly more expensive than the bus. In larger cities, dolmuş stops are marked by signs; look for a 'D' and text reading *'Dolmuş İndirme Bindirme Yeri'* (Dolmuş Boarding and Alighting Place). Stops are usually conveniently located near major squares, terminals and intersections.

Metro

Several cities have underground metros, including İstanbul, İzmir, Bursa and Ankara. These are usually quick and simple to use, although you may have to go through the ticket barriers to find a route map. Most metros require you to buy a *jeton* (transport token; around ₺2) and insert it into the ticket barrier.

Taxi

Turkish taxis are fitted with digital meters. If your driver doesn't start his, mention it right away by saying *'saatiniz'* (your meter). Check your driver is running the right rate, which varies from city to city. The *gece* (night) rate is 50% more than the *gündüz* (daytime) rate, but some places, including İstanbul, do not have a night rate.

Some taxi drivers – particularly in İstanbul – try to demand a flat payment from foreigners. In this situation, drivers sometimes offer a decent fare; for example to take you to an airport, where they can pick up a good fare on the return journey. It is more often the case that they demand an exorbitant amount, give you grief and refuse to run the meter. If this happens find another cab and, if convenient, complain to the police. Generally, only when you are using a taxi for a private tour involving waiting time (eg to an archaeological site) should you agree on a set fare, which should work out cheaper than using the meter. Taxi companies normally have set fees for longer journeys written in a ledger at the rank – they can be haggled down a little. Always confirm such fares in advance to avoid argument later.

Tram

Several cities have *tramvays* (trams), which are a quick and efficient way of getting around, and normally cost around ₺2 to use.

Tours

Every year we receive complaints from travellers who feel they have been fleeced by local travel agents, especially some of those operating in Sultanahmet, İstanbul. However, there are plenty of good agents alongside the sharks. Figure out a ballpark figure for doing the same trip yourself, and shop around before committing.

Operators

Amber Travel (☑0242-836 1630; www.ambertravel.com) British-run adventure travel company specialising in hiking, biking and sea kayaking.

Bougainville Travel (Map p356; ☑0242-836 3737; www.bougainville-turkey. com; İbrahim Serin Caddesi 10, Kaş) Long-established English-Turkish tour operator based in Kaş, offering a range of Mediterranean activities and tours.

Crowded House Tours (☑0286-814 1565; www. crowdedhousegallipoli.com; Zubeyde Hanim Meydani 28, Eceabat) Tours of the Gallipoli Peninsula and other areas, including Cappadocia and Ephesus. Based in Eceabat.

Eastern Turkey Tours (☑0530 349 2793, 0432-215 2092; www.easternturkeytour. org; Ordu Caddesi, Van) Recommended Van-based outfit specialising in eastern Anatolia, Georgia and Armenia.

Fez Travel (☑0212-520 0434; www.feztravel.com) Tours around Turkey, including the Gallipoli Peninsula and *gület* cruises. Has four offices in western Turkey.

Hassle Free Travel Agency (☑0286-213 5969; www. anzachouse.com; Cumhuriyet Meydanı 59, Çanakkale) Tours of the Gallipoli Peninsula and other parts of western Turkey, plus *gület* cruises. Based in Çanakkale and İstanbul.

Kirkit Voyage (📞0384-511 3259; www.kirkit.com; Atatürk Caddesi 50, Avanos) Cappadocia specialists offering customised tours around Turkey, including İstanbul and Ephesus. French spoken, too.

Train

Train travel through Turkey is becoming increasingly popular as improvements are made, with high-speed lines such as İstanbul–Ankara appearing.

If you're on a budget, an overnight train journey is a great way to save accommodation costs. Many fans also appreciate no-rush travel experiences such as the stunning scenery rolling by and meeting fellow passengers. Occasional unannounced hold-ups and toilets gone feral by the end of the long journey are all part of the adventure.

Classes

Following a modernisation effort, Turkish trains are mostly as good as regular trains in Western Europe. Most have carpeted air-conditioned carriages with reclining Pullman seats; some have six-seat compartments. Riding the 250km/h *Yüksek Hızlı Treni* (high-speed trains, known as YHT) is a treat, with two classes to choose between and a cafeteria car.

Many regular trains have restaurant cars and *küşet* (couchette) wagons with shared four-person compartments with seats that fold down into shelf-like beds. Bedding is not provided unless it's an *örtülü küşetli* ('covered' couchette). A *yataklı vagon* (sleeping car) has one- and two-bed compartments, with a washbasin, bedding, fridge and even a shared shower; the best option for women travelling alone on overnight trips.

Costs

Train tickets are usually about half the price of bus tickets, with the exception of high-speed services. A return ticket is 20% cheaper than two singles. Students (though you may need a Turkish student card), ISIC cardholders and seniors (60 years plus) get a 20% discount. Children under eight travel free.

InterRail Global and One Country passes and Balkan Flexipass cover the Turkish railway network, as do the Eurail Global and Select passes. Train Tour Cards, available at major stations, allow unlimited travel on Turkish inter-city trains for a month. There are also Tour Cards covering just high-speed trains, inter-city trains (apart from sleeping and couchette wagons) or couchettes and sleeping cars.

Long-Distance Trips

The following trains depart from Ankara:

➡ Adana via Kayseri

➡ Diyarbakır via Kayseri, Sivas and Malatya

➡ İzmir via Eskişehir

➡ Kars via Kayseri, Sivas and Erzurum

➡ Kurtalan (near Hasankeyf) via Kayseri, Sivas, Malatya and Diyarbakır

➡ Tatvan (Lake Van) via Kayseri, Sivas and Malatya

Network

The **Turkish State Railways** (📞444 8233; www.tcdd.gov.tr) network covers the country fairly well, with the notable exception of the coastlines. For the Aegean and Mediterranean coasts you can travel by train to either İzmir or Konya, and take the bus from there.

At the time of writing, to access Turkish State Railways' Anatolian network from İstanbul, you had to cross the city to Pendik (25km southeast of the centre near Sabiha Gökçen International Airport, reached via metro to Kartal and bus or taxi from there). From Pendik, high-speed trains run to Ankara via Eskişehir. Alternatively, catch a ferry across the Sea of Marmara to Bandırma, from where trains depart to İzmir. Trains to eastern Anatolia depart from Ankara. For updates visit www.seat61.com/Turkey2.

High-speed routes:

➡ Ankara–Konya

➡ Eskişehir–Konya

➡ İstanbul Pendik–Eskişehir–Ankara

Other useful routes:

➡ İstanbul–İzmir (including ferry to/from Bandırma)

➡ İzmir–Selçuk-Denizli

Reservations

It is wise to reserve your seat at least a few days before travelling, although they can be paid for shortly before departure. For the *yataklı* wagons, reserve as far in advance as possible, especially if a religious or public holiday is looming. Weekend trains tend to be busiest.

You can buy tickets at stations (only major stations for sleeping car tickets), through travel agencies and, with more difficulty, at www.tcdd.gov.tr. The website www.seat61.com/Turkey2.htm gives step-by-step instructions for navigating the transaction.

Timetables

You can double-check train departure times, which do change, at www.tcdd.gov.tr.

Timetables sometimes indicate stations rather than cities, eg Basmane rather than İzmir.

Health

BEFORE YOU GO

Recommended Vaccinations

The following are recommended as routine for travellers, regardless of the region they are visiting:

➡ diphtheria-tetanus-pertussis (whooping cough)
➡ influenza
➡ measles-mumps-rubella (MMR)
➡ polio
➡ varicella (chickenpox)

The following are also recommended for travellers to Turkey:

➡ hepatitis A and B
➡ typhoid

Rabies is endemic in Turkey, so if you will be travelling off the beaten track, consider an antirabies vaccination.

Malaria is found from May to October in the provinces of Diyarbakır, Mardin and Şanlıurfa.

Get vaccinations four to eight weeks before departure, and ask for an International Certificate of Vaccination or Prophylaxis (ICVP or 'yellow card'), listing all the vaccinations you've received.

Medical Checklist

Consider packing the following in your medical kit:

➡ acetaminophen/paracetamol (Tylenol) or aspirin
➡ adhesive or paper tape
➡ antibacterial cream or ointment
➡ antibiotics (if travelling off the beaten track)
➡ antidiarrhoeal drugs (eg loperamide)
➡ antihistamines (for hay fever and allergic reactions)
➡ anti-inflammatory drugs (eg ibuprofen)
➡ bandages, gauze and gauze rolls
➡ DEET-based insect repellent for the skin
➡ insect spray for clothing, tents and bed nets
➡ water purification tablets
➡ oral rehydration salts (eg Dioralyte)
➡ pocket knife, scissors, safety pins and tweezers
➡ steroid cream or cortisone
➡ sunblock (it's expensive in Turkey)
➡ syringes and sterile needles (if travelling to remote areas)
➡ thermometer

Websites

Consult your government's travel health website before departure, if one is available. The Health section at www.lonelyplanet.com/turkey has further information.

IN TURKEY

Prevention is the key to staying healthy while travelling in Turkey. Infectious diseases here are usually associated with poor living conditions and poverty, and can be avoided with a few precautions.

INSURANCE

Turkish doctors generally expect payment in cash. Find out in advance if your travel insurance will reimburse you for overseas health expenditures or, less likely, pay providers directly. If you are required to pay upfront, keep all documentation. Some policies ask you to call a centre in your home country (reverse charges) for an immediate assessment of your problem. It's also worth ensuring your insurance covers ambulances and transport. Not all policies cover emergency medical evacuation home or to a hospital in a major city, which may be necessary in a serious emergency.

Availability & Cost of Health Care

Getting Treated

If you need basic care for problems such as cuts, bruises and jabs, you could ask for the local *sağulık ocağuı* (health centre), but don't expect anyone to speak anything but Turkish.

If your hotel can't recommend the nearest source of medical help, try the travel assistance provided by your insurance or, in an emergency, your embassy or consulate.

Standards

The best private hospitals in İstanbul and Ankara offer world-class service, but they are expensive. Elsewhere, even private hospitals don't always have high standards of care and their state-run equivalents even less so.

Hospitals & clinics Medicine, and even sterile dressings or intravenous fluids, may need to be bought from a local pharmacy. Nursing care is frequently limited or rudimentary, as family and friends often look after Turkish patients.

Dentists Standards vary and there is a risk of hepatitis B and HIV transmission via poorly sterilised equipment, so watch the tools in use carefully. Travel insurance will usually only cover emergency dental treatment.

Pharmacists For minor illnesses, pharmacists can often provide advice and sell over-the-counter medication, including drugs that would require a prescription in your home country. They can also advise when more specialised help is needed.

Infection Diseases

Diphtheria

Spread through Close respiratory contact.

Symptoms & effects A high temperature and severe sore throat. Sometimes a membrane forms across the throat, requiring a tracheotomy to prevent suffocation.

Prevention The vaccine is given as an injection, normally with tetanus and in many countries as a routine childhood jab. Recommended for those likely to be in close contact with the local population in infected areas.

Hepatitis A

Spread through Contaminated food (particularly shellfish) and water.

Symptoms & effects Jaundice, dark urine, a yellow colour to the whites of the eyes, fever and abdominal pain. Although rarely fatal, it can cause prolonged lethargy and delayed recovery.

Prevention Vaccine given as an injection, with a booster extending the protection offered. Available in some countries as a combined single-dose vaccine with hepatitis B or typhoid.

Hepatitis B

Spread through Infected blood, contaminated needles and sexual intercourse.

Symptoms & effects Jaundice and liver problems (occasionally failure).

Prevention The vaccine is worth considering for Turkey, where the disease is endemic. Many countries give it as part of routine childhood vaccinations.

Leishmaniasis

Spread through The bite of an infected sandfly or dog. More prevalent in areas bordering Syria.

Symptoms & effects A slowly growing skin lump or ulcer. It may develop into a serious, life-threatening fever, usually accompanied by anaemia and weight loss.

Leptospirosis

Spread through The excreta of infected rodents, especially rats. It is unusual for travellers to be affected unless living in poor sanitary conditions.

Symptoms & effects Fever, jaundice, and hepatitis and renal failure that may be fatal.

Malaria

Spread through Mosquito bites. Check with your doctor if you are considering travelling to southeastern Turkey. Elsewhere, the risk is minimal to zero.

Symptoms & effects Malaria almost always starts with marked shivering, fever and sweating. Muscle pain, headache and vomiting are common. Symptoms may occur anywhere from a few days to three weeks after a bite by an infected mosquito. The illness can start while you are taking preventative tablets, if they are not fully effective, or after you have finished taking your tablets. Malaria symptoms can be mistaken for flu by travellers who return home during winter.

Prevention Taking antimalarial tablets is inconvenient, but malaria can kill. You must take them if the risk is significant.

Rabies

Spread through Bites or licks on broken skin from an infected animal.

Symptoms & effects Initially, pain or tingling at the site of the bite, with fever, loss of appetite and headache. With 'furious' rabies, there is a growing sense of anxiety, jumpiness, disorientation, neck stiffness, sometimes seizures or convulsions, and fear of water. 'Dumb' rabies (less common) affects the spinal cord, causing muscle paralysis then heart and lung failure. If untreated, both forms are fatal.

TAP WATER

It's not wise to drink tap water if you're only in Turkey on a short visit. Stick to bottled water, boil tap water for 10 minutes or use purification tablets or a filter.

Do not drink river or lake water, which may lead to diarrhoea or vomiting.

TRAVELLER'S DIARRHOEA

To prevent diarrhoea, avoid tap water unless it has been boiled, filtered or chemically disinfected (with iodine or purification tablets). Eat fresh fruit or vegetables only if they're cooked or you have peeled them yourself, and avoid dairy products that might contain unpasteurised milk. Buffet meals are risky since food may not be kept hot enough; meals freshly cooked in front of you in a busy restaurant are safer.

If you develop diarrhoea, drink plenty of fluids, and preferably an oral rehydration solution containing salt and sugar. A few loose stools don't require treatment, but if you start having more than four or five motions a day, you should take an antidiarrhoeal agent (such as loperamide) or, if that's unavailable, an antibiotic (usually a quinolone drug). If diarrhoea is bloody, persists for more than 72 hours or is accompanied by fever, shaking chills or severe abdominal pain, you should seek medical attention.

Prevention People travelling to remote areas, where a reliable source of post-bite vaccine is not available within 24 hours, should be vaccinated. Any bite, scratch or lick from a warm-blooded, furry animal should immediately be thoroughly cleaned. If you have not been vaccinated and you get bitten, you will need a course of injections starting as soon as possible after the injury. Vaccination does not provide immunity, it merely buys you more time to seek medical help.

Tuberculosis

Spread through Close respiratory contact and, occasionally, infected milk or milk products.

Symptoms & effects Can be asymptomatic, although symptoms can include a cough, weight loss or fever months or even years after exposure. An X-ray is the best way to confirm if you have tuberculosis.

Prevention BCG vaccine is recommended for those likely to be mixing closely with the local population – visiting family, planning a long stay, or working as a teacher or healthcare worker. As it's a live vaccine, it should not be given to pregnant women or immunocompromised individuals.

Typhoid

Spread through Food or water contaminated by infected faeces.

Symptoms & effects Initially, usually a fever or a pink rash on the abdomen. Septicaemia (blood poisoning) may also occur.

Prevention Vaccination given by injection. In some countries, an oral vaccine is available.

Environmental Hazards

Heat Illness

Causes Sweating heavily, fluid loss and inadequate replacement of fluids and salt. Particularly common when you exercise outside in a hot climate.

Symptoms & effects Headache, dizziness and tiredness.

Prevention Drink sufficient water (you should produce pale, diluted urine). By the time you are thirsty, you are already dehydrated.

Treatment Replace fluids by drinking water, fruit juice or both, and cool down with cold water and fans. Treat salt loss by consuming salty fluids, such as soup or broth, and adding a little more table salt to foods.

Heatstroke

Causes Extreme heat; high humidity; dehydration; drug or alcohol use or physical exertion in the sun. Occurs when the body's heat-regulating mechanism breaks down.

Symptoms & effects Sweating stops; an excessive rise in body temperature; irrational and hyperactive behaviour; and eventually loss of consciousness and death.

Treatment Rapidly cool down by spraying the body with water and a fan. Emergency fluid intake and replacing electrolytes by intravenous drip are usually also required.

Insect Bites & Stings

Causes Mosquitoes, sandflies (located around the Mediterranean beaches), scorpions (found in arid or dry climates), bees and wasps (in the Aegean and Mediterranean coastal areas, particularly around Marmaris), and centipedes.

Symptoms & effects Even if mosquitoes do not carry malaria, they can cause irritation and infected bites. Sandflies have a nasty, itchy bite, and occasionally carry leishmaniasis or Pappataci fever. Turkey's small white scorpions can give a painful sting that will bother you for up to 24 hours.

Prevention DEET-based insect repellent. Citronella candles. Cover up with light-coloured clothing. Avoid riversides and marshy areas from late afternoon onwards. Take a mosquito head net and bed net.

Treatment Antihistamine cream to sooth and reduce inflammation.

Snake Bites

Prevention Do not walk barefoot or stick your hands into holes or cracks when exploring nature or touring overgrown ruins and little-visited historic sites.

Treatment Do not panic: half of those bitten by venomous snakes are not actually injected with poison (envenomed). Immobilise the bitten limb with a splint (eg a stick) and bandage the site with firm pressure. Do not apply a tourniquet, or cut or suck the bite. Note the snake's appearance for identification purposes, and get medical help as soon as possible so that antivenene can be given.

Language

Turkish belongs to the Ural-Altaic language family. It's the official language of Turkey and Northern Cyprus, and has approximately 70 million speakers worldwide.

Pronouncing Turkish is pretty simple for English speakers as most Turkish sounds are also found in English. If you read our coloured pronunciation guides as if they were English, you should be understood just fine. Note that the symbol ew represents the sound 'ee' pronounced with rounded lips (as in 'few'), and that the symbol uh is pronounced like the 'a' in 'ago'. The Turkish r is always rolled and v is pronounced a little softer than in English.

Word stress is quite light in Turkish – in our pronunciation guides the stressed syllables are in italics.

BASICS

Hello.
Merhaba.   mer·ha·ba

Goodbye.
Hoşçakal.   hosh·cha·kal
(said by person leaving)

Güle güle.   gew·le gew·le
(said by person staying)

Yes.
Evet.   e·vet

No.
Hayır.   ha·yuhr

WANT MORE?

For in-depth language information and handy phrases, check out Lonely Planet's *Turkish Phrasebook*. You'll find it at **shop.lonelyplanet.com**.

Excuse me.
Bakar mısınız.   ba·kar muh·suh·nuhz

Sorry.
Özür dilerim.   er·zewr dee·le·reem

Please.
Lütfen.   lewt·fen

Thank you.
Teşekkür ederim.   te·shek·kewr e·de·reem

You're welcome.
Birşey değil.   beer·shay de·eel

How are you?
Nasılsınız?   na·suhl·suh·nuhz

Fine, and you?
İyiyim, ya siz?   ee·yee·yeem ya seez

What's your name?
Adınız nedir?   a·duh·nuhz ne·deer

My name is ...
Benim adım ...   be·neem a·duhm ...

Do you speak English?
İngilizce   een·gee·leez·je
konuşuyor   ko·noo·shoo·yor
musunuz?   moo·soo·nooz

I understand.
Anlıyorum.   an·luh·yo·room

I don't understand.
Anlamıyorum.   an·la·muh·yo·room

ACCOMMODATION

Where can I find a ...?	Nerede ... bulabilirim?	ne·re·de ... boo·la·bee·lee·reem
campsite	kamp yeri	kamp ye·ree
guesthouse	misafirhane	mee·sa·feer·ha·ne
hotel	otel	o·tel
pension	pansiyon	pan·see·yon
youth hostel	gençlik hosteli	gench·leek hos·te·lee

How much is it per night/person?
Geceliği/Kişi   ge·je·lee·ee/kee·shee
başına ne kadar?   ba·shuh·na ne ka·dar

Is breakfast included?
Kahvaltı dahil mi?   kah·val·tuh da·heel mee

Do you have a ...?	... *odanız var mı?*	... o·da·nuz var muh
single room	*Tek kişilik*	tek kee·shee·leek
double room	*İki kişilik*	ee·kee kee·shee·leek

air conditioning	*klima*	klee·ma
bathroom	*banyo*	ban·yo
window	*pencere*	pen·je·re

DIRECTIONS

Where is ...?
... nerede?   ... ne·re·de

What's the address?
Adresi nedir?   ad·re·see ne·deer

Could you write it down, please?
Lütfen yazar   lewt·fen ya·zar
mısınız?   muh·suh·nuhz

Can you show me (on the map)?
Bana (haritada)   ba·na (ha·ree·ta·da)
gösterebilir   gers·te·re·bee·leer
misiniz?   mee·seen·neez

It's straight ahead.
Tam karşıda.   tam kar·shuh·da

at the traffic lights
trafik   tra·feek
ışıklarından   uh·shuhk·la·ruhn·dan

at the corner	*köşeden*	ker·she·den
behind	*arkasında*	ar·ka·suhn·da
far (from)	*uzak*	oo·zak
in front of	*önünde*	er·newn·de
near (to)	*yakınında*	ya·kuh·nuhn·da
opposite	*karşısında*	kar·shuh·suhn·da
Turn left.	*Sola dön.*	so·la dern
Turn right.	*Sağa dön.*	sa·a dern

EATING & DRINKING

What would you recommend?
Ne tavsiye   ne tav·see·ye
edersiniz?   e·der·see·neez

What's in that dish?
Bu yemekte neler var?   boo ye·mek·te ne·ler var

I don't eat ...
... yemiyorum.   ... ye·mee·yo·room

Cheers!
Şerefe!   she·re·fe

KEY PATTERNS

To get by in Turkish, mix and match these simple patterns with words of your choice:

When's (the next bus)?
(Sonraki otobüs)   (son·ra·kee o·to·bews)
ne zaman?   ne za·man

Where's (the market)?
(Pazar yeri) nerede?   (pa·zar ye·ree) ne·re·de

Where can I (buy a ticket)?
Nereden (bilet   ne·re·den (bee·let
alabilirim)?   a·la·bee·lee·reem)

I have (a reservation).
(Rezervasyonum)   (re·zer·vas·yo·noom)
var.   var

Do you have (a map)?
(Haritanız)   (ha·ree·ta·nuhz)
var mı?   var muh

Is there (a toilet)?
(Tuvalet) var mı?   (too·va·let) var muh

I'd like (the menu).
(Menüyü)   (me·new·yew)
istiyorum.   ees·tee·yo·room

I want to (make a call).
(Bir görüşme   (beer ger·rewsh·me
yapmak)   yap·mak)
istiyorum.   ees·tee·yo·room

Do I have to (declare this)?
(Bunu beyan   (boo·noo be·yan
etmem) gerekli mi?   et·mem) ge·rek·lee mee

I need (assistance).
(Yardıma)   (yar·duh·ma)
ihtiyacım var.   eeh·tee·ya·juhm var

That was delicious!
Nefisti!   ne·fees·tee

The bill/check, please.
Hesap lütfen.   he·sap lewt·fen

I'd like a table for ...	... *bir masa ayırtmak istiyorum.*	... beer ma·sa a·yuhrt·mak ees·tee·yo·room
(eight) o'clock	*Saat (sekiz) için*	sa·at (se·keez) ee·cheen
(two) people	*(İki) kişilik*	(ee·kee) kee·shee·leek

Key Words

appetisers	*mezeler*	me·ze·ler
bottle	*şişe*	shee·she
bowl	*kase*	ka·se
breakfast	*kahvaltı*	kah·val·tuh
(too) cold	*(çok) soğuk*	(chok) so·ook

cup	fincan	feen·jan
delicatessen	şarküteri	shar·kew·te·ree
dinner	akşam yemeği	ak·sham ye·me·ee
dish	yemek	ye·mek
food	yiyecek	yee·ye·jek
fork	çatal	cha·tal
glass	bardak	bar·dak
grocery	bakkal	bak·kal
halal	helal	he·lal
highchair	mama sandalyesi	ma·ma san·dal·ye·see
hot (warm)	sıcak	suh·jak
knife	bıçak	buh·chak
kosher	koşer	ko·sher
lunch	öğle yemeği	er·le ye·me·ee
main courses	ana yemekler	a·na ye·mek·ler
market	pazar	pa·zar
menu	yemek listesi	ye·mek lees·te·see
plate	tabak	ta·bak
restaurant	restoran	res·to·ran
spicy	acı	a·juh
spoon	kaşık	ka·shuhk
vegetarian	vejeteryan	ve·zhe·ter·yan

Meat & Fish

anchovy	hamsi	ham·see
beef	sığır eti	suh·uhr e·tee
calamari	kalamares	ka·la·ma·res
chicken	piliç/ tavuk	pee·leech/ ta·vook
fish	balık	ba·luhk
lamb	kuzu	koo·zoo
liver	ciğer	jee·er
mussels	midye	meed·ye
pork	domuz eti	do·mooz e·tee
veal	dana eti	da·na e·tee

Fruit & Vegetables

apple	elma	el·ma
apricot	kayısı	ka·yuh·suh
banana	muz	mooz
capsicum	biber	bee·ber
carrot	havuç	ha·vooch
cucumber	salatalık	sa·la·ta·luhk
fruit	meyve	may·ve
grape	üzüm	ew·zewm
melon	kavun	ka·voon

olive	zeytin	zay·teen
onion	soğan	so·an
orange	portakal	por·ta·kal
peach	şeftali	shef·ta·lee
potato	patates	pa·ta·tes
spinach	ıspanak	uhs·pa·nak
tomato	domates	do·ma·tes
watermelon	karpuz	kar·pooz

Other

bread	ekmek	ek·mek
cheese	peynir	pay·neer
egg	yumurta	yoo·moor·ta
honey	bal	bal
ice	buz	booz
pepper	kara biber	ka·ra bee·ber
rice	pirinç/ pilav	pee·reench/ pee·lav
salt	tuz	tooz
soup	çorba	chor·ba
sugar	şeker	she·ker
Turkish delight	lokum	lo·koom

Drinks

beer	bira	bee·ra
coffee	kahve	kah·ve
(orange) juice	(portakal) suyu	(por·ta·kal soo·yoo)
milk	süt	sewt
mineral water	maden suyu	ma·den soo·yoo
soft drink	alkolsüz içecek	al·kol·sewz ee·che·jek
tea	çay	chai
water	su	soo
wine	şarap	sha·rap
yoghurt	yoğurt	yo·oort

Signs

Açık	Open
Bay	Male
Bayan	Female
Çıkışı	Exit
Giriş	Entrance
Kapalı	Closed
Sigara İçilmez	No Smoking
Tuvaletler	Toilets
Yasak	Prohibited

EMERGENCIES

Help!
İmdat! — eem·dat

I'm lost.
Kayboldum. — kai·bol·*doom*

Leave me alone!
Git başımdan! — geet ba·shuhm·*dan*

There's been an accident.
Bir kaza oldu. — beer ka·za ol·*doo*

Can I use your phone?
Telefonunuzu — te·le·fo·noo·noo·*zoo*
kullanabilir miyim? — kool·la·*na*·bee·leer mee·*yeem*

Call a doctor!
Doktor çağırın! — dok·*tor* cha·uh·ruhn

Call the police!
Polis çağırın! — po·*lees* cha·uh·ruhn

I'm ill.
Hastayım. — has·*ta*·yuhm

It hurts here.
Burası ağrıyor. — boo·ra·*suh* a·ruh·yor

I'm allergic to (nuts).
(Çerezlere) — (che·rez·le·re)
alerjim var. — a·ler·*zheem* var

SHOPPING & SERVICES

I'd like to buy ...
... almak istiyorum. — ... al·*mak* ees·*tee*·yo·room

I'm just looking.
Sadece bakıyorum. — sa·de·je ba·*kuh*·yo·room

May I look at it?
Bakabilir miyim? — ba·*ka*·bee·leer mee·*yeem*

The quality isn't good.
Kalitesi iyi değil. — ka·lee·te·*see* ee·*yee* de·*eel*

How much is it?
Ne kadar? — ne ka·*dar*

It's too expensive.
Bu çok pahalı. — boo chok pa·ha·*luh*

Do you have something cheaper?
Daha ucuz birşey — da·ha oo·*jooz* beer·*shay*
var mı? — var muh

There's a mistake in the bill.
Hesapta bir — he·sap·*ta* beer
yanlışlık var. — yan·luhsh·*luhk* var

Question Words

How?	*Nasıl?*	na·*seel*
What?	*Ne?*	ne
When?	*Ne zaman?*	ne za·*man*
Where?	*Nerede?*	ne·re·de
Which?	*Hangi?*	han·*gee*
Who?	*Kim?*	keem
Why?	*Neden?*	ne·den

ATM	*bankamatik*	ban·ka·ma·*teek*
credit card	*kredi kartı*	kre·dee kar·*tuh*
post office	*postane*	pos·*ta*·ne
signature	*imza*	eem·za
tourist office	*turizm*	too·reezm
	bürosu	bew·ro·soo

TIME & DATES

What time is it? *Saat kaç?* — sa·at kach
It's (10) o'clock. *Saat (on).* — sa·at (on)
Half past (10). *(On) buçuk.* — (on) boo·*chook*

in the morning	*öğleden evvel*	er·le·den ev·vel
in the afternoon	*öğleden sonra*	er·le·den son·ra
in the evening	*akşam*	ak·sham
yesterday	*dün*	dewn
today	*bugün*	boo·gewn
tomorrow	*yarın*	ya·ruhn

Monday	*Pazartesi*	pa·zar·te·see
Tuesday	*Salı*	sa·luh
Wednesday	*Çarşamba*	char·sham·ba
Thursday	*Perşembe*	per·shem·be
Friday	*Cuma*	joo·ma
Saturday	*Cumartesi*	joo·mar·te·see
Sunday	*Pazar*	pa·zar

January	*Ocak*	o·jak
February	*Şubat*	shoo·bat
March	*Mart*	mart
April	*Nisan*	nee·san
May	*Mayıs*	ma·yuhs
June	*Haziran*	ha·zee·ran
July	*Temmuz*	tem·mooz
August	*Ağustos*	a·oos·tos
September	*Eylül*	ay·lewl
October	*Ekim*	e·keem
November	*Kasım*	ka·suhm
December	*Aralık*	a·ra·luhk

TRANSPORT

Public Transport

At what time does the ... leave/arrive?	*... ne zaman kalkacak/ varır?*	... ne za·man kal·ka·jak/ va·ruhr
boat	*Vapur*	va·poor
bus	*Otobüs*	o·to·bews
plane	*Uçak*	oo·chak
train	*Tren*	tren

Numbers

1	bir	beer
2	iki	ee·kee
3	üç	ewch
4	dört	dert
5	beş	besh
6	altı	al·tuh
7	yedi	ye·dee
8	sekiz	se·keez
9	dokuz	do·kooz
10	on	on
20	yirmi	yeer·mee
30	otuz	o·tooz
40	kırk	kuhrk
50	elli	el·lee
60	altmış	alt·muhsh
70	yetmiş	et·meesh
80	seksen	sek·sen
90	doksan	dok·san
100	yüz	yewz
1000	bin	been

Does it stop at (Maltepe)?
(Maltepe'de) durur mu? — (mal·te·pe·de) doo·roor moo

What's the next stop?
Sonraki durak hangisi? — son·ra·kee doo·rak han·gee·see

Please tell me when we get to (Beşiktaş).
(Beşiktaş'a) vardığımızda lütfen bana söyleyin. — (be·sheek·ta·sha) var·duh·uh·muhz·da lewt·fen ba·na say·le·yeen

I'd like to get off at (Kadıköy).
(Kadıköy'de) inmek istiyorum. — (ka·duh·kay·de) een·mek ees·tee·yo·room

I'd like a ... ticket to (Bostancı).	(Bostancı'ya) ... bir bilet lütfen.	(bos·tan·juh·ya) ... beer bee·let lewt·fen
1st-class	Birinci mevki	bee·reen·jee mev·kee
2nd-class	İkinci mevki	ee·keen·jee mev·kee
one-way	Gidiş	gee·deesh
return	Gidiş-dönüş	gee·deesh-der·newsh

first	ilk	eelk
last	son	son
next	geleçek	ge·le·jek

I'd like a/an ... seat.	... bir yer istiyorum.	... beer yer ees·tee·yo·room
aisle	Koridor tarafında	ko·ree·dor ta·ra·fuhn·da
window	Cam kenarı	jam ke·na·ruh

cancelled	iptal edildi	eep·tal e·deel·dee
delayed	ertelendi	er·te·len·dee
platform	peron	pe·ron
ticket office	bilet gişesi	bee·let gee·she·see
timetable	tarife	ta·ree·fe
train station	istasyon	ees·tas·yon

Driving & Cycling

I'd like to hire a ...	Bir ... kiralamak istiyorum.	beer ... kee·ra·la·mak ees·tee·yo·room
4WD	dört çeker	dert che·ker
bicycle	bisiklet	bee·seek·let
car	araba	a·ra·ba
motorcycle	motosiklet	mo·to·seek·let

bike shop	bisikletçi	bee·seek·let·chee
child seat	çocuk koltuğu	cho·jook kol·too·oo
diesel	dizel	dee·zel
helmet	kask	kask
mechanic	araba tamircisi	a·ra·ba ta·meer·jee·see
petrol/gas	benzin	ben·zeen
service station	benzin istasyonu	ben·zeen ees·tas·yo·noo

Is this the road to (Taksim)?
(Taksim'e) giden yol bu mu? — (tak·see·me) gee·den yol boo moo

(How long) Can I park here?
Buraya (ne kadar süre) park edebilirim? — boo·ra·ya (ne ka·dar sew·re) park e·de·bee·lee·reem

The car/motorbike has broken down (at Osmanbey).
Arabam/Motosikletim (Osmanbey'de) bozuldu. — a·ra·bam/mo·to·seek·le·teem (os·man·bay·de) bo·zool·doo

I have a flat tyre.
Lastiğim patladı. — las·tee·eem pat·la·duh

I've run out of petrol.
Benzinim bitti. — ben·zee·neem beet·tee

GLOSSARY

acropolis – hilltop citadel and temples of a classical Hellenic city

ada(sı) – island

agora – open space for commerce and politics in a Greco-Roman city

Anatolia – the Asian part of Turkey; also called *Asia Minor*

arabesk – Arabic-style Turkish music

arasta – row of shops near a mosque, the rent from which supports the mosque

Asia Minor – see *Anatolia*

bahçe(si) – garden

bedesten – vaulted, fireproof market enclosure where valuable goods are kept

belediye (sarayı) – municipal council, town hall

bey – polite form of address for a man; follows the name

bilet – ticket

bouleuterion – place of assembly, council meeting place in a classical Hellenic city

bulvar(ı) – boulevard or avenue; often abbreviated to 'bul'

cadde(si) – street; often abbreviated to 'cad'

cami(i) – mosque

caravanserai – large fortified way-station for (trade) caravans

çarşı(sı) – market, bazaar; sometimes town centre

çay bahçesi – tea garden

çayı – stream

çeşme – spring, fountain

Cilician Gates – a pass in the Taurus Mountains in southern Turkey

dağ(ı) – mountain

deniz – sea

dervish – member of Mevlevi Muslim brotherhood

dolmuş – shared taxi; can be a minibus or sedan

döviz (bürosu) – currency exchange (office)

emir – Turkish tribal chieftain

eski – old (thing, not person)

ev pansiyonu – pension in a private home

eyvan – vaulted hall opening into a central court in a *medrese* or mosque; balcony

fasıl – Ottoman classical music, usually played by gypsies

GAP – Southeastern Anatolia Project, a mammoth hydroelectric and irrigation project

geçit, geçidi – (mountain) pass

gişe – ticket kiosk

göl(ü) – lake

gület – traditional Turkish wooden yacht

hamam(ı) – Turkish bathhouse

han(ı) – see *caravanserai*

hanım – polite form of address for a woman

haremlik – family/women's quarters of a residence; see also *selamlık*

heykel – statue

hisar(ı) – fortress or citadel

Hittites – nation of people inhabiting Anatolia during 2nd millennium BC

hükümet konağı – government house, provincial government headquarters

imam – prayer leader, Muslim cleric

imaret(i) – soup kitchen for the poor, usually attached to a *medrese*

indirim – discount

iskele(si) – jetty, quay

jeton – transport token

kale(si) – fortress, citadel

kapı(sı) – door, gate

kaplıca – thermal spring or baths

Karagöz – shadow-puppet theatre

kaya – cave

KDV – katma değer vergisi, Turkey's value-added tax

kebapçı – place selling kebaps

kervansaray(ı) – Turkish for *caravanserai*

kilim – flat-weave rug

kilise(si) – church

köfte – meatballs

köfteci – *köfte* maker or seller

konak, konağı – mansion, government headquarters

köprü(sü) – bridge

köşk(ü) – pavilion, villa

köy(ü) – village

kule(si) – tower

külliye(si) – mosque complex including seminary, hospital and soup kitchen

kümbet – vault, cupola, dome; tomb topped by this

liman(ı) – harbour

lokanta – eatery serving ready-made food

mağara(sı) – cave

mahalle(si) – neighbourhood, district of a city

medrese(si) – Islamic theological seminary or school attached to a mosque

mescit, mescidi – prayer room, small mosque

Mevlâna – also known as Celaleddin Rumi, a great mystic and poet (1207–73), founder of the Mevlevi whirling *dervish* order

meydan(ı) – public square, open place

meyhane – tavern, wine shop

mihrab – niche in a mosque indicating the direction of Mecca

milli parkı – national park

mimber – pulpit in a mosque

müze(si) – museum

nargile – traditional water pipe (for smoking); hookah

necropolis – city of the dead, cemetery

oda(sı) – room

otobüs – bus

otogar – bus station

Ottoman – of or pertaining to the Ottoman Empire, which lasted from the end of the 13th century to the end of WWI

pansiyon – pension, B&B, guesthouse

paşa – general, governor

pastane – pastry shop (patisserie); also *pastahane*

pazar(ı) – weekly market, bazaar

peribacalar – fairy chimneys (rock formation)

pideci – pide maker or seller

plaj – beach

PTT – Posta, Telefon, Telegraf; post, telephone and telegraph office

Ramazan – Islamic holy month of fasting

saat kulesi – clock tower

şadırvan – fountain where Muslims perform ritual ablutions

saray(ı) – palace

sedir – bench seating that doubled as a bed in Ottoman houses

şehir – city; municipality

selamlık – public/men's quarters of a residence; see also *haremlik*

Seljuk – of or pertaining to the Seljuk Turks, the first Turkish state to rule Anatolia from the 11th to 13th centuries

sema – *dervish* ceremony

semahane – hall where whirling *dervish* ceremonies are held

servis – shuttle minibus service to and from the *otogar*

sinema – cinema

sokak, sokağı – street or lane; often abbreviated to 'sk'

Sufi – Muslim mystic, member of a mystic *(dervish)* brotherhood

TCDD – Turkish State Railways

tekke(si) – *dervish* lodge

tersane – shipyard

Thrace – the European part of Turkey

tramvay – tram

TRT – Türkiye Radyo ve Televizyon, Turkish broadcasting corporation

tuff, tufa – soft stone laid down as volcanic ash

türbe(si) – tomb, grave, mausoleum

valide sultan – mother of the reigning sultan

vilayet, valilik, valiliği – provincial government headquarters

yalı – grand waterside residence

yayla – highland pastures

yeni – new

yol(u) – road, way

Behind the Scenes

SEND US YOUR FEEDBACK

We love to hear from travellers – your comments keep us on our toes and help make our books better. Our well-travelled team reads every word on what you loved or loathed about this book. Although we cannot reply individually to your submissions, we always guarantee that your feedback goes straight to the appropriate authors, in time for the next edition. Each person who sends us information is thanked in the next edition – the most useful submissions are rewarded with a selection of digital PDF chapters.

Visit **lonelyplanet.com/contact** to submit your updates and suggestions or to ask for help. Our award-winning website also features inspirational travel stories, news and discussions.

Note: We may edit, reproduce and incorporate your comments in Lonely Planet products such as guidebooks, websites and digital products, so let us know if you don't want your comments reproduced or your name acknowledged. For a copy of our privacy policy visit lonelyplanet.com/privacy.

OUR READERS

Many thanks to the travellers who used the last edition and wrote to us with helpful hints, useful advice and interesting anecdotes: Ayla Sevim, David Mateparae, Diego Salazar, Eric Böhm, Gary Stocker, Hans von Fintel, Hylary Kingham, Jacqueline Hodge, Jascha de Ridder, Jason Nunan, Nick Galvin, Nina Hagel, Robert Brimlow, Roscoe Ward, Sain Alizada, Suzie Magnus

AUTHOR THANKS

James Bainbridge

Çok teşekkürler to my İstanbullu friends old and new who helped me discover the best of the city, and to everyone on the Turquoise Coast for the hospitality and help. Every time I visit Turkey I love it a little more, largely thanks to the brilliant people I meet along the way. On the home front, thanks to Leigh-Robin, Oliver, tiny Thomas and in-laws Pierre and Rhea for all the support and coffee. Last but not least, cheers to my coauthors and everyone at LP.

Brett Atkinson

Thanks to Birsen and family in Eğirdir – it was great catching up after eight years. Also in Eğirdir, thank you to Ibrahim for all the information. In Pamukkale, çok teşekkürler to Mehmet and Ummu for the company and conversation, and across the country in Van, my heartfelt thanks to the wonderful Alkan family. At LP, cheers to my fellow scribes and the hardworking editors and cartos, and final thanks to Carol for holding the fort back in Yeni Zelanda.

Steve Fallon

Çok teşekkürler to those who provided assistance, ideas and/or hospitality along the way in the South Aegean, including: Justine and Melih Kavak in Akyaka; Captain Mehmet Nazmi Nurel and the Endorfina crew and Mustafa and Selda Kaya in Bodrum; Karina and Müslüm Tokur in Datça; Hasan Değirmenci in Kuşadası; Mithat and Oktay Serçin on Lake Bafa; Erdal Kahya and Nazmi Uyanik, Hüseyin and Candy Çağıran and Mehmet and Christine Esenkaya in Selçuk; and Jenny and Salih Orhan in Selimiye. My partner, Michael Rothschild, was – as always – a patient and helpful travelling companion.

Jessica Lee

A huge çok teşekkürler to Deniz Aşık and family; Uğur Bağcı; the fantastic staff at both Safranbolu and Konya tourist offices; Nil Tuncer, Ceyda Yelkalan, Pat Yale and Yvette Koç for cultural queries; Jodie Redding for last-minute cross-checking; Yılmaz and Angela Şisman; Diane Nelson; Ruth Lockwood; and Vicky Burke.

Virginia Maxwell

Many thanks to Pat Yale, Mehmet Umur, Emel Güntaş, Faruk Boyacı, Atilla Tuna, Görgün

Taner, Tahir Karabaş, Jen Hartin, Eveline Zoutendijk, George Grundy, Ann Nevans, Tina Nevans, Jennifer Gaudet, Özlem Tuna, Monica Fritz, Leon Yildirimer, Luca Fritz, Teoman Göral, Meltem İnce Okvuran, Nurullah Çınar, Deniz Ova, Zeynep Unanç, Antony Doucet, Sabiha Apaydın, Saliha Yavuz, İlknur Bodur, Nüket Franco, Nesim Bencoya, Zafer Acar, Oliver Gareis and the many others who shared their knowledge and love of Turkey with me.

Hugh McNaughtan
Thanks to my editor Clifton Wilkinson, to the kind people I met in Turkey, and, most importantly, to Tasmin, Maise and Willa.

John Noble
Extra special thanks to Vedat Akçayöz, Kenan Kara, Celil Ersözoğlu, Yakup Bastem, Süleyman Bolat, Idris Duman, Demet Alba, Virginia Maxwell, Pat Yale and Brett Atkinson.

ACKNOWLEDGEMENTS
Climate map data adapted from Peel MC, Finlayson BL & McMahon TA (2007) 'Updated World Map of the Köppen-Geiger Climate Classification', Hydrology and Earth System Sciences, 11, 163344.

Illustrations pp68-9, pp78-9 and pp228-9 by Javier Zarracina.

Cover photograph: Turkish çay (tea), Luca Da Ros/4Corners ©.

BEHIND THE SCENES

THIS BOOK
This 15th edition of Lonely Planet's *Turkey* guidebook was researched and written by James Bainbridge, Brett Atkinson, Steve Fallon, Jessica Lee, Virginia Maxwell, Hugh McNaughtan and John Noble. The previous edition was also written by James, Brett, Steve, Jessica and Virginia, along with Stuart Butler and Will Gourlay.

This guidebook was produced by the following:
Destination Editors Clifton Wilkinson, Lorna Parkes, Tom Stainer
Product Editor Joel Cotterell
Senior Cartographer Corey Hutchison
Book Designer Jessica Rose
Assisting Editors Andrew Bain, Melanie Dankel, Kate James, Kate Morgan, Charlotte Orr, Susan Paterson, Monique Perrin, Chris Pitts
Assisting Cartographer Diana Von Holdt
Cover Researcher Naomi Parker
Thanks to Kate Chapman, Bruce Evans, Andi Jones, Anne Mason, Kate Mathews, Claire Naylor, Karyn Noble, Martine Power, Kathryn Rowan, Tony Wheeler

Index

Map Legend

Sights
- Beach
- Bird Sanctuary
- Buddhist
- Castle/Palace
- Christian
- Confucian
- Hindu
- Islamic
- Jain
- Jewish
- Monument
- Museum/Gallery/Historic Building
- Ruin
- Shinto
- Sikh
- Taoist
- Winery/Vineyard
- Zoo/Wildlife Sanctuary
- Other Sight

Activities, Courses & Tours
- Bodysurfing
- Diving
- Canoeing/Kayaking
- Course/Tour
- Sento Hot Baths/Onsen
- Skiing
- Snorkelling
- Surfing
- Swimming/Pool
- Walking
- Windsurfing
- Other Activity

Sleeping
- Sleeping
- Camping

Eating
- Eating

Drinking & Nightlife
- Drinking & Nightlife
- Cafe

Entertainment
- Entertainment

Shopping
- Shopping

Information
- Bank
- Embassy/Consulate
- Hospital/Medical
- Internet
- Police
- Post Office
- Telephone
- Toilet
- Tourist Information
- Other Information

Geographic
- Beach
- Gate
- Hut/Shelter
- Lighthouse
- Lookout
- Mountain/Volcano
- Oasis
- Park
- Pass
- Picnic Area
- Waterfall

Population
- Capital (National)
- Capital (State/Province)
- City/Large Town
- Town/Village

Transport
- Airport
- Border crossing
- Bus
- Cable car/Funicular
- Cycling
- Ferry
- Metro station
- Monorail
- Parking
- Petrol station
- S-Bahn/Subway station
- Taxi
- T-bane/Tunnelbana station
- Train station/Railway
- Tram
- Tube station
- U-Bahn/Underground station
- Other Transport

Note: Not all symbols displayed above appear on the maps in this book

Routes
- Tollway
- Freeway
- Primary
- Secondary
- Tertiary
- Lane
- Unsealed road
- Road under construction
- Plaza/Mall
- Steps
- Tunnel
- Pedestrian overpass
- Walking Tour
- Walking Tour detour
- Path/Walking Trail

Boundaries
- International
- State/Province
- Disputed
- Regional/Suburb
- Marine Park
- Cliff
- Wall

Hydrography
- River, Creek
- Intermittent River
- Canal
- Water
- Dry/Salt/Intermittent Lake
- Reef

Areas
- Airport/Runway
- Beach/Desert
- Cemetery (Christian)
- Cemetery (Other)
- Glacier
- Mudflat
- Park/Forest
- Sight (Building)
- Sportsground
- Swamp/Mangrove

Jessica Lee

Ankara & Central Anatolia, Cappadocia After four years leading adventure tours across Turkey, Jessica moved there to live in 2011 and Turkey has been home ever since. This is the third edition of the Turkey guide she has worked on and for this edition she made a welcome return to central Anatolia's creaky Ottoman back streets and pulled on her hiking boots to trek the Ala Dağlar. She also wrote the Turkey's Outdoors chapter and the Understand features covering Architecture, Arts, People and Environment. Read more about Jess at: https://auth. lonelyplanet.com/profiles/jessicalee1.

Virginia Maxwell

İstanbul (Bazaar District, Beyoğlu, Kadıköy and Ferry Trips), İzmir & the North Aegean Although based in Australia, Virginia spends part of each year in Turkey. As well as authoring LP's *İstanbul* city guide, she also writes Lonely Planet's *Pocket İstanbul*.

Hugh McNaughtan

Black Sea Coast, Eastern Mediterranean A former English lecturer, Hugh swapped grant applications for visa applications, and turned his love of travel into a full-time thing. Having done a bit of restaurant-reviewing in his home town (Melbourne) he jumped at the opportunity to eat his way around the Black Sea Coast and Eastern Mediterranean. He's never happier than when on the road with his two daughters. Except perhaps on the cricket field...

John Noble

Eastern Anatolia John has been travelling since his teens and doing so as a Lonely Planet writer since the 1980s. The number of LP titles he's written or co-written is well into three figures, covering a somewhat random selection of countries scattered across the globe, predominantly ones where Spanish, Russian or English are spoken (usually alongside numerous local languages). He still gets as excited as ever about heading out on the road to unfamiliar experiences, people and destinations, especially remote, off-the-beaten-track ones. Above all, he loves mountains, from the English Lake District to the Himalaya. See his pics on Instagram: @johnnoble11.

OUR STORY

A beat-up old car, a few dollars in the pocket and a sense of adventure. In 1972 that's all Tony and Maureen Wheeler needed for the trip of a lifetime – across Europe and Asia overland to Australia. It took several months, and at the end – broke but inspired – they sat at their kitchen table writing and stapling together their first travel guide, *Across Asia on the Cheap*. Within a week they'd sold 1500 copies. Lonely Planet was born.

Today, Lonely Planet has offices in Franklin, London, Melbourne, Oakland, Dublin, Beijing and Delhi, with more than 600 staff and writers. We share Tony's belief that 'a great guidebook should do three things: inform, educate and amuse'.

OUR WRITERS

James Bainbridge

Coordinating Author; İstanbul (Sultanahmet & Around, Western Districts, Beşiktaş, Ortaköy & Nişantaşı); Antalya & the Turquoise Coast James is a British writer based in Cape Town, South Africa, where he contributes to publications worldwide. He has been working on Lonely Planet projects for over a decade, including coordinating five editions of *Turkey* and writing the first edition of *Discover Turkey*. He was extremely happy to return to İstanbul, where he once lived and took a Turkish-language course, and to the Mediterranean, having previously passed through while researching a feature for *Lonely Planet Traveller* magazine. James also wrote most of the Plan Your Trip chapters, the Turkey Today and History essays and Survival Guide chapters for this edition. Read more about James at: https://auth.lonelyplanet.com/profiles/james_bains.

Brett Atkinson

Thrace & Marmara, Western Anatolia Since first visiting Turkey in 1985, Brett has returned regularly to one of his favourite countries. For his fifth Lonely Planet trip to Turkey he explored the astounding Ottoman architecture of Bursa and Edirne, the poignant Anzac history of the Gallipoli Peninsula, and surprising destinations including laidback Gökçeada and cosmopolitan Eskişehir. Brett's contributed to Lonely Planet guidebooks spanning Europe, Asia and the Pacific, and covered over 50 countries as a food and travel writer. See www.brett-atkinson.net for his latest adventures.

Steve Fallon

Ephesus, Bodrum & the South Aegean With a house in Kalkan on the Turquoise Coast of the Mediterranean, Steve considers Turkey to be a second home. This assignment took him to that other coast, the South Aegean one, where he stepped back in time at Ephesus, joined a sailing regatta off Bodrum and rediscovered the beauty of the Datça and Bozburun Peninsulas. OK, *Türkçe'yi hala mağara adamı gibi konuşuyor* (he still speaks Turkish like a caveman), but no Turk has called him Tarzan. At least not yet. Find Steve at www.steveslondon.com.

OVER PAGE MORE WRITERS

Published by Lonely Planet Global Limited
CRN 554153
15th edition – February 2017
ISBN 978 1 78657 235 6
© Lonely Planet 2017   Photographs © as indicated 2017
10 9 8 7 6 5 4 3 2 1
Printed in China

Although the authors and Lonely Planet have taken all reasonable care in preparing this book, we make no warranty about the accuracy or completeness of its content and, to the maximum extent permitted, disclaim all liability arising from its use.